Index of American Periodical Verse: 1986

Rafael Catalá
and
James D. Anderson
assisted by
Sarah Park Anderson
and
Martha Park Sollberger

The Scarecrow Press, Inc.
Metuchen, N.J., & London
1988

Library of Congress Catalog Card No. 73-3060
ISBN 0-8108-2149-4
Copyright © 1988 by Rafael Catalá and James D. Anderson
Manufactured in the United States of America

Contents

Preface

This, the sixteenth annual volume of the *Index of American Periodical Verse*, was produced with the cooperation of 246 participating English and Spanish language periodicals from Canada, the United States, and Puerto Rico. Nearly 6,000 entries for individual poets and translators are included, with more than 16,000 entries for individual poems and 16,000 title or first line entries.

The importance of the *Index* grows as its necessity becomes more apparent in circles of contemporary poetry research. The increasing demand for inclusion corroborates this fact. The *Index* constitutes an objective measure of poetry in North America, recording not only the publication of our own poets in Canada, the U.S. and Puerto Rico, but also those from other lands and cultures and from other times. Of course, the *Index*'s primary purpose is to show what poems have been published by particular poets, what poems have been translated by particular translators, and who wrote poems with particular titles or first lines. But taken together, the *Index* reveals trends and influences: the ebb and flow of particular poets, as well as the influence of cultures of other lands and times as represented by their poets published in North American journals.

James D. Anderson has made a major contribution to the *Index* by designing and refining computer programs that have greatly facilitated the indexing process, control of necessary cross references, and typesetting. Also, I want to express my sincere appreciation to Sarah Park Anderson and Martha Park Sollberger for their valuable assistance.

Rafael Catalá
Co-Editor

Introduction

Compilation

The 1986 *Index* was compiled on an Osborne 4 Vixen microcomputer using the Wordstar wordprocessing program. Once all indexing was complete, entries, including cross-references, were transferred to an IBM AT personal computer for sorting by a new program, "IOTA Big Sort," written by Fred A. Rowley. Title entries were then extracted, and formatted author and title entries were transferred to a Macintosh computer with lazer printer for typesetting and page formatting.

The principal advantage of computer-based compilation is the elimination of repetitive data entry. Within a single issue of a journal, for example, the journal citation will be the same for every poem, yet with the old card-based method, the citation had to be rewritten on every card. With the computer, it is simply copied, without re-keying, to each entry. Similarly, translations no longer call for a completely new entry for the translator. Instead, the original entry is simply modified, moving the name of the translator to the lead position, and the author to the note.

Persons interested in the precise details of compilation, including the computer programs used, should write to the editors at P.O. Box 38, New Brunswick, NJ 08903-0038. The 1982, 1983, 1984, 1985 and 1986 *Indexes* are available from the editors on 5-1/4" floppy disks.

Names and Cross References

With the addition of many more poets with compound surnames and surnames containing various prefixes, we have recognized the need for systematic cross references from alternative forms of surname to the form chosen for entry in the *Index*. We have included these references whenever the form used for entry did not fall under the last element. In addition, many poets publish under different forms of the same name, for example, with or without a middle initial. Often these forms will file next to each other in the *index*. When it is not possible to determine with assurance whether it is the same poet or different poets with similar names, both names may be used. In such cases, "see also" cross references are added to headings to remind users to check the variant name forms which possibly refer to the same poet. When the poets are known to use different forms of the same name, alternative forms may be indicated by using the format authorized by the *Anglo-American Cataloguing Rules*, Second Edition. For example:

WHEATLEY, Pat (Patience)

This heading indicates that this poet has poems published under two forms of name: Pat Wheatley and Patience Wheatley.

Format and Arrangement of Entries

The basic format and style of the *Index* remain unchanged. Poets are arranged alphabetically by surname and forenames. In creating this alphabetical sequence, we have adopted principles of the filing rules issued in 1980 by the American Library Association and the Library of Congress. Names are arranged on the basis of their spelling, rather than their pronunciation, so that, for example, names beginning with 'Mac' and 'Mc' are no longer interfiled. Similarly, the space consistently counts as a filing element, so that similar compound and prefixed surnames are often separated by some distance, as illustrated in the following examples. Note that "De BOLT" precedes "DeBEVOISE" by a considerable number of entries.

De ANGELIS	Van BRUNT
De BOLT	Van DUYN
De GRAVELLES	Van HALTEREN
De LOACH	Van TOORN
De PALCHI	Van TROYER
De RONSARD	Van WERT
De VAUL	Van WINCKEL
DEAL	VANCE
DeBEVOISE	Vander DOES
DeFOE	VANDERBEEK
DEGUY	VanDEVENTER
Del VECCHIO	
DeLISLE	
DeMOTT	
DENNISON	
Der HOVANESSIAN	
DESY	
DeYOUNG	

Abbreviations are also arranged on the basis of spelling, rather than pronunciation, so that "ST. JOHN" is *not* filed as "SAINT JOHN", but as "S+T+space+JOHN". Punctuation is not considered; a hyphen is filed as if it were a space and apostrophes and accents are ignored for purposes of filing. Finally, numerals are arranged in numerical order preceding alphabetical letters rather than as if they were spelled out.

Under each poet's name, poems are arranged alphabetically by title or, if there is no title, by first line. Initial articles in the major languages are ignored in the arrangement. Poem titles and first lines are placed within quotation marks. All significant words of titles are capitalized, but in first lines, only the first word and proper nouns are capitalized. Incomplete excerpts from larger works are followed by the note "Excerpt" or, if they consist of complete sections, by "Selection". The title, first line or number of the excerpt follows if given in the publication. For example:

WALCOTT, Derek
"Midsummer" (Selections: XXXIV-XXXVI). [Agni] (18) 83, p. 5-7.

WEBB, Phyllis
"The Vision Tree" (Selection: "I Daniel"). [PoetryCR] (5:2) Wint 83-84, p. 11.

WAINWRIGHT, Jeffrey
"Heart's Desire" (Excerpt: "Some Propositions and Part of a Narrative"). [Agni] (18) 83, p. 37.

WATTEN, Barret
"One Half" (Excerpts). [ParisR] (24:86) Wint 82, p. 112-113.

If an excerpt is a complete "sub-work", it receives an independent entry, with reference to the larger work in a note. For example:

ANDERSON, Jack
"Magnets" (from The Clouds of That Country). [PoNow] (7:2, #38) 83, p. 23.

Notes about dedications, joint authors, translators, and sources follow the title, enclosed in parentheses. A poem with more than one author is entered under each author. Likewise, a translated poem is entered under each translator, as well as its author(s). Each entry includes the names of all authors and all translators. Multiple authors or translators are indicated by the abbreviation "w.", standing for "with". Translators are indicated by the abbreviation "tr. by", standing for "translated by", and original authors are indicated by the abbreviation "tr. of", standing for "translation of". For example:

AGGESTAM, Rolf
"Old Basho" (tr. by Erland Anderson and Lars Nordström). [NewRena] (16) Spr 83, p. 25.

ANDERSON, Erland
"Old Basho" (tr. of Rolf Aggestam, w. Lars Nordström). [NewRena] (16) Spr 83, p. 25.

NORDSTRÖM, Lars
"Old Basho" (tr. of Rolf Aggestam, w. Erland Anderson). [NewRena] (16) Spr 83, p. 25.

The journal citation includes an abbreviation standing for the journal title, followed by volume and issue numbers, date, and pages. The journal abbreviation is enclosed in square brackets. An alphabetical list of these journal abbreviations is included at the front of the volume, followed by the full journal title, name of editor(s), address, the numbers of the issues indexed for this volume of the *Index*, and subscription information. A separate list of indexed periodicals is arranged by full journal title, with a reference to the abbreviated title. Volume and issue numbers are included within parentheses, e.g., (16:5) stands for volume 16, number 5; (21) refers to issue 21 for a journal which does not use volume numbers. Dates are given using abbreviations for months and seasons. Year of publication is indicated by the last two digits of the year, e.g., 86. Please see the separate list of abbreviations.

Compiling this year's *Index* has been an adventure into the wealth and variety of poetry published in U. S., Puerto Rican and Canadian periodicals as well as the intricacies of bringing this wealth together and organizing it into a consistent index. The world of poetry publication is a dynamic one, with new journals appearing, older journals declining, dying, reviving and thriving. This year saw the loss of eighteen journals and the addition of forty new ones, with a net gain of 22 journals. Both deleted and newly added journals are listed at the front of the volume. Keeping up with these changes is a big job, and we solicit our readers' suggestions as to journals which should be included in future volumes of the *Index*, and also, journals which could be dropped. Editors who would like their journals considered for inclusion in future volumes should send sample issues to:

Rafael Catalá, Editor
Index of American Periodical Verse
P.O. Box 38
New Brunswick, NJ 08903-0038

Although indexing is indispensable for the organization of any literature so that particular works can be found when needed and scholarship and research facilitated, it is a tedious business. I know that we have made mistakes. We solicit your corrections and suggestions, which you may send to me at the above address.

James D. Anderson
Co-Editor

Abbreviations

dir., dirs.	director, directors
ed., eds.	editor, editors
(for.)	price for foreign countries
(ind.)	price for individuals
(inst.)	price for institutions
(lib.)	price for libraries
NS	new series
p.	page, pages
po. ed.	poetry editor
pub.	publisher
(stud.)	price for students
tr. by	translated by
tr. of	translation of
U.	University
w.	with

Months

Ja	January	Jl	July
F	February	Ag	August
Mr	March	S	September
Ap	April	O	October
My	May	N	November
Je	June	D	December

Seasons

Aut	Autumn	Spr	Spring
Wint	Winter	Sum	Summer

Years

83	1983	85	1985
84	1984	86	1986

Periodicals Added

Periodical acronyms are followed by the titles.

Acts: ACTS
AnotherCM: ANOTHER CHICAGO MAGAZINE
BellArk: BELLOWING ARK
BellR: THE BELLINGHAM REVIEW
BostonR: BOSTON REVIEW
Boulevard: BOULEVARD
Caliban: CALIBAN
CentralP: CENTRAL PARK
ColR: COLORADO REVIEW
Contact: CONTACT II
CrescentR: THE CRESCENT REVIEW
Electrum: ELECTRUM MAGAZINE
Event: EVENT: Journal of the Contemporary Arts
Farm: FARMER'S MARKET
FloridaR: THE FLORIDA REVIEW
HayF: HAYDEN'S FERRY REVIEW
HeliconN: HELICON NINE: The Journal of Women's Arts & Letters
HighP: HIGH PLAINS LITERARY REVIEW
Interim: INTERIM
InterPR: INTERNATIONAL POETRY REVIEW
Jacaranda: THE JACARANDA REVIEW
LakeSR: THE LAKE STREET REVIEW
Lips: LIPS
ManhatPR: MANHATTAN POETRY REVIEW
NewAW: NEW AMERICAN WRITING
Notus: NOTUS, New Writing
Pax: PAX: A Journal for Peace through Culture
Pembroke: PEMBROKE MAGAZINE
PennR: THE PENNSYLVANIA REVIEW
Puerto: PUERTO DEL SOL
RedBass: RED BASS
RevICP: REVISTA DEL INSTITUTO DE CULTURA PUERTORRIQUENA
SingHM: SING HEAVENLY MUSE!: Women's Poetry and Prose
Sink: SINK
SinW: SINISTER WISDOM
SlipS: SLIPSTREAM
Sonora: SONORA REVIEW
Translation: TRANSLATION, The Journal of Literary Translation
WillowS: WILLOW SPRINGS
WritersF: WRITERS' FORUM

Periodicals Deleted

The following periodicals have been deleted from the Index because (1) we have been notified that publication has ceased; (2) the periodical no longer publishes poetry; (3) no 1985 or 1986 issues have been received after repeated requests, or (4) it falls outside the scope of the *Index*.

13thM: 13TH MOON, Marilyn Hacker, ed., P.O. Box 309, Cathedral Station, New York, NY 10025. No 1985 or 1986 issues received.

Annex: ANNEX 21, Patrick Worth Gray, ed., UNO-Community Writer's Workshop, University of Nebraska at Omaha, Omaha, NE 68182. No 1984, 1985, or 1986 issues received.

BlueBuf: BLUE BUFFALO, Roberts Hilles, David Maulsby, et al., eds., c/o Dandelion, 922 - 9 Avenue, S.E., Calgary, Alberta, Canada, T2G 0S4. Withdrawn from Index by publisher.

CropD: CROP DUST, Edward C. Lynskey, ed., Route 5, Box 75, Warrenton, VA 22186. No 1984 or 1985 issues published; No 1986 isses received.

FourQt: FOUR QUARTERS, John Christopher Kleis, ed., Richard Lautz, po. ed., La Salle U., 20th & Olney Aves., Philadelphia, PA 19141. No 1985 or 1986 issues received.

Kayak: KAYAK, George Hitchcock, Marjorie Simon, Gary Fisher, eds., 325 Ocean View Ave., Santa Cruz, CA 95062. No longer published.

LittleR: THE LITTLE REVIEW, John McKernan, ed., Little Review Press, Box 205, Marshall U., Huntington, WV 25701. No 1984, 1985 or 1986 issues received.

Metam: METAMORFOSIS, Lauro Flores, Director, Centro de Estudios Chicanos, GN-80, U. of Washington, Seattle, WA 98195. No 1985 or 1986 issues received.

Mund: MUNDUS ARTIUM, Rainer Schulte, ed., U. of Texas at Dallas, Box 830688, MS J031, Richardson, TX 75080-0688. No longer published.

Oink: OINK!, Maxine Chernoff and Paul Hoover, eds., 1446 Jarvis, Chicago, IL 60626. No longer published. Superseded by New American Writing, first issue, 1987. See NewAW.

Paunch: PAUNCH, Arthur Efron, ed., Mili Clark, po. ed., 123 Woodward Ave., Buffalo, NY 14214. No 1985 or 1986 issues received.

Peb: PEBBLE, Greg Kuzma, ed., The Best Cellar Press, Dept. of English, U. of Nebraska, Lincoln, NE 68588. No 1985 or 1986 issues received.

Playb: PLAYBOY, Hugh M. Hefner, ed./pub., 919 N. Michigan Ave., Chicago, IL 60611. No longer publishes poetry.

PoetryR: POETRY REVIEW, A magazine of poetry, translations of poetry, and essays, Poetry Society of America, Jerome Mazzaro, ed., 15 Gramercy Park, New York, NY 10003. No longer published.

SinN: SIN NOMBRE, Nilita Vientós Gastón, Dir., Box 4391, San Juan, PR 00905-4391. No longer published.

Stepp: STEPPINGSTONE, James B. Gwyne, ed., Box 1856, Harlem, NY 10027. No 1985 or 1986 issues received.

Swallow: SWALLOW'S TALE, Joe Taylor, ed., P.O. Box 4328, Tallahassee, FL 32315-4328. No longer published.

Veloc: VELOCITIES, Andrew Joron, ed., 1509 Le Roy Ave., Berkeley, CA 94708. No 1985 or 1986 issues received.

Periodicals Indexed

Arranged by acronym, with names of editors, addresses, issues indexed, and subscription information. New titles added to the Index in 1986 are marked with an asterisk (*).

Abraxas: ABRAXAS, Ingrid Swanberg, ed., 2518 Gregory St., Madison, WI 53711. Issues indexed: (34). Subscriptions: $12/4 issues; Single issues: $3..

*Acts: ACTS: A Journal of New Writing, David Levi Strauss, ed., 514 Guerrero St., San Franisco, CA 94110. Issues indexed: (5). Subscriptions: $12/yr. (2 issues, ind.), $16/yr. (2 issues, inst. & for.); $20/2 yrs. (4 issues, ind.), $28/2 yrs. (4 issues, inst. & for.); Single issues: $5-$6.

Agni: THE AGNI REVIEW, Mary Morris, Sharon Dunn, eds., P.O. Box 660, Amherst, MA 01004. Issues indexed: (23). Subscriptions: $21/3 yrs., $15/2 yrs., $8/yr., plus $1/yr. (for.); Single issues: $5.

Amelia: AMELIA, Frederick A. Raborg, Jr., ed., 329 "E" St., Bakersfield, CA 93304. Issues indexed: (3:1-4). Subscriptions: US, Canada, Mexico, $40/3 yrs., $28/2 yrs., $15/yr.; $75/3 yrs., $52/2 yrs., $27/yr. (for. air mail); Single issues: $4.75, $7 (for. air mail).

Americas: THE AMERICAS REVIEW, A Review of Hispanic Literature and Art of the USA (formerly Revista Chicano-Requeña), Julián Olivares, ed., U. of Houston, University Park, Houston, TX 77004. Issues indexed: (14:1-2). Subscriptions: $15/yr. (ind.), $20/yr. (inst.); Single issues: $5.

AmerPoR: THE AMERICAN POETRY REVIEW, David Bonanno, Stephen Berg, Arthur Vogelsang, eds., World Poetry, Inc., Temple U Center City, 1616 Walnut St., Room 405, Philadelphia, PA 19103. Issues indexed: (15:1-6). Subscriptions: $25/3 yrs., $30/3 yrs. (for.), $17/2 yrs., $21/2 yrs. (for.), $9.50/yr., $11.50/yr. (for.); classroom rate $6/yr. per student; Single issues: $1.95.

AmerS: THE AMERICAN SCHOLAR, Joseph Epstein, ed., United Chapters of Phi Beta Kappa, 1811 Q St. NW, Washington, DC 20009. Issues indexed: (55:1-4). Subscriptions: $39/3 yrs., $16/yr. plus $3/yr. (for.); Single issues: $4.75.

AmerV: THE AMERICAN VOICE, Frederick Smock, ed., The Kentucky Foundation for Women, Inc., Heyburn Bldg., Suite 1215, Broadway at 4th Ave., Lousiville, KY 40202. Issues indexed: (2-5). Subscriptions: $12/yr. Single issues: $4.

*AnotherCM: ANOTHER CHICAGO MAGAZINE, Lee Webster & Barry Silesky, eds., Box 11223, Chicago, IL 60611. Issues indexed: (15-16). Subscriptions: $9/yr., $40/5 yrs., $150/lifetime; Single issues: $5.

Antaeus: ANTAEUS, Daniel Halpern, ed., The Ecco Press, 18 W. 30th St., New York, NY 10001. Issues indexed: (56-57). Subscriptions: $20/4 issues, $37/8 issues, $53/12 issues; plus $3 per issue (for., surface mail), $6 per issue (for. air mail); Single issues: $10.

AntigR: THE ANTIGONISH REVIEW, George Sanderson, ed., St. Francis Xavier U., Antigonish, Nova Scotia B2G 1C0 Canada. Issues indexed: (64-66/67). Subscriptions: $14/4 issues; Single issues: $4.

AntR: THE ANTIOCH REVIEW, Robert S. Fogarty, ed., David St. John, po. ed., P.O. Box 148, Yellow Springs, OH 45387. Issues indexed: (44:1-4). Subscriptions: $18/yr., $34/2 yrs., $48/3 yrs. (ind.); $25/yr., $48/2 yrs., $69/3 yrs. (inst.); plus $5/yr. (for.); Single issues: $4.75.

Periodicals Indexed

Areito: AREITO, Max Azicri, Emilio Bejel, et al., eds., GPO Box 2174, New York, NY 10116. Issues indexed: No 1986 issues received. Subscriptions: $18/yr. (inst.), $12/yr. (ind)., $20/yr. (for.); Single issues: $3; Back issues: $3.50.

ArizQ: ARIZONA QUARTERLY, Albert Frank Gegenheimer, ed., U. of Arizona, Tucson, AZ 85721. Issues indexed: (42:1-4). Subscriptions: $10/3 yrs., $5/yr.; Single issues: $1.50.

Ascent: ASCENT, Daniel Curley, et al., eds., English Dept., U. of Illinois, 608 South Wright St., Urbana, IL 61801. Issues indexed: (11:2-3, 12:1). Subscriptions: $3/yr. (3 issues), $4.50/yr. (for.); Single issues: $1 (bookstore), $1.50 (mail).

Atlantic: THE ATLANTIC, William Whitworth, ed., Peter Davison, po. ed., 8 Arlington St., Boston, MA 02116. Issues indexed: (257:1-6, 258:1-6). Subscriptions: $29.95/3 yrs., $15.95/2 yrs., $9.95/yr., plus $3/yr. (Canada), $5/yr. (for.); Single issues: $2.

BallSUF: BALL STATE UNIVERSITY FORUM, Bruce W. Hozeski, Frances Mayhew Rippy, eds., Darlene Mathis-Eddy, po. ed., Ball State U., Muncie, IN 47306. Issues indexed: (26:3-4, 27:1-4). Subscriptions: (vol. 26) $10/yr., Single issues: $3.; (vol. 27) $15/yr., Single issues: $4.50; (vol. 28-) $20/yr., Single issues: $6.

*BellArk: BELLOWING ARK, A Literary Tabloid, Robert R. Ward, ed., P.O. Box 45637, Seattle, WA 98145. Issues indexed: (2:1-6). Subscriptions: $12/yr.; Single issues: $2.

*BellR: THE BELLINGHAM REVIEW, Randy Jay Landon, ed., 932 Monitor Avenue, Wenatchee, WA 98801. Issues indexed: (9:1-2). Subscriptions: $4/yr. (2 issues), $7.50/2 yrs., $10.50/3 yrs.; Single issues: $2.

BelPoJ: THE BELOIT POETRY JOURNAL, Marion K. Stocking, ed., RFD 2, Box 154, Ellsworth, ME 04605. Issues indexed: (36:3-4, 37:1-2). Subscriptions: $17/3 yrs., $6/yr.; Single issues: $1.50.

BilingR: THE BILINGUAL REVIEW/LA REVISTA BILINGUE, Gary D. Keller, ed., Hispanic Research Center, Arizona State U., Tempe, AZ 85287. Issues indexed: (12:1/2). Subscriptions: $15/yr., $28/2 yrs., $39/3 yrs. (ind.); $24/yr. (inst.).

BlackALF: BLACK AMERICAN LITERATURE FORUM, Joe Weixlmann, ed., Sterling Plumpp, po. ed., Parsons Hall 237, Indiana State U., Terre Haute, IN 47809. Issues indexed: (20:1-4). Subscriptions: $15/yr. (ind.), $21/yr. (inst.), $18/yr. (for.), $24 (for. inst.). Single issues: $6.

BlackWR: BLACK WARRIOR REVIEW, Janet McAdams, ed., Mary Anne Ellis, po. ed., U. of Alabama, P.O. Box 2936, Tuscaloosa, AL 35487-2936. Issues indexed: (12:2, 13:1). Subscriptions: $6.50/yr. (ind.), $9/yr. (inst.); Single issues: $3.50 plus $.75 postage.

BlueBldgs: BLUE BUILDINGS: An International Magazine of Poetry and Translations, Tom Urban, Ruth Doty et al., eds., Dept. of English, Drake U., Des Moines, IA 50311. Issues indexed: No 1986 issues received. Subscriptions: $4/2 issues; Single issues: $2.

Blueline: BLUELINE, Alice Gilborn, ed. & publisher; Jane Z. Carroll & Gary McLouth, po. eds. Blue Mountain Lake, NY 12812. Issues indexed: (7:2, 8:1). Subscriptions: $5/yr. (U.S. & Canada), $6/yr. (for.); Back issues: $2.75; The Chauncy Press / Blue Line, P.O. Box 830, Saranac Lake, NY 12983.

Bogg: BOGG, John Elsberg, ed., 422 N. Cleveland St., Arlington, VA 22201; George Cairncross, ed., 31 Belle Vue St., Filey, N. Yorkshire YO14 9HU, UK. Issues indexed: (55-56). Subscriptions: $8/3 issues; Single issues: $3.

*BostonR: BOSTON REVIEW, Mark Silk, ed., 33 Harrison Ave., Boston, MA 02111. Issues indexed: (11:1-6). Subscriptions: $9/yr., $15/2 yrs. (ind.); $10.50/yr., $17/2 yrs. (inst.); plus $6/yr. (for.); Single issues: $3.

*Boulevard: BOULEVARD, David Brezovic, executive ed., Richard Burgin, ed., Opojaz, Inc. Suite 9R, 4 Washington Square Village, New York, NY 10012. Issues indexed: (1:1-3). Subscriptions: $7/yr., $11/2 yrs., $15/3 yrs.; Single issues: $4-$4.50.

Periodicals Indexed

Bound: BOUNDARY 2, William V. Spanos, ed., Dept. of English, State U. of New York, Binghamton, NY 13901. Issues indexed: No 1986 issues received. Subscriptions: $25/yr. (inst.), $15/yr. (ind.), $13/yr (stud.), plus $2 (for.); Single issues: $8, Double issues: $10.

*Caliban: CALIBAN, Lawrence R. Smith, ed., P.O. Box 4321, Ann Arbor, MI 48106. Issues indexed: (1). Subscriptions: $8/yr. (ind.), $15/yr. (inst.); Single issues: $5.

Callaloo: CALLALOO: A Tri-Annual Journal of Afro-American and African Arts and Letters, Charles H. Rowell, ed., Dept. of English, Wilson Hall, U. of Virginia, Charlottesville, VA 22903. Issues indexed: (8:3, 9:1-3; #25-28). Subscriptions: $15/yr. (ind.), $30/yr. (inst.); plus $5 (Canada, Mexico); plus $12 (outside North America); The Johns Hopkins University Press, Journals Publishing Division, 701 W. 40th St., Suite 275, Baltimore, MD 21211.

CalQ: CALIFORNIA QUARTERLY, Elliot L. Gilbert, ed., Carlos Rodriguez, po. ed., 100 Sproul Hall, U. of California, Davis, CA 95616. Issues indexed: (27/29). Subscriptions: $10/yr. (4 issues); Single issues: $2.50.

Calyx: CALYX: A Journal of Art and Literature by Women, Margarita Donnelly, Managing ed., P.O. Box B, Corvallis, OR 97339-0539. Issues indexed: (9:2/3, 10:1). Subscriptions: $18/yr., $32/2 yrs., $42/3 yrs., plus $4/yr. (for.), $9/yr. (for. airmail); $22.50/yr. (inst.); $15/yr. (low income individual); Single issue: $6.50-$12.

CanLit: CANADIAN LITERATURE, W. H. New, ed., U. of British Columbia, 2029 West Mall, Vancouver, B.C. V6T 1W5 Canada. Issues indexed: (108-111). Subscriptions: $20/yr. (ind.), $25/yr. (inst.) plus $5/yr. outside Canada; Single issues: $7.50.

CapeR: THE CAPE ROCK, Harvey Hecht, et al ., eds., Southeast Missouri State U., Cape Girardeau, MO 63701. Issues indexed: (21:1-2). Subscriptions: $3/yr.; Single issues: $2.

CapilR: THE CAPILANO REVIEW, Dorothy Jantzen, ed., Sharon Thesen, po. ed., Capilano College, 2055 Purcell Way, North Vancouver, B.C. V7J 3H5 Canada. Issues indexed: (38-41). Subscriptions: $22/8 issues (ind.), $12/4 issues (ind.), $14/4 issues (lib.); plus $1/4 issues (for.); Single issues: $5.

CarolQ: CAROLINA QUARTERLY, Emily Stockard, ed., Margaret Bockting po. ed., Greenlaw Hall 066-A, U. of North Carolina, Chapel Hill, NC 27514. Issues indexed: (38:2-3, 39:1). Subscriptions: $12/yr. (inst.), $10/yr. (ind.), $11/yr. (for.); Single issues: $4, Back issues: $4, plus $1 postage.

CentR: THE CENTENNIAL REVIEW, Linda Wagner-Martin, ed., 110 Morrill Hall, Michigan State U., East Lansing, MI 48824-1036. Issues indexed: (30:1-4). Subscriptions: $10/2 yrs., $6/yr., plus $3/yr. (for.); Single issues: $2.

*CentralP: CENTRAL PARK, Stephen-Paul Martin, Richard Royal, Eve Ensler, eds., Box 1446, New York, NY 10023. Issues indexed: (9-10). Subscriptions: $9/yr. (ind.), $10/yr. (inst.); Single issues: $5 (ind), $5.50 (inst).

CharR: THE CHARITON REVIEW, Jim Barnes, ed., Division of Language and Literature, Northeast Missouri State U., Kirksville, MO 63501. Issues indexed: (12:1-2). Subscriptions: $7/4 issues; Single issues: $2.

Chelsea: CHELSEA, Sonia Raiziss, ed., P.O. Box 5880, Grand Central Station, New York, NY 10163. Issues indexed: (45). Subscriptions: $9/2 issues or double issue, $10 (for.); Single issues: $5, $5.50 (for.).

ChiR: CHICAGO REVIEW, Robert Sitko, ed., Paul Baker & Michael Donaghy, po. eds., U. of Chicago, Faculty Exchange, Box C, Chicago, IL 60637. Issues indexed: (35:3). Subscriptions: $54/3 yrs., $36/2 yrs., $18/yr., $14/yr. (ind.), plus $4/yr. (for.); Single issues: $4.50.

ChrC: THE CHRISTIAN CENTURY, James M. Wall, ed., 407 S. Dearborn St., Chicago, IL 60605. Issues indexed: (103:1-40). Subscriptions: $28/yr.; Single issues: $1.25.

4

CimR: CIMARRON REVIEW, Neil J. Hackett, ed., Michael J. Bugeja, po. ed., 208 Life Sciences East, Oklahoma State U., Stillwater, OK 74078-0273. Issues indexed: (74-77). Subscriptions: $10/yr.; Single issues: $2.50.

ClockR: CLOCKWATCH REVIEW, James Plath, ed., 737 Penbrook Way, Hartland, WI 53029. Issues indexed: (3:1-2). Subscriptions: $6/yr.; Single issues: $3.

ColEng: COLLEGE ENGLISH, National Council of Teachers of English, James C. Raymond, ed., James Tate, po. ed., P.O. Drawer AL, Tuscaloosa, AL 35487. Issues indexed: (48:1-8). Subscriptions: $35/yr. (inst.), $30/yr. (ind.), plus $4/yr. (for.); Single issues: $4; NCTE, 1111 Kenyon Rd., Urbana, IL 61801.

*ColR: COLORADO REVIEW, Bill Tremblay, po. ed., English Dept., Colorado State U., 360 Liberal Arts, Fort Collins, CO 80523. Issues indexed: (NS 13:1-2). Subscriptions: $5/yr; Single issues: $3; Back issues: $1.50.

Comm: COMMONWEAL, Peter Steinfels, ed., Rosemary Deen, po. ed., 15 Dutch St., New York, NY 10038. Issues indexed: (113:1-22). Subscriptions: $49/2 yrs., $53/2 yrs. (Canada), $59/2 yrs. (for.), $28/yr., $30/yr. (Canada), $33/yr. (for.); Single issues: $1.50.

ConcPo: CONCERNING POETRY, Diane Ostrom, Ellwood Johnson, eds., Robert Huff, po. ed., Dept. of English, Western Washington U., Bellingham, WA 98225. Issues indexed: (19). Subscriptions: $8/yr. (USA, Canada), $10/yr. (for.).

Cond: CONDITIONS, Cheryl Clarke, Dorothy Randall Gray, Randye Lordon, Annette Peláez, Sabrina, eds., P.O. Box 56, Van Brunt Station, Brooklyn, NY 11215. Issues indexed: (13). Subscriptions: $28/3 issues (inst.), $18/3 issues (ind), $12/3 issues "hardship" rate, plus $2.50 (for.); free to women in prisons and mental institutions; Single issues: $7 (ind.), $10 (inst.), plus $.50 (for.).

Confr: CONFRONTATION, Martin Tucker, ed., English Dept., C. W. Post College, Long Island U., Greenvale, NY 11548. Issues indexed: (32, 33/34). Subscriptions: $20/3 yrs., $15/2 yrs., $8/yr.; Single issues: $5-6.

Conjunc: CONJUNCTIONS, Bradford Morrow, ed., 33 West 9th St., New York, NY 10011. Issues indexed: (9). Subscriptions: $16/yr. (2 issues), $30/2 yrs.; $20/yr., $40/2 yrs. (inst., for.); $45/yr., $85/ 2 yrs. (cloth binding); Single issues: $8.95.

ConnPR: THE CONNECTICUT POETRY REVIEW, J. Clair White, James Wm. Chichetto, eds., P.O. Box 3783, Amity Station, New Haven, CT 06525. Issues indexed: (4:1, 5:1). Single issues: $3 (including postage).

*Contact: CONTACT II, Maurice Kenny, J. G. Gosciak, eds., P.O. Box 451, Bowling Green, New York, NY 10004. Issues indexed: (7:38/39/40, 8:41/42/43). Subscriptions: $8/yr. (ind.); $14/yr. (inst.); Single issues: $6.

CrabCR: CRAB CREEK REVIEW, Linda Clifton, ed., 806 N. 42nd, Seattle WA 98103. Issues indexed: (3:2-3, 4:1). Subscriptions: $15/2 yrs., $8/yr.; Single issues: $3.

Crazy: CRAZYHORSE, Russell Murphy, managing ed., Ralph Burns, po. ed., Dept. of English, U. of Arkansas, Little Rock, AR 72204. Issues indexed: (30-31). Subscriptions: $8/yr., $15/2 yrs., $22/3 yrs. Single issues: $4.

CreamCR: CREAM CITY REVIEW, Peter Blewett, ed., Marcia Hesselman, po. ed., English Dept., P.O. Box 413, U. of Wisconsin-Milwaukee, 53201. Issues indexed: (11:1). Single issues: $4.50; Double issues: $7.50.

*CrescentR: THE CRESCENT REVIEW, Shirley Anders, po. ed., P.O. Box 15065, Winston-Salem, NC 27113. Issues indexed: (4:1-2). Subscriptions: $7.50/yr. (2 issues); Single issues: $4.

CrossC: CROSS-CANADA WRITERS' QUARTERLY, Ted Plantos, ed., George Swede, po. ed., Box 277, Station F, Toronto, Ontario M4Y 2L7 Canada. Issues indexed: (8:1-3/4). Subscriptions: $14/yr. (ind.), $16/yr. (inst.), $18/yr (for.); Single issues: $3.95.

Periodicals Indexed

CrossCur: CROSSCURRENTS, Linda Brown Michelson, ed., Elizabeth Bartlett, po. ed., 2200 Glastonbury Road, Westlake Village, CA 91361. Issues indexed: (5:4/6:1, 6:2-3). Subscriptions: $15/yr., $22.50/2 yrs.; Single issues: $5.

CumbPR: CUMBERLAND POETRY REVIEW, The Editors, Poetics, Inc., P.O. Box 120128, Acklen Station, Nashville, TN 37212. Issues indexed: (5:2, 6:1). Subscriptions: $12/yr, $22/2 yrs. (ind.); $15/yr., $27/2 yrs. (inst.); $21/yr., $33/2 yrs. (for.); Single issue: $6.

CutB: CUTBANK, Pamela Uschuk, ed., Dept. of English, U. of Montana, Missoula, MT 59812. Issues indexed: (25-26). Subscriptions: $13/2 yrs., $7/yr.; Single issues: $3.75.

Dandel: DANDELION, Robert Hilles & John McDermid, eds., John McDermid & Claire Harris, po. eds., Alexandra Centre, 922 - 9th Ave., S.E., Calgary, Alberta T2G 0S4 Canada. Issues indexed: (13:1). Subscriptions: $15/2 yrs., $8/yr., $12/yr. (inst.); Single issues: $4.

DekalbLAJ: THE DEKALB LITERARY ARTS JOURNAL, Frances S. Ellis, ed., DeKalb College, 555 N. Indian Creek Dr., Clarkston, GA 30021. Issues indexed: (19:1-3/4). Subscriptions: $10/volume, $12/volume (for.)

DenQ: DENVER QUARTERLY, David Milofsky, ed., U. of Denver, Denver, CO 80208. Issues indexed: (20:3, 20:4/21:1). Subscriptions: $28/2 yrs., $15/yr., $18/yr. (inst.), plus $1/yr. (for.); Single issues: $5.

Descant: DESCANT, Karen Mulhallen, ed., P.O. Box 314, Station P, Toronto M5S 2S8, Ontario, Canada. Issues indexed: (17:2-17:41, issues 53-55). Subscriptions: $18/yr (ind.), $26/yr. (inst.); Single issues: $8.

*Electrum: ELECTRUM MAGAZINE, Roger Suva, ed., 2222 Silk Tree Drive, Tustin, CA 92680-7129. Issues indexed: (38). Subscriptions: $10/4 issues, $17/8 issues, plus $5 (for.); Single issues: $3.

EngJ: ENGLISH JOURNAL, National Council of Teachers of English, Alleen Pace Nilsen, Ken Donelson, eds., College of Education, Arizona State U., Tempe, AZ 85287. Issues indexed: (75:1-8). Subscriptions: $40/yr. (inst.), $35/yr. (ind.), plus $4/yr. (for.); Single issues: $4; NCTE, 1111 Kenyon Rd., Urbana, IL 61801.

Epoch: EPOCH, C. S. Giscombe, ed., 251 Goldwin Smith Hall, Cornell U., Ithaca, NY 14853-3201. Issues indexed: (35:1-3). Subscriptions: $9.50/yr.; Single issues: $3.50.

*Event: EVENT: Journal of the Contemporary Arts, Dale Zieroth, ed., Douglas College, P.O. Box 2503, New Westminster, B.C., V3L 5B2 Canada. Issues indexed: (15:1-2). Subscriptions: $8/yr., $15/2 yrs.; $17/2 yrs. (lib.); Single issue: $5.

EvergR: EVERGREEN REVIEW, Barney Rosset & Fred Jordan, eds., c/o Grove Press, 196 W. Houston St., New York, NY 10014; Issues indexed: "Suspended until 1987"; Single issues: $5.95.

*Farm: FARMER'S MARKET, Jean C. Lee, John E. Hughes, Gail Nichols, eds., Midwest Farmer's Market, Inc., P.O. Box 1272, Galesburg, IL 61402. Issues indexed: (3:1-2). Subscriptions: $7/yr. (2 issues).

Field: FIELD: Contemporary Poetry and Poetics, Stuart Friebert, David Young, eds., Rice Hall, Oberlin College, Oberlin, OH 44074. Issues indexed: (33-35). Subscriptions: $14/2 yrs., $8/yr.; Single issues: $4.; Back issues: $10.

*FloridaR: THE FLORIDA REVIEW, Pat Rushin, ed., Judith Hemschemeyer, po. ed., Dept. of English, U. of Central Florida, Orlando, FL 32816. Issues indexed: (14:1-2). Subscriptions: $6/yr., $10/2 yrs.; Single issues: $3.50.

Gargoyle: GARGOYLE MAGAZINE, Richard Peabody, Jr., ed./pub., Gretchen Johnsen, po. ed., Paycock Press, P.O. Box 3567, Washington, DC 20007. Issues indexed: Nos. 28 & 29 consist of cassette sound recordings and were not indexed. Subscriptions: $10/yr., 2 issues (ind.), $12/yr., 2 issues (inst.). Single issues: $5.95-7.95.

Periodicals Indexed

GeoR: GEORGIA REVIEW, Stanley W. Lindberg, ed., U. of Georgia, Athens, GA 30602. Issues indexed: (40:1-4). Subscriptions: $15/2 yrs., $9/yr., plus $3/yr. (for.); Single issues: $4.

Germ: GERMINATION, Allan Cooper, ed. & pub., Leigh Faulkner, Assoc. ed., 428 Yale Ave., Riverview, New Brunswick E1B 2B5, Canada. Issues indexed: (10:1) Subscriptions: $6/2 issues (ind.), $8/2 issues (inst.); Single issues: $3.50.

GrahamHR: GRAHAM HOUSE REVIEW, Peter Balakian & Bruce Smith, eds., Colgate U. Press, Box 5000, Colgate U., Hamilton, NY 13346; Issues indexed: No 1986 issues published; Subscriptions: $17/2 yrs; Single issues: $4.50.

Grain: GRAIN, Saskatchewan Writers Guild, Brenda Riches, ed., Garry Radison, po. ed., Box 1154, Regina, Saskatchewan S4P 3B4 Canada. Issues indexed: (14:1-4). Subscriptions: $20/2 yrs., $12/yr.; Single issues: $4.

GrandS: GRAND STREET, Ben Sonnenberg, ed., 50 Riverside Dr., New York, NY 10024. Issues indexed: (5:2-4, 6:1). Subscriptions: $20/yr. (ind.), $24/yr. (for.); $24/yr. (inst.), $28/yr. (for. inst.); Single issues: $5; Back issues, $6..

GreenfR: GREENFIELD REVIEW, Joseph Bruchac III, ed., R.D. 1, Box 80, Greenfield Center, NY 12833. Issues indexed: (13:3/4). Subscriptions: $10/2 double issues; $12 (lib.); Single issues: $5.

GWR: THE G. W. REVIEW, The Editor, Box 20, Marvin Center, The George Washington U., 800 21st St., N.W., Washington, DC 20052 (Editor changes annually). Issues indexed: (6:2). Subscriptions: $6/yr.; Single copies: $1.50.

HangL: HANGING LOOSE, Robert Hershon, Dick Lourie, Mark Pawlak, Ron Schreiber, eds., 231 Wyckoff St., Brooklyn, NY 11217. Issues indexed: (49). Subscriptions: $25/9 issues, $17/6 issues, $9/3 issues; Single issues: $3.50.

Harp: HARPER'S MAGAZINE, Lewis H. Lapham, ed., 666 Broadway, New York, NY 10012. Issues indexed: (272:1628-1633, 273:1634-1639). Subscriptions: $18/yr., plus $2/yr. (USA possessions, Canada), plus $3/yr. (for.); Single issues: $2; P.O. Box 1937, Marion, OH 43305.

HarvardA: THE HARVARD ADVOCATE, Catherine Herridge, Managing ed., Drea Maier, po. ed., 21 South St., Cambridge, MA 02138. Issues indexed: (119:3-4, 120:1); 119:3, March 1986, is numbered 120:3 in error. Subscriptions: $15/yr. (ind.), $17/yr. (inst.), $20/yr. (for.).

HawaiiR: HAWAII REVIEW, Zdenek Kluzak, ed., Dean Honma, po. ed., U. of Hawaii at Manoa, Dept. of English, 1733 Donaghho Rd., Honolulu, HI 06822. Issues indexed: Spring 1986 (19) issue received too late for indexing; will be included in 1987 volume. Subscriptions: $6/yr.; Single issue: $3.

*HayF: HAYDEN'S FERRY REVIEW, John Graves Morris, Paul Morris, po. eds., Student Publications, Matthews Center, Arizona State U., Tempe, AZ 85287. Issues indexed: (1). Subscriptions: $4/yr. (1 issue).

*HeliconN: HELICON NINE: The Journal of Women's Arts & Letters, Gloria Vando Hickok, ed., P.O. Box 22412, Kansas City, MO 64113. Issues indexed: (14/15, 16). Subscriptions: $18/yr., plus $1/issue (for.); Single issues: $8-10.

*HighP: HIGH PLAINS LITERARY REVIEW, Robert O. Greer, Jr., ed., Joy Harjo, po. ed., 180 Adams St., Suite 250, Denver, CO 80206. Issues indexed: (1:1). Subscriptions: $20/yr., $38/2 yrs., plus $5/yr. (for.); Single issues: $7.

HiramPoR: HIRAM POETRY REVIEW, English Dept., Hiram College, Hale Chatfield & Carol Donley, eds., P.O. Box 162, Hiram, OH 44234. Issues indexed: (40-41). Subscriptions: $4/yr.; Single issues: $2.

HolCrit: THE HOLLINS CRITIC, John Rees Moore, ed., Hollins College, VA 24020. Issues indexed: (23:1-5). Subscriptions: $5/yr., $9/2 yrs., $13/3 yrs.; $6.50/yr., $10.50/2 yrs.,

7

$14.50/3 yrs. (for.).

Hudson: THE HUDSON REVIEW, Paula Deitz, Frederick Morgan, eds., 684 Park Ave., New York, NY 10021. Issues indexed: (38:4, 39:1-3). Subscriptions: $18/yr., $34/2 yrs., $50/3 yrs., plus $3/yr. (for.); Single issues: $5.

Imagine: IMAGINE: International Chicano Poetry Journal, Tino Villanueva, ed., 89 Mass. Ave., Suite 270, Boston, MA 02115. Issues indexed: No 1986 issues received. Subscriptions: $8/yr., $14/2 yrs. (ind.); $12/yr., $18/2 yrs. (inst.); plus $1/yr. (for.); Single issues: $5.50-$8.

IndR: INDIANA REVIEW, Pamela Wampler, ed., Christopher Cokinos, Elizabeth Dodd, James Harmes, po. eds., 316 N. Jordan Ave., Bloomington, IN 47405. Issues indexed: (9:1-3). Subscriptions: $10/3 issues, $12/3 issues (inst.); $18/6 issues (ind.), $20/6 issues (inst.); Single issues: $4.

*Interim: INTERIM, A. Wilber Stevens, ed., Dept. of English, U. of Nevada, Las Vegas, NV 89154. Issues indexed: (5:1-2). Subscriptions: $5/yr. (ind.), $8/yr. (inst.), $10/yr. (for.); Single issues: $3.

*InterPR: INTERNATIONAL POETRY REVIEW, Evalyn P. Gill, Raymond Tyner, eds., Box 2047, Greensboro, NC 27402. Issues indexed: (12:1-2). Subscriptions: $6/yr.; Single issues: $3.

Inti: INTI, Revista de Literatura Hispanica, Roger B. Carmosino, ed., Dept. of Modern Languages, Providence College, Providence, RI 02918. Issues indexed: (21). Subscriptions: $20/yr. (ind.), $25/yr. (for.); $25/yr. (inst.), $30/yr. (for. inst.); Single issues: $12 (ind.), $14 (for.), $18 (special issues).

Iowa: IOWA REVIEW, David Hamilton, ed., 308 EPB, U. of Iowa, Iowa City, IA 52242. Issues indexed: (16:1-3). Subscriptions: $20/yr. (inst.), $15/yr. (ind.), plus $3/yr. (for.); Single issues: $6.95.

*Jacaranda: THE JACARANDA REVIEW, Laurence Roth, ed., Reed Wilson, Gregory Castle, po. eds., Dept. of English, U. of California, Los Angeles, 90024. Issues indexed: (2:1). Subscriptions: $5/yr. (2 issues), $9/2 yrs. (4 issues) (ind.); $8/yr. (inst.).

JamesWR: THE JAMES WHITE REVIEW, A Gay Men's Literary Quarterly, Phil Willkie, David Lindahl, Greg Baysans, eds., P.O. Box 3356, Traffic Station, Minneapolis, MN 55403. Issues indexed: (3:2-4, 4:1). Subscriptions: $8/yr., $14/2 yrs.; $10/yr. (Canada); $13/yr. (other for.); $10/yr.(inst.); Single issues: $2.

JINJPo: THE JOURNAL OF NEW JERSEY POETS, Marjorie Keyishian, Managing ed., English Dept., Fairleigh Dickinson U., 285 Madison Ave., Madison, NJ 07940. Issues indexed: (9:1). Subscriptions: $3/2 issues; Single issues: $1.50.

Kaleid: KALEIDOSCOPE, International Magazine of Literature, Fine Arts, and Disability; Darshan Perusek, ed., Chris Hewitt (228 W. 71 St., Apt. F, New York, NY 10023), po. ed., United Cerebral Palsy and Services for the Handicapped, 326 Locust St., Akron, OH 44302. Issues indexed: (12-13); No. 13 (Fall-Sum 86) not numbered. Subscriptions: $8/yr. (2 issues); $9/yr. (for.); Single issues: $4; $5 (for.); Back issues: $3; $4 (for.).

KanQ: KANSAS QUARTERLY, Harold Schneider, et al., eds., Dept. of English, Denison Hall, Kansas State U., Manhattan, KS 66506. Issues indexed: (18:1/2-4). Subscriptions: $27/2 yrs., $15/yr. (USA, Canada, Latin America); $29/2 yrs., $16/yr. (other countries); Single issues: $4.

KenR: KENYON REVIEW, Philip D. Church, Galbraith M. Crump, eds., Kenyon College, Gambier, OH 43022. Issues indexed: (NS 7:1-4, 8:1-4). Subscriptions: Kenyon Review, P.O. Box 1308 L, Fort Lee, NJ 07024; $15/yr., $28/2 yrs., $39/3 yrs. (ind.); $18/yr. (inst.); +$5 (for.); Single issues: $6.50; Back issues: $3.

*LakeSR: THE LAKE STREET REVIEW, Kevin FitzPatrick, ed., Box 7188, Powderhorn Station, Minneapolis, MN 55407. Issues indexed: (20). Subscriptions: $4/2 yrs. (2 issues); Single issues: $2.

Periodicals Indexed

LaurelR: LAUREL REVIEW, Mark DeFoe, ed., David McAleavey, et al. , po. eds., Dept. of English, West Virginia Wesleyan College, Buckhannon, WV 26201. Issues indexed: No 1986 issues received. Subscriptions: $8/yr. (2 issues); Single issues: $4.

LetFem: LETRAS FEMENINAS, Asociación de Literatura Femenina Hispánica, Dr. Adelaida López de Martínez, Directora., Dept. of Modern Languages, Texas A & M U., College Station, TX 77843-4238. Issues indexed: (10:1-2, 12:1/2) -- 11:1/2 was indexed in the 1985 index. Membership/Subscription: $20/yr; $25/yr. (lib.).

LindLM: LINDEN LANE MAGAZINE, Belkis Cuza Male, ed., P.O. Box 2384, Princeton, NJ 08543-2384. Issues indexed: (5:1-4). Subscriptions: $10/yr. (ind.), $16/yr. (inst.), $20/yr. (for.); Single issues: $2.

*Lips: LIPS, Laura Boss, ed., P.O. Box 1345, Montclair, NJ 07042. Issues indexed: (12). Subscriptions: $9/yr. (3 issues), $12/yr. (inst).; Single issues: $3, $4 (inst.).

LitR: THE LITERARY REVIEW, Walter Cummins, ed., Fairleigh Dickinson U., 285 Madison Ave., Madison, NJ 07940. Issues indexed: (29:2-4, 30:1). Subscriptions: $12/yr., $15/yr. (for.); $22/2 yrs., $28/2 yrs. (for.); Single issues: $4.50, $5.50 (for.).

LittleBR: THE LITTLE BALKANS REVIEW, Gene DeGruson, po. ed., The Little Balkans Press, Inc., 601 Grandview Heights Terr., Pittsburg, KS 66762. Issues indexed: No 1986 issues received. Subscriptions: $10/yr.; Single issues: $3.50.

LittleM: THE LITTLE MAGAZINE, Kathryn Cramer, et al ., eds, Dragon Press, P.O. Box 78, Pleasantville, NY 10570. Issues Indexed: (15:1-2); the 1985 index lists 15:1, but it is indexed here, not in the 1985 index. Subscriptions: $16/4 issues; Single issues: $4.95.

Mairena: MAIRENA: Revista de Crítica y Poesía, Manuel de la Puebla, director, Himalaya 257, Urbanización Monterrey, Río Piedras, PR 00926. Issues indexed: (8:21-22). Subscriptions: $6/yr., $10/yr. (inst.), $10/yr. (for.), $15/yr. (for. inst.).

MalR: THE MALAHAT REVIEW, Constance Rooke, ed., P.O. Box 1700, Victoria, B. C., Canada V8W 2Y2. Issues indexed: (73-77). Subscriptions: $40/3 yrs., $15/yr. (USA, Canada), $50/3 yrs., $20/yr. (other countries), $10/yr. (stud.); Single issues: $7 (USA, Canada), $8 (other countries).

*ManhatPR: MANHATTAN POETRY REVIEW, Elaine Reiman-Fenton, ed., 11-D, 36 Sutton Place South, New York, NY 10022. Issues indexed: (6-8). Subscriptions: $10/yr.

ManhatR: THE MANHATTAN REVIEW, Philip Fried, ed., 304 Third Ave., Apt. 4A, New York, NY 10010. Issues indexed: (4:1). Subscriptions: $8/2 issues (ind.), $12/2 issues (inst.), plus $2.50/2 issues (outside USA & Canada); Back issues: $4.

MassR: THE MASSACHUSETTS REVIEW, Mary Heath, John Hicks, Fred Robinson, eds., Anne Halley, Paul Jenkins, po. eds., Memorial Hall, U. of Massachusetts, Amherst, MA 01003. Issues indexed: (27:1-1, 3/4). Subscriptions: $12/yr., $14/yr. (for.); Single issues: $4.

MemphisSR: MEMPHIS STATE REVIEW, William Page, ed., Dept. of English, Memphis State U., Memphis, TN 38152. Issues indexed: (6:1/2, 7:1). Subscriptions: $3/yr.; Single issues: $2.

Mester: MESTER, Maria-Luiza Carrano, ed., Dept. of Spanish and Portuguese, U. of California, Los Angeles, CA 90024. Issues indexed: (15:1-2); 14:2 contains no poetry. Subscriptions: $17/yr. (inst.), $10/yr. (ind.), $6/yr. (stud.); Single issues: $7 (inst.), $4 (ind.)

MichQR: MICHIGAN QUARTERLY REVIEW, Laurence Goldstein, ed., 3032 Rackham Bldg., U. of Michigan, Ann Arbor, MI 48109. Issues indexed: (25:1-4). Subscriptions: $24/2 yr., $13/yr. (ind.), $15/yr. (inst.); Single issues: $3.50; Back issues: $2.

MidAR: MID-AMERICAN REVIEW, Robert Early, ed., Sally Kraine, po. ed., 106 Hanna Hall, Dept. of English, Bowling Green State U., Bowling Green, OH 43403. Issues indexed: (6:1-2, 7:1). Subscriptions: $6/yr. (2 issues), $10/2 yrs., $14/3 yrs.

Periodicals Indexed

MidwQ: THE MIDWEST QUARTERLY, James B. M. Schick, ed., Stephen E. Meats, po. ed., Pittsburg State U., Pittsburg, KS 66762-5889. Issues indexed: (27:2-4, 28:1). Subscriptions: $8/yr. plus $2 (for.); Single issues: $2.50.

MinnR: THE MINNESOTA REVIEW, Helen Cooper, Michael Sprinker, Susan Squier, eds, Helen Cooper, po. ed., Dept. of English, SUNY--Stony Brook, Stony Brook, NY 11794. Issues Indexed: (NS 26-27). Subscriptions: $24/2 yrs. (inst. & for.), $12/2 yrs. (ind.); $14/yr. (inst. & for.), $7/yr. (ind.); Single issues: $4.

MissouriR: THE MISSOURI REVIEW, Speer Morgan, ed., Sherod Santos & Garrett Kaoru Hongo, po. eds., Dept. of English, 231 Arts and Science, U. of Missouri, Columbia, MO 65211. Issues indexed: (9:1-3). Subscriptions: $21/2 yrs. (6 issues), $12/yr. (3 issues). Single issues: $5.

MissR: MISSISSIPPI REVIEW, Frederick Barthelme, ed., The Center for Writers, U. of Southern Mississippi, Southern Station, Box 5144, Hattiesburg, MS 39406-5144. Issues indexed: (42-/44). Subscriptions: $26/3 yrs., $18/2 yrs., $10/yr., plus $2/yr. (for.); Single issues: usually $5.

MoodySI: MOODY STREET IRREGULARS, Joy Walsh, ed., P.O. Box 157, Clarence Center, NY 14032. Issues indexed: (16/17). Subscriptions: $7/3 issues (ind.), $9/3 issues (lib.); Single issues: $3.

MSS: MSS, L. M. Rosenberg, ed., Box 530, State U. of NY at Binghamton, Binghamton, NY 13901. Issues indexed: (5:1). Subscriptions: $18/2 yrs. (ind.), $25/2 yrs. (lib.); $10/yr. (ind.), $15/yr. (lib.); Single issues: $4., Double issues: $6.

Nat: THE NATION, Victor Navasky, ed., Grace Schulman, po. ed., 72 Fifth Ave., New York, NY 10011. Issues indexed: (242:1-25, 243:1-22). Subscriptions: $67/2 yrs., $36/yr., plus $9/yr. (for.); Single issues: $1.25; P.O. Box 1953, Marion, OH 43305.

NegC: NEGATIVE CAPABILITY, Sue Walker, ed., 6116 Timberly Road North, Mobile, AL 36609. Issues indexed: (6:1, 2/3, 4). Subscriptions: $12/yr. (ind.), $16/yr. (inst., for.); Single issues: $4.

*NewAW: NEW AMERICAN WRITING, Paul Hoover, Maxine Chernoff, eds., OINK! Press, 1446 West Jarvis, Chicago, IL 60626. First issue dated 1987. Subscriptions: $6/issue.

NewEngR: NEW ENGLAND REVIEW AND BREAD LOAF QUARTERLY, Sydney Lea, Jim Schley, eds., Box 170, Hanover, NH 03755. Issues indexed: (8:3-4, 9:1-2). Subscriptions: $12/yr.; Single issues: $4; 13 Dartmouth College Highway, Lyme, NH 03768.

NewL: NEW LETTERS, James McKinley, ed., U. of Missouri-Kansas City, 5216 Rockhill Rd., Kansas City, MO 64110. Issues indexed: (52:2/3, 4, 53:1). Subscriptions: $50/5 yrs., $25/2 yrs., $15/yr. (ind.); $60/5 yrs., $30/2 yrs., $18/yr. (lib.); Single issues: $4.

NewOR: NEW ORLEANS REVIEW, John Biguenet, John Mosier, eds., Box 195, Loyola U., New Orleans, LA 70118. Issues indexed: (13:1-4). Subscriptions: $25/yr. (ind.), $30/yr. (inst.), $35/yr. (for.); Single issues: $7.

NewRena: THE NEW RENAISSANCE, Louise T. Reynolds, ed., Stanwood Bolton, po. ed., 9 Heath Road, Arlington, MA 02174. Issues indexed: (6:3, #20). Subscriptions: $20/6 issues, $10.50/3 issues; $24/6 issues, $12.50/3 issues (Canada, Mexico, Europe); $26/6 issues, $13.50/3 issues (elsewhere); Single issues: $5.90; $6.15 (Canada, Mexico & Europe); $6.25 (Elsewhere).

NewRep: THE NEW REPUBLIC, Martin Peretz, ed., 1220 19th St. N.W., Washington, DC 20036. Issues indexed: (194:1-26, 195:1-26). Subscriptions: $56/yr., $70 (Canada), $81 (elsewhere). Back issues: $2.50. Single issues: $2.25. Subscription Service Dept., The New Republic, P.O. Box 56515, Boulder, CO 80322.

NewYorker: THE NEW YORKER, 25 W. 43rd St., New York, NY 10036. Issues indexed: (61:46-52, 62:1-45). Subscriptions: $52/2 yrs., $32/yr.; $50/yr. (Canada); $56/yr. (other for.); Single issues: $1.50; Box 56447, Boulder, CO 80322.

NewYRB: THE NEW YORK REVIEW OF BOOKS, Robert B. Silvers, Barbara Epstein, eds., 250 W. 57th St., New York, NY 10107. Issues indexed: (32:21/22, 33:1-20). Subscriptions: $34/yr., $64/2 yrs, $95/3 yrs; plus $6/yr. (N. & S. America); plus $8 (other for.); Single issues: $2; Subscription Service Dept., P.O. Box 940, Farmingdale, NY 11737.

Nimrod: NIMROD, Francine Ringold, ed., Joan Flint, Manly Johnson, Chris Seid, po. eds., Arts and Humanities Council of Tulsa, 2210 S. Main St., Tulsa, OK 74114. Issues indexed: (29:2, 30:1). Subscriptions: $10/yr., $13/yr. (for.); Single issues: $5.50, $7 (for.).

NoAmR: THE NORTH AMERICAN REVIEW, Robley Wilson, Jr., ed., Peter Cooley, po. ed., U. of Northern Iowa, Cedar Falls, IA 50614. Issues indexed: (271:1-4). Subscriptions: $11/yr., $12/yr. (Canada, Latin America), $14/yr. (elsewhere); Single issues: $3.

NoDaQ: NORTH DAKOTA QUARTERLY, Robert W. Lewis, ed., Jay Meek, po. ed., Box 8237, U. of North Dakota, Grand Forks, ND 58202. Issues indexed: (54:1-4). Subscriptions: $10/yr.; Single issues: $4.

Northeast: NORTHEAST, John Judson, ed., Juniper Press, 1310 Shorewood Dr., La Crosse, WI 54601. Issues indexed: (Ser. 4:3-4). Subscriptions: $30 (ind.), $35 (inst.); Single issues: $3.

*Notus: NOTUS, New Writing, Pat Smith, ed., 2420 Walter Dr., Ann Arbor, MI 48103. Issues indexed: (1:1). Subscriptions: $10/yr., 2 issues, U.S. & Canada (ind.), $14/yr. (elsewhere), $20/yr. (inst.).

NowestR: NORTHWEST REVIEW, John Witte, ed. & po. ed., 369 PLC, U. of Oregon, Eugene, OR 97403. Issues indexed: (24:1-3). Subscriptions: $30/3 yrs., $21/2 yrs., $11/yr.; $20/2 yrs., $10/yr. (stud.); plus $2/yr. (for.); Single issues: $4.

Obs: OBSIDIAN II: Black Literature in Review, Gerald Barrax, ed., Dept. of English, Box 8105, North Carolina State University, Raleigh, NC 27695-8105. Issues indexed: (1:1/2). Subscriptions: $10/yr., $18/2 yrs.; $11/yr. (Canada), $13/yr. (other for.); Single issues: $4; Double issues: $8.

OhioR: THE OHIO REIVEW, Wayne Dodd, ed., Ellis Hall, Ohio U., Athens, OH 45701-2979. Issues indexed: (36-37). Subscriptions: $30/3 yrs. (9 issues), $12/yr. (3 issues); Single issues: $4.25.

Oink: OINK!, Maxine Chernoff and Paul Hoover, eds., 1446 Jarvis, Chicago, IL 60626. No longer published. Superseded by New American Writing, first issue, 1987. See NewAW.

OntR: ONTARIO REVIEW, Raymond J. Smith, ed., 9 Honey Brook Dr., Princeton, NJ 08540. Issues indexed: (24-25). Subscriptions: $21/3 yrs., $15/2 yrs., $8/yr., plus $1/yr. (for.); Single issues: $3.95.

Open24: OPEN 24 HOURS, Kate Pipkin and Chris Toll, eds, 702 Homestead St., Baltimore, MD 21218. Issues indexed: No 1986 issues received. Subscriptions: $7/3 issues; Single issues: $3.

OP: OPEN PLACES, Eleanor M. Bender, ed., Box 2085, Stephens College, Columbia, MO 65215. Issues indexed: (41, 42/43). Final issue published in 1987.

Origin: ORIGIN. National Poetry Foundation. Cid Corman, ed., Michael Heller, USA ed., P.O. Box 981, Stuyvesant Sta., New York, NY 10009. Issues indexed: No 1986 issues received. Subscriptions: $12/4 issues, $15/4 issues (Canadian currency), $21/4 issues (for.). Business Office: 305 Neville Hall, U. of Maine, Orono, ME 04469-0122.

OroM: ORO MADRE, Loss and Jan Glazier, eds., 4429 Gibraltar Dr., Fremont, CA 94536. Issues indexed: (4:1/4) = All's Normal Here: A Charles Bukowski Primer (Ruddy Duck

11

Periodicals IndexedPeriodicals Indexed

Press, 1985). Subscriptions: $12/4 issues; Single issues: $3.95.

Os: OSIRIS, Andrea Moorhead, ed., Box 297, Deerfield, MA 01342. Issues indexed: (22-23). Subscriptions: $7/2 issues (USA, Canada, Mexico), $8/2 issues (elsewhere, surface mail); Single issues: $3.50.

Outbr: OUTERBRIDGE, Charlotte Alexander, ed., English Dept. (A323), College of Staten Island, 715 Ocean Terrace, Staten Island, NY 10301. Issues indexed: (16/17). Sub-scriptions: $4/yr.; Single issues: $2.

Paint: PAINTBRUSH: A Journal of Poetry, Translations, and Letters, Ben Bennani, ed., Division of Language and Literature, Northeast Missouri State U., Kirksville, MO 63501. Issues indexed: (13:25/26). Subscriptions: $6/yr. (ind.), $8/yr. (inst.); Single issues: $5; Back issues: $5.

PaintedB: PAINTED BRIDE QUARTERLY, Louis Camp, Joanna DiPaolo, Louis McKee, eds., Painted Bride Art Center, 230 Vine St., Philadelphia, PA 19106. Issues indexed: (28-29). Subscriptions: $12/yr., $20/2 yrs., $16/yr. (lib, inst.); Single issues: $5. Distributed free to inmates.

ParisR: THE PARIS REVIEW, George A. Plimpton, et al ., eds., Jonathan Galassi, po. ed., 541 East 72nd St., New York, NY 10021. Issues indexed: 99-101. Subscriptions: $2500/life, $48/12 issues, $32/8 issues, $16/4 issues, plus $4/4 issues (for.); Single issues: $5; 45-39 171 Place, Flushing, NY 11358.

PartR: PARTISAN REVIEW, William Phillips, ed., Boston U., 141 Bay State Rd., Boston, MA 02215. Issues indexed: (53:2-4). Subscriptions: $39/3 yrs., $29/2 yrs., $16/yr.; $33/2 yrs., $18/yr. (for.); $22/yr. (inst.); Single issues: $4.50.

PassN: PASSAGES NORTH, Elinor Benedict, ed., Bay Arts Writers' Guild of the William Bonifas Fine Arts Center, Inc., Escanaba, MI 49829. Issues indexed: (7:1-2). Subscriptions: $2/yr., $5/3 yrs; Single issues: $1.50.

*Pax: PAX: A Journal for Peace through Culture, Bryce Milligan, ed., Center for Peace through Culture, 217 Pershing Ave., San Antonio, TX 78209. Issues indexed: (3:1/2). Subscriptions: $15/3 issues (U.S., Canada, Mexico); $20/3 issues (inst.); $25/3 issues (other for.).

*Pembroke: PEMBROKE MAGAZINE, Shelby Stephenson, ed., Box 60, Pembroke State U., Pembroke, NC 28372. Issues indexed: (18). Subscriptions: $3/issue (USA, Canada, Mexico), $3.50/issue (for.).

*PennR: THE PENNSYLVANIA REVIEW, Lee Gutkind, executive ed., James Gyure, po. ed., Writing Program, English Dept., 526 Cathedral of Learning, U. of Pittsburgh, Pittsburgh, PA 15260. Issues indexed: (1:1-2, 2:1); Inaugural ed. (1:1) has no vol. or number. Subscriptions: $9/yr., $15/2 yrs.; Single issues: $5.

Pequod: PEQUOD, Mark Rudman, ed., Dept. of English, Room 200, New York U., 19 University Place, New York, NY 10003. Issues indexed: (22). Subscriptions: $17/2 yrs. (4 issues), $9/yr. (2 issues) (ind.); $30/2 yrs., $15/yr. (inst).; plus $3/yr. (for.); Single issues: $5. The National Poetry Foundation, 305 Neville Hall, U. of Maine, Orono, ME 04469-0122.

Pig: PIG IRON, Rose Sayre & Jim Villani, eds., Pig Iron Press, P.O. Box 237, Youngstown, OH 44501. Issues indexed: No 1986 issues received. Single issues: $5.95.

PikeF: THE PIKESTAFF FORUM, Robert D. Sutherland, James R. Scrimgeour, eds./pubs., P.O. Box 127, Normal, IL 61761. Issues indexed: (7). Subscriptions: $10/6 issues; Single issues: $2; Back issues: $2.

Ploughs: PLOUGHSHARES, DeWitt Henry, Peter O'Malley, Directors, Div. of Writing, Publishing and Literature, Emerson College, 100 Beacon St., Boston, MA 02116; 214A Waverly Ave., Watertown, MA 02172. Issues indexed: (12:1/2, 3-4). Subscriptions: $15/yr. (ind.), $18/yr. (for. ind.); $16/yr. (inst.), $19/yr. (for. inst.). Single issues: $6.50.

Poem: POEM, Huntsville Literary Association, Nancy Frey Dillard, eds., c/o English Dept., U. of Alabama, Huntsville, AL 35899. Issues indexed: (55-56). Subscriptions: $7.50/yr., $10/yr. (for.); Back issues: $5; Huntsville Literary Association, P.O. Box 919,, Huntsville, AL 35804.

PoetC: POET AND CRITIC, Michael Martone, ed., Mary Swander, Anita Helle, po eds., 203 Ross Hall, Iowa State U., Ames, IA 50011. Issues indexed: (17:2-3, 18:1). Subscriptions: 12/yr., plus $3/yr. (for.); Single issues: $4; Iowa State U. Press, South State St., Ames, IA 50010.

PoeticJ: POETIC JUSTICE: Contemporary American Poetry, Alan Engebretsen, ed., 8220 Rayford Dr., Los Angeles, CA 90045. Issues indexed: (13-16). Subscriptions: $10/yr.; Single issues: $3.

PoetL: POET LORE, Philip K. Jason, Barbara Lefcowitz, Roland Flint, Executive eds., Heldref Publications, 4000 Albemarle St., N.W., Washington, DC 20016. Issues indexed: (80:4, 81:1-2). Subscriptions: $12/yr., $20/yr. (inst.), plus $6/yr. (for.); Single issues: $5.

Poetry: POETRY, Joseph Parisi, ed., 601 S. Morgan St., P.O. Box 4348, Chicago, IL 60680. Issues indexed: (147:4-6, 148:1-6, 149:1-3). Subscriptions: $22/yr., $27/yr. (for.); Single issues: $2.50 plus $.75 postage; Back issues: $3 plus $.75 postage.

PoetryCR: POETRY CANADA REVIEW, Robert Billings, ed., 307 Coxwell Ave., Toronto, Ontario M4L 3B5 Canada. Issues indexed: No 1986 issues received. Subscriptions: $14/yr., $26/2 yrs. (ind.); $30/yr. $56/2 yrs. (inst.); Single issues: $2.50.

PoetryE: POETRY EAST, Richard Jones, Kate Daniels, eds., Star Route 1, Box 50, Earlysville, VA 22936. Issues indexed: (19-20/21). Subscriptions: $10/yr.; Single issues: $3.50-$6.

PoetryNW: POETRY NORTHWEST, David Wagoner, ed., U. of Washington, 4045 Brooklyn Ave., NE, Seattle, WA 98105. Issues indexed: (27:1-4). Subscriptions: $10/yr., $12/yr. (for.); Single issues: $3, $3.50 (for.).

PortLES: THE PORTABLE LOWER EAST SIDE, Kurt Hollander, ed., 463 West St., #344, New York, NY 10014. Issues indexed: No 1986 issues received. Subscriptions: $8/yr. (2 issues); Single issues: $4.

PottPort: THE POTTERSFIELD PORTFOLIO, Peggy Amirault, Barbara Cottrell, Robin Metcalfe, Donalee Moulton-Barrett, eds., Crazy Quilt Press, c/o 19 Oakhill Drive, Halifax, Nova Scotia B3M 2V3 Canada. Issues indexed: (8). Subscriptions: $12/3 yrs. (ind.), $15/3 yrs. (inst.); $15/3 yrs. (USA, for. ind.), $18/3 yrs. (USA, for. inst., USA).

PraF: PRAIRIE FIRE, Andris Taskans, ed., Kristjana Gunnars, po. ed., 208-100 Arthur Street, Winnipeg, Manitoba R3B 1H3 Canada. Issues indexed: (7:1-4). Subscriptions: $18/yr. (ind.), $24/yr. (inst.), plus $6 (for.); Single issues: $4.95.

PraS: PRAIRIE SCHOONER, Hugh Luke, ed., Hilda Raz, po. ed., 201 Andrews Hall, U. of Nebraska, Lincoln, NE 68588. Issues indexed: (60:1-4). Subscriptions: $29/3 yrs., $20/2 yrs., $11/yr. (ind.); $15/yr. (lib.); Single issues: $3.25.

Prima: PRIMAVERA, Ann Grearen, Lisa Grayson, Jeanne Krinsley, Karen Frankfather Peterson, Julie Weissman, Ruth Young, eds., 1212 East 59th, Chicago, IL 60637. Issues indexed: (10). Single issues: $5.

*Puerto: PUERTO DEL SOL, Joe Somoza, po. ed., English Dept., Box 3E, New Mexico State U., Las Cruces, NM 88003. Issues indexed: (21:2, 22:1). Subscriptions: $7.75/yr. (2 issues), $15/2 yrs., $22/3 yrs.; Single issues: $4.

Quarry: QUARRY, Bob Hilderley, ed., Box 1061, Kingston, Ontario K7L 4Y5 Canada. Issues indexed: (35:1-4). Subscriptions: $16/yr. (4 issues), $28/2 yrs. (8 issues); Single issues: $4.

13

Periodicals Indexed

QRL: QUARTERLY REVIEW OF LITERATURE, T. & R. Weiss, 26 Haslet Ave., Princeton, NJ 08540. Issues indexed: Poetry series 7, vol. 26. Subscriptions: $15/2 volumes (paper), $35/2 volumes (cloth, inst.).

QW: QUARTERLY WEST, Christopher Merrill, Ann Snodgrass, eds.; Kevin Cantwell, Karen Propp, po. eds., 317 Olpin Union, U. of Utah, Salt Lake City, UT 84112. Issues indexed: (22-23). Subscriptions: $16/2 yrs. (4 issues), $8.50/yr. (2 issues); Single issues: $4.50.

Raccoon: RACCOON, David Spicer, ed., 3387 Poplar Ave., Suite 205, Memphis, TN 38111. Issues indexed: (19-21). Subscriptions: $12.50/yr.; Single issues: $2-5.

RagMag: RAG MAG, Beverly Voldseth, ed., Box 12, Goodhue, MN 55027. Issues indexed: (5:1-2). Subscriptions: $5/yr.; Single issues: $3.

Rampike: RAMPIKE, Karl Jirgens, ed., 95 Rivercrest Road, Toronto, Ontario M6S 4H7 Canada. Issues indexed: (5:1-2). Subscriptions: $12/2 issues; Single issues: $6.

Raritan: RARITAN, Richard Poirier, ed., Rutgers U., 165 College Ave., New Brunswick, NJ 08903. Issues indexed: (5:3-4, 6:1-2). Subscriptions: $16/yr., $26/2 yrs. (ind.); $20/yr., $30/2 yrs. (inst.); plus $4/yr (for.); Single issues: $5; Back issues: $6.

*RedBass: RED BASS, Jay Murphy, ed., P.O. Box 10258, Tallahassee, FL 32302. Issues indexed: (10-11). Subscriptions: $6/4 issues (ind.), $10/4 issues (inst.); Single issues: $1.25.

RevChic: REVISTA CHICANO-RIQUENA. See Americas: THE AMERICAS REVIEW.

*RevICP: REVISTA DEL INSTITUTO DE CULTURA PUERTORRIQUENA, Marta Aponte Alsina, Directora, Apartado 4184, San Juan, PR. Issues indexed: (88-91). Subscriptions: $6/yr.; Single issues: $2.

RiverS: RIVER STYX, Carol J. Pierman, ed., 14 South Euclid, St. Louis, MO 63108. Issues indexed: (19-21). Subscriptions: $14/yr. (3 issues, ind.); $24/yr. (3 issues, inst.); Single issues: $5.

Salm: SALMAGUNDI, Robert Boyers, ed., Skidmore College, Saratoga Springs, NY 12866. Issues indexed: (70/71). Subscriptions: $12/yr., $18/2 yrs. (ind.); $16/yr., $25/2 yrs. (inst.); Plus $1.50/yr. (for.); Single issues: $4-10.

Sam: SAMISDAT, Merritt Clifton, ed., Box 129, Richford, VT 05476. Issues indexed: (43:4-46:2, releases 172-182). Subscriptions: $150/all future and available backissues, $25/1000 pages, $15/500 pages.

SanFPJ: SAN FERNANDO POETRY JOURNAL, Richard Cloke, ed., 18301 Halsted St., Northridge, CA 91325. Issues indexed: (8:1-4, 9:1). Subscriptions: $10/yr. (4 issues), $18/2 yrs., $25/3 yrs.; Single issues: $3; Sample back issues: $2.

SecC: SECOND COMING, A. D. Winans, ed./pub., Box 31249, San Francisco, CA 94131. Issues indexed: (14:1-2). Subscriptions: $8.50/yr. (lib.), $6/yr. (ind.), $11 (for.).

SenR: SENECA REVIEW, Deborah Tall, ed., Hobart & William Smith Colleges, Geneva, NY 14456. Issues indexed: (16:1-2). Subscriptions: $6/yr., $10/2 yrs.; Single issues: $3.50.

SewanR: THE SEWANEE REVIEW, George Core, ed., U. of the South, Sewanee, TN 37375. Issues indexed: (94:1-4). Subscriptions: $48/3 yrs., $33/2 yrs., $18/yr. (inst.); $28/3 yrs., $20/2 yrs., $12/yr. (ind.); plus $3/yr. (for.); Single issues: $4; Back issues: $5-10, plus $1/copy postage & handling.

Shen: SHENANDOAH, James Boatwright, ed., Richard Howard, po. ed., Washington and Lee U., Box 722, Lexington, VA 24450. Issues indexed: (36:2-4). Subscriptions: $25/3 yrs., $18/2 yrs., $11/yr.; $33/3 yrs., $24/2 yrs., $14/yr. (for.); Single issues: $3.50; Back issues: $6.

14

Periodicals Indexed

SilverFR: SILVERFISH REVIEW, Rodger Moody, ed., P.O. Box 3541, Eugene, OR 97403. Issues indexed: (11-13). Subscriptions: $9/3 issues (ind.), $12/3 issues (inst.), Single issues: $4.

*SingHM: SING HEAVENLY MUSE!: Women's Poetry and Prose, Sue Ann Martinson, ed., P.O. Box 13299, Minneapolis, MN 55414. Issues indexed: (13-14). Subscriptions: $17/3 issues (ind.), $21/3 issues (inst.); Single issues: $6 + $1.50 postage & handling.

*Sink: SINK, Spencer Selby, ed., P.O. Box 590095, San Francisco, CA 94159. Issues indexed: (1-2). Subscriptions: $12/3 issues; Single issues: $4.

*SinW: SINISTER WISDOM, Melanie Kaye/Kantrowitz, ed., P.O. Box 1308, Montpelier, VT 05602. Issues indexed: (29/30) = The Tribe of Dina: A Jewish Women's Anthology. Subscriptions: $15/yr. (4 issues), $27/2 yrs. (ind.); $28/yr. (inst.); $17/yr. (for.); $6/yr. (hardship); Free on request to women in prisons and mental institutions; Single issues: $5.95-9.95.

*SlipS: SLIPSTREAM, Robert Borgatti, Dan Sicoli, eds., Box 2071, New Market Station, Niagara Falls, NY 14301. Issues indexed: (6). Subscriptions: $5.50/2 issues; Single issues: $3.

SmPd: THE SMALL POND MAGAZINE OF LITERATURE, Napoleon St. Cyr, ed./pub., P.O. Box 664, Stratford, CT 06497. Issues indexed: (23:1-3, issues 66-68). Subscriptions: $6.25/yr. (3 issues), $11.50/2 yrs., $16.75/3 yrs.; Single issues: $2.50.

SnapD: SNAPDRAGON, Gail Eckwright, Tina Foriyes, Ron McFarland, Margaret Snyder, eds., Library-Humanities, U. of Idaho, Moscow, ID 83843. Issues indexed: (9:2). Subscriptions: $3.50 (ind.), $4.50 (inst.).

*Sonora: SONORA REVIEW, Alison Hicks, Scott Wigton, eds, Elizabeth Price, po. ed., Dept. of English, U. of Arizona, Tucson, AZ 85721. Issues indexed: (10-11). Subscriptions: $6/yr. (2 issues); Single issues: $4.

SoCaR: SOUTH CAROLINA REVIEW, Richard J. Calhoun, ed., Dept. of English, Clemson U., Clemson, SC 29634-1503. Issues indexed: (18:2, 19:1). Subscriptions: $9/2 yrs., $5/yr. (USA, Canada, Mexico); $10/2 yrs., $5.50/yr. (elsewhere); Back issues: $5.

SoDakR: SOUTH DAKOTA REVIEW, John R. Milton, ed., Dept. of English, U. of South Dakota, Box 111, U. Exchange, Vermillion, SD 57069. Issues indexed: (24:1-4). Subscriptions: $17/2 yrs., $10/yr. (USA, Canada); $20/2 yrs., $12/yr. (elsewhere); Single issues: $3.

SouthernHR: SOUTHERN HUMANITIES REVIEW, Dan R. Latimer, Thomas L. Wright, eds., 9088 Haley Center, Auburn U., Auburn, AL 36849. Issues indexed: (20:1-4). Subscriptions: $12/yr.; Single issues: $4.

SouthernPR: SOUTHERN POETRY REVIEW, Robert Grey, ed., English Dept., U. of North Carolina, Charlotte, NC 28223. Issues indexed: (26:1-2). Subscriptions: $5/yr.; Single issues: $3.

SouthernR: SOUTHERN REVIEW, James Olney, Lewis P. Simpson, eds., Louisiana State U., 43 Allen Hall, Baton Rouge, LA 70803. Issues indexed: (22:1-4). Subscriptions: $30/3 yrs., $21/2 yrs., $12/yr.; Single issues: $5.

SouthwR: SOUTHWEST REVIEW, Willard Spiegelman, ed., Southern Methodist U., Box 4374, Dallas, TX 75275. Issues indexed: (71:1-4). Subscriptions: $36/3 yrs., $25/2 yrs., $14/yr.; Single issues: $4.

Sparrow: SPARROW PRESS POVERTY PAMPHLETS, Felix Stefanile, ed./Pub., Sparrow Press, 103 Waldron St., West Lafayette, IN 47906. Issues indexed: (50); No. 51 contained "only prose (essays and notes)" and was not submitted for indexing. Subscriptions: $7.50/3 issues; Single issues: $2.50.

Spirit: THE SPIRIT THAT MOVES US, Morty Sklar, ed., P.O. Box 1585, Iowa City, IA 52244. Issues indexed: No 1985 or 1986 issues published; next issue (8:2) published in

Periodicals Indexed

1987. Subscriptions: Vol. 8 -- $14.80 (paper), $26 (cloth); Vol. 9 -- $10.80 (paper), $20.40 (cloth).

SpiritSH: SPIRIT, David Rogers, ed., Seton Hall U., South Orange, NJ 07079. Issues indexed: (52). Subscriptions: $4/yr.; Single issues: $2.

SpoonRQ: THE SPOON RIVER QUARTERLY, David R. Pichaske, ed., P.O. Box 1443, Peoria, IL 61655. Issues indexed: (11:2-4). Subscriptions: $10/yr.; Single issues: $3.

Stand: STAND, Jon Silkin, Lorna Tracy, Michael Blackburn, eds., 179 Wingrove Road, Newcastle upon Tyne NE4 9DA, U.K.; Howard Fink, Canadian ed., 4054 Melrose Ave., Montreal, Quebec H4A 2S4 Canada; Issues indexed: (27:1-4). Subscriptions: $13/yr.; $10.50/yr. (students, unwaged); Single issues: $3; Stand Magazine USA, P.O. Box 648, Concord, MA 01742,

StoneC: STONE COUNTRY, Judith Neeld, ed., The Nathan Mayhew Seminars of Martha's Vineyard, P.O. Box 132, Menemsha, MA 02552. Issues indexed: (13:1/2, 14:1/2). Subscriptions: $15/4 issues, $8/2 issues; Single issues: $4.50; Back issues: $3.50.

Sulfur: SULFUR, Clayton Eshleman, ed., English Dept., Eastern Michigan U., Ypsilanti, MI 48197. Issues indexed: (5:3. 6:1-2, issues 15-17). Subscriptions: $22/yr. - 3 issues (inst.), $15/yr. - 3 issues (ind.), plus $3/yr. (for.) or $12 for airmail postage; Single issues: $6.

TarRP: TAR RIVER POETRY, Peter Makuck, ed., Dept. of English, Austin Bldg., East Carolina U., Greenville, NC 27858-4353. Issues indexed: (24:2, 25:1-2, 26:1). Subscriptions: $6/yr., $10/2 yrs.; Single issues: $3.

Temblor: TEMBLOR, Contemporary Poets, Leland Hickman, ed., 4624 Cahuenga Blvd., #307, North Hollywood, CA 91602. Issues indexed: (3-4). Subscriptions: $16/2 issues, $30/4 issues (ind.); $20/2 issues, $40/4 issues (inst.); plus $2.50/issue (for.); Single issues: $7.50.

Tendril: TENDRIL, George E. Murphy, Jr., managing ed., Box 512, Green Harbor, MA 02041. Issues indexed: No 1986 issues received. Subscriptions: $27/9 issues, $19/6 issues, $12/3 issues (ind.); $14/yr. (inst.); Single issues: $5.95-$10.95.

TexasR: TEXAS REVIEW, Paul Ruffin, ed., Division of English and Foreign Language, Sam Houston State U., Huntsville, TX 77341. Issues indexed: (7:1/2). Subscriptions: $4/yr., $4.25/yr. (Canada), $4.50/yr. (for.); Single issues: $2.

ThRiPo: THREE RIVERS POETRY JOURNAL, Gerald Costanzo, ed., Three Rivers Press, P.O. Box 21, Carnegie-Mellon U., Pittsburgh, PA 15213. Issues indexed: (27/28). Subscriptions: $10/4 issues; Single issues: $2.50; Double issues: $5.

Thrpny: THE THREEPENNY REVIEW, Wendy Lesser, ed./pub., P.O. Box 9131, Berkeley, CA 94709. Issues indexed: (24-27). Subscriptions: $13/2 yrs., $8/yr., $16/yr. (surface for.), $24/yr. (airmail for.); Single issues: $2.

*Translation: TRANSLATION, The Journal of Literary Translation, Lane Dunlop, Yu Li Hua, Frank MacShane, eds., The Translation Center, 307A Mathematics Bldg., Columbia U., New York, NY 10027. Issues indexed: (16-17). Subscriptions: $15/yr. (2 issues), $25/2 yrs., plus $1/yr. postage; plus $2/yr. (for. except Canada, Mexico); Single issues: $8.

TriQ: TRIQUARTERLY, Reginald Gibbons, ed., Northwestern U., 1735 Benson Ave., Evanston, IL 60201. Issues indexed: (65-67). Subscriptions: $150/life (ind.), $300/life (inst.), $28/2 yrs. (ind.), $44/2 yrs. (inst.), $16/yr. (ind.), $26/yr. (inst.), plus $4/yr. (for.); Single issues: usually $6.95-8.95; Sample copies: $4.

US1: US 1 WORKSHEETS, US 1 Poets Cooperative, 21 Lake Dr., Roosevelt, NJ 08555. Issues indexed: No 1986 issues received. Subscriptions: $5/4 issues; Single issues: $2.50; Back issues: Prices on request.

Verse: VERSE, Henry Hart, U. S. ed., Dept. of English, College of William and Mary, Williamsburg, VA 23185. Issues indexed: (5-6, 3:3). Subscriptions: $9/3 issues; Single

Alphabetical List of Journals Indexed, with Acronyms

Abraxas : Abraxas
Acts: A Journal of New Writing : Acts
The Agni Review : Agni
Amelia : Amelia
The American Poetry Review : AmerPoR
The American Scholar : AmerS
The American Voice : AmerV
The Americas Review : Americas
Another Chicago Magazine : AnotherCM
Antaeus : Antaeus
The Antigonish Review : AntigR
The Antioch Review : AntR
Areito : Areito
Arizona Quarterly : ArizQ
Ascent : Ascent
The Atlantic : Atlantic

Ball State University Forum : BallSUF
The Bellingham Review : BellR
Bellowing Ark : BellArk
The Beloit Poetry Journal : BelPoJ
The Bilingual Review/La Revista Bilingue : BilingR
Black American Literature Forum : BlackALF
Black Warrior Review : BlackWR
Blue Buildings: An International Magazine of Poetry and Translations : BlueBldgs
Blueline : Blueline
Bogg : Bogg
Boston Review : BostonR
Boulevard : Boulevard
Boundary 2 : Bound

Caliban : Caliban
California Quarterly : CalQ
Callaloo: A Tri-annual Journal of Afro-american and African Arts and Letters : Callaloo
Calyx: A Journal of Art and Literature by Women : Calyx
Canadian Literature : CanLit
The Cape Rock : CapeR
The Capilano Review : CapilR
Carolina Quarterly : CarolQ
The Centennial Review : CentR
Central Park : CentralP
The Chariton Review : CharR
Chelsea : Chelsea
Chicago Review : ChiR
The Christian Century : ChrC
Cimarron Review : CimR
Clockwatch Review : ClockR
College English : ColEng
Colorado Review : ColR
Commonweal : Comm
Concerning Poetry : ConcPo
Conditions : Cond
Confrontation : Confr
Conjunctions : Conjunc
The Connecticut Poetry Review : ConnPR
Contact II : Contact

Crab Creek Review : CrabCR
Crazyhorse : Crazy
Cream City Review : CreamCR
The Crescent Review : CrescentR
Cross-Canada Writers' Quarterly : CrossC
Crosscurrents : CrossCur
Cumberland Poetry Review : CumbPR
Cutbank : CutB

Dandelion : Dandel
The Dekalb Literary Arts Journal : DekalbLAJ
Denver Quarterly : DenQ
Descant : Descant

Electrum Magazine : Electrum
English Journal : EngJ
Epoch : Epoch
Event: Journal of the Contemporary Arts : Event
Evergreen Review : EvergR

Farmer's Market : Farm
Field: Contemporary Poetry and Poetics : Field
The Florida Review : FloridaR

The G. W. Review : GWR
Gargoyle Magazine : Gargoyle
Georgia Review : GeoR
Germination : Germ
Graham House Review : GrahamHR
Grain : Grain
Grand Street : GrandS
Greenfield Review : GreenfR

Hanging Loose : HangL
Harper's Magazine : Harp
The Harvard Advocate : HarvardA
Hawaii Review : HawaiiR
Hayden's Ferry Review : HayF
Helicon Nine: The Journal of Women's Arts & Letters : HeliconN
High Plains Literary Review : HighP
Hiram Poetry Review : HiramPoR
The Hollins Critic : HolCrit
The Hudson Review : Hudson

Imagine: International Chicano Poetry Journal : Imagine
Indiana Review : IndR
Interim : Interim
International Poetry Review : InterPR
Inti : Inti
Iowa Review : Iowa

The Jacaranda Review : Jacaranda
The James White Review : JamesWR
The Journal Of New Jersey Poets : JlNJPo

Kaleidoscope : Kaleid
Kansas Quarterly : KanQ
Kenyon Review : KenR

The Lake Street Review : LakeSR
Laurel Review : LaurelR
Letras Femeninas : LetFem
Linden Lane Magazine : LindLM
Lips : Lips
The Literary Review : LitR

The Little Balkans Review : LittleBR
The Little Magazine : LittleM

Mairena: Revista de Crítica y Poesía : Mairena
The Malahat Review : MalR
Manhattan Poetry Review : ManhatPR
The Manhattan Review : ManhatR
The Massachusetts Review : MassR
Memphis State Review : MemphisSR
Mester : Mester
Michigan Quarterly Review : MichQR
Mid-American Review : MidAR
The Midwest Quarterly : MidwQ
The Minnesota Review : MinnR
Mississippi Review : MissR
The Missouri Review : MissouriR
Moody Street Irregulars : MoodySI
Mss : MSS

The Nation : Nat
Negative Capability : NegC
New American Writing : NewAW
New England Review and Bread Loaf Quarterly : NewEngR
New Letters : NewL
New Orleans Review : NewOR
The New Renaissance : NewRena
The New Republic : NewRep
The New York Review of Books : NewYRB
The New Yorker : NewYorker
Nimrod : Nimrod
The North American Review : NoAmR
North Dakota Quarterly : NoDaQ
Northeast : Northeast
Northwest Review : NowestR
Notus : Notus

Obsidian II: Black Literature in Review : Obs
The Ohio Reivew : OhioR
Oink! : Oink
Ontario Review : OntR
Open 24 Hours : Open24
Open Places : OP
Origin : Origin
Oro Madre : OroM
Osiris : Os
Outerbridge : Outbr

Paintbrush: A Journal of Poetry : Paint
Painted Bride Quarterly : PaintedB
The Paris Review : ParisR
Partisan Review : PartR
Passages North : PassN
Pax: A Journal for Peace through Culture : Pax
Pembroke Magazine : Pembroke
The Pennsylvania Review : PennR
Pequod : Pequod
Pig Iron : Pig
The Pikestaff Forum : PikeF
Ploughshares : Ploughs
Poem : Poem
Poet and Critic : PoetC
Poet Lore : PoetL
Poetic Justice: Contemporary American Poetry : PoeticJ
Poetry : Poetry
Poetry Canada Review : PoetryCR

Poetry East : PoetryE
Poetry Northwest : PoetryNW
The Portable Lower East Side : PortLES
The Pottersfield Portfolio : PottPort
Prairie Fire : PraF
Prairie Schooner : PraS
Primavera : Prima
Puerto Del Sol : Puerto

Quarry : Quarry
Quarterly Review of Literature : QRL
Quarterly West : QW

Raccoon : Raccoon
Rag Mag : RagMag
Rampike : Rampike
Raritan : Raritan
Red Bass : RedBass
Revista Chicano-Riqueña : *See* The Americas Review
Revista del Instituto de Cultura Puertorriqueña : RevICP
River Styx : RiverS

Salmagundi : Salm
Samisdat : Sam
San Fernando Poetry Journal : SanFPJ
Second Coming : SecC
Seneca Review : SenR
The Sewanee Review : SewanR
Shenandoah : Shen
Silverfish Review : SilverFR
Sing Heavenly Muse!: Women's Poetry and Prose : SingHM
Sink : Sink
Sinister Wisdom : SinW
Slipstream : SlipS
The Small Pond Magazine of Literature : SmPd
Snapdragon : SnapD
Sonora Review : Sonora
South Carolina Review : SoCaR
South Dakota Review : SoDakR
Southern Humanities Review : SouthernHR
Southern Poetry Review : SouthernPR
Southern Review : SouthernR
Southwest Review : SouthwR
Sparrow Press Poverty Pamphlets : Sparrow
Spirit : SpiritSH
The Spirit That Moves Us : Spirit
The Spoon River Quarterly : SpoonRQ
Stand : Stand
Stone Country : StoneC
Sulfur : Sulfur

Tar River Poetry : TarRP
Temblor : Temblor
Tendril : Tendril
Texas Review : TexasR
Three Rivers Poetry Journal : ThRiPo
The Threepenny Review : Thrpny
Translation : Translation
Triquarterly : TriQ

Us 1 Worksheets : US1

Verse : Verse
The Virginia Quarterly Review : VirQR
Visions : Vis

Waves : Waves
Webster Review : WebR
West Branch : WestB
West Coast Review : WestCR
Western Humanities Review : WestHR
Willow Springs : WillowS
Wind : Wind
The Windless Orchard : WindO
Wooster Review : WoosterR
World Order : WorldO
The Wormwood Review : WormR
Writ : Writ
Writers' Forum : WritersF
Writer's Lifeline : WritersL

The Yale Review : YaleR
Yellow Silk : YellowS
Yet Another Small Magazine : YetASM

Zyzzyva: The Last Word : Zyzzyva

The Author Index

1. AAL, Katharyn Machan
"Daughter: Helen Wall." [NegC] (6:1) Wint 86, p. 72.
"The Difference between North." [BelPoJ] (36:3) Spr 86, p. 14-15.
"Someone Warm, You Know Him." [BelPoJ] (36:3) Spr 86, p. 16.
2. AARON, Jonathan
"The Fourth Grade" (for Tom Lux). [Ploughs] (12:3) 86, p. 112-113.
"Then." [Ploughs] (12:3) 86, p. 110-111.
3. ABBEY, Lloyd
"Home from Hospital: Holiday." [MalR] (77) D 86, p. 71.
"Humpback Whales." [AntigR] (66/67) Sum-Aut 86, p. 40-42.
4. ABBOTT, Franklin
"Little Ease." [JamesWR] (3:2) Wint 86, p. 5.
5. ABBOTT, Steve
"Brothers in Drag." [JamesWR] (4:1) Fall 86, p. 4.
"Poem in St. Paul." [JamesWR] (4:1) Fall 86, p. 4.
6. ABBOTT, Tony
"Finding It." [PennR] (2:1) Fall-Wint 86, p. 65-66.
7. ABERCROMBIE, Denise
"The Moose Club." [MinnR] (NS 26) Spr 86, p. 12.
8. ABINADER, Elmaz
"Although the Sky." [Amelia] (3:4) Fall 86, p. 24.
"Walking at Sunset." [Blueline] (8:1) Sum-Fall 86, p. 19.
"What We Leave Behind." [Farm] (3:1) Fall 85, p. 17.
"Young Women" (to mother). [PennR] (1:2) Fall 85, p. 17.
9. ABNOUDY, Abderrahman
"Old Man Lampo died in Spain" (tr. by Susan Slyomovics). [SenR] (16:1) 86, p.
84-90.
10. ABRAMS, Fred
"Yes Sergeant!" [NewL] (52:2/3) Wint-Spr 86, p. 99.
11. ABRAMS, M. H.
"Ambivalence Reexammoned." [Pembroke] (18) 86, p. 27.
12. ABRELAT, Paul
"Petulant Requiem." [DeKalbLAJ] (19:3/4) 86, p. 112.
13. ABSE, Dannie
"Bedtime Story." [GeoR] (40:3) Fall 86, p. 619-620.
"Crepuscolo." [TriQ] (67) Fall 86, p. 116-117.
"Last Visit to 198 Cathedral Road." [TriQ] (67) Fall 86, p. 118.
"A Winter visit." [GeoR] (40:3) Fall 86, p. 620.
14. ABSHER, Tom
"Childhood." [Nat] (242:15) 19 Ap 86, p. 559.
"Open Country" (for Naomi Nye). [SenR] (16:2) 86, p. 69-70.
ACEVEDO, Manuel Silva
See SILVA ACEVEDO, Manuel
15. ACHTERBERG, Gerrit
"Dream Ballad" (tr. by Pleuke Boyce). [LitR] (29:3) Spr 86, p. 360.
16. ACHUGAR, Hugo
"Angel Triptych" (tr. by Reginald Gibbons and the author). [TriQ] (66) Spr-Sum 86, p.
161-162.
"Family Portrait" (tr. by Reginald Gibbons and the author). [TriQ] (66) Spr-Sum 86, p.
160.
"Inscription" (tr. by Reginald Gibbons and the author). [TriQ] (66) Spr-Sum 86, p.
158-159.
17. ACKER, Paul
"Skating in the Rooms of a Half-Built House." [PennR] (1:2) Fall 85, p. 47.
18. ACKER, Peter
"On Hearing of a Man's Death in a Hang Glider Accident." [GreenfR] (13:3/4)
Sum-Fall 86, p. 1.

19. ACKERMAN, Diane
    "Air Show in Barbados." [Chelsea] (45) 86, p. 119-121.
    "Amber." [KenR] (NS 8:3) Sum 86, p. 89.
    "Halley's Comet." [Atlantic] (257:5) My 86, p. 79.
    "Intensive Care." [KenR] (NS 8:3) Sum 86, p. 87-89.
    "White Flag." [Chelsea] (45) 86, p. 122-123.
    "You Will Think This a Dream" (headline to an article about the invention of electricity,
        ... 1915). [Chelsea] (45) 86, p. 118-119.
20. ACKERMAN, Vivian Marie
    "First Communion." [YetASM] (5) 86, p. 2.
21. ACORN, Milton
    "The Dolphin-Walk." [GreenfR] (13:3/4) Sum-Fall 86, p. 3.
    "A Good Sight of Andromeda." [GreenfR] (13:3/4) Sum-Fall 86, p. 3.
    "Gull Passage by Moonlight." [GreenfR] (13:3/4) Sum-Fall 86, p. 4.
    "A Mass for the Unborn New Dead." [AntigR] (65) Spr 86, p. 15.
22. ACOS, Anrique Paco d'
    "Carnival" (tr. by Bradley R. Strahan). [Vis] (22) 86, p. 17.
23. ADAMCZYK, Terri
    "Leaving Lenola." [ColEng] (48:1) Ja 86, p. 40-41.
24. ADAMS, B. B.
    "The 7:31 Hoboken Train." [Confr] (32) Spr-Sum 86, p. 138.
25. ADAMS, Barbara
    "Babyskin: Notes for a Grandchild." [NegC] (6:1) Wint 86, p. 68.
26. ADAMS, Gail Galloway
    "Three Women on a Porch." [AmerV] (2) Spr 86, p. 29.
ADAMS, Lily Jean Lee
    See LEE-ADAMS, Lily Jean
27. ADAMSSON, Slade
    "Poem-by-Numbers." [Bogg] (56) 86, p. 46.
28. ADCOCK, Betty
    "New South." [SouthernPR] (26:1) Spr 86, p. 47-48.
    "Nothing Happened." [GeoR] (40:3) Fall 86, p. 621.
    "White Rhinoceros." [SouthernR] (22:4) O 86, p. 799-800.
29. ADDONIZIO, Kim
    "Getting Back." [BelPoJ] (37:1) Fall 86, p. 1.
30. ADEN, Carlin
    "Ode to Otis Roebuck." [BellR] (9:1) Spr 86, p. 18.
31. ADLER, Carol
    "My House." [BallSUF] (26:4) Aut 85, p. 51.
32. ADLER, Fran
    "Signals." [CentR] (30:4) Fall 86, p. 475-476.
33. ADLER, Lorica
    "In Lakeview." [MidAR] (7:1) 86, p. 143.
ADORNO, Pedro López
    See LOPEZ ADORNO, Pedro
34. AGGESTAM, Rolf
    "And Eternity?" (in Swedish & English, tr. by Lars Nordström and Erland Anderson).
        [InterPR] (12:1) Spr 86, p. 10-11.
    "Encounter" (in Swedish & English, tr. by Lars Nordström and Erland Anderson).
        [InterPR] (12:1) Spr 86, p. 10-11.
    "The Future Sleeps" (in Swedish & English, tr. by Lars Nordström and Erland
        Anderson). [InterPR] (12:1) Spr 86, p. 14-15.
    "I Came to Uncle Axel But Could Not Find Him" (in Swedish & English, tr. by Lars
        Nordström and Erland Anderson). [InterPR] (12:1) Spr 86, p. 12-13.
    "Song of the Shaman in Our Time" (in Swedish & English, tr. by Lars Nordström and
        Erland Anderson). [InterPR] (12:1) Spr 86, p. 6-7.
    "Three Tons of Rock a Day" (in Swedish & English, tr. by Lars Nordström and Erland
        Anderson). [InterPR] (12:1) Spr 86, p. 8-9.
    "Troll Eye" (in Swedish & English, tr. by Lars Nordström and Erland Anderson).
        [InterPR] (12:1) Spr 86, p. 18-19.
    "You Shall Stare Down" (in Swedish & English, tr. by Lars Nordström and Erland
        Anderson). [InterPR] (12:1) Spr 86, p. 16-17.
AGHA SHAHID ALI
    See ALI, Agha Shahid
35. AGOOS, Julie
    "American Patriotic." [PoetryNW] (27:3) Aut 86, p. 33-34.

"At Ponte a Mensola." [Pequod] (22) 86, p. 37-39.
"Florence Interlude." [YaleR] (76:1) Aut 86, p. 42-43.
36. AGOSIN, Marjorie
"The Course of the Lettuce" (tr. by S. Jill Levine). [Cond] (13) 86, p. 82.
"Deja Que la Vida Sea Tuya." [Mairena] (8:22) 86, p. 111.
"Mi Estomago (My Belly)" (tr. by Cola Franzen). [Calyx] (9:2/3) Wint 86, p. 110-111.
"Mi Estomago (My Belly)" (tr. by Cola Franzen). [Cond] (13) 86, p. 83.
"She Conjured Up Returnings" (tr. by Cola Franzen). [WebR] (11:2) Fall 86, p. 33.
37. AGOSTINI, Juan Antonio
"Cuando caiga mi estrella." [Mairena] (8:22) 86, p. 88.
38. AGRAIT LLADO, Francisco R.
"Estos Dias Azules." [Mairena] (8:22) 86, p. 110.
39. AGRICOLA, Sandra
"Bone Scan." [OhioR] (37) 86, p. 38-39.
"Chit Chat." [CharR] (12:1) Spr 86, p. 70-72.
"Courting Grandaddy Longlegs." [DenQ] (20:4/21:1) Spr-Sum 86, p. 124-125.
"Domestication of Flies." [DenQ] (20:4/21:1) Spr-Sum 86, p. 126-127.
"Genesis of Strip Poker." [OhioR] (37) 86, p. 36-37.
40. AGUILAR, Mila D.
"Haikus in Solitary Confinement." [RedBass] (11) 86, p. 6.
"Rain." [Calyx] (10:1) Sum 86, p. 43.
"Researcher Reporting on the Dumagats." [Calyx] (10:1) Sum 86, p. 40-42.
41. AGUIRRE MOLINA, Roberto
"Abril en Vos." [Mairena] (8:21) 86, p. 110.
42. AHARONI, Ada
"Green Seedlings" (tr. of Shara Halfon). [InterPR] (12:2) Fall 86, p. 45.
"Is It Possible to Love You?" (tr. of Shara Halfon). [InterPR] (12:2) Fall 86, p. 47.
"The Turtle" (tr. of Shara Halfon). [InterPR] (12:2) Fall 86, p. 43.
43. AHERN, Maureen
"First Penmanship Lesson" (tr. of Cecilia Bustamante). [RedBass] (10) 86, p. 6.
"Maestro Lezama" (tr. of Juan Gustavo Cobo Borda). [ColR] (NS 13:1) Fall 85, p. 39.
"On the Death of Remedios Varo" (tr. of Rosario Castellanos). [RedBass] (10) 86, p. 7.
"Wasting My Life?" (For Peter Shultze-Kraft, tr. of Juan Gustavo Cobo Borda). [ColR] (NS 13:1) Fall 85, p. 38.
44. AHLUWALIA, Usha
"All My Travels" (From Idylles, tr. of Jean Clarence Lambert). [Vis] (22) 86, p. 6.
"Summer" (From Idylles, tr. of Jean Clarence Lambert). [Vis] (22) 86, p. 6.
45. AHMED, Christine Choi
"It's about What I Lost." [PraF] (7:2) Sum 86, p. 51.
46. AHO, Margaret
"Carpal Bones." [NowestR] (24:1) 86, p. 28.
"Pause at Forty." [NowestR] (24:1) 86, p. 27.
47. AI
"Blue Suede Shoes" (A Fiction). [Callaloo] (9:1, #26) Wint 86, p. 1-5.
"The Emigré." [Agni] (23) 86, p. 98-100.
"The Journalist." [MissouriR] (9:1) 85-86, p. 66-69.
"Reunions with a Ghost" (for Jim Davis). [QW] (23) 86, p. 141-142.
48. AI, Qing
"On the Massacre at Longhua" (tr. by Robert Dorsett). [SenR] (16:1) 86, p. 100.
49. AIELLO, Kate
"Aphrodisiac." [Bogg] (56) 86, p. 20.
50. AIGLA, Jorge H.-
"Sublunarly away from God." [Puerto] (22:1) Fall 86, p. 69.
51. AIKEN, Conrad
"The Walk." [GeoR] (40:3) Fall 86, p. 622.
52. AIKEN, David
"Aspiration." [DeKalbLAJ] (19:1) 86, p. 25.
53. AINSWORTH, J. Alan
"Not Knowing." [FloridaR] (14:2) Fall-Wint 86, p. 107.
54. AITENBICHLER, Ulrike
"In the Blue Signature of the Ice Bird" (Poems in German & English, tr. of Reiner Kunze, w. Thomas Edwards and Ken Letko). [MidAR] (7:1) 86, p. 73-101.
"Nowhere Is Near So Far" (Poems in German & English, tr. of Ulrich Schacht, w. Thomas Edwards and Ken Letko). [MidAR] (6:2) 86, p. 49-86.

55. AKHMATOVA, Anna
    "I finally wrote down the words" ("An Untitled Poem," tr. by Judith Hemschemeyer).
        [Boulevard] (1:1/2) Wint 86, p. 153.
AKIKO, Takemoto
    See TAKEMOTO, Akiko
AKIKO, Yosano
    See YOSANO, Akiko
56. AKWII-WANGUSA, Hellen G.
    "Grandmother's Advice." [SouthernR] (22:1) Ja 86, p. 147.
57. Al-ARRAFAT, Ibn
    "What am I?" (tr. by Will Kirkland). [NewOR] (13:4) Wint 86, p. 38.
58. Al-ATTAR, Amin Ibn Ibrahim
    "The Fool, Let them say what they want" (tr. by Will Kirkland). [NewOR] (13:4) Wint
        86, p. 29.
59. Al-HARBI, Muhammad Ubaid
    "Bedouin Lament at the Gates . . ." (tr. by Diana Der Hovanessian, w. Lena Jayyusi).
        [Translation] (17) Fall 86, p. 264-267.
60. Al MAGUT, Mohamed
    "O Tourist" (tr. by Saheb Meshtet and Beth Tornes). [SenR] (16:1) 86, p. 72.
    "Orphan" (tr. by Saheb Meshtet and Beth Tornes). [SenR] (16:1) 86, p. 69.
    "Tattoo" (tr. by Saheb Meshtet and Beth Tornes). [SenR] (16:1) 86, p. 70-71.
61. AL-MASKARY, Shaikha
    "The Arabian Mountains." [Pax] (3:1/2) Wint 85-86, p. 143.
    "A Bedouin Daughter." [Pax] (3:1/2) Wint 85-86, p. 141.
    "The Flower." [Pax] (3:1/2) Wint 85-86, p. 144.
    "Suddenly One Night." [Pax] (3:1/2) Wint 85-86, p. 142.
62. Al-NAWWAB, Mozaffar
    "Night-Strings" (Excerpts, tr. by Adnan Haydar and Michael Beard). [MinnR] (NS 26)
        Spr 86, p. 44-55.
63. ALABAU, Magaly
    "La memoria ausente." [Mairena] (8:22) 86, p. 89.
ALBA, Guillermina P. Moore
    See MOORE ALBA, Guillermina P.
64. ALBAN, Laureano
    "Fields of Memory" (tr. by Frederick H. Fornoff). [Sonora] (11) Fall 86 [c87], p. 85,
        87.
    "The Green Dominion" (tr. by Frederick H. Fornoff). [Sonora] (11) Fall 86 [c87], p.
        81, 83.
    "Prados de la Memoria." [Sonora] (11) Fall 86 [c87], p. 84, 86.
    "La Verde Potestad." [Sonora] (11) Fall 86 [c87], p. 80, 82.
65. ALBERS, Margie
    "The Temple of the Sun Tiger" (Tribute to Dr. Sun Yat-sen). [DeKalbLAJ] (19:3/4) 86,
        p. 112.
66. ALBERT, Matilde
    "Otra vez." [Mairena] (8:22) 86, p. 98.
67. ALBERTI, Rafael
    "Telegram" (tr. by Robert Lima). [Vis] (22) 86, p. 18.
68. ALBIZUREZ PALMA, Francisco
    "Se quedaron en el camino." [Mairena] (8:22) 86, p. 119.
69. ALDAN, Daisy
    "The Earth Is a Being Who Deserves to Be Loved." [Pax] (3:1/2) Wint 85-86, p. 140.
    "They Sailed for Home." [Pax] (3:1/2) Wint 85-86, p. 138-139.
70. ALDANA, Felipe
    "El poema era tan delicadamente triste." [Mairena] (8:22) 86, p. 47.
71. ALDRICH, Marcia
    "White Cherries" (In memory of Louise Bogan). [LitR] (30:1) Fall 86, p. 42.
72. ALESHIRE, Joan
    "Blue Bird Cab." [VirQR] (62:3) Sum 86, p. 429-430.
    "Crossing." [VirQR] (62:3) Sum 86, p. 428-429.
73. ALEXANDER, Elizabeth
    "Alice at One Hundred and Two." [Calyx] (9:2/3) Wint 86, p. 126.
    "The Dirt-Eaters." [Callaloo] (9:1, #26) Wint 86, p. 7-8.
    "Letter: Blues." [Callaloo] (9:1, #26) Wint 86, p. 6.
74. ALEXANDER, Floyce
    "From the Free World." [Contact] (8:41/42/43) Fall-Wint 86-87, p. 66.
    "San Diego 1971, Managua 1983." [Contact] (8:41/42/43) Fall-Wint 86-87, p. 68-69.

"Words That Are Hard to Say." [Contact] (8:41/42/43) Fall-Wint 86-87, p. 67.
75. ALEXANDER, Francis W.
"The Blind Citizens." [SanFPJ] (8:3) 85, p. 14.
"A Dream Vanquished." [SanFPJ] (8:3) 85, p. 8.
"Five Years Hence." [SanFPJ] (8:4) 85, p. 6.
"Kiddie Logic." [SanFPJ] (8:4) 85, p. 6.
"Philosophy Zero Hundred." [SanFPJ] (8:4) 85, p. 7.
"The Thumping Dominoes Theory." [SanFPJ] (8:3) 85, p. 9.
76. ALEXANDER, Pamela
"Howard Hughes Leaves Managua: Peacetime, 1972." [NewYorker] (62:43) 15 D 86,
    p. 46.
77. ALEXANDER, Paul
"The Swimmers." [Poetry] (148:4) Jl 86, p. 223-224.
78. ALFARO, Rosanna Yamagiwa
"Her Twenty-Seventh Birthday." [AntigR] (64) Wint 86, p. 116.
ALFONSO, Antonio d'
    See D'ALFONSO, Antonio
79. ALI, Agha Shahid
"Hansel's Game." [Interim] (5:1) Spr 86, p. 37-38.
"Houses." [Shen] (36:2) 86, p. 66.
"I Dream It Is Afternoon When I Return to Delhi." [QW] (23) 86, p. 74-75.
"The Rain of Stones" (adaption of Faiz Ahmed Faiz). [LitR] (29:3) Spr 86, p. 361.
"Snowmen." [QW] (23) 86, p. 73.
"Solitude" (adaption of Faiz Ahmed Faiz). [LitR] (29:3) Spr 86, p. 361.
"Story of a Silence." [QW] (23) 86, p. 76-77.
"The Tourist." [Interim] (5:1) Spr 86, p. 38.
80. ALIBERTI, Antonio
"Ella." [Mairena] (8:21) 86, p. 89.
"La Lluvia." [Mairena] (8:21) 86, p. 90.
"Señas Personales." [Mairena] (8:21) 86, p. 90.
81. ALICE, Joyletta A.
"Quilt Poem #1." [PraS] (60:2) Sum 86, p. 74.
82. ALIESAN, Jody
"Lightning near the Tower" (Selections: II, IV). [Contact] (8:41/42/43) Fall-Wint
    86-87, p. 18-19.
ALIGHIERI, Dante
    See DANTE ALIGHIERI
83. ALKALAY-GUT, Karen
"Another Song on Absalom" (tr. of Natan Yonathan). [PoetL] (81:2) Sum 86, p. 90.
"Family Vacation at Banias" (Golan Heights, 1982, tr. by the author). [MassR] (27:2)
    Sum 86, p. 200-201.
"I'm So Glad" (tr. by the author). [MassR] (27:2) Sum 86, p. 201.
"On Rabbi Kook's Street" (tr. of Yehuda Amichai). [MassR] (27:2) Sum 86, p. 194.
"Our Blood is the World's Petrol" (tr. of Asher Reich). [MassR] (27:2) Sum 86, p.
    193.
"Parting in Tivon" (tr. of Eyal Megged). [PoetL] (81:2) Sum 86, p. 114.
"Practical Poems" (tr. of David Avidan). [MassR] (27:2) Sum 86, p. 195.
"Script" (tr. of Natan Zach). [MassR] (27:2) Sum 86, p. 196-197.
"Terminal" (tr. of Natan Yonatan). [MassR] (27:2) Sum 86, p. 198-199.
"When I Wrote My Name" (tr. of Eyal Megged). [PoetL] (81:2) Sum 86, p. 113.
84. ALKAZRAJI, Paul
"I Saw a Photograph of You in Someone Else's Album." [Bogg] (56) 86, p. 54.
85. ALLARDT, Linda
"Signs." [NegC] (6:4) Fall 86, p. 53.
86. ALLARY, Jennifer
"A Visit to the Armoury Museum at Shilo: a Child's View." [Event] (15:2) 86, p. 179.
87. ALLBERY, Debra
"Forgiveness." [Poetry] (147:6) Mr 86, p. 315.
"Money." [PraS] (60:4) Wint 86, p. 20-21.
"Second Sight." [PraS] (60:4) Wint 86, p. 18-20.
"Walking below Zero You Tell Yourself." [Poetry] (147:6) Mr 86, p. 313-314.
88. ALLEGRE, Marla Rowe
"Hothouse." [YetASM] (5) 86, p. 3.
89. ALLEN, Barbara
"Elvis, Elvis." [BellArk] (2:3) My-Je 86, p. 14.

90. ALLEN, Blair (Blair H.)
  "Blue Thunder." [Vis] (20) 86, p. 29.
  "Rusted Sea Oranges." [Electrum] (38) Spr 86, p. 15.
91. ALLEN, Dick
  "Adirondack Town: An Idyll." [Hudson] (39:1) Spr 86, p. 97-98.
  "Backstroking at Thrushwood Lake." [OntR] (24) Spr-Sum 86, p. 100-101.
  "Crows and Windmills." [Hudson] (39:1) Spr 86, p. 99-100.
  "The Flutist." [NewYorker] (61:48) 20 Ja 86, p. 32.
  "If You Visit Our Country." [NoAmR] (271:2) Je 86, p. 43.
  "The Postmaster." [Hudson] (39:1) Spr 86, p. 98-99.
92. ALLEN, Gilbert
  "Burning Brush on Sunday Morning in the Bible Belt." [Amelia] (3:2) Spr 86, p. 100.
  "The Husband's Letter, 1969." [ManhatPR] (8) Wint 86-87, p. 10-11.
  "The Romantic Tradition for A.R. Ammons." [Pembroke] (18) 86, p. 86.
  "A Simple Reverence." [ManhatPR] (8) Wint 86-87, p. 11.
  "Visitation: 7 P.M." [CumbPR] (6:1) Fall 86, p. 75.
  "What Frightens Me." [KanQ] (18:1/2) Wint-Spr 86, p. 132.
93. ALLEN, Heather
  "The Cartographers." [GeoR] (40:3) Fall 86, p. 623-624.
94. ALLEN, Robert
  "Sunrising Behind Me." [MalR] (73) Ja 86, p. 98-99.
  "Young Boy at His Father's Funeral." [MalR] (73) Ja 86, p. 100.
95. ALLEN, Roberta
  "Africa." [HeliconN] (16) Wint 86, p. 49.
  "The Pear." [HeliconN] (16) Wint 86, p. 48.
  "Spoiled." [HeliconN] (16) Wint 86, p. 50.
  "The Terrace." [HeliconN] (16) Wint 86, p. 51.
96. ALLEN, William
  "The Loon." [SouthernPR] (26:2) Fall 86, p. 33-34.
97. ALLEY, Rewi
  "Fruit" (tr. of Lu Li). [Verse] (6) 86, p. 48.
  "Memory" (tr. of Shao Yanxiang). [Verse] (6) 86, p. 47.
98. ALLISON, Gay
  "About My Birth." [CrossC] (8:2) 86, p. 15.
  "I Want to Write about Women" (for Viviene). [CrossC] (8:2) 86, p. 16.
  "This Is the Way It Begins" (for Dorie). [CrossC] (8:2) 86, p. 15.
99. ALLMAN, John
  "Five Cats and a Discussion of the Soul after a Trip to South Carolina." [MemphisSR]
    (7:1) Fall 86, p. 8-9.
  "Mechanics." [MemphisSR] (7:1) Fall 86, p. 10.
  "Transplants." [MemphisSR] (7:1) Fall 86, p. 9.
100. ALMAND, Betty
  "A Head in the News." [DeKalbLAJ] (19:3/4) 86, p. 66.
  "Side Trip from Dying." [DeKalbLAJ] (19:3/4) 86, p. 67.
101. ALMEIDA, Jovita de
  "A Orillas del Palmar." [LetFem] (10:2) Fall 84 [c1985], p. 94.
  "No Ha Muerto el Charrua." [LetFem] (10:2) Fall 84 [c1985], p. 95.
102. ALMELA, Harry
  "Grillo." [LindLM] (5:2) Ap-Je 86, p. 7.
  "Me acuesto desnudo cada noche." [LindLM] (5:2) Ap-Je 86, p. 7.
103. ALMOG, Aharon
  "The Summer Is Over" (tr. by Hillel Halkin). [PoetL] (81:2) Sum 86, p. 96.
  "Yet Thirty Days" (tr. by Hillel Halkin). [PoetL] (81:2) Sum 86, p. 95.
ALONSO, Agustín Garcia
  See GARCIA ALONSO, Agustín
104. ALTER, Michael
  "Thanksgiving." [HiramPoR] (41) Fall-Wint 86-87, p. 6.
105. ALVAREZ, Griselda
  "Above the Sea" (tr. by Elizabeth Bartlett). [WebR] (11:2) Fall 86, p. 34.
106. ALVAREZ, Maria Auxiliadora
  "11. Conozco el tiempo de cocción de las legumbres." [LindLM] (5:2) Ap-Je 86, p. 9.
  "22. Es injusto que duermas." [LindLM] (5:2) Ap-Je 86, p. 9.
107. ALVAREZ, Maria de la Fe
  "Comienzo por Tu Nombre." [Mairena] (8:21) 86, p. 91.
  "Comunion." [Mairena] (8:21) 86, p. 92.
  "Creacion." [Mairena] (8:21) 86, p. 91.

"La Huella de los Cisnes." [Mairena] (8:21) 86, p. 92.
"Lluvia sin Ventanas." [Mairena] (8:21) 86, p. 91.
"Perfil en Sombras." [Mairena] (8:21) 86, p. 92.
108. ALVAREZ MERLO, Rafael
"La Palabra." [Mairena] (8:22) 86, p. 7.
109. ALVES, Antonio de Castro
"Tragedy at Sea: The Slave Ship" (tr. by Amy Peterson). [Translation] (17) Fall 86, p. 268-274.
110. AMATO, Joseph
"Helmet" (A Poem to France). [SpoonRQ] (11:4) Fall 86, p. 36-39.
111. AMERY, Al
"Crucifixion." [SanFPJ] (9:1) 86, p. 65.
"Greedy Enterprise." [SanFPJ] (8:4) 85, p. 32.
"Growth." [SanFPJ] (8:2) 85, p. 81-82.
"June Boon." [SanFPJ] (8:4) 85, p. 31.
"Letter from Spain." [SanFPJ] (8:4) 85, p. 45-46.
"No Picnic." [SanFPJ] (9:1) 86, p. 40.
"Rule or Ruin." [SanFPJ] (8:2) 85, p. 84.
112. AMICHAI, Yehuda
"Autobiography, 1952" (tr. by Stephen Mitchell). [PartR] (53:2) 86, p. 232-233.
"Ballad of the Washed Hair." [Atlantic] (257:1) Ja 86, p. 60.
"A Girl Called Sarah" (tr. by Stephen Mitchell). [PoetL] (81:2) Sum 86, p. 77.
"God's Hand in the World." [Atlantic] (257:1) Ja 86, p. 60.
"In a Leap Year" (tr. by Chana Bloch). [Field] (34) Spr 86, p. 63.
"Inside the Apple" (tr. by Chana Bloch). [NewRep] (194:18) 5 My 86, p. 38.
"Jasmine" (tr. by Chana Bloch). [Shen] (36:3) 86, p. 90.
"Love Is Finished Again" (tr. by Chana Bloch). [Field] (34) Spr 86, p. 64.
"Of Three or Four in a Room" (tr. by Stephen Mitchell). [Nat] (242:15) 19 Ap 86, p. 559.
"On Rabbi Kook's Street" (tr. by Karen Alkalay-Gut). [MassR] (27:2) Sum 86, p. 194.
"Relativity" (tr. by Chana Bloch). [Field] (34) Spr 86, p. 65.
"Songs of Zion the Beautiful" (Selection: 12, 14, tr. by Chana Bloch). [PoetL] (81:2) Sum 86, p. 75-76.
"Summer or Its End" (tr. by Stephen Mitchell). [Nat] (242:15) 19 Ap 86, p. 558.
113. AMIR, Ibn Musa
"Yes, certainly the land you offer me is better, richer than my own" (tr. by Will Kirkland). [NewOR] (13:4) Wint 86, p. 31.
114. AMISON, Les
"The Grinders." [Sam] (44:2 release 174) 86, p. 43.
"Plumbing." [Sam] (44:3 release 175) 86, p. 35.
115. AMMONS, A. R.
"Autonomy." [Pembroke] (18) 86, p. 13.
"Backcasting." [Pembroke] (18) 86, p. 20.
"Breaking for the Broken." [Pembroke] (18) 86, p. 25.
"Cold Rheum." [Pembroke] (18) 86, p. 16.
"Could Be." [Pembroke] (18) 86, p. 17.
"Course Work." [Pembroke] (18) 86, p. 19.
"The Dwelling." [Pembroke] (18) 86, p. 14-15.
"Eidos." [Pembroke] (18) 86, p. 10.
"Entranceways." [Pembroke] (18) 86, p. 20-21.
"Evasive Actions." [Pembroke] (18) 86, p. 24.
"Hairy Belly." [Pembroke] (18) 86, p. 19.
"The Hubbub." [Pembroke] (18) 86, p. 12-13.
"Ithaca, N.Y." [Pembroke] (18) 86, p. 208-209.
"Liquidities." [Pembroke] (18) 86, p. 16.
"Long Sorrowing." [NewYorker] (62:35) 20 O 86, p. 48.
"Marking Time." [Pembroke] (18) 86, p. 15.
"Milepost." [Pembroke] (18) 86, p. 26.
"Night Post." [Pembroke] (18) 86, p. 26.
"Noted Imposition." [Pembroke] (18) 86, p. 21.
"Over and Done With." [Pembroke] (18) 86, p. 24.
"Permanence." [Pembroke] (18) 86, p. 13.
"Regards Regardless." [Pembroke] (18) 86, p. 22-23.
"Rosy Transients." [Pembroke] (18) 86, p. 14.
"So I Said I Am Ezra." [Pembroke] (18) 86, p. 209.

"Some Any." [Pembroke] (18) 86, p. 18.
"Spring Cleaning." [Pembroke] (18) 86, p. 26.
"Summer Fashion." [Pembroke] (18) 86, p. 23.
"Superstars." [Pembroke] (18) 86, p. 18.
"Telling Moves." [Pembroke] (18) 86, p. 17.
"Their Sex Life." [Pembroke] (18) 86, p. 26.
"Trivial Means." [Pembroke] (18) 86, p. 11.
"Working Out." [Pembroke] (18) 86, p. 10-11.
"The Yucca Moth." [Pembroke] (18) 86, p. 134-135.
116. AMOR, Alicia
"Puntualidad de Golondrinas" (Al Dr. Juan Grau). [LetFem] (12:1/2)
Primavera-Otoño 86, p. 163-164.
AMOUR, Michèle d'
See D'AMOUR, Michèle
117. AMPRIMOZ, Alexandre (Alexandre L.)
"Alba." [PraF] (7:4) Wint 86-87, p. 13.
"Knitting the Invisible." [PraF] (7:4) Wint 86-87, p. 12.
"Like April in Paris." [CanLit] (111) Wint 86, p. 129.
"The Poem That Fall." [WestCR] (20:4) Ap 86, p. 41.
"Rain in Their Shoes." [WestCR] (20:4) Ap 86, p. 40.
"Risorgimento." [WestCR] (20:4) Ap 86, p. 42.
"Social Conventions." [Rampike] (5:1) 86, p. 76-77.
"A Voice at the Zoo." [WestCR] (20:4) Ap 86, p. 39.
"Waves." [PraF] (7:4) Wint 86-87, p. 13.
118. ANAPORTE, Jean Easton
"Touch." [YellowS] (21) Wint 86, p. 7.
119. ANASTACIO, Michael
"October Is Walking." [AntigR] (65) Spr 86, p. 58.
120. ANDAY, Melih Cevdet
"Are We Going to Live Without Aging?" (tr. by Talat Sait Halman). [Vis] (22) 86, p.
22.
121. ANDERMAN, Joan
"Some nights some rooms are swathed in comfort." [Amelia] (3:4) Fall 86, p. 46.
122. ANDERS, Shirley B.
"Letter to A.R. Ammons." [Pembroke] (18) 86, p. 233-234.
123. ANDERSON, Barbara
"Is It You." [Sonora] (10) Spr 86, p. 8-9.
"Tough Love." [Sonora] (10) Spr 86, p. 6-7.
124. ANDERSON, Bobby
"Aladdin." [Ploughs] (12:4) 86, p. 97.
125. ANDERSON, Colleen
"Calhoun County, September." [CarolQ] (38:2) Wint 86, p. 76.
126. ANDERSON, Douglas
"Site of the First Self-Sustaining Controlled Nuclear Chain Reaction, December 2,
1942." [LittleM] (15:2) 86, p. 7.
127. ANDERSON, Erland
"And Eternity?" (tr. of Rolf Aggestam, w. Lars Nordström). [InterPR] (12:1) Spr 86,
p. 11.
"Encounter" (tr. of Rolf Aggestam, w. Lars Nordström). [InterPR] (12:1) Spr 86, p.
11.
"The Future Sleeps" (tr. of Rolf Aggestam, w. Lars Nordström). [InterPR] (12:1) Spr
86, p. 15.
"I Came to Uncle Axel But Could Not Find Him" (tr. of Rolf Aggestam, w. Lars
Nordström). [InterPR] (12:1) Spr 86, p. 13.
"Psychological Experiments." [CharR] (12:2) Fall 86, p. 68-70.
"Song of the Shaman in Our Time" (tr. of Rolf Aggestam, w. Lars Nordström).
[InterPR] (12:1) Spr 86, p. 7.
"Three Tons of Rock a Day" (tr. of Rolf Aggestam, w. Lars Nordström). [InterPR]
(12:1) Spr 86, p. 9.
"Troll Eye" (tr. of Rolf Aggestam, w. Lars Nordström). [InterPR] (12:1) Spr 86, p.
19.
"You Shall Stare Down" (tr. of Rolf Aggestam, w. Lars Nordström). [InterPR] (12:1)
Spr 86, p. 17.
128. ANDERSON, J. S.
"Beyond the 100th Meridian." [Poem] (56) N 86, p. 26.
"Circumspect beneath the Senses." [Poem] (56) N 86, p. 27.

"Time Was Nothing." [Poem] (56) N 86, p. 28.
129. ANDERSON, Jack
"Around Here." [LittleM] (15:2) 86, p. 5-6.
"How We Are Born." [Caliban] (1) 86, p. 43-44.
"Life on the Moon." [Caliban] (1) 86, p. 44.
"Street Talk." [Caliban] (1) 86, p. 43.
"Voice from a Future." [LittleM] (15:2) 86, p. 4.
130. ANDERSON, Kath
"Bellini's Models: *Madonna and Saints*" (San Zaccaria, Venice). [Ploughs] (12:4) 86, p. 77-78.
131. ANDERSON, Ken
"The Phone." [ConnPR] (5:1) 86, p. 27.
132. ANDERSON, Lori
"Adhering." [SingHM] (13) 86, p. 76.
133. ANDERSON, Maggie
"The Artist." [MissouriR] (9:2) 86, p. 11.
"Before Winter." [PennR] (2:1) Fall-Wint 86, p. 61.
"Civilization." [AmerPoR] (15:4) Jl-Ag 86, p. 10.
"Long Story." [PoetryE] (20/21) Fall 86, p. 96-97.
"To Carry All of Us." [AmerPoR] (15:4) Jl-Ag 86, p. 10.
134. ANDERSON, Mark
"The Magnificence of Big Trees." [CimR] (76) Jl 86, p. 18.
ANDERSON, Maxine S. Petry
See PETRY-ANDERSON, Maxine S.
135. ANDERSON, Mia
"Château Puits '81." [Quarry] (35:1) Wint 86, p. 89-94.
"The Milky Way Goes into the Food Processor" (A Ghazal). [Rampike] (5:1) 86, p. 64.
"The Nature Store." [MalR] (74) Mr 86, p. 96-101.
136. ANDERSON, Michael
"Another Bedside History of Angst." [WormR] (26:1, issue 101) 86, p. 26-27.
"Aubade in Cow Country." [Wind] (16:58) 86, p. 2-3.
"The Oregonization of Rain." [WormR] (26:1, issue 101) 86, p. 25-26.
"Reunion at Galapagos High." [Wind] (16:58) 86, p. 1-2.
137. ANDERSON, Rod
"Susan." [Waves] (14:3) Wint 86, p. 60.
"Understanding." [Quarry] (35:4) Aut 86, p. 34.
"Waves." [Quarry] (35:4) Aut 86, p. 35-36.
138. ANDERSON, Teresa
"Kneading Bread" (for Denis on a day when there is no money). [SingHM] (13) 86, p. 78-79.
139. ANDINA, Peter T.
"Time Change." [Wind] (16:57) 86, p. 1.
140. ANDRADE, Carlos Drummond de
"Song for That Man of the People Charlie Chaplin" (tr. by Thomas Colchie). [ParisR] (28:100) Sum-Fall 86, p. 152-159.
141. ANDRADE, Eugenio de
"As If There Were Still Leaves" (tr. by Alexis Levitin). [PennR] (1:2) Fall 85, p. 49.
"Concerns of Summer" (tr. by Alexis Levitin). [Confr] (32) Spr-Sum 86, p. 106.
"Exercises with Vowels" (tr. by Alexis Levitin). [IndR] (9:2) Spr 86, p. 24.
"A friend is sometimes desert" (tr. by Alexis Levitin). [Verse] (3:3) N 86, p. 11.
"No, it is not yet the troubled light of March" (tr. by Alexis Levitin). [Verse] (3:3) N 86, p. 11.
"Upon Desire" (tr. by Alexis Levitin). [Confr] (32) Spr-Sum 86, p. 106.
"While I Was Writing" (tr. by Alexis Levitin). [IndR] (9:2) Spr 86, p. 25.
142. ANDREI, Cristian
"Postmeridian" (tr. of Nina Cassian, w. the author and Naomi Lazard). [NewYorker] (62:38) 10 N 86, p. 45.
143. ANDRESEN, Sophia de Mello Breyner
"Coral" (Excerpt, tr. by Lisa Sapinkopf). [AnotherCM] (15) 86, p. 5.
"Dead, How bright you are" (tr. by Lisa Sapinkopf). [WebR] (11:1) Spr 86, p. 34-35.
"Graphic" (tr. by Lisa Sapinkopf). [AnotherCM] (15) 86, p. 6.
144. ANDREWS, Bruce
"Don't Write Down Your Thoughts." [Sink] (1) 86, p. 52-53.

"I Don't Have Any Paper So Shut Up (or, Social Realism)" (Selections: 4 poems). [Temblor] (4) 86, p. 67-74.
"Only the Ego Can Pick Up a Pencil." [Sink] (1) 86, p. 50-51.
145. ANDREWS, Linda
"Fogbound, Sailing Toward Buoy #6." [TarRP] (25:2) Spr 86, p. 37.
"Shared Custody" (for Carrie). [TarRP] (25:2) Spr 86, p. 38.
146. ANDREWS, M. S.
"Sisters." [YetASM] (5) 86, p. 4.
147. ANDREWS, Michael
"Body Bags" (Excerpt, for the 5th Cavalry to the tune of 'Camptown Ladies'). [Sam] (46:2 release 182) 86, p. 5-6.
"Boy on Curb" (San Cristobal de las Casa, Mexico). [DeKalbLAJ] (19:1) 86, p. 26.
"For 2 Cents." [DeKalbLAJ] (19:1) 86, p. 27.
"The Man in the Mural" (Toluca, Mexico). [CapeR] (21:2) Fall 86, p. 20-21.
"Stones." [ArizQ] (42:3) Aut 86, p. 285.
"A Telegram, Unsigned." (Chapbook issue). [Sam] (45:1, release 177) 86, 20 p.
"VIPS, Paseo de la Reforma, Mexico City." [Lips] (12) 86, p. 25-27.
148. ANDREWS, Nancy
"Mine Shaft." [ConnPR] (5:1) 86, p. 26.
149. ANDREWS, Susan
"For Patrick." [PraF] (7:3) Aut 86, p. 73.
"Non-Violence." [CanLit] (108) Spr 86, p. 39.
150. ANDREWS, Tom
"By a Bend in the Kanawha River" (for Jack Ridl). [PassN] (7:2) Spr-Sum 86, p. 4.
"Clay." [Wind] (16:58) 86, p. 4.
"Evening Song." [AntR] (44:4) Fall 86, p. 435.
"May I Read You a Few Lines from Pepys' Diary?" (for Guy Davenport and Charles Wright). [MissouriR] (9:2) 86, p. 155-157.
"Paul Celan." [Field] (34) Spr 86, p. 40-41.
"Prayer in Gratitude." [Wind] (16:58) 86, p. 4.
"Three for Slugs." [Wind] (16:58) 86, p. 5.
151. ANDROLA, Ron
"Day." [Bogg] (55) 86, p. 35.
"Rick's Halloween." [SlipS] (6) 86, p. 39.
152. ANDRUS, David
"Interruption." [Quarry] (35:3) Sum 86, p. 27-28.
"The Machine." [Quarry] (35:3) Sum 86, p. 26-27.
153. ANDRUS, R. Blain
"As I Climbed Up." [Amelia] (3:2) Spr 86, p. 30.
154. ANGEL, Ralph
"Headlights Trail Away." [ColEng] (48:7) N 86, p. 683.
"Long Shadows, Many Footsteps." [MissouriR] (9:2) 86, p. 206-207.
"The Privilege of Silence." [AmerPoR] (15:2) Mr-Ap 86, p. 48.
"Subliminal Birds." [ColEng] (48:7) N 86, p. 681.
"Unspeakable." [ColEng] (48:7) N 86, p. 682-683.
"Waves." [MissouriR] (9:2) 86, p. 205.
155. ANGELL, Robert
"Greetings, Friends!" [NewYorker] (62:45) 29 D 86, p. 23.
ANGELO, Anna d'
See D'ANGELO, Anna
156. ANGKUW, Rietje M. (Rietje Marie)
"Correspondence." [AntigR] (66/67) Sum-Aut 86, p. 68-69.
"There Is Nothing." [NegC] (6:4) Fall 86, p. 109.
157. ANGLESEY, Zoe
"Evocation of Carmen Miranda" (tr. of Luz Méndez de la Vega). [MassR] (27:3/4) Fall-Wint 86, p. 660.
"Home Rivers." [Ploughs] (12:4) 86, p. 44-45.
"I Want to Find, Desparately I Look" (tr. of Bertalicia Peralta). [MassR] (27:3/4) Fall-Wint 86, p. 570.
"It Is." [OP] (42/43) Wint 86-87, p. 137.
"It Is Certain That We Are Constructing a World" (tr. of Rosario Murillo). [MassR] (27:3/4) Fall-Wint 86, p. 643-645.
"The Man Who Boxes" (tr. of Ana Istarú). [MassR] (27:3/4) Fall-Wint 86, p. 528-530.
"The Recent Future." [OP] (42/43) Wint 86-87, p. 136.

"Sudden Death" (Selections: 1-6, tr. of Etelvina Astrada). [MassR] (27:3/4) Fall-Wint
   86, p. 458-460.
"This Country Is in a Dream" (tr. of Ana Istarú). [MassR] (27:3/4) Fall-Wint 86, p.
   526-528.
"Uncertainty" (to my old man, tr. of Bessy Reyna). [MassR] (27:3/4) Fall-Wint 86, p.
   643-645.
158. ANNHARTE
"Hudson Bay Bill." [Cond] (13) 86, p. 94.
"Moon Bear." [PraF] (7:4) Wint 86-87, p. 66.
"Warrior Woman." [Cond] (13) 86, p. 93.
159. ANONYMOUS
"All My Words" (tr. from Bangla by Abu Zafar Obaidullah). [Pax] (3:1/2) Wint
   85-86, p. 194-198.
"Canto del Fuego" (Poesia Tradicional Africana). [Mairena] (8:22) 86, p. 31.
"La Doncella Guerrera" (Judeo-Español romança). [SinW] (29/30) 86, p. 27.
"The Fig Tree's Leaves Have Returned" (tr. from the Malagasy by Leonard Fox).
   [Translation] (16) Spr 86, p. 179.
"Hymns from the Time of the Conquest" (in English & Quechua, tr. by Grady
   Hillman). [Pax] (3:1/2) Wint 85-86, p. 62-66.
"I am neither Arab nor Jew" (Palestinian Song, tr. by Will Kirkland). [NewOR]
   (13:4) Wint 86, p. 28.
"I Am the Friendless Child" (tr. from the Malagasy by Leonard Fox). [Translation]
   (16) Spr 86, p. 180.
"If you've been married once" (from "The Palatine Anthology, tr. by John Gill).
   [YellowS] (21) Wint 86, p. 24.
"Limbic Chill." [SanFPJ] (9:1) 86, p. 36.
"The Mourning Songs of Greece" (tr. by Konstantinos Lardas). [BlackWR] (13:1)
   Fall 86, p. 26-34.
"The Mourning Songs of Greece" (tr. by Konstantinos Lardas). [LitR] (30:1) Fall 86,
   p. 81-83.
"The Mourning Songs of Greece" (tr. by Konstantinos Lardas). [SenR] (16:2) 86, p.
   101-112.
"Par'ó era 'Strellero" (Judeo-Español romança). [SinW] (29/30) 86, p. 29.
"Quechua Poetry" (Four poems tr. by Miriam Joel). [WebR] (11:2) Fall 86, p. 40.
"The Rape of Dina" (tr. of anonymous Judeo-Español romança). [SinW] (29/30) 86,
   p. 26.
"El Robo de Dina" (Judeo-Español romança). [SinW] (29/30) 86, p. 26.
"The Seafarer" (tr. from Old English by Antony Oldknow). [NoDaQ] (54:4) Fall 86,
   p. 18-21.
"Sol la Saddika" (Judeo-Español romança). [SinW] (29/30) 86, p. 28.
"Sol the Righteous" (tr. of anonymous Judeo-Español romança). [SinW] (29/30) 86,
   p. 28.
"Song" (from *Kanteletar*, collected by Lonnrot in the 19th century, tr. by Jascha
   Kessler and Kirsti Simonsuuri). [MalR] (77) D 86, p. 45.
"The Story-Teller of Messer Azzolino" (tr. by Felix Stefanile). [Sparrow] (50) 86, p.
   16-20.
"Style." [Bogg] (56) 86, p. 24.
"Tell the Clouds to Wait" (tr. from the Malagasy by Leonard Fox). [Translation] (16)
   Spr 86, p. 179.
"Thirteen Ahau" (from the Book of Chilam Balam, a Mayan volume of prophecy, tr.
   by Steve Wilson). [WebR] (11:1) Spr 86, p. 43.
"Tian Wen: A Chinese Book of Origins" (Selections: Parts I-II, tr. by Stephen Field).
   [Translation] (17) Fall 86, p. 275-282.
"The Wanderer" (tr. from Old English by Antony Oldknow). [NoDaQ] (54:4) Fall 86,
   p. 21-24.
"The Warrior Maiden" (tr. of anonymous Judeo-Español romança). [SinW] (29/30)
   86, p. 27-28.
"We can argue about whether I am a Jew or an Israeli" (A dialogue, translated from
   the Ladino by Will Kirkland). [NewOR] (13:4) Wint 86, p. 36.
"When Paroah Gazed at the Stars" (tr. of anonymous Judeo-Español romança).
   [SinW] (29/30) 86, p. 29.
"When you were a green grape you refused me" (from "The Palatine Anthology, tr. by
   John Gill). [YellowS] (21) Wint 86, p. 24.
"Wine, Women & Weddings." [Bogg] (55) 86, p. 51.
"You ought to stop this search for perverse pleasure" (from "The Palatine Anthology,
   tr. by John Gill). [YellowS] (21) Wint 86, p. 24.

160. ANSON, John
"Old Fish Eye." [Thrpny] (25) Spr 86, p. 5.
ANTAS, Guillermo Argar de
See ARGAR DE ANTAS, Guillermo
161. ANTHONY, Frank
"The Plan." [NegC] (6:2/3) Spr-Sum 86, p. 48.
162. ANTON, Ted
"Street Glance." [JINJPo] (9:1) 86, p. 5.
163. ANZAI, Hitoshi
"The Ancient Pine Tree on Mt. Tempai" (tr. by James Kirkup and Akiko Takemoto).
[Translation] (17) Fall 86, p. 116.
"My Eye" (tr. by James Kirkup and Akiko Takemoto). [Translation] (17) Fall 86, p.
115.
164. APPEL, Cathy
"Legacy." [PraS] (60:4) Wint 86, p. 101.
"Letters." [Raccoon] (20) Ap 86, p. 38.
"Observations." [Raccoon] (20) Ap 86, p. 37.
165. APPEL, Dori
"Savings Account." [NewRena] (6:3, #20) Spr 86, p. 108-109.
166. APPELL, M. R.
"Totem at Skidegate." [AntigR] (65) Spr 86, p. 165-166.
167. APPLEBAUM, Mika
"Seedling." [PoeticJ] (14) 86, p. 29.
168. APPLEMAN, Philip
"Heading North." [Poetry] (149:1) O 86, p. 27.
"In the Summer of '36." [IndR] (9:1) Wint 86, p. 87-90.
169. APPLEWHITE, James
"The Hard Role." [SouthernR] (22:2) Ap 86, p. 357-358.
"The Other, Nature." [SouthernR] (22:2) Ap 86, p. 359.
"Southern Voices." [SouthernR] (22:2) Ap 86, p. 356-357.
170. APSCHE, Jack
"After the War." [Sam] (46:2 release 182) 86, p. 118.
171. ARBERY, Glenn Cannon
"Honeymoon, All Soul's." [KenR] (NS 7:1) Wint 85, p. 54-65.
ARCY, Michael James d'
See D'ARCY, Michael James
172. ARENAS, Rosa Maria
"At Buck and Mary's." [PassN] (7:1) Fall-Wint 85-86, p. 26.
173. ARGAR DE ANTAS, Guillermo
"La Esquina." [Mairena] (8:22) 86, p. 28.
174. ARGUELLES, Ivan
"Artificial Paranoia." [SilverFR] (11) Sum 86, p. 5.
"Black Pomegranate." [YellowS] (19) Sum 86, p. 17.
"Capital of the World." [Sink] (1) 86, p. 62.
"The Death of Stalin." [Abraxas] (34) 86, p. 16-17.
"Diplomacy." [Sink] (1) 86, p. 61.
"Fame & Fortune." [StoneC] (14:1/2) Fall-Wint 86-87, p. 43.
"For Max: Six Years After." [SilverFR] (11) Sum 86, p. 8.
"The Form of Salome the Shape of Shekinah." [YellowS] (19) Sum 86, p. 16.
"Hero and Leander." [Sink] (1) 86, p. 63.
"Higher Education." [NowestR] (24:2) 86, p. 19.
"History of Pier Paolo Pasolini." [Caliban] (1) 86, p. 6.
"Hylas." [YellowS] (19) Sum 86, p. 15.
"In the Place Where Time Stops." [YellowS] (20) Aut 86, p. 25.
"Labyrinthesis." [YellowS] (19) Sum 86, p. 16.
"Life's Undelivered Letter." [AmerPoR] (15:5) S-O 86, p. 35.
"Marginalia." [RedBass] (11) 86, p. 24.
"The Masque of the Red Death." [Abraxas] (34) 86, p. 18.
"Mysteries of the Orgasm." [YellowS] (20) Aut 86, p. 23.
"Orlando Innamorato." [YellowS] (20) Aut 86, p. 24.
"The Poet to His Wife." [NowestR] (24:2) 86, p. 20.
"Portrait of Alfred." [Interim] (5:1) Spr 86, p. 46.
"Shafts of Agony." [Caliban] (1) 86, p. 4.
"Tartara." [RedBass] (11) 86, p. 24.
"The Temple of Mars." [Caliban] (1) 86, p. 5.
"Undressing the Hangman." [SilverFR] (11) Sum 86, p. 6-7.

"La Vita Nuova: An Interpretation." [Electrum] (38) Spr 86, p. 16.
"Warning to Orpheus." [Lips] (12) 86, p. 21.
175. ARGYROS, Alex
"Dirge for My Father, August 31, 1983." [Grain] (14:4) N 86, p. 75-77.
"Early April." [Grain] (14:4) N 86, p. 68-69.
"In the Valley of the Roundout." [Grain] (14:4) N 86, p. 73-74.
"Partition." [Grain] (14:4) N 86, p. 71-72.
"The Second Time." [LitR] (29:3) Spr 86, p. 282.
"Stéphane's Fowl." [Grain] (14:4) N 86, p. 70.
"The White Mountain." [LitR] (29:3) Spr 86, p. 283.
176. ARIAS, Olga
"He padecido." [Mairena] (8:22) 86, p. 9.
177. ARIDJIS, Homero
"Persephone" (Excerpt, tr. by Betty Ferber). [Translation] (16) Spr 86, p. 226-233.
178. ARIF, Ahmet
"In Prison" (tr. by Ozcan Yalim, William Fielder & Dionis Riggs). [InterPR] (12:1)
    Spr 86, p. 65.
179. ARIZA, René
"Fragmentos." [Mairena] (8:22) 86, p. 84.
180. ARKELL, C.
"Under the Reach of the Sky" (tr. of Eugene Dubnov, w. the author). [AntigR] (65)
    Spr 86, p. 34.
181. ARMAND, Octavio
"Confess, 1220-50" (tr. by Carol Maier). [IndR] (9:2) Spr 86, p. 26.
182. ARMANTROUT, Rae
"The Garden." [Sulfur] (6:1, issue 16) 86, p. 54.
"Labors." [Sink] (2) 86, p. 13-14.
"On Location." [Sink] (2) 86, p. 15.
"Sense." [Sulfur] (6:1, issue 16) 86, p. 54-55.
183. ARMAS, Edda
"Así camine sin sentido ni desmarcando los rayados." [LindLM] (5:2) Ap-Je 86, p.
    10.
"El hombre camina esta calle del día sin ocupar los ojos en el paisaje." [LindLM] (5:2)
    Ap-Je 86, p. 10.
184. ARMER, Sondra
"Home Movies." [NegC] (6:1) Wint 86, p. 80-81.
"The Passover Set Was Glass." [YetASM] (5) 86, p. 5.
"Safari." [YetASM] (4) 85, insert.
185. ARMIJO, Richard
"The fabulous butterflies!" [Contact] (7:38/39/40) Wint-Spr 86, p. 87.
186. ARMITAGE, Barri
"Fall Ritual." [Poetry] (148:6) S 86, p. 336.
"Replay." [GeoR] (40:4) Wint 86, p. 968-969.
"Weights." [Poetry] (148:6) S 86, p. 337.
187. ARMSTRONG, Gene
"Blocked Out in Yellow." [BellArk] (2:4) Jl-Ag 86, p. 16.
"Signs of Summer." [BellArk] (2:4) Jl-Ag 86, p. 8.
188. ARMSTRONG, Lewis, Jr.
"13 years and still smoking." [Wind] (16:57) 86, p. 2.
"Another year enters." [Wind] (16:57) 86, p. 2.
189. ARMSTRONG, Tim
"The first dead leaves fall." [Bogg] (55) 86, p. 43.
190. ARNEY, Helen Troisi
"To Paul." [SpoonRQ] (11:2) Spr 86, p. 37.
191. ARNOUX, Gale Coffin
"Triptych: Bryn Athyn, Philadelphia, the Farm." [NewL] (52:2/3) Wint-Spr 86, p.
    238.
192. ARPIN, Roger C.
"The First Day of Winter." [CapeR] (21:2) Fall 86, p. 29.
ARPINO, Tony d'
    See D'ARPINO, Tony
193. ARRAIZ LUCCA, Rafael
"I. Era el sitio del perdón." [LindLM] (5:2) Ap-Je 86, p. 3.
"IV. En un día podían ocurrir tranquilamente." [LindLM] (5:2) Ap-Je 86, p. 3.
194. ARROWSMITH, William
"Agave on the Rocks" (tr. of Eugenio Montale). [AmerPoR] (15:4) Jl-Ag 86, p. 25.

"Autumn Cellars" (tr. of Eugenio Montale). [ParisR] (28:101) Wint 86, p. 231.
"Cape Mesco" (tr. of Eugenio Montale). [Translation] (17) Fall 86, p. 234.
"Cliffside" (tr. of Eugenio Montale). [AmerPoR] (15:4) Jl-Ag 86, p. 26.
"Cuttlefish Bones" (tr. of Eugenio Montale). [AmerPoR] (15:4) Jl-Ag 86, p. 22-24.
"Delta" (tr. of Eugenio Montale). [AmerPoR] (15:4) Jl-Ag 86, p. 27.
"Elegy of Pico Farnese" (tr. of Eugenio Montale). [Translation] (17) Fall 86, p. 231-233.
"House by the Sea" (tr. of Eugenio Montale). [AmerPoR] (15:4) Jl-Ag 86, p. 27.
"The Lemon Trees" (tr. of Eugenio Montale). [NewYRB] (33:3) 27 F 86, p. 26.
"Minstrels" (from C. Debussy, tr. of Eugenio Montale). [AmerPoR] (15:4) Jl-Ag 86, p. 27.
"Moiré" (tr. of Eugenio Montale). [AmerPoR] (15:4) Jl-Ag 86, p. 26.
"Palio" (tr. of Eugenio Montale). [Translation] (17) Fall 86, p. 235-236.
"Pool" (tr. of Eugenio Montale). [AmerPoR] (15:4) Jl-Ag 86, p. 27.
"Rejoice: this breeze entering the orchard" (tr. of Eugenio Montale). [AmerPoR] (15:4) Jl-Ag 86, p. 21.
"Sarcophagi" (tr. of Eugenio Montale). [Translation] (16) Spr 86, p. 129-131.
"To Liuba, Leaving" (tr. of Eugenio Montale). [ParisR] (28:101) Wint 86, p. 231.
"Wind and Banners" (tr. of Eugenio Montale). [AmerPoR] (15:4) Jl-Ag 86, p. 25.
195. ARROYO VICENTE, Arminda
"Poeta de Poetas!." [Mairena] (8:21) 86, p. 53.
"Quiero Cantar." [Mairena] (8:22) 86, p. 103.
196. ARTHUR, Delna
"Can You Imagine?" [SanFPJ] (8:2) 85, p. 35.
"Secy. Udall Looks at a Nuclear Dumpsite." [SanFPJ] (8:3) 85, p. 7.
197. ARVEY, Michael
"Annie." [Farm] (3:1) Fall 85, p. 29.
"Artaud, Don't Let It Snow." [CutB] (25) Fall-Wint 86, p. 33.
"The Carnival Barker's Son." [CrabCR] (3:3) Sum 86, p. 25.
"Note." [CutB] (25) Fall-Wint 86, p. 32.
198. ARVIO, Sarah
"It Can Happen" (tr. of Vicente Huidobro). [MassR] (27:3/4) Fall-Wint 86, p. 422.
199. ASBRIDGE, N. S.
"Battle Honours." [Bogg] (55) 86, p. 34.
200. ASCHMANN, Charles
"An Old Man's Song in Winter." [DeKalbLAJ] (19:2) 86, p. 10.
"To Rest." [DeKalbLAJ] (19:2) 86, p. 10.
201. ASCLEPIADES
"If you're thirsty, snow in summer is sweet" (from "The Palatine Anthology, tr. by John Gill). [YellowS] (21) Wint 86, p. 24.
"I'm only twenty-one and life is already a burden" (from "The Palatine Anthology, tr. by John Gill). [YellowS] (21) Wint 86, p. 25.
202. ASH, John
"In the Street." [ParisR] (28:101) Wint 86, p. 60.
"A Long Encounter" (for Maggie Paley). [ParisR] (28:101) Wint 86, p. 58.
"The Monuments." [ParisR] (28:100) Sum-Fall 86, p. 52-53.
"Party Damage." [ParisR] (28:101) Wint 86, p. 59.
"Unwilling Suspension." [NewYorker] (62:10) 28 Ap 86, p. 38.
203. ASH, Karin
"Winter's Note." [NewL] (53:1) Fall 86, p. 102.
204. ASHANTI, Asa Paschal
"After the Second War." [Obs] (NS 1:1/2) Spr-Sum 86, p. 109-110.
"Drowning in the Del Gap." [Obs] (NS 1:1/2) Spr-Sum 86, p. 110-111.
"Washington Monument, September 18, 1976." [Obs] (NS 1:1/2) Spr-Sum 86, p. 111-112.
"Where Have You Gone Jackie Robinson." [Obs] (NS 1:1/2) Spr-Sum 86, p. 108-109.
205. ASHBERY, John
"Alone in the Lumber Business." [NewYorker] (62:1) 24 F 86, p. 34.
"Märchenbilder." [GeoR] (40:3) Fall 86, p. 625-626.
"Posture of Unease." [Verse] (3:3) N 86, p. 3.
"A Sermon: Amos 8:11-14." [HarvardA] (119:4) My 86, p. 27.
"Vaucanson." [NewYorker] (62:43) 15 D 86, p. 40.
"Whether It Exists." [GeoR] (40:3) Fall 86, p. 626.
206. ASHEAR, Linda
"Anthem." [BellR] (9:1) Spr 86, p. 28.

"In the Shadow of the Goat." [Amelia] (3:4) Fall 86, p. 64-65.
207. ASKINS, Justin
"The Lesson" (for Herb Leibowitz). [Jacaranda] (2:1) Fall 86, p. 37.
208. ASPENSTROM, Werner
"You and I and the World" (tr. by Siv Cedering). [PoetryE] (20/21) Fall 86, p. 78.
209. ASPINWALL, Dorothy (Dorothy B.)
"Crayfish" (tr. of Pierre Mathias). [CumbPR] (5:2) Spr 86, p. 79.
"The Difficult Journey" (tr. of Jules Supervielle). [WebR] (11:2) Fall 86, p. 28.
"Forgetting My Body" (tr. of Jules Supervielle). [WebR] (11:2) Fall 86, p. 29.
"I am like you, O Wind!" ("Untitled", tr. of Ilarie Voronca). [WebR] (11:2) Fall 86,
    p. 26.
"In the Kingdom of Moles: Death" (tr. of Tristan Klingsor). [WebR] (11:2) Fall 86, p.
    25.
"The Point of a Flame" (tr. of Jules Supervielle). [WebR] (11:2) Fall 86, p. 28.
"Stele of the Way of the Soul" (tr. of Victor Segalen). [WebR] (11:2) Fall 86, p. 27.
"Tale (Fragment)" (tr. of Ilarie Voronca). [CrabCR] (4:1) Fall-Wint 86, p. 4.
"To Get Lost Daily" (tr. of Victor Segelen). [CrabCR] (4:1) Fall-Wint 86, p. 5.
210. ASSAD, Maria
"Waldsterben." [Os] (22) 86, p. 6.
211. ASTOR, Susan
"Air Raid." [GWR] (6:2) 86, p. 24.
"Consenting to Night." [GWR] (6:2) 86, p. 26.
"Marriage." [GWR] (6:2) 86, p. 25.
212. ASTRACHAN, John Mann
"Barren." [NegC] (6:4) Fall 86, p. 113.
213. ASTRADA, Etelvina
"Muerte Arrebatada" (Selections: Poem 1-3, 8, 15, tr. by Timothy J. Rogers).
    [WebR] (11:1) Spr 86, p. 5-15.
"Sudden Death" (Selections: 1-6, tr. by Zoe Anglesey). [MassR] (27:3/4) Fall-Wint
    86, p. 458-460.
214. ATKINSON, Alan
"Mosquitoes." [Wind] (16:56) 86, p. 1-2.
215. ATKINSON, Charles
"Concert, After a Friend's Death." [DenQ] (20:4/21:1) Spr-Sum 86, p. 118-119.
"The Need for Coffee Break at Lockheed." [SouthwR] (71:4) Aut 86, p. 441.
"Scavenge after the Flood." [DenQ] (20:4/21:1) Spr-Sum 86, p. 120-121.
216. ATKINSON, Donald
"In Search of the Kreen-Akrore (an Anthropological Expedition)." [Stand] (27:2) Spr
    86, p. 46-47.
217. ATKINSON, Jennifer
"Choosing Happiness" (For Bob and Margie). [Poetry] (148:3) Je 86, p. 125-126.
"Exposures" (after reading the notebooks of Thomas Hardy). [Sonora] (11) Fall 86
    [c87], p. 73-74.
"Haddam in August." [PennR] (1:1) 85, p. 57.
218. ATUNGAYE, Manifa
"Lullaby and Sweet Goodnight." [BlackALF] (20:3) Fall 86, p. 312-313.
219. ATWOOD, Margaret
"Aging Female Poet Sits on the Balcony." [MalR] (75) Je 86, p. 25.
"An Angel." [MalR] (74) Mr 86, p. 61-62.
"At the Tourist Centre in Boston." [CrossCur] (6:3) 86, p. 24-25.
"Cave Series" (Excerpt). [GreenfR] (13:3/4) Sum-Fall 86, p. 5.
"Christmas Carols." [CrossCur] (6:3) 86, p. 60-61.
"Last Poem." [CrossCur] (6:3) 86, p. 73-74.
"Marrying the Hangman." [CrossCur] (6:3) 86, p. 47-51.
"Nightshade on the Way to School." [MalR] (75) Je 86, p. 27-28.
"Porcupine Tree." [MalR] (75) Je 86, p. 26.
"The Rest." [MalR] (75) Je 86, p. 29.
"There Is Only One of Everything." [CrossCur] (6:3) 86, p. 71-72.
"Three Praises." [MalR] (75) Je 86, p. 24.
"True Stories." [CrossCur] (6:3) 86, p. 21-23.
"Variations on the Word *Love*." [CrossCur] (6:3) 86, p. 58-59.
"Woman Skating." [CrossCur] (6:3) 86, p. 27-28.
"Women's Novels." [CrossCur] (6:3) 86, p. 29-32.
220. AUBERT, Alvin
"All Singing in a Pie." [Callaloo] (9:1, #26) Wint 86, p. 9.
"A Light Outside." [Callaloo] (9:1, #26) Wint 86, p. 11.

"Van der Zee Extrapolation #1." [Callaloo] (9:1, #26) Wint 86, p. 10.
221. AUBREY, Keith
"An Aesthetic of Autumn." [Pembroke] (18) 86, p. 249-250.
"The Ancient Circle" (Priest River valley, seven miles north of Jasper Mountain. One for Mark). [HolCrit] (23:5) D 86, p. 19.
222. AUER, Benedict
"Four White on Blacks: Thoughts on Photos by Ansel Adams." [CapeR] (21:2) Fall 86, p. 27.
"Mirror Maze." [PoeticJ] (16) Fall 86, p. 8.
223. AUERBACH, Emily
"To a Writer." [EngJ] (75:4) Ap 86, p. 28.
224. AUGUSTINE, Jane
"Rock, Cloud, Scroll" (in the Colorado mountains, meditating on H. D.). [Iowa] (16:3) Fall 86, p. 222-228.
225. AUSLANDER, Jay
"Epistemology." [InterPR] (12:2) Fall 86, p. 65.
"Ether." [InterPR] (12:2) Fall 86, p. 66.
"Metaphysic: A Dramatic 'Transcendalogue'." [InterPR] (12:2) Fall 86, p. 67.
"To a Soon-to-Be Mother." [InterPR] (12:2) Fall 86, p. 66.
226. AUSONIUS
"Three Epitaphs" (27, 31, 35, tr. by Joseph Salemi). [Translation] (17) Fall 86, p. 322-323.
227. AUSTIN, Kathy
"Playing Tag with the Moon." [Kaleid] (13) Sum-Fall 86, p. 55.
228. AUSTIN, Penelope
"How Not to Die." [AmerPoR] (15:3) My-Je 86, p. 16.
"Mrs. Walker's Injunction Becomes a Desire." [AmerPoR] (15:3) My-Je 86, p. 16.
AVE JEANNE
See JEANNE, Ave
229. AVERILL, Kelly
"St. Louis Cemetery." [SmPd] (23:3, #68) Fall 86, p. 30.
230. AVIDAN, David
"Practical Poems" (tr. by Karen Alkalay-Gut). [MassR] (27:2) Sum 86, p. 195.
231. AVISON, Margaret
"Goal Far and Near." [GreenfR] (13:3/4) Sum-Fall 86, p. 7.
"Setting for the Portrait." [GreenfR] (13:3/4) Sum-Fall 86, p. 8.
232. AWAD, Joseph (Joseph F.)
"Black Holes." [Vis] (20) 86, p. 11.
"A Novena for My Mother." [NegC] (6:1) Wint 86, p. 19-23.
"Orestes." [HolCrit] (23:1) F 86, p. 16.
"Remembering Washington." [KanQ] (18:1/2) Wint-Spr 86, p. 59.
233. AXELROD, David
"Cutthroat." [CrabCR] (3:3) Sum 86, p. 4.
"In the Jewish Community Cemetery." [ColR] (NS 13:1) Fall 85, p. 20.
"Incident at Moonville." [ColR] (NS 13:1) Fall 85, p. 21.
"Regarding a Nude on Diamond Mountain." [WillowS] (18) Sum 86, p. 24-25.
"This Morning in Detroit." [ColR] (NS 13:1) Fall 85, p. 19.
234. AXINN, Donald Everett
"Desert, Tucson to Phoenix." [WritersF] (12) Fall 86, p. 169-170.
235. AYCOCK, Shirley
"Pop" (4/30/1895 - 12/17/75). [PoeticJ] (16) Fall 86, p. 25.
"The Sisters." [YetASM] (4) 85, p. 7.
236. AYERS, Esther
"The Asparagus Eaters." [PassN] (7:1) Fall-Wint 85-86, p. 13.
237. AYUKAWA, Nobuo
"A Thought in Autumn" (tr. by James Kirkup and Akiko Takemoto). [Translation] (17) Fall 86, p. 200.
238. AZAD, Abid
"Her Eyes" (tr. by Kabir Chowdhury). [Pax] (3:1/2) Wint 85-86, p. 145.
239. AZZOUNI, Jody
"Amateur Theology." [HolCrit] (23:5) D 86, p. 16.
"Cancer Can Be Fatal." [Amelia] (3:1) Ja 86, p. 89.
"No Use Crying over Spilt Sap." [Amelia] (3:1) Ja 86, p. 89.

41

240. BAATZ, Ronald
"In Some Future Conversation." [YellowS] (21) Wint 86, p. 40.
"Second Hand" (Special Section). [WormR] (26:4, issue 104) 86, p. 135-146.
241. BABAD, Katharine Heath
"Anza Borrego." [CapeR] (21:1) Spr 86, p. 13.
"Behind Our Eyes." [CapeR] (21:1) Spr 86, p. 15.
"In Südtirol, in Answering." [CapeR] (21:1) Spr 86, p. 14.
242. BABICKY, Charlotte L.
"Last Moments." [YetASM] (4) 85, p. 3.
243. BACA, Jimmy Santiago
"I Have Always Compared the White Man to Snow." [BilingR] (12:1/2) Ja-Ag 85
[c1987], p. 116-117.
"Martin" (Excerpt). [QW] (22) Spr-Sum 86, p. 29.
"Since You've Come." [BilingR] (12:1/2) Ja-Ag 85 [c1987], p. 115.
244. BACHAM, Paul
"Back to the Caves." [SanFPJ] (8:4) 85, p. 51.
"Bargain Day / 1943." [SanFPJ] (8:4) 85, p. 50.
"Memorial Day." [SanFPJ] (8:4) 85, p. 52.
245. BACHLER, Wolfgang
"Villa Serpentara" (in German & English, tr. by Rainer Schulte). [RiverS] (20) 86, p.
38.
246. BACIU, Stefan
"Elegia en Sibiu para Lucian Blaga." [LindLM] (5:3) Jl-S 86, p. 5.
"Ernesto Mejia Sanchez" (Se nos mueren los amigos, E.M.S.). [LindLM] (5:3) Jl-S
86, p. 5.
"Exilio." [LindLM] (5:3) Jl-S 86, p. 5.
247. BADDOUR, Margaret Boothe
"Land of Is." [StoneC] (13:3/4) Spr-Sum 86, p. 63.
248. BAEZA FLORES, Alberto
"La soledad se hace a veces una delgada lámina de plata." [Mairena] (8:22) 86, p. 12.
249. BAGINSKY, Sigmund
"Jehova, if you exist, make the earth turn faster" (tr. by Will Kirkland). [NewOR]
(13:4) Wint 86, p. 33.
250. BAHAN, Lee Harlin
"Early Spring in the Settlers' Cemetery, Heighton Hill." [SpoonRQ] (11:4) Fall 86, p.
31.
251. BAHLKE, Kate
"Suburban Spring." [Amelia] (3:2) Spr 86, p. 105.
252. BAILEY, Alfred
"University Reading Room." [AntigR] (64) Wint 86, p. 103.
253. BAILEY, Don
"Every Day Life." [WestCR] (21:1) Je 86, p. 12.
"Everyday Living." [WestCR] (21:1) Je 86, p. 18.
"The Future." [WestCR] (21:1) Je 86, p. 17.
"Notes to Myself." [WestCR] (21:1) Je 86, p. 19.
"The Past." [WestCR] (21:1) Je 86, p. 15.
"The Present." [WestCR] (21:1) Je 86, p. 16.
"Thanksgiving" (a persona poem). [WestCR] (21:1) Je 86, p. 11.
"Therapy." [WestCR] (21:1) Je 86, p. 13.
"The Therapy of Joseph Small." [Quarry] (35:1) Wint 86, p. 30-38.
"Visitations." [WestCR] (21:1) Je 86, p. 14.
254. BAILEY, Donald
"America Was Promises." [SanFPJ] (8:3) 85, p. 76.
"Marie" (pianist). [KanQ] (18:4) Fall 86, p. 88.
"TV News." [SanFPJ] (8:3) 85, p. 69.
255. BAILEY, Rebecca
"Signs." [AntR] (44:2) Spr 86, p. 196.
256. BAILEY, Rick
"Word from Anzio." [ColEng] (48:8) D 86, p. 800.
257. BAILEY-WOFFORD, Jan
"Alzheimer's." [CrescentR] (4:2) Fall 86, p. 42.
"Upon the Anniversary of Her Son's Death." [SoCaR] (19:1) Fall 86, p. 47.
258. BAIRD, Bonnie
"Close Coffins." [PottPort] (8) 86-87, p. 28.
"Seasons Change." [PottPort] (8) 86-87, p. 28.

259. BAKER, Beverly
"Suburban Clytemnestra." [EngJ] (75:6) O 86, p. 56.
"Unprepared." [EngJ] (75:2) F 86, p. 57.
260. BAKER, David (Dave)
"Murder: Crows." [QW] (23) 86, p. 107.
"Sunbathing." [Poetry] (148:3) Je 86, p. 147.
"Survey: Last Reading." [MissouriR] (9:2) 86, p. 148-149.
261. BAKER, Donald W.
"Flat Box with Glass Cover." [TarRP] (25:1) Fall 85, p. 16.
BAKER, Marie
See ANNHARTE
262. BAKKEN, Dick
"Kathleen's Advice." [BellR] (9:2) Fall 86, p. 53.
263. BALAZS, Mary
"New Year." [KanQ] (18:1/2) Wint-Spr 86, p. 162-163.
"Respite." [KanQ] (18:1/2) Wint-Spr 86, p. 163.
264. BALCOMB, John
"At a Rebel Base in the Hindu Kush" (tr. of Gu Cheng). [Nimrod] (29:2) Spr-Sum
        86, p. 27.
"A Feeling" (tr. of Gu Cheng). [Nimrod] (29:2) Spr-Sum 86, p. 26.
"Near and Far" (tr. of Gu Cheng). [Nimrod] (29:2) Spr-Sum 86, p. 25.
"One Generation" (tr. of Gu Cheng). [Nimrod] (29:2) Spr-Sum 86, p. 25.
265. BALDERSTON, Jean
"City Park." [SingHM] (14) 86, p. 49.
266. BALDWIN, Barbara
"Huerfano." [NegC] (6:1) Wint 86, p. 95-96.
267. BALDWIN, Joseph
"Wood-note, Domestic." [PraS] (60:4) Wint 86, p. 42-43.
268. BALDWIN, Laura
"Honey." [Bogg] (56) 86, p. 49.
269. BALK, Christianne
"Before I Learned to Say Goodbye." [Sonora] (10) Spr 86, p. 33-36.
"The Holding Rocks" (For Paul, 1953-1979). [Crazy] (31) Fall 86, p. 58-62.
270. BALL, Angela
"House." [Poetry] (149:1) O 86, p. 12.
"How I Know." [Boulevard] (1:1/2) Wint 86, p. 150.
"Nina's Evanescent Loves: Clement." [IndR] (9:2) Spr 86, p. 60-61.
"Nina's Evanescent Loves: Philip." [MalR] (74) Mr 86, p. 65-66.
"There." [MemphisSR] (6:1/2) Spr 86, p. 26.
271. BALL, Joseph H.
"Due Thursday." [EngJ] (75:6) O 86, p. 74.
"Lines." [MidAR] (6:1) 86?, p. 90.
272. BALL, Richard
"Poem for A.R. Ammons." [Pembroke] (18) 86, p. 234-235.
273. BALLARD, Richard
"The Modern Dance." [LittleM] (15:1) 86, p. 50-51.
"Supermarket Crimes." [LittleM] (15:1) 86, p. 52.
"Trunk Diving." [LittleM] (15:1) 86, p. 49.
274. BALLENTINE, Lee
"His Pandemonium." [Vis] (20) 86, p. 28.
"In event of my death." [Abraxas] (34) 86, p. 49.
275. BALLIRO, Lenore
"After the Dujinsheng Silk Factory, Zhejiang Province." [MinnR] (NS 27) Fall 86, p.
        41-43.
276. BALOIAN
"Permanent Arrangement." [MidwQ] (27:4) Sum 86, p. 457.
"Up to Mezey's" (for Bob Mezey). [SpiritSH] (52) 86, p. 22.
277. BANDEIRA, Manuel
"Death" (tr. by Manoel Cardozo). [Vis] (21) 86, p. 33.
278. BANERJEE, Ron D. K.
"From Bozena Nemcová's Fan" (tr. of Jaroslav Seifert). [InterPR] (12:1) Spr 86, p.
        41-47.
279. BANGERT, Sharon
"Days" (tr. of Bei Dao). [RiverS] (20) 86, p. 7.
"Degrees of Arc" (tr. of Gu Cheng). [RiverS] (20) 86, p. 9.
"My Graveyard" (tr. of Gu Cheng). [RiverS] (20) 86, p. 8.

43

"Rain Walk" (tr. of Gu Cheng). [RiverS] (20) 86, p. 9.
"Remembered" (tr. of Bei Dao). [RiverS] (20) 86, p. 8.
280. BANGS, Carol Jane
    "Walking on Blood at North Beach." [Ploughs] (12:4) 86, p. 198-199.
281. BANKS, Loy
    "Near the Interstate." [Wind] (16:57) 86, p. 3.
    "Pull-Back." [DeKalbLAJ] (19:3/4) 86, p. 67-68.
    "Wear." [CrabCR] (3:2) Spr 86, p. 17.
282. BANKS, Stanley E.
    "A Black and Blue Woman." [NewL] (52:2/3) Wint-Spr 86, p. 211.
Bar YOSEF, Hamutal
    See YOSEF, Hamutal bar
283. BARAKA, Amiri
    "1929: Y You Ask?" [PoetryE] (20/21) Fall 86, p. 47-48.
    "Death Parallels" (Work Song). [PoetryE] (20/21) Fall 86, p. 38-42.
    "There Was Something I Wanted to Tell You. Why?" [PoetryE] (20/21) Fall 86, p.
        43-46.
284. BARANCHUK, Adrian
    "Duelo." [Mairena] (8:22) 86, p. 73.
285. BARANCZAK, Stanislaw
    "Anyone Can Stand" (tr. by Antony Graham and Reginald Gibbons). [TriQ] (65)
        Wint 86, p. 88.
    "Curriculum Vitae" (tr. by Reginald Gibbons). [SouthwR] (71:4) Aut 86, p. 436.
    "Do Not Want to Die for Us" (tr. of Ryszard Krynicki, w. Clare Cavanagh). [TriQ]
        (67) Fall 86, p. 129.
    "From a Window" (tr. of Ryszard Krynicki, w. Clare Cavanagh). [TriQ] (67) Fall 86,
        p. 129.
    "I Can't Help You" (tr. of Ryszard Krynicki, w. Clare Cavanagh). [TriQ] (67) Fall
        86, p. 128.
    "I'd Forgotten" (tr. of Ryszard Krynicki, w. Clare Cavanagh). [TriQ] (67) Fall 86, p.
        128.
    "The Morning After" (tr. by Magnus J. Krynski and Robert A. Maguire). [TriQ] (65)
        Wint 86, p. 87.
    "The New World" (tr. by the author w. Reginald Gibbons). [AmerPoR] (15:5) S-O
        86, p. 44.
    "A Second Nature" (tr. by the author w. Reginald Gibbons). [AmerPoR] (15:5) S-O
        86, p. 44.
    "Setting the Hand Brake" (tr. by Reginald Gibbons). [SouthwR] (71:4) Aut 86, p.
        437-438.
    "Sleep Well" (tr. of Ryszard Krynicki, w. Clare Cavanagh). [TriQ] (67) Fall 86, p.
        129.
    "Small Talk" (tr. by Reginald Gibbons). [SouthwR] (71:4) Aut 86, p. 437.
    "Some Day, Years from Now" (tr. by the author w. Reginald Gibbons). [AmerPoR]
        (15:5) S-O 86, p. 44.
    "We Drew the Proper Conclusions from the Events" (tr. by Frank Kujawinski and
        Reginald Gibbons). [TriQ] (65) Wint 86, p. 89.
    "Yes, She Says" (tr. of Ryszard Krynicki, w. Clare Cavanagh). [TriQ] (67) Fall 86,
        p. 128.
286. BARANOW, Joan
    "Dedicated to My Creative Writing Students." [MSS] (5:1) 86, p. 76-79.
287. BARANSZKY, László
    "Diary: December, 1944, January-February, 1945." [PartR] (53:1) 86, p. 95-96.
    "My Mirror Image." [PartR] (53:1) 86, p. 94-95.
288. BARATTA, Edward
    "Hosanna in the Highest." [MassR] (27:2) Sum 86, p. 238.
    "Mr. World." [MassR] (27:2) Sum 86, p. 239.
289. BARBARESE, J. T.
    "Get Up." [IndR] (9:1) Wint 86, p. 61-63.
    "Through the Windows at Walt's." [CarolQ] (38:2) Wint 86, p. 8-11.
290. BARBER, David
    "Worldly Goods." [Sonora] (11) Fall 86 [c87], p. 70-72.
291. BARBOUR, Douglas
    "Autobiographical." [GreenfR] (13:3/4) Sum-Fall 86, p. 9.
    "The Image Repetition" (for Stephen Scobie, in memory perhaps). [GreenfR] (13:3/4)
        Sum-Fall 86, p. 10.

BARCIA, José Rubia
   See RUBIA BARCIA, José
292. BARCLAY, Sydney J.
   "Who Is in Charge?" [SanFPJ] (9:1) 86, p. 63.
293. BARDEN, Tom
   "On Teaching *On the Road* in 1984." [MoodySI] (16/17) Sum 86, p. 21-23.
294. BARDSLEY, Beverly
   "Phaedra" (To Yannis Tsarouchis, tr. of Yannis Ritsos, w. Peter Green).
      [SouthernHR] (20:3) Sum 86, p. 227-247.
295. BARGAD, Warren
   "Australia" (tr. of Dahlia Ravikovitch). [PoetL] (81:2) Sum 86, p. 99-100.
   "Drawing Nearer" (tr. of Yona Wollach). [PoetL] (81:2) Sum 86, p. 115.
   "I Couldn't" (tr. of Yona Wollach). [PoetL] (81:2) Sum 86, p. 116.
   "Impoverishment" (tr. of Dahlia Ravikovitch). [PoetL] (81:2) Sum 86, p. 101.
296. BARGEN, Walter
   "Adam at Thirty-Three." [CapeR] (21:2) Fall 86, p. 48.
   "Adam Despairs." [Farm] (3:2) Spr-Sum 86, p. 57-58.
   "Adam Hears Wendell Berry Lecture on Milton and Dante." [Farm] (3:2) Spr-Sum 86,
      p. 59.
   "Adam to Armageddon." [CapeR] (21:2) Fall 86, p. 49.
   "Afternudes" (By Thomas Hart Benton). [CharR] (12:2) Fall 86, p. 76-77.
   "Already Two Hours Late." [Wind] (16:56) 86, p. 4-5.
   "Debris." [Vis] (20) 86, p. 5-6.
   "Passing Through Walls." [Wind] (16:56) 86, p. 3-4.
   "Rumors in Florist Shops." [Puerto] (22:1) Fall 86, p. 37-38.
297. BARGER, Rita
   "Therapy." [PoeticJ] (14) 86, p. 10.
298. BARKAN, Stanley H.
   "Brighton Beach Vegetarian Cafeteria" (for Celia — Tsivia — the best thing there!).
      [Lips] (12) 86, p. 35.
299. BARKER, David
   "Donut Shop." [WormR] (26:3, issue 103) 86, p. 118.
   "Helper." [WormR] (26:3, issue 103) 86, p. 118.
   "Henry Miller's Bathrobe." [WormR] (26:3, issue 103) 86, p. 120.
   "Just in Case I Become a World Traveler." [WormR] (26:3, issue 103) 86, p. 119.
   "Three Cats." [WormR] (26:3, issue 103) 86, p. 119.
300. BARKER, Wendy
   "The Navy Blue Chair." [Poetry] (148:1) Ap 86, p. 23-24.
   "Red Chair at the Piano Recital." [Poetry] (148:1) Ap 86, p. 24-25.
301. BARKS, Coleman
   "The Last Rebirth." [GeoR] (40:3) Fall 86, p. 627-628.
   "The Premise" (Winner, NER/BLQ Narrative Poetry Competition). [NewEngR] (9:1)
      Aut 86, p. 50-57.
302. BARLOW, George
   "A Dream of the Ring: The Great Jack Johnson." [Iowa] (16:1) Wint 86, p. 49.
   "A Rosary" (for Little Ray). [Iowa] (16:1) Wint 86, p. 48.
303. BARNARD, Mary
   "Song for the Northern Quarter." [ParisR] (28:99) Spr 86, p. 166-168.
304. BARNES, Jim
   "Crow White." [Chelsea] (45) 86, p. 38.
   "Crow's Firesticks." [Chelsea] (45) 86, p. 39.
   "International Student Union Coffee Shoppe: Ramadan." [KanQ] (18:1/2) Wint-Spr
      86, p. 96-97.
   "La Plata, Missouri: Turkey Season." [OhioR] (37) 86, p. 102.
   "Shaving the Dead." [Interim] (5:1) Spr 86, p. 25-28.
   "Ubi Sunt." [KanQ] (18:1/2) Wint-Spr 86, p. 96.
   "Vesperal." [KanQ] (18:1/2) Wint-Spr 86, p. 97.
305. BARNES, Tim
   "The Uncoiling, April in Oregon." [CrabCR] (3:2) Spr 86, p. 28.
306. BARNSTONE, Tony
   "After a Night" (tr. of Mang Ke, w. Willis Barnstone and Gu Zhong Xing). [Nimrod]
      (29:2) Spr-Sum 86, p. 42.
   "By the Dream Ocean" (tr. of Gu Cheng, w. Tang Chao). [Nimrod] (29:2) Spr-Sum
      86, p. 28.
   "Climbing Nanyue Mountain at Night and Waiting for Sunrise at the Summit" (tr. of
      Chou Ping, w. the author). [Nimrod] (29:2) Spr-Sum 86, p. 34.

45

"Declining Years" (tr. of Mang Ke, w. Willis Barnstone and Gu Zhong Xing).
[Nimrod] (29:2) Spr-Sum 86, p. 45.
"Drunk and Playing *Go* under the White Lady, the Moon" (tr. of Chou Ping, w. the
author). [Nimrod] (29:2) Spr-Sum 86, p. 31.
"Early Morning after Rain" (tr. of Mang Ke, w. Willis Barnstone and Gu Zhong
Xing). [Nimrod] (29:2) Spr-Sum 86, p. 43.
"I Don't Need It" (tr. of Bei Ling, w. Xi Chuan). [Nimrod] (29:2) Spr-Sum 86, p.
94.
"Many Years" (tr. of Bei Dao, w. Tang Chao). [Nimrod] (29:2) Spr-Sum 86, p. 96.
"Memory" (on an exhibition of Ling Fengmian's paintings, tr. of Tang Qi, w. Tang
Chao). [Nimrod] (29:2) Spr-Sum 86, p. 35.
"Night in the Snowfield" (tr. of Mang Ke, w. Willis Barnstone and Gu Zhong Xing).
[Nimrod] (29:2) Spr-Sum 86, p. 40.
"Poems in October" (tr. of Mang Ke, w. Willis Barnstone and Gu Zhong Xing).
[Nimrod] (29:2) Spr-Sum 86, p. 46-47.
"Spring" (tr. of Mang Ke, w. Willis Barnstone and Gu Zhong Xing). [Nimrod] (29:2)
Spr-Sum 86, p. 44.
"Suffering from Heat" (tr. of Wang Wei, w. Willis Barnstone and Xu Haixin).
[Nimrod] (29:2) Spr-Sum 86, p. 20.
"Sunflower in the Sun" (tr. of Mang Ke, w. Willis Barnstone and Gu Zhong Xing).
[Nimrod] (29:2) Spr-Sum 86, p. 66.
"There Beyond the River" (tr. of Xi Chuan, w. the author). [Nimrod] (29:2) Spr-Sum
86, p. 70.
"These Days" (tr. of Mang Ke, w. Willis Barnstone and Gu Zhong Xing). [Nimrod]
(29:2) Spr-Sum 86, p. 39.
"To Jeffers" (tr. of Bei Ling, w. Xi Chuan). [Nimrod] (29:2) Spr-Sum 86, p. 95.
"Twilight Has No Voice" (tr. of Bei Ling, w. Xi Chuan). [Nimrod] (29:2) Spr-Sum
86, p. 93.
"Visiting the Mountain Courtyard . . ." (tr. of Wang Wei, w. Willis Barnstone and Xu
Haixin). [Nimrod] (29:2) Spr-Sum 86, p. 23.
"Weeping for Ying Yao" (tr. of Wang Wei, w. Willis Barnstone and Xu Haixin).
[Nimrod] (29:2) Spr-Sum 86, p. 22.
"Wind Rising from the Water's Back" (tr. of Mang Ke, w. Willis Barnstone and Gu
Zhong Xing). [Nimrod] (29:2) Spr-Sum 86, p. 44.
"Written When Climbing the City Tower . . ." (tr. of Wang Wei, w. Willis Barnstone
and Xu Haixin). [Nimrod] (29:2) Spr-Sum 86, p. 23.
307. BARNSTONE, Willis
"After a Night" (tr. of Mang Ke, w. Tony Barnstone and Gu Zhong Xing). [Nimrod]
(29:2) Spr-Sum 86, p. 42.
"Declining Years" (tr. of Mang Ke, w. Tony Barnstone and Gu Zhong Xing).
[Nimrod] (29:2) Spr-Sum 86, p. 45.
"Early Morning after Rain" (tr. of Mang Ke, w. Tony Barnstone and Gu Zhong
Xing). [Nimrod] (29:2) Spr-Sum 86, p. 43.
"Night in the Snowfield" (tr. of Mang Ke, w. Tony Barnstone and Gu Zhong Xing).
[Nimrod] (29:2) Spr-Sum 86, p. 40.
"Poems in October" (tr. of Mang Ke, w. Tony Barnstone and Gu Zhong Xing).
[Nimrod] (29:2) Spr-Sum 86, p. 46-47.
"Spring" (tr. of Mang Ke, w. Tony Barnstone and Gu Zhong Xing). [Nimrod] (29:2)
Spr-Sum 86, p. 44.
"Suffering from Heat" (tr. of Wang Wei, w. Tony Barnstone and Xu Haixin).
[Nimrod] (29:2) Spr-Sum 86, p. 20.
"Sunflower in the Sun" (tr. of Mang Ke, w. Tony Barnstone and Gu Zhong Xing).
[Nimrod] (29:2) Spr-Sum 86, p. 66.
"These Days" (tr. of Mang Ke, w. Tony Barnstone and Gu Zhong Xing). [Nimrod]
(29:2) Spr-Sum 86, p. 39.
"Visiting the Mountain Courtyard . . ." (tr. of Wang Wei, w. Tony Barnstone and Xu
Haixin). [Nimrod] (29:2) Spr-Sum 86, p. 23.
"Weeping for Ying Yao" (tr. of Wang Wei, w. Tony Barnstone and Xu Haixin).
[Nimrod] (29:2) Spr-Sum 86, p. 22.
"Wind Rising from the Water's Back" (tr. of Mang Ke, w. Tony Barnstone and Gu
Zhong Xing). [Nimrod] (29:2) Spr-Sum 86, p. 44.
"Written When Climbing the City Tower . . ." (tr. of Wang Wei, w. Tony Barnstone
and Xu Haixin). [Nimrod] (29:2) Spr-Sum 86, p. 23.
308. BARON, Enid L.
"Chicks." [YetASM] (5) 86, p. 2.
"Father." [YetASM] (4) 85, p. 8.

309. BARON, Todd
   "Clearing." [Sink] (2) 86, p. 69.
   "The Rooms" (Excerpts). [Sink] (2) 86, p. 66-67.
   "The Rooms" (Selections: 2 poems). [Acts] (5) 86, p. 77-78.
   "Velocity or Pause." [Sink] (2) 86, p. 68.
310. BARONE, Dennis (Denis)
   "In the Center of All Things." [Confr] (32) Spr-Sum 86, p. 114.
   "What He Thinks." [Pax] (3:1/2) Wint 85-86, p. 146.
311. BARONE, Frank
   "Clown." [EngJ] (75:5) S 86, p. 69.
   "How to Report on What You've Seen or Read." [EngJ] (75:8) D 86, p. 36.
312. BARQUET, Jesús
   "Trilogia de la Nieve." [Mairena] (8:22) 86, p. 116.
313. BARR, Allan
   "In the Garden of King Richard the Third." [Grain] (14:2) My 86, p. 37-40.
314. BARR, John
   "Restoration." [PassN] (7:2) Spr-Sum 86, p. 16.
   "Terrapin." [Amelia] (3:3) Sum 86, p. 49.
315. BARR, Tina
   "Arizona: The Watcher." [PaintedB] (28) Ap 86, p. 52.
   "Between the House and the Sky." [PaintedB] (28) Ap 86, p. 50.
   "Center Line, Route 1, Brooklin." [PaintedB] (28) Ap 86, p. 54-55.
   "The Decade's Lesson." [PaintedB] (28) Ap 86, p. 51.
   "Easter, Vineland, New Jersey." [PaintedB] (28) Ap 86, p. 56-57.
   "For Alice." [PaintedB] (28) Ap 86, p. 61.
   "In the Firehouse." [PaintedB] (28) Ap 86, p. 53-54.
   "October." [PaintedB] (28) Ap 86, p. 57.
   "Summer, St. Gerard des Laurentides." [PaintedB] (28) Ap 86, p. 62.
   "Two Women." [PaintedB] (28) Ap 86, p. 60.
   "Voice of a Dancer: Making an Aesthetic" (for Christine Vilardo). [PaintedB] (28) Ap
       86, p. 59-60.
316. BARRACK, Jack
   "Junk Mail." [Confr] (33/34) Fall-Wint 86-87, p. 211.
317. BARRAX, Gerald (Gerald W.)
   "The Competitors." [GeoR] (40:3) Fall 86, p. 629-630.
   "Not Often Near Such Water." [Callaloo] (9:1, #26) Wint 86, p. 12-14.
318. BARRECA, Regina
   "Nighttime Fires." [MinnR] (NS 27) Fall 86, p. 5.
319. BARRERA, Alberto
   "Amor Que por Demás Eres Ajeno." [LindLM] (5:2) Ap-Je 86, p. 6.
320. BARRESI, Dorothy
   "The Hole in the Ceiling." [Ploughs] (12:4) 86, p. 74-75.
   "How It Comes." [Ploughs] (12:4) 86, p. 72-73.
   "In Waking Words." [SouthernPR] (26:2) Fall 86, p. 22-23.
   "Pure Jesus, Early Morning Shift." [SouthernPR] (26:2) Fall 86, p. 21.
321. BARRETO, Igor
   "Ciudad Alianza." [LindLM] (5:2) Ap-Je 86, p. 8.
322. BARRETO, Nestor
   "El Deseo." [RevICP] (89) Jul-Sep 85, p. 64-65.
323. BARRETO-RIVERA, Rafael
   "Shredded What" (A Whitman Serial). [Rampike] (5:1) 86, p. 40-41.
324. BARRETT, Carol
   "After My Death." [ConcPo] (19) 86, p. 74.
   "Benediction." [StoneC] (13:3/4) Spr-Sum 86, p. 25.
   "Flight of the Geese" (for Angela). [CapeR] (21:1) Spr 86, p. 18.
   "Shelling the Peas" (for Alice Hart Blackburn and the women we both know).
       [WoosterR] (6) Fall 86, p. 6-7.
   "Stopping in the Cornfield." [CapeR] (21:1) Spr 86, p. 19.
BARRETT, Donalee Moulton
   See MOULTON-BARRETT, Donalee
325. BARRETT, Herb
   "Haiku: A stack of old poems." [Bogg] (55) 86, p. 49.
326. BARRINGER, Margaret
   "The Farmer's Wife." [Boulevard] (1:1/2) Wint 86, p. 114-119.
327. BARRON, Lori
   "Postcard from Jupiter." [Vis] (20) 86, p. 15.

47

BARRON

328. BARRON, Monica
    "Getting Past This." [CharR] (12:2) Fall 86, p. 58-59.
    "Going Somewhere Right Here." [CharR] (12:2) Fall 86, p. 58.
    "Homage to Alice Neel." [CharR] (12:2) Fall 86, p. 56-57.
329. BARRY, Jan
    "In the Footsteps of Ghengis Khan." [Sam] (46:2 release 182) 86, p. 12.
330. BARRY, Sandra
    "Fun House." [AntigR] (64) Wint 86, p. 42.
331. BARST, Fran
    "Appalachia." [Poem] (55) Mr 86, p. 30-31.
    "Birdswings." [Poem] (55) Mr 86, p. 32-34.
    "Black Mountain." [Poem] (55) Mr 86, p. 26-27.
    "Family Portrait." [Poem] (55) Mr 86, p. 28-29.
    "Snow Sleep." [LittleM] (15:2) 86, p. 35.
332. BARTH, R. L.
    "The Lighter That Never Fails." [Sam] (46:2 release 182) 86, p. 52.
    "Observation Post." [Sam] (46:2 release 182) 86, p. 41.
333. BARTHOLOMEW, Hillary
    "Ameri- Might." [SanFPJ] (8:4) 85, p. 84.
    "Apartheid." [SanFPJ] (8:4) 85, p. 82.
    "Countdown." [SanFPJ] (8:4) 85, p. 92.
    "Death March." [SanFPJ] (8:3) 85, p. 94.
    "Death Watch." [SanFPJ] (8:4) 85, p. 17.
    "Untouched." [SanFPJ] (8:4) 85, p. 28.
334. BARTKOWECH, R.
    "Composition." [Outbr] (16/17) Fall 85-Spr 86, p. 12.
    "Five Embarrassing Laws of Physics." [Outbr] (16/17) Fall 85-Spr 86, p. 10-11.
335. BARTLETT, Elizabeth
    "1 x 1 x 1 x 1." [StoneC] (14:1/2) Fall-Wint 86-87, p. 47.
    "Above the Sea" (tr. of Griselda Alvarez). [WebR] (11:2) Fall 86, p. 34.
    "Fifty Seasons in the Sun." [StoneC] (14:1/2) Fall-Wint 86-87, p. 46-47.
    "A New Image." [StoneC] (14:1/2) Fall-Wint 86-87, p. 46.
    "Pentimento." [AntigR] (64) Wint 86, p. 132.
    "Travelogue." [SanFPJ] (8:1) 85, p. 54-56.
336. BARTLEY, Nellis M.
    "Hidden Exhibits" (observation of a 6 year old). [Wind] (16:58) 86, p. 45.
337. BARTON, Fred
    "Fishing Men." [SouthernPR] (26:1) Spr 86, p. 38.
338. BARTON, John
    "Envoi." [GreenfR] (13:3/4) Sum-Fall 86, p. 12.
    "Housebound." [CanLit] (108) Spr 86, p. 15.
    "Metropolitan Life." [GreenfR] (13:3/4) Sum-Fall 86, p. 11-12.
339. BASILE, Giambattista
    "Belluccia" (Little Pretty, from *Pentameron*, III, 6, tr. by Felix Stefanile). [Sparrow] (50) 86, p. 1-15.
340. BASSEN, Lois Shapley
    "Mortal." [EngJ] (75:3) Mr 86, p. 65.
341. BASSO, Eric
    "The Moment After." [CentralP] (9) Spr 86, p. 31.
342. BASTIEN, Mark
    "Last Week a Woman on Latham Island." [Event] (15:1) 86, p. 112-113.
343. BASTONS, Liliana
    "Poema Inaugural." [Mairena] (8:21) 86, p. 93.
    "Violencia." [Mairena] (8:21) 86, p. 93-94.
344. BASU, Anjana
    "Paris Autumn." [Pax] (3:1/2) Wint 85-86, p. 147.
345. BATEMAN, Claire
    "Bestowal: Recollection of a Summer Night." [SingHM] (14) 86, p. 36.
    "Pilfering the Moon." [SingHM] (14) 86, p. 36.
346. BATES, Kyle
    "It's Waving, That's What" (for Julie Greenfield). [Electrum] (38) Spr 86, p. 42.
347. BATHANTI, Joseph
    "Paulo Mia." [ManhatPR] (6) Wint-Spr 85-86, p. 54-55.
    "Whiteville" (For A.R. Ammons). [Pembroke] (18) 86, p. 165.
348. BATISTA, Liony E.
    "Coming Home" (for Kenia). [Lips] (12) 86, p. 4-5.

48

BATISTA

"Conversations with My Father." [Lips] (12) 86, p. 3.
"This Life." [Lips] (12) 86, p. 6-7.
349. BATTILANA, Carlos
"A veces las palabras." [Mairena] (8:22) 86, p. 84.
350. BAUCH, Susan Charles
"Wasted Lands." [SecC] (14:1) 86, p. 22-23.
351. BAUDELAIRE, Charles
"The Blind" ("Les Aveugles," tr. by James McGowan). [HiramPoR] (40) Spr-Sum
86, p. 51.
352. BAUER, Grace
"C'Est la Vie." [ColR] (NS 13:1) Fall 85, p. 30-31.
"Reunion" (for Ella). [ColR] (NS 13:1) Fall 85, p. 32-33.
353. BAUER, Lois Browning
"The Search." [WritersL] (1986:6), p. 21.
354. BAUER, Nona Kilgore
"Left Behind." [KanQ] (18:3) Sum 86, p. 22.
355. BAUER, Steven
"Grass." [PraS] (60:4) Wint 86, p. 37-38.
"Intro to Poetry." [PraS] (60:1) Spr 86, p. 60.
"The Man Who Knew Too Much." [PraS] (60:1) Spr 86, p. 61.
"Vagrant." [PraS] (60:4) Wint 86, p. 38-40.
356. BAUMBACH, Jonathan
"Invasion of the Body Snatchers." [Boulevard] (1:1/2) Wint 86, p. 148.
"The Wrong Man." [Boulevard] (1:1/2) Wint 86, p. 149.
357. BAUSCH, Victor H.
"Leftovers." [Sam] (46:2 release 182) 86, p. 110.
"Playboy Meets the Virgin Mary." [SlipS] (6) 86, p. 47.
"Suffocation." [Sam] (46:2 release 182) 86, p. 112-113.
358. BAWER, Bruce
"Beach" (For Brian). [Poetry] (148:4) Jl 86, p. 225-227.
"Fur." [Boulevard] (1:3) Fall 86, p. 40.
359. BAXTER, Charles
"How She Knew It Was Over: A Summary." [DenQ] (20:4/21:1) Spr-Sum 86, p.
158.
"The Man Who Sold His Bed" (Translation from an Unknown Language). [Caliban]
(1) 86, p. 76.
"Midwestern Poetics." [Poetry] (148:1) Ap 86, p. 26.
"The Passionate Shopping Mall." [Caliban] (1) 86, p. 77.
360. BAYSANS, Greg
"All I Dare Say, or: Another AIDS Poem." [JamesWR] (3:2) Wint 86, p. 10.
361. BEACH, Mary
"Bob Kaufman" (to Eileen & Parker, tr. of Claude Pelieu). [RedBass] (11) 86, p. 10.
362. BEAKE, Fred
"Out of control the dove of fire." [Bogg] (55) 86, p. 55.
363. BEAMISH, Mark
"Seconds." [Rampike] (5:1) 86, p. 68.
364. BEARD, Michael
"Night-Strings" (Excerpts, tr. of Mozaffar Al-Nawwab, w. Adnan Haydar). [MinnR]
(NS 26) Spr 86, p. 44-55.
365. BEARDEN, Nancy
"Things I can't See." [TarRP] (26:1) Fall 86, p. 20.
366. BEARDSLEY, Doug
"The Fifth Song" (for Richard Strauss). [MalR] (77) D 86, p. 118.
"Mahler's Pastorale." [MalR] (77) D 86, p. 116-117.
367. BEASLEY, Bruce
"Autumn." [CrabCR] (4:1) Fall-Wint 86, p. 3.
"Prayers." [SenR] (16:2) 86, p. 98-100.
368. BEASLEY, Sherry
"August." [SouthernPR] (26:1) Spr 86, p. 33-34.
"Play." [WoosterR] (6) Fall 86, p. 66-67.
369. BEAUCHAMP, Steve
"The Potter." [SoCaR] (19:1) Fall 86, p. 32.
"The Robins." [SoCaR] (19:1) Fall 86, p. 32-34.
370. BEAUSOLEIL, Claude
"Chant I" (tr. by Andrea Moorhead). [AmerPoR] (15:3) My-Je 86, p. 30.
"Chant III" (tr. by Andrea Moorhead). [AmerPoR] (15:3) My-Je 86, p. 30.

"Chant VI" (tr. by Andrea Moorhead). [AmerPoR] (15:3) My-Je 86, p. 30.
"Chant XVIII" (tr. by Andrea Moorhead). [AmerPoR] (15:3) My-Je 86, p. 31.
"Chant XXIII" (tr. by Andrea Moorhead). [AmerPoR] (15:3) My-Je 86, p. 31.
"City at Night" (for Nicole Smith, tr. by Andrea Moorhead). [Translation] (16) Spr 86, p. 198-199.
"Cordoba" (tr. by Andrea Moorhead). [Translation] (16) Spr 86, p. 197.
371. BEAZER, Danielle
"An Awakening." [TarRP] (25:2) Spr 86, p. 36.
372. BECKER, Robin
"Taos Pow-Wow." [Ploughs] (12:4) 86, p. 37.
373. BECKER, Therese
"Pomegranate." [PassN] (7:2) Spr-Sum 86, p. 16.
374. BECKWITH, Merle Ray
"Greatest Peace." [WritersL] (1986:4), p. 12.
"Nature's Lore." [WritersL] (1986:5), p. 32.
"On Dignity." [WritersL] (1986:5), p. 32.
"Peace and Conciliation." [WritersL] (1986:5), p. 32.
"Sweet Peace." [WritersL] (1986:2), p. 18.
375. BEGIN, Tom
"Yarded Deer." [PottPort] (8) 86-87, p. 51.
376. BEHAN, Marie
"Camphor." [ManhatPR] (8) Wint 86-87, p. 38-39.
377. BEHLEN, Charles
"The Drunken Boat" (adaption of Arthur Rimbaud). [Pax] (3:1/2) Wint 85-86, p. 108-110.
378. BEHM, Richard
"Child Sleeping." [Amelia] (3:2) Spr 86, p. 101.
"Getting Al Kaline's Autograph." [MichQR] (25:2) Spr 86, p. 350.
"The Horses of Morning." [KenR] (NS 7:3) Sum 85, p. 99.
"Nightfall, Holy Redeemer Cemetery." [Amelia] (3:1) Ja 86, p. 46.
"Recalling a Conversation with My Daughter." [KenR] (NS 7:3) Sum 85, p. 98.
"St. Joseph's Grade School." [CimR] (76) Jl 86, p. 36.
"Three Prophecies for the Other Hemisphere." [Amelia] (3:1) Ja 86, p. 46-47.
379. BEHN, Bettina
"Gradually" (tr. by Stuart Friebert). [Field] (35) Fall 86, p. 104.
"What They Told the Child" (tr. by Stuart Friebert). [Field] (35) Fall 86, p. 103.
380. BEHN, Robin
"The Earth's a Little Lighter" (Florence Behn 1894-1984). [Iowa] (16:1) Wint 86, p. 6.
"Elegy for the New Year." [Farm] (3:2) Spr-Sum 86, p. 43.
"Paper Bird." [Iowa] (16:1) Wint 86, p. 4-5.
"To Rise, So Suddenly" (for Phil Mark). [GeoR] (40:3) Fall 86, p. 631.
"Winter Poem." [Farm] (3:2) Spr-Sum 86, p. 44-45.
381. BEHRENDT, Stephen C.
"Farm Auction." [PraS] (60:2) Sum 86, p. 48-49.
"For the Teenagers Who Stoned the Zoo Bear." [SoCaR] (18:2) Spr 86, p. 93.
"Transients on the Campus Mall." [KanQ] (18:4) Fall 86, p. 23.
382. BEHUNIN, Judy
"Catfishing at the Bay." [PoeticJ] (16) Fall 86, p. 32.
"A Day Like This." [PoeticJ] (16) Fall 86, p. 27.
"September Magic." [PoeticJ] (15) Sum 86, p. 26.
"Waiting." [PoeticJ] (15) Sum 86, p. 11.
383. BEI, Dao
"Boat Ticket" (tr. by Bonnie S. McDougall). [Verse] (6) 86, p. 49.
"Days" (tr. by Sharon Bangert). [RiverS] (20) 86, p. 7.
"Many Years" (tr. by Tony Barnstone and Tang Chao). [Nimrod] (29:2) Spr-Sum 86, p. 96.
"Remembered" (tr. by Sharon Bangert). [RiverS] (20) 86, p. 8.
384. BEI, Ling
"I Don't Need It" (tr. by Tony Barnstone and Xi Chuan). [Nimrod] (29:2) Spr-Sum 86, p. 94.
"To Jeffers" (tr. by Tony Barnstone and Xi Chuan). [Nimrod] (29:2) Spr-Sum 86, p. 95.
"Twilight Has No Voice" (tr. by Tony Barnstone and Xi Chuan). [Nimrod] (29:2) Spr-Sum 86, p. 93.

385. BEJERANO, Maya
"The Ostrich" (tr. by Lisa Fliegal). [PoetL] (81:2) Sum 86, p. 122.
386. BELAMICH, André
"El Amor Duerme en el Pecho del Poeta" (French tr. of Federico García Lorca).
[Mairena] (8:21) 86, p. 45.
387. BELFIELD, Judy
"Freeze-Frame." [YetASM] (4) 85, p. 7.
388. BELFORD, November
"Moving." [BlackALF] (20:3) Fall 86, p. 265.
"Spit Mirror." [BlackALF] (20:3) Fall 86, p. 264.
389. BELIELE, Kelvin
"Chubby Chaser." [JamesWR] (3:3) Spr 86, p. 14.
"Fog Boy." [JamesWR] (3:2) Wint 86, p. 9.
390. BELIN, Mel
"Audrey Rose." [Wind] (16:57) 86, p. 10.
"Pas de Deux." [PoetL] (80:4) Wint 86, p. 200.
391. BELISLE, Jeanne
"For Our Times." [SanFPJ] (8:3) 85, p. 27.
"Helicopters." [SanFPJ] (8:3) 85, p. 26.
"On the Death of John Lennon." [SanFPJ] (8:2) 85, p. 8.
392. BELL, Bill
"Torture — A Found Poem" (found in Amnesty International's 1984 Report on
International Torture). [SanFPJ] (8:1) 85, p. 58-59.
393. BELL, John
"Footprints." [AntigR] (64) Wint 86, p. 122.
"Historic Properties, Halifax." [AntigR] (64) Wint 86, p. 121-122.
394. BELL, Linda R.
"Before the Days of Divorce." [PoeticJ] (14) 86, p. 3.
"Dinner Companion." [PoeticJ] (14) 86, p. 43-44.
"Handfuls of Your Heart." [PoeticJ] (15) Sum 86, p. 12.
"My Grandfather." [PoeticJ] (13) 86, p. 36.
"Sandpaintings." [PoeticJ] (14) 86, p. 14.
"Southward Seagulls." [PoeticJ] (14) 86, p. 14.
395. BELL, Mae Woods
"Cicada Summer" (For A.R. Ammons). [Pembroke] (18) 86, p. 218.
396. BELL, Marvin
"Classified." [Iowa] (16:1) Wint 86, p. 125.
"In My Nature: 3 Corrective Dialogues." [QW] (23) 86, p. 48-51.
"The Pill." [QW] (23) 86, p. 53-54.
"The Politics of an Object." [QW] (23) 86, p. 52.
"Wednesday." [NewYorker] (62:36) 27 O 86, p. 44.
"Where He Stood: Schulze's Portfolio." [Iowa] (16:1) Wint 86, p. 124-125.
397. BELL, Melissa
"Last Week's Woman." [Vis] (22) 86, p. 36.
398. BELLA DONNA
"Jose: d. 1985." [CentralP] (9) Spr 86, p. 40.
399. BELLAMY, Joe David
"The End of Archeology." [Boulevard] (1:1/2) Wint 86, p. 113.
"The Frozen Sea." [Boulevard] (1:1/2) Wint 86, p. 112.
"Jogging at Evergreen Cemetery." [TarRP] (25:1) Fall 85, p. 32-36.
"Leningrad 1942." [IndR] (9:2) Spr 86, p. 19.
"The Light's True Inertia." [IndR] (9:2) Spr 86, p. 14-15.
"Lost in the Junkyard." [TarRP] (25:1) Fall 85, p. 36.
"The Moth's Attraction to the Light." [IndR] (9:2) Spr 86, p. 16.
400. BELLEAU, Janick
"Cauchemar : L'une." [PraF] (7:3) Aut 86, p. 52.
"Walden's à Edmonton." [PraF] (7:3) Aut 86, p. 53.
401. BELLI, Gioconda
"Dressed in Dynamite" (tr. by Regina McCarthy). [MassR] (27:3/4) Fall-Wint 86, p.
608.
402. BELLIARD, Madeleine E.
"De repente le vi robándome la mente." [Mairena] (8:22) 86, p. 119.
403. BELLINGER, Celia
"Plot." [LitR] (29:2) Wint 86, p. 193.
404. BELLSCHEIDT, Eric
"Elegy for a Sofa of Two Generations." [BellR] (9:1) Spr 86, p. 8.

"Not What You Said But How." [BellR] (9:1) Spr 86, p. 9.
BEN-ZVI, Moshe
    See MOSHE-BEN-ZVI
405. BENARDO, Margot
    "It Is Hatred I Feel" (tr. of Víctor Carrillo). [Electrum] (38) Spr 86, p. 31.
BENAVIDES, Manuel Terrin
    See TERRIN BENAVIDES, Manuel
406. BENBOW-NIEMIER, Glynis
    "1932." [Farm] (3:2) Spr-Sum 86, p. 35.
407. BENDALL, Molly
    "The Need for Shoes." [GeoR] (40:2) Sum 86, p. 474.
408. BENDER, Sheila
    "At Mono Lake." [BellArk] (2:4) Jl-Ag 86, p. 8.
    "Flight" (for Scott and Libba). [BellArk] (2:3) My-Je 86, p. 4.
    "Home Tides." [BellArk] (2:4) Jl-Ag 86, p. 6.
    "On Location." [BellArk] (2:4) Jl-Ag 86, p. 4.
409. BENEDICT, Elinor
    "Announcement." [PennR] (1:1) 85, p. 38.
    "A Bridge to China." [HeliconN] (14/15) Sum 86, p. 116.
    "Evidence." [PennR] (2:1) Fall-Wint 86, p. 67.
    "In a Far City." [HeliconN] (14/15) Sum 86, p. 118.
    "Two Women Leaving Peking." [HeliconN] (14/15) Sum 86, p. 116-117.
410. BENEDIKT, Michael
    "Alice's Wants" (Midst a prolonged divorcement . . . From *Family Blessings, Family
        Curses*). [Lips] (12) 86, p. 44-54.
    "Grandfather's Impositions, and How They Grew." [LitR] (30:1) Fall 86, p. 41.
411. BENFEY, Christopher
    "Expecting." [ParisR] (28:101) Wint 86, p. 186.
BENITO, Juan Luis Pla
    See PLA BENITO, Juan Luis
412. BENNANI, Benjamin
    "Easter in Southwest Georgia." [DeKalbLAJ] (19:2) 86, p. 11.
413. BENNETT, Allyson
    "Father Who Speaks Not My Language." [SmPd] (23:1, #66) Wint 86, p. 35.
414. BENNETT, Bruce
    "Eating Crow." [SenR] (16:2) 86, p. 90-91.
    "The Handsome Poet." [TarRP] (24:2) Spr 85, p. 15-16.
    "The Poem." [TarRP] (24:2) Spr 85, p. 14.
415. BENNETT, John
    "Toiletseat." [Rampike] (5:1) 86, p. 65.
416. BENNETT, Karen
    "Valence." [PaintedB] (28) Ap 86, p. 31.
    "Waves." [PaintedB] (28) Ap 86, p. 32.
417. BENNETT, Maria
    "Breaking the Cup." [StoneC] (14:1/2) Fall-Wint 86-87, p. 48.
    "Looking for Galileo." [CrossCur] (5:4/6:1) 86, p. 152-153.
    "What Women Carry." [StoneC] (14:1/2) Fall-Wint 86-87, p. 48.
418. BENNETT, Vicky L.
    "Mother." [SmPd] (23:3, #68) Fall 86, p. 31.
419. BENSEN, Robert
    "Club at the Halcyon Beach" (Castries, St. Lucia). [ThRiPo] (27/28) 86, p. 29.
    "Standing By." [PartR] (53:4) 86, p. 593.
    "Wargames." [MinnR] (NS 27) Fall 86, p. 27.
420. BENSKO, John
    "The Elk Gets a Photography Lesson." [MemphisSR] (7:1) Fall 86, p. 46.
    "The Elk on Mutability." [MemphisSR] (7:1) Fall 86, p. 47.
    "Virginia Beach" (for Rosemary). [ForidaR] (14:1) Spr-Sum 86, p. 51.
421. BENSKO, Rosemary
    "Bronwen, Painter of Miccasukee Street." [MemphisSR] (7:1) Fall 86, p. 43.
422. BENSON, Joan
    "Thick Skins." [PassN] (7:2) Spr-Sum 86, p. 11.
    "Three Women in a Winter Kitchen." [PassN] (7:1) Fall-Wint 85-86, p. 9.
423. BENSON, Robert
    "Borinquen." [LitR] (30:1) Fall 86, p. 53.
    "Très Riches Heures." [LitR] (30:1) Fall 86, p. 53.

52

424. BENSON, Steve
    "The Stand-In Under Duress." [Temblor] (3) 86, p. 111-116.
425. BENTLEY, Jon Gill
    "The Feel of the Field" (for Andy & Claire). [YellowS] (21) Wint 86, p. 7.
426. BENTLEY, Nelson
    "Tracking the Transcendental Moose" (Book One: Childhood at Elm). [BellArk] (2:3)
        My-Je 86, p. 9-12.
    "Tracking the Transcendental Moose" (Book Two: The Lindbergh Helmet). [BellArk]
        (2:4) Jl-Ag 86, p. 9-12.
    "Tracking the Transcendental Moose" (Book Three: The Daily Blah). [BellArk] (2:5)
        S-O 86, p. 8-14.
    "Tracking the Transcendental Moose" (Book Four: The Old Dutch Mill and the
        Wolverine). [BellArk] (2:6) N-D 86, p. 9-15.
427. BENTLEY, Roy
    "The Heart as Second Child." [OhioR] (37) 86, p. 98.
    "On Board the Scirocco, Errol Flynn Asks John Barrymore Why Luck Follows One
        Man and Not Another." [MidAR] (7:1) 86, p. 171-173.
    "The Orchard the Dry Year." [MidAR] (7:1) 86, p. 174-175.
428. BENTTINEN, Ted
    "After the Pleiades Shower." [StoneC] (13:3/4) Spr-Sum 86, p. 17.
    "Fernando at the 'Paradise Bar'." [HangL] (49) Spr 86, p. 3-4.
    "New England Koan." [StoneC] (13:3/4) Spr-Sum 86, p. 17.
    "Snow, Blue Cloth and Fire." [LitR] (29:3) Spr 86, p. 312-313.
    "The Talons in the Waiting Room of the Dead." [SouthernR] (22:1) Ja 86, p. 125.
    "Vinland Journeys, Stone and Paper." [SouthernR] (22:1) Ja 86, p. 123-124.
BERCEDONIZ, Jorge María Ruscalleda
    See RUSCALLEDA BERCEDONIZ, Jorge María
429. BERG, Arie van den
    "Owl" (tr. by Scott Rollins). [Vis] (21) 86, p. 17.
    "Rondo" (tr. by James S. Holmes and Scott Rollins). [BostonR] (11:5) O 86, p. 18.
430. BERG, Lora
    "For Joy Adamson." [Shen] (36:2) 86, p. 54.
    "Lessons." [Vis] (21) 86, p. 4.
    "Samuel." [CarolQ] (39:1) Fall 86, p. 82-84.
431. BERG, Sharon
    "Asking for My Hand." [CrossC] (8:2) 86, p. 9.
    "The Birth Poem." [GreenfR] (13:3/4) Sum-Fall 86, p. 13.
    "Breastfeeding at the Art Gallery of Ontario Alex Colville Retrospective, 1983."
        [GreenfR] (13:3/4) Sum-Fall 86, p. 13-17.
432. BERG, Stephen
    "Big Mood." [AntR] (44:1) Wint 86, p. 68.
    "Now and Then." [AntR] (44:1) Wint 86, p. 69.
    "One." [AntR] (44:1) Wint 86, p. 70.
    "The Visit." [AntR] (44:1) Wint 86, p. 71.
433. BERGAMIN, José
    "Close My Eyes" (tr. by David Garrison). [WebR] (11:1) Spr 86, p. 32.
    "The Echo of Your Voice" (tr. by David Garrison). [LitR] (29:3) Spr 86, p. 346.
    "Hidden in the Dark Night" (tr. by David Garrison). [LitR] (29:3) Spr 86, p. 346.
    "In This Dark Night" (tr. by David Garrison). [WebR] (11:1) Spr 86, p. 33.
    "When a Hand of Shadow" (tr. by David Garrison). [WebR] (11:1) Spr 86, p. 32.
434. BERGAMINI, L. J.
    "The Wild Garden." [Blueline] (8:1) Sum-Fall 86, p. 3.
435. BERGAN, Brooke
    "Poem for Carla Reading." [AnotherCM] (15) 86, p. 9-11.
436. BERGE, H. C. ten
    "Brassempouy" (tr. by Theo Hermans and Paul Vincent). [Stand] (27:2) Spr 86, p.
        22.
    "Lübeck" (tr. by Theo Hermans and Paul Vincent). [Stand] (27:2) Spr 86, p. 23.
437. BERGER, Aishe
    "Nose Is a Country, I Am the Second Generation" (for Emma Eckstein). [SinW]
        (29/30) 86, p. 126-130.
438. BERGER, Bruce
    "Transmigration." [Poetry] (148:5) Ag 86, p. 276.
439. BERGER, Jacqueline
    "Americans." [NowestR] (24:3) 86, p. 13.

53

440. BERGER, Jim
"Growing Up." [BellR] (9:1) Spr 86, p. 63.
"Octopus." [BellR] (9:1) Spr 86, p. 62.
"Promises." [BellR] (9:1) Spr 86, p. 63.
"So, What Else Is New?" [BellR] (9:1) Spr 86, p. 62.
441. BERGERON, Alain
"Position Politique de la Société de Conservation du Present . . ." (w. Jean Dubé &
Philippe Coté). [Rampike] (5:2) 86, p. 60.
442. BERGIN, Thomas G.
"In Praise of Curves." [SouthwR] (71:2) Spr 86, p. 179.
443. BERGLAND, Martha
"Accommodations." [Prima] (10) 86, p. 12.
444. BERGMAN, David
"Bonzai for Beginners." [Poetry] (149:3) D 86, p. 139-142.
"Cardiogram." [KenR] (NS 7:1) Wint 85, p. 83-84.
"The Dedicant" (for Gordon Lester-Massman). [KenR] (NS 7:1) Wint 85, p. 80-83.
"In the Waiting Room." [Poetry] (149:3) D 86, p. 136-138.
"A Part for Horn." [Raritan] (6:2) Fall 86, p. 77-80.
445. BERGMAN, James P.
"A.W.O.L." [Sam] (46:2 release 182) 86, p. 97.
"Buffalo Bill Revisited." [Sam] (46:2 release 182) 86, p. 35-36.
"Vietnam." [Sam] (46:2 release 182) 86, p. 96.
"Water buffalo." [Sam] (46:2 release 182) 86, p. 68.
446. BERGON, Holly St. John
"The Witch of Teopisca." [Pequod] (22) 86, p. 90-91.
"World without End" (for Francisco Rivera, "Paquirri," killed . . . at Pozoblanco,
Sept. 26, 1984). [Pequod] (22) 86, p. 92.
447. BERGSTROM, Vera
"Here I Am." [Bogg] (55) 86, p. 35.
448. BERKE, Judith
"Courtesan." [DenQ] (20:4/21:1) Spr-Sum 86, p. 76.
"Fable of the Two Widowed Sisters." [MalR] (74) Mr 86, p. 107.
"Last Tango" (for John). [NewOR] (13:1) Spr 86, p. 10.
"Oedipus." [KenR] (NS 8:4) Fall 86, p. 107.
"The Return." [CarolQ] (38:2) Wint 86, p. 51.
"White Night" (Juan les Pins, 1958). [NewEngR] (8:4) Sum 86, p. 469-470.
449. BERKSON, Bill
"A Head at the Covers." [Zyzzyva] (2:2) Sum 86, p. 136-137.
450. BERLAND, Dinah
"Reflections" (for Adam). [NewL] (53:1) Fall 86, p. 83.
451. BERNAL, Esmeralda
"My Womb." [Americas] (14:1) Spr 86, p. 49.
"No Busco la Luna." [Americas] (14:1) Spr 86, p. 48.
"Remember." [Americas] (14:1) Spr 86, p. 50.
452. BERNARD, April
"The Way We Live Now." [ParisR] (28:101) Wint 86, p. 182-184.
453. BERNARD, Kenneth
"A Dream about Love in Public." [Confr] (33/34) Fall-Wint 86-87, p. 138.
454. BERNDT, John
"Pataphysics." [Rampike] (5:2) 86, p. 71.
455. BERNICHON, Janet
"The Laundramat." [SmPd] (23:1, #66) Wint 86, p. 17.
456. BERNIER, Jack
"Cordless Telephones." [SanFPJ] (8:3) 85, p. 44.
"Epilogue." [SanFPJ] (8:4) 85, p. 76.
"His Sign Is Pisces." [SanFPJ] (8:3) 85, p. 50.
"Let's Break It In." [SanFPJ] (8:2) 85, p. 51.
"Liberation." [SanFPJ] (9:1) 86, p. 25.
"Lottery Ticket." [NegC] (6:4) Fall 86, p. 93.
"Not Approved." [SanFPJ] (8:2) 85, p. 50.
"Origo." [SanFPJ] (8:3) 85, p. 41.
"Our Computer Has Selected You." [SanFPJ] (8:3) 85, p. 51.
"Read Between the Lines." [SanFPJ] (8:2) 85, p. 52.
"The Zodiac." [SanFPJ] (8:4) 85, p. 73.
457. BERNLEF, Henk
"Jan Van Goyen 1982" (tr. by Scott Rollins). [Caliban] (1) 86, p. 41.

"Rustle" (tr. by Heleen Mendl-Schrama). [Caliban] (1) 86, p. 42.
458. BERNLEF, J.
"Uncle Carl: a Home Movie" (tr. by Scott Rollins). [Stand] (27:2) Spr 86, p. 24.
459. BERNSTEIN, Charles
"Epiphanies of Suppression (3)." [Sink] (1) 86, p. 8-9.
"Factotum." [Rampike] (5:2) 86, p. 28.
"Fear of Flipping." [Sulfur] (6:1, issue 16) 86, p. 117-120.
"Like DeCLAraTionS in a HymIE CEMetEry." [SouthernHR] (20:1) Wint 86, p. 50-51.
"Special Pleading." [SouthernHR] (20:3) Sum 86, p. 220-221.
"We Sell Ice Picks, Don't We?" [Sink] (1) 86, p. 9.
460. BERNSTEIN, Lisa
"The Airplane." [YellowS] (21) Wint 86, p. 39.
"Husbandry." [YellowS] (21) Wint 86, p. 38.
"Night Swimmer." [YellowS] (21) Wint 86, p. 39.
461. BERRIS, Sandra
"Onion Evenings." [MidwQ] (27:4) Sum 86, p. 458.
462. BERRY, D. C.
"Cathedral." [IndR] (9:1) Wint 86, p. 33.
"Hawk." [SouthernR] (22:4) O 86, p. 778.
"Snake." [SouthernR] (22:4) O 86, p. 779.
463. BERRY, Wendell
"One of Us." [AmerV] (2) Spr 86, p. 24.
"Sabbaths" (Excerpt). [Verse] (3:3) N 86, p. 9.
"Sabbaths" (Selections: I-III). [VirQR] (62:3) Sum 86, p. 422-426.
"Sabbaths" (Selections: I-VI). [NewEngR] (8:3) Spr 86, p. 361-365.
"Sabbaths" (Selections: II, III, IV, VIII). [CutB] (26) Spr-Sum 86, p. 8-11.
464. BERRYMAN, John
"Two Dream Songs." [YaleR] (75:2) Wint 86, p. 319-320.
465. BERSSENBRUGGE, Mei-mei
"The Background." [Contact] (7:38/39/40) Wint-Spr 86, p. 32.
"The Carmelites." [Temblor] (3) 86, p. 47.
"Forms of Politeness." [Conjunc] (9) 86, p. 92-97.
466. BERTOLINO, James
"First Credo" (For Lois, & with thanks to my teachers). [QRL] (Poetry series 6:26) 86, 84 p.
"Inventing Buddha." [AnotherCM] (16) 86, p. 5.
467. BERTONE, Concepción
"Las Palabras." [Mairena] (8:22) 86, p. 56.
468. BERZINS, Rai
"The Plumber Waxes Morbid." [Event] (15:1) 86, p. 65.
469. BESCHTA, Jim
"Carnival." [SnapD] (9:2) Spr 86, p. 7-9.
"For My Mother." [SnapD] (9:2) Spr 86, p. 10-11.
470. BESKIN, Lisa
"Sneakers." [PaintedB] (28) Ap 86, p. 66.
471. BETTS, Gregory
"Hearing Heaney Read." [GreenfR] (13:3/4) Sum-Fall 86, p. 18.
"Stormwatch: Fogo Island." [GreenfR] (13:3/4) Sum-Fall 86, p. 19.
472. BEVAN, Maggie
"One Evening." [Bogg] (55) 86, p. 38.
473. BEYER, Christine D.
"America the Beautiful." [SanFPJ] (8:2) 85, p. 24.
474. BEYER, Richard G.
"Distant Object." [NegC] (6:4) Fall 86, p. 120.
"Reunion." [Outbr] (16/17) Fall 85-Spr 86, p. 79.
"To Marjorie, Eight Years Gone" (A Beymorlin Sonnet for Marjorie Lees Linn). [Outbr] (16/17) Fall 85-Spr 86, p. 80.
475. BEYER, William
"A Mother's Death: In Retrospect." [NegC] (6:4) Fall 86, p. 118.
476. BEZIAT, Richard
"Col. Mustard in the Lounge with the Lead Pipe." [SouthernHR] (20:3) Sum 86, p. 264-265.
477. BEZNER, Kevin
"Fishing with Grandfather: July 1958." [AntigR] (64) Wint 86, p. 113.

55

BHATT

478. BHATT, Sujata
"The Kama Sutra Retold." [YellowS] (18) Spr 86, p. 12.
479. BIALOSKY, Jill
"Cold Heart." [PartR] (53:1) 86, p. 92-93.
480. BIALOSTOTSKY, B. J.
"Autumn" (tr. by Aaron Kramer). [Vis] (21) 86, p. 24.
481. BIANCHI, Luigi M.
"The Labyrinth" (tr. of Giorgio Chiesura, w. Roger Greenwald). [Writ] (18) 86, c87,
p. 127-134.
482. BIANUCCI, Patrick
"Means to an End." [Electrum] (38) Spr 86, p. 27.
483. BICKNELL, John
"Casablanca." [KanQ] (18:1/2) Wint-Spr 86, p. 120.
484. BIEKER, Judith
"In a Cornfield at Dusk." [CapeR] (21:2) Fall 86, p. 42.
485. BIENKOWSKI, Marek
"I, Peter" (tr. by Daniel Bourne). [LitR] (29:3) Spr 86, p. 353.
"Icarus Descending" (tr. by Daniel Bourne). [LitR] (29:3) Spr 86, p. 353.
"A Pre-Christmas Toast" (tr. by Daniel Bourne). [LitR] (29:3) Spr 86, p. 354.
"The Word and the Flesh" (tr. by Daniel Bourne). [LitR] (29:3) Spr 86, p. 355.
486. BIENVENU, Roberta
"This Garden." [Ploughs] (12:3) 86, p. 88-89.
487. BIERDS, Linda
"The Klipsan Stallions." [NewYorker] (62:19) 30 Je 86, p. 36.
488. BIGBIE, Nina Juel
"Blood sight" (tr. of Thomas Bruun, w. Erik Porret). [Os] (23) 86, p. 24-25.
"Bound up in blood" (from Masker Uden Navne, tr. of Claus Carstensen, w. Erik
Porret). [Os] (23) 86, p. 38-39.
"Come to me" (tr. of Thomas Bruun, w. Erik Porret). [Os] (23) 86, p. 24-25.
"Copperkisses" (tr. of Claus Carstensen, w. Erik Porret). [Os] (23) 86, p. 20.
"Echoes arose in the room" (from Totenbuch, tr. of Claus Carstensen, w. Erik
Porret). [Os] (23) 86, p. 28.
"Even Further" (tr. of Pia Tafdrup, w. Erik Porret). [Os] (23) 86, p. 30-31.
"The Formlessness of Death" (tr. of Claus Carstensen, w. Erik Porret). [Os] (23) 86,
p. 38-39.
"Polaroid" (tr. of Claus Carstensen, w. Erik Porret). [Os] (23) 86, p. 36-37.
"Reading Piece" (from Totenbuch, tr. of Claus Carstensen, w. Erik Porret). [Os] (23)
86, p. 36-37.
"Shrapnel in flight" (tr. of Thomas Bruun, w. Erik Porret). [Os] (23) 86, p. 22-23.
"The Skin" (tr. of Pia Tafdrup, w. Erik Porret). [Os] (23) 86, p. 34-35.
"Spring Flood" (tr. of Pia Tafdrup, w. Erik Porret). [Os] (23) 86, p. 32-33.
"With a knife" (tr. of Thomas Bruun, w. Erik Porret). [Os] (23) 86, p. 26-27.
489. BILES, David
"Dragon's Jaw." [Sam] (46:2 release 182) 86, p. 31-32.
"Pleiku." [Sam] (46:2 release 182) 86, p. 8.
490. BILGERE, George
"Belle Plaine." [IndR] (9:3) Sum 86, p. 38-39.
"Bennett's Star" (discovered in 1886). [KenR] (NS 8:1) Wint 86, p. 50.
"Coming to Earth." [SewanR] (94:3) Sum 86, p. 373.
"Deep-Sea Fishing." [KenR] (NS 8:1) Wint 86, p. 49-50.
"The Folks Perform." [AntigR] (66/67) Sum-Aut 86, p. 53.
"Intersection." [SewanR] (94:3) Sum 86, p. 371.
"Night Drive." [KenR] (NS 8:1) Wint 86, p. 49.
"The Trout Farm." [CumbPR] (6:1) Fall 86, p. 73.
"What It Gives." [CumbPR] (6:1) Fall 86, p. 74.
"Windmill." [SewanR] (94:3) Sum 86, p. 372.
491. BILICKE, Tom
"Haiku: August afternoon." [Bogg] (56) 86, p. 25.
492. BILLET, Bonnie
"Ordinary Life." [KanQ] (18:3) Sum 86, p. 50.
493. BILLINGS, Robert
"At Billings' Bridge Graveyard." [GreenfR] (13:3/4) Sum-Fall 86, p. 20.
494. BINGHAM, Ginger
"Bright Birds." [Sonora] (11) Fall 86 [c87], p. 60.
"The Cake That Holds a City." [Sonora] (11) Fall 86 [c87], p. 58.
"Home." [Sonora] (11) Fall 86 [c87], p. 59.

BINGJUN, Pang
    See PANG, Bingjun
495. BIRCH, Michele
    "Firewalk." [Ploughs] (12:4) 86, p. 92-93.
    "For Linda, Off on a Cruise, Me in Penobscot Taking Care of Her Kids." [Ploughs]
        (12:4) 86, p. 94-96.
496. BIRKS, Ian C.
    "Van Gogh." [JamesWR] (3:3) Spr 86, p. 4.
497. BIRNBAUM, Saul
    "The Hardest Task." [SanFPJ] (8:4) 85, p. 81-82.
498. BIRNEY, Earle
    "Again and Again." [Waves] (14:3) Wint 86, p. 43.
    "Canada: Case History No. 3 (1985)." [Interim] (5:2) Fall 86, p. 7.
    "Dear Biographer." [Interim] (5:2) Fall 86, p. 6.
    "Deckhand on a Limey Freighter." [Interim] (5:2) Fall 86, p. 5-6.
    "In Port: The Lifeboat." [Waves] (14:3) Wint 86, p. 42.
    "Rot Below Adam's Peak" (Sri Lanka). [GreenfR] (13:3/4) Sum-Fall 86, p. 23-24.
    "Still Life near Bangalore." [GreenfR] (13:3/4) Sum-Fall 86, p. 22-23.
499. BISHOP, Bonnie
    "The Lucy Poems." [MalR] (75) Je 86, p. 97-100.
500. BISHOP, W. (Wendy)
    "After Crossing the Sahara." [ManhatPR] (8) Wint 86-87, p. 58-59.
    "The Bread Sellers, Kano City, Nigeria." [CapeR] (21:1) Spr 86, p. 36.
    "Family Furniture." [GWR] (6:2) 86, p. 16-17.
    "The Getting Ready." [LitR] (29:3) Spr 86, p. 288.
    "Netting the Pond." [CapeR] (21:1) Spr 86, p. 37.
    "Piano Player in a Whorehouse." [BellR] (9:2) Fall 86, p. 52.
    "El Radio." [CutB] (25) Fall-Wint 86, p. 27.
    "Second Chances." [TarRP] (25:1) Fall 85, p. 23.
    "The Southwest: O'Keeffe and Stieglitz." [SouthwR] (71:1) Wint 86, p. 63.
    "Twelve Year Old Bridge." [BellR] (9:2) Fall 86, p. 52.
    "Your Apple Tree." [DenQ] (20:4/21:1) Spr-Sum 86, p. 134-136.
501. BISSETT, Bill
    "Dew Yu Know." [GreenfR] (13:3/4) Sum-Fall 86, p. 27.
    "Looking for th Innr Life in 100 Mile." [GreenfR] (13:3/4) Sum-Fall 86, p. 25-26.
    "Th First Terrorism." [Rampike] (5:1) 86, p. 58.
    "Th Lovr Sighs If It All Revolvs around Yu." [GreenfR] (13:3/4) Sum-Fall 86, p.
        26-27.
    "Wintr Solstis Song, Famine in Afrika, Crescent Moons." [Rampike] (5:1) 86, p. 58.
502. BITZ, Gregory W.
    "Lost." [LakeSR] (20) 86, p. 21.
    "October 28, Don't Know the Year." [LakeSR] (20) 86, p. 22.
    "Pretty Big Deal." [LakeSR] (20) 86, p. 21.
    "Wood." [LakeSR] (20) 86, p. 22.
503. BIZZARO, Patrick
    "The Product." [ColEng] (48:7) N 86, p. 685.
504. BLACK, Charles
    "Oremus pro Ignotis." [ArizQ] (42:4) Wint 86, p. 304.
505. BLACK, Sharon
    "The Old Woman." [PaintedB] (28) Ap 86, p. 27.
506. BLACK, Sophia C.
    "On the Last Day of the World: Waiting on the Roof." [Atlantic] (258:6) D 86, p. 45.
507. BLACK, Star
    "Eleanor by Harry Callahan." [AmerPoR] (15:2) Mr-Ap 86, p. 42.
    "Really." [AmerPoR] (15:2) Mr-Ap 86, p. 42.
    "With Running Water and Fast Food." [AmerPoR] (15:2) Mr-Ap 86, p. 42.
508. BLACK ELK
    "Black Elk Speaks Again" (tr. by the son of Black Elk). [Paint] (13:25/26) Spr-Aut
        86, p. 29.
509. BLACKBURN, Cathy
    "Going Home." [NegC] (6:1) Wint 86, p. 78-79.
510. BLACKBURN, Michael
    "Icarus." [Stand] (27:2) Spr 86, p. 25.
511. BLACKSHEAR-PETER, Melanie
    "I'm Saying Goodbye." [FloridaR] (14:1) Spr-Sum 86, p. 110.
    "Postcard from Before the Freeze." [FloridaR] (14:1) Spr-Sum 86, p. 109.

512. BLADES, Joe
"Where the Sky Should Be." [PottPort] (8) 86-87, p. 52.
513. BLAIR, John
"In the Swimmer's Dressing Room at the Y." [CimR] (75) Ap 86, p. 38.
"The Lightning." [NewL] (53:1) Fall 86, p. 22-23.
514. BLAKE, William
"America: A Prophecy" (Selection: "A Prophecy"). [AmerPoR] (15:2) Mr-Ap 86, p.
    6.
515. BLAKER, Margaret
"Pueblo Mother" (After a reminiscence by Tristram Beresford). [PassN] (7:2)
    Spr-Sum 86, p. 15.
516. BLANCHARD, Lucile
"The Cliffs of Puyé." [MidwQ] (27:2) Wint 86, p. 195.
517. BLANCHETTE, Stephen, Jr.
"Thoughts on a Sunday Afternoon." [Amelia] (3:1) Ja 86, p. 43.
518. BLAND, Celia
"The Map." [Verse] (6) 86, p. 40.
519. BLANKENBURG, Gary
"Mr. Electric." [Puerto] (21:2) Spr 86, p. 34-36.
"Mr. Electric." [Wind] (16:57) 86, p. 30.
520. BLASER, Robin
"Advice: find someplace where." [WestCR] (20:4) Ap 86, p. 11.
"Home for Boys and Girls." [WestCR] (20:4) Ap 86, p. 13.
"To whom it may concern." [WestCR] (20:4) Ap 86, p. 12.
521. BLASING, Randy
"An Album Family." [Poetry] (149:1) O 86, p. 9.
"Richfield." [Poetry] (149:1) O 86, p. 10-11.
"Squid." [LitR] (30:1) Fall 86, p. 61.
522. BLAUNER, Laurie
"The Flamboyance of Memory." [PennR] (1:2) Fall 85, p. 72.
"When Marriage Isn't All It Could Be." [BlackWR] (13:1) Fall 86, p. 68.
523. BLAZEK, Douglas
"Argument." [Abraxas] (34) 86, p. 44-45.
"Obituary." [Abraxas] (34) 86, p. 43.
524. BLEHERT, Dean
"Deanotations" (9 selections). [Bogg] (56) 86, p. 48.
525. BLENGIO PINTO, José Rafael
"Un Hombre Levanta o Repara Su Casa." [Mairena] (8:22) 86, p. 99.
526. BLESSING, Marlene
"Heart Break." [PoetryNW] (27:1) Spr 86, p. 4-5.
"Identity Crisis at One." [QW] (22) Spr-Sum 86, p. 28.
"Moving Day." [PoetryNW] (27:1) Spr 86, p. 4.
"Passing Away." [PoetryNW] (27:1) Spr 86, p. 3.
527. BLESSING, Tom
"I Take These Words." [PoeticJ] (16) Fall 86, p. 21.
"On the Need for Slang to Revive Dying Languages, or Why We don't Talk Like
    Hamlet." [PoeticJ] (16) Fall 86, p. 21.
"UAW Haiku." [Bogg] (55) 86, p. 6.
528. BLESSINGTON, Francis
"Boustrophedon." [CumbPR] (6:1) Fall 86, p. 61.
"Incident." [Wind] (16:57) 86, p. 20.
"The Lisbon Poem." [DenQ] (20:4/21:1) Spr-Sum 86, p. 145-146.
"Rape." [SouthernHR] (20:1) Wint 86, p. 38.
"Samphire." [CumbPR] (5:2) Spr 86, p. 72.
"Speaking of Gravel." [CumbPR] (5:2) Spr 86, p. 71.
529. BLOCH, Chana
"In a Leap Year" (tr. of Yehuda Amichai). [Field] (34) Spr 86, p. 63.
"Inside the Apple" (tr. of Yehuda Amichai). [NewRep] (194:18) 5 My 86, p. 38.
"Jasmine" (tr. of Yehuda Amichai). [Shen] (36:3) 86, p. 90.
"Love Is Finished Again" (tr. of Yehuda Amichai). [Field] (34) Spr 86, p. 64.
"Relativity" (tr. of Yehuda Amichai). [Field] (34) Spr 86, p. 65.
"Songs of Zion the Beautiful" (Selection: 12, 14, tr. of Yehuda Amichai). [PoetL]
    (81:2) Sum 86, p. 75-76.
530. BLODGETT, E. D.
"Hypothesis of Doves." [MalR] (74) Mr 86, p. 111-119.

531. BLOMAIN, Karen
"Aria." [ManhatPR] (8) Wint 86-87, p. 46.
"Generations." [Blueline] (8:1) Sum-Fall 86, p. 39.
"Listen." [PassN] (7:2) Spr-Sum 86, p. 15.
"The Molly D. Mine." [PaintedB] (29) Ag 86, p. 17.
"Sepia." [PaintedB] (29) Ag 86, p. 18.
532. BLOSSOM, Laurel
"Daylight Savings." [AmerPoR] (15:1) Ja-F 86, p. 20.
"What's Wrong." [AmerPoR] (15:1) Ja-F 86, p. 20.
533. BLOSSOM, Lavina
"Marginal World." [LitR] (29:3) Spr 86, p. 313.
534. BLOUNT, Richard
"Learning to Be Married." [Puerto] (22:1) Fall 86, p. 1.
535. BLUE, Jane
"Cinéma Vérité." [CarolQ] (38:3) Spr 86, p. 7-8.
"Digression." [CarolQ] (39:1) Fall 86, p. 51.
"Epithalamion." [CarolQ] (39:1) Fall 86, p. 52.
536. BLUMBERG, Michele
"Coming Back to Earth." [PassN] (7:1) Fall-Wint 85-86, p. 14.
537. BLUMENTHAL, Michael
"The Pleasures of Abstraction." [Verse] (5) 86, p. 33.
538. BLY, Robert
"The Busy Man Speaks." [Raccoon] (19) 86, p. 9.
"Canadian Geese." [VirQR] (62:3) Sum 86, p. 434.
"A Chunk of Amethyst." [Chelsea] (45) 86, p. 41.
"For My Son Noah, Ten Years Old." [Raccoon] (19) 86, p. 32-33.
"The Hawk." [VirQR] (62:3) Sum 86, p. 435-436.
"Prayer Service in an English Church." [GeoR] (40:3) Fall 86, p. 632.
"Remaining Asleep." [VirQR] (62:3) Sum 86, p. 434-435.
"Snowbanks North of the House." [Raccoon] (19) 86, p. 31-32.
"The Teeth Mother Naked at Last" (Selection: Section II). [AmerPoR] (15:2) Mr-Ap
86, p. 5-6.
"Unrest." [Raccoon] (19) 86, p. 18.
539. BOBES, Marylin
"No vayas a decirle que he llorado." [Mairena] (8:22) 86, p. 56.
540. BOBROWSKI, Johannes
"Intelligence Report" (tr. by Paul Morris). [Translation] (16) Spr 86, p. 234.
"Joseph Conrad" (tr. by Paul Morris). [Translation] (16) Spr 86, p. 236.
"Mozart" (tr. by Paul Morris). [Translation] (16) Spr 86, p. 235.
541. BOBYSHEV, Dmitry V.
"Proceeding to Hell Together" (In Russian & English, tr. by Donald Davie).
[CumbPR] (6:1) Fall 86, p. 22-27.
542. BOCCIA, Michael
"Ha" (A translation/interpretation of "God's Seven Laughs." Text: Papyrus XIII in
Papyri Graecae Magicae). [WebR] (11:1) Spr 86, p. 44.
543. BOCK, Caroline
"Ripe." [Ploughs] (12:4) 86, p. 30.
544. BOCK/PALLANT, Layeh
"Poems and Fragments" (from the Amatory Epigrams of the Parnassian Anthology, tr.
of Myrrha). [YellowS] (19) Sum 86, p. 18.
545. BOE, Deborah
"Breaking Down." [Poetry] (147:6) Mr 86, p. 318.
"Factory Work." [Poetry] (147:6) Mr 86, p. 316-317.
"The Mother in the Pictures." [HangL] (49) Spr 86, p. 5-11.
"Still-Life." [Poetry] (147:6) Mr 86, p. 316.
546. BOE, Marilyn J.
"Coal." [PassN] (7:2) Spr-Sum 86, p. 18.
"Garage Door." [SingHM] (14) 86, p. 51.
BOER, David C. den
See DenBOER, David C.
547. BOES, Don
"The Rendezvous." [Puerto] (22:1) Fall 86, p. 60.
"Supper's Over." [Puerto] (22:1) Fall 86, p. 61.
548. BOGEN, Don
"The Pageant." [Poetry] (147:6) Mr 86, p. 324-325.
"The Pond." [Poetry] (147:6) Mr 86, p. 327.

59

"Romanesque." [Poetry] (147:6) Mr 86, p. 325-326.
549. BOGEN, Laurel Ann
"Love Poem for the Confused." [Electrum] (38) Spr 86, p. 45.
550. BOGIN, George
"The Kiss." [Confr] (33/34) Fall-Wint 86-87, p. 27.
"On Hearing an Aluminum Disc Again of My Voice in 1938." [OhioR] (36) 86, p. 94.
"Runaway." [LitR] (29:3) Spr 86, p. 316.
"Snapshot." [LitR] (29:3) Spr 86, p. 315.
"The Stone." [LitR] (29:3) Spr 86, p. 314.
551. BOGIN, Nina
"Initiation." [KenR] (NS 8:3) Sum 86, p. 63.
"Through Marshland." [KenR] (NS 8:3) Sum 86, p. 62.
"Wild Plums in August." [KenR] (NS 8:3) Sum 86, p. 61.
552. BOIDO, Guillermo
"Sea Voyages" (tr. by John Oliver Simon). [InterPR] (12:1) Spr 86, p. 21.
"Viajes de la Marea" (from *Voces y Fragmentos: Poesia Argentina de Hoy*, 1981).
    [InterPR] (12:1) Spr 86, p. 20.
BOIS, Barbara R. du
    See DuBOIS, Barbara R.
553. BOISSEAU, Michelle
"A Marriage." [OhioR] (37) 86, p. 82-83.
"Tennyson under the Yews." [GeoR] (40:2) Sum 86, p. 487-488.
554. BOISVERT, Yves
"L'homme vient justement de traverser la rue" ("Sans Titre"). [Rampike] (5:2) 86, p.
    59.
BOIX, Amaro Gomez
    See GOMEZ BOIX, Amaro
555. BOJANOWSKI, Ted
"Timetables." [KanQ] (18:1/2) Wint-Spr 86, p. 225.
556. BOLAND, Eavan
"Fond Memory." [SenR] (16:1) 86, p. 63.
"The Glass King." [SenR] (16:1) 86, p. 59-60.
"The Journey." [ChiR] (35:3) Spr 86, p. 62-65.
"Mise Eire." [SenR] (16:1) 86, p. 61-62.
"Nocturne." [Verse] (6) 86, p. 14.
"The Oral Tradition." [SenR] (16:1) 86, p. 53-56.
"Two Worlds." [SenR] (16:1) 86, p. 57-58.
"The Unlived Life." [Verse] (6) 86, p. 13.
"The Wild Spray" (for Kevin). [SenR] (16:1) 86, p. 64-65.
557. BOLEN, Brian
"All My Life." [PraF] (7:1) Spr 86, p. 53.
558. BOLLIER, E. P.
"The Fly." [NegC] (6:4) Fall 86, p. 64-65.
"A Garland of Clerihews, Political and Otherwise." [NegC] (6:4) Fall 86, p. 68.
"A Missed Opportunity." [NegC] (6:4) Fall 86, p. 63.
"'Modernism' Revisited." [NegC] (6:4) Fall 86, p. 66-67.
559. BOLLS, Imogene (Imogene L.)
"A Particular Death: Cimarron National Grasslands." [TarRP] (26:1) Fall 86, p.
    42-43.
"Rock Collector." [SoDakR] (24:3) Aut 86, p. 22.
"Who Only Stand and Wait" (On *Faithful*, a painting by Nicolai Fechin, 1881-1955).
    [SoDakR] (24:3) Aut 86, p. 157.
560. BOLTON, Joe
"After Rain." [MissouriR] (9:2) 86, p. 201.
"Black Water." [QW] (22) Spr-Sum 86, p. 30-31.
"Party." [Crazy] (31) Fall 86, p. 34-36.
"Sonnet." [CumbPR] (5:2) Spr 86, p. 32.
"Speaking of the South, 1961." [MissouriR] (9:2) 86, p. 202-203.
"Three Scenes from the Provinces of Blood." [Crazy] (31) Fall 86, p. 32-33.
"Towards Twenty-Four." [BlackWR] (13:1) Fall 86, p. 69-70.
"The Woman with the Blue Bandana." [CumbPR] (5:2) Spr 86, p. 33.
561. BOLZ, Barbara
"Before Stillbirth." [NegC] (6:4) Fall 86, p. 114.
562. BOMBA, Bernard
"Dismissal" (Summer, downtown Trenton). [JINJPo] (9:1) 86, p. 6.
"The Eiger's North Face, Unclimbed." [Confr] (33/34) Fall-Wint 86-87, p. 160-161.

"Estuary." [LitR] (29:2) Wint 86, p. 235.
"Homestead Burning, Galicia, 1895." [JINJPo] (9:1) 86, p. 7.
BOMBARD, Joan La
    See LaBOMBARD, Joan
563. BONA, Cele
    "When Robert Creeley Read His Poems beside His Hat." [LittleM] (15:1) 86, p. 36-38.
564. BOND, Bruce
    "Messiaen." [GeoR] (40:4) Wint 86, p. 952.
565. BOND, Joan
    "Maiden Aunt Felicity." [PottPort] (8) 86-87, p. 32.
566. BOND, Morris
    "Final Groove." [Ploughs] (12:4) 86, p. 91.
567. BONETTI, Ed
    "For Tom McAfee, from a Letter That Was Never Sent." [NewL] (52:2/3) Wint-Spr 86, p. 35-38.
568. BONNEFOY, Yves
    "The Beautiful Summer" (tr. by Lisa Sapinkopf). [StoneC] (13:3/4) Spr-Sum 86, p. 19.
    "Le Bel Eté." [StoneC] (13:3/4) Spr-Sum 86, p. 18.
    "Delphes du Second Jour." [StoneC] (13:3/4) Spr-Sum 86, p. 18.
    "Delphi the Second Day" (tr. by Lisa Sapinkopf). [StoneC] (13:3/4) Spr-Sum 86, p. 19.
    "The lamp burned low" ("Untitled", tr. by Lisa Sapinkopf). [AnotherCM] (15) 86, p. 8.
    "Shore of Another Death" (tr. by Lisa Sapinkopf). [NewOR] (13:2) Sum 86, p. 88-89.
    "To a Sadness" (from Réqnant Désert, tr. by Lisa Sapinkopf). [AnotherCM] (15) 86, p. 7.
    "A Voice" (tr. by Lisa Sapinkopf). [WebR] (11:1) Spr 86, p. 36.
569. BONNELL, Paula
    "Chinoiserie, Before the Wars." [ManhatPR] (7) Sum 86, p. 44.
    "Montaña Rusa" (reprinted to correct error in issue 3). [YetASM] (4) 85, p. 3.
570. BONNER, Deborah
    "The Cripple" (El mutilat, tr. of Gabriel Ferrater). [SenR] (16:1) 86, p. 34-35.
    "Expect No Omens" (tr. of Miquel Marti i Pol). [Translation] (16) Spr 86, p. 52.
    "Idols" (tr. of Gabriel Ferrater). [SenR] (16:1) 86, p. 33.
    "Joy" (tr. of Miquel Marti i Pol). [Translation] (16) Spr 86, p. 54.
    "Proclamation" (tr. of Miquel Marti i Pol). [Translation] (16) Spr 86, p. 56.
    "The Shadow of the Sea" (tr. of Miquel Marti i Pol). [Translation] (16) Spr 86, p. 52.
    "Slower Than Falling" (tr. of Miquel Marti i Pol). [Translation] (16) Spr 86, p. 55.
    "Their Eyes Always Open" (tr. of Miquel Marti i Pol). [Translation] (16) Spr 86, p. 55.
    "The Wind's Code" (tr. of Miquel Marti i Pol). [Translation] (16) Spr 86, p. 53.
    "With People of Highly Diverse Origins" (tr. of Miquel Marti i Pol). [Translation] (16) Spr 86, p. 53.
BONTE, Karen La
    See LaBONTE, Karen
571. BONVENTRE, Peter, FSC
    "Caravaggio at the Metropoitan 1985: A Second Visit." [EngJ] (75:5) S 86, p. 70.
572. BOOK, M. K.
    "Horizon" (2 poems: 1 & 2). [WormR] (26:2, issue 102) 86, p. 52.
573. BOOKER, Fred
    "Blue Notes of a White Girl" (for Monique, selections: 28-30, 32-37, 39). [Quarry] (35:1) Wint 86, p. 55.
574. BOONE, Gene
    "A Voice on the Wind." [WritersL] (1986:3), p. 23.
575. BOOSE, Maryetta Kelsick
    "An Attempt to Repeat." [SanFPJ] (8:4) 85, p. 12.
    "Discrepancy." [SanFPJ] (8:4) 85, p. 12.
    "In a Tattered Plaid Shirt." [SanFPJ] (8:1) 85, p. 45.
    "Living Off Their Backs." [SanFPJ] (8:4) 85, p. 57.
    "Now They Are Shooting the Children." [SanFPJ] (8:4) 85, p. 57.
    "The Prize." [SanFPJ] (8:4) 85, p. 9-10.
    "The Teenage Strut." [BlackALF] (20:3) Fall 86, p. 309.
    "Torn Lives." [SanFPJ] (8:2) 85, p. 36.

"With Sunglasses Hiding Her Tears." [SanFPJ] (8:1) 85, p. 46.
"A Woman Tired at 55." [SanFPJ] (8:1) 85, p. 47.
576. BOOTH, Philip
"Figuring How." [Ploughs] (12:4) 86, p. 178-179.
"Fire on the Island." [AmerPoR] (15:2) Mr-Ap 86, p. 39.
"Pick-Up." [AmerPoR] (15:2) Mr-Ap 86, p. 39.
"Relations: Old Light / New Sun / Postmistress / Earth / 04421." [AmerPoR] (15:2)
   Mr-Ap 86, p. 40.
"Relations: Old Light / New Sun / Postmistress / Earth / 04421." [NewEngR] (9:2)
   Wint 86, p. 157-158.
"Room 310." [AmerPoR] (15:2) Mr-Ap 86, p. 40.
"Saying It." [NewEngR] (9:2) Wint 86, p. 146-148.
"Short Day." [AmerPoR] (15:2) Mr-Ap 86, p. 40.
"Stonington." [AmerPoR] (15:2) Mr-Ap 86, p. 40.
"This Day after Yesterday" (Robert Trail Spence Lowell, 1917-1977). [GeoR] (40:3)
   Fall 86, p. 633-636.
"Wedge." [AmerPoR] (15:2) Mr-Ap 86, p. 40.
BORDA, Juan Gustavo Cobo
   See COBO BORDA, Juan Gustavo
577. BORDAO, Rafael
"Fabula de la Cucaracha." [LindLM] (5:3) Jl-S 86, p. 13.
578. BORDKEY, Harold
"The Garden." [NewYorker] (62:13) 19 My 86, p. 36.
579. BORGATTI, Robert
"Lights Out." [SlipS] (6) 86, p. 74.
"Shower Scene." [SlipS] (6) 86, p. 75.
580. BORGES, Jorge Luis
"Haiku" (4 poems, tr. by Paul Scott Derrick). [Verse] (3:3) N 86, p. 50.
"Mi Vida Entera." [Mairena] (8:21) 86, p. 68.
"The Web" (tr. by Alastair Reid). [NewYorker] (62:15) 2 Je 86, p. 32.
581. BORICH, Barrie
"He Brings You Part Way." [SingHM] (13) 86, p. 74-75.
582. BORROFF, Marie
"Understanding Poetry." [Poetry] (148:4) Jl 86, p. 194.
583. BORSON, Roo
"City." [GreenfR] (13:3/4) Sum-Fall 86, p. 29.
584. BORUCH, Marianne
"Angels." [Field] (35) Fall 86, p. 91-92.
"The Doctor Far from Home." [Field] (35) Fall 86, p. 94.
"The Heart, for Weldon Kees." [NoAmR] (271:4) D 86, p. 20.
"Light" (after Edward Hopper). [Field] (35) Fall 86, p. 95.
"Memory Biscuit." [Field] (34) Spr 86, p. 90.
"The Moon Losing Its Color All Over the Street." [Field] (34) Spr 86, p. 90-91.
"Raising Lumber." [Field] (35) Fall 86, p. 93.
585. BOSS, Laura
"Firsts, Seconds, and Thirds." [Lips] (12) 86, p. 43.
586. BOSTON, Bruce
"Coats." [Vis] (20) 86, p. 26.
587. BOSWELL, Virgina E.
"Julie Benning (a Spoon River Epitaph)." [EngJ] (75:5) S 86, p. 70.
588. BOSWORTH, Martha
"Walking on Space." [ManhatPR] (8) Wint 86-87, p. 16.
589. BOTTOMS, David
"Awake" (for Barry Hannah). [MissouriR] (9:2) 86, p. 227.
"The Guitar." [Poetry] (148:3) Je 86, p. 131-132.
"Homage to Little Roy Lewis." [KenR] (NS 8:1) Wint 86, p. 52-53.
"In Louisiana." [SouthernR] (22:4) O 86, p. 772-773.
"The Offering." [MissouriR] (9:2) 86, p. 228.
"The Resurrection." [Poetry] (148:3) Je 86, p. 133-134.
"A Row of Eagles." [CutB] (26) Spr-Sum 86, p. 12-13.
"Shingling the New Roof." [SouthernR] (22:4) O 86, p. 773-774.
"Under the Vulture-Tree" (for Mary Oliver). [Atlantic] (257:2) F 86, p. 58.
"White Swan." [KenR] (NS 8:1) Wint 86, p. 51-52.
590. BOUCHER, Alan
"Burning Face" (from the Icelandic poem cycle "Time and Water", tr. of Steinn
   Steinarr). [Vis] (22) 86, p. 13.

62

BOUCHER

"The Skies Rain" (tr. of Steinn Steinarr). [Vis] (20) 86, p. 8.
"Space Travel" (tr. of Olafur Johann Sigurdsson). [Vis] (20) 86, p. 9.
"Transparent Wings" (tr. of Steinn Steinarr). [Vis] (21) 86, p. 31.
591. BOUCHERON, Robert
"Pavane pour les Bains Défunts." [JamesWR] (3:4) Sum 86, p. 9.
"Poems 50" (tr. of Catullus). [JamesWR] (4:1) Fall 86, p. 7.
592. BOUIS, Antonina W.
"Fuku" (Fragment, tr. of Yevgeny Yevtushenko). [Nat] (242:11) 22 Mr 86, p. 365.
593. BOULGER, Lynn
"The Power of Bridges" (for Jeffrey). [Ploughs] (12:3) 86, p. 71-73.
594. BOULTING, Jonathan
"Like this one sees the poem like the meadow" (tr. of Robert Marteau). [Verse] (6) 86,
    p. 43.
"Lovers, you with less than a bed for land" (tr. of Robert Marteau). [Verse] (6) 86, p.
    43.
595. BOURASSA, Alan
"A Critique of Capitalism." [AntigR] (66/67) Sum-Aut 86, p. 74.
"The Torturer." [AntigR] (66/67) Sum-Aut 86, p. 74.
596. BOURNE, Daniel
"I, Peter" (tr. of Marek Bienkowski). [LitR] (29:3) Spr 86, p. 353.
"Icarus Descending" (tr. of Marek Bienkowski). [LitR] (29:3) Spr 86, p. 353.
"A Pre-Christmas Toast" (tr. of Marek Bienkowski). [LitR] (29:3) Spr 86, p. 354.
"Rafters." [YellowS] (19) Sum 86, p. 6.
"Salamanders." [YellowS] (19) Sum 86, p. 7.
"Solstice." [YellowS] (19) Sum 86, p. 6.
"Surviving the First Litter." [PikeF] (7) Spr 86, p. 12.
"The Word and the Flesh" (tr. of Marek Bienkowski). [LitR] (29:3) Spr 86, p. 355.
597. BOWDEN, Michael
"Flying Cloud." [MidAR] (6:1) 86?, p. 102-103.
598. BOWDRING, Paul
"To a Friend after Long Absence." [PottPort] (8) 86-87, p. 32.
"The View from Beaver Mountain" (August 6, 1985). [PottPort] (8) 86-87, p. 32.
599. BOWEN, Melody
"Appalachian Sonnet." [ManhatPR] (7) Sum 86, p. 46.
600. BOWERING, George
"Berlin." [MalR] (76) S 86, p. 135-141.
BOWERS, Cathy Smith
See SMITH-BOWERS, Cathy
601. BOWERS, Neal
"As the Crow Flies." [CumbPR] (5:2) Spr 86, p. 24.
"Bring Pies." [Poetry] (148:2) My 86, p. 70.
"The Dance" (For Nancy). [Poetry] (148:2) My 86, p. 68.
"For the Heart." [Poetry] (148:2) My 86, p. 69.
"A Kind of Love." [SewanR] (94:3) Sum 86, p. 375.
"Looking Out." [NewYorker] (62:11) 5 My 86, p. 46.
"The Message." [CumbPR] (5:2) Spr 86, p. 22.
"Mixed Pairs." [SewanR] (94:3) Sum 86, p. 374.
"The Necklace" (for Nancy). [CumbPR] (5:2) Spr 86, p. 23.
602. BOWIE, Robert
"Favorite Fishing Hole." [NoDaQ] (54:1) Wint 86, p. 59.
"Footprints." [Amelia] (3:4) Fall 86, p. 57.
"In the Wind." [PoetL] (81:1) Spr 86, p. 43.
603. BOWMAN, Maurice G.
"A Woodwren's Fall." [PoeticJ] (15) Sum 86, p. 25.
604. BOWMAN, Melanie
"Permanent Address." [AmerPoR] (15:1) Ja-F 86, p. 28.
"Saving Père David's Deer." [AmerPoR] (15:1) Ja-F 86, p. 28.
"When You Feel Strong." [AmerPoR] (15:1) Ja-F 86, p. 28.
BOWMAN, Sallie McCormick de
See DeBOWMAN, Sallie McCormick
605. BOYCE, Pleuke
"Dream Ballad" (tr. of Gerrit Achterberg). [LitR] (29:3) Spr 86, p. 360.
"Our Old Neighbour." [AntigR] (64) Wint 86, p. 92.
"Writing a Letter to My Brother." [AntigR] (64) Wint 86, p. 91.
606. BOYCE, Robert C.
"Beer Strike" (Victorian-style). [Bogg] (55) 86, p. 60.

"An Ever-Expanding Universe." [Bogg] (55) 86, p. 55.
607. BOYD, Carolyn Lee
"The Aphrodisiac." [LittleM] (15:1) 86, p. 41.
"Corazón a Corazón." [LittleM] (15:1) 86, p. 42.
608. BOYD, Greg
"The Lowest Form of Chicanery." [WormR] (26:4, issue 104) 86, p. 134.
"One Day." [WormR] (26:4, issue 104) 86, p. 134.
609. BOYD, W.
"Wednesday's Child." [YetASM] (4) 85, p. 5.
610. BOYDEN, Teresa
"Bolts." [CrabCR] (3:3) Sum 86, p. 11.
611. BOYER, Patsy
"Apocryphal Journalism" (tr. of Kato Molinari, w. Mary Crow). [MidAR] (6:1) 86?,
p. 69, 71.
612. BOYLE, Kevin
"Natural." [DenQ] (20:4/21:1) Spr-Sum 86, p. 45-47.
613. BOZANIC, Nick
"The Lake" (Honorable mention, 1986 Poetry Competition). [PassN] (7:2) Spr-Sum
86, p. 4.
"On Empty." [PassN] (7:1) Fall-Wint 85-86, p. 14.
614. BRACKETT, Donald
"What's for Dinner?" [Rampike] (5:1) 86, p. 69.
615. BRADEN, Dennis
"The Creative Writing Teacher Exhorts One of His Students." [BallSUF] (27:4) Aut
86, p. 54.
616. BRADLEY, George
"As the Romans Do." [NewRep] (194:23) 9 Je 86, p. 40.
"The Lines Between the Stars." [Shen] (36:3) 86, p. 20.
617. BRADLEY, John
"A Few Things You Should Know about Roberto." [MidAR] (6:2) 86, p. 10-11.
"So This Is the World: Biloxi, 1943." [Puerto] (22:1) Fall 86, p. 35-36.
"Vanity of the Hanged Man" (for Li Ho). [MidAR] (7:1) 86, p. 57-62.
618. BRADT, David
"Gerard David" (from *Al Partir de Manhattan*, tr. of Enrique Lihn). [CumbPR] (6:1)
Fall 86, p. 65.
"Monet's Years at Giverny" (from *Al Partir de Manhattan*, tr. of Enrique Lihn).
[CumbPR] (6:1) Fall 86, p. 69-71.
"Short Litany in a Low Voice" (tr. of Herib Campos Cervera). [Vis] (21) 86, p. 35.
619. BRADY, Dan
"I remember, I remember him." [SmPd] (23:1, #66) Wint 86, p. 25.
620. BRADY, Stephen (*See also* BRADY, Steven)
"Gravity and the Snow Storm." [BellArk] (2:5) S-O 86, p. 7.
"Set Theory." [BellArk] (2:5) S-O 86, p. 4.
621. BRADY, Steven (*See also* BRADY, Stephen)
"The Worship of Steel." [PikeF] (7) Spr 86, p. 24.
622. BRAGDON, Jane
"The Island." [StoneC] (13:3/4) Spr-Sum 86, p. 57.
623. BRAINBOW, Tez
"From underneath the radioactive mushroom." [WritersL] (1986:1), p. 6.
624. BRAMSON, Betty
"Ed." [Amelia] (3:1) Ja 86, p. 33.
625. BRAND, Alice (Alice G.)
"The Last Generation to Remember a Response to the Scrolls of Fire, 1943." [Event]
(15:2) 86, p. 170-171.
"The Twist of the Place." [SingHM] (13) 86, p. 29.
"Words." [Nimrod] (30:1) Fall-Wint 86, p. 108.
626. BRAND, Helena (Sister)
"Complaint: Dream Journal Assignment." [EngJ] (75:6) O 86, p. 74.
627. BRANDER, John
"Mistake." [Amelia] (3:1) Ja 86, p. 83.
628. BRANDI, John
"Conversations in Rangoon." [Pax] (3:1/2) Wint 85-86, p. 158-171.
"The Source of the Personification of Shiva." [Pax] (3:1/2) Wint 85-86, p. 152-157.
"Visible Sound." [Pax] (3:1/2) Wint 85-86, p. 149-152.
"Yes to the Universe." [Contact] (8:41/42/43) Fall-Wint 86-87, p. 60-61.

BRANDLER

629. BRANDLER, Marcielle
"America: At Your Service." [SanFPJ] (8:3) 85, p. 17.
"The Civilian, the Siege." [SanFPJ] (8:3) 85, p. 73.
"What a Girl Told Me in the Ladies Room" (To Bag Ladies). [SanFPJ] (8:3) 85, p. 17.
630. BRANDON, Sherry
"The Diamond Cutter." [PoeticJ] (14) 86, p. 9.
631. BRANDT, Di
"The crippled woman in my bed with the hole." [PraF] (7:3) Aut 86, p. 30.
"Valkyrie Song." [PraF] (7:3) Aut 86, p. 29.
632. BRANDT, P. M.
"To Jerome, in Hull." [Bogg] (55) 86, p. 8.
633. BRANDVOLD, Peter
"Color." [Raccoon] (20) Ap 86, p. 39.
634. BRAVARD, Robert S.
"Species" (For Dr. James H. Mitchell). [LittleM] (15:2) 86, p. 11.
635. BRAVERMAN, Kate
"By the Second." [Electrum] (38) Spr 86, p. 44.
636. BRAXTON, Charlie R.
"The King Uncrowned." [BlackALF] (20:3) Fall 86, p. 261.
637. BRAYMEN-CLEARY, Lee
"Once Again Blackberry Warheads." [Poem] (55) Mr 86, p. 44.
"The Tanning Salon Coupon." [Poem] (55) Mr 86, p. 45.
638. BREBNER, Diana
"Black and White Kimonos." [MalR] (77) D 86, p. 101.
"Meditations on the Serene Blue Shirt" (2 selections, variations on a poem by Margaret Atwood). [Grain] (14:2) My 86, p. 44-45.
"When You Settle All in a White Chair." [MalR] (77) D 86, p. 100.
"You, of All White Women I Have Loved." [Quarry] (35:3) Sum 86, p. 14.
639. BRECHT, Stefan
"8th Avenue." [Confr] (33/34) Fall-Wint 86-87, p. 193.
640. BREEDEN, David
"Going Under the Porch." [YetASM] (5) 86, p. 3.
641. BREEN, Nancy
"Dancing on a Bum Leg." [Amelia] (3:2) Spr 86, p. 63.
642. BREGA, Jorge
"We Were Brave" (tr. by Thorpe Running). [ColR] (NS 13:1) Fall 85, p. 47.
643. BRENNAN, Karen
"My Mother and the Shepherdess." [Sonora] (10) Spr 86, p. 1-2.
"Nijinsky at the Windshield." [Sonora] (10) Spr 86, p. 3.
"The Wondrousness of Light and Other Problems." [Sonora] (10) Spr 86, p. 4-5.
644. BRENNAN, Matthew
"August Morning in Bloom's Bay." [Wind] (16:57) 86, p. 26.
"First Cold Night of Fall." [BallSUF] (27:4) Aut 86, p. 45.
"Snowblind" (for Tim). [BallSUF] (27:4) Aut 86, p. 26.
645. BRESLIN, Paul
"The Scale." [TriQ] (67) Fall 86, p. 134.
646. BRETT, Peter
"Ghost of Snow." [Electrum] (38) Spr 86, p. 10.
"The Invitation of Time." [Farm] (3:1) Fall 85, p. 40.
"Walking the Central Valley." [KanQ] (18:3) Sum 86, p. 102-103.
647. BREWER, Kenneth
"Faces Like Houses." [Wind] (16:56) 86, p. 6-7.
"Light of the Moon / Dark of the Moon." [Wind] (16:56) 86, p. 6.
648. BREWSTER, Elizabeth
"For H.D., Imagiste." [OntR] (24) Spr-Sum 86, p. 71.
"Hilda Doolittle Analyzes Sigmund Freud." [OntR] (24) Spr-Sum 86, p. 72-78.
"Is the Pathetic Fallacy True?" [GreenfR] (13:3/4) Sum-Fall 86, p. 30-31.
"Poem for My Sixty-Third Birthday." [OntR] (24) Spr-Sum 86, p. 79-80.
649. BREWSTER, Marty
"Leah's Specialty." [Wind] (16:57) 86, p. 31.
BREYNER, Sophia de Mello
See ANDRESEN, Sophia de Mello Breyner
BREYNER ANDRESEN, Sophia de Mello
See ANDRESEN, Sophia de Mello Breyner

650. BRIDGFORD, Kim
  "After the Waiting." [Event] (15:1) 86, p. 114.
  "The Only Reason." [KanQ] (18:3) Sum 86, p. 51.
651. BRILL, Victoria A.
  "Todo el mundo cree que está a salvo." [Mairena] (8:22) 86, p. 90.
652. BRIND, Susan
  "Go Round" (tr. of Amal Donqal). [SenR] (16:1) 86, p. 92.
  "Roses" (tr. of Amal Donqal). [SenR] (16:1) 86, p. 91.
  "Song of Baramhat" (tr. of Salah Jahin). [SenR] (16:1) 86, p. 93-96.
653. BRINGHURST, Robert
  "The Beauty of Weapons" (El-Arish, 1967). [CrabCR] (4:1) Fall-Wint 86, p. 7.
  "The Book of Silences" (Selections: Six Poems). [CutB] (26) Spr-Sum 86, p. 38-45.
  "For the Bones of Josef Mengele, Disinterred June 1985." [CutB] (26) Spr-Sum 86,
    p. 51.
  "Of the Snaring of Birds" (from *Antigone* by Sophocles, a version in memory of
    Martin Heidegger). [CrabCR] (4:1) Fall-Wint 86, p. 6.
  "Poem about Crystal." [CrabCR] (4:1) Fall-Wint 86, p. 6.
  "A Quadratic Equation." [CrabCR] (4:1) Fall-Wint 86, p. 6.
  "Rubus Ursinus: A Prayer for the Blackberry Harvest." [CutB] (26) Spr-Sum 86, p.
    49.
  "Study for an Ecumenical Window." [CrabCR] (4:1) Fall-Wint 86, p. 8.
  "Sunday Morning" (for Don McKay & Jan Zwicky). [ParisR] (28:100) Sum-Fall 86,
    p. 54-55.
  "Sutra of the Heart." [CutB] (26) Spr-Sum 86, p. 46-48.
  "Tending the Fire." [CutB] (26) Spr-Sum 86, p. 52-58.
  "Thirty Words." [CutB] (26) Spr-Sum 86, p. 50.
654. BRINKMAN, Marilyn Salzl
  "August." [RagMag] (5:2) Fall 86, p. 4.
  "The Blackbird Call." [RagMag] (5:1) Spr 86, p. 17.
  "The Promise of Others." [RagMag] (5:1) Spr 86, p. 15.
  "The Rock Pile." [RagMag] (5:2) Fall 86, p. 5.
  "Sleep Fences." [RagMag] (5:1) Spr 86, p. 15.
655. BRISTOL, David
  "Warm Night with Pig." [KanQ] (18:1/2) Wint-Spr 86, p. 39.
656. BROADHEAD, Marlis Manley
  "On Things Predictable." [MidwQ] (28:1) Aut 86, p. 88-89.
657. BROCK, James
  "One Size Fits Most." [ForidaR] (14:1) Spr-Sum 86, p. 101.
658. BROCK, Randall
  "Inside I Am." [JamesWR] (3:2) Wint 86, p. 5.
659. BROCK, Van K.
  "Crete." [SouthernPR] (26:1) Spr 86, p. 8-9.
  "For a Whitewaterer — On His 16th Birthday." [SouthernR] (22:4) O 86, p. 797-798.
  "The Hunger." [SouthernR] (22:4) O 86, p. 796.
660. BROCK-BROIDO, Lucie
  "After the Grand Perhaps." [Ploughs] (12:3) 86, p. 90-91.
  "The Future as a Cow." [MissR] (15:1/2, #43/44) Fall-Wint 86, p. 42-43.
  "Lucie & Her Sisters." [MissR] (15:1/2, #43/44) Fall-Wint 86, p. 44-45.
  "Ten Years' Apprenticeship in Fantasy." [Ploughs] (12:3) 86, p. 92-94.
661. BROCKLEY, Michael
  "Cottonwoods." [SpoonRQ] (11:2) Spr 86, p. 21.
  "Hiding." [SpoonRQ] (11:2) Spr 86, p. 19.
  "The Hourglass Mirror." [Wind] (16:57) 86, p. 4.
  "Jody Hips a Cocktail." [Wind] (16:57) 86, p. 4-5.
  "Sanctus Bells." [BallSUF] (26:4) Aut 85, p. 55.
  "Wednesday After Being Laid-Off." [SpoonRQ] (11:2) Spr 86, p. 20.
662. BRODEY, Jim
  "Anselm Hollo." [LittleM] (15:1) 86, p. 35.
  "Frank O'Hara 2." [LittleM] (15:1) 86, p. 34.
  "Peter Orlovsky." [LittleM] (15:1) 86, p. 33.
663. BRODKEY, Harold
  "On First Being Published" (for Joanna Brown). [ParisR] (28:100) Sum-Fall 86, p.
    56-57.
664. BRODSKY, Joseph
  "History of the Twentieth Century" (A Roadshow). [PartR] (53:3) 86, p. 327-343.

BRODSKY

665. BRODSKY, Louis Daniel
"Earthly Rewards." [BallSUF] (26:4) Aut 85, p. 46-47.
"Guilty Until Proven Innocent." [SouthernR] (22:3) Sum 86, p. 558.
"A Renewal of Faith." [BallSUF] (26:4) Aut 85, p. 45.
"Young Willy Services Two Major Accounts." [SouthernR] (22:3) Sum 86, p. 559.
666. BRODY, Farrell
"Max Trujillo, the One-Band Man." [Puerto] (22:1) Fall 86, p. 79-80.
667. BRODY, Harry
"The Hero." [Wind] (16:56) 86, p. 8.
"In the Small Iowa Town the Only Officer on Graveyard . . ." [Wind] (16:56) 86, p. 8-9.
"Leaving Work in Light Rain." [StoneC] (13:3/4) Spr-Sum 86, p. 49.
"Lines for One As Yet Unnamed." [Electrum] (38) Spr 86, p. 17.
"On Learning I'm to Be a Father Again." [ConnPR] (5:1) 86, p. 41.
"On the Way to Them." [WebR] (11:1) Spr 86, p. 87.
"Only Felt Just Now." [DeKalbLAJ] (19:2) 86, p. 12.
"Written in the Stars." [Bogg] (55) 86, p. 24.
BROIDO, Lucie Brock
    See BROCK-BROIDO, Lucie
668. BROMIGE, David
"Moves in England's Queen and Peasant Tongue" (Selections: 1-5). [Sink] (1) 86, p. 39-41.
669. BROMLEY, Anne C.
"The Northerners at Homosassa Springs, Florida." [CarolQ] (38:2) Wint 86, p. 56-57.
"There Are Ripe Moments That Sing." [CutB] (25) Fall-Wint 86, p. 26.
670. BROOKS, Alan
"Cascade Canyon." [BelPoJ] (36:3) Spr 86, p. 30-35.
671. BROOKS, Andrew
"For Barbara." [GreenfR] (13:3/4) Sum-Fall 86, p. 32.
672. BROOKS, Pamela Barlow
"I'd like to take you home with me" (visual poem). [WestCR] (20:4) Ap 86, p. 53.
"Sometimes the wolves are silent" (visual poem). [WestCR] (20:4) Ap 86, p. 52.
"Wanting" (visual poem). [WestCR] (20:4) Ap 86, p. 54.
673. BROSMAN, Catharine Savage
"The Blinded Man at Night." [SouthernR] (22:3) Sum 86, p. 551-552.
"Crows." [SouthernR] (22:3) Sum 86, p. 552.
"Falling at Mont Saint Michel." [SouthernR] (22:3) Sum 86, p. 550-551.
"Moving into Summer." [SoDakR] (24:2) Sum 86, p. 81.
674. BROSSA, Joan
"Corrected Perspective" (tr. by Gregory Rabassa). [Translation] (16) Spr 86, p. 25.
"Hamlet" (for the poet Stephen Spender, in remembrance of London, tr. by Gregory Rabassa). [Translation] (16) Spr 86, p. 26.
"Joana" (tr. by Gregory Rabassa). [Translation] (16) Spr 86, p. 29.
"The People Don't Realize" (tr. by Gregory Rabassa). [Translation] (16) Spr 86, p. 28.
"Revolutionary Artist" (tr. by Gregory Rabassa). [Translation] (16) Spr 86, p. 28.
"Sack of Blood" (A Small Tale, tr. by Gregory Rabassa). [Translation] (16) Spr 86, p. 27.
"Untitled Short Poems" (tr. by Gregory Rabassa). [Translation] (16) Spr 86, p. 24-25.
675. BROSSARD, Iris
"Country Wedding" (for Jeremy Cole and Shelly Ganberg). [ManhatPR] (6) Wint-Spr 85-86, p. 61.
676. BROUGHTON, James
"Here I Am." [JamesWR] (4:1) Fall 86, p. 5.
"The Sorrows of Befuddlement." [Zyzzyva] (2:4) Wint 86-87, p. 137.
677. BROUGHTON, T. Alan
"Caretaker." [KanQ] (18:1/2) Wint-Spr 86, p. 72-73.
"Don Giovanni in Retirement." [QW] (22) Spr-Sum 86, p. 25-27.
"For Leviathan" (to arn chorn). [Northeast] (series 4:4) Wint 86-87, p. 17.
"Ice Fisher." [LitR] (29:2) Wint 86, p. 170-172.
"A Winter." [TarRP] (25:2) Spr 86, p. 29-30.
678. BROUMAS, Olga
"Abroad." [OP] (42/43) Wint 86-87, p. 18-19.

"Anoint the Ariston" (Selections: VIII-X, tr. of Odysseas Elytis). [AmerV] (5) Wint 86, p. 11-12.
"Eros." [Calyx] (10:1) Sum 86, p. 15-18.
"Famous Night" (tr. of Odysseas Elytis). [AmerPoR] (15:5) S-O 86, p. 19.
"Jai Alai." [OP] (42/43) Wint 86-87, p. 20.
"The Monogram" (Selections: III, IV, tr. of Odysseas Elytis). [AmerPoR] (15:5) S-O 86, p. 18.
"Native." [OP] (42/43) Wint 86-87, p. 17-18.
"Périsprit." [OP] (42/43) Wint 86-87, p. 19.
679. BROUN, Hob
"Hollywood Canteen." [Zyzzyva] (2:4) Wint 86-87, p. 105.
680. BROWN, Allan
"Moss-wind." [Quarry] (35:1) Wint 86, p. 104-110.
"On Hearing Vivaldi" (largo e sostenuto). [Quarry] (35:3) Sum 86, p. 36.
681. BROWN, Bebe
"Cinder Peace." [SanFPJ] (8:2) 85, p. 64.
"Communication." [SanFPJ] (8:4) 85, p. 71.
"Contingency plans." [SanFPJ] (8:4) 85, p. 71.
"A dog eat dog world." [SanFPJ] (8:4) 85, p. 46.
"Justification?" [SanFPJ] (8:4) 85, p. 71.
"Menu for an International Bar-B-Que." [SanFPJ] (8:4) 85, p. 48.
"A new world order." [SanFPJ] (8:4) 85, p. 71.
"Proliferation." [SanFPJ] (8:4) 85, p. 71.
682. BROWN, Berkeley
"Delta." [AmerV] (3) Sum 86, p. 94-95.
683. BROWN, Beth
"Eulogy for James Weldon Jones." [Callaloo] (9:1, #26) Wint 86, p. 16-17.
"Father." [Callaloo] (9:1, #26) Wint 86, p. 15.
684. BROWN, Beverly
"Turn Out." [WebR] (11:1) Spr 86, p. 76-77.
685. BROWN, Christopher (*See also* BROWN, Christopher N.)
"Wind in My Mind." [WritersL] (1986:1), p. 6.
686. BROWN, Christopher N. (*See also* BROWN, Christopher)
"Black Irish." [ManhatPR] (8) Wint 86-87, p. 21.
687. BROWN, Emerson
"Retro San Francisco." [SanFPJ] (8:2) 85, p. 92.
"Ronald's Regular Rap." [SanFPJ] (8:2) 85, p. 76.
"Sun City Sonnet." [SanFPJ] (8:2) 85, p. 88.
"Young Black Joe." [SanFPJ] (8:2) 85, p. 89.
BROWN, Iris J. Johnson
See JOHNSONBROWN, Iris J.
688. BROWN, Jeffrey M.
"Mistaken Identity." [SecC] (14:1) 86, p. 20.
BROWN, Joseph A., S.J.
See LUKE (JOSEPH A. BROWN, S.J.)
689. BROWN, Judith Bradshaw
"Working Out." [EngJ] (75:7) N 86, p. 35.
690. BROWN, Marilyn
"Imagination, from a Corpse." [RagMag] (5:1) Spr 86, p. 6.
"Sky, from October." [RagMag] (5:1) Spr 86, p. 4-5.
691. BROWN, P. J. L.
"Polyphony." [NewRena] (6:3, #20) Spr 86, p. 101.
692. BROWN, Robert
"Walking on Water." [Sam] (46:5 [i.e. 46:1] release 181) 86, p. 50-51.
693. BROWN, Ronnie
"The Jumpers." [Quarry] (35:1) Wint 86, p. 85-88.
694. BROWN, Simon
"The Child." [Bogg] (55) 86, p. 48.
695. BROWN, Stuart C.
"The Calligraphy of the Taut Line." [SouthernPR] (26:1) Spr 86, p. 37-38.
"Grinning Over Breakfast." [HayF] (1) Spr 86, p. 14.
"Notes from the Weekend, Osage River, 1901." [SouthernPR] (26:2) Fall 86, p. 70-71.
696. BROWN, Victor H.
"Sawdust Circle." [CrossCur] (5:4/6:1) 86, p. 135.

697. BROWN, Vincent J.
　　"Birthday Forenoon." [EngJ] (75:3) Mr 86, p. 80.
698. BROWN-DAVIDSON, Terri L.
　　"Slow Pan of a *Guernica*-Cityscape." [SanFPJ] (8:1) 85, p. 23.
699. BROWNE, Michael Dennis
　　"Mengele." [Iowa] (16:1) Wint 86, p. 117.
　　"To Show Peter the World." [Iowa] (16:1) Wint 86, p. 118-119.
700. BROWNING, Patricia
　　"Nuclear Medicine." [Interim] (5:1) Spr 86, p. 42.
　　"Trapeze Artist." [Interim] (5:1) Spr 86, p. 41.
701. BROWNSTEIN, Andrea
　　"Studies." [EngJ] (75:7) N 86, p. 91.
702. BRUCE, Debra
　　"Father, Son, Grandson." [PassN] (7:2) Spr-Sum 86, p. 19.
　　"For Roxeanna in Summer." [Calyx] (10:1) Sum 86, p. 22.
　　"For Roxeanna in Winter." [Calyx] (10:1) Sum 86, p. 23.
　　"Mother and Daughter." [NegC] (6:4) Fall 86, p. 51.
　　"Never Married." [NegC] (6:4) Fall 86, p. 50.
　　"Notes toward a Sermon." [LitR] (30:1) Fall 86, p. 44.
703. BRUCE, George
　　"Old Man and Sea." [Interim] (5:2) Fall 86, p. 8.
　　"Rembrandt in Age" (Self-portrait in the National Gallery of Scotland, as seen in
　　　　English and in Scots). [Interim] (5:2) Fall 86, p. 9.
704. BRUCE, Lennart
　　"New" (tr. of Eva Runefelt, w. Sonja Bruce). [Translation] (17) Fall 86, p. 309-310.
　　"The Slaughterhouse" (tr. of Eva Runefelt, w. Sonja Bruce). [Translation] (17) Fall
　　　　86, p. 307-308.
705. BRUCE, Sonja
　　"New" (tr. of Eva Runefelt, w. Lennart Bruce). [Translation] (17) Fall 86, p.
　　　　309-310.
　　"The Slaughterhouse" (tr. of Eva Runefelt, w. Lennart Bruce). [Translation] (17) Fall
　　　　86, p. 307-308.
706. BRUCHAC, Joseph
　　"At the Old Dog's Grave." [CrossCur] (6:2) 86, p. 46-47.
　　"Buson's Ashes." [TexasR] (7:1/2) Spr-Sum 86, p. 16.
　　"The Flint from Mississquoi." [PennR] (1:2) Fall 85, p. 67.
　　"Leaving Oregon" (for Bill Stafford). [PaintedB] (29) Ag 86, p. 32.
　　"Maskwa." [PoetryE] (20/21) Fall 86, p. 193.
　　"Tangled Lines." [PaintedB] (29) Ag 86, p. 33.
707. BRUGALETTA, John J.
　　"Dead in the Water." [NegC] (6:4) Fall 86, p. 40.
　　"The Fat Lady's Knee." [NegC] (6:4) Fall 86, p. 41.
　　"People of the Dog." [NegC] (6:4) Fall 86, p. 37-39.
708. BRUHWILER, Ryland
　　"Poplar and Evergreen." [Raccoon] (20) Ap 86, p. 9.
　　"Tines." [MemphisSR] (7:1) Fall 86, p. 42.
709. BRUMMELS, J. V.
　　"Beyond Our Words." [HolCrit] (23:1) F 86, p. 17.
　　"Weather in the Bones." [PraS] (60:2) Sum 86, p. 45-48.
710. BRUNER, Deborah
　　"Gathering Pasts." [Zyzzyva] (2:1) Spr 86, p. 27-28.
711. BRUNK, Juanita
　　"Fortune." [SouthernPR] (26:1) Spr 86, p. 43.
BRUNT, H. L. van
　　See Van BRUNT, H. L.
BRUNT, Lloyd van
　　See Van BRUNT, Lloyd
712. BRUSH, Thomas
　　"Chalk." [TarRP] (25:2) Spr 86, p. 41.
　　"Signs." [PoetryNW] (27:4) Wint 86-87, p. 28-29.
713. BRUTEN, Avril
　　"The Months in the Breviary Grimani." [Verse] (5) 86, p. 48.
714. BRUUN, Thomas
　　"Blood sight" (in Danish and English, tr. by Nina Juel Bigbie and Erik Porret). [Os]
　　　　(23) 86, p. 24-25.

"Come to me" (in Danish and English, tr. by Nina Juel Bigbie and Erik Porret). [Os]
(23) 86, p. 24-25.
"Shrapnel in flight" (in Danish and English, tr. by Nina Juel Bigbie and Erik Porret).
[Os] (23) 86, p. 22-23.
"With a knife" (in Danish and English, tr. by Nina Juel Bigbie and Erik Porret). [Os]
(23) 86, p. 26-27.
715. BRYAN, Sharon
"Abiding Love." [Ploughs] (12:4) 86, p. 50-57.
"Bad News." [PoetryNW] (27:2) Sum 86, p. 28.
"Hopper's *Early Sunday Morning*." [WestHR] (40:3) Aut 86, p. 212.
"If Nobody Dies It's a Comedy." [WestHR] (40:4) Wint 86, p. 350-351.
716. BRYAN, Tom
"Of Fine Cloth Made: A Rant." [Bogg] (56) 86, p. 21-22.
"Poetic Licence." [Bogg] (56) 86, p. 12.
717. BUCK, Wilfred
"Did I see you wading in the dawn" ("Untitled"). [PraF] (7:1) Spr 86, p. 73.
718. BUCKHOLTS, Claudia
"The Dream Animal." [Paint] (13:25/26) Spr-Aut 86, p. 20.
719. BUCKLEY, Christopher
"Evening in Santorini." [Poetry] (148:3) Je 86, p. 136-137.
"For a Friend Lacking Faith" (Santa Barbara, 1983). [PennR] (1:2) Fall 85, p. 35-36.
"Poem on a Birthday." [ThRiPo] (27/28) 86, p. 30-31.
"The Roadrunner" (for Glover Davis). [MissouriR] (9:1) 85-86, p. 18.
"Walking Out the Appian Way Past the Circus of Maxentius." [Poetry] (148:3) Je 86,
p. 135-136.
720. BUCKLEY, Mignonne
"Renewed." [BellR] (9:2) Fall 86, p. 6.
"A Spherical Cow." [BellR] (9:2) Fall 86, p. 7.
721. BUCKNER, Sally
"Holcomb County Poems" ("The Guv," "Maintenance"). [CrabCR] (4:1) Fall-Wint
86, p. 17-21.
"White Water." [ChrC] (103:8) 5 Mr 86, p. 238.
722. BUDENZ, Julia
"Flora Baum, Historian." [SouthwR] (71:3) Sum 86, p. 380-382.
"The Gardens of Flora Baum" (Excerpt from "Floralia," Part 2 of "Rome").
[BostonR] (11:5) O 86, p. 8.
723. BUDY, Andrea Hollander
"Pigs." [GeoR] (40:3) Fall 86, p. 637.
724. BUELL, Frederick
"History Lesson." [LittleM] (15:1) 86, p. 9-14.
"Hunt." [LittleM] (15:2) 86, p. 8-10.
"March Day-End" (Honorable Mention Poem, 1985/1986). [KanQ] (18:1/2) Wint-Spr
86, p. 23.
"The Marshlands." [NoAmR] (271:3) S 86, p. 5.
"Sloatsburg." [KanQ] (18:1/2) Wint-Spr 86, p. 23-25.
725. BUELL, Tom
"Householding." [BellArk] (2:1) Ja-F 86, p. 8.
726. BUETTNER, Shirley
"Birthday." [PraS] (60:2) Sum 86, p. 66.
"Dear Harland." [Northeast] (series 4:3) Spr 86, p. 4.
"In Cottonwood Township." [PraS] (60:2) Sum 86, p. 67.
"Recovering the Corm." [PraS] (60:2) Sum 86, p. 68.
"To Bones That Rocked Me." [Northeast] (series 4:3) Spr 86, p. 3.
727. BUFFET, Jimmy
"Incommunicado." [ClockR] (3:2) 86, p. 33.
728. BUGDEN, Jocelyn
"In Slow Motion" (Selections). [Quarry] (35:1) Wint 86, p. 71-74.
729. BUGEJA, Michael (Michael J.)
"Campout in Paradise." [Wind] (16:56) 86, p. 10.
"Dying, He Curses the Comet." [PoetL] (81:1) Spr 86, p. 49.
"Fontanelle." [NegC] (6:4) Fall 86, p. 34.
"Harmony." [Amelia] (3:4) Fall 86, p. 36.
"The Life We Share." [BallSUF] (26:4) Aut 85, p. 54.
"Mary's Heaven." [NewEngR] (8:3) Spr 86, p. 313.
"Mothers." [KenR] (NS 8:3) Sum 86, p. 55.

"On the Anniversary of Her First Stillborn, Divine Intervention." [BallSUF] (27:4)
  Aut 86, p. 36.
"The Present" (To Marsha Caldwell, nurse). [KenR] (NS 8:3) Sum 86, p. 54-55.
"The Prodigy" (for Heidi Miller). [LakeSR] (20) 86, p. 33.
"Redefining the Blues" (For Terry Hummer). [NegC] (6:1) Wint 86, p. 18.
"Snake, Rock: A Poem I Cannot Write." [KenR] (NS 8:3) Sum 86, p. 56.
"Warnings." [NegC] (6:4) Fall 86, p. 35.
"Words That Will Terrify Our Children." [QW] (22) Spr-Sum 86, p. 49.
730. BUISSON, Justine
"Access" (Honorable Mention Poem, 1985/1986). [KanQ] (18:1/2) Wint-Spr 86, p.
  14.
"My Father Brooding." [NegC] (6:1) Wint 86, p. 74.
731. BUKOWSKI, Charles
"About the Love Poems of the Cat." [OroM] (4:1-4) My 85, p. 86.
"Barred from the Polo Lounge." [OroM] (4:1-4) My 85, p. 87-89.
"Dark Night Poems" (#1-12). [Amelia] (3:2) Spr 86, p. 18-27.
"Don't Play It Again, Sam." [WormR] (26:4, issue 104) 86, p. 158.
"For A.D." [OroM] (4:1-4) My 85, p. 95.
"For the Foxes, the Defamers, the Tap Dancers and the Dreamers of Ballet." [WormR]
  (26:3, issue 103) 86, p. 87.
"Gallery." [WormR] (26:1, issue 101) 86, p. 36-37.
"Hands." [WormR] (26:1, issue 101) 86, p. 38.
"Here I Am." [OroM] (4:1-4) My 85, p. 90.
"The History of a Tough Motherfucker." [WormR] (26:4, issue 104) 86, p. 156-157.
"Hot Night." [SlipS] (6) 86, p. 43-44.
"The House." [OroM] (4:1-4) My 85, p. 5-6.
"If You Want Justice, Take the Knife." [SecC] (14:1) 86, p. 12-13.
"The Joke Is on the Sun." [SecC] (14:1) 86, p. 11.
"Love Crushed Like a Dead Fly." [SecC] (14:1) 86, p. 14-19.
"The Lucky Ones." [WormR] (26:2, issue 102) 86, p. 77-78.
"A Man for the Centuries." [SecC] (14:1) 86, p. 10.
"My Friend." [WormR] (26:3, issue 103) 86, p. 89-90.
"Oh, to Be Young." [SlipS] (6) 86, p. 44-46.
"Poem for My 43rd Birthday." [OroM] (4:1-4) My 85, p. 4.
"A Poem Is a City." [OroM] (4:1-4) My 85, p. 27.
"Result." [WormR] (26:3, issue 103) 86, p. 88-89.
"Rhyming Poem." [OroM] (4:1-4) My 85, p. 16.
"Same Old Thing, Shakespeare Through Mailer." [OroM] (4:1-4) My 85, p. 17.
"Shut Out." [WormR] (26:3, issue 103) 86, p. 88.
"Style." [OroM] (4:1-4) My 85, p. 29-30.
"This Is Free, Take It, and Feel Better." [WormR] (26:2, issue 102) 86, p. 78-79.
"You Can't Tell a Turkey by Its Feathers." [WormR] (26:3, issue 103) 86, p. 90-91.
732. BULLIS, Jerald
"Brilliant Afternoon." [BostonR] (11:6) D 86, p. 7.
"Cooleemee Plantation." [BostonR] (11:6) D 86, p. 7.
"Headland." [BostonR] (11:6) D 86, p. 7.
"Home." [BostonR] (11:6) D 86, p. 7.
"Ozark Lullaby." [BostonR] (11:6) D 86, p. 7.
"Up the Creek." [BostonR] (11:6) D 86, p. 7.
733. BUNDY, Alison F.
"Travels with Mine Roan." [Nimrod] (30:1) Fall-Wint 86, p. 109-110.
734. BUNIN, Ivan Alekseyevitch
"The Grave of Rachel" (tr. by Moshe Spiegel). [WebR] (11:1) Spr 86, p. 42.
735. BURAK, Kathryn
"Letter from My Sister, the Tattooist." [HolCrit] (23:2) Ap 86, p. 19.
736. BURD, Jennifer J.
"Coming Of." [BellArk] (2:4) Jl-Ag 86, p. 4.
"Romance." [BellArk] (2:5) S-O 86, p. 5.
737. BURFORD, William
"Late at Night, Walking in Washington." [Pax] (3:1/2) Wint 85-86, p. 7.
738. BURGESON, Joseph
"Recipe for Recidivism." [PoeticJ] (14) 86, p. 24.
BURGOS, Juan Saez
  See SAEZ BURGOS, Juan

739. BURKARD, Michael
"2 Poems on the Same Theme." [AmerPoR] (15:5) S-O 86, p. 3.
"8 Hour Voyage." [AmerPoR] (15:5) S-O 86, p. 4.
"At the Gate of the Headless Sunset." [QW] (23) 86, p. 55.
"Black and Green." [AmerPoR] (15:5) S-O 86, p. 5.
"Breathless Storm." [AmerPoR] (15:5) S-O 86, p. 4.
"The Brothers." [Ploughs] (12:4) 86, p. 209.
"I have a silence in the rain" ("Untitled"). [AmerPoR] (15:5) S-O 86, p. 5.
"If I See the Lost." [QW] (23) 86, p. 56-57.
"Little Final Sunlight." [Ploughs] (12:4) 86, p. 214.
"Moon's Rule." [Ploughs] (12:4) 86, p. 211.
"One Don't." [Sonora] (11) Fall 86 [c87], p. 61-62.
"Secret Warning." [QW] (22) Spr-Sum 86, p. 47-48.
"Sleigh on Hire." [AmerPoR] (15:5) S-O 86, p. 4.
"The Summer of the Thief." [Ploughs] (12:4) 86, p. 210.
"Too Many Drops." [Ploughs] (12:4) 86, p. 212-213.
"The World at Dusk." [Ploughs] (12:4) 86, p. 215-216.
740. BURKE, Anne
"The Beginning of the Sky." [PraF] (7:1) Spr 86, p. 25.
"Icarus in Big Hill Country." [PraF] (7:1) Spr 86, p. 26.
741. BURKE, William T.
"Fat Cat's Motto." [SanFPJ] (9:1) 86, p. 13.
"They've Nuked You Without Asking Me." [SanFPJ] (9:1) 86, p. 16.
742. BURKS, Charlie
"Boswell likes you." [Contact] (8:41/42/43) Fall-Wint 86-87, p. 17.
743. BURLAND, Brian
"A Few Words for Malcolm Lowry, Echoes from the Ebro." [NewL] (52:2/3)
    Wint-Spr 86, p. 157-159.
744. BURLINGAME, Robert
"For Robert Walser Who Voluntarily Entered a Mental Asylum in 1929." [Puerto]
    (21:2) Spr 86, p. 72.
"Old Story." [Puerto] (21:2) Spr 86, p. 74.
"On a Sort of Work." [Puerto] (21:2) Spr 86, p. 73.
"Once Again — Time." [Puerto] (21:2) Spr 86, p. 71.
"Pair of Whiskers." [Puerto] (21:2) Spr 86, p. 69.
"Wobbling" (for Patricia). [Puerto] (21:2) Spr 86, p. 70.
745. BURN, Skye
"Storm Watch." [BellArk] (2:2) Mr-Ap 86, p. 4.
746. BURNETT, Norman
"Lines." [Amelia] (3:3) Sum 86, p. 88.
747. BURNHAM, Clint
"I Hitchhike Without Hope." [Event] (15:1) 86, p. 19.
748. BURNHAM, Deborah
"Cutting the Pear Tree." [WoosterR] (6) Fall 86, p. 58.
749. BURNS, Gerald
"Twenty Four Gnomic Poems." [Temblor] (3) 86, p. 59-71.
750. BURNS, Michael
"The August Casualties." [MidwQ] (27:4) Sum 86, p. 459.
"Territory" (for my brother). [NewOR] (13:1) Spr 86, p. 32-33.
751. BURNS, Ralph
"The Comfort of a Woman." [Poetry] (147:5) F 86, p. 262.
"Debris." [Poetry] (147:5) F 86, p. 261-262.
"Luck." [Field] (33) Fall 85, p. 82-84.
"Mozart's Starling." [Field] (35) Fall 86, p. 97-98.
"Texas Aubade." [Field] (35) Fall 86, p. 96.
752. BURROWS, E. G.
"Fault." [WestCR] (21:2) O 86, p. 56-57.
"Going toward Memphis." [PassN] (7:1) Fall-Wint 85-86, p. 9.
"The House on First Hill." [WestCR] (21:2) O 86, p. 55-56.
"Living at the Edge of the Ice." [ManhatPR] (8) Wint 86-87, p. 20.
"The Market." [PoetryNW] (27:3) Aut 86, p. 38.
"Mercenary." [WestCR] (21:2) O 86, p. 58.
"Planted Too Close." [Paint] (13:25/26) Spr-Aut 86, p. 21.
"Political Weathers: A Love Song." [Ascent] (11:2) 86, p. 13.
"Sleeping Close." [CrabCR] (3:2) Spr 86, p. 16.

"Surprised by Trees." [WestCR] (21:2) O 86, p. 59.
753. BURSK, Chris (Christopher)
"First Love." [ManhatR] (4:1) Fall 86, p. 37.
"Grey Sand." [ManhatR] (4:1) Fall 86, p. 38.
"Lib Bristol's." [ManhatR] (4:1) Fall 86, p. 39.
"Rowing Cutthroat Creek." [Poetry] (148:2) My 86, p. 92.
"Sisters." [Poetry] (148:2) My 86, p. 90.
"The Trees Keeping Their Place, Saying Nothing." [Poetry] (148:2) My 86, p. 91.
"Wings." [ManhatR] (4:1) Fall 86, p. 32-36.
754. BURT, John
"Andrew Ramsay at the Somme." [Shen] (36:2) 86, p. 98.
"Paolo and Francesca." [Shen] (36:2) 86, p. 97.
"St. Francis and the Wolf." [Shen] (36:2) 86, p. 96.
"Waiting for Birds." [Shen] (36:2) 86, p. 95.
755. BURT, Kathryn
"The Decoy." [Farm] (3:1) Fall 85, p. 19.
"To Where There's Never Been." [Farm] (3:1) Fall 85, p. 18.
756. BUSAILAH, R. (Raja-e, Reja-e)
"Ali of Lydda." [TexasR] (7:1/2) Spr-Sum 86, p. 56.
"At an Old Market." [CrossCur] (6:2) 86, p. 141.
"At the Battlefront." [Interim] (5:2) Fall 86, p. 39.
"A Slice of Palestine." [Interim] (5:2) Fall 86, p. 38.
"Tease." [DeKalbLAJ] (19:3/4) 86, p. 68.
757. BUSCH, Trent
"Round Rock Creek." [StoneC] (13:3/4) Spr-Sum 86, p. 70-71.
"The Sighter." [NoAmR] (271:2) Je 86, p. 45.
758. BUSHELLE, David
"Emerge." [StoneC] (13:3/4) Spr-Sum 86, p. 66.
759. BUSHKOWSKY, Aaron
"A Dream of Sorts." [WestCR] (21:1) Je 86, p. 84-85.
"A Field of Lines." [MalR] (77) D 86, p. 69-70.
"In the Late Evening." [AntigR] (66/67) Sum-Aut 86, p. 67.
"Mabel Brushes Her Hair." [MalR] (77) D 86, p. 67.
"Prairie Sleep." [WestCR] (21:1) Je 86, p. 85.
"Taken Up." [MalR] (77) D 86, p. 68.
"Time for Tea." [MalR] (77) D 86, p. 65-66.
760. BUSIA, Abena
"Achimota: From the Story My Mother Taught Me." [Cond] (13) 86, p. 95-96.
761. BUSTAMANTE, Cecilia
"Contraseña." [Americas] (14:1) Spr 86, p. 47.
"First Penmanship Lesson" (To my son Leonardo, tr. by Maureen Ahern). [RedBass]
(10) 86, p. 6.
"Noche de Santa Lucía." [Americas] (14:1) Spr 86, p. 46.
"Y en el Tercer Día" (a José María Arguedas). [Americas] (14:1) Spr 86, p. 45.
762. BUTCHER, Grace
"Farmer in the Dell." [HiramPoR] (40) Spr-Sum 86, p. 37-38.
"Let Me Tell You about My Operation." [PassN] (7:2) Spr-Sum 86, p. 22.
"Once." [HiramPoR] (40) Spr-Sum 86, p. 35-36.
"Refuge." [CapeR] (21:2) Fall 86, p. 7.
"Simon Sez." [HiramPoR] (40) Spr-Sum 86, p. 39-40.
763. BUTLER, Ken
"War Memorial." [Wind] (16:56) 86, p. 27.
764. BUTSCHER, Edward
"Spring Harvest." [ConnPR] (5:1) 86, p. 36.
765. BUTTERFIELD, Martha
"Corriere della Sera, Siena 1926." [MalR] (75) Je 86, p. 82.
"Mise en Scène." [MalR] (75) Je 86, p. 83.
766. BUTTRESS, Derrick
"Broxtowe Estate." [Bogg] (55) 86, p. 42.
767. BYER, Kathryn Stripling
"All Hallows Eve." [GeoR] (40:3) Fall 86, p. 638.
768. BYLAND, Pat
"Rose." [WritersL] (1986:2), p. 11.
"Take My Hand." [WritersL] (1986:3), p. 20.

73

BYRNE

769. BYRNE, Edward
     "Aubade: For a Dancer." [MissouriR] (9:2) 86, p. 58-59.
     "Homecoming." [MissouriR] (9:2) 86, p. 56-57.
770. BYRNE, Elena Karina
     "Because in This Hour." [MidAR] (7:1) 86, p. 142.
C., R.
     See R. C.
771. CABALQUINTO, Luis
     "Alignment." [Contact] (7:38/39/40) Wint-Spr 86, p. 30.
     "Beach Lights." [RiverS] (20) 86, p. 34.
     "Bongao Wedding." [RiverS] (20) 86, p. 34.
     "Web." [RiverS] (20) 86, p. 34.
CABAN, David Cortes
     See CORTES-CABAN, David
772. CABRAL, Manuel del
     "Aire Durando." [Mairena] (8:22) 86, p. 62.
     "Carta a Mi Padre." [Mairena] (8:22) 86, p. 61.
     "Nuestro canto no cabe en las banderas." [Mairena] (8:22) 86, p. 55.
     "Poesia." [Mairena] (8:22) 86, p. 14.
CABRERA, Pedro Garcia
     See GARCIA CABRERA, Pedro
773. CACCIUTTO, Frank
     "Circling David" (For Melissa Green, my student). [EngJ] (75:2) F 86, p. 80.
CACHO, Manuel Joglar
     See JOGLAR CACHO, Manuel
774. CADER, Teresa
     "The Cloth Factory." [PraS] (60:4) Wint 86, p. 63-64.
     "Farm Accident." [StoneC] (14:1/2) Fall-Wint 86-87, p. 26.
     "Letter from Paris" (for Ahuva and Yehuda Arie). [PraS] (60:4) Wint 86, p. 65.
     "Not a Sound." [PraS] (60:4) Wint 86, p. 66.
     "The Outsider." [TriQ] (67) Fall 86, p. 131-132.
     "Sailing." [PraS] (60:4) Wint 86, p. 62-63.
775. CADNUM, Michael
     "Beauty." [GeoR] (40:4) Wint 86, p. 882.
     "The Courtesan in Old Age." [Amelia] (3:2) Spr 86, p. 81-82.
     "A Dislike for Flowers." [GeoR] (40:3) Fall 86, p. 639.
     "Privacy." [CentR] (30:3) Sum 86, p. 353-354.
     "Spring in a Foreign Country." [Amelia] (3:2) Spr 86, p. 82.
776. CADSBY, Heather
     "From the Immense Curriculum." [AntigR] (65) Spr 86, p. 70.
     "Glimpse." [AntigR] (65) Spr 86, p. 69.
     "Nothing Really." [AntigR] (65) Spr 86, p. 69.
     "Wednesday's Child." [Waves] (14:3) Wint 86, p. 61.
777. CADY, Joseph
     "Conferring." [MassR] (27:2) Sum 86, p. 240.
     "January 1981: Some Gay Men Watch the Inauguration Events." [MinnR] (NS 26)
          Spr 86, p. 8.
778. CAIN, Richard
     "A Villanelle for the Balance." [KanQ] (18:4) Fall 86, p. 130.
779. CAIRNS, Scott
     "The Book of Forms." [WestHR] (40:2) Sum 86, p. 115.
     "Revisiting." [CharR] (12:1) Spr 86, p. 23.
     "You Wreck Your Car." [CharR] (12:1) Spr 86, p. 22.
780. CALABRESE, John Michael
     "Dust." [JamesWR] (3:2) Wint 86, p. 1.
     "To Carve Out the Lion." [JamesWR] (3:2) Wint 86, p. 1.
781. CALANDRO, Ann
     "On the Roof" (for Susan Packer). [WebR] (11:1) Spr 86, p. 84.
     "Photograph of a Friend." [WebR] (11:1) Spr 86, p. 85.
782. CALDWELL, John
     "O Starry Night." [InterPR] (12:1) Spr 86, p. 97.
     "We Only Meet at Funerals Anymore." [InterPR] (12:1) Spr 86, p. 96.
783. CALHOUN, Nadine
     "Country." [WritersL] (1986:6), p. 26.
     "Ending." [WritersL] (1986:6), p. 26.
     "Love." [WritersL] (1986:2), p. 11.

"Supper." [WritersL] (1986:3), p. 11.
"Visions." [WritersL] (1986:4), p. 22.
784. CALHOUN, Tim
"The Death of the Philosopher from Paros." [ManhatPR] (6) Wint-Spr 85-86, p. 62.
"Holding Back the Flame." [ManhatPR] (6) Wint-Spr 85-86, p. 63.
785. CALLAGHAN, Barry
"Assonance." [GreenfR] (13:3/4) Sum-Fall 86, p. 34.
"Mother and Son." [GreenfR] (13:3/4) Sum-Fall 86, p. 34.
"Snowfall." [GreenfR] (13:3/4) Sum-Fall 86, p. 33.
"So It Was Done." [GreenfR] (13:3/4) Sum-Fall 86, p. 33.
786. CALLIMACHUS
"I detest long-winded poetry" (from "The Palatine Anthology, tr. by John Gill).
[YellowS] (21) Wint 86, p. 24.
787. CALVILLO, M. Kimberly
"Coon Rapids." [PraS] (60:2) Sum 86, p. 51-52.
"'Cottonwood County' Backflap" (for the big hummers K & K). [PraS] (60:2) Sum
86, p. 51.
"Evening Chores" (for Ellen in Center, Nebraska). [PraS] (60:2) Sum 86, p. 50.
"Gotta Getta Block." [PraS] (60:2) Sum 86, p. 53.
788. CAMERON, Nancy
"Flying into Dusk." [Event] (15:1) 86, p. 27.
789. CAMERON, Norman
"A Bowl of Wine." [CumbPR] (6:1) Fall 86, p. 49.
"Lucifer." [CumbPR] (6:1) Fall 86, p. 59.
"Naked among the Trees." [CumbPR] (6:1) Fall 86, p. 57.
"Pretty Maids All in a Row" (From a hand-book of advice to travellers). [CumbPR]
(6:1) Fall 86, p. 55.
"The Thespians at Thermopylae." [CumbPR] (6:1) Fall 86, p. 56.
"Via Maestranze." [CumbPR] (6:1) Fall 86, p. 58.
790. CAMPBELL, Anne
"Mixed Memory." [PraF] (7:2) Sum 86, p. 28.
"Trade Off." [PraF] (7:2) Sum 86, p. 27.
"Vacant Image." [PraF] (7:2) Sum 86, p. 28.
791. CAMPBELL, Arthur
"Urban Blender." [Sam] (44:3 release 175) 86, p. 54.
792. CAMPBELL, Katie
"Cathedral." [PraF] (7:3) Aut 86, p. 108.
"Recently I've Been Thinking of Blue." [PraF] (7:3) Aut 86, p. 109.
793. CAMPBELL, Mary Belle
"Caux-sur-Montreux." [InterPR] (12:2) Fall 86, p. 32.
"Caux-sur-Montreux" (tr. by the author). [InterPR] (12:2) Fall 86, p. 33.
"Purple Distance." [Pembroke] (18) 86, p. 206-207.
794. CAMPBELL, Nicholas
"Tableau." [CrossCur] (6:2) 86, p. 129-130.
795. CAMPBELL, Rick
"Draft Resister." [Sam] (44:3 release 175) 86, p. 38.
"Endings" (for James Wright). [ConnPR] (5:1) 86, p. 33.
"For One Who Jumped from the New Blue Heron Bridge." [Sam] (44:3 release 175)
86, p. 48.
796. CAMPOS CERVERA, Herib
"Short Litany in a Low Voice" (tr. by David Bradt). [Vis] (21) 86, p. 35.
797. CANADAY, John
"Some Things Are a Bright Flash." [Nimrod] (30:1) Fall-Wint 86, p. 69-77.
798. CANAN, Janine
"Saint Hildegarde." [ManhatPR] (6) Wint-Spr 85-86, p. 17.
"Singer." [ManhatPR] (6) Wint-Spr 85-86, p. 16.
799. CANCEL, Mario R.
"Los libros" (Selections: I, II, V, VI). [Mairena] (8:21) 86, p. 56-57.
800. CANDEGABE, Nelly
"Adan Tu Mismo." [Mairena] (8:22) 86, p. 30.
801. CANDELARIA, Fred
"Berkeley." [WestCR] (21:1) Je 86, p. 68.
"Lemmings at the Edge of Land" (Vancouver, 1986). [WestCR] (21:1) Je 86, p. 69.
"Nocturne." [WestCR] (21:1) Je 86, p. 65.
"A Time Ago." [WestCR] (21:1) Je 86, p. 66.
"Time Passes." [WestCR] (21:1) Je 86, p. 67.

802. CANHAM, Stephen
"Wasted" (Saigon, 1969). [Sam] (46:2 release 182) 86, p. 67.
803. CANNON, Janet
"Vietnamese Girl." [HeliconN] (14/15) Sum 86, p. 119.
804. CANTONI, Louis J.
"Now That You Are Gone." [PoeticJ] (13) 86, p. 28-29.
805. CANTSIN, Monty
"My Gold Bust" (by Monty Cantsin, a.k.a. Istvan Kantor). [Rampike] (5:2) 86, p. 24-25.
806. CANTWELL, Kevin
"Late Night Replay at Buddy's Exxon." [CutB] (25) Fall-Wint 86, p. 24-25.
807. CARABAJAL, Alicia
"Cancion de Invierno." [LetFem] (10:1) Spr 84, p. 110.
"Nocturno." [LetFem] (10:1) Spr 84, p. 111.
CARBEAU, Mitchell les
   See LesCARBEAU, Mitchell
808. CARDENAL, Ernesto
"At the Tomb of the Guerrilla" (tr. by Jonathan Cohen). [Agni] (23) 86, p. 80.
"Barricade" (tr. by Sesshu Foster). [RedBass] (11) 86, p. 10.
"For Those Dead, Our Dead" (tr. by Jonathan Cohen). [AmerV] (2) Spr 86, p. 100-101.
"Founding of the Latin American Association for Human Rights" (tr. by Jonathan Cohen). [Agni] (23) 86, p. 75-76.
"New Ecology" (tr. by Jonathan Cohen). [Agni] (23) 86, p. 78-79.
"The Parrots" (tr. by Jonathan Cohen). [Agni] (23) 86, p. 77.
"The Price of Bras" (tr. by Jonathan Cohen). [MassR] (27:3/4) Fall-Wint 86, p. 510.
"Vision from the Blue Plane-Window" (tr. by Jonathan Cohen). [Agni] (23) 86, p. 74.
"Visit to Weimar" (tr. by Ellen Watson). [MassR] (27:3/4) Fall-Wint 86, p. 506-509.
809. CARDILLO, Joe
"It Is Morning." [Vis] (21) 86, p. 39.
"Maybe Tonight." [CrabCR] (3:2) Spr 86, p. 9.
810. CARDOZO, Manoel
"Death" (tr. of Manuel Bandeira). [Vis] (21) 86, p. 33.
"The Ex(orbit)ant Voyage" (tr. of Cassiano Ricardo). [Vis] (20) 86, p. 16-18.
"Future, 4" (tr. of Pericles Eugenio da Silva Ramos). [Vis] (20) 86, p. 7.
"Guitar" (tr. of Cecilia Meireles). [Vis] (21) 86, p. 34.
811. CARDUCCI, Lisa
"Passeggiata Tridimensionale." [Os] (23) 86, p. 5.
812. CAREY, Barbara
"Crack the Whip." [PraF] (7:4) Wint 86-87, p. 38.
"Mr. Fix It." [Event] (15:1) 86, p. 62-63.
"Sovereign States." [PraF] (7:4) Wint 86-87, p. 37.
813. CAREY, Michael A.
"Country School: Donegal." [CapeR] (21:1) Spr 86, p. 25.
"Working-Class Children: Newark, New Jersey." [CapeR] (21:1) Spr 86, p. 24.
814. CARLETON, Augustus
"Beethoven and Goethe Once Met in Teplitz." [Epoch] (35:2) 86-87, p. 184-185.
"An Economy of Fulfillment." [Epoch] (35:2) 86-87, p. 186-187.
"Wedding." [Epoch] (35:2) 86-87, p. 182-183.
815. CARLILE, Henry
"Camouflage." [Poetry] (148:2) My 86, p. 98.
"Four Variations on the Invisible Bittern." [Crazy] (31) Fall 86, p. 14-16.
"In Oceans, in Rivers" (For Raymond Carver). [Poetry] (148:2) My 86, p. 96-97.
"November Memo." [Crazy] (31) Fall 86, p. 17.
"Singles Bar." [Crazy] (31) Fall 86, p. 19.
"To a Journalist in Sweden." [Crazy] (31) Fall 86, p. 18.
816. CARLISLE, C. R.
"Juana de Asbaje." [LetFem] (10:2) Fall 84 [c1985], p. 89.
817. CARLISLE, Thomas John
"Emily Dickinson and the Burglar." [ChrC] (103:17) 14 My 86, p. 484.
818. CARLSON, Barbara Siegel
"Before the Solstice." [HolCrit] (23:3) Je 86, p. 16.
819. CARLSON, Helen
"This Winter's Nightmare." [MidAR] (7:1) 86, p. 103.

820. CARLSON, R. S.
    "Deux ex Machina." [SilverFR] (11) Sum 86, p. 31.
    "Walking the Wall." [HolCrit] (23:1) F 86, p. 18.
821. CARLSON, Sharon
    "First Anniversary: Divorce." [Quarry] (35:4) Aut 86, p. 32-33.
    "Widower: Year Two." [Quarry] (35:4) Aut 86, p. 33.
822. CARLSON, Thomas C.
    "And You Are Here Now" (for Christine Nielson). [JINJPo] (9:1) 86, p. 8.
CARMEN, Aisha Eshe
    See ESHE-CARMEN, Aisha
823. CARMI, T.
    "By Which to Lydda?" (Selections: 19 poems, tr. by Grace Schulman). [PoetL] (81:2)
        Sum 86, p. 83-89.
    "Two-Faced Woman" (tr. by Marcia Falk). [PoetL] (81:2) Sum 86, p. 89.
824. CARNER, Josep
    "Between You and Me" (En mig de tu i de mi, tr. by David H. Rosenthal). [SenR]
        (16:1) 86, p. 23.
825. CARNEY, Jeanne
    "There'll Always Be." [Amelia] (3:3) Sum 86, p. 33.
826. CAROL, Luiza
    "That Rock." [Amelia] (3:3) Sum 86, p. 38.
827. CARPENTER, Bogdana
    "Transformation of Livy" (tr. of Zbigniew Herbert, w. John Carpenter). [NewYRB]
        (33:17) 6 N 86, p. 10.
828. CARPENTER, Carol
    "The Odyssey." [CapeR] (21:1) Spr 86, p. 46-47.
    "Sexual Division." [CapeR] (21:1) Spr 86, p. 45.
829. CARPENTER, J. D.
    "Our Northern Tour." [CanLit] (111) Wint 86, p. 40-46.
830. CARPENTER, John
    "Transformation of Livy" (tr. of Zbigniew Herbert, w. Bogdana Carpenter).
        [NewYRB] (33:17) 6 N 86, p. 10.
831. CARPER, Thomas
    "The Beauty of Poetry." [Poetry] (148:5) Ag 86, p. 249.
    "Heavenly Park." [Poetry] (148:5) Ag 86, p. 252.
    "Oh Keep the Poet Hence." [Poetry] (148:5) Ag 86, p. 250.
    "What People Make." [Poetry] (148:5) Ag 86, p. 251.
832. CARR, John
    "At the End of the Sixties." [HolCrit] (23:2) Ap 86, p. 18.
833. CARRADICE, Phil
    "Artful Arthur." [Bogg] (55) 86, p. 52.
    "Magic Maggie." [Bogg] (55) 86, p. 43.
    "What We Had to Sell." [Bogg] (55) 86, p. 58.
834. CARREGA, Gordon
    "The Older Woman." [YellowS] (20) Aut 86, p. 32.
835. CARRIE, LeAnn Jackson
    "Nightmare." [Electrum] (38) Spr 86, p. 24.
836. CARRIER, Warren
    "The Diver." [QRL] (Poetry series 6:26) 86, 48 p.
837. CARRILLO, Víctor
    "Es Odio Lo Que Siento." [Electrum] (38) Spr 86, p. 31.
    "It Is Hatred I Feel" (tr. by Margot Benardo). [Electrum] (38) Spr 86, p. 31.
838. CARRINO, Michael
    "What the Persian Cat and the Woman Know." [NewL] (52:2/3) Wint-Spr 86, p. 210.
839. CARRUTH, Hayden
    "A Backyard in California." [WestB] (18) 86, p. 41.
    "Continuo." [WestB] (18) 86, p. 40.
    "Cyclist." [WestB] (18) 86, p. 40.
    "Dancing as Vestigia and Other Considerations." [SouthernR] (22:2) Ap 86, p. 362.
    "The Ethics of Altruism in Altoona." [NewEngR] (9:2) Wint 86, p. 126.
    "I've Never Seen Such a Real Hard Time Before: Three-Part Invention." [NewEngR]
        (9:2) Wint 86, p. 127.
    "Meditation in the Presence of 'Ostrich Walk'." [NewEngR] (9:2) Wint 86, p. 125.
    "Survival as Tao, Beginning at 5:00 AM." [SouthernR] (22:2) Ap 86, p. 360-361.
    "To Know in Reverie the Only Phenomenology of the Absolute." [NewEngR] (9:2)
        Wint 86, p. 128.

77

CARSON

840. CARSON, Anne
    "A stranger is poor, voracious and turbulent." [NoDaQ] (54:4) Fall 86, p. 47.
    "A stranger is someone who." [NoDaQ] (54:4) Fall 86, p. 48.
    "What is the holiness of the citizen?" [NoDaQ] (54:4) Fall 86, p. 46.
841. CARSON, Mike
    "Double." [BelPoJ] (37:2) Wint 86-87, p. 14-15.
    "Match-Up." [BelPoJ] (37:2) Wint 86-87, p. 15-16.
842. CARSON, Ricks
    "If I Should Undertake to Say." [CharR] (12:2) Fall 86, p. 80.
    "Samaritan." [CharR] (12:2) Fall 86, p. 81.
843. CARSTENSEN, Claus
    "Bound up in blood" (from Masker Uden Navne, in Danish and English, tr. by Nina
        Juel Bigbie and Erik Porret). [Os] (23) 86, p. 38-39.
    "Copperkisses" (in Danish and English, tr. by Nina Juel Bigbie and Erik Porret). [Os]
        (23) 86, p. 20.
    "Echoes arose in the room" (from Totenbuch, in Danish and English, tr. by Nina Juel
        Bigbie and Erik Porret). [Os] (23) 86, p. 28.
    "The Formlessness of Death" (in Danish and English, tr. by Nina Juel Bigbie and Erik
        Porret). [Os] (23) 86, p. 38-39.
    "Polaroid" (in Danish and English, tr. by Nina Juel Bigbie and Erik Porret). [Os] (23)
        86, p. 36-37.
    "Reading Piece" (from Totenbuch, in Danish and English, tr. by Nina Juel Bigbie and
        Erik Porret). [Os] (23) 86, p. 36-37.
844. CARTELLI, Mary Anne
    "XV. From the bedroom with the door closed." [LittleM] (15:1) 86, p. 58.
    "The Lacuna." [LittleM] (15:1) 86, p. 61.
    "The Pink Palace." [LittleM] (15:1) 86, p. 62-63.
    "The Power of Things." [LittleM] (15:1) 86, p. 60.
    "The Restless Sleeper." [LittleM] (15:1) 86, p. 59.
    "Urban Pastoral." [LittleM] (15:1) 86, p. 63.
845. CARTER, Jared
    "Blueprints." [Hudson] (39:3) Aut 86, p. 461-462.
    "Isinglass" (for Glen Buzzard). [SenR] (16:2) 86, p. 46-47.
846. CARTER, Stephen
    "Prana." [Wind] (16:58) 86, p. 15.
847. CARTLEDGE-HAYES, Mary
    "Missionary" (For Anne Herbert). [ChrC] (103:23) 30 Jl-6 Ag 86, p. 668.
    "The Tower of Babel." [ChrC] (103:24) 13-20 Ag 86, p. 708.
848. CARTUNE, Suzan
    "Flea Market" (The Phantoms Come Close). [YetASM] (5) 86, p. 5.
849. CARVER, Raymond
    "Asia." [NowestR] (24:1) 86, p. 61.
    "The Autopsy Room." [OntR] (24) Spr-Sum 86, p. 45.
    "The Cobweb." [Caliban] (1) 86, p. 102.
    "Cutlery." [NewYorker] (62:5) 24 Mr 86, p. 38.
    "Egress." [NowestR] (24:1) 86, p. 57-58.
    "From the East, Light." [NowestR] (24:1) 86, p. 56.
    "His Bathrobe Pockets Stuffed with Notes." [Caliban] (1) 86, p. 96-98.
    "Hope." [ParisR] (28:100) Sum-Fall 86, p. 58-59.
    "Its Course." [OntR] (24) Spr-Sum 86, p. 46-47.
    "Limits." [NowestR] (24:1) 86, p. 59-60.
    "The Mail." [TriQ] (66) Spr-Sum 86, p. 145.
    "Migration." [OntR] (24) Spr-Sum 86, p. 48-49.
    "The Phone Booth." [NowestR] (24:1) 86, p. 52-53.
    "Powder-Monkey." [NowestR] (24:1) 86, p. 55.
    "The Projectile" (for Haruki Murakami). [OhioR] (37) 86, p. 60-61.
    "The River." [Poetry] (148:3) Je 86, p. 127.
    "Scale" (for Richard Marius). [Caliban] (1) 86, p. 99-100.
    "Shooting." [Caliban] (1) 86, p. 101.
    "Simple." [OhioR] (37) 86, p. 59.
    "Sinew." [Atlantic] (258:5) N 86, p. 112.
    "Sleeping." [ParisR] (28:100) Sum-Fall 86, p. 60.
    "Sweet Light." [TriQ] (66) Spr-Sum 86, p. 144.
    "A Tall Order." [Poetry] (148:3) Je 86, p. 128.
    "What I Can Do." [NowestR] (24:1) 86, p. 54.

850. CASADESUS, José
    "Volveras?" [Mairena] (8:22) 86, p. 39.
851. CASE, Edward
    "As Grammarians." [AmerS] (55:1) Wint 85-86, p. 43.
    "The Business of the Dancer" (for Balanchine). [AmerS] (55:2) Spr 86, p. 226.
852. CASE, Robert
    "Heartland Credo." [BallSUF] (27:4) Aut 86, p. 17.
853. CASEY, Crysta
    "Fire." [BellArk] (2:5) S-O 86, p. 14.
    "First Grade, Austin, 1958." [BellArk] (2:3) My-Je 86, p. 7.
    "Homecoming." [BellArk] (2:2) Mr-Ap 86, p. 2.
    "Prayer at 3 A.M." [BellArk] (2:2) Mr-Ap 86, p. 6.
    "Runaway." [BellArk] (2:3) My-Je 86, p. 4.
854. CASEY, Deb
    "Blue Pool." [Ploughs] (12:4) 86, p. 208.
    "What to Tell Betsy Besides *We Tried*." [RiverS] (20) 86, p. 40-41.
855. CASH, Les
    "A Bang-Up Christmas." [Amelia] (3:4) Fall 86, p. 34-36.
856. CASSELLS, Cyrus
    "After the Trees" (tr. of Salvador Espriu). [Translation] (16) Spr 86, p. 82.
    "Autumn" (tr. of Salvador Espriu). [Translation] (16) Spr 86, p. 84.
    "Beginning of the Temple Hymn" (Inici de càntic en el temple, tr. of Salvador Espriu).
        [SenR] (16:1) 86, p. 32.
    "From the Same Theater" (tr. of Salvador Espriu). [Translation] (16) Spr 86, p. 84.
    "Memory" (tr. of Salvador Espriu). [Translation] (16) Spr 86, p. 83.
    "Possible Introduction to an Epithalamium" (wedding of friends, in Sinera, tr. of
        Salvador Espriu). [Translation] (16) Spr 86, p. 81.
    "Sinera Cemetery" (Excerpts, tr. of Salvador Espriu). [Translation] (16) Spr 86, p.
        79-80.
    "Sinera Cemetery" (tr. of Salvador Espriu). [Translation] (16) Spr 86, p. 83.
    "These Are Not Brushstrokes" (in homage to Picasso's Guernica, after a viewing in
        Madrid). [Callaloo] (9:1, #26) Wint 86, p. 24-25.
    "To the Cypress Again and Again" (for Salvador Espriu, 1913-1985). [Callaloo] (9:1,
        #26) Wint 86, p. 18-23.
    "The Wait" (tr. of Salvador Espriu). [Translation] (16) Spr 86, p. 82.
857. CASSELMAN, Barry
    "The Gates of Atonement Opening." [Abraxas] (34) 86, p. 52-53.
858. CASSIAN, Nina
    "Postmeridian" (tr. by the author, Cristian Andrei and Naomi Lazard). [NewYorker]
        (62:38) 10 N 86, p. 45.
859. CASSIE, David Susumu
    "The Piping Crows of Chattahoochee." [Contact] (7:38/39/40) Wint-Spr 86, p. 39.
860. CASSIN, Maxine
    "Molar, Second from the Left, a Farewell." [NewOR] (13:3) Fall 86, p. 65.
861. CASSITY, Turner
    "The Autoscopic Experience." [Poetry] (148:4) Jl 86, p. 205.
    "Berlin-to-Baghdad" (Constantinople, 1986). [SewanR] (94:2) Spr 86, p. 205-206.
    "Hedy Lamarr and a Chocolate Bar." [SewanR] (94:2) Spr 86, p. 206.
    "Inducted." [Poetry] (148:4) Jl 86, p. 206-207.
862. CASTAÑO, Wilfredo
    "Orchid." [SecC] (14:1) 86, p. 4.
863. CASTELLANOS, Rosario
    "On the Death of Remedios Varo" (tr. by Maureen Ahern). [RedBass] (10) 86, p. 7.
864. CASTILLO, Jerónimo
    "Lobo de Amor." [Mairena] (8:22) 86, p. 96.
865. CASTILLO, Ofelia
    "They" (for Oscar Sola, tr. by H. E. Francis). [AmerV] (4) Fall 86, p. 59-60.
866. CASTILLO ZAPATA, Rafael
    "V. Me están doliendo de golpe." [LindLM] (5:2) Ap-Je 86, p. 10.
867. CASTLEMAN, D.
    "Dignity Blushes." [Bogg] (56) 86, p. 13.
868. CASTRO, Jesse
    "Figuring Out the Automatic." [Pax] (3:1/2) Wint 85-86, p. 15.
    "Hand me down from the stars, gently." [Pax] (3:1/2) Wint 85-86, p. 14.
869. CASTRO, Michael
    "After Vallejo." [RiverS] (20) 86, p. 24-25.

870. CASTRO, Robert Clayton
"The Country of Women" (after seeing Judy Chicago's "The Dinner Party"). [Waves]
(14:3) Wint 86, p. 46-47.
"The Phosphorus." [Waves] (14:3) Wint 86, p. 48-49.
"Rotten Elegy." [Waves] (14:3) Wint 86, p. 47.
CASTRO ALVES, Antonio de
See ALVES, Antonio de Castro
871. CASTY, Deborah A.
"Retribution." [WritersL] (1986:5), p. 12.
"Soul Food." [WritersL] (1986:4), p. 13.
872. CASULLO, Joanne
"The Accident." [PraS] (60:2) Sum 86, p. 110.
"The Harvest." [PraS] (60:2) Sum 86, p. 107.
"Madame Kind-heart." [PraS] (60:2) Sum 86, p. 108.
"The Needle, the Bowl" (for Loren). [PraS] (60:2) Sum 86, p. 109.
873. CASWELL, Donald
"Seeking the Visible World." [MidAR] (6:2) 86, p. 99-101.
874. CATALANO, Kristen
"Bedtime Story for a Past Lover." [HayF] (1) Spr 86, p. 59-60.
875. CATINA, Ray
"Job Action." [Sam] (46:2 release 182) 86, p. 30.
"Wise Guys." [Sam] (46:2 release 182) 86, p. 40.
876. CATLIN, Alan
"Jim Carroll and Friends Performing at J.B. Scott's: A Still Life, Albany, N.Y."
[Bogg] (56) 86, p. 46.
"Liar's Poker." [WoosterR] (5) Spr 86, p. 52.
"A Long Day's Journey." [Puerto] (22:1) Fall 86, p. 67-68.
"The Man with the Sunday Suit." [Puerto] (22:1) Fall 86, p. 65-66.
877. CATULLUS
"He is like a god" (LI, tr. by Sam Hamill). [CrabCR] (3:2) Spr 86, p. 15.
"Poems 50" (tr. by Robert Boucheron). [JamesWR] (4:1) Fall 86, p. 7.
"Porki and Socration, sinister thugs for Piso" (XLVII, tr. by Sam Hamill). [CrabCR]
(3:2) Spr 86, p. 15.
"Surely, you'll dine with me, my Fabulle" (XIII, tr. by Sam Hamill). [CrabCR] (3:2)
Spr 86, p. 15.
878. CAU, Jacques
"The Hand" (tr. by Roch C. Smith). [InterPR] (12:2) Fall 86, p. 31.
"La Main." [InterPR] (12:2) Fall 86, p. 30.
879. CAUCCI, Frank
"Red." [AntigR] (66/67) Sum-Aut 86, p. 66.
880. CAVAFY, C. P.
"Of the Ship" (tr. by David Mason). [Translation] (16) Spr 86, p. 142.
881. CAVANAGH, Clare
"Do Not Want to Die for Us" (tr. of Ryszard Krynicki, w. Stanislaw Baranczak).
[TriQ] (67) Fall 86, p. 129.
"From a Window" (tr. of Ryszard Krynicki, w. Stanislaw Baranczak). [TriQ] (67)
Fall 86, p. 129.
"I Can't Help You" (tr. of Ryszard Krynicki, w. Stanislaw Baranczak). [TriQ] (67)
Fall 86, p. 128.
"I'd Forgotten" (tr. of Ryszard Krynicki, w. Stanislaw Baranczak). [TriQ] (67) Fall
86, p. 128.
"Sleep Well" (tr. of Ryszard Krynicki, w. Stanislaw Baranczak). [TriQ] (67) Fall 86,
p. 129.
"Yes, She Says" (tr. of Ryszard Krynicki, w. Stanislaw Baranczak). [TriQ] (67) Fall
86, p. 128.
882. CAVITCH, Joanna Byrne
"Number 2 Holly Village." [MichQR] (25:4) Fall 86, p. 659.
883. CAWLEY, Kevin
"Cold." [LittleM] (15:1) 86, p. 53.
"Uncool." [LittleM] (15:1) 86, p. 53.
884. CAYLE
"A Man Against a Wall" (to Deborah Lynne Hunter, September 1982). [NegC] (6:4)
Fall 86, p. 96.
885. CECIL, Richard
"Ballad of Dead Actresses." [Poetry] (149:1) O 86, p. 24-26.
"The Siren." [Poetry] (149:1) O 86, p. 26.

886. CEDERING, Siv
"You and I and the World" (tr. of Werner Aspenstrom). [PoetryE] (20/21) Fall 86, p. 78.
887. CELAN, Paul
"Confidence" (tr. by Michael Hamburger). [Stand] (27:1) Wint 85-86, p. 54.
"Last Poems" (Selections, tr. by Katharine Washburn and Margret Guillemin). [AmerPoR] (15:3) My-Je 86, p. 3-5.
"Rubble Barge" (tr. by Michael Hamburger). [Stand] (27:1) Wint 85-86, p. 54.
"Sprachgitter" (Selections: 3 poems in German & English, tr. by Michael Hamburger). [SouthernHR] (20:1) Wint 86, p. 27-30.
CERDA, Hernan Lavin
See LAVIN CERDA, Hernan
888. CERNUDA, Luis
"Nevada" (tr. by Robert Lima). [Vis] (22) 86, p. 18.
889. CERRATO, Laura
"I Keep Punctuating My Madness" (tr. by Thorpe Running). [ColR] (NS 13:1) Fall 85, p. 49.
"Without Your Presence" (tr. by Thorpe Running). [ColR] (NS 13:1) Fall 85, p. 48.
890. CERVANTES, James
"Make the Turtle Whole." [HayF] (1) Spr 86, p. 82.
CERVERA, Herib Campos
See CAMPOS CERVERA, Herib
891. CESARANO, James
"The Distance between Us." [NegC] (6:1) Wint 86, p. 98.
892. CHABRE, Virgil
"It Was." [SanFPJ] (8:3) 85, p. 21.
893. CHACE, Joel
"Beethoven." [SmPd] (23:1, #66) Wint 86, p. 8.
"Time Rime — for A.R. Ammons." [Pembroke] (18) 86, p. 139.
894. CHAFFIN, Lillie D.
"Captain America." [Wind] (16:58) 86, p. 7.
"Fullness." [Wind] (16:58) 86, p. 6-7.
"The Place, My Son: There Must be a Place Somewhere That Nobody Else Can Go." [Wind] (16:58) 86, p. 6.
895. CHALLENDER, Craig
"It's 2 A.M." [TarRP] (26:1) Fall 86, p. 36-37.
"Lone Swimmer." [SoCaR] (18:2) Spr 86, p. 103.
896. CHALPIN, Lila
"Mother at 88." [BallSUF] (26:4) Aut 85, p. 35.
897. CHAMBERLAIN, Karen
"Groundhog Sees Its Shadow." [Nat] (242:4) 1 F 86, p. 123.
898. CHAMBERS, Carole
"The Apples of Eden." [YellowS] (19) Sum 86, p. 13.
"Dream Life of a Border Guard." [Event] (15:2) 86, p. 36-37.
"Heteromobila." [YellowS] (19) Sum 86, p. 12.
"The Worms Song." [YellowS] (19) Sum 86, p. 12.
899. CHAMBERS, George
"It's Just a Story." [Rampike] (5:2) 86, p. 72-73.
900. CHAMLEE, Kenneth
"Housefire." [ColEng] (48:2) F 86, p. 142.
901. CHANDLER, Janet Carncross
"Something Reassuring." [CapeR] (21:2) Fall 86, p. 50.
902. CHANDLER, Michael J.
"Starving on Light Years." [Bogg] (55) 86, p. 13.
903. CHANDLER, Tom
"Andrew Maksimuk." [CarolQ] (39:1) Fall 86, p. 87.
"Shiloh Cemetery." [DeKalbLAJ] (19:2) 86, p. 14-15.
"Sudden As Wonder." [DeKalbLAJ] (19:2) 86, p. 15.
"The Troubador." [DeKalbLAJ] (19:2) 86, p. 16.
904. CHANDONNET, Ann Fox
"Alexandra." [CrossCur] (6:2) 86, p. 127.
905. CHANDRA, G. S. Sharat
"Aliens." [NewL] (52:2/3) Wint-Spr 86, p. 62-66.
"Glass Bells." [MissR] (15:1/2, #43/44) Fall-Wint 86, p. 51.
"Sanskrit Love Poem Retold." [Interim] (5:2) Fall 86, p. 40-41.

906. CHANG, Diana
    "Ah Yes Wisdom." [Contact] (7:38/39/40) Wint-Spr 86, p. 51.
907. CHAO, Meng-fu
    "Fisherman's Lyric" (tr. by Jonathan Chaves). [Translation] (17) Fall 86, p. 327.
    "In the Ancient Manner" (tr. by Jonathan Chaves). [Translation] (17) Fall 86, p. 327.
    "Living in Retirement at Te-Ch'ing" (tr. by Jonathan Chaves). [Translation] (17) Fall
        86, p. 328.
908. CHAO, Rosa Lentini
    "Ciertas Meigas." [Inti] (21) Primavera 85, p. 117-118.
    "Homenaje." [Inti] (21) Primavera 85, p. 118.
    "Reposo." [Inti] (21) Primavera 85, p. 118-119.
    "El Tapiz." [Inti] (21) Primavera 85, p. 117.
CHAO, Tang
    See TANG, Chao
909. CHAPMAN, D.
    "No Time." [WritersL] (1986:2), p. 13.
910. CHAPMAN, Jane Autenrieth
    "Little Lightning Death." [SoDakR] (24:2) Sum 86, p. 117.
    "Twelve Glass Doors." [SoDakR] (24:2) Sum 86, p. 116.
911. CHAPMAN, R. S.
    "D = R x T." [NewL] (52:2/3) Wint-Spr 86, p. 97.
912. CHAPPELL, Fred
    "The Betrayal." [ColEng] (48:5) S 86, p. 458.
    "Earthsleep." [GeoR] (40:3) Fall 86, p. 640-641.
    "The Embitterment of Charity." [ColEng] (48:5) S 86, p. 458.
    "A Glorious Twilight." [ColEng] (48:5) S 86, p. 457.
    "Humility." [BostonR] (11:1) F 86, p. 11.
    "Meanwhile" (A Prologue to Tolstoy's *The Death of Ivan Ilych*). [CreamCR] (11:1)
        86?, p. 37.
    "Messages." [Boulevard] (1:1/2) Wint 86, p. 15.
    "My Father's Hurricane" (Excerpt). [BostonR] (11:1) F 86, p. 11.
    "My Grandmother Washes Her Feet" (Excerpt). [BostonR] (11:1) F 86, p. 11.
    "Photography" (Ansel Adams: "White Branches, Moon Lake, California, 1947).
        [TarRP] (25:2) Spr 86, p. 14.
    "Pierrot Escapes." [CreamCR] (11:1) 86?, p. 38-39.
    "A Prologue to the *Georgics*." [GeoR] (40:2) Sum 86, p. 411-412.
    "The Recall." [TarRP] (25:2) Spr 86, p. 15-16.
    "Recovery of Sexual Desire after a Bad Cold." [BostonR] (11:1) F 86, p. 11.
    "Slow Harbor." [Boulevard] (1:1/2) Wint 86, p. 14.
    "Spitballer." [BostonR] (11:1) F 86, p. 11.
    "The Story." [BostonR] (11:1) F 86, p. 11.
913. CHAPPUIS, Pierre
    "Alentour, Intermittents." [Os] (22) 86, p. 28-31.
914. CHAR, René
    "Aversions" (tr. by Charles Guenther). [Paint] (13:25/26) Spr-Aut 86, p. 27.
    "Good Neighbors" (tr. by Charles Guenther). [Paint] (13:25/26) Spr-Aut 86, p. 27.
    "October's Judgment" (tr. by Charles Guenther). [Paint] (13:25/26) Spr-Aut 86, p.
        24.
    "Outer Possessions" (tr. by Charles Guenther). [Paint] (13:25/26) Spr-Aut 86, p. 25.
    "Wrestlers" (tr. by Charles Guenther). [Paint] (13:25/26) Spr-Aut 86, p. 26.
915. CHARD, John V.
    "What the Stones Know." [JlNJPo] (9:1) 86, p. 9.
CHARITY, Ralph la
    See La CHARITY, Ralph
916. CHARLES, Susan
    "Fear." [SanFPJ] (8:1) 85, p. 30.
    "Moving Out." [SanFPJ] (8:1) 85, p. 48.
    "Wasted Lands." [SanFPJ] (8:1) 85, p. 31-32.
917. CHARLTON, Lindsey D.
    "It Doesn't Get Any Better." [AntigR] (64) Wint 86, p. 90.
918. CHARTIER, David
    "The Flooding of the Swift River Valley." [RiverS] (20) 86, p. 51-53.
    "Your Hometown." [RiverS] (20) 86, p. 53.
919. CHASE, Karen
    "I Tell You Stories." [AntigR] (66/67) Sum-Aut 86, p. 108.

920. CHASEK, Ruth M.
    "The Frog." [NegC] (6:1) Wint 86, p. 81-82.
921. CHATFIELD, Hale
    "The Famous Dog Explosion." [HiramPoR] (40) Spr-Sum 86, p. 44-45.
    "Reprise." [HiramPoR] (40) Spr-Sum 86, p. 41.
    "Why There Is No True Artificial Intelligence" (after an argument by John
        Haugeland). [HiramPoR] (40) Spr-Sum 86, p. 42-43.
922. CHATTOPADJYA, Shakti
    "I May Leave, But Why Shall I Leave?" (tr. by Rabiul Hasan). [Amelia] (3:3) Sum
        86, p. 100.
923. CHAUDHURI, Mrinal Basu
    "Defiled Nose-Ring" (tr. by Abhik Gupta). [Pax] (3:1/2) Wint 85-86, p. 172-173.
    "Rose is a kind of flower." [Pax] (3:1/2) Wint 85-86, p. 172.
924. CHAVES, Jonathan
    "After Reading the Poems of Master Han Shan" (Two poems, tr. of Wang Chiu-ssu).
        [Translation] (17) Fall 86, p. 329.
    "Cheng-Tao Temple" (tr. of Tai Piao-yüan). [Translation] (17) Fall 86, p. 326.
    "Fisherman's Lyric" (tr. of Chao Meng-fu). [Translation] (17) Fall 86, p. 327.
    "Fog at Liang-Hsiang" (tr. of Yuan Mei). [Translation] (17) Fall 86, p. 331.
    "In the Ancient Manner" (tr. of Chao Meng-fu). [Translation] (17) Fall 86, p. 327.
    "Living in Retirement at Te-Ch'ing" (tr. of Chao Meng-fu). [Translation] (17) Fall 86,
        p. 328.
    "Living in the Woods" (In the Manner of Yao Ho, tr. of Wang Chiu-ssu).
        [Translation] (17) Fall 86, p. 330.
    "The Next Day the Fog Was Even Worse" (tr. of Yuan Mei). [Translation] (17) Fall
        86, p. 331.
    "The Robber of Kuan-Shan" (tr. of Wang Chiu-ssu). [Translation] (17) Fall 86, p.
        330.
    "Things Seen" (tr. of Yuan Mei). [Translation] (17) Fall 86, p. 332.
    "Things Seen on Spring Days" (tr. of Yuan Mei). [Translation] (17) Fall 86, p. 332.
925. CHAVSKY, Salomon
    "Night time still" (tr. by Will Kirkland). [NewOR] (13:4) Wint 86, p. 30.
926. CHAZAL, Malcolm de
    "Sens-Plastique" (Selections, tr. by Irving Weiss). [Rampike] (5:1) 86, p. 27.
927. CHECK, David Hovan
    "Acid Rain" (for the Adirondacks, Eastern Canada, and New England). [SanFPJ]
        (8:1) 85, p. 91.
    "Atomic Priesthood." [SanFPJ] (8:1) 85, p. 63.
    "Did You Know?" [SanFPJ] (9:1) 86, p. 19.
    "The Drowning Island." [SanFPJ] (9:1) 86, p. 74-75.
    "The Folkie Blues." [SanFPJ] (8:1) 85, p. 92.
    "High Society." [SanFPJ] (8:2) 85, p. 45.
    "Lost Revelations." [SanFPJ] (9:1) 86, p. 86-87.
    "Sinister Satellites." [SanFPJ] (8:1) 85, p. 62.
    "Space: The Final Fear." [SanFPJ] (9:1) 86, p. 90-92.
    "Steerage." [SanFPJ] (8:2) 85, p. 71.
928. CHENG, Anne A.
    "Fisher Day." [HeliconN] (14/15) Sum 86, p. 13.
    "One Gesture." [HeliconN] (14/15) Sum 86, p. 12.
    "Seven Dreams of a Housewife." [HeliconN] (14/15) Sum 86, p. 11-12.
CHENG, Gu
    See GU, Cheng
929. CHERNOW, Ann
    "Larva." [DeKalbLAJ] (19:3/4) 86, p. 69.
930. CHERRY, Kelly
    "The Daughter Who Visits the Green River Singing." [MidwQ] (27:2) Wint 86, p.
        196.
    "Epithalamium" (For my parents' Golden Anniversary, 1983). [PraS] (60:1) Spr 86,
        p. 86.
    "Facing the Truth about Yourself." [CrossCur] (6:2) 86, p. 92.
    "In the Place Where the Corridors Watch Your Every Move." [DenQ] (20:4/21:1)
        Spr-Sum 86, p. 43-44.
    "Letter to a Censor." [GeoR] (40:3) Fall 86, p. 642-643.
    "The Photojournalist." [PraS] (60:1) Spr 86, p. 85-86.
    "The Redemptorists." [LitR] (29:3) Spr 86, p. 317.
    "The Relation That Art Bears to Silence." [MidwQ] (27:2) Wint 86, p. 197.

"Someone Is Stealing the People." [LitR] (29:2) Wint 86, p. 195.
"The Voyage." [NewL] (52:2/3) Wint-Spr 86, p. 68.
"A Warning." [LitR] (29:3) Spr 86, p. 317.
"Where the Songs Are As Smooth-Running As Water." [Raccoon] (20) Ap 86, back
    cover.
931. CHESS, Richard
    "What to Say When You're Depressed." [BelPoJ] (36:4) Sum 86, p. 18.
932. CHESTER, Laura
    "In Regard to Him." [Notus] (1:1) Fall 86, p. 70-71.
933. CHEVAKO, Mari Reitsma
    "Dark Birds." [MissouriR] (9:2) 86, p. 205.
    "Postals." [ClockR] (3:2) 86, p. 17-20.
CHI, Lu
    See LU, Chi
934. CHIBEAU, Edmond
    "Oxherding." [Confr] (32) Spr-Sum 86, p. 59.
935. CHICHETTO, James Wm.
    "The Bakers' Wind" (Excerpt). [ConnPR] (4:1) 85, p. 34-37.
    "Fantasy on John Updike." [ConnPR] (5:1) 86, p. 8-9.
    "Holocaust Poems" (Selections: "The Dodge," "The Funeral"). [ConnPR] (5:1) 86, p.
        24-25.
936. CHICKADEL, Carmine F.
    "Tangles." [ParisR] (28:101) Wint 86, p. 273.
937. CHIDESTER, Leon
    "And You'll Break Your Mother's Back." [WillowS] (17) Wint 86, p. 54.
    "Most Things Break." [WillowS] (17) Wint 86, p. 53.
    "Son." [WillowS] (17) Wint 86, p. 55.
938. CHIESA, Carmen
    "Arpa sin Voces." [Mairena] (8:22) 86, p. 43.
939. CHIESURA, Giorgio
    "The Escape" (tr. by Rina Ferrarelli). [WebR] (11:1) Spr 86, p. 30.
    "The Illness" (tr. by Rina Ferrarelli). [WebR] (11:1) Spr 86, p. 31.
    "The Labyrinth" (tr. by Luigi M. Bianchi and Roger Greenwald). [Writ] (18) 86, c87,
        p. 127-134.
940. CHILD, Abigail
    "Fallout" (for Steve Benson). [Sink] (1) 86, p. 36-38.
941. CHILDERS, Joanne
    "The Long Distance." [CumbPR] (5:2) Spr 86, p. 73-74.
    "Two Deaf Girls on the Trailway Bus." [FloridaR] (14:2) Fall-Wint 86, p. 72-73.
942. CHILDISH, Billy
    "15 Quid." [Bogg] (56) 86, p. 26.
CHIMAKO, Tada
    See TADA, Chimako
943. CHIN, Marilyn
    "Beauty, My Sisters, Is Not Regalia." [YellowS] (18) Spr 86, p. 36.
    "A Dream in the Life of Playboy John." [YellowS] (18) Spr 86, p. 35.
    "I Am Not Rich, But for You." [YellowS] (18) Spr 86, p. 36.
    "Love Poem from Nagasaki." [YellowS] (18) Spr 86, p. 34.
    "So Lost in Him." [YellowS] (18) Spr 86, p. 34.
944. CHIN-AN, Li
    "The Poem" (tr. by Lora Dewey Finley and the author). [Nimrod] (29:2) Spr-Sum 86,
        p. 95.
CHING, Ines Asinc Ramos de
    See RAMOS de CHING, Ines Asinc
CHIU-SSU, Wang
    See WANG, Chiu-ssu
945. CHMIELARZ, Sharon
    "Leaning Away from the Sun." [SingHM] (13) 86, p. 55.
946. CHOCK, Eric
    "3 A.M. Waikiki." [Contact] (7:38/39/40) Wint-Spr 86, p. 47.
    "Strawberries." [Zyzzyva] (2:4) Wint 86-87, p. 111-112.
947. CHOO, Mary E.
    "Cat Town." [Amelia] (3:4) Fall 86, p. 100.
948. CHOPPA, Danielle
    "Green River." [CrabCR] (4:1) Fall-Wint 86, p. 16.
    "Skipping Stones." [BellArk] (2:1) Ja-F 86, p. 3.

"The Trail Down to Prescott." [BellArk] (2:2) Mr-Ap 86, p. 4.
949. CHORLTON, David
"The Connoisseur." [WebR] (11:2) Fall 86, p. 50.
"Hugo Wolf Wanders Through Nocturnal Vienna Asking the Way to Himself."
[WebR] (11:2) Fall 86, p. 51.
"Kino's Teaching." [DeKalbLAJ] (19:3/4) 86, p. 69-70.
950. CHOU, Ping
"Climbing Nanyue Mountain at Night and Waiting for Sunrise at the Summit" (tr. by
Tony Barnstone and the author). [Nimrod] (29:2) Spr-Sum 86, p. 34.
"A Dream." [Nimrod] (29:2) Spr-Sum 86, p. 29.
"Dream of an Island" (tr. of Shu Ting). [Nimrod] (29:2) Spr-Sum 86, p. 97.
"Drunk and Playing Go under the White Lady, the Moon" (tr. by Tony Barnstone and
the author). [Nimrod] (29:2) Spr-Sum 86, p. 31.
"A Letter" (tr. of Zhou, Jia-ti). [Nimrod] (29:2) Spr-Sum 86, p. 68-69.
"Man, Do You Have a Notebook?" [Nimrod] (29:2) Spr-Sum 86, p. 32.
"Passing by a Village on Foot in Summer, I Was Amused by a Group of Children
Playing . . ." [Nimrod] (29:2) Spr-Sum 86, p. 33.
"You Stand There." [Nimrod] (29:2) Spr-Sum 86, p. 32.
951. CHOUDHURY, Kabir (Chowdhury, Kabir)
"Fish" (tr. of Abdul Mannan Syed). [Pax] (3:1/2) Wint 85-86, p. 205.
"Her Eyes" (tr. of Abid Azad). [Pax] (3:1/2) Wint 85-86, p. 145.
"Moonlight Like a Ghost Stands at the Door" (tr. of Abdul Mannan Syed). [SenR]
(16:1) 86, p. 78.
952. CHOYCE, Lesley
"Chasing Flies with a Vacuum Cleaner." [Event] (15:2) 86, p. 29.
"A Deaf Hitchhiker at Sunset." [PottPort] (8) 86-87, p. 19.
"Encounter with an Immortal." [PottPort] (8) 86-87, p. 19.
"Smoke and Mirrors" (for Michael Clugston). [AntigR] (66/67) Sum-Aut 86, p.
13-14.
953. CHRISTAKOS, Margaret
"It becomes my room after someone else has slept here." [PraF] (7:3) Aut 86, p. 52.
"Of all the senses vision most informs us of separateness." [PraF] (7:3) Aut 86, p. 49.
"Today it is these interior spaces which have no consistency." [PraF] (7:3) Aut 86, p.
50.
"When I wrote these words it was because I could not speak." [PraF] (7:3) Aut 86, p.
51.
954. CHRISTENSEN, Erleen
"Winstons." [MemphisSR] (6:1/2) Spr 86, p. 53.
955. CHRISTENSEN, Paul
"Choosing." [Nimrod] (30:1) Fall-Wint 86, p. 111.
CHRISTHILF, Mark
See CRISTHILF, Mark
956. CHRISTIAN, Eddena
"Duet for One." [PoeticJ] (14) 86, p. 38.
"The Elder Heart." [PoeticJ] (15) Sum 86, p. 29.
"Hear Me." [PoeticJ] (15) Sum 86, p. 29.
"Tale of an Extra Tail." [PoeticJ] (14) 86, p. 38.
957. CHRISTIAN, Sandra Hart
"Planting." [MemphisSR] (6:1/2) Spr 86, p. 25.
958. CHRISTINA, Martha
"A Second Dose of Madness." [PassN] (7:2) Spr-Sum 86, p. 9.
959. CHRISTMAN, Rick
"Asylum." [WormR] (26:1, issue 101) 86, p. 2-3.
"Six Lucky Men." [WormR] (26:1, issue 101) 86, p. 1-2.
960. CHRISTOPHER, Nicholas
"Construction Site, Windy Night." [RiverS] (19) 86, p. 48.
"Elegy for E—." [RiverS] (19) 86, p. 47.
"Green Animals." [NewYorker] (62:11) 5 My 86, p. 40.
"The Hottest Night of the Year." [Shen] (36:4) 86, p. 51-52.
"Passing through the Torrid Zone." [OP] (42/43) Wint 86-87, p. 103-106.
"Postcard from Albania." [OP] (42/43) Wint 86-87, p. 106-107.
"A Short History of the Island of Butterflies." [OP] (42/43) Wint 86-87, p. 101-103.
961. CHRISTOPHERSEN, Bill
"April Limes." [KanQ] (18:4) Fall 86, p. 86.
"Autumn." [KanQ] (18:4) Fall 86, p. 87.
"The Drifter." [KanQ] (18:4) Fall 86, p. 86.

"Wintering." [KanQ] (18:4) Fall 86, p. 87.
CHUAN, Xi
    See XI, Chuan
962. CHUBBS, Boyd
    "The Juggler Is the Nimble Wind." [PottPort] (8) 86-87, p. 27.
CHUILLEANAIN, Eilean ni
    See Ni CHUILLEANAIN, Eilean
963. CHURA, David
    "On My Father's Birthday." [YetASM] (5) 86, p. 6.
964. CHUTE, Robert M.
    "Arthur Bernard Deacon (1905-1927)." [Northeast] (series 4:3) Spr 86, p. 36.
    "Ice Fisherman." [SmPd] (23:3, #68) Fall 86, p. 13.
    "Lot's Wife." [SmPd] (23:3, #68) Fall 86, p. 12.
    "Magician of the Charnel House" (George Cuvier discovers extinction). [BallSUF]
        (26:4) Aut 85, p. 64.
    "The Pantry." [BallSUF] (27:4) Aut 86, p. 41.
    "Proper Snow." [HiramPoR] (41) Fall-Wint 86-87, p. 7.
    "Pussy Willows." [CapeR] (21:2) Fall 86, p. 34.
965. CHYET, Stanley F.
    "Next Year" (tr. of Dahlia Ravikovitch). [PoetL] (81:2) Sum 86, p. 98-99.
966. CIARDI, John
    "Always While Nothing Happens the Same Again." [NewL] (52:2/3) Wint-Spr 86, p.
        41-42.
    "The Logician's Nocturne." [NewL] (52:2/3) Wint-Spr 86, p. 42.
    "A Trenta-Sei of the Pleasure We Take in the Early Death of Keats." [Poetry] (148:5)
        Ag 86, p. 281-282.
967. CIESZYNSKI, Wladyslaw
    "The Potatoes Were Large." [CreamCR] (11:1) 86?, p. 56.
968. CIORDIA, Javier
    "Ritual." [Mairena] (8:22) 86, p. 89.
969. CIRINO, Leonard
    "The Desert Rock" (after Atsuhiro Sawai). [Amelia] (3:1) Ja 86, p. 81.
    "Examination." [Amelia] (3:1) Ja 86, p. 81-82.
    "Matrice." [SmPd] (23:3, #68) Fall 86, p. 32.
    "Nearly Everyone Speaks for the Maryknolls." [Amelia] (3:2) Spr 86, p. 77.
970. CITINO, David
    "The Cremations." [NewL] (53:1) Fall 86, p. 74.
    "The Devil's Bath, Melancholy." [SoDakR] (24:3) Aut 86, p. 134-135.
    "Feeding the Vipers at the Columbus Zoo." [LitR] (30:1) Fall 86, p. 29.
    "The History of Human Sacrifice." [Interim] (5:2) Fall 86, p. 24.
    "Learning the Sounds Trees Make in Wind." [PennR] (2:1) Fall-Wint 86, p. 62.
    "The Man with the Loud Mind." [LitR] (30:1) Fall 86, p. 30-31.
    "May 20: San Bernardino." [SouthernHR] (20:2) Spr 86. p. 114.
    "Meditation, during Another Hostage Crisis, on Randomness at the Subatomic Level."
        [CharR] (12:1) Spr 86, p. 91.
    "On Looking into Homer for the First Time Since Becoming a Father." [NoDaQ]
        (54:2) Spr 86, p. 84.
    "On the Nature of the Beast." [KanQ] (18:1/2) Wint-Spr 86, p. 40.
    "The Politics of Falling." [SoDakR] (24:3) Aut 86, p. 136-138.
    "Possum." [PennR] (1:1) 85, p. 39.
    "The Sea of Kansas, Ohio Tundra, Time Still Running Out." [CimR] (74) Ja 86, p.
        46-47.
    "Sister Mary Appassionata Lectures the Health Class: To Keep the Blood from
        Running Cold." [CrabCR] (3:2) Spr 86, p. 12.
    "Sister Mary Appassionata Lectures the History Class: *Doctrines of Memory*." [DenQ]
        (20:4/21:1) Spr-Sum 86, p. 22-23.
    "Sister Mary Appassionata Lectures the Science-for-Non-Majors Class." [DenQ]
        (20:4/21:1) Spr-Sum 86, p. 20-21.
    "Sister Mary Appassionata to the Home Ec Class." [SoCaR] (19:1) Fall 86, p. 48-49.
    "Staking the Garden." [CentR] (30:2) Spr 86, p. 136.
    "Tales of Trickster: The Flood." [Confr] (33/34) Fall-Wint 86-87, p. 222.
    "Trickster Invents Time." [MemphisSR] (6:1/2) Spr 86, p. 7.
    "Trickster, Three Pools, the Law." [MemphisSR] (6:1/2) Spr 86, p. 6.
    "Vagrant Found Dead Near River." [WestB] (18) 86, p. 76-77.
    "Your Dream House." [CharR] (12:1) Spr 86, p. 90.

971. CIUPUREANU, Ionel
"Along the Tracks" (tr. by Isabella Stefanescu). [Descant] (17:2, #53) Sum 86, p. 115.
"L'Ecume des Jours" (tr. by Isabella Stefanescu). [Descant] (17:2, #53) Sum 86, p. 116.

972. CLAMPITT, Amy
"Alice." [NewRep] (194:17) 28 Ap 86, p. 40.
"An Anatomy of Migraine." [NewYorker] (62:25) 11 Ag 86, p. 24-25.
"At the Grave of George Eliot." [NewYorker] (62:42) 8 D 86, p. 46.
"Dorothy and William at Rydal Mount." [ParisR] (28:100) Sum-Fall 86, p. 61-63.
"Margaret Fuller, 1847." [NewYorker] (62:29) 8 S 86, p. 38.
"Medusa at Broadstairs." [GrandS] (5:4) Sum 86, p. 47-48.
"The Odessa Steps." [YaleR] (75:4) Sum 86, p. 532.
"Perseus to Atlas." [SouthwR] (71:4) Aut 86, p. 463-464.

973. CLAPS, Robert
"Card Game at the Italian Club." [TarRP] (26:1) Fall 86, p. 32.

974. CLARK, Alison
"Transformations." [Verse] (5) 86, p. 18.

975. CLARK, Cecily
"Upton Grant." [Blueline] (8:1) Sum-Fall 86, p. 24.

976. CLARK, G. O.
"The Official View: Central America.." [Sam] (45:4 release 180) 86, p. 47.
"Somebody's Daughter." [Sam] (46:5 [i.e. 46:1] release 181) 86, p. 35.

977. CLARK, J. Wesley
"An A.E.F. Poet in the Argonne" (September 1918). [Wind] (16:58) 86, p. 8.
"Annapolis." [Bogg] (55) 86, p. 7.
"Initiation." [Bogg] (56) 86, p. 26.

978. CLARK, Kevin
"Widow under a New Moon." [GeoR] (40:3) Fall 86, p. 644-645.

979. CLARK, Marie
"Metaphor." [Rampike] (5:1) 86, p. 69.

980. CLARK, Miriam Marty
"Kirigami" (the Japanese art of paper cutting). [SouthernHR] (20:1) Wint 86, p. 14.

981. CLARK, Naomi
"The Kingdom" (4 Selections). [Nimrod] (30:1) Fall-Wint 86, p. 56-59.

982. CLARK, Patricia
"Commencement Bay." [MissouriR] (9:2) 86, p. 154.
"Elegy near the Bitterroot Range." [NewEngR] (8:4) Sum 86, p. 467.
"The Lodge Meadow." [MissouriR] (9:2) 86, p. 153.

983. CLARK, Steven C.
"I Don't Write Love Poems." [SanFPJ] (8:2) 85, p. 90-91.

984. CLARKE, Cheryl
"Committed Sex." [Cond] (13) 86, p. 110.
"Indira." [AmerV] (3) Sum 86, p. 20-22.

985. CLARKE, George Elliott
"The Boy Dreams His Destiny." [PottPort] (8) 86-87, p. 11.
"The Lover's Argument with Shelley." [PottPort] (8) 86-87, p. 11.

986. CLARKE, Gerald
"Grackles and Regrets." [NegC] (6:1) Wint 86, p. 92-93.

987. CLARKE, John
"Aeonic Residue." [Acts] (5) 86, p. 83.
"Climbing the Statue of Liberty Prior to Her Repair." [Temblor] (3) 86, p. 49.
"Daughter of the Mind." [Temblor] (3) 86, p. 49.
"Dead Pan." [Temblor] (3) 86, p. 48.
"December News." [TarRP] (25:1) Fall 85, p. 37.
"Dim All the Lights." [Temblor] (3) 86, p. 50.
"Enough, or Way Too Much." [Acts] (5) 86, p. 82.
"Fuck the New syntax." [Acts] (5) 86, p. 80.
"God, the Urgent Requisite." [Temblor] (3) 86, p. 50.
"I Thought Literature Was an Interior Store?" [Acts] (5) 86, p. 79.
"If I Were a Painter like Delacroix . . ." [Acts] (5) 86, p. 81.
"Neolithic Man Without a Fravarti." [Temblor] (3) 86, p. 48.
"Our Asters." [TarRP] (25:1) Fall 85, p. 37.

988. CLARY, Killarney
"After work, after meals for Raul and her mother." [BostonR] (11:3) Je 86, p. 11.
"Don't tell me you give up here." [BostonR] (11:3) Je 86, p. 11.

"Have we proved our wealth or kindness?" [IndR] (9:2) Spr 86, p. 86.
"I drop the day like a damp towel." [BostonR] (11:3) Je 86, p. 11.
"I lean on Sunday morning." [BostonR] (11:3) Je 86, p. 11.
"I was thinking of a different hand." [BostonR] (11:3) Je 86, p. 11.
"I'm sorry I brought it up." [BostonR] (11:3) Je 86, p. 11.
"Life is boundless." [BostonR] (11:3) Je 86, p. 11.
"Sounds are a puzzle for her to figure." [BostonR] (11:3) Je 86, p. 11.
"There is no way to know what I miss." [IndR] (9:2) Spr 86, p. 87.
"This isn't my life." [BostonR] (11:3) Je 86, p. 11.
"We are always asleep." [BostonR] (11:3) Je 86, p. 11.
"What can anything stand for." [BostonR] (11:3) Je 86, p. 11.
CLEARY, Lee Braymen
    See BRAYMEN-CLEARY, Lee
989. CLEARY, Suzanne
    "Amaryllis" (for Brian). [PraS] (60:3) Fall 86, p. 52.
    "Pencil and Charcoal Nectarine." [PraS] (60:3) Fall 86, p. 54.
    "What Could Be." [PraS] (60:3) Fall 86, p. 53-54.
990. CLEMENTE, Concepción
    "Marina III." [LetFem] (12:1/2) Primavera-Otoño 86, p. 160.
    "Marina IV." [LetFem] (12:1/2) Primavera-Otoño 86, p. 160-161.
991. CLEMENTE, Vince
    "Basho Awake at Night." [BlackWR] (13:1) Fall 86, p. 71.
992. CLEMENTS, Susan L.
    "Penance." [NegC] (6:1) Wint 86, p. 79-80.
993. CLEMONS, Brian Douglas
    "The Cure." [JamesWR] (3:3) Spr 86, p. 13.
    "Living" (after Jim Carroll). [JamesWR] (3:3) Spr 86, p. 14.
    "Thrashback." [JamesWR] (4:1) Fall 86, p. 3.
994. CLEVELAND, Odessa
    "Lifeless Heart." [BlackALF] (20:3) Fall 86, p. 314.
995. CLEVELAND, Pamela
    "Ice Crystals." [ManhatPR] (8) Wint 86-87, p. 48.
996. CLEVER, Bertolt
    "Widows Travel." [MidAR] (7:1) 86, p. 20.
997. CLEWELL, David
    "Back to Life." [Poetry] (147:5) F 86, p. 272-277.
998. CLIFFORD, James
    "The Unbridled Line (André Masson)" (tr. of Michel Leiris). [Sulfur] (5:3, issue 15)
        86, p. 25-26.
999. CLIFTON, Harry
    "Euclid Avenue" (after Hart Crane). [Verse] (6) 86, p. 17.
    "Vladimir and Estragon." [Verse] (6) 86, p. 16-17.
1000. CLIFTON, Merritt
    "The 16-Year-Old Suicide Bomber." [Sam] (45:4 release 180) 86, p. 22.
    "Center." [Sam] (46:5 [i.e. 46:1] release 181) 86, p. 25.
1001. CLIFTON, Nicole
    "For a Woman in Texas." [Sam] (44:3 release 175) 86, back cover.
1002. CLIMENHAGA, Joel
    "Do Not Tell Me the Child Is Dead in Me." [KanQ] (18:4) Fall 86, p. 55.
    "Everybody Has Reason." [KanQ] (18:4) Fall 86, p. 54.
    "If Charles Olson Were Alive Now, He'd Know." [KanQ] (18:4) Fall 86, p. 54.
1003. CLINE, Michael
    "A Primary Color." [CrescentR] (4:2) Fall 86, p. 93.
1004. CLINTON, DeWitt
    "X." [RiverS] (19) 86, p. 53.
1005. CLODFELTER, Michael D.
    "Monsoon." [Sam] (46:2 release 182) 86, p. 66.
    "Piss Tubes." [Sam] (46:2 release 182) 86, p. 33.
1006. CLOKE, Richard (*See also* R. C.)
    "Bombs fell somewhere." [SanFPJ] (9:1) 86, p. 40.
    "Nelson Mandela." [SanFPJ] (8:1) 85, p. 14-16.
    "Nuclear Winter." [SanFPJ] (9:1) 86, p. 62-63.
1007. CLOSSON, Paula
    "Los Padres Perdidos." [WestB] (18) 86, p. 78.
    "Textile Mill on the Charles." [WestB] (18) 86, p. 80.
    "Whitefish Railyard Invention." [WestB] (18) 86, p. 78-79.

88

1008. CLOUD, Darrah
"Waitress, West Texas." [Amelia] (3:1) Ja 86, p. 86.
1009. COBEAN, Charles S.
"Borrowed Things." [Jacaranda] (2:1) Fall 86, p. 7.
1010. COBIAN, Ricardo
"Un día Me Quede Sólo" (Balada). [RevICP] (89) Jul-Sep 85, p. 63.
1011. COBO BORDA, Juan Gustavo
"Henry James" (tr. by Gary Emmons). [Pequod] (22) 86, p. 122.
"Maestro Lezama" (tr. by Maureen Ahern). [ColR] (NS 13:1) Fall 85, p. 39.
"Wasting My Life?" (For Peter Shultze-Kraft, tr. by Maureen Ahern). [ColR] (NS 13:1) Fall 85, p. 38.
1012. COCHRAN, Brian
"The House on the Tip of My Tongue." [SouthernPR] (26:2) Fall 86, p. 73.
"The Man in the Cell." [WestHR] (40:1) Spr 86, p. 39-40.
1013. CODRESCU, Andrei
"The Other End." [Sulfur] (6:1, issue 16) 86, p. 10-25.
1014. CODY, Cornelia F.
"After a Dark Winter." [Blueline] (7:2) Wint-Spr 86, p. 46.
1015. COFER, Judith Ortiz
"Una Mujer Loca." [Americas] (14:2) Sum 86, p. 41.
"El Olvido" (según las madres). [Americas] (14:2) Sum 86, p. 39.
"Origen." [Americas] (14:2) Sum 86, p. 40.
"So Much for Mañana." [Americas] (14:2) Sum 86, p. 42.
"Spring" (for Sue Ellen Thompson). [SouthernPR] (26:1) Spr 86, p. 13.
"What We Feared." [SouthernPR] (26:2) Fall 86, p. 29.
1016. COFFIN, Lyn (Lynn)
"Analysis." [InterPR] (12:2) Fall 86, p. 80.
"A Genealogical Allegory." [InterPR] (12:2) Fall 86, p. 79.
"Molto Vivace" (for Ned). [Confr] (32) Spr-Sum 86, p. 94.
"The Widower Grows Lustful." [MidAR] (6:1) 86?, p. 39.
COFFIN RIGGS, Dionis
See RIGGS, Dionis Coffin
1017. COGSWELL, Fred
"The Great Blue Heron." [AntigR] (64) Wint 86, p. 11.
"Puppet Show." [AntigR] (64) Wint 86, p. 11.
1018. COHEN, Diana
"The Conversation." [Pax] (3:1/2) Wint 85-86, p. 173.
"Moonlight Mime." [Pax] (3:1/2) Wint 85-86, p. 173.
1019. COHEN, Gerald
"British Museum Library." [CumbPR] (5:2) Spr 86, p. 77.
1020. COHEN, Ira
"The Hidden Tear" (for Arden). [LittleM] (15:2) 86, p. 41-42.
1021. COHEN, Jonathan
"At the Tomb of the Guerrilla" (tr. of Ernesto Cardenal). [Agni] (23) 86, p. 80.
"For Those Dead, Our Dead" (tr. of Ernesto Cardenal). [AmerV] (2) Spr 86, p. 100-101.
"Founding of the Latin American Association for Human Rights" (tr. of Ernesto Cardenal). [Agni] (23) 86, p. 75-76.
"New Ecology" (tr. of Ernesto Cardenal). [Agni] (23) 86, p. 78-79.
"The Parrots" (tr. of Ernesto Cardenal). [Agni] (23) 86, p. 77.
"The Price of Bras" (tr. of Ernesto Cardenal). [MassR] (27:3/4) Fall-Wint 86, p. 510.
"Vision from the Blue Plane-Window" (tr. of Ernesto Cardenal). [Agni] (23) 86, p. 74.
1022. COHEN, Miriam A.
"Madame M's Description of What Could Happen to Your Body After You Die." [SanFPJ] (8:1) 85, p. 57.
"To Yet Another New Actress Here." [Wind] (16:57) 86, p. 6.
1023. COLAKIS, Marianthe
"Agamemnon" (tr. of Yannis Ritsos). [WebR] (11:1) Spr 86, p. 12-28.
1024. COLANDER, Valerie Nieman
"The Baptists Cut a Tree." [YetASM] (5) 86, p. 7.
1025. COLBURN, Don
"Bank Building." [Vis] (21) 86, p. 13.
1026. COLBY, Joan
"The Coming of Blindness." [Interim] (5:2) Fall 86, p. 35.

89

"Cut-Off." [ConnPR] (4:1) 85, p. 26.
"The Lonely Hearts Killers" (Special Chapbook edition). [SpoonRQ] (11:3) Sum 86, 73 p.
"Reversals." [Interim] (5:2) Fall 86, p. 34-35.
"Target Fixation." [Poetry] (148:2) My 86, p. 82-83.
1027. COLCHIE, Thomas
"Song for That Man of the People Charlie Chaplin" (tr. of Carlos Drummond de Andrade). [ParisR] (28:100) Sum-Fall 86, p. 152-159.
1028. COLE, Duff
"Bad-Mouthed." [Sam] (46:2 release 182) 86, p. 39.
1029. COLE, Henri
"Cape Cod Elegy." [Poetry] (149:3) D 86, p. 133-134.
"Dorothy's Fossils." [Hudson] (38:4) Wint 86, p. 634-635.
"Midnight Sailing on the Chesapeake." [SouthernR] (22:2) Ap 86, p. 363-367.
1030. COLE, James
"Decoration Day." [ManhatPR] (7) Sum 86, p. 24.
"Faculty Offices, Circa 1985." [Poetry] (148:4) Jl 86, p. 195.
"Glimpse from the Classroom." [ParisR] (28:101) Wint 86, p. 275.
"Great-Grandma." [ManhatPR] (7) Sum 86, p. 25.
1031. COLE, Kevin
"Autistic Boy." [Poetry] (148:4) Jl 86, p. 221.
"Indoor Pool." [Poetry] (148:4) Jl 86, p. 222.
1032. COLE, Michael
"Babel." [NegC] (6:1) Wint 86, p. 85.
"Flight: Listening to Brubeck, Reading Aksyanov." [HiramPoR] (41) Fall-Wint 86-87, p. 9.
"The Footbridge" (for Emily, my daughter). [HiramPoR] (41) Fall-Wint 86-87, p. 10.
"He looks in the distance for his destination" (tr. of Pentii Saarikoski, w. Karen Kimball). [Chelsea] (45) 86, p. 124.
"The Mental Universe" (after a painting by Magritte). [HiramPoR] (41) Fall-Wint 86-87, p. 8.
"The wind is coming up" (tr. of Pentii Saarikoski, w. Karen Kimball). [Chelsea] (45) 86, p. 125.
"The world's idea that you can see the world" (tr. of Pentti Saarikoski, w. Karen Kimball). [WebR] (11:1) Spr 86, p. 29.
1033. COLE, Norma
"Letters of Discipline." [Temblor] (4) 86, p. 131-138.
"Paper House" (Part One, a-o). [Sulfur] (6:2, issue 17) 86, p. 50-55.
"Parabolic Texts" (after Vittoria Colonna and Veronica Gambara). [Acts] (5) 86, p. 41-44.
1034. COLE, Peter
"Alphabet." [Conjunc] (9) 86, p. 63.
"Isaac: A Poise." [Conjunc] (9) 86, p. 64-65.
"Knowing Is." [Conjunc] (9) 86, p. 65-66.
"Leviticus." [Conjunc] (9) 86, p. 53-62.
"Torches." [Conjunc] (9) 86, p. 63.
1035. COLE, Sylvia
"Roundabout." [WoosterR] (6) Fall 86, p. 57.
"Synchronized Swimmers" (A poem for Liz). [WoosterR] (5) Spr 86, p. 82.
1036. COLEMAN, Arthur
"On His Blindness" (Dadaist Sonnet in Memory of Tristan Tsara). [Confr] (33/34) Fall-Wint 86-87, p. 139.
1037. COLEMAN, Jane
"Folk Tales." [WestB] (19) 86, p. 64.
"Poor Will's Widow." [WestB] (19) 86, p. 65-66.
1038. COLEMAN, Mary Ann
"Photographs, Lives." [Comm] (113:1) 17 Ja 86, p. 25.
1039. COLEMAN, Wanda
"African Sleeping Sickness" (for Anna Halprin). [AnotherCM] (16) 86, p. 6-9.
"Auguries (2)." [Caliban] (1) 86, p. 8.
"Auguries (6)." [Caliban] (1) 86, p. 9.
"Bakersfield U.S.A." [Caliban] (1) 86, p. 7.
"Cafe Society" (the autobiography of the night). [SlipS] (6) 86, p. 9.
"Casting Call." [MichQR] (25:3) Sum 86, p. 536.
"Emmett Till." [Callaloo] (9:2, #27) Spr 86, p. 295-299.

"Invitation to a Gunfighter." [MichQR] (25:3) Sum 86, p. 535.
"Motel." [SlipS] (6) 86, p. 10.
"Old Black Lady Next Door, Walking." [Electrum] (38) Spr 86, p. 41.
"Shop of Signs" (on Manchester Av. in Los Angeles). [Obs] (NS 1:1/2) Spr-Sum
      86, p. 52.
"Some of Us." [Event] (15:1) 86, p. 58-59.
"The Third Party." [Obs] (NS 1:1/2) Spr-Sum 86, p. 53-54.
1040. COLES, Don
      "Photo." [GreenfR] (13:3/4) Sum-Fall 86, p. 35.
1041. COLES, Katharine
      "At a Sidewalk Cafe." [Vis] (21) 86, p. 8-11.
      "Heirlooms." [Vis] (21) 86, p. 5-6.
      "Hurricane from a Distance." [Vis] (21) 86, p. 12.
      "In Absence." [Vis] (21) 86, p. 7.
1042. COLLECOTT, Diana
      "A Double Matrix: Re-reading H. D." [Iowa] (16:3) Fall 86, p. 93-124.
1043. COLLIER, Phyllis K.
      "Daylilies" (For Peter Wilhelm, b. 5/5/69, d. 5/6/69). [PoetryNW] (27:2) Sum 86,
            p. 29-30.
      "The Hay Wife" (For Anna Louise Strong). [PoetryNW] (27:2) Sum 86, p. 31.
1044. COLLINS, Billy
      "The Blue." [WoosterR] (6) Fall 86, p. 43.
      "Grand Central Station." [WoosterR] (6) Fall 86, p. 45.
      "Indoors." [WoosterR] (6) Fall 86, p. 44.
      "Morning." [WoosterR] (6) Fall 86, p. 42.
      "The Unreal McCoy." [LitR] (30:1) Fall 86, p. 43.
1045. COLLINS, Martha
      "Iris." [MidwQ] (27:2) Wint 86, p. 198.
      "Lent." [Agni] (23) 86, p. 59.
      "Martin Luther King Day." [Agni] (23) 86, p. 60.
      "Outside." [Agni] (23) 86, p. 58.
      "Traveling Poem." [NoDaQ] (54:4) Fall 86, p. 149.
      "White Room." [ConnPR] (4:1) 85, p. 23.
1046. COLON RUIZ, José O.
      "Caras y Espejos, Lisa." [Mairena] (8:22) 86, p. 112.
1047. COLSON, Theodore
      "Domain of Porcupines." [AntigR] (64) Wint 86, p. 114.
1048. COLTMAN, Paul
      "Delphi." [CumbPR] (5:2) Spr 86, p. 27-28.
1049. COMBER, Nesta
      "Mayday." [NewL] (53:1) Fall 86, p. 73.
1050. CONATSER, Lema
      "Threes." [PoeticJ] (14) 86, p. 6-7.
1051. CONCANNON, Carey
      "On the Truck Route in Eastern Oregon." [PoetryNW] (27:2) Sum 86, p. 22-23.
1052. CONDINI, Ned E.
      "What You Knew about Me" (tr. of Eugenio Montale). [MissR] (15:1/2, #43/44)
            Fall-Wint 86, p. 49.
1053. CONKLING, Helen
      "Austin Dickinson, Listening to Mrs. Todd Play Scarlatti." [LittleM] (15:2) 86, p.
            28.
      "An Old Man." [LittleM] (15:2) 86, p. 29.
      "There Was an Angel." [LittleM] (15:2) 86, p. 30.
      "Vivaldi" (For Claudia Maria Forestieri, September, 1985). [LittleM] (15:2) 86, p.
            25-27.
1054. CONN, Jan
      "Double Vision." [Quarry] (35:3) Sum 86, p. 84-85.
      "Learn from the Wind" (for Ryuchi Matsuda). [Quarry] (35:3) Sum 86, p. 85-86.
1055. CONN, Lewis
      "On Reading Chekhov." [NewL] (53:1) Fall 86, p. 29.
1056. CONNELLY, Karen
      "It's Easy for Them." [Grain] (14:4) N 86, p. 28.
      "Words I Never Heard." [Grain] (14:4) N 86, p. 26-27.
1057. CONNELLY, Mark
      "The Day." [SanFPJ] (8:2) 85, p. 86.
      "Waiting." [SanFPJ] (8:2) 85, p. 87.

1058. CONNER, Don
    "To Kenneth Rexroth." [Amelia] (3:1) Ja 86, p. 67.
1059. CONNOLLY, Carol
    "Baggage." [LakeSR] (20) 86, p. 7.
    "Ode to a Message." [LakeSR] (20) 86, p. 8.
1060. CONNOLLY, Geraldine
    "Food for the Winter." [Nimrod] (30:1) Fall-Wint 86, p. 45-47.
    "The House." [CrossCur] (6:2) 86, p. 60.
    "Summer." [PennR] (2:1) Fall-Wint 86, p. 41.
    "What We Are Carrying." [CrossCur] (6:2) 86, p. 59.
1061. CONOLEY, Gillian
    "After the Baptism." [ThRiPo] (27/28) 86, p. 33.
    "Correctional House." [AmerPoR] (15:6) N-D 86, p. 47.
    "Murder in a Small Town." [AmerPoR] (15:6) N-D 86, p. 47.
    "Premature Reincarnation." [NoAmR] (271:3) S 86, p. 21.
    "The Sky Fills Everything." [ThRiPo] (27/28) 86, p. 32.
    "Suddenly the Graves." [Ploughs] (12:4) 86, p. 76.
1062. CONOVER, Carl
    "Azaleas and the Circus." [SoCaR] (18:2) Spr 86, p. 65.
    "Matriarch." [StoneC] (14:1/2) Fall-Wint 86-87, p. 34.
    "Patrimony." [CumbPR] (5:2) Spr 86, p. 70.
1063. CONRAD, Nick
    "A Man in Late Autumn." [StoneC] (13:3/4) Spr-Sum 86, p. 66.
1064. CONSTANTINE, David
    "At Kirtlington Quarry" (For Simon). [Verse] (5) 86, p. 44.
1065. CONTE, Joseph M.
    "Lyric Construction." [ManhatR] (4:1) Fall 86, p. 40.
1066. CONTI, Edmund
    "Being God Is No Picnic." [RagMag] (5:2) Fall 86, p. 6.
    "New Nose Is Good Nose." [Bogg] (55) 86, p. 26.
1067. CONTOSKI, Victor
    "Conversation over Hot Coffee." [KanQ] (18:1/2) Wint-Spr 86, p. 94.
    "The Liar." [Caliban] (1) 86, p. 115-116.
    "My Father's Ties." [KanQ] (18:1/2) Wint-Spr 86, p. 95.
    "A Note from a Friend" (for Ed Rune). [Caliban] (1) 86, p. 117.
    "The Things of the Dead." [KanQ] (18:1/2) Wint-Spr 86, p. 95.
1068. COOK, Jane W.
    "Harvested Words." [DeKalbLAJ] (19:2) 86, p. 17.
    "Harvested Words" (reprinted because of error in Vol. XIX, no. 2). [DeKalbLAJ]
        (19:3/4) 86, p. 118.
    "My Choice." [WoosterR] (6) Fall 86, p. 77.
1069. COOK, Joie
    "Habitat." [RagMag] (5:2) Fall 86, p. 7.
1070. COOK, Paul
    "Fossils." [CharR] (12:1) Spr 86, p. 83.
    "The Scene of My Death." [CharR] (12:1) Spr 86, p. 84-85.
1071. COOK, R. L.
    "Epitaph." [ArizQ] (42:1) Spr 86, p. 36.
    "How Can I Find You." [BallSUF] (27:4) Aut 86, p. 42.
    "Migrating Geese." [NegC] (6:4) Fall 86, p. 90.
    "On Blackford Hill." [BallSUF] (27:4) Aut 86, p. 6.
    "Summer Is Over." [BallSUF] (26:4) Aut 85, p. 23.
1072. COOK-DARBY, Candice
    "Rebirth." [Blueline] (8:1) Sum-Fall 86, p. 4.
1073. COOKSHAW, Marlene
    "The Blind Leading." [CanLit] (111) Wint 86, p. 47.
    "Cupboards" (from *The Whole Elephant*). [MalR] (74) Mr 86, p. 36.
    "Egg in a Teacup" (from *The Whole Elephant*). [MalR] (74) Mr 86, p. 34-35.
    "Flying Home from the Prairies" (from *The Whole Elephant*). [MalR] (74) Mr 86, p.
        37-38.
    "The Grassy Verge" (from *The Whole Elephant*). [MalR] (74) Mr 86, p. 32-33.
    "Intricate Play." [CanLit] (111) Wint 86, p. 66.
    "Poisons." [MalR] (74) Mr 86, p. 72-73.
    "The Porter." [MalR] (74) Mr 86, p. 70-71.
1074. COOLEY, Dennis
    "Confectionary." [Rampike] (5:1) 86, p. 39.

"Trails in His Head." [CanLit] (108) Spr 86, p. 103-104.
"What's Good for General Motors." [CanLit] (108) Spr 86, p. 105.
1075. COOLEY, Peter
"Afterward." [Ploughs] (12:4) 86, p. 98.
"Ararat." [GeoR] (40:3) Fall 86, p. 646.
"Augustine Boulin: La Berceuse." [NegC] (6:4) Fall 86, p. 31.
"Detritus." [MemphisSR] (6:1/2) Spr 86, p. 5.
"Keeping, Here." [KanQ] (18:1/2) Wint-Spr 86, p. 57.
"Least Sandpiper." [KanQ] (18:1/2) Wint-Spr 86, p. 58.
"Sleep and Poetry." [KanQ] (18:1/2) Wint-Spr 86, p. 58.
"The Suppliant." [MemphisSR] (6:1/2) Spr 86, p. 5.
"Van Gogh, 'Fishing Boats on the Beach at Saint-Marie'." [VirQR] (62:2) Spr 86, p. 263.
"Van Gogh, 'Landscape with Ploughed Fields'." [SouthernR] (22:1) Ja 86, p. 137.
"Van Gogh, 'Olive Orchard'." [Northeast] (series 4:4) Wint 86-87, p. 15.
"Van Gogh, 'Pavement Cafe at Night'." [Interim] (5:1) Spr 86, p. 15.
"Van Gogh, 'Self-Portrait with Soft Felt Hat'." [VirQR] (62:2) Spr 86, p. 264.
"Van Gogh, 'Stairway at Auvers'." [VirQR] (62:2) Spr 86, p. 263-264.
"Van Gogh, 'Sunflowers'." [Northeast] (series 4:4) Wint 86-87, p. 14.
"Van Gogh, 'Tarascon Diligence'." [Ploughs] (12:4) 86, p. 99.
"Van Gogh, 'The Bedroom at Arles'." [SouthernR] (22:1) Ja 86, p. 138.
"Van Gogh, 'The Last Self-Portrait'." [Northeast] (series 4:4) Wint 86-87, p. 16.
"Van Gogh, 'Undergrowth with Two Figures'." [SouthernR] (22:1) Ja 86, p. 136.
1076. COOLIDGE, Clark
"Another Life." [Temblor] (3) 86, p. 3-15.
"The Brought Book." [Sink] (2) 86, p. 3-4.
"Figures." [Notus] (1:1) Fall 86, p. 10.
"In Cell." [Caliban] (1) 86, p. 122-123.
"The Insect the Lady Is Interested In." [Notus] (1:1) Fall 86, p. 12.
"The Liquid Up in the Sky." [Sink] (2) 86, p. 5-6.
"Notebook." [Notus] (1:1) Fall 86, p. 11.
"An Open Else." [Sulfur] (6:2, issue 17) 86, p. 121.
"The Secret." [Caliban] (1) 86, p. 125.
"Shied Witnesses." [Sulfur] (6:2, issue 17) 86, p. 120.
"A Slight Report." [Sink] (2) 86, p. 7.
"Somehow to Be Able to Say" (for M.P.). [Caliban] (1) 86, p. 124.
"We Leave What We Know Behind Desire." [Notus] (1:1) Fall 86, p. 9.
1077. COOLIDGE, Miles
"Overheard." [HarvardA] (120, i.e. 119:3) Mr 86, p. 33.
1078. COON, Tom
"Endings." [NegC] (6:4) Fall 86, p. 91.
1079. COOPER, Adrienne
"Don't think that I have changed" ("Untitled", tr. of Anna Margolin). [SinW] (29/30) 86, p. 151.
"Full of Night and Weeping" (tr. of Anna Margolin). [SinW] (29/30) 86, p. 148.
"Mother Earth, Well Worn, Sun Washed" (tr. of Anna Margolin). [SinW] (29/30) 86, p. 150.
"My Ancestors Speak" (tr. of Anna Margolin). [SinW] (29/30) 86, p. 148-149.
"Not Happy" (tr. of Anna Margolin). [SinW] (29/30) 86, p. 150.
"The Proud Poem" (tr. of Anna Margolin). [SinW] (29/30) 86, p. 151.
1080. COOPER, Bernard
"Atlantis." [MichQR] (25:4) Fall 86, p. 699-700.
"Childless." [IndR] (9:2) Spr 86, p. 52-53.
1081. COOPER, Daniel
"The Autonomous Splendor of Deities." [AmerPoR] (15:3) My-Je 86, p. 32.
"Her Father Dying." [AmerPoR] (15:3) My-Je 86, p. 32.
"The Marriage." [AmerPoR] (15:3) My-Je 86, p. 32.
1082. COOPER, Jane (See also COOPER, Jane Todd)
"Childhood in Jacksonville, Florida." [Iowa] (16:1) Wint 86, p. 51.
"Class" (Jacksonville 1934). [Iowa] (16:1) Wint 86, p. 50.
"Estrangement." [Iowa] (16:1) Wint 86, p. 50.
1083. COOPER, Jane Todd (See also COOPER, Jane)
"Touching Women." [WebR] (11:1) Spr 86, p. 79.
1084. COOPER, M. Truman
"Against Odds" (for Nancy). [LitR] (29:3) Spr 86, p. 289.
"Ashes." [PoetryNW] (27:2) Sum 86, p. 27.

"Becoming Homeless." [NegC] (6:4) Fall 86, p. 98-99.
"Inside the Wind" (for David). [MinnR] (NS 27) Fall 86, p. 40.
"Piece Work." [MinnR] (NS 27) Fall 86, p. 39.
"The Waiting Room." [TarRP] (26:1) Fall 86, p. 24.
"The Well-Dressed Chair." [PoetryNW] (27:2) Sum 86, p. 26-27.
1085. COOPER, Wyn
"David Copperfield Sees It All." [CimR] (75) Ap 86, p. 48.
"Posterity." [MidAR] (6:1) 86?, p. 83.
"The River." [PraS] (60:3) Fall 86, p. 121.
"The Tenant" (for Larry Levis). [MidAR] (6:1) 86?, p. 84.
1086. COOPERMAN, Robert
"Achilles in Hades Laments His Life." [NoDaQ] (54:4) Fall 86, p. 36-37.
"The Bassist Runs Amok." [ConcPo] (19) 86, p. 132-133.
"Boswell on Dr. Johnson's Friend, Mrs. Anna Williams." [AntigR] (64) Wint 86, p. 101-102.
"Cassandra." [CimR] (74) Ja 86, p. 45.
"Counting the Sheep." [Poem] (55) Mr 86, p. 64.
"Early Memory." [HolCrit] (23:5) D 86, p. 15.
"Easter Sunday, 1984." [Poem] (55) Mr 86, p. 60-61.
"From the Ballad of 'The Two Corbies'" ("Where Shall We Gine and Dine Today?"). [WillowS] (17) Wint 86, p. 79-80.
"Glorying in the Wind They Stir." [MidAR] (6:1) 86?, p. 40.
"Growing Up." [DeKalbLAJ] (19:3/4) 86, p. 70-71.
"Helena." [HiramPoR] (41) Fall-Wint 86-87, p. 11.
"J.S. Bach Remembers Frederica Henrietta, Wife of Prince Leopold." [TarRP] (26:1) Fall 86, p. 39-40.
"Lady Mortmain Remembers Her Wedding Night." [CumbPR] (5:2) Spr 86, p. 75-76.
"Mikhail Tukhachevsky." [PoeticJ] (16) Fall 86, p. 33.
"The Mother of the Girl with Down's Syndrome." [TarRP] (24:2) Spr 85, p. 8-9.
"Mrs. Hudson Remembers Sherlock Holmes." [InterPR] (12:1) Spr 86, p. 108-109.
"Playing Basketball with the Boys." [CapeR] (21:1) Spr 86, p. 26.
"Sir Patrick Spens." [WillowS] (17) Wint 86, p. 81-82.
"Sister of the Pregnant Woman." [CimR] (76) Jl 86, p. 35.
"Six Months after the Happy Ending of *The Merchant of Venice*." [MidAR] (7:1) 86, p. 23-26.
"Sleeping Alone." [SoCaR] (19:1) Fall 86, p. 80.
"Thersites, after His Tirade at Agamemnon." [CimR] (74) Ja 86, p. 61-62.
"Tongue Twister." [Poem] (55) Mr 86, p. 62.
"The Valdez Earthquake and Tidal Wave." [InterPR] (12:1) Spr 86, p. 107.
"The Valdez Earthquake and Tidal Wave" (Corrected reprint). [InterPR] (12:2) Fall 86, p. 92-93.
"The Way to Your Heart." [InterPR] (12:2) Fall 86, p. 93.
"Why the Chinese Never Discovered Europe." [TexasR] (7:1/2) Spr-Sum 86, p. 14-15.
"The Wife of Ramon." [CimR] (77) O 86, p. 26-27.
"The Wild, Soft Air." [StoneC] (13:3/4) Spr-Sum 86, p. 32-33.
"The Wild Years." [LakeSR] (20) 86, p. 23.
"The Witches of Salem." [WillowS] (17) Wint 86, p. 83.
"The Zebra Foal." [Poem] (55) Mr 86, p. 63.
1087. COOPERSTEIN, Claire
"On Safari with Abercrombie and Kent." [Amelia] (3:3) Sum 86, p. 50.
1088. COPE, Steven R.
"Flight." [StoneC] (13:3/4) Spr-Sum 86, p. 12.
"Sacred Cows." [StoneC] (13:3/4) Spr-Sum 86, p. 12.
1089. COPELAND, R. F.
"Untitled #36." [JamesWR] (3:3) Spr 86, p. 6.
1090. CORBEN, Beverly
"Images." [PoeticJ] (16) Fall 86, p. 4.
"Lines on Mother's Day." [PoeticJ] (16) Fall 86, p. 5.
1091. CORBETT, William
"East Mauch Chunk — Jim Thorpe." [Sulfur] (6:1, issue 16) 86, p. 38-47.
"Philip Guston, 1913-1980." [Ploughs] (12:3) 86, p. 95-100.
1092. CORCOBA HERRERO, Víctor
"Luto en Fabero del Bierzo." [Mairena] (8:22) 86, p. 54.

1093. CORDING, Robert
    "A Cottage in the Country." [Poetry] (149:3) D 86, p. 143.
    "Cranberry Island." [Nimrod] (30:1) Fall-Wint 86, p. 51-53.
    "Dr. Johnson: From the Western Isles." [SewanR] (94:4) Fall 86, p. 519-520.
    "Elegy for John, My Student Dead of AIDS." [Poetry] (149:3) D 86, p. 143-144.
    "Evenings in Cromane." [MissouriR] (9:2) 86, p. 152.
    "Exterior View with Goldfinches" (after seeing Fairfield Porter's works). [TarRP]
        (26:1) Fall 86, p. 15.
    "Fall." [TarRP] (25:1) Fall 85, p. 21-22.
    "Letter." [Crazy] (31) Fall 86, p. 66-67.
    "Like." [GeoR] (40:2) Sum 86, p. 404.
    "Monet: 'The Luncheon'." [QW] (23) 86, p. 14.
    "Monet's 'Peace under the Lilacs'." [KenR] (NS 8:1) Wint 86, p. 71.
    "Party." [TarRP] (26:1) Fall 86, p. 16.
    "Rock of Ages." [Poetry] (149:3) D 86, p. 145.
    "Visit." [TarRP] (25:1) Fall 85, p. 22.
1094. COREY, Chet
    "The Classicist." [SpoonRQ] (11:4) Fall 86, p. 27.
    "Intersection at Sub-Zero." [SpoonRQ] (11:2) Spr 86, p. 24.
    "The Last Time Up." [SpoonRQ] (11:4) Fall 86, p. 50.
    "Molting." [LakeSR] (20) 86, p. 19.
    "Mother." [SpoonRQ] (11:2) Spr 86, p. 23.
1095. COREY, Stephen
    "The Blooming of Sentimentality." [Poetry] (147:5) F 86, p. 251-252.
    "Bread" (for Susan). [GeoR] (40:3) Fall 86, p. 647-648.
    "Epitaphs" (In memory of John Hamilton Reynolds, 1794-1852 . . .). [TarRP]
        (24:2) Spr 85, p. 17-18.
    "Reasons for Love." [YellowS] (21) Wint 86, p. 4.
    "Remaking Love." [YellowS] (21) Wint 86, p. 5.
CORMIER-SHEKERJIAN, Regina de
    See DeCORMIER-SHEKERJIAN, Regina
1096. CORN, Alfred
    "Apartment on 22nd St." (for Darragh Park). [ParisR] (28:100) Sum-Fall 86, p. 64.
    "The Candlelight Burglary." [YaleR] (75:4) Sum 86, p. 536-537.
    "Dogwood." [Jacaranda] (2:1) Fall 86, p. 1.
    "Light Tasks." [Pequod] (22) 86, p. 123.
    "Lost and Found." [ParisR] (28:101) Wint 86, p. 239-240.
    "Old Lang Synes." [Jacaranda] (2:1) Fall 86, p. 2.
    "Tercina: Winter in Vermont." [Pequod] (22) 86, p. 124.
    "Wild Carrot." [NewYorker] (62:17) 16 Je 86, p. 34.
1097. CORNELL, Brian R.
    "In a Letter from Home" (#6, #10). [AntigR] (65) Spr 86, p. 167-168.
1098. CORRALES, Jose
    "13 de Junio de 1985." [LindLM] (5:3) Jl-S 86, p. 15.
    "Decidido se levantó temprano." [LindLM] (5:3) Jl-S 86, p. 15.
1099. CORRIGAN, Paul
    "Elegy in March." [Blueline] (7:2) Wint-Spr 86, p. 48-49.
    "John L. Regan, Killed in Korea, 1950, His Hunting Pals." [YetASM] (4) 85, p. 3.
1100. CORTES, Carlos
    "Diptico para Cuando Tus Senos Terminen de Despedirse." [Mairena] (8:22) 86, p.
        121.
1101. CORTES-CABAN, David
    "Hay Frente al Tiempo." [Mairena] (8:22) 86, p. 117.
1102. CORTEZ, Jayne
    "I See Chano Pozo." [OP] (41) Spr 86, p. 34-36.
    "If the Drum Is a Woman." [OP] (41) Spr 86, p. 32-33.
    "When I Look at Wifredo Lam's Paintings." [Callaloo] (9:1, #26) Wint 86, p.
        26-27.
1103. CORY, Jim
    "For Mary the Hat." [JamesWR] (3:4) Sum 86, p. 6.
1104. COSBY, Dee
    "All in All." [Contact] (7:38/39/40) Wint-Spr 86, p. 90.
1105. COSEM, Michel
    "Demain le temps sera inutilement sombre." [Os] (22) 86, p. 19.
    "Qu'ai-je à marcher." [Os] (22) 86, p. 18.

1106. COSENS, Susan M.
  "Picking Berries — Rochester, Minnesota." [RagMag] (5:2) Fall 86, p. 8.
1107. COSIER, Tony
  "Always a Storm, and No Two Storms Alike." [Dandel] (13:1) Spr-Sum 86, p. 23.
  "The Berry Gatherers." [Dandel] (13:1) Spr-Sum 86, p. 22.
  "Einstein at Camp Cromer." [Dandel] (13:1) Spr-Sum 86, p. 20-21.
  "The Mountains (1882)." [CanLit] (109) Sum 86, p. 31-32.
  "The Novelist Draws the Line." [CanLit] (109) Sum 86, p. 32-33.
1108. COSMA, Flavia
  "How Long" (tr. by Jim Roberts and Roger Greenwald, w. the author). [Writ] (18)
      86, c87, p. 109.
  "If I could Be" (tr. by Jim Roberts and Roger Greenwald, w. the author). [Writ] (18)
      86, c87, p. 108.
  "On the Sea Float Chestnut Trees" (tr. by Roger Greenwald, w. the author). [Writ]
      (18) 86, c87, p. 106.
  "Toil" (tr. by Jim Roberts and Roger Greenwald, w. the author). [Writ] (18) 86,
      c87, p. 107.
1109. COSTA, Marithelma
  "Persecucion Primera." [Mairena] (8:22) 86, p. 117.
  "Reaganianas." [RevICP] (90) Oct-Dic 85, p. 51-52.
1110. COSTA, Pere Oriol
  "On the Way into Exile" (El camí de l'exili, tr. by Nathaniel Smith). [SenR] (16:1)
      86, p. 44.
1111. COSTANZO, Gerald
  "Snake" (for Susan Petrie). [OhioR] (36) 86, p. 21.
1112. COTE, Philippe
  "Position Politique de la Société de Conservation du Present . . ." (w. Jean Dubé &
      Alain Bergeron). [Rampike] (5:2) 86, p. 60.
1113. COTHARY, Jean
  "The Trade." [EngJ] (75:2) F 86, p. 54.
  "White Train." [SanFPJ] (8:1) 85, p. 19.
  "World Burn." [SanFPJ] (8:2) 85, p. 48.
1114. COTNOIR, Louise
  "With the Desire to Die" (Selections: 3, 4). [Os] (23) 86, p. 10-11.
1115. COTTER, James Finn
  "Memory." [Hudson] (39:2) Sum 86, p. 283.
1116. COTTERILL, Sarah
  "Blue Wing." [Ploughs] (12:3) 86, p. 77-78.
1117. COUCH, Larry
  "The Amazon" (tr. of Joyce Mansour). [Vis] (20) 86, p. 28.
  "Fever" (tr. of Joyce Mansour). [Vis] (22) 86, p. 9.
  "Wild Animals on the Blacktop" (tr. of Joyce Mansour). [Vis] (22) 86, p. 9.
1118. COULETTE, Henri
  "Memoir." [Iowa] (16:1) Wint 86, p. 7.
  "Newfangleness." [Iowa] (16:1) Wint 86, p. 8.
1119. COULOMBE, Gerard
  "Marguerite." [YetASM] (5) 86, p. 5.
1120. COULTHARD, Leslie Jean
  "Enter the Wolves." [Comm] (113:21) 5 D 86, p. 658.
1121. COUNCILMAN, Emily Sargent
  "Double Sonata." [InterPR] (12:2) Fall 86, p. 77.
  "More Than Interim Between." [InterPR] (12:2) Fall 86, p. 76.
1122. COUTO, Nancy Vieira
  "The Face in the Water." [PoetryNW] (27:4) Wint 86-87, p. 20-23.
  "Rouen Cathedral, West Façade, Strobe Light." [PoetryNW] (27:4) Wint 86-87, p.
      18-19.
1123. COX, Andrew
  "The Swimmer in His Head." [LitR] (30:1) Fall 86, p. 87.
1124. COX, Lori
  "Women's Work." [PottPort] (8) 86-87, p. 3.
1125. COX, Rosemary D.
  "The Hermit." [DeKalbLAJ] (19:2) 86, p. 18.
  "Watercress." [DeKalbLAJ] (19:2) 86, p. 19.
1126. COX, Terrance
  "Roll over McFadden (78)." [CanLit] (111) Wint 86, p. 115-116.

1127. COYLE, Charles
"Though I'll Not Say It." [StoneC] (13:3/4) Spr-Sum 86, p. 60.
CRABBE, Chris Wallace
See WALLACE-CRABBE, Chris
1128. CRAGO, William
"Thanatopsis 1001." [Wind] (16:58) 86, p. 42.
1129. CRAIG, David
"The Fugitive Years." [Wind] (16:58) 86, p. 23.
"Sojourner." [NegC] (6:1) Wint 86, p. 73.
1130. CRAIG, Ray
"Sacramento." [Contact] (7:38/39/40) Wint-Spr 86, p. 31.
1131. CRAMER, A. E.
"Blue Dreams." [Blueline] (7:2) Wint-Spr 86, p. 28-29.
1132. CRAMER, Steven
"Etude." [BostonR] (11:6) D 86, p. 4.
"Marie's Snow." [Sonora] (10) Spr 86, p. 37-39.
1133. CRASE, Douglas
"Theme Park." [ParisR] (28:100) Sum-Fall 86, p. 65.
1134. CREELEY, Robert
"Common." [Notus] (1:1) Fall 86, p. 25.
"For Richard Eberhart." [NegC] (6:2/3) Spr-Sum 86, p. 47.
"Go Float the Boat." [Notus] (1:1) Fall 86, p. 23.
"Interior." [Notus] (1:1) Fall 86, p. 22.
"Not Much." [Notus] (1:1) Fall 86, p. 24.
1135. CRENNER, James
"Young Hormones Madrigal." [Iowa] (16:1) Wint 86, p. 130-131.
CREW, Louie
See LI, Min Hua
1136. CREWE, Jennifer
"Encounter." [TarRP] (25:2) Spr 86, p. 33.
"Herons." [TarRP] (25:2) Spr 86, p. 34.
"Poison." [ManhatPR] (7) Sum 86, p. 45.
1137. CREWS, Jacquelyn
"The Crystal Ball." [Amelia] (3:2) Spr 86, p. 17.
1138. CREWS, John
"How." [CumbPR] (6:1) Fall 86, p. 17.
"Of the Dead So Little Recognized." [CumbPR] (6:1) Fall 86, p. 18.
1139. CREWS, Judson
"An Arching Grossness of Uncut Stems Is." [WormR] (26:3, issue 103) 86, p. 84-85.
"The Conjunctions the Dead Converge Upon Beyond." [WritersF] (12) Fall 86, p. 76.
"Crews, Judson "Your Cracked Hero Worship for Men." [WormR] (26:3, issue 103) 86, p. 86.
"I Had Thought of This Camp-Out Engage." [WormR] (26:3, issue 103) 86, p. 83-84.
"If Bulltoven's Reputation Got Worse Yet." [WormR] (26:3, issue 103) 86, p. 85.
"In New York, According to E. B. White's." [Wind] (16:57) 86, p. 7.
"It Was Not That Bulltoven Was Going Deaf." [WormR] (26:3, issue 103) 86, p. 86.
"Let Us Figure It Out Sometime in the Calm." [Amelia] (3:2) Spr 86, p. 91.
"The Old Stallion Has His Black Cock Out." [WormR] (26:3, issue 103) 86, p. 85.
"Ringed in a Circle of Singing so Soundless." [WritersF] (12) Fall 86, p. 76-77.
"The Sweep-down of Tawny Grasses As If." [Wind] (16:57) 86, p. 7.
"Tepid Tea Since the Samovar Would not." [WormR] (26:3, issue 103) 86, p. 82-83.
"There Are Salt Marshes Here That Seem to." [Amelia] (3:2) Spr 86, p. 91.
"This Is the Nub of It, You Force Your Will." [WormR] (26:3, issue 103) 86, p. 84.
"Time for Prayer, Brothers, Berryman Cried." [Interim] (5:2) Fall 86, p. 11.
"Tradition Has It the Mature Gandhi." [SecC] (14:1) 86, p. 21.
"We Were Fetched by a Small Plane Over." [AnotherCM] (15) 86, p. 14.
1140. CRIST, Vonnie
"Chess." [SanFPJ] (8:2) 85, p. 60.
"Sleep Tight." [SanFPJ] (8:2) 85, p. 49.
1141. CRISTHILF, Mark (CHRISTHILF, Mark)
"Elder." [SoDakR] (24:2) Sum 86, p. 34.

"Mountains." [PennR] (2:1) Fall-Wint 86, p. 63.
"Nobody." [SoDakR] (24:2) Sum 86, p. 35.
1142. CROCKER, Jean-Marie J.
"Testament." [BallSUF] (26:4) Aut 85, p. 39.
1143. CRONIN, Richard
"Inside the City." [SanFPJ] (8:3) 85, p. 34-35.
"The Power of the Word." [SanFPJ] (8:3) 85, p. 37.
1144. CRONWALL, Brian
"Beginning to Understand Vegetarianism" (Olga's Kitchen Restaurant, East Lansing,
Michigan, May 10, 1985). [LakeSR] (20) 86, p. 8.
1145. CROOKER, Barbara
"The Iris Work in the Year's Rhythm." [HiramPoR] (40) Spr-Sum 86, p. 7.
"Raspberries." [HiramPoR] (40) Spr-Sum 86, p. 6.
"Unclaimed Salvage & Freight." [WestB] (19) 86, p. 85.
"The Wine Tasting." [WestB] (19) 86, p. 84.
1146. CROSBY, Philip D.
"Freedom." [PoeticJ] (13) 86, p. 26.
"Late Snow." [PoeticJ] (13) 86, p. 27.
1147. CROSHAW, Michael
"Madame Arcadia." [Bogg] (55) 86, p. 47.
1148. CROSSON, Robert
"On Spicer & Other Poems." [Temblor] (4) 86, p. 89-108.
1149. CROW, Mary
"Alice in Nightmareland" (tr. of Enrique Lihn). [MassR] (27:3/4) Fall-Wint 86, p.
472.
"Apocryphal Journalism" (tr. of Kato Molinari, w. Patsy Boyer). [MidAR] (6:1)
86?, p. 69, 71.
"Hospital in Barcelona" (tr. of Enrique Lihn). [MidAR] (6:1) 86?, p. 67.
"I Row Against the Night" (tr. of Olga Orozco). [MidAR] (6:1) 86?, p. 61, 63, 65.
"Layers." [CentralP] (9) Spr 86, p. 79.
"Night Snow" (tr. of Jorge Teillier). [InterPR] (12:1) Spr 86, p. 39.
"Poem 2" (tr. of José Donoso). [MidAR] (6:1) 86?, p. 75.
"Prelude" (tr. of José Donoso). [MidAR] (6:1) 86?, p. 73.
"The Real Thing." [MidAR] (6:2) 86, p. 117-118.
"Rose Red." [BelPoJ] (36:3) Spr 86, p. 18.
"Seated Before the Fire" (tr. of Jorge Teillier). [InterPR] (12:1) Spr 86, p. 37.
"Translation." [CentralP] (9) Spr 86, p. 56.
1150. CROZIER, Lorna
"Angels of Snow." [GreenfR] (13:3/4) Sum-Fall 86, p. 36.
"Childhood." [AntigR] (64) Wint 86, p. 77.
"Gorky's Childhood." [GreenfR] (13:3/4) Sum-Fall 86, p. 37-38.
"If a Poem Could Walk." [MalR] (73) Ja 86, p. 60.
"Love Poem, after Rain." [AntigR] (64) Wint 86, p. 78.
"Put a Finger to Your Lips." [MalR] (73) Ja 86, p. 61.
"The Simple Acts" (after reading Primo Levi). [Event] (15:2) 86, p. 166.
1151. CRUZ, Pedro Oscar
"Quisiera descansar." [Mairena] (8:22) 86, p. 59.
1152. CRUZKATZ, Ida
"Nails." [ManhatPR] (7) Sum 86, p. 42.
1153. CSAMER, Mary Ellen
"In the End." [WestCR] (21:2) O 86, p. 71.
"Once." [WestCR] (21:2) O 86, p. 75.
"Rug Dancing." [AntigR] (65) Spr 86, p. 74.
"There Are Poems." [Event] (15:1) 86, p. 102-103.
"This Was Lost." [WestCR] (21:2) O 86, p. 74.
"The Unblending" (for David). [WestCR] (21:2) O 86, p. 72.
"The Visitation." [AntigR] (65) Spr 86, p. 73.
"The Visitor." [WestCR] (21:2) O 86, p. 73.
1154. CSOORI, Sándor
"E.K.'s Will" (tr. by Jascha Kessler, w. Maria Körösy). [MissouriR] (9:1) 85-86,
p. 197.
"Summer, Haloed" (tr. by Jascha Kessler, w. Maria Körösy). [MissouriR] (9:1)
85-86, p. 195.
"Sunday before Christmas" (tr. by Jascha Kessler, w. Maria Körösy). [MissouriR]
(9:1) 85-86, p. 196.

"You Were Still the Sun's There" (tr. by Jascha Kessler, w. Maria Körösy). [MissouriR] (9:1) 85-86, p. 194.
1155. CUADRA, Pablo Antonio
"Poem of the Foreigners' Moment in Our Jungle" (for several voices, tr. by Steven White). [AmerV] (5) Wint 86, p. 107-109.
1156. CUENCA, Luis Alberto de
"El Poeta a Su Amada para que No Le Tire Bombas." [Mairena] (8:22) 86, p. 41.
1157. CUENCA, Mike
"Rue de la Paix?" [NegC] (6:4) Fall 86, p. 71.
1158. CULLIMORE, Jason
"A cloud and a tree." [Grain] (14:2) My 86, p. 32.
"Darkness." [Grain] (14:2) My 86, p. 29.
"No-one knows where the world has gone." [Grain] (14:2) My 86, p. 30.
"There Once was a thing named Fred." [Grain] (14:2) My 86, p. 30.
"Warm Fuzzy." [Grain] (14:2) My 86, p. 31.
1159. CULLY, Barbara
"Finally." [SouthernPR] (26:2) Fall 86, p. 25.
"Three Potatoes." [OP] (42/43) Wint 86-87, p. 181-182.
"When Beauty Speaks, She Is Harsh and Disappointing." [SouthernPR] (26:1) Spr 86, p. 17.
CUMBA, Israel Ruiz
See RUIZ CUMBA, Israel
1160. CUMMINGS, Darcy
"My Father, Standing at a Snowy Bus Stop" (January, 1946). [PoetryNW] (27:1) Spr 86, p. 33-34.
"Still Life: Shipyard, September, 1950." [PaintedB] (29) Ag 86, p. 22.
1161. CUNNINGHAM, Gloria
"Arugamama" (from Japanese: accepting reality as it is). [Amelia] (3:3) Sum 86, p. 52.
1162. CUNNINGHAM, Shaun
"Asian Festival." [Grain] (14:4) N 86, p. 51.
"Boot Tracks." [Grain] (14:4) N 86, p. 49-50.
"Korean Postcard." [Grain] (14:4) N 86, p. 45.
"Racing Angels." [Grain] (14:4) N 86, p. 46-48.
1163. CURRAN, Ann
"Even the Stones Speak." [ThRiPo] (27/28) 86, p. 34.
1164. CURRIER, Douglas K.
"Abuelo" (for Vincente Ojeda). [PennR] (1:1) 85, p. 36-37.
1165. CURTIS, Linda Lee
"Cook." [PoeticJ] (14) 86, p. 34.
"Hot Bread." [PoeticJ] (15) Sum 86, p. 37.
"Magician." [PoeticJ] (15) Sum 86, p. 33.
"On Past Yuma." [PoeticJ] (15) Sum 86, p. 33.
1166. CURTIS, Tony
"Ivy." [NewYorker] (62:7) 7 Ap 86, p. 88.
1167. CUSHING, George
"Attila József" (tr. of Attila József, w. Edwin Morgan). [Verse] (5) 86, p. 50.
"Culture" (tr. of Attila József, w. Edwin Morgan). [Verse] (5) 86, p. 50.
"In the End" (tr. of Attila József, w. Edwin Morgan). [Verse] (5) 86, p. 51.
"It Is a Fine Summer Evening" (tr. of Attila József, w. Edwin Morgan). [Verse] (5) 86, p. 53.
"Sorrow" (tr. of Attila József, w. Edwin Morgan). [Verse] (5) 86, p. 52.
"A True Man" (tr. of Attila József, w. Edwin Morgan). [Verse] (5) 86, p. 54.
1168. CUTLER, Bruce
"Angelita" (October, 1943. From The Book of Naples). [KanQ] (18:3) Sum 86, p. 64-69.
"Captain Diver's Dinner" (October, 1943, from: The Book of Naples). [BelPoJ] (37:1) Fall 86, p. 5-9.
1169. CUTLER, Charles
"Amazonas, Land of Water" (Excerpt, tr. of Thiago de Mello). [MassR] (27:3/4) Fall-Wint 86, p. 693, 698.
1170. CUZA MALE, Belkis
"The Angry Woman Who Married God" (to Sister Juana Inés de la Cruz, tr. by William T. Lawlor). [NegC] (6:4) Fall 86, p. 199.
"Mujer Brava Que Caso con Dios" (A Sor Juana Inés de la Cruz). [NegC] (6:4) Fall 86, p. 198.

1171. CZAPLA, Cathy Young
"Champlain." [Blueline] (7:2) Wint-Spr 86, p. 33.
"Driving through Sherburne, Vermont." [Sam] (46:5 [i.e. 46:1] release 181) 86, p. 8.
"Midway Diner." [SlipS] (6) 86, p. 29.
"Stillborn." [Sam] (46:5 [i.e. 46:1] release 181) 86, p. 31.
1172. CZURY, Craig
"The Hole in the Wall." [PaintedB] (28) Ap 86, p. 68.
"Legend." [PaintedB] (28) Ap 86, p. 69.
"Theorem" (for Karen & Kyoto). [PaintedB] (28) Ap 86, p. 67.
Da SILVA RAMOS, Pericles Eugenio
See RAMOS, Pericles Eugenio da Silva
1173. DABNEY, Stuart
"1943." [DenQ] (20:4/21:1) Spr-Sum 86, p. 130-131.
"Don't Look Back." [DenQ] (20:4/21:1) Spr-Sum 86, p. 128-129.
1174. DABROCK, Martha
"The Offering." [NegC] (6:4) Fall 86, p. 104-105.
1175. DABYDEEN, Cyril
"Farewell." [GreenfR] (13:3/4) Sum-Fall 86, p. 39.
1176. DACEY, Philip
"Army Hospital." [SpoonRQ] (11:4) Fall 86, p. 22.
"Charis Wilson" (from "The Edward Weston Poems"). [AmerPoR] (15:2) Mr-Ap 86, p. 7.
"The Day Irony Died." [SpoonRQ] (11:4) Fall 86, p. 24.
"First Kisses" (for Linda). [PoetryNW] (27:3) Aut 86, p. 28-29.
"Lat. *Mittere*, to Send." [PaintedB] (29) Ag 86, p. 79.
"Libyan Pantoum." [PoetryNW] (27:4) Wint 86-87, p. 14.
"The Musician." [SouthernPR] (26:2) Fall 86, p. 54.
"My Son, the Drummer." [SouthernPR] (26:2) Fall 86, p. 53-54.
"The Nuns." [SpoonRQ] (11:4) Fall 86, p. 23.
"Squeak." [PennR] (2:1) Fall-Wint 86, p. 38-39.
"The Story." [SpoonRQ] (11:4) Fall 86, p. 51.
"Upon Sending His Child Support Check to L. L. Bean . . . ." [Poetry] (148:6) S 86, p. 328-329.
"The Woman in the Laundromat" (for Dave Etter). [RagMag] (5:2) Fall 86, p. 9.
"You'll Come Out of This Smelling Like a Rose." [PaintedB] (29) Ag 86, p. 78.
D'ACOS, Anrique Paco
See ACOS, Anrique Paco d'
1177. DACRON, Ron
"Sarah Dallas." [Contact] (8:41/42/43) Fall-Wint 86-87, p. 10.
1178. DAHL, Chris
"The Domestic Transformation Ruling My Life." [PoetryNW] (27:4) Wint 86-87, p. 6-7.
1179. DAILEY, Joel
"Dog Food." [Bogg] (55) 86, p. 20.
"The Photographers." [WormR] (26:1, issue 101) 86, p. 16.
1180. DAILY, Patrick
"The Dishwasher Drains His Sink." [PoetL] (80:4) Wint 86, p. 212-213.
"The Dishwasher's Meditation." [PoetL] (80:4) Wint 86, p. 211-212.
"The Dishwasher's Wife Speaks." [PoetL] (80:4) Wint 86, p. 211.
"Rib Bones." [PoetL] (80:4) Wint 86, p. 213-214.
1181. DAKESSIAN, Sylvia
"Hold Me." [Jacaranda] (2:1) Fall 86, p. 14.
1182. DALE, Karen
"Two-Wheeler." [Thrpny] (27) Fall 86, p. 20.
1183. DALE, Peter
"Canto Three: Dante's Inferno" (Excerpt). [AntigR] (66/67) Sum-Aut 86, p. 80-81.
1184. D'ALFONSO, Antonio
"Perseverance." [GreenfR] (13:3/4) Sum-Fall 86, p. 40.
1185. DALI, Salvador
"Le Grand Masturbateur" (Excerpt, tr. by Frank C. Lewis and Sonja A. Rein). [ClockR] (3:1) 85, p. 61-62.
"Metamorphosis of Narcissus" (tr. by Francis Scarpe). [ClockR] (3:1) 85, p. 5-9.
"Sonnet to Mallarme's Commode" (tr. by Eleanor R. Morse). [ClockR] (3:1) 85, p. 59.

"Sonnet to the Pupils of Velazquez' Eyes, Gala of My Eyes" (tr. by Eleanor R. Morse). [ClockR] (3:1) 85, p. 11.
"Surrealism." [ClockR] (3:1) 85, back cover.

1186. DALLAS, Mark
"Moon Pull." [FloridaR] (14:2) Fall-Wint 86, p. 105.

1187. DALTON, Roque
"Agreed: It's True That You Look Like May Britt" (tr. by Roberto Márquez). [MassR] (27:3/4) Fall-Wint 86, p. 443-444.
"Sayings" (tr. by Roberto Márquez). [MassR] (27:3/4) Fall-Wint 86, p. 442.

1188. DALTON, Sheila
"Naming Song." [CrossC] (8:2) 86, p. 12.

1189. DALVEN, Rae
"Take Care My Child" (tr. of Lydia Stephanou). [Confr] (33/34) Fall-Wint 86-87, p. 115.
"The Teacher" (tr. of Sophia Mavroeidi Papadaky). [Confr] (33/34) Fall-Wint 86-87, p. 114.

1190. DAMALI, Nia
"Birth of a Poet." [BlackALF] (20:3) Fall 86, p. 303-305.
"I Am Natural." [SanFPJ] (9:1) 86, p. 45.
"Indigo." [SanFPJ] (9:1) 86, p. 6.
"Real Lovin'." [BlackALF] (20:3) Fall 86, p. 305.
"Sassafras U.S.A." [BlackALF] (20:3) Fall 86, p. 305.
"Victory." [SanFPJ] (9:1) 86, p. 7.

1191. DAME, Enid
"Cinderella." [LittleM] (15:1) 86, p. 17-18.
"Ethel Rosenberg: A Sestina." [SinW] (29/30) 86, p. 254-255.
"Harriet's Song." [PikeF] (7) Spr 86, p. 7.
"Lilith's Sestina." [SinW] (29/30) 86, p. 55-56.
"Lot's Wife Revisited." [LittleM] (15:1) 86, p. 15-16.
"Lot's Wife Revisited." [SinW] (29/30) 86, p. 168.
"Ms. Lot Makes a Political Statement." [SinW] (29/30) 86, p. 169.
"Vildeh Chaya." [SinW] (29/30) 86, p. 170.

1192. D'AMOUR, Michèle
"Incantation for the Worry Stone." [BellArk] (2:4) Jl-Ag 86, p. 3.
"Old Wives' Tales." [BellArk] (2:4) Jl-Ag 86, p. 16.

1193. DANA, Robert
"Bad Heart." [Iowa] (16:1) Wint 86, p. 37.
"Everything Else You Can Get You Take." [Iowa] (16:1) Wint 86, p. 36.
"My Kind." [PoetryE] (20/21) Fall 86, p. 173.
"Tenements." [PoetryE] (20/21) Fall 86, p. 172.
"Victor." [Iowa] (16:1) Wint 86, p. 38.

1194. D'ANGELO, Anna
"Why Kids Shouldn't Wear Braces." [Event] (15:2) 86, p. 106.

1195. DANIEL, David
"Blue Ridge at 223,353 Hours." [AntR] (44:4) Fall 86, p. 432.
"Self-Portrait without Woman." [AntR] (44:4) Fall 86, p. 433.
"Station to Station." [AntR] (44:4) Fall 86, p. 434.

1196. DANIEL, Hal J., III
"Berwick upon Tweed." [CrescentR] (4:2) Fall 86, p. 65.
"Camouflage." [Bogg] (56) 86, p. 43.
"David." [JamesWR] (3:4) Sum 86, p. 4.
"Holy Eucharist with Dick." [JamesWR] (3:2) Wint 86, p. 5.
"Milton Berle and the Sparkle Bugs." [Vis] (22) 86, p. 37.
"Raymond." [YetASM] (4) 85, p. 4.
"Why I Like My Father." [YetASM] (5) 86, p. 10.

1197. DANIEL, John
"At Thirty-Five." [SouthwR] (71:2) Spr 86, p. 203.

1198. DANIELL, Rosemary
"Fort Bragg" (for Zane, and the soldiers of the peacetime Army). [AmerV] (5) Wint 86, p. 102-106.
"Loss of the Soul, & Other Sicknesses." [AmerV] (3) Sum 86, p. 38-40.

1199. DANIELS, Celia (Celia A.)
"Hostage." [SpoonRQ] (11:4) Fall 86, p. 49.
"Old Trails." [MidwQ] (27:4) Sum 86, p. 462.
"Suicide." [MidwQ] (27:4) Sum 86, p. 460-461.

101

1200. DANIELS, Gabrielle
    "The Man Who Has Breasts." [YellowS] (20) Aut 86, p. 16.
1201. DANIELS, Jim
    "5000 Apply for 100 Jobs." [CentR] (30:1) Wint 86, p. 67-68.
    "Belle Isle Park, Detroit." [WoosterR] (5) Spr 86, p. 38.
    "Delivering Pizzas." [WestB] (18) 86, p. 46.
    "Digger Goes on Vacation, #2." [MidAR] (6:2) 86, p. 39-40.
    "Digger's Lawn-Care Philosophy." [MidAR] (6:2) 86, p. 38.
    "Driving Detroit, 1985." [WoosterR] (5) Spr 86, p. 39-40.
    "Fire." [BellR] (9:1) Spr 86, p. 35.
    "Intro to Foreman Psych." [WoosterR] (5) Spr 86, p. 43.
    "Joy Ride" (for my brother Mike in Detroit). [MichQR] (25:2) Spr 86, p. 363.
    "Midnight Date." [QW] (22) Spr-Sum 86, p. 57-58.
    "Not Working." [QW] (22) Spr-Sum 86, p. 59.
    "Out of Work." [WoosterR] (5) Spr 86, p. 42.
    "Racing Cars, 1972." [WoosterR] (5) Spr 86, p. 41.
    "Steady as a Rock." [Contact] (8:41/42/43) Fall-Wint 86-87, p. 56.
    "Wild Country." [PennR] (1:1) 85, p. 64.
DANIELSON, Anita Endrezze
    See ENDREZZE-DANIELSON, Anita
1202. DANON, Ruth
    "Afterimage." [BostonR] (11:1) F 86, p. 20.
    "Changing Weather at the Point of Departure." [AnotherCM] (15) 86, p. 15.
    "Keeping Track." [ParisR] (28:99) Spr 86, p. 142-144.
    "Refugee." [ParisR] (28:99) Spr 86, p. 141.
    "Vocation." [ParisR] (28:99) Spr 86, p. 139-140.
1203. DANTE ALIGHIERI
    "Canto Three: Dante's Inferno" (Excerpt, tr. by Peter Dale). [AntigR] (66/67) Sum-Aut 86, p. 80-81.
1204. DANYS, Milda
    "Mr. Bilevicius in the Cactus Garden." [Descant] (17:2, #53) Sum 86, p. 87-93.
DAO, Bei
    See BEI, Dao
DAO, Jia
    See JIA, Dao
1205. DAOUST, Jean-Paul
    "Animal Story." [Rampike] (5:1) 86, p. 13.
DARBY, Candice Cook
    See COOK-DARBY, Candice
1206. D'ARCY, Michael James
    "Spring on Town Cove." [StoneC] (13:3/4) Spr-Sum 86, p. 26.
1207. DARLING, Charles
    "1952." [ClockR] (3:2) 86, p. 32.
    "In the Time before Names." [ChrC] (103:35) 19 N 86, p. 1034.
    "The Last Will of Mad Anthony Wayne: His Bones." [PennR] (2:1) Fall-Wint 86, p. 42.
    "Undivided Attention." [TarRP] (26:1) Fall 86, p. 44.
    "The Walkers." [Wind] (16:58) 86, p. 9.
1208. DARLINGTON, Andrew
    "From Monochrome/ to Circuits on Full Gush." [Bogg] (55) 86, p. 39.
1209. D'ARPINO, Tony
    "Concerning Earthquakes." [Vis] (20) 86, p. 25-26.
    "Stairway Door Company." [Vis] (22) 86, p. 34.
1210. DARRAGH, Tina
    "A Perfect One of Those" (for the Doctors Foye, Ed & Barbara). [Sink] (2) 86, p. 19-23.
1211. DARRIGRAND, Jacqueline
    "Cleaving." [YellowS] (21) Wint 86, p. 31.
    "Daughter." [YellowS] (21) Wint 86, p. 30.
1212. DASSANOWSKY-HARRIS, Robert von
    "Im Kursalon, Wien 1914." [Os] (22) 86, p. 5.
    "Last Things." [Vis] (22) 86, p. 29.
    "Marbledress" (To the German People). [Vis] (22) 86, p. 30.
    "Triebhaus." [Os] (22) 86, p. 4.
1213. DAUGHERTY, Michael
    "Trains." [Bogg] (55) 86, p. 47.

1214. DAUMAL, René
"The Desertion" (tr. by Richard Zenith). [Translation] (17) Fall 86, p. 305.
"The Disillusion" (tr. by Richard Zenith). [Translation] (17) Fall 86, p. 306.
"I'm Dead" (tr. by Richard Zenith). [Translation] (17) Fall 86, p. 304.

1215. DAUNT, Jon
"American Gothic." [MidAR] (6:2) 86, p. 15-16.
"The Carolers." [ConnPR] (5:1) 86, p. 19.
"Church Service, 1962." [HiramPoR] (40) Spr-Sum 86, p. 8.

1216. DAVEY, Frank
"India Poems." [Rampike] (5:1) 86, p. 18.

1217. DAVID, Almitra
"Notes from Delmira." [BelPoJ] (36:3) Spr 86, p. 4-9.

1218. DAVID, Michael
"Love drills through one skin." [Amelia] (3:3) Sum 86, p. 73.

1219. DAVIDSON, Lisa
"Babel." [BellArk] (2:2) Mr-Ap 86, p. 15.
"Babel." [BellArk] (2:3) My-Je 86, p. 7.
"Escape of the Carpet Souls." [BellArk] (2:2) Mr-Ap 86, p. 14.
"Escape of the Carpet Souls." [BellArk] (2:3) My-Je 86, p. 4.
"Madam, Your Daughter Is Molting." [BellArk] (2:3) My-Je 86, p. 15.
"Madam, Your Daughter Is Moulting." [BellArk] (2:2) Mr-Ap 86, p. 1.

1220. DAVIDSON, Scott
"Words to Say Before Leaving." [PikeF] (7) Spr 86, p. 13.

DAVIDSON, Terri L. Brown
See BROWN-DAVIDSON, Terri L.

1221. DAVIDSON-SHADDOX, Brenda
"España: Feeling the History." [Pax] (3:1/2) Wint 85-86, p. 23-24.
"Lessons." [Pax] (3:1/2) Wint 85-86, p. 23.

1222. DAVIE, Donald
"Proceeding to Hell Together" (tr. of Dmitry V. Bobyshev). [CumbPR] (6:1) Fall
86, p. 25-27.
"Though Dry, Not Dry" (For Dorren). [SewanR] (94:1) Wint 86, p. 92-93.

1223. DAVIE, Sharon
"Night Visit." [CumbPR] (5:2) Spr 86, p. 18.

1224. DAVIES, Hilary
"Elmstead Woods Station." [Hudson] (39:1) Spr 86, p. 105.

1225. DAVIS, Albert
"What They Wrote on the Bathhouse Walls last Summer, Yen's Marina, Chinese
Bayou, LA." [SouthernR] (22:4) O 86, p. 775-777.

1226. DAVIS, Catherine
"The Passing of Eden: Pomona, California." [Iowa] (16:1) Wint 86, p. 126.

1227. DAVIS, Christopher
"His Prayer." [DenQ] (20:4/21:1) Spr-Sum 86, p. 90-91.
"The Only Pasture We Can Graze In." [DenQ] (20:4/21:1) Spr-Sum 86, p. 92-93.
"Song about a Meadow in Sunset." [DenQ] (20:4/21:1) Spr-Sum 86, p. 94-95.

1228. DAVIS, David
"For James Dickey." [Amelia] (3:2) Spr 86, p. 59.
"There's a difference between" ("Untitled"). [Amelia] (3:1) Ja 86, p. 84.

1229. DAVIS, Ed
"Chamber Music" (For the Colorado String Quartet). [CapeR] (21:2) Fall 86, p. 17.
"Night Stalker." [Sam] (46:5 [i.e. 46:1] release 181) 86, p. 7.

1230. DAVIS, Frances
"Thirteenth Summer, Sooke Inlet, B. C." [AntigR] (64) Wint 86, p. 113.

1231. DAVIS, Jon
"At Home in a Paradise of Objects." [MalR] (75) Je 86, p. 87.
"The Body in Question." [KanQ] (18:1/2) Wint-Spr 86, p. 133.
"Bubo: The Great Horned Owl" (for Phil, 1950-1969). [KanQ] (18:1/2) Wint-Spr
86, p. 134-135.
"Driving in the Age of Rock 'n' Roll" (for Rob). [KanQ] (18:1/2) Wint-Spr 86, p.
134.
"Notes for an Essay on Poetry." [Wind] (16:57) 86, p. 8.

1232. DAVIS, Marilyn
"Departure." [Kaleid] (12) Wint 86, p. 49.
"The Departure." [Kaleid] (12) Wint 86, p. 48.

1233. DAVIS, Norma Ruiz
"The Class of '44." [Puerto] (22:1) Fall 86, p. 48.

103

DAVIS

"Edith." [Puerto] (22:1) Fall 86, p. 49.
1234. DAVIS, Robert H.
"Change of Season." [Contact] (8:41/42/43) Fall-Wint 86-87, p. 65.
"Naming the Old Woman." [Contact] (8:41/42/43) Fall-Wint 86-87, p. 65.
1235. DAVIS, Thadious
"News Clips: Black Women Today." [BlackALF] (20:3) Fall 86, p. 299-302.
1236. DAVIS, William Virgil
"Another Castle." [SouthernPR] (26:2) Fall 86, p. 50.
"Aspidistra." [NewOR] (13:3) Fall 86, p. 57.
"A Clear Day and No Clouds." [ArizQ] (42:3) Aut 86, p. 238.
"Cwmdonkin Drive and Park." [LitR] (29:2) Wint 86, p. 193.
"Early One Morning My Son and I Take a Short Drive." [BallSUF] (26:4) Aut 85, p. 24.
"An Evening in Berlin." [NoDaQ] (54:4) Fall 86, p. 154.
"Gulls." [ArizQ] (42:4) Wint 86, p. 330.
"Perspectives." [ManhatPR] (7) Sum 86, p. 22.
"Poetry of Statement." [Event] (15:1) 86, p. 18.
"A Rainy Day in Maine." [ManhatPR] (7) Sum 86, p. 22.
"Tapestry." [Hudson] (39:2) Sum 86, p. 284.
"A Wedding in Hallstatt." [CharR] (12:1) Spr 86, p. 89.
"The Wind." [ConnPR] (5:1) 86, p. 42.
1237. DAVISON, Neil R.
"The Mantis." [CimR] (7O) O 86, p. 33-34.
"To an Unborn Child." [Abraxas] (34) 86, p. 22.
1238. DAWE, Gerald
"The Comedians." [Verse] (3:3) N 86, p. 45.
"Little Palaces." [Verse] (3:3) N 86, p. 46.
1239. DAWSON, Hester Jewell
"October." [StoneC] (14:1/2) Fall-Wint 86-87, p. 34.
1240. DAY, Cynthia
"Loving." [LitR] (29:2) Wint 86, p. 222-223.
"Not Sleeping on Summer Nights." [DenQ] (20:4/21:1) Spr-Sum 86, p. 122.
1241. DAY, David
"The Unicorn." [CanLit] (108) Spr 86, p. 13-14.
De . . .
    See also names beginning with "De" without the following space, filed below in their
        alphabetic positions, e.g., DeFOE.
De ALMEIDA, Jovita
    See ALMEIDA, Jovita de
De ANDRADE, Eugenio
    See ANDRADE, Eugenio de
1242. De ANGELIS, Milo
"July Arrives for the Dead" (tr. by Lawrence Venuti). [Stand] (27:3) Sum 86, p. 17.
"The Slowness" (tr. by Lawrence Venuti). [Stand] (27:3) Sum 86, p. 17.
De ANTAS, Guillermo Argar
    See ARGAR DE ANTAS, Guillermo
De CASTRO ALVES, Antonio
    See ALVES, Antonio de Castro
De CHAZAL, Malcolm
    See CHAZAL, Malcolm de
De CHING, Ines Asinc Ramos
    See RAMOS de CHING, Ines Asinc
De CUENCA, Luis Alberto
    See CUENCA, Luis Alberto de
1243. De GRAZIA, Emilio
"Retributions." [HiramPoR] (41) Fall-Wint 86-87, p. 12-13.
"Tennis Lessons." [CimR] (75) Ap 86, p. 4.
De HOYOS, Angela
    See HOYOS, Angela de
De HOYOS, Ramón Ruiz
    See RUIZ DE HOYOS, Ramón
De JESUS, Dionisio
    See JESUS, Dionisio de
De la FONTAINE, Jean
    See La FONTAINE, Jean de

De LUIS, Leopoldo
    See LUIS, Leopoldo de
1244. De MARIS, Ron
    "Apples." [NewL] (52:2/3) Wint-Spr 86, p. 213.
    "Hot Soup." [AmerPoR] (15:1) Ja-F 86, p. 34.
    "Nets." [AmerPoR] (15:1) Ja-F 86, p. 34.
    "The Watch Maker." [AmerPoR] (15:1) Ja-F 86, p. 35.
De MEDRANO, Francisco
    See MEDRANO, Francisco de
1245. De MELLO, Thiago
    "Amazonas, Land of Water" (Excerpt, tr. by Charles Cutler). [MassR] (27:3/4)
        Fall-Wint 86, p. 693, 698.
De PEREZ, Ilma Valenzuela
    See PEREZ, Ilma Valenzuela de
De PIZAN, Christine
    See PIZAN, Christine de
De RIOS, Maria Eloísa Segovia de
    See SEGOVIA DE RIOS, Maria Eloísa
1246. De ROUS, Peter
    "They Want." [Bogg] (55) 86, p. 43.
De SOTO, Gladys Pagan
    See PAGAN DE SOTO, Gladys
1247. De SOUZA, Eunice
    "Conversation Piece." [LitR] (29:4) Sum 86, p. 436.
    "Idyll." [LitR] (29:4) Sum 86, p. 436.
1248. De VITO, E. B.
    "Absence." [CrossCur] (6:2) 86, p. 142.
    "Interval." [CrossCur] (6:2) 86, p. 143.
    "Something in You." [Comm] (113:1) 17 Ja 86, p. 25.
1249. De VRIES, Carrow
    "Let Us Call It, the American Language." [WindO] (47) Sum 86, p. 21.
    "Marvin De Vries." [WindO] (47) Sum 86, p. 22.
1250. De VRIES, Peter (*See also* DeVRIES, Peter Hugh)
    "To His Importunate Mistress" (Andrew Marvell Updated). [NewYorker] (62:1) 24
        F 86, p. 40.
1251. DEAHL, James
    "The Passing" (for Terry Barker). [GreenfR] (13:3/4) Sum-Fall 86, p. 42-43.
    "Petite-Matane, Gaspé." [AntigR] (66/67) Sum-Aut 86, p. 10.
    "Scientia" (for Werner Heisenberg, Richard Diebenkorn, Helen Frankenthaler).
        [MalR] (77) D 86, p. 51-52.
    "The Slender Yard" (for Shoju-rojin, Japanese poet, 1642-1721). [MalR] (77) D 86,
        p. 49-50.
    "The Story of Rain." [AntigR] (66/67) Sum-Aut 86, p. 11.
    "Unexpectedly, the Clear Sky" (in memory of Chuang Tzu). [AntigR] (66/67)
        Sum-Aut 86, p. 12.
1252. DEAN, Harry
    "Believing's Use." [CumbPR] (6:1) Fall 86, p. 72.
1253. DEAN, Larry O.
    "The Social Contract Rewritten." [PassN] (7:2) Spr-Sum 86, p. 18.
1254. DEANE, John F.
    "Molokai" (tr. of Tomas Transtromer). [Verse] (6) 86, p. 18-19.
    "Sunflowers." [Verse] (6) 86, p. 18.
1255. DEANE, Seamus
    "Power Cut." [Verse] (6) 86, p. 19.
    "Qui Vivent en Marge." [Verse] (6) 86, p. 20.
1256. DEANS, G. N.
    "Then & Now." [Bogg] (55) 86, p. 50.
1257. DeBOWMAN, Sallie McCormick
    "Magician." [YetASM] (5) 86, p. 3.
1258. DECARNIN, Camilla
    "After 'Lady, Weeping at the Crossroads': Women to W.H. Auden." [LittleM]
        (15:1) 86, p. 46.
    "Harmonica." [LittleM] (15:1) 86, p. 45.
1259. DECELLES, Paul
    "Crickets." [KanQ] (18:3) Sum 86, p. 30.

1260. DECEMBER, John
"Letters from a Season." [Wind] (16:56) 86, p. 11-12.
1261. DeCORMIER-SHEKERJIAN, Regina
"The Fragile Construct." [CrossCur] (6:2) 86, p. 13.
"Grandmother." [GWR] (6:2) 86, p. 38-39.
"Jalisco Woman" (Clay figure: Jalisco, Mexico, circa A.D. 1100-1400?). [PassN]
(7:1) Fall-Wint 85-86, p. 21.
"Learning to Read." [CrossCur] (6:2) 86, p. 11-12.
"Realities, Homage to Chagall." [Comm] (113:11) 6 Je 86, p. 347.
"Salut!" (D. B. — The Barnes, 1892-1982). [AmerV] (5) Wint 86, p. 119-121.
1262. DEERING, Christopher
"Flashback." [Sam] (44:3 release 175) 86, p. 36.
1263. DeFOE, Mark
"Lament of the Convenience Store Clerk." [GWR] (6:2) 86, p. 22-23.
"Letter from My Porch." [CumbPR] (5:2) Spr 86, p. 83-84.
"On Arbor Day Mrs. Zonn Plucks Out a Maple Which Has Offended Her." [WestB]
(18) 86, p. 60-61.
"Photo: Father and Son Before a War." [MemphisSR] (7:1) Fall 86, p. 49.
"Podiatry." [KanQ] (18:1/2) Wint-Spr 86, p. 145-146.
"Song of the Lady in the Skin-Tight Jeans." [KanQ] (18:1/2) Wint-Spr 86, p.
144-145.
"Sonnet for an Old Cat, Dead at 16." [CumbPR] (5:2) Spr 86, p. 86.
"Sunday." [TarRP] (25:1) Fall 85, p. 44.
"Ten Marriages / The Reasons." [FloridaR] (14:2) Fall-Wint 86, p. 38-39.
"The White Bread Sandwich." [CumbPR] (5:2) Spr 86, p. 85.
1264. DeFORD, Sheri
"Hard Enough." [SpoonRQ] (11:2) Spr 86, p. 46-47.
1265. DeFREES, Madeline
"After the Winter Solstice." [NowestR] (24:2) 86, p. 74.
"The Auger Kaleidoscope" (for Andrew Fetler). [NowestR] (24:2) 86, p. 70-71.
"Dumb Cane." [NowestR] (24:2) 86, p. 72-73.
"English Teachers' Convention for the Sixties" (for Dorothy Barresi). [PoetryNW]
(27:4) Wint 86-87, p. 38-39.
"From the People's Memorial Association." [PoetryNW] (27:4) Wint 86-87, p. 37.
"Imaginary Ancestors: The Giraffe Women of Burma." [NowestR] (24:2) 86, p.
68-69.
"In the Locker Room." [NowestR] (24:2) 86, p. 65-66.
"In the Whirlpool." [NowestR] (24:2) 86, p. 67.
"On the Freeway, Getting the Big Picture." [NowestR] (24:2) 86, p. 64.
1266. DeGENNARO, Lorraine S.
"Stony Point 1985 / 1779." [PoeticJ] (13) 86, p. 11.
1267. DeGRAVELLES, Charles
"The Accident." [SouthernR] (22:4) O 86, p. 770-771.
"Microwave and the New Mythology" (for Ed Lakin). [KanQ] (18:1/2) Wint-Spr 86,
p. 202-203.
"The Prophecy." [KanQ] (18:1/2) Wint-Spr 86, p. 203-204.
"The Sound of It." [SmPd] (23:2, issue 67) Spr 86, p. 9-10.
1268. DeGROOTE, Judith
"My Father's Garden." [YetASM] (5) 86, p. 5.
1269. DEGUY, Michel
"Gisants" (Selections, Three poems: "Convoy," "Tale," "Dialogues," tr. by
Nathaniel Tarn). [Conjunc] (9) 86, p. 24-26.
1270. DEKIN, Timothy
"At the Family Plot." [AmerS] (55:1) Wint 85-86, p. 96.
"Community Hospital." [AmerS] (55:1) Wint 85-86, p. 96.
"The Condolence." [TriQ] (67) Fall 86, p. 133.
"The Errand." [Thrpny] (26) Sum 86, p. 17.
Del CABRAL, Manuel
See CABRAL, Manuel del
Del MAR, María
See MAR, María del
Del ROSARIO MARQUEZ, Nieves
See MARQUEZ, Nieves del Rosario
Del VALLE, Máximo Gonzalez
See GONZALEZ DEL VALLE, Máximo

1271. DELANO, Page (Page D.)
"Address to a Friend about Writing." [LitR] (30:1) Fall 86, p. 58-59.
"Shucking Oysters, 1905." [AntR] (44:1) Wint 86, p. 74-76.
1272. DeLAURENTIS, Louise Budde
"Death Should Be Easy in This Kind of Climate." [Poem] (56) N 86, p. 11.
"Fit for Survival?" [KanQ] (18:1/2) Wint-Spr 86, p. 201.
1273. DELETANT, Andrea
"Absurd Chess" (tr. of Mircea Dinescu, w. Brenda Walker). [Translation] (16) Spr
86, p. 215.
"Cold Comfort" (tr. of Mircea Dinescu, w. Brenda Walker). [Translation] (16) Spr
86, p. 215.
"A Couple" (tr. of Mircea Dinescu, w. Brenda Walker). [Translation] (16) Spr 86, p.
214.
"How the Natives on the Reservation Lost the Right . . ." (tr. of Mircea Dinescu, w.
Brenda Walker). [Translation] (16) Spr 86, p. 216.
1274. DELFIS, Fivos
"A Bark at the Moon" (To my good friend Yu Suwa, tr. by Charles Guenther).
[Paint] (13:25/26) Spr-Aut 86, p. 36.
"A Bird Calls" (tr. by Charles Guenther). [Paint] (13:25/26) Spr-Aut 86, p. 41.
"Death of Adonis" (tr. by Charles Guenther). [Paint] (13:25/26) Spr-Aut 86, p. 38.
"Dog Barks at Moon" (tr. by Charles Guenther). [Paint] (13:25/26) Spr-Aut 86, p.
35.
"Flint" (tr. by Charles Guenther). [Paint] (13:25/26) Spr-Aut 86, p. 40.
"The Hours of Lyric Sighs" (tr. by Charles Guenther). [Paint] (13:25/26) Spr-Aut
86, p. 39.
"I Am the Same" (tr. by Charles Guenther). [Paint] (13:25/26) Spr-Aut 86, p. 37.
"The Wing of Springtime" (tr. by Charles Guenther). [Paint] (13:25/26) Spr-Aut 86,
p. 42.
1275. DELGADO, Juan
"Campesinos." [ConnPR] (5:1) 86, p. 21-22.
"The Slowness of Noon." [ConnPR] (5:1) 86, p. 23.
DELIZ, Wenceslao Serra
See SERRA DELIZ, Wenceslao
1276. DELP, Michael
"Bloodtrail" (for Jack Driscoll). [PoetryNW] (27:1) Spr 86, p. 44-45.
"Driving Home from the East Branch." [PassN] (7:1) Fall-Wint 85-86, p. 6.
"Fathers." [PassN] (7:1) Fall-Wint 85-86, p. 7.
"The Graves of Two Horses" (for Tom. First prize, 1986 Poetry Competition).
[PassN] (7:2) Spr-Sum 86, p. 3.
"Mothers." [SouthernPR] (26:1) Spr 86, p. 19-20.
"Poem for My Mother." [PassN] (7:1) Fall-Wint 85-86, p. 6.
"Ratman." [PoetryNW] (27:3) Aut 86, p. 12-13.
"Running the Corn" (the day after Reagan's re-election). [PassN] (7:1) Fall-Wint
85-86, p. 6.
"Shooting the Horse" (for Jim Tipton). [PassN] (7:1) Fall-Wint 85-86, p. 6.
1277. DEMPSEY, Ivy
"In the Open." [CharR] (12:2) Fall 86, p. 79.
"West from Amarillo." [CharR] (12:2) Fall 86, p. 79.
1278. DEMPSTER, Barry
"A Tropic of Bookshelves." [CanLit] (108) Spr 86, p. 65-66.
Den BERG, Arie van
See BERG, Arie van den
1279. DENBERG, Ken
"Tractors and Rhyme." [CharR] (12:2) Fall 86, p. 14.
1280. DenBOER, David C.
"Adolescence." [MSS] (5:1) 86, p. 112.
"Desire." [KanQ] (18:1/2) Wint-Spr 86, p. 98.
"Welcome." [KanQ] (18:1/2) Wint-Spr 86, p. 98.
1281. DENBY, Edwin
"At first sight, not Pollock." [GrandS] (5:2) Wint 86, p. 77.
"In a hotelroom a madman." [GrandS] (5:2) Wint 86, p. 77.
1282. DENDINGER, Lloyd
"R.E. — Literalist of the Imagination." [NegC] (6:2/3) Spr-Sum 86, p. 54-55.
1283. DeNIORD, Chard
"Swimming Lesson." [NegC] (6:4) Fall 86, p. 111.

107

1284. DENNIS, Carl
"Distance." [GeoR] (40:2) Sum 86, p. 408-409.
"An Entry in Mary's Diary." [NewRep] (194:7) 17 F 86, p. 36.
"Fairy Tales." [Poetry] (149:1) O 86, p. 22-23.
"Fenton Road." [PraS] (60:1) Spr 86, p. 55-56.
"The List." [GeoR] (40:3) Fall 86, p. 649.
"Taking Both Sides." [GeoR] (40:2) Sum 86, p. 409-410.
"The Task." [Poetry] (149:1) O 86, p. 21.
1285. DENNIS, Michael
"Portrait of the Artist 1985" (for the twister). [PraF] (7:2) Sum 86, p. 49.
"RCR, Royal Canadian Regiment, 1956." [PraF] (7:2) Sum 86, p. 48.
"Why I Wear the Socks I Do" (for jana). [CanLit] (109) Sum 86, p. 86.
1286. DEPPE, Theodore
"Altenbrücken." [BelPoJ] (36:4) Sum 86, p. 14.
"The Garden of St. Dymphna." [SouthernPR] (26:2) Fall 86, p. 18-20.
"Riding with the Prophet." [Wind] (16:58) 86, p. 10.
"Walking Fast." [Comm] (113:12) 20 Je 86, p. 373.
1287. DEPTA, Victor M.
"Who Said Nothing Lasts Forever." [LitR] (30:1) Fall 86, p. 68.
1288. Der HOVANESSIAN, Diana
"Bedouin Lament at the Gates . . ." (tr. of Muhammad Ubaid al-Harbi, w. Lena Jayyusi). [Translation] (17) Fall 86, p. 264-267.
"Kitchen Poem." [NegC] (6:4) Fall 86, p. 201.
"Portrait" (tr. of Andrei Voznesensky). [AmerPoR] (15:6) N-D 86, p. 23.
1289. DERGE, William
"After the Wedding." [BellR] (9:2) Fall 86, p. 29.
"Paring Nails." [BellR] (9:1) Spr 86, p. 34.
"The Real Ones." [BellR] (9:2) Fall 86, p. 30.
1290. DERRICK, Curtis
"Eugene Smith, Bluecollar Mute." [BelPoJ] (36:4) Sum 86, p. 6-7.
"The Palm Reading." [BelPoJ] (36:4) Sum 86, p. 6.
"Surrendering Arcady." [BelPoJ] (36:4) Sum 86, p. 7.
1291. DERRICK, Paul Scott
"Haiku" (4 poems, tr. of Jorge Luis Borges). [Verse] (3:3) N 86, p. 50.
1292. DERRICOTTE, Toi
"Fears of the Eighth Grade." [Callaloo] (9:1, #26) Wint 86, p. 29.
"For a Woman Who Lowered Her Head." [AmerV] (5) Wint 86, p. 22.
"Hamtramck: The Polish Women." [Callaloo] (9:1, #26) Wint 86, p. 30.
"Letter to Miss Glasser." [Callaloo] (9:1, #26) Wint 86, p. 28.
1293. DERRY, Alice
"Anguish of the Heart" (for Dawn Chin, a student from Korea). [Ploughs] (12:4) 86, p. 205-207.
"Hunger." [TarRP] (25:2) Spr 86, p. 31-32.
"Like Vine Maple Red in the Fir." [Ploughs] (12:4) 86, p. 200-201.
"Masques." [Ploughs] (12:4) 86, p. 204.
"We Drive toward Lewiston." [PraS] (60:3) Fall 86, p. 69-70.
"You Are My First Brother." [Ploughs] (12:4) 86, p. 202-203.
1294. DeRUGERIS, C. K.
"Prima Donna." [JamesWR] (4:1) Fall 86, p. 11.
1295. DESMOND, Walter
"Trees Like American Writers." [WindO] (47) Sum 86, p. 16.
1296. DESNOS, Robert
"XI. Night Suicide" (tr. by James Kates). [Vis] (22) 86, p. 8.
"XIII. Night Falls" (tr. by James Kates). [Vis] (22) 86, p. 7.
"At the End of the World" (tr. by J. Kates). [StoneC] (13:3/4) Spr-Sum 86, p. 45.
"Au Bout du Monde." [StoneC] (13:3/4) Spr-Sum 86, p. 44.
"Couplet du Verre du Vin." [StoneC] (13:3/4) Spr-Sum 86, p. 44.
"Demain." [StoneC] (13:3/4) Spr-Sum 86, p. 46.
"The Glass of Wine" (tr. by J. Kates). [StoneC] (13:3/4) Spr-Sum 86, p. 45.
"In the Time of Dungeons" (tr. by J. Kates). [RedBass] (11) 86, p. 29.
"Men on This Earth" (tr. by J. Kates). [RedBass] (11) 86, p. 6.
"Tomorrow" (tr. by J. Kates). [StoneC] (13:3/4) Spr-Sum 86, p. 47.
1297. DesRUISSEAUX, Pierre
"Entre tout corps." [Os] (23) 86, p. 7.
"L'immense éloignement des mots." [Os] (23) 86, p. 6.
"Un mot qui brusque matière." [Os] (23) 86, p. 6.

"Perte avant tout." [Os] (23) 86, p. 7.
1298. DESY, Peter
"At a Poetry Reading at Larry's Bar." [Poem] (56) N 86, p. 5.
"Family." [CrabCR] (3:3) Sum 86, p. 10.
"Father Cowboy." [CimR] (74) Ja 86, p. 48.
"Idiots." [Poem] (56) N 86, p. 6-7.
"In a Dark Cage" (Chapbook issue). [Sam] (43:4 release 172) 86, 16 p.
1299. DEUTSCH, Laynie Tzena
"Model/Actress Drowns Self, Page 15." [HeliconN] (14/15) Sum 86, p. 169.
1300. DeVALL, Sally
"Concealed." [PoeticJ] (15) Sum 86, p. 13.
"Survivors." [PoeticJ] (16) Fall 86, p. 34.
1301. DEVERELL, Ramsay
"The Ballad of Emotion." [Grain] (14:2) My 86, p. 14.
"The Ballad of Insane Love." [Grain] (14:2) My 86, p. 14.
"The Ballad of Riddle." [Grain] (14:2) My 86, p. 13.
"Ghazal with Cartoon and Caption." [Grain] (14:2) My 86, p. 13.
"A Note." [Grain] (14:2) My 86, p. 12.
"Tis your end coming where magic does loom." [Grain] (14:2) My 86, p. 12.
"War." [Grain] (14:2) My 86, p. 14.
"Writing." [Grain] (14:2) My 86, p. 12.
1302. DEVET, Rebecca McClanahan
"Ancient Weaving: The Mistress to the Wife." [CarolQ] (38:2) Wint 86, p. 7.
1303. DeVRIES, Peter Hugh (See also De VRIES, Peter)
"To Katie at Eighty." [AmerS] (55:4) Aut 86, p. 476.
1304. DeVRIES, Rachel (Rachel Guido)
"Burning the Bed." [Blueline] (7:2) Wint-Spr 86, p. 14.
"Scavenging Apples." [Cond] (13) 86, p. 92.
1305. DEWDNEY, Christopher
"The Lateshow Diorama." [GreenfR] (13:3/4) Sum-Fall 86, p. 44.
"Winter Central." [GreenfR] (13:3/4) Sum-Fall 86, p. 45.
1306. DHARWADKER, Vinay
"The Myth of the Good Prince" (Dara Shikoh, 1615-1659). [Hudson] (38:4) Wint
    86, p. 620-622.
DHOMHNAILL, Nuala NI
    See Ni DHOMHNAILL, Nuala
1307. DHURJATI
"For the Lord of the Animals" (Excerpt, tr. by Hank Heifetz and Velcheru Narayana
    Rao). [Translation] (16) Spr 86, p. 200-202.
Di . . .
    See also names beginning with "Di" without the following space, filed below in their
        alphabetic positions, e.g., DiFALCO
DI, Xin
    See XIN, Di
1308. Di LEO, Michael, Jr.
"In the bright sun" ("Untitled"). [Amelia] (3:4) Fall 86, p. 65.
1309. Di MICHELE, Mary
"My Hands in Purdah." [GreenfR] (13:3/4) Sum-Fall 86, p. 60.
1310. Di PIERO, W. S.
"The Adoration." [TriQ] (67) Fall 86, p. 72-73.
"The Apricot Trees." [TriQ] (67) Fall 86, p. 69-70.
"At the Well." [SouthernR] (22:1) Ja 86, p. 126-127.
"The Bugler." [TriQ] (67) Fall 86, p. 74.
"The Cellar Twenty Years Later." [TriQ] (67) Fall 86, p. 71.
"The Gemini." [TriQ] (67) Fall 86, p. 78.
"Ice Plant in Bloom." [SouthernR] (22:1) Ja 86, p. 130.
"Leopardi's 'Alla Luna'." [TriQ] (67) Fall 86, p. 75.
"Modo, Mahu." [SouthernR] (22:1) Ja 86, p. 128-129.
"The Reading." [TriQ] (67) Fall 86, p. 76-77.
"South." [SouthernR] (22:1) Ja 86, p. 127-128.
1311. DIAL, Stephen A.
"Delayed Stress Etiquette." [BellArk] (2:1) Ja-F 86, p. 4.
1312. DIAZ, Benito Luis
"Afuera la vida nos llama." [Mairena] (8:21) 86, p. 58-59.
1313. DIAZ-DIOCARETZ, Myriam
"El Arco, la Flecha, el Blanco." [LetFem] (12:1/2) Primavera-Otoño 86, p. 139-141.

1314. DICKENSON, Joan
"Girls Get Pregnant in the Hills." [Blueline] (8:1) Sum-Fall 86, p. 35-36.
1315. DICKEY, James
"Spring-Shock." [ParisR] (28:100) Sum-Fall 86, p. 66-67.
1316. DICKEY, William
"Windows." [GeoR] (40:3) Fall 86, p. 650.
1317. DICKINSON, Emily
"More life went out, when he went." [YaleR] (75:2) Wint 86, p. 224.
"Somehow myself survived the night." [YaleR] (75:2) Wint 86, p. 224.
1318. DICKSON, Charles B.
"Deer." [Amelia] (3:4) Fall 86, p. 31.
"Fingers." [PoeticJ] (15) Sum 86, p. 24.
"Magnet." [PoeticJ] (14) 86, p. 17.
"The Silent Summons." [PoeticJ] (16) Fall 86, p. 30.
"Two Haiku." [Amelia] (3:3) Sum 86, p. 55.
1319. DICKSON, John
"Finding the Wallet." [SpoonRQ] (11:4) Fall 86, p. 20.
"House Guest." [SpoonRQ] (11:4) Fall 86, p. 21.
"Hypothermia." [SpoonRQ] (11:4) Fall 86, p. 19.
"Reader and Adviser." [SpoonRQ] (11:2) Spr 86, p. 40.
1320. DICKSON, Lawrence Michael
"My Father Is Not Senile." [Amelia] (3:2) Spr 86, p. 106-107.
1321. DICKSON, Nick
"Cocoon" (to Lee and Norma Schweikert). [CarolQ] (39:1) Fall 86, p. 71.
1322. DICKSON, Ray Clark
"Juan Pico and the Acequia Madre." [BelPoJ] (37:1) Fall 86, p. 10.
"A Night with Borstal Boy." [BelPoJ] (37:1) Fall 86, p. 12.
"Poem for Doc Ernst's Abalone Recipe." [BelPoJ] (37:1) Fall 86, p. 11.
1323. DIDSBURY, Peter
"Cider Story." [Verse] (5) 86, p. 45.
1324. DiFALCO, Salvatore
"Caught in the Sky." [WestCR] (20:4) Ap 86, p. 44.
"Consorto in Mar." [Dandel] (13:1) Spr-Sum 86, p. 12-13.
"Evasion." [WestCR] (20:4) Ap 86, p. 43.
"It Was Not Raining." [Dandel] (13:1) Spr-Sum 86, p. 16-17.
"My Sister and Picassos." [Writ] (17) 85, c86, p. 13.
"Rite by Stream." [Writ] (17) 85, c86, p. 14-15.
"Sadly He Waved." [Dandel] (13:1) Spr-Sum 86, p. 14-15.
1325. DIGGES, Deborah
"First Fire of the Season." [NewYorker] (62:39) 17 N 86, p. 46.
"In Exile." [NewYorker] (61:52) 17 F 86, p. 30.
"Milk." [MissouriR] (9:2) 86, p. 9.
"Secrets." [NewYorker] (62:44) 22 D 86, p. 38.
"To the Angels." [NewYorker] (62:20) 7 Jl 86, p. 28.
"The Transmigration of Souls." [MissouriR] (9:2) 86, p. 10.
1326. DIGMAN, Steven M.
"Marriage." [Amelia] (3:4) Fall 86, p. 96.
1327. DILLARD, Annie
"Language for Everyone" (from *Language for Everyone* — Leonard Bloomfield,
1933). [SouthwR] (71:4) Aut 86, p. 488-492.
1328. DILLARD, Gavin
"Out in the desert." [ConnPR] (5:1) 86, p. 20.
1329. DILLARD, R. H. W.
"The Great Dream of Henri Rousseau." [DenQ] (20:4/21:1) Spr-Sum 86, p. 7-9.
1330. DILLON, Andrew
"In the Woods behind the Duke Chapel" (for William Stafford). [KanQ] (18:4) Fall
86, p. 72.
"Night after Long Practice." [InterPR] (12:2) Fall 86, p. 91.
"The Pelvis of the Shark." [Nimrod] (30:1) Fall-Wint 86, p. 114.
"Poland: May 1983" (for Grzegory Przemyk, 19). [ConnPR] (5:1) 86, p. 14.
"Shakespeare's Kings." [ArizQ] (42:1) Spr 86, p. 76.
"What We've Had Shot at Us." [InterPR] (12:2) Fall 86, p. 90.
1331. DILLON, Enoch
"Telling My Granddaughter about the Tillamook Burn." [SanFPJ] (8:2) 85, p.
14-16.
"The Wimp." [SanFPJ] (8:2) 85, p. 25.

1332. DiMAGGIO, Jill
"Annette — the Ninth Month." [PoeticJ] (15) Sum 86, p. 35.
"Love Poem." [YetASM] (5) 86, p. 7.
1333. DiMAINA, Susan
"The Perils of the High Wire." [EngJ] (75:7) N 86, p. 88.
1334. DINESCU, Mircea
"Absurd Chess" (tr. by Andrea Deletant and Brenda Walker). [Translation] (16) Spr 86, p. 215.
"Cold Comfort" (tr. by Andrea Deletant and Brenda Walker). [Translation] (16) Spr 86, p. 215.
"A Couple" (tr. by Andrea Deletant and Brenda Walker). [Translation] (16) Spr 86, p. 214.
"How the Natives on the Reservation Lost the Right . . ." (tr. by Andrea Deletant and Brenda Walker). [Translation] (16) Spr 86, p. 216.
DIOCARETZ, Myriam Diaz
See DIAZ-DIOCARETZ, Myriam
1335. DION, Marc
"South Dakota.." [Sam] (45:4 release 180) 86, p. 37.
"To Any Readers I Ever Have in Belgium." [Sam] (46:5 [i.e. 46:1] release 181) 86, p. 48.
1336. DIPALMA, Ray
"Eyeload and Mirrorstone." [Sink] (1) 86, p. 60.
"Poem: Resperation's grateful magnet." [Sink] (1) 86, p. 59.
"Rumours Film Island." [Sink] (1) 86, p. 59.
1337. DiPIETRO, Marylou
"Advent." [SouthernPR] (26:1) Spr 86, p. 18.
1338. DiSANTO, Grace
"The Color Red, Excess and Unshelled Peas" (for Archie Ammons). [Pembroke] (18) 86, p. 188-189.
"Paper Moons" (A.R. Ammons Art Show, Winston-Salem, NC June 1981). [Pembroke] (18) 86, p. 192.
1339. DISCH, Tom
"MCMLXXXIV." [ParisR] (28:100) Sum-Fall 86, p. 68-73.
"After Péguy." [Shen] (36:2) 86, p. 23.
"The Argument Resumed, or, Up Through Tribeca." [Poetry] (148:5) Ag 86, p. 255.
"Coming To." [Boulevard] (1:1/2) Wint 86, p. 106-108.
"The Dot on the i." [Poetry] (148:4) Jl 86, p. 198-199.
"Dueling Platitudes." [GrandS] (6:1) Aut 86, p. 100-101.
"Gilda: An Entr'acte." [Shen] (36:4) 86, p. 48.
"Happy Mediocrity: A Patriotic Sestina" (for Roman Hruska). [MinnR] (NS 26) Spr 86, p. 6-7.
"In Defense of Forest Lawn." [Poetry] (148:5) Ag 86, p. 253-254.
"Indian Spring." [Boulevard] (1:3) Fall 86, p. 36-37.
"Juliet, Voice Over" (for Sir Kenneth). [Boulevard] (1:3) Fall 86, p. 35.
"Lives of Great Men All Remind Us." [NewRep] (195:18) 3 N 86, p. 36.
"To the Young Mercenaries." [Poetry] (148:4) Jl 86, p. 202.
"The Viewers and the Viewed: Eurailpass Verses, 1985." [Poetry] (148:4) Jl 86, p. 200-201.
"Zsa-Zsa, In Defense of Her Pearls." [NewRep] (195:25) 22 D 86, p. 40.
1340. DISCHELL, Stuart
"Little Foot." [Ploughs] (12:3) 86, p. 105.
1341. DITCHOFF, Pamela
"Rally." [YetASM] (5) 86, p. 5.
1342. DITSKY, John
"Adultery." [Puerto] (21:2) Spr 86, p. 143.
"Cellars." [ThRiPo] (27/28) 86, p. 35.
"Feeding the Toads." [Chelsea] (45) 86, p. 84.
"The Floating World." [MalR] (77) D 86, p. 48.
"Hiatuses." [AntigR] (66/67) Sum-Aut 86, p. 82.
"In Touch." [Chelsea] (45) 86, p. 85.
"Landscape with Slowing Clock." [Confr] (33/34) Fall-Wint 86-87, p. 167.
"A Melancholy of Anatomy." [TexasR] (7:1/2) Spr-Sum 86, p. 83.
"Prismatics." [WritersF] (12) Fall 86, p. 204.
"Raking Poem." [MemphisSR] (7:1) Fall 86, p. 28.
"Regional Theatre." [MemphisSR] (7:1) Fall 86, p. 28.

111

DITSKY

"Season of Pentecost." [Confr] (32) Spr-Sum 86, p. 22.
"Tonight, for Instance." [Puerto] (21:2) Spr 86, p. 142.
1343. DITZANI, Rami
"A Brand Snatched from Anti-Tank Fire" (in . . . Ramban Hospital, Haifa, tr. by
Ruth Whitman). [PoetL] (81:2) Sum 86, p. 134-135.
1344. DIXON, Melvin
"The Alchemist's Dilemma." [Callaloo] (9:1, #26) Wint 86, p. 31-33.
"Place, Places." [Callaloo] (9:1, #26) Wint 86, p. 34.
1345. DJANIKIAN, Gregory
"Agami Beach" (Alexandria, 1955). [Iowa] (16:2) Spr-Sum 86, p. 117-119.
"Beethoven: Sonata No. 14" (for Roma). [Iowa] (16:2) Spr-Sum 86, p. 122-124.
"Clouds." [Poetry] (148:3) Je 86, p. 164-165.
"Gathering Hay" (Vermont, 1982). [Iowa] (16:2) Spr-Sum 86, p. 116-117.
"Grandmother's Rugs" (Alexandria, 1953). [Poetry] (148:3) Je 86, p. 165-166.
"Great-Grandfather's Nurse" (Alexandria, 1954). [Iowa] (16:2) Spr-Sum 86, p.
121-122.
"Mme. Sperides" (Alexandria, 1956, after the nationalization of the Suez Canal and
all foreign capital). [Iowa] (16:2) Spr-Sum 86, p. 119-120.
1346. DJERASSI, Carl
"Catalyst." [KenR] (NS 8:1) Wint 86, p. 93-94.
"The Clock Runs Backwards." [KenR] (NS 8:1) Wint 86, p. 91-93.
"The Next Birthday." [KenR] (NS 8:1) Wint 86, p. 94.
1347. DOAR, Harriet
"Oldfield." [SouthernPR] (26:1) Spr 86, p. 45-46.
1348. DOBLER, Patricia
"1066." [PoetryNW] (27:2) Sum 86, p. 41-42.
"Alternative Universe." [PoetryNW] (27:2) Sum 86, p. 42.
1349. DOBLER, Stephanie
"Photograph of a Minamata Disease Victim." [PennR] (2:1) Fall-Wint 86, p. 94.
1350. DOBYNS, Stephen
"Amazing Story." [Iowa] (16:1) Wint 86, p. 182-183.
"Boneyard." [Ploughs] (12:3) 86, p. 76.
"Bowlers' Anonymous." [Raccoon] (20) Ap 86, p. 8.
"Cemetery Nights II." [NewEngR] (8:4) Sum 86, p. 486.
"Cemetery Nights V." [Poetry] (147:5) F 86, p. 279-280.
"Charity." [NewL] (52:2/3) Wint-Spr 86, p. 102.
"Cheap Vase." [QW] (23) 86, p. 138.
"The Children." [Ploughs] (12:3) 86, p. 74.
"The Day the World Ends." [Ploughs] (12:3) 86, p. 75.
"Faces." [QW] (22) Spr-Sum 86, p. 24.
"Funeral." [QW] (22) Spr-Sum 86, p. 23.
"The Invitation." [Poetry] (147:5) F 86, p. 278-279.
"Leaving Winter." [SilverFR] (11) Sum 86, p. 45.
"Marsyas, Midas and the Barber." [AmerPoR] (15:6) N-D 86, p. 32.
"Natural Talent." [Raccoon] (20) Ap 86, p. 7.
"The Nihilist." [AmerPoR] (15:6) N-D 86, p. 30.
"On the Famous Painting by Rousseau." [NewEngR] (8:4) Sum 86, p. 482-483.
"Parachutes." [QW] (23) 86, p. 139-140.
"The Party." [IndR] (9:3) Sum 86, p. 71.
"Prime Mover." [NewEngR] (8:4) Sum 86, p. 484-485.
"Querencia." [Poetry] (147:5) F 86, p. 283-286.
"Selection Process." [Raccoon] (20) Ap 86, p. 5-6.
"Street Corner Romance" (For Karin Ash). [NewL] (52:2/3) Wint-Spr 86, p.
100-101.
"Theseus within the Labyrinth" (For Stratis Haviaras). [Poetry] (147:5) F 86, p.
281-283.
"To Pull into Oneself As into a Locked Room." [AmerPoR] (15:6) N-D 86, p. 30.
"Tomatoes." [AmerPoR] (15:1) Ja-F 86, p. 48.
"Warning." [IndR] (9:3) Sum 86, p. 72.
"White Pig." [AmerPoR] (15:6) N-D 86, p. 31.
"Wolves in the Street." [Verse] (3:3) N 86, p. 9.
1351. DODD, Bill
"The Two-Lane Chisholm Trail." [Puerto] (22:1) Fall 86, p. 45-47.
1352. DODD, Elizabeth
"Sometimes We Want to Sound the Alarm But Nothing Has Happened." [TarRP]
(25:2) Spr 86, p. 16-17.

1353. DODD, Wayne
"And What Shall We Gather to Us." [DenQ] (20:4/21:1) Spr-Sum 86, p. 149-152.
"Deer Tracks in March." [OntR] (24) Spr-Sum 86, p. 93-94.
"Glacier Trail: Rainbow Trout" (Erratum: Penultimate line should read "are is
     permanent"). [WestB] (18) 86, p. 22-23.
"Of Sitting Bear" (from *The General Mule Poems*). [GeoR] (40:3) Fall 86, p. 652.
"Sometimes Music Rises." [GeoR] (40:3) Fall 86, p. 651-651.
DOLEGA, Christine Lahey
     See LAHEY-DOLEGA, Christine
1354. DOLGORUKOV, Florence
"How the Ground Rises!" [InterPR] (12:2) Fall 86, p. 60.
"Old War Movie (Tora, Tora, Tora)." [BallSUF] (27:4) Aut 86, p. 69.
"River Scene." [InterPR] (12:2) Fall 86, p. 59.
"The Small Monkey Mountain." [BallSUF] (27:4) Aut 86, p. 14.
"The Stone People." [InterPR] (12:2) Fall 86, p. 61.
1355. DOLIN, Sharon
"Family Rites." [PennR] (1:1) 85, p. 71.
"Limbo, 1." [ManhatPR] (8) Wint 86-87, p. 49.
1356. DOLMATZ, Steven
"Pharoahs." [SouthernPR] (26:2) Fall 86, p. 49-50.
1357. DOMENECH, Sylvia
"A Mi Vientre." [Mairena] (8:22) 86, p. 106.
1358. DOMINA, Lynn
"A Basket of Eggs." [PoetryNW] (27:1) Spr 86, p. 17-18.
"Bats." [CimR] (74) Ja 86, p. 24.
1359. DOMINGUEZ, Pedro Juan
"De las Aguilas y el Mercurio." [Mairena] (8:22) 86, p. 77.
1360. DONAHUE, Joseph
"Lenny Bruce." [Acts] (5) 86, p. 99-100.
"Parrhesia." [Acts] (5) 86, p. 101.
1361. DONAHUE, Neal R.
"If There Were No Bombs." [SanFPJ] (8:2) 85, p. 18-19.
"SAC Bomber." [SanFPJ] (9:1) 86, p. 15.
"Tattoo." [SanFPJ] (8:2) 85, p. 41.
"There Is No Advocate for Down and Out." [SanFPJ] (9:1) 86, p. 14.
1362. DONALDSON, Dick
"Factory Disclaimer." [LakeSR] (20) 86, p. 40.
1363. DONALDSON, Jeffery
"Nearing the Gate of Horn." [PartR] (53:4) 86, p. 586-588.
"An Old Map of Somewhere." [GreenfR] (13:3/4) Sum-Fall 86, p. 62.
1364. DONLAN, John
"Steam Engineer (Retired)." [AntigR] (66/67) Sum-Aut 86, p. 107.
"Three Sonnets for Farmer Head." [Quarry] (35:4) Aut 86, p. 55-56.
DONNA, Bella
     See BELLA DONNA
1365. DONNELLY, Marilyn
"Visiting My Children." [Comm] (113:17) 10 O 86, p. 535.
1366. DONNELLY, Paul
"Soup." [Bogg] (55) 86, p. 41.
1367. DONNELLY, Susan
"The Garden Statues." [MassR] (27:1) Spr 86, p. 97-101.
1368. DONOSO, José
"Poem 2" (tr. by Mary Crow). [MidAR] (6:1) 86?, p. 75.
"Poema 2." [MidAR] (6:1) 86?, p. 74.
"Prelude" (tr. by Mary Crow). [MidAR] (6:1) 86?, p. 73.
"Preludio." [MidAR] (6:1) 86?, p. 72.
1369. DONOVAN, Laurence
"After Many Years." [SpiritSH] (52) 86, p. 9.
"The Arrival." [SpiritSH] (52) 86, p. 11-12.
"Late Night." [SpiritSH] (52) 86, p. 8-9.
"Talisman." [SpiritSH] (52) 86, p. 12-13.
"Two Young Poets at Night" (for Eugene Rosenblum). [SpiritSH] (52) 86, p.
     10-11.
"Winds." [SpiritSH] (52) 86, p. 8.
1370. DONOVAN, Loretta
"The Time of Faces." [Vis] (22) 86, p. 35.

1371. DONQAL, Amal
"Go Round" (tr. by Susan Brind). [SenR] (16:1) 86, p. 92.
"Roses" (tr. by Susan Brind). [SenR] (16:1) 86, p. 91.
1372. DOOLEY, David
"Journey." [MidwQ] (28:1) Aut 86, p. 78-79.
1373. DOR, Moshe
"Letters" (tr. by the author, Erella Hadar and Myra Sklarew). [PoetL] (81:2) Sum 86, p. 103.
"Responsibility" (tr. by the author, Erella Hadar and Myra Sklarew). [PoetL] (81:2) Sum 86, p. 104.
1374. DORAN, Heather
"Barnacle Dick." [BellArk] (2:1) Ja-F 86, p. 16.
1375. DORESKI, William
"Meteor Shower." [ColR] (NS 13:1) Fall 85, p. 52.
"A Neighbor's Goat Reminds Me of Socrates." [KanQ] (18:1/2) Wint-Spr 86, p. 281-282.
"Neither Victim Nor Muse." [ColR] (NS 13:1) Fall 85, p. 51.
"Old Pajamas, New Law." [PoetL] (81:1) Spr 86, p. 48.
"The Oswego Mills Burning." [KanQ] (18:1/2) Wint-Spr 86, p. 280.
"Starkboro." [ColR] (NS 13:1) Fall 85, p. 53-54.
"Thanksgiving, Growing Older." [GeoR] (40:3) Fall 86, p. 653-654.
"Thinking of Literary Friends." [StoneC] (13:3/4) Spr-Sum 86, p. 48-49.
1376. DORFMAN, Ariel
"Two Plus Two" (tr. by Kent Johnson). [RedBass] (11) 86, p. 6.
1377. DORION, Hélène
"Les Amorces de l'Emoi" (Excerpts). [Os] (23) 86, p. 8-9.
1378. DORMAN, Sonya
"Deep Sleep." [CrabCR] (3:2) Spr 86, p. 11.
"Geraniums." [ManhatPR] (6) Wint-Spr 85-86, p. 24.
"Walking to Work in Portland." [ManhatPR] (6) Wint-Spr 85-86, p. 25.
1379. DORN, Alfred
"Blue." [Hudson] (38:4) Wint 86, p. 628.
"Masks" (For Joseph Campbell). [Hudson] (38:4) Wint 86, p. 627-628.
D'ORS, Eugeni
See ORS, Eugeni d'
1380. DORSETT, Robert
"Another Dawn." [LitR] (29:3) Spr 86, p. 335.
"Dusk" (tr. of Wen Yi-duo). [SenR] (16:1) 86, p. 97.
"First Ice." [Poem] (56) N 86, p. 9.
"Her Little Elegy Ending with a Line by Nizami." [InterPR] (12:1) Spr 86, p. 91.
"In Tintoretto's Eve." [BallSUF] (27:4) Aut 86, p. 33.
"Last Day" (tr. of Wen Yi-duo). [SenR] (16:1) 86, p. 99.
"Mallarmé Dusk" (de l'éternel azur la sereine ironie). [BallSUF] (26:4) Aut 85, p. 9.
"Myth as a Persian Rug." [Poem] (56) N 86, p. 8.
"On the Massacre at Longhua" (tr. of Ai Qing). [SenR] (16:1) 86, p. 100.
"Ondine." [InterPR] (12:1) Spr 86, p. 92.
"Parable of the Poet and Time." [Interim] (5:2) Fall 86, p. 46.
"Quiet Night" (tr. of Wen Yi-duo). [SenR] (16:1) 86, p. 98.
"Two Landscapes That Include the Artist." [LitR] (29:3) Spr 86, p. 334.
"Willard's Coat, by Andrew Wyeth." [SouthwR] (71:3) Sum 86, p. 357.
1381. DORSETT, Thomas
"An Encounter." [InterPR] (12:2) Fall 86, p. 88.
"La Femme de Néant." [JINJPo] (9:1) 86, p. 10.
"The Insects." [InterPR] (12:2) Fall 86, p. 89.
1382. DOTY, Mark
"Hair." [PoetryNW] (27:3) Aut 86, p. 46-47.
1383. DOUBIAGO, Sharon
"Oedipus Drowned" (Selection: 7. "How Do I Love Thee? Let Me Count the Ways"). [Calyx] (10:1) Sum 86, p. 10-14.
"South America" (for Shawn). [Electrum] (38) Spr 86, p. 6-8.
"South America Mi Hija" (Selection: 1. "Descent: La Violencia"). [OP] (42/43) Wint 86-87, p. 132-135.
1384. DOUGHERTY, Jay
"Cheating." [YetASM] (5) 86, p. 10.
"Counselor Good As Any." [Bogg] (56) 86, p. 42.
"Koan Sense." [SmPd] (23:3, #68) Fall 86, p. 34.

"Working On." [Bogg] (55) 86, p. 10.
1385. DOUGLAS, Ann
"The Inheritance." [Ploughs] (12:4) 86, p. 58.
"Rousseau's Virgin Forest with Panther." [CutB] (25) Fall-Wint 86, p. 21.
"The Web." [PaintedB] (29) Ag 86, p. 63.
"Without Distinction." [BelPoJ] (36:4) Sum 86, p. 19.
1386. DOUGLAS, Charles
"Anima Poems" (for C.D.). [Writ] (17) 85, c86, p. 28-34.
"Butterfly." [Writ] (17) 85, c86, p. 33.
"Constant Thought." [Writ] (17) 85, c86, p. 34.
"Epithalamium with Two Pakcs of Wolves." [Writ] (17) 85, c86, p. 29.
"The Force of Transformation." [Writ] (17) 85, c86, p. 31.
"The Smile." [Writ] (17) 85, c86, p. 28.
"TTC (No. 1)." [Writ] (17) 85, c86, p. 30.
"TTC (No. 2)." [Writ] (17) 85, c86, p. 32.
1387. DOUGLASS, Karen
"Selective Perjury." [Atlantic] (257:3) Mr 86, p. 79.
1388. DOUSKEY, Franz
"Old Terror." [Abraxas] (34) 86, p. 11.
1389. DOVE, Rita
"After Storm." [HayF] (1) Spr 86, p. 84.
"Anniversary." [Callaloo] (9:1, #26) Wint 86, p. 46.
"Canary" (for Michael S. Harper). [TriQ] (67) Fall 86, p. 113.
"Company." [Callaloo] (9:1, #26) Wint 86, p. 50.
"Genie's Prayer Under the Kitchen Sink." [TriQ] (67) Fall 86, p. 114-115.
"Headdress." [Callaloo] (9:1, #26) Wint 86, p. 47.
"The House on Bishop Street." [Callaloo] (9:1, #26) Wint 86, p. 45.
"Lucille, Post-Operative Years." [GeoR] (40:4) Wint 86, p. 937.
"Motherhood." [Callaloo] (9:1, #26) Wint 86, p. 44.
"Nightmare." [Callaloo] (9:1, #26) Wint 86, p. 49.
"One Volume Missing." [Callaloo] (9:1, #26) Wint 86, p. 39.
"Parsley." [BlackALF] (20:3) Fall 86, p. 227-229.
"Parsley." [TriQ] (65) Wint 86, p. 63-64.
"Promises." [Callaloo] (9:1, #26) Wint 86, p. 43.
"Receiving the Stigmata." [GeoR] (40:3) Fall 86, p. 655.
"Recovery." [Callaloo] (9:1, #26) Wint 86, p. 48.
"Roast Possum." [Callaloo] (9:1, #26) Wint 86, p. 41-42.
"Straw Hat." [Callaloo] (9:1, #26) Wint 86, p. 37.
"This Life." [Callaloo] (9:1, #26) Wint 86, p. 63.
"Under the Viaduct, 1932." [Callaloo] (9:1, #26) Wint 86, p. 38.
"Variation on Gaining a Son." [Callaloo] (9:1, #26) Wint 86, p. 40.
"Your Death." [SenR] (16:2) 86, p. 64.
1390. DOWD, Nicholas
"Instinct." [Wind] (16:57) 86, p. 9-10.
"Outside Torrington Wyoming at 3am." [Wind] (16:57) 86, p. 9.
1391. DOWNES, Claire Van Breemen
"Hereditary Virtues." [LakeSR] (20) 86, p. 31.
"Mulberry Creek." [LakeSR] (20) 86, p. 32.
1392. DOWNES, G. V. (Gwladys)
"At the Terminal." [Event] (15:1) 86, p. 101.
"On the Driveway." [MalR] (73) Ja 86, p. 33.
"On the Sundeck." [MalR] (73) Ja 86, p. 32.
"Pastoral." [Event] (15:1) 86, p. 100.
"Poem as Iceberg." [Event] (15:1) 86, p. 99.
"Stone Garden with Wasp." [MalR] (73) Ja 86, p. 34.
"TV Interview." [MalR] (73) Ja 86, p. 31.
1393. DOWNIE, Glen
"The Art of Survival." [MalR] (73) Ja 86, p. 92.
"Immortality." [Event] (15:2) 86, p. 119.
"Skywriting." [Event] (15:2) 86, p. 118.
1394. DOWNSBROUGH, Julie
"Seascape." [WritersL] (1986:1), p. 27.
1395. DOXEY, W. S.
"Spring—At Last." [Amelia] (3:2) Spr 86, p. 9.
1396. DOYLE, Catherine S.
"Our Wandering Love." [WritersL] (1986:1), p. 15.

1397. DOYLE, James
  "The Altarboy." [BellR] (9:1) Spr 86, p. 61.
  "The Children." [BellR] (9:1) Spr 86, p. 60.
  "Civilized." [MidwQ] (28:1) Aut 86, p. 77.
  "Common to This Climate." [BellR] (9:1) Spr 86, p. 60.
  "For You." [BellR] (9:1) Spr 86, p. 61.
  "The Tool." [Paint] (13:25/26) Spr-Aut 86, p. 17.
  "The Trinkets." [Pembroke] (18) 86, p. 255-256.
1398. DOZIER, Brent
  "In the pejorative snow." [SanFPJ] (8:2) 85, p. 29.
  "Nov. the 9th." [SanFPJ] (8:2) 85, p. 72.
1399. DRAGU, Margaret
  "Hot about Beans." [Rampike] (5:1) 86, p. 44.
1400. DRAIME, Douglas
  "Worship." [SecC] (14:1) 86, p. 24.
1401. DRAKE, Jack
  "Two Children, 1985." [NegC] (6:4) Fall 86, p. 115.
1402. DREW, George
  "Fishing with Scudder Bates." [Blueline] (7:2) Wint-Spr 86, p. 30-31.
1403. DRISCOLL, Frances
  "Os." [NegC] (6:1) Wint 86, p. 40-41.
  "Talk to Me: Carol." [GWR] (6:2) 86, p. 13-15.
  "Vaginal Discharge" (for Carolyn Matsumoto, 1959-1984). [Ploughs] (12:4) 86, p. 48-49.
  "Why Plates Are Round." [Ploughs] (12:4) 86, p. 46-47.
  "Your Wickedness' Friend Grace Still Not Getting Any." [YellowS] (21) Wint 86, p. 19.
  "Your Wickedness' Sex Life." [YellowS] (21) Wint 86, p. 19.
1404. DRISCOLL, Jack
  "Farm Wedding." [PassN] (7:1) Fall-Wint 85-86, p. 13.
  "Leaving for Outer Space." [PennR] (2:1) Fall-Wint 86, p. 91.
  "Look Park: Florence, Massachusetts, 1958." [CutB] (25) Fall-Wint 86, p. 40.
  "Look Park: Florence, Massachusetts, 1958." [ThRiPo] (27/28) 86, p. 36.
  "Meeting Again at the Ballpark." [PassN] (7:1) Fall-Wint 85-86, p. 13.
  "My Brother's Shoulder Holster." [PennR] (1:2) Fall 85, p. 50.
  "Shooting Pool at Sledder's Inn." [TarRP] (26:1) Fall 86, p. 31.
1405. DRISCOLL, Mary
  "How It Goes On." [ManhatPR] (8) Wint 86-87, p. 50-51.
1406. DRISKELL, Leon V.
  "And Have Been All This While." [TarRP] (24:2) Spr 85, p. 11-12.
1407. DROPKIN, Celia
  "Adam" (tr. by Grace Schulman). [Translation] (17) Fall 86, p. 250.
  "The Circus Dancer" (tr. by Grace Schulman). [Translation] (17) Fall 86, p. 249.
  "The Filth of Your Suspicion" (tr. by Grace Schulman). [Translation] (17) Fall 86, p. 250.
1408. DRURY, John
  "The Refugee Camp." [OP] (42/43) Wint 86-87, p. 38-56.
  "Weeping Fig." [KanQ] (18:1/2) Wint-Spr 86, p. 243.
1409. DU, Fu
  "Autumn Song" (tr. by James F. Maybury). [Hudson] (38:4) Wint 86, p. 632.
  "House Cricket" (tr. by J. P. Seaton). [CarolQ] (39:1) Fall 86, p. 70.
  "Trawler's lantern" (ed. by H. F. Noyes, tr. by W. S. Merwin). [Amelia] (3:2) Spr 86, p. 47.
1410. DUBE, Jean
  "Position Politique de la Société de Conservation du Present . . ." (w. Philippe Coté & Alain Bergeron). [Rampike] (5:2) 86, p. 60.
1411. DUBIE, Norman
  "Groom Falconer." [AmerPoR] (15:2) Mr-Ap 86, p. 4.
  "Lamentations." [AmerPoR] (15:2) Mr-Ap 86, p. 3.
  "Sanctuary." [AmerPoR] (15:2) Mr-Ap 86, p. 4.
  "The Train." [HayF] (1) Spr 86, p. 79.
  "The Williamstown Gulf." [AmerPoR] (15:2) Mr-Ap 86, p. 3.
1412. DUBIELAK, C. A.
  "Walleye." [MidAR] (6:2) 86, p. 43-44.
1413. DUBNOV, Eugene
  "Autumn" (tr. by the author and Derek Mahon). [CentR] (30:4) Fall 86, p. 474.

"Bent Is the Grass" (tr. by C. Newman). [Confr] (32) Spr-Sum 86, p. 109.
"By Cramond Shore" (For R. Robertson). [PartR] (53:1) 86, p. 91-92.
"Canadian Lines" (For Rachel Eaves, tr. by the author and C. Newman). [CanLit]
    (110) Fall 86, p. 44.
"Outside Yet Another New Window" (In Russian and English, tr. by the author and
    Chris Newman). [BelPoJ] (37:2) Wint 86-87, p. 29.
"Over the Fields of Alsace" (tr. of Maksimilian Voloshin w. John Heath-Stubbs).
    [Event] (15:2) 86, p. 115.
"Partakers in the Blood" (tr. by the author and John Heath-Stubbs). [Interim] (5:2)
    Fall 86, p. 45.
"Snapshot" (tr. by the author and John Heath-Stubbs). [Confr] (32) Spr-Sum 86, p.
    107-108.
"The time has arrived for the light-pinioned burden of combat" (tr. by the author and
    John Heath-Stubbs). [Interim] (5:2) Fall 86, p. 44.
"Under the Reach of the Sky" (tr. by the author and C. Arkell). [AntigR] (65) Spr
    86, p. 34.
"The Way the Leaves Crackle" (for T. Graham, tr. by the author). [AntigR] (65) Spr
    86, p. 33.
1414. DuBOIS, Barbara R.
    "Vote with Your Feet." [EngJ] (75:3) Mr 86, p. 50.
1415. DUDEK, Louis
    "As May Flowers" (For Bernhard Beutler). [Germ] (10:1) Spr-Sum 86, p. 48.
    "To a Young Woman." [GreenfR] (13:3/4) Sum-Fall 86, p. 63.
1416. DUEMER, Joseph
    "Letter Home." [MidAR] (6:2) 86, p. 148-149.
    "Streambed." [MidAR] (6:2) 86, p. 146-147.
    "Supplication." [HolCrit] (23:4) O 86, p. 19.
1417. DUER, David
    "Paris Love." [SmPd] (23:1, #66) Wint 86, p. 19.
1418. DUESING, Laurie
    "Send Picture, You Said." [YellowS] (21) Wint 86, p. 42.
1419. DUGGAN, Laurie
    "South Coast Haiku." [Verse] (5) 86, p. 18.
1420. DUGGIN, Lorraine
    "Miracle at Stink Creek." [PraS] (60:2) Sum 86, p. 70-71.
1421. DUGUAY, Denise
    "A Room of My Own." [WritersL] (1986:4), p. 24.
1422. DUHAMEL, Denise
    "That Summer." [PraF] (7:3) Aut 86, p. 191.
1423. DUMBRAVEANU, Anghel
    "Landscape in White" (tr. by Adam J. Sorkin and Irina Grigorescu). [LitR] (30:1)
        Fall 86, p. 24.
    "The Sailor's Window" (tr. by Adam J. Sorkin and Irina Grigorescu). [LitR] (30:1)
        Fall 86, p. 25.
1424. DUNBAR, Mark
    "Circumstance." [Outbr] (16/17) Fall 85-Spr 86, p. 9.
1425. DUNCAN, Ginnie
    "Breakthrough." [PoeticJ] (15) Sum 86, p. 21.
1426. DUNCAN, Graham
    "Resting in a Private Cemetery in Vermont." [Wind] (16:57) 86, p. 11.
    "Tattoo." [WebR] (11:2) Fall 86, p. 63.
1427. DUNHAM, Vera
    "Autolithography" (tr. of Andrei Voznesensky, w. William Jay Smith). [AmerPoR]
        (15:6) N-D 86, p. 27.
1428. DUNLAP, Caroline
    "Burning Babies." [PassN] (7:2) Spr-Sum 86, p. 21.
1429. DUNN, Ethel
    "Garden Scene." [Kaleid] (13) Sum-Fall 86, p. 59.
1430. DUNN, Millard
    "But She's Not You." [KanQ] (18:3) Sum 86, p. 104.
    "Patio, November, First Snow." [Wind] (16:58) 86, p. 11.
    "Seeing Porpoises for the First Time." [KanQ] (18:3) Sum 86, p. 103.
1431. DUNN, Sharon
    "Back Then." [Confr] (33/34) Fall-Wint 86-87, p. 201.
1432. DUNN, Stephen
    "Aerial in the Pines." [Poetry] (147:5) F 86, p. 256.

117

"All That We Have" (to John Jay Osborn, Jr.). [Poetry] (147:5) F 86, p. 253-254.
"Aubade" (After Philip Dacey). [PaintedB] (28) Ap 86, p. 12.
"Because We Are Not Taken Seriously." [GeoR] (40:3) Fall 86, p. 657.
"The Department Store in the Mall." [PoetryNW] (27:2) Sum 86, p. 19-20.
"Enough Time" (for Lyn Harrison). [GeoR] (40:3) Fall 86, p. 656.
"Impediment." [MemphisSR] (7:1) Fall 86, p. 39.
"Just Fascinated." [PraS] (60:1) Spr 86, p. 25-26.
"Long Term." [PraS] (60:1) Spr 86, p. 27.
"Money for the Dead" (For Christine Martens). [PraS] (60:1) Spr 86, p. 24.
"On the Greyhound." [PraS] (60:1) Spr 86, p. 22-23.
"Sacred." [NewEngR] (9:2) Wint 86, p. 212.
"The Sensualist's Fast." [PaintedB] (28) Ap 86, p. 11.
"Sleeping with Ghosts." [Poetry] (147:5) F 86, p. 255.
"Waiting." [Nat] (242:15) 19 Ap 86, p. 559.
1433. DUNNE, Carol
"To the Mother in My Lenitive Dream." [SmPd] (23:2, issue 67) Spr 86, p. 32.
1434. DUNNING, Stephen
"Golden Rule, 3 Ways." [PennR] (1:1) 85, p. 28-29.
"Sister." [IndR] (9:2) Spr 86, p. 88-89.
1435. DUNPHY, Ron
"Sight." [Outbr] (16/17) Fall 85-Spr 86, p. 15-18.
1436. DUO, Duo
"Dead, Ten Dead" (tr. by Penelope Kwang). [Nimrod] (29:2) Spr-Sum 86, p. 56.
"In Northern Fields Lying Fallow Is a Plough Which Brings Me Pain" (tr. by
    Penelope Kwang). [Nimrod] (29:2) Spr-Sum 86, p. 61.
"Moment" (tr. by Penelope Kwang). [Nimrod] (29:2) Spr-Sum 86, p. 60.
"Northern Sea" (tr. by Penelope Kwang). [Nimrod] (29:2) Spr-Sum 86, p. 57-58.
"Wake Up" (tr. by Penelope Kwang). [Nimrod] (29:2) Spr-Sum 86, p. 58.
1437. DuPLESSIS, Rachel Blau
"Afterimage." [Temblor] (4) 86, p. 19-22.
1438. DUPRE, Delia
"Bench Warmers." [Abraxas] (34) 86, p. 29.
1439. DuPREE, Don Keck
"Bourbon and Firelight" (for Andrew Lytle: November 9, 1978). [SouthernR] (22:1)
    Ja 86, p. 155.
"Stanzas on a Recurring Theme." [SouthernR] (22:1) Ja 86, p. 156.
1440. DUPREY, Meryl
"Dirt World." [Event] (15:1) 86, p. 64.
1441. DUQUE, Aquilino
"Punto de Luz." [Mairena] (8:22) 86, p. 65.
1442. DURBIN, Libby A.
"Caught in the Act." [Calyx] (9:2/3) Wint 86, p. 116.
"Woman in Dialysis: Enroute to the Clinic." [Calyx] (9:2/3) Wint 86, p. 117.
1443. DURBIN, Roman
"Prison Poems and Drawings" (tr. of Irina Ratushinskaya, w. Reginald Gibbons).
    [TriQ] (66) Spr-Sum 86, p. 152-157.
1444. DURBIN, William
"Photographs." [Confr] (33/34) Fall-Wint 86-87, p. 212.
1445. DUTTON, Paul
"Alpha / Omega." [Rampike] (5:1) 86, p. 69.
1446. DUVAL, Quinton
"Mayflies." [CutB] (25) Fall-Wint 86, p. 15.
"Rare." [CutB] (25) Fall-Wint 86, p. 14.
DUYN, Mona van
    See Van DUYN, Mona
1447. DWORZAN, Hélène
"New York Summer." [ManhatR] (4:1) Fall 86, p. 52-56.
1448. DWYER, Cynthia Brown
"The Frogs of Chile." [NewL] (53:1) Fall 86, p. 75.
1449. DWYER, David
"Metaphysics." [VirQR] (62:4) Aut 86, p. 611-613.
1450. DYAK, Miriam
"I have finally learned that I don't like icecream." [YellowS] (21) Wint 86, p. 32.
"Lovers Who Don't" (for J and R). [YellowS] (21) Wint 86, p. 32.
"When I Say I Love You." [YellowS] (21) Wint 86, p. 32.

1451. DYBEK, Stuart
"Angelus." [Poetry] (149:3) D 86, p. 158.
"Autobiography." [Poetry] (149:3) D 86, p. 161-164.
"Benediction." [MissouriR] (9:1) 85-86, p. 188-189.
"Fingerprints." [Pequod] (22) 86, p. 126.
"Flies." [Pequod] (22) 86, p. 125.
"King Midas." [Pequod] (22) 86, p. 126-127.
"Merle." [Pequod] (22) 86, p. 127.
"Naked Maja." [Pequod] (22) 86, p. 125.
"Night Walk." [Poetry] (149:3) D 86, p. 160.
"Tomorrow." [Poetry] (149:3) D 86, p. 159.
1452. DYC, Gloria
"Before the Sweat a Grandmother Gives Advice." [SoDakR] (24:2) Sum 86, p. 20-21.
"Lament for the Waning Female Moons." [SoDakR] (24:2) Sum 86, p. 22.
"Picking Tea in Grass Mountain" (For David and Rita (Means) Halmi). [SingHM] (13) 86, p. 87.
1453. DYE, Bru
"Consequent Women." [SanFPJ] (8:3) 85, p. 95-96.
"Dynamite." [JamesWR] (4:1) Fall 86, p. 7.
1454. EADY, Cornelius
"Knowledge." [BellR] (9:2) Fall 86, p. 24.
"The Professor Tries to Inspire His Students." [BellR] (9:2) Fall 86, p. 25.
"U.S. Involvement in Latin America." [BellR] (9:2) Fall 86, p. 26.
"Victims of the Latest Dance Craze." [Harp] (273:1637) O 86, p. 31-33.
1455. EAGLETON, Terry
"The Ballad of English Literature." [Harp] (273:1636) S 86, p. 32.
1456. EARLY, Gerald
"Amagideon, or When Lee Andrews and the Hearts Sang Only for Me." [AmerPoR] (15:5) S-O 86, p. 53.
"Autobiographies of Ex-Colored Men, Part I" (for boxers Jack Johnson and Joe Louis). [AmerPoR] (15:5) S-O 86, p. 55.
"Consensus Vessels" (for Ida). [NegC] (6:4) Fall 86, p. 86-87.
"Four Songs at the End of Winter" (for Thelonious Monk). [AmerPoR] (15:5) S-O 86, p. 54.
"Lawrence Talbot: King of the B Movies" (for Lon Chaney, Jr.). [TarRP] (25:1) Fall 85, p. 25.
"Prizefighting and the Modern World." [AmerPoR] (15:5) S-O 86, p. 55.
"Soon, One Morning: The Last Stand of Andy Bowen." [AmerPoR] (15:5) S-O 86, p. 54.
"Tribute to the Art of the Chest" (for Jo Jones and Philly Joe Jones). [TarRP] (25:1) Fall 85, p. 24.
"With Ida at the Pacific Ocean." [AmerPoR] (15:5) S-O 86, p. 55.
1457. EASE, Lynda Lou
"To My First Lover. To Ruthie." [Cond] (13) 86, p. 117-121.
1458. EASON, Wayne
"Phenomenology" (for A.R. Ammons). [Pembroke] (18) 86, p. 139-140.
1459. EASTMAN, Bruce
"Ouija." [Thrpny] (24) Wint 86, p. 20.
"Stopping for Camels." [CharR] (12:1) Spr 86, p. 74-75.
1460. EASTMAN, Jon
"Boarding at Porta Nuova, Verona." [CharR] (12:1) Spr 86, p. 80.
"Delivering Papers on the Moon." [CharR] (12:1) Spr 86, p. 82.
"First Fountains." [CharR] (12:1) Spr 86, p. 81.
1461. EATON, Charles Edward
"Biography of a Still Life." [GeoR] (40:3) Fall 86, p. 658.
"Black Magic." [CharR] (12:1) Spr 86, p. 92.
"The Clamp." [ConnPR] (4:1) 85, p. 29-30.
"Dead End." [CharR] (12:1) Spr 86, p. 93.
"The Dream Book." [SouthernPR] (26:1) Spr 86, p. 61.
"The Factory." [DeKalbLAJ] (19:2) 86, p. 20.
"Latchstring." [DenQ] (20:4/21:1) Spr-Sum 86, p. 14-15.
"The Pump." [ConnPR] (5:1) 86, p. 40.
"Sack Race." [WebR] (11:1) Spr 86, p. 78.
"Snapback." [SouthernPR] (26:1) Spr 86, p. 62-63.
"The Speculum." [MemphisSR] (6:1/2) Spr 86, p. 24.

119

"Trade Winds." [Paint] (13:25/26) Spr-Aut 86, p. 18-19.
1462. EATON, Philip
"After a Thousand Children." [WillowS] (18) Sum 86, p. 14.
"This Dead of Winter." [WillowS] (18) Sum 86, p. 13.
"Winter Day." [WillowS] (18) Sum 86, p. 12.
1463. EBERHART, Richard
"Breathing." [Paint] (13:25/26) Spr-Aut 86, p. 5.
"Care and Love." [NegC] (6:2/3) Spr-Sum 86, p. 127.
"Deep Fishing." [KenR] (NS 8:2) Spr 86, p. 24-25.
"Growing Up: The Jungle, the Orchard, the River." [NegC] (6:2/3) Spr-Sum 86, p.
122-124.
"Hornets by the Sill." [MichQR] (25:3) Sum 86, p. 540.
"Just So Everybody Comes Up to Bat." [Paint] (13:25/26) Spr-Aut 86, p. 6.
"Laocoon." [NegC] (6:2/3) Spr-Sum 86, p. 118.
"Moment That Stays, But Passes." [NegC] (6:2/3) Spr-Sum 86, p. 119-120.
"Pursuit." [Interim] (5:2) Fall 86, p. 7.
"Summer Incident." [NegC] (6:2/3) Spr-Sum 86, p. 125-126.
"That Final Meeting." [NegC] (6:2/3) Spr-Sum 86, p. 128.
"Vignette: Achievement, Ninth Symphony" (For Philip Booth). [NegC] (6:2/3)
Spr-Sum 86, p. 121.
1464. EBERLY, David
"Late Letter to William Carlos Williams." [JamesWR] (3:3) Spr 86, p. 4.
1465. ECHEVERRI MEJIA, Oscar
"El Mar en Cartagena." [Mairena] (8:22) 86, p. 41.
1466. ECKEL, Martha Charlier
"The spider." [Amelia] (3:3) Sum 86, p. 9.
EDDY, Darlene Mathis
See MATHIS-EDDY, Darlene
1467. EDDY, Gary
"Desire." [GeoR] (40:3) Fall 86, p. 659.
1468. EDDY, James
"The Name of Loneliness Is a Dingy Bar" (La soledat té nom de bar ombrívol, tr. of
Ponç Pons). [SenR] (16:1) 86, p. 49.
"Remembered Roses" (Roses recordades, tr. of Salvador Espriu). [SenR] (16:1) 86,
p. 30.
"Thanatos" (tr. of Salvador Espriu). [SenR] (16:1) 86, p. 31.
1469. EDDY, Lynn R.
"Mellowing." [DeKalbLAJ] (19:3/4) 86, p. 71.
1470. EDELMAN, David
"Cliff-Climbing at the Stuckomish." [Raccoon] (20) Ap 86, p. 18.
"Sheep." [Raccoon] (20) Ap 86, p. 16-17.
"Staying Home." [Raccoon] (20) Ap 86, p. 19-20.
1471. EDELMAN, Elaine
"Song of Myselves." [CapeR] (21:1) Spr 86, p. 29.
1472. EDELSON, Shereen F.
"Special Delivery." [YetASM] (5) 86, p. 2.
1473. EDELSTEIN, Wendy
"Mohini." [Pax] (3:1/2) Wint 85-86, p. 175.
1474. EDKINS, Anthony
"Astronomy." [SpiritSH] (52) 86, p. 45.
"Craftsman." [WestCR] (20:4) Ap 86, p. 45.
"Hamlet in the Market-Place" (tr. of Santiago E. Sylvester). [WebR] (11:1) Spr 86,
p. 29.
"On Assignment." [WestCR] (20:4) Ap 86, p. 47.
"Post Mortem." [SpiritSH] (52) 86, p. 45.
"Ringmaster." [WestCR] (20:4) Ap 86, p. 46.
1475. EDMANDS, Trevor
"The Painting Without a Title." [TriQ] (66) Spr-Sum 86, p. 39-40.
"The Safe." [TriQ] (66) Spr-Sum 86, p. 42-43.
"The Salon." [TriQ] (66) Spr-Sum 86, p. 40.
1476. EDMOND, Lauris
"Exodus." [Verse] (3:3) N 86, p. 8.
"Orthopaedic Ward." [Stand] (27:3) Sum 86, p. 27.
"Tempo." [Verse] (3:3) N 86, p. 7-8.
1477. EDMUNDS, Susan H.
"Mother." [Wind] (16:58) 86, p. 12.

1478. EDMUNDSON, Gary
      "Classics." [Pax] (3:1/2) Wint 85-86, p. 30.
EDOM, Obed
      See OBED-EDOM
1479. EDSON, Russell
      "The Breast." [Ploughs] (12:3) 86, p. 65.
      "My Head" (Excerpt). [IndR] (9:2) Spr 86, p. 7.
      "The Theory." [Ploughs] (12:3) 86, p. 63-64.
      "The Tree." [Ploughs] (12:3) 86, p. 65.
1480. EDWARDS, Dennis
      "Hear." [RagMag] (5:2) Fall 86, p. 10.
      "Medicine Woman." [RagMag] (5:2) Fall 86, p. 10.
EDWARDS, Lucille King
      See KING-EDWARDS, Lucille
1481. EDWARDS, Martin
      "Children of Albion" (For Michael Horovitz). [Bogg] (55) 86, p. 41.
1482. EDWARDS, Nancy
      "Tiger Eye." [Amelia] (3:2) Spr 86, p. 83.
1483. EDWARDS, Robert
      "Departure." [InterPR] (12:1) Spr 86, p. 104.
      "The Driver." [InterPR] (12:1) Spr 86, p. 106.
      "Litany from Oregon" (for Ed Edmo). [InterPR] (12:1) Spr 86, p. 103.
      "Professor Higgins at Fifty-Five" (for Pat McManus). [InterPR] (12:1) Spr 86, p.
            105.
      "A Written Divorce." [InterPR] (12:1) Spr 86, p. 102.
1484. EDWARDS, Sd
      "Thinking of Mum." [Event] (15:2) 86, p. 114.
1485. EDWARDS, Stephanie
      "A Lesser Death." [RagMag] (5:2) Fall 86, p. 11.
1486. EDWARDS, Thomas
      "In the Blue Signature of the Ice Bird" (Poems in German & English, tr. of Reiner
            Kunze, w. Ulrike Aitenbichler and Ken Letko). [MidAR] (7:1) 86, p. 73-101.
      "Nowhere Is Near So Far" (Poems in German & English, tr. of Ulrich Schacht, w.
            Ulrike Aitenbichler and Ken Letko). [MidAR] (6:2) 86, p. 49-86.
1487. EFRAT, Israel
      "In a Public Restaurant" (tr. by Bernhard Frank). [ColR] (NS 13:1) Fall 85, p. 44.
1488. EGERMEIER, Virginia
      "Memorial Service." [CrossCur] (5:4/6:1) 86, p. 108.
      "On the Olympic Peninsula" (for Ruth McFarland). [CrossCur] (5:4/6:1) 86, p. 107.
1489. EHRHART, W. D.
      "Apples" (for Tran Kinh Chi, Hanoi, 16 December 1985). [Sam] (45:4 release 180)
            86, p. 33.
      "Coming Home." [Sam] (46:2 release 182) 86, p. 99.
      "For Mrs. Na" (Cu Chi District, 28 December 1985). [Sam] (46:5 [i.e. 46:1] release
            181) 86, p. 33.
      "The Next Step." [Sam] (46:2 release 182) 86, p. 55.
      "One Night on Guard Duty." [Sam] (46:2 release 182) 86, p. 34.
      "POW/MIA." [ConnPR] (5:1) 86, p. 16-18.
      "Rules of the Club." [SanFPJ] (8:1) 85, p. 20.
1490. EHRLICH, Shelley
      "Bird Watching." [DenQ] (20:4/21:1) Spr-Sum 86, p. 88.
      "Crowding in to Hear the Doctor." [DenQ] (20:4/21:1) Spr-Sum 86, p. 86-87.
      "Early Losses." [QW] (22) Spr-Sum 86, p. 9.
      "February Love" (for a 33rd anniversary). [Northeast] (series 4:4) Wint 86-87, p.
            11-13.
1491. EHRMAN, Sally
      "Highway Department." [YetASM] (5) 86, p. 6.
1492. EIGNER, Larry
      "Birds." [Sink] (1) 86, p. 30-32.
1493. EIGO, J.
      "Diviner" (Excerpt). [Sink] (2) 86, p. 16-18.
1494. EILENBERG, Mara
      "Calm for Breakfast." [Bogg] (56) 86, p. 54.
1495. EIMERS, Nancy
      "The End of the Season." [Sonora] (11) Fall 86 [c87], p. 77.

121

1496. EINBOND, Bernard Lionel
"Images This Night." [Bogg] (56) 86, p. 23.
1497. EINZIG, Barbara
"Life Moves Outside." [Temblor] (3) 86, p. 98-104.
"Reentry." [Pequod] (22) 86, p. 61.
1498. EISENBERG, Ruth F.
"My Grandson Reaches." [PoeticJ] (14) 86, p. 30.
"Sitters." [PoeticJ] (15) Sum 86, p. 28.
"That." [PoeticJ] (14) 86, p. 35.
1499. EISIMINGER, Skip
"A Father Reads His Son's First College Composition" (for Shane). [BallSUF]
(27:4) Aut 86, p. 53.
"Going to the Wall: At the Viet Nam Veterans Memorial." [BallSUF] (26:4) Aut 85,
p. 25.
"Steady Cries from the North Woods" (for Edvard Munch). [BallSUF] (26:4) Aut
85, p. 19.
1500. EKLUND, George
"Kissing Each Other's Crimes" (Selections: 8, 12, 14, 21, 22, 25, 33). [PoetC]
(18:1) 86, p. 3-9.
1501. ELDER, Karl
"Titicut Follies." [PikeF] (7) Spr 86, p. 3.
1502. ELIAS, Karen
"Two Poems for My Son." [Cond] (13) 86, p. 122-123.
1503. ELIAS, Megan
"The foolish animal." [HangL] (49) Spr 86, p. 56.
"Full round bowls of flowers." [HangL] (49) Spr 86, p. 55.
1504. ELIASON, Ginny
"The Speech of the World." [NewEngR] (9:2) Wint 86, p. 211.
1505. ELIOT, Katie
"Avowal." [BellArk] (2:6) N-D 86, p. 1.
"Four Songs for the Impermanent" (w. Blair Rossner). [BellArk] (2:6) N-D 86, p.
3.
ELK, Black
See BLACK ELK
1506. ELKIND, Sue Saniel
"As Related to Me by a Wife After Her Husband Had Shock Therapy." [SanFPJ]
(9:1) 86, p. 10.
"Ashes in the Adirondack Mountains." [CrossCur] (6:2) 86, p. 88.
"Come to Me." [DeKalbLAJ] (19:3/4) 86, p. 72.
"Hoping for a Thaw." [CentR] (30:1) Wint 86, p. 57.
"HUD-Section 231/8: Federal Housing for the Elderly." [SanFPJ] (8:1) 85, p. 87.
"In My Dream." [SanFPJ] (9:1) 86, p. 11.
"Man's Descent." [SanFPJ] (9:1) 86, p. 12.
"Mistake." [NegC] (6:4) Fall 86, p. 116.
"Pittsburgh." [SanFPJ] (8:1) 85, p. 86.
"Sisters." [Calyx] (9:2/3) Wint 86, p. 121.
"Snow Storm." [CrossCur] (6:2) 86, p. 87.
"The Story." [SanFPJ] (8:1) 85, p. 88.
"Tribute." [SanFPJ] (9:1) 86, p. 50.
"Two Little Girls." [SanFPJ] (8:1) 85, p. 85.
"White / Red / Black." [SanFPJ] (9:1) 86, p. 9.
"A Whore." [SlipS] (6) 86, p. 18.
1507. ELLEDGE, Jim
"Paul Blackburn, Again." [SpoonRQ] (11:4) Fall 86, p. 25.
1508. ELLEN
"Dance." [Wind] (16:58) 86, p. 13.
ELLEN, Patricia Ver
See VerELLEN, Patricia
1509. ELLENBOGEN, Miriam
"I. Father." [Electrum] (38) Spr 86, p. 30.
"II. Lover." [Electrum] (38) Spr 86, p. 30.
1510. ELLENTUCK, Rebeca
"October Night." [LindLM] (5:4) O-D 86, p. 19.
"Precious." [LindLM] (5:4) O-D 86, p. 19.
"Sofian." [LindLM] (5:4) O-D 86, p. 19.
"William Waking." [LindLM] (5:4) O-D 86, p. 19.

1511. ELLINGSON, Alice
"Bird Talk." [Vis] (22) 86, p. 34.
1512. ELLIOT, Priscilla
"Vivid Spring: 1 A.M." [Bogg] (55) 86, p. 53.
1513. ELLIOTT, Andrew
"A Visit." [BostonR] (11:4) Ag 86, p. 4.
1514. ELLIOTT, Gail S.
"Time Warp." [ChrC] (103:23) 30 Jl-6 Ag 86, p. 681.
"Twilight Ride." [ChrC] (103:15) 30 Ap 86, p. 435.
1515. ELLIOTT, Harley
"White Boys in Control." [Raccoon] (20) Ap 86, p. 15.
1516. ELLIOTT, Roselyn
"Autumn." [Blueline] (8:1) Sum-Fall 86, p. 45.
1517. ELLIOTT, William D.
"First Shell." [Abraxas] (34) 86, p. 53.
1518. ELLIS, Mayne
"Prognosis improving." [Cond] (13) 86, p. 129.
1519. ELLIS, Millen
"Dickinson and Faulkner — A Short Study in Literary Parallels." [EngJ] (75:3) Mr
86, p. 37.
1520. ELLISON, Jesse T.
"Canaletto - 49 Plates in Full Color." [WindO] (47) Sum 86, p. 42.
"Tina." [WindO] (47) Sum 86, p. 42.
1521. ELLISON, Julie
"Connecticut Valley Flood." [SouthwR] (71:4) Aut 86, p. 473.
1522. ELON, Florence
"Underworld." [SouthernPR] (26:2) Fall 86, p. 16-17.
1523. ELSBERG, John
"Candles: A Rhyme." [Amelia] (3:4) Fall 86, p. 87.
"Exiles." [Wind] (16:56) 86, p. 13.
1524. ELYTIS, Odysseas
"Anoint the Ariston" (Selections: VIII-X, tr. by Olga Broumas). [AmerV] (5) Wint
86, p. 11-12.
"Famous Night" (tr. by Olga Broumas). [AmerPoR] (15:5) S-O 86, p. 19.
"The Monogram" (Selections: III, IV, tr. by Olga Broumas). [AmerPoR] (15:5) S-O
86, p. 18.
1525. EMANS, Elaine V.
"Bonus." [BallSUF] (27:4) Aut 86, p. 5.
"Choosing a Water Color." [BallSUF] (26:4) Aut 85, p. 10.
"I Remember." [DeKalbLAJ] (19:2) 86, p. 21.
"On a Clear Night." [BallSUF] (26:4) Aut 85, p. 65.
"Pelican." [BallSUF] (27:4) Aut 86, p. 50.
1526. EMANUEL, Lynn
"Getting Born." [NewEngR] (9:1) Aut 86, p. 25.
"Imagining Rio at Sixteen." [NewEngR] (9:1) Aut 86, p. 24.
"The Technology of Inspiration." [NewEngR] (9:1) Aut 86, p. 26.
"The Technology of Love." [AmerPoR] (15:5) S-O 86, p. 17.
"The Technology of Spring." [AmerPoR] (15:5) S-O 86, p. 17.
"You Tell Me." [GeoR] (40:3) Fall 86, p. 660.
1527. EMERSON, Helen
"Forgive Me, Grandma." [BallSUF] (26:4) Aut 85, p. 28-29.
1528. EMERY, Michael J.
"Science Fiction Convention." [JamesWR] (3:4) Sum 86, p. 4.
1529. EMERY, Thomas
"California Indians." [Ploughs] (12:4) 86, p. 153-154.
1530. EMIN, Gevorg
"At the Barber's" (tr. by Martin Robbins). [WebR] (11:1) Spr 86, p. 62-64.
"Come On, Tonight Let's Have Fun" (tr. by Martin Robbins). [WebR] (11:1) Spr
86, p. 64.
"The Firefly" (tr. by Martin Robbins). [InterPR] (12:1) Spr 86, p. 68.
"Say 'Good Morning' to the Old Ones" (tr. by Martin Robbins). [WebR] (11:1) Spr
86, p. 65.
"Twentieth Century" (tr. by Martin Robbins). [WebR] (11:1) Spr 86, p. 59-61.
"Winter Scene" (tr. by Martin Robbins). [InterPR] (12:1) Spr 86, p. 67.
"Your Hands" (tr. by Martin Robbins). [InterPR] (12:1) Spr 86, p. 66.

123

1531. EMMET, Peter
"I Place Each Word." [Stand] (27:3) Sum 86, p. 41.
"The Toad." [Stand] (27:3) Sum 86, p. 41.
1532. EMMONDS, David
"War in an Urban Setting (Stalingrad)." [Event] (15:2) 86, p. 31-33.
1533. EMMONS, Gary
"Henry James" (tr. of Juan Gustavo Cobo Borda). [Pequod] (22) 86, p. 122.
"My Family Toyed with a Borrowed Violin" (tr. of Juan Manuel Roca). [Pequod] (22) 86, p. 62.
1534. ENCARNACION, Alred
"Reading at Sedenger's Bookstore, Of [sic] in Huntingdon Valley." [Wind] (16:56) 86, p. 12.
1535. ENDERS, Alvin C.
"Consume Comes to the Self's Room." [PoeticJ] (15) Sum 86, p. 5.
1536. ENDREZZE-DANIELSON, Anita
"Fox-Woman Goes Man-Hunting." [WillowS] (18) Sum 86, p. 80-82.
1537. ENGEBRETSEN, Alan C.
"The Grammar of Tomorrow." [Amelia] (3:2) Spr 86, p. 109.
"Those Who Remember." [SanFPJ] (8:1) 85, p. 44.
"Truth to Tell." [SanFPJ] (8:1) 85, p. 44.
1538. ENGEL, Mary
"The Photograph." [SanFPJ] (8:1) 85, p. 21.
1539. ENGELS, John
"The Harbor." [GeoR] (40:3) Fall 86, p. 661.
"Patterns of Sleep." [NewEngR] (8:4) Sum 86, p. 445-446.
"The Silence." [NewEngR] (8:4) Sum 86, p. 444.
"Snowy Owl." [NewEngR] (8:4) Sum 86, p. 447.
1540. ENGLE, Paul
"Door." [Iowa] (16:1) Wint 86, p. 132-133.
1541. ENGLER, Robert Klein
"Costumes" (for the Sawyers). [BallSUF] (27:4) Aut 86, p. 23-25.
"Out from Winter Half Singing." [Wind] (16:58) 86, p. 14-15.
"The Perfect Flower of Human Time." [SoDakR] (24:2) Sum 86, p. 60-61.
1542. ENLOE, Glen
"Catfish." [Wind] (16:58) 86, p. 16.
1543. ENSLER, Eve
"Ireland: Surviving." [CentralP] (9) Spr 86, p. 86.
1544. ENSLIN, Theodore
"Motet." [Conjunc] (9) 86, p. 205-208.
1545. ENTREKIN, Charles
"Yes." [NowestR] (24:1) 86, p. 29.
1546. EPSTEIN, Daniel Mark
"Cygnus Musicus." [AmerS] (55:4) Aut 86, p. 520.
"Gifts." [PraS] (60:3) Fall 86, p. 64.
"Lateness." [VirQR] (62:1) Wint 86, p. 47-48.
"Silence." [PraS] (60:3) Fall 86, p. 63.
1547. EPSTEIN, Henrietta
"From the Shore: Toronto." [PassN] (7:1) Fall-Wint 85-86, p. 20.
1548. EPSTEIN, Richard
"And So to Bed." [BallSUF] (26:4) Aut 85, p. 50.
"A Short Course in Theology." [BallSUF] (27:4) Aut 86, p. 19.
1549. EQUI, Elaine
"A Bouquet of Objects." [AmerV] (2) Spr 86, p. 85.
1550. ERBES, Cynthia K.
"Hearing Impaired." [Kaleid] (12) Wint 86, p. 51.
"I hold the funnel changing colors" ("Untitled"). [Kaleid] (12) Wint 86, p. 51.
"My Mother's Illness." [Kaleid] (12) Wint 86, p. 50.
1551. ERICKSON, Elizabeth
"Moons." [SingHM] (14) 86, p. xi.
1552. ERICKSON, Lorene
"Common Cabbage." [PassN] (7:2) Spr-Sum 86, p. 22.
1553. ERNST, Myron
"Lagoon-Laguna." [SmPd] (23:3, #68) Fall 86, p. 35.
"On Going Nowhere on a Bicycle into the Endless Mountains of Pennsylvania." [SmPd] (23:2, issue 67) Spr 86, p. 33-34.
"Truck Watching." [SmPd] (23:3, #68) Fall 86, p. 36.

1554. ESHE, Aisha
"Lookin' for His Wife He Kills Himself." [Obs] (NS 1:1/2) Spr-Sum 86, p. 74-75.
"Suicide Abated." [SingHM] (14) 86, p. 18.
"Sunset." [SingHM] (14) 86, p. 18.
1555. ESHE-CARMEN, Aisha
"She Came to Life." [Amelia] (3:4) Fall 86, p. 109.
"Therapy." [HeliconN] (14/15) Sum 86, p. 143.
1556. ESHLEMAN, Clayton
"Anxiety of Signs" (tr. of Juan Larrea, w. José Rubia Barcia). [Sulfur] (6:1, issue 16) 86, p. 123.
"Apotheosis." [Caliban] (1) 86, p. 121.
"The Bill." [Sulfur] (6:2, issue 17) 86, p. 56-61.
"Galactite" (In memory of Ana Mendieta). [RiverS] (20) 86, p. 36-37.
"A Night with Hamlet" (Excerpt, tr. of Vladimir Holan, w. Frantisek Galan). [Sulfur] (6:1, issue 16) 86, p. 130-137.
"On Vacation Like a Stone" (tr. of Juan Larrea, w. José Rubia Barcia). [Sulfur] (6:1, issue 16) 86, p. 122-123.
"Our Journey around the Drowned City of Is" (Excerpt). [AnotherCM] (16) 86, p. 10-12, 14.
"Postcards from Carnac." [AnotherCM] (16) 86, p. 13.
"Risk Attraction" (tr. of Juan Larrea, w. José Rubia Barcia). [Sulfur] (6:1, issue 16) 86, p. 122.
"Thorns in the Snow" (tr, of Juan Larrea, w. José Rubia Barcia). [Sulfur] (6:1, issue 16) 86, p. 121-122.
1557. ESPADA, Martin
"Grito for Nicaragua" (para Mauricio y barrio Rene Cisneros, Managua). [HangL] (49) Spr 86, p. 12.
"Operation Bootstrap: San Juan, 1985." [HangL] (49) Spr 86, p. 12.
1558. ESPAILLAT, Rhina P.
"In Praise of Boxes." [Amelia] (3:3) Sum 86, p. 75.
"Museum Exhibit: The Siege of Hasanlu, Ninth Century B.C." [ManhatPR] (6) Wint-Spr 85-86, p. 64.
"Possession." [Amelia] (3:3) Sum 86, p. 29.
"A Sestina Made to Order." [Amelia] (3:3) Sum 86, p. 74-75.
"Willows Leaning." [Amelia] (3:4) Fall 86, p. 14.
1559. ESPINO, Alfredo Ernesto
"And Then" (tr. by Mark Smith-Soto). [InterPR] (12:2) Fall 86, p. 17.
"De Alguien Que No Soy Yo." [InterPR] (12:2) Fall 86, p. 18.
"Nadie Se Ahoga Eva." [InterPR] (12:2) Fall 86, p. 14.
"Noboby Drowns Eve" (tr. by Mark Smith-Soto). [InterPR] (12:2) Fall 86, p. 15.
"Of Someone Who Is Not I" (tr. by Mark Smith-Soto). [InterPR] (12:2) Fall 86, p. 19.
"Toulouse Lautrec." [InterPR] (12:2) Fall 86, p. 12.
"Toulouse Lautrec" (tr. by Mark Smith-Soto). [InterPR] (12:2) Fall 86, p. 13.
"Tu Ropa." [InterPR] (12:2) Fall 86, p. 10.
"Y Luego." [InterPR] (12:2) Fall 86, p. 16.
"Your Clothing" (tr. by Mark Smith-Soto). [InterPR] (12:2) Fall 86, p. 11.
1560. ESPINOLA, Lourdes
"Sor Juana, Mujer." [LetFem] (10:2) Fall 84 [c1985], p. 90.
1561. ESPINOZA, Xiomara
"Juan Erre" (tr. by Kent Johnson). [NowestR] (24:1) 86, p. 113.
1562. ESPOSITO, Nancy
"Camping across the Border." [Nat] (242:25) 28 Je 86, p. 898.
1563. ESPRIU, Salvador
"After the Trees" (tr. by Cyrus Cassells). [Translation] (16) Spr 86, p. 82.
"Autumn" (tr. by Cyrus Cassells). [Translation] (16) Spr 86, p. 84.
"Beginning of the Temple Hymn" (Inici de càntic en el temple, tr. by Cyrus Cassells). [SenR] (16:1) 86, p. 32.
"From the Same Theater" (tr. by Cyrus Cassells). [Translation] (16) Spr 86, p. 84.
"Memory" (tr. by Cyrus Cassells). [Translation] (16) Spr 86, p. 83.
"Possible Introduction to an Epithalamium" (wedding of friends, in Sinera, tr. by Cyrus Cassells). [Translation] (16) Spr 86, p. 81.
"Remembered Roses" (Roses recordades, tr. by James Eddy). [SenR] (16:1) 86, p. 30.
"Sinera Cemetery" (Excerpts, tr. by Cyrus Cassells). [Translation] (16) Spr 86, p. 79-80.

125

ESPRIU

"Sinera Cemetery" (tr. by Cyrus Cassells). [Translation] (16) Spr 86, p. 83.
"Thanatos" (tr. by James Eddy). [SenR] (16:1) 86, p. 31.
"The Wait" (tr. by Cyrus Cassells). [Translation] (16) Spr 86, p. 82.
1564. ESPY, Brent
"From the Source, We Flow" (for a special friend). [PoeticJ] (15) Sum 86, p. 3.
1565. ESRIG, Mark
"Oriental Ghost." [Outbr] (16/17) Fall 85-Spr 86, p. 24-25.
1566. ESTELLES, Vicent Andrés
"I Won't Tell You" (No et diré, tr. by Nathaniel Smith). [SenR] (16:1) 86, p. 36.
"The Lovers" (Els amants, tr. by Nathaniel Smith). [SenR] (16:1) 86, p. 39.
"The Mud, the Rain" (El fang, la pluja, tr. by Nathaniel Smith). [SenR] (16:1) 86, p. 37.
"Secretly and Very Chastely" (Horatians, XLVI: Secretament i molt castament, tr. by Nathaniel Smith). [SenR] (16:1) 86, p. 38.
1567. ESTES, Angie
"The Iron's Credo." [NegC] (6:4) Fall 86, p. 52.
1568. ESTESS, Sybil
"Flight." [ManhatPR] (6) Wint-Spr 85-86, p. 58.
1569. ESTEVE, Jean
"Our Hero." [ForidaR] (14:1) Spr-Sum 86, p. 108.
1570. ETTER, Carol A.
"An Understanding." [PikeF] (7) Spr 86, p. 20.
1571. ETTER, Dave
"Black Russians" (for Sarah). [SpoonRQ] (11:2) Spr 86, p. 5.
"Community Hospital." [WritersF] (12) Fall 86, p. 170-171.
"Doorbell." [SpoonRQ] (11:2) Spr 86, p. 8.
"Rhonda, the Full Moon, and Richard Brautigan." [SpoonRQ] (11:2) Spr 86, p. 6-7.
"Snake." [MidAR] (6:1) 86?, p. 87.
"What's Missing Now." [MidAR] (6:1) 86?, p. 86.
1572. EURIPIDES
"Chorus — The Bacchae" (tr. by C. K. Williams and Herbert Golder). [Translation] (16) Spr 86, p. 254-262.
1573. EVANS, Bradford
"Crossing Patagonia." [MidAR] (6:2) 86, p. 127-128.
"Journey to Nowhere." [CrossCur] (5:4/6:1) 86, p. 34-35.
"Underneath the Shirt." [JamesWR] (4:1) Fall 86, p. 5.
1574. EVANS, George
"Lightning." [Thrpny] (25) Spr 86, p. 18.
1575. EVANS, Jack
"Evening on Camp Street." [ManhatPR] (6) Wint-Spr 85-86, p. 46-47.
1576. EVANS, James
"The Buxton Woods, Being a Poem for My Wife." [KanQ] (18:1/2) Wint-Spr 86, p. 172-173.
"Song for July." [KanQ] (18:1/2) Wint-Spr 86, p. 172.
"The Wish." [KanQ] (18:1/2) Wint-Spr 86, p. 171.
1577. EVANS, Judson
"Directions." [AntigR] (66/67) Sum-Aut 86, p. 110-111.
"Father Tongue" (from Lignum Vitae). [AntigR] (66/67) Sum-Aut 86, p. 109-110.
"Montauk." [Poem] (55) Mr 86, p. 56-59.
"Owls." [Poem] (55) Mr 86, p. 54-55.
1578. EVANS, Kathy
"Twilight." [YellowS] (19) Sum 86, p. 39.
1579. EVANS, Kevin
"Poem, Preoccupation II." [CarolQ] (39:1) Fall 86, p. 25.
1580. EVERETT, Joann Marie
"Instead." [SanFPJ] (8:2) 85, p. 80.
"A Living Whole." [SanFPJ] (8:2) 85, p. 80.
1581. EWART, Gavin
"The Difference." [ParisR] (28:99) Spr 86, p. 101.
"Kingsley Has a Go at a Latin Poem." [GrandS] (5:2) Wint 86, p. 113-114.
"Kipper." [GrandS] (5:4) Sum 86, p. 177-178.
"Miles Williamson-Noble" (De Mortuis). [ParisR] (28:99) Spr 86, p. 98-99.
"Putney OAPs in 1985." [ParisR] (28:99) Spr 86, p. 100.
"Sally." [ParisR] (28:99) Spr 86, p. 96-97.
"Screaming Venus." [ParisR] (28:99) Spr 86, p. 102.
"Trying to Interest John Fuller in American Breakfasts." [Verse] (6) 86, p. 5.

1582. FACKNITZ, Mark A. R.
    "Topography." [GeoR] (40:3) Fall 86, p. 662.
1583. FAERSTEIN, Howard
    "After de Kooning." [PaintedB] (28) Ap 86, p. 44.
    "December Women." [Confr] (32) Spr-Sum 86, p. 74.
    "The Things I Did" (after Marvin Bell, for David Dunn). [PaintedB] (28) Ap 86, p. 45.
1584. FAGLES, Robert
    "Aerial Reconnaissance." [GrandS] (5:4) Sum 86, p. 213-215.
    "The Scream" (after the painting by Munch). [KenR] (NS 7:2) Spr 85, p. 67.
    "To the Parents of Our Adopted Children." [KenR] (NS 7:2) Spr 85, p. 67-68.
1585. FAHEY, Diane
    "Lullaby" (For Kyle). [BelPoJ] (36:4) Sum 86, p. 36.
1586. FAHEY, W. A.
    "Invention of a Raindrop." [Confr] (32) Spr-Sum 86, p. 111.
    "Landscape for Georgia O'Keefe." [Confr] (33/34) Fall-Wint 86-87, p. 141.
1587. FAHRBACH, Helen
    "It's a Matter of Architecture." [RagMag] (5:1) Spr 86, p. 36.
1588. FAIRCHILD, B. H.
    "Canada." [Caliban] (1) 86, p. 133.
    "The Jazz Musician." [Electrum] (38) Spr 86, p. 12.
    "A Man in His Garage." [Caliban] (1) 86, p. 132.
    "Vuillard: The Painter Ker-Xavier Roussel and His Daughter." [MemphisSR] (6:1/2) Spr 86, p. 33.
1589. FAIZ, Faiz Ahmed
    "Be Near Me" (tr. by Naomi Lazard). [SenR] (16:1) 86, p. 77.
    "The Day Death Comes" (tr. by Daud Kamal). [Vis] (21) 86, p. 34.
    "Don't Look at Them" (tr. by Naomi Lazard). [CentralP] (9) Spr 86, p. 60.
    "The Hour of Faithlessness" (tr. by Naomi Lazard). [AmerPoR] (15:5) S-O 86, p. 36.
    "If My Suffering Found a Voice" (tr. by Naomi Lazard). [CentralP] (9) Spr 86, p. 59.
    "Paris" (tr. by Naomi Lazard). [SenR] (16:1) 86, p. 76.
    "The Rain of Stones" (adapted by Agha Shahid Ali). [LitR] (29:3) Spr 86, p. 361.
    "Solitude" (adapted by Agha Shahid Ali). [LitR] (29:3) Spr 86, p. 361.
    "Three Quatrains" (tr. by Naomi Lazard). [CentralP] (9) Spr 86, p. 61.
    "Travelogue" (tr. by Naomi Lazard). [AmerPoR] (15:5) S-O 86, p. 36.
    "The War Cemetery in Leningrad" (tr. by N. Lazard). [CentralP] (9) Spr 86, p. 62.
1590. FALCO, Edward
    "Frost as Morning Goes On." [ColEng] (48:1) Ja 86, p. 41.
    "St. Francis Protecting This World." [IndR] (9:2) Spr 86, p. 18.
1591. FALCO, Raphael
    "After the Prizes." [ManhatPR] (7) Sum 86, p. 35.
    "The Dead Architect." [ManhatPR] (7) Sum 86, p. 34-35.
    "The Weightlifter." [ManhatPR] (7) Sum 86, p. 34.
FALCO, Salvatore di
    See DiFALCO, Salvatore
1592. FALCON, Aristides
    "II. Alguien nos espera nos escucha." [LindLM] (5:3) Jl-S 86, p. 15.
1593. FALDET, David
    "Noah's Raven." [MidAR] (6:2) 86, p. 34.
1594. FALK, Marcia
    "Arrived" (tr. of Malka Heifetz Tussman). [AmerPoR] (15:6) N-D 86, p. 20.
    "Dear Monsters" (tr. of Anna Margolin). [AmerPoR] (15:6) N-D 86, p. 21.
    "Epitaph" (tr. of Anna Margolin). [AmerPoR] (15:6) N-D 86, p. 21.
    "Girls in Crotona Park" (tr. of Anna Margolin). [AmerPoR] (15:6) N-D 86, p. 21.
    "In the Dry Riverbed" (tr. of Zelda). [AmerPoR] (15:6) N-D 86, p. 20.
    "Then My Soul Cried Out" (tr. of Zelda). [AmerPoR] (15:6) N-D 86, p. 20.
    "Thou Shalt Not" (for Yudka, tr. of Malka Heifetz Tussman). [AmerPoR] (15:6) N-D 86, p. 20.
    "Two-Faced Woman" (tr. of T. Carmi). [PoetL] (81:2) Sum 86, p. 89.
1595. FALKENBERG, Betty
    "Jacob" (tr. of Else Lasker-Schüler). [InterPR] (12:2) Fall 86, p. 41.
    "My People" (tr. of Else Lasker-Schüler). [InterPR] (12:2) Fall 86, p. 39.
    "Pharaoh and Joseph" (tr. of Else Lasker-Schüler). [InterPR] (12:2) Fall 86, p. 35.
    "To God" (tr. of Else Lasker-Schüler). [InterPR] (12:2) Fall 86, p. 37.

1596. FALKOFF, Fontaine
"In Autumn." [PoeticJ] (16) Fall 86, p. 40.
"Small Predator." [PoeticJ] (15) Sum 86, p. 30.
"To Nickie in the Rain." [PoeticJ] (15) Sum 86, p. 30.
1597. FALLON, Peter
"Brothers." [Field] (34) Spr 86, p. 59-60.
"Carnaross 2." [Verse] (6) 86, p. 22.
"Dipping Day." [Field] (34) Spr 86, p. 57.
"The Meadow." [Verse] (6) 86, p. 21.
"The Rag-Tree, Boherard." [Field] (34) Spr 86, p. 58.
"Sabbath." [Field] (34) Spr 86, p. 61-62.
1598. FALUDY, George
"Northern Summer." [Harp] (273:1635) Ag 86, p. 30.
1599. FANDL, John
"AMDG." [Comm] (113:21) 5 D 86, p. 660.
1600. FARLEY, Blanche
"Alder Moon" (for Mary Downs). [SingHM] (14) 86, p. 8.
"Requirements for Anyone Attending a Van Gogh Exhibition." [ForidaR] (14:1)
    Spr-Sum 86, p. 49-50.
1601. FARLEY, Joseph
"At My Brother's Grave." [RagMag] (5:2) Fall 86, p. 12.
"Chasing the Ice Cream Truck." [SlipS] (6) 86, p. 10.
"Visiting." [YetASM] (4) 85, p. 7.
1602. FARNSWORTH, Robert
"Almost Family." [PoetryNW] (27:3) Aut 86, p. 5.
"Blueprint." [MissouriR] (9:2) 86, p. 152.
"Broadcast." [CarolQ] (39:1) Fall 86, p. 2.
"For William Cowper." [MissouriR] (9:2) 86, p. 150-151.
"Mimesis." [CarolQ] (39:1) Fall 86, p. 3.
"The Pose." [MichQR] (25:3) Sum 86, p. 508-510.
1603. FARR, Judith
"In the Gallery" (Selections: 1-3). [ManhatPR] (7) Sum 86, p. 10-12.
1604. FARRAR, Winifred Hamrick
"Apocalypse." [NegC] (6:4) Fall 86, p. 70.
1605. FARRELL, Kate
"How Can I Miss You If You Won't Go Away." [AntigR] (66/67) Sum-Aut 86, p.
    118.
"Using My Eyes Can I Convince You I'm Right?" [AntigR] (66/67) Sum-Aut 86, p.
    117.
1606. FARRELL, M. A. (Mary Ann)
"Burning the Cane." [HolCrit] (23:3) Je 86, p. 15-16.
"Leolord's Gabardines." [Outbr] (16/17) Fall 85-Spr 86, p. 88-89.
"Lucika's Man." [Outbr] (16/17) Fall 85-Spr 86, p. 90-91.
"A Neon Body." [Pembroke] (18) 86, p. 262-263.
"On Sundays." [CapeR] (21:1) Spr 86, p. 21.
"Place of the Tiger." [CutB] (25) Fall-Wint 86, p. 22-23.
"Place of the Tiger." [InterPR] (12:1) Spr 86, p. 84-85.
"Voyage." [InterPR] (12:1) Spr 86, p. 83.
1607. FASEL, Ida
"Gardener in Spring." [ChrC] (103:16) 7 My 86, p. 453.
"In Weimar." [PoeticJ] (13) 86, p. 17.
"Nursery Rhyme." [PoeticJ] (14) 86, p. 8.
"Those Days." [PoeticJ] (16) Fall 86, p. 11.
"Twide." [ChrC] (103:35) 19 N 86, p. 1030.
1608. FATTORI, Ross
"Lost Heroes." [WritersL] (1986:3), p. 10.
1609. FAUCHER, Real
"The Distant Light." [WritersL] (1986:2), p. 8.
"Egyptian Princess Undergoes X-Rays." [SecC] (14:1) 86, p. 26-28.
"The Flood of '82." [Sam] (44:3 release 175) 86, p. 60.
"Growth." [Wind] (16:56) 86, p. 14-15.
"Nude in Centerfold." [SecC] (14:1) 86, p. 25.
"Riding a Dream to the End." [WritersL] (1986:6), p. 31.
"Slaves and Masters." [WritersL] (1986:5), p. 32.
"When I Asked Her." [Sam] (44:2 release 174) 86, p. 16.

1610. FAULKNER, Pete
"Ghost Town Supermarkets" (Excerpt). [Bogg] (56) 86, p. 45.
"October Poem for Kerouac." [Bogg] (56) 86, p. 25.
1611. FAULKS, Lana
"Cowtown." [ManhatPR] (7) Sum 86, p. 47.
1612. FAVEREY, Hans
"Girolamo Cavazzoni, Who Disappeared in Context" (Selections: 2, 5, tr. by Francis
Redvers Jones). [Stand] (27:2) Spr 86, p. 21.
1613. FAY, Julie
"Geography." [RiverS] (20) 86, p. 33.
"Postcard: Paris, Au Temps Jadis — l'Eglise Eustache." [RiverS] (20) 86, p. 32-33.
1614. FEELA, David J.
"Subliminal." [PennR] (1:2) Fall 85, p. 65.
1615. FEENY, Thomas
"Los Cementerios de Palmeras" (for Silvia). [Event] (15:2) 86, p. 102-103.
"Cousin Nettie." [HiramPoR] (40) Spr-Sum 86, p. 9.
"In the Night, Waiting." [Event] (15:1) 86, p. 118-119.
1616. FEIGEN, Gerald M.
"Amsterdam." [AntigR] (64) Wint 86, p. 115.
1617. FEINBERG, Robert
"Tenth Fragment, Curtain of Sound." [CrossCur] (5:4/6:1) 86, p. 121.
1618. FEINSTEIN, Robert N.
"Curator's Curse." [Amelia] (3:4) Fall 86, p. 75.
"Heaven Can't Wait." [Poetry] (148:5) Ag 86, p. 259.
"Season's Greetings!" [Amelia] (3:1) Ja 86, p. 90.
1619. FEIRSTEIN, Frederick
"Family History: A Narrative Poem." [QRL] (Poetry series 6:26) 86, 68 p.
1620. FELDMAN, Alan
"Fish." [ColEng] (48:3) Mr 86, p. 269.
"Last Class." [ColEng] (48:3) Mr 86, p. 270.
1621. FELDMAN, Irving
"All of Us Here" (On the plaster sculptures of George Segal. Selections: 3 poems).
[GrandS] (5:3) Spr 86, p. 43-46.
"All of Us Here" (Poems on the plaster sculptures of George Segal: 3 Selections).
[SouthwR] (71:2) Spr 86, p. 180-185.
"All of Us Here" (Poems on the plaster sculptures of George Segal: Excerpt).
[YaleR] (75:3) Spr 86, p. 368-369.
"The Call." [NewRep] (194:20) 19 My 86, p. 38.
"Epilogue" (tr. of Zishe Landau). [Translation] (17) Fall 86, p. 253.
"The Little Pig" (tr. of Zishe Landau). [Translation] (17) Fall 86, p. 253.
"Of Course, We Would Wish" (from All of Us Here, Poems on the plaster
sculptures of George Segal). [Confr] (32) Spr-Sum 86, p. 28.
"Simple Outlines, Human Shapes" (from All of Us Here, Poems on the plaster
sculptures of George Segal). [Confr] (32) Spr-Sum 86, p. 29.
"The Strikover Rabbi" (tr. of Zishe Landau). [Translation] (17) Fall 86, p. 251.
"This Evening" (tr. of Zishe Landau). [Translation] (17) Fall 86, p. 252.
1622. FELDMAN, Ruth
"Aquarium Fish" (tr. of Piera Simeoni). [NewRena] (6:3, #20) Spr 86, p. 55.
"August at Grassano" (for Carlo Levi, tr. of Rocco Scotellaro, w. Brian Swann).
[NewRena] (6:3, #20) Spr 86, p. 51.
"Cueva de las Manos" (tr. of Margherita Guidacci). [InterPR] (12:2) Fall 86, p. 7, 9.
"Fragments." [ConnPR] (5:1) 86, p. 35-36.
"The Orange Tree" (tr. of Rocco Scotellaro, w. Brian Swann). [NewRena] (6:3,
#20) Spr 86, p. 53.
1623. FELL, Mary
"Mowing." [PaintedB] (29) Ag 86, p. 30.
"Tuning Up." [PaintedB] (29) Ag 86, p. 29.
1624. FELLMAN, Stanley A.
"Picked Feathers and Blind Gardens." [MidAR] (7:1) 86, p. 118.
1625. FELTS, Diana J.
"Lines Down a Borrowed Field." [Farm] (3:2) Spr-Sum 86, p. 29.
1626. FERBER, Betty
"Persephone" (Excerpt, tr. of Homero Aridjis). [Translation] (16) Spr 86, p.
226-233.
1627. FEREBEE, Gideon, Jr.
"Refugee." [BlackALF] (20:3) Fall 86, p. 311.

129

1628. FERGUSON, Moira
"Women's Weeds." [PraS] (60:3) Fall 86, p. 26-28.
1629. FERLINGHETTI, Lawrence
"Let Us Pray." [RedBass] (11) 86, p. 6.
1630. FERNANDEZ GILL, Alicia
"Puertas." [Mairena] (8:22) 86, p. 101.
1631. FERRARELLI, Rina
"The Escape" (tr. of Giorgio Chiesura). [WebR] (11:1) Spr 86, p. 30.
"The Illness" (tr. of Giorgio Chiesura). [WebR] (11:1) Spr 86, p. 31.
1632. FERRATER, Gabriel
"Autumn Room" (tr. by Arthur Terry). [Translation] (16) Spr 86, p. 113.
"The Cripple" (El mutilat, tr. by Deborah Bonner). [SenR] (16:1) 86, p. 34-35.
"Idols" (tr. by Deborah Bonner). [SenR] (16:1) 86, p. 33.
"Landscape with Figures" (tr. by Arthur Terry). [Translation] (16) Spr 86, p. 117.
"Maîtresse de Poète" (tr. by Arthur Terry). [Translation] (16) Spr 86, p. 118.
"October" (tr. by Arthur Terry). [Translation] (16) Spr 86, p. 116.
"A Small War" (tr. by Arthur Terry). [Translation] (16) Spr 86, p. 114.
"Solstice" (tr. by Arthur Terry). [Translation] (16) Spr 86, p. 112.
"Time Was" (tr. by Arthur Terry). [Translation] (16) Spr 86, p. 119.
"An Uncertain Step" (tr. by Arthur Terry). [Translation] (16) Spr 86, p. 115.
1633. FERRE, Rosario
"Requiem para Rock Hudson." [Mairena] (8:22) 86, p. 94.
1634. FERREIRA, Roberto
"Conversacion." [Mairena] (8:21) 86, p. 61.
"Esta bola de cristal líquida." [Mairena] (8:21) 86, p. 61.
"Septiembre Mes de la Patria." [Mairena] (8:21) 86, p. 60-61.
1635. FERRELLI, R. J.
"No Less Than Ever." [Rampike] (5:2) 86, p. 68-69.
FERREYRA, Silvia
See PEREYRA, Silvina L.
1636. FERRY, David
"Adapted from the Latin of Samuel Johnson." [Raritan] (5:4) Spr 86, p. 146.
"The Rhyme." [Raritan] (5:4) Spr 86, p. 146.
1637. FERTIG, Mona
"A Political Poem." [CrossC] (8:2) 86, p. 14.
1638. FIALKOWSKI, Barbara
"Our Adopted Son." [NewL] (52:2/3) Wint-Spr 86, p. 236-237.
1639. FIELD, Robert
"Seasons Where I Love." [CentR] (30:4) Fall 86, p. 478-479.
1640. FIELD, Stephen
"Tian Wen: A Chinese Book of Origins" (Selections: Parts I-II, tr. of anonymous
work). [Translation] (17) Fall 86, p. 275-282.
1641. FIELDER, William
"In Prison" (tr. of Ahmet Arif, w. Ozcan Yalim & Dionis Riggs). [InterPR] (12:1)
Spr 86, p. 65.
"Such Love" (tr. of Attilâ Ilhan, w. Dionis Coffin Riggs and Ozcan Yalim). [StoneC]
(14:1/2) Fall-Wint 86-87, p. 16.
1642. FIELDS, Kenneth
"Apology." [WritersF] (12) Fall 86, p. 64.
"Imprisoned Lover Singing Freedom." [WritersF] (12) Fall 86, p. 63-64.
"In the Place of Stories." [WritersF] (12) Fall 86, p. 62.
"La Salamandre" (for Yves Bonnefoy). [WritersF] (12) Fall 86, p. 65.
"Tangled." [WritersF] (12) Fall 86, p. 63.
1643. FIET, Lowell
"To Build a House." [ManhatPR] (8) Wint 86-87, p. 34-35.
1644. FIFER, Ken
"Birthday on the Great Divide." [PaintedB] (28) Ap 86, p. 74.
1645. FIGMAN, Elliot
"On Turning Thirty-Five." [Lips] (12) 86, p. 20.
"Snow." [Lips] (12) 86, p. 20.
FIGUEROA, Eduardo Rangel
See RANGEL FIGUEROA, Eduardo
1646. FILES, Meg
"Jungle Walking." [MidAR] (7:1) 86, p. 140-141.
"Late summer, tarnished." [Amelia] (3:3) Sum 86, p. 79.

1647. FILIP, Ray (Raymond)
"Apsara." [CapilR] (39) 86, p. 60.
"Happy Masks Cost More." [CapilR] (39) 86, p. 61.
"Watching Whales Watching Us." [GreenfR] (13:3/4) Sum-Fall 86, p. 64.
1648. FILIPKOWSKI, Zoe
"You Have Your Life on Backwards." [MidwQ] (27:4) Sum 86, p. 463.
1649. FILKINS, Peter
"For Rilke, for Us." [HiramPoR] (41) Fall-Wint 86-87, p. 16.
"The Muskrat." [HiramPoR] (41) Fall-Wint 86-87, p. 17-18.
"The Wall" (for Peter Carpenter). [HiramPoR] (41) Fall-Wint 86-87, p. 14-15.
1650. FILSON, B. K.
"The Full Moon Follows." [AntigR] (66/67) Sum-Aut 86, p. 119.
1651. FINALE, Frank
"All Hallow's Eve." [NegC] (6:4) Fall 86, p. 78.
1652. FINBOND, Bernard Lionel
"Images This Night." [Bogg] (55) 86, p. 25.
1653. FINCH, A. R. C.
"No Snake." [SoDakR] (24:2) Sum 86, p. 62.
1654. FINCH, Roger
"The Color of Skin." [Quarry] (35:3) Sum 86, p. 15.
"Cows in Moonlight" (to Anne-Marie Bove). [Poem] (55) Mr 86, p. 4.
"Door-to-Door Salesmen." [HiramPoR] (41) Fall-Wint 86-87, p. 20.
"A Few Weeks before Hallowe'en." [AntigR] (66/67) Sum-Aut 86, p. 120.
"Floating Town." [Waves] (14:3) Wint 86, p. 67.
"How We Are Diminished by the Deaths of Strangers." [Event] (15:2) 86, p. 28.
"Looking for Ezra Pound's Grave." [HiramPoR] (41) Fall-Wint 86-87, p. 22.
"The Love-Stricken Heart" (Late 15th Century). [HiramPoR] (41) Fall-Wint 86-87,
    p. 23.
"Music Alcove, Northside Public Library." [HiramPoR] (41) Fall-Wint 86-87, p.
    19.
"One of Japan's Earliest Musical Instruments, the Biwa." [WormR] (26:4, issue
    104) 86, p. 122-123.
"One of the World's Five Most Exciting Professions." [WormR] (26:4, issue 104)
    86, p. 121-122.
"A Strange New Beast." [HiramPoR] (41) Fall-Wint 86-87, p. 21.
"The Structure of the *Décoration des Nymphéas*." [WormR] (26:4, issue 104) 86, p.
    123.
"T Is for Tailor." [HiramPoR] (40) Spr-Sum 86, p. 10.
"Visitors from *The Red Shoes*" (to Lloyd and Carol Kropp). [MidAR] (7:1) 86, p.
    56.
"We Will Not See the Cave." [WormR] (26:4, issue 104) 86, p. 124.
"Why the Word 'Homesick' Cannot Be Translated." [DeKalbLAJ] (19:1) 86, p. 28.
1655. FINCH, Steven
"For Gene Kelly." [JamesWR] (3:2) Wint 86, p. 4.
"The Message." [JamesWR] (4:1) Fall 86, p. 1.
1656. FINCKE, Gary
"After Arriving from Germany." [CapeR] (21:1) Spr 86, p. 3.
"Another Foot of Water in the Basement." [LitR] (30:1) Fall 86, p. 54.
"Blood Ties." [CapeR] (21:1) Spr 86, p. 2.
"Dan Sickles' Leg." [SouthernPR] (26:1) Spr 86, p. 31-32.
"During the First Semester." [ThRiPo] (27/28) 86, p. 37.
"Elements." [CimR] (77) O 86, p. 48-49.
"The Green Rack." [PoetL] (81:1) Spr 86, p. 45.
"Hanging the Elephant." [PennR] (1:2) Fall 85, p. 48.
"In Emerico's Bar." [MidAR] (7:1) 86, p. 106-107.
"Just before Christmas, Her Letter." [LitR] (30:1) Fall 86, p. 55.
"Manitou Springs." [InterPR] (12:2) Fall 86, p. 110.
"The Merge Arrow." [BelPoJ] (36:4) Sum 86, p. 37-38.
"Moving." [SouthernPR] (26:2) Fall 86, p. 43-44.
"Shoveling the Beans." [Outbr] (16/17) Fall 85-Spr 86, p. 13-14.
"The Ten-Inch Ordinance." [InterPR] (12:2) Fall 86, p. 109-110.
"What Argument Was Beginning?" [IndR] (9:2) Spr 86, p. 99.
1657. FINK, Janie
"For Our Wedding." [VirQR] (62:1) Wint 86, p. 48-49.
"Love Poem." [VirQR] (62:1) Wint 86, p. 49.

1658. FINK, Robert A.
    "Consider." [Poetry] (148:2) My 86, p. 84.
    "Mother's Day." [Poetry] (148:2) My 86, p. 85.
    "The Need for Order." [Poetry] (148:2) My 86, p. 86.
1659. FINK, Tom
    "Come Closer." [ManhatPR] (7) Sum 86, p. 39.
    "On the Birthday of Wallace Stevens." [ManhatPR] (7) Sum 86, p. 38.
1660. FINKEL, Donald
    "San Miguel, 1985." [OntR] (25) Fall-Wint 86-87, p. 30-33.
1661. FINLAY, John
    "The Graves by the Sea" (tr. of Paul Valery). [SouthernR] (22:1) Ja 86, p. 118-122.
1662. FINLAYSON, Douglas
    "Northern Lights." [DeKalbLAJ] (19:2) 86, p. 22.
1663. FINLEY, C. Stephen
    "The Leave-Taking." [Wind] (16:58) 86, p. 17.
    "Refugees." [Wind] (16:58) 86, p. 17.
1664. FINLEY, Lora Dewey
    "The Poem" (tr. of Chin-An Li, w. the author). [Nimrod] (29:2) Spr-Sum 86, p. 95.
1665. FINLEY, Michael
    "A Drive in the Country." [ParisR] (28:101) Wint 86, p. 274.
    "I Feel Sorry for My Fish." [Wind] (16:56) 86, p. 16.
    "The Woman in the Blue Dress." [Wind] (16:56) 86, p. 16.
1666. FINNEGAN, James
    "Out for the Evening." [MissouriR] (9:2) 86, p. 46-47.
1667. FINNELL, Dennis
    "On the Lookout for Neighbors." [DenQ] (20:4/21:1) Spr-Sum 86, p. 84-85.
    "Over Voice of America." [DenQ] (20:4/21:1) Spr-Sum 86, p. 82-83.
FIRMAT, Gustavo Pérez
    See PEREZ FIRMAT, Gustavo
1668. FISET, Joan
    "Visiting My Father's Grave." [CrabCR] (4:1) Fall-Wint 86, p. 26.
1669. FISH, Karen
    "Florida." [FloridaR] (14:2) Fall-Wint 86, p. 22.
    "The Good Return" (the name of my great-great grandfather's trading ship — middle
        1800s). [NoAmR] (271:4) D 86, p. 9.
    "When the Soul Leaves the Body." [FloridaR] (14:2) Fall-Wint 86, p. 21.
1670. FISHBEIN, Julie Deane
    "Electra." [AntR] (44:4) Fall 86, p. 436.
    "Man from Purulha." [AntR] (44:4) Fall 86, p. 437.
1671. FISHER, Adam D.
    "P.S. 101." [ManhatPR] (8) Wint 86-87, p. 37.
1672. FISHER, Allen
    "Boogie Woogie." [Sink] (1) 86, p. 5-7.
1673. FISHER, Lori H.
    "Driving West on Route 7, New York." [Blueline] (7:2) Wint-Spr 86, p. 38-39.
1674. FISHER, Nancy
    "The Vatican." [YetASM] (5) 86, p. 4.
1675. FISHMAN, Charles
    "Breather" (tr. of Sarah Kirsch, w. Marina Roscher). [Vis] (22) 86, p. 11.
    "The Corpse Lily." [Pembroke] (18) 86, p. 252-253.
    "Gentle Fright" (tr. of Sarah Kirsch, w. Marina Roscher). [HolCrit] (23:5) D 86, p.
        14.
    "Nigh Noon Summer" (after Ammons' *Tape for the Turn of the Year*). [Pembroke]
        (18) 86, p. 156-157.
    "Rainy Season" (tr. of Sarah Kirsch, w. Marina Roscher). [Vis] (22) 86, p. 11.
1676. FITTERMAN, Robert
    "Counting." [Acts] (5) 86, p. 108.
    "Just for a second" (Untitled). [Acts] (5) 86, p. 111.
    "Make a point across the lake" (Untitled). [Acts] (5) 86, p. 109.
    "Siim." [Acts] (5) 86, p. 107.
    "To You, Anyone." [Acts] (5) 86, p. 110.
1677. FITZGERALD, Judith
    "Food for Thought." [Rampike] (5:1) 86, p. 38.
    "Newsmakers" (For Nick Hills). [CrossC] (8:1) 86, p. 8.
1678. FLANAGAN, Joanne
    "Cabin Fever." [Sam] (46:5 [i.e. 46:1] release 181) 86, p. 29.

FLANAGAN

132

1679. FLANAGAN, Katherine
"In This Darkening Room." [RagMag] (5:1) Spr 86, p. 3.
"Kwik Wash Monday Night." [Electrum] (38) Spr 86, p. 43.
1680. FLANDERS, Jane
"Big Cars." [NewEngR] (9:1) Aut 86, p. 73.
"Daughters." [PraS] (60:3) Fall 86, p. 49.
"Eating Flowers." [Confr] (33/34) Fall-Wint 86-87, p. 168.
"Falling." [WestB] (19) 86, p. 92-93.
"Flowering Privet." [Nat] (243:5) 30 Ag 86, p. 154.
"Messengers." [NewEngR] (9:1) Aut 86, p. 72.
"Nightingales in America." [PraS] (60:3) Fall 86, p. 50-51.
"The Origin of Romanticism" (A Scene from "Der Freischütz"). [WestB] (19) 86, p. 93.
"Planting Onions." [PraS] (60:3) Fall 86, p. 50.
"Spin the Bottle at Eleanor Hartle's." [MassR] (27:1) Spr 86, p. 131-132.
"Testimony." [PraS] (60:3) Fall 86, p. 51.
1681. FLECKENSTEIN, Mark
"Truce." [SouthernPR] (26:1) Spr 86, p. 66.
1682. FLEESON, Tyler
"At the Center." [AnotherCM] (15) 86, p. 16.
"Catch." [NowestR] (24:2) 86, p. 15.
"Paronomasia." [AnotherCM] (15) 86, p. 17.
1683. FLEISHMAN, Gustav
"Ballad of a Sabra" (tr. by Will Kirkland). [NewOR] (13:4) Wint 86, p. 42.
1684. FLEMING, Deborah
"Bagomoyo, 1862." [PennR] (1:2) Fall 85, p. 20.
"The Falls of Panga-Ni." [YetASM] (4) 85, p. 8.
"Pemba." [PennR] (1:2) Fall 85, p. 21.
1685. FLEMING, Gerald
"Wapello, Iowa, 1956." [IndR] (9:2) Spr 86, p. 56-57.
1686. FLEMING, Robert Alan
"Sea Sick." [DeKalbLAJ] (19:3/4) 86, p. 72.
1687. FLETCHER, Luellen
"Memorandum." [BlackWR] (13:1) Fall 86, p. 99.
"Story." [BlackWR] (13:1) Fall 86, p. 100-101.
1688. FLETCHER, Tessie
"Agua de Rio." [LetFem] (12:1/2) Primavera-Otoño 86, p. 157-158.
"Dialogo." [LetFem] (12:1/2) Primavera-Otoño 86, p. 158-159.
"Dream?" [LetFem] (12:1/2) Primavera-Otoño 86, p. 159.
1689. FLIEGEL, Lisa
"Johnny" (tr. of Ronnie Someck). [PoetL] (81:2) Sum 86, p. 123.
"The Ostrich" (tr. of Maya Bejerano). [PoetL] (81:2) Sum 86, p. 122.
"Welders Street. She Sings at Weddings" (tr. of Ronnie Someck). [PoetL] (81:2) Sum 86, p. 124.
1690. FLINT, Roland
"At Bernards'." [NewL] (52:2/3) Wint-Spr 86, p. 241.
"Cinema." [NewL] (52:2/3) Wint-Spr 86, p. 239-240.
"For Gabriel's Hands." [PraS] (60:4) Wint 86, p. 53-54.
"Jim." [TriQ] (66) Spr-Sum 86, p. 133-134.
"A Letter Home." [TriQ] (66) Spr-Sum 86, p. 129-132.
"Measure for Elizabeth." [DenQ] (20:4/21:1) Spr-Sum 86, p. 104.
"Nocturne." [DenQ] (20:4/21:1) Spr-Sum 86, p. 105-106.
"What I Have Tried to Say to You." [PraS] (60:4) Wint 86, p. 54-55.
1691. FLINTOFF, Eddie
"Homage to Jose Garcia Villa." [Bogg] (55) 86, p. 52.
1692. FLOOK, Maria
"Child Burial." [Poetry] (148:6) S 86, p. 341.
"The Sapling." [Poetry] (148:1) Ap 86, p. 21-22.
FLORES, Alberto Baeza
See BAEZA FLORES, Alberto
FLORIDO, Jorge J. Rodriguez
See RODRIGUEZ-FLORIDO, Jorge J.
1693. FLYNN, David
"Bed Time." [Confr] (32) Spr-Sum 86, p. 251.
"The House in the Woods." [Wind] (16:56) 86, p. 17.
"The Night Is Enough." [Wind] (16:56) 86, p. 17.

133

FLYNN

"Things Once Human." [StoneC] (14:1/2) Fall-Wint 86-87, p. 43.
1694. FLYNN, Richard
"The Evolution of Darkness" (for Rebecca Brown). [GWR] (6:2) 86, p. 11.
FOE, Mark de
See DeFOE, Mark
1695. FOERSTER, Richard
"The Steel Ring." [TarRP] (26:1) Fall 86, p. 38.
"To an Escaped Parakeet." [ManhatPR] (6) Wint-Spr 85-86, p. 40.
1696. FOGEL, Alice B.
"Snowstorm." [Ploughs] (12:3) 86, p. 103-104.
1697. FOGELIN, Florence
"Parabola." [NegC] (6:4) Fall 86, p. 200.
1698. FOIX, J. V.
"Alone and Dressed in Mourning" (Sol i de dol, tr. by David H. Rosenthal). [SenR]
(16:1) 86, p. 29.
"I Got to That Town, They All Greeted Me, . . ." (tr. by M. L. Rosenthal).
[Translation] (16) Spr 86, p. 68-69.
"I Like, at Random" (Em plau, d'atzar, tr. by David H. Rosenthal). [SenR] (16:1)
86, p. 28.
"It Was Growing Dark and We Stared at the Hides Scattered About . . ." (tr. by M.
L. Rosenthal). [Translation] (16) Spr 86, p. 66.
"It's When I Sleep That I See Clearly" (tr. by M. L. Rosenthal). [Translation] (16)
Spr 86, p. 67.
1699. FOLEY, Hugh
"News Hooks." [DeKalbLAJ] (19:3/4) 86, p. 73.
1700. FOLEY, Louis
"Dancing the Night Away." [Bogg] (56) 86, p. 44.
1701. FOLEY, Michael
"Investigating Subsidence." [Verse] (3:3) N 86, p. 46.
1702. FOLKESTAD, Marilyn
"Speaking in Tongues." [Calyx] (10:1) Sum 86, p. 30-31.
1703. FOLLIN-JONES, Elizabeth
"Hobo Trains." [PennR] (2:1) Fall-Wint 86, p. 88.
1704. FOLSOM, Eric
"Ave." [AntigR] (64) Wint 86, p. 61.
"Fouling the Nest." [Event] (15:2) 86, p. 116-117.
"Still Life with Diffidence." [Event] (15:1) 86, p. 66.
1705. FONT, María Cecilia
"La Espada Mas Aguda" (Homenaje a Jorge Luis Borges. Selections: III, IV).
[Mairena] (8:22) 86, p. 87.
1706. FONTENOT, Ken
"Trouble." [NewL] (52:2/3) Wint-Spr 86, p. 160-161.
1707. FOOTE, Gerry
"Cultural Exchange." [EngJ] (75:2) F 86, p. 57.
"Still Learning My Colors at 33" (for Tye)." [EngJ] (75:7) N 86, p. 66.
1708. FORCE, Kathy
"Shelter." [RagMag] (5:2) Fall 86, p. 13.
"The Woman Who Writes." [RagMag] (5:2) Fall 86, p. 13.
1709. FORD, Charles Henri
"The Minotaur Sutra" (Excerpt). [Caliban] (1) 86, p. 128-129.
FORD, Sheri de
See DeFORD, Sheri
1710. FORD, Terri
"Romancing the Carolinas." [SingHM] (14) 86, p. 42.
"The Yearly Vacation" (for my Father's Second Wife). [SingHM] (14) 86, p. 40-41.
1711. FORD, William
"Country Crime, a Tale." [ThRiPo] (27/28) 86, p. 39-40.
"Her Last Doll." [PennR] (1:1) 85, p. 35.
"To His Daughter in Malibu." [PennR] (2:1) Fall-Wint 86, p. 83.
"The Woman at the Well." [ThRiPo] (27/28) 86, p. 38.
1712. FORNOFF, Frederick H.
"Fields of Memory" (tr. of Laureano Alban). [Sonora] (11) Fall 86 [c87], p. 85, 87.
"The Green Dominion" (tr. of Laureano Alban). [Sonora] (11) Fall 86 [c87], p. 81,
83.
1713. FORSTER, Louis
"The Young Doctor and I." [CutB] (25) Fall-Wint 86, p. 41.

1714. FORSTHOFFER, J. P.
"The Air Show" (for Mark Johnson, Dayton, Ohio). [Farm] (3:1) Fall 85, p. 24.
"Trio for Hearts and Water." [CimR] (77) O 86, p. 40.
1715. FORTIN, Célyne
"Revoir l'Abitibi." [Os] (22) 86, p. 27.
1716. FORTNER, Ethel N.
"For We Are Many" (St. Mark 5:9). [Calyx] (9:2/3) Wint 86, p. 118-119.
"In November." [Calyx] (9:2/3) Wint 86, p. 119.
1717. FORTNEY, Steven
"Freud and Jung." [YetASM] (4) 85, p. 7.
1718. FORTUNATO, Peter
"Every Wizard" (for Alfredo Fortunao, Second Prize, Pablo Neruda Prize for
Poetry). [Nimrod] (30:1) Fall-Wint 86, p. 39-43.
1719. FOSTER, Robert
"For St. Francis." [Dandel] (13:1) Spr-Sum 86, p. 35.
1720. FOSTER, Sesshu
"Barricade" (tr. of Ernesto Cardenal). [RedBass] (11) 86, p. 10.
"California Roll" (for Umeko Agawa). [Jacaranda] (2:1) Fall 86, p. 41-42.
"Letter before Leaving for a Reforestation Brigade." [MinnR] (NS 26) Spr 86, p.
58-60.
"Of Man by Man" (tr. of Arnoldo Garcia, w. the author). [Contact] (8:41/42/43)
Fall-Wint 86-87, p. 21-22.
"On Los Leones Avenue" (tr. of Carlos Pineda). [CentralP] (9) Spr 86, p. 82-83.
1721. FOSTER, Susannah
"Someone watches the green bench until." [Electrum] (38) Spr 86, p. 41.
1722. FOURNIER, Merci
"My Father, with a Soul Like Honey." [Waves] (14:3) Wint 86, p. 57.
"My Mother Is Leaving." [Waves] (14:3) Wint 86, p. 56.
1723. FOUSHEE, Sandra
"Body of a Man" (after Neruda). [PraS] (60:4) Wint 86, p. 99.
"The Right to Turbary." [PraS] (60:4) Wint 86, p. 98-99.
1724. FOWLER, Anne Carroll
"Afternoon at the MCZ." [NewRena] (6:3, #20) Spr 86, p. 69.
"Guindi, Dying." [KanQ] (18:1/2) Wint-Spr 86, p. 310.
"Still Life." [CumbPR] (5:2) Spr 86, p. 25.
1725. FOWLER, Karen Joy
"Pietà" (for the mothers of husbands). [CentR] (30:1) Wint 86, p. 62.
"Solomon's Child." [Prima] (10) 86, p. 8.
1726. FOWLER, Russell T.
"Settling." [MidwQ] (27:4) Sum 86, p. 464.
1727. FOX, Anne Valley
"Certainty." [AmerV] (3) Sum 86, p. 9-10.
1728. FOX, Hugh
"Clots." [Vis] (20) 86, p. 35.
"Homage to Bukowski." [OroM] (4:1-4) My 85, p. 53-54.
1729. FOX, Leonard
"The Fig Tree's Leaves Have Returned" (anonymous, tr. from the Malagasy).
[Translation] (16) Spr 86, p. 179.
"I Am the Friendless Child" (anonymous, tr. from the Malagasy). [Translation] (16)
Spr 86, p. 180.
"Tell the Clouds to Wait" (anonymous, tr. from the Malagasy). [Translation] (16)
Spr 86, p. 179.
1730. FOY, John F.
"Letter to the Board." [AntigR] (66/67) Sum-Aut 86, p. 122.
"The Shinglekill." [AntigR] (66/67) Sum-Aut 86, p. 121.
1731. FRALEY, Michael
"Letting Go." [PoeticJ] (15) Sum 86, p. 39.
"Recurring Arboreal Dream." [PoeticJ] (13) 86, p. 7.
"Return to the Forest." [PoeticJ] (16) Fall 86, p. 35.
1732. FRANCIS, David
"My Sister and I Hunted Bugs." [Blueline] (8:1) Sum-Fall 86, p. 20.
1733. FRANCIS, H. E.
"They" (for Oscar Sola, tr. of Ofelia Castillo). [AmerV] (4) Fall 86, p. 59-60.
1734. FRANCIS, Robert
"Late Fire Late Snow." [MassR] (27:2) Sum 86, p. 220.
"Nostalgia." [MassR] (27:2) Sum 86, p. 218.

"Surf." [MassR] (27:2) Sum 86, p. 219.
1735. FRANCISCO, Edward
"Alvin Goines." [InterPR] (12:2) Fall 86, p. 81-85.
"Noise." [InterPR] (12:2) Fall 86, p. 86.
"Pendragon." [InterPR] (12:2) Fall 86, p. 87.
1736. FRANCOEUR, Lucien
"Les Nourritures Terrestres" (à Langue de Feu pour le *naked lunch* littéraire).
[Rampike] (5:1) 86, p. 59.
1737. FRANK, Bernhard
"In a Public Restaurant" (tr. of Israel Efrat). [ColR] (NS 13:1) Fall 85, p. 44.
1738. FRANKLIN, George
"The Old Songs." [Thrpny] (24) Wint 86, p. 10.
1739. FRANKLIN, Lurlynn
"New Law." [SanFPJ] (8:3) 85, p. 36.
"To Quote Gloria Steinum: 'Black Women Have Always Been Leaders.'" [SanFPJ]
(8:1) 85, p. 10-11.
1740. FRANKLIN, Walt
"The Laundramat." [YetASM] (5) 86, p. 2.
"Lost Lead Mine." [Blueline] (7:2) Wint-Spr 86, p. 13.
"Raccoons." [PoeticJ] (13) 86, p. 18-19.
1741. FRANTOM, Marcy
"Lake Turning Over." [Nimrod] (30:1) Fall-Wint 86, p. 79-81.
"Ruby and the Bridal Wreath." [BlackWR] (13:1) Fall 86, p. 64-65.
1742. FRANZEN, Cola
"Grasp" (tr. of Saúl Yurkievich). [Conjunc] (9) 86, p. 201-203.
"Mi Estomago (My Belly)" (tr. of Marjorie Agosin). [Calyx] (9:2/3) Wint 86, p.
110-111.
"Mi Estomago (My Belly)" (tr. of Marjorie Agosin). [Cond] (13) 86, p. 83.
"She Conjured Up Returnings" (tr. of Marjorie Agosin). [WebR] (11:2) Fall 86, p.
33.
"So Then" (tr. of Saúl Yurkievich). [Conjunc] (9) 86, p. 203-204.
1743. FRASER, Kathleen
"Botticelli: From Bryher's Imagined Notes." [Iowa] (16:3) Fall 86, p. 72-74.
"Electric Railway, 1922, Two Women" (for Susan Gevirtz). [Iowa] (16:3) Fall 86,
p. 74-76.
1744. FRATE, Frank (Frank C.)
"Billie." [Sam] (46:5 [i.e. 46:1] release 181) 86, p. 22.
"Mary's Cat." [Wind] (16:56) 86, p. 18.
1745. FRATUS, David
"Lindbergh's Ghosts." [HiramPoR] (40) Spr-Sum 86, p. 46.
"Love Song." [HiramPoR] (40) Spr-Sum 86, p. 48.
"The Oral Interpretation of Literature." [HiramPoR] (40) Spr-Sum 86, p. 47.
"Word Wars I." [HiramPoR] (40) Spr-Sum 86, p. 49.
1746. FRAZEE, James
"Elegy for a Child." [Wind] (16:56) 86, p. 19.
"The Pickpocket of Torre Bermeja." [MissouriR] (9:2) 86, p. 223-225.
"Under the Alder Trees." [SouthernPR] (26:2) Fall 86, p. 26.
1747. FRAZER, Vernon
"Shana's Going to Disney World!" [Sam] (44:2 release 174) 86, p. 10.
1748. FRAZIER, Jane
"Journey." [DeKalbLAJ] (19:1) 86, p. 28.
"Scourings." [DeKalbLAJ] (19:2) 86, p. 23.
1749. FRAZIER, Mark
"Chimney Sparrows." [Prima] (10) 86, p. 38.
1750. FRAZIER, Robert
"Passing by the Black Hole at Cygnus X-1." [Vis] (20) 86, p. 11.
1751. FREDERICK, Charles
"Summertime." [JamesWR] (3:3) Spr 86, p. 6.
1752. FREDERIKSEN, Nancy
"Coming Home" (for D. J. M.). [SpoonRQ] (11:4) Fall 86, p. 48.
1753. FREED, Florence W.
"Lament of the Astronaut's Teenage Daughter." [SingHM] (14) 86, p. 34-35.
1754. FREEDMAN, William
"The Dwarf." [LitR] (29:3) Spr 86, p. 333.

1755. FREEMAN, John P.
"Church Paintings: In the Garden of Gethsemane." [ChrC] (103:10) 19-26 Mr 86, p. 298.

FREES, Madeline de
See DeFREES, Madeline

1756. FREIDINGER, Paul
"Upon Contemplating the Greenhouse Effect." [StoneC] (14:1/2) Fall-Wint 86-87, p. 37.
"Whatever You Have Come to Know." [FloridaR] (14:2) Fall-Wint 86, p. 55-56.

1757. FREISINGER, Randall R.
"Goose Farmer, 1936: A Photograph by Roman Vishniac." [Interim] (5:1) Spr 86, p. 21.
"Stalking Prairie: Madison, South Dakota." [Interim] (5:1) Spr 86, p. 22.
"Thirty-Fifth Bombing Mission, Cerignola, Italy" (for Richard Hugo). [Interim] (5:1) Spr 86, p. 23.

FRENCH, Davy James
See JAMES-FRENCH, Davy

1758. FRESCO, Ana María
"Soneto de Ausencia." [LetFem] (10:1) Spr 84, p. 109.

1759. FREY, Cecelia
"Birth of Sacrifice." [MalR] (73) Ja 86, p. 93.
"Homecoming." [AntigR] (64) Wint 86, p. 56.

1760. FRIEBERT, Stuart
"At the Office." [PraS] (60:1) Spr 86, p. 62.
"Fundamentum Divisionis." [Lips] (12) 86, p. 42.
"Gradually" (tr. of Bettina Behn). [Field] (35) Fall 86, p. 104.
"Heading East, Early Morning." [PennR] (2:1) Fall-Wint 86, p. 43.
"I'll Be Frank with You." [ConnPR] (4:1) 85, p. 28.
"One Dog, One Rabbit." [PennR] (1:2) Fall 85, p. 66.
"Safe for Now." [MSS] (5:1) 86, p. 114.
"Somewhere in East Germany." [PennR] (1:1) 85, p. 67.
"St. Sebastian." [NoDaQ] (54:2) Spr 86, p. 118.
"Tunisian Holiday." [Amelia] (3:2) Spr 86, p. 20.
"What They Told the Child" (tr. of Bettina Behn). [Field] (35) Fall 86, p. 103.

1761. FRIED, Philip
"The Demiurge's Troops." [ChiR] (35:3) Spr 86, p. 17.
"The hanged teddy bear with his red bow." [ChiR] (35:3) Spr 86, p. 19.
"The Kite." [CrabCR] (3:3) Sum 86, p. 26.
"Little God." [ChiR] (35:3) Spr 86, p. 18.
"A Round for the Dry Cleaner." [MemphisSR] (7:1) Fall 86, p. 13.
"Theogony." [ConnPR] (5:1) 86, p. 15.

1762. FRIEDMAN, Dorothy
"Miracle." [Wind] (16:58) 86, p. 18.
"Murder of a Poem." [CrossCur] (5:4/6:1) 86, p. 55.
"The Trip." [Wind] (16:58) 86, p. 18-19.

1763. FRIEDMAN, Jeff
"Reflexive." [IndR] (9:3) Sum 86, p. 78.

1764. FRIEDMAN, Nancy Bengis
"I Knew It Was a Boy." [Amelia] (3:4) Fall 86, p. 86-87.

1765. FRIEDMAN, S. L.
"Green Fruit." [YetASM] (4) 85, p. 7.
"No Certitude, No Peace." [DeKalbLAJ] (19:2) 86, p. 24.

1766. FRIEDMAN, Sari
"The Daughter at a 'Fathers and Sons' Poetry Reading." [ManhatPR] (7) Sum 86, p. 33.
"Diseases of the Poor." [ManhatPR] (7) Sum 86, p. 32.
"Fragment." [Amelia] (3:3) Sum 86, p. 68.
"Home Movies." [Amelia] (3:3) Sum 86, p. 68.
"When I Draw You." [ManhatPR] (7) Sum 86, p. 32.

1767. FRIEND, Robert
"The Return" (tr. of Dalia Hertz). [PoetL] (81:2) Sum 86, p. 102.

1768. FRIMAN, Alice
"The Boy in the Black Leather Jacket." [Confr] (33/34) Fall-Wint 86-87, p. 45.
"Girls" (for Lillian). [TexasR] (7:1/2) Spr-Sum 86, p. 72-73.
"The Magician's Daughter." [NoDaQ] (54:1) Wint 86, p. 60-61.
"The Reckoning." [GeoR] (40:3) Fall 86, p. 663.

"Walking in Holcomb Gardens" (to my mother). [TexasR] (7:1/2) Spr-Sum 86, p. 70-71.
1769. FRIST, Ron
"Not yours to know." [PoeticJ] (16) Fall 86, p. 9.
1770. FRITZ, Mary Ellen
"In Praise of Madness." [WebR] (11:2) Fall 86, p. 73.
1771. FROST, Carol
"Carousel." [WestB] (18) 86, p. 21.
"A Field Full of Black Cats." [PraS] (60:3) Fall 86, p. 106-107.
"The Gardener Envies Henri Rousseau." [DenQ] (20:4/21:1) Spr-Sum 86, p. 100.
"Harriet St." [GeoR] (40:4) Wint 86, p. 896.
"Hounding the Myth." [KanQ] (18:1/2) Wint-Spr 86, p. 27.
"Notes to the Cold." [QW] (22) Spr-Sum 86, p. 50-51.
"The Snake Skins." [PraS] (60:3) Fall 86, p. 108.
"The Whispering Geese" (Honorable Mention Poem, 1985/1986). [KanQ] (18:1/2) Wint-Spr 86, p. 26.
1772. FROST, Robert
"The Bearer of Evil Tidings." [YaleR] (75:2) Wint 86, p. 227-228.
"Departmental." [YaleR] (75:2) Wint 86, p. 226-227.
"Design." [Pembroke] (18) 86, p. 134.
"From a Milkweed Pod." [GeoR] (40:3) Fall 86, p. 664-665.
"Moon Compasses." [YaleR] (75:2) Wint 86, p. 225.
"Neither Out Far Nor In Deep." [YaleR] (75:2) Wint 86, p. 225.
1773. FROST, Robert A.
"Astronomer." [MidwQ] (28:1) Aut 86, p. 80.
1774. FRUMKIN, Gene
"Humiliation as Grist." [Chelsea] (45) 86, p. 45.
"Selective History." [Chelsea] (45) 86, p. 44.
1775. FRY, Cassandra
"Ballet Class." [YetASM] (4) 85, p. 2.
1776. FRY, Nan
"Openings." [CrossCur] (5:4/6:1) 86, p. 45.
1777. FRYER, Sarah
"Single Mother's Vita." [CentR] (30:1) Wint 86, p. 63-67.
FU, Du
      See DU, Fu
FU, Tu
      See DU, Fu
1778. FUERTES, Gloria
"No Writing Allowed" (tr. by Christopher Sawyer-Lauçanno). [AmerPoR] (15:4) Jl-Ag 86, p. 48.
"The Thin Women" (tr. by Christopher Sawyer-Lauçanno). [AmerPoR] (15:4) Jl-Ag 86, p. 48.
1779. FUGATE, Terry
"What She Was Trying to Say." [CumbPR] (5:2) Spr 86, p. 56-57.
1780. FUJINO, David
"Lines." [Contact] (7:38/39/40) Wint-Spr 86, p. 51.
1781. FULKER, Tina
"If I was in love today." [Bogg] (55) 86, p. 51.
"It will be no miracle." [Bogg] (55) 86, p. 40.
1782. FULLEN, George
"Outside of Eden" (A Verse Dialogue). [InterPR] (12:1) Spr 86, p. 70-77.
1783. FULLER, John
"Mirra Lake, August 17th." [SmPd] (23:3, #68) Fall 86, p. 28.
1784. FULLER, Roy
"Chemistry for Old Men." [SewanR] (94:4) Fall 86, p. 571.
"Old Poets." [SewanR] (94:4) Fall 86, p. 571.
"Old Puzzles." [SewanR] (94:4) Fall 86, p. 572.
1785. FULLER, William
"Harsh of France." [Sink] (2) 86, p. 8-12.
1786. FULLER, Winston
"Anger." [IndR] (9:2) Spr 86, p. 62.
"Defeat." [IndR] (9:2) Spr 86, p. 63.
1787. FULTON, Alice
"Another Troy." [Poetry] (147:6) Mr 86, p. 322-323.
"Behavioral Geography." [PoetryE] (20/21) Fall 86, p. 214-216.

"The Body Opulent." [Poetry] (147:6) Mr 86, p. 319-321.
"Dance Script with Electric Ballerina." [GeoR] (40:3) Fall 86, p. 666-668.
"The New Affluence." [NewYorker] (62:7) 7 Ap 86, p. 40.
"Peripheral Vision" (For David Lehman). [SouthwR] (71:1) Wint 86, p. 64-66.
"When Bosses Sank Steel Islands." [VirQR] (62:1) Wint 86, p. 42-43.
"The Wreckage Entrepreneur." [BostonR] (11:4) Ag 86, p. 25.
1788. FULTON, Keith Louise
"Breaking the Sound Barrier" (Hiroshima Day, 1985). [PraF] (7:3) Aut 86, p. 145.
"A Plea for Higher Education." [PraF] (7:3) Aut 86, p. 146-147.
1789. FULTON, Leah Shelleda
"Don't put all your eggs in one basket." [Comm] (113:6) 28 Mr 86, p. 163.
"Eddie My Love, a Ballad of the '50's." [BellR] (9:1) Spr 86, p. 7.
"The Wizard and the Lover." [BellR] (9:1) Spr 86, p. 7.
1790. FULTON, Suzy
"Houston, 1984" (for J.H.K.). [Pax] (3:1/2) Wint 85-86, p. 37.
1791. FUNGE, Robert
"Birds of Youth." [KanQ] (18:4) Fall 86, p. 148.
"A Cold Place." [SpoonRQ] (11:2) Spr 86, p. 42.
"Forty Hours." [SpoonRQ] (11:4) Fall 86, p. 41-42.
"John / Henry"" (Excerpt). [SoDakR] (24:2) Sum 86, p. 38.
"John / Henry, Four from Mpls." (Selections: I, IV). [SoDakR] (24:2) Sum 86, p. 36-37.
"The Meaning of Life." [CharR] (12:2) Fall 86, p. 64.
"Onan Bound." [CharR] (12:2) Fall 86, p. 63-64.
"The Unicorn." [HolCrit] (23:5) D 86, p. 13.
"Wine, Women & 'Dream Song 291'." [SpoonRQ] (11:2) Spr 86, p. 41.
1792. FUNK, Allison
"Elegy" (Jerusalem, 1978). [Poetry] (147:5) F 86, p. 265.
"Explaining a Death to My Son." [PoetryNW] (27:1) Spr 86, p. 7.
"Forms of Conversion." [Poetry] (147:5) F 86, p. 264.
"The Ghost of Elinor Wylie." [Poetry] (147:5) F 86, p. 263.
1793. FUNSTEN, Kenneth
"At Tom's #5." [SlipS] (6) 86, p. 7-8.
"The Ball Park." [Bogg] (55) 86, p. 27.
"Down by the Water I took You." [SlipS] (6) 86, p. 6.
"Yeah!" [Bogg] (55) 86, p. 33.
1794. FUQUA, C. S.
"Saturday." [Amelia] (3:1) Ja 86, p. 65.
1795. FURLONG, Waltrina
"Caliente, Nevada, 1937." [Interim] (5:2) Fall 86, p. 37.
"Modern Wedding." [Interim] (5:2) Fall 86, p. 36.
1796. FUSEK, Serena
"At 11 PM the Temperature is 85." [PoeticJ] (15) Sum 86, p. 31.
1797. FUTORANSKY, Luisa
"Probable Olvido de Itaca." [Mairena] (8:22) 86, p. 12.
1798. GABBARD, G. N.
"Film Clip from an Epic" (A free translation from the prelude of Beowulf, lines 1-53). [LitR] (30:1) Fall 86, p. 84-86.
"Hai-Kuhn." [Bogg] (55) 86, p. 31.
1799. GABIS, Rita
"The Potato Field." [MassR] (27:1) Spr 86, p. 68.
"The Scientist's Widow." [MassR] (27:1) Spr 86, p. 69.
1800. GAERTNER, Ken
"Prophet." [ChrC] (103:12) 9 Ap 86, p. 352.
1801. GALAN, Frantisek
"A Night with Hamlet" (Excerpt, tr. of Vladimir Holan, w. Clayton Eshleman). [Sulfur] (6:1, issue 16) 86, p. 130-137.
1802. GALASSI, Jonathan
"Elegy" (For J. T. G. lost 5/26/83). [SouthwR] (71:2) Spr 86, p. 244-245.
"Girl on a Bike" (Block Island). [SouthwR] (71:2) Spr 86, p. 244.
"Lateness." [ParisR] (28:100) Sum-Fall 86, p. 160.
"To a Classic Poet." [Thrpny] (25) Spr 86, p. 8.
1803. GALATI, Graziano
"Herald to Poetry." [WritersL] (1986:3), p. 11.
1804. GALE, Joseph Michael
"Red Wood." [PottPort] (8) 86-87, p. 52.

1805. GALEANO, Juan Carlos
    "Despedida." [Mester] (15:1) Spr 86, p. 48.
    "Estuvo Aquí." [Mester] (15:1) Spr 86, p. 50.
    "H2 O." [Mester] (15:1) Spr 86, p. 49.
    "Poética." [Mester] (15:1) Spr 86, p. 52.
    "Reloj." [Mester] (15:1) Spr 86, p. 51.
1806. GALIOTO, Salvatore
    "The Bronx." [SanFPJ] (9:1) 86, p. 30.
    "Independence Day." [SanFPJ] (9:1) 86, p. 32.
    "Memory Manager." [SanFPJ] (9:1) 86, p. 31.
    "Ms. Bag Lady's Choice." [SanFPJ] (8:3) 85, p. 70-71.
    "Poundian Debate N. II." [SanFPJ] (9:1) 86, p. 79-80.
    "Terricciola 1968." [SanFPJ] (9:1) 86, p. 78.
    "Terrorism II." [SanFPJ] (9:1) 86, p. 41.
    "Vietnam." [SanFPJ] (8:3) 85, p. 74-75.
1807. GALLAGHER, Tess
    "Accordingly." [Iowa] (16:1) Wint 86, p. 87-88.
1808. GALLARDO, Sara
    "Juliano Stampa" (tr. by Soledad H-D Jasin). [NewOR] (13:3) Fall 86, p. 58.
    "On the Puna" (tr. by Soledad H-D Jasin). [NewOR] (13:3) Fall 86, p. 80.
1809. GALLAS, John
    "Lincolnshire in a Hot Car." [Bogg] (56) 86, p. 55.
GALLAS, Louisa Loveridge
    See LOVERIDGE-GALLAS, Louisa
1810. GALLER, David
    "Antigua." [Confr] (32) Spr-Sum 86, p. 62.
    "As after a Great Illness." [Confr] (32) Spr-Sum 86, p. 62.
    "Looking at a Poet's Photo on His Book's Cover Before Beginning to Read."
        [Wind] (16:57) 86, p. 12.
    "Someone Somehow." [Wind] (16:57) 86, p. 12-13.
1811. GALT, Margot Kriel
    "Galleries — To Helena at Fourteen." [SingHM] (13) 86, p. 56-57.
1812. GALVIN, Brendan
    "An American Describes a New Sect" (1760). [TriQ] (67) Fall 86, p. 111-112.
    "Cougar." [TarRP] (25:1) Fall 85, p. 2.
    "Fog Township." [Poetry] (148:2) My 86, p. 63-64.
    "Greenhorns." [Verse] (5) 86, p. 39-40.
    "Letter Accompanying the Specimen of an Amazing Bird" (1763). [GeoR] (40:4)
        Wint 86, p. 909-912.
    "Looking for Captain Teabag." [TarRP] (25:1) Fall 85, p. 4-5.
    "Mayflies." [Poetry] (148:2) My 86, p. 66-67.
    "Old Map of Barnstable County." [GeoR] (40:3) Fall 86, p. 670-671.
    "Pole Beans." [Poetry] (148:2) My 86, p. 64-65.
    "Saying Her Name." [GeoR] (40:3) Fall 86, p. 669-670.
    "Sea Fogs at the Chequammitt Inn." [NewYorker] (62:4) 17 Mr 86, p. 101.
    "Summer School." [TarRP] (25:1) Fall 85, p. 3-4.
    "Town Pier Parking Lot." [TarRP] (25:1) Fall 85, p. 1.
1813. GALVIN, James
    "Coming into His Shop from a Bright Afternoon." [Iowa] (16:1) Wint 86, p. 180.
    "A Man's Vocation Is Nobody's Business." [GeoR] (40:3) Fall 86, p. 672.
    "Not So Much on the Land As in the Wind." [MissouriR] (9:1) 85-86, p. 22.
    "What We Said the Light Said." [PartR] (53:1) 86, p. 97-98.
1814. GANDER, Forrest
    "Cat, Clarinet, and Two Women." [StoneC] (14:1/2) Fall-Wint 86-87, p. 66-67.
    "The Face of Another." [StoneC] (14:1/2) Fall-Wint 86-87, p. 67-68.
    "Text, White Paper." [StoneC] (14:1/2) Fall-Wint 86-87, p. 66.
1815. GANGEL, Barbara L.
    "The Man Who Rapes Children." [YetASM] (5) 86, p. 7.
1816. GANGEMI, Kenneth
    "Names." [Ploughs] (12:4) 86, p. 161-162.
    "Random Reading in a Small Library." [Confr] (33/34) Fall-Wint 86-87, p. 36.
1817. GANGOPADHYA, Sunil
    "I Hang Around" (tr. by Rabiul Hasan). [Amelia] (3:3) Sum 86, p. 101.
1818. GANICK, Peter
    "The Password Is Elegance." [Sink] (1) 86, p. 35.
    "A Real Tool." [Sink] (1) 86, p. 34.

"Realm of Control." [Sink] (1) 86, p. 33.
"Twisted from an Identity of Relata" (Selection: sixth part). [Sink] (2) 86, p. 31-35.
"Vestigial Promises." [Sink] (1) 86, p. 35.
1819. GANSZ, David C. D.
"Animadversions" (Selections). [Notus] (1:1) Fall 86, p. 58-62.
1820. GARCIA, Arnoldo
"El Hombre por el Hombre." [Contact] (8:41/42/43) Fall-Wint 86-87, p. 20.
"Of Man by Man" (tr. by Sesshu Foster, w. the author). [Contact] (8:41/42/43)
      Fall-Wint 86-87, p. 21-22.
1821. GARCIA, Reloy
"Pen." [KanQ] (18:1/2) Wint-Spr 86, p. 309-310.
1822. GARCIA ALONSO, Agustín
"Pezones." [Mairena] (8:22) 86, p. 21.
1823. GARCIA CABRERA, Pedro
"Isla y Mujer." [Mairena] (8:22) 86, p. 76.
1824. GARCIA LORCA, Federico
"El Amor Duerme en el Pecho del Poeta" (original, French tr. by André Belamich,
      and Spanish tr. of the French by Jesús Tomé). [Mairena] (8:21) 86, p. 44-46.
1825. GARDINIER, Suzanne
"Cutting." [NewRep] (195:10) 8 S 86, p. 40.
"Letter to My Mother." [Shen] (36:4) 86, p. 33-34.
"Natural Forces." [Shen] (36:4) 86, p. 34-35.
1826. GARDNER, Eric
"Everything the Good Lord Ever Wrote Was in 12-Bar." [PikeF] (7) Spr 86, p. 22.
1827. GARDNER, Geoffrey
"Counting." [CharR] (12:1) Spr 86, p. 85.
"Shadow." [CharR] (12:1) Spr 86, p. 85.
1828. GARDNER, Stephen
"Cheap Shot: Confessional Poetry at 4 A.M." [KanQ] (18:1/2) Wint-Spr 86, p. 48.
"For Stephanie, My Niece, Age 3." [CrescentR] (4:2) Fall 86, p. 139.
"Knife." [KanQ] (18:1/2) Wint-Spr 86, p. 46-47.
"Spring, Saturday Suburbia." [KanQ] (18:1/2) Wint-Spr 86, p. 47.
1829. GARFITT, Roger
"Skara Brae." [Stand] (27:4) Aut 86, p. 46-47.
1830. GARGANO, Elizabeth
"At the Day Care Center." [SingHM] (13) 86, p. 77.
1831. GARIN, Marita
"At the Nursing Home." [CrescentR] (4:1) Spr 86, p. 104.
"Dissolution." [Hudson] (39:3) Aut 86, p. 464-465.
"Taken near the Jocko River, Montana — 1932." [Hudson] (39:3) Aut 86, p.
      465-466.
"A Yard near Elizabethton, Tennessee." [KenR] (NS 7:3) Sum 85, p. 100.
1832. GARMON, John
"Touch Your Sleeves Gently and Say Thanks." [PassN] (7:2) Spr-Sum 86, p. 8.
1833. GARRETT, Charlotte
"At Long Hill Farm." [SouthernR] (22:3) Sum 86, p. 556-557.
"In Lieu of a Letter to Ndutu" (for P.D.M.). [SouthernR] (22:3) Sum 86, p.
      553-554.
"Snowbirds." [SouthernR] (22:3) Sum 86, p. 555.
1834. GARRETT, Lorene V.
"Broken Friend." [BlackALF] (20:3) Fall 86, p. 306.
"Undying Treachery." [BlackALF] (20:3) Fall 86, p. 306.
"Winter Green." [BlackALF] (20:3) Fall 86, p. 306-307.
1835. GARRISON, David
"Close My Eyes" (tr. of José Bergamín). [WebR] (11:1) Spr 86, p. 32.
"The Echo of Your Voice" (tr. of José Bergamín). [LitR] (29:3) Spr 86, p. 346.
"Hidden in the Dark Night" (tr. of José Bergamín). [LitR] (29:3) Spr 86, p. 346.
"In This Dark Night" (tr. of José Bergamín). [WebR] (11:1) Spr 86, p. 33.
"When a Hand of Shadow" (tr. of José Bergamín). [WebR] (11:1) Spr 86, p. 32.
1836. GARSON, Karl
"The Return." [CreamCR] (11:1) 86?, p. 53.
1837. GARTON, Victoria
"Boughten Rooms." [Farm] (3:2) Spr-Sum 86, p. 54.
"If a Lizard Should Dream." [Poem] (55) Mr 86, p. 1.
1838. GARZA, San Juanita
"Smugglers of Middle." [SecC] (14:1) 86, p. 64.

1839. GASPAR, Frank
   "August." [KenR] (NS 8:3) Sum 86, p. 51.
   "Catechism." [KenR] (NS 8:3) Sum 86, p. 52-53.
   "Leaving Pico." [KenR] (NS 8:3) Sum 86, p. 49.
   "Passing." [KenR] (NS 8:3) Sum 86, p. 50.
1840. GASSER, Ann
   "It Just Happened." [Amelia] (3:3) Sum 86, p. 58.
1841. GATES, Bea
   "Afterdeaths." [Raccoon] (20) Ap 86, p. 41.
   "Small World" (for Jean). [Raccoon] (20) Ap 86, p. 40.
1842. GATES, Bob
   "At the Nude." [Bogg] (56) 86, p. 27.
1843. GATES, Edward
   "Subbing for the Art Teacher." [PottPort] (8) 86-87, p. 51.
GATTUTA, Margo la
   See LaGATTUTA, Margo
1844. GAUER, Jim
   "Will This Thought Do?" [ParisR] (28:100) Sum-Fall 86, p. 161-162.
1845. GAUTREAU, Anne L.
   "Mind Snack." [EngJ] (75:6) O 86, p. 39.
1846. GAVER, James
   "It Just So Happens." [Sulfur] (6:1, issue 16) 86, p. 33.
   "No One Feels Like I Do." [Sulfur] (6:1, issue 16) 86, p. 34.
1847. GAVRILIS, Nancy
   "Windward in the Rubble" (Selection: "The Sweetness of Pears"). [Nimrod] (30:1)
      Fall-Wint 86, p. 54-55.
1848. GAY, Tom
   "Summer Haste." [TarRP] (26:1) Fall 86, p. 43.
1849. GAZINSKI, Joanne
   "Haiku" (3 poems). [Northeast] (series 4:4) Wint 86-87, p. 18.
1850. GEAREN, Ann
   "Good Friday in the Islands: A Meditation on Death." [Prima] (10) 86, p. 36-37.
1851. GEDDES, Gary
   "The Apprenticeship." [CanLit] (110) Fall 86, p. 78.
   "Gail Pollock." [CanLit] (110) Fall 86, p. 60.
   "Hong Kong" (Excerpt). [Event] (15:2) 86, p. 22-23.
1852. GEHRING, Wes D.
   "Red Skelton: A One Man Band of Comedy." [BallSUF] (27:4) Aut 86, p. 51-52.
1853. GELBURD, Sue Russell
   "The Fear." [PennR] (1:1) 85, p. 72.
1854. GELDMAN, Mordechai
   "A Bird" (tr. by Harold Schimmel). [PoetL] (81:2) Sum 86, p. 111.
   "My Father in His Youth" (tr. by Harold Schimmel). [PoetL] (81:2) Sum 86, p. 112.
   "With Long Hooks" (tr. by Harold Schimmel). [PoetL] (81:2) Sum 86, p. 111-112.
1855. GELLIS, Barrie
   "Heaven Is." [YellowS] (19) Sum 86, p. 43.
1856. GELMI, Alexa
   "When I find a pair of panties in the street." [MidAR] (7:1) 86, p. 136.
1857. GEMINDER, Kathleen
   "Death Songs for My Daughter." [AntigR] (64) Wint 86, p. 62-64.
   "Swan Lake." [MinnR] (NS 27) Fall 86, p. 78-80.
1858. GENEGA, Paul
   "Death and the Sculptor." [CrossCur] (6:2) 86, p. 70-71.
   "The Fairy Tale Fathers." [LitR] (29:3) Spr 86, p. 284.
   "Safe Places." [LitR] (29:3) Spr 86, p. 285.
GENGYE, Luo
   See LUO, Gengye
1859. GENTLEMAN, Dorothy Corbett
   "After the Service." [AntigR] (66/67) Sum-Aut 86, p. 151.
   "Disturbed Poet." [WritersL] (1986:6), p. 13.
   "Dream." [AntigR] (66/67) Sum-Aut 86, p. 150.
   "Freezing Rain." [CanLit] (111) Wint 86, p. 26.
   "Here Is the Sea." [Quarry] (35:3) Sum 86, p. 21.
   "Himself the Poet." [WritersL] (1986:2), p. 28.
   "Night Fire." [Event] (15:1) 86, p. 116.
   "Winter Solstice." [Event] (15:1) 86, p. 117.

1860. GEORGE, Alice (*See also* GEORGE, Alice Rose)
"Love That Needs Leaving." [ManhatPR] (7) Sum 86, p. 59.
"Note to a Rescuer." [ManhatPR] (7) Sum 86, p. 58.
1861. GEORGE, Alice Rose (*See also* GEORGE, Alice)
"Success." [ParisR] (28:101) Wint 86, p. 271-272.
1862. GEORGE, Anne
"Why We Have Daughters." [NegC] (6:1) Wint 86, p. 64-66.
1863. GEORGE, Diana Hume
"A Genesis." [NegC] (6:1) Wint 86, p. 25-30.
1864. GEORGICK, Lily
"Demeter Calls to Persephone." [ManhatPR] (7) Sum 86, p. 53.
1865. GERBER, Dan
"In the Winter Dark." [GeoR] (40:3) Fall 86, p. 673.
1866. GERGELY, Agnes
"Prayer before Turning Off the Light" (tr. by Jascha Kessler, w. Maria Körösy).
[NewL] (53:1) Fall 86, p. 25.
1867. GERMAN, Norman
"Ergo." [SanFPJ] (8:1) 85, p. 36.
"More Than a Haiku." [SanFPJ] (8:1) 85, p. 35.
1868. GERRY, David
"Memorial." [NoDaQ] (54:1) Wint 86, p. 62-63.
"Peach." [JamesWR] (3:3) Spr 86, p. 13.
GERTH, Miguel Gonzales
See GONZALEZ-GERTH, Miguel
1869. GERTLER, Pesha
"The Season of Bitter Root and Snake Venom." [Calyx] (9:2/3) Wint 86, p. 87.
1870. GERVAIS, C. H.
"To Marc Chagall in Jerusalem." [CrossC] (8:1) 86, p. 6.
"To Reno Bertoia." [CrossC] (8:1) 86, p. 6.
1871. GERZ, Jochen
"Objects Are Withdrawing from Me More and More" (Malmö 1973/75, San
Francisco 1986). [Acts] (5) 86, p. 52.
1872. GETTLER, Andrew
"Family Ties." [PoeticJ] (15) Sum 86, p. 8-9.
1873. GETTY, Sarah
"Getting Clearer." [NewRep] (195:6/7) 11-18 Ag 86, p. 40.
1874. GEWANTER, David
"Oda" (tr. of Francisco de Medrano). [CumbPR] (5:2) Spr 86, p. 55.
1875. GEYER, William
"Not Winter, on the Central Flyway." [SoDakR] (24:2) Sum 86, p. 98.
1876. GHIRADELLA, Robert
"Farmers." [CrossCur] (5:4/6:1) 86, p. 122.
"Language" (for Jack Spicer). [CrossCur] (5:4/6:1) 86, p. 123.
"Photograph." [Confr] (33/34) Fall-Wint 86-87, p. 141.
1877. GHISELIN, Brewster
"A Celebration." [WillowS] (17) Wint 86, p. 51-52.
"Elemental." [QW] (23) 86, p. 98-103.
"Leone Traverso" (in Italian & English, tr. by the author). [WillowS] (17) Wint 86,
p. 48-49.
"Llewelyn Powys" (Spring, 1929). [WillowS] (17) Wint 86, p. 50.
1878. GIANNATTASIO, Edward M.
"Bad Lands." [SanFPJ] (8:4) 85, p. 91.
"Coming Attractions." [SanFPJ] (8:4) 85, p. 70-71.
"Dishpan Hands." [SanFPJ] (9:1) 86, p. 69.
"Duel in the Sun." [SanFPJ] (8:4) 85, p. 83.
"Freedom's Child." [SanFPJ] (8:4) 85, p. 7.
"Hi Ho." [SanFPJ] (8:3) 85, p. 10-12.
"The Last Upper." [SanFPJ] (8:2) 85, p. 12.
"Medium Rare Rump State." [SanFPJ] (8:4) 85, p. 90.
"My Piano Keys." [SanFPJ] (9:1) 86, p. 22-23.
"The Secretary of State." [SanFPJ] (8:3) 85, p. 31.
"The Security of Our Nation." [SanFPJ] (8:2) 85, p. 10-11.
1879. GIANOLI, Paul
"The Child." [SoDakR] (24:2) Sum 86, p. 123.
1880. GIBB, Robert
"Among the Successions." [WillowS] (17) Wint 86, p. 27-28.

143

"At Newswanger's." [PraS] (60:1) Spr 86, p. 83.
"Dillingersville Road." [PoetryNW] (27:1) Spr 86, p. 45-46.
"Listening to the Ballgame." [WillowS] (17) Wint 86, p. 29-30.
"The Nestling." [Wind] (16:56) 86, p. 21.
"Poem to the Dutch Cartographer, Andreas Cellarius." [SnapD] (9:2) Spr 86, p. 59.
"Pruning the Orchard." [Wind] (16:56) 86, p. 20-21.
"Sitting in the Dark." [PraS] (60:1) Spr 86, p. 84-85.
"Turtle Shell." [Wind] (16:56) 86, p. 20.
"Working in the Yard I Think of Thoreau Who Opposed the Mexican War."
    [PoetryNW] (27:1) Spr 86, p. 46-47.
1881. GIBBONS, Kaye
    "June Bug." [CarolQ] (38:2) Wint 86, p. 55.
1882. GIBBONS, Reginald
    "Angel Triptych" (tr. of Hugo Achugar, w. the author). [TriQ] (66) Spr-Sum 86, p.
        161-162.
    "Anyone Can Stand" (tr. of Stanislaw Baranczak, w. Antony Graham). [TriQ] (65)
        Wint 86, p. 88.
    "Away from You." [Nat] (242:13) 5 Ap 86, p. 494.
    "Curriculum Vitae" (tr. of Stanislaw Baranczak). [SouthwR] (71:4) Aut 86, p. 436.
    "Family Portrait" (tr. of Hugo Achugar, w. the author). [TriQ] (66) Spr-Sum 86, p.
        160.
    "Inscription" (tr. of Hugo Achugar, w. the author). [TriQ] (66) Spr-Sum 86, p.
        158-159.
    "The New World" (tr. of Stanislaw Baranczak, w. the author). [AmerPoR] (15:5)
        S-O 86, p. 44.
    "No Matter What Has Happened This May." [Raccoon] (20) Ap 86, p. 24-25.
    "Prison Poems and Drawings" (tr. of Irina Ratushinskaya, w. Roman Durbin).
        [TriQ] (66) Spr-Sum 86, p. 152-157.
    "A Second Nature" (tr. of Stanislaw Baranczak, w. the author). [AmerPoR] (15:5)
        S-O 86, p. 44.
    "Setting the Hand Brake" (tr. of Stanislaw Baranczak). [SouthwR] (71:4) Aut 86, p.
        437-438.
    "Small Talk" (tr. of Stanislaw Baranczak). [SouthwR] (71:4) Aut 86, p. 437.
    "Some Day, Years from Now" (tr. of Stanislaw Baranczak, w. the author).
        [AmerPoR] (15:5) S-O 86, p. 44.
    "We Drew the Proper Conclusions from the Events" (tr. of Stanislaw Baranczak, w.
        Frank Kujawinski). [TriQ] (65) Wint 86, p. 89.
    "Wildflowers." [PartR] (53:1) 86, p. 102.
1883. GIBBONS, Robert James
    "Bag Lady Marsupials." [BallSUF] (26:4) Aut 85, p. 14.
1884. GIBSON, Margaret
    "Darkroom Nights." [Iowa] (16:2) Spr-Sum 86, p. 141-142.
    "Green Pepper." [MissouriR] (9:2) 86, p. 206.
    "Home." [Iowa] (16:2) Spr-Sum 86, p. 140-141.
    "In the Market." [Iowa] (16:2) Spr-Sum 86, p. 143-144.
    "Retreat to the Future." [Iowa] (16:2) Spr-Sum 86, p. 146-149.
    "Soledad." [Iowa] (16:2) Spr-Sum 86, p. 144-146.
1885. GIBSON, Morgan
    "A Defense of Poetry — 1" (for Karl Young). [CrossCur] (6:2) 86, p. 114.
1886. GIBSON, Stephen M.
    "American Primitive." [Chelsea] (45) 86, p. 78.
    "The Answer." [Chelsea] (45) 86, p. 79.
    "Arsenic." [BlackWR] (12:2) Spr 86, p. 68.
    "Family" (a photograph of Kansas). [Chelsea] (45) 86, p. 40.
    "The Odyssey at Horn and Hardart." [Chelsea] (45) 86, p. 80.
    "Rubbings." [MidAR] (6:1) 86?, p. 89.
    "View of the Paris Communard Dead Murdered by Versailles Troops . . ., 1871."
        [SouthernHR] (20:1) Wint 86, p. 23-26.
1887. GILBERT, Celia
    "Behind Doors." [DenQ] (20:4/21:1) Spr-Sum 86, p. 99.
    "Moonscapes." [DenQ] (20:4/21:1) Spr-Sum 86, p. 98.
1888. GILBERT, David
    "Less than 100" (Selections). [Sink] (2) 86, p. 56-57.
1889. GILBERT, Gerry
    "Sex and the Single Mushroom" (Selections: 4 poems). [Rampike] (5:1) 86, p. 11.

"Tonight in Vancouver Would Be Impossible Without You, Bob" (for Robert
Creeley, 16 May 1986). [WestCR] (21:2) O 86, p. 31-36.
1890. GILBERT, Marie
"The Magic of Two." [InterPR] (12:2) Fall 86, p. 73.
"On Watching Challenger" (January 28, 1986). [InterPR] (12:2) Fall 86, p. 71.
"Recompense." [InterPR] (12:2) Fall 86, p. 72.
1891. GILBERT, Sandra M.
"For Beethoven." [MissouriR] (9:2) 86, p. 112-113.
"Gull." [MissouriR] (9:2) 86, p. 110.
"Hooked Rug." [MissouriR] (9:2) 86, p. 111.
1892. GILBERT, Virginia
"On the Nolichucky." [MSS] (5:1) 86, p. 70-72.
1893. GILCHRIST, Ellen
"A Mother's Dream." [PraS] (60:1) Spr 86, p. 21.
"Song in January." [PraS] (60:1) Spr 86, p. 20.
"There's Some Stuff That Is Always Poetry." [PraS] (60:1) Spr 86, p. 19.
1894. GILDNER, Gary
"A Gathering Off the Avenue Victor Hugo." [MalR] (73) Ja 86, p. 35-38.
"Pies." [CentR] (30:2) Spr 86, p. 137-138.
"Wheat." [GeoR] (40:3) Fall 86, p. 674-676.
1895. GILGUN, John
"Political Consciousness 1986." [Raccoon] (21) Je 86, p. 15.
"The Spirit of Irony." [Raccoon] (21) Je 86, p. 16.
"The Spirit of the Other Manifests Himself in Des Moines, Iowa, Christmas, 1983."
[Raccoon] (20) Ap 86, p. 10-11.
GILL, Alicia Fernandez
See FERNANDEZ GILL, Alicia
1896. GILL, John
"I detest long-winded poetry" (from "The Palatine Anthology, tr. of Callimachus).
[YellowS] (21) Wint 86, p. 24.
"If you're thirsty, snow in summer is sweet" (from "The Palatine Anthology, tr. of
Asclepiades). [YellowS] (21) Wint 86, p. 24.
"If you've been married once" (anonymous translation from "The Palatine
Anthology). [YellowS] (21) Wint 86, p. 24.
"I'm only twenty-one and life is already a burden" (from "The Palatine Anthology,
tr. of Asclepiades). [YellowS] (21) Wint 86, p. 25.
"Nothing is sweeter than love" (from "The Palatine Anthology, tr. of Nossis).
[YellowS] (21) Wint 86, p. 24.
"Now you're ready!" (from "The Palatine Anthology, tr. of Strato). [YellowS] (21)
Wint 86, p. 24.
"They say a man bitten by a rabid dog" (from "The Palatine Anthology, tr. of Paulus
Silentiarius). [YellowS] (21) Wint 86, p. 24.
"When you were a green grape you refused me" (anonymous translation from "The
Palatine Anthology). [YellowS] (21) Wint 86, p. 24.
"Yesterday, in the baths" (from "The Palatine Anthology, tr. of Strato). [YellowS]
(21) Wint 86, p. 24.
"You ought to stop this search for perverse pleasure" (anonymous translation from
"The Palatine Anthology). [YellowS] (21) Wint 86, p. 24.
1897. GILL, Rosalind
"Ciudad de Mexico" (tr. of Jean-Claude Masson). [Writ] (18) 86, c87, p. 102.
"Honduras" (tr. of Jean-Claude Masson). [Writ] (18) 86, c87, p. 104.
"Past Present" (tr. of Jean-Claude Masson). [Writ] (18) 86, c87, p. 101.
"Scherzo" (tr. of Jean-Claude Masson). [Writ] (18) 86, c87, p. 103.
1898. GILL, Stephen
"I Have Seen." [WritersL] (1986:5), p. 9.
"To War-Mongers." [WritersL] (1986:6), p. 8.
1899. GILLAM, Brian M.
"Summerhouse." [PottPort] (8) 86-87, p. 38.
1900. GILLAN, Maria
"Arturo." [Lips] (12) 86, p. 30-31.
"Christmas Shopping for My Mother: December, 1985." [Lips] (12) 86, p. 32-33.
1901. GILLATT, D.
"There is a rough compassion in the rain." [Verse] (5) 86, p. 17.
1902. GILLESPIE, Mary
"Gardens and Walkways." [KanQ] (18:3) Sum 86, p. 98.
"Gray River, Far Shore." [CapeR] (21:1) Spr 86, p. 9.

"Modern Day Meditation." [LittleM] (15:1) 86, p. 39-40.
"San Simeon." [KanQ] (18:3) Sum 86, p. 102.
1903. GILLILAND, Mary
"Five Teeth Grin on the Gnawed Jawbone." [StoneC] (14:1/2) Fall-Wint 86-87, p.
42.
1904. GILLIS, Don
"Writers in an Oral Tradition." [AntigR] (66/67) Sum-Aut 86, p. 112.
1905. GILMORE, John C.
"Reasons Before & After the Fact." [Sam] (46:2 release 182) 86, p. 26.
1906. GILMORE, Patricia
"Child." [CapeR] (21:1) Spr 86, p. 6.
"December." [PassN] (7:2) Spr-Sum 86, p. 14.
1907. GIMENEZ, Nelly E.
"Casi Nada." [Mairena] (8:21) 86, p. 96.
"Gris." [Mairena] (8:21) 86, p. 96.
"Poema de las Luces." [Mairena] (8:21) 86, p. 96.
"Las Postas." [Mairena] (8:21) 86, p. 95.
"Testimoniamos sombra." [Mairena] (8:21) 86, p. 95-96.
1908. GINSBERG, Allen
"Black Shroud." [Sulfur] (6:2, issue 17) 86, p. 22-24.
"I Love Old Whitman So." [Atlantic] (258:1) Jl 86, p. 66.
"Quatrains." [ParisR] (28:100) Sum-Fall 86, p. 163.
"Reading Bai Juyi." [Sulfur] (6:2, issue 17) 86, p. 17-22.
"Things I Don't Know." [Sulfur] (6:2, issue 17) 86, p. 24-25.
"Written in My Dream by W. C. Williams." [Poetry] (148:5) Ag 86, p. 256-257.
1909. GIOIA, Dana
"An Emigré in Autumn." [Boulevard] (1:1/2) Wint 86, p. 10.
"The End of a Season." [Hudson] (38:4) Wint 86, p. 614.
"Equations of the Light." [NewYorker] (62:19) 30 Je 86, p. 32.
"Five Speeches for Pygmalion." [SouthwR] (71:1) Wint 86, p. 42-44.
"For Joe Weaver in Minneapolis." [Boulevard] (1:1/2) Wint 86, p. 9.
"The Homecoming." [Boulevard] (1:1/2) Wint 86, p. 11.
"In Cheever Country." [Hudson] (38:4) Wint 86, p. 609-611.
"Los Angeles after the Rain." [Hudson] (38:4) Wint 86, p. 612-613.
"Maze without a Minotaur." [Hudson] (38:4) Wint 86, p. 613-614.
"Pornotopia." [SouthwR] (71:1) Wint 86, p. 42.
"A Short History of Tobacco." [Hudson] (38:4) Wint 86, p. 611-612.
"The Silence of the Poets." [SouthwR] (71:1) Wint 86, p. 44-45.
"Sleeping on the River." [Boulevard] (1:1/2) Wint 86, p. 12-13.
1910. GIOSEFFI, Daniela
"Answer to 'The Suicide'." [ManhatPR] (6) Wint-Spr 85-86, p. 34.
1911. GIRARD, Linda Walvoord
"Exodus." [PraS] (60:4) Wint 86, p. 74-77.
"Magi." [PraS] (60:4) Wint 86, p. 73-74.
1912. GIROUX, Roger
"Ailleurs." [InterPR] (12:1) Spr 86, p. 54.
"As from the Shadows" (tr. by Richard Zenith). [InterPR] (12:1) Spr 86, p. 49.
"By Itself" (tr. by Richard Zenith). [InterPR] (12:1) Spr 86, p. 55.
"Cette Phrase Qui Doute." [InterPR] (12:1) Spr 86, p. 56.
"Comme des Ombres." [InterPR] (12:1) Spr 86, p. 55.
"De Soi Comme Sable Toujours." [InterPR] (12:1) Spr 86, p. 54.
"Here a Lake, Blue" (tr. by Richard Zenith). [InterPR] (12:1) Spr 86, p. 51.
"Un Lac Est Ici, Bleu." [InterPR] (12:1) Spr 86, p. 50.
"Night Passes through the Heart" (tr. by Richard Zenith). [InterPR] (12:1) Spr 86,
p. 53.
"Nous Ne Saurons Jamais." [InterPR] (12:1) Spr 86, p. 52.
"Par le Coeur la Nuit Passe." [InterPR] (12:1) Spr 86, p. 52.
"Quel Est Ce Lieu Qui Ne Me Parle Pas." [InterPR] (12:1) Spr 86, p. 58.
"Somewhere" (tr. by Richard Zenith). [InterPR] (12:1) Spr 86, p. 55.
"This Phrase Which Doubts" (tr. by Richard Zenith). [InterPR] (12:1) Spr 86, p. 57.
"We Will Never Know" (tr. by Richard Zenith). [InterPR] (12:1) Spr 86, p. 53.
"What Is This Place?" (tr. by Richard Zenith). [InterPR] (12:1) Spr 86, p. 59.
1913. GJESDAL, Dyane
"Devil's Island." [PottPort] (8) 86-87, p. 3.

1914. GJUZEL, Bogomil
"On the Way Back" (tr. by Carolyn Kizer, w. the author). [WillowS] (17) Wint 86, p. 72.
"Prostitution" (tr. by Carolyn Kizer, w. the author). [WillowS] (17) Wint 86, p. 73.
"When I Came Back" (tr. by Carolyn Kizer, w. the author). [WillowS] (17) Wint 86, p. 71.
1915. GLADDING, Jody
"To Archie Ammons from Pescadero Beach, Ca." [Pembroke] (18) 86, p. 147.
1916. GLADHART, Amalia R.
"Shooting Hoops Before Rain." [WoosterR] (5) Spr 86, p. 20.
1917. GLADING, Jan
"Monterey Pine Cone, Fallen from an Aged Tree." [Kaleid] (13) Sum-Fall 86, p. 55.
1918. GLADUN, Chris
"Ballad of the Table" (tr. of Kazimierz Wierzynski). [Writ] (18) 86, c87, p. 138-140.
"Fair Play, a Morality Play" (tr. of Kazimierz Wierzynski). [Writ] (18) 86, c87, p. 137.
"Like One Who Knows." [Writ] (17) 85, c86, p. 10.
"Near-Death Experience II." [Writ] (17) 85, c86, p. 5-6.
"The Orphanage at Zamitan." [Writ] (17) 85, c86, p. 8-9.
"The Purser's Dream." [Writ] (17) 85, c86, p. 7.
"Scientific Expedition" (tr. of Kazimierz Wierzynski). [Writ] (18) 86, c87, p. 136.
1919. GLANCY, Diane
"Clothes Horse." [CutB] (25) Fall-Wint 86, p. 72-73.
"Evolution of the Sacred Dog." [CutB] (25) Fall-Wint 86, p. 71.
"I Was." [Puerto] (22:1) Fall 86, p. 25-26.
"Over blue pines." [MidwQ] (27:4) Sum 86, p. 46.
"Oyster Bed." [Puerto] (22:1) Fall 86, p. 27-28.
"Philbrook Art Gallery, Tulsa" (Selections: "Fortitude," "Write on Two Sticks," "Winnifred"). [Nimrod] (30:1) Fall-Wint 86, p. 47-50.
"Red Moonwalking Woman." [Ploughs] (12:4) 86, p. 148.
"The River Bridge." [Confr] (33/34) Fall-Wint 86-87, p. 144.
"Salvador." [MidwQ] (27:4) Sum 86, p. 466.
"The Sign Writer." [MidwQ] (27:4) Sum 86, p. 465.
"Someone Has to Drive" (For Olga). [Abraxas] (34) 86, p. 42.
"Sunday Storm, March Eighteenth." [LitR] (29:2) Wint 86, p. 236-237.
1920. GLANG, Gabriele
"Consider the Horseradish" (For Gillian, In Memoriam). [NewL] (53:1) Fall 86, p. 103.
1921. GLASER, Elton
"Cradlesong" (For Bob and Carol Pope). [CharR] (12:1) Spr 86, p. 63.
"Deathbed Edition." [CharR] (12:1) Spr 86, p. 58-60.
"El Rancho Roacho." [LittleM] (15:1) 86, p. 43-44.
"Elegant Solutions." [PoetryNW] (27:3) Aut 86, p. 9-10.
"Misery by My Gauge" (tr. of Raymond Queneau). [ColR] (NS 13:1) Fall 85, p. 40.
"Orpheus at the Orpheum." [CharR] (12:1) Spr 86, p. 61-62.
"Vacation." [CharR] (12:1) Spr 86, p. 62.
1922. GLASER, Michael S.
"Leaving Things Behind." [ChrC] (103:12) 9 Ap 86, p. 356.
"Nightwatch." [Poem] (56) N 86, p. 30.
1923. GLASS, Jesse
"In Winter." [CreamCR] (11:1) 86?, p. 46-47.
1924. GLASS, Malcolm
"How the Moon Got Its Handle." [MidwQ] (27:2) Wint 86, p. 199.
"Logic, Like Weather." [CreamCR] (11:1) 86?, p. 42.
"Mockingbird." [NegC] (6:4) Fall 86, p. 69.
1925. GLAZE, Andrew
"Smith" (to Richard Eberhart). [NegC] (6:2/3) Spr-Sum 86, p. 64.
1926. GLAZER, Jane
"Another Wedding." [BellArk] (2:5) S-O 86, p. 5.
"Photography Workshop." [Poem] (55) Mr 86, p. 52.
"Short Rations." [BellArk] (2:5) S-O 86, p. 7.
"Vanishing Point." [BellArk] (2:4) Jl-Ag 86, p. 8.
"Veterinarian's Daughter." [BellArk] (2:4) Jl-Ag 86, p. 3.
"We Will Build a Fire, Now." [BellArk] (2:5) S-O 86, p. 6.
"Woman Carrying Plum Blossoms." [BellArk] (2:4) Jl-Ag 86, p. 6.

"Yi-Feng Dreams of a New Life." [Poem] (55) Mr 86, p. 53.
1927. GLAZIER, Jan Riley
"I've Come Too Near." [OroM] (4:1-4) My 85, p. 52.
1928. GLAZIER, Loss Pequeño
"Banana leaves." [Os] (23) 86, p. 4.
"Unwritten poem." [OroM] (4:1-4) My 85, p. 47-48.
1929. GLEASON, Paul
"Karmauac." [MoodySI] (16/17) Sum 86, p. 41.
1930. GLEN, Emilie
"New Paint." [DeKalbLAJ] (19:3/4) 86, p. 73.
"Sound Pennies." [Amelia] (3:4) Fall 86, p. 72.
1931. GLENN, Laura
"After Me." [StoneC] (13:3/4) Spr-Sum 86, p. 27.
"Out on a Limb." [SnapD] (9:2) Spr 86, p. 61.
"While You're Away." [Ascent] (11:3) 86, p. 14.
1932. GLENN, Wendy
"Those Melons." [Electrum] (38) Spr 86, p. 20.
1933. GLICKMAN, Susan
"For My Students in English 108 Who Complain That All Modern Literature Is Too
Depressing." [MalR] (75) Je 86, p. 103.
"The Romance of Language." [MalR] (75) Je 86, p. 101.
"Sassafras" (To the memory of William Carlos Williams). [GreenfR] (13:3/4)
Sum-Fall 86, p. 65.
"Saxifrage" (To the memory of William Carlos Williams). [MalR] (75) Je 86, p.
102.
1934. GLOVER, Albert
"Song." [Contact] (7:38/39/40) Wint-Spr 86, p. 87.
1935. GLOVER, Jon
"Microscopes and Flora." [Stand] (27:4) Aut 86, p. 60.
1936. GLUCK, Robert
"APR." [Acts] (5) 86, p. 104.
"Bataille." [Acts] (5) 86, p. 105.
"Business." [Acts] (5) 86, p. 103.
"Violette LeDuc." [Acts] (5) 86, p. 102.
1937. GLUCK, Tereze
"Preponderance of the Small." [Chelsea] (45) 86, p. 17-19.
1938. GODFREY, John
"Bath." [LittleM] (15:2) 86, p. 14.
"Conveyances." [LittleM] (15:1) 86, p. 23-24.
"Eff." [LittleM] (15:2) 86, p. 13.
"Fur." [LittleM] (15:1) 86, p. 26.
"In the Chamber." [LittleM] (15:1) 86, p. 22-23.
"Old Guitar." [LittleM] (15:1) 86, p. 25.
"Pink Eye." [LittleM] (15:2) 86, p. 12.
1939. GOEDICKE, Patricia
"Against Death." [QW] (23) 86, p. 96.
"American Exercises." [AnotherCM] (15) 86, p. 22-23.
"The Emperor's Nightingale." [DenQ] (20:4/21:1) Spr-Sum 86, p. 113-115.
"Last Mornings." [WillowS] (18) Sum 86, p. 22-23.
"The One with the Spoon in Her Mouth." [PoetryNW] (27:2) Sum 86, p. 12-13.
"Passports." [TarRP] (25:1) Fall 85, p. 12-14.
"So Long." [TarRP] (25:1) Fall 85, p. 14-16.
"Time Zones: Sister to Sister." [SenR] (16:2) 86, p. 72-74.
"Under Ben Bulben, 1984." [Interim] (5:1) Spr 86, p. 31-32.
"Worst Is Not" (for Emily Dickinson). [PoetryE] (20/21) Fall 86, p. 104.
1940. GOFF, Charles Rice, III
"Lessening Lesson." [SanFPJ] (8:2) 85, p. 61.
"Make Sense to Me by Telling Me No One Really Believes This Stuff." [SanFPJ]
(8:2) 85, p. 9.
"Spots in the Swirl." [SanFPJ] (8:2) 85, p. 8.
1941. GOFREED, Howard
"Challenger." [NegC] (6:4) Fall 86, p. 119.
1942. GOLD, Edward
"Breathing." [CrabCR] (4:1) Fall-Wint 86, p. 4.
"First." [SmPd] (23:3, #68) Fall 86, p. 18.

1943. GOLDBARTH, Albert
    "Again." [Poetry] (149:1) O 86, p. 13-20.
    "The Alias: A Survey." [IndR] (9:1) Wint 86, p. 28-29.
    "At Death." [TarRP] (25:2) Spr 86, p. 5.
    "Atavism/Bowl." [BelPoJ] (37:1) Fall 86, p. 26-30.
    "The Cover, the Contents." [PoetryNW] (27:1) Spr 86, p. 22-23.
    "Elbee Novelty Company Inc., 1985." [OntR] (24) Spr-Sum 86, p. 38-39.
    "The Elements." [NewEngR] (8:3) Spr 86, p. 297-298.
    "For Years." [PraS] (60:1) Spr 86, p. 65-66.
    "Fossil Music." [BlackWR] (12:2) Spr 86, p. 11.
    "Giotto: *Saint Francis Preaching to the Birds*: About 1300." [SenR] (16:2) 86, p.
        77-78.
    "Good Even." [IndR] (9:2) Spr 86, p. 103-107.
    "The Greek Islands." [TarRP] (25:2) Spr 86, p. 5.
    "He Was Reading the Great Jewish Mystics." [TarRP] (25:2) Spr 86, p. 6.
    "Here." [IndR] (9:1) Wint 86, p. 30-32.
    "How It Begins." [TarRP] (25:2) Spr 86, p. 7.
    "Human Time." [BlackWR] (12:2) Spr 86, p. 7-10.
    "Intermediaries." [CarolQ] (38:3) Spr 86, p. 52.
    "A Monument." [Poetry] (148:5) Ag 86, p. 260-261.
    "The More Modest the Definition of Heaven, the Oftener We're There." [Poetry]
        (148:5) Ag 86, p. 264.
    "Of Ontology." [CarolQ] (38:3) Spr 86, p. 53-54.
    "On the Grave." [PoetryNW] (27:4) Wint 86-87, p. 46-47.
    "The Opposition." [SenR] (16:2) 86, p. 79-82.
    "Pete's Yahoo Neighbor . . ." (for JM in Japan). [OntR] (24) Spr-Sum 86, p. 34-37.
    "Red: The Blue Moon." [MissouriR] (9:1) 85-86, p. 48-49.
    "Seeing." [Poetry] (148:5) Ag 86, p. 262-263.
    "*Shawabty, Ushabi*, or *Shabti* Figures." [YaleR] (76:1) Aut 86, p. 124.
    "Suddenly, Reading *The Book of the Griffin*." [TarRP] (25:2) Spr 86, p. 6.
    "What Doesn't Happen." [BelPoJ] (37:1) Fall 86, p. 22-25.
    "Winter." [IndR] (9:2) Spr 86, p. 108-109.
    "Zenbu" (for Judy, far away). [BlackWR] (12:2) Spr 86, p. 12-13.
1944. GOLDBERG, Barbara
    "Erendira Remembers." [StoneC] (14:1/2) Fall-Wint 86-87, p. 60-61.
    "A Question of Aesthetics." [AmerS] (55:1) Wint 85-86, p. 112.
    "The Succulent Edge." [StoneC] (14:1/2) Fall-Wint 86-87, p. 62.
1945. GOLDBERG, Beckian (Beckian Fritz)
    "Birth." [HayF] (1) Spr 86, p. 28-29.
    "Hartford County." [NoAmR] (271:4) D 86, p. 54.
    "Keeping Warm in New York." [HayF] (1) Spr 86, p. 24-25.
    "Mr. Lucky's." [HayF] (1) Spr 86, p. 23.
    "Paris." [HayF] (1) Spr 86, p. 21-22.
    "Salvation." [HayF] (1) Spr 86, p. 26-27.
1946. GOLDBERG, Bonni
    "As a Patient at the Clinic." [ForidaR] (14:1) Spr-Sum 86, p. 26.
    "How's the City Treating You." [ForidaR] (14:1) Spr-Sum 86, p. 24-25.
    "Letter from a Friend." [ForidaR] (14:1) Spr-Sum 86, p. 27.
1947. GOLDBLATT, Eli
    "A sonnet says joy." [AnotherCM] (16) 86, p. 50.
1948. GOLDENSOHN, Barry
    "Emily Dickinson's Room, Main Street, Amherst." [NewRep] (194:11) 17 Mr 86, p.
        36.
    "Midsummer Night's Marriage." [AntR] (44:2) Spr 86, p. 204.
    "Summer." [MSS] (5:1) 86, p. 113.
    "To Prospero" (on setting Ariel free). [AntR] (44:2) Spr 86, p. 205.
    "The Toy." [Poetry] (147:5) F 86, p. 289-290.
1949. GOLDER, Herbert
    "Chorus — The Bacchae" (tr. of Euripides, w. C. K. Williams). [Translation] (16)
        Spr 86, p. 254-262.
1950. GOLDERMAN, Cynthia R.
    "The Black Chrysanthemum." [SanFPJ] (9:1) 86, p. 94-95.
    "The Forgotten Kingdom of Quality." [SanFPJ] (8:2) 85, p. 67-68.
    "Just the Beginning." [SanFPJ] (8:2) 85, p. 38-39.
1951. GOLDMAN, Edward M.
    "David, Running the 100 Meter Dash." [InterPR] (12:2) Fall 86, p. 106.

"Summer Gift." [InterPR] (12:2) Fall 86, p. 105.
1952. GOLDMAN, Judy
"Humoresque." [Poem] (56) N 86, p. 29.
1953. GOLDSMITH, Ann S.
"Like Lakes and Hemlocks." [HeliconN] (16) Wint 86, p. 35.
"Woman in the Shape of a Memoir" (In Response to the Drawing, *Triptych*, by
Camille Cox). [HeliconN] (16) Wint 86, p. 34-35.
1954. GOLDSTEIN, Fran Avnet
"No Star-dust." [MidwQ] (28:1) Aut 86, p. 81.
1955. GOLDSTEIN, Sanford
"Records of a Well-Polished Satchel, #3: Zones of Emptiness." [Northeast] (series
4:3) Spr 86, p. 20-22.
1956. GOM, Leona
"Arthritis." [CanLit] (108) Spr 86, p. 46-47.
1957. GOMANN, David
"Chagall Knows These Wings" (for Deborah). [Quarry] (35:3) Sum 86, p. 32.
"Ishmael." [Quarry] (35:3) Sum 86, p. 33.
GOMEZ, Victoria Sales
See SALES-GOMEZ, Victoria
1958. GOMEZ BOIX, Amaro
"De un Diccionario Apocrifo." [LindLM] (5:3) Jl-S 86, p. 30.
1959. GOMEZ GLEASON, M. T.
"A veces pasa el amor como un ala." [LetFem] (12:1/2) Primavera-Otoño 86, p.
155-156.
1960. GOMORI, George
"Autumn Breakfast" (tr. of Dezsö Kosztolányi, w. Clive Wilmer). [Verse] (5) 86, p.
55.
"Snapshot" (tr. of Zsuzsa Rakovszky, w. Clive Wilmer). [Verse] (5) 86, p. 56.
"What Man Can Do on This Planet" (tr. of László Kálnoky, w. Clive Wilmer).
[Verse] (5) 86, p. 55-56.
1961. GONET, Jill
"40-Year-Old Picture." [Ploughs] (12:4) 86, p. 146-147.
"Primer." [Ploughs] (12:4) 86, p. 144-145.
"Sea-Maid." [Ploughs] (12:4) 86, p. 143.
1962. GONZALES, Ray
"Christmas Day, El Paso, 1984." [CutB] (26) Spr-Sum 86, p. 15.
1963. GONZALEZ, John
"All Was Not Madness." [Bogg] (55) 86, p. 48.
1964. GONZALEZ, José
"Relacion de la Primera Muerte de los Hombres de la Tierra." [Mairena] (8:22) 86, p.
114.
1965. GONZALEZ, Josemilio
"A Francisco Matos Paoli" (Al leer el libro *Vestido para la Denudez*). [Mairena]
(8:21) 86, p. 54.
1966. GONZALEZ, Oscar
"Fragmento de Visita del Arcangel Gardel." [Mairena] (8:22) 86, p. 79.
1967. GONZALEZ, Rafael Jesús
"The Hands" (to Victor Jara). [SecC] (14:1) 86, p. 33.
"Sowers of Visions." [SecC] (14:1) 86, p. 34-35.
1968. GONZALEZ, Ray
"Excited by an Old Manuscript." [MidAR] (6:2) 86, p. 104.
1969. GONZALEZ DEL VALLE, Máximo
"Retorno" (Para José Jurado Morales desde su poemario *Ayer Huerto Florido*).
[Mairena] (8:22) 86, p. 93.
1970. GONZALEZ-GERTH, Miguel
"Ashes of the Dead." [Pax] (3:1/2) Wint 85-86, p. 38-39.
"Winter Journey." [Pax] (3:1/2) Wint 85-86, p. 39-40.
1971. GOOCH, Brad
"Church Music." [ParisR] (28:99) Spr 86, p. 150-152.
"H." [ParisR] (28:99) Spr 86, p. 145-146.
"Rip Tide." [ParisR] (28:99) Spr 86, p. 147-149.
1972. GOOD, Regan
"Flower Picking with Vincent van Gogh." [MidwQ] (27:3) Spr 86, p. 311.
"The Perpetual Tea I." [MidwQ] (27:3) Spr 86, p. 312.
1973. GOOD, Ruth
"Bulletin 1." [MidwQ] (27:3) Spr 86, p. 313.

1974. GOODENOUGH, J. B.
    "Apples in January." [RagMag] (5:2) Fall 86, p. 14.
    "Applesauce." [Puerto] (21:2) Spr 86, p. 154.
    "Arrival of the Prince." [ConcPo] (19) 86, p. 20.
    "Auntie Emma Stews a Squirrel." [Blueline] (8:1) Sum-Fall 86, p. 5.
    "Bass Harbor" (January). [CrossCur] (5:4/6:1) 86, p. 31.
    "The Blind Mice." [CumbPR] (5:2) Spr 86, p. 12.
    "Bok and the Tree." [ChiR] (35:3) Spr 86, p. 27.
    "Burying the Magician." [ChiR] (35:3) Spr 86, p. 28.
    "The Children." [TexasR] (7:1/2) Spr-Sum 86, p. 57.
    "Cowbird." [Puerto] (21:2) Spr 86, p. 152.
    "Esterhanz the Hermit, Sleeping." [NoDaQ] (54:2) Spr 86, p. 135.
    "Going North." [WindO] (47) Sum 86, p. 46.
    "Ground Rules." [LitR] (29:2) Wint 86, p. 173.
    "Harvest." [SpoonRQ] (11:2) Spr 86, p. 35.
    "Harvest in the Plague Year." [DeKalbLAJ] (19:1) 86, p. 29.
    "Husband and Wife." [SpoonRQ] (11:2) Spr 86, p. 36.
    "Hymn-Singer." [StoneC] (14:1/2) Fall-Wint 86-87, p. 39.
    "In Passing." [LitR] (29:3) Spr 86, p. 337.
    "Kansas Sunflower." [CharR] (12:1) Spr 86, p. 78.
    "Marker." [CharR] (12:1) Spr 86, p. 78-79.
    "Masque." [InterPR] (12:2) Fall 86, p. 78.
    "The Mer-Wife." [CumbPR] (5:2) Spr 86, p. 11.
    "Old Man My Father." [Pembroke] (18) 86, p. 252.
    "The Oracles." [WindO] (47) Sum 86, p. 46.
    "Passing Through." [ArizQ] (42:2) Sum 86, p. 156.
    "Picaroon." [CumbPR] (5:2) Spr 86, p. 13.
    "Provisions in the Will." [Blueline] (8:1) Sum-Fall 86, p. 5.
    "Pursuit." [DeKalbLAJ] (19:3/4) 86, p. 74.
    "Raree Show." [CumbPR] (5:2) Spr 86, p. 14.
    "A Ring of Keys." [LitR] (29:2) Wint 86, p. 173.
    "Spencer's Pond, Sunset." [CapeR] (21:1) Spr 86, p. 31.
    "Spy." [DeKalbLAJ] (19:1) 86, p. 29.
    "The Things That Catch the Fish." [ManhatPR] (7) Sum 86, p. 27.
    "Want Not." [StoneC] (14:1/2) Fall-Wint 86-87, p. 38.
    "The Woodcutter and His Wife." [Puerto] (21:2) Spr 86, p. 153.
GOODENOUGH, Judith B.
    See GOODENOUGH, J. B.
1975. GOODIER, Sharon
    "Unicorn." [GreenfR] (13:3/4) Sum-Fall 86, p. 66.
1976. GOODMAN, Dottie
    "Insulation." [PoeticJ] (15) Sum 86, p. 18.
    "Once Bonded." [PoeticJ] (16) Fall 86, p. 26.
1977. GOODMAN, Michael
    "Crossing the East River after 15 Years I Fall into Memory's Web" (for Don
        Carlson). [BlackWR] (13:1) Fall 86, p. 75.
    "Little Neck Bay." [PraS] (60:3) Fall 86, p. 95.
    "The Testimony" (The Hotel Irving, Grammercy Park, NY). [PraS] (60:3) Fall 86,
        p. 96.
1978. GOODMAN, Ryah Tumarkin
    "Ancestors." [Confr] (32) Spr-Sum 86, p. 81.
1979. GOODWIN, Joseph P.
    "When Love Is Plagued by Doubt and Harbors Fears." [BallSUF] (27:4) Aut 86, p.
        38.
1980. GORDETT, Marea
    "Taos Flores." [AntR] (44:3) Sum 86, p. 332-333.
1981. GORDON, Carol
    "The Birthday Birds." [CrabCR] (3:3) Sum 86, p. 16.
    "Calling Out the Names." [Calyx] (9:2/3) Wint 86, p. 120.
1982. GORDON, Mark
    "The Meeting." [GreenfR] (13:3/4) Sum-Fall 86, p. 67.
1983. GORDON, Sarah
    "Always." [FloridaR] (14:2) Fall-Wint 86, p. 109.
1984. GORDON, Sonia
    "How Will You Know It's Eden?" [CrabCR] (4:1) Fall-Wint 86, p. 16.

1985. GORHAM, Sarah
"Evolution in Connecticut." [KanQ] (18:1/2) Wint-Spr 86, p. 303.
"Ice on Her Lips." [PoetryNW] (27:3) Aut 86, p. 15.
"Implant." [PoetryNW] (27:3) Aut 86, p. 14.
"My Father Leaving: Chincateaque, 1972." [KanQ] (18:1/2) Wint-Spr 86, p. 302.
"Nap." [CarolQ] (38:3) Spr 86, p. 34.
"The Sixth Finger." [NewL] (53:1) Fall 86, p. 85.
"Washing Her Hair." [PoetryNW] (27:3) Aut 86, p. 14-15.
"A Whistle Heard Twice." [CarolQ] (38:3) Spr 86, p. 35.
1986. GORMAN, Leroy
"Outside St Jacobs." [Quarry] (35:3) Sum 86, p. 79-80.
1987. GORRIZ LERGA, Jesús
"De Arte Poetica (I y II)." [Mairena] (8:22) 86, p. 20.
1988. GOSTAS, Theodore W.
"Vietnam P.O.W. Camp." [Sam] (46:2 release 182) 86, p. 54.
1989. GOTT, George
"Herman and Elise." [YetASM] (4) 85, p. 6.
"Waking in Salto." [Wind] (16:58) 86, p. 32.
1990. GOULD, Alan
"Fire Eater." [Verse] (5) 86, p. 17.
1991. GOULD, S. V.
"Coin of the Realm" (An essay in presidential sleight-of-tongue). [SanFPJ] (8:3) 85,
p. 72.
"Zbigniew, Herm, and Daniel Sing the Lullabye of the Great Transition." [SanFPJ]
(8:3) 85, p. 81.
1992. GOURLAY, Elizabeth
"Happy Days" (After Samuel Beckett). [MalR] (73) Ja 86, p. 41.
"Poems, with Colour, for Scriabin." [MalR] (76) S 86, p. 78-91.
"Through an Ordinary Aperture." [MalR] (73) Ja 86, p. 39.
"Up in the Attic." [MalR] (73) Ja 86, p. 40.
1993. GOW, Maureen
"Going Home." [PottPort] (8) 86-87, p. 11.
1994. GOWLAND, Marylee
"Friday Morning." [RagMag] (5:2) Fall 86, p. 15.
1995. GRABILL, James
"A Fall." [MidAR] (6:2) 86, p. 8-9.
1996. GRACE, Patricia J.
"The Thread That Binds." [WritersL] (1986:5), p. 25.
1997. GRAFTON, Grace
"Trip." [YellowS] (20) Aut 86, p. 8.
1998. GRAHAM, Antony
"Anyone Can Stand" (tr. of Stanislaw Baranczak, w. Reginald Gibbons). [TriQ]
(65) Wint 86, p. 88.
1999. GRAHAM, David
"Breaking and Entering." [PaintedB] (28) Ap 86, p. 22.
"The Day I Cannot Stop Crying." [Poetry] (148:5) Ag 86, p. 269-270.
"The Editorial We." [Poetry] (147:4) Ja 86, p. 206.
"The Garden and Its Owners." [PassN] (7:2) Spr-Sum 86, p. 21.
"Landscape of Domestic Life." [GeoR] (40:3) Fall 86, p. 677.
"Letter with Blurred Postmark." [ColEng] (48:8) D 86, p. 802.
"Margin of Error." [MinnR] (NS 26) Spr 86, p. 11.
"Marriage of the Magician." [PaintedB] (28) Ap 86, p. 23.
"Midnight Special." [PennR] (2:1) Fall-Wint 86, p. 37.
"Planxty Beethoven." [Ploughs] (12:4) 86, p. 32.
"Rough Air." [Ploughs] (12:4) 86, p. 31.
"Self-Portrait with Nostalgia." [Poetry] (147:4) Ja 86, p. 203-204.
"Self-Portrait with Self-Doubt." [Poetry] (147:4) Ja 86, p. 205.
"Self-Portrait with Stage Fright." [Poetry] (148:5) Ag 86, p. 271.
"Trouble at the Twin Altars of Work and Love." [MinnR] (NS 26) Spr 86, p. 24-25.
"The Valley Where We Live." [CutB] (25) Fall-Wint 86, p. 38.
"Village Eccentric." [Blueline] (7:2) Wint-Spr 86, p. 50-51.
2000. GRAHAM, Desmond
"I Dreamt I Was in England." [Stand] (27:3) Sum 86, p. 5.
"In Warsaw." [Stand] (27:3) Sum 86, p. 4.
2001. GRAHAM, Jorie
"Breakdancing." [AmerPoR] (15:5) S-O 86, p. 27.

"Description." [ParisR] (28:100) Sum-Fall 86, p. 164-166.
"Expulsion." [AmerPoR] (15:5) S-O 86, p. 31.
"Haying." [GeoR] (40:3) Fall 86, p. 679.
"Headlights." [DenQ] (20:4/21:1) Spr-Sum 86, p. 50-53.
"Jackpot." [GeoR] (40:3) Fall 86, p. 678.
"The Lovers." [AmerPoR] (15:5) S-O 86, p. 32.
"Of Forced Sightes and Trusty Ferefulness." [ParisR] (28:101) Wint 86, p. 66-67.
"Orpheus and Eurydice." [AmerPoR] (15:5) S-O 86, p. 30-31.
"Pietà." [DenQ] (20:4/21:1) Spr-Sum 86, p. 54-55.
"Pollock and Canvas." [AmerPoR] (15:5) S-O 86, p. 33-35.
"Room-Tone." [AmerPoR] (15:5) S-O 86, p. 28.
"Self Portrait as Apollo and Daphne." [ParisR] (28:101) Wint 86, p. 61-65.
"Self Portrait as Hurry and Delay" (Penelope at her loom). [AmerPoR] (15:5) S-O
     86, p. 29.
"To the Reader." [AmerPoR] (15:5) S-O 86, p. 25-26.
"The Veil." [AmerPoR] (15:5) S-O 86, p. 26.
"Vertigo." [AmerPoR] (15:5) S-O 86, p. 32.
2002. GRAHAM, Loren
"Memory." [SouthernHR] (20:4) Fall 86, p. 344.
"Three Things Surprise Me in the Fall." [DeKalbLAJ] (19:1) 86, p. 30.
2003. GRAHAM, Matthew
"Indiana." [CumbPR] (5:2) Spr 86, p. 30-31.
2004. GRAHAM, Neile
"Lakeside Inventory." [Calyx] (10:1) Sum 86, p. 35.
"Map of Vancouver Island." [GreenfR] (13:3/4) Sum-Fall 86, p. 68.
2005. GRANATO, Carol
"Strange Lullabye." [Poem] (56) N 86, p. 38.
GRANIELLA RODRIGUEZ, Magda
     See RODRIGUEZ, Magda Graniella
2006. GRANT, Paul
"Burying." [CarolQ] (38:3) Spr 86, p. 64.
"Forgiveness." [CarolQ] (38:3) Spr 86, p. 73.
"Yellow Dog Blues." [CarolQ] (38:3) Spr 86, p. 74.
2007. GRANT, Sharon M.
"Dreams That Blister Sleep." [PraF] (7:3) Aut 86, p. 135.
"No One Under Eighteen Admitted." [PraF] (7:3) Aut 86, p. 129.
GRAVELLES, Charles de
     See DeGRAVELLES, Charles
2008. GRAVES, Colin
"The Children's Hospital, January 1942." [ManhatPR] (8) Wint 86-87, p. 28.
"Colin." [ManhatPR] (8) Wint 86-87, p. 28.
2009. GRAVES, Michael
"Outside St. Jude's." [HolCrit] (23:5) D 86, p. 14.
2010. GRAVES, Robert
"Judgement of Paris." [GeoR] (40:3) Fall 86, p. 680.
2011. GRAY, Beth
"Ashes: A Chronicle for David." [BellArk] (2:1) Ja-F 86, p. 13.
"Crater Lake, Washington, July." [BellArk] (2:3) My-Je 86, p. 3.
"Edge." [BellArk] (2:3) My-Je 86, p. 15.
"Going Home." [BellArk] (2:4) Jl-Ag 86, p. 2.
"How the Waiting Ends." [BellArk] (2:5) S-O 86, p. 2.
"Oysterville." [BellArk] (2:3) My-Je 86, p. 1.
2012. GRAY, James
"Coup de Grasp." [Rampike] (5:2) 86, p. 64-65.
2013. GRAY, Jan
"Rain." [SouthernHR] (20:2) Spr 86, p. 124.
2014. GRAY, Janet
"I Spent My Infancy in a Used Clothing Warehouse." [Amelia] (3:1) Ja 86, p. 77.
"Item 158 (True)." [RagMag] (5:2) Fall 86, p. 17.
"The Thing We Fear the Most Has Already Happened (3)." [RagMag] (5:2) Fall 86,
     p. 16.
"Thinking on Medicine Street." [Abraxas] (34) 86, p. 48.
"You Have to Project an Image." [Abraxas] (34) 86, p. 47.
2015. GRAYSON, Lisa
"Museum Babies." [Prima] (10) 86, p. 43.

GRAZIA, Emilio de
    See De GRAZIA, Emilio
2016. GRAZIANO, Frank
    "Self-Portrait with Daughter" (for Jessica). [MemphisSR] (6:1/2) Spr 86, p. 8-11.
2017. GREATHOUSE, Florence
    "Driving to Elk River." [NewRena] (6:3, #20) Spr 86, p. 102-103.
    "End of an Era." [NewRena] (6:3, #20) Spr 86, p. 103.
    "Forgetting." [WillowS] (17) Wint 86, p. 61-62.
    "Gogol." [NewRena] (6:3, #20) Spr 86, p. 104.
2018. GREEN, Amelia
    "Slide Show of a Trip to Nicaragua New Years Day, 1985." [SanFPJ] (8:1) 85, p. 24.
2019. GREEN, Coppie
    "Approaching." [TriQ] (66) Spr-Sum 86, p. 169.
    "The Father Visits." [TriQ] (66) Spr-Sum 86, p. 168.
2020. GREEN, David
    "Epistle to a Lady." [CarolQ] (39:1) Fall 86, p. 36.
2021. GREEN, George
    "Grumjian Entertains an Audience of Weeds." [OntR] (24) Spr-Sum 86, p. 50.
2022. GREEN, Joseph
    "The Lone Somnambulist." [BellR] (9:1) Spr 86, p. 6.
    "To William Carlos Williams in Heaven." [BellR] (9:1) Spr 86, p. 6.
2023. GREEN, Karen
    "Editing a Vapor Trail." [BellR] (9:2) Fall 86, p. 23.
2024. GREEN, Leigh
    "Facing Death." [Kaleid] (12) Wint 86, p. 52.
    "Mickey." [Kaleid] (12) Wint 86, p. 52.
2025. GREEN, Lori Susan
    "February, 1982." [Amelia] (3:1) Ja 86, p. 5.
2026. GREEN, Paul
    "Four Poems." [Sink] (2) 86, p. 36.
    "The Manufacture." [Sink] (2) 86, p. 37.
2027. GREEN, Peter
    "Phaedra" (To Yannis Tsarouchis, tr. of Yannis Ritsos, w. Beverly Bardsley). [SouthernHR] (20:3) Sum 86, p. 227-247.
2028. GREEN, William H.
    "Captain John Dill Godwin, C.S.A." [SouthernR] (22:4) O 86, p. 768.
    "The Last Battle" (Fought in Girard, Alabama, April 16, 1865). [SouthernR] (22:4) O 86, p. 769.
    "Letter in Early March." [YellowS] (21) Wint 86, p. 6.
    "The Phone Interrupts His Wife's Bath." [LitR] (29:3) Spr 86, p. 291.
    "Under the Crematorium." [Lips] (12) 86, p. 36.
2029. GREENBAUM, Jessica
    "Why Women Cry When Plates Break." [Nat] (242:17) 3 My 86, p. 621.
2030. GREENBERG, Alvin
    "Cutting Birch." [OhioR] (37) 86, p. 96.
    "Standing in the Doorway." [OhioR] (37) 86, p. 97.
2031. GREENBERG, Sara
    "In Vitro." [Amelia] (3:4) Fall 86, p. 82.
2032. GREENBURG, Candace
    "Waiting for the Days of Grace." [HayF] (1) Spr 86, p. 63-64.
2033. GREENE, James
    "Pietà." [Verse] (5) 86, p. 41-42.
    "Special Effects." [Verse] (5) 86, p. 41.
2034. GREENE, Jeffrey
    "On Augusta." [AntR] (44:4) Fall 86, p. 438.
    "On Crossing the Mojave." [MemphisSR] (6:1/2) Spr 86, p. 35.
    "Sabbatical." [MemphisSR] (6:1/2) Spr 86, p. 34-35.
    "St. Valentine's Day at the Charity Hospital." [MSS] (5:1) 86, p. 111.
2035. GREENHOOD, David
    "Cargo and Complement." [SoDakR] (24:3) Aut 86, p. 172.
    "The Jest." [SoDakR] (24:3) Aut 86, p. 172.
    "Night-Blooming Prophecy." [SoDakR] (24:3) Aut 86, p. 171.
2036. GREENING, John
    "Cromwell to His Wife Elizabeth." [Stand] (27:4) Aut 86, p. 45.

154

GREENLEY

2037. GREENLEY, Emily
"20 Nov, Fake Spring." [HarvardA] (120, i.e. 119:3) Mr 86, p. 31.
"Garden." [HarvardA] (120:1) D 86, p. 48.
"The Quiet Man." [HarvardA] (120, i.e. 119:3) Mr 86, p. 32.
2038. GREENWALD, Robert
"Artist Unknown" (for David). [Kaleid] (12) Wint 86, p. 55.
2039. GREENWALD, Roger
"Barbed-wire Winter" (tr. of Rolf Jacobsen). [Writ] (18) 86, c87, p. 47.
"Did I Know You?" (tr. of Rolf Jacobsen). [Writ] (18) 86, c87, p. 49.
"The Fireflies" (tr. of Rolf Jacobsen). [Writ] (18) 86, c87, p. 51.
"How Long" (tr. of Flavia Cosma, w. Jim Roberts and the author). [Writ] (18) 86,
    c87, p. 109.
"If I could Be" (tr. of Flavia Cosma, w. Jim Roberts and the author). [Writ] (18) 86,
    c87, p. 108.
"It Was Here" (tr. of Rolf Jacobsen). [Writ] (18) 86, c87, p. 50.
"The Labyrinth" (tr. of Giorgio Chiesura, w. Luigi M. Bianchi). [Writ] (18) 86, c87,
    p. 127-134.
"On the Sea Float Chestnut Trees" (tr. of Flavia Cosma, w. the author). [Writ] (18)
    86, c87, p. 106.
"Room 301" (tr. of Rolf Jacobsen). [Writ] (18) 86, c87, p. 46.
"The Sewing Machine" (tr. of Rolf Jacobsen). [Writ] (18) 86, c87, p. 48.
"Thoughts at Lake Sjodal" (tr. of Rolf Jacobsen). [Writ] (18) 86, c87, p. 45.
"Toil" (tr. of Flavia Cosma, w. Jim Roberts and the author). [Writ] (18) 86, c87, p.
    107.
"Trees in Autumn" (tr. of Rolf Jacobsen). [Writ] (18) 86, c87, p. 44.
2040. GREENWAY, William
"Acclaim." [CumbPR] (5:2) Spr 86, p. 37-38.
"The Best Days of Your Life." [Poetry] (148:5) Ag 86, p. 273.
"Our Father Who Art on Third." [Poetry] (148:5) Ag 86, p. 272.
"Sea Change." [ForidaR] (14:1) Spr-Sum 86, p. 100.
"Senior Year." [CumbPR] (5:2) Spr 86, p. 39.
2041. GREGER, Debora
"Action." [DenQ] (20:4/21:1) Spr-Sum 86, p. 155-157.
"Ever After." [YaleR] (76:1) Aut 86, p. 44-45.
"The Penguin Jane Austen." [YaleR] (76:1) Aut 86, p. 43-44.
"The Second Violinist's Son." [GeoR] (40:3) Fall 86, p. 681.
2042. GREGERSON, Linda
"For My Father, Who Would Rather Stay Home." [PartR] (53:4) 86, p. 577-580.
"Whale Washed Ashore at Ancona" (anonymous engraving, 1601). [Iowa] (16:1)
    Wint 86, p. 178-179.
2043. GREGG, Linda
"After the Beginning." [ParisR] (28:101) Wint 86, p. 56.
"Closeness at the Goodwill." [QW] (22) Spr-Sum 86, p. 6.
"The Dark Shining." [OP] (42/43) Wint 86-87, p. 24-25.
"Greece When Nobody's Looking." [OP] (42/43) Wint 86-87, p. 26.
"Happiness and White Sky." [QW] (22) Spr-Sum 86, p. 4.
"It Is the Rising I Love." [ParisR] (28:101) Wint 86, p. 57.
"Made to Ring." [QW] (23) 86, p. 7.
"Not Tearing My Dress." [OP] (42/43) Wint 86-87, p. 24.
"Part of Me Wanting Everything to Live." [ParisR] (28:100) Sum-Fall 86, p. 167.
"Return to Paros." [ParisR] (28:101) Wint 86, p. 55.
"The Single Music Flooding Forward." [QW] (23) 86, p. 6.
"Supposed to Be Happy." [OP] (42/43) Wint 86-87, p. 25.
"Women in Winter." [QW] (22) Spr-Sum 86, p. 5.
2044. GREGOR, Arthur
"Art Songs" (Selections: 2, 5, 6). [Interim] (5:2) Fall 86, p. 32-33.
"Not Occurred." [Interim] (5:2) Fall 86, p. 33.
2045. GRENNAN, Eamon
"At Home in Winter." [Poetry] (149:2) N 86, p. 66-67.
"Bright and Dark." [BellR] (9:1) Spr 86, p. 27.
"The Coming Day." [Poetry] (149:2) N 86, p. 65-66.
"Four Deer." [NewYorker] (62:40) 24 N 86, p. 46.
"Houseplants in Winter." [Poetry] (149:2) N 86, p. 68-69.
"Jewel Box." [LitR] (30:1) Fall 86, p. 64-65.
"Men Roofing." [NewYorker] (62:18) 23 Je 86, p. 23.
"Morning, the Twenty-second of March." [NewYorker] (62:18) 23 Je 86, p. 23.

155

"My Daughter, Growing." [LitR] (30:1) Fall 86, p. 65-66.
"St. Patrick's Hospital." [BellR] (9:1) Spr 86, p. 26.
"Totem." [ParisR] (28:101) Wint 86, p. 243-244.
"Widow Garden." [BellR] (9:1) Spr 86, p. 26.
"Wing Road." [NewYorker] (62:18) 23 Je 86, p. 23.
2046. GREVEN, Leonardo
"Coma Berenice" (tr. by Kevin Mathewson). [AmerPoR] (15:3) My-Je 86, p. 48.
2047. GREY, John
"Madame Tussaud's." [DeKalbLAJ] (19:3/4) 86, p. 75.
2048. GRIER, Jennifer
"One Shining Day." [SanFPJ] (8:1) 85, p. 39.
2049. GRIFFIN, Walter
"Aunt Ida and Lord Byron." [WritersF] (12) Fall 86, p. 132.
"Fetal Position." [StoneC] (13:3/4) Spr-Sum 86, p. 35.
"Fish Leaves." [CarolQ] (38:2) Wint 86, p. 49.
"Fish Leaves." [WritersF] (12) Fall 86, p. 131-132.
"Heritage." [AmerV] (2) Spr 86, p. 86.
"Homesick." [MidAR] (6:1) 86?, p. 108.
"Homesick." [Wind] (16:56) 86, p. 22.
"In Italy, Sons Kiss Their Fathers." [StoneC] (13:3/4) Spr-Sum 86, p. 34.
"Me and Scarpatti." [Vis] (21) 86, p. 25.
"The Poet Reads in Front of His Son for the First Time." [Wind] (16:56) 86, p. 23.
"Transient: Open Ward." [Wind] (16:56) 86, p. 22-23.
2050. GRIGORESCU, Irina
"Landscape in White" (tr. of Anghel Dumbraveanu, w. Adam J. Sorkin). [LitR] (30:1) Fall 86, p. 24.
"The Sailor's Window" (tr. of Anghel Dumbraveanu, w. Adam J. Sorkin). [LitR] (30:1) Fall 86, p. 25.
2051. GRIMALDI, A. J.
"42nd & 8th." [SlipS] (6) 86, p. 47.
"George Murphy." [YetASM] (5) 86, p. 10.
2052. GRIMSHAW, James A., Jr.
"Morning After the Night of the Red Moon." [SouthernR] (22:4) O 86, p. 780-781.
2053. GRINDAL, Gracia
"The Scar." [SingHM] (13) 86, p. 43.
2054. GRISWOLD, Jay
"At the Sanitorium." [NegC] (6:4) Fall 86, p. 60.
"Doors Opening Outward." [MidAR] (7:1) 86, p. 165.
"Guido's Last Poem." [NegC] (6:4) Fall 86, p. 62.
"Hyacinth." [WindO] (47) Sum 86, p. 44.
"Meditations for the Year of the Horse." [WestHR] (40:4) Wint 86, p. 329-331.
"More News." [NegC] (6:4) Fall 86, p. 61.
"The Tyranny of Stones." [StoneC] (14:1/2) Fall-Wint 86-87, p. 41.
"Working." [BlackWR] (13:1) Fall 86, p. 72-73.
2055. GROL, Lini R.
"Fading Footsteps." [WritersL] (1986:4), p. 13.
"Portrait of a Matriarch." [WritersL] (1986:4), p. 13.
2056. GROOMS, Anthony
"Grandaddy." [DeKalbLAJ] (19:2) 86, p. 25-27.
GROOTE, Judith de
See DeGROOTE, Judith
2057. GROSHOLZ, Emily
"Another Song." [Boulevard] (1:3) Fall 86, p. 107.
"Dialogue of Body and Soul." [PraS] (60:4) Wint 86, p. 46-47.
"The gold Earrings." [CumbPR] (6:1) Fall 86, p. 76-77.
"In the Abruzzi." [PraS] (60:4) Wint 86, p. 44-45.
"On the Untersberg" (Salzburg). [SouthwR] (71:3) Sum 86, p. 378.
"The Purblind Letter" (Pienso en ti mi vida). [SouthwR] (71:3) Sum 86, p. 378-379.
"Summer Lightning." [NewEngR] (9:1) Aut 86, p. 68.
"Two Variations on a Theme." [MichQR] (25:4) Fall 86, p. 733-735.
"Via della Lungaretta, 74." [PraS] (60:4) Wint 86, p. 43-44.
2058. GROSS, Jim
"Pocket Watch." [AntigR] (66/67) Sum-Aut 86, p. 229.
"The Tilting Wall." [AntigR] (66/67) Sum-Aut 86, p. 228.
2059. GROSS, Pamela
"Apsis." [Raccoon] (20) Ap 86, p. 13-14.

"The Cache." [WillowS] (17) Wint 86, p. 60.
"To a Poet Making Good at the PCC." [Calyx] (10:1) Sum 86, p. 36-37.
GROSS, Sonja Kravanja
    See KRAVANJA-GROSS, Sonja
2060. GROSS, Steven
    "Sober." [KanQ] (18:1/2) Wint-Spr 86, p. 124.
2061. GROSSMAN, Allen
    "Poland of Death (II)." [GrandS] (5:2) Wint 86, p. 34-35.
2062. GROSSMAN, Andrew J.
    "Certain Thoughts." [BellArk] (2:6) N-D 86, p. 4.
    "The Efficient Nurses of Florida." [Lips] (12) 86, p. 8-9.
    "The Efficient Nurses of Florida." [Wind] (16:58) 86, p. 20-21.
    "Manic." [DeKalbLAJ] (19:1) 86, p. 32.
2063. GROSSMAN, Florence
    "Country Auction." [TarRP] (25:1) Fall 85, p. 41.
    "Rainbow." [ManhatPR] (8) Wint 86-87, p. 29.
2064. GROSSMAN, K. Margaret
    "Telephone Poets." [PoetryNW] (27:4) Wint 86-87, p. 29.
2065. GROSSMAN, Richard
    "The Larval War." [Hudson] (39:1) Spr 86, p. 103-104.
2066. GROTH, Brian J.
    "Bravo." [SanFPJ] (9:1) 86, p. 76.
    "For the Children." [SanFPJ] (9:1) 86, p. 67.
    "Forty Years After Hiroshima." [SanFPJ] (9:1) 86, p. 73.
    "History Repeats Itself." [SanFPJ] (8:1) 85, p. 12.
    "Into the Mirage." [SanFPJ] (8:4) 85, p. 19.
    "Mad." [SanFPJ] (9:1) 86, p. 66.
    "Passing Cat City." [PoeticJ] (13) 86, p. 4.
    "Rich and Famous." [SanFPJ] (8:4) 85, p. 86.
    "Who Lied?" [SanFPJ] (9:1) 86, p. 44.
2067. GROTH, Patricia Celley
    "Of Apple Tree and Tree House." [StoneC] (14:1/2) Fall-Wint 86-87, p. 56-57.
    "Wild Apples." [StoneC] (14:1/2) Fall-Wint 86-87, p. 55-56.
2068. GROVER-ROGOFF, Jay
    "The Barn Owl." [ChiR] (35:3) Spr 86, p. 20.
    "First Hand" (Selections: Four Poems). [KanQ] (18:1/2) Wint-Spr 86, p. 199-201.
    "Hogan's Bar, Galway." [PraS] (60:4) Wint 86, p. 84.
    "Inishmore Cuckoo." [PraS] (60:4) Wint 86, p. 82.
    "Teaching My Students Prosody." [GeoR] (40:3) Fall 86, p. 775-776.
    "The Wedding Sermon." [PraS] (60:4) Wint 86, p. 83.
2069. GROW, Eric
    "I Was Not a Bunny." [WormR] (26:1, issue 101) 86, p. 9-10.
    "Strawberry Lip Gloss." [WormR] (26:1, issue 101) 86, p. 8-9.
2070. GRUE, Lee Meitzen
    "Signed Poem: For the Women Poets." [TexasR] (7:1/2) Spr-Sum 86, p. 94-95.
2071. GRUPP, Art
    "Quiet Men Working." [SanFPJ] (8:3) 85, p. 58-59.
    "Quiet Men Working." [SanFPJ] (8:4) 85, p. 26-27.
    "Recruiting at the Airport." [SanFPJ] (8:4) 85, p. 87-88.
2072. GU, Cheng
    "At a Rebel Base in the Hindu Kush" (In Chinese & English, tr. by John Balcomb).
        [Nimrod] (29:2) Spr-Sum 86, p. 27.
    "By the Dream Ocean" (tr. by Tang Chao). [Verse] (6) 86, p. 50.
    "By the Dream Ocean" (tr. by Tony Barnstone and Tang Chao). [Nimrod] (29:2)
        Spr-Sum 86, p. 28.
    "Degrees of Arc" (tr. by Sharon Bangert). [RiverS] (20) 86, p. 9.
    "A Feeling" (In Chinese & English, tr. by John Balcomb). [Nimrod] (29:2) Spr-Sum
        86, p. 26.
    "My Graveyard" (tr. by Sharon Bangert). [RiverS] (20) 86, p. 8.
    "Near and Far" (tr. by John Balcomb). [Nimrod] (29:2) Spr-Sum 86, p. 25.
    "One Generation" (In Chinese & English, tr. by John Balcomb). [Nimrod] (29:2)
        Spr-Sum 86, p. 25.
    "Rain Walk" (tr. by Sharon Bangert). [RiverS] (20) 86, p. 9.
2073. GU, Zhong Xing
    "After a Night" (tr. of Mang Ke, w. Tony Barnstone and Willis Barnstone).
        [Nimrod] (29:2) Spr-Sum 86, p. 42.

"Declining Years" (tr. of Mang Ke, w. Tony Barnstone and Willis Barnstone). [Nimrod] (29:2) Spr-Sum 86, p. 45.
"Early Morning after Rain" (tr. of Mang Ke, w. Tony Barnstone and Willis Barnstone). [Nimrod] (29:2) Spr-Sum 86, p. 43.
"Night in the Snowfield" (tr. of Mang Ke, w. Tony Barnstone and Willis Barnstone). [Nimrod] (29:2) Spr-Sum 86, p. 40.
"Poems in October" (tr. of Mang Ke, w. Tony Barnstone and Willis Barnstone). [Nimrod] (29:2) Spr-Sum 86, p. 46-47.
"Spring" (tr. of Mang Ke, w. Tony Barnstone and Willis Barnstone). [Nimrod] (29:2) Spr-Sum 86, p. 44.
"Sunflower in the Sun" (tr. of Mang Ke, w. Tony Barnstone and Willis Barnstone). [Nimrod] (29:2) Spr-Sum 86, p. 66.
"These Days" (tr. of Mang Ke, w. Tony Barnstone and Willis Barnstone). [Nimrod] (29:2) Spr-Sum 86, p. 39.
"Wind Rising from the Water's Back" (tr. of Mang Ke, w. Tony Barnstone and Willis Barnstone). [Nimrod] (29:2) Spr-Sum 86, p. 44.
GUARDIA, Armando Rojas
   See ROJAS GUARDIA, Armando
2074. GUDE, Michael
   "Nightcrawlers." [HayF] (1) Spr 86, p. 46-47.
2075. GUELERMAN, Jose
   "El Cantaro Roto." [Mairena] (8:21) 86, p. 97.
   "Los Pinos y la Noche." [Mairena] (8:21) 86, p. 98.
   "Tiwanacu." [Mairena] (8:21) 86, p. 98.
2076. GUENTHER, Charles
   "Aversions" (tr. of René Char). [Paint] (13:25/26) Spr-Aut 86, p. 27.
   "A Bark at the Moon" (To my good friend Yu Suwa, tr. of Fivos Delfis). [Paint] (13:25/26) Spr-Aut 86, p. 36.
   "A Bird Calls" (tr. of Fivos Delfis). [Paint] (13:25/26) Spr-Aut 86, p. 41.
   "Death of Adonis" (tr. of Fivos Delfis). [Paint] (13:25/26) Spr-Aut 86, p. 38.
   "Dog Barks at Moon" (tr. of Fivos Delfis). [Paint] (13:25/26) Spr-Aut 86, p. 35.
   "Flint" (tr. of Fivos Delfis). [Paint] (13:25/26) Spr-Aut 86, p. 40.
   "Good Neighbors" (tr. of René Char). [Paint] (13:25/26) Spr-Aut 86, p. 27.
   "The Hours of Lyric Sighs" (tr. of Fivos Delfis). [Paint] (13:25/26) Spr-Aut 86, p. 39.
   "I Am the Same" (tr. of Fivos Delfis). [Paint] (13:25/26) Spr-Aut 86, p. 37.
   "October's Judgment" (tr. of René Char). [Paint] (13:25/26) Spr-Aut 86, p. 24.
   "Outer Possessions" (tr. of René Char). [Paint] (13:25/26) Spr-Aut 86, p. 25.
   "The Wing of Springtime" (tr. of Fivos Delfis). [Paint] (13:25/26) Spr-Aut 86, p. 42.
   "Wrestlers" (tr. of René Char). [Paint] (13:25/26) Spr-Aut 86, p. 26.
2077. GUERIN, Christopher D.
   "The Vietnam War Memorial." [WindO] (47) Sum 86, p. 45.
GUERNELLI, Adelaida Lugo
   See LUGO-GUERNELLI, Adelaida
2078. GUERNSEY, Bruce
   "The Search." [SoDakR] (24:3) Aut 86, p. 65.
   "The Thief." [SoDakR] (24:3) Aut 86, p. 66.
2079. GUERRA TEJADA, Maria
   "A Mi Padre" (from *Cinco Botellas al Mar*, 1985). [InterPR] (12:1) Spr 86, p. 28.
   "To My Father" (tr. by John Oliver Simon). [InterPR] (12:1) Spr 86, p. 29.
2080. GUEST, Barbara
   "The Rose Marble Table." [Conjunc] (9) 86, p. 209-210.
   "The View from Kandinsky's Window." [ParisR] (28:100) Sum-Fall 86, p. 168.
2081. GUIDACCI, Margherita
   "Cueva de las Manos." [InterPR] (12:2) Fall 86, p. 6, 8.
   "Cueva de las Manos" (tr. by Ruth Feldman). [InterPR] (12:2) Fall 86, p. 7, 9.
2082. GUILFORD, Charles
   "Vanishing Point." [StoneC] (14:1/2) Fall-Wint 86-87, p. 35.
2083. GUILLEMIN, Margret
   "Last Poems" (Selections, tr. of Paul Celan, w. Katharine Washburn). [AmerPoR] (15:3) My-Je 86, p. 3-5.
2084. GUIMERA, Angel
   "The Man Condemned to Death" (Reu de mort, tr. by Nathaniel Smith and Lynette McGrath). [SenR] (16:1) 86, p. 19-20.

158

GUIN

GUIN, Ursula K. le
    See Le GUIN, Ursula K.
2085. GUINTA, Bill
    "Anthropometric Summer Landscape." [PaintedB] (29) Ag 86, p. 62.
    "Outskirts of Lancaster." [PaintedB] (29) Ag 86, p. 62.
2086. GUITART, Jorge
    "Dos Tangos Ontologicos." [LindLM] (5:3) Jl-S 86, p. 14.
    "Retazos de la Vida." [LindLM] (5:3) Jl-S 86, p. 14.
2087. GULLEDGE, Jo
    "The Barn." [TexasR] (7:1/2) Spr-Sum 86, p. 18.
    "Fall in the Pisgah." [TarRP] (24:2) Spr 85, p. 24-25.
2088. GULLIKSEN, G. S.
    "The Real Pain." [WindO] (47) Sum 86, p. 40-41.
2089. GUNDERSON, Joanna
    "A Lot of Things Added Up." [Rampike] (5:2) 86, p. 70-71.
2090. GUNDERSON, Valerie
    "A Few Days After." [ManhatPR] (8) Wint 86-87, p. 52.
2091. GUNDY, Jeff
    "Class Reunion." [WoosterR] (6) Fall 86, p. 78-79.
2092. GUNN, Genni
    "From the M.P.'s Office." [Event] (15:1) 86, p. 104-105.
2093. GUNN, Thom
    "Nasturtium." [Thrpny] (26) Sum 86, p. 9.
    "A Sketch of the Great Dejection." [Thrpny] (27) Fall 86, p. 11.
2094. GUPTA, Abhik
    "Defiled Nose-Ring" (tr. of Mrinal Basu Chaudhuri). [Pax] (3:1/2) Wint 85-86, p.
        172-173.
2095. GUREVITCH, Zali
    "Memory of This Very Moment from a Distance of Years Ahead" (tr. by Gabriel
        Levin). [PoetL] (81:2) Sum 86, p. 120.
    "Sleep" (In the army, 6/82, tr. by Gabriel Levin). [PoetL] (81:2) Sum 86, p. 119.
    "This Too, the Place Where I Live" (tr. by Gabriel Levin). [PoetL] (81:2) Sum 86,
        p. 121.
2096. GURLEY, James
    "Dust." [Sonora] (11) Fall 86 [c87], p. 68-69.
2097. GURMANKIN, Arthur
    "Chocolate Aspirations." [PoeticJ] (13) 86, p. 35.
    "Love in the Rain." [PoeticJ] (13) 86, p. 35.
2098. GURNEY, Peter
    "Aubade." [BellArk] (2:2) Mr-Ap 86, p. 15.
    "Hunt." [CrabCR] (3:2) Spr 86, p. 3.
2099. GUSS, David
    "Colonel Morris's Fancy Turning Windward." [Pequod] (22) 86, p. 80.
    "To Speak and Feel" (for H.N., after H. D. Brumble's "Indian Sacred Materials").
        [Pequod] (22) 86, p. 81.
2100. GUSTAFSON, Ralph
    "Anatomy of Melancholy." [GreenfR] (13:3/4) Sum-Fall 86, p. 70.
    "At the Ocean's Verge Again." [CanLit] (108) Spr 86, p. 12.
    "The Broken Pianola" (for Heitor Villa-Lobos). [GreenfR] (13:3/4) Sum-Fall 86, p.
        71.
    "Psalm 151." [CanLit] (108) Spr 86, p. 67.
2101. GUSTAVSON, Jeffrey
    "Curator Visiting Zoo." [GrandS] (5:4) Sum 86, p. 97-98.
GUT, Karen Alkalay
    See ALKALAY-GUT, Karen
2102. GUTIERREZ, Guillermo
    "Ser de la Luz." [Mairena] (8:22) 86, p. 107.
2103. GUTIERREZ MORALES, Guillermo
    "Los Espejos de Borges." [Mairena] (8:21) 86, p. 70.
2104. GUY, Buddy
    "Stone Crazy." [ClockR] (3:1) 85, p. 29.
2105. GWILYM, Dafydd ap
    "The Dream" (tr. by Leslie Norris). [QW] (23) 86, p. 148-149.
2106. GWYNN, R. S.
    "1916." [SewanR] (94:2) Spr 86, p. 181-185.

2107. GYURE, James
"My Grandfather's Tongue." [PennR] (1:2) Fall 85, p. 45.
H., Wf
See WF. H.
HA, Jin
See JIN, Ha
2108. HACKER, Marilyn
"After Assumption." [RiverS] (19) 86, p. 32.
"And Tuesday." [Contact] (8:41/42/43) Fall-Wint 86-87, p. 81.
"And Tuesday II." [Contact] (8:41/42/43) Fall-Wint 86-87, p. 81.
"And Tuesday III." [Contact] (8:41/42/43) Fall-Wint 86-87, p. 81.
"Another Sunday." [YellowS] (21) Wint 86, p. 16.
"Aubade I." [Calyx] (10:1) Sum 86, p. 20.
"Aubade II." [Calyx] (10:1) Sum 86, p. 21.
"Bayswater." [Atlantic] (258:3) S 86, p. 77.
"Bloomingdale's I." [ManhatPR] (7) Sum 86, p. 15.
"Bloomingdale's II." [ManhatPR] (7) Sum 86, p. 15.
"Bloomingdale's III." [ManhatPR] (7) Sum 86, p. 16.
"Conversation in the Park." [Shen] (36:2) 86, p. 49.
"The Dark Night of the 747" (5 poems, I-V). [MassR] (27:1) Spr 86, p. 102-104.
"Denim and silk pooled at our feet upstairs." [Contact] (8:41/42/43) Fall-Wint 86-87,
   p. 81.
"Eight Days in August." [OP] (42/43) Wint 86-87, p. 97-100.
"First I want to make you come in my hand." [Cond] (13) 86, p. 105.
"Four Sonnets." [RiverS] (19) 86, p. 30-31.
"Friday Morning." [YellowS] (21) Wint 86, p. 14.
"Market Day." [PraS] (60:3) Fall 86, p. 46-48.
"Monday, Monday." [Contact] (8:41/42/43) Fall-Wint 86-87, p. 80.
"Monday, Monday II." [Contact] (8:41/42/43) Fall-Wint 86-87, p. 80.
"Monday, Monday III." [Contact] (8:41/42/43) Fall-Wint 86-87, p. 80.
"Nights of 1962: The River Merchant's Wife." [GrandS] (6:1) Aut 86, p. 199-201.
"Queensway." [YaleR] (75:4) Sum 86, p. 533.
"Rondeau." [YaleR] (75:4) Sum 86, p. 533.
"Rondeau After." [YellowS] (21) Wint 86, p. 16.
"Saturday Morning." [YellowS] (21) Wint 86, p. 13.
"Saturday Night." [YellowS] (21) Wint 86, p. 13.
"Saturday Night Song." [YellowS] (21) Wint 86, p. 14.
"Sonnet September." [Boulevard] (1:3) Fall 86, p. 91.
"Sunday Night." [YellowS] (21) Wint 86, p. 13.
"Then." [YellowS] (21) Wint 86, p. 15.
"Though sometimes, now, we sound like fiancées." [Cond] (13) 86, p. 104.
"Trajectory." [ManhatPR] (7) Sum 86, p. 14.
"Le Travail Rajeunit." [OP] (42/43) Wint 86-87, p. 96-97.
"Wagers." [YellowS] (21) Wint 86, p. 12.
"What You Might Answer." [Cond] (13) 86, p. 106.
2109. HACTHOUM, A.
"Las Estaciones." [LindLM] (5:4) O-D 86, p. 31.
"Llegas." [LindLM] (5:4) O-D 86, p. 31.
2110. HADAR, Erella
"Letters" (tr. of Moshe Dor, w. the author and Myra Sklarew). [PoetL] (81:2) Sum
   86, p. 103.
"Responsibility" (tr. of Moshe Dor, w. the author and Myra Sklarew). [PoetL]
   (81:2) Sum 86, p. 104.
2111. HADAS, Rachel
"Answer to a Letter from Boulder." [SouthwR] (71:1) Wint 86, p. 72-73.
"The End of Summer." [Agni] (23) 86, p. 29-30.
"First Night Back." [Boulevard] (1:3) Fall 86, p. 83-85.
"Lying under a Quilt." [Boulevard] (1:1/2) Wint 86, p. 151-152.
"Odds Against." [LitR] (29:3) Spr 86, p. 280-281.
"Pass It On." [SouthwR] (71:1) Wint 86, p. 76-77.
"Pass It On, III." [PartR] (53:2) 86, p. 236-237.
"Philoctetes." [LitR] (29:3) Spr 86, p. 281.
"Telling." [CumbPR] (5:2) Spr 86, p. 10.
"Two and One." [SouthwR] (71:1) Wint 86, p. 74-76.
"The Visit." [ColEng] (48:5) S 86, p. 461.

2112. HAEDER, Paul
"Cozumel: An Island with a Wall and High Forms of Life." [SmPd] (23:3, #68) Fall 86, p. 11-12.
"Getting a Handle on the Border." [SmPd] (23:3, #68) Fall 86, p. 8-10.
2113. HAGEDORN, Jessica
"Arts & Leisure." [OP] (41) Spr 86, p. 57-59.
"The Mummy." [RiverS] (19) 86, p. 33-36.
"The Song of Bullets." [OP] (41) Spr 86, p. 54-56.
2114. HAGINS, Jerry
"Morning Glory." [PaintedB] (29) Ag 86, p. 37.
"Yes." [PaintedB] (29) Ag 86, p. 37.
2115. HAHN, Kimiko
"Spring." [Contact] (7:38/39/40) Wint-Spr 86, p. 46.
2116. HAHN, Oscar
"Hearbreak Hotel" (Music of Elvis Presley, R.I.P., tr. by Steven F. White). [SilverFR] (11) Sum 86, p. 13.
"Hotel de las Nostalgias" (Música de Elvis Presley, Q.E.P.D.). [SilverFR] (11) Sum 86, p. 12.
"Reencarnacion de los Carniceros." [SilverFR] (11) Sum 86, p. 10.
"Reincarnation of the Butchers" (tr. by Steven F. White). [SilverFR] (11) Sum 86, p. 11.
2117. HAHN, Susan
"Given Name." [TriQ] (66) Spr-Sum 86, p. 148.
"If I Set Up the Chairs." [TriQ] (66) Spr-Sum 86, p. 150.
"The *Lamedvovniks*." [TriQ] (66) Spr-Sum 86, p. 146-147.
"Movie Star." [TriQ] (66) Spr-Sum 86, p. 149.
"Psalm." [TriQ] (66) Spr-Sum 86, p. 151.
2118. HAI-JEW, Dianne
"Rachel." [Contact] (7:38/39/40) Wint-Spr 86, p. 42.
2119. HAI-JEW, Shalin
"Father's Belt." [BellR] (9:2) Fall 86, p. 21.
"Reciprocation." [BellR] (9:2) Fall 86, p. 22.
2120. HAIGHT, Robert
"The Source of Bear Creek, Manistee County, Michigan." [PassN] (7:2) Spr-Sum 86, p. 20.
2121. HAINES, John
"On a Certain Field on Auvers." [PoetryE] (20/21) Fall 86, p. 80-82.
"Paolo and Francesca." [NewEngR] (9:2) Wint 86, p. 210.
HAIXIN, Xu
See XU, Haixin
2122. HALEY, Michael Cabot
"Rabies." [TexasR] (7:1/2) Spr-Sum 86, p. 17.
2123. HALEY, Vanessa
"Letters from a Lost Brother." [SouthernPR] (26:1) Spr 86, p. 25-27.
2124. HALFON, Shara
"Green Seedlings" (in Hebrew & English, tr. by Ada Aharoni). [InterPR] (12:2) Fall 86, p. 44-45.
"Is It Possible to Love You?" (in Hebrew & English, tr. by Ada Aharoni). [InterPR] (12:2) Fall 86, p. 46-47.
"The Turtle" (in Hebrew & English, tr. by Ada Aharoni). [InterPR] (12:2) Fall 86, p. 42-43.
2125. HALKIN, Hillel
"One Hundred Years of Jewish Settlement Later" (tr. of Aryeh Sivan). [PoetL] (81:2) Sum 86, p. 78-79.
"The Summer Is Over" (tr. of Aharon Almog). [PoetL] (81:2) Sum 86, p. 96.
"An Unpleasant Incident at a Memorial" (tr. of Aryeh Sivan). [PoetL] (81:2) Sum 86, p. 79.
"Yet Thirty Days" (tr. of Aharon Almog). [PoetL] (81:2) Sum 86, p. 95.
2126. HALL, Daniel
"Incident at the Lotus Pool." [Nat] (242:17) 3 My 86, p. 621.
"Long Nguyen." [SouthwR] (71:4) Aut 86, p. 517-518.
"Rainy Season." [Jacaranda] (2:1) Fall 86, p. 33.
2127. HALL, Donald
"The Day I Was Older." [Stand] (27:1) Wint 85-86, p. 22-23.
"For an Exchange of Rings." [MissouriR] (9:2) 86, p. 43.
"My Friend Felix." [ParisR] (28:99) Spr 86, p. 169-170.

"Richard." [Ploughs] (12:3) 86, p. 122.
"Shrubs Burned Away." [KenR] (NS 8:2) Spr 86, p. 1-9.
"Sums." [Poetry] (148:2) My 86, p. 93.
2128. HALL, Gene
"A Tribute to T.S. Eliot and Sixty." [DeKalbLAJ] (19:3/4) 86, p. 75.
2129. HALL, James B.
"Aloft the Hang Glider Meditates." [Interim] (5:2) Fall 86, p. 12.
"Orphans: Under Siege." [Interim] (5:2) Fall 86, p. 13.
2130. HALL, James Baker
"Home Movies." [KenR] (NS 8:1) Wint 86, p. 107-110.
"Local Weight." [PoetryNW] (27:2) Sum 86, p. 44-45.
"Reading Palms" (for Margaret Gibson). [PoetryNW] (27:2) Sum 86, p. 45.
"Washing My Cup in the Last Light." [SouthernPR] (26:2) Fall 86, p. 76.
2131. HALL, Jim
"Cheering." [KanQ] (18:1/2) Wint-Spr 86, p. 56.
"Old Bats." [OhioR] (37) 86, p. 115.
"One-Liners." [Poetry] (148:2) My 86, p. 74.
"Ourselves." [Poetry] (148:2) My 86, p. 76.
"Scatology." [KanQ] (18:1/2) Wint-Spr 86, p. 55.
"Tennis Elbow." [Poetry] (148:2) My 86, p. 77-78.
"Working to the Top." [Poetry] (148:2) My 86, p. 75.
2132. HALL, Judith
"Fragments of an Eve" (scraps from her album). [Shen] (36:4) 86, p. 83-97.
2133. HALL, Kathryn
"The Listening Tree." [NewRena] (6:3, #20) Spr 86, p. 105.
"A Toast for a Wedding." [AntR] (44:3) Sum 86, p. 337.
2134. HALL, Phil
"The Holes in the Trees." [Event] (15:2) 86, p. 38-39.
2135. HALL, Shelly L.
"When Earth Comes to Water." [Callaloo] (9:1, #26) Wint 86, p. 71.
2136. HALLAM, C.
"Jailhouse Tattoo." [Vis] (21) 86, p. 32.
2137. HALLERMAN, Victoria
"The Road Home." [Poetry] (148:2) My 86, p. 88.
"A Sculpture by George Segal." [Poetry] (148:2) My 86, p. 87.
"Slippage: A Writing-Room Idyll." [Poetry] (148:2) My 86, p. 89.
"Wind Unlashes." [SouthernPR] (26:2) Fall 86, p. 48.
2138. HALLEY, Anne
"Grieving for Mary." [HeliconN] (14/15) Sum 86, p. 48.
"On Dannenberg, in Paddelbourne, near Bleifeld." [SouthernPR] (26:1) Spr 86, p.
6-7.
2139. HALLGREN, Stephanie
"Checkers." [GeoR] (40:4) Wint 86, p. 894-895.
"Imaginary Numbers." [GeoR] (40:4) Wint 86, p. 891-893.
"The Mekong River Poem." [BlackWR] (12:2) Spr 86, p. 25-26.
"Miss Papago Indian Nation." [NegC] (6:1) Wint 86, p. 36-37.
2140. HALLIDAY, Mark
"Green Pants On." [NewEngR] (9:2) Wint 86, p. 190.
"Population." [NewEngR] (9:2) Wint 86, p. 191-192.
"Why the HG Is Holy." [MichQR] (25:1) Wint 86, p. 104.
2141. HALLORAN, Florence Ngoc
"My Grandmother." [DeKalbLAJ] (19:1) 86, p. 32-33.
2142. HALMAN, Talat S. (Talat Sait)
"Are We Going to Live Without Aging?" (tr. of Melih Cevdet Anday). [Vis] (22) 86,
p. 22.
"History of the Vanquished" (tr. of Ulkü Tamer). [Verse] (5) 86, p. 49.
2143. HALPERIN, Joan
"Fatherly Love: The Obsession." [CimR] (74) Ja 86, p. 4.
2144. HALPERIN, Mark
"Passion." [CrabCR] (4:1) Fall-Wint 86, p. 28.
2145. HALPERN, Daniel
"At Dante's Tomb." [OP] (42/43) Wint 86-87, p. 111.
"Bar Escargot: A Story." [ColEng] (48:6) O 86, p. 551-553.
"Caravaggio." [DenQ] (20:4/21:1) Spr-Sum 86, p. 48-49.
"Child Running." [NoAmR] (271:3) S 86, p. 25.
"Dark Night." [OP] (42/43) Wint 86-87, p. 110-111.

"An Early Death." [Shen] (36:3) 86, p. 17-19.
"The Hobbyist" (for my mother). [ColEng] (48:6) O 86, p. 556-557.
"Hotel Carlton, Tangier: The Old City." [OP] (42/43) Wint 86-87, p. 109.
"Local." [OP] (42/43) Wint 86-87, p. 112.
"Monterchi." [Verse] (5) 86, p. 37.
"Scars." [OP] (42/43) Wint 86-87, p. 113.
"Stazione." [Ploughs] (12:3) 86, p. 51-52.
"Tango." [Ploughs] (12:3) 86, p. 49-50.
"The Title." [OntR] (25) Fall-Wint 86-87, p. 41-42.
"Visitors." [ColEng] (48:6) O 86, p. 554-555.
2146. HALSALL, Jalaine
"Four Women." [MinnR] (NS 27) Fall 86, p. 81-82.
2147. HALSTEAD, Carol
"A Triumph of Tulips." [Quarry] (35:1) Wint 86, p. 64-65.
2148. HAMBLIN, Robert W.
"Spring Warfare." [CapeR] (21:2) Fall 86, p. 22.
2149. HAMBURGER, Michael
"Confidence" (tr. of Paul Celan). [Stand] (27:1) Wint 85-86, p. 54.
"Rubble Barge" (tr. of Paul Celan). [Stand] (27:1) Wint 85-86, p. 54.
"Sprachgitter" (Selections: 3 poems, tr. of Paul Celan). [SouthernHR] (20:1) Wint 86, p. 27-30.
"To Bridge a Lull" (i. m. George Oppen). [SouthernHR] (20:1) Wint 86, p. 12-13.
2150. HAMER, Mike
"Ambush at Wilike" (Nicarague). [Sam] (44:3 release 175) 86, p. 46-47.
"At the Comedor Infantil" (Nicaragua). [Sam] (44:3 release 175) 86, p. 41.
"Death Valley Days." [Sam] (44:3 release 175) 86, p. 43.
"The New Jerusalem" (Nicaragua). [Sam] (44:3 release 175) 86, p. 44-45.
"Returning from Bocana de Paiwas" (Nicaragua). [Sam] (44:3 release 175) 86, p. 40.
2151. HAMILL, Paul
"The Flight of Starlings." [GeoR] (40:4) Wint 86, p. 986-989.
2152. HAMILL, Sam
"Black Marsh Eclogue." [CutB] (25) Fall-Wint 86, p. 18.
"Elder-trees that thrushes have sown" (tr. of Jaan Kaplinski, w. the author and Riina Tamm). [WillowS] (18) Sum 86, p. 77.
"He is like a god" (LI, tr. of Catullus). [CrabCR] (3:2) Spr 86, p. 15.
"I could have said: I stepped from the bus" (tr. of Jaan Kaplinski, w. the author and Riina Tamm). [WillowS] (18) Sum 86, p. 75.
"It gets cold in the evening" (tr. of Jaan Kaplinski, w. the author and Riina Tamm). [WillowS] (18) Sum 86, p. 76.
"Listen, Ianni." [Zyzzyva] (2:3) Fall 86, p. 110-111.
"Naming the Beast." [PoetryE] (20/21) Fall 86, p. 60-64.
"Once I got a postcard from the Fiji Islands" (tr. of Jaan Kaplinski, w. the author and Riina Tamm). [WillowS] (18) Sum 86, p. 74.
"Porki and Socration, sinister thugs for Piso" (XLVII, tr. of Catullus). [CrabCR] (3:2) Spr 86, p. 15.
"Surely, you'll dine with me, my Fabulle" (XIII, tr. of Catullus). [CrabCR] (3:2) Spr 86, p. 15.
"Wen Fu (The Art of Writing)" (tr. of Lu Chi). [AmerPoR] (15:3) My-Je 86, p. 23-27.
2153. HAMILTON, Alfred Starr
"Of Joan of Arc." [Lips] (12) 86, p. 22.
"Wilderness." [NewL] (53:1) Fall 86, p. 29.
2154. HAMILTON, Carol
"Arts Festival." [PoeticJ] (16) Fall 86, p. 24.
"Fallen Angel." [CapeR] (21:2) Fall 86, p. 32.
"Heroine of Zanesville." [BellR] (9:2) Fall 86, p. 51.
"Leona." [Amelia] (3:1) Ja 86, p. 19.
2155. HAMILTON, Fritz
"1:30 AM Delusion." [DeKalbLAJ] (19:2) 86, p. 28.
"Above the Sea at Sunset!." [Kaleid] (13) Sum-Fall 86, p. 56.
"All Day Walking / No Bananas." [Kaleid] (13) Sum-Fall 86, p. 56.
"At the Oakland Arts Festival." [Kaleid] (13) Sum-Fall 86, p. 56.
"Boy Poem." [Kaleid] (13) Sum-Fall 86, p. 57.
"Upon Receiving 13 Boxes!" [HiramPoR] (41) Fall-Wint 86-87, p. 24-25.

2156. HAMILTON, Horace
"From the Walls." [SouthernR] (22:1) Ja 86, p. 148-149.
"My Name Is Nohbdy." [SouthernR] (22:1) Ja 86, p. 149-151.
2157. HAMILTON, Laura
"Industry and Water Don't Mix." [SanFPJ] (8:1) 85, p. 9.
"Remnants." [SanFPJ] (8:2) 85, p. 40.
"Sigh." [SanFPJ] (8:2) 85, p. 37.
2158. HAMILTON, Suzan G.
"Another Way of Seeing." [PoetryNW] (27:3) Aut 86, p. 18-20.
"Knitting." [PoetryNW] (27:3) Aut 86, p. 18.
2159. HAMMER, Margaret B.
"This Is for Ernie, Because He Gave Me Angels." [PottPort] (8) 86-87, p. 38-39.
2160. HAMMER, Patrick, Jr.
"November, 1880" (a Found Poem from the floor of today's Xerox room).
[JamesWR] (4:1) Fall 86, p. 7.
2161. HAMMOND, Karla M.
"The Myth of Breath." [YetASM] (5) 86, p. 5.
2162. HAMMOND, Mary Stewart
"Communion." [NewYorker] (62:6) 31 Mr 86, p. 32.
"Slow Dancing in the Living Room: Thanksgiving." [NewYorker] (62:41) 1 D 86,
p. 40.
2163. HAMMOND, Ralph
"The Cyclone Tail of Cow." [NegC] (6:4) Fall 86, p. 208.
"Death-Watch on the Nile." [Amelia] (3:1) Ja 86, p. 51.
HAN, Yu
See YU, Han
2164. HANEN, Edythe Anstey
"Secrets." [PraF] (7:2) Sum 86, p. 29.
2165. HANFT-MARTONE, Marjorie
"Leaving Oklahoma." [Calyx] (10:1) Sum 86, p. 34.
2166. HANKINS, Liz Porter
"Circles." [MemphisSR] (6:1/2) Spr 86, p. 49.
"Planting for the Kill." [Raccoon] (20) Ap 86, p. 42.
"Red Tulips and Windmills." [MemphisSR] (6:1/2) Spr 86, p. 48.
2167. HANKLA, Cathryn
"Puritan." [DenQ] (20:4/21:1) Spr-Sum 86, p. 132-133.
2168. HANNERS, LaVerne
"For Felix E. Goodson Jr." (my brother, who told me this). [BallSUF] (27:4) Aut
86, p. 65.
"Ice." [BallSUF] (27:4) Aut 86, p. 68.
"Lost Continent." [BallSUF] (27:4) Aut 86, p. 66-67.
2169. HANNON, Michael
"Clouds & Rivers." [WillowS] (18) Sum 86, p. 33-37.
2170. HANNS, Genine
"Legend of the Red Rose." [WritersL] (1986:6), p. 21.
2171. HANSEN, Joseph
"The Honor." [Zyzzyva] (2:1) Spr 86, p. 133.
2172. HANSEN, Matthew
"Still Alive." [NewYorker] (61:52) 17 F 86, p. 34.
2173. HANSEN, Tom
"Accepting Whatever Words Come." [BelPoJ] (36:4) Sum 86, p. 2.
"Chopping Down the Bodhi Tree." [BelPoJ] (36:4) Sum 86, p. 3-4.
"Emblem" (drawing by Christopher, age 7). [DeKalbLAJ] (19:2) 86, p. 30.
"Reflections of Wittgenstein." [KanQ] (18:4) Fall 86, p. 71.
2174. HANSEN, Twyla
"Airing Out." [PraS] (60:2) Sum 86, p. 34.
"The Call." [SpoonRQ] (11:4) Fall 86, p. 47.
"Nuance." [PraS] (60:2) Sum 86, p. 35.
2175. HANSON, Harold P.
"At a Painter's" (tr. of Georg Johannesen). [Vis] (22) 86, p. 16.
"Flight Preparation" (tr. of Georg Johannesen). [Vis] (22) 86, p. 15.
"The Jester's Greeting" (tr. of Georg Johannesen). [Vis] (22) 86, p. 16.
"Poster in a Condominium" (tr. of Georg Johannesen). [Vis] (22) 86, p. 15.
2176. HANSON, Julie Jordan
"At Last." [SoDakR] (24:2) Sum 86, p. 111-115.

2177. HANSON, Katherine
"Lineage" (tr. of Olav H. Hauge, w. Ron Wakefield and the author). [LitR] (29:3)
Spr 86, p. 357.
2178. HANSON, Kenneth O.
"Poem: In Venice — city built on mud." [Interim] (5:2) Fall 86, p. 27.
"Ritsos." [Interim] (5:2) Fall 86, p. 28.
"They Needed Each Other Song." [Interim] (5:2) Fall 86, p. 25-26.
2179. HANSON, Michael
"Cat-Strength." [DeKalbLAJ] (19:3/4) 86, p. 76.
"Mr. Everett" (Remembering Everett Renew, Remembering my first job).
[DeKalbLAJ] (19:3/4) 86, p. 77.
2180. HANZLICEK, C. G.
"Cemetery in Dolni Dobrouc, Czechoslovakia." [AntR] (44:1) Wint 86, p. 62.
"Under Stars." [AntR] (44:1) Wint 86, p. 61.
HAO-JAN, Mong
See MONG, Hao-Jan
2181. HARAS, Deborah L.
"Gentle Lover." [PottPort] (8) 86-87, p. 4.
2182. HARD, Rob
"Remembering." [JamesWR] (4:1) Fall 86, p. 1.
2183. HARDENBROOK, Yvonne M.
"Newly stacked firewood." [Amelia] (3:3) Sum 86, p. 46.
2184. HARDESTY, Harley C.
"I Give Up, We Win." [SanFPJ] (8:3) 85, p. 33.
2185. HARDING, Dew
"Of Men and Women." [RagMag] (5:2) Fall 86, p. 19.
2186. HARDING, Robert
"Boundaries." [AntigR] (65) Spr 86, p. 145.
"Cleaning Up." [AntigR] (66/67) Sum-Aut 86, p. 227.
2187. HARDING-RUSSELL, R. F. Gillian
"Opal's Dream." [CapilR] (39) 86, p. 53-59.
2188. HARDY, Isabeth
"For the Early Morning Students" (at Escuela Alberto Correa, Sept. 19, 1985,
Mexico City D.F.). [Pax] (3:1/2) Wint 85-86, p. iv-v.
2189. HARE, Madeline
"Plea." [PottPort] (8) 86-87, p. 51.
2190. HARJO, Joy
"Meeting." [CutB] (25) Fall-Wint 86, p. 51.
"Summer Night." [CutB] (25) Fall-Wint 86, p. 57.
2191. HARLOW, Robert
"The Comet." [MidwQ] (28:1) Aut 86, p. 90-92.
"Guided Tour." [MidwQ] (27:2) Wint 86, p. 204.
"Heartland." [MidwQ] (27:2) Wint 86, p. 202-203.
"Home." [MidwQ] (27:2) Wint 86, p. 200-201.
2192. HARMLESS, William, S.J.
"Ezekiel's Voice." [CumbPR] (5:2) Spr 86, p. 67.
2193. HARMON, Joan
"Herding." [PottPort] (8) 86-87, p. 11.
2194. HARMON, William
"If Anything Will Stand You Up Cold, Winter Will: Laconic Section for a February
Festival." [Pembroke] (18) 86, p. 67-70.
"Prose Poem." [PartR] (53:1) 86, p. 98-99.
2195. HARMS, James
"Mexican Christmas." [Poetry] (149:3) D 86, p. 156-157.
2196. HARNACK, Curtis
"Each Release." [Confr] (33/34) Fall-Wint 86-87, p. 165.
"Red Snow." [Confr] (33/34) Fall-Wint 86-87, p. 166.
2197. HARNESS, Ann
"Cafe." [PoeticJ] (14) 86, p. 13.
2198. HARPER, Michael (Michael S.)
"Archives" (Cooperstown, N.Y.). [TriQ] (65) Wint 86, p. 115-116.
"Arthritis Dance" (for Boyd Wright). [Callaloo] (9:1, #26) Wint 86, p. 75.
"Cousins." [Agni] (23) 86, p. 69-70.
"The Deer" (Election Day, 1984). [TriQ] (65) Wint 86, p. 111-112.
"Fanny's Kitchen." [Callaloo] (9:2, #27) Spr 86, p. 324-325.
"A Father's Song." [Callaloo] (9:1, #26) Wint 86, p. 72.

"Fifty." [Caliban] (1) 86, p. 15-16.
"Flight to Canada" (for Nancy). [MissouriR] (9:2) 86, p. 188-189.
"Free Association: Some Practical Symbols." [Callaloo] (9:2, #27) Spr 86, p. 328-330.
"Heat" (Brown University, 1985). [TriQ] (65) Wint 86, p. 117-118.
"Hinton's Silkscreens." [Callaloo] (9:2, #27) Spr 86, p. 326-327.
"Leaps from Prison." [Caliban] (1) 86, p. 17-18.
"Loyalty." [Callaloo] (9:1, #26) Wint 86, p. 73-74.
"Portrait of James Weldon Johnson" (Atlanta Archives). [Caliban] (1) 86, p. 14-15.
"Presidential Quotes" (Brown University). [TriQ] (65) Wint 86, p. 109-110.
"Studs" (for Shirley). [Caliban] (1) 86, p. 18-19.
"Study Windows." [TriQ] (65) Wint 86, p. 113-114.
"Zimmerhouse." [MissouriR] (9:2) 86, p. 186-187.
2199. HARRIAGUE, Magdalena
      "Poema: El ha llegado." [Mairena] (8:22) 86, p. 30.
2200. HARRINGTON, Ann
      "Advice and Comfort for a Newly-Divorced Woman." [YellowS] (21) Wint 86, p. 18.
2201. HARRIS, Bertha
      "A Philosopher in Love." [Pembroke] (18) 86, p. 262.
2202. HARRIS, Betty Donley
      "His Pillow." [Calyx] (9:2/3) Wint 86, p. 83.
2203. HARRIS, Claire
      "Coming to Terms" (With the White Visibility of Death). [Waves] (14:3) Wint 86, p. 50-53.
2204. HARRIS, Craig G.
      "Sacrificial Cock." [CentralP] (9) Spr 86, p. 16-17.
2205. HARRIS, Gail
      "Men." [MalR] (73) Ja 86, p. 57-58.
      "My Ego-Man." [MalR] (73) Ja 86, p. 59.
      "Three-legged Dogs." [MalR] (77) D 86, p. 31-32.
2206. HARRIS, Jana
      "The Potlatch RV Resort." [Lips] (12) 86, p. 29.
      "Shipwrecked in Useless Bay" (2 selections: "On Sunday, Blind Ray," "What Saved Him That Night"). [OntR] (25) Fall-Wint 86-87, p. 25-29.
2207. HARRIS, Jeane
      "Negotiations." [StoneC] (13:3/4) Spr-Sum 86, p. 24.
2208. HARRIS, Joseph
      "An Epitaph, of Sorts." [Amelia] (3:2) Spr 86, p. 51.
      "Landscape with Barn." [NegC] (6:4) Fall 86, p. 121.
      "Watching Marcel Marceau." [CrossCur] (6:2) 86, p. 144.
2209. HARRIS, Peter
      "Gravely Elegy." [ColEng] (48:2) F 86, p. 143.
      "Our Names Are Contraband." [OP] (41) Spr 86, p. 63-64.
      "Some Songs Women Sing." [OP] (41) Spr 86, p. 60-62.
2210. HARRIS, Rennick W.
      "Paradise Last." [Amelia] (3:1) Ja 86, p. 61-62.
2211. HARRIS, Robert
      "Fertile Yarn." [CapeR] (21:2) Fall 86, p. 44.
      "Forgotten Relations." [CapeR] (21:2) Fall 86, p. 45.
      "When the Twigs Nearly Split." [InterPR] (12:2) Fall 86, p. 74.
HARRIS, Robert von Dassanowsky
      See DASSANOWSKY-HARRIS, Robert von
2212. HARRISON, Jeffrey
      "Arrival at the Cabin." [MissouriR] (9:2) 86, p. 68.
      "Butterflies." [MissouriR] (9:2) 86, p. 73.
      "Crossing the Mississippi in a U-Haul." [LitR] (30:1) Fall 86, p. 71.
      "For a Friend in the Hospital." [MissouriR] (9:2) 86, p. 67.
      "Hornets' Nest." [MissouriR] (9:2) 86, p. 69.
      "Living near Trains." [LitR] (30:1) Fall 86, p. 70-71.
      "The Peacock Flounder" (The Boston Aquarium). [MissouriR] (9:2) 86, p. 74.
      "Poem: Like those spider webs strung across a path." [MissouriR] (9:2) 86, p. 72.
      "Returning to Cuttyhunk." [MissouriR] (9:2) 86, p. 70-71.
      "Via Yugoslavia." [LitR] (30:1) Fall 86, p. 69.
2213. HARRISON, Jim
      "The Theory and Practice of Rivers." [NewL] (52:2/3) Wint-Spr 86, p. 177-199.

2214. HARRISON, Richard
"Edgar." [AntigR] (65) Spr 86, p. 156-157.
"Footage." [Event] (15:2) 86, p. 20-21.
"Verrocchio." [GreenfR] (13:3/4) Sum-Fall 86, p. 72.
2215. HARRISON, Tony
"Y." [Verse] (6) 86, p. 3-4.
2216. HARROD, Lois Marie
"Three Haiku to Coming Spring." [Amelia] (3:2) Spr 86, p. 56.
2217. HARRYMAN, Carla
"The fate of my own fanaticism" ("Untitled"). [Temblor] (3) 86, p. 106-110.
2218. HARSHMAN, Marc
"Turning Back." [PassN] (7:1) Fall-Wint 85-86, p. 9.
2219. HART, Henry
"Bald Mountain Cemetery" (For A.R. Ammons). [Pembroke] (18) 86, p. 130-131.
"Leif Speaks of Vinland." [CumbPR] (5:2) Spr 86, p. 1-2.
"A Prairie Woman Remembers Kansas." [CumbPR] (5:2) Spr 86, p. 5-6.
"Winter Meditations (Boston, 1693)." [CumbPR] (5:2) Spr 86, p. 3-4.
2220. HART, John
"Annunciation." [Interim] (5:1) Spr 86, p. 35-36.
"Kitten." [Interim] (5:1) Spr 86, p. 36.
2221. HART, Jonathan (Jonathan Locke)
"Dug in the Bottom of My Skull." [Quarry] (35:3) Sum 86, p. 75-76.
"When a Man Gets Drunk." [Quarry] (35:3) Sum 86, p. 75.
"When I Stand Here with You." [Grain] (14:2) My 86, p. 28.
2222. HART, Kevin
"Approaching Sleep." [Verse] (5) 86, p. 11.
"The Map." [Verse] (5) 86, p. 10.
2223. HARTER, Linda Bohrer
"I Dream Poems." [EngJ] (75:7) N 86, p. 60.
2224. HARTMAN, Charles O.
"The Difference Engine" (1985 John Williams Andrews Prize Co-winner). [PoetL]
(81:1) Spr 86, p. 5-15.
"The Done Without." [Pequod] (22) 86, p. 75-76.
"A Succession of Acts." [Pequod] (22) 86, p. 77-79.
2225. HARTMAN, James D.
"Equals." [Sam] (46:2 release 182) 86, p. 40.
"Laundromat Eulogies." [Sam] (46:2 release 182) 86, p. 47.
2226. HARTMAN, Yuki
"Office." [Contact] (7:38/39/40) Wint-Spr 86, p. 32.
2227. HARTWICH, Jacqueline
"Ensemble Performance at Silver Lake" (Honorable Mention Poem, 1985/1986).
[KanQ] (18:1/2) Wint-Spr 86, p. 28.
2228. HARVEY, Gayle Elen
"Dracula's Bride." [Prima] (10) 86, p. 44.
"Family Photograph, c. 1912." [YetASM] (4) 85, p. 4.
"The Miner's Wife." [StoneC] (14:1/2) Fall-Wint 86-87, p. 23.
2229. HARVEY, Kay
"The Killdeer." [PoeticJ] (16) Fall 86, p. 15.
"The Orchard." [PoeticJ] (16) Fall 86, p. 28.
2230. HARVEY, Ken J.
"The Horizon." [PraF] (7:2) Sum 86, p. 49.
"Picasso's Death." [PraF] (7:2) Sum 86, p. 12.
2231. HARWAY, Judith
"Fontanelle." [CapeR] (21:1) Spr 86, p. 40.
"Geese." [CapeR] (21:1) Spr 86, p. 41.
"Living with Cancer." [SouthernPR] (26:1) Spr 86, p. 30.
2232. HASAN, Rabiul
"A Glass Face in the Rain." [WritersF] (12) Fall 86, p. 222-223.
"I Hang Around" (tr. of Sunil Gangopadhya). [Amelia] (3:3) Sum 86, p. 101.
"I May Leave, But Why Shall I Leave?" (tr. of Shatki Chattopadjya). [Amelia] (3:3)
Sum 86, p. 100.
2233. HASKINS, Lola
"At the Pittsburgh Airport." [MidwQ] (27:3) Spr 86, p. 303-304.
"The Hidden Flower" (after the Chinese). [MidwQ] (27:3) Spr 86, p. 302.
"Momotaro — A folk Tale." [MidwQ] (27:3) Spr 86, p. 295-301.

"Northern Light, Northern Dark" (Solvadal, Greenland 1000AD). [MidwQ] (27:3)
Spr 86, p. 305-310.
"Over the Dark Fishes." [BelPoJ] (36:4) Sum 86, p. 22-29.
2234. HASLAM, Thomas
"The Waste Lane, Rev." (for T.S. Eliot, il miglior fabbro & all that). [PaintedB] (29)
Ag 86, p. 28.
2235. HASS, Robert
"Father CH., Many Years Later" (tr. of Czeslaw Milosz, w. the author). [NewYRB]
(33:5) 27 Mr 86, p. 38.
"Lauda" (tr. of Czeslaw Milosz, w. the author). [ParisR] (28:100) Sum-Fall 86, p.
104-131.
2236. HASSLER, Donald M.
"Two Dozen Lines for Rich." [TarRP] (26:1) Fall 86, p. 30.
2237. HATCHER-MAYS, David
"Dissolving." [PoetryNW] (27:3) Aut 86, p. 34-36.
2238. HATHAWAY, Jeanine
"Death and Tracking." [Northeast] (series 4:3) Spr 86, p. 18.
"The Name of God Is." [GeoR] (40:3) Fall 86, p. 682.
2239. HATHAWAY, William
"At the Jet Show." [TarRP] (25:2) Spr 86, p. 10-11.
"Catfish Grumble" (for Jim Borck). [CharR] (12:2) Fall 86, p. 72-74.
"Cayuga Heights Crows" (for Archie). [Pembroke] (18) 86, p. 104.
"December Eighth." [QW] (22) Spr-Sum 86, p. 54-55.
"The Giants' Game." [MidAR] (7:1) 86, p. 18-19.
"In Each Day" (For Lisa Ress). [Poetry] (148:4) Jl 86, p. 203-204.
"Riding the Lions." [ColR] (NS 13:1) Fall 85, p. 58-59.
"Salt Treatment." [NoAmR] (271:4) D 86, p. 58-59.
2240. HATLEN, Burton
"Eight San Joaquin Valley Variations on a Midwestern Photograph by Art
Sensabaugh" (Midwestern Landscape #23). [BelPoJ] (37:1) Fall 86, p. 13-20.
2241. HATTERSLEY, Geoff
"A Bad Day." [Bogg] (55) 86, p. 45.
"Relax." [Bogg] (56) 86, p. 23.
2242. HATTON, Bill
"Ambition." [LakeSR] (20) 86, p. 14.
"Power Trip" (from a counselling session for delayed stress at the V.A. Hospital).
[LakeSR] (20) 86, p. 14.
2243. HAUG, James
"1951." [BellR] (9:2) Fall 86, p. 16.
"Edges." [IndR] (9:3) Sum 86, p. 79.
"Terminal Hotel." [Ascent] (12:1) 86, p. 26.
"This Must Be the Place." [PennR] (2:1) Fall-Wint 86, p. 44.
"Whenever You Go Away" (for Laurie). [LittleM] (15:1) 86, p. 19.
2244. HAUGE, Olav H.
"Lineage" (tr. by Ron Wakefield, Katherine Hanson and the author). [LitR] (29:3)
Spr 86, p. 357.
2245. HAUSER, Gwen
"Dream." [WestCR] (21:1) Je 86, p. 46-48.
"Meditations on Xango" (on hearing Cocada play). [Quarry] (35:1) Wint 86, p.
81-84.
"No Grass Grows" (autobiographical poem). [WestCR] (21:1) Je 86, p. 45.
2246. HAUSER, Susan
"August: Blueberry Moon." [SingHM] (14) 86, p. 70.
"December: Frost on the Windows Forever Moon." [SingHM] (14) 86, p. 73.
"July: Raspberry Moon." [SingHM] (14) 86, p. 70.
"June: Strawberry Moon." [SingHM] (14) 86, p. 69.
"May: Wildflower Moon." [SingHM] (14) 86, p. 69.
"November: Frozen Water Moon." [SingHM] (14) 86, p. 72.
"October: Falling Leaf Moon." [SingHM] (14) 86, p. 72.
"September: Wild Rice Moon." [SingHM] (14) 86, p. 71.
"Thirteenth Moon." [SingHM] (14) 86, p. 73.
2247. HAVEMANN, Leo
"A Ghazal." [Grain] (14:2) My 86, p. 57.
"The Light Within." [Grain] (14:2) My 86, p. 58.
"Opposing Forces." [Grain] (14:2) My 86, p. 56.
"A Villanelle." [Grain] (14:2) My 86, p. 57.

2248. HAVIRD, David
"In the White Room." [SouthernPR] (26:2) Fall 86, p. 24-25.
HAWK, Red
See RED HAWK
2249. HAWKINS, H. S., Jr.
"Notes to a Daughter." [Amelia] (3:1) Ja 86, p. 84.
2250. HAWKINS, Hunt
"The Prejohn." [GeoR] (40:3) Fall 86, p. 683-684.
2251. HAWLEY, James
"John Greenleaf Whittier." [ManhatPR] (6) Wint-Spr 85-86, p. 44.
2252. HAXTON, Brooks
"Serenade Airborne." [SouthernR] (22:4) O 86, p. 792-795.
2253. HAYASHI, R. T.
"Dusty." [Poem] (55) Mr 86, p. 37.
2254. HAYDAR, Adnan
"Night-Strings" (Excerpts, tr. of Mozaffar Al-Nawwab, w. Michael Beard).
[MinnR] (NS 26) Spr 86, p. 44-55.
2255. HAYDEN, Dolores
"Authorities Tolerate Isolated Fires" (for Florence Luscombe). [YetASM] (4) 85, p.
6.
"Yesterday I Learned the Earth Is Flat." [ManhatPR] (8) Wint 86-87, p. 7.
2256. HAYDEN, Robert
"Those Winter Sundays." [TriQ] (65) Wint 86, p. 62.
2257. HAYES, Ann
"Song for an Old Wife." [Confr] (32) Spr-Sum 86, p. 48.
"Sun Dance." [Confr] (33/34) Fall-Wint 86-87, p. 142.
HAYES, Mary Cartledge
See CARTLEDGE-HAYES, Mary
2258. HAYNES, Robert (Robert E.)
"Father Poem." [HiramPoR] (41) Fall-Wint 86-87, p. 27.
"From Evansville to Hollywood." [Farm] (3:2) Spr-Sum 86, p. 55.
"My Only Ode to Walt Whitman." [Vis] (22) 86, p. 32.
"She Who Had Nothing to Lose." [HiramPoR] (41) Fall-Wint 86-87, p. 28-29.
"The Swamp Thing." [HiramPoR] (41) Fall-Wint 86-87, p. 26.
2259. HAYS, Janice
"The Neo-Life Temple of Health Shop." [WritersF] (12) Fall 86, p. 223.
2260. HAYS, Robert
"Love Song of Day 1, Time 00:00:10 -10." [MidwQ] (28:1) Aut 86, p. 82.
2261. HAYS, Terry E.
"Admittance." [FloridaR] (14:2) Fall-Wint 86, p. 37.
2262. HAYWARD, Camille
"Charcoal Drawing." [BellArk] (2:3) My-Je 86, p. 1.
"Foxgloves." [BellArk] (2:2) Mr-Ap 86, p. 7.
"Geography." [BellArk] (2:1) Ja-F 86, p. 1.
"Let There Be Words." [BellArk] (2:1) Ja-F 86, p. 8.
"Man on a Ladder." [BellArk] (2:3) My-Je 86, p. 15.
"Oranges." [BellArk] (2:5) S-O 86, p. 4.
"Theology." [BellArk] (2:1) Ja-F 86, p. 8.
HE, Jiang
See JIANG, He
2263. HEABERLIN, Hal
"Sweet Revenge." [EngJ] (75:7) N 86, p. 75.
2264. HEAD, Gwen
"Bait." [PraS] (60:1) Spr 86, p. 28.
"Columbus." [PraS] (60:1) Spr 86, p. 29.
"The Dream of Dancing" (for Rebecca). [PraS] (60:1) Spr 86, p. 30-32.
2265. HEAD, Linda Weasel
"The Stone Woman." [CutB] (25) Fall-Wint 86, back cover.
2266. HEAL, Edith
"Cancer." [Lips] (12) 86, p. 24.
2267. HEALY, Sophie
"Nuevo Leon." [Pax] (3:1/2) Wint 85-86, p. 176-177.
2268. HEANEY, Seamus
"Clearances" (Selections: II, III, V, VII, VIII). [Field] (34) Spr 86, p. 44-46.
"A Daylight Art" (for Norman MacCaig). [CumbPR] (5:2) Spr 86, p. 43-44.
"Hailstones." [SenR] (16:2) 86, p. 40-41.

"The Haw Lantern." [Verse] (6) 86, p. 23.
"The Stone Grinder." [Verse] (6) 86, p. 24.
"Two Quick Notes." [Verse] (6) 86, p. 23.
"Wolfe Tone." [Verse] (6) 86, p. 24.
2269. HEARLE, Kevin J.
"Approaching the Door." [Sonora] (10) Spr 86, p. 23.
"West 7th Street." [Sonora] (10) Spr 86, p. 24.
2270. HEARST, James
"The Hurt of Pleasure." [Farm] (3:2) Spr-Sum 86, p. 26.
"Not the Day to Listen." [Farm] (3:2) Spr-Sum 86, p. 27.
"Winter Reverie." [Farm] (3:2) Spr-Sum 86, p. 25.
2271. HEATH-STUBBS, John
"The New Dance of Death." [Interim] (5:1) Spr 86, p. 3-6.
"Over the Fields of Alsace" (tr. of Maksimilian Voloshin w. Eugene Dubnov).
[Event] (15:2) 86, p. 115.
"Partakers in the Blood" (tr. of Eugene Dubnov, w. the author). [Interim] (5:2) Fall
86, p. 45.
"Snapshot" (tr. of Eugene Dubnov, w. the author). [Confr] (32) Spr-Sum 86, p.
107-108.
"The time has arrived for the light-pinioned burden of combat" (tr. of Eugene
Dubnov, w. the author). [Interim] (5:2) Fall 86, p. 44.
2272. HEBALD, Carol
"At the Zoo" (To Walt Witcover). [Confr] (32) Spr-Sum 86, p. 60.
"Branches, Scattered, Strewn: I Lie Alone." [DeKalbLAJ] (19:3/4) 86, p. 78.
2273. HECHT, Anthony
"Envoi." [YaleR] (76:1) Aut 86, p. 127.
"The Feast of Stephen." [GeoR] (40:3) Fall 86, p. 685-686.
"Humoresque." [ParisR] (28:100) Sum-Fall 86, p. 169.
2274. HECHT, Janice
"Survival." [YetASM] (4) 85, p. 7.
2275. HECHT, Jennifer
"Albert and Sidney." [WebR] (11:2) Fall 86, p. 56.
"Repairs." [WebR] (11:2) Fall 86, p. 55.
2276. HEDGES, David
"The Coldest Day." [Sam] (45:4 release 180) 86, p. 21.
"A Question of Whales." [YetASM] (5) 86, p. 10.
2277. HEDGES, Warren
"An Ozark Baptist Looks for Limestone." [WoosterR] (5) Spr 86, p. 83.
2278. HEDIN, Robert
"Flyers." [Pembroke] (18) 86, p. 262.
"On the Twenty-Fifth Anniversary of the Mother Superior's Drowning." [Germ]
(10:1) Spr-Sum 86, p. 27.
2279. HEFFERNAN, Michael
"Saturday." [AmerPoR] (15:4) Jl-Ag 86, p. 9.
HEHIR, Diana O'
See O'HEHIR, Diana
2280. HEIFETZ, Fabiana L.
"Diciembre." [Mairena] (8:22) 86, p. 70.
2281. HEIFETZ, Hank
"For the Lord of the Animals" (Excerpt, tr. of Dhurjati, w. Velcheru Narayana Rao).
[Translation] (16) Spr 86, p. 200-202.
2282. HEIGHTON, Steven
"Endurance" (for J.H.). [Quarry] (35:3) Sum 86, p. 55.
"Ferry at Melbourne." [Grain] (14:2) My 86, p. 53.
"Grave by Rapids" (dated 1892, Rifle Chutes, Madawaska). [Quarry] (35:3) Sum
86, p. 55-56.
"The Machine-Gunner." [Event] (15:2) 86, p. 123-124.
"Near Pulpit Rock." [Grain] (14:2) My 86, p. 55.
HEIICHI, Sugiyama
See SUGIYAMA, Heiichi
2283. HEIMLER, Charles
"The Beauty of Research." [Sam] (46:5 [i.e. 46:1] release 181) 86, p. 52.
HEINE, Lala Koehn
See KOEHN-HEINE, Lala
2284. HEINE, Thomas
"Respite." [CumbPR] (6:1) Fall 86, p. 44.

2285. HEINEMAN, W. F.
"Concerned That I Am Not." [DeKalbLAJ] (19:1) 86, p. 33.
"Festival around the Nets." [CapeR] (21:1) Spr 86, p. 38.
"The Moonrise." [CarolQ] (39:1) Fall 86, p. 72.
"Mountain Winter." [BallSUF] (26:4) Aut 85, p. 8.
"The Old Dog." [DeKalbLAJ] (19:1) 86, p. 33.
"Opening the Door at Night." [BallSUF] (26:4) Aut 85, p. 21.
"Taking Our Shadows." [CarolQ] (39:1) Fall 86, p. 73.
"The Watch." [CentR] (30:1) Wint 86, p. 60.
"Where Night Is Quarried." [BallSUF] (27:4) Aut 86, p. 10.
"A Woman Arguing." [DeKalbLAJ] (19:1) 86, p. 33.
2286. HEISLER, Eva
"The Banks Brigade" (First Award Poem, 1985/1986). [KanQ] (18:1/2) Wint-Spr
86, p. 11-12.
"The Death of Psyche." [SouthernPR] (26:2) Fall 86, p. 10-15.
"Teed." [IndR] (9:2) Spr 86, p. 50-51.
2287. HEJINIAN, Lyn
"The Person" (Excerpt). [Sulfur] (6:1, issue 16) 86, p. 79-85.
"The Person" (Selections: 9 poems). [Temblor] (4) 86, p. 33-41.
2288. HEJNA, James
"Soaps." [MissouriR] (9:1) 85-86, p. 50.
2289. HELDT, Barbara
"Behind me someone" (tr. of Tatyana Momonova). [Pax] (3:1/2) Wint 85-86, p.
191.
"I entrust myself to her" (tr. of Tatyana Momonova). [Pax] (3:1/2) Wint 85-86, p.
191.
"I will return" (tr. of Tatyana Momonova). [Pax] (3:1/2) Wint 85-86, p. 190.
"No letters" (tr. of Tatyana Momonova). [Pax] (3:1/2) Wint 85-86, p. 190.
"Rebirth on the edge of worry" (tr. of Tatyana Momonova). [Pax] (3:1/2) Wint
85-86, p. 191.
2290. HELIE, Leonard
"No One Has Told the Tiger." [Amelia] (3:3) Sum 86, p. 97.
"Oak leaves dry and gnarled." [Amelia] (3:4) Fall 86, p. 10.
2291. HELLER, Liane
"Coma." [GreenfR] (13:3/4) Sum-Fall 86, p. 73.
2292. HELLEW, Joyce
"Elegy for My Cat." [HolCrit] (23:4) O 86, p. 19.
2293. HELLMAN, Sheila
"Progression." [StoneC] (14:1/2) Fall-Wint 86-87, p. 22.
2294. HELLUS, Al
"Abandoning Florida." [Caliban] (1) 86, p. 29.
"I Drink to Bukowski's Nose." [Caliban] (1) 86, p. 27-28.
2295. HELWIG, Maggie
"Columbus at Night." [GreenfR] (13:3/4) Sum-Fall 86, p. 74.
"New World Overture." [Quarry] (35:1) Wint 86, p. 39-49.
2296. HEMINGWAY, Anne
"Gato in the Rain." [ClockR] (3:2) 86, p. 43.
2297. HEMP, Christine E.
"No Question Mark, Please." [WebR] (11:1) Spr 86, p. 73.
"To Build a Poem." [WebR] (11:1) Spr 86, p. 71-72.
2298. HEMPHILL, Essex
"The Edge." [Callaloo] (9:1, #26) Wint 86, p. 76-78.
"The Note." [Callaloo] (9:2, #27) Spr 86, p. 302.
2299. HEMSCHEMEYER, Judith
"I finally wrote down the words" ("An Untitled Poem," tr. of Anna Akhmatova).
[Boulevard] (1:1/2) Wint 86, p. 153.
2300. HENDERSON, Brian
"Finally, You Begin." [AntigR] (66/67) Sum-Aut 86, p. 197.
"Nightfall by the River." [GreenfR] (13:3/4) Sum-Fall 86, p. 75.
"Standing in Starlight." [AntigR] (66/67) Sum-Aut 86, p. 196.
"This Begins at the Edge." [AntigR] (66/67) Sum-Aut 86, p. 195.
2301. HENDERSON, Cindy S.
"Dear Robert." [EngJ] (75:3) Mr 86, p. 66.
"Proofreading Joshua." [EngJ] (75:5) S 86, p. 69.
2302. HENDERSON, David
"The Destroying Angels" (The White Amanita). [PoetryNW] (27:3) Aut 86, p. 17.

"The First One." [Ploughs] (12:4) 86, p. 166-167.
2303. HENDLER, Sue
"On the Making of Bread." [Quarry] (35:4) Aut 86, p. 61.
2304. HENKE, Mark
"Hillsboro 1966." [SoDakR] (24:2) Sum 86, p. 119.
"Legacy." [CapeR] (21:1) Spr 86, p. 20.
"NATO 1961." [MidAR] (7:1) 86, p. 138-139.
2305. HENN, Mary Ann
"Big Question." [SanFPJ] (8:1) 85, p. 8.
"Brother Francis." [PoeticJ] (16) Fall 86, p. 10.
"Clear It Up" (A Karina). [SanFPJ] (8:3) 85, p. 15.
"Good News Is the Novelty" (To Lenny). [SanFPJ] (8:2) 85, p. 95.
"How's That Again?" [SanFPJ] (8:1) 85, p. 93.
"I Know the Immediate." [Amelia] (3:2) Spr 86, p. 115.
"Nun in a Bar." [Bogg] (56) 86, p. 52.
"The Pendulum Swings" (A Karina). [SanFPJ] (8:1) 85, p. 25.
"Praise." [Wind] (16:57) 86, p. 42.
"Quick Kill." [SanFPJ] (8:4) 85, p. 20.
"Quick! Tell Me!" [SanFPJ] (8:2) 85, p. 94.
"Remember, That's Us." [SanFPJ] (8:1) 85, p. 94.
"So Many Times" (A Karina). [SanFPJ] (8:3) 85, p. 13.
"Tied to Earth." [PoeticJ] (16) Fall 86, p. 31.
"White for Tears." [SanFPJ] (8:3) 85, p. 16.
"Who Could Doubt?" [SanFPJ] (8:1) 85, p. 6.
"You Ain't Seen Nuthin' Yet." [SanFPJ] (8:1) 85, p. 7.
2306. HENNING, Dianna
"Squirrels Running over New Spring Grass." [CapeR] (21:1) Spr 86, p. 23.
2307. HENRIKSON, Carol
"Marriages." [SouthernHR] (20:1) Wint 86, p. 52.
2308. HENRY, Daniel
"Finally, One for Frost" (to Mary Burgess). [EngJ] (75:3) Mr 86, p. 40.
2309. HENRY, Gordon
"Message from the Kingdom of Intellect." [Raccoon] (20) Ap 86, p. 43.
2310. HENRY, Laurie
"As They Start at the Top of the Orchard." [KanQ] (18:1/2) Wint-Spr 86, p. 184.
"A Former Dispatcher's Comment." [MissouriR] (9:1) 85-86, p. 190.
"Leaks" (for John). [KanQ] (18:1/2) Wint-Spr 86, p. 183.
2311. HENRY, Michael
"Tax Collector." [Bogg] (55) 86, p. 55.
2312. HENRY, Tim
"On First Looking into Walker's Negatives" (Volume 5, Number III). [NegC] (6:4)
Fall 86, p. 209.
2313. HENSHAW, Tyler
"Dreaming of Teamsters." [MidAR] (6:1) 86?, p. 36.
"The Rites of Garbage Day." [CapeR] (21:2) Fall 86, p. 40.
2314. HENSON, David
"The Grass Back Home Is Knee-Deep under the Walnut Tree." [PikeF] (7) Spr 86,
p. 3.
"Her Husband Keeps the Swords." [PikeF] (7) Spr 86, p. 3.
"Marriage (Last Week We Saw an Eel with Wings)." [GWR] (6:2) 86, p. 28.
"The Old Woman Keeps Two Big Dogs." [GWR] (6:2) 86, p. 27.
"Til Jack-in-the-Boxes Pop All Around Us." [PikeF] (7) Spr 86, p. 3.
2315. HENTZ, Robert R.
"The Analyst." [SanFPJ] (9:1) 86, p. 72.
"Consensus." [SanFPJ] (8:4) 85, p. 61.
"The Demagogue." [SanFPJ] (9:1) 86, p. 72.
"Election Night." [SanFPJ] (8:1) 85, p. 73.
"Viet Nam — A Retrospect." [SanFPJ] (8:4) 85, p. 74-75.
2316. HERBERT, Joyce
"The Forge." [Stand] (27:2) Spr 86, p. 49.
"Sanctuary Wood, Ypres." [Stand] (27:2) Spr 86, p. 48.
2317. HERBERT, Zbigniew
"Transformation of Livy" (tr. by John Carpenter and Bogdana Carpenter).
[NewYRB] (33:17) 6 N 86, p. 10.

2318. HERMANS, Theo
"Brassempouy" (tr. of H. C. ten Berge, w. Paul Vincent). [Stand] (27:2) Spr 86, p. 22.
"Lübeck" (tr. of H. C. ten Berge, w. Paul Vincent). [Stand] (27:2) Spr 86, p. 23.
2319. HERNANDEZ, Roberto
"Amor: Camino de Laberinto" (fragmento). [Mairena] (8:22) 86, p. 100.
2320. HERNANDEZ, Samuel
"Learning Revolution." [Stand] (27:1) Wint 85-86, p. 56-57.
2321. HERNANDEZ MURIEL, Rodrigo
"Cuando Murio Vicente Aleixandre." [Mairena] (8:22) 86, p. 118.
2322. HEROY, Susan
"To Calgary." [PraS] (60:4) Wint 86, p. 28-29.
"Veiling, Unveiling." [PraS] (60:4) Wint 86, p. 25-28.
"Veronika." [PraS] (60:4) Wint 86, p. 23-25.
2323. HERPORT, Susan Hall
"I Name These Things." [TarRP] (25:2) Spr 86, p. 32-33.
HERRERO, Víctor Corcoba
    See CORCOBA HERRERO, Víctor
2324. HERRIN, Sally
"Down on the Farm in Heaven, Nebraska." [PraS] (60:2) Sum 86, p. 105.
"The Love of a Good Woman." [PraS] (60:2) Sum 86, p. 106.
"When Science and Religion Coalesce." [Wind] (16:56) 86, p. 38.
2325. HERRINGTON
"It Didn't Rhyme, But Still Means Something." [Dandel] (13:1) Spr-Sum 86, p. 18.
"The Leaves Are Falling." [Dandel] (13:1) Spr-Sum 86, p. 19.
2326. HERRON, Mick
"A Month of Ice." [Verse] (5) 86, p. 44-45.
2327. HERSHON, Robert
"Evergreen and Covert." [PoetryNW] (27:1) Spr 86, p. 19.
"Real Estate." [RiverS] (20) 86, p. 39.
"Where to Eat in Goderich, 'The Prettiest Town in Canada'." [PoetryNW] (27:1) Spr 86, p. 19-20.
2328. HERTZ, Dalia
"The Return" (tr. by Robert Friend). [PoetL] (81:2) Sum 86, p. 102.
2329. HERZBERG, Judith
"Gulls" (tr. by Shirley Kaufman). [Field] (34) Spr 86, p. 70.
"Over There" (tr. by Shirley Kaufman). [Field] (34) Spr 86, p. 66.
"Program" (tr. by Shirley Kaufman). [Field] (34) Spr 86, p. 71.
"A Strange Map" (tr. by Shirley Kaufman). [Field] (34) Spr 86, p. 67-69.
2330. HERZING, Albert
"Arachnid." [KanQ] (18:1/2) Wint-Spr 86, p. 245-246.
"Nazi Lampshades." [SouthwR] (71:4) Aut 86, p. 536-537.
"Peakload Labor." [KanQ] (18:1/2) Wint-Spr 86, p. 244-245.
2331. HESFORD, Wendy S.
"The Concurrian River." [Abraxas] (34) 86, p. 28.
2332. HESSELMAN, Marcia
"Budgies." [Farm] (3:2) Spr-Sum 86, p. 47.
2333. HESTER, M. L.
"The Mother of the Thundering Brood." [FloridaR] (14:2) Fall-Wint 86, p. 92.
"The Poet, in February." [LitR] (29:3) Spr 86, p. 340.
"The Poet, Ready to Get Religion." [LitR] (29:3) Spr 86, p. 340.
"The Poet, Walking Down Main Street." [LitR] (29:3) Spr 86, p. 340.
"To Another Outpatient." [Wind] (16:57) 86, p. 14.
2334. HETTICH, Michael
"Down at the Docks." [IndR] (9:2) Spr 86, p. 102.
"Lost Lake." [SmPd] (23:1, #66) Wint 86, p. 18.
"Making Plans." [YetASM] (4) 85, p. 6.
"Mother." [BelPoJ] (37:2) Wint 86-87, p. 20-21.
2335. HEWITT, Christopher
"The Bicyclist" (in memory of Jackson Burgess). [Kaleid] (12) Wint 86, p. 53.
"The Watch." [Kaleid] (12) Wint 86, p. 53.
2336. HEWMAN, Wade
"Divorce and Continuum." [Confr] (32) Spr-Sum 86, p. 140.
2337. HEYECK, Bryan
"Alone in the cold you sit." [Zyzzyva] (2:1) Spr 86, p. 151.

173

2338. HEYEN, William
"In a Ching Dynasty Painting by Chu Lien." [SouthernHR] (20:2) Spr 86, p. 170.
"A Long Island Fish Story." [PaintedB] (29) Ag 86, p. 34.
"The Nuclear Plant at Shoreham." [SenR] (16:2) 86, p. 63.
"Plague Sermon." [GeoR] (40:3) Fall 86, p. 687-688.
"While We Are Still Alive." [SouthernHR] (20:4) Fall 86, p. 316.
2339. HEYL, AnneLiese
"I Miss You Too" (for Manon). [PikeF] (7) Spr 86, p. 20.
2340. HEYL, Stephanie
"I Knew the Woman." [PikeF] (7) Spr 86, p. 22.
"Mama's Sick." [PikeF] (7) Spr 86, p. 22.
2341. HEYMAN, Ann
"Genetics." [DeKalbLAJ] (19:1) 86, p. 44.
"Gossip." [DeKalbLAJ] (19:3/4) 86, p. 54.
"Gravis." [DeKalbLAJ] (19:3/4) 86, p. 54.
"Housework." [DeKalbLAJ] (19:3/4) 86, p. 54.
"The Invalid." [DeKalbLAJ] (19:1) 86, p. 44-45.
"Vanity." [DeKalbLAJ] (19:1) 86, p. 45.
2342. HIBBARD, Tom
"Voices." [DeKalbLAJ] (19:2) 86, p. 32.
2343. HICKS, John V.
"Schematic." [CanLit] (109) Sum 86, p. 100.
HIDE, Oshiro
   See OSHIRO, Hide
2344. HIESTAND, Emily
"On Nothing." [Hudson] (39:2) Sum 86, p. 289-290.
"Planting in Tuscaloosa." [Hudson] (39:2) Sum 86, p. 288-289.
2345. HIGH, Maura
"The Bird Called Halcyon." [MissouriR] (9:2) 86, p. 55.
"The Four Corners." [MissouriR] (9:2) 86, p. 54.
"The Gun." [DenQ] (20:4/21:1) Spr-Sum 86, p. 111-112.
2346. HILBERRY, Conrad
"Cretan Dawn: A Metaphor." [KenR] (NS 8:2) Spr 86, p. 39.
"Crickets and the Rain." [ThRiPo] (27/28) 86, p. 42.
"Heraclitus on Fire." [KenR] (NS 8:2) Spr 86, p. 41.
"Night Sky with Tree." [VirQR] (62:1) Wint 86, p. 47.
"On the Promontory." [KenR] (NS 8:2) Spr 86, p. 40.
"Self Portrait in Smoke." [VirQR] (62:1) Wint 86, p. 46.
"Six Poems from Crete." [TarRP] (25:2) Spr 86, p. 3-5.
"Sorting the Smoke." [VirQR] (62:1) Wint 86, p. 45-46.
"Talk." [KenR] (NS 8:2) Spr 86, p. 40.
"Waves." [ThRiPo] (27/28) 86, p. 41.
2347. HILDEBIDLE, John
"To Accompany a Gift of Flowers." [PennR] (1:2) Fall 85, p. 41.
2348. HILL, Crag
"Spirit" (visual poem). [WindO] (47) Sum 86, p. 27.
2349. HILL, Daniel
"Smokey Water Doubled Over." [CutB] (26) Spr-Sum 86, p. 20-24.
2350. HILL, Gerald
"Conversation with Nader Ghermezian" (A developer, with his brothers, of the West Edmonton Mall). [PraF] (7:4) Wint 86-87, p. 62-63.
2351. HILL, Hyacinthe
"Lullanye for Mother's Day." [SingHM] (14) 86, p. 4.
2352. HILL, Jack
"Despite all the training." [Sam] (46:2 release 182) 86, p. 25.
"Having been issued immortality." [Sam] (46:2 release 182) 86, p. 60.
"Hill 190, August '69." [Sam] (46:2 release 182) 86, p. 37.
"In the morning he came for me." [Sam] (46:2 release 182) 86, p. 96.
2353. HILL, John Meredith
"Home and Away." [AntR] (44:2) Spr 86, p. 208.
"Selling." [ManhatPR] (7) Sum 86, p. 56.
2354. HILL, Kathleen
"In Time." [IndR] (9:2) Spr 86, p. 85.
2355. HILL, R. Nemo
"Children's Story." [Sulfur] (6:1, issue 16) 86, p. 36.
"Self-Portrait." [Sulfur] (6:1, issue 16) 86, p. 35.

"Slow Men." [MidAR] (6:2) 86, p. 122.
"The Tip of the Tongue." [Sulfur] (6:1, issue 16) 86, p. 37.
2356. HILL, Sarah
"Fence-building." [MidAR] (7:1) 86, p. 17.
"The Year of the Cicada." [MidAR] (7:1) 86, p. 16.
2357. HILLARD, Jeffrey
"At the Top of the Stairs" (for Dan and Jeff). [WritersF] (12) Fall 86, p. 241-242.
"Rain Rising." [WritersF] (12) Fall 86, p. 242-243.
2358. HILLES, Robert
"Against Mountains." [AntigR] (65) Spr 86, p. 14-15.
"Dead Eyes." [PraF] (7:1) Spr 86, p. 15.
"Emergency." [PraF] (7:1) Spr 86, p. 18.
"Tender Glass." [PraF] (7:1) Spr 86, p. 16.
"This Poem Will Not Harm You." [AntigR] (66/67) Sum-Aut 86, p. 73.
"Where Beauty Goes." [PraF] (7:1) Spr 86, p. 17.
2359. HILLINGA, Helena M.
"The Asking." [BellArk] (2:3) My-Je 86, p. 14.
"Collectibles." [BellArk] (2:4) Jl-Ag 86, p. 4.
"The Craft of Welding." [BellArk] (2:3) My-Je 86, p. 1.
"On Calling Fore-Mother Down from the Dining Room Wall." [BellArk] (2:4) Jl-Ag
86, p. 8.
"Planting the Mountain Ash." [BellArk] (2:5) S-O 86, p. 1.
"Punk Bird." [BellArk] (2:6) N-D 86, p. 8.
2360. HILLIS, Rick
"Deconstruction." [PraF] (7:2) Sum 86, p. 46.
"Photographer of Snow." [Descant] (17:2, #53) Sum 86, p. 123-132.
"Pushing Bush." [AntigR] (66/67) Sum-Aut 86, p. 70-72.
2361. HILLMAN, Brenda
"Amanuensis." [Thrpny] (26) Sum 86, p. 12.
"Crooked Bridge." [Thrpny] (27) Fall 86, p. 18.
"Eucalyptus Grove." [TarRP] (25:2) Spr 86, p. 34-35.
"Four O'Clock Fugue." [HayF] (1) Spr 86, p. 80-81.
"Scott on Flight 559." [Ploughs] (12:1/2) 86, p. 150-151.
2362. HILLMAN, Elizabeth
"Hopi Morning." [Amelia] (3:2) Spr 86, p. 6.
"Watcher." [Amelia] (3:2) Spr 86, p. 6.
2363. HILLMAN, Grady
"Hymns from the Time of the Conquest" (tr. of anonymous Quechua poems). [Pax]
(3:1/2) Wint 85-86, p. 62-66.
"Lightning fell like bombs last night." [Pax] (3:1/2) Wint 85-86, p. 61.
"When Death Came." [Pax] (3:1/2) Wint 85-86, p. 61.
2364. HILLRINGHOUSE, Mark
"Ending in Gloucester." [ManhatPR] (6) Wint-Spr 85-86, p. 41.
2365. HILTON, David
"Thousand-Legger." [HangL] (49) Spr 86, p. 13-14.
2366. HILTY, Peter
"Sonnet on Receipt of an Old Photograph." [CapeR] (21:2) Fall 86, p. 2.
2367. HIMMIRSKY, Krassin
"Native Homes" (tr. by the author). [Vis] (21) 86, p. 16.
2368. HINDMARCH, Gladys
"Third Person Singular" (Excerpt). [Event] (15:2) 86, p. 24.
2369. HINES, Carrie
"Assyria." [SmPd] (23:1, #66) Wint 86, p. 22.
"Marie Antoinette's Kitten." [SmPd] (23:1, #66) Wint 86, p. 20.
2370. HIRSCH, Edward
"The Enforcer." [RiverS] (20) 86, p. 28-29.
"Loon." [MissouriR] (9:1) 85-86, p. 71.
"Omen." [MissouriR] (9:1) 85-86, p. 70.
"Portrait of the Artist with John Egner" (Detroit, 1984). [AmerPoR] (15:4) Jl-Ag 86,
p. 28.
2371. HIRSCH, Wendy
"Leaving Home." [KanQ] (18:1/2) Wint-Spr 86, p. 136.
"Night in a Bus." [KanQ] (18:1/2) Wint-Spr 86, p. 136.
2372. HIRSHFIELD, Jane
"A Different Rising." [YellowS] (18) Spr 86, p. 4.
"Evening, Late Fall." [ParisR] (28:101) Wint 86, p. 188.

"Needles of Pine, of Morning." [Sonora] (11) Fall 86 [c87], p. 75.
"On Reading Brecht." [NewL] (52:2/3) Wint-Spr 86, p. 162.
"On the Current Events." [NewL] (52:2/3) Wint-Spr 86, p. 162-163.
"The Song." [Atlantic] (257:5) My 86, p. 48.
"To Heat the Falling World." [ParisR] (28:101) Wint 86, p. 189.
2373. HIRZEL, David
"A Blueprint." [MidAR] (6:1) 86?, p. 104.
"I Knew It Would Come to This." [SanFPJ] (8:1) 85, p. 84.
"Images." [CapeR] (21:1) Spr 86, p. 27.
"In Winter." [CumbPR] (6:1) Fall 86, p. 28.
"P. O. W." [SanFPJ] (8:1) 85, p. 81.
2374. HITCHCOCK, George
"The Questions Which Occur along This Dreamflecked Avenue." [Caliban] (1) 86, p.
88.
HITOSHI, Anzai
See ANZAI, Hitoshi
2375. HIX, H. L. (Harvey)
"Autumn." [NegC] (6:4) Fall 86, p. 77.
"House of Mirrors." [Crazy] (31) Fall 86, p. 37-40.
"The One Is Neither at Rest Nor in Motion" (Plato *Parmenides*). [CumbPR] (6:1)
Fall 86, p. 21.
"The Snake" (for Sheila). [NegC] (6:4) Fall 86, p. 76-77.
"Walking the Harbor." [SouthernHR] (20:2) Spr 86, p. 169.
2376. HJALMARSSON, Jóhann
"Dark Destination" (tr. by Gregory C. Richter). [Paint] (13:25/26) Spr-Aut 86, p.
30.
2377. HOAGLAND, Bill
"December Spearing." [WritersF] (12) Fall 86, p. 243-244.
"Falling in a Photograph." [SnapD] (9:2) Spr 86, p. 6.
2378. HOAGLAND, Tony
"A Dowry" (for David Rivard). [AmerPoR] (15:2) Mr-Ap 86, p. 10.
"Freud's Secret Notebook." [AmerPoR] (15:2) Mr-Ap 86, p. 10.
"Poem for Men Only" (for Robert Boswell). [Ploughs] (12:4) 86, p. 110-111.
"Sweet Ruin." [Crazy] (31) Fall 86, p. 43-45.
2379. HOBEN, Sandra
"Badlands." [AntR] (44:1) Wint 86, p. 66.
"Connecticut, 1966." [AntR] (44:1) Wint 86, p. 67.
2380. HOBSON, Christopher Z.
"Aftermath of a Shooting." [MinnR] (NS 26) Spr 86, p. 9-10.
2381. HOCHMAN, William S.
"After Seeing 'Wisdom and Strength' by Veronese at the Frick." [ManhatPR] (8)
Wint 86-87, p. 47.
2382. HODGE, Margaret
"A Bicycling Road Blessing" (for my son Randall Nordfors at the start of a bike trip
across the country). [BellArk] (2:1) Ja-F 86, p. 8.
"Cedarn" (adj. meaning of cedar or cedars, for Herb). [BellArk] (2:1) Ja-F 86, p. 4.
"For Mr. Brooks' Thursdays." [BellArk] (2:3) My-Je 86, p. 7.
"Living Room" (to Herb). [BellArk] (2:4) Jl-Ag 86, p. 1.
"Throwing the Hammer." [BellArk] (2:3) My-Je 86, p. 5.
2383. HODGES, Gregg
"Calypso." [Puerto] (22:1) Fall 86, p. 2-3.
"Refusing to Translate Lobster." [Puerto] (22:1) Fall 86, p. 4-5.
2384. HODGSON, Graeme
"Institution." [Stand] (27:3) Sum 86, p. 26.
2385. HOEFLER, Walter
"Is There Anyone" (tr. by Steven White). [NewOR] (13:2) Sum 86, p. 31.
"The Place You Inhabit" (tr. by Steven White). [NewOR] (13:2) Sum 86, p. 57.
"Survivor" (tr. by Steven White). [NewOR] (13:2) Sum 86, p. 48.
2386. HOEFT, Robert D.
"Beach Item." [CrossCur] (6:2) 86, p. 85.
2387. HOEPER, Alex
"Hot Lunch." [JamesWR] (4:1) Fall 86, p. 4.
2388. HOEY, Allen
"Alba." [Poem] (55) Mr 86, p. 49.
"Anniversary." [BelPoJ] (36:3) Spr 86, p. 22-26.
"Driving at Night." [MidAR] (6:2) 86, p. 102.

"A Husband Pleads His Case." [Blueline] (7:2) Wint-Spr 86, p. 40.
"Hymns to a Tree." [WillowS] (17) Wint 86, p. 39-44.
"Optima Dies." [SouthernHR] (20:4) Fall 86, p. 364.
"South Sandy Creek" (for Ed Falco). [Poem] (55) Mr 86, p. 48.
"Teaching My Son Solitude." [MidAR] (6:2) 86, p. 103.
2389. HOFER, Mariann
　　"Last Summer." [Wind] (16:57) 86, p. 15.
2390. HOFF, Muriel
　　"Progressions." [InterPR] (12:2) Fall 86, p. 69.
2391. HOFFER, William
　　"Days Have No Lovers." [AntigR] (65) Spr 86, p. 160.
　　"The Motives." [AntigR] (65) Spr 86, p. 158-159.
2392. HOFFMAN, Daniel
　　"Asleep." [OntR] (25) Fall-Wint 86-87, p. 98.
　　"A Barn Burnt in Ohio." [OntR] (25) Fall-Wint 86-87, p. 99.
　　"Essay on Style." [Hudson] (39:3) Aut 86, p. 449-451.
　　"A Felled Tree." [Boulevard] (1:3) Fall 86, p. 39.
　　"The Finish." [Shen] (36:3) 86, p. 87-88.
　　"Possession." [Boulevard] (1:3) Fall 86, p. 38.
　　"Stop the Deathwish! Stop It! Stop!" [SouthernR] (22:1) Ja 86, p. 145-146.
　　"Who Done It?" [NewRep] (195:15) 13 O 86, p. 38.
2393. HOFFMAN, Helen
　　"The Soldier." [PassN] (7:1) Fall-Wint 85-86, p. 22.
　　"Three Meditations on a Bunch of Red Flowers." [PassN] (7:1) Fall-Wint 85-86, p.
　　　　22.
2394. HOFFMAN, Jill
　　"Anonymous." [HeliconN] (14/15) Sum 86, p. 49.
　　"Never-Never-Land." [HeliconN] (14/15) Sum 86, p. 49.
2395. HOFFMANN, Roald
　　"The Devil Teaches Thermodynamics." [WebR] (11:2) Fall 86, p. 41-42.
　　"Napkin Engineering." [ManhatR] (4:1) Fall 86, p. 3-4.
2396. HOFSTADTER, Marc Elihu
　　"Spring Showers." [Confr] (32) Spr-Sum 86, p. 110.
2397. HOGAN, Linda
　　"Get Up, Go AWOL!" [PraS] (60:4) Wint 86, p. 70-71.
　　"Night Wind." [PraS] (60:4) Wint 86, p. 69-70.
　　"Scorpion." [PraS] (60:4) Wint 86, p. 71-73.
2398. HOGAN, Wayne
　　"My Mother's Quilt." [YetASM] (5) 86, p. 4.
　　"Ricochet Radio." [Amelia] (3:1) Ja 86, p. 68.
2399. HOGGARD, James
　　"A Little Ceremony / Ronda, Spain." [Pax] (3:1/2) Wint 85-86, p. 69.
　　"Mandala." [Pax] (3:1/2) Wint 85-86, p. 69.
　　"Walking in Heat, Alien to Rain." [CapeR] (21:1) Spr 86, p. 44.
2400. HOLAN, Vladimir
　　"A Night with Hamlet" (Excerpt, tr. by Clayton Eshleman and Frantisek Galan).
　　　　[Sulfur] (6:1, issue 16) 86, p. 130-137.
2401. HOLDEN, Jonathan
　　"An American Boyhood." [TarRP] (26:1) Fall 86, p. 1-2.
　　"Cutting Beetle-Blighted Ponderosa Pine." [GeoR] (40:3) Fall 86, p. 689.
　　"The Edge." [TarRP] (26:1) Fall 86, p. 6-7.
　　"Falling from Stardom" (for S.). [TarRP] (26:1) Fall 86, p. 13-14.
　　"The History of the Wedge." [KenR] (NS 8:1) Wint 86, p. 32-33.
　　"Hotel Kitchen." [MinnR] (NS 26) Spr 86, p. 23.
　　"An Introduction to New Jersey." [KenR] (NS 8:1) Wint 86, p. 29.
　　"Jealousy." [KenR] (NS 8:1) Wint 86, p. 31-32.
　　"Junk." [TarRP] (26:1) Fall 86, p. 10-11.
　　"A Personal History of the Curve Ball." [Harp] (272:1631) Ap 86, p. 32-33.
　　"A Personal History of the Curveball." [KenR] (NS 8:1) Wint 86, p. 27-28.
　　"Seventeen." [TarRP] (26:1) Fall 86, p. 4.
　　"Ulysses and the Sirens." [KenR] (NS 8:1) Wint 86, p. 30.
2402. HOLDER, Barbara
　　"Do You Know, Father." [PoeticJ] (13) 86, p. 3.
　　"Feathers." [YetASM] (5) 86, p. 12.
2403. HOLDSTOCK, P. J.
　　"Hagar." [MalR] (74) Mr 86, p. 67-69.

2404. HOLENDER, Barbara D.
"Collage." [HeliconN] (14/15) Sum 86, p. 87.
"Judith Prepares to Meet Holofernes." [HeliconN] (16) Wint 86, p. 20.
"The Little Mermaid." [HeliconN] (14/15) Sum 86, p. 86.
"Straw into Gold (A Middle Age Romance)." [HeliconN] (14/15) Sum 86, p. 86-87.
2405. HOLINGER, Richard
"Evolution." [Interim] (5:2) Fall 86, p. 43.
"The Wicked One." [SpoonRQ] (11:2) Spr 86, p. 48-49.
2406. HOLLADAY, Hilary
"Cornstalks in Snow." [WestB] (19) 86, p. 28.
2407. HOLLAHAN, Eugene
"Two Singers: For Patricia, at the Met." [KanQ] (18:4) Fall 86, p. 112.
2408. HOLLAND, Barbara A.
"These Friendly Streets." [Lips] (12) 86, p. 28.
2409. HOLLAND-WHEATON, Heather
"Moi/Nous" (for d.j.). [SlipS] (6) 86, p. 30.
"Whirlpool Eyes (Quick! Suck Me Under!)." [SlipS] (6) 86, p. 31.
2410. HOLLANDER, Benjamin
"The Book of Who Are Was" (Excerpts, from a reading at New College of
California, December 13, 1985). [Acts] (5) 86, p. 124-134.
"A Commentary (Cut after Edmond Jabès) for Michael Palmer." [Acts] (5) 86, p.
133.
"Translation Orders" (in 3 Sets, from "The Book of Who Are Was"). [Temblor] (3)
86, p. 87-92.
2411. HOLLANDER, Gad
"Dissolution (For Three Hands)" (from "And Becomes 130 Ultimate Sentences").
[Temblor] (4) 86, p. 139-143.
"World Without Catastrophe" (from "And Becomes 130 Ultimate Sentences").
[Temblor] (3) 86, p. 85-86.
2412. HOLLANDER, John
"Ballade for Richard Wilbur." [NewRep] (194:21) 26 My 86, p. 40.
"By the Gulf." [ParisR] (28:100) Sum-Fall 86, p. 170-171.
"In Time" (Selections: 7 poems). [SouthwR] (71:3) Sum 86, p. 358-362.
"An Introduction to Absence." [PartR] (53:1) 86, p. 89-90.
"Monuments" (for Natalie Charkow). [GeoR] (40:3) Fall 86, p. 690-692.
"A Talk in the Park." [PartR] (53:1) 86, p. 90-91.
"To a Sculptor" (An Essay on the Origin and Nature of Relief). [GrandS] (5:3) Spr
86, p. 55-58.
2413. HOLLANDER, Martha
"Ogata Korin on His Field of Irises" (Kyoto, c. 1701). [PartR] (53:4) 86, p.
584-586.
2414. HOLLO, Anselm
"Only the Snow Stays" (tr. of Tomaz Salamun, w. Sonja Kravanja-Gross). [Vis]
(22) 86, p. 27.
"The White Angel" (tr. of Tomaz Salamun, w. Sonja Kravanja-Gross). [Vis] (22)
86, p. 26.
2415. HOLLOWAY, Glenna
"Commuter Train Riders." [ManhatPR] (6) Wint-Spr 85-86, p. 65.
2416. HOLLOWAY, John
"From Small Beginnings." [KenR] (NS 8:2) Spr 86, p. 90.
"The Hermit Gets to the Heart of It." [Hudson] (39:3) Aut 86, p. 455.
"Non-Event." [Hudson] (39:3) Aut 86, p. 458.
"An Old Master." [Hudson] (39:3) Aut 86, p. 457.
"Remember." [Hudson] (39:3) Aut 86, p. 456.
2417. HOLMES, James S.
"Rondo" (tr. of Arie van den Berg, w. Scott Rollins). [BostonR] (11:5) O 86, p. 18.
2418. HOLMES, Nancy
"Grace in a Cool June." [Descant] (17:2, #53) Sum 86, p. 83.
"Valancy and the New World." [Descant] (17:2, #53) Sum 86, p. 81-82.
2419. HOLSTEIN, Michael
"Museum Safari Guide." [Grain] (14:4) N 86, p. 44.
"Poem Hawker." [Amelia] (3:2) Spr 86, p. 67-68.
"Zen Lesson." [SmPd] (23:2, issue 67) Spr 86, p. 10.
2420. HOLT, Christopher E.
"Eating Butterflies in the Dark." [SanFPJ] (9:1) 86, p. 81-84.

2421. HOLT, Rochelle Lynn
"Old Russia." [CrossCur] (6:2) 86, p. 111.
"A song of geese." [Amelia] (3:4) Fall 86, p. 92.
2422. HOLUB, Miroslav
"Crush Syndrome" (tr. by David Young, with the author). [Field] (33) Fall 85, p. 77.
"Hemophilia" (tr. by David Young, with the author). [Field] (33) Fall 85, p. 80-81.
"Vanishing Lung Syndrome" (tr. by David Young, with the author). [Field] (33) Fall 85, p. 78-79.
2423. HOLZAPFEL, Rudi
"Now Is the Autumn Failing." [WritersF] (12) Fall 86, p. 105.
"Those Green Fuzzy-Looking Plants." [WritersF] (12) Fall 86, p. 104-105.
2424. HOMER, Art
"Forecast." [PraS] (60:2) Sum 86, p. 113.
"I-80 with Charles Darwin." [PraS] (60:2) Sum 86, p. 112-113.
2425. HOMER, Janet
"Looking for the Circle." [CutB] (25) Fall-Wint 86, p. 67.
"Poem for a Small Piece of Paper." [PassN] (7:1) Fall-Wint 85-86, p. 13.
2426. HONDA, Jun
"High-Pressure Chart" (tr. by James Kirkup and Akiko Takemoto). [Translation] (17) Fall 86, p. 210-211.
2427. HONGO, Garrett Kaoru
"The Cadence of Silk." [RiverS] (20) 86, p. 26-27.
"A Far Galaxy" (for Grey Pape). [Pequod] (22) 86, p. 35-36.
"O-Bon: Dance for the Dead." [Field] (35) Fall 86, p. 110-111.
"Redress: Thinking It Through." [Contact] (7:38/39/40) Wint-Spr 86, p. 72-73.
"The Sound of Water." [Pequod] (22) 86, p. 33-34.
"The Unreal Dwelling: My Years in Volcano." [Field] (33) Fall 85, p. 89-92.
2428. HONIG, Edwin
"Making It" (for James Schevill). [MichQR] (25:3) Sum 86, p. 537.
"Moles Progress." [ConnPR] (4:1) 85, p. 13-19.
2429. HONIGFELD, Gilbert
"Cameo." [DeKalbLAJ] (19:2) 86, p. 33.
"The Game." [SlipS] (6) 86, p. 29.
"Growing Up." [Poem] (55) Mr 86, p. 50-51.
"Luxuries of the Poor." [JINJPo] (9:1) 86, p. 11-12.
"Na-Ja-Da." [SlipS] (6) 86, p. 28.
"Tattoo" (Six poems). [PoetL] (80:4) Wint 86, p. 201-206.
2430. HOOD, Michael
"Christmas Day" (Worcester). [ColR] (NS 13:1) Fall 85, p. 36.
2431. HOOGESTRAAT, Jane
"Learning the Language." [KanQ] (18:4) Fall 86, p. 56.
2432. HOOPER, Edward L.
"In My Wheelchair, Not Despising Stairs." [Kaleid] (12) Wint 86, p. 50.
"Snowramp." [Kaleid] (12) Wint 86, p. 25.
2433. HOOVER, Paul
"Brazil." [Lips] (12) 86, p. 10.
"The Kiss." [Lips] (12) 86, p. 11.
"Tribal Item." [Lips] (12) 86, p. 12-13.
2434. HOPE, Akua Lezli
"Leaving Is a Little Death." [BlackALF] (20:3) Fall 86, p. 262-263.
2435. HOPES, David
"Carolina Wren." [KanQ] (18:1/2) Wint-Spr 86, p. 99.
"A Dream of Adonis." [ManhatR] (4:1) Fall 86, p. 17-31.
"Driving Home." [KanQ] (18:1/2) Wint-Spr 86, p. 100.
"From the Infinite Names of the Center." [Vis] (21) 86, p. 18-20.
"In the Shadow of *The Yorktown*." [ManhatR] (4:1) Fall 86, p. 13-14.
"Loosestrife." [StoneC] (13:3/4) Spr-Sum 86, p. 16.
"Love in the Holocene." [StoneC] (13:3/4) Spr-Sum 86, p. 13-14.
"Not Listening to the Blues." [WestB] (19) 86, p. 18-19.
"On Marrying the Poet." [ManhatR] (4:1) Fall 86, p. 11-13.
"Oppenheimer's Ghost Glides by Night to Trinity." [ManhatR] (4:1) Fall 86, p. 15-16.
"Prospectus." [StoneC] (13:3/4) Spr-Sum 86, p. 15.
"To a Sort of Disciple." [KanQ] (18:1/2) Wint-Spr 86, p. 99.
"Unaccountably by Night." [Vis] (21) 86, p. 20.

2436. HOPKINS, Lea
   "Hallelujah Lady." [HeliconN] (14/15) Sum 86, p. 166-167.
   "The Mammy." [HeliconN] (14/15) Sum 86, p. 167.
   "The Yipper." [HeliconN] (14/15) Sum 86, p. 166.
2437. HORACE
   "I.9." [CumbPR] (5:2) Spr 86, p. 58.
   "II.8." [CumbPR] (5:2) Spr 86, p. 60.
   "Horace, I.9" (tr. by Joseph Salemi). [CumbPR] (5:2) Spr 86, p. 59.
   "Horace, II.8" (tr. by Joseph Salemi). [CumbPR] (5:2) Spr 86, p. 61.
2438. HORAN, Elizabeth
   "How to Write a Grandmother Poem" (for Diane). [PoetL] (80:4) Wint 86, p.
      207-208.
2439. HORD, Fred L.
   "Belly Dancer." [BlackALF] (20:3) Fall 86, p. 270.
   "The Black Axe: Cleaving for Song." [BlackALF] (20:3) Fall 86, p. 268-269.
   "How Could I Not Love You?" [BlackALF] (20:3) Fall 86, p. 267-268.
   "Nuptials." [BlackALF] (20:3) Fall 86, p. 267.
2440. HOREVITZ, Alice
   "Two Poems." [SpoonRQ] (11:4) Fall 86, p. 46.
HORMAZABAL, Candelas Ranz
   See RANZ HORMAZABAL, Candelas
2441. HORNE, Lewis
   "4th Avenue." [Quarry] (35:4) Aut 86, p. 31.
   "Another Clarity." [OntR] (24) Spr-Sum 86, p. 98-99.
   "Being — Not So Simply." [TarRP] (25:1) Fall 85, p. 18-19.
   "Bess's Husband." [OntR] (24) Spr-Sum 86, p. 95-96.
   "North Alma School Road." [OntR] (24) Spr-Sum 86, p. 97.
2442. HORNER, Carl S.
   "Water Color." [MidAR] (7:1) 86, p. 51.
2443. HORNER, David
   "A Little Night Music." [Bogg] (55) 86, p. 49.
2444. HORNER, Davis
   "The Joint Where Sin Is Kept." [MidAR] (7:1) 86, p. 168-169.
2445. HORSTING, Eric
   "Mud Hole Trail on Great Wass Island." [BelPoJ] (37:2) Wint 86-87, p. 3.
2446. HORTON, Barbara
   "Doves." [Wind] (16:57) 86, p. 37.
2447. HOSKIN, William (William D.)
   "Afternoon Was Fading." [HiramPoR] (40) Spr-Sum 86, p. 11.
   "Amish Horse." [HiramPoR] (41) Fall-Wint 86-87, p. 30.
   "Connections." [HiramPoR] (41) Fall-Wint 86-87, p. 32.
   "Morning in Troy, N.Y." [HiramPoR] (41) Fall-Wint 86-87, p. 31.
2448. HOTALING, Debra
   "The Good Night." [ManhatPR] (8) Wint 86-87, p. 54.
   "A.M. at Zuider Zee." [ManhatPR] (8) Wint 86-87, p. 54.
2449. HOTCHKISS, Karen L.
   "Mid-Morning." [Puerto] (21:2) Spr 86, p. 56-57.
   "Ode to an Unfertilized Egg." [Puerto] (21:2) Spr 86, p. 58.
2450. HOUGHTON, Tim (Timothy)
   "Elegy" (in memory of my father). [CarolQ] (38:2) Wint 86, p. 65-66.
   "Fall at Night" (After Tanguy). [PennR] (1:1) 85, p. 58.
   "High Bridges." [TarRP] (25:2) Spr 86, p. 23-24.
   "Sleeping Face" (for my wife, Barbara). [ColEng] (48:7) N 86, p. 684.
   "What I Saw When I Closed My Eyes to Sleep." [CarolQ] (39:1) Fall 86, p. 50.
   "What I Saw When I Closed My Eyes to Sleep." [Stand] (27:4) Aut 86, p. 61.
2451. HOUSE, Tom
   "Art?" [Bogg] (55) 86, p. 10.
   "I Drop in the Turf Last Fri. Night." [SlipS] (6) 86, p. 5.
2452. HOUSER, Gordon
   "Praying at a Missile Site." [KanQ] (18:1/2) Wint-Spr 86, p. 254-255.
2453. HOUSTON, Beth
   "Thin Ice." [MinnR] (NS 27) Fall 86, p. 75-77.
2454. HOUSTON, Opie R.
   "The burly fullback." [Amelia] (3:4) Fall 86, p. 112.
HOVANESSIAN, Diana der
   See Der HOVANESSIAN, Diana

2455. HOWARD, Ben
"1985." [Poetry] (148:5) Ag 86, p. 266.
"Because You Asked for a Bedtime Story." [Poetry] (148:5) Ag 86, p. 265.
"Clearing." [KenR] (NS 8:1) Wint 86, p. 54.
"Losing Ground." [PraS] (60:4) Wint 86, p. 100.
"Monaghan Quartet" (i.m. Patrick Kavanagh, 1904-1967). [NewEngR] (8:4) Sum
   86, p. 510-512.
"Near." [KenR] (NS 8:1) Wint 86, p. 54.
"Remembering the Names." [KenR] (NS 8:1) Wint 86, p. 55.
"Swarming." [PennR] (2:1) Fall-Wint 86, p. 17.
"A Thing Forgotten." [KenR] (NS 8:1) Wint 86, p. 55.
2456. HOWARD, Eugene
"The Ancestors Smile" (for Sumi Tonooka). [PaintedB] (29) Ag 86, p. 50.
"The Fool of the Dark Goddess Utters One of Her Many Names." [PaintedB] (29)
   Ag 86, p. 52-53.
"A Group of Three Elderly African American Women Waiting at a Bus Stop in Cold
   January." [PaintedB] (29) Ag 86, p. 49.
"In the Dark." [PaintedB] (29) Ag 86, p. 55.
"Piano Player." [PaintedB] (29) Ag 86, p. 47-48.
"Reading Robert Hayden on a Quiet Morning." [PaintedB] (29) Ag 86, p. 51.
"A Silent e in Praise of the Blues" (Gut bucket jelly belly juke jam). [PaintedB] (29)
   Ag 86, p. 43-45.
2457. HOWARD, Richard
"Oracles" (To the memory of Vera Lachmann, 1905-1985). [GrandS] (6:1) Aut 86,
   p. 52-72.
"Stanzas in Bloomsbury: Mrs. Woolf Entertains the Notion of a Novel about Lord
   Byron." [ParisR] (28:100) Sum-Fall 86, p. 187-188.
"Stitching in Time: Dorothy Ruddick." [GeoR] (40:3) Fall 86, p. 693-694.
2458. HOWE, Fanny
"Scattered Light." [Temblor] (3) 86, p. 51-53.
"Secondary Indifferents." [Ploughs] (12:3) 86, p. 59-62.
2459. HOWE, Marie
"Apology." [Poetry] (147:5) F 86, p. 288.
"Lullaby." [Poetry] (147:5) F 86, p. 287.
2460. HOWE, Susan
"12 Poems from a Work in Progress." [Temblor] (3) 86, p. 16-27.
"Heliopathy." [Temblor] (4) 86, p. 42-54.
"Two Poems for H. D. 1886/1986." [Iowa] (16:3) Fall 86, p. 229-231.
2461. HOWELL, Christopher
"At Friday Harbor near Christmas." [NowestR] (24:3) 86, p. 50.
"For the Fishermen." [NowestR] (24:3) 86, p. 46.
"The God in Central Park." [NowestR] (24:3) 86, p. 48.
"If the House." [DenQ] (20:4/21:1) Spr-Sum 86, p. 69.
"I've Never Told You This." [DenQ] (20:4/21:1) Spr-Sum 86, p. 68.
"Listening." [NowestR] (24:3) 86, p. 47.
"Metamorphosis." [DenQ] (20:4/21:1) Spr-Sum 86, p. 70.
"Nefertiti." [BlackWR] (13:1) Fall 86, p. 89.
"Philosopher's Rose." [BlackWR] (13:1) Fall 86, p. 91.
"Violets." [NowestR] (24:3) 86, p. 44-45.
"Wisdom's Silver." [BlackWR] (13:1) Fall 86, p. 90.
"With the Distance." [NowestR] (24:3) 86, p. 49.
2462. HOWELL, Robert
"Richard Eberhart: April 2, 1986" (Poetry at Jacksonville University). [NegC]
   (6:2/3) Spr-Sum 86, p. 56-57.
2463. HOWES, Barbara
"The Field of the Cloth of Gold" (for John Lemon). [MemphisSR] (6:1/2) Spr 86, p.
   4.
2464. HOWES, Kelly King
"What of Love." [CarolQ] (39:1) Fall 86, p. 24.
2465. HOYOS, Angela de
"The Artist." [Pax] (3:1/2) Wint 85-86, p. 26-27.
"At the Hospital." [Pax] (3:1/2) Wint 85-86, p. 28-29.
"En el Hospital." [Pax] (3:1/2) Wint 85-86, p. 27-28.
"For Marsha." [Pax] (3:1/2) Wint 85-86, p. 25-26.
"Some People Sing." [Pax] (3:1/2) Wint 85-86, p. 29.

HOYOS, Ramón Ruiz de
     See RUIZ DE HOYOS, Ramón
2466. HRYCIUK, Marshall
     "On the Passing of Heidegger." [GreenfR] (13:3/4) Sum-Fall 86, p. 78-80.
HUA, Li Min
     See LI, Min Hua
2467. HUANG, Parker Po-fei
     "Autumn Scenes" (tr. by the author). [Nimrod] (29:2) Spr-Sum 86, p. 55.
     "A Morning Stroll in Early Fall." [Nimrod] (29:2) Spr-Sum 86, p. 55.
     "Spring" (In Chinese & English, tr. by the author). [Nimrod] (29:2) Spr-Sum 86, p.
          53.
2468. HUBINGER, Bert
     "Nancy Reagan Looks to the East and Turns to Salt." [Vis] (22) 86, p. 33.
2469. HUDDLESON, Tom
     "The Platte Thaws before the Flood." [PraS] (60:2) Sum 86, p. 111.
2470. HUDECHEK, Robin
     "Soldier Story." [Caliban] (1) 86, p. 103-104.
2471. HUDGINS, Andrew
     "All of Us Beneath Red Cowboy Hats." [Poetry] (147:4) Ja 86, p. 194.
     "From Commerce to the Capitol: Montgomery, Alabama." [Iowa] (16:1) Wint 86, p.
          52-54.
     "The Green Christ." [Poetry] (147:4) Ja 86, p. 195.
     "Love Letter from the Grave: Sidney Lanier, 1881." [SouthernR] (22:4) O 86, p.
          766-767.
     "Two Ember Days in Alabama." [Shen] (36:4) 86, p. 36-37.
2472. HUDSON, J.
     "Massage." [FloridaR] (14:2) Fall-Wint 86, p. 76.
2473. HUDSON, Marc
     "The Garden and the Sea: An Essay for Helen." [KenR] (NS 8:3) Sum 86, p.
          112-119.
     "My Son Is Ferried by Copter over the Okanogan on His Birth Night." [PraS] (60:1)
          Spr 86, p. 32-35.
     "Pytheas Reports from Thule." [PraS] (60:1) Spr 86, p. 36.
     "The Songs of Sorgwud." [PraS] (60:1) Spr 86, p. 37-40.
     "Wiglaf's Tale." [SewanR] (94:3) Sum 86, p. 347-351.
2474. HUETTEMAN, Susan
     "Introduction." [YetASM] (4) 85, p. 8.
2475. HUFF, Robert
     "Carried Away." [Interim] (5:2) Fall 86, p. 23.
     "Taking Her Sides on Immortality" (March 30, 1979). [WestHR] (40:3) Aut 86, p.
          255-258.
2476. HUFF, Steven
     "The Library Reading Room, Batavia, New York." [MSS] (5:1) 86, p. 37.
2477. HUFFSTICKLER, Albert
     "At the Cafe du Jour." [PaintedB] (28) Ap 86, p. 36.
     "Breakfast Stop in Gallup." [Pax] (3:1/2) Wint 85-86, p. 70-71.
     "Champion" (from a dream). [PaintedB] (28) Ap 86, p. 35.
     "Fossil." [Pax] (3:1/2) Wint 85-86, p. 71.
     "Levels." [ClockR] (3:2) 86, p. 11.
     "Summer of '72." [PaintedB] (28) Ap 86, p. 33-34.
2478. HUFFSTUTTER, Robert L.
     "Dreams of Relief: When the Mind and Soul Go Their Own Way." [KanQ] (18:1/2)
          Wint-Spr 86, p. 161.
     "The Party." [KanQ] (18:1/2) Wint-Spr 86, p. 162.
2479. HUGGAN, Isabel
     "The End of August." [Quarry] (35:4) Aut 86, p. 8.
2480. HUGGINS, Peter
     "Tenuous Mortality." [NoDaQ] (54:4) Fall 86, p. 108.
     "The Waving Girl on the Bull Street Docks." [NoDaQ] (54:4) Fall 86, p. 109.
2481. HUGHES, Carolyn J. Fairweather
     "Vows." [YetASM] (5) 86, p. 3.
2482. HUGHES, Deborah
     "Depression." [HangL] (49) Spr 86, p. 57.
2483. HUGHES, Mary Gray
     "Art." [Confr] (33/34) Fall-Wint 86-87, p. 167.
     "Like Two Dogs Barking." [TriQ] (67) Fall 86, p. 135-136.

2484. HUGHES, Sophie
   "Case History." [HolCrit] (23:4) O 86, p. 18.
2485. HUGHES, Ted
   "Halfway Head." [GrandS] (6:1) Aut 86, p. 16.
   "Lamenting Head." [GrandS] (6:1) Aut 86, p. 14.
   "Reckless Head." [GrandS] (6:1) Aut 86, p. 15.
   "Sacrificed Head." [GrandS] (6:1) Aut 86, p. 17.
2486. HUGO, Richard
   "Last Words to James Wright." [GeoR] (40:3) Fall 86, p. 695-696.
HUIDOBRO, Matías Montes
   See MONTES HUIDOBRO, Matías
2487. HUIDOBRO, Vicente
   "It Can Happen" (tr. by Sarah Arvio). [MassR] (27:3/4) Fall-Wint 86, p. 422.
2488. HUK, Roma
   "The Confession of Lemuel" (The Berlin Stopped in the Night, tr. of Oscar V. de L.
      Milosz). [AnotherCM] (15) 86, p. 72-74.
2489. HULBERT, Gary
   "Appreciation for City Music." [BelPoJ] (37:2) Wint 86-87, p. 1.
   "Lovecraft." [BelPoJ] (36:3) Spr 86, p. 38.
   "Morning." [BelPoJ] (36:3) Spr 86, p. 36.
   "Theresa." [BelPoJ] (36:3) Spr 86, p. 37.
2490. HULL, Bob
   "Heat." [CumbPR] (5:2) Spr 86, p. 29.
2491. HULL, Lynda
   "1933." [Crazy] (31) Fall 86, p. 20-22.
   "Accretion." [Crazy] (31) Fall 86, p. 23-24.
   "Arias, 1971." [Crazy] (31) Fall 86, p. 25-26.
   "The Bookkeeper." [AntR] (44:2) Spr 86, p. 202-203.
   "Chinese New Year." [Poetry] (148:3) Je 86, p. 150-151.
   "The Fitting." [PoetryNW] (27:3) Aut 86, p. 36-38.
   "Harbor Lights." [MSS] (5:1) 86, p. 35-36.
   "Hollywood Jazz." [Sonora] (10) Spr 86, p. 30-32.
   "Insect Life of Florida." [Poetry] (148:3) Je 86, p. 148-149.
   "Little Elegies." [AntR] (44:2) Spr 86, p. 198-199.
   "Maquillage." [AntR] (44:2) Spr 86, p. 200-201.
   "Night Waitress." [MissouriR] (9:2) 86, p. 190-191.
   "Preparing the Estate Sale." [IndR] (9:3) Sum 86, p. 42-43.
   "Remington." [IndR] (9:3) Sum 86, p. 40-41.
2492. HULY, Ann M.
   "The Hour." [Kaleid] (12) Wint 86, p. 49.
   "The Water's Edge." [Kaleid] (12) Wint 86, p. 49.
2493. HUMES, Harry
   "Caught in the Woods in the Dark." [WestB] (19) 86, p. 69.
   "Frozen Lake at Midnight." [WestB] (19) 86, p. 70-71.
   "Gathering Watercress in the Hex Country." [KanQ] (18:1/2) Wint-Spr 86, p. 121.
   "On Mountaineering." [SnapD] (9:2) Spr 86, p. 12-13.
   "Shadow Matter." [WestB] (19) 86, p. 68.
   "The Snow Snake." [PoetryNW] (27:3) Aut 86, p. 45-46.
   "Throwing Away the Comapss" (Chapbook). [SilverFR] (13) 86, unpaged.
   "Water." [SnapD] (9:2) Spr 86, p. 14-15.
2494. HUMMA, John
   "My Grandmother ('Berchie'), 98, As Spring Approaches." [SouthernHR] (20:4)
      Fall 86, p. 356.
2495. HUMMER, T. R.
   "Cancer Rising" (a dream of walking). [KenR] (NS 7:2) Spr 85, p. 17-19.
   "Dogma: Pigmeat and Whiskey" (For Fred Chappell). [KenR] (NS 7:2) Spr 85, p.
      10-15.
   "The Ideal" (for John Hales and Joe Battaglia). [KenR] (NS 8:3) Sum 86, p. 26-31.
   "The Moon and Constellations." [KenR] (NS 7:2) Spr 85, p. 15-17.
   "The Real." [KenR] (NS 8:3) Sum 86, p. 31-35.
   "The Second Story." [GeoR] (40:3) Fall 86, p. 697-700.
   "Winter, a Walk in Pinewoods" (For Theo, on her seventh birthday). [KenR] (NS
      7:2) Spr 85, p. 20.
2496. HUMPHREY, James
   "This Day Has Sung to Itself." [SmPd] (23:1, #66) Wint 86, p. 28.

2497. HUMPHRIES, Dwight E.
"Waters." [DeKalbLAJ] (19:2) 86, p. 34.
2498. HUMPHRIES, Jefferson
"Aurora Australis." [SouthernR] (22:4) O 86, p. 784-785.
"Home, Early Summer." [SouthernR] (22:4) O 86, p. 782-783.
2499. HUNT, Leigh
"Do Tell." [Amelia] (3:2) Spr 86, p. 52-54.
"Hands Across the Water" (A Poem for the people of Irkutsk, USSR). [SanFPJ]
(8:3) 85, p. 42-43.
2500. HUNT, Nan
"Angel in the House" (from Virginia Woolf). [Electrum] (38) Spr 86, p. 25.
"Old Taos Pueblo, Christmas Eve." [BelPoJ] (37:1) Fall 86, p. 37-38.
"The Wrong Bride" (In memory: Frances Pribyl, Prague, Bohemia 1888-Camarillo,
California 1975). [BelPoJ] (37:1) Fall 86, p. 38-40.
2501. HUNT, Ralph
"The Beauty Mark." [WindO] (47) Sum 86, p. 33.
"Consolation." [WindO] (47) Sum 86, p. 32.
"My Youthful Self." [WindO] (47) Sum 86, p. 31.
"Snow." [WindO] (47) Sum 86, p. 34.
2502. HUNT, William
"By the Water." [AmerPoR] (15:3) My-Je 86, p. 15.
"Looking Ahead." [AmerPoR] (15:3) My-Je 86, p. 15.
"Seeing What Isn't There." [TriQ] (67) Fall 86, p. 130.
"Seeing You Undressing." [YellowS] (20) Aut 86, p. 9.
2503. HUNTER, Bruce
"Ten Thousand Jaws." [Waves] (14:3) Wint 86, p. 59.
"The Young Widow." [Waves] (14:3) Wint 86, p. 58-59.
2504. HUNTER, Catherine
"III. Waiting for the doctor." [PraF] (7:3) Aut 86, p. 64.
"IV. I have been here a time now." [PraF] (7:3) Aut 86, p. 65.
2505. HUNTER, Dennis
"How I long to return." [StoneC] (14:1/2) Fall-Wint 86-87, p. 29.
2506. HUNTER, Donnell
"At the Wedding." [Interim] (5:2) Fall 86, p. 18.
"Final Testament." [Interim] (5:2) Fall 86, p. 19.
"Spiders." [CapeR] (21:1) Spr 86, p. 34.
2507. HUNTER, Nancy
"The Man Who Saw Birds." [CrabCR] (4:1) Fall-Wint 86, p. 27.
2508. HUNTSBERRY, Randy
"Cottontail" (for David Swift who once stoned a coyote). [BallSUF] (26:4) Aut 85,
p. 20.
2509. HURLEY, Thomas
"Waking." [StoneC] (14:1/2) Fall-Wint 86-87, p. 15.
2510. HURLOW, Marcia L.
"Elyce." [Paint] (13:25/26) Spr-Aut 86, p. 22.
"Still Life with Alley" (for Jack C. Hurlow, 1924-1981). [PoetryNW] (27:2) Sum
86, p. 46.
2511. HURVITZ, Ya'ir
"And Not Wind from There" (tr. by Harold Schimmel). [PoetL] (81:2) Sum 86, p.
117.
"And Still I Love" (tr. by Harold Schimmel). [PoetL] (81:2) Sum 86, p. 118.
"At the Hour of Brightening" (tr. by Harold Schimmel). [PoetL] (81:2) Sum 86, p.
117-118.
2512. HUSTVEDT, Siri
"Along the leaf-nerves" (tr. of Tor Ulven). [Writ] (18) 86, c87, p. 65.
"I try to write faster" (tr. of Tor Ulven). [Writ] (18) 86, c87, p. 64.
"Let the door stand wide open" (tr. of Tor Ulven). [Writ] (18) 86, c87, p. 63.
"Slush" (tr. of Tor Ulven). [Writ] (18) 86, c87, p. 62.
"They dance far into the woods" (tr. of Tor Ulven). [Writ] (18) 86, c87, p. 60.
"You can't be silent enough" (tr. of Tor Ulven). [Writ] (18) 86, c87, p. 61.
2513. HUTCHINGS, Pat
"The First of May." [CrabCR] (3:3) Sum 86, p. 5.
"Five Things for a Friend Who Wants a Poem for His Painting." [AnotherCM] (16)
86, p. 54-55.
"Home Movies." [SouthernHR] (20:3) Sum 86, p. 226.
"In a House with Ashtrays." [Northeast] (series 4:3) Spr 86, p. 7.

"Living in the Here and Now." [KanQ] (18:1/2) Wint-Spr 86, p. 279.
"Not a Theory of Dreams" (and not for Freud). [SouthernHR] (20:3) Sum 86, p. 261.
"Old Woman Observed through a Window." [CrabCR] (3:3) Sum 86, p. 5.
"Refinishing." [ClockR] (3:1) 85, p. 43.
"Sun in the New Place." [Northeast] (series 4:3) Spr 86, p. 8.
2514. HUTCHINSON, Jeremy
"Jeff." [PikeF] (7) Spr 86, p. 20.
HUTCHINSON, Joseph
See HUTCHISON, Joseph
2515. HUTCHISON, Joseph
"Cape Kidnappers, New Zealand" (After a photograph by Linda Pohle). [SoDakR] (24:2) Sum 86, p. 149-150.
"From the Family Album." [SoDakR] (24:2) Sum 86, p. 150.
"Recurring Dream." [ColR] (NS 13:1) Fall 85, p. 57.
"A Story about Fall" (for Ted Kooser). [Northeast] (series 4:3) Spr 86, p. 44.
2516. HUTCHMAN, Laurence
"Nelligan." [GreenfR] (13:3/4) Sum-Fall 86, p. 76-77.
2517. HUTH, Geof A.
"Muqdisho, Mogadiscio, Mogadishu." [PoetryNW] (27:4) Wint 86-87, p. 45-46.
"Plummage." [PoetryNW] (27:4) Wint 86-87, p. 45.
2518. HUYETT, Pat
"Peach Preserves." [SingHM] (14) 86, p. 20-21.
2519. HUYLER, Frank
"The Retiree." [Verse] (6) 86, p. 39.
2520. HYETT, Barbara Helfgott
"Emergence of a Monarch Butterfly." [Nat] (242:21) 31 My 86, p. 770.
"The Workingman's Bird." [Nat] (243:20) 13 D 86, p. 682.
2521. HYKIN, Susan
"Carolina." [MalR] (77) D 86, p. 106.
"Grapes." [MalR] (77) D 86, p. 107.
"Inventory Man." [MalR] (77) D 86, p. 105.
2522. IACIOFANO, Carol
"The Dream." [Calyx] (10:1) Sum 86, p. 38.
2523. IACOBELLI, Luciano
"Chimney Smoke." [Descant] (17:2, #53) Sum 86, p. 95.
"Prima Materia" (dedicated to Giorgio Di Cicco). [Descant] (17:2, #53) Sum 86, p. 94.
2524. IBARGOYEN, Saúl
"A Single Syllable" (tr. by John Oliver Simon). [InterPR] (12:1) Spr 86, p. 23.
"Una Sola Silaba" (from Palabra por Palabra, 1979). [InterPR] (12:1) Spr 86, p. 22.
IBARRA, Beatriz M. Santiago
See SANTIAGO-IBARRA, Beatriz M.
2525. IGNACIO-ZIMARDI, Joselyn
"River Requiem." [Contact] (7:38/39/40) Wint-Spr 86, p. 33.
2526. IGNATOW, David
"And Now." [VirQR] (62:2) Spr 86, p. 269.
"The Bay." [ManhatPR] (6) Wint-Spr 85-86, p. 6.
"Dear Sir." [Agni] (23) 86, p. 68.
"Finally." [Caliban] (1) 86, p. 87.
"The Fly." [MichQR] (25:4) Fall 86, p. 701.
"Have Mercy." [Chelsea] (45) 86, p. 33.
"If." [ManhatPR] (6) Wint-Spr 85-86, p. 6.
"The Image." [VirQR] (62:2) Spr 86, p. 269-270.
"In My Childhood." [VirQR] (62:2) Spr 86, p. 267-268.
"In Retrospect." [PaintedB] (29) Ag 86, p. 5.
"It Is." [VirQR] (62:2) Spr 86, p. 267.
"Knowledge." [SouthernHR] (20:2) Spr 86, p. 126.
"A Lesser Hamlet." [Chelsea] (45) 86, p. 36-37.
"Lives." [Lips] (12) 86, p. 1-2.
"The Living." [SouthernHR] (20:1) Wint 86, p. 13.
"A Memory." [Caliban] (1) 86, p. 85.
"Newborn." [Caliban] (1) 86, p. 85.
"On Broadcasting." [Caliban] (1) 86, p. 86.
"On Quantitative Analysis." [Chelsea] (45) 86, p. 34.
"Overhead." [ColEng] (48:4) Ap 86, p. 351.

"The Ride." [Chelsea] (45) 86, p. 35.
"The Saint." [PaintedB] (29) Ag 86, p. 6.
"Silence." [Caliban] (1) 86, p. 86.
"A Time of Night." [MichQR] (25:4) Fall 86, p. 702.
"Together." [ColEng] (48:4) Ap 86, p. 352.
"Wait." [VirQR] (62:2) Spr 86, p. 268.
2527. IGNATOW, Yaedi
"Your Happiness Is Mine." [Lips] (12) 86, p. 38-39.
2528. IKEDA, Patricia
"Conversation." [Contact] (7:38/39/40) Wint-Spr 86, p. 44.
"Riding to Coldwater, Michigan in Mid-August." [Contact] (7:38/39/40) Wint-Spr
86, p. 44.
2529. ILES, Steven
"Quarterpounder." [Bogg] (55) 86, p. 45.
2530. ILHAN, Attilâ
"Böyle Bir Sevmek." [StoneC] (14:1/2) Fall-Wint 86-87, p. 17.
"Such Love" (tr. by Dionis Coffin Riggs, William Fielder, and Ozcan Yalim).
[StoneC] (14:1/2) Fall-Wint 86-87, p. 16.
2531. ILLO, Maria
"Vision." [WritersL] (1986:6), p. 20.
2532. INADA, Lawson Fusao
"Choreography" (World Premier, State Ballet of Oregon Fund-Raising Benefit,
1983). [Contact] (7:38/39/40) Wint-Spr 86, p. 68-70.
"Going by the Music." [OP] (41) Spr 86, p. 37-44.
"Winter in Michigan" (For Dorothy Yoshimori). [Caliban] (1) 86, p. 105-107.
2533. INDREEIDE, Erling
"Does Life Extend?" (tr. by Deborah Tannen). [Vis] (22) 86, p. 14.
2534. INEZ, Colette
"Advice to a Writer Imagining Conception and Birth." [MemphisSR] (7:1) Fall 86,
p. 6.
"The Dream Forest." [MemphisSR] (7:1) Fall 86, p. 5.
"Escape from the Iron Gates." [PoetryNW] (27:4) Wint 86-87, p. 36.
"Gascogne Journey." [VirQR] (62:1) Wint 86, p. 50-51.
"Glenn." [HeliconN] (14/15) Sum 86, p. 26.
"Going Far." [Caliban] (1) 86, p. 83.
"The Happy Child." [Caliban] (1) 86, p. 84.
"Lady in the Stacks." [ManhatPR] (6) Wint-Spr 85-86, p. 14-15.
"The Leavetaking" (for Jenny). [MemphisSR] (7:1) Fall 86, p. 4.
"Lost Letters." [NewL] (53:1) Fall 86, p. 31.
"Mirror." [WestB] (19) 86, p. 20.
"Musing on Large Questions in a Small Corner of England." [WestB] (19) 86, p. 21.
"Northern Words." [VirQR] (62:1) Wint 86, p. 53.
"On the Moon Viewing Terrace." [MemphisSR] (7:1) Fall 86, p. 7.
"Red August Letter." [VirQR] (62:1) Wint 86, p. 51-52.
"Seaspools for Two Voices." [HeliconN] (14/15) Sum 86, p. 25.
"The Sisters." [HeliconN] (14/15) Sum 86, p. 26-27.
"Writing Letters to My Mother." [HeliconN] (14/15) Sum 86, p. 27-28.
2535. INFUSINO, Jorge
"Ausencia." [Mairena] (8:22) 86, p. 86.
2536. INKSTER, Tim
"The Birth of Scepticism." [Descant] (17:2, #53) Sum 86, p. 110.
"Free Information." [Descant] (17:2, #53) Sum 86, p. 110.
"Hazel." [Descant] (17:2, #53) Sum 86, p. 111.
"Rosemary's Poem." [Descant] (17:2, #53) Sum 86, p. 111.
2537. INMAN, Will
"Our Armors Carry Names." [ArizQ] (42:3) Aut 86, p. 260.
2538. INNES, Chris
"Membrane Triptych." [JINJPo] (9:1) 86, p. 13.
2539. INNES, Stephanie
"The Tree." [Grain] (14:2) My 86, p. 27.
2540. INOSTROZA, Raúl
"El Agujero de la Muerte." [LindLM] (5:1) Ja-Mr 86, p. 33.
"En el Teatro del Mundo." [LindLM] (5:1) Ja-Mr 86, p. 33.
2541. IOANNOU, Susan
"Convalescence." [Quarry] (35:3) Sum 86, p. 83.
"Last Photographs" (for Merla). [Quarry] (35:3) Sum 86, p. 81-82.

"Mothering Days." [CrossC] (8:2) 86, p. 13.
2542. IRARRAZABAL YAÑEZ, Juan José
"Flor Inesperada." [Mairena] (8:22) 86, p. 91.
2543. IRIE, Kevin
"Cottage Country." [BallSUF] (27:4) Aut 86, p. 56.
"Immigrants: The Second Generation." [Contact] (7:38/39/40) Wint-Spr 86, p. 37.
2544. IRION, Mary Jean
"In Winter Sun." [ChrC] (103:1) 1-8 Ja 86, p. 4.
"Who We Are." [ChrC] (103:21) 2-9 Jl 86, p. 614.
2545. IRWIN, Judith
"The Racing Man in the Wall of China." [BellR] (9:2) Fall 86, p. 17.
"Rocks Play for Keeps." [BellR] (9:2) Fall 86, p. 17.
2546. IRWIN, Mark
"Against the Meanwhile" (To David St. John). [KenR] (NS 7:3) Sum 85, p. 21-35.
2547. ISAACS, Robert Martin
"The Magic Age." [StoneC] (13:3/4) Spr-Sum 86, p. 64-65.
2548. ISGRO, Gustavo Raúl
"A Veces." [Mairena] (8:22) 86, p. 114.
2549. ISHIGAKI, Rin
"At the Public Bath" (tr. by Harold Wright). [Translation] (17) Fall 86, p. 13.
"In the Stomachs of One Hundred Persons" (tr. by Harold Wright). [Translation]
(17) Fall 86, p. 10.
"Land & House" (tr. by Harold Wright). [Translation] (17) Fall 86, p. 14.
"Song" (tr. by Harold Wright). [Translation] (17) Fall 86, p. 11.
"Tsuetsuki Pass" (tr. by Harold Wright). [Translation] (17) Fall 86, p. 12.
2550. ISHII, Roger
"No Deposit, No Return." [Amelia] (3:1) Ja 86, p. 48.
"On the bridge." [Amelia] (3:3) Sum 86, p. 63.
2551. ISHIKAWA, Takuboku
"Do Not Get Up" (tr. by James Kirkup and Akiko Takemoto). [Translation] (17) Fall
86, p. 186.
"Fist" (tr. by James Kirkup and Akiko Takemoto). [Translation] (17) Fall 86, p.
187.
2552. ISLAS, Maya
"Ahora comprendo cómo nos duele." [Mairena] (8:22) 86, p. 121.
2553. ISSENHUTH, Jean-Pierre
"Noé" (à Charlotte Melançon). [Os] (22) 86, p. 9.
"Le Roi Pêcheur." [Os] (22) 86, p. 8.
2554. ISTARU, Ana
"The Man Who Boxes" (tr. by Zoe Anglesey). [MassR] (27:3/4) Fall-Wint 86, p.
528-530.
"This Country Is in a Dream" (tr. by Zoe Anglesey). [MassR] (27:3/4) Fall-Wint 86,
p. 526-528.
2555. IUPPA, M. J.
"Blessings." [PennR] (2:1) Fall-Wint 86, p. 40.
"The Gift." [Amelia] (3:4) Fall 86, p. 7.
2556. IVEREM, Esther
"Some Places in America Scare You More." [BlackALF] (20:3) Fall 86, p. 256.
"The Time." [BlackALF] (20:3) Fall 86, p. 254-255.
"Tsunami." [BlackALF] (20:3) Fall 86, p. 255-256.
2557. IVES, Rich
"The Consequences of Color." [MissR] (15:1/2, #43/44) Fall-Wint 86, p. 53.
"In Preparation for Setting a Watch." [MissR] (15:1/2, #43/44) Fall-Wint 86, p. 54.
"A New Jacket." [MissR] (15:1/2, #43/44) Fall-Wint 86, p. 55.
"Notes for a Folktale." [MissR] (15:1/2, #43/44) Fall-Wint 86, p. 52.
2558. IVES, Robert W.
"Exploration." [KanQ] (18:1/2) Wint-Spr 86, p. 238.
"From far inside what only I can know" ("Untitled"). [KanQ] (18:1/2) Wint-Spr 86,
p. 238.
IZUMI, Shikibu
See SHIKIBU, Izumi
2559. JABES, Edmond
"The Book of Dialogue" (Selections, tr. by Rosmarie Waldrop). [Notus] (1:1) Fall
86, p. 3-8.
2560. JACCOTTET, Philippe
"In the Steps of the Moon" (tr. by Derek Mahon). [Verse] (6) 86, p. 29.

"Patience" (tr. by Derek Mahon). [Verse] (6) 86, p. 29.
"Portovenere" (tr. by Derek Mahon). [Verse] (6) 86, p. 29.
"The Tenant" (tr. by Derek Mahon). [Verse] (6) 86, p. 29.
2561. JACINTO, Jaime
"A Death" (tr. of Ines Asinc Ramos de Ching, w. V. Sales-Gomez & J. Tagami).
[Contact] (7:38/39/40) Wint-Spr 86, Supplement p. 10.
"Defining" (tr. of Ines Asinc Ramos de Ching, w. V. Sales-Gomez & J. Tagami).
[Contact] (7:38/39/40) Wint-Spr 86, Supplement p. 12.
"Farewell" (tr. of Rafael Yamasato, w. V. Sales-Gomez & J. Tagami). [Contact]
(7:38/39/40) Wint-Spr 86, Supplement p. 22.
"Imitation of Watanabe" (tr. of Rafael Yamasato, w. V. Sales-Gomez & J. Tagami).
[Contact] (7:38/39/40) Wint-Spr 86, Supplement p. 23.
"Letter to a Brother Prisoner" (tr. of Ines Asinc Ramos de Ching, w. V.
Sales-Gomez & J. Tagami). [Contact] (7:38/39/40) Wint-Spr 86, Supplement
p. 8.
"Noriko" (tr. of Rafael Yamasato, w. V. Sales-Gomez & J. Tagami). [Contact]
(7:38/39/40) Wint-Spr 86, Supplement p. 16-17.
"The Snow and the Male Flower" (tr. of Rafael Yamasato, w. V. Sales-Gomez & J.
Tagami). [Contact] (7:38/39/40) Wint-Spr 86, Supplement p. 21.
"Well of Desires" (tr. of Rafael Yamasato, w. V. Sales-Gomez & J. Tagami).
[Contact] (7:38/39/40) Wint-Spr 86, Supplement p. 20.
"With Doubtful Comic Achievements" (tr. of Jose Watanabe, w. V. Sales-Gomez &
J. Tagami). [Contact] (7:38/39/40) Wint-Spr 86, Supp. p. 28-29.
"With Regard to Misadjustments . . ." (tr. of Jose Watanabe, w. V. Sales-Gomez &
J. Tagami). [Contact] (7:38/39/40) Wint-Spr 86, Supp. p. 26.
2562. JACKSON, Angela
"Miz Rosa Rides the Bus." [TriQ] (65) Wint 86, p. 129-130.
"RockandRoll Monster: Down Home Blues Goes to Hollywood" (for 5527 and the
television tribe). [RiverS] (19) 86, p. 17-18.
"Transformable Prophecy." [RiverS] (19) 86, p. 19.
2563. JACKSON, Fleda Brown
"Home of the Razorbacks." [DeKalbLAJ] (19:1) 86, p. 34.
"Rabbits." [BelPoJ] (36:4) Sum 86, p. 15.
"Saving a Life." [PoetryNW] (27:3) Aut 86, p. 16.
"Sky Watch." [MidwQ] (28:1) Aut 86, p. 93-94.
2564. JACKSON, Gale
"Needles. Threads." [Callaloo] (9:2, #27) Spr 86, p. 314-323.
JACKSON, Haywood
See JACKSON, William (Haywood)
2565. JACKSON, John
"Memento Mori." [ParisR] (28:101) Wint 86, p. 185.
2566. JACKSON, Reuben M.
"The Murder City Blues." [BlackALF] (20:3) Fall 86, p. 308.
2567. JACKSON, Richard
"The Gift." [TarRP] (24:2) Spr 85, p. 6-7.
"Greenwood." [GeoR] (40:3) Fall 86, p. 701.
"Out of Sight." [TarRP] (25:2) Spr 86, p. 17-19.
"The Promise of Light." [GeoR] (40:2) Sum 86, p. 405-407.
"A Sense of Direction." [PraS] (60:4) Wint 86, p. 48-49.
"Things We Could Have Been." [TarRP] (24:2) Spr 85, p. 7-8.
"The Waterfall." [PoetryNW] (27:1) Spr 86, p. 39.
"Web." [PraS] (60:4) Wint 86, p. 47-48.
2568. JACKSON, William (Haywood)
"The Cranes, 1964." [Sam] (44:2 release 174) 86, p. 58-60.
"Long Lunch and the Sudden Boss Angry." [Bogg] (55) 86, p. 15.
"A Measure of the Party." [PaintedB] (28) Ap 86, p. 65.
2569. JACOBIK, Gray
"Evening, East of Wheeling." [TarRP] (26:1) Fall 86, p. 26.
2570. JACOBOWITZ, Judah
"Dream-Tales." [CumbPR] (6:1) Fall 86, p. 42-43.
2571. JACOBS, Lucky
"Slow" (poem written after reading that Faulkner flunked grammar in high school).
[Confr] (33/34) Fall-Wint 86-87, p. 125.
2572. JACOBS, Maria
"Just War." [GreenfR] (13:3/4) Sum-Fall 86, p. 81.

2573. JACOBSEN, Josephine
"The Presences." [Poetry] (148:3) Je 86, p. 161-163.
2574. JACOBSEN, Rolf
"Barbed-wire Winter" (tr. by Roger Greenwald). [Writ] (18) 86, c87, p. 47.
"Did I Know You?" (tr. by Roger Greenwald). [Writ] (18) 86, c87, p. 49.
"The Fireflies" (tr. by Roger Greenwald). [Writ] (18) 86, c87, p. 51.
"It Was Here" (tr. by Roger Greenwald). [Writ] (18) 86, c87, p. 50.
"Room 301" (tr. by Roger Greenwald). [Writ] (18) 86, c87, p. 46.
"The Sewing Machine" (tr. by Roger Greenwald). [Writ] (18) 86, c87, p. 48.
"Thoughts at Lake Sjodal" (tr. by Roger Greenwald). [Writ] (18) 86, c87, p. 45.
"Trees in Autumn" (tr. by Roger Greenwald). [Writ] (18) 86, c87, p. 44.
2575. JACOBSON, Jean
"The Dry Tortugas." [Shen] (36:3) 86, p. 114-115.
2576. JAECH, Stephen
"Le Dernier Cri Gallery." [WebR] (11:1) Spr 86, p. 80-81.
2577. JAEGER, Ann
"Chinese Puzzle Box." [Epoch] (35:1) 85-86, p. 50.
"MN." [Epoch] (35:1) 85-86, p. 49.
2578. JAFFE, Carrie
"The Gift." [LittleM] (15:2) 86, p. 45-46.
"Sitting Next to Angelina." [LittleM] (15:2) 86, p. 47.
2579. JAFFE, Maggie
"In Cafe del Rey Moro." [SanFPJ] (8:4) 85, p. 79-80.
"Vigilante." [SanFPJ] (8:4) 85, p. 77-78.
"Vigilante" (April 8, 1985). [SanFPJ] (9:1) 86, p. 17-18.
2580. JAFFER, Frances
"Any Time Now" (Excerpt). [Iowa] (16:3) Fall 86, p. 249-250.
"Great Day for the Virgin." [Iowa] (16:3) Fall 86, p. 246-249.
"Milk Song" (Excerpt). [Iowa] (16:3) Fall 86, p. 250-251.
2581. JAGODZINSKE, Marcia
"Spring Bomb." [MinnR] (NS 27) Fall 86, p. 97-98.
2582. JAHIN, Salah
"Song of Baramhat" (tr. by Susan Brind). [SenR] (16:1) 86, p. 93-96.
2583. JAMES, Ashwini
"Two Ghazals." [Grain] (14:2) My 86, p. 47.
2584. JAMES, David
"The Accident." [CentR] (30:3) Sum 86, p. 348-349.
"Lost in the Storm." [PennR] (1:2) Fall 85, p. 70.
"Of All Things." [MidAR] (7:1) 86, p. 170.
"This Far" (Second prize, 1986 Poetry Competition). [PassN] (7:2) Spr-Sum 86, p.
3.
"A Topology of Contemplation." [WormR] (26:2, issue 102) 86, p. 41-44.
"What Do You Want to Be." [CentR] (30:3) Sum 86, p. 347-348.
2585. JAMES, Sibyl
"Don't Cry for Me, Argentina" (for Eva Peron). [Contact] (8:41/42/43) Fall-Wint
86-87, p. 12.
"How I'll Live Then." [Calyx] (9:2/3) Wint 86, p. 88.
"Learning the Road." [WillowS] (17) Wint 86, p. 70.
"Poem for Samantha and Me." [Calyx] (9:2/3) Wint 86, p. 89.
"Short Wave in Shanghai." [Event] (15:2) 86, p. 34-35.
"Washington Pass." [CrabCR] (3:2) Spr 86, p. 3.
"A Well in Chad." [WillowS] (17) Wint 86, p. 69.
2586. JAMES, Tom
"Anybody Home?" [Bogg] (56) 86, p. 22.
"Four Minutes Left." [SanFPJ] (8:2) 85, p. 96.
"Postamble." [SanFPJ] (8:3) 85, p. 84.
"Spring." [SanFPJ] (8:3) 85, p. 86-87.
2587. JAMES-FRENCH, Davy
"About Mr. V." [AntigR] (66/67) Sum-Aut 86, p. 171.
"Breakfast in Betws-y-coed." [AntigR] (66/67) Sum-Aut 86, p. 170.
2588. JAMIESON, Lee
"Two-Tone." [YetASM] (5) 86, p. 3.
2589. JAMIESON, Leland
"Kallaia." [YetASM] (4) 85, p. 2.

189

JAMIS

2590. JAMIS, Fayad
"The New Day Dazzles You" (For Gustavo Eguren, tr. by John Oliver Simon).
[InterPR] (12:1) Spr 86, p. 33-35.
"El Nuevo Día Te Deslumbra" (trom *Abri la Verga de Hierro*, 1973). [InterPR]
(12:1) Spr 86, p. 32, 34.
2591. JAMISON, Barbara
"Love Life." [AnotherCM] (15) 86, p. 46-47.
2592. JAMPOLE, Marc
"Every Firefly Is." [NegC] (6:1) Wint 86, p. 91.
2593. JANIK, Phyllis
"C'mon, Donna! Show Us What You're Made Of!" (Contemplation after the foetus
hears a reading from Richard Selzer's Mortal Lessons). [NewL] (52:2/3)
Wint-Spr 86, p. 92-93.
"Compass Rose." [NewL] (52:2/3) Wint-Spr 86, p. 94-95.
2594. JANOWITZ, Phyllis
"The Blood." [Jacaranda] (2:1) Fall 86, p. 27-28.
"Keepers of the Flame." [Boulevard] (1:1/2) Wint 86, p. 146-147.
"Perch." [PraS] (60:4) Wint 86, p. 90-91.
"Summer Place." [Jacaranda] (2:1) Fall 86, p. 26.
2595. JARMAN, Mark
"As Good as Dead." [DenQ] (20:4/21:1) Spr-Sum 86, p. 140-141.
"At the Zane Grey Pueblo Hotel." [QW] (23) 86, p. 63-64.
"The Black Riviera." [NewYorker] (62:13) 19 My 86, p. 40.
"The Cure, an Anecdote" (For Chase Twichell). [NewEngR] (9:1) Aut 86, p. 11-14.
"A Drawer of Scarves." [Crazy] (31) Fall 86, p. 10-13.
"Madrigal." [Crazy] (31) Fall 86, p. 7.
"The Mystic." [MissouriR] (9:2) 86, p. 202-204.
"An Occasion in Summer." [TarRP] (25:1) Fall 85, p. 31-32.
"The Pendulum's Weight." [Crazy] (31) Fall 86, p. 8-9.
2596. JARRELL, Randall
"The Bad Music." [Field] (35) Fall 86, p. 8-9.
"Bats." [Field] (35) Fall 86, p. 50.
"The Death of the Ball Turret Gunner." [Field] (35) Fall 86, p. 14.
"Field and Forest." [Field] (35) Fall 86, p. 55-56.
"The House in the Wood." [Field] (35) Fall 86, p. 62-63.
"Moving." [Field] (35) Fall 86, p. 21-22.
"Nestus Gurley." [Field] (35) Fall 86, p. 43-45.
"Seele Im Raum." [Field] (35) Fall 86, p. 30-32.
"The Truth." [Field] (35) Fall 86, p. 37-38.
2597. JASIN, Soledad H-D
"Juliano Stampa" (tr. of Sara Gallardo). [NewOR] (13:3) Fall 86, p. 58.
"On the Puna" (tr. of Sara Gallardo). [NewOR] (13:3) Fall 86, p. 80.
2598. JASINSKI, Jay
"Car Trouble." [JamesWR] (3:2) Wint 86, p. 9.
"Stuck." [MalR] (74) Mr 86, p. 108.
2599. JAY, Leilani
"Door Running." [HayF] (1) Spr 86, p. 83.
2600. JAYYUSI, Lena
"Bedouin Lament at the Gates . . ." (tr. of Muhammad Ubaid al-Harbi, w. Diana Der
Hovanessian). [Translation] (17) Fall 86, p. 264-267.
2601. JEANNE, Ave
"Abortion / of the Corn." [SecC] (14:1) 86, p. 36.
"American Music: The Refrain." [SanFPJ] (8:2) 85, p. 60.
"The Collage / Gray Haired Man & Trumpet." [PaintedB] (29) Ag 86, p. 26.
"Eating Another Loophole." [SanFPJ] (8:2) 85, p. 57.
"Finally / the Marigolds." [SanFPJ] (9:1) 86, p. 54.
"Music Learned from Viet Nam" (a round). [SanFPJ] (8:2) 85, p. 57.
"Picture Postcard / Philadelphia 1985." [SanFPJ] (9:1) 86, p. 55.
"A rabbit." [Electrum] (38) Spr 86, p. 47.
"Resewing My Spangles." [Bogg] (55) 86, p. 18.
"Retirement." [SecC] (14:1) 86, p. 42.
"Still Life / Greener Pastures." [SanFPJ] (9:1) 86, p. 51.
2602. JENA, Bibek
"Calcutta" (tr. by Bibhu Padhi). [RiverS] (20) 86, p. 55.
2603. JENKINS, Edith
"On Seeing Berlioz' *Les Troyens*." [Thrpny] (25) Spr 86, p. 16.

2604. JENKINS, Louis
"Cirrus." [Ascent] (11:3) 86, p. 1-2.
"The Dead of Winter." [Ascent] (11:3) 86, p. 3.
"October." [IndR] (9:2) Spr 86, p. 94.
"Spring Ice." [IndR] (9:2) Spr 86, p. 95.
2605. JENKINS, Patricia M.
"Legacy." [ManhatPR] (8) Wint 86-87, p. 25.
2606. JENKINS, Paul
"Let's Make a Baby." [PoetryNW] (27:4) Wint 86-87, p. 13.
"Special Police." [PoetryNW] (27:4) Wint 86-87, p. 11-12.
2607. JENKINS, Shane
"Grandpa Davis." [PikeF] (7) Spr 86, p. 22.
2608. JENNINGS, Kate
"She Dreams about Voodoo." [LitR] (30:1) Fall 86, p. 62.
"Stagnant Water." [LitR] (30:1) Fall 86, p. 63.
2609. JENNINGS, Lane
"Companions." [Vis] (20) 86, p. 22.
"Second Honeymoon (AD 2150)." [Vis] (20) 86, p. 19.
"Shakespearean Brag." [Vis] (20) 86, p. 24.
2610. JENSEN, Laura
"Army Jets." [Field] (34) Spr 86, p. 97.
"China." [QW] (22) Spr-Sum 86, p. 12-13.
"Come Up to My House." [PoetryNW] (27:2) Sum 86, p. 4-5.
"Corsage — to the Order of Runeberg." [Ploughs] (12:4) 86, p. 16-17.
"A Fairy Tale of Flowers." [PoetryNW] (27:2) Sum 86, p. 3-4.
"Gray Area." [Field] (34) Spr 86, p. 99-101.
"Heidegger" (for Benjamin Moloise). [Field] (34) Spr 86, p. 6.
"A Meditation on the Position of the Head." [Field] (34) Spr 86, p. 7-8.
"Morning." [QW] (22) Spr-Sum 86, p. 11.
"Pony Farm." [Field] (34) Spr 86, p. 5.
"Possessions." [Ploughs] (12:4) 86, p. 18-19.
"Separate." [Field] (34) Spr 86, p. 98-99.
"The Shadow Specialists." [QW] (23) 86, p. 8-9.
"Shelter." [CutB] (26) Spr-Sum 86, p. 107-108.
"The Storm." [CutB] (26) Spr-Sum 86, p. 106-107.
"Swimming." [Field] (35) Fall 86, p. 108-109.
2611. JENTZ, Jeff
"Dream Letter." [NoDaQ] (54:1) Wint 86, p. 65.
"Harvest Psalm" (for Karen). [NoDaQ] (54:1) Wint 86, p. 64-65.
"Two Weeks Bride in Early March." [NoDaQ] (54:1) Wint 86, p. 64.
2612. JERVEY, Evelyn
"Clothes." [PaintedB] (28) Ap 86, p. 30.
2613. JESSON, Mary Ellen
"Writing a Poem." [EngJ] (75:4) Ap 86, p. 50.
2614. JESUS, Dionisio de
"El Azar Organiza los Sueños" (A Jorge Luis Borges). [Mairena] (8:22) 86, p. 74.
JET WIMP
   See WIMP, Jet
JEW, Dianne Hai
   See HAI-JEW, Dianne
2615. JEWELL, David
"I Wait for You." [YetASM] (5) 86, p. 11.
2616. JEWELL, Terri L.
"The Buddy System." [SanFPJ] (8:3) 85, p. 32.
"Closed Case." [Obs] (NS 1:1/2) Spr-Sum 86, p. 55.
"Covenant." [BlackALF] (20:3) Fall 86, p. 259-260.
"Felled Shadows." [Calyx] (9:2/3) Wint 86, p. 90.
"Gasoline on the Roof." [BlackALF] (20:3) Fall 86, p. 257-259.
"God Bless." [SanFPJ] (8:3) 85, p. 12.
"Outside Johannesburg." [SanFPJ] (8:3) 85, p. 93.
"Sistah Flo." [Calyx] (9:2/3) Wint 86, p. 91.
"Taken by Michael Depores." [Obs] (NS 1:1/2) Spr-Sum 86, p. 56.
2617. JIA, Dao
"Longing for Zheng Congzhi" (In Chinese & English, tr. by Miles W. Murphy).
   [NewL] (53:1) Fall 86, p. 55.

"On a Hermit's Hut" (In Chinese & English, tr. by Miles W. Murphy). [NewL] (53:1) Fall 86, p. 54.
JIA-TI, Zhou
        See ZHOU, Jia-ti
2618. JIANG, He
        "Begin from Here" (from the poem-cycle, Part V, tr. by John Minford, Pang Bingjun *et al.*). [Nimrod] (29:2) Spr-Sum 86, p. 123-124.
2619. JIMENEZ, Miguel Antonio
        "Concierto Despojos" (a León Felipe). [Mairena] (8:22) 86, p. 55.
2620. JIN, Ha
        "The Dead Soldier's Talk." [ParisR] (28:101) Wint 86, p. 245-246.
JIN, Xuefei
        See JAN, Ha
JIN-XUAN, Sun
        See SUN, Jin-xuan
2621. JIRGENS, Karl
        "Dugong Song" (An Ocean "Rap-ture"). [Rampike] (5:1) 86, p. 47.
2622. JOEL, Miriam
        "Quechua Poetry" (tr. of four anonymous poems). [WebR] (11:2) Fall 86, p. 40.
2623. JOENS, Harley
        "The Blues Mouth." [Northeast] (series 4:3) Spr 86, p. 19.
        "Last Poem." [Northeast] (series 4:4) Wint 86-87, p. 26.
2624. JOGLAR CACHO, Manuel
        "Clara Lair está sola en la desierta." [Mairena] (8:22) 86, p. 50.
        "Contigo va mi voz." [Mairena] (8:22) 86, p. 49.
        "Un pájaro gorjea en la alta rosa." [Mairena] (8:22) 86, p. 24.
        "Sonetos" (Del Poema en preparación, "Cien Campanas en una Sola Torre"). [RevICP] (88) Abril-Junio 85, p. 55.
        "Y mi afán estas cosas aún remueve." [Mairena] (8:22) 86, p. 14.
2625. JOHANNES, Joan C.
        "The Nisse and the Cat." [BallSUF] (26:4) Aut 85, p. 30.
2626. JOHANNESEN, Georg
        "At a Painter's" (tr. by Harold P. Hanson). [Vis] (22) 86, p. 16.
        "Flight Preparation" (tr. by Harold P. Hanson). [Vis] (22) 86, p. 15.
        "The Jester's Greeting" (tr. by Harold P. Hanson). [Vis] (22) 86, p. 16.
        "Poster in a Condominium" (tr. by Harold P. Hanson). [Vis] (22) 86, p. 15.
2627. JOHANNESSEN, Matthías
        "June 26" (tr. by Gregory C. Richter). [Paint] (13:25/26) Spr-Aut 86, p. 31.
2628. JOHANSEN, J. G.
        "At the Autumn Equinox." [ChrC] (103:37) 3 D 86, p. 1088.
2629. JOHLER, Walt
        "Chain Saw." [SpoonRQ] (11:2) Spr 86, p. 58.
        "Honest As Old Abe." [SpoonRQ] (11:2) Spr 86, p. 59.
2630. JOHNSON, Bernard
        "War" (tr. of Miodrag Pavlovic). [Verse] (6) 86, p. 51.
2631. JOHNSON, Bruce
        "Walla Walla Sweets." [CrabCR] (3:3) Sum 86, p. 3.
2632. JOHNSON, Colin
        "Granny Mary Came Our Way." [MassR] (27:2) Sum 86, p. 365-366.
        "Song Twelve." [MassR] (27:2) Sum 86, p. 363-364.
        "Song Twenty-Nine." [MassR] (27:2) Sum 86, p. 364-365.
        "Song Two." [MassR] (27:2) Sum 86, p. 363.
        "Under an Aboriginal Tree." [MassR] (27:2) Sum 86, p. 366.
2633. JOHNSON, David
        "Immigrant." [KanQ] (18:1/2) Wint-Spr 86, p. 237.
2634. JOHNSON, Denis
        "Grey Day in Miami." [MissouriR] (9:2) 86, p. 208.
        "The Heavens." [MissouriR] (9:2) 86, p. 210.
        "The Risen." [MissouriR] (9:2) 86, p. 209.
2635. JOHNSON, Doug
        "Hay Stacks." [RagMag] (5:1) Spr 86, p. 46.
        "In the Tamarack Swamp." [RagMag] (5:1) Spr 86, p. 46.
        "Nightfall, Rusk County, Wisconsin." [RagMag] (5:1) Spr 86, p. 47.
        "Things Found on a Path." [RagMag] (5:1) Spr 86, p. 47.
2636. JOHNSON, Elizabeth
        "From Room to Room." [SingHM] (13) 86, p. 58.

2637. JOHNSON, Hamilton
"To Comfort Bess." [DeKalbLAJ] (19:2) 86, p. 35.
2638. JOHNSON, Jean Youell
"Mind Slash." [Bogg] (55) 86, p. 32.
2639. JOHNSON, Jenny
"Mother, Daughter." [Stand] (27:4) Aut 86, p. 5.
"The Nursery." [Stand] (27:4) Aut 86, p. 4.
2640. JOHNSON, Jodi
"The Sale." [Jacaranda] (2:1) Fall 86, p. 17-19.
2641. JOHNSON, Kate Knapp
"Yes" (for Eva). [Raccoon] (20) Ap 86, p. 44.
2642. JOHNSON, Keith Cowell
"Decals." [CentralP] (9) Spr 86, p. 38.
2643. JOHNSON, Kent
"Ah, That You Escape" (tr. of Jose Lezama Lima). [ClockR] (3:1) 85, p. 57.
"Discovery of Stone" (tr. of Miguel Otero Silva). [ClockR] (3:1) 85, p. 56.
"Huatesca Woman" (tr. of Octavio Paz). [ClockR] (3:1) 85, p. 55.
"Juan Erre" (tr. of Xiomara Espinoza). [NowestR] (24:1) 86, p. 113.
"The Last Day of Somoza's Liberal Party" (tr. of Juan Antonio Lira). [CentralP] (9)
Spr 86, p. 81.
"Two Plus Two" (tr. of Ariel Dorfman). [RedBass] (11) 86, p. 6.
2644. JOHNSON, Kristopher
"Boat Made of Water." [Hudson] (39:1) Spr 86, p. 106.
2645. JOHNSON, Larry
"Earth." [Poem] (55) Mr 86, p. 41.
"Pollution." [Poem] (55) Mr 86, p. 42.
"The Self-Torturer." [Poem] (55) Mr 86, p. 43.
2646. JOHNSON, Manly
"Autumn" (tr. of Sun Jin-xuan, w. Xu Yaoping). [Nimrod] (29:2) Spr-Sum 86, p.
37.
"The Winter Snow" (tr. of Sun Jin-xuan, w. Xu Yaoping). [Nimrod] (29:2)
Spr-Sum 86, p. 38.
2647. JOHNSON, Mark Allan
"Into Motionless Love." [BellArk] (2:2) Mr-Ap 86, p. 5.
"Morning Watch." [BellArk] (2:2) Mr-Ap 86, p. 1.
"Nightlight." [BellArk] (2:4) Jl-Ag 86, p. 8.
"The River." [BellArk] (2:1) Ja-F 86, p. 8.
"Shadow Fish." [BellArk] (2:3) My-Je 86, p. 4.
"Sorcery & Salmon." [BellArk] (2:2) Mr-Ap 86, p. 5.
"The Trail." [BellArk] (2:3) My-Je 86, p. 4.
"Visions of October: Lines Composed the Day after Attending a Nelson Bentley
Poetry Reading." [BellArk] (2:1) Ja-F 86, p. 3.
2648. JOHNSON, Michael L.
"Ein Aschenbecher für Aschenbach." [Amelia] (3:2) Spr 86, p. 102.
"Comet P/Halley." [KanQ] (18:4) Fall 86, p. 43.
"For Margie." [CentR] (30:3) Sum 86, p. 352.
"Henri Rousseau's *Sleeping Gypsy*." [ManhatPR] (8) Wint 86-87, p. 15.
"Interior" (tr. of Paul Valéry). [Amelia] (3:4) Fall 86, p. 99.
"Modigliani." [KanQ] (18:4) Fall 86, p. 44.
"Some Common Weeds of Kansas." [KanQ] (18:4) Fall 86, p. 44.
"To Harry Crews." [KanQ] (18:4) Fall 86, p. 42-43.
"To My Dying Grandmother." [CentR] (30:3) Sum 86, p. 352-353.
"Wyeth's Pentimenti." [HighP] (1:1) Wint 86, p. 39.
2649. JOHNSON, Peter
"Mud Season." [ColEng] (48:8) D 86, p. 799.
"The Pessimist." [IndR] (9:2) Spr 86, p. 64.
2650. JOHNSON, Robert K.
"Autumn Mood." [WebR] (11:1) Spr 86, p. 70.
"Home." [WebR] (11:1) Spr 86, p. 69.
"A Moment on the Tennis Court." [WebR] (11:1) Spr 86, p. 69.
"Through Darkness." [PoeticJ] (15) Sum 86, p. 27.
"The Touch of Rose Petals." [PoeticJ] (14) 86, p. 15.
2651. JOHNSON, Robin
"Catteries in Rome." [ManhatPR] (6) Wint-Spr 85-86, p. 48.
2652. JOHNSON, Ronald
"Ark 54, Starspire" (for Bucky Fuller). [Sulfur] (6:2, issue 17) 86, p. 26-28.

"The Imaginary Menagerie" (Selections: 5 poems). [Acts] (5) 86, p. 106.
2653. JOHNSON, Sören
    "The Letter." [Puerto] (22:1) Fall 86, p. 58-59.
    "Love." [BellR] (9:1) Spr 86, p. 36.
    "So Young Once." [BellR] (9:1) Spr 86, p. 37.
2654. JOHNSON, Thomas
    "Not the Sea." [VirQR] (62:4) Aut 86, p. 600.
    "Rooted." [VirQR] (62:4) Aut 86, p. 601.
2655. JOHNSON, Tom
    "Sailing after Supper." [SewanR] (94:1) Wint 86, p. 94-95.
    "Summertime." [SewanR] (94:1) Wint 86, p. 96.
2656. JOHNSON, W. R.
    "Endymion." [LitR] (29:3) Spr 86, p. 279.
    "Jason." [LitR] (29:3) Spr 86, p. 279.
    "Orpheus." [Poem] (56) N 86, p. 52.
    "A Scribe of Monte Cassino" (per signa ad signata). [Poem] (56) N 86, p. 53.
    "Sophocles." [Poem] (56) N 86, p. 51.
2657. JOHNSON, William
    "Moose." [QW] (22) Spr-Sum 86, p. 56.
2658. JOHNSONBROWN, Iris J.
    "Stairs." [PraS] (60:2) Sum 86, p. 115-116.
    "Wishing." [PraS] (60:2) Sum 86, p. 114.
2659. JOHNSTON, Carole
    "To the Writing Teacher." [EngJ] (75:3) Mr 86, p. 89.
2660. JOHNSTON, Craig
    "Once Removed." [KanQ] (18:1/2) Wint-Spr 86, p. 226.
2661. JOHNSTON, Fred
    "Alphabets of Brass" (for my daughter Saoirse Deirdre Johnston on her 7th
        birthday). [Descant] (17:2, #53) Sum 86, p. 112-113.
    "Cantata." [SpiritSH] (52) 86, p. 40-41.
    "Cruinniú Na Mbád." [SpiritSH] (52) 86, p. 42.
    "Towards Winter." [SpiritSH] (52) 86, p. 41.
    "Visiting Hours." [Descant] (17:2, #53) Sum 86, p. 114.
2662. JOHNSTON, Gordon
    "Catullus 46." [AntigR] (65) Spr 86, p. 68.
2663. JOHNSTON, Jean
    "A Fine Line." [Cond] (13) 86, p. 124.
    "What Mother Never Saw." [Cond] (13) 86, p. 125.
2664. JOHNSTON, Marilyn
    "Candid Photograph" (for Jane Ayres). [SmPd] (23:3, #68) Fall 86, p. 29.
2665. JOHNSTON, Mark
    "A Different Girl" (for Elizabeth). [BallSUF] (27:4) Aut 86, p. 29-31.
    "Jamaica: Cattle with Egrets." [StoneC] (14:1/2) Fall-Wint 86-87, p. 30.
    "Jealousy" (After the photograph by Moholy-Nagy). [CarolQ] (39:1) Fall 86, p. 38.
    "List of Chores." [BallSUF] (27:4) Aut 86, p. 39-40.
    "Riddles with No Solutions." [CarolQ] (39:1) Fall 86, p. 37.
    "Slides for the Weather Show." [BallSUF] (27:4) Aut 86, p. 27-28.
2666. JONES
    "On the Beach in Puerto Angel." [GreenfR] (13:3/4) Sum-Fall 86, p. 82.
2667. JONES, Alonzo Augustus
    "A Day As This." [WritersL] (1986:3), p. 11.
2668. JONES, Andrew M.
    "Street Silence." [Pax] (3:1/2) Wint 85-86, p. 72.
2669. JONES, Arlene (Arlene S., Arlene Swift)
    "Country Hospital." [Calyx] (9:2/3) Wint 86, p. 98-99.
    "Poussin's "The Martyrdom of St. Erasmus" (The Vatican Exhibit at the
        Metropolitan Museum, NYC). [TarRP] (26:1) Fall 86, p. 40-41.
    "Rheumatoid Arthritis" (for Drs. CLS, CSR, The Hospital for Special Surgery,
        NYC). [Calyx] (9:2/3) Wint 86, p. 100.
    "Vintage" (On Being in the Hospital). [Calyx] (9:2/3) Wint 86, p. 101.
2670. JONES, D. G.
    "Musica Ficta." [GreenfR] (13:3/4) Sum-Fall 86, p. 84-86.
    "A Sort of Blues." [GreenfR] (13:3/4) Sum-Fall 86, p. 87.
    "Victoria." [CanLit] (108) Spr 86, p. 45-46.
JONES, Elizabeth Follin
    See FOLLIN-JONES, Elizabeth

2671. JONES, Francis Redvers
"Girolamo Cavazzoni, Who Disappeared in Context" (Selections: 2, 5, tr. of Hans
Faverey). [Stand] (27:2) Spr 86, p. 21.
2672. JONES, Patricia
"Landlocked." [OP] (41) Spr 86, p. 18-20.
"Tuesday Evening." [OP] (41) Spr 86, p. 21.
2673. JONES, Paul
"Bamboo." [SouthernHR] (20:4) Fall 86, p. 341.
"The Sower" (for JJ). [CrescentR] (4:1) Spr 86, p. 75.
"Toward the Source of the Amazon" (for A.R.A.). [Pembroke] (18) 86, p. 195.
2674. JONES, Paula
"Daffodils." [BellArk] (2:4) Jl-Ag 86, p. 4.
"Pot of Heather." [BellArk] (2:3) My-Je 86, p. 5.
"Song of Yellow Tulips." [BellArk] (2:3) My-Je 86, p. 6.
"Tulips." [ManhatPR] (8) Wint 86-87, p. 17.
"The Walk." [YellowS] (20) Aut 86, p. 17.
2675. JONES, Richard
"The Fire." [CharR] (12:1) Spr 86, p. 50.
"The Idle Fleet, James River, Virginia." [WillowS] (17) Wint 86, p. 25.
"The Wounded One." [WillowS] (17) Wint 86, p. 26.
2676. JONES, Richard A.
"Amtrak — Chicago to Martinsburg West Virginia." [WritersF] (12) Fall 86, p.
237-238.
"Thirty-Fifth Birthday." [WritersF] (12) Fall 86, p. 238.
2677. JONES, Robert
"Conundrums" (for Joseph Monniger). [PoetryNW] (27:1) Spr 86, p. 18.
2678. JONES, Roger
"Again: A Kinser Dream." [CimR] (77) O 86, p. 50-51.
"Goodwill." [DeKalbLAJ] (19:3/4) 86, p. 79.
"Not Ready Yet." [SmPd] (23:3, #68) Fall 86, p. 10.
"Whippoorwill, Remembered." [TexasR] (7:1/2) Spr-Sum 86, p. 55.
2679. JONES, Seaborn
"Literature." [Amelia] (3:1) Ja 86, p. 27.
"The Red Army." [Amelia] (3:1) Ja 86, p. 27.
"Religion." [Amelia] (3:1) Ja 86, p. 27.
2680. JONES, Walt
"Seekers of Freedom." [Sam] (46:2 release 182) 86, p. 53.
2681. JORDAN, June
"An Always Lei of Ginger Blossoms for the First Lady of Hawaii: Queen
Liliuokalani." [Callaloo] (9:1, #26) Wint 86, p. 79-80.
"Poem for Buddy" (Dedicated to André Morgan, 3/29/86). [Callaloo] (9:2, #27) Spr
86, p. 341-344.
2682. JORIS, Pierre
"Canto Diurno" (Sunday, February 23rd, 1986). [Temblor] (4) 86, p. 109-121.
2683. JOSEPH, Lawrence
"In Angel Park." [PennR] (1:2) Fall 85, p. 64.
"London." [ParisR] (28:100) Sum-Fall 86, p. 189-190.
"Sand Nigger." [MichQR] (25:2) Spr 86, p. 366-368.
2684. JOSEPH, Margaret A.
"Heartshaped on the Highway." [Pax] (3:1/2) Wint 85-86, p. 73.
2685. JOTAMARIO
"Film Short" (tr. by Ellen Watson). [MassR] (27:3/4) Fall-Wint 86, p. 626-628.
"We Misfits Don't Forget You, Marilyn" (tr. by Ellen Watson). [MassR] (27:3/4)
Fall-Wint 86, p. 624-626.
2686. JOYCE, Alisa
"Begin from Here" (from the poem-cycle, Part V, tr. of Jiang He, w. John Minford
et al.). [Nimrod] (29:2) Spr-Sum 86, p. 123-124.
2687. JOZSEF, Attila
"Attila József" (tr. by Edwin Morgan and George Cushing). [Verse] (5) 86, p. 50.
"Culture" (tr. by Edwin Morgan and George Cushing). [Verse] (5) 86, p. 50.
"In the End" (tr. by Edwin Morgan and George Cushing). [Verse] (5) 86, p. 51.
"It Is a Fine Summer Evening" (tr. by Edwin Morgan and George Cushing). [Verse]
(5) 86, p. 53.
"Sorrow" (tr. by Edwin Morgan and George Cushing). [Verse] (5) 86, p. 52.
"A True Man" (tr. by Edwin Morgan and George Cushing). [Verse] (5) 86, p. 54.

2688. JUARROZ, Roberto
    "After half a life or maybe all of it" (tr. by W. S. Merwin). [SenR] (16:2) 86, p. 45.
    "The last light always welds itself to the hand" (tr. by W. S. Merwin). [SenR] (16:2)
        86, p. 43.
    "On a night that should have been rain" (tr. by W. S. Merwin). [SenR] (16:2) 86, p.
        42.
    "Twelve Untitled Poems" (tr. by W. S. Merwin). [Translation] (17) Fall 86, p.
        283-290.
    "We'll bury it all" (tr. by W. S. Merwin). [SenR] (16:2) 86, p. 44.
2689. JUDSON, John
    "1952." [NoAmR] (271:3) S 86, p. 16.
    "Husbanding." [Confr] (32) Spr-Sum 86, p. 27.
2690. JUERGENSEN, Hans
    "'Woman II' by Willem De Kooning." [NewL] (53:1) Fall 86, p. 101.
2691. JUGDEO, Naveen
    "Track." [Grain] (14:2) My 86, p. 42.
JUKICHI, Yagi
    See YAGI, Jukichi
2692. JULIUS, Richard Todd
    "City Streets at Night." [SanFPJ] (9:1) 86, p. 88.
    "Riot." [SanFPJ] (8:1) 85, p. 89.
    "The Sound." [SanFPJ] (9:1) 86, p. 85.
    "The Way to War." [SanFPJ] (8:1) 85, p. 28.
JUN, Honda
    See HONDA, Jun
2693. JUNKINS, Donald
    "The Veil." [AmerPoR] (15:6) N-D 86, p. 22.
JUNKO, Yoshida
    See YOSHIDA, Junko
2694. JURADO MORALES, José
    "Del manantial." [Mairena] (8:22) 86, p. 15.
    "Homenaje a Antonio Machado." [Mairena] (8:22) 86, p. 82.
    "Me llega en mi remanso la armonía." [Mairena] (8:22) 86, p. 25.
    "Soneto de Amor." [Mairena] (8:22) 86, p. 81.
2695. JURCZAK, Kate
    "For Sol Newman, Wherever He Finds Lui-Même." [Jacaranda] (2:1) Fall 86, p.
        8-9.
2696. JUSSAWALLA, Adil
    "The Exile's Story." [LitR] (29:4) Sum 86, p. 452-453.
2697. JUSTICE, Donald
    "Elegy for Cello and Piano." [Iowa] (16:1) Wint 86, p. 2-3.
    "Henry James at the Pacific" (Coronado Beach, California, March, 1905). [Atlantic]
        (257:1) Ja 86, p. 78.
    "In Memory of Mrs. Snow, My First Piano Teacher." [Atlantic] (258:5) N 86, p.
        122.
    "Last Evening" (after Rilke). [Nat] (243:1) 5-12 Jl 86, p. 27.
    "Manhattan Dawn." [Nat] (243:16) 15 N 86, p. 530.
    "The Pupil." [NewYorker] (62:32) 29 S 86, p. 46.
    "Purgatory." [Nat] (243:1) 5-12 Jl 86, p. 27.
2698. JUSTICE, Jack
    "The Art of Bartering." [SlipS] (6) 86, p. 66.
    "Bean Farm." [StoneC] (13:3/4) Spr-Sum 86, p. 31.
    "Embers." [Sam] (46:5 [i.e. 46:1] release 181) 86, p. 41.
    "Home Again." [Sam] (45:4 release 180) 86, p. 11.
    "Installing Cable Lines on 43rd Street After the Rain Stops." [Sam] (46:5 [i.e. 46:1]
        release 181) 86, p. 49.
    "Walking the Child Who Knows Too Much." [Sam] (45:4 release 180) 86, p. 7.
2699. KACHE, Saraswati
    "Waterfall." [PikeF] (7) Spr 86, p. 21.
2700. KACHINSKE, Timothy
    "The Olive Bush" (tr. of József Konczek). [ColR] (NS 13:1) Fall 85, p. 42.
    "To Mayakovsky, in Place of an Introduction" (tr. of Endre Rozsa). [Stand] (27:1)
        Wint 85-86, p. 24-25.
2701. KAGAN, Tara
    "Ode to Attila." [Pax] (3:1/2) Wint 85-86, p. 174.

2702. KAGEYAMA, Yuri
"Love Poems for Isaku / IV." [RiverS] (20) 86, p. 57.
2703. KAHANEY, Phyllis
"Germany, 1981." [WoosterR] (5) Spr 86, p. 53.
2704. KAI, Nubia
"The Boat Skin Bag." [Obs] (NS 1:1/2) Spr-Sum 86, p. 57-58.
2705. KAISER-MARTIN, Billie
"Acidity." [SanFPJ] (9:1) 86, p. 96.
"Developmental Economics." [SanFPJ] (8:3) 85, p. 62.
"Felon." [SanFPJ] (8:3) 85, p. 61.
"The Modern Penal System." [SanFPJ] (8:3) 85, p. 61.
"Violence." [SanFPJ] (8:1) 85, p. 41.
"A Yearly Assessment." [SanFPJ] (8:3) 85, p. 63.
2706. KALAMARAS, George
"Beware the Insistence of Gravity, Or Upon Waking in the Body of Cesar Vallejo."
[MinnR] (NS 27) Fall 86, p. 89-91.
"Easter, 1940." [Germ] (10:1) Spr-Sum 86, p. 31.
"For Costas" (Sunday night, late). [Germ] (10:1) Spr-Sum 86, p. 34-35.
"The Mud beneath the River" (for Richard Hugo). [CrabCR] (4:1) Fall-Wint 86, p.
15.
"The Return." [MidAR] (6:2) 86, p. 152-156.
"Tonight, the Memories." [Germ] (10:1) Spr-Sum 86, p. 32.
"Who Has Spent the Light." [MidAR] (6:2) 86, p. 97-98.
"Zakynthos, When the Wind Blows." [Germ] (10:1) Spr-Sum 86, p. 33.
2707. K'ALANDADZE, Ana
"By the Aragvi" (1980, tr. by Kevin Tuite). [LitR] (30:1) Fall 86, p. 21.
"The Cathedral Glowed" (1960, tr. by Kevin Tuite). [LitR] (30:1) Fall 86, p. 23.
"A Cool Spring's Cut-Crystal" (tr. by Kevin Tuite). [LitR] (30:1) Fall 86, p. 23.
"January Flowers at Uplistesikhe" (1961, tr. by Kevin Tuite). [LitR] (30:1) Fall 86,
p. 21.
"Speak, Ladybug!" (1945, tr. by Kevin Tuite). [LitR] (30:1) Fall 86, p. 22.
2708. KALIKOFF, Beth
"The Discovery of Chili." [AnotherCM] (15) 86, p. 48.
2709. KALMUS, Morris A.
"Ex Leftist." [SanFPJ] (8:1) 85, p. 60.
"The Immigrant Soldier." [SanFPJ] (8:4) 85, p. 58.
"The Return of Prometheus." [SanFPJ] (8:1) 85, p. 68.
2710. KALNOKY, László
"The Glass Hat" (tr. by Jascha Kessler, w. Maria Körösy). [LitR] (29:3) Spr 86, p.
356.
"What Man Can Do on This Planet" (tr. by Clive Wilmer and George Gömöri).
[Verse] (5) 86, p. 55-56.
2711. KAMAL, Daud
"The Day Death Comes" (tr. of Faiz Ahmad Faiz). [Vis] (21) 86, p. 34.
"Stone Bridge." [Pax] (3:1/2) Wint 85-86, p. 179.
"The Sunset Bridge." [Pax] (3:1/2) Wint 85-86, p. 178-179.
"Thirst." [Pax] (3:1/2) Wint 85-86, p. 178.
KAMARI, Shyam
See KUMARI, Shyam
2712. KAMENETZ, Rodger
"For Balthus." [Shen] (36:2) 86, p. 79.
"Moving Distances." [Shen] (36:2) 86, p. 78-79.
"Parsley." [Shen] (36:3) 86, p. 113-114.
"What Turns But Doesn't Move." [MissR] (15:1/2, #43/44) Fall-Wint 86, p. 50.
2713. KAMINSKY, Marc
"Broker." [CentralP] (9) Spr 86, p. 74-75.
"Defense" (Black Out of the Architect Joe Stylianos). [CentralP] (9) Spr 86, p.
69-73.
"News of the Abolition of Nuclear Weapons." [CentralP] (9) Spr 86, p. 13-15.
2714. KAMLAKANTO
"Argil's Prayer." [WritersL] (1986:5), p. 21.
"Kinship." [WritersL] (1986:5), p. 20.
"A Question." [WritersL] (1986:5), p. 20.
2715. KAMMEL, Edward Paul
"Nightwalker." [Contact] (7:38/39/40) Wint-Spr 86, p. 86.

2716. KAMPLEY, Linda
   "Nine A.M. Sunday." [DeKalbLAJ] (19:3/4) 86, p. 80-81.
2717. KANAZAWA, Teru
   "Harvard Square." [Contact] (7:38/39/40) Wint-Spr 86, p. 50.
   "In Memoriam." [Contact] (7:38/39/40) Wint-Spr 86, p. 50.
2718. KANE, Katherine
   "Celia Gray." [VirQR] (62:4) Aut 86, p. 609.
   "To a Staghorn Fern." [VirQR] (62:4) Aut 86, p. 610-611.
2719. KANE, Paul
   "A Moment's Notice." [Shen] (36:4) 86, p. 47-48.
2720. KANEKO, Lonny
   "October on Green Lake." [Contact] (7:38/39/40) Wint-Spr 86, p. 42.
2721. KANEKO, Mitsuharu
   "Mount Fuji" (tr. by James Kirkup and Akiko Takemoto). [Translation] (17) Fall 86,
      p. 188-189.
2722. KANGAS, J. R.
   "Agnus Dei." [JamesWR] (3:4) Sum 86, p. 10.
   "Desire." [SoCaR] (18:2) Spr 86, p. 76-77.
   "Lines in Summer." [Bogg] (56) 86, p. 26.
   "Out of the Mouths of Ample Women." [SoCaR] (18:2) Spr 86, p. 77.
2723. KANTCHEV, Nicolai
   "Medusa: Selected Poems" (tr. by Jascha Kessler and Alexander Shurbanov). [QRL]
      (Poetry series 6:26) 86, 38 p.
KANTROWITZ, Melanie Kaye
   See KAYE/KANTROWITZ, Melanie
2724. KAPLAN, B. David
   "Eucalyptus Bark Only." [Poem] (55) Mr 86, p. 38-39.
2725. KAPLAN, Issac
   "They offered us some of the finest sites in the world" (tr. by Will Kirkland).
      [NewOR] (13:4) Wint 86, p. 40-41.
2726. KAPLAN, Richard
   "I Always Thought of You as a Delicate Vase." [Jacaranda] (2:1) Fall 86, p. 38.
2727. KAPLAN, Susan
   "The Servant's Choice." [Poetry] (148:5) Ag 86, p. 274-275.
2728. KAPLINSKI, Jaan
   "Elder-trees that thrushes have sown" (tr. by the author, Riina Tamm, and Sam
      Hamill). [WillowS] (18) Sum 86, p. 77.
   "I could have said: I stepped from the bus" (tr. by the author, Riina Tamm, and Sam
      Hamill). [WillowS] (18) Sum 86, p. 75.
   "It gets cold in the evening" (tr. by the author, Riina Tamm, and Sam Hamill).
      [WillowS] (18) Sum 86, p. 76.
   "Once I got a postcard from the Fiji Islands" (tr. by the author, Riina Tamm, and
      Sam Hamill). [WillowS] (18) Sum 86, p. 74.
2729. KAPOOR, Neil
   "A Ghazal." [Grain] (14:2) My 86, p. 41.
   "A Villanelle without Rhyme." [Grain] (14:2) My 86, p. 41.
2730. KAPOOR, Pam
   "Monarch." [Grain] (14:2) My 86, p. 48.
2731. KAPUR, Kamal
   "Death Is the Spring in Every Dancer's Toes." [YellowS] (21) Wint 86, p. 23.
   "I Have Announced Our Love." [YellowS] (21) Wint 86, p. 22.
   "In That Stillness Before the Pounce." [YellowS] (21) Wint 86, p. 23.
   "It's Not That I." [YellowS] (21) Wint 86, p. 22.
   "The Message Was Mine." [YellowS] (21) Wint 86, p. 23.
   "Plonk in the Middle Of." [YellowS] (21) Wint 86, p. 22.
2732. KARAFEL, Lorraine
   "Heroines." [NewRep] (195:2/3) 14-21 Jl 86, p. 36.
2733. KARAVATOS, Nicholas
   "Modern Java Man." [SanFPJ] (8:4) 85, p. 59-60.
2734. KARLINS, Mark
   "Dear Comrade." [Sulfur] (6:1, issue 16) 86, p. 4-5.
   "Greybeard in Ring." [Sulfur] (6:1, issue 16) 86, p. 6.
   "In the dream of the glass cliff." [Sulfur] (6:1, issue 16) 86, p. 4.
   "Like oracles." [Sulfur] (6:1, issue 16) 86, p. 5.
   "Mastery Is the Power to Stop Writing (Blanchot)." [Sulfur] (6:1, issue 16) 86, p. 9.
   "Naming the Animals." [Sulfur] (6:1, issue 16) 86, p. 7-9.

"Narrative." [Sulfur] (6:1, issue 16) 86, p. 7.
"Sam Spade Exceeds Us Humanly." [Sulfur] (6:1, issue 16) 86, p. 6.
2735. KARP, Vickie
"The Consequences of Waking." [AntR] (44:3) Sum 86, p. 330-331.
"Dust." [NewYorker] (62:41) 1 D 86, p. 44.
2736. KARR, Mary
"The Lynched Man." [Ploughs] (12:3) 86, p. 82-83.
"Soft Mask." [Poetry] (148:6) S 86, p. 330.
2737. KASPER, Vancy
"August 11 Has Come and Gone" (for Jan). [Quarry] (35:3) Sum 86, p. 22.
"Coming Home" (for Ray Singer). [Quarry] (35:3) Sum 86, p. 23.
2738. KATES, J. (James)
"XI. Night Suicide" (tr. of Robert Desnos). [Vis] (22) 86, p. 8.
"XIII. Night Falls" (tr. of Robert Desnos). [Vis] (22) 86, p. 7.
"At the End of the World" (tr. of Robert Desnos). [StoneC] (13:3/4) Spr-Sum 86, p.
    45.
"The Glass of Wine" (tr. of Robert Desnos). [StoneC] (13:3/4) Spr-Sum 86, p. 45.
"The Hammock." [MidAR] (6:1) 86?, p. 88.
"In the Time of Dungeons" (tr. of Robert Desnos). [RedBass] (11) 86, p. 29.
"Letter to Etheridge." [FloridaR] (14:2) Fall-Wint 86, p. 106.
"Men on This Earth" (tr. of Robert Desnos). [RedBass] (11) 86, p. 6.
"To Dissuade a Suicide." [Outbr] (16/17) Fall 85-Spr 86, p. 77-78.
"Tomorrow" (tr. of Robert Desnos). [StoneC] (13:3/4) Spr-Sum 86, p. 47.
2739. KATROVAS, Richard
"Put Your Fingers Down My Throat." [NewL] (52:2/3) Wint-Spr 86, p. 208-209.
2740. KATSIMPALIS, Melissa
"Solstice." [WebR] (11:2) Fall 86, p. 54.
KATSUKO, Nishio
    See NISHIO, Katsuko
2741. KATZ, Susan A.
"The Ache to Dream." [ManhatPR] (7) Sum 86, p. 20.
"The Trip." [ManhatPR] (6) Wint-Spr 85-86, p. 21.
"Why She Died." [ManhatPR] (7) Sum 86, p. 21.
2742. KAUFFMAN, Janet
"Without Papers." [Caliban] (1) 86, p. 20-21.
2743. KAUFMAN, Shirley
"Bellagio." [OP] (42/43) Wint 86-87, p. 61-62.
"Calendar"" (tr. of Dan Pagis). [PoetL] (81:2) Sum 86, p. 82.
"Changing the Order" (tr. of Abba Kovner, w. Dan Laor). [PoetL] (81:2) Sum 86,
    p. 72-73.
"Cineraria." [OP] (42/43) Wint 86-87, p. 59-60.
"Diagnosis"" (tr. of Dan Pagis). [PoetL] (81:2) Sum 86, p. 81.
"Drifting." [PoetL] (81:2) Sum 86, p. 125-127.
"Driving Through Delhi." [OP] (42/43) Wint 86-87, p. 58.
"Everyone Who Comes" (tr. of Abba Kovner, w. Dan Laor). [PoetL] (81:2) Sum
    86, p. 73-74.
"Falling Rocks" (tr. of Abba Kovner). [Field] (34) Spr 86, p. 9-17.
"Gulls" (tr. of Judith Herzberg). [Field] (34) Spr 86, p. 70.
"Initials" (tr. of Avner Treinin). [PoetL] (81:2) Sum 86, p. 91.
"Kitchen Table" (tr. of Hamutal bar Yosef, w. Rivka Ma'oz). [PoetL] (81:2) Sum
    86, p. 97.
"The lawns of Delhi." [OP] (42/43) Wint 86-87, p. 59.
"Living in Jerusalem." [OP] (42/43) Wint 86-87, p. 60-61.
"On the Way" (tr. of Abba Kovner, w. Dan Laor). [PoetL] (81:2) Sum 86, p. 74.
"Over There" (tr. of Judith Herzberg). [Field] (34) Spr 86, p. 66.
"Palestine" (tr. of Hamutal bar Yosef, w. Rivka Ma'oz). [PoetL] (81:2) Sum 86, p.
    97.
"Potash" (tr. of Avner Treinin). [PoetL] (81:2) Sum 86, p. 92.
"Program" (tr. of Judith Herzberg). [Field] (34) Spr 86, p. 71.
"The Recurrence Theorem (Poincaré Cycle)" (tr. of Avner Treinin). [PoetL] (81:2)
    Sum 86, p. 92-94.
"A Strange Map" (tr. of Judith Herzberg). [Field] (34) Spr 86, p. 67-69.
2744. KAUNE, Gayle Rogers
"Blue Bridge" (Correction). [CrabCR] (3:2) Spr 86, p. 2.
2745. KAVANAGH, P. J.
"A Father Reorganizes." [GrandS] (5:2) Wint 86, p. 62-63.

209

2746. KAY, David P. L.
"Mpaka Afternoon." [Grain] (14:4) N 86, p. 52-53.
2747. KAY, John
"The Real McCoy." [OroM] (4:1-4) My 85, p. 44.
2748. KAYE, Frances W.
"Crocheting at the Arts Festival." [KanQ] (18:3) Sum 86, p. 52.
"Pond." [KanQ] (18:3) Sum 86, p. 52.
2749. KAYE/KANTROWITZ, Melanie
"Jerusalem Shadow." [SinW] (29/30) 86, p. 93-97.
2750. KAZANTZIS, Judith
"Nebuchadnezzar. A Gloss on a Picture by William Blake." [Stand] (27:2) Spr 86,
p. 7.
KAZUE, Shinkawa
See SHINKAWA, Kazue
2751. KAZUK, A. R.
"Badlands." [Dandel] (13:1) Spr-Sum 86, p. 37.
"Café." [Dandel] (13:1) Spr-Sum 86, p. 36.
"Separation." [AntigR] (66/67) Sum-Aut 86, p. 246.
"Wisdom." [AntigR] (66/67) Sum-Aut 86, p. 246.
2752. KAZUO, Ryu
"House of the Grieving Dogs" (Exceprt, tr. by Tom Koehne and the author).
[CarolQ] (38:2) Wint 86, p. 64.
KE, Mang
See MANG, Ke
2753. KEARNS, Josie
"Water Witching." [PassN] (7:1) Fall-Wint 85-86, p. 27.
2754. KEARSEY, Greg
"The Settlement." [Quarry] (35:4) Aut 86, p. 37.
KEATING, Helane Levine
See LEVINE-KEATING, Helane
2755. KEEFER, Janice Kulyk
"Adam and Eve: Rembrandt's Etching." [MalR] (76) S 86, p. 113.
"Children's Drawings on the Theme of Peace." [Event] (15:2) 86, p. 78-79.
"Eden." [Grain] (14:2) My 86, p. 28.
"Homecoming for Gonzalo." [MalR] (76) S 86, p. 112.
2756. KEELER, Greg
"Brook Trout behind a Beaver Dam." [RiverS] (19) 86, p. 58.
"Making It in Time." [RiverS] (19) 86, p. 59.
2757. KEELER, Julia
"His Matisses, 1938." [GreenfR] (13:3/4) Sum-Fall 86, p. 88-89.
2758. KEELEY, Edmund
"Apollo's First Altar" (tr. of Yannis Ritsos). [NewRep] (194:12) 24 Mr 86, p. 40.
"The Decay of the Argo" (tr. of Yannis Ritsos). [NewRep] (194:12) 24 Mr 86, p.
40.
"Requiem on Poros" (tr. of Yannis Ritsos). [NewRep] (194:12) 24 Mr 86, p. 40.
2759. KEENAN, Terrance
"The Nameless Stream." [Blueline] (7:2) Wint-Spr 86, p. 3.
2760. KEENER, LuAnn
"Force Fields." [CapeR] (21:1) Spr 86, p. 12.
"Hearth." [CapeR] (21:1) Spr 86, p. 11.
"Night Train." [Pembroke] (18) 86, p. 251-252.
"You're Here." [CapeR] (21:1) Spr 86, p. 10.
2761. KEITH, Ann
"Ghazal: I'd have left you ashore." [Confr] (33/34) Fall-Wint 86-87, p. 175.
2762. KELLER, Beverly
"Low Life." [AmerV] (3) Sum 86, p. 117.
2763. KELLER, David
"Absence." [SouthernPR] (26:2) Fall 86, p. 36.
"The Animals of That Country" (for H.P.). [PoetryNW] (27:4) Wint 86-87, p.
15-16.
"The Applicants for the Correspondence Course." [Poetry] (148:4) Jl 86, p.
196-197.
"In the Garden." [PoetryNW] (27:4) Wint 86-87, p. 16-17.
"Mussels." [OhioR] (37) 86, p. 112.
"Spring Storm." [OhioR] (37) 86, p. 113.

2764. KELLEY, Janine
    "Bhopal." [SanFPJ] (8:1) 85, p. 29.
    "Los Desaparecidos" (por los madres de Argentina). [SanFPJ] (8:1) 85, p. 71.
    "A Letter to Nietzsche." [SanFPJ] (8:1) 85, p. 70.
    "The Match Children." [SanFPJ] (8:1) 85, p. 90.
    "Shooting Star." [HeliconN] (14/15) Sum 86, p. 165.
    "Whispers" (for Vanessa). [HeliconN] (14/15) Sum 86, p. 164.
2765. KELLEY, Shannon Keith
    "Floating." [CapeR] (21:1) Spr 86, p. 4.
    "Hilderman's Store, Cape Girardeau, Missouri." [KanQ] (18:4) Fall 86, p. 24.
    "Safe." [CapeR] (21:1) Spr 86, p. 5.
2766. KELLEY, Tina
    "The First Autumn after Your Death." [StoneC] (13:3/4) Spr-Sum 86, p. 67.
2767. KELLY, Brigit Pegeen
    "Imagining Their Own Hymns." [NewEngR] (9:1) Aut 86, p. 27.
    "The Leaving." [PraS] (60:3) Fall 86, p. 45.
    "Percival." [WestB] (19) 86, p. 63.
    "Queen Elizabeth and the Blind Girl, or Music for the Dead Children." [PraS] (60:3)
        Fall 86, p. 42-44.
    "Those Who Wrestle with the Angel for Us." [GeoR] (40:4) Wint 86, p. 878-879.
    "Young Wife's Lament." [Nat] (242:17) 3 My 86, p. 620.
KELLY, Janine
    See KELLEY, Janine
2768. KELLY, Joan Auer
    "The Acid Rain." [SanFPJ] (9:1) 86, p. 38-39.
    "The Drowned Haitian: Florida, 1981." [FloridaR] (14:2) Fall-Wint 86, p. 71.
    "The Masque of the White Death." [SanFPJ] (9:1) 86, p. 57-59.
    "A Poet's Roots." [SanFPJ] (9:1) 86, p. 34.
    "Survivors." [SanFPJ] (9:1) 86, p. 29.
    "Unholy Harvest." [SanFPJ] (9:1) 86, p. 52.
2769. KELLY, Robert
    "Allemande" (for Mary Moore Goodlett). [Notus] (1:1) Fall 86, p. 38-39.
    "Her Hair on Fire" (for Elizabeth Robinson). [Notus] (1:1) Fall 86, p. 36-37.
    "The Maze." [Temblor] (3) 86, p. 28-35.
    "Sequana." [PaintedB] (28) Ap 86, p. 29.
    "Text Beginning with a Sequence from *Imagines*" (for Richard Marshall). [Notus]
        (1:1) Fall 86, p. 40.
2770. KELLY, Robert A.
    "Petrified Boy." [AntigR] (66/67) Sum-Aut 86, p. 235.
2771. KEMP, Penny
    "You paint pictures of angels" ("Untitled Poem"). [CrossC] (8:2) 86, p. 11.
2772. KEMPHER, Ruth Moon
    "The Antigone." [YetASM] (4) 85, p. 6.
    "The Gypsy Lady Pens a Closing Song Like a Grace Note, for the Accomplice, C."
        [YetASM] (5) 86, p. 3.
    "Scents, Like a Voice." [DeKalbLAJ] (19:1) 86, p. 34-35.
    "Too Klutzy to Dream Myself a Real Ballerina, But." [Bogg] (55) 86, p. 27.
2773. KENDALL, Robert
    "In Her Breasts." [RiverS] (20) 86, p. 50.
    "Sea Variations." [NegC] (6:1) Wint 86, p. 16-17.
2774. KENDIG, Diane
    "Elegy for My Pet, Gerard Turtle Hopkins." [EngJ] (75:3) Mr 86, p. 115.
    "I've Recovered My Tenderness by Long Looking" (Roethke). [HiramPoR] (41)
        Fall-Wint 86-87, p. 33.
    "Notwithstanding" (After James Wright). [HiramPoR] (41) Fall-Wint 86-87, p. 34.
2775. KENDLER, Helene
    "Instruction from the Village Holy Man." [NewL] (52:2/3) Wint-Spr 86, p. 67.
2776. KENNEDY, Chris
    "Gold." [Ploughs] (12:4) 86, p. 174.
    "The Miracle." [Ploughs] (12:4) 86, p. 175.
    "Occlusion in Long Rain" (for my father). [Ploughs] (12:4) 86, p. 176-177.
2777. KENNEDY, Terry
    "After Boot Camp Graduation." [SecC] (14:1) 86, p. 43.
    "Night, Tonight." [Electrum] (38) Spr 86, p. 28.
2778. KENNEDY, X. J.
    "Amazing Grace." [Interim] (5:1) Spr 86, p. 7.

"Epigrams." [Interim] (5:1) Spr 86, p. 8.
2779. KENNEY, Richard
"Richard Eberhart." [NegC] (6:2/3) Spr-Sum 86, p. 45.
2780. KENNY, Adele
"Water from the Moon." [SingHM] (14) 86, p. 12-13.
2781. KENNY, Maurice
"In the Vines" (For Oakley in Wisconsin, At Oneida Nation). [Abraxas] (34) 86, p. 32.
"Molly." [OP] (41) Spr 86, p. 45-46.
"Molly's Likeness (Smallpox)." [OP] (41) Spr 86, p. 47-48.
2782. KENYON, Jane
"April Walk." [VirQR] (62:3) Sum 86, p. 432-433.
"At the Summer Solstice." [Iowa] (16:2) Spr-Sum 86, p. 67.
"Back from the City." [KenR] (NS 7:1) Wint 85, p. 95-96.
"Breakfast at the Mount Washington Hotel." [Iowa] (16:2) Spr-Sum 86, p. 63.
"Deer Season." [Iowa] (16:2) Spr-Sum 86, p. 64.
"The Hermit." [Iowa] (16:2) Spr-Sum 86, p. 64-65.
"Ice Storm." [VirQR] (62:3) Sum 86, p. 431-432.
"Main Street: Tilton, New Hampshire." [VirQR] (62:3) Sum 86, p. 430-431.
"Siesta: Barbados." [KenR] (NS 7:1) Wint 85, p. 95.
"Song." [NewYorker] (62:11) 5 My 86, p. 105.
"Staying at Grandma's." [Ploughs] (12:3) 86, p. 54.
"Sun and Moon" (for Donald Clark). [Iowa] (16:2) Spr-Sum 86, p. 65-66.
"Twilight: After Haying." [KenR] (NS 7:1) Wint 85, p. 94.
"With the Dog at Sunrise" (in memory of Stephen Blos). [Ploughs] (12:3) 86, p. 53.
2783. KENYON, Michael (Michael C.)
"Orange Rind" (for five voices). [CapilR] (39) 86, p. 62-69.
"Pinocchio's Wife." [MalR] (74) Mr 86, p. 39-52.
2784. KEPHART, Andrew J., Jr.
"Whiskey Poem #1" (To Bubba: a Best Friend). [Poem] (56) N 86, p. 39.
2785. KERCHEVAL, Jesse Lee
"De la Photographie." [CapeR] (21:1) Spr 86, p. 1.
"Mama." [BallSUF] (26:4) Aut 85, p. 38.
2786. KERLEY, Gary
"The Moon's Own." [ConnPR] (4:1) 85, p. 27.
2787. KERLIKOWSKE, Elizabeth
"Report from the New World" (found . . . on the blackboard of a Denver elementary school). [PassN] (7:1) Fall-Wint 85-86, p. 24.
"Why I Got Pregnant in 1984." [PennR] (1:1) 85, p. 54.
2788. KERNER, David
"The Tree of Self-Knowledge." [MidwQ] (27:4) Sum 86, p. 468.
2789. KERR, Don
"The Fight for the Family Poet." [AntigR] (66/67) Sum-Aut 86, p. 207-208.
2790. KERSLAKE, Susan
"1969." [PottPort] (8) 86-87, p. 12-13.
2791. KESLER, Russell
"Mr. and Mrs." [FloridaR] (14:2) Fall-Wint 86, p. 41.
"On Two Feet." [FloridaR] (14:2) Fall-Wint 86, p. 40.
2792. KESSLER, Clyde
"Yuan." [DeKalbLAJ] (19:1) 86, p. 35.
2793. KESSLER, Jascha
"Bibliothèque Nationale" (tr. of Kirsti Simonsuuri, w. the author). [Writ] (18) 86, c87, p. 70.
"Dreaming of the Castle" (tr. of Endre Veszi, w. Maria Korosy). [Vis] (22) 86, p. 12.
"E.K.'s Will" (tr. of Sándor Csoóri, w. Maria Körösy). [MissouriR] (9:1) 85-86, p. 197.
"For Bowie" (tr. of Kirsti Simonsuuri, w. the author). [MalR] (77) D 86, p. 46.
"The Glass Hat" (tr. of László Kálnoky, w. Maria Körösy). [LitR] (29:3) Spr 86, p. 356.
"A Headboard to Headboards" (tr. of László Nagy, w. Maria Körösy). [VirQR] (62:2) Spr 86, p. 255-257.
"The Little Jesus of the Barren" (tr. of László Nagy, w. Maria Körösy). [MalR] (75) Je 86, p. 35-36.
"The Little Jesus of the Barren" (tr. of László Nagy, w. Maria Körösy). [VirQR] (62:2) Spr 86, p. 253-254.

"Medusa: Selected Poems" (tr. of Nicolai Kantchev, w. Alexander Shurbanov). [QRL] (Poetry series 6:26) 86, 38 p.
"A Monk" (tr. of Kirsti Simonsuuri, w. the author). [Writ] (18) 86, c87, p. 68.
"Moving" (tr. of Kirsti Simonsuuri, w. the author). [Writ] (18) 86, c87, p. 73.
"Mythos" (tr. of Kirsti Simonsuuri, w. the author). [MalR] (77) D 86, p. 47.
"A Poetry Reading" (tr. of Kirsti Simonsuuri, w. the author). [Writ] (18) 86, c87, p. 71-72.
"Prayer before Turning Off the Light" (tr. of Agnes Gergely, w. Maria Körösy). [NewL] (53:1) Fall 86, p. 25.
"Some Definite Laws" (tr. of Kirsti Simonsuuri, w. the author). [Writ] (18) 86, c87, p. 69.
"Song" (from *Kanteletar*, collected by Lonnrot in the 19th c., tr. of anonymous poem, w. Kirsti Simonsuuri). [MalR] (77) D 86, p. 45.
"Summer, Haloed" (tr. of Sándor Csoöri, w. Maria Körösy). [MissouriR] (9:1) 85-86, p. 195.
"Sunday before Christmas" (tr. of Sándor Csoöri, w. Maria Körösy). [MissouriR] (9:1) 85-86, p. 196.
"Taproot" (tr. of Otto Orban, w. Maria Körösy). [MalR] (77) D 86, p. 79.
"Taproot" (tr. of Ottó Orbán, w. Maria Körösy). [MichQR] (25:1) Wint 86, p. 103-104.
"There Is No Southern Island" (tr. László Nagy, w. Maria Körösy). [LitR] (29:2) Wint 86, p. 208.
"Travelling Light" (tr. of Kirsti Simonsuuri, w. the author). [Writ] (18) 86, c87, p. 67.
"You Were Still the Sun's There" (tr. of Sándor Csoöri, w. Maria Körösy). [MissouriR] (9:1) 85-86, p. 194.
2794. KESSLER, Rod
"Apartheid." [Ploughs] (12:4) 86, p. 191-192.
"Fall Term, the Course Begins." [Interim] (5:1) Spr 86, p. 35.
2795. KESTIN, Leslie
"A.M. Rebeccaspitpark." [Writ] (17) 85, c86, p. 20.
"It's a Fairly Long Way to Gordonsville." [Writ] (17) 85, c86, p. 19-20.
"Tale of a Thousand Grandmothers." [Writ] (17) 85, c86, p. 18.
KETHLEY, Fiona Pitt
See PITT-KETHLEY, Fiona
2796. KEVAN, Martin
"Congratulations." [CanLit] (108) Spr 86, p. 59-60.
2797. KEWLEY, Dorothea
"Defrosting the Refrigerator." [WindO] (47) Sum 86, p. 30.
"A Sunday Morning Bus Ride." [WindO] (47) Sum 86, p. 30.
2798. KEYES, Claire
"Subterranean." [PassN] (7:2) Spr-Sum 86, p. 14.
2799. KHLEBNIKOV, Velimir
"On Swan Land" (tr. by Paul Schmidt). [Temblor] (4) 86, p. 84-88.
2800. KHOSLA, Maya
"City K." [InterPR] (12:2) Fall 86, p. 98.
"Friends." [InterPR] (12:2) Fall 86, p. 99.
2801. KICKNOSWAY, Faye
"The Bed He Dreamed Himself Into." [OntR] (24) Spr-Sum 86, p. 40-42.
2802. KIDDER, Cheryl
"Autumn Piece 1." [Amelia] (3:4) Fall 86, p. 90.
"Autumn Piece 2." [Amelia] (3:4) Fall 86, p. 90.
2803. KIEFER, Rita (Rita B.)
"Ilse's Poem." [AntigR] (66/67) Sum-Aut 86, p. 245.
"Snow White." [CrossCur] (5:4/6:1) 86, p. 119.
"Switchbacks." [Ploughs] (12:4) 86, p. 149-152.
"Torn Photo." [AntigR] (66/67) Sum-Aut 86, p. 244.
2804. KIERNAN, Rebecca Lu
"Canopy." [Amelia] (3:1) Ja 86, p. 88.
"September, Brighton." [Amelia] (3:1) Ja 86, p. 88.
2805. KIJEWSKI, Bruce
"The Unpronounceable Face of God." [Jacaranda] (2:1) Fall 86, p. 29-30.
2806. KIKUCHI, Carl
"Cancer." [PaintedB] (28) Ap 86, p. 73.
"Prenatal." [PassN] (7:2) Spr-Sum 86, p. 20.

203

KILGOREKILGORE

2807. KILGORE, James C.
"She Told Me." [Obs] (NS 1:1/2) Spr-Sum 86, p. 77.
"Where No Rainbow Had Hung for Years." [Obs] (NS 1:1/2) Spr-Sum 86, p. 76.
2808. KILLIAN, Kevin
"The Push." [JamesWR] (3:4) Sum 86, p. 10.
2809. KIM, Myung Mi
"The Days She Came To." [AntR] (44:3) Sum 86, p. 328.
"Pleasure As Steadfast." [AntR] (44:3) Sum 86, p. 327.
2810. KIM, Will Yee
"In this heat" ("Untitled"). [Contact] (7:38/39/40) Wint-Spr 86, p. 33.
2811. KIMBALL, Arthur
"Hiroshige's 'Hiratsuka: Path through a Paddy Field'." [SmPd] (23:2, issue 67) Spr
    86, p. 19.
"Tsuyu (Rainy Season)." [CrabCR] (3:3) Sum 86, p. 4.
2812. KIMBALL, Karen
"He looks in the distance for his destination" (tr. of Pentii Saarikoski, w. Michael
    Cole). [Chelsea] (45) 86, p. 124.
"The wind is coming up" (tr. of Pentii Saarikoski, w. Michael Cole). [Chelsea] (45)
    86, p. 125.
"The world's idea that you can see the world" (tr. of Pentti Saarikoski, w. Michael
    Cole). [WebR] (11:1) Spr 86, p. 29.
2813. KIME, Peter
"From a Younger Brother." [Ascent] (11:2) 86, p. 39.
2814. KIMMET, Gene
"Night Runner." [PikeF] (7) Spr 86, p. 23.
"Ohio Foundry." [PikeF] (7) Spr 86, p. 12.
"Pictures in a Cherry County Museum." [SpoonRQ] (11:4) Fall 86, p. 40.
2815. KIMRON, Eliahn
"The night is falling, filtering in from Jordan" (tr. by Will Kirkland). [NewOR]
    (13:4) Wint 86, p. 39.
2816. KINCAID, Joan Payne
"Small Audience." [PoeticJ] (16) Fall 86, p. 14.
2817. KING, Dean
"On a Warm Night." [Sam] (46:2 release 182) 86, p. 50-51.
2818. KING, Kenneth
"The House of Laryngitis." [PoetryNW] (27:1) Spr 86, p. 20.
2819. KING, Lyn
"A Man Like You." [MalR] (75) Je 86, p. 16-23.
2820. KING, R. D.
"Blue Shoes Downtown." [NowestR] (24:2) 86, p. 12.
"Jazz Nebraska." [NowestR] (24:2) 86, p. 11.
2821. KING, Robert
"April in a Northern Latitude." [CapeR] (21:1) Spr 86, p. 50.
"Brief." [BellR] (2:6) N-D 86, p. 2.
"The Car at the Edge of the Woods." [NoDaQ] (54:2) Spr 86, p. 143.
"Ornamental Fish." [BellArk] (2:5) S-O 86, p. 6.
"What I Was Thinking About" (for Robin). [BellArk] (2:5) S-O 86, p. 4.
2822. KING, Robert S.
"If God Permits." [KenR] (NS 7:3) Sum 85, p. 102.
"The Juggler Tells His Children of Dreams." [NegC] (6:4) Fall 86, p. 112.
"A Wingbeat of Hope." [KenR] (NS 7:3) Sum 85, p. 101.
2823. KING, Susan Deborah
"Quilts." [PraS] (60:3) Fall 86, p. 68.
2824. KING-EDWARDS, Lucille
"Blue Lake Graveyard." [CapilR] (39) 86, p. 11-12.
"Entre Chien et Loup." [CapilR] (39) 86, p. 13.
2825. KINKEAD, Joyce
"Computer Expert." [EngJ] (75:6) O 86, p. 68.
2826. KINNE, Kaci
"Elegy: Tom's Rape." [SingHM] (13) 86, p. 89.
2827. KINNELL, Galway
"Last Holy Fragrance" (In Memoriam James Wright). [KenR] (NS 7:4) Fall 85, p.
    15-17.
2828. KINSELLA, Thomas
"It Is Well for Small Birds" (tr. of Gaelic folk poetry, from *Poems of the
    Dispossessed*). [ManhatR] (4:1) Fall 86, p. 61.

"My Own Dark Head" (tr. of Gaelic folk poetry, from *Poems of the Dispossessed*).
[ManhatR] (4:1) Fall 86, p. 61.
"Remember That Night" (tr. of Gaelic folk poetry, from *Poems of the
Dispossessed*). [ManhatR] (4:1) Fall 86, p. 62.
"Songs of the Psyche" (Selections: I, VIII, XIII, "Brotherhood," "Talent and
Friendship"). [ManhatR] (4:1) Fall 86, p. 57-60.
2829. KINSOLVING, Susan
"Cubes on a Curve." [GrandS] (5:2) Wint 86, p. 201.
"Off Standard Time." [AntR] (44:4) Fall 86, p. 430.
2830. KINZE, Reiner
"In the Blue Signature of the Ice Bird" (Poems in German & English, tr. by Thomas
Edwards, assisted by Ulrike Aitenbichler and Ken Letko). [MidAR] (7:1) 86,
p. 73-101.
2831. KINZIE, Mary
"Catacomb" (To the gentlemen of the Universal Library, Reclam Verlag, Stuttgart).
[Shen] (36:3) 86, p. 47.
"Elegiacs for the Old Year." [SouthwR] (71:2) Spr 86, p. 204-205.
"The Fables" (after the drawing by Virgil Burnett). [SouthernR] (22:1) Ja 86, p.
131-132.
"A Note Correcting the Hour for Dinner" (after a theme by Christopher Boffey).
[SouthernR] (22:1) Ja 86, p. 132.
"Tar Roof." [SouthwR] (71:2) Spr 86, p. 204.
2832. KIRBY, David
"Complicity." [KanQ] (18:1/2) Wint-Spr 86, p. 111.
"Fathers and Sons." [KanQ] (18:1/2) Wint-Spr 86, p. 110-111.
"You Can't Always Get What You Want." [MidAR] (6:1) 86?, p. 18.
2833. KIRCHDORFER, Ulf
"Mountain Village of Belief." [Pax] (3:1/2) Wint 85-86, p. 74.
2834. KIRCHER, Pamela
"The Intimate Earth." [GeoR] (40:3) Fall 86, p. 702.
2835. KIRCHHOFF, Steve
"Homage to an Unknown Self." [LitR] (29:2) Wint 86, p. 194.
2836. KIRK, James
"Cows in Snow." [Ploughs] (12:3) 86, p. 114-115.
2837. KIRKLAND, Will
"The 39 Prohibitions for Saturday" (tr. of Frances H. Melziner). [NewOR] (13:4)
Wint 86, p. 34.
"Ballad of a Sabra" (tr. of Gustav Fleishman). [NewOR] (13:4) Wint 86, p. 42.
"The Fool, Let them say what they want" (tr. of Amin Ibn Ibrahim Al-Attar).
[NewOR] (13:4) Wint 86, p. 29.
"I am neither Arab nor Jew" (tr. of anonymous Palestinian Song). [NewOR] (13:4)
Wint 86, p. 28.
"I have come this far" (tr. of Manoce Mohrenwitz). [NewOR] (13:4) Wint 86, p. 32.
"Jehova, if you exist, make the earth turn faster" (tr. of Sigmund Baginsky).
[NewOR] (13:4) Wint 86, p. 33.
"A man says: sweet" (tr. of Ali Fakum Nazzar). [NewOR] (13:4) Wint 86, p. 27.
"The Mirror" (tr. of Frances H. Melziner). [NewOR] (13:4) Wint 86, p. 35.
"The night is falling, filtering in from Jordan" (tr. of Eliahn Kimron). [NewOR]
(13:4) Wint 86, p. 39.
"Night time still" (tr. of Salomon Chavsky). [NewOR] (13:4) Wint 86, p. 30.
"They offered us some of the finest sites in the world" (tr. of Issac Kaplan).
[NewOR] (13:4) Wint 86, p. 40-41.
"To Yevgeny Yevtushenko" (tr. of Selomo Weitzel (Jasper Reid)). [NewOR] (13:4)
Wint 86, p. 37.
"We can argue about whether I am a Jew or an Israeli" (Anonymous dialogue,
translated from the Ladino). [NewOR] (13:4) Wint 86, p. 36.
"What am I?" (tr. of Ibn Al-Arrafat). [NewOR] (13:4) Wint 86, p. 38.
"Yes, certainly the land you offer me is better, richer than my own" (tr. of Ibn Musa
Amir). [NewOR] (13:4) Wint 86, p. 31.
2838. KIRKUP, James
"The Ancient Pine Tree on Mt. Tempai" (tr. of Hitoshi Anzai, w. Akiko Takemoto).
[Translation] (17) Fall 86, p. 116.
"Appetite" (tr. of Sachiko Yoshihara, w. Akiko Takemoto). [Translation] (17) Fall
86, p. 207.
"At a Cannery" (tr. of Katsuko Nishio, w. Akiko Takemoto). [Translation] (17) Fall
86, p. 202.

205

"A Dirge" (tr. of Chimako Tada, w. Akiko Takemoto). [Translation] (17) Fall 86, p. 203.
"Do Not Get Up" (tr. of Takuboku Ishikawa, w. Akiko Takemoto). [Translation] (17) Fall 86, p. 186.
"Early Winter" (tr. of Mokuo Nagayama, w. Akiko Takemoto). [Translation] (17) Fall 86, p. 209.
"The Electric Car" (tr. of Masao Nakagiri, w. Akiko Takemoto). [Translation] (17) Fall 86, p. 199.
"Emperor" (tr. of Ryuichi Tamura, w. Akiko Takemoto). [Translation] (17) Fall 86, p. 201.
"Ennui" (tr. of Heiichi Sugiyama, w. Akiko Takemoto). [Translation] (17) Fall 86, p. 197.
"Fist" (tr. of Takuboku Ishikawa, w. Akiko Takemoto). [Translation] (17) Fall 86, p. 187.
"Frozen Love" (tr. of Mokuo Nagayama, w. Akiko Takemoto). [Translation] (17) Fall 86, p. 208.
"Going Down" (tr. of Heiichi Sugiyama, w. Akiko Takemoto). [Translation] (17) Fall 86, p. 198.
"The Governor" (tr. of Shigeharu Nakano, w. Akiko Takemoto). [Translation] (17) Fall 86, p. 194.
"Gray Gulls" (tr. of Tatsuji Miyoshi, w. Akiko Takemoto). [Translation] (17) Fall 86, p. 192-193.
"High-Pressure Chart" (tr. of Jun Honda, w. Akiko Takemoto). [Translation] (17) Fall 86, p. 210-211.
"How to Cook Women" (tr. of Kyozo Takagi, w. Michio Nakano). [Translation] (17) Fall 86, p. 33.
"Monstrous Fish" (tr. of Tozaburo Ono, w. Akiko Takemoto). [Translation] (17) Fall 86, p. 196.
"Mount Fuji" (tr. of Mitsuharu Kaneko, w. Akiko Takemoto). [Translation] (17) Fall 86, p. 188-189.
"My Eye" (tr. of Hitoshi Anzai, w. Akiko Takemoto). [Translation] (17) Fall 86, p. 115.
"My Father" (tr. of Jukichi Yagi, w. Akiko Takemoto). [Translation] (17) Fall 86, p. 191.
"The Name" (tr. of Sachiko Yoshihara, w. Akiko Takemoto). [Translation] (17) Fall 86, p. 206.
"Never Bind Me" (tr. of Kazue Shinkawa, w. Akiko Takemoto). [Translation] (17) Fall 86, p. 204-205.
"One Day" (tr. of Jukichi Yagi, w. Akiko Takemoto). [Translation] (17) Fall 86, p. 190.
"Overhang" (tr. of Mokuo Nagayama, w. Akiko Takemoto). [Translation] (17) Fall 86, p. 209.
"Rain" (tr. of Jukichi Yagi, w. Akiko Takemoto). [Translation] (17) Fall 86, p. 191.
"A Skyline — New Year's Day" (tr. of Kyozo Takagi, w. Michio Nakano). [Translation] (17) Fall 86, p. 32.
"Snowy Night" (tr. of Kyozo Takagi, w. Michio Nakano). [Translation] (17) Fall 86, p. 31.
"Sorrow" (tr. of Jukichi Yagi, w. Akiko Takemoto). [Translation] (17) Fall 86, p. 190.
"Sorrow Piling Up Within Me" (tr. of Jukichi Yagi, w. Akiko Takemoto). [Translation] (17) Fall 86, p. 190.
"A Thought in Autumn" (tr. of Nobuo Ayukawa, w. Akiko Takemoto). [Translation] (17) Fall 86, p. 200.
"To the Sea" (tr. of Kyozo Takagi, w. Michio Nakano). [Translation] (17) Fall 86, p. 34.
"Tomorrow" (tr. of Tozaburo Ono, w. Akiko Takemoto). [Translation] (17) Fall 86, p. 195.
"Whale Spouting" (tr. of Kotaro Takamura, w. Akiko Takemoto). [Translation] (17) Fall 86, p. 184-185.
2839. KIRSCH, Sarah
"Breather" (tr. by Marina Roscher and Charles Fishman). [Vis] (22) 86, p. 11.
"Gentle Fright" (tr. by Marina Roscher and Charles Fishman). [HolCrit] (23:5) D 86, p. 14.
"Rainy Season" (tr. by Marina Roscher and Charles Fishman). [Vis] (22) 86, p. 11.
2840. KIRSTEIN, Lincoln
"Buttons." [ParisR] (28:99) Spr 86, p. 39-41.

"Hustler." [ParisR] (28:99) Spr 86, p. 28-30.
"Interview." [Raritan] (5:3) Wint 86, p. 76-78.
"Look, Ma! I'm Dancing!" [ParisR] (28:99) Spr 86, p. 35-38.
"Sunny Jim." [ParisR] (28:99) Spr 86, p. 33-34.
"Taxi." [ParisR] (28:99) Spr 86, p. 31-32.
2841. KITCHEN, Judith
    "Perennials." [GeoR] (40:3) Fall 86, p. 703-704.
2842. KITSON, Herb
    "Velvet Thoughts." [NegC] (6:1) Wint 86, p. 94.
2843. KITTELL, Linda
    "Along the Blackfoot." [CarolQ] (38:3) Spr 86, p. 36-37.
2844. KITTELL, Ronald Edward
    "O Give Me Something to Live For." [RagMag] (5:2) Fall 86, p. 20.
    "Shadows." [YetASM] (4) 85, p. 2.
2845. KIWUS, Karin
    "Alienation Through Work" (tr. by Christopher Middleton). [SouthernHR] (20:2)
        Spr 86, p. 156-157.
2846. KIZER, Carolyn
    "?.!" (tr. of Shu Ting). [Zyzzyva] (2:2) Sum 86, p. 56-57.
    "Crime and Punishment." [TarRP] (25:2) Spr 86, p. 8.
    "Final Meeting." [MichQR] (25:4) Fall 86, p. 655-656.
    "Horseback" (for Raymond Carver). [Shen] (36:2) 86, p. 50-51.
    "Not Writing Poems About Children." [WebR] (11:2) Fall 86, p. 89-90.
    "On the Way Back" (tr. of Bogomil Gjuzel, w. the author). [WillowS] (17) Wint 86,
        p. 72.
    "Pearl." [Poetry] (148:6) S 86, p. 318-320.
    "Prostitution" (tr. of Bogomil Gjuzel, w. the author). [WillowS] (17) Wint 86, p.
        73.
    "Rebellion" (tr. of Han Yu, 768-824 A.D.). [TarRP] (25:2) Spr 86, p. 8-9.
    "Threatening Letter." [WebR] (11:2) Fall 86, p. 94-95.
    "To an Unknown Poet." [MichQR] (25:4) Fall 86, p. 657-658.
    "Translation" (for Lars Gustafsson). [TarRP] (25:2) Spr 86, p. 7.
    "When I Came Back" (tr. of Bogomil Gjuzel, w. the author). [WillowS] (17) Wint
        86, p. 71.
2847. KLAUSE, Annette Curtis
    "The Ambassador Speaks of Courtship on Zinnia." [Vis] (20) 86, p. 13.
2848. KLAVAN, Andrew
    "Cumberland Island." [Amelia] (3:1) Ja 86, p. 63-64.
    "Mengele." [SouthernPR] (26:2) Fall 86, p. 30.
    "Morning Meditation." [Amelia] (3:1) Ja 86, p. 63.
2849. KLEIN, Jim
    "1940-1980." [WormR] (26:4, issue 104) 86, p. 128.
    "An Exquisite Ombré Effect." [WormR] (26:4, issue 104) 86, p. 131.
    "Grandfather." [WormR] (26:4, issue 104) 86, p. 127.
    "Imagine German Beachcombers." [WormR] (26:4, issue 104) 86, p. 128-129.
    "In One of My Mother's Tiny Pictures." [WormR] (26:4, issue 104) 86, p. 128.
    "Inarticulate People." [WormR] (26:4, issue 104) 86, p. 129-130.
    "My Daughter Asks If I Have a Philosophy." [WormR] (26:4, issue 104) 86, p.
        129.
    "Paulina." [NoDaQ] (54:2) Spr 86, p. 144.
    "Travel." [WormR] (26:4, issue 104) 86, p. 130-131.
2850. KLEINSCHMIDT, Edward
    "Commas in Comas." [KanQ] (18:1/2) Wint-Spr 86, p. 109.
    "December Poem." [LitR] (29:3) Spr 86, p. 285.
    "Equinox." [Confr] (32) Spr-Sum 86, p. 113.
    "How Now Brown Cow." [LittleM] (15:2) 86, p. 52.
    "Many Windows." [LittleM] (15:2) 86, p. 50.
    "Organon." [LittleM] (15:2) 86, p. 51-52.
    "To Sleep." [KanQ] (18:1/2) Wint-Spr 86, p. 109.
    "University of Iowa Hospital, 1976." [Poetry] (147:6) Mr 86, p. 333-334.
    "Watching the Geese Storm the Summertime." [LittleM] (15:2) 86, p. 53.
    "Winter Fathers, 1963." [Poetry] (147:6) Mr 86, p. 331.
    "Without Thinking." [Poetry] (147:6) Mr 86, p. 332.
2851. KLEINZAHLER, August
    "The Fourth of July." [Ploughs] (12:1/2) 86, p. 154-155.
    "Pinned." [Zyzzyva] (2:3) Fall 86, p. 77.

207

"What It Takes." [Thrpny] (26) Sum 86, p. 17.
2852. KLEPETAR, Steve
"The Weary Man Attends a Conference." [LitR] (29:3) Spr 86, p. 290-291.
"The Weary Man Meets Medusa." [Poem] (56) N 86, p. 47.
"The Weary Man Speaks of His Hair." [Poem] (56) N 86, p. 44.
"The Weary Man Turns." [Poem] (56) N 86, p. 46.
"The Weary Man's Skywriting." [Poem] (56) N 86, p. 45.
2853. KLEPFISZ, Irena
"Di Rayze Aheym / The Journey Home." [SinW] (29/30) 86, p. 49-52.
"Etlekhe Verter oyf Mame-Loshn / A Few Words in the Mother Tongue." [SinW] (29/30) 86, p. 77-78.
"Fradel Schtok." [SinW] (29/30) 86, p. 152-153.
2854. KLINGSOR, Tristan
"In the Kingdom of Moles: Death" (tr. by Dorothy Aspinwall). [WebR] (11:2) Fall 86, p. 25.
2855. KLOEFKORN, William
"At the Red Lion Tavern, Saturday Night." [SpoonRQ] (11:4) Fall 86, p. 4-5.
"Country Western" (for Jenny Wood). [SpoonRQ] (11:4) Fall 86, p. 6.
"Cycle." [TarRP] (25:2) Spr 86, p. 22-23.
"Distances." [CarolQ] (39:1) Fall 86, p. 49.
"Eating Prime Rib Shortly After Being Advised to Stay the Hell Away from All Red Meat." [SpoonRQ] (11:4) Fall 86, p. 8.
"A Feeling of Generosity." [TarRP] (25:2) Spr 86, p. 21-22.
"Gathering Eggs." [SpoonRQ] (11:4) Fall 86, p. 7.
"Learning It." [WestB] (18) 86, p. 56.
"Nebraska, Early March" (for Eloise Ann). [PraS] (60:2) Sum 86, p. 117.
"Summer 1946." [WestB] (18) 86, p. 58-59.
"Swapping Gum." [WestB] (18) 86, p. 57-58.
"Taking the Milk to Grandmother." [GeoR] (40:3) Fall 86, p. 705-706.
"Two Older People Petting Heavily in a Parked Car." [SpoonRQ] (11:4) Fall 86, p. 9.
"Up to Omaha" (for Boley Crawford). [SpoonRQ] (11:4) Fall 86, p. 2-3.
"Vegas." [SpoonRQ] (11:4) Fall 86, p. 1.
"You Have Lived Long Enough." [SoDakR] (24:2) Sum 86, p. 33.
2856. KLOSE, Robert T.
"The Dance of Gideon Wechselstrom." [BelPoJ] (36:3) Spr 86, p. 20-21.
2857. KLUTTS, Randy
"New Mall Restaurant." [Bogg] (56) 86, p. 27.
2858. KNAUTH, Stephen
"Andromeda." [ManhatPR] (6) Wint-Spr 85-86, p. 26.
"Sledding." [Puerto] (22:1) Fall 86, p. 50-51.
2859. KNICKERBOCKER, Harry E.
"Night Wind in Arroyo Hondo." [Amelia] (3:4) Fall 86, p. 103.
2860. KNIGHT, Arthur Winfield
"Dawn." [Wind] (16:57) 86, p. 17.
"Empty Spaces." [WormR] (26:1, issue 101) 86, p. 33.
"Giant Steps." [SpoonRQ] (11:2) Spr 86, p. 43.
"Little Agonies." [WormR] (26:1, issue 101) 86, p. 32.
"The Power of Prayer." [Wind] (16:57) 86, p. 16.
"Spanish Fly." [SlipS] (6) 86, p. 68-69.
"The Subway." [Bogg] (55) 86, p. 36.
"Too Late." [YetASM] (4) 85, p. 5.
"Unreal Things." [SpoonRQ] (11:2) Spr 86, p. 44-45.
"Where Dreams Come True." [Amelia] (3:1) Ja 86, p. 69-70.
2861. KNIGHT, Cranston Sedrick
"Tour of Duty: Vietnam in the Words of Those Who Were There" (edited by C. S. Knight). [Sam] (46:2 release 182) 86, 135 p.
2862. KNIGHT, Etheridge
"Circling the Daughter" (for Tandi). [PaintedB] (28) Ap 86, p. 43.
"Eat Helen B Happy" (a found poem). [AmerPoR] (15:4) Jl-Ag 86, p. 31.
"Genesis II." [AmerPoR] (15:4) Jl-Ag 86, p. 31.
"On the Removal of the Fascist American Right from Power." [AmerPoR] (15:4) Jl-Ag 86, p. 31.
"Sigh, cry, broken hearted." [AmerPoR] (15:4) Jl-Ag 86, p. 31.
"Various Protestations from Various People." [PaintedB] (28) Ap 86, p. 42.

2863. KNIGHT, Kit
"Betrayal." [WormR] (26:1, issue 101) 86, p. 14-15.
2864. KNOEPFLE, John
"Kickapoo Burial, Remembrance South of Ellsworth, Illinois." [PikeF] (7) Spr 86,
p. 18.
"Kickapoo Dance." [PikeF] (7) Spr 86, p. 18.
2865. KNOLL, John
"Trinity." [Sam] (46:2 release 182) 86, p. 101.
2866. KNOTT, Bill
"Childhood: the Offense of History." [Caliban] (1) 86, p. 1-2.
"I Meet an Andy." [Caliban] (1) 86, p. 1.
"Title: Free Me or Worship Me." [Caliban] (1) 86, p. 2.
"Vague Consoles." [Caliban] (1) 86, p. 3.
2867. KNOX, Ann B.
"Freight." [CumbPR] (5:2) Spr 86, p. 40.
"A New Language." [CumbPR] (5:2) Spr 86, p. 41-42.
2868. KNOX, Caroline
"The Stone Calendar." [NewRep] (195:5) 4 Ag 86, p. 38.
2869. KOCH, Kenneth
"Impressions of Africa" (Selections: "1/Madagascar. Subcontinent," "5/Kenya.
Savanna"). [Boulevard] (1:1/2) Wint 86, p. 64-88.
2870. KOEHN-HEINE, Lala
"Letter to an Exile" (For Halinka Kopkowicz-Kostyra and my People). [GreenfR]
(13:3/4) Sum-Fall 86, p. 90-91.
2871. KOEHNE, Tom
"House of the Grieving Dogs" (Exceprt, tr. of Ryu Kazuo, w. the author). [CarolQ]
(38:2) Wint 86, p. 64.
2872. KOERNER, Edgar
"Blind." [ManhatPR] (7) Sum 86, p. 31.
"Grandfather Ernst at Ebbets Field." [ManhatPR] (6) Wint-Spr 85-86, p. 49.
"Prince Genji in Massachusetts" (for Eileen). [ManhatPR] (7) Sum 86, p. 30.
2873. KOERTGE, Ron
"Getaway." [WormR] (26:3, issue 103) 86, p. 110-111.
"Girl Talk." [WormR] (26:3, issue 103) 86, p. 113-114.
"If You Lived Here You'd Be Home Now." [WormR] (26:3, issue 103) 86, p. 115.
"I'm Amazed." [WormR] (26:3, issue 103) 86, p. 111-112.
"Just Imagine That Jesus Were With You" (— my Sunday School teacher).
[WormR] (26:3, issue 103) 86, p. 112.
"Missing Persons." [WormR] (26:3, issue 103) 86, p. 112-113.
"Obsessed with Sex" (— a critic). [WormR] (26:3, issue 103) 86, p. 114.
"Rapunzel." [WormR] (26:3, issue 103) 86, p. 114-115.
"Some Say I Ran Guns to Cuban Rebels." [WormR] (26:3, issue 103) 86, p. 111.
"What a Varied Place the World Is, How Trusting and Strange, So Deserving of
Love and Praise." [WormR] (26:3, issue 103) 86, p. 110.
2874. KOESTENBAUM, Wayne
"A Limousine for Auden." [Confr] (33/34) Fall-Wint 86-87, p. 176.
"The Moving Occupations" (after seeing Caravaggio's "Bacchus"). [Shen] (36:3) 86,
p. 48-49.
"Tea Dance." [Epoch] (35:2) 86-87, p. 206-209.
"A Visit." [MissouriR] (9:1) 85-86, p. 125.
"Where I Lived, and What I Lived For." [BostonR] (11:3) Je 86, p. 4.
2875. KOGAWA, Joy
"Fish Poem." [GreenfR] (13:3/4) Sum-Fall 86, p. 93.
"July in Coaldale." [Contact] (7:38/39/40) Wint-Spr 86, p. 49.
"Minerals from Stone." [GreenfR] (13:3/4) Sum-Fall 86, p. 93.
"My Father's Poem." [Contact] (7:38/39/40) Wint-Spr 86, p. 49.
2876. KOHLER, Sandra
"What the Children Say." [PaintedB] (28) Ap 86, p. 13.
2877. KOLLAR, Sybil
"The Nap." [Confr] (33/34) Fall-Wint 86-87, p. 161.
2878. KOLODZIEJ, Krysia
"Keeping Time in Avignon." [LindLM] (5:1) Ja-Mr 86, p. 27.
"Oracle Bones Rattle Me Awake" (V). [LindLM] (5:4) O-D 86, p. 19.
2879. KOLOTKAR, Arun Balkrishna
"Ajamil and the Tigers." [LitR] (29:4) Sum 86, p. 454-455.

209

2880. KOLUMBAN, Nicholas
"A Native Tourist in Hungary." [LindLM] (5:4) O-D 86, p. 19.
2881. KOMACHI, Ono no
"The cherry blossoms fade." [YellowS] (18) Spr 86, p. 33.
"On such a dark night he will not come." [YellowS] (18) Spr 86, p. 33.
"This inn on the road to Iwanoue." [YellowS] (18) Spr 86, p. 43.
2882. KOMUNYAKAA, Yusef
"Boy Wearing a Dead Man's Clothes." [Callaloo] (9:1, #26) Wint 86, p. 81-82.
"The Brain to the Heart." [ColR] (NS 13:1) Fall 85, p. 35.
"Camouflaging the Chimera." [AmerV] (4) Fall 86, p. 40-41.
"Communiqué." [Callaloo] (9:1, #26) Wint 86, p. 83-84.
"Crescent City Blues" (Excerpt). [Callaloo] (9:2, #27) Spr 86, p. 301.
"How I See Things." [MissouriR] (9:1) 85-86, p. 120-121.
"Jonestown: More Eyes for *Jadwiga's Dream*" (after Rousseau). [NewOR] (13:1)
Spr 86, p. 19.
"Lightshow." [Callaloo] (9:1, #26) Wint 86, p. 86.
"Nothing Big." [Callaloo] (9:1, #26) Wint 86, p. 85.
"A Song the Gong Makes, a Question the Wind Asks." [ColR] (NS 13:1) Fall 85, p.
34.
"Too Pretty for Serious Business." [MissouriR] (9:1) 85-86, p. 122.
"Two Cranial Murals." [Callaloo] (9:2, #27) Spr 86, p. 300.
2883. KONCZEK, József
"The Olive Bush" (tr. by Timothy Kachinske). [ColR] (NS 13:1) Fall 85, p. 42.
2884. KONG, Ann
"The Seal." [Amelia] (3:1) Ja 86, p. 10.
2885. KOONTZ, Tom
"Family Portrait: Summer 1945." [SpoonRQ] (11:4) Fall 86, p. 15.
2886. KOOSER, Ted
"Just Now." [GeoR] (40:3) Fall 86, p. 707.
"Territories" (A Correspondence with Leonard Nathan: 8 poems). [PraS] (60:3) Fall
86, p. 101-105.
2887. KOPPERL, Helga
"The Thing You Love Most" (in the voice of William Burroughs). [HayF] (1) Spr
86, p. 41-43.
2888. KOROSY, Maria
"Dreaming of the Castle" (tr. of Endre Veszi, w. Jascha Kessler). [Vis] (22) 86, p.
12.
"E.K.'s Will" (tr. of Sándor Csoöri, w. Jascha Kessler). [MissouriR] (9:1) 85-86,
p. 197.
"The Glass Hat" (tr. of László Kálnoky, w. Jascha Kessler). [LitR] (29:3) Spr 86,
p. 356.
"A Headboard to Headboards" (tr. of László Nagy, w. Jascha Kessler). [VirQR]
(62:2) Spr 86, p. 255-257.
"The Little Jesus of the Barren" (tr. of László Nagy, w. Jascha Kessler). [MalR]
(75) Je 86, p. 35-36.
"The Little Jesus of the Barren" (tr. of László Nagy, w. Jascha Kessler). [VirQR]
(62:2) Spr 86, p. 253-254.
"Prayer before Turning Off the Light" (tr. of Agnes Gergely, w. Jascha Kessler).
[NewL] (53:1) Fall 86, p. 25.
"Summer, Haloed" (tr. of Sándor Csoöri, w. Jascha Kessler). [MissouriR] (9:1)
85-86, p. 195.
"Sunday before Christmas" (tr. of Sándor Csoöri, w. Jascha Kessler). [MissouriR]
(9:1) 85-86, p. 196.
"Taproot" (tr. of Otto Orban, w. Jascha Kessler). [MalR] (77) D 86, p. 79.
"Taproot" (tr. of Ottó Orbán, w. Jascha Kessler). [MichQR] (25:1) Wint 86, p.
103-104.
"There Is No Southern Island" (tr. László Nagy, w. Jascha Kessler). [LitR] (29:2)
Wint 86, p. 208.
"You Were Still the Sun's There" (tr. of Sándor Csoöri, w. Jascha Kessler).
[MissouriR] (9:1) 85-86, p. 194.
2889. KORSMO, Fae L.
"In Charlottesville." [CrabCR] (3:3) Sum 86, p. 28.
2890. KORT, Ellen
"I Sing My Name Around the Moon." [RagMag] (5:2) Fall 86, p. 23-25.
2891. KOSER, Ted
"A Poetry Reading." [PraS] (60:2) Sum 86, p. 118.

2892. KOST, Holly Hunt
"A Housewife Thinks of Damascus." [SouthernR] (22:1) Ja 86, p. 153-154.
"Lines on the Delta: Where the Worst Isn't Always Over." [SouthernR] (22:1) Ja 86,
p. 152-153.
2893. KOSTELANETZ, Richard
"Duets, Trios, & Choruses" (Excerpt). [ConnPR] (4:1) 85, p. 31.
"Lovings" (Selections). [CentralP] (9) Spr 86, p. 8-15.
"Sketchy Stories" (To be read as a whole, or in parts, in any order). [NewL] (53:1)
Fall 86, p. 33-35.
"Wasting." [Rampike] (5:1) 86, p. 20.
2894. KOSZTOLANYI, Dezsö
"Autumn Breakfast" (tr. by Clive Wilmer and George Gömöri). [Verse] (5) 86, p.
55.
KOTARO, Takamura
See TAKAMURA, Kotaro
2895. KOTARY, Judith
"The Catfish Song." [BelPoJ] (36:3) Spr 86, p. 3.
"Heads." [BelPoJ] (36:3) Spr 86, p. 2-3.
2896. KOTZIN, Miriam N.
"Lois Lane Courts Death." [Boulevard] (1:3) Fall 86, p. 88.
"Lycanthropy." [Boulevard] (1:1/2) Wint 86, p. 168-169.
2897. KOVACIC, Kristin
"Flooding Pittsburgh, 1985." [WestB] (18) 86, p. 96-97.
2898. KOVACS, Steven
"Second Eclogue" (tr. of Miklos Radnoti). [RedBass] (11) 86, p. 26.
2899. KOVNER, Abba
"Changing the Order" (tr. by Shirley Kaufman, w. Dan Laor). [PoetL] (81:2) Sum
86, p. 72-73.
"Everyone Who Comes" (tr. by Shirley Kaufman, w. Dan Laor). [PoetL] (81:2)
Sum 86, p. 73-74.
"Falling Rocks" (tr. by Shirley Kaufman). [Field] (34) Spr 86, p. 9-17.
"On the Way" (tr. by Shirley Kaufman, w. Dan Laor). [PoetL] (81:2) Sum 86, p.
74.
2900. KOWAL, Fedorio
"De este lado de la luz me quedo solo." [Mairena] (8:21) 86, p. 99.
2901. KOWIT, Steve
"Jack Kerouac Died." [MoodySI] (16/17) Sum 86, p. 40.
2902. KOZAK, Roberta
"Wheat Ears." [OhioR] (36) 86, p. 34-35.
2903. KOZER, José
"La Evidencia (1)." [Mairena] (8:22) 86, p. 39.
2904. KRAFT, Kelley
"Racers." [RagMag] (5:2) Fall 86, p. 27.
"Skins and Bones." [RagMag] (5:2) Fall 86, p. 26.
2905. KRAMER, Aaron
"Autumn" (tr. of B. J. Bialostotsky). [Vis] (21) 86, p. 24.
"Biography." [Wind] (16:58) 86, p. 22.
"Blue Square." [Wind] (16:58) 86, p. 22.
"In-Laws." [CumbPR] (6:1) Fall 86, p. 60.
"News Item." [Wind] (16:58) 86, p. 22-23.
"Progress." [Vis] (20) 86, p. 24.
"What Has Become of" (tr. of Rajzel Zychlinsky). [Vis] (21) 86, p. 24.
2906. KRAMER, Joan
"Cape May Beach House." [Vis] (21) 86, p. 15.
2907. KRAMER, Larry
"A Book of Hours" (Excerpt). [MissouriR] (9:1) 85-86, p. 23.
"Hunter in the Snow." [MissouriR] (9:1) 85-86, p. 24-25.
2908. KRAPF, Norbert
"Daniel and the Dust." [Confr] (33/34) Fall-Wint 86-87, p. 143.
"Expectant." [CrossCur] (5:4/6:1) 86, p. 139.
2909. KRATT, Mary
"The Fourth of July Hungarian." [StoneC] (14:1/2) Fall-Wint 86-87, p. 12.
2910. KRAUSS, Janet
"On Hearing the Quick Sad Music of the 30's." [Wind] (16:56) 86, p. 44.

2911. KRAVANJA-GROSS, Sonja
"Only the Snow Stays" (tr. of Tomaz Salamun, w. Anselm Hollo). [Vis] (22) 86, p. 27.
"The White Angel" (tr. of Tomaz Salamun, w. Anselm Hollo). [Vis] (22) 86, p. 26.
2912. KREBS, Adele
"Premonitions of Death" (tr. by Lucie Weinstein and Jennifer Krebs). [SinW] (29/30) 86, p. 101.
"Todesahnen." [SinW] (29/30) 86, p. 101.
2913. KREBS, Jennifer
"Premonitions of Death" (tr. of Adele Krebs, w. Lucie Weinstein). [SinW] (29/30) 86, p. 101.
"Short Black Hair." [SinW] (29/30) 86, p. 98-100.
2914. KRECHEL, Ursula
"The Old World" (tr. by David Scrase). [ColR] (NS 13:1) Fall 85, p. 41.
2915. KREITER-KURYLO, Carolyn
"Crows over the Fields of Auvers." (Third prize, 1986 Poetry Competition). [PassN] (7:2) Spr-Sum 86, p. 3.
"A Former Teacher Said It Is Not Easy to Become a Poet." [EngJ] (75:3) Mr 86, p. 57.
2916. KRESH, David
"At the Winter Solstice." [MissR] (15:1/2, #43/44) Fall-Wint 86, p. 48.
"Silence." [MissR] (15:1/2, #43/44) Fall-Wint 86, p. 46-47.
2917. KRESS, Leonard
"Napoleon's Arrival into Lithuania" (from Pan Tadeusz, tr. of Adam Mickiewicz). [WebR] (11:1) Spr 86, p. 45-49.
2918. KRETZ, T. (Thomas)
"Androgynous." [Amelia] (3:2) Spr 86, p. 104-105.
"Asking in Metaphor." [KanQ] (18:1/2) Wint-Spr 86, p. 112.
"Deep into When Nothing Becomes No One." [Wind] (16:58) 86, p. 24.
"Dormant." [WestCR] (21:1) Je 86, p. 44.
"Experiment 31." [Amelia] (3:2) Spr 86, p. 104.
"Graviton." [SpoonRQ] (11:4) Fall 86, p. 32.
"The Reason Why Graces Fervently Said." [Rampike] (5:1) 86, p. 60.
"Rubbing Cells without Key." [HolCrit] (23:3) Je 86, p. 14.
"Running Out of Old Shoes." [RagMag] (5:2) Fall 86, p. 28.
2919. KRINSLEY, Jeanne
"Cryptograms." [Prima] (10) 86, p. 7.
"Outside the Knesset." [Prima] (10) 86, p. 14-15.
2920. KRITSCH, Holly
"The Lobster." [AntigR] (65) Spr 86, p. 35.
"Old Woman in Nursing Home." [AntigR] (65) Spr 86, p. 36.
2921. KROETSCH, Robert
"Excerpts from the Real World" (Selections). [CanLit] (108) Spr 86, p. 36-38.
2922. KROK, Peter
"The Bocce Players." [PaintedB] (29) Ag 86, p. 38-39.
2923. KROLL, Ernest
"The Great Del Orti." [LitR] (30:1) Fall 86, p. 67.
"London Company." [WebR] (11:2) Fall 86, p. 86.
"Paging Robinson Jeffers." [WebR] (11:2) Fall 86, p. 86.
"Train Wreck." [DeKalbLAJ] (19:2) 86, p. 36.
2924. KROMBEL, Raymond M.
"The Fallen Masters." [DeKalbLAJ] (19:2) 86, p. 37.
2925. KRONEN, Steve
"Aleister Crowley Meets with the American Theosophists, Philadelphia, 1908." [AmerPoR] (15:1) Ja-F 86, p. 35.
"The Island of Glassblowers." [AmerPoR] (15:1) Ja-F 86, p. 35.
"A Scientist aboard the Titanic Says Good-bye to His Wife in His Head." [AmerS] (55:3) Sum 86, p. 364.
2926. KRONENBERG, Mindy (Mindy H.)
"A Belief in Pain." [CumbPR] (5:2) Spr 86, p. 69.
"Close-Up." [YetASM] (5) 86, p. 2.
"The Widow." [CumbPR] (5:2) Spr 86, p. 68.
"Wish Bone." [CapeR] (21:2) Fall 86, p. 39.
2927. KRONENFELD, Judy
"Long Marriage." [Electrum] (38) Spr 86, p. 47.
"Next Year in Jerusalem." [HiramPoR] (40) Spr-Sum 86, p. 12-13.

"The Romance of the Family." [HiramPoR] (40) Spr-Sum 86, p. 14.
2928. KRUSOE, James
"Four Last Songs." [Zyzzyva] (2:2) Sum 86, p. 94-96.
2929. KRYNICKI, Ryszard
"Do Not Want to Die for Us" (tr. by Stanislaw Baranczak and Clare Cavanagh).
[TriQ] (67) Fall 86, p. 129.
"From a Window" (tr. by Stanislaw Baranczak and Clare Cavanagh). [TriQ] (67)
Fall 86, p. 129.
"I Can't Help You" (tr. by Stanislaw Baranczak and Clare Cavanagh). [TriQ] (67)
Fall 86, p. 128.
"I'd Forgotten" (tr. by Stanislaw Baranczak and Clare Cavanagh). [TriQ] (67) Fall
86, p. 128.
"Sleep Well" (tr. by Stanislaw Baranczak and Clare Cavanagh). [TriQ] (67) Fall 86,
p. 129.
"Yes, She Says" (tr. by Stanislaw Baranczak and Clare Cavanagh). [TriQ] (67) Fall
86, p. 128.
2930. KRYNSKI, Magnus J.
"The Morning After" (tr. of Stanislaw Baranczak, w. Robert A. Maguire). [TriQ]
(65) Wint 86, p. 87.
2931. KRYSL, Marilyn
"Are You the Malthus Ma or the Marxist Ma?" [OP] (42/43) Wint 86-87, p. 141-142.
"The Back." [AnotherCM] (16) 86, p. 56.
"Grandmother." [HeliconN] (14/15) Sum 86, p. 84.
"Matraphobia." [HighP] (1:1) Wint 86, p. 16-18.
"Reciprocal." [HeliconN] (14/15) Sum 86, p. 85.
"Sestina Rima: She Laments Her Rotten Luck." [DenQ] (20:4/21:1) Spr-Sum 86, p.
60.
"Snapshot, Tianjin, 1982: The Extended Sestina." [OP] (42/43) Wint 86-87, p.
142-143.
2932. KRYSTON, Vic
"Students Writing." [EngJ] (75:2) F 86, p. 67.
2933. KUCHINSKY, Walter
"Her Hands." [Wind] (16:57) 86, p. 18.
2934. KUDERKO, Lynne (Lynne M.)
"Fishing Black River, Wisconsin, 1953." [PoetryNW] (27:3) Aut 86, p. 23.
"Gathering Eggs on My Grandfather's Farm When I Was Eight or So." [SingHM]
(14) 86, p. 19.
"Gathering Eggs on My Grandfather's Farm When I Was Eight or So."
[SouthernPR] (26:1) Spr 86, p. 42.
"Love Letter Written on the Outskirts of a Small Town." [Ascent] (11:2) 86, p.
23-24.
"Noah." [Ascent] (11:2) 86, p. 24.
"Winter in the First Month." [PoetryNW] (27:3) Aut 86, p. 21-23.
2935. KUJAWINSKI, Frank
"We Drew the Proper Conclusions from the Events" (tr. of Stanislaw Baranczak, w.
Reginald Gibbons). [TriQ] (65) Wint 86, p. 89.
2936. KULIK, Ted
"Heavyweight Champion of the Wood." [AntigR] (65) Spr 86, p. 32.
"The Silence of Barns." [AntigR] (65) Spr 86, p. 31.
2937. KUMARI, Shyam
"The Bride." [WritersL] (1986:2), p. 16.
"Dream-Scape." [WritersL] (1986:2), p. 28.
"One Day." [WritersL] (1986:3), p. 23.
2938. KUMIN, Maxine
"A Calling." [Poetry] (148:4) Jl 86, p. 193.
"The Festung, Salzburg." [Poetry] (148:4) Jl 86, p. 189.
"Night Launch" (Canaveral Seashore National Park). [Poetry] (148:4) Jl 86, p.
190-191.
"On Reading an Old Baedeker in Schloss Leopoldskron" (Salzburg, Austria).
[Poetry] (148:4) Jl 86, p. 187-188.
"Orb." [GeoR] (40:3) Fall 86, p. 708.
"'Primitivism' Exhibit" (Museum of Modern Art, 1984). [Poetry] (148:4) Jl 86, p.
192.
"Spree." [PennR] (1:1) 85, p. 68-69.
2939. KUNTZ, Laurie
"Tropism" (for Steven). [CrossCur] (5:4/6:1) 86, p. 151.

2940. KUO, Alex
"Fishing at Night." [NowestR] (24:3) 86, p. 17-18.
2941. KURESHI, Salman Tarik
"Switchboard." [Vis] (20) 86, p. 36-38.
2942. KURIS, Edward S.
"Your Name in Vein." [WestCR] (21:2) O 86, p. 70.
2943. KURT, Ronald
"His Depression." [PraF] (7:4) Wint 86-87, p. 51.
KURYLO, Carolyn Kreiter
See KREITER-KURYLO, Carolyn
2944. KUSHNER, Dale (Dale M.)
"La Mer / After H. D." (for Susan Stanford Friedman). [Iowa] (16:3) Fall 86, p. 57.
"Recovery." [OhioR] (37) 86, p. 84-85.
"Sleeping Beauty." [BlackWR] (13:1) Fall 86, p. 74.
2945. KUTCHINS, Laurie
"Kadoka Needs Another Doctor." [MidAR] (6:2) 86, p. 12-13.
"Welcome to Heet." [MidAR] (6:2) 86, p. 14.
2946. KUTNEY, Bruce
"Swampfire" (for Dawn). [KanQ] (18:1/2) Wint-Spr 86, p. 267.
2947. KUZMA, Greg
"The Great Poems." [GeoR] (40:3) Fall 86, p. 709.
"Mother." [PennR] (1:2) Fall 85, p. 42-43.
"Notes." [MSS] (5:1) 86, p. 168-169.
"The Photograph." [PennR] (2:1) Fall-Wint 86, p. 92-93.
"The Return." [Puerto] (22:1) Fall 86, p. 81-84.
"Translations from the English" (4 Selections). [Poetry] (148:5) Ag 86, p. 277-280.
2948. KVAM, Wayne
"The Apples" (Leipzig). [Amelia] (3:3) Sum 86, p. 70.
"Die Lehre der Schlange" (Leipzig). [Amelia] (3:3) Sum 86, p. 70.
2949. KWANG, Penelope
"Dead, Ten Dead" (tr. of Duo Duo). [Nimrod] (29:2) Spr-Sum 86, p. 56.
"In Northern Fields Lying Fallow Is a Plough Which Brings Me Pain" (tr. of Duo
Duo). [Nimrod] (29:2) Spr-Sum 86, p. 61.
"Moment" (tr. of Duo Duo). [Nimrod] (29:2) Spr-Sum 86, p. 60.
"Northern Sea" (tr. of Duo Duo). [Nimrod] (29:2) Spr-Sum 86, p. 57-58.
"Wake Up" (tr. of Duo Duo). [Nimrod] (29:2) Spr-Sum 86, p. 58.
2950. KYLE, Carol
"The Thunderbolt." [SouthernPR] (26:1) Spr 86, p. 21.
KYOKO, Mori
See MORI, Kyoko
KYOZO, Takagi
See TAKAGI, Kyozo
2951. L. C. S.
"Sea of Pain." [SanFPJ] (8:2) 85, p. 16.
La . . .
See also names beginning with "La" without the following space, filed below in their
alphabetic positions, e.g., LaRUE.
2952. La CHARITY, Ralph
"Gravity's Graven Erupt Eneanympic Ganpan." [Contact] (8:41/42/43) Fall-Wint
86-87, p. 16.
"The Teaching." [Contact] (8:41/42/43) Fall-Wint 86-87, p. 17.
2953. La FONTAINE, Jean de
"Fables" (Selections, tr. by Norman R. Shapiro. Texas Review Poetry Award
Chapbook). [TexasR] (7:1/2) Spr-Sum 86, p. 33-48.
2954. La ROQUE, Catherine
"The 20th Century." [SanFPJ] (8:4) 85, p. 13-14.
"American Lament." [SanFPJ] (8:4) 85, p. 14.
"Landscape." [SanFPJ] (8:4) 85, p. 15.
"White Man." [SanFPJ] (8:4) 85, p. 16.
2955. LaBOMBARD, Joan
"July." [ManhatPR] (6) Wint-Spr 85-86, p. 43.
2956. LaBONTE, Karen
"About Grief." [MidAR] (7:1) 86, p. 52.
"Tideline." [MidAR] (7:1) 86, p. 53.
2957. LACASA, Cristina
"Nadie Escape a la Vida." [Mairena] (8:22) 86, p. 10.

2958. LACHOWSKI, Cheryl Schaff
"Pa'ndau: Flower Cloth." [CarolQ] (39:1) Fall 86, p. 80-81.
2959. LAGAN, Miriam
"Leaving the Temple." (Chapbook issue). [Sam] (43:3, release 171) 84, hand
corrected to 44:4 release 176) [86], 20 p.
2960. LaGATTUTA, Margo
"Pretending to Be a Barn." [PassN] (7:1) Fall-Wint 85-86, p. 9.
2961. LAGIER, Jennifer
"Black and White Window into the Past." [ColEng] (48:8) D 86, p. 801.
2962. LAGO, David
"La Tarde" (Sobre un verso de Antonio Desquirón). [LindLM] (5:3) Jl-S 86, p. 26.
2963. LAGOMARSINO, Nancy
"Family Pride." [NegC] (6:1) Wint 86, p. 77.
"Moon-Struck." [SingHM] (14) 86, p. 50.
2964. LAHEY-DOLEGA, Christina (Christine)
"Afterglow" (Written after seeing *Tales of Ordinary Madness*, based on Bukowski).
[OroM] (4:1-4) My 85, p. 50.
"Do It in Detroit." [MichQR] (25:2) Spr 86, p. 386.
"Hot July Night." [OroM] (4:1-4) My 85, p. 51.
2965. LAKE, Paul
"The Age of Terror." [PartR] (53:1) 86, p. 93-94.
"Blue Jay." [AmerS] (55:4) Aut 86, p. 448.
"Crime and Punishment." [Thrpny] (25) Spr 86, p. 5.
"Imagine a Book." [CumbPR] (5:2) Spr 86, p. 50.
"Jogging in Ouita Park." [CumbPR] (5:2) Spr 86, p. 52.
"An Open Form." [CumbPR] (5:2) Spr 86, p. 51.
2966. LALAN SHAH PHAKIR
"Songs" (in Bengali & English, tr. by Carol Salomon). [BellArk] (2:1) Ja-F 86, p.
5.
2967. LALLY, Margaret
"Seven Horses Feeding in the Sun" (for Patrick). [OhioR] (36) 86, p. 75.
2968. LaMANNA, Richard
"Visiting Hours." [Wind] (16:57) 86, p. 13.
2969. LAMAR, Paul
"Conversation with a Photograph." [MidAR] (6:1) 86?, p. 41-42.
2970. LAMB, Margaret
"For Martha." [Blueline] (8:1) Sum-Fall 86, p. 16.
"For Martha, II." [Blueline] (8:1) Sum-Fall 86, p. 17.
2971. LAMBERT, Jean Clarence
"All My Travels" (From Idylles, tr. by Usha Ahluwalia). [Vis] (22) 86, p. 6.
"Summer" (From Idylles, tr. by Usha Ahluwalia). [Vis] (22) 86, p. 6.
2972. LAMPHEAR, Lynn
"Two Haiku." [Amelia] (3:3) Sum 86, p. 14.
2973. LANAM, Jeff
"The Cobble Stone Road." [BallSUF] (26:4) Aut 85, p. 27.
2974. LANCE, Jeanne
"Hegira." [HangL] (49) Spr 86, p. 15.
2975. LAND, Thomas
"I Took the Sea-Eyed Goddess." [Amelia] (3:4) Fall 86, p. 50.
2976. LANDALE, Zoë
"Beginnings." [MalR] (73) Ja 86, p. 62.
2977. LANDAU, Julie
"Five Tz'u" (tr. of Su Shih). [Translation] (17) Fall 86, p. 324-325.
2978. LANDAU, Zishe
"Epilogue" (tr. by Irving Feldman). [Translation] (17) Fall 86, p. 253.
"The Little Pig" (tr. by Irving Feldman). [Translation] (17) Fall 86, p. 253.
"The Strikover Rabbi" (tr. by Irving Feldman). [Translation] (17) Fall 86, p. 251.
"This Evening" (tr. by Irving Feldman). [Translation] (17) Fall 86, p. 252.
2979. LANDGRAF, Susan
"Blood and Berries." [WoosterR] (5) Spr 86, p. 71.
"What If, Today, You Came Home?" [Ploughs] (12:4) 86, p. 183.
2980. LANE, Dixie
"The Life of Flowers." [RiverS] (19) 86, p. 46-47.
2981. LANE, John
"Duo." [StoneC] (14:1/2) Fall-Wint 86-87, p. 35.

2982. LANE, M. Travis
"Farther North." [GreenfR] (13:3/4) Sum-Fall 86, p. 94.
"King's Landing." [GreenfR] (13:3/4) Sum-Fall 86, p. 95-96.
"Must Get on Going." [AntigR] (65) Spr 86, p. 160.
2983. LANE, Patrick
"And of Song, Its Terrible Order" (for Sean Virgo). [MalR] (74) Mr 86, p. 87.
"Dante's Angels." [GreenfR] (13:3/4) Sum-Fall 86, p. 98.
"Harvest." [MalR] (74) Mr 86, p. 89.
"Nunc Dimittis" (for Mary Drover). [GreenfR] (13:3/4) Sum-Fall 86, p. 97.
"The Rose." [MalR] (74) Mr 86, p. 88.
2984. LANE, Pinkie Gordon
"Children." [BlackALF] (20:3) Fall 86, p. 293.
"Poems to My Father." [BlackALF] (20:3) Fall 86, p. 289-293.
2985. LANE, Walter
"Blindly." [Wind] (16:58) 86, p. 16.
"In the Eye of the Sun." [Wind] (16:58) 86, p. 5.
2986. LANG, Warren
"The Blessings." [Northeast] (series 4:3) Spr 86, p. 38-39.
"The Old Ones." [Abraxas] (34) 86, p. 51.
2987. LANGBIEN, Bruce
"For Frank (5-70)." [Sam] (46:2 release 182) 86, p. 61.
2988. LANGE, Kathleen Faith
"Heads or Tails." [SanFPJ] (8:1) 85, p. 65-68.
2989. LANGTON, Daniel J.
"1949-1983." [StoneC] (13:3/4) Spr-Sum 86, p. 69.
"A Bird." [ManhatPR] (6) Wint-Spr 85-86, p. 36.
"Except in Sleep." [StoneC] (13:3/4) Spr-Sum 86, p. 68.
"The Parts of Speech." [BallSUF] (27:4) Aut 86, p. 49.
"What's New?" [StoneC] (13:3/4) Spr-Sum 86, p. 68.
"When My Friend Francis Was a Boy." [PennR] (1:2) Fall 85, p. 40.
2990. LANIER, Parks
"Knee Surgery." [NewL] (52:2/3) Wint-Spr 86, p. 97.
2991. LANTHIER, Kateri
"Dream Scars." [GreenfR] (13:3/4) Sum-Fall 86, p. 99.
2992. LAOR, Dan
"Changing the Order" (tr. of Abba Kovner, w. Shirley Kaufman). [PoetL] (81:2)
Sum 86, p. 72-73.
"Everyone Who Comes" (tr. of Abba Kovner, w. Shirley Kaufman). [PoetL] (81:2)
Sum 86, p. 73-74.
"On the Way" (tr. of Abba Kovner, w. Shirley Kaufman). [PoetL] (81:2) Sum 86,
p. 74.
2993. LAPIDUS, Jacqueline
"The Borrowed Poem." [Cond] (13) 86, p. 89-90.
"Hunger." [Cond] (13) 86, p. 91.
"In Spite of, and Because." [Cond] (13) 86, p. 84-88.
2994. LAPINGTON, S. C.
"Spring Owl." [Stand] (27:2) Spr 86, p. 6.
2995. LARA, Omar
"Deseos." [SilverFR] (11) Sum 86, p. 16.
"Wishing" (tr. by Steven F. White). [SilverFR] (11) Sum 86, p. 17.
2996. LARBES, R. J.
"On Making a Difference." [EngJ] (75:3) Mr 86, p. 45.
2997. LARDAS, Konstantinos
"Adelphic." [WillowS] (17) Wint 86, p. 58.
"Fragments." [Poem] (56) N 86, p. 54.
"Gloria." [WillowS] (17) Wint 86, p. 56-57.
"Marvels." [WillowS] (17) Wint 86, p. 59.
"Mirrorings." [Poem] (56) N 86, p. 55.
"The Mourning Songs of Greece" (tr. of anonymous poems). [BlackWR] (13:1) Fall
86, p. 26-34.
"The Mourning Songs of Greece" (tr. of anonymous poems). [LitR] (30:1) Fall 86,
p. 81-83.
"The Mourning Songs of Greece" (tr. of anonymous poems). [SenR] (16:2) 86, p.
101-112.
"Seers." [Poem] (56) N 86, p. 56.

2998. LARDNER, Ted
"Bare Hands." [ColR] (NS 13:1) Fall 85, p. 60-62.
2999. LARKIN, Philip
"Continuing to Live." [NewYRB] (32:21/22) 16 Ja 86, p. 21.
3000. LaROCQUE, Emma
"An Evening Walk." [PraF] (7:1) Spr 86, p. 72-73.
3001. LARREA, Juan
"Anxiety of Signs" (tr. by José Rubia Barcia and Clayton Eshleman). [Sulfur] (6:1, issue 16) 86, p. 123.
"On Vacation Like a Stone" (tr. by José Rubia Barcia and Clayton Eshleman). [Sulfur] (6:1, issue 16) 86, p. 122-123.
"Risk Attraction" (tr. by José Rubia Barcia and Clayton Eshleman). [Sulfur] (6:1, issue 16) 86, p. 122.
"Thorns in the Snow" (tr. by José Rubia Barcia and Clayton Eshleman). [Sulfur] (6:1, issue 16) 86, p. 121-122.
3002. LARSEN, Wendy
"Into Marsh Blinds." [ManhatPR] (8) Wint 86-87, p. 6.
3003. LARSON, Kathryn
"Just Before Winter." [SanFPJ] (8:2) 85, p. 74-75.
"Poem Written in Derby, Connecticut." [SanFPJ] (8:2) 85, p. 42-43.
3004. LARSON, Norita Dittberner
"The Peaceable Kingdom." [SingHM] (13) 86, p. 92-93.
3005. LARSON, R. A.
"Communion at Smith Rock Near Terrebonne" (for Tim Barnes). [SilverFR] (11) Sum 86, p. 27.
"Satus Messages." [SilverFR] (11) Sum 86, p. 26.
3006. LaRUE, Dorie
"The Afghan from My Sister." [RagMag] (5:2) Fall 86, p. 36-37.
"Don't Talk to Me." [RagMag] (5:2) Fall 86, p. 30.
"Exotica." [RagMag] (5:2) Fall 86, p. 31.
"Finger Curls." [RagMag] (5:2) Fall 86, p. 33.
"Hill Street, the First Walls I Slept In." [RagMag] (5:2) Fall 86, p. 38-39.
"Into the Killing Jar." [RagMag] (5:2) Fall 86, p. 29.
"Retrospect." [RagMag] (5:2) Fall 86, p. 32.
"The Turn Row." [RagMag] (5:2) Fall 86, p. 34-35.
3007. LARUM, Glen
"Birthday in October." [Pax] (3:1/2) Wint 85-86, p. 74-75.
3008. LASARTE, Javier
"Casablanca." [LindLM] (5:2) Ap-Je 86, p. 6.
3009. LASHER, Darlene
"Resonance." [Prima] (10) 86, p. 10.
3010. LASHER, Susan
"Narcissus." [PartR] (53:4) 86, p. 582-583.
3011. LASKER-SCHULER, Else
"An Gott." [InterPR] (12:2) Fall 86, p. 36.
"Jacob" (tr. by Betty Falkenberg). [InterPR] (12:2) Fall 86, p. 41.
"Jakob." [InterPR] (12:2) Fall 86, p. 40.
"Mien Volk." [InterPR] (12:2) Fall 86, p. 38.
"My People" (tr. by Betty Falkenberg). [InterPR] (12:2) Fall 86, p. 39.
"Pharao und Joseph." [InterPR] (12:2) Fall 86, p. 34.
"Pharaoh and Joseph" (tr. by Betty Falkenberg). [InterPR] (12:2) Fall 86, p. 35.
"To God" (tr. by Betty Falkenberg). [InterPR] (12:2) Fall 86, p. 37.
3012. LASKIN, Pam (Pamela L.)
"Grand Central Station." [BallSUF] (26:4) Aut 85, p. 15.
"Munch's Scream." [YetASM] (5) 86, p. 4.
3013. LASSELL, Michael
"Cold Heat." [LitR] (30:1) Fall 86, p. 72.
"For John, Since I Cannot Be His Lover." [HangL] (49) Spr 86, p. 16-19.
"How to Be a Hedonist." [Amelia] (3:1) Ja 86, p. 12-15.
"Intersections." [JamesWR] (3:3) Spr 86, p. 13.
"Late Dinner." [Amelia] (3:1) Ja 86, p. 18.
"Man Wearing Laurels" (oil on canvas, 1880, John Singer Sargent, American, 1856-1925). [Amelia] (3:1) Ja 86, p. 16-17.
"Winter Vacation." [JamesWR] (3:2) Wint 86, p. 9.
3014. LASTRA, Pedro
"Ave Nocturna." [Inti] (21) Primavera 85, p. 113-114.

217

"Noticias de Roque Dalton" (A Rigas Kappatos). [Inti] (21) Primavera 85, p. 114-115.
"Peligro." [Inti] (21) Primavera 85, p. 113.
"Pez Volador y Tigre de Bengala." [Inti] (21) Primavera 85, p. 114.
3015. LATIOLAIS, P. M.
"Root Beer" (for Margery Buck Latiolais). [OhioR] (36) 86, p. 95-96.
3016. LATTA, John
"For Robert Assaf & Dominique Hausfater." [Epoch] (35:2) 86-87, p. 200.
"Poem (My Feelings)." [Jacaranda] (2:1) Fall 86, p. 12-13.
3017. LATTIMORE, Elaine
"Cathy." [YetASM] (4) 85, p. 2.
3018. LAU, Carolyn
"Metaphysics, a Kind of Curse." [CreamCR] (11:1) 86?, p. 36.
3019. LAU, Evelyn
"Memories of a Math Classroom." [HangL] (49) Spr 86, p. 59.
"Separations." [HangL] (49) Spr 86, p. 58.
LAUCANNO, Christopher Sawyer
See SAWYER-LAUCANNO, Christopher
3020. LAUGHLIN, James
"Being Much Too Tall." [Interim] (5:1) Spr 86, p. 11.
"Her Line Will be Busy." [Interim] (5:1) Spr 86, p. 10.
"A Night at the Opera." [ParisR] (28:100) Sum-Fall 86, p. 191.
LAURENTIS, Louise Budde de
See DeLAURENTIS, Louise Budde
3021. LAUTERBACH, Ann
"A Documentary." [QW] (23) 86, p. 10.
"Dominion in February" (for Ronald Bladen). [Conjunc] (9) 86, p. 165.
3022. LAUTERMILCH, Steven
"Poem: My friend, I can see your picture." [CentR] (30:1) Wint 86, p. 60-61.
3023. LAUTURE, Denizé
"The Gift of Creativity." [BlackALF] (20:3) Fall 86, p. 252.
"A Green Star for the Bard." [BlackALF] (20:3) Fall 86, p. 251-252.
"Necropsying." [BlackALF] (20:3) Fall 86, p. 252-253.
3024. LAUX, Dorianne
"Ghosts." [Zyzzyva] (2:1) Spr 86, p. 101-103.
"The Nurse." [Electrum] (38) Spr 86, p. 21.
"Sunday." [Zyzzyva] (2:4) Wint 86-87, p. 50-51.
3025. LaVIGNE, Steven
"I Saunter Down Main Street." [SanFPJ] (8:3) 85, p. 18.
"Ladies and Gentlemen, the President of the United States." [SanFPJ] (8:3) 85, p. 19.
3026. LAVIN CERDA, Hernan
"A Cadena Perpetua." [Inti] (21) Primavera 85, p. 105-106.
"Círculos Concéntricos." [Inti] (21) Primavera 85, p. 103-104.
"Una Sombra en Auschwitz." [Inti] (21) Primavera 85, p. 106-107.
"La Visión Objetiva." [Inti] (21) Primavera 85, p. 107-108.
"Una Vista al Matadero." [Inti] (21) Primavera 85, p. 104-105.
3027. LAVOIE, Steven
"Cloud Spots." [Sink] (1) 86, p. 44.
"Unity Communique." [Sink] (1) 86, p. 42-44.
3028. LAW, L. Bradley
"High Canyon Recital." [Amelia] (3:2) Spr 86, p. 70.
"Private Stock." [Amelia] (3:4) Fall 86, p. 75.
3029. LAWDER, Donald
"To a Certain Lady Who I Hope Is Fair." [YellowS] (20) Aut 86, p. 6.
3030. LAWDER, Douglas
"Foot Hold." [StoneC] (13:3/4) Spr-Sum 86, p. 39-40.
"Measures" (for Theresa). [StoneC] (13:3/4) Spr-Sum 86, p. 43.
"The New World" (for Clara and Bob). [StoneC] (13:3/4) Spr-Sum 86, p. 41-43.
"Triangulations." [StoneC] (13:3/4) Spr-Sum 86, p. 38-39.
3031. LAWLER, Patrick
"Dwarfs' Concerto." [Verse] (5) 86, p. 40.
"Elagabalus, Roman Emperor, Trickster Too." [AmerPoR] (15:5) S-O 86, p. 19.
"Making Ends Meet." [Confr] (32) Spr-Sum 86, p. 110.
"Nine Times the Space." [LitR] (29:3) Spr 86, p. 286.
"Phrenology." [MemphisSR] (7:1) Fall 86, p. 29.

218

LAWLER

"Two Stories." [LitR] (29:3) Spr 86, p. 287.
3032. LAWLOR, William T.
"The Angry Woman Who Married God" (to Sister Juana Inés de la Cruz, tr. of Belkis Cuza Male). [NegC] (6:4) Fall 86, p. 199.
3033. LAWRENCE, Kirk L.
"School Girl-Lady." [WritersL] (1986:1), p. 21.
3034. LAWRENCE, Robert
"Barra." [GreenfR] (13:3/4) Sum-Fall 86, p. 100.
3035. LAWRENCE, William B.
"Epiphany." [ChrC] (103:40) 24-31 D 86, p. 1167.
3036. LAWRY, Mercedes
"The Heart of the Matter." [NegC] (6:1) Wint 86, p. 96-97.
"Sullen Skies." [BellArk] (2:4) Jl-Ag 86, p. 4.
"Wrestling." [CutB] (25) Fall-Wint 86, p. 39.
3037. LAWSON, D. S.
"The One Who Tells." [JamesWR] (4:1) Fall 86, p. 5.
3038. LAYTON, Irving
"Anglo-Canadian." [PraF] (7:4) Wint 86-87, p. 29.
"Boschka Layton 1921-1984." [GreenfR] (13:3/4) Sum-Fall 86, p. 102.
"Casa Cacciatore." [AntigR] (66/67) Sum-Aut 86, p. 199.
"Dionysians in a Bad Time." [GreenfR] (13:3/4) Sum-Fall 86, p. 103.
"Final Reckoning: After Theognis." [AntigR] (66/67) Sum-Aut 86, p. 198.
"A Madrigal for Anna." [AntigR] (66/67) Sum-Aut 86, p. 200.
3039. LAZARD, Naomi
"Be Near Me" (tr. of Faiz Ahmed Faiz). [SenR] (16:1) 86, p. 77.
"Don't Look at Them" (tr. of Faiz Ahmed Faiz). [CentralP] (9) Spr 86, p. 60.
"The Hour of Faithlessness" (tr. of Faiz Ahmed Faiz). [AmerPoR] (15:5) S-O 86, p. 36.
"If My Suffering Found a Voice" (tr. of Faiz Ahmed Faiz). [CentralP] (9) Spr 86, p. 59.
"Paris" (tr. of Faiz Ahmed Faiz). [SenR] (16:1) 86, p. 76.
"Postmeridian" (tr. of Nina Cassian, w. the author and Cristian Andrei). [NewYorker] (62:38) 10 N 86, p. 45.
"Three Quatrains" (tr. of Faiz Ahmed Faiz). [CentralP] (9) Spr 86, p. 61.
"Travelogue" (tr. of Faiz Ahmed Faiz). [AmerPoR] (15:5) S-O 86, p. 36.
"The War Cemetery in Leningrad" (tr. of Faiz Ahmed Faiz). [CentralP] (9) Spr 86, p. 62.
3040. LAZZARA, Edward J.
"Apuro del Poeta." [Mester] (15:1) Spr 86, p. 68.
Le . . .
See also names beginning with "Le" without the following space, filed below in their alphabetic positions, e.g., LeFEBVRE.
3041. Le GUIN, Ursula K.
"At the Party." [Calyx] (9:2/3) Wint 86, p. 85.
"Ella Peavy's Birthday." [NowestR] (24:3) 86, p. 20.
"His Daughter." [Calyx] (10:1) Sum 86, p. 9.
"The Light." [Calyx] (9:2/3) Wint 86, p. 84.
"The Menstrual Lodge." [Calyx] (10:1) Sum 86, p. 8-9.
"Northern B.C." [NowestR] (24:3) 86, p. 19.
"A Private Ceremony of Public Mourning for the Language of the People Called Wappo." [Calyx] (10:1) Sum 86, p. 6-7.
3042. Le SUEUR, Meridel
"Rites of Ancient Ripening." [Calyx] (9:2/3) Wint 86, p. 10-13.
3043. LEA, Sydney
"Another Autumn, And." [NewYorker] (62:35) 20 O 86, p. 44.
"The Art of the Son." [NegC] (6:4) Fall 86, p. 24-26.
"December 7th." [Verse] (6) 86, p. 41-42.
"Dusk." [NewYorker] (62:9) 21 Ap 86, p. 50.
"Horn." [GeoR] (40:3) Fall 86, p. 710-713.
"How to Leave Nothing." [Crazy] (31) Fall 86, p. 55-57.
"In the Blind: For Tommy, My Oldest Friend." [MissouriR] (9:1) 85-86, p. 191-193.
"Leonora's Kitchen." [NewYorker] (62:21) 14 Jl 86, p. 28.
"The Light Going Down." [PartR] (53:2) 86, p. 239-241.
"No Sign." [Crazy] (31) Fall 86, p. 52-54.
"Yet Unharmed." [PraS] (60:3) Fall 86, p. 118-120.

3044. LEACH, Chet
    "My Favorite Fable." [CentR] (30:4) Fall 86, p. 473-474.
3045. LEAF, Mindy
    "My Glasses Hurt." [Amelia] (3:3) Sum 86, p. 80.
3046. LEARDI, Jeanette
    "Covering Tracks." [LittleM] (15:2) 86, p. 31.
    "Night Flower." [TexasR] (7:1/2) Spr-Sum 86, p. 98.
3047. LEASE, Joseph
    "The Blue Face Suite." [Boulevard] (1:3) Fall 86, p. 41.
3048. LEAVITT, Penelope
    "Ashes, Ashes." [Comm] (113:7) 11 Ap 86, p. 220.
3049. LECKIE, Ross
    "Turning Once to Look Back." [GreenfR] (13:3/4) Sum-Fall 86, p. 104.
3050. LEE, Alice
    "Fear of Failing." [KanQ] (18:4) Fall 86, p. 72.
3051. LEE, David
    "Alpine Pond, Cedar Breaks." [WillowS] (17) Wint 86, p. 1-2.
    "Kaiparowits Plateau." [WillowS] (17) Wint 86, p. 5.
    "South Gorge, Moab." [WillowS] (17) Wint 86, p. 3-4.
3052. LEE, Deborah
    "Haiku for Leah." [Contact] (7:38/39/40) Wint-Spr 86, p. 46.
3053. LEE, Dennis
    "New Lives for Old." [Event] (15:1) 86, p. 28-29.
    "Riffs" (Excerpts from a Work in Progress). [GreenfR] (13:3/4) Sum-Fall 86, p.
        105-107.
    "Try Panic." [Event] (15:1) 86, p. 30.
    "Unlucky Once." [Event] (15:1) 86, p. 31.
3054. LEE, Ginger
    "Begin from Here" (from the poem-cycle, Part V, tr. of Jiang He, w. John Minford
        et al.). [Nimrod] (29:2) Spr-Sum 86, p. 123-124.
3055. LEE, John B.
    "Ash." [WritersL] (1986:5), p. 27.
    "Horses 'nd Asses." [Event] (15:2) 86, p. 156-157.
    "She Too Is a Kind of Clock." [Quarry] (35:4) Aut 86, p. 7.
3056. LEE, Li-Young
    "My Indigo." [AmerPoR] (15:5) S-O 86, p. 20.
    "My Sleeping Loved Ones." [AmerPoR] (15:5) S-O 86, p. 20.
3057. LEE, Myra
    "Agile." [Puerto] (21:2) Spr 86, p. 144-145.
3058. LEE-ADAMS, Lily Jean
    "The Friendship Only Lasted a Few Seconds." [Sam] (46:2 release 182) 86, p. 58.
    "I Thought They Would Listen." [Sam] (46:2 release 182) 86, p. 56.
3059. LEEMAN, Reva
    "Waiting to Sort Things Out." [Calyx] (9:2/3) Wint 86, p. 103.
3060. LEER, Norman
    "The Beach at Rockport." [SpoonRQ] (11:2) Spr 86, p. 18.
3061. LEET, Judith
    "The Inner Outer Fine Line." [OntR] (25) Fall-Wint 86-87, p. 74-75.
    "Lyman's Shade Garden." [OntR] (25) Fall-Wint 86-87, p. 76-77.
    "Painter of Forsythia." [OntR] (25) Fall-Wint 86-87, p. 78-79.
    "Winter Walk." [OntR] (25) Fall-Wint 86-87, p. 70-73.
3062. LEFCOWITZ, Barbara F.
    "Rosie's Banquet" (for Rose Lefcowitz, 1907-1984). [WebR] (11:1) Spr 86, p. 68.
    "Turning 50." [WebR] (11:1) Spr 86, p. 67.
3063. LEFEBURE, Stephen
    "The Guilt." [KanQ] (18:1/2) Wint-Spr 86, p. 73.
3064. LEFEBVRE, Michel
    "Escarmouche de Féerie Mondiale." [Rampike] (5:2) 86, p. 62-63.
3065. LEHMAN, David
    "Beyond Is Anything." [Boulevard] (1:1/2) Wint 86, p. 111.
    "Enigma Variations." [ParisR] (28:100) Sum-Fall 86, p. 192-193.
    "Fear." [Shen] (36:2) 86, p. 22.
    "The Master of Ceremonies." [GrandS] (5:3) Spr 86, p. 228-229.
    "Our Hero." [NewRep] (195:26) 29 D 86, p. 36.
    "Peripheral Vision" (For Alice Fulton). [SouthwR] (71:1) Wint 86, p. 66-67.
    "Reverse Angle." [Agni] (23) 86, p. 151.

"The True Philosopher" (for Sheila McCullough). [Boulevard] (1:1/2) Wint 86, p. 109-110.
3066. LEHNER, Frank
"Goodness Returning" (For Larry Powell). [PennR] (1:2) Fall 85, p. 34.
3067. LEIGHT, Peter
"Mirror." [CapeR] (21:1) Spr 86, p. 22.
3068. LEINART, Virginia
"Herself." [Ploughs] (12:4) 86, p. 104-107.
"Transported." [Ploughs] (12:4) 86, p. 108.
3069. LEIPER, Esther M.
"Nathan Hall." [Amelia] (3:4) Fall 86, p. 40.
3070. LEIRIS, Michel
"The Unbridled Line (André Masson)" (tr. by James Clifford). [Sulfur] (5:3, issue 15) 86, p. 25-26.
3071. LEITHAUSER, Brad
"On the Lea Side" (Cape Breton, Nova Scotia). [NewRep] (194:4) 27 Ja 86, p. 38.
3072. LEIVICK, H.
"Sanitorium" (tr. by Cynthia Ozick). [Translation] (17) Fall 86, p. 254-255.
3073. LEM, Carol
"White Out." [Contact] (7:38/39/40) Wint-Spr 86, p. 41.
3074. LEMLEY, Bill
"The Chosen." [ChrC] (103:17) 14 My 86, p. 477.
3075. LEMM, Pat
"Metamorphosis II (The Saga Continues)." [Amelia] (3:4) Fall 86, p. 92.
3076. LEMM, Richard
"Samaria Gorge." [Event] (15:2) 86, p. 176-177.
3077. LENIHAN, Dan
"Ruth and Ellis and Friends" (Special section). [WormR] (26:2, issue 102) 86, p. 53-68.
3078. LENNON, M.
"Flash Flood." [Contact] (8:41/42/43) Fall-Wint 86-87, p. 15.
"The Four Powers." [Contact] (8:41/42/43) Fall-Wint 86-87, p. 15.
3079. LENSE, Edward
"Glass Skin." [HiramPoR] (40) Spr-Sum 86, p. 15.
3080. LENT, John
"The Bad Days." [AntigR] (64) Wint 86, p. 54-55.
3081. LENTINI, Javier
"La Externa Morada (I)" (Respuesta a Santa Teresa). [Mairena] (8:22) 86, p. 75.
LEO, Michael di, Jr.
See Di LEO, Michael, Jr.
3082. LEONE, Angela Tehaan
"Springsong." [Wind] (16:56) 86, p. 2.
3083. LEONHARD, Zigi
"The Frogprince Servant or How to Reach Happiness by Identification." [RagMag] (5:1) Spr 86, p. 53.
"What Would You Say, Marcel?" [RagMag] (5:1) Spr 86, p. 50-52.
"When She Made Tea." [RagMag] (5:1) Spr 86, p. 49.
3084. LEPORE, Dominick J.
"Pity." [ArizQ] (42:1) Spr 86, p. 16.
3085. LEPOVETSKY, Lisa
"Girl and Father (From Hine's Photo - 1908)." [Interim] (5:1) Spr 86, p. 33.
"Robotics." [Vis] (20) 86, p. 14.
3086. LEPSON, Ruth
"Sleeping on the Couch." [HeliconN] (16) Wint 86, p. 73.
LERGA, Jesús Gorriz
See GORRIZ LERGA, Jesús
3087. LERNER, Elizabeth
"Calories and Other Counts." [WebR] (11:2) Fall 86, p. 79-80.
"Name It After Me." [WebR] (11:2) Fall 86, p. 81-82.
"Sociobiology." [WebR] (11:2) Fall 86, p. 80.
"This Little Piggy." [WebR] (11:2) Fall 86, p. 82.
3088. LERNER, Eve
"Un Ange un Peu Fou." [SmPd] (23:2, issue 67) Spr 86, p. 22.
3089. LESANDRINI, Jay
"My Quartz-Dialed Life." [Bogg] (55) 86, p. 6.

3090. LesCARBEAU, Mitchell
"Afterthoughts on *The Expulsion* of Masaccio." [Interim] (5:2) Fall 86, p. 15.
"Duchamp's Birthday Gift." [Interim] (5:2) Fall 86, p. 14.
"Inside the *Crown and Anchor*." [NewRena] (6:3, #20) Spr 86, p. 68.
"Rilke's Angels." [CarolQ] (38:3) Spr 86, p. 50-51.
3091. LESLIE, Naton
"Broken Leg." [IndR] (9:2) Spr 86, p. 59.
"Twister." [ThRiPo] (27/28) 86, p. 43.
3092. LESSER, Rika
"Blue Ripening" (tr. of Göran Sonnevi). [Writ] (18) 86, c87, p. 75.
"Dyron, 1981" (Two Poems, tr. of Göran Sonnevi). [Chelsea] (45) 86, p. 126-128.
"I said to you" (tr. of Göran Sonnevi). [Writ] (18) 86, c87, p. 76.
"The wound bleeding" (tr. of Göran Sonnevi). [Writ] (18) 86, c87, p. 77.
3093. LESSING, Karin
"The Slate Opening." [Temblor] (4) 86, p. 122-123.
3094. LETKO, Ken
"In the Blue Signature of the Ice Bird" (Poems in German & English, tr. of Reiner
Kunze, w. Thomas Edwards and Ulrike Aitenbichler). [MidAR] (7:1) 86, p.
73-101.
"Nowhere Is Near So Far" (Poems in German & English, tr. of Ulrich Schacht, w.
Thomas Edwards and Ulrike Aitenbichler). [MidAR] (6:2) 86, p. 49-86.
3095. LEUCHTENBERG, Myles
"XXXII. Here are the minerals, ashes." [ManhatPR] (6) Wint-Spr 85-86, p. 59.
3096. LEV, Donald
"City Life." [Confr] (32) Spr-Sum 86, p. 73.
"The Dry Spell." [ManhatPR] (8) Wint 86-87, p. 36.
"Epiphany in Grand Central." [Lips] (12) 86, p. 34.
3097. LEVENSON, Christopher
"Virginia and the Cow." [Event] (15:1) 86, p. 106.
3098. LEVENTHAL, Ann Z.
"Mending Time." [PassN] (7:2) Spr-Sum 86, p. 18.
3099. LEVER, Bernice
"As If Carbon Is Nothing." [GreenfR] (13:3/4) Sum-Fall 86, p. 108.
3100. LEVERTOV, Denise
"Carapace." [Agni] (23) 86, p. 91-92.
"Embrasure." [PoetryE] (20/21) Fall 86, p. 13.
"Every Day." [PoetryE] (20/21) Fall 86, p. 14.
"To One Steeped in Bitterness." [PoetryE] (20/21) Fall 86, p. 11.
"Variation on a Theme by Rilke" (The Book of Hours, Bk I, 1). [PoetryE] (20/21)
Fall 86, p. 12.
3101. LEVETT, John
"Snap." [AntigR] (65) Spr 86, p. 45.
"Tomato." [AntigR] (65) Spr 86, p. 43.
"Zig-Zag." [AntigR] (65) Spr 86, p. 44.
3102. LEVI, Steven C.
"That ain' a blowout, boy, that just natural." [MidAR] (6:2) 86, p. 41.
3103. LEVI, Toni Mergentime
"End of the Season." [KanQ] (18:1/2) Wint-Spr 86, p. 60.
"Hanging Out." [Electrum] (38) Spr 86, p. 18-19.
"Spring Thaw." [Blueline] (7:2) Wint-Spr 86, p. 41.
3104. LEVIN, Ephraim
"Afterward." [SanFPJ] (8:2) 85, p. 58.
"Politicians." [SanFPJ] (8:2) 85, p. 59.
"What Right." [SanFPJ] (8:2) 85, p. 53.
3105. LEVIN, Gabriel
"Letter from Outremer." [PoetL] (81:2) Sum 86, p. 129.
"Memory of This Very Moment from a Distance of Years Ahead" (tr. of Zali
Gurevitch). [PoetL] (81:2) Sum 86, p. 120.
"Sleep" (In the army, 6/82, tr. of Zali Gurevitch). [PoetL] (81:2) Sum 86, p. 119.
"Songs of Innocence." [PoetL] (81:2) Sum 86, p. 128.
"This Too, the Place Where I Live" (tr. of Zali Gurevitch). [PoetL] (81:2) Sum 86,
p. 121.
3106. LEVIN, Harriet
"In Grandfather's Stamproom." [NewL] (53:1) Fall 86, p. 72-73.
3107. LEVIN, Phillis
"Chalk and Ash." [Boulevard] (1:1/2) Wint 86, p. 165.

"The Skaters." [GrandS] (6:1) Aut 86, p. 211.
3108. LEVINE, David Z.
"Oral Care." [HiramPoR] (40) Spr-Sum 86, p. 19-20.
"The Quiet Boy." [HiramPoR] (40) Spr-Sum 86, p. 16-18.
3109. LEVINE, Miriam
"David at Fifteen." [Confr] (32) Spr-Sum 86, p. 31.
"The Green Tunnel" (In memory of R.S., 1961-1982). [Confr] (32) Spr-Sum 86, p. 30.
3110. LEVINE, Philip
"28: At 28 I was still faithless." [NewYorker] (62:28) 1 S 86, p. 30-31.
"Any Night." [GeoR] (40:3) Fall 86, p. 714-715.
"Coming Home from the Post Office." [GeoR] (40:4) Wint 86, p. 950-951.
"The Last Shift." [MichQR] (25:2) Spr 86, p. 333-334.
"Last Song of the Angel of Bad Luck." [GeoR] (40:3) Fall 86, p. 715.
"Making It Work." [MichQR] (25:2) Spr 86, p. 335.
"Making Light of It." [NewYorker] (62:32) 29 S 86, p. 40.
"Picture Postcard from the Other World." [Ploughs] (12:3) 86, p. 15-17.
"Waking in March." [PartR] (53:2) 86, p. 233-234.
"Who." [GeoR] (40:3) Fall 86, p. 716.
"The Whole Soul." [Poetry] (149:3) D 86, p. 131-132.
"Winter Words" (For Tu Fu). [Poetry] (149:3) D 86, p. 127-130.
3111. LEVINE, S. Jill
"The Course of the Lettuce" (tr. of Marjorie Agosin). [Cond] (13) 86, p. 82.
3112. LEVINE-KEATING, Helane
"Anne Frank's House." [CentralP] (9) Spr 86, p. 49.
3113. LEVITIN, Alexis
"As If There Were Still Leaves" (tr. of Eugenio de Andrade). [PennR] (1:2) Fall 85, p. 49.
"Concerns of Summer" (tr. of Eugenio de Andrade). [Confr] (32) Spr-Sum 86, p. 106.
"Exercises with Vowels" (tr. of Eugenio de Andrade). [IndR] (9:2) Spr 86, p. 24.
"A friend is sometimes desert" (tr. of Eugenio de Andrade). [Verse] (3:3) N 86, p. 11.
"No, it is not yet the troubled light of March" (tr. of Eugenio de Andrade). [Verse] (3:3) N 86, p. 11.
"Upon Desire" (tr. of Eugenio de Andrade). [Confr] (32) Spr-Sum 86, p. 106.
"While I Was Writing" (tr. of Eugenio de Andrade). [IndR] (9:2) Spr 86, p. 25.
3114. LEVITZ, Linda
"Island Poem." [YetASM] (4) 85, p. 6.
3115. LEVY, Carlo
"Maurice and Helen's Son Dreams Two Dreams, One Night." [CrabCR] (3:3) Sum 86, p. 17.
3116. LEVY, Ellen
"Rec Room." [NewYRB] (33:15) 9 O 86, p. 20.
3117. LEVY, Robert J.
"On the Pythagorean Theorem." [Chelsea] (45) 86, p. 104-105.
"The Palace at 4 A.M." (after Giacometti). [GeoR] (40:2) Sum 86, p. 415.
"Whistle Maker." [GeoR] (40:2) Sum 86, p. 413-415.
3118. LEVY, Thurber, Jr.
"One More Winter on Sinclair." [BellArk] (2:1) Ja-F 86, p. 7.
3119. LEWANDOWSKI, Antonia
"For My Student, Dead in a Car Crash." [EngJ] (75:7) N 86, p. 32.
3120. LEWANDOWSKI, Stephen
"Early Morning Driving / After Passage of the 'Peacekeeper'." [Wind] (16:58) 86, p. 25-26.
"Letter to Lynn." [Wind] (16:58) 86, p. 25.
3121. LEWIN, Rebecca
"Errant Moon." [Sam] (44:2 release 174) 86, p. 22.
3122. LEWIN, Vivian
"Falling: The First Time." [Field] (35) Fall 86, p. 90.
"A Mild Christmas." [Field] (35) Fall 86, p. 88-89.
3123. LEWINSOHN, Alberto
"Esta Bien." [Mairena] (8:22) 86, p. 122.
3124. LEWIS, Bill
"Red Guitar" (for Victor Jara). [Bogg] (56) 86, p. 61.

3125. LEWIS, Frank C.
"Le Grand Masturbateur" (Excerpt, tr. of Salvador Dali, w. Sonja A. Rein).
[ClockR] (3:1) 85, p. 61-62.
3126. LEWIS, Lisa
"Bottles." [KenR] (NS 7:2) Spr 85, p. 37-39.
"Cloudlight." [MissouriR] (9:2) 86, p. 132.
"The Innocent Embrace." [MissouriR] (9:2) 86, p. 134-137.
"Oats." [KenR] (NS 7:2) Spr 85, p. 40.
"Red Ribbon." [MissouriR] (9:2) 86, p. 127-129.
"Winter Wheat." [MissouriR] (9:2) 86, p. 130-131.
3127. LEWIS, Melvyn J.
"Returning Again." [PoeticJ] (15) Sum 86, p. 16.
3128. LEWIS, Pamela
"Newly Installed Still a Novelty." [Bogg] (55) 86, p. 53.
3129. LEWIS, Rob
"Expedition on Onion Creek" (Fantasy on a Photograph by Ed Buffaloe). [Pax]
(3:1/2) Wint 85-86, p. 76-78.
3130. LEZAMA LIMA, Jose
"Ah, That You Escape" (tr. by Kent Johnson). [ClockR] (3:1) 85, p. 57.
LI, Chin-An
See CHIN-AN, Li
LI, Lu
See LU, Li
3131. LI, Min Hua
"Found in the Supreme Court." [Sam] (45:4 release 180) 86, p. 44.
"I've Got a Sweet Heart." [Wind] (16:56) 86, p. 24.
"Salem Revisited, 1980s." [Amelia] (3:2) Spr 86, p. 90.
"View from My Study." [Amelia] (3:2) Spr 86, p. 90.
3132. LI, Po
"Quiet Night Thoughts" (tr. by Joseph McLeod). [Waves] (14:3) Wint 86, p. 71.
"Quite Night" (tr. by Joseph McLeod). [Waves] (14:3) Wint 86, p. 71.
"A Reply to the Vulgar" (tr. by Joseph McLeod). [Waves] (14:3) Wint 86, p. 71.
LI-YOUNG, Lee
See LEE, Li-Young
3133. LIBBEY, Elizabeth
"Stars on a Cloudy Night." [PartR] (53:2) 86, p. 237-238.
3134. LIDDELL, Eleanor P.
"Hardware Store." [PoeticJ] (14) 86, p. 33.
"Ram's Skull." [PoeticJ] (13) 86, p. 8.
"Survivor." [PoeticJ] (13) 86, p. 9.
"Translating." [PoeticJ] (14) 86, p. 26.
3135. LIEBER, Ron
"Gare Montparnasse (The Melancholy of Departure), 1914, 1983." [SenR] (16:2)
86, p. 93-95.
3136. LIEBERMAN, Beatrice
"Judas Tree." [SinW] (29/30) 86, p. 88.
3137. LIEBERT, Dan (Daniel)
"Migraine." [Comm] (113:20) 21 N 86, p. 633.
"Reasons." [Puerto] (22:1) Fall 86, p. 64.
"Running in Place." [SoCaR] (19:1) Fall 86, p. 34.
3138. LIEBMAN, Maura
"Cool Water Afternoon." [PoeticJ] (15) Sum 86, p. 19.
"Fever." [Bogg] (55) 86, p. 14.
"Redwing Morning." [PoeticJ] (15) Sum 86, p. 19.
"Shadow on the Path." [PoeticJ] (15) Sum 86, p. 6.
"The Stillness." [Bogg] (56) 86, p. 52.
3139. LIETZ, Robert
"Pistols." [MidAR] (6:2) 86, p. 125-126.
"Preparations." [PraS] (60:3) Fall 86, p. 116-117.
"Weekend on State Land." [CrescentR] (4:2) Fall 86, p. 123.
"Widower, New Hampshire, 1954." [SoCaR] (18:2) Spr 86, p. 104.
3140. LIFSHIN, Lyn
"47 8 O Clock August Morning." [RagMag] (5:1) Spr 86, p. 18.
"1040 Madonna." [Bogg] (55) 86, p. 36.
"Anger Madonna." [YetASM] (4) 85, p. 5.

"Another Young Woman Disappears in the Trees." [Confr] (33/34) Fall-Wint 86-87, p. 194.
"Back Aches Like Certain Men." [WormR] (26:1, issue 101) 86, p. 13.
"Ballet Class." [RagMag] (5:1) Spr 86, p. 21.
"Bastille Day." [Wind] (16:57) 86, p. 20.
"Below Zero Madonna." [WormR] (26:3, issue 103) 86, p. 105.
"Bikini Madonna." [WormR] (26:3, issue 103) 86, p. 104.
"The Bottle Woman." [WormR] (26:1, issue 101) 86, p. 13.
"Bridge Over the Arno Madonna." [WormR] (26:3, issue 103) 86, p. 106.
"Burn Out Madonna." [WormR] (26:3, issue 103) 86, p. 105.
"Camel Madonna." [WormR] (26:3, issue 103) 86, p. 105.
"Cardinals in the Walnuts." [Farm] (3:2) Spr-Sum 86, p. 50.
"Chair Full of Leaves." [SanFPJ] (8:4) 85, p. 29.
"Chameleon Madonna, 1." [WormR] (26:3, issue 103) 86, p. 105.
"Chicago World's Fair 1893." [WormR] (26:1, issue 101) 86, p. 12.
"Cowboy's Madonna." [Bogg] (56) 86, p. 9.
"Depression." [RagMag] (5:1) Spr 86, p. 20.
"The Engineer on Her Sculptures, Terra Cotta Torsos." [WormR] (26:3, issue 103) 86, p. 109.
"Fallen Leaf Madonna." [WormR] (26:3, issue 103) 86, p. 105.
"Fat Madonna." [WormR] (26:3, issue 103) 86, p. 106.
"Film Madonna, 1." [WormR] (26:3, issue 103) 86, p. 106.
"Fool's Gold Madonna." [WormR] (26:3, issue 103) 86, p. 105.
"Football Addicts Madonna." [NewL] (52:2/3) Wint-Spr 86, p. 243.
"He Was Always Leaving When I Was Coming Around." [Wind] (16:57) 86, p. 19.
"Hearing about It." [Amelia] (3:4) Fall 86, p. 70.
"High Interest Rate Madonna." [WormR] (26:3, issue 103) 86, p. 106.
"Holding Animals." [WebR] (11:2) Fall 86, p. 65.
"Hooked on Ballet Madonna." [WormR] (26:3, issue 103) 86, p. 106.
"The Hotel Lifshin." [Bogg] (55) 86, p. 33.
"Hydroponic Madonna." [WormR] (26:3, issue 103) 86, p. 109.
"In That House." [Grain] (14:2) My 86, p. 51.
"In That Room." [Grain] (14:2) My 86, p. 50.
"In the Grey Front Living Room the Walls Stained the Chairs Unravelling." [Lips] (12) 86, p. 16-17.
"In the Hospital at Night." [SlipS] (6) 86, p. 11.
"In the Story Now I'm." [Contact] (8:41/42/43) Fall-Wint 86-87, p. 59.
"In Venice, That November and December." [WebR] (11:2) Fall 86, p. 66.
"It Was Like." [Amelia] (3:3) Sum 86, p. 97.
"It Was Like." [WormR] (26:1, issue 101) 86, p. 12.
"The Jesuit Sees Sex in the Olive Trees." [SecC] (14:1) 86, p. 44.
"Laryngitis Madonna." [DeKalbLAJ] (19:2) 86, p. 38.
"Lasagna Madonna." [WormR] (26:3, issue 103) 86, p. 106.
"Leech Madonna." [WormR] (26:3, issue 103) 86, p. 106.
"Like a Lover." [YetASM] (5) 86, p. 11.
"Like Being Called 'Cat' That Saturday in Montreal." [FloridaR] (14:2) Fall-Wint 86, p. 23.
"Locket Madonna." [WormR] (26:3, issue 103) 86, p. 107.
"Lost Glove Madonna." [WormR] (26:3, issue 103) 86, p. 106.
"Madonna of the Before TV Comes On." [WormR] (26:3, issue 103) 86, p. 109.
"Madonna of the Blahs and Flaws." [Farm] (3:2) Spr-Sum 86, p. 49.
"Madonna of the Man Who Writes Boring Letters." [WormR] (26:1, issue 101) 86, p. 14.
"Madonna of the Over Reactions." [WormR] (26:1, issue 101) 86, p. 13.
"Madonna of the Relationships She Doesn't Know When to Get Out of." [WormR] (26:3, issue 103) 86, p. 106.
"Madonna of the Submissions." [WormR] (26:3, issue 103) 86, p. 106.
"Madonna Who Goes Over the Manuscripts to Take Out the Dirty Words." [WormR] (26:3, issue 103) 86, p. 105.
"Madonna Who Is Tired of Changing Her Thighs for Every Lover." [Event] (15:1) 86, p. 111.
"Madonna Who Lives It Up." [WormR] (26:3, issue 103) 86, p. 106.
"Madonna Whose Mother Keeps Her on a Rope." [WormR] (26:3, issue 103) 86, p. 107.
"Madonna with Too Much Too Tightly Scheduled." [WormR] (26:3, issue 103) 86, p. 104.

225

LIFSHIN

"Madonna's Response to Ann Landers' '70 Percent of Women Would Prefer
  Cuddling and Hugging to "it"'." [WormR] (26:1, issue 101) 86, p. 14.
"Mafiosa Madonna." [WormR] (26:3, issue 103) 86, p. 105.
"Momentum Madonna." [WormR] (26:3, issue 103) 86, p. 105.
"My Mother and the Heat." [PennR] (2:1) Fall-Wint 86, p. 85.
"My Mother and the Marquis Ring." [Lips] (12) 86, p. 14-15.
"My Mother and the Oranges." [HangL] (49) Spr 86, p. 20-21.
"My Mother, Her Foot Banging the Side of the Bed in a Way I'd Never." [WormR]
  (26:3, issue 103) 86, p. 107.
"My Mother, Straightening Pots and Pans." [WormR] (26:3, issue 103) 86, p. 108.
"My Sister Wants to Sue the Trees." [WormR] (26:3, issue 103) 86, p. 108.
"The Name and Address in Your Wallet." [RagMag] (5:1) Spr 86, p. 20.
"Next Day Madonna." [Amelia] (3:1) Ja 86, p. 37.
"Nifty Fifty Madonna." [WormR] (26:3, issue 103) 86, p. 105.
"Oh Yes." [WormR] (26:1, issue 101) 86, p. 13.
"Old Map Madonna, 1." [WormR] (26:3, issue 103) 86, p. 106.
"On the Edge." [CapeR] (21:1) Spr 86, p. 35.
"The Poem Like Pirouettes." [WormR] (26:1, issue 101) 86, p. 13.
"Politician's Madonna." [Bogg] (56) 86, p. 42.
"Screw Madonna." [Bogg] (56) 86, p. 33.
"She Said I'll Never Forget One Evening." [Contact] (8:41/42/43) Fall-Wint 86-87,
  p. 58.
"She Said I'll Never Forget One Evening." [MinnR] (NS 27) Fall 86, p. 25-26.
"She Said It Was the Chestnuts You And." [DeKalbLAJ] (19:3/4) 86, p. 81.
"She Wore Blue Contact Lenses." [WormR] (26:1, issue 101) 86, p. 13.
"Short Term Madonna." [WormR] (26:3, issue 103) 86, p. 105.
"Sick of the Stage Door Madonna." [WormR] (26:3, issue 103) 86, p. 109.
"The Smell, Digging Up Bodies in Mass Graves." [Sam] (44:3 release 175) 86, p.
  18.
"Snow Madonna." [WormR] (26:3, issue 103) 86, p. 104.
"Steepletop Millay Colony." [WormR] (26:3, issue 103) 86, p. 109.
"Thinking It's Monday, Waking Up Alone." [WormR] (26:1, issue 101) 86, p. 12.
"Those Mondays." [FloridaR] (14:2) Fall-Wint 86, p. 24.
"The Thought of It." [LitR] (29:2) Wint 86, p. 223.
"Thursday 9:15." [RagMag] (5:1) Spr 86, p. 19.
"Tomato Sandwiches." [Abraxas] (34) 86, p. 31.
"Train Man's Madonna." [Bogg] (55) 86, p. 36.
"Used Up Madonna." [WormR] (26:3, issue 103) 86, p. 104.
"Vietnam." [SanFPJ] (8:4) 85, p. 29.
"Water Always Pleases Children." [PraF] (7:2) Sum 86, p. 30.
"We Still Call It." [WormR] (26:3, issue 103) 86, p. 108.
LIFSON, Martha Ronk
    See RONK-LIFSON, Martha
3141. LIGNELL, Kathleen
    "The Range of Light" (First Prize, Pablo Neruda Prize for Poetry). [Nimrod] (30:1)
      Fall-Wint 86, p. 7-15.
    "So This Is Obsidian." [SouthernPR] (26:2) Fall 86, p. 41.
3142. LIHN, Enrique
    "Alice in Nightmareland" (tr. by Mary Crow). [MassR] (27:3/4) Fall-Wint 86, p.
      472.
    "Gerard David" (from Al Partir de Manhattan, in Spanish & English, tr. by David
      Bradt). [CumbPR] (6:1) Fall 86, p. 64-65.
    "Hospital de Barcelona." [MidAR] (6:1) 86?, p. 66.
    "Hospital in Barcelona" (tr. by Mary Crow). [MidAR] (6:1) 86?, p. 67.
    "Monet's Years at Giverny" (from Al Partir de Manhattan, in Spanish & English, tr.
      by David Bradt). [CumbPR] (6:1) Fall 86, p. 66-71.
3143. LILBURNE, Geoffrey R.
    "Eleven O'Clock Sunday Morning." [ChrC] (103:11) 2 Ap 86, p. 324.
    "Looking Out to Sea." [Wind] (16:58) 86, p. 27.
3144. LILLO-MORO, Eduarda
    "Ubi Sunt" (En recuerdo de Carmen Amaya). [Mairena] (8:22) 86, p. 77-78.
3145. LILLY, Elaine
    "Before Any Plans" (Abans de qualsevol projecte, tr. of Miquel Martí i Pol). [SenR]
      (16:1) 86, p. 43.
LILLYWHITE, Eileen Silver
    See SILVER-LILLYWHITE, Eileen

3146. LIM, Genny
"If Sartre Was a Whore." [Contact] (7:38/39/40) Wint-Spr 86, p. 28.
3147. LIM, Shirley
"Pigeons." [Contact] (7:38/39/40) Wint-Spr 86, p. 47.
3148. LIMA, Robert
"Nevada" (tr. of Luis Cernuda). [Vis] (22) 86, p. 18.
"Telegram" (tr. of Rafael Alberti). [Vis] (22) 86, p. 18.
3149. LIN, Paul J.
"April" (tr. by the author). [Nimrod] (29:2) Spr-Sum 86, p. 52.
"Autumn Thoughts" (In Chinese & English, tr. by the author). [Nimrod] (29:2)
     Spr-Sum 86, p. 50.
"Childhood" (tr. by the author). [Nimrod] (29:2) Spr-Sum 86, p. 51.
"Farewell" (Song of the Feather, tr. by the author). [Nimrod] (29:2) Spr-Sum 86, p.
     48.
3150. LINDBERG, Judy
"Canoeing the Comstock" (Academy of American Poets Prize, 1985). [PennR] (1:1)
     85, p. 1-2.
"Three Steel Mill Pins." [PennR] (1:1) 85, p. 53.
3151. LINDHOLDT, Paul
"Traveler to the Colonies." [SewanR] (94:1) Wint 86, p. 1-3.
3152. LINDNER, Carl
"Spring Pruning." [KanQ] (18:1/2) Wint-Spr 86, p. 143.
3153. LINDO, Hugo
"Only the Voice" (Excerpt, tr. by Elizabeth Gamble Miller). [NewOR] (13:2) Sum
     86, p. 74-75.
3154. LINDOW, Sandra
"August Sacrament: William Meier Sings the Mass As He Combines the North
     Forty." [Farm] (3:1) Fall 85, p. 21-23.
LING, Bei
    See BEI, Ling
3155. LINTHICUM, John
"Epistle of Mother Teresa to the Holy Father." [LitR] (29:3) Spr 86, p. 276-278.
3156. LINTON, David
"Our Trains Are Nothing More Than Coupled Cars." [WindO] (47) Sum 86, p. 24.
3157. LIOTTA, P.
"Dakota Borealis." [PassN] (7:2) Spr-Sum 86, p. 16.
3158. LIPMAN, Joel
"Elena." [YellowS] (20) Aut 86, p. 11.
"Innuendoes of, I Dare Not Describe." [YellowS] (21) Wint 86, p. 37.
"My Love Is." [YellowS] (20) Aut 86, p. 10.
"No More Love Poem." [YellowS] (21) Wint 86, p. 37.
"Song of the Vulgar Refrigerator." [YellowS] (20) Aut 86, p. 11.
3159. LIPSITZ, David
"Sunrise Daughter." [PoeticJ] (15) Sum 86, p. 15.
3160. LIPSITZ, Lou
"After Chagall." [Wind] (16:56) 86, p. 26-27.
"Down the Block" (Crown St., Brooklyn, 1948). [Wind] (16:56) 86, p. 26.
"Nude Descending a Staircase" (for Sandy). [SouthernPR] (26:2) Fall 86, p. 37-39.
"Rain Poem for The New Yorker." [Wind] (16:56) 86, p. 25.
"Word." [SouthernPR] (26:2) Fall 86, p. 39.
3161. LIRA, Juan Antonio
"The Last Day of Somoza's Liberal Party" (tr. by Kent Johnson). [CentralP] (9) Spr
     86, p. 81.
3162. LISHAN, Stuart
"Sandy Koufax Is Telling Us These Things." [NewEngR] (8:4) Sum 86, p.
     501-502.
3163. LISOWSKI, Joseph
"The Funeral." [NegC] (6:4) Fall 86, p. 117.
"Roofing." [Wind] (16:56) 86, p. 39.
"Sunday News." [Wind] (16:56) 86, p. 17.
3164. LITTLE, Geraldine (Geraldine C.)
"A Brother Dies of Lupus." [SenR] (16:2) 86, p. 53-54.
"Concerning Rock." [StoneC] (13:3/4) Spr-Sum 86, p. 56-57.
"Creek Rites." [SenR] (16:2) 86, p. 51-52.
"Lines for Hwang Chin-I (1506-1544)" (The most famous of all Korean women
     poets). [StoneC] (14:1/2) Fall-Wint 86-87, p. 52-53.

"Mary Ludwig in Old Age" (Whom history knows as Molly Pitcher). [StoneC]
     (14:1/2) Fall-Wint 86-87, p. 53-55.
"One of the Suitors' Harlots." [Shen] (36:2) 86, p. 47-48.
"Reminiscences: Victorious Life, Olive Schreiner." [MinnR] (NS 27) Fall 86, p.
     94-96.
3165. LIU, Stephen S. N. (Steve)
     "The Naked Guest." [Contact] (7:38/39/40) Wint-Spr 86, p. 37.
     "Old Moon, New Hampshire." [NegC] (6:1) Wint 86, p. 95.
     "Photographing a Naked Woman on Rocks." [NoDaQ] (54:1) Wint 86, p. 67.
     "Thunderstorms in Peterborough." [NoDaQ] (54:1) Wint 86, p. 66.
     "To a Snowy Egret." [NoDaQ] (54:1) Wint 86, p. 66-67.
LIU, Tao
     See TAO, Liu
3166. LIVESAY, Dorothy
     "The Ancestors: A Suite." [GreenfR] (13:3/4) Sum-Fall 86, p. 110-114.
     "Celebrant." [WestCR] (21:2) O 86, p. 10.
     "The Differences." [WestCR] (21:2) O 86, p. 7.
     "Gloria." [WestCR] (21:2) O 86, p. 11.
     "Unmusical Bird" (blue heron). [WestCR] (21:2) O 86, p. 8.
     "The Whole Sun." [WestCR] (21:2) O 86, p. 9.
LLADO, Francisco R. Agrait
     See AGRAIT LLADO, Francisco R.
LLOSA, Ricardo Pau
     See PAU-LLOSA, Ricardo
3167. LLOVET, María
     "La Amistad." [Mairena] (8:22) 86, p. 36.
3168. LLOYD, D. H.
     "Common Frame of Reference." [WormR] (26:1, issue 101) 86, p. 16.
     "Madonna House." [WormR] (26:1, issue 101) 86, p. 25.
3169. LLUCH MORA, Francisco
     "Aqui, Aqui la Frente Despejada." [Mairena] (8:22) 86, p. 65.
3170. LOCKE, Duane
     "A Blue Shadow." [MidwQ] (27:2) Wint 86, p. 205-206.
     "The Bridge." [Os] (22) 86, p. 26.
     "The Famous Angel's Brother." [ManhatPR] (6) Wint-Spr 85-86, p. 22.
     "The Named." [Os] (22) 86, p. 24-25.
     "Prayer." [MidwQ] (27:2) Wint 86, p. 207.
     "Venus with the Organ Player." [ManhatPR] (6) Wint-Spr 85-86, p. 23.
     "Winter." [LitR] (29:3) Spr 86, p. 336-337.
3171. LOCKE, Karen
     "Looking for Dad." [Ploughs] (12:4) 86, p. 137.
3172. LOCKLIN, Gerald
     "L'Age d'Aluminum." [Abraxas] (34) 86, p. 45.
     "Bestsellers." [Bogg] (55) 86, p. 31.
     "Bukowski at His Best." [OroM] (4:1-4) My 85, p. 37-38.
     "The Cable." [BellR] (9:1) Spr 86, p. 32-33.
     "Ceremonial." [WormR] (26:1, issue 101) 86, p. 29.
     "The Common Grave." [BellR] (9:1) Spr 86, p. 30.
     "Easy Enough for You, Jean-Paul Sartre, to Turn Down the Goddamn Nobel Prize."
          [WormR] (26:1, issue 101) 86, p. 29-30.
     "A Fad with Consequences, or Who Needs Whom?" [WormR] (26:3, issue 103) 86,
          p. 95-96.
     "The Fog Comes In on Free Verse." [WormR] (26:1, issue 101) 86, p. 28-29.
     "Getting Involved." [WormR] (26:2, issue 102) 86, p. 76-77.
     "Harsh Realtiy." [WormR] (26:2, issue 102) 86, p. 76.
     "Hey, hank." [OroM] (4:1-4) My 85, p. 42-43.
     "How to Get Along with Charles Bukowski." [OroM] (4:1-4) My 85, p. 56.
     "How You Get an Appointment at the Pre-Paid Health Care Center." [WormR]
          (26:2, issue 102) 86, p. 75-76.
     "John Gardner." [WormR] (26:3, issue 103) 86, p. 93-94.
     "The Little Atlas of Modern English Lit." [WormR] (26:3, issue 103) 86, p. 96.
     "My Retiring Colleagues." [WormR] (26:1, issue 101) 86, p. 30-31.
     "On the Beach." [Abraxas] (34) 86, p. 46.
     "One Threat Aborted, One Not." [BellR] (9:1) Spr 86, p. 30.
     "Oregon Crisis Hotline." [WormR] (26:1, issue 101) 86, p. 27-28.
     "Patty." [WormR] (26:4, issue 104) 86, p. 154-155.

"People Say Bukowski Has Sold Out." [WormR] (26:2, issue 102) 86, p. 75.
"Quo Vadis, M.F.A.?" [WormR] (26:3, issue 103) 86, p. 94.
"A Secular Salvation." [WormR] (26:3, issue 103) 86, p. 92.
"She Loves the Ring of It." [WormR] (26:3, issue 103) 86, p. 92.
"Some Women Still Like Men to Like Each Other." [WormR] (26:4, issue 104) 86,
   p. 155.
"A Spoil-Sport." [WormR] (26:4, issue 104) 86, p. 156.
"A T. Coraghessan Boyle Character Once Said That He Didn't Care How He Died . .
   ." [Abraxas] (34) 86, p. 47.
"They Don't Put the Same Value on Human Life As We Do." [BellR] (9:1) Spr 86,
   p. 33.
"Totally Unoriginal Poem." [BellR] (9:1) Spr 86, p. 30.
"An Underrated Conditioned Response." [WormR] (26:4, issue 104) 86, p. 155.
"Untitled Because It Doesn't Deserve One." [WormR] (26:1, issue 101) 86, p. 32.
"The Value of Poetry Readings." [Bogg] (55) 86, p. 17.
"We're Entitled." [BellR] (9:1) Spr 86, p. 31-32.
"Working Girls." [WormR] (26:3, issue 103) 86, p. 94-95.
"You Probably Have to Put Down a Deposit on the Silverware." [WormR] (26:3,
   issue 103) 86, p. 95.
3173. LOCKWOOD, Sandra
   "Buying Spring." [Waves] (14:3) Wint 86, p. 68.
3174. LOGAN, Thean
   "Aquarius in August." [Wind] (16:58) 86, p. 28.
   "Haircut." [AntigR] (65) Spr 86, p. 52.
   "Hole to China." [WestB] (18) 86, p. 62.
   "Love Chapped." [Wind] (16:58) 86, p. 28-29.
   "White Roses." [WestB] (18) 86, p. 63.
3175. LOGAN, William
   "Britain without Baedeker." [NewRep] (195:17) 27 O 86, p. 49.
   "Convention of Liars." [SewanR] (94:4) Fall 86, p. 573-574.
   "Disease and Etiquette." [YaleR] (75:4) Sum 86, p. 589-591.
   "The Duck Pond." [ParisR] (28:101) Wint 86, p. 238.
   "The Great Wildlife of the Church." [Shen] (36:4) 86, p. 49-51.
   "The Imitative Fallacy." [ParisR] (28:100) Sum-Fall 86, p. 194.
   "Major James." [SewanR] (94:4) Fall 86, p. 574-575.
   "Nocturne Revolutionnaire." [Agni] (23) 86, p. 71-72.
3176. LOGUE, Christopher
   "Walking." [ParisR] (28:100) Sum-Fall 86, p. 195.
3177. LOMAS, Herbert
   "Letters in the Dark" (Selections). [Hudson] (38:4) Wint 86, p. 615-619.
3178. LONERGAN, Frank
   "The Judgment of Stones." [KanQ] (18:1/2) Wint-Spr 86, p. 122.
   "Old Folks Visit." [KanQ] (18:1/2) Wint-Spr 86, p. 123.
3179. LONG, Keith
   "My Birds: Wise Birds." [CimR] (77) O 86, p. 52.
3180. LONG, Priscilla
   "Nuclear Patchwork." [Vis] (20) 86, p. 33.
3181. LONG, Richard
   "A Change in the Way of Life" (for A.S.). [Poem] (55) Mr 86, p. 47.
   "Looking for Treasure." [Poem] (55) Mr 86, p. 46.
   "Minor Notes on June in November." [MidAR] (7:1) 86, p. 112-117.
3182. LONG, Robert
   "Found and Lost." [IndR] (9:3) Sum 86, p. 49.
   "Time and Its Double." [IndR] (9:3) Sum 86, p. 47-48.
3183. LONG, Robert Hill
   "Rosa Mundi." [IndR] (9:2) Spr 86, p. 68.
3184. LONGLEY, Judy
   "Glass Harp at Jackson Square." [SouthernPR] (26:2) Fall 86, p. 69.
3185. LOONEY, George
   "By Instinct." [TarRP] (25:2) Spr 86, p. 30-31.
   "The Dream of a Language." [MidwQ] (27:2) Wint 86, p. 208.
   "Fireflies." [IndR] (9:3) Sum 86, p. 70.
   "Halley's Comet." [MidwQ] (28:1) Aut 86, p. 95-97.
   "The Last Vision of Light." [PraS] (60:3) Fall 86, p. 97-99.
   "Release." [TexasR] (7:1/2) Spr-Sum 86, p. 96-97.

3186. LOOTS, Barbara
"Advice to a Younger Woman." [HeliconN] (16) Wint 86, p. 54.
3187. LOPEZ, Adelaida
"Si bajo la luz de las escaleras." [Mairena] (8:22) 86, p. 122.
LOPEZ, Carolie Parker
See PARKER-LOPEZ, Carolie
3188. LOPEZ, Christopher
"Before Motel 6." [HarvardA] (119:4) My 86, p. 30.
LOPEZ, Joaquín Lopez
See LOPEZ LOPEZ, Joaquín
3189. LOPEZ, Julio César
"La Mano." [Mairena] (8:22) 86, p. 101.
3190. LOPEZ, Karen Braithwaite
"Angel." [EngJ] (75:3) Mr 86, p. 66.
3191. LOPEZ, Raymond M.
"The Rape." [Electrum] (38) Spr 86, p. 22-23.
3192. LOPEZ ADORNO, Pedro
"Donde el Escribiente Trama la Reconciliacion de Dos Entidades Opuestas."
[Mairena] (8:22) 86, p. 66.
3193. LOPEZ LOPEZ, Joaquín
"Adios a Federico." [Mairena] (8:21) 86, p. 19-20.
3194. LOPEZ MASS, Jesus Efrain
"En Granada" (En la muerte de Federico García Lorca). [Mairena] (8:21) 86, p.
35-36.
"Mi Novia." [Mairena] (8:21) 86, p. 42.
"Romance de Ella y Yo." [Mairena] (8:21) 86, p. 40.
"Romance de la Princesa y el Doncel." [Mairena] (8:21) 86, p. 36-37.
"Se Fue." [Mairena] (8:21) 86, p. 38-40.
"El Viejo Viejo." [Mairena] (8:21) 86, p. 41-42.
3195. LOPEZ SURIA, Violeta
"Eres la Sombra Clara" (A Jorge Luis Morales, al acogerse a retiro, en la
Universidad). [Mairena] (8:22) 86, p. 98.
"Laura y Georgina" (para Ana Aida Astol de Antúnez). [RevICP] (88) Abril-Junio
85, p. 57.
LORCA, Federico Garcia
See GARCIA LORCA, Federico
3196. LORD, Alan
"Three Simple Pieces." [Rampike] (5:2) 86, p. 58.
3197. LORD, Ted
"Hobbled." [IndR] (9:3) Sum 86, p. 77.
3198. LORDAHL, J. A.
"Art Deco." [YetASM] (4) 85, p. 6.
3199. LORDE, Audre
"Berlin Is Hard on Colored Girls." [Callaloo] (9:1, #26) Wint 86, p. 89.
"Sisters in Arms." [Callaloo] (9:1, #26) Wint 86, p. 87-88.
3200. LOTT, Clarinda Harriss
"Veronica's Song." [Calyx] (10:1) Sum 86, p. 24-25.
3201. LOTT, Rick
"The Face in the Mirror." [CarolQ] (39:1) Fall 86, p. 35.
"Incident at Blue Lake." [CimR] (76) Jl 86, p. 54-55.
"Nocturne for Autumn." [Poetry] (149:1) O 86, p. 7-8.
3202. LOUCAREAS, Dale
"The Informer." [WritersL] (1986:5), p. 14.
"The Pursuit of Poetry." [WritersL] (1986:5), p. 14.
3203. LOUGHRY, Ron
"Upon Arrival." [Wind] (16:57) 86, p. 21.
3204. LOUIS, Frank W.
"Coda" (For My Father). [YetASM] (4) 85, p. 2.
3205. LOVE, B. D.
"Carp." [SouthernPR] (26:2) Fall 86, p. 74-76.
"Grace." [KanQ] (18:4) Fall 86, p. 88.
3206. LOVELOCK, Yann
"Sentence Analysis." [Stand] (27:3) Sum 86, p. 23-25.
3207. LOVERDE, James
"Fantomas Whiles Away" (tr. of Ernst Moerman). [Vis] (22) 86, p. 5.

3208. LOVERIDGE-GALLAS, Louisa
"Now That I'm Truly Old." [CreamCR] (11:1) 86?, p. 50-51.
3209. LOW, Denise
"An Ice Age Ghost Story." [KanQ] (18:3) Sum 86, p. 34.
"Ptolemy's *Tetrabiblos*: Comets." [MidwQ] (28:1) Aut 86, p. 98.
3210. LOW, Jackson Mac
"Pieces o' Six — XXII." [Sulfur] (6:2, issue 17) 86, p. 105-107.
"Pieces o' Six — XXIV." [Sulfur] (6:2, issue 17) 86, p. 4-6.
"Pieces O' Six" (Five Prose Pieces: XV-XIX). [Chelsea] (45) 86, p. 61-75.
3211. LOWE, Frederick
"The Satyr." [YellowS] (18) Spr 86, p. 42.
3212. LOWELL, Robert
"The Public Garden." [YaleR] (75:2) Wint 86, p. 318-319.
3213. LOWERY, Joanne
"The Werewolf." [ManhatPR] (7) Sum 86, p. 49.
3214. LOWEY, Mark
"Birdsong for the Dying." [Dandel] (13:1) Spr-Sum 86, p. 29.
"The Builder." [Dandel] (13:1) Spr-Sum 86, p. 30-31.
"Don't Call It Sadness." [Dandel] (13:1) Spr-Sum 86, p. 28.
3215. LOWRY, Betty
"At Knossos." [DeKalbLAJ] (19:2) 86, p. 39.
3216. LOWRY, Charlene
"Wagluh' Ta Tapi." [RiverS] (19) 86, p. 60-61.
3217. LOWRY, John
"Day of Infamy." [HangL] (49) Spr 86, p. 22.
"The Hand of the Potter." [WormR] (26:1, issue 101) 86, p. 5.
"Point of Disorder." [HangL] (49) Spr 86, p. 23.
"Sleeping Dogs." [WormR] (26:1, issue 101) 86, p. 4.
"So Help Me God." [WormR] (26:1, issue 101) 86, p. 4-5.
"Think Japanese." [WormR] (26:1, issue 101) 86, p. 4.
3218. LOWRY, Mary Ann
"Harvest Time." [YetASM] (4) 85, p. 2.
3219. LU, Chi
"Wen Fu (The Art of Writing)" (tr. by Sam Hamill). [AmerPoR] (15:3) My-Je 86, p. 23-27.
3220. LU, Li
"Fruit" (tr. by Rewi Alley). [Verse] (6) 86, p. 48.
3221. LUBETSKY, Elsen
"Blessings on Their Little Heads." [PoeticJ] (16) Fall 86, p. 6.
"Connections." [SanFPJ] (8:2) 85, p. 30.
"Growing Up." [PoeticJ] (14) 86, p. 31.
"However Did You Guess?" [PoeticJ] (16) Fall 86, p. 7.
"I, Rachel, Take Thee, Grandma." [PoeticJ] (13) 86, p. 30.
"Migrants." [SanFPJ] (8:2) 85, p. 73.
"Nicaraguan." [SanFPJ] (8:2) 85, p. 31.
"No More Myths." [YetASM] (4) 85, p. 3.
"The Perils of Nursery School." [PoeticJ] (13) 86, p. 31.
"A Place in the Heart." [PoeticJ] (16) Fall 86, p. 2.
"Second Birthday. So Soon?" [PoeticJ] (13) 86, p. 31.
"S'more Rachel." [PoeticJ] (13) 86, p. 30.
"Statistically Speaking." [PoeticJ] (16) Fall 86, p. 6.
"That Uncertain Age." [PoeticJ] (14) 86, p. 31.
"Uhuru." [SanFPJ] (8:2) 85, p. 32.
3222. LUCAS, Dennis
"Irony." [Amelia] (3:4) Fall 86, p. 20.
3223. LUCAS, Lawrence A.
"West of Fortville." [BallSUF] (26:4) Aut 85, p. 31.
LUCCA, Rafael Arraiz
See ARRAIZ LUCCA, Rafael
3224. LUCHT, Dave
"The Jerry Jeff Walker Poem" (for Walt Cieszynski). [CreamCR] (11:1) 86?, p. 54-55.
3225. LUCIA, Joseph
"Foundation." [LitR] (29:3) Spr 86, p. 345.
"To Ben, for Watering My Garden." [SouthernHR] (20:3) Sum 86, p. 266.
"Turning Toward, Turning Away." [Wind] (16:57) 86, p. 22.

3226. LUCINA, Mary (Sister)
    "Calling you." [Comm] (113:14) 15 Ag 86, p. 436.
    "How They Build Their Fires." [Amelia] (3:3) Sum 86, p. 102.
    "If It Was." [Nimrod] (30:1) Fall-Wint 86, p. 113.
    "Returning." [MidAR] (7:1) 86, p. 110.
    "The Trains Are Farther Away." [MidAR] (7:1) 86, p. 111.
3227. LUDVIGSON, Susan
    "Dangers." [SouthernPR] (26:2) Fall 86, p. 28.
    "From the Beginning." [MichQR] (25:1) Wint 86, p. 23-24.
    "Hypochondria." [SoCaR] (19:1) Fall 86, p. 31.
    "I Arrive in a Small Boat, Alone." [GeoR] (40:3) Fall 86, p. 718.
    "Lesson." [GeoR] (40:3) Fall 86, p. 717.
    "The Origami Heart." [MissouriR] (9:2) 86, p. 48.
    "Point of Disappearance." [Verse] (5) 86, p. 38.
    "The Room." [AntR] (44:1) Wint 86, p. 63-65.
    "The Sudden Approach of Trees." [SouthernPR] (26:2) Fall 86, p. 27-28.
3228. LUDWIN, Peter
    "Losing It." [Sam] (44:3 release 175) 86, p. 50-51.
    "The Vietnam Veterans Parade, Manhattan." [Sam] (44:3 release 175) 86, p. 39.
    "Walking Point — 'Nam." [Sam] (44:3 release 175) 86, p. 36.
3229. LUEBBE, James
    "First Blizzard, Worst Blizzard." [PraS] (60:2) Sum 86, p. 131.
    "White Ground." [PraS] (60:2) Sum 86, p. 130.
3230. LUGN, Kristina
    "It Doesn't Look Nice" (tr. by Daniel Ogden). [Vis] (22) 86, p. 19.
    "Telephones That Ring" (tr. by Daniel Ogden). [Vis] (22) 86, p. 19.
3231. LUGO, Samuel
    "Agro-Cosmico." [RevICP] (90) Oct-Dic 85, p. 33.
    "Alba." [RevICP] (90) Oct-Dic 85, p. 30.
    "Fantasia de Amor a lo Infinito." [RevICP] (90) Oct-Dic 85, p. 32.
    "Mireya." [RevICP] (90) Oct-Dic 85, p. 30.
    "No Des al Mar Tus Limoneros." [RevICP] (90) Oct-Dic 85, p. 31.
    "Perspectiva." [RevICP] (90) Oct-Dic 85, p. 33.
    "Yumbra." [RevICP] (90) Oct-Dic 85, p. 31.
3232. LUGO-GUERNELLI, Adelaida
    "Tu Soledad." [Mairena] (8:22) 86, p. 103.
3233. LUIS, Leopoldo de
    "Homenaje a Jacobson." [Mairena] (8:22) 86, p. 24.
3234. LUKAS, Susan G.
    "September 29, Bath, Maine." [SmPd] (23:1, #66) Wint 86, p. 9.
3235. LUKASIK, Gail Kalina
    "A Fairy Tale." [Prima] (10) 86, p. 51.
3236. LUKE (JOSEPH A. BROWN, S.J.)
    "At the Edge." [Callaloo] (9:1, #26) Wint 86, p. 93.
    "Stories about Chrone." [Callaloo] (9:1, #26) Wint 86, p. 90-92.
3237. LUKEMAN, Mark
    "Above the Solomons." [Wind] (16:57) 86, p. 23.
    "Doctor Sax Says Boo" (243rd Chorus). [MoodySI] (16/17) Sum 86, p. 11.
    "Tarawa, 1943." [Wind] (16:57) 86, p. 23.
3238. LUM, Wing Tek
    "On the First Proper Sunday of Ching Ming." [Contact] (7:38/39/40) Wint-Spr 86,
        p. 27.
    "Subway Scene." [Contact] (7:38/39/40) Wint-Spr 86, p. 27.
    "What Pyjamas Were." [MinnR] (NS 27) Fall 86, p. 83.
3239. LUNDE, David
    "Morgan & Fate." [BallSUF] (26:4) Aut 85, p. 49.
    "Morgan Cruising." [BallSUF] (26:4) Aut 85, p. 48.
    "Morgan Mowing" (for Harold Tinkle, with thanks to George Peele). [BallSUF]
        (26:4) Aut 85, p. 48.
    "Morgan's Mirror." [BallSUF] (26:4) Aut 85, p. 49.
    "Morganwelt." [BallSUF] (26:4) Aut 85, p. 48.
    "Poem for Our Birthday." [RagMag] (5:1) Spr 86, p. 38.
3240. LUNDE, Diane
    "The Hudson River." [Blueline] (7:2) Wint-Spr 86, p. 32.
    "We, the True Believers." [PoetryNW] (27:2) Sum 86, p. 43-44.

3241. LUNDQUIST, Kaye
"Flora Obbligata." [BellArk] (2:3) My-Je 86, p. 6.
"Morning Journey." [BellArk] (2:3) My-Je 86, p. 5.
"So Little Time." [BellArk] (2:6) N-D 86, p. 2.
3242. LUNDY, Gary
"In Time They Speak." [ClockR] (3:2) 86, p. 63.
"Insurance." [BelPoJ] (37:2) Wint 86-87, p. 17.
3243. LUNN, Jean
"Lions." [ManhatPR] (6) Wint-Spr 85-86, p. 50.
3244. LUO, Gengye
"Train through Qin Mountains" (tr. by John Minford and Pang Bingjun). [Nimrod]
        (29:2) Spr-Sum 86, p. 108-111.
3245. LUTHER, Susan M.
"Seventeen Months after One Death and Seven Months after Another." [CumbPR]
        (6:1) Fall 86, p. 29.
3246. LUX, Thomas
"Barracuda." [Field] (33) Fall 85, p. 87.
"Bodo." [Field] (35) Fall 86, p. 69-70.
"Cellar Stairs." [Field] (35) Fall 86, p. 68.
"Kwashiorkor, Marasmus." [Ploughs] (12:3) 86, p. 26.
"Old Man Shovelling Snow." [Ploughs] (12:3) 86, p. 24-25.
"On Visiting Herbert Hoover's Birth and Burial Place." [Ploughs] (12:3) 86, p. 23.
"Traveling Exhibit of Torture Instruments." [Field] (33) Fall 85, p. 88.
"Ultima Thule." [Ploughs] (12:3) 86, p. 27-28.
3247. LUZZARO, Susan
"La Fleur Sauvage." [CentR] (30:4) Fall 86, p. 476-477.
"Full Circle." [TarRP] (26:1) Fall 86, p. 27-28.
"To the Third Power." [TarRP] (26:1) Fall 86, p. 28-29.
3248. LYLES, Peggy (Peggy Willis)
"Books close buds" (Haiku). [WindO] (47) Sum 86, p. 3.
"New address book." [Amelia] (3:1) Ja 86, p. 8.
3249. LYNCH, Janice (Janice M.)
"The Apartment Is Centrally Located." [Vis] (21) 86, p. 14.
"Sixty-Four Caprices for a Long-Distance Swimmer: Notes on Swimming 100
        Miles." [BelPoJ] (37:1) Fall 86, p. 32-37.
3250. LYNCH, Jennifer
"Letters to John Berryman." [ThRiPo] (27/28) 86, p. 44-46.
3251. LYNCH, Michael
"Across the Room from the Sobbing Man in a Yarmulka." [Contact] (7:38/39/40)
        Wint-Spr 86, p. 80-81.
"From the Air" (on the death of a friend with AIDS: Selections). [Contact]
        (7:38/39/40) Wint-Spr 86, p. 80-82.
"Giving Up the Ghost." [Contact] (7:38/39/40) Wint-Spr 86, p. 81-82.
"The News about Ray." [Contact] (7:38/39/40) Wint-Spr 86, p. 80.
3252. LYNCH, Thomas
"The Sin-Eater." [BostonR] (11:6) D 86, p. 22.
3253. LYNGSTAD, Sverre
"Minoan Ruins" (Selections: I, III, tr. of Nicole Mace). [WebR] (11:2) Fall 86, p.
        31-32.
3254. LYNNE, Sondraya
"I am great American dying." [SanFPJ] (8:2) 85, p. 21.
"The Murder of Innocence." [SanFPJ] (8:2) 85, p. 24.
3255. LYNSKEY, Edward C.
"The Lame Shall Enter First." [SouthernPR] (26:1) Spr 86, p. 32.
"The Later Days." [Wind] (16:57) 86, p. 24.
"The Night Light." [MidAR] (7:1) 86, p. 104.
"The Strange Case of Doctor Mudd." [MidAR] (7:1) 86, p. 105.
3256. LYON, George Ella
"Mother's Day at the Air Force Museum." [AmerV] (4) Fall 86, p. 109-111.
3257. LYON, Hillary
"The Diagnosis." [MidwQ] (27:4) Sum 86, p. 469.
"Enola in New Mexico." [MidwQ] (27:4) Sum 86, p. 471.
"Outwitting Thieves." [PoetryNW] (27:3) Aut 86, p. 20.
"Pick Up the Prisoners." [MidwQ] (27:4) Sum 86, p. 470.
3258. LYON, Mark
"Tomorrow." [PikeF] (7) Spr 86, p. 22.

233

3259. LYON, Michael
"We Are an Insane People." [KanQ] (18:3) Sum 86, p. 19-22.
3260. LYON, Richard
"Burning the Meadows." [AmerPoR] (15:3) My-Je 86, p. 18.
"One Other Thing." [AmerPoR] (15:3) My-Je 86, p. 18.
"Stone Fence Post." [AmerPoR] (15:3) My-Je 86, p. 18.
3261. LYON, W. (Wendy)
"Domestic Discomfort." [PoetryNW] (27:2) Sum 86, p. 18-19.
"Gathering." [Amelia] (3:2) Spr 86, p. 99.
"Honey Locust." [LitR] (29:3) Spr 86, p. 292.
"Meditation." [PoetryNW] (27:2) Sum 86, p. 17.
"Prayer." [PoetryNW] (27:2) Sum 86, p. 18.
"Saturday Afternoon." [LitR] (29:3) Spr 86, p. 292.
3262. LYONS, Richard
"Chiemsee." [Nat] (242:21) 31 My 86, p. 768.
"Constellation." (For Glenn). [Poetry] (147:4) Ja 86, p. 219-220.
"A Season." [DenQ] (20:4/21:1) Spr-Sum 86, p. 123.
3263. LYONS, Robert
"In the Reeds." [BellArk] (2:4) Jl-Ag 86, p. 7.
"The Return." [BellArk] (2:5) S-O 86, p. 6.
Mac . . .
    See also names beginning with Mc . . .
MAC LOW, Jackson
    See LOW, Jackson Mac
3264. MacAFEE, Norman
"Pictures from Bosch." [LittleM] (15:2) 86, p. 48-49.
3265. MacBETH, George
"The Pigeon." [Stand] (27:1) Wint 85-86, p. 55.
3266. MacCAIG, Norman
"Hotel Room, 12th Floor." [Confr] (33/34) Fall-Wint 86-87, p. 292.
"In Peace Time." [Confr] (33/34) Fall-Wint 86-87, p. 291.
"Painting — 'The Blue Jar'." [Confr] (33/34) Fall-Wint 86-87, p. 290.
3267. MacDONALD, Cynthia
"A Critical Age." [NewRep] (195:24) 15 D 86, p. 36.
3268. MACDONALD, D.
"Hands" (for David Resch, sculptor). [NegC] (6:4) Fall 86, p. 140.
3269. MacDONALD, Errol
"Aviva at the Crossroads." [Quarry] (35:3) Sum 86, p. 29-30.
"Discussions That Work." [Quarry] (35:3) Sum 86, p. 29.
"Mauve Descending." [Quarry] (35:3) Sum 86, p. 30-31.
3270. MACE, Nicole
"Minoan Ruins" (Selections: I, III, tr. by Sverre Lyngstad). [WebR] (11:2) Fall 86,
    p. 31-32.
3271. MACEBUH, Sandy
"Dust." [WritersL] (1986:6), p. 14.
"He Ain't Heavy and I'm Surprised." [WritersL] (1986:3), p. 20.
"A Shining Star." [WritersL] (1986:2), p. 14.
MACEBUSH, Sandy
    See MACEBUH, Sandy
3272. MacEWEN, Gwendolyn
"The Death of the Loch Ness Monster." [GreenfR] (13:3/4) Sum-Fall 86, p. 123.
"Grey Owl's Poem." [GreenfR] (13:3/4) Sum-Fall 86, p. 125.
"The Names." [GreenfR] (13:3/4) Sum-Fall 86, p. 124.
"November." [WestCR] (21:2) O 86, p. 37.
3273. MACHADO, Antonio
"The Flies" (tr. by Pamela Uschuk). [AnotherCM] (16) 86, p. 101-102.
3274. MACHOS, Angie
"I wish I could go to Paris on one ski in one hour." [QW] (23) 86, p. 117.
3275. MACHOS, Leah
"If I was a lightbulb." [QW] (23) 86, p. 117.
3276. MacINNES, Mairi
"The Fields of Light." [TriQ] (67) Fall 86, p. 120-121.
"I Look for You Everywhere." [NewYorker] (62:38) 10 N 86, p. 50.
3277. MacISAAC, Dan
"La Brea Woman." [Quarry] (35:3) Sum 86, p. 52-53.
"Footprints at Laetoli, Tanzania." [Quarry] (35:3) Sum 86, p. 53.

3278. MACK, Joe
"Beirut." [SanFPJ] (8:4) 85, p. 66-67.
"Literary Suicide." [SanFPJ] (8:4) 85, p. 49.
"Upbeat Protest." [SanFPJ] (8:4) 85, p. 23.
3279. MacKENZIE, Gareth Morgan
"Fragmented Letter." [JamesWR] (3:4) Sum 86, p. 1.
3280. MACKEY, Nathaniel
"Dogon Eclipse." [Callaloo] (9:1, #26) Wint 86, p. 96-97.
"The Sleeping Rocks" (for Wilson Harris). [Callaloo] (9:1, #26) Wint 86, p. 94-95.
"Solomon's Outer Wall." [Callaloo] (9:1, #26) Wint 86, p. 98-99.
"Song of the Andoumboulou, 10." [Temblor] (3) 86, p. 37.
"Song of the Andoumboulou, 11." [Temblor] (3) 86, p. 38.
"Uninhabited Angel." [Temblor] (3) 86, p. 36.
3281. MACKIE, James
"Letter to a Woman in a Wheat Field." [Wind] (16:58) 86, p. 30.
"Two Men with Blue Bedrolls." [Wind] (16:58) 86, p. 30.
3282. MACKRIDGE, Peter
"Foresight" (tr. of Titos Patrikios). [Verse] (5) 86, p. 57.
"Half-Finished Letter" (tr. of Titos Patrikios). [Verse] (5) 86, p. 58.
"The Mountains" (tr. of Titos Patrikios). [Verse] (5) 86, p. 57.
"Secret Life" (tr. of Titos Patrikios). [Verse] (5) 86, p. 57.
3283. MACLEOD, Norman
"An Apology to Wallace Stevens." [Pembroke] (18) 86, p. 259.
"The Descent." [Pembroke] (18) 86, p. 260.
"The Lord Gets around a Lot." [Pembroke] (18) 86, p. 259.
"Something of Blind Benefit." [Pembroke] (18) 86, p. 257-258.
"TV's Latest Massacre of the Past." [Pembroke] (18) 86, p. 258.
"Wireless: To All Gaelic Gulls." [Pembroke] (18) 86, p. 257.
MACLOW, Jackson
See LOW, Jackson Mac
3284. MACOMBER, Megan
"At the Ob-Gyn Associates." [WoosterR] (6) Fall 86, p. 40-41.
"Daybreak in the Locker Room." [WoosterR] (6) Fall 86, p. 36.
"Epithalamion on the Marriage of My Middle Sister." [HeliconN] (14/15) Sum 86, p. 168.
"Solstice." [WoosterR] (6) Fall 86, p. 37.
"Stray." [WoosterR] (6) Fall 86, p. 38-39.
3285. MacPHERSON, Jay
"Dead Languages." [GreenfR] (13:3/4) Sum-Fall 86, p. 126-127.
3286. MacSWEEN, R. J.
"Corners." [AntigR] (64) Wint 86, p. 38.
"If Clarity Returns." [AntigR] (64) Wint 86, p. 39.
"In the Quiet Fields." [AntigR] (64) Wint 86, p. 36-37.
"Jerome." [AntigR] (65) Spr 86, p. 46-47.
"Looking at Some Czéch Words." [AntigR] (66/67) Sum-Aut 86, p. 204-205.
"On a Journey." [AntigR] (65) Spr 86, p. 49.
"Reading the Great Poets." [AntigR] (66/67) Sum-Aut 86, p. 206.
"Waiting." [AntigR] (65) Spr 86, p. 48.
3287. MADDEN, John E., IV
"Poetry and Bath." [Bogg] (55) 86, p. 19.
3288. MADGETT, Naomi Long
"Images." [MichQR] (25:2) Spr 86, p. 312.
3289. MADSON, Arthur
"Vine-Covered." [CrossCur] (5:4/6:1) 86, p. 175-176.
3290. MADUENO, Amalio
"A Note on Musical Pitch." [LakeSR] (20) 86, p. 25.
"Thistle." [LakeSR] (20) 86, p. 24.
3291. MADZELAN, Pete
"Unvarnished Lies." [SanFPJ] (8:4) 85, p. 43.
"Where Have the Farmers Gone." [SanFPJ] (8:4) 85, p. 44.
3292. MAGAR, Donald
"This Short Odyssey about Edison Who Created More Light . . ." (tr. of Vítezslav Nezval). [NewOR] (13:3) Fall 86, p. 66-76.
MAGARITY, Brenda Najimian
See NAJIMIAN-MAGARITY, Brenda

3293. MAGEE, Kevin
"The Broken Boy." [AnotherCM] (16) 86, p. 57.
"A Time of Sundering." [AntR] (44:4) Fall 86, p. 431.
3294. MAGUIRE, Robert A.
"The Morning After" (tr. of Stanislaw Baranczak, w. Magnus J. Krynski). [TriQ]
(65) Wint 86, p. 87.
MAGUT, Mohamed Al
See Al MAGUT, Mohamed
3295. MAGYAR, Rose
"My Life Was Rich." [SinW] (29/30) 86, p. 155-156.
3296. MAHAPATRA, Jayanta
"Afternoon Ceremonies." [KenR] (NS 8:4) Fall 86, p. 49.
"Ann." [Hudson] (39:1) Spr 86, p. 95.
"Crossworlds." [KenR] (NS 8:4) Fall 86, p. 51.
"Days." [Hudson] (39:1) Spr 86, p. 96.
"A Death." [KenR] (NS 8:4) Fall 86, p. 52.
"Father." [Hudson] (39:1) Spr 86, p. 94.
"From Star to Star." [KenR] (NS 8:4) Fall 86, p. 50.
"Light." [KenR] (NS 8:4) Fall 86, p. 54.
"Nakedness." [KenR] (NS 8:4) Fall 86, p. 53.
"Shadows." [KenR] (NS 8:4) Fall 86, p. 48.
"Summer Afternoons." [CrossCur] (5:4/6:1) 86, p. 9.
"The Time Afterward." [CrossCur] (5:4/6:1) 86, p. 12.
"To a Young Girl." [CrossCur] (5:4/6:1) 86, p. 13.
"When You Need to Play Act." [KenR] (NS 8:4) Fall 86, p. 47-48.
"With Broken Wings." [CrossCur] (5:4/6:1) 86, p. 10-11.
3297. MAHLER-SUSSMAN, Leona
"Berry Rich." [SmPd] (23:1, #66) Wint 86, p. 24.
"Span." [SmPd] (23:1, #66) Wint 86, p. 34.
3298. MAHON, Derek
"Autumn" (tr. of Eugene Dubnov, w. the author). [CentR] (30:4) Fall 86, p. 474.
"In the Steps of the Moon" (after the French of Philippe Jaccottet). [Verse] (6) 86, p.
29.
"Patience" (after the French of Philippe Jaccottet). [Verse] (6) 86, p. 29.
"Portovenere" (after the French of Philippe Jaccottet). [Verse] (6) 86, p. 29.
"The Tenant" (after the French of Philippe Jaccottet). [Verse] (6) 86, p. 29.
3299. MAHON, Jeanne
"Grace." [WestB] (19) 86, p. 23-24.
"Joining the Mourners." [CutB] (26) Spr-Sum 86, p. 34-35.
"Stonehenge." [WestB] (19) 86, p. 22.
3300. MAIA
"Give Me the Moon." [SingHM] (14) 86, p. 38-39.
"Pieces of the Moon." [SingHM] (14) 86, p. 37.
3301. MAIER, Carol
"Confess, 1220-50" (tr. of Octavio Armand). [IndR] (9:2) Spr 86, p. 26.
MAINA, Susan di
See DiMAINA, Susan
3302. MAINO, Jeannette (Jeannette Gould)
"Afternoon Television" (a rondeau). [KanQ] (18:4) Fall 86, p. 41.
"Autumn Rain." [BallSUF] (27:4) Aut 86, p. 15.
"In Mountains at Night." [BallSUF] (27:4) Aut 86, p. 11.
"Iva." [BallSUF] (27:4) Aut 86, p. 32.
"Journey, 1842" (for my grandfather in Maine). [BallSUF] (27:4) Aut 86, p. 22.
"Sonnet Sequence." [KanQ] (18:3) Sum 86, p. 31-33.
3303. MAJOR, Devorah
"A Crowded Table." [Zyzzyva] (2:3) Fall 86, p. 105-108.
3304. MAKEEVER, Anne T.
"Seduction." [HeliconN] (16) Wint 86, p. 52-53.
3305. MAKOFSKE, Mary
"They Keep House." [WoosterR] (5) Spr 86, p. 72.
3306. MAKUCK, Peter
"Feeders." [Poetry] (149:1) O 86, p. 29.
"Historic Present" (Loire Valley, 1975). [SouthernPR] (26:2) Fall 86, p. 51-52.
"Owl and Heron, Months Apart." [Hudson] (38:4) Wint 86, p. 631-632.
MALDONADO, Manuel Martinez
See MARTINEZ MALDONADO, Manuel

MALE, Belkis Cuza
    See CUZA MALE, Belkis
3307. MALINA, Judith
    "Every One of the Cleaning Women." [RedBass] (10) 86, p. 21.
3308. MALLAVARAPU, Anita
    "A Ghazal." [Grain] (14:2) My 86, p. 49.
    "Paper Life." [Grain] (14:2) My 86, p. 48.
    "Time." [Grain] (14:2) My 86, p. 49.
    "Without Seclusion." [Grain] (14:2) My 86, p. 49.
3309. MALLORY, Norman
    "Love in the Library." [AntigR] (64) Wint 86, p. 22.
    "Three Poems on Jupiter's Red Spot" (on seeing the spacecraft "Galileo"). [AntigR]
        (64) Wint 86, p. 23.
3310. MALONE, Pamela Altfeld
    "The Model." [Chelsea] (45) 86, p. 25-28.
    "Springtime in Leonia." [BellArk] (2:2) Mr-Ap 86, p. 8.
    "Time." [BellArk] (2:2) Mr-Ap 86, p. 15.
3311. MALONEY, Dennis
    "The Stones of Chile" (Selections: 9 poems, tr. of Pablo Neruda). [WillowS] (18)
        Sum 86, p. 41-57.
    "Tangled Hair: Poems" (tr. of Akiko Yosano, w. Hide Oshiro). [YellowS] (18) Spr
        86, p. 24-25.
3312. MALPEZZI, Frances
    "Professor Sid Snivelley Addresses His Medieval Literature Class." [NegC] (6:4)
        Fall 86, p. 73.
3313. MALTMAN, Kim
    "Installation #17." [Dandel] (13:1) Spr-Sum 86, p. 32.
    "Installation #33." [MalR] (76) S 86, p. 76.
    "Installation #37 (Sudden Pain)." [MalR] (76) S 86, p. 77.
    "Long Narrow Roadway." [GreenfR] (13:3/4) Sum-Fall 86, p. 128-129.
    "The Technology of Disquiet and Distance." [Dandel] (13:1) Spr-Sum 86, p. 34.
    "The Technology of Introspection." [MalR] (76) S 86, p. 75.
    "The Technology of Metal, Turning." [MalR] (76) S 86, p. 74.
    "The Technology of Nausea, and Ecstacy, Which, Having Flared a Moment, Remain
        Like a Blue Flame . . ." [Dandel] (13:1) Spr-Sum 86, p. 33.
3314. MALYON, Carol
    "The Colville Paintings" (Selections). [Quarry] (35:1) Wint 86, p. 68-70.
3315. MAMBER, Ellie
    "Don't Laugh, It's Serious, She Says." [Calyx] (9:2/3) Wint 86, p. 112.
3316. MANCINI, Ronald
    "Going on Convention." [WindO] (47) Sum 86, p. 19.
3317. MANDEL, Charlotte
    "Bahia." [StoneC] (14:1/2) Fall-Wint 86-87, p. 13.
    "Going to Work." [WestB] (19) 86, p. 108-109.
    "In Quantum Mechanics, Marriage Is." [ClockR] (3:1) 85, p. 42.
    "My Father at Ninety-Two, Splitting the Days." [SenR] (16:2) 86, p. 84.
3318. MANDEL, Eli
    "June #! 21/84* a Poem with Mistakes Included." [GreenfR] (13:3/4) Sum-Fall 86,
        p. 131.
3319. MANDEL, Oscar
    "And the Lord God Planted a Garden." [KenR] (NS 7:2) Spr 85, p. 87-114.
3320. MANDEL, Tom
    "Mute Canto II." [Sink] (2) 86, p. 70-72.
3321. MANDELBAUM, Allen
    "The *Savantasse* of Montparnasse" (Selections: "First Light," "The Ayre of Albion").
        [DenQ] (20:4/21:1) Spr-Sum 86, p. 28-35.
3322. MANDRELL, James
    "Disarticulations." [AntR] (44:3) Sum 86, p. 336.
    "Hands." [PartR] (53:1) 86, p. 99-101.
    "The Postcard." [AntR] (44:3) Sum 86, p. 334-335.
3323. MANESS, Norma
    "Dance Forsythia." [ForidaR] (14:1) Spr-Sum 86, p. 80.
3324. MANG, Ke
    "After a Night" (tr. by Tony Barnstone, Willis Barnstone and Gu Zhong Xing).
        [Nimrod] (29:2) Spr-Sum 86, p. 42.

237

"Declining Years" (tr. by Tony Barnstone, Willis Barnstone and Gu Zhong Xing).
[Nimrod] (29:2) Spr-Sum 86, p. 45.
"Early Morning after Rain" (tr. by Tony Barnstone, Willis Barnstone and Gu Zhong
Xing). [Nimrod] (29:2) Spr-Sum 86, p. 43.
"Night in the Snowfield" (tr. by Tony Barnstone, Willis Barnstone and Gu Zhong
Xing). [Nimrod] (29:2) Spr-Sum 86, p. 40.
"Poems in October" (tr. by Tony Barnstone, Willis Barnstone and Gu Zhong Xing).
[Nimrod] (29:2) Spr-Sum 86, p. 46-47.
"Spring" (tr. by Tony Barnstone, Willis Barnstone and Gu Zhong Xing). [Nimrod]
(29:2) Spr-Sum 86, p. 44.
"Sunflower in the Sun" (tr. by Tony Barnstone, Willis Barnstone and Gu Zhong
Xing). [Nimrod] (29:2) Spr-Sum 86, p. 66.
"These Days" (tr. by Tony Barnstone, Willis Barnstone and Gu Zhong Xing).
[Nimrod] (29:2) Spr-Sum 86, p. 39.
"Wind Rising from the Water's Back" (tr. by Tony Barnstone, Willis Barnstone and
Gu Zhong Xing). [Nimrod] (29:2) Spr-Sum 86, p. 44.
3325. MANGAN, Kathy
"Filament." [PennR] (2:1) Fall-Wint 86, p. 60.
3326. MANICOM, David
"Cement." [AntigR] (65) Spr 86, p. 169-170.
"Water and Light." [MalR] (77) D 86, p. 18.
3327. MANILLA, Saul
"Look Homeward Angels." [WormR] (26:4, issue 104) 86, p. 134.
"The Old Man and the Pea Fowls." [WormR] (26:4, issue 104) 86, p. 134.
3328. MANN, Charles
"Death." [Vis] (21) 86, p. 33.
"Father." [Wind] (16:58) 86, p. 31.
3329. MANN, Jeff
"The Princeton Omelet Shoppe" (for Rhonda). [JamesWR] (4:1) Fall 86, p. 4.
3330. MANNES, Marya
"An Die Musik." [HeliconN] (16) Wint 86, p. 75.
"Sonnets." [HeliconN] (16) Wint 86, p. 74.
3331. MANNING, Lynn
"Field Forever" (For the Migrant Strawberry Pickers). [SanFPJ] (8:4) 85, p. 63-64.
"Outward Appearances." [Kaleid] (13) Sum-Fall 86, p. 59.
"A Question in Passing." [SanFPJ] (8:4) 85, p. 62.
"This Is Me." [SanFPJ] (8:4) 85, p. 62.
3332. MANRIQUE, Jaime
"Elegía al Cisne." [LindLM] (5:1) Ja-Mr 86, p. 28.
"El Fantasma de Mi Padre en Dos Paisajes." [LindLM] (5:1) Ja-Mr 86, p. 28.
3333. MANSELL, Chris
"Overtime." [Amelia] (3:4) Fall 86, p. 101.
3334. MANSOUR, Joyce
"The Amazon" (tr. by Larry Couch). [Vis] (20) 86, p. 28.
"Fever" (tr. by Larry Couch). [Vis] (22) 86, p. 9.
"Mother's Fruit." [RedBass] (11) 86, p. 6.
"Wild Animals on the Blacktop" (tr. by Larry Couch). [Vis] (22) 86, p. 9.
3335. MANUS, Fay Whitman
"Brooklyn Bread." [ManhatPR] (8) Wint 86-87, p. 26-27.
3336. MA'OZ, Rivka
"Kitchen Table" (tr. of Hamutal bar Yosef, w. Shirley Kaufman). [PoetL] (81:2)
Sum 86, p. 97.
"Palestine" (tr. of Hamutal bar Yosef, w. Shirley Kaufman). [PoetL] (81:2) Sum 86,
p. 97.
3337. MAR, Laureen
"The Lull." [Contact] (8:41/42/43) Fall-Wint 86-87, p. 9.
3338. MAR, María del
"Amor." [LetFem] (12:1/2) Primavera-Otoño 86, p. 138.
"Paisaje Nocturno" (A Federico García Lorca, en el cincuentenario de su muerte).
[LetFem] (12:1/2) Primavera-Otoño 86, p. 137.
3339. MARAGALL, Joan
"The Blind Cow" (La vaca cega, tr. by Nathaniel Smith). [SenR] (16:1) 86, p. 21.
3340. MARANISS, James
"All of a sudden: — Look!" (tr. of Jorge Valls). [AmerPoR] (15:3) My-Je 86, p. 29.
"Discovery" (tr. of Jorge Valls). [AmerPoR] (15:3) My-Je 86, p. 29.

"I spoke that word to create it from the air" (tr. of Jorge Valls). [AmerPoR] (15:3) My-Je 86, p. 29.

"Like a wounded beast" (tr. of Jorge Valls). [AmerPoR] (15:3) My-Je 86, p. 29.

"Where I am there is no light" (tr. of Jorge Valls). [AmerPoR] (15:3) My-Je 86, p. 29.

3341. MARÇAL, Maria Mercè
"Bonfire Joana" (Foguera Joana, selections tr. by Kathleen McNerney). [SenR] (16:1) 86, p. 47-48.
"Fiery Blades" (Foc de pales, selections tr. by Kathleen McNerney). [SenR] (16:1) 86, p. 45-46.

3342. MARCANO MONTAÑEZ, Jaime
"Amo ahora cantar" (Al leer el libro *Vestido para la Denudez*). [Mairena] (8:21) 86, p. 54.
"Canto a la America Hispana." [Mairena] (8:22) 86, p. 67.

3343. MARCELLO, Leo Luke
"Buying Cheese." [SouthernR] (22:4) O 86, p. 786-788.
"Villanelle on the Suicide of a Young Belgian Teacher Soon to Be Naturalized." [SouthernR] (22:4) O 86, p. 789.

3344. MARCHAMPS, Guy
"Sédiments de l'Amnésie" (Excerpts). [Os] (22) 86, p. 10-11.

3345. MARCHAND, Richard
"Le Beau Eurasien." [PottPort] (8) 86-87, p. 3.

3346. MARCHANT, Fred
"El Meson del Marques" (in Vallodolid). [StoneC] (13:3/4) Spr-Sum 86, p. 67.

3347. MARCHESE, Joan
"Jocks." [YetASM] (5) 86, p. 4.

3348. MARCILIO, Haydee
"Eternidades." [Mairena] (8:21) 86, p. 101-102.
"Signos." [Mairena] (8:21) 86, p. 102.
"Solo Poema." [Mairena] (8:21) 86, p. 101.

3349. MARCOS PADUA, Reynaldo
"Praxis." [RevICP] (88) Abril-Junio 85, p. 56.
"Prolegomenos al Estudio del Afan de Jimenez." [RevICP] (88) Abril-Junio 85, p. 56.
"Teosofica." [RevICP] (88) Abril-Junio 85, p. 56.

3350. MARCUS, Harold
"The Dinosaurs." [Lips] (12) 86, p. 37.

3351. MARCUS, Mordecai
"Drunken Luck." [ClockR] (3:1) 85, p. 63.
"Entering a Liquor Store." [Interim] (5:1) Spr 86, p. 45.
"A Farewell to My Thursday Night Poetry Writing Class." [BallSUF] (26:4) Aut 85, p. 42-44.
"Finding Our Names." [SoDakR] (24:2) Sum 86, p. 80.
"A Furnished Room." [Amelia] (3:2) Spr 86, p. 89.
"In Passing." [Amelia] (3:2) Spr 86, p. 88.
"Lab Report." [Amelia] (3:2) Spr 86, p. 88-89.
"Poisonous Berries." [ManhatPR] (6) Wint-Spr 85-86, p. 30.

3352. MARCUS, Morton
"Gratitude: A Folk Tale." [TriQ] (67) Fall 86, p. 137-138.

3353. MAREK, Jayne
"Teenagers Cruise This Street Saturday Nights." [WindO] (47) Sum 86, p. 43.

3354. MARGOLIN, Anna
"Dear Monsters" (tr. by Marcia Falk). [AmerPoR] (15:6) N-D 86, p. 21.
"Don't think that I have changed" ("Untitled", in Yiddish & English, tr. by Adrienne Cooper). [SinW] (29/30) 86, p. 151.
"Epitaph" (tr. by Marcia Falk). [AmerPoR] (15:6) N-D 86, p. 21.
"Full of Night and Weeping" (tr. by Adrienne Cooper). [SinW] (29/30) 86, p. 148.
"Girls in Crotona Park" (tr. by Marcia Falk). [AmerPoR] (15:6) N-D 86, p. 21.
"Mother Earth, Well Worn, Sun Washed" (tr. by Adrienne Cooper). [SinW] (29/30) 86, p. 150.
"My Ancestors Speak" (tr. by Adrienne Cooper). [SinW] (29/30) 86, p. 148-149.
"Not Happy" (tr. by Adrienne Cooper). [SinW] (29/30) 86, p. 150.
"The Proud Poem" (In Yiddish & English, tr. by Adrienne Cooper). [SinW] (29/30) 86, p. 151.

3355. MARGOLIS, Gary
"The Anniversary of Fidelity." [PennR] (1:2) Fall 85, p. 38.

"Away from Any Uniform." [Poetry] (147:4) Ja 86, p. 207-208.
"Cocaine, Sex or Food." [NoAmR] (271:3) S 86, p. 30.
"Crescent Beach, Florida." [OhioR] (37) 86, p. 109.
"Happy." [Crazy] (31) Fall 86, p. 70.
"Having Watched 'The Day After'." [Poetry] (147:4) Ja 86, p. 208-209.
"If You Asked." [Poetry] (147:4) Ja 86, p. 209-210.
"To the Young Woman Looking for the Eating Disorder Workshop Who found a
    Poetry Reading Instead." [PoetryNW] (27:1) Spr 86, p. 26-27.
3356. MARGOLIS, Richard J.
"Letting Go" (a sonnet for Harriet). [Blueline] (7:2) Wint-Spr 86, p. 45.
3357. MARGOSHES, Dave
"Trees." [CanLit] (109) Sum 86, p. 99-100.
"White Fruit" (for Judy on her 50th birthday). [CanLit] (109) Sum 86, p. 15-16.
3358. MARIE, Tydal
"The Man with the Plow" (William Franklin Longmire). [NegC] (6:1) Wint 86, p.
    75.
3359. MARINARA, Martha
"March Seventeenth." [BallSUF] (27:4) Aut 86, p. 46.
3360. MARINO, Gigi
"Earth Shine Sisters." [SingHM] (14) 86, p. 26-27.
3361. MARION, Elizabeth
"Skyscrapers." [CrossCur] (5:4/6:1) 86, p. 87.
3362. MARIS, Maria (Maria R.)
"Deceleration Exercise." [KanQ] (18:1/2) Wint-Spr 86, p. 184.
"Joinings." [Wind] (16:57) 86, p. 25-26.
"Running Backward." [WindO] (47) Sum 86, p. 36-37.
MARIS, Ron de
    See De MARIS, Ron
3363. MARKS, Gigi
"When It Begins." [StoneC] (13:3/4) Spr-Sum 86, p. 53.
3364. MARLATT, Daphne
"Ana Historic" (Excerpt). [CapilR] (41) 86, p. 14-21.
"Ana Historic" (Excerpts). [MalR] (77) D 86, p. 19-20.
3365. MARLIS, Stefanie
"Banner of Fish." [MassR] (27:2) Sum 86, p. 332.
"Fruit." [MassR] (27:2) Sum 86, p. 332.
"Shift." [Sonora] (10) Spr 86, p. 21.
"Starlight." [Sonora] (10) Spr 86, p. 19.
"Zoo Keeper." [Sonora] (10) Spr 86, p. 20.
3366. MARMON, Sharon
"One Bitch Grieves Another." [SouthernPR] (26:1) Spr 86, p. 41.
3367. MARPLE, Vivian
"Map for the Journey That Takes 6 Days." [MalR] (76) S 86, p. 61-63.
3368. MARQUART, Barbara
"Gold at the Rainbow's End." [ManhatPR] (6) Wint-Spr 85-86, p. 53.
MARQUEZ, Alberto Martinez
    See MARTINEZ MARQUEZ, Alberto
3369. MARQUEZ, Nieves del Rosario
"Similitud Bajo el Claro de Luna" (Estampa de Acapulco, México). [LetFem]
    (12:1/2) Primavera-Otoño 86, p. 142-143.
"Sueños de Xochimilco." [LetFem] (12:1/2) Primavera-Otoño 86, p. 143.
3370. MARQUEZ, Roberto
"Agreed: It's True That You Look Like May Britt" (tr. of Roque Dalton). [MassR]
    (27:3/4) Fall-Wint 86, p. 443-444.
"Sayings" (tr. of Roque Dalton). [MassR] (27:3/4) Fall-Wint 86, p. 442.
3371. MARRIOTT, Anne
"On Reading That I Am 'Elderly'." [CrossC] (8:1) 86, p. 9.
"On That Beach." [CrossC] (8:1) 86, p. 9.
3372. MARRODAN, Mario Angel
"Invitacion a la Esperanza." [Mairena] (8:22) 86, p. 58.
3373. MARSH, Donald
"Curve of Air." [ManhatPR] (7) Sum 86, p. 55.
"Eine Kleine Nacht Parking Lot." [Outbr] (16/17) Fall 85-Spr 86, p. 94-95.
"The Man Who Shaved Clark Gable." [Outbr] (16/17) Fall 85-Spr 86, p. 96.
"A Real Pool Player." [ManhatPR] (7) Sum 86, p. 54.
"Sunny Side of the Street." [Outbr] (16/17) Fall 85-Spr 86, p. 93.

"Vanishings." [Outbr] (16/17) Fall 85-Spr 86, p. 92.
3374. MARSH, William
"The Driver's Seat." [WormR] (26:2, issue 102) 86, p. 46-47.
"Get Back." [WormR] (26:2, issue 102) 86, p. 47.
"Marsh, William "Kimberley and Frank." [WormR] (26:2, issue 102) 86, p. 48.
"Pandemonium." [WormR] (26:2, issue 102) 86, p. 45-46.
"The Spirit of Seventy-Six." [WormR] (26:2, issue 102) 86, p. 46.
"Use Your Imagination." [WormR] (26:2, issue 102) 86, p. 45.
"Wrap." [WormR] (26:2, issue 102) 86, p. 44-45.
3375. MARSHALL, J. M.
"Early Snow." [KanQ] (18:1/2) Wint-Spr 86, p. 261.
"Elegy." [KanQ] (18:1/2) Wint-Spr 86, p. 260-261.
"Long Seasons of Fathers." [KanQ] (18:1/2) Wint-Spr 86, p. 256.
3376. MARSHALL, Jack
"After Rumi." [AmerPoR] (15:1) Ja-F 86, p. 3-5.
"Arabian Nights." [Zyzzyva] (2:1) Spr 86, p. 56-57.
"Self-Portrait, Cézanne." [AmerPoR] (15:3) My-Je 86, p. 42.
3377. MARSHALL, John
"Broken Water." [Dandel] (13:1) Spr-Sum 86, p. 39-44.
"Broken Water, White Air" (for Anne Biss, Chestnut Street, Winnipeg, February 13, 1983). [Event] (15:1) 86, p. 55-57.
3378. MARSHALL, Quitman
"Save the Amazon." [SouthernPR] (26:2) Fall 86, p. 46-47.
3379. MARSHBURN, Sandra
"At Forty." [TarRP] (25:1) Fall 85, p. 42.
"A Body of Water." [WestB] (19) 86, p. 73.
"Low Water Line." [TarRP] (26:1) Fall 86, p. 23.
"Record Breaking Cold." [TarRP] (26:1) Fall 86, p. 22.
"Traffic." [WoosterR] (6) Fall 86, p. 30.
"When She Needs Them." [WestB] (19) 86, p. 72.
3380. MARSICANO, Julie
"Invitation to Tea, Omaha, Nebraska, 1957." [SingHM] (13) 86, p. 30-31.
3381. MARTEAU, Robert
"Le 16 Janvier 1986 au Pont Royal à Paris." [Os] (22) 86, p. 16.
"Like this one sees the poem like the meadow" (tr. by Jonathan Boulting). [Verse] (6) 86, p. 43.
"Lovers, you with less than a bed for land" (tr. by Jonathan Boulting). [Verse] (6) 86, p. 43.
3382. MARTI I POL, Miquel
"Autobiography" (Autobiografia, tr. by Nathaniel Smith and Lynette McGrath). [SenR] (16:1) 86, p. 40.
"Before Any Plans" (Abans de qualsevol projecte, tr. by Elaine Lilly). [SenR] (16:1) 86, p. 43.
"Expect No Omens" (tr. by Deborah Bonner). [Translation] (16) Spr 86, p. 52.
"Joy" (tr. by Deborah Bonner). [Translation] (16) Spr 86, p. 54.
"Metamorphosis-I" (Metamòrfosi-I, tr. by Nathaniel Smith and Lynette McGrath). [SenR] (16:1) 86, p. 41.
"Proclamation" (tr. by Deborah Bonner). [Translation] (16) Spr 86, p. 56.
"The Shadow of the Sea" (tr. by Deborah Bonner). [Translation] (16) Spr 86, p. 52.
"Slower Than Falling" (tr. by Deborah Bonner). [Translation] (16) Spr 86, p. 55.
"Their Eyes Always Open" (tr. by Deborah Bonner). [Translation] (16) Spr 86, p. 55.
"We Speak of You" (Parlem de tu, tr. by Nathaniel Smith and Lynette McGrath). [SenR] (16:1) 86, p. 42.
"The Wind's Code" (tr. by Deborah Bonner). [Translation] (16) Spr 86, p. 53.
"With People of Highly Diverse Origins" (tr. by Deborah Bonner). [Translation] (16) Spr 86, p. 53.
3383. MARTIALIS, Marcus Valerius
"III.65. The breath of a young girl, biting an apple" (tr. by Joseph Salemi). [Paint] (13:25/26) Spr-Aut 86, p. 32.
MARTIN, Billie Kaiser
   See KAISER-MARTIN, Billie
3384. MARTIN, Charles
"A Burial at Shanidar." [Boulevard] (1:1/2) Wint 86, p. 102-103.
"The Housatonic at Falls Village." [NewYorker] (62:33) 6 O 86, p. 42.
"If I Were Fire, I Would Torch the World." [Boulevard] (1:1/2) Wint 86, p. 104.

"Speech against Stone." [Hudson] (38:4) Wint 86, p. 629-630.
3385. MARTIN, D. Roger
"Minor League Veteran." (Chapbook issue). [Sam] (45:2, release 178) 86, 11 p.
3386. MARTIN, J. F. D.
"After Work." [CrabCR] (3:3) Sum 86, p. 8.
3387. MARTIN, James
"The Trouble with the Moon." [Raccoon] (20) Ap 86, p. 45.
3388. MARTIN, Jennifer
"Post-Time." [ManhatPR] (8) Wint 86-87, p. 53.
3389. MARTIN, Lynn
"The Blue Bowl." [TarRP] (25:2) Spr 86, p. 9.
"Elegy." [YetASM] (5) 86, p. 8.
"Four Snows" (For Judy Marquardt, 1938-1984). [SouthernPR] (26:1) Spr 86, p.
57-59.
"Gdansk, 1982" (for Grazyna Kapral and Ursula Mielczarek). [TarRP] (25:2) Spr
86, p. 10.
MARTIN, Manuel San
See SAN MARTIN, Manuel
3390. MARTIN, Mary E.
"Tableau." [CimR] (76) Jl 86, p. 26.
3391. MARTIN, Richard
"Love Poem." [YellowS] (21) Wint 86, p. 32-33.
"Plastic Frames." [AnotherCM] (15) 86, p. 49-50.
3392. MARTINDALE, Sheila
"Final Confrontation." [GreenfR] (13:3/4) Sum-Fall 86, p. 143.
3393. MARTINEZ, Jan
"El Lagartijo, las Alas y la Luz." [RevICP] (89) Jul-Sep 85, p. 68-69.
3394. MARTINEZ, Ramón E.
"Cantinflas Puppet." [BilingR] (12:1/2) Ja-Ag 85 [c1987], p. 119.
"The Emperor of Helados." [BilingR] (12:1/2) Ja-Ag 85 [c1987], p. 118-119.
"July in the Desert." [CapeR] (21:2) Fall 86, p. 19.
"Unveiling." [CapeR] (21:2) Fall 86, p. 18.
3395. MARTINEZ, Ruben
"I Want a Lucid Witness from You" (tr. of Jaime Suarez Quemain). [RedBass] (11)
86, p. 8.
"Like This" (tr. of Joaquin Meza). [RedBass] (11) 86, p. 7.
"With a Butcher from My Village" (tr. of Rafael Mendoza). [RedBass] (11) 86, p. 7.
3396. MARTINEZ CUITIÑO, Luis
"Recorres la Palabra" (Excerpt, tr. by Thorpe Running). [ColR] (NS 13:1) Fall 85,
p. 46.
3397. MARTINEZ MALDONADO, Manuel
"Duermevela." [LindLM] (5:1) Ja-Mr 86, p. 27.
3398. MARTINEZ MARQUEZ, Alberto (Alberto A.)
"Caminos." [Mairena] (8:21) 86, p. 62-63.
"Huesped de las Sombras." [Mairena] (8:22) 86, p. 109.
"Tiempos Redondos." [Mairena] (8:21) 86, p. 62.
3399. MARTONE, John
"Hemps." [AnotherCM] (16) 86, p. 58-59.
MARTONE, Marjorie Hanft
See HANFT-MARTONE, Marjorie
3400. MARTONE, Michael
"Limited." [IndR] (9:2) Spr 86, p. 54-55.
3401. MARTY, Sid
"Chanson du Dejeuner Gratis." [Rampike] (5:1) 86, p. 10.
MARY LUCINA, Sister
See LUCINA, Mary (Sister)
3402. MARZANO, Nick
"Mathematics." [JamesWR] (3:2) Wint 86, p. 4.
"Meeting Nathan Unexpectedly." [JamesWR] (3:4) Sum 86, p. 8.
"This Particular Moment." [JamesWR] (3:4) Sum 86, p. 8.
MASAO, Nakagiri
See NAKAGIRI, Masao
MASAO, Nonagase
See NONAGASE, Masao
3403. MASARIK, Al
"Lure." [PaintedB] (28) Ap 86, p. 39.

"On Turning Forty." [PaintedB] (28) Ap 86, p. 37.
"Some Place." [PaintedB] (28) Ap 86, p. 38-39.
3404. MASCARO, John
"What It Has Been." [Jacaranda] (2:1) Fall 86, p. 36.
3405. MASEFIELD, John
"The Will to Perfection." [YaleR] (75:2) Wint 86, p. viii.
3406. MASINI, Donna
"Fran." [Cond] (13) 86, p. 115.
"Hole in the Wall." [Cond] (13) 86, p. 116.
MASKARY, Shaikha Al
See AL-MASKARY, Shaikha
3407. MASON, David
"Of the Ship" (tr. of C. P. Cavafy). [Translation] (16) Spr 86, p. 142.
"Upstate Cottage." [Boulevard] (1:3) Fall 86, p. 42.
"Xanthoula" (tr. of Dionysios Solomos). [Translation] (16) Spr 86, p. 143-144.
MASS, Jesus Efrain Lopez
See LOPEZ MASS, Jesus Efrain
3408. MASSA, Ron
"What Are We to Think?" [ArizQ] (42:4) Wint 86, p. 292.
3409. MASSEY, Tom
"The Seeker." [MidAR] (6:2) 86, p. 19-20.
3410. MASSON, Jean-Claude
"Ciudad de Mexico" (tr. by Rosalind Gill). [Writ] (18) 86, c87, p. 102.
"Honduras" (tr. by Rosalind Gill). [Writ] (18) 86, c87, p. 104.
"Past Present" (tr. by Rosalind Gill). [Writ] (18) 86, c87, p. 101.
"Scherzo" (tr. by Rosalind Gill). [Writ] (18) 86, c87, p. 103.
3411. MASTERS, Dexter
"Graffiti for a Particle Accelerator." [GeoR] (40:3) Fall 86, p. 719.
3412. MASTERS, Marcia Lee
"Unsuspecting Morning." [SpoonRQ] (11:2) Spr 86, p. 50-51.
3413. MASTERSON, Dan
"Those Who Trespass." [Raccoon] (20) Ap 86, p. 29-36.
3414. MATHEWSON, Kevin
"Coma Berenice" (tr. of Leonardo Greven). [AmerPoR] (15:3) My-Je 86, p. 48.
3415. MATHIAS, Pierre
"Crayfish" (tr. by Dorothy B. Aspinwall). [CumbPR] (5:2) Spr 86, p. 79.
"Les Ecrevisses." [CumbPR] (5:2) Spr 86, p. 78.
3416. MATHIS, Cleopatra
"Against April." [DenQ] (20:4/21:1) Spr-Sum 86, p. 107-108.
"Cremation." [Field] (34) Spr 86, p. 74.
"For Richard Eberhart's Felled Trees, and for Alexandra." [NegC] (6:2/3) Spr-Sum
  86, p. 62-63.
"Runner in March Rain." [CutB] (25) Fall-Wint 86, p. 16.
"Running at Nightfall on the Last Day." [DenQ] (20:4/21:1) Spr-Sum 86, p.
  109-110.
"A Seasonal Record." [Ploughs] (12:3) 86, p. 36-41.
"Tell Me." [Field] (34) Spr 86, p. 75.
3417. MATHIS-EDDY, Darlene
"A Bone of Doggerel for the Dons." [Amelia] (3:4) Fall 86, p. 104-106.
3418. MATLIN, David
"Udan Adan" (Excerpt). [Acts] (5) 86, p. 88.
"Udan Adan" (Selections: 4 poems). [Notus] (1:1) Fall 86, p. 63-68.
3419. MATOS PAOLI, Francisco
"A Manuel del Cabral." [Mairena] (8:22) 86, p. 86.
"Biografia de un Poeta." [Mairena] (8:21) 86, p. 52.
MATRE, Connie van
See Van MATRE, Connie
3420. MATSON, Suzanne
"In Rovaniemi, Finland, Twenty-Fifth Birthday." [PoetryNW] (27:1) Spr 86, p.
  11-12.
3421. MATSUDA, Sumio
"Views of an American Writer." [GeoR] (40:3) Fall 86, p. 720.
3422. MATTE, Robert, Jr.
"Boot Hill." [BellR] (9:2) Fall 86, p. 31.
"The Lazy D." [BellR] (9:2) Fall 86, p. 32.

3423. MATTHEWS, Jack
"The People in These Houses." [GeoR] (40:3) Fall 86, p. 721.
3424. MATTHEWS, Sharon
"A Capacity for Leaping." [YellowS] (18) Spr 86, p. 29.
3425. MATTHEWS, Tede
"Gidget LaRue." [JamesWR] (3:4) Sum 86, p. 1.
3426. MATTHEWS, William
"Cabbage." [NewEngR] (9:1) Aut 86, p. 91.
"Construction." [GeoR] (40:2) Sum 86, p. 490.
"Days beyond Recall." [NewEngR] (9:1) Aut 86, p. 88.
"Dust above the Roads." [NewEngR] (9:1) Aut 86, p. 89.
"Egg and Daughter Night, April, 1951." [DenQ] (20:4/21:1) Spr-Sum 86, p. 57.
"Fairbanks, the Summer Solstice, 1983." [QW] (23) 86, p. 134.
"Fellow Oddballs." [Crazy] (31) Fall 86, p. 50.
"Flood." [GeoR] (40:3) Fall 86, p. 722-723.
"Leipzig, 1894." [PartR] (53:2) 86, p. 238-239.
"Liver Cancer." [Field] (34) Spr 86, p. 39.
"Mail Order Catalogs." [DenQ] (20:4/21:1) Spr-Sum 86, p. 56.
"Men in Dark Suits." [Crazy] (31) Fall 86, p. 51.
"Minuscule Things." [NewYorker] (61:51) 10 F 86, p. 104.
"The Scalpel." [Caliban] (1) 86, p. 134.
"Schoolboys with Dog, Winter." [Ploughs] (12:3) 86, p. 35.
"Self-Knowledge." [Ploughs] (12:3) 86, p. 34.
"Stubble." [PartR] (53:2) 86, p. 239.
"Torch Song." [NewEngR] (9:1) Aut 86, p. 90.
"Worm Sonnet." [ColEng] (48:3) Mr 86, p. 269.
"Writer-in-Residence." [ColEng] (48:3) Mr 86, p. 268.
3427. MATTHIAS, Mohn
"An East Anglian Diptych: Ley Lines, Rivers." [AnotherCM] (15) 86, p. 51-67.
3428. MATUZAK, Joseph
"Woman Casting a Lion's Shadow." [KanQ] (18:3) Sum 86, p. 92.
3429. MATYAS, Cathy
"Bromeliad." [GreenfR] (13:3/4) Sum-Fall 86, p. 144.
"Nile (I)." [GreenfR] (13:3/4) Sum-Fall 86, p. 145.
3430. MATYSHAK, Stanley
"Another for the Same." [KanQ] (18:1/2) Wint-Spr 86, p. 148.
3431. MAURA (SISTER)
"Litany for the Living." [AntigR] (66/67) Sum-Aut 86, p. 54.
3432. MAURICE, Carlotta
"Sleeping Beauty." [Chelsea] (45) 86, p. 96-98.
"Sonnet: Inlet." [Chelsea] (45) 86, p. 99.
3433. MAVIGLIA, Joseph
"Paolo Dipietro." [GreenfR] (13:3/4) Sum-Fall 86, p. 146.
3434. MAY, Kathy
"Weeds." [TarRP] (25:1) Fall 85, p. 40-41.
3435. MAY, Kerry Paul
"Autumn." [ThRiPo] (27/28) 86, p. 49.
"Leaving Madrid." [SilverFR] (11) Sum 86, p. 32-33.
"Remember." [ThRiPo] (27/28) 86, p. 48.
"Test Flight." [ThRiPo] (27/28) 86, p. 47.
3436. MAYBURY, James F.
"Autumn Song" (tr. of Du Fu). [Hudson] (38:4) Wint 86, p. 632.
3437. MAYHALL, Jane
"Florida, 1984." [Hudson] (39:1) Spr 86, p. 102.
"Mourner." [AmerS] (55:1) Wint 85-86, p. 74.
"What's New in Appalachia." [Hudson] (39:1) Spr 86, p. 101.
"Wyoming Stop-off." [Hudson] (39:1) Spr 86, p. 101-102.
3438. MAYHEW, Lenore
"Haiku" (3 poems). [WindO] (47) Sum 86, p. 3.
3439. MAYHOOD, Clifton Ralph
"I Know Now I Will Never Finish College." [JamesWR] (4:1) Fall 86, p. 7.
"Into the Snow" (a poem in four parts in memory of James L. White. Selections: I,
    IV). [JamesWR] (3:3) Spr 86, p. 4.
3440. MAYNE, Seymour
"Jerusalem As She Is" (tr. of Shlomo Vinner). [Writ] (18) 86, c87, p. 117-125.

"Pneumatic Drills on the Ninth of Ab" (tr. of Shlomo Vinner). [PoetL] (81:2) Sum 86, p. 105.

MAYS, David Hatcher
    See HATCHER-MAYS, David

3441. MAZEIKA, Jurate
    "The Work of Mirrors" (tr. of Henrikas Radauskas). [Vis] (22) 86, p. 14.

3442. MAZUR, Gail
    "Dog Days, Sweet Everlasting." [BostonR] (11:1) F 86, p. 15.
    "Pears." [Pequod] (22) 86, p. 56-57.
    "Spring Planting." [Poetry] (148:1) Ap 86, p. 5-6.

3443. MAZZA, Antonio
    "Ars Poetica." [CanLit] (111) Wint 86, p. 25.
    "Doors." [CanLit] (111) Wint 86, p. 26.
    "Forest." [CanLit] (111) Wint 86, p. 25.
    "Night." [CanLit] (111) Wint 86, p. 26.
    "Psychoanalysts." [CanLit] (111) Wint 86, p. 26.

3444. MAZZARO, Jerome
    "Packing Away This Kylix." [Hudson] (39:2) Sum 86, p. 278.
    "Tontons Macoutes: The Bogymen." [NewRep] (195:23) 8 D 86, p. 35.

3445. MBUTHIA, Waithira
    "Childhood Revisited." [CrossCur] (6:2) 86, p. 45.
    "Like crumbled stale bread" ("Untitled"). [LitR] (29:2) Wint 86, p. 237.

Mc . . .
    See also names beginning with Mac . . .

3446. McADAM, Rhona
    "After the Revolution." [Event] (15:2) 86, p. 162.
    "Domestic Hazard." [Event] (15:2) 86, p. 163.
    "First Snow." [Quarry] (35:4) Aut 86, p. 9.
    "Nose Poem." [Event] (15:1) 86, p. 16.
    "Overseas Mail." [Event] (15:1) 86, p. 14-15.
    "Putting Food By." [Dandel] (13:1) Spr-Sum 86, p. 38.
    "Vive la Révolution." [Event] (15:2) 86, p. 158.

3447. McAFEE, Thomas
    "Being Dull." [NewL] (52:2/3) Wint-Spr 86, p. 35.

3448. McAULEY, James J.
    "Ten-Mile Run." [PoetryNW] (27:2) Sum 86, p. 32-36.

3449. McBRIDE, Elizabeth
    "The Bible: The Book That Most Influenced My Life." [Chelsea] (45) 86, p. 54.
    "Open Marriage: The Book That Most Influenced My Life." [Chelsea] (45) 86, p. 53.
    "Preface." [Chelsea] (45) 86, p. 49-52.

3450. McBRIDE, Mekeel
    "After Solstice." [Pequod] (22) 86, p. 99.
    "Alien in Control." [Pequod] (22) 86, p. 98.
    "Annunciation." [Ploughs] (12:3) 86, p. 47.
    "Once Upon a Time." [GeoR] (40:3) Fall 86, p. 724.
    "Taking Pleasure." [Ploughs] (12:3) 86, p. 48.

3451. McCAFFERY, Steve
    "Ba-Lue Bolivar Ba-Lues Are." [Temblor] (4) 86, p. 55-56.
    "The Black Debt" (Excerpt). [Temblor] (4) 86, p. 57-59.
    "Lag." [Temblor] (4) 86, p. 60-61.

3452. McCALLISTER, Rick
    "En el Corazón de el Salvador." [Pax] (3:1/2) Wint 85-86, p. 188-189.
    "Nica-Anáhuac: Recuerdos de un Viaje por Nicaragua durante la Guerra Civil." [Americas] (14:1) Spr 86, p. 38-44.

3453. McCALLUM, Mary B.
    "On Contemplating Retirement." [EngJ] (75:6) O 86, p. 68.

3454. McCALLUM, Paddy
    "Gargoyle Song." [MalR] (73) Ja 86, p. 78.
    "Letter from Moscow." [Event] (15:2) 86, p. 30.
    "Red Tide." [MalR] (73) Ja 86, p. 79.

3455. McCANN, Janet
    "Cat's." [BallSUF] (26:4) Aut 85, p. 62.
    "Foul Weather Friends." [Poem] (55) Mr 86, p. 10.
    "Reasons for Leaving." [CrescentR] (4:2) Fall 86, p. 64.
    "The Vendor." [CrescentR] (4:2) Fall 86, p. 64.

3456. McCANN, Richard
    "In the Health Room." [VirQR] (62:4) Aut 86, p. 606.
    "One of the Reasons." [VirQR] (62:4) Aut 86, p. 604-605.
3457. McCARRISTON, Linda
    "Barn Fire" (for Mike). [TarRP] (24:2) Spr 85, p. 45.
    "Caritas." [TarRP] (24:2) Spr 85, p. 44.
3458. McCARTHY, Dermot
    "Love in the North." [Quarry] (35:3) Sum 86, p. 48.
3459. McCARTHY, Regina
    "Dressed in Dynamite" (tr. of Gioconda Belli). [MassR] (27:3/4) Fall-Wint 86, p.
        608.
3460. McCARTHY, Suzanne M.
    "Crow." [Waves] (14:3) Wint 86, p. 69.
3461. McCARTHY, Thomas
    "Arland Ussher." [Verse] (6) 86, p. 26.
    "A Daughter's Cry." [Verse] (6) 86, p. 26.
    "The Dying Synagogue at South Terrace." [Field] (34) Spr 86, p. 53-54.
    "The Gathering of Waves" (for Catherine). [Verse] (6) 86, p. 25.
    "Seven Orange Tulips." [Field] (34) Spr 86, p. 52.
3462. McCASLIN, Susan
    "A Dream of William Blake." [BellArk] (2:2) Mr-Ap 86, p. 5.
    "In Time Alone" (for Reverend Gordon Nakayama). [WestCR] (21:1) Je 86, p. 80.
    "Old News." [WestCR] (21:1) Je 86, p. 81.
    "Orpheus in Vancouver." [BellArk] (2:6) N-D 86, p. 8.
    "Palimpsest." [BellArk] (2:2) Mr-Ap 86, p. 7.
    "Salmon." [BellArk] (2:5) S-O 86, p. 6.
    "Sympathy for the Flesh." [BellArk] (2:5) S-O 86, p. 1.
    "Trillium and Unicorn." [WestCR] (21:1) Je 86, p. 79.
    "Wings." [BellArk] (2:2) Mr-Ap 86, p. 1.
3463. McCLANE, Kenneth A.
    "Elm Taking" (For A.R. Ammons). [Pembroke] (18) 86, p. 230.
3464. McCLEARY, Joy
    "The Night before the First Day of School." [EngJ] (75:2) F 86, p. 54.
3465. McCLELLAN, Jane
    "Making Syrup with Mary, Sarah, Magdalene, Jewell, and Shalisha." [BallSUF]
        (26:4) Aut 85, p. 68-69.
    "Mr Pons Sees His Life as Less Than Tragic." [Poem] (56) N 86, p. 43.
    "Mr Pons Sees Something Astonishing." [Poem] (56) N 86, p. 42.
3466. McCLELLAND, Bruce
    "At Its Heart Is an Adder." [Sulfur] (6:1, issue 16) 86, p. 75-78.
    "Because the body is so slow to notice." [Epoch] (35:2) 86-87, p. 145.
    "The Cost of Memory" (Excerpt). [Epoch] (35:2) 86-87, p. 146.
3467. McCLURE, Michael
    "The Bulks of Heart." [Conjunc] (9) 86, p. 109-110.
    "Dark Brown Eyes of Seals." [Zyzzyva] (2:3) Fall 86, p. 48-49.
    "The Torture Murders Upstate in Calaveras County." [Conjunc] (9) 86, p. 108-109.
3468. McCOMBS, Judith
    "After I Leave, First Night Home." [Calyx] (10:1) Sum 86, p. 33.
    "In the Week of Your Leaving." [Calyx] (10:1) Sum 86, p. 32.
3469. McCONNEL, Frances
    "Aerials." [BellArk] (2:1) Ja-F 86, p. 6.
    "Easter" (for John). [BellArk] (2:2) Mr-Ap 86, p. 8.
3470. McCORKLE, James
    "The Accident of Seasons." [AntR] (44:3) Sum 86, p. 329.
    "After Chardin." [LittleM] (15:2) 86, p. 34.
3471. McCORMACK, Catherine Savoy
    "Bought by the N.R.A." [SanFPJ] (8:2) 85, p. 83.
    "Have You Found a Spare Missle?" [SanFPJ] (8:2) 85, p. 44.
    "Secret Cravings." [Amelia] (3:4) Fall 86, p. 102.
    "That November." [Amelia] (3:1) Ja 86, p. 60.
3472. McCORMACK, Karen
    "Only Hours in Wadi Halfa." [Rampike] (5:1) 86, p. 60.
3473. McCREDIE, Marcia
    "Sandy Creek Condos." [Pembroke] (18) 86, p. 266.
3474. McCROSKEY, Gretchen
    "A Foothold on the Land." [Wind] (16:57) 86, p. 44.

3475. McCROSSIN, Dana L.
"This Canyon." [Sam] (46:5 [i.e. 46:1] release 181) 86, p. 15.
"Walking with Rain." [Sam] (45:4 release 180) 86, p. 45.
3476. McCUE, Edward Patrick
"City Landscape: Order." [ArizQ] (42:3) Aut 86, p. 196.
3477. McCULLOUGH, Ken
"Cal." [NewL] (52:2/3) Wint-Spr 86, p. 98-99.
"Joey." [Stand] (27:4) Aut 86, p. 7.
3478. McCURRY, Jim
"Cold Water." [Farm] (3:2) Spr-Sum 86, p. 36.
"Condo" (for the late Donald Drummond). [WritersF] (12) Fall 86, p. 172.
"The Doves." [WritersF] (12) Fall 86, p. 171.
"The Summer of Summers, My Old Flame — the Type & Idea of Longest Days."
    [Farm] (3:2) Spr-Sum 86, p. 37.
3479. McDANIEL, Wilma Elizabeth
"Lonnie Wickersham." [WormR] (26:4, issue 104) 86, p. 133.
"Marty Fedderman in California." [WormR] (26:4, issue 104) 86, p. 133.
"Pastor for a Day." [HangL] (49) Spr 86, p. 25-26.
"Priorities." [HangL] (49) Spr 86, p. 24.
3480. McDONALD, Sara
"Aside." [Grain] (14:1) F 86, p. 56.
"Minneapolis." [Grain] (14:1) F 86, p. 53.
"Picadilly Circus." [Grain] (14:1) F 86, p. 52.
"Separation Anxiety." [Grain] (14:1) F 86, p. 50.
"The Squatter." [Grain] (14:1) F 86, p. 49.
"Two Part Harmony." [Grain] (14:1) F 86, p. 51.
"Wish You Were Here." [Grain] (14:1) F 86, p. 54.
3481. McDONALD, Walter
"After Eden." [PoetL] (80:4) Wint 86, p. 227-228.
"Another Kind of Outdoor Game." [PoetL] (80:4) Wint 86, p. 230-231.
"Backpacking the San Juan." [SenR] (16:2) 86, p. 71.
"Between the Moon and Me." [Ascent] (12:1) 86, p. 45.
"Bloodhounds." [Abraxas] (34) 86, p. 35.
"Breathe Deeply, and Relax." [TarRP] (26:1) Fall 86, p. 25.
"A Brief, Familiar Story of Winter." [KanQ] (18:3) Sum 86, p. 121.
"Building on Hardscrabble." [Confr] (33/34) Fall-Wint 86-87, p. 213.
"Catfish at Lake Buchanan." [SilverFR] (11) Sum 86, p. 4.
"Caught in a Squall near Matador." [ColR] (NS 13:1) Fall 85, p. 55-56.
"Changing the Dressing." [MemphisSR] (6:1/2) Spr 86, p. 52.
"Chili at the Rattlesnake Roundup." [Wind] (16:56) 86, p. 28.
"Closure." [Event] (15:1) 86, p. 60.
"Crashes Real and Imagined." [MidAR] (6:2) 86, p. 119.
"Drilling on Hardscrabble." [SilverFR] (11) Sum 86, p. 3.
"Driving Home to the Plains." [PoetL] (80:4) Wint 86, p. 228-229.
"The Dunes South of Brownfield." [CrossCur] (6:2) 86, p. 159.
"Dying in Blizzards." [Outbr] (16/17) Fall 85-Spr 86, p. 5.
"Each in Its Element." [Interim] (5:1) Spr 86, p. 14.
"Fathers and Sons." [Event] (15:1) 86, p. 61.
"The Fears of Horses." [WillowS] (18) Sum 86, p. 72.
"Fences." [AntigR] (66/67) Sum-Aut 86, p. 218.
"First Solo." [HiramPoR] (41) Fall-Wint 86-87, p. 35.
"First Solo in Thunderstorms." [MemphisSR] (7:1) Fall 86, p. 32.
"Following the Dog to Water." [Descant] (17:2, #53) Sum 86, p. 109.
"The Food Pickers of Saigon." [TriQ] (67) Fall 86, p. 122-123.
"Going." [DeKalbLAJ] (19:3/4) 86, p. 82.
"Going Away Together." [PoetL] (80:4) Wint 86, p. 232-233.
"Honky-Tonk Blues." [Outbr] (16/17) Fall 85-Spr 86, p. 4.
"Hunting Doves at Matador." [PraS] (60:1) Spr 86, p. 41.
"Hunting on Hardscrabble." [Descant] (17:2, #53) Sum 86, p. 108.
"Ice Fishing." [MalR] (77) D 86, p. 72.
"In the Bunker." [Event] (15:2) 86, p. 27.
"In the shallows." [Wind] (16:56) 86, p. 29-30.
"Learning to Sit Tight." [DeKalbLAJ] (19:3/4) 86, p. 83.
"Living on Hardscrabble." [AntigR] (66/67) Sum-Aut 86, p. 217.
"Living on Hardscrabble." [Ascent] (12:1) 86, p. 44.
"Living on Hardscrabble." [PennR] (2:1) Fall-Wint 86, p. 64.

"Living on Open Plains." [WillowS] (18) Sum 86, p. 73.
"Llano Estacado Orchards." [WestB] (19) 86, p. 107.
"Making Do." [CumbPR] (5:2) Spr 86, p. 7.
"Midnight Near Pecos." [WillowS] (18) Sum 86, p. 71.
"The Neighbors." [Interim] (5:1) Spr 86, p. 13.
"New Guy, 1969." [Event] (15:2) 86, p. 26.
"Night of the Bonfire Club." [MidAR] (6:1) 86?, p. 85.
"Nights in the San Juan." [ColEng] (48:4) Ap 86, p. 354.
"Nights in the San Juan." [Puerto] (21:2) Spr 86, p. 162.
"No Matter How Many Dinosaurs." [YetASM] (5) 86, p. 7.
"The Norther" (Winner, The Pennsylvania Review Prize in Poetry, 1985). [PennR]
     (1:1) 85, p. 23.
"Old Men Fishing at Brownwood." [MissouriR] (9:2) 86, p. 226.
"On a Busy Street in a Nation's Capital." [Event] (15:2) 86, p. 25.
"Opening the Cabin in April." [ThRiPo] (27/28) 86, p. 50.
"Out of the Whirlwind." [Puerto] (21:2) Spr 86, p. 160-161.
"Owls and Uncle Bubba." [Outbr] (16/17) Fall 85-Spr 86, p. 3.
"Prairie Dog Fork of the Brazos." [BelPoJ] (36:3) Spr 86, p. 19.
"Praying for Rain in the Rockies." [ColEng] (48:4) Ap 86, p. 355.
"Principles of Flight." [TarRP] (25:1) Fall 85, p. 11.
"Reasons for Taking Risks." [PraS] (60:1) Spr 86, p. 42.
"Retrievers in Winter." [KenR] (NS 8:4) Fall 86, p. 83.
"Scenes of Childhood." [YetASM] (4) 85, p. 5.
"Searching." [PoetL] (80:4) Wint 86, p. 229.
"Setting the Torch to Stubble." [NewOR] (13:2) Sum 86, p. 21.
"Sleeping at the Edge of High Tide." [Wind] (16:56) 86, p. 29.
"Smoke and Aspen Ashes." [PikeF] (7) Spr 86, p. 13.
"Spinning." [PoetL] (80:4) Wint 86, p. 227.
"Tracking on Hardscrabble." [KenR] (NS 8:4) Fall 86, p. 82-83.
"The Truth Trees Know." [MidAR] (6:2) 86, p. 120.
"Witching." [SoDakR] (24:3) Aut 86, p. 24.
3482. MCDOUGALL, Bonnie S.
     "Boat Ticket" (tr. of Bei Dao). [Verse] (6) 86, p. 49.
3483. McDOUGALL, Jo
     "Act." [Nimrod] (30:1) Fall-Wint 86, p. 115.
     "At the Vietnam War Memorial for the American Dead." [SouthernPR] (26:2) Fall
          86, p. 7.
     "A Farm Wife Laments Her Husband's Absence." [Nimrod] (30:1) Fall-Wint 86, p.
          115.
3484. McELROY, Colleen J.
     "With Bill Pickett at the 101 Ranch." [Callaloo] (9:1, #26) Wint 86, p. 100.
3485. McELROY, James
     "Marvellous and the Manqué." [InterPR] (12:1) Spr 86, p. 80-82.
3486. McFADDEN, David
     "Angels and Lovers." [Descant] (17:2, #53) Sum 86, p. 104.
     "Consciousness." [Descant] (17:2, #53) Sum 86, p. 106-107.
     "Conversation with a Small Herd of Cattle." [Descant] (17:2, #53) Sum 86, p.
          100-101.
     "Elephants on Television." [MalR] (76) S 86, p. 126-127.
     "Heading towards Buchenwald" (After Baudelaire's "La Chambre Double"). [MalR]
          (76) S 86, p. 124-125.
     "How to Be Your Own Butcher." [CanLit] (108) Spr 86, p. 60-61.
     "How to Be Your Own Butcher" (corrected printing). [CanLit] (110) Fall 86, p. 7.
     "Jellyfish of Light" (After Baudelaire's "Le Chien et le Flaçon"). [MalR] (76) S 86,
          p. 122-123.
     "The Kamikaze Pilots of Japan." [Rampike] (5:2) 86, p. 47-48.
     "Monkey on My Back" (After Baudelaire's "Chacun Sa Chimère"). [MalR] (76) S
          86, p. 128.
     "My Own True Nature." [Descant] (17:2, #53) Sum 86, p. 99.
     "The Robe of Your Intelligence." [Descant] (17:2, #53) Sum 86, p. 102-103.
     "The Two of Cups." [Descant] (17:2, #53) Sum 86, p. 105.
     "Windsurfers." [Descant] (17:2, #53) Sum 86, p. 98.
3487. McFARLAND, G. E. C.
     "Aftermath." [Amelia] (3:3) Sum 86, p. 20.
     "Rain World." [PassN] (7:2) Spr-Sum 86, p. 22.

3488. McFARLAND, Joanne
"August." [Obs] (NS 1:1/2) Spr-Sum 86, p. 23.
"Baked." [Obs] (NS 1:1/2) Spr-Sum 86, p. 24-25.
"Birth." [Obs] (NS 1:1/2) Spr-Sum 86, p. 22-23.
"Deliverance." [Obs] (NS 1:1/2) Spr-Sum 86, p. 25.
"The Injustice of Injustice" (or why women can't fly). [Obs] (NS 1:1/2) Spr-Sum
    86, p. 24.
"Late-Night." [Obs] (NS 1:1/2) Spr-Sum 86, p. 28.
"The Politics of Rouge." [Obs] (NS 1:1/2) Spr-Sum 86, p. 27.
"Renaissance." [Obs] (NS 1:1/2) Spr-Sum 86, p. 22.
"Staying In." [Obs] (NS 1:1/2) Spr-Sum 86, p. 26.
"Yellow Brick." [Obs] (NS 1:1/2) Spr-Sum 86, p. 26.
3489. McFARLAND, Ron
"Walking Around the Block with My Daughter." [OhioR] (37) 86, p. 114.
3490. McFEE, Michael
"Cold Quilt." [Poetry] (149:1) O 86, p. 28.
"The Elm." [CrescentR] (4:1) Spr 86, p. 30-37.
"Hints for Pilgrimage." [OntR] (24) Spr-Sum 86, p. 43-44.
3491. McFERREN, Martha (Martha A.)
"The Barometric Witch" (for Nancy Harris). [SingHM] (14) 86, p. 1-2.
"Her Side of It." [SoCaR] (18:2) Spr 86, p. 44.
"I Can't Sleep." [SoCaR] (18:2) Spr 86, p. 45.
"Mountain Soprano." [GeoR] (40:3) Fall 86, p. 725-736.
"O Raccoon." [WormR] (26:4, issue 104) 86, p. 132-133.
"Only the Order of Events Has Been Changed." [WormR] (26:4, issue 104) 86, p.
    131-132.
"Train/Time/Train." [ColEng] (48:1) Ja 86, p. 144.
"Update for That Biographer." [NegC] (6:4) Fall 86, p. 204-205.
"We Know Where" (for George Macdonald). [StoneC] (14:1/2) Fall-Wint 86-87, p.
    24-25.
3492. McGANN, Mary
"Waiting for the Plows in Winter." [Blueline] (7:2) Wint-Spr 86, p. 15.
3493. McGARRY, Jean
"World with a Hard K." [Temblor] (4) 86, p. 156-157.
3494. McGEE, Lynn
"The Executive." [WestCR] (21:2) O 86, p. 13.
"The Huntress." [WestCR] (21:2) O 86, p. 12.
"The 'No'." [WestCR] (21:2) O 86, p. 14.
"The Parking Lot Attendant." [WestCR] (21:2) O 86, p. 15.
"The Tightrope Walker." [CrossCur] (5:4/6:1) 86, p. 67.
3495. McGLYNN, Brian
"Country Ride." [Wind] (16:56) 86, p. 7.
"Motorcycle." [Wind] (16:56) 86, p. 7.
3496. McGOVERN, Martin
"For Charles and Mary Lamb." [Poetry] (149:2) N 86, p. 86-91.
"Summer Garden." [AntR] (44:1) Wint 86, p. 72-73.
3497. McGOWAN, James
"The Blind" (tr. of "Les Aveugles," by Charles Baudelaire). [HiramPoR] (40)
    Spr-Sum 86, p. 51.
"Christmas Sestina" (for Caitlin). [HiramPoR] (40) Spr-Sum 86, p. 52-53.
"Moline, Illinois: Settling in at Lock & Dam #14." [HiramPoR] (40) Spr-Sum 86, p.
    50.
3498. McGOWAN, Les
"The Jacaranda Tree" (Anti-War Memorial Day 1978). [SanFPJ] (9:1) 86, p. 21.
"Ladies of the Black Sash." [SanFPJ] (9:1) 86, p. 20.
"Space Vision." [SanFPJ] (9:1) 86, p. 24.
3499. McGRATH, Campbell
"Rifle, Colorado." [OhioR] (36) 86, p. 76.
"Silt, Colorado." [OhioR] (36) 86, p. 77.
3500. McGRATH, Lynette
"Autobiography" (Autobiografia, tr. of Miquel Martí i Pol, w. Nathaniel Smith).
    [SenR] (16:1) 86, p. 40.
"How Like a Kite My Star Is" (Quina grua el meu estel, tr. of Joan Salvat-Papasseit,
    w. Nathaniel Smith). [SenR] (16:1) 86, p. 26-27.
"The Man Condemned to Death" (Reu de mort, tr. of Angel Guimerà, w. Nathaniel
    Smith). [SenR] (16:1) 86, p. 19-20.

"Metamorphosis-I" (Metamòrfosi-I, tr. of Miquel Martí i Pol, w. Nathaniel Smith).
    [SenR] (16:1) 86, p. 41.
"We Speak of You" (Parlem de tu, tr. of Miquel Martí i Pol, w. Nathaniel Smith).
    [SenR] (16:1) 86, p. 42.
3501. McGRATH, Thomas
    "Inside the Papal Ring." [AnotherCM] (16) 86, p. 62.
    "The Migration of Cities." [PoetryE] (20/21) Fall 86, p. 24-25.
    "Nuclear Winter." [PoetryE] (20/21) Fall 86, p. 27.
    "The Underground." [AnotherCM] (16) 86, p. 60-61.
3502. McGUCKIAN, Medbh
    "Four O'Clock, Summer Street." [Field] (34) Spr 86, p. 47.
    "Goya." [Field] (34) Spr 86, p. 48.
    "On Ballycastle Beach." [Verse] (6) 86, p. 27.
    "The Stone-Hitter." [Verse] (6) 86, p. 28.
    "Suivez Moi." [Verse] (6) 86, p. 28.
    "To a Cuckoo at Coolnalough." [Verse] (6) 86, p. 28.
3503. McGUINN, Rex
    "The Astronomer beside His Telescope Looks with His Eyes Out His Window" (2nd
        Award Poem, 1985/86). [KanQ] (18:1/2) Wint-Spr 86, p. 13.
3504. McHALE, Kathleen
    "Apis Mellifera" (with thanks to Maurice Maeterlinck and Karl Von Frisch). [AntigR]
        (64) Wint 86, p. 19.
    "Mississippi" (Haiku series). [AntigR] (64) Wint 86, p. 20.
3505. McHUGH, Heather
    "Artifactual." [Sonora] (11) Fall 86 [c87], p. 66-67.
    "The Night." [BostonR] (11:2) Ap 86, p. 18.
    "Shades." [PaintedB] (29) Ag 86, p. 14.
    "Three Times." [Sonora] (11) Fall 86 [c87], p. 63-64.
    "What the Typewriter's Good For." [Sonora] (11) Fall 86 [c87], p. 65.
    "Where." [PaintedB] (29) Ag 86, p. 16.
    "Whose Move." [PaintedB] (29) Ag 86, p. 15.
3506. McINNES, Nadine
    "Atlantis." [Quarry] (35:1) Wint 86, p. 99-103.
3507. McKAY, Don
    "Drinking Lake Superior." [CapilR] (39) 86, p. 18.
    "Finding Silence." [CapilR] (39) 86, p. 19.
    "Midnight Dip." [CapilR] (39) 86, p. 20.
    "Sturnus Vulgaris." [CapilR] (39) 86, p. 14-17.
    "Trouble in Paradise." [CapilR] (39) 86, p. 21.
3508. McKAY, Linda Back
    "Nam Man." [AntigR] (66/67) Sum-Aut 86, p. 48.
    "Primer." [AntigR] (66/67) Sum-Aut 86, p. 49.
3509. McKAY, Matthew
    "Mayflies." [Wind] (16:57) 86, p. 27.
    "We Were Building a Fire." [Wind] (16:57) 86, p. 27-28.
3510. McKEAN, James
    "Breakneck." [PoetryNW] (27:1) Spr 86, p. 29-30.
    "Composing a Black and White Photograph, Lake McBride, Iowa." [CimR] (75) Ap
        86, p. 56.
    "Correspondence." [Iowa] (16:1) Wint 86, p. 89-90.
    "Headlong." [Poetry] (148:1) Ap 86, p. 27-28.
    "Rented Room." [PoetryNW] (27:1) Spr 86, p. 28-29.
    "Stump Farm" (For my brother). [Poetry] (148:1) Ap 86, p. 28.
    "To the Cats of Crete." [CimR] (75) Ap 86, p. 32-33.
3511. McKEE, Louis
    "The Bath." [PaintedB] (28) Ap 86, p. 14.
    "Bebop." [BallSUF] (26:4) Aut 85, p. 13.
    "Following Tracks" (for Etheridge Knight). [BallSUF] (26:4) Aut 85, p. 33.
    "The Gift of Whales." [Amelia] (3:1) Ja 86, p. 68.
    "Graduation Exercises." [PaintedB] (28) Ap 86, p. 15.
    "In Our Hands." [PaintedB] (28) Ap 86, p. 16.
    "Last Call" (For Etheridge Knight). [SouthernHR] (20:2) Spr 86, p. 158.
    "Off Balance." [CentR] (30:3) Sum 86, p. 351.
    "Symphony of Silence." [NegC] (6:2/3) Spr-Sum 86, p. 53.
3512. McKEEVER, Herman
    "Work — Night Comes." [BlackALF] (20:3) Fall 86, p. 310

3513. McKENNA, James
"Dr. Charles Cobb" (The Dover Jail). [NegC] (6:4) Fall 86, p. 94-95.
"John Dills." [LitR] (30:1) Fall 86, p. 28.
"Thomas Hartley." [LitR] (30:1) Fall 86, p. 26-27.
3514. McKERNAN, Llewellyn
"For My Grandmother Who Knows How." [SouthernPR] (26:1) Spr 86, p. 44.
"Your Own History." [Amelia] (3:3) Sum 86, p. 66-67.
3515. McKIERNAN, Ethna
"Catch." [LakeSR] (20) 86, p. 4.
3516. McKINLEY, Mary Ann
"On Editor's Advice I Fix My Poem about Tom McAfee." [NewL] (52:2/3) Wint-Spr
86, p. 39.
3517. McKINNON, Patrick
"32 Below." [RagMag] (5:1) Spr 86, p. 26.
"The Bill Burroughs Poem." [RagMag] (5:1) Spr 86, p. 31.
"Chicago." [RagMag] (5:1) Spr 86, p. 29.
"Duluth Minnesota America." [RagMag] (5:1) Spr 86, p. 26.
"Esther the Brick Lady." [RagMag] (5:2) Fall 86, p. 40.
"Fishing." [RagMag] (5:1) Spr 86, p. 26.
"Im Writing This." [SlipS] (6) 86, p. 36.
"Inside a Barmaids Head." [SlipS] (6) 86, p. 36.
"Last Time I Was Thru Montana." [RagMag] (5:2) Fall 86, p. 41.
"Lets All Live Beneath Thumbscrews." [SanFPJ] (8:1) 85, p. 82-83.
"Lunch Counter in the Old Depot, Pueblo Colorado" (for Okie tony moffeit).
[RagMag] (5:1) Spr 86, p. 32.
"Lunch Counter in the Old Depot, Pueblo Colorado" (for okie tony moffeit).
[YetASM] (5) 86, p. 9.
"Night/Day." [SlipS] (6) 86, p. 35.
"On Wednesday." [RagMag] (5:1) Spr 86, p. 28.
"Pitching Coach." [Bogg] (56) 86, p. 53.
"Ripe Fruit." [RagMag] (5:1) Spr 86, p. 29.
"Soup." [RagMag] (5:2) Fall 86, p. 42.
"Starfish." [RagMag] (5:1) Spr 86, p. 30.
"Today a Guy." [RagMag] (5:1) Spr 86, p. 28.
"Work Poem." [RagMag] (5:1) Spr 86, p. 27.
"The Worst Date I Ever Had." [Bogg] (55) 86, p. 32.
"The Writer, Everyday." [YetASM] (4) 85, p. 5.
3518. McKINSEY, Martin
"In a Large Cambridge Bookstore, A.D. 1985" (after Cavafy). [BostonR] (11:2) Ap
86, p. 4.
MCKNIGHT, Juilene Osborne
See OSBORNE-McKNIGHT, Juilene
3519. McLAREN, Jason
"Imagine." [Grain] (14:2) My 86, p. 35.
"Two Ghazals." [Grain] (14:2) My 86, p. 35.
3520. McLAUGHLIN, Catherine
"Belfast Winter: February 1985." [MidAR] (7:1) 86, p. 166-167.
3521. McLAUGHLIN, William
"Trying to See What Hart Crane Saw in Tepotzotlán." [PoetryNW] (27:1) Spr 86, p.
32-33.
3522. McLAURIN, Ken
"No Bones about It." [SouthernPR] (26:2) Fall 86, p. 35.
3523. McLEOD, Joseph
"Quiet Night Thoughts" (tr. of Li Po). [Waves] (14:3) Wint 86, p. 71.
"Quite Night" (tr. of Li Po). [Waves] (14:3) Wint 86, p. 71.
"A Reply to the Vulgar" (tr. of Li Po). [Waves] (14:3) Wint 86, p. 71.
"Waiting for the Menu." [Rampike] (5:1) 86, p. 61.
3524. McLEOD, Milt
"Thirst." [LitR] (29:3) Spr 86, p. 339.
3525. McMAHON, Lynne
"Faith." [Field] (35) Fall 86, p. 113-115.
"Father." [Field] (35) Fall 86, p. 112.
"Furlough." [Field] (35) Fall 86, p. 118.
"The Ghostly Beatitudes." [OP] (42/43) Wint 86-87, p. 92-93.
"Like Toy Animals Arranging Themselves." [OP] (42/43) Wint 86-87, p. 93-94.
"The New Days" (for my son). [BlackWR] (12:2) Spr 86, p. 36-40.

"Night Sweat." [OP] (42/43) Wint 86-87, p. 91.
"Patois" (Père Lachaise Cemetery, Paris). [Field] (35) Fall 86, p. 116-117.
"Toussaint." [OP] (42/43) Wint 86-87, p. 90.
3526. McMAHON, Michael
"Deer and Ghosts in Orchards." [Farm] (3:1) Fall 85, p. 44.
"Laura's Harvest" (for my grandmother). [Farm] (3:1) Fall 85, p. 41.
"Silences, and the Silence of Deer." [Farm] (3:1) Fall 85, p. 42-43.
"What Our Failed Farms Will Be Next, I Think." [Farm] (3:1) Fall 85, p. 45.
3527. McMICHAEL, James
"I want her sense of me to be wrong." [MissouriR] (9:2) 86, p. 27.
"Impatience, most of all." [MissouriR] (9:2) 86, p. 26.
"She likes to be out." [MissouriR] (9:2) 86, p. 28.
"She's at the mirror." [MissouriR] (9:2) 86, p. 25.
"Three years not so much of squabbles as of routine." [MissouriR] (9:2) 86, p. 29.
3528. McMULLAN, Hugh
"The Lost Lands." [Bogg] (55) 86, p. 50.
3529. McMULLEN, Richard E.
"Getting Over Death." [SouthernPR] (26:1) Spr 86, p. 36.
3530. McNALLY, John
"An Exercise in Describing Snow." [Bogg] (56) 86, p. 11.
3531. McNAMARA, Eugene
"Cellar Door." [AntigR] (66/67) Sum-Aut 86, p. 51.
"Song Sung at the Top of the Voice." [AntigR] (66/67) Sum-Aut 86, p. 50.
3532. McNAMARA, Peter
"David Hockney." [Wind] (16:58) 86, p. 32.
3533. McNEIL, Maureen
"Home." [ManhatPR] (8) Wint 86-87, p. 45.
"Night Horse." [ManhatPR] (8) Wint 86-87, p. 45.
3534. McNERNEY, Joan
"Wildflowers bobbing in open fields." [SmPd] (23:3, #68) Fall 86, p. 18.
3535. McNERNEY, Kathleen
"Bonfire Joana" (Foguera Joana, selections tr. of Maria Mercè Marçal). [SenR]
    (16:1) 86, p. 47-48.
"Fiery Blades" (Foc de pales, selections tr. of Maria Mercè Marçal). [SenR] (16:1)
    86, p. 45-46.
3536. McPHERRON, Till
"Front Porch." [KanQ] (18:1/2) Wint-Spr 86, p. 38.
"Kansas Flint Hills." [KanQ] (18:1/2) Wint-Spr 86, p. 39.
"The Spring Lamb Ram Show." [KanQ] (18:1/2) Wint-Spr 86, p. 38.
3537. McPHERSON, Sandra
"At the Grave of Hazel Hall." [TriQ] (66) Spr-Sum 86, p. 135-138.
"Big Flowers." [AmerPoR] (15:2) Mr-Ap 86, p. 18.
"The Danger Is." [Field] (35) Fall 86, p. 81-82.
"Deep Grass, May." [AmerPoR] (15:2) Mr-Ap 86, p. 16.
"Douglas's Meadow Foam, False Mermaid." [TriQ] (66) Spr-Sum 86, p. 139-140.
"Eve." [AmerPoR] (15:2) Mr-Ap 86, p. 17.
"The Fidelity." [AmerPoR] (15:2) Mr-Ap 86, p. 17.
"Flowering Plum." [Zyzzyva] (2:2) Sum 86, p. 23-24.
"Fox" (After an observation by Gerald Durrell). [WestHR] (40:2) Sum 86, p.
    123-124.
"Letter Resembling Things" (to Walter Pavlich). [Field] (35) Fall 86, p. 83-84.
"Maureen Morris, Mother of Five, Eats a Pansy from the Garden of a Fancy
    Restaurant in Aspen." [Iowa] (16:1) Wint 86, p. 86.
"Moth Mullein." [AmerPoR] (15:2) Mr-Ap 86, p. 10.
"The Senses." [TriQ] (66) Spr-Sum 86, p. 141-143.
"Streamers." [AmerPoR] (15:2) Mr-Ap 86, p. 18-19.
"Wild Radish." [YaleR] (75:3) Spr 86, p. 422-423.
"Yellow Sand Verbena." [YaleR] (75:3) Spr 86, p. 423-424.
"YWCA, Wilder Avenue, Honolulu." [GrandS] (5:4) Sum 86, p. 69-70.
3538. McQUILKIN, Rennie
"Bird in the Belvedere." [MalR] (77) D 86, p. 75-76.
"Burial." [BelPoJ] (36:4) Sum 86, p. 12-13.
"Cecropia." [BelPoJ] (36:4) Sum 86, p. 11-12.
"Eviction." [Poetry] (147:4) Ja 86, p. 201-202.
"First Snow in the Garden of the Geishas." [SouthernPR] (26:2) Fall 86, p. 31-32.
"Henri Raymond Marie de Toulouse-Lautrec-Montfa." [Chelsea] (45) 86, p. 81-83.

"The Son." [MalR] (77) D 86, p. 73-74.
"A Sort of Summer Storm." [SouthwR] (71:1) Wint 86, p. 71.
3539. McRAY, Paul
"This Is No Painting." [StoneC] (14:1/2) Fall-Wint 86-87, p. 27.
3540. McSEVENEY, Angela
"My Breasts." [Verse] (6) 86, p. 40.
3541. MEAD, Jane
"And All These Things Are So." [Ploughs] (12:4) 86, p. 38.
"Bach, Winter." [Ploughs] (12:4) 86, p. 39.
"Paradise Consists of Forty-nine Rotating Spheres" (C. G. Jung on archetypal dream
    imagery). [Ploughs] (12:4) 86, p. 40-41.
"Where the Zinfandel Pass Their Seasons in Mute Rows." [Ploughs] (12:4) 86, p.
    42-43.
3542. MEAD, Stephen X.
"The Reliquary Room." [CrabCR] (4:1) Fall-Wint 86, p. 12-13.
3543. MEADE, Mary Ann
"Dream of Soldiers." [StoneC] (13:3/4) Spr-Sum 86, p. 21.
"Nesting." [FloridaR] (14:2) Fall-Wint 86, p. 74.
"Night Field." [FloridaR] (14:2) Fall-Wint 86, p. 75.
3544. MEADE, Robert
"May Day." [EngJ] (75:6) O 86, p. 44.
3545. MEANS-YBARRA, Ricardo
"East L.A." [CrossCur] (6:2) 86, p. 69.
3546. MEATS, Stephen
"Let Now the Stargazers." [MidwQ] (27:4) Sum 86, p. 472.
"Waiting for the Pale Eagle." [KanQ] (18:1/2) Wint-Spr 86, p. 49.
3547. MECKEL, Christoph
"End of the World" (tr. by Magda Osterhuber). [Chelsea] (45) 86, p. 48.
"Tear Animals" (tr. by Magda Osterhuber). [Chelsea] (45) 86, p. 46-47.
3548. MEDCALF, Robert Randolph, Jr.
"Under Strange Stars." [Vis] (20) 86, p. 13.
3549. MEDINA, Oquendo
"Cosas Vistas." [Mairena] (8:22) 86, p. 36.
3550. MEDINA, Pablo
"Cuban Lullaby." [Pax] (3:1/2) Wint 85-86, p. 189.
"Sam's Deli, South Broad." [TarRP] (25:1) Fall 85, p. 19.
3551. MEDINA SANCHEZ, Bethoven
"Al Temblor de la Esperanza." [Mairena] (8:21) 86, p. 64.
"Mar, Tendida Mano Azul." [Mairena] (8:21) 86, p. 65.
3552. MEDOWS, Debra F.
"Astral Projection (in Parenthesis)." [Pax] (3:1/2) Wint 85-86, p. 83-84.
"Aunt Lula's Hands." [Pax] (3:1/2) Wint 85-86, p. 80-81.
"Loretta." [Pax] (3:1/2) Wint 85-86, p. 81-82.
3553. MEDRANO, Francisco de
"Oda." [CumbPR] (5:2) Spr 86, p. 54.
"Oda" (tr. by David Gewanter). [CumbPR] (5:2) Spr 86, p. 55.
3554. MEDRANO, Marianela'
"Gestacion." [Mairena] (8:22) 86, p. 68.
3555. MEEK, Ed
"Bartending Bears in Roxbury." [ManhatPR] (7) Sum 86, p. 43.
"Your High Heels." [Wind] (16:57) 86, p. 24.
3556. MEEK, Jay
"At the New England Aquarium." [ThRiPo] (27/28) 86, p. 51-52.
"Coming Down to the Water." [PoetryNW] (27:2) Sum 86, p. 16.
"The House with Blue Windows." [Raccoon] (20) Ap 86, p. 46-47.
"Life Sources." [PoetryNW] (27:2) Sum 86, p. 14-15.
"Meeting." [MemphisSR] (6:1/2) Spr 86, p. 12.
"A Station on the Commuter Line." [OhioR] (37) 86, p. 100-101.
"Two Boys Playing Catch." [TarRP] (25:2) Spr 86, p. 40.
"Vending Display, Roanoke Bus Station." [PoetryNW] (27:2) Sum 86, p. 13-14.
"Walking the Estate." [OhioR] (37) 86, p. 99.
3557. MEGGED, Eyal
"Parting in Tivon" (tr. by Karen Alkalay-Gut). [PoetL] (81:2) Sum 86, p. 114.
"When I Wrote My Name" (tr. by Karen Alkalay-Gut). [PoetL] (81:2) Sum 86, p.
    113.

3558. MEHROTRA, Arvind Krishna
"Continuities." [LitR] (29:4) Sum 86, p. 471-472.
MEI, Yuan
See YUAN, Mei
3559. MEIER, Kay
"Island Belle." [EngJ] (75:4) Ap 86, p. 27.
3560. MEINEMA, Clarence
"Dracula's Daughter." [Bogg] (56) 86, p. 53.
3561. MEINKE, Peter
"50 on 50." [GeoR] (40:3) Fall 86, p. 737-738.
"Divorce." [NegC] (6:4) Fall 86, p. 29.
"Pink Giraffes." [PennR] (1:1) 85, p. 31.
"The Slow Child." [SouthernPR] (26:2) Fall 86, p. 42.
"Stille Nacht, Heilege Nacht." [PennR] (1:1) 85, p. 30.
3562. MEIRELES, Cecilia
"Guitar" (tr. by Manoel Cardozo). [Vis] (21) 86, p. 34.
3563. MEISSNER, Bill
"Living in Houses Too Near the River: Four Explanations of Home." [SouthernPR]
(26:2) Fall 86, p. 72-73.
"So Many Americans, Driving Late on Country Roads." [Poetry] (148:5) Ag 86, p.
267-268.
"Wings of Dust." [Chelsea] (45) 86, p. 20-24.
3564. MEISTER, Shirley Vogler
"Park Promise." [PoeticJ] (16) Fall 86, p. 18.
"To the Newborn." [PoeticJ] (16) Fall 86, p. 19.
MEJIA, Oscar Echeverri
See ECHEVERRI MEJIA, Oscar
3565. MEKETA, Rebecca
"Bestiality." [YellowS] (19) Sum 86, p. 4.
3566. MELARTIN, Riikka
"Casting." [OntR] (25) Fall-Wint 86-87, p. 34.
3567. MELE, Kate
"The Veil." [MinnR] (NS 27) Fall 86, p. 71-72.
3568. MELFI, Mary
"The end of the world." [WritersL] (1986:2), p. 33.
"The first thing I noticed." [WritersL] (1986:5), p. 17.
"How Suicide Fails to Seduce Dr. Rose" (Excerpt, an interior monologue in three
voices). [Event] (15:2) 86, p. 112-113.
"The Trainee." [CrossC] (8:1) 86, p. 8.
3569. MELGAR, Christine
"The Children." [SanFPJ] (8:3) 85, p. 48.
3570. MELHUSE, Christine
"Snake Bite." [WormR] (26:2, issue 102) 86, p. 52.
"Sylvia." [WormR] (26:2, issue 102) 86, p. 52.
"Two of a Kind." [WormR] (26:2, issue 102) 86, p. 51.
3571. MELLARD, Joan
"Starting to Rite." [EngJ] (75:2) F 86, p. 54.
MELLO, Thiago de
See De MELLO, Thiago
3572. MELZINER, Frances H.
"The 39 Prohibitions for Saturday" (tr. by Will Kirkland). [NewOR] (13:4) Wint 86,
p. 34.
"The Mirror" (tr. by Will Kirkland). [NewOR] (13:4) Wint 86, p. 35.
3573. MEMMOTT, David
"Clean Up." [CrabCR] (3:3) Sum 86, p. 23.
3574. MENASHE, Samuel
"Family Plot." [Thrpny] (25) Spr 86, p. 15.
3575. MENDEZ de la VEGA, Luz
"Evocation of Carmen Miranda" (tr. by Zoe Anglesey). [MassR] (27:3/4) Fall-Wint
86, p. 660.
3576. MENDL-SCHRAMA, Heleen
"Rustle" (tr. of Henk Bernlef). [Caliban] (1) 86, p. 42.
3577. MENDOZA, Rafael
"With a Butcher from My Village" (tr. by Ruben Martinez). [RedBass] (11) 86, p. 7.
3578. MENEBROKER, Ann
"Backstore Neighbors." [Bogg] (55) 86, p. 11.

"The Repetition of Morning & Death & Six O'Clock." [OroM] (4:1-4) My 85, p. 45.
"When There Is Reason to Destroy." [OroM] (4:1-4) My 85, p. 46.
"White Dress." [Bogg] (56) 86, p. 10.
3579. MENFI, John
"Dogwood Tree in the Morning." [NegC] (6:4) Fall 86, p. 32.
"Four-Poster Bed as Muse." [NegC] (6:4) Fall 86, p. 33.
MENG-FU, Chao
See CHAO, Meng-fu
3580. MENGDEN, Carol
"Morning Light." [Pax] (3:1/2) Wint 85-86, p. 85.
"Mothering." [Pax] (3:1/2) Wint 85-86, p. 87.
"Rites of Passage." [Pax] (3:1/2) Wint 85-86, p. 86.
3581. MENNIS, Bernice
"The Miracle." [SinW] (29/30) 86, p. 175.
3582. MERA, Karen
"A Perfect Picture." [PikeF] (7) Spr 86, p. 20.
3583. MERASTY, Billy
"Potential." [PraF] (7:1) Spr 86, p. 64.
"Radio Alone." [PraF] (7:1) Spr 86, p. 64.
"Reminiscence." [PraF] (7:1) Spr 86, p. 63.
3584. MERCER, Lianne
"Sentenced by a Short Story." [NegC] (6:1) Wint 86, p. 91.
3585. MERCER, Trudy
"Confession." [Contact] (8:41/42/43) Fall-Wint 86-87, p. 13.
"Dissent." [Contact] (8:41/42/43) Fall-Wint 86-87, p. 13.
3586. MERCHANT, Norris
"Heroic Males, Pre-Armageddon, Prepare for Macho Worst, Defense of the Higher
Culture." [SanFPJ] (8:4) 85, p. 38-39.
"Osmosis." [SanFPJ] (8:4) 85, p. 40.
"Upbeat Reject." [RagMag] (5:1) Spr 86, p. 45.
MERLO, Rafael Alvarez
See ALVAREZ MERLO, Rafael
3587. MERRILL, James
"Arabian Night." [NewYorker] (62:26) 18 Ag 86, p. 26.
"Cornwall." [DenQ] (20:4/21:1) Spr-Sum 86, p. 153-154.
"David's Watercolor." [NewYorker] (62:8) 14 Ap 86, p. 36.
"Hindu Illumination." [NewYorker] (61:46) 6 Ja 86, p. 26.
"Lipstick, 1935." [NewYRB] (33:1) 30 Ja 86, p. 40.
"Losing the Marbles." [NewYorker] (62:3) 10 Mr 86, p. 42-43.
"Page from the Koran." [GeoR] (40:3) Fall 86, p. 739.
"Philip Larkin (1922-1985)." [NewYRB] (32:21/22) 16 Ja 86, p. 21.
"The Ponchielli Complex." [YaleR] (75:4) Sum 86, p. 587-588.
"A Room at the Heart of Things." [ParisR] (28:100) Sum-Fall 86, p. 196-199.
"Serenade." [NewYorker] (61:51) 10 F 86, p. 38.
3588. MERRILL, Michael E.
"Being a Vietnam Veteran." [Sam] (46:2 release 182) 86, p. 117.
3589. MERRIN, Jeredith
"The Right Words." [Thrpny] (24) Wint 86, p. 9.
3590. MERWIN, W. S.
"After half a life or maybe all of it" (tr. of Roberto Juarroz). [SenR] (16:2) 86, p. 45.
"The boatman's song" (tr. of Mong Hao-Jan, ed. by H. F. Noyes). [Amelia] (3:2)
Spr 86, p. 47.
"Fate." [GeoR] (40:3) Fall 86, p. 741.
"History." [NewYorker] (62:31) 22 S 86, p. 36.
"The last light always welds itself to the hand" (tr. of Roberto Juarroz). [SenR]
(16:2) 86, p. 43.
"More." [PartR] (53:1) 86, p. 88-89.
"Notes from a Journey." [GrandS] (5:2) Wint 86, p. 22-25.
"On a night that should have been rain" (tr. of Roberto Juarroz). [SenR] (16:2) 86,
p. 42.
"Pastures." [GrandS] (5:4) Sum 86, p. 31-33.
"The Play." [OhioR] (36) 86, p. 66.
"Seeing the Cliffs." [OhioR] (36) 86, p. 67.
"Snow." [PartR] (53:1) 86, p. 88.
"Stairs." [GeoR] (40:3) Fall 86, p. 740.
"Term." [OhioR] (36) 86, p. 68-69.

"Trawler's lantern" (tr. of Tu Fu, ed. by H. F. Noyes). [Amelia] (3:2) Spr 86, p. 47.
"Twelve Untitled Poems" (tr. of Roberto Juarroz). [Translation] (17) Fall 86, p. 283-290.
"Waking to the Rain." [Nat] (242:18) 10 My 86, p. 660.
"We'll bury it all" (tr. of Roberto Juarroz). [SenR] (16:2) 86, p. 44.
3591. MERZ, Sandra
"Confinement." [WritersL] (1986:4), p. 20.
"Faces." [WritersL] (1986:5), p. 14.
"One from the East and One from the West." [WritersL] (1986:1), p. 11.
3592. MERZLAK, Regina
"Florida — Full Moonrise." [SpiritSH] (52) 86, p. 39.
"Metamorphosis." [SpiritSH] (52) 86, p. 39-40.
3593. MESA, Lauren
"Wheat Harvest, August 1565" (after Pieter Brueghel). [Sonora] (11) Fall 86 [c87], p. 78.
3594. MESHTET, Saheb
"O Tourist" (tr. of Mohamed Al Magut, w. Beth Tornes). [SenR] (16:1) 86, p. 72.
"Orphan" (tr. of Mohamed Al Magut, w. Beth Tornes). [SenR] (16:1) 86, p. 69.
"Tattoo" (tr. of Mohamed Al Magut, w. Beth Tornes). [SenR] (16:1) 86, p. 70-71.
3595. MESSERLI, Douglas
"Maxims from My Mother's Milk" (Selections: 2 poems). [Temblor] (4) 86, p. 83.
3596. METCALFE, Robin
"The Moscow Circus Flies Home." [Event] (15:2) 86, p. 40-41.
3597. METRAS, Gary
"Adam, Returning." [PoeticJ] (13) 86, p. 12-13.
"The Children Meeting Poets." [Sam] (44:3 release 175) 86, p. 22-23.
"One Way It Happens." [CrossCur] (5:4/6:1) 86, p. 33.
"A Week of Dreams" (Selection: "Night 2"). [ConnPR] (5:1) 86, p. 28.
3598. METZGER, Deena
"In the Morning, Walking." [Electrum] (38) Spr 86, p. 38-40.
3599. MEURY, Janet S.
"A Return." [ForidaR] (14:1) Spr-Sum 86, p. 99.
3600. MEYER, Bruce
"Blind at Dieppe." [Event] (15:2) 86, p. 172.
"Blue Willow." [Shen] (36:2) 86, p. 52.
"Private Thomas Kelly." [Event] (15:2) 86, p. 173.
"The Rivermen." [Shen] (36:2) 86, p. 53.
3601. MEYER, Marilyn
"Metaphors on Old Shoes." [BellArk] (2:1) Ja-F 86, p. 7.
"Trying on Maternity Clothes in Front of a Full-Length Mirror." [BellArk] (2:3) My-Je 86, p. 6.
3602. MEYER, Thomas
"From a Crown of Sonnets." [Conjunc] (9) 86, p. 211-215.
3603. MEYER, William (William E., Jr.)
"The February American Flag." [NewRena] (6:3, #20) Spr 86, p. 49.
"Camp-Meeting Girl." [DeKalbLAJ] (19:3/4) 86, p. 83.
"Galveston by Dark." [BallSUF] (27:4) Aut 86, p. 60.
"Gulf of Mexico." [Amelia] (3:2) Spr 86, p. 36.
"Haiku" (3 poems). [WindO] (47) Sum 86, p. 3.
"Man on White Hourse." [SlipS] (6) 86, p. 70-71.
"Prayer to My Grandfather: Wm. Young, Blacksmith, A.D. 1879-1977." [BallSUF] (26:4) Aut 85, p. 36.
"To Eve." [DeKalbLAJ] (19:2) 86, p. 40.
3604. MEZA, Joaquin
"Like This" (tr. by Ruben Martinez). [RedBass] (11) 86, p. 7.
3605. MEZEY, Robert
"Couplets" (Selections: 7, 9, 10, 15, 20). [Iowa] (16:1) Wint 86, p. 83-85.
"Mercy." [MemphisSR] (7:1) Fall 86, p. 40.
"School Bells." [MemphisSR] (7:1) Fall 86, p. 41.
3606. MICHAUX, Henri
"Façons d'Endormi, Façons d'Eveillé" (Selections, tr. by James Wanless). [Notus] (1:1) Fall 86, p. 72-75.
MICHELE, Mary di
See Di MICHELE, Mary

3607. MICHELINE, Jack
   "Long After Midnight." [OroM] (4:1-4) My 85, p. 35-36.
3608. MICHELSON, Max
   "Towards the End." [Bogg] (56) 86, p. 15.
3609. MICHELUTTI, Dorina
   "Father." [Writ] (17) 85, c86, p. 26.
   "She." [Writ] (17) 85, c86, p. 27.
MICHIO, Nakano
   See NAKANO, Michio
3610. MICKIEWICZ, Adam
   "Napoleon's Arrival into Lithuania" (from Pan Tadeusz, tr. by Leonard Kress).
      [WebR] (11:1) Spr 86, p. 45-49.
3611. MIDDLETON, Christopher
   "Alienation Through Work" (tr. of Karin Kiwus). [SouthernHR] (20:2) Spr 86, p.
      156-157.
   "Lento." [SouthernHR] (20:2) Spr 86, p. 125.
MIELES, Edgardo Nieves
   See NIEVES MIELES, Edgardo
3612. MIKI, Roy
   "Emblem." [Rampike] (5:2) 86, p. 23.
3613. MIKULEC, Patrick B.
   "Mrs. Roger's Science Class." [EngJ] (75:7) N 86, p. 45.
3614. MILBURN, Michael
   "Condemned Man Dies in Florida Chair." [NewL] (53:1) Fall 86, p. 99.
3615. MILES, Ron
   "Secretary." [CanLit] (110) Fall 86, p. 97.
3616. MILLAN, Gonzalo
   "60. El anciano se mira el espejo." [SilverFR] (11) Sum 86, p. 20, 22.
   "The City" (Selection: Poem 60, tr. by Steven F. White). [SilverFR] (11) Sum 86,
      p. 21, 23.
3617. MILLAY, Edna St. Vincent
   "What Lips My Lips Have Kissed." [Sam] (46:2 release 182) 86, p. 70.
3618. MILLER, A. McA.
   "Foreclosed, It's." [BelPoJ] (36:4) Sum 86, p. 20-21.
3619. MILLER, Carolyn Reynolds
   "Maiden Aunts and the Cello." [PoetryNW] (27:4) Wint 86-87, p. 43-44.
   "Mildred and the Minotaur." [PoetryNW] (27:4) Wint 86-87, p. 40-41.
   "Walks in Winter." [PoetryNW] (27:4) Wint 86-87, p. 41-43.
3620. MILLER, Derek
   "Letter to Me of a Year Ago." [HangL] (49) Spr 86, p. 63.
   "Sleepless Restaurant." [HangL] (49) Spr 86, p. 61-62.
   "When I'm alone in my room in the dark" ("Untitled"). [HangL] (49) Spr 86, p. 62.
   "You Can't Even Fake It." [HangL] (49) Spr 86, p. 60.
3621. MILLER, E. Ethelbert
   "Francisco." [OP] (41) Spr 86, p. 7.
   "A Question of Faith." [OP] (41) Spr 86, p. 7.
   "The stars sit on the back porch." [OP] (41) Spr 86, p. 6.
3622. MILLER, Elizabeth Gamble
   "Only the Voice" (Excerpt, tr. of Hugo Lindo). [NewOR] (13:2) Sum 86, p. 74-75.
3623. MILLER, Frances
   "When the People Dream" (for the Guatemalan Dolls). [StoneC] (14:1/2) Fall-Wint
      86-87, p. 13.
3624. MILLER, Hugh
   "After the Opera II" (for Marilyn). [AntigR] (65) Spr 86, p. 146.
3625. MILLER, James A.
   "American Gothic." [BellArk] (2:3) My-Je 86, p. 5.
   "Amishman at the New World." [BellArk] (2:2) Mr-Ap 86, p. 3.
   "Emergency Room." [BellArk] (2:6) N-D 86, p. 2.
   "High Holiday at Mt. Hope." [BellArk] (2:1) Ja-F 86, p. 8.
   "Invocation." [BellArk] (2:1) Ja-F 86, p. 1.
   "Isle" (for Ellen & John). [BellArk] (2:6) N-D 86, p. 7.
   "More Real than Dream." [BellArk] (2:2) Mr-Ap 86, p. 8.
   "On Not Going Gentle into That Good Night." [BellArk] (2:1) Ja-F 86, p. 16.
   "Passim." [BellArk] (2:2) Mr-Ap 86, p. 6.
   "Saturday Evening, the Idea of Order on Canal Street." [BellArk] (2:5) S-O 86, p. 6.
   "Time Will Have to Come." [CrabCR] (3:2) Spr 86, p. 7.

3626. MILLER, Jane
"American Odalisque" (American Haiku). [Sonora] (10) Spr 86, p. 27-28.
"Centripetal." [Agni] (23) 86, p. 128-129.
"Fiesta." [Sonora] (10) Spr 86, p. 29.
"The Mate to the Plum." [PartR] (53:2) 86, p. 230-232.
"Miami Heart." [OP] (42/43) Wint 86-87, p. 170-171.
"Peace Lyric." [ParisR] (28:99) Spr 86, p. 175-176.
"The Stagger of the Wind That I Think Is Your Turning." [GeoR] (40:3) Fall 86, p. 742.
"To Remember Every Hour." [OP] (42/43) Wint 86-87, p. 169.
"Video Rain." [Sonora] (10) Spr 86, p. 25-26.
3627. MILLER, Jauren
"A Week on the Madison." [Wind] (16:57) 86, p. 29-30.
3628. MILLER, John (John N.)
"Charisma." [Sam] (45:4 release 180) 86, p. 18-19.
"Denouement." [WebR] (11:2) Fall 86, p. 62.
"Eating Their Words." [WebR] (11:2) Fall 86, p. 61.
3629. MILLER, Leslie Adrienne
"Afternoon at Pettaquanscutt Rock." [Prima] (10) 86, p. 60.
"All the Rooms of the House." [AntR] (44:4) Fall 86, p. 442-443.
"Backyard Lyric." [YellowS] (19) Sum 86, p. 5.
"An Early Meeting with Men." [NegC] (6:1) Wint 86, p. 14-15.
"The Future of Beauty." [AntR] (44:4) Fall 86, p. 441.
"Lost Flamingo." [AntR] (44:4) Fall 86, p. 439.
"Owning a Bar." [AntR] (44:4) Fall 86, p. 440.
"Saturday Night, Almost Thirty." [SouthernPR] (26:1) Spr 86, p. 64-65.
3630. MILLER, Michael
"The Bird Feeder." [SouthwR] (71:1) Wint 86, p. 41.
"The Crow." [PennR] (1:1) 85, p. 40.
"First Kingdom." [KenR] (NS 7:3) Sum 85, p. 96-97.
"The Mallard." [KanQ] (18:1/2) Wint-Spr 86, p. 76.
"Red-Wing." [ManhatPR] (6) Wint-Spr 85-86, p. 39.
3631. MILLER, Philip
"And the Story Continues." [Bogg] (55) 86, p. 9.
"Catalogue." [Raccoon] (20) Ap 86, p. 21.
"Daysleeper." [Vis] (21) 86, p. 22.
"Drinking Alone with Father." [SmPd] (23:3, #68) Fall 86, p. 33.
"The Old Woman Who Jumped in a Well." [Wind] (16:56) 86, p. 31.
"Pacing Like a Caged Wolf." [CapeR] (21:1) Spr 86, p. 48.
"Photos of Father." [CapeR] (21:1) Spr 86, p. 49.
"Rat Snake." [ColEng] (48:2) F 86, p. 145.
"Sunday Sunset." [Puerto] (22:1) Fall 86, p. 62.
3632. MILLER, Shane
"World Stop." [RagMag] (5:1) Spr 86, p. 7.
3633. MILLER, Vassar
"Subterfuge." [Kaleid] (12) Wint 86, p. 47.
3634. MILLER, Warren C.
"Senility Check." [Bogg] (56) 86, p. 62.
3635. MILLER, William
"Among Roots" (Delta, AL). [DeKalbLAJ] (19:2) 86, p. 41.
"Laugharne." [Poem] (56) N 86, p. 1.
"Waking" (After Emerson). [Poem] (56) N 86, p. 2.
"Writer's Block." [DeKalbLAJ] (19:2) 86, p. 41.
3636. MILLETT, John
"Curlew." [Vis] (21) 86, p. 17.
"Jonathan Apples." [Amelia] (3:3) Sum 86, p. 31.
"Old House on Lytton Hill." [Amelia] (3:3) Sum 86, p. 32.
"Oral Testimony." [Vis] (21) 86, p. 36.
3637. MILLIS, Christopher
"Ceremony." [CutB] (26) Spr-Sum 86, p. 16.
"Inside the Iguanodon." [BellR] (9:1) Spr 86, p. 51.
"Messages." [BellR] (9:1) Spr 86, p. 50-51.
"On First Seeing My Wife's Lover." [YetASM] (5) 86, p. 7.
3638. MILLMAN, Lawrence
"A Child's Guide to Latin American Politics." [Agni] (23) 86, p. 93.
"Shells." [CrossCur] (6:2) 86, p. 91.

MILLS, Elizabeth Randall
    See RANDALL-MILLS, Elizabeth
3639. MILLS, George
    "Chairs, Hats, Water." [StoneC] (13:3/4) Spr-Sum 86, p. 22-23.
3640. MILLS, Laurel
    "The Dance of the Gulls." [RagMag] (5:2) Fall 86, p. 45.
    "Lime Kiln at High Cliff." [RagMag] (5:2) Fall 86, p. 46.
    "To the Woman Who Sleeps under the Cupola." [RagMag] (5:2) Fall 86, p. 47.
3641. MILLS, Ralph J., Jr.
    "4/18." [SpoonRQ] (11:2) Spr 86, p. 28.
    "Ailanthus, Yes." [TarRP] (25:1) Fall 85, p. 39.
    "Clouds & A." [SpoonRQ] (11:2) Spr 86, p. 27.
    "Clouds & A." [SpoonRQ] (11:4) Fall 86, p. 18.
    "How." [SpoonRQ] (11:2) Spr 86, p. 26.
    "Lit." [TarRP] (25:1) Fall 85, p. 38.
    "Wind / Switch." [SpoonRQ] (11:2) Spr 86, p. 29.
3642. MILLS, Robert
    "Coastal Reverie." [SpoonRQ] (11:4) Fall 86, p. 30.
3643. MILLS, Sparling
    "The Claras I Have Known." [CrossC] (8:1) 86, p. 25.
    "A Dog Story." [AntigR] (64) Wint 86, p. 100.
3644. MILLS, Stephen R.
    "Rending of AIDS." [JamesWR] (3:4) Sum 86, p. 9.
3645. MILOSZ, Czeslaw
    "Father Ch., Many Years Later" (tr. by the author and Robert Hass). [NewYRB]
        (33:5) 27 Mr 86, p. 38.
    "In a Jar" (tr. by the author). [NewYorker] (62:16) 9 Je 86, p. 42.
    "Incantation" (tr. by the author and Robert Pinsky). [YaleR] (76:1) Aut 86, p. 1.
    "Lauda" (tr. by the author and Robert Hass). [ParisR] (28:100) Sum-Fall 86, p.
        104-131.
    "Preparation." [Harp] (272:1628) Ja 86, p. 31.
3646. MILOSZ, Oscar V. de L.
    "The Confession of Lemuel" (The Berlin Stopped in the Night, tr. by Roma Huk).
        [AnotherCM] (15) 86, p. 72-74.
3647. MINAR, Scott
    "Luminare." [GeoR] (40:3) Fall 86, p. 743-744.
    "The Nexus of Rain" (Chapbook of Poems, Dedicated to Walter Byrd Minar and to
        Nancy Ann Minar). [OhioR] (36) 86, p. 49-64.
3648. MINARIK, John Paul
    "December Snow." [Confr] (32) Spr-Sum 86, p. 115.
3649. MINCZESKI, John
    "Asparagus." [Abraxas] (34) 86, p. 37-40.
    "Blue." [AnotherCM] (15) 86, p. 75.
    "Native Tongue." [AnotherCM] (15) 86, p. 77.
    "Phelps Municipal Dump" (for ACH). [Abraxas] (34) 86, p. 36.
    "Sparrow." [LakeSR] (20) 86, p. 5.
3650. MINFORD, John
    "Begin from Here" (from the poem-cycle, Part V, tr. of Jiang He, w. Pang Bingjun
        et al.). [Nimrod] (29:2) Spr-Sum 86, p. 123-124.
    "Train through Qin Mountains" (tr. Luo Gengye, w. Pang Bingjun). [Nimrod]
        (29:2) Spr-Sum 86, p. 108-111.
MINGSHAN, Xia
    See XIA, Mingshan
3651. MINISTSOOS, Charles
    "Nine Years Old." [PraF] (7:1) Spr 86, p. 74-75.
    "Remembering Jackson Beardy." [PraF] (7:1) Spr 86, p. 75-76.
3652. MINOR, James
    "Haiku" (3 poems). [Northeast] (series 4:3) Spr 86, p. 35.
3653. MINOR, William
    "Translation from Mandelstam." [HangL] (49) Spr 86, p. 27.
3654. MINTON, Helena
    "Next Door." [FloridaR] (14:2) Fall-Wint 86, p. 93.
    "The People Who Come to Save Me." [BelPoJ] (37:2) Wint 86-87, p. 4-5.
    "The Wall." [BelPoJ] (37:2) Wint 86-87, p. 5.
3655. MINTY, Judith
    "The Gypsy." [Caliban] (1) 86, p. 75.

"The Harpist." [Caliban] (1) 86, p. 74.
"Trees." [Caliban] (1) 86, p. 72-73.
MIRANDA, Stella Selva
    See SELVA MIRANDA, Stella
3656. MIRIKITANI, Janice
    "A Love Poem" (For Cecil). [Contact] (7:38/39/40) Wint-Spr 86, p. 71.
3657. MIROLLA, Michael
    "Beyond the Appian Way." [WestCR] (21:2) O 86, p. 62.
    "Ghosts." [WestCR] (21:2) O 86, p. 60.
    "Love." [WestCR] (21:2) O 86, p. 61.
3658. MISHKIN, Julia
    "Cruel Duet" (For my mother and father). [QRL] (Poetry series 6:26) 86, 74 p.
    "Sleeper Abandoned." [PennR] (1:1) 85, p. 32.
MISHKOVSKY, Shneurson
    See ZELDA (Shneurson Mishkovsky)
3659. MISHLER, Richard M.
    "Dark Friend." [Sam] (46:2 release 182) 86, p. 59.
    "Medals." [Sam] (46:2 release 182) 86, p. 124.
3660. MITCHAM, Judson
    "About Women." [GeoR] (40:2) Sum 86, p. 518-519.
    "A Knowledge of Water." [GeoR] (40:2) Sum 86, p. 519.
    "Where We Are." [GeoR] (40:3) Fall 86, p. 745-746.
3661. MITCHELL, Andrew
    "Saltaire." [Stand] (27:3) Sum 86, p. 40.
3662. MITCHELL, Ben
    "We Go Along Together." [PassN] (7:1) Fall-Wint 85-86, p. 23.
    "Yesterday, Why I Didn't Call." [PassN] (7:1) Fall-Wint 85-86, p. 23.
3663. MITCHELL, Hugh P.
    "Four Quarters of the World" (From Loren McIntyre, "The Lost Empire of the
        Incas"). [BallSUF] (27:4) Aut 86, p. 62-64.
3664. MITCHELL, Peyton
    "Poems." [Amelia] (3:3) Sum 86, p. 102.
3665. MITCHELL, Roger
    "Rubble." [PoetryNW] (27:4) Wint 86-87, p. 7.
    "The Two Secretaries." [PennR] (1:1) 85, p. 55-56.
3666. MITCHELL, Stephen
    "Autobiography, 1952" (tr. of Yehuda Amichai). [PartR] (53:2) 86, p. 232-233.
    "A Girl Called Sarah" (tr. of Yehuda Amichai). [PoetL] (81:2) Sum 86, p. 77.
    "The Grand Duke of New York" (tr. of Dan Pagis). [PoetL] (81:2) Sum 86, p. 80.
    "Of Three or Four in a Room" (tr. of Yehuda Amichai). [Nat] (242:15) 19 Ap 86, p.
        559.
    "Summer or Its End" (tr. of Yehuda Amichai). [Nat] (242:15) 19 Ap 86, p. 558.
3667. MITCHELL, Susan
    "Bus Trip." [Atlantic] (258:2) Ag 86, p. 46.
3668. MITCHELL, Wendy
    "Observations." [NegC] (6:1) Wint 86, p. 84-85.
MITSUHARU, Kaneko
    See KANEKO, Mitsuharu
3669. MIYOSHI, Tatsuji
    "Gray Gulls" (tr. by James Kirkup and Akiko Takemoto). [Translation] (17) Fall 86,
        p. 192-193.
3670. MIZRAHHI, Nava
    "Gevalt Poem." [SinW] (29/30) 86, p. 212.
    "In the 'Unlimited Opportunity Land'." [SinW] (29/30) 86, p. 154.
    "To Be an Arab Jew." [SinW] (29/30) 86, p. 211-212.
3671. MLADINIC, Peter
    "Invisible Friends" (from a sequence). [MSS] (5:1) 86, p. 170.
3672. MODIC, John L.
    "Tunisia - 1943." [WindO] (47) Sum 86, p. 10-12.
3673. MOERMAN, Ernst
    "Fantomas Whiles Away" (tr. by James Loverde). [Vis] (22) 86, p. 5.
3674. MOFFAT, Napoléon
    "It May Be a Question of Time Before, or The Shadow of Nothing Will Behave As
        Such." [Rampike] (5:2) 86, p. 60.
3675. MOFFEIT, Tony
    "Anadarko." [YetASM] (4) 85, p. 2.

"Answer." [CrabCR] (3:3) Sum 86, p. 15.
"Crazy Horse." [PoeticJ] (15) Sum 86, p. 23.
"Dancing on the Edge." [PoeticJ] (16) Fall 86, p. 22.
"El Paso." [Amelia] (3:4) Fall 86, p. 76.
"Fever Water Bed of Fire." [SlipS] (6) 86, p. 12.
"James Dean: Like coyote you had your secrets." [PoeticJ] (14) 86, p. 21.
"James Dean: You raced the devil." [PoeticJ] (14) 86, p. 23.
"Johnny Ace." [CrabCR] (3:3) Sum 86, p. 15.
"Mexican Ber." [SlipS] (6) 86, p. 11.
"The Moon My Flesh, the Stars My Teeth." [PoeticJ] (14) 86, p. 22.
"My Blood Is Dark Rain." [PoeticJ] (16) Fall 86, p. 23.
"My Bones Are Dice Thrown to the Sky." [Amelia] (3:4) Fall 86, p. 76.
"No Hurry No Worry." [PoeticJ] (15) Sum 86, p. 22.
"La Nortenita." [CrabCR] (3:3) Sum 86, p. 13-14.
3676. MOFFI, Larry
    "Black and White Tulips" (in memorium, S. L.). [TriQ] (67) Fall 86, p. 119.
3677. MOFFITT, John
    "At Nanzen-Ji" (Kyoto). [NegC] (6:1) Wint 86, p. 87-90.
    "Confluence." [NegC] (6:4) Fall 86, p. 47.
    "Skirting Riddles." [NegC] (6:4) Fall 86, p. 46.
3678. MOHRENWITZ, Manoce
    "I have come this far" (tr. by Will Kirkland). [NewOR] (13:4) Wint 86, p. 32.
MOKUO, Nagayama
    See NAGAYAMA, Mokuo
MOLINA, Roberto Aguirre
    See AGUIRRE MOLINA, Roberto
3679. MOLINARI, Kato
    "Apocryphal Journalism" (tr. by Mary Crow and Patsy Boyer). [MidAR] (6:1) 86?,
        p. 69, 71.
    "Periodismo Apocrifo." [MidAR] (6:1) 86?, p. 68, 70.
3680. MOLLOHAN, Terrie
    "Our Minister Was a Young Widower" (God Save His Soul). [Amelia] (3:2) Spr 86,
        p. 98.
3681. MOLLOY, Barbara
    "Force." [BlackWR] (12:2) Spr 86, p. 29-30.
3682. MOLLOY-OLUND, Barbara
    "Blockstarken." [Field] (35) Fall 86, p. 74-75.
    "Heirloom." [Field] (35) Fall 86, p. 80.
    "In Favor of Lightning." [Field] (35) Fall 86, p. 76-77.
    "Knot." [PoetryNW] (27:3) Aut 86, p. 26.
    "On the Porch in the Evening." [Field] (35) Fall 86, p. 78-79.
3683. MOLODOWSKY, Kadia
    "God of Mercy" (tr. by Moshe Spiegel). [WebR] (11:1) Spr 86, p. 41-42.
3684. MOLONEY, Karen M.
    "Emily Rose" (Ascott under Wychwood, Oxfordshire). [Jacaranda] (2:1) Fall 86, p.
        20.
3685. MOMADAY, N. Scott
    "Concession." [ParisR] (28:99) Spr 86, p. 161.
    "The Hotel 1829" (For An Painter). [ParisR] (28:99) Spr 86, p. 160.
    "Sonnet for a Mottled-Breasted Girl." [ParisR] (28:99) Spr 86, p. 162.
3686. MOMONOVA, Tatyana
    "Behind me someone" (tr. by Barbara Heldt). [Pax] (3:1/2) Wint 85-86, p. 191.
    "I entrust myself to her" (tr. by Barbara Heldt). [Pax] (3:1/2) Wint 85-86, p. 191.
    "I will return" (tr. by Barbara Heldt). [Pax] (3:1/2) Wint 85-86, p. 190.
    "No letters" (tr. by Barbara Heldt). [Pax] (3:1/2) Wint 85-86, p. 190.
    "Rebirth on the edge of worry" (tr. by Barbara Heldt). [Pax] (3:1/2) Wint 85-86, p.
        191.
3687. MONAGHAN, Patricia
    "Coming Home." [CrossCur] (6:2) 86, p. 57.
    "Death Cammas: A Manual." [SingHM] (14) 86, p. 22.
    "Running with Whales." [SingHM] (14) 86, p. 23.
3688. MONAHAN, Jean
    "The Bones of Potter's Field." [NewRep] (195:21) 24 N 86, p. 50.
    "O orange cat do your chameleon act." [WebR] (11:2) Fall 86, p. 48-49.
    "The Voice of Thy Brother's Blood." [WebR] (11:2) Fall 86, p. 43-46.
    "The Way the Yellow." [WebR] (11:2) Fall 86, p. 47-48.

3689. MONFREDO, Louise
"Grandmothering." [CentR] (30:1) Wint 86, p. 58-59.
"October." [Calyx] (9:2/3) Wint 86, p. 105.
3690. MONG, Hao-Jan
"The boatman's song" (ed. by H. F. Noyes, tr. by W. S. Merwin). [Amelia] (3:2)
Spr 86, p. 47.
3691. MONROE, Kent, Jr.
"Winter Evenings." [NewEngR] (8:4) Sum 86, p. 499-500.
3692. MONTAGUE, John
"The Broken Doll" (tr. of Nuala ni Dhomhnaill). [Verse] (3:3) N 86, p. 48.
"By the Lighthouse Dome, or Roethke's Ghost at Roche's Point." [Verse] (3:3) N
86, p. 47.
3693. MONTAKHAB, Behrouz
"Ritual." [Amelia] (3:3) Sum 86, p. 23.
3694. MONTALE, Eugenio
"Agave on the Rocks" (tr. by William Arrowsmith). [AmerPoR] (15:4) Jl-Ag 86, p.
25.
"Autumn Cellars" (tr. by William Arrowsmith). [ParisR] (28:101) Wint 86, p. 231.
"Cape Mesco" (tr. by William Arrowsmith). [Translation] (17) Fall 86, p. 234.
"Cliffside" (tr. by William Arrowsmith). [AmerPoR] (15:4) Jl-Ag 86, p. 26.
"Cuttlefish Bones" (tr. by William Arrowsmith). [AmerPoR] (15:4) Jl-Ag 86, p.
22-24.
"Delta" (tr. by William Arrowsmith). [AmerPoR] (15:4) Jl-Ag 86, p. 27.
"Elegy of Pico Farnese" (tr. by William Arrowsmith). [Translation] (17) Fall 86, p.
231-233.
"House by the Sea" (tr. by William Arrowsmith). [AmerPoR] (15:4) Jl-Ag 86, p.
27.
"The Lemon Trees" (tr. by William Arrowsmith). [NewYRB] (33:3) 27 F 86, p. 26.
"Minstrels" (from C. Debussy, tr. by William Arrowsmith). [AmerPoR] (15:4) Jl-Ag
86, p. 27.
"Moiré" (tr. by William Arrowsmith). [AmerPoR] (15:4) Jl-Ag 86, p. 26.
"Palio" (tr. by William Arrowsmith). [Translation] (17) Fall 86, p. 235-236.
"Pool" (tr. by William Arrowsmith). [AmerPoR] (15:4) Jl-Ag 86, p. 27.
"Rejoice: this breeze entering the orchard" (tr. by William Arrowsmith). [AmerPoR]
(15:4) Jl-Ag 86, p. 21.
"Sarcophagi" (tr. by William Arrowsmith). [Translation] (16) Spr 86, p. 129-131.
"To Liuba, Leaving" (tr. by William Arrowsmith). [ParisR] (28:101) Wint 86, p.
231.
"What You Knew about Me" (tr. by Ned E. Condini). [MissR] (15:1/2, #43/44)
Fall-Wint 86, p. 49.
"Wind and Banners" (tr. by William Arrowsmith). [AmerPoR] (15:4) Jl-Ag 86, p.
25.
3695. MONTALVO, Berga G.
"Una Noche de Contrastes." [LindLM] (5:4) O-D 86, p. 23.
MONTANEZ, Jaime Marcano
See MARCANO MONTANEZ, Jaime
3696. MONTEIRO, George
"A Cross? On the Door of the Tobacco Shop?" (tr. of Fernando Pessoa).
[Translation] (17) Fall 86, p. 225.
"The God Pan Did Not Die" (tr. of Fernando Pessoa). [Translation] (17) Fall 86, p.
226.
"An Instantly Venerable Sonnet" (tr. of Fernando Pessoa). [Translation] (17) Fall
86, p. 229.
"Self-Analysis" (tr. of Fernando Pessoa). [Translation] (17) Fall 86, p. 230.
"Today I Read Nearly Two Pages" (tr. of Fernando Pessoa). [Translation] (17) Fall
86, p. 227.
"Tripe, Porto Style" (tr. of Fernando Pessoa). [Translation] (17) Fall 86, p. 228.
3697. MONTERO-PAULSON, Daria J.
"Elegía." [Mester] (15:2) Fall 86, p. 51.
3698. MONTES HUIDOBRO, Matías
"Haiku." [Mairena] (8:22) 86, p. 99.
3699. MONTGOMERY, George
"Sweet Charity." [SecC] (14:1) 86, p. 45.
3700. MONTGOMERY, Marion
"The Second Year." [GeoR] (40:3) Fall 86, p. 747-748.

3701. MONTUORI, Deborah
"Divertimento (One for Salieri)." [PassN] (7:1) Fall-Wint 85-86, p. 24.
3702. MOODY, Rodger
"The Last Summer." [IndR] (9:1) Wint 86, p. 82.
3703. MOONEY, Sharon
"Is Every Kitchen Sink under a Window?" [Calyx] (9:2/3) Wint 86, p. 108-109.
"Middle Womon." [Calyx] (9:2/3) Wint 86, p. 106-107.
3704. MOORE, Barbara
"Hanging Loose." [HolCrit] (23:3) Je 86, p. 15.
"Homing." [KanQ] (18:3) Sum 86, p. 50.
"Seeing." [AmerPoR] (15:2) Mr-Ap 86, p. 7.
3705. MOORE, Berwyn
"Discovering Patience in My 31st Year." [StoneC] (14:1/2) Fall-Wint 86-87, p. 36.
"Living the Magic" (for Mark). [KanQ] (18:1/2) Wint-Spr 86, p. 173.
3706. MOORE, Dennis
"The Girl of Rue Joli." [Sam] (46:2 release 182) 86, p. 90.
"Somewhere Near the Mekong River, 1966." [Sam] (46:2 release 182) 86, p. 71-74.
"The Train." [Sam] (46:2 release 182) 86, p. 48-49.
3707. MOORE, Jacqueline
"Ox-Shoe." [SingHM] (14) 86, p. 24.
3708. MOORE, Janice Townley
"Anne Frank Dreams at Bergen-Belsen." [ForidaR] (14:1) Spr-Sum 86, p. 52.
"A Woman's Baseball Poem." [NegC] (6:4) Fall 86, p. 103.
3709. MOORE, Lenard D.
"Dinin' Out at the Midway Café, 1975." [BlackALF] (20:3) Fall 86, p. 266.
"I See Snow" (For A.R. Ammons). [Pembroke] (18) 86, p. 164.
"I'm Listening." [CrossCur] (6:2) 86, p. 90.
"Songlet to A.R. Ammons." [Pembroke] (18) 86, p. 164.
"Two Sides of the Road." [CrossCur] (6:2) 86, p. 89.
"The Way I Think It Should Be" (for Marcille Lynn Moore). [BlackALF] (20:3) Fall
86, p. 266.
3710. MOORE, Marianne
"Ezra Pound." [YaleR] (75:3) Spr 86, p. 351.
3711. MOORE, Richard
"Influences." [ManhatPR] (7) Sum 86, p. 26.
"The Poet." [NegC] (6:4) Fall 86, p. 28.
"Resolution." [NegC] (6:4) Fall 86, p. 28.
"Singer." [ManhatPR] (7) Sum 86, p. 26.
"The Spirits of Middle Air." [CumbPR] (6:1) Fall 86, p. 32.
"To Sit on the Grass." [NegC] (6:4) Fall 86, p. 27.
3712. MOORE, Todd
"He Was Leaning." [Wind] (16:56) 86, p. 41.
"Jerry." [SlipS] (6) 86, p. 12.
"She Wanted." [Bogg] (55) 86, p. 24.
"The Way." [Bogg] (56) 86, p. 56.
3713. MOORE ALBA, Guillermina P.
"De la Vida." [Mairena] (8:21) 86, p. 103.
"De los Cielos Internos." [Mairena] (8:21) 86, p. 103.
"Para Mi Ciudad." [Mairena] (8:21) 86, p. 104.
3714. MOORHEAD, Andrea
"Acton Vale." [Os] (22) 86, p. 20-23.
"The Body Invisible." [Os] (23) 86, p. 15.
"Chant I" (tr. of Claude Beausoleil). [AmerPoR] (15:3) My-Je 86, p. 30.
"Chant III" (tr. of Claude Beausoleil). [AmerPoR] (15:3) My-Je 86, p. 30.
"Chant VI" (tr. of Claude Beausoleil). [AmerPoR] (15:3) My-Je 86, p. 30.
"Chant XVIII" (tr. of Claude Beausoleil). [AmerPoR] (15:3) My-Je 86, p. 31.
"Chant XXIII" (tr. of Claude Beausoleil). [AmerPoR] (15:3) My-Je 86, p. 31.
"City at Night" (for Nicole Smith, tr. of Claude Beausoleil). [Translation] (16) Spr
86, p. 198-199.
"Cordoba" (tr. of Claude Beausoleil). [Translation] (16) Spr 86, p. 197.
"February Bloom." [StoneC] (14:1/2) Fall-Wint 86-87, p. 42.
"First Light." [Os] (23) 86, p. 13.
"For Susan." [StoneC] (13:3/4) Spr-Sum 86, p. 11.
"For Susan" (The Phillips Poetry Award — Spring/Summer 1986). [StoneC]
(14:1/2) Fall-Wint 86-87, p. 2.
"Hiroshima Blooms." [Os] (23) 86, p. 16.

"Portrait." [Os] (23) 86, p. 17.
"Retina of Joy." [Os] (23) 86, p. 14.
3715. MOOSE, Ruth
"10 AM" (For A.R. Ammons). [Pembroke] (18) 86, p. 76-77.
"August Storm." [ManhatPR] (8) Wint 86-87, p. 19.
"House in the Horseshoe." [CrescentR] (4:2) Fall 86, p. 55-56.
"Nothing Has Changed" (For A.R. Ammons). [Pembroke] (18) 86, p. 77.
"Original Knowledge" (A confession of sorts). [SingHM] (14) 86, p. 3.
"Weatherside" (After Andrew Wyeth). [ManhatPR] (8) Wint 86-87, p. 18.
3716. MOOTRY, Maria K.
"To Winnie on Ecumenical Day, October, 1985." [OP] (41) Spr 86, p. 65-69.
MORA, Francisco Lluch
See LLUCH MORA, Francisco
3717. MORA, Pat
"Marriage II." [Pax] (3:1/2) Wint 85-86, p. 89.
"Unnatural Deeds" (for Vicki Ruiz). [Pax] (3:1/2) Wint 85-86, p. 88.
3718. MORAFF, Barbara
"Coincidence." [WormR] (26:2, issue 102) 86, p. 48.
"Craft." [WormR] (26:2, issue 102) 86, p. 49.
"Light (Culinary) Touch in a Heavy Book." [WormR] (26:2, issue 102) 86, p. 49.
"Smoke rises catches." [WormR] (26:2, issue 102) 86, p. 49.
"To the Lady #10." [WormR] (26:2, issue 102) 86, p. 50-51.
MORALES, Guillermo Gutierrez
See GUTIERREZ MORALES, Guillermo
MORALES, José Jurado
See JURADO MORALES, José
3719. MORALES ROSADO, Beatriz
"Anhelo." [LetFem] (10:2) Fall 84 [c1985], p. 92.
"Cuerpos." [LetFem] (10:2) Fall 84 [c1985], p. 93.
"Pajaro invencible el de mis vuelos de poeta." [LetFem] (10:2) Fall 84 [c1985], p. 91.
3720. MORAN, Moore
"Ord." [Thrpny] (24) Wint 86, p. 7.
3721. MORAN, Ronald
"The Mazda Effect." [Northeast] (series 4:3) Spr 86, p. 5.
3722. MORDENSKI, Jan
"Basia." [YetASM] (5) 86, p. 7.
"In October." [CapeR] (21:2) Fall 86, p. 46.
"November Morning." [CapeR] (21:2) Fall 86, p. 47.
"Quilting Bees." [PassN] (7:1) Fall-Wint 85-86, p. 20.
3723. MOREAU, June
"Mojave." [StoneC] (13:3/4) Spr-Sum 86, p. 51.
3724. MOREHEAD, Barbara
"Right On." [Calyx] (9:2/3) Wint 86, p. 102.
3725. MORELLI, Miguel Angel
"Elogio de la Locura." [Mairena] (8:21) 86, p. 106.
"Holderlin." [Mairena] (8:21) 86, p. 105.
"Muertes y Contramuertes" (tango en el exilio). [Mairena] (8:21) 86, p. 105.
3726. MORGAN, Dale
"Hot Summer Day." [OhioR] (36) 86, p. 39.
3727. MORGAN, Edwin
"Attila József" (tr. of Attila József, w. George Cushing). [Verse] (5) 86, p. 50.
"Culture" (tr. of Attila József, w. George Cushing). [Verse] (5) 86, p. 50.
"In the End" (tr. of Attila József, w. George Cushing). [Verse] (5) 86, p. 51.
"It Is a Fine Summer Evening" (tr. of Attila József, w. George Cushing). [Verse] (5) 86, p. 53.
"Sorrow" (tr. of Attila József, w. George Cushing). [Verse] (5) 86, p. 52.
"A True Man" (tr. of Attila József, w. George Cushing). [Verse] (5) 86, p. 54.
3728. MORGAN, Frederick
"The Body." [AmerS] (55:4) Aut 86, p. 492-493.
"The Gorge." [SouthernR] (22:1) Ja 86, p. 142-144.
"Greenwich 1930's, II." [AmerS] (55:1) Wint 85-86, p. 75.
3729. MORGAN, Jean
"Lookout" (For A.R. Ammons). [Pembroke] (18) 86, p. 131-132.
"Offstage" (For A.R. Ammons). [Pembroke] (18) 86, p. 133.

"University of Maryland Spring Break Said Song" (as told to me by R.J., for A.R. Ammons). [Pembroke] (18) 86, p. 132.
3730. MORGAN, John
"The Beach Walk at Port Townsend, WA" (for Nancy). [NoAmR] (271:3) S 86, p. 80.
"A Dirt Road West of Fairbanks." [Chelsea] (45) 86, p. 114-115.
"Revolutionary Poets." [Chelsea] (45) 86, p. 117.
"The Urn." [Chelsea] (45) 86, p. 116.
3731. MORGAN, Robert
"Absence of History" (For A.R. Ammons). [Pembroke] (18) 86, p. 105.
"Bellrope." [KenR] (NS 8:4) Fall 86, p. 97.
"Blizzard." [MissouriR] (9:2) 86, p. 210.
"Blowing Cave." [MichQR] (25:3) Sum 86, p. 539.
"The Body of Elisha Mitchell." [Epoch] (35:1) 85-86, p. 17.
"The Burnt Corn Manifesto." [Rampike] (5:1) 86, p. 19.
"The Charge." [Poetry] (148:2) My 86, p. 71.
"Deer Stands." [KenR] (NS 8:4) Fall 86, p. 96.
"Ernest." [KenR] (NS 8:4) Fall 86, p. 97-98.
"Full of the Moon." [VirQR] (62:3) Sum 86, p. 426-427.
"Hatch." [MichQR] (25:3) Sum 86, p. 538.
"Hearth." [Epoch] (35:1) 85-86, p. 18.
"Inertia." [ColEng] (48:4) Ap 86, p. 353.
"Jugs in the Smokehouse." [VirQR] (62:3) Sum 86, p. 427-428.
"Linesman." [Verse] (3:3) N 86, p. 10.
"Memory's Front" (For A.R. Ammons). [Pembroke] (18) 86, p. 105.
"Ninety-Six Line." [MissouriR] (9:2) 86, p. 208-209.
"Numinescent." [ColEng] (48:4) Ap 86, p. 354.
"Oxbow Lakes." [ParisR] (28:101) Wint 86, p. 187.
"Pilot Light." [VirQR] (62:3) Sum 86, p. 428.
"Rapture." [ColEng] (48:4) Ap 86, p. 353.
"Sigodlin." [Atlantic] (258:6) D 86, p. 80.
"Sleeping Tower." [ColEng] (48:4) Ap 86, p. 352.
"Visitors." [Poetry] (148:2) My 86, p. 72.
3732. MORGAN, S. K.
"4-30-79, 11:28 p.m." [SlipS] (6) 86, p. 71.
"Aiding and Abetting." [WormR] (26:4, issue 104) 86, p. 151-152.
"Bricks." [WormR] (26:4, issue 104) 86, p. 150-151.
"Civil War Summer." [WormR] (26:4, issue 104) 86, p. 152.
"I Find Poetry." [WormR] (26:4, issue 104) 86, p. 153.
"I'm Standing Alone." [WormR] (26:4, issue 104) 86, p. 148-149.
"Life in the Fast Lane." [Bogg] (55) 86, p. 23.
"Loving Ohio University's Outstanding Senior Independent Woman of 1966-67" (for Judy Brown). [WormR] (26:4, issue 104) 86, p. 148.
"The Olympics." [YetASM] (4) 85, p. 8.
"Rubbing It." [WormR] (26:4, issue 104) 86, p. 151.
"Tell Me You Love Me, Jean-Paul Sartre." [WormR] (26:4, issue 104) 86, p. 149-150.
"Wearing Jeans at the Grand Traverse Resort." [WormR] (26:4, issue 104) 86, p. 149.
3733. MORI, Kyoko
"A Day in the Country" (the Art Institute Museum, December, 1984). [NowestR] (24:1) 86, p. 20-21.
"Every Woman." [DenQ] (20:4/21:1) Spr-Sum 86, p. 24-27.
3734. MORIARTY, Laura
"Four Rondeaux." [Conjunc] (9) 86, p. 40-41.
3735. MORIN, Edward
"Badger on the Loose." [NegC] (6:1) Wint 86, p. 99.
3736. MORISON, Ted
"Epistle to Williams." [NegC] (6:4) Fall 86, p. 54.
3737. MORITZ, A. F.
"The Bone Hunter" (Red Deer River badlands, Alberta, Canada). [MemphisSR] (6:1/2) Spr 86, p. 21.
"Childhood of a Scientist." [GreenfR] (13:3/4) Sum-Fall 86, p. 147-148.
"Entropy." [KanQ] (18:1/2) Wint-Spr 86, p. 295-296.
"Song without Words." [KanQ] (18:1/2) Wint-Spr 86, p. 295.

3738. MORLEY, Hilda
    "The Lizard." [PartR] (53:2) 86, p. 234-235.
    "Quayside, Ibiza, August." [TriQ] (66) Spr-Sum 86, p. 163-164.
    "The Shadow." [TriQ] (66) Spr-Sum 86, p. 165-166.
3739. MORLEY, Marjorie
    "Captain Quinn." [BellArk] (2:2) Mr-Ap 86, p. 4.
    "Mt. St. Helens' Ash Zone, 1985." [BellArk] (2:2) Mr-Ap 86, p. 7.
MORO, Eduarda Lillo
    See LILLO-MORO, Eduarda
3740. MORRIS, Herbert
    "Film." [Agni] (23) 86, p. 124-127.
    "The Five Rooms of the Dream." [Shen] (36:2) 86, p. 67-77.
    "A Photograph by August Sander" (Young Girl in a Circus Wagon, Düren, 1932).
        [KenR] (NS 7:4) Fall 85, p. 47-53.
    "Reading to the Children." [Hudson] (39:2) Sum 86, p. 272-276.
3741. MORRIS, John N.
    "The Old Hand." [NewYorker] (62:42) 8 D 86, p. 50.
3742. MORRIS, Matt
    "Black Windows." [Wind] (16:56) 86, p. 15.
3743. MORRIS, Paul
    "The Cargo Cults." [HayF] (1) Spr 86, p. 44.
    "The Coastwatcher, 1943." [HayF] (1) Spr 86, p. 45.
    "Crib Death." [BlackWR] (13:1) Fall 86, p. 96.
    "Eve" (tr. of Rainer Maria Rilke). [WebR] (11:1) Spr 86, p. 9.
    "The Insane" (tr. of Rainer Maria Rilke). [WebR] (11:1) Spr 86, p. 10.
    "Intelligence Report" (tr. of Johannes Bobrowski). [Translation] (16) Spr 86, p.
        234.
    "Joseph Conrad" (tr. of Johannes Bobrowski). [Translation] (16) Spr 86, p. 236.
    "The Last Supper" (tr. of Rainer Maria Rilke). [WebR] (11:1) Spr 86, p. 10.
    "Leaving Guatemala" (for Sr. Darlene Nigorski). [BlackWR] (13:1) Fall 86, p.
        97-98.
    "Letter from Berlin." [BlackWR] (13:1) Fall 86, p. 94-95.
    "Mozart" (tr. of Johannes Bobrowski). [Translation] (16) Spr 86, p. 235.
    "Neighbor" (tr. of Rainer Maria Rilke). [WebR] (11:1) Spr 86, p. 9.
    "People at Night" (tr. of Rainer Maria Rilke). [WebR] (11:1) Spr 86, p. 11.
3744. MORRIS, Peter
    "Critique." [WormR] (26:2, issue 102) 86, p. 71-72.
    "Dragsters Down in Jersey." [WormR] (26:2, issue 102) 86, p. 72-73.
    "Egg Salad Sandwich." [WormR] (26:2, issue 102) 86, p. 74.
    "Her Things Don't Define Her." [WormR] (26:2, issue 102) 86, p. 73.
    "Lincoln's Bar Mitzvah." [WormR] (26:2, issue 102) 86, p. 70.
    "Mister Involvement." [WormR] (26:2, issue 102) 86, p. 70.
    "Portrait of Juan." [WormR] (26:2, issue 102) 86, p. 71.
    "Something Constructive." [JINJPo] (9:1) 86, p. 15-16.
    "To Beat a Chiquita." [WormR] (26:2, issue 102) 86, p. 70-71.
    "What's Important." [WormR] (26:2, issue 102) 86, p. 74.
    "The White Sand." [JlNJPo] (9:1) 86, p. 14.
3745. MORSE, Carl
    "Inmates." [JamesWR] (3:3) Spr 86, p. 13.
3746. MORSE, Cheryl
    "Abalone Woman Experiments" (for Edna Jackson). [Calyx] (10:1) Sum 86, p. 44.
3747. MORSE, Eleanor R.
    "Sonnet to Mallarme's Commode" (tr. of Salvador Dali). [ClockR] (3:1) 85, p. 59.
    "Sonnet to the Pupils of Velazquez' Eyes, Gala of My Eyes" (tr. of Salvador Dali).
        [ClockR] (3:1) 85, p. 11.
3748. MORSE, Ruth
    "21/5/48 to 21/7/07." [CumbPR] (5:2) Spr 86, p. 45.
    "Departures: II" (after Christine de Pisan, "Cent Ballades XIV"). [CumbPR] (5:2)
        Spr 86, p. 47.
    "Letter to a Dying Scholar" (for Judson Boyce Allen, d. 23 July 1985). [CumbPR]
        (5:2) Spr 86, p. 48-49.
3749. MORTON, Carl (Carl P.)
    "Lockstep." [NegC] (6:4) Fall 86, p. 202-203.
    "Tracks." [NegC] (6:1) Wint 86, p. 92.
3750. MOSBY, Katherine
    "Easter 1964." [DenQ] (20:4/21:1) Spr-Sum 86, p. 101-103.

MOSES

3751. MOSES, Daniel David
"The Persistence of Songs." [Waves] (14:3) Wint 86, p. 64.
"A Shaman Song Predicting Winter." [AntigR] (65) Spr 86, p. 112.
"Snow White." [AntigR] (65) Spr 86, p. 113.
"Song at the Second Flood." [Waves] (14:3) Wint 86, p. 65.
"Song Sobering Up." [AntigR] (65) Spr 86, p. 114.
3752. MOSES, W. R.
"A Kind of Epistle." [Northeast] (series 4:3) Spr 86, p. 27-34.
"Old Theme." [GeoR] (40:3) Fall 86, p. 749.
3753. MOSHE-BEN-ZVI
"Bird." [InterPR] (12:2) Fall 86, p. 104.
"I Know My Heart." [InterPR] (12:2) Fall 86, p. 103.
3754. MOSS, Howard
"Einstein's Bathrobe." [Nat] (243:13) 25 O 86, p. 413.
"The Moon." [NewYorker] (62:2) 3 Mr 86, p. 34.
"Morning Glory" (For Lee Krasner). [Nat] (243:13) 25 O 86, p. 414.
"No Harm." [Nat] (243:13) 25 O 86, p. 414.
"Rules of Sleep." [Nat] (243:13) 25 O 86, p. 414.
"Seven Odes of Departure." [YaleR] (76:1) Aut 86, p. 122-123.
"The Wars." [Nat] (243:13) 25 O 86, p. 413.
3755. MOSS, Melissa
"Crossing the Line." [HangL] (49) Spr 86, p. 28-32.
3756. MOSS, Sylvia
"1913." [NewL] (52:2/3) Wint-Spr 86, p. 164.
"The Idea of North" (Glenn Gould, 1932-1982). [HeliconN] (14/15) Sum 86, p. 171.
"Proof" (for my daughter). [HeliconN] (14/15) Sum 86, p. 170.
"Steamer to Feodosiya." [NewL] (52:2/3) Wint-Spr 86, p. 164-165.
3757. MOSS, Thylias
"More Lessons from a Mirror." [Callaloo] (9:1, #26) Wint 86, p. 106.
"A Reconsideration of the Blackbird." [Callaloo] (9:1, #26) Wint 86, p. 107.
"The Road to Todos Santos Is Closed." [Callaloo] (9:1, #26) Wint 86, p. 101.
"Timex Remembered." [Callaloo] (9:1, #26) Wint 86, p. 104-105.
"To Eliminate Vagueness" (for Gary and the English 401 staff). [Callaloo] (9:1, #26) Wint 86, p. 102-103.
3758. MOTT, Elaine
"Ariadne." [Prima] (10) 86, p. 61.
"Moons and Blood." [Abraxas] (34) 86, p. 30.
"Night Work." [Nimrod] (30:1) Fall-Wint 86, p. 116.
"Summer House at Cragsmoor, New York, 1899." [WestB] (18) 86, p. 42-43.
"The Zen Master's Answer." [NegC] (6:4) Fall 86, p. 79.
3759. MOTT, Michael
"Birdless." [TarRP] (25:2) Spr 86, p. 2.
"Cabin Between Creeks." [TarRP] (25:2) Spr 86, p. 1-2.
"Don Juan in Winter." [GeoR] (40:3) Fall 86, p. 750.
"Driving Through the Wilderness, North Virginia, in a Blizzard to Rachmaninov." [Verse] (3:3) N 86, p. 44.
3760. MOULTON, Gordon
"Below the Fear Lurks a Feeling." [PottPort] (8) 86-87, p. 39.
3761. MOULTON-BARRETT, Donalee
"Lot 4701." [AntigR] (66/67) Sum-Aut 86, p. 23.
3762. MOURE, Erin
"Ocean Poem." [Descant] (17:2, #53) Sum 86, p. 119.
"Pure Writing Is a Notion beyond the Pen." [Descant] (17:2, #53) Sum 86, p. 122.
"Sodality." [CanLit] (108) Spr 86, p. 38-39.
"Speaking in Tongues." [GreenfR] (13:3/4) Sum-Fall 86, p. 149.
"Three Versions." [Descant] (17:2, #53) Sum 86, p. 120-121.
MOYANO, José Repiso
   See REPISO MOYANO, José
3763. MOYER, Jennifer
"Paris." [SpoonRQ] (11:2) Spr 86, p. 25.
3764. MOYLES, Lois
"What Have You?" [ManhatPR] (8) Wint 86-87, p. 8-9.
MU, Yang
   See YANG, Mu

3765. MUELLER, Lisel
"Acts of Mourning" (Vincent Van Gogh). [QW] (23) 86, p. 13.
"The Exhibit." [WillowS] (18) Sum 86, p. 58.
"Magnolia." [QW] (23) 86, p. 12.
"Milkweed Pods in Winter." [GeoR] (40:3) Fall 86, p. 751.
"Paper-White Narcissus." [QW] (23) 86, p. 11.
"Southpaw." [GeoR] (40:3) Fall 86, p. 752.
3766. MUELLER, Marnie
"Train Ride to Tule Lake Internment Camp" (May 1942). [MinnR] (NS 27) Fall 86,
p. 22.
3767. MUELLER, Michael
"Letter from Mother." [PassN] (7:1) Fall-Wint 85-86, p. 19.
3768. MUKHERJEE, Sarat Kumar
"That Evening in a Fair." [Pax] (3:1/2) Wint 85-86, p. 192.
3769. MUKHOPADHYAYA, Vijaya
"Let Fear Invade" (tr. by the author). [SenR] (16:1) 86, p. 74.
"My Home Had Left the Place" (tr. by the author). [SenR] (16:1) 86, p. 73.
3770. MULDOON, Paul
"Meeting the British." [Field] (34) Spr 86, p. 49.
"Paul Klee *They're Biting.*" [Field] (34) Spr 86, p. 51.
"The Wishbone." [Field] (34) Spr 86, p. 50.
3771. MULDOON, Virginia
"Lower Manhattan Lullaby." [PoeticJ] (14) 86, p. 39.
3772. MULLEN, Harryette
"Fable." [Callaloo] (9:1, #26) Wint 86, p. 108.
"Unspoken." [Callaloo] (9:2, #27) Spr 86, p. 345-346.
3773. MULLEN, K. G.
"Tuesday." [Vis] (20) 86, p. 15.
3774. MULLEN, Laura
"Home." [DenQ] (20:4/21:1) Spr-Sum 86, p. 38-39.
"In the Late Nineteenth Century, the Art Critic's Autobiography." [Thrpny] (26)
Sum 86, p. 16.
"Museum Garden Café." [Sonora] (10) Spr 86, p. 22.
3775. MULLIGAN, J. B.
"Cars of Separation." [Wind] (16:57) 86, p. 31.
3776. MULLINS, Cecil J.
"At the Movies." [CapeR] (21:2) Fall 86, p. 24.
"Generation Gap." [CapeR] (21:2) Fall 86, p. 25.
3777. MULLOY, Marcia
"The Way Two Times May Happen Together." [ManhatPR] (6) Wint-Spr 85-86, p.
60.
3778. MUMFORD, Erika
"India Notebook." [Hudson] (39:2) Sum 86, p. 279-282.
"Mosaic: Sophie Scholl, 1921-1943" (1985 John Williams Andrews Prize
Co-winner). [PoetL] (81:1) Spr 86, p. 16-42.
"Objet d'Art." [Ploughs] (12:4) 86, p. 195.
"Some Flowers." [Ploughs] (12:4) 86, p. 193-194.
"Words for Myself." [Ploughs] (12:4) 86, p. 196-197.
3779. MUNCIE, Mary
"The Poetry Reading" (Karl Rakosi). [Bogg] (55) 86, p. 51.
3780. MUNFORD, David
"Reminiscence." [Poem] (55) Mr 86, p. 6.
"Star Nosed Mole." [Poem] (55) Mr 86, p. 5.
3781. MUÑOZ, Martin
"Two Grains of Sand." [LindLM] (5:1) Ja-Mr 86, p. 27.
3782. MURABITO, Stephen
"Testing the Tomatoes." [BellR] (9:1) Spr 86, p. 53-55.
3783. MURATORI, Fred
"Hometown Oak." [MidAR] (6:1) 86?, p. 19-20.
"Lineage and Fear." [NowestR] (24:1) 86, p. 22-23.
"The Moment After." [ManhatPR] (7) Sum 86, p. 51.
"Practical Advice for Travellers Who Don't Get Out of the USA Very Much . . ."
[MidAR] (6:1) 86?, p. 21-22.
3784. MURAWSKI, Elisabeth
"Climbing the Family Tree." [Comm] (113:4) 28 F 86, p. 114.
"Coup." [OhioR] (36) 86, p. 22.

"Drawing Down Rain." [LitR] (29:2) Wint 86, p. 174.
"The Embrace." [SouthernPR] (26:1) Spr 86, p. 65.
"Gauguin the Unfortunate." [ManhatPR] (6) Wint-Spr 85-86, p. 56.
"Hired Man, the (Life and)." [CrabCR] (3:2) Spr 86, p. 17.
"Keepsake." [CarolQ] (39:1) Fall 86, p. 20.
"Long Slow Advances on the Primitive." [GrandS] (5:3) Spr 86, p. 85.
"Passing Trees by Twilight." [OhioR] (36) 86, p. 23.
"Reaching Darien." [Comm] (113:11) 6 Je 86, p. 347.
"Replica Medieval Wooden Matrix." [AmerPoR] (15:3) My-Je 86, p. 31.
"Swans at Berryville." [LitR] (29:2) Wint 86, p. 175.
"Violets" (For Emily Dickinson). [MSS] (5:1) 86, p. 137-138.
MURIEL, Rodrigo Hernandez
   See HERNANDEZ MURIEL, Rodrigo
3785. MURILLO, Rosario
   "It Is Certain That We Are Constructing a World" (tr. by Zoe Anglesey). [MassR]
      (27:3/4) Fall-Wint 86, p. 643-645.
3786. MURPHEY, Joseph Colin
   "Conceptions." [Pax] (3:1/2) Wint 85-86, p. 90-91.
   "On Being Fully Armored." [Pax] (3:1/2) Wint 85-86, p. 92.
   "Villanelle of Youth and Age Caught in a Dream of Truth." [Pax] (3:1/2) Wint 85-86,
      p. 93.
3787. MURPHY, Carole
   "Lunch at Dixie Kitchen." [Wind] (16:56) 86, p. 32.
   "Uncle kit." [Wind] (16:56) 86, p. 32.
3788. MURPHY, Dorothy
   "Man in the Middle." [SanFPJ] (9:1) 86, p. 53.
   "Young Oregon Woman." [SanFPJ] (9:1) 86, p. 46-47.
3789. MURPHY, Katherine
   "Seattle to Minneapolis, 1946." [MidAR] (7:1) 86, p. 50.
3790. MURPHY, Kay
   "Accidents." [AnotherCM] (16) 86, p. 64.
   "What May Be Prayer." [AnotherCM] (16) 86, p. 63.
3791. MURPHY, Miles W.
   "Longing for Zheng Congzhi" (tr. of Jia Dao). [NewL] (53:1) Fall 86, p. 55.
   "On a Hermit's Hut" (tr. of Jia Dao). [NewL] (53:1) Fall 86, p. 54.
3792. MURPHY, Peter E.
   "Shaping Up." [BelPoJ] (37:2) Wint 86-87, p. 22-28.
3793. MURPHY, Rich (Richard)
   "Anthem." [GrandS] (6:1) Aut 86, p. 120.
   "The Forty-Year Journey on Essence." [GrandS] (6:1) Aut 86, p. 121.
   "The Om and Dance Man." [SmPd] (23:3, #68) Fall 86, p. 19.
   "The Petrifying Situation." [GrandS] (6:1) Aut 86, p. 120-121.
   "Sri Lanka." [NewYRB] (33:8) 8 My 86, p. 8.
3794. MURPHY, Sheila E.
   "Blue Transparencies." [DeKalbLAJ] (19:3/4) 86, p. 84.
   "France." [FloridaR] (14:2) Fall-Wint 86, p. 104.
   "Haibun 236." [ForidaR] (14:1) Spr-Sum 86, p. 111.
   "The Media." [Puerto] (21:2) Spr 86, p. 118.
   "The Mountain and the Professor." [Puerto] (22:1) Fall 86, p. 53.
   "Regression." [Amelia] (3:2) Spr 86, p. 34.
   "Retracing." [Chelsea] (45) 86, p. 30.
   "A Saxophone Wind Presses." [Chelsea] (45) 86, p. 31.
   "A Secretary." [Puerto] (22:1) Fall 86, p. 52.
   "Status Quo." [YetASM] (5) 86, p. 11.
   "This Clown." [DeKalbLAJ] (19:2) 86, p. 42.
   "Visualization." [Chelsea] (45) 86, p. 31.
   "Waking Up and Not Remembering." [DeKalbLAJ] (19:3/4) 86, p. 85.
3795. MURPHY, Sheila K.
   "Night Poet." [YetASM] (4) 85, p. 5.
3796. MURRAY, G. E.
   "Flying Low, near France, among Birds." [Poetry] (148:2) My 86, p. 81.
   "For Drunks, in the Nighttime" (To lost friends on a blue burn). [PoetryNW] (27:3)
      Aut 86, p. 7-8.
   "Northern Exposures" (For Richard Hugo). [Poetry] (148:2) My 86, p. 79-80.
3797. MURRAY, Joan
   "The Public Service." [OntR] (25) Fall-Wint 86-87, p. 94-95.

"What the Sun Really Is." [OntR] (25) Fall-Wint 86-87, p. 96-97.
3798. MURRAY, Les (Les A.)
"1980 in a Street of Federation Houses" (Chatswood 1985). [Verse] (5) 86, p. 4.
"At the Aquatic Carnival." [AmerPoR] (15:2) Mr-Ap 86, p. 26.
"The Dream of Wearing Shorts Forever." [AmerPoR] (15:2) Mr-Ap 86, p. 23.
"Easter 1984." [AmerPoR] (15:2) Mr-Ap 86, p. 25.
"The Edgeless." [AmerPoR] (15:2) Mr-Ap 86, p. 27.
"Physiognomy on the Savage Manning River." [AmerPoR] (15:2) Mr-Ap 86, p. 24-25.
"The Sleepout." [AmerPoR] (15:2) Mr-Ap 86, p. 27.
"The Sleepout." [Verse] (5) 86, p. 5.
"Tropical Window." [AmerPoR] (15:2) Mr-Ap 86, p. 27.
"Tropical Window." [Verse] (5) 86, p. 3.
"The Vol Sprung from Heraldry." [AmerPoR] (15:2) Mr-Ap 86, p. 26.
3799. MURRAY, Philip
"Poisson d'Avril, or: the Quintessential Russian Anecdote." [AmerS] (55:2) Spr 86, p. 194.
3800. MURRAY, Yvette R.
"Armaggedon Blues." [SanFPJ] (8:1) 85, p. 77.
"Two." [SanFPJ] (8:1) 85, p. 80.
3801. MUSGRAVE, Susan
"Breakfast Anytime." [CrossC] (8:2) 86, p. 8.
"Breakfast Anytime." [MalR] (74) Mr 86, p. 29.
"Elisa and Mary." [CrossC] (8:2) 86, p. 10.
"Imagine" (For Patrick Lane). [CrossC] (8:2) 86, p. 6.
"Imagine" (for Patrick Lane). [MalR] (74) Mr 86, p. 31.
"Nobody Gets Over Me." [MalR] (74) Mr 86, p. 30.
"The Small Night So Alone Out There." [CrossC] (8:2) 86, p. 8.
"Something Has to Give in a Life." [CrossC] (8:2) 86, p. 8.
3802. MUSICK, Martin
"Eclipsed." [PoeticJ] (13) 86, p. 32.
"School Days." [PoeticJ] (13) 86, p. 32.
"Stay." [PoeticJ] (13) 86, p. 32.
3803. MUSKAT, Timothy
"Log." [CapeR] (21:2) Fall 86, p. 9.
"Of Bones." [CapeR] (21:2) Fall 86, p. 10.
"To the Beauty Sleeping." [CapeR] (21:2) Fall 86, p. 8.
3804. MUSKE, Carol
"Immunity." [MissouriR] (9:1) 85-86, p. 20-21.
"Solar Machinery." [MissouriR] (9:1) 85-86, p. 19.
"Sounding" (Annie Cameron). [Field] (34) Spr 86, p. 87-88.
"Summer Cold." [NewYorker] (62:12) 12 My 86, p. 76.
3805. MUTH, Carol Sue
"Plaint of the Wife of the Fifth Generation Family-Farmer." [Amelia] (3:2) Spr 86, p. 11.
3806. MYCUE, Edward
"Stick It Against." [JamesWR] (3:4) Sum 86, p. 5.
3807. MYERS, Christopher A.
"Between Dreams." [Amelia] (3:2) Spr 86, p. 44.
3808. MYERS, Gary
"Invitation from a Deceased Spanish Poet." [Poetry] (148:4) Jl 86, p. 215-216.
"Ode to Sleep." [Poetry] (148:4) Jl 86, p. 216-217.
3809. MYERS, George, Jr.
"Models: Cloud, Forest." [SmPd] (23:1, #66) Wint 86, p. 11.
3810. MYERS, Jack
"Beating Back Death with a Lilac Bush." [DenQ] (20:4/21:1) Spr-Sum 86, p. 139.
"Domestic Poem." [CharR] (12:2) Fall 86, p. 78.
"The Wild and Real Agency." [DenQ] (20:4/21:1) Spr-Sum 86, p. 137-138.
3811. MYERS, Joan Rohr
"Breakthrough." [ChrC] (103:2) 15 Ja 86, p. 43.
"Diaspora." [ChrC] (103:19) 4-11 Je 86, p. 549.
"Exchange." [DeKalbLAJ] (19:1) 86, p. 36.
"Vigil Light." [ChrC] (103:18) 21-28 My 86, p. 522.
"Watching" (for Rachel). [ChrC] (103:30) 15 O 86, p. 884.
3812. MYERS, Neil
"Poems on Hebrew Themes — II." [CharR] (12:2) Fall 86, p. 59-62.

"Vladimir Nabokov, Aging, in Montreux." [CharR] (12:2) Fall 86, p. 62-63.
3813. MYLES, Eileen
    "Dad's Bag." [LittleM] (15:2) 86, p. 36-38.
3814. MYRRHA
    "Poems and Fragments" (from the Amatory Epigrams of the Parnassian Anthology,
        tr. by Layeh Bock/Pallánt). [YellowS] (19) Sum 86, p. 18.
MYUNG, Mi Kim
    See KIM, Myung Mi
3815. NADIG, Sumatheendra
    "Gorgon" (tr. by the author). [SenR] (16:1) 86, p. 79.
    "The Parrots" (tr. of M. Govinda Pai). [SenR] (16:1) 86, p. 75.
    "The Python" (tr. by the author). [SenR] (16:1) 86, p. 80.
3816. NAGAI-ROTHE, Tomi
    "The Chanting Will Keep Us Up for Years" (for Melissa). [OP] (42/43) Wint 86-87,
        p. 147-148.
    "Lit Like Candles, Tokyo 1945" (for Obaasan). [OP] (42/43) Wint 86-87, p. 147.
    "Lunacy, Moon Viewing." [OP] (42/43) Wint 86-87, p. 146.
3817. NAGAYAMA, Mokuo
    "Early Winter" (tr. by James Kirkup and Akiko Takemoto). [Translation] (17) Fall
        86, p. 209.
    "Frozen Love" (tr. by James Kirkup and Akiko Takemoto). [Translation] (17) Fall
        86, p. 208.
    "Overhang" (tr. by James Kirkup and Akiko Takemoto). [Translation] (17) Fall 86,
        p. 209.
3818. NAGLE, Alice
    "What Remains." [SouthernPR] (26:2) Fall 86, p. 40.
3819. NAGY, László
    "A Headboard to Headboards" (tr. by Jascha Kessler, w. Maria Körösy). [VirQR]
        (62:2) Spr 86, p. 255-257.
    "The Little Jesus of the Barren" (tr. by Jascha Kessler, w. Maria Körösy). [MalR]
        (75) Je 86, p. 35-36.
    "The Little Jesus of the Barren" (tr. by Jascha Kessler, w. Maria Körösy). [VirQR]
        (62:2) Spr 86, p. 253-254.
    "There Is No Southern Island" (tr. by Jascha Kessler, w. Maria Körösy). [LitR]
        (29:2) Wint 86, p. 208.
3820. NAGY, Paul
    "Images Textuelles." [Rampike] (5:2) 86, p. 50-54.
3821. NAJARIAN, Pete
    "Daughters of Memory" (Selections). [Zyzzyva] (2:1) Spr 86, p. 19-25.
3822. NAJIMIAN-MAGARITY, Brenda
    "Count a Joy." [SingHM] (14) 86, p. 52-53.
3823. NAKAGIRI, Masao
    "The Electric Car" (tr. by James Kirkup and Akiko Takemoto). [Translation] (17)
        Fall 86, p. 199.
3824. NAKANO, Michio
    "How to Cook Women" (tr. of Kyozo Takagi, w. James Kirkup). [Translation] (17)
        Fall 86, p. 33.
    "A Skyline — New Year's Day" (tr. of Kyozo Takagi, w. James Kirkup).
        [Translation] (17) Fall 86, p. 32.
    "Snowy Night" (tr. of Kyozo Takagi, w. James Kirkup). [Translation] (17) Fall 86,
        p. 31.
    "To the Sea" (tr. of Kyozo Takagi, w. James Kirkup). [Translation] (17) Fall 86, p.
        34.
3825. NAKANO, Shigeharu
    "The Governor" (tr. by James Kirkup and Akiko Takemoto). [Translation] (17) Fall
        86, p. 194.
3826. NALBANDIAN, Dana
    "Imagination." [PikeF] (7) Spr 86, p. 22.
3827. NAMEROFF, Rochelle
    "The Accident." [PoetryNW] (27:2) Sum 86, p. 8-9.
    "The Boulevard of Broken Dreams" (for my mother). [MidAR] (6:2) 86, p. 32-33.
    "Jellyfish." [PoetryNW] (27:2) Sum 86, p. 9-10.
    "Poem for François Truffaut." [MalR] (75) Je 86, p. 84-85.
    "Runaway." [PoetryNW] (27:2) Sum 86, p. 10-11.
    "The Sky So Much Closer." [CutB] (25) Fall-Wint 86, p. 42-43.
    "Still Life with Invasion of Privacy." [MalR] (75) Je 86, p. 86.

3828. NAMJOSHI, Suniti
"Killer Dyke." [LitR] (29:4) Sum 86, p. 507.
"Nasty Story." [LitR] (29:4) Sum 86, p. 507.
3829. NANDAN, Satendra P.
"My Father's Son." [LitR] (29:4) Sum 86, p. 508-511.
3830. NANI, Nora
"Los Desaparecidos." [Mairena] (8:21) 86, p. 107.
"Reconstruccion del Ala." [Mairena] (8:21) 86, p. 107.
"Las Tres Soledades del Juego." [Mairena] (8:21) 86, p. 108.
3831. NARDOZA, Edward
"First Snow at Freezing Point." [ManhatPR] (7) Sum 86, p. 36.
"A Questionable Quest." [ManhatPR] (7) Sum 86, p. 37.
3832. NASH, Roger
"Please Write to Me in This Poem." [MalR] (77) D 86, p. 77.
"Schubert's Lessons for Clarinet in an Old Trapper's Hut." [Quarry] (35:1) Wint 86,
    p. 56-57.
"Uncle Lennie's Third Proof of the Existence of a Question." [MalR] (77) D 86, p.
    78.
"Waiting and Waiting for Her in the Park." [WestCR] (21:2) O 86, p. 38.
3833. NASH, Valery
"From a Room over the Creek." [Prima] (10) 86, p. 13.
"The Net." [Prima] (10) 86, p. 59.
"Process." [StoneC] (13:3/4) Spr-Sum 86, p. 55.
3834. NASIO, Brenda
"Black Crows." [Amelia] (3:1) Ja 86, p. 26.
"Close Call." [Amelia] (3:1) Ja 86, p. 25.
"In a Brownstone on East Fifty-First." [CrabCR] (3:2) Spr 86, p. 10-11.
"My, My." [Amelia] (3:1) Ja 86, p. 24.
"This I How We Say Goodbye." [CrabCR] (3:2) Spr 86, p. 10.
"Toronto, Late February." [CrabCR] (3:2) Spr 86, p. 10.
3835. NASON, Jim
"Meditation." [WritersL] (1986:5), p. 30.
"Sibling Song." [WritersL] (1986:5), p. 18.
3836. NATHAN, Leonard
"From the Cave." [ThRiPo] (27/28) 86, p. 53-54.
"The Most Wonderful Thing of All." [NewEngR] (8:3) Spr 86, p. 388-392.
"The Night You Came Home." [Zyzzyva] (2:2) Sum 86, p. 43.
"One Rainy Saturday Morning." [CrossCur] (6:2) 86, p. 43.
"Territories" (A Correspondence with Ted Kooser: 8 poems). [PraS] (60:3) Fall 86,
    p. 101-105.
3837. NATHAN, Norman
"Allegory." [SpiritSH] (52) 86, p. 34.
"Antropolis." [SpiritSH] (52) 86, p. 32.
"Flora." [SpiritSH] (52) 86, p. 33.
"I Do." [SpiritSH] (52) 86, p. 31.
"Often Our Eyes Met." [SpiritSH] (52) 86, p. 33-34.
3838. NATT, Gregory
"How the Poet Works." [YetASM] (5) 86, p. 6.
3839. NAUGLER, Chris
"Between Us." [PottPort] (8) 86-87, p. 44.
3840. NAWAZ, Shuja
"The Well at Mohenjodaro" (2500 B.C.). [AmerS] (55:1) Wint 85-86, p. 106.
NAWWAB, Mozaffar Al
    See Al-NAWWAB, Mozaffar
3841. NAZZAR, Ali Fakum
"A man says: sweet" (tr. by Will Kirkland). [NewOR] (13:4) Wint 86, p. 27.
3842. NEELD, Judith
"Variation on a Theme of Incest." [MidAR] (6:2) 86, p. 121.
3843. NEELIN, David
"The Gospel of St. Boniface, Chapter 22." [Shen] (36:4) 86, p. 32.
"Home." [NewRep] (194:24) 16 Je 86, p. 41.
"Recall." [Shen] (36:4) 86, p. 31.
"Waiting." [Shen] (36:4) 86, p. 30.
3844. NEELON, Ann
"Kaya-Magan" (Ode to the Accompaniment of African Harp, tr. of Léopold Sédar
    Senghor). [AmerPoR] (15:1) Ja-F 86, p. 19.

"Old Cronies." [OP] (42/43) Wint 86-87, p. 163-164.
"When a Porch Is Obliterated by a Hurricane." [OP] (42/43) Wint 86-87, p. 162-163.
3845. NEGRI, Sharon
"Dead Lines." [SlipS] (6) 86, p. 32.
"That Electricshock Glow." [SlipS] (6) 86, p. 31.
"Working the Corner." [SlipS] (6) 86, p. 32.
3846. NEKOLA, Charlotte
"Alphabet." [MassR] (27:2) Sum 86, p. 330.
"Before Her Life." [MassR] (27:2) Sum 86, p. 331.
"Now We Live by the Sea." [NewL] (52:2/3) Wint-Spr 86, p. 245.
"Trapeze Song." [NewL] (52:2/3) Wint-Spr 86, p. 244.
3847. NELLES, Andrea
"The Bay Bus." [MalR] (73) Ja 86, p. 89.
"Lash House." [MalR] (73) Ja 86, p. 88.
"Rich Red Bole with Leaf." [MalR] (73) Ja 86, p. 90.
"Sal and Andy." [MalR] (73) Ja 86, p. 91.
3848. NELMS, Sheryl L.
"Bullfrog." [YetASM] (5) 86, p. 11.
"Double Exposure." [YetASM] (4) 85, p. 8.
"Every Night." [Bogg] (56) 86, p. 44.
"Ho." [Bogg] (56) 86, p. 10.
3849. NELSON, Eric
"Deeper Channels." [WestB] (19) 86, p. 95-96.
"The Measure." [WestB] (19) 86, p. 94-95.
3850. NELSON, Howard
"Love-Making in the Eighth Month." [WestB] (18) 86, p. 18.
"Night and Joy." [WestB] (18) 86, p. 20.
"Ninth Month." [WestB] (18) 86, p. 19.
"Singing into the Belly." [WestB] (18) 86, p. 17.
3851. NELSON, Jo
"Critical." [SanFPJ] (8:1) 85, p. 78.
"Unable." [SanFPJ] (8:1) 85, p. 78.
"Wait!" [SanFPJ] (8:1) 85, p. 79.
3852. NELSON, John S.
"Daughters." [SoDakR] (24:2) Sum 86, p. 118.
NELSON, Katharine Whitcomb
   See WHITCOMB-NELSON, Katharine
3853. NELSON, Lonnie
"Brave Poets." [SanFPJ] (8:2) 85, p. 6-7.
"Farm Women." [SanFPJ] (8:2) 85, p. 62-63.
"On Turning 50 Years." [SanFPJ] (8:2) 85, p. 66.
"A U.S. Mother's Message." [SanFPJ] (8:2) 85, p. 22-23.
3854. NELSON, Nils
"Putting Out the Fire." [SilverFR] (11) Sum 86, p. 24-25.
3855. NELSON, Paul
"Fathoms." [ColR] (NS 13:1) Fall 85, p. 64-65.
"The Nature of Prayer." [ColR] (NS 13:1) Fall 85, p. 63.
"Night Work." [ColR] (NS 13:1) Fall 85, p. 68-69.
"Shark." [ColR] (NS 13:1) Fall 85, p. 66-67.
3856. NELSON, Sandra
"Dear Marge." [SingHM] (14) 86, p. 11.
"Fire." [BlackALF] (20:3) Fall 86, p. 315.
"The Girl by the Water." [SingHM] (14) 86, p. 10.
"The Mate." [BlackALF] (20:3) Fall 86, p. 316.
"Message to the Country Poets." [BlackALF] (20:3) Fall 86, p. 316.
3857. NELSON, Shannon
"The Carbon River." [WillowS] (17) Wint 86, p. 24.
"Deep Water, Wide River." [CutB] (25) Fall-Wint 86, p. 34-35.
3858. NEMEROV, Howard
"The Biographer's Mandate." [SewanR] (94:2) Spr 86, p. 209.
"A Cabinet of Seeds Displayed." [GeoR] (40:3) Fall 86, p. 753.
"D-Day + All the Years." [SewanR] (94:2) Spr 86, p. 207.
"Drowning the Book." [SouthwR] (71:4) Aut 86, p. 510-511.
"Freezing the Rain." [SewanR] (94:2) Spr 86, p. 208-209.
"Night Operations, Coastal Command RAF." [ParisR] (28:101) Wint 86, p. 237.

"On Reading *King Lear* Again, 1984." [SewanR] (94:2) Spr 86, p. 207-208.
"A Reader of Mysteries." [KenR] (NS 8:3) Sum 86, p. 74-75.
"Theater of the Absurd." [KenR] (NS 8:3) Sum 86, p. 75.
"The Three Towns." [GeoR] (40:3) Fall 86, p. 754.
"To Dante." [KenR] (NS 8:3) Sum 86, p. 76.
"Two-Person / Zero-Sum." [KenR] (NS 8:3) Sum 86, p. 74.
"The War in the Air." [ParisR] (28:100) Sum-Fall 86, p. 200.
3859. NEPO, Mark
"Blood for Mercy." [MidAR] (7:1) 86, p. 144-148.
"Burning Odor of Mint." [SewanR] (94:3) Sum 86, p. 378.
"Driving the Sunlight." [KenR] (NS 8:2) Spr 86, p. 63-64.
"Earth Made of Stars." [SewanR] (94:3) Sum 86, p. 376-377.
"Ecology." [KenR] (NS 8:2) Spr 86, p. 62-63.
"Passion." [Blueline] (8:1) Sum-Fall 86, p. 37-38.
"The Quarrel Remains Unknown." [Chelsea] (45) 86, p. 100-103.
"Voicings." [NegC] (6:4) Fall 86, p. 84-85.
"Water on the Heart." [MidAR] (6:2) 86, p. 105-106.
3860. NERUDA, Pablo
"For All to Know" (tr. by William O'Daly). [AnotherCM] (16) 86, p. 67.
"Gautama Christ" (tr. by William O'Daly). [AmerPoR] (15:5) S-O 86, p. 56.
"Love Sonnets" (Selections: II, VI, XXII, XXXIII, tr. by Stephen Tapscott). (for
    Mary Oliver). [Atlantic] (257:2) F 86, p. 62-63.
"Modestly" (tr. by William O'Daly). [AnotherCM] (16) 86, p. 65.
"Ode to Numbers" (tr. by Margaret Sayers Peden). [MassR] (27:3/4) Fall-Wint 86,
    p. 464-466.
"Ode to the Americas" (tr. by Margaret Sayers Peden). [MassR] (27:3/4) Fall-Wint
    86, p. 461-463.
"One Hundred Love Sonnets" (Selections: I, XX, LI, LII, XCII, C, tr. by Stephen
    Tapscott). [AmerPoR] (15:3) My-Je 86, p. 21-22.
"The Stones of Chile" (Selections: 9 poems tr. by Dennis Maloney). [WillowS] (18)
    Sum 86, p. 41-57.
"With Quevedo, in Springtime" (tr. by William O'Daly). [AnotherCM] (16) 86, p.
    66.
3861. NESTOR, Jack
"Quasimodo." [Wind] (16:58) 86, p. 33-34.
3862. NETTLEMAN, Robert
"Green." [PassN] (7:1) Fall-Wint 85-86, p. 27.
3863. NEUER, Kathleen
"The Alps Quartet." [MalR] (76) S 86, p. 116-117.
"Boy on a Ledge." [Thrpny] (26) Sum 86, p. 9.
"In Praise of Palm Trees." [MSS] (5:1) 86, p. 73-74.
"Late Bloomer." [MalR] (76) S 86, p. 114.
"Laundry." [MalR] (76) S 86, p. 115.
"The Runaways." [BlackWR] (13:1) Fall 86, p. 66-67.
3864. NEUFELDT, Leonard
"Extravagances in Ruidoso, New Mexico" (For Ted Weiss and "The Theory of
    Repetition"). [CharR] (12:1) Spr 86, p. 63-68.
"Seafair Seattle." [CharR] (12:1) Spr 86, p. 68-69.
3865. NEUMAN, Scott
"Ars Poetica / Love Poem." [WindO] (47) Sum 86, p. 9.
3866. NEURON, Vesta
"And Memory Enshrouded." [PoeticJ] (13) 86, p. 23.
"Patchwork." [PoeticJ] (16) Fall 86, p. 37.
3867. NEW, Joan
"Martha." [SenR] (16:2) 86, p. 75-76.
"The Platter." [NoDaQ] (54:2) Spr 86, p. 169.
3868. NEWCOMB, P. F.
"Blackbirds in December." [CapeR] (21:2) Fall 86, p. 31.
3869. NEWCOMER, Katarzyna W.
"On the wave." [SanFPJ] (8:3) 85, p. 89.
3870. NEWELL, James
"Famine in Modern Civilized Times." [SanFPJ] (8:3) 85, p. 53-54.
"An Odd Age." [SanFPJ] (8:3) 85, p. 55-56.
3871. NEWLOVE, John
"The Attempt." [Grain] (14:4) N 86, p. 54.
"Bugdancing" (a work-in-progress). [MalR] (77) D 86, p. 10-15.

"The Candy-Maker's Song." [Descant] (17:2, #53) Sum 86, p. 117.
"A Crescent." [Descant] (17:2, #53) Sum 86, p. 118.
"Driving." [GreenfR] (13:3/4) Sum-Fall 86, p. 151.
"The Weather." [GreenfR] (13:3/4) Sum-Fall 86, p. 152.
"White Philharmonic Novels." [MalR] (73) Ja 86, p. 5-12.
3872. NEWMAN, C. (Chris)
"Bent Is the Grass" (tr. of Eugene Dubnov). [Confr] (32) Spr-Sum 86, p. 109.
"Canadian Lines" (For Rachel Eaves, tr. of Eugene Dubnov, w. the author).
[CanLit] (110) Fall 86, p. 44.
"Outside Yet Another New Window" (tr. of Eugene Dubnow, w. the author).
[BelPoJ] (37:2) Wint 86-87, p. 29.
3873. NEWMAN, C. V.
"Translation." [Epoch] (35:1) 85-86, p. 39-43.
3874. NEWMAN, Debbie
"Ghazals" (5 poems). [Grain] (14:2) My 86, p. 36.
3875. NEWMAN, Dwight
"Two Ghazals." [Grain] (14:2) My 86, p. 47.
3876. NEWMAN, Gail
"A.M." [YellowS] (20) Aut 86, p. 18.
"House Near the Sea." [YellowS] (20) Aut 86, p. 14.
"Red Dress." [Sam] (44:2 release 174) 86, p. 32-33.
3877. NEWMAN, P. B.
"Fourth of July Sparklers." [CarolQ] (38:2) Wint 86, p. 75.
"The Orb." [SouthernPR] (26:1) Spr 86, p. 9.
"Westons' Farm." [HiramPoR] (41) Fall-Wint 86-87, p. 36.
3878. NEZVAL, Vítezslav
"This Short Odyssey about Edison Who Created More Light . . ." (tr. by Donald
Magar). [NewOR] (13:3) Fall 86, p. 66-76.
3879. Ni CHUILLEANAIN, Eilean
"Letter from the Italian Kitchen." [Verse] (6) 86, p. 15.
"Recovery." [Verse] (6) 86, p. 15.
3880. Ni DHOMHNAILL, Nuala
"The Broken Doll" (tr. by John Montague). [Verse] (3:3) N 86, p. 48.
3881. NIATUM, Duane
"Eurydice to Narcissus" (an imaginary dialogue on F. Morgan's poem "Orpheus to
Eurydice"). [AnotherCM] (15) 86, p. 77-81.
3882. NICCUM, Terri
"Chandleresque." [Electrum] (38) Spr 86, p. 19.
3883. NICHOL, B. P.
"From Translating Translating Apollinaire." [Rampike] (5:2) 86, p. 6-7.
"Organ Music" (Selections: "Sum of the Parts," "The Fingers"). [MalR] (76) S 86,
p. 31-38.
3884. NICHOLAS, John
"Minor Poet." [Bogg] (55) 86, p. 51.
3885. NICHOLS, Martha
"The First Time." [YellowS] (19) Sum 86, p. 8.
"The Three." [Rampike] (5:1) 86, p. 53.
3886. NICHOLSON, Joseph
"Buffalo Gal." [WormR] (26:3, issue 103) 86, p. 116.
"Fictry." [WormR] (26:3, issue 103) 86, p. 116.
"Hanging Around the House." [WormR] (26:3, issue 103) 86, p. 117.
"Sorry for My Elf." [WormR] (26:3, issue 103) 86, p. 117.
3887. NICHOLSON, Ruth
"Expedition" (corrected version of poem in 6:2 Sum 85). [PassN] (7:1) Fall-Wint
85-86, p. 30.
3888. NICKERSON, Sheila
"Illumination." [CrabCR] (3:3) Sum 86, p. 8.
"Return to the Wisconsin Homestead." [CrabCR] (3:3) Sum 86, p. 6.
3889. NICOL, Alfred
"An After-Image of the Opening Scene." [NewEngR] (9:2) Wint 86, p. 183.
"My Boy's Close Friend." [NewEngR] (9:2) Wint 86, p. 184.
3890. NICOLLS, Alix
"Bone's Edge." [Wind] (16:58) 86, p. 35.
3891. NIDITCH, B. Z.
"Anna Akhmatova." [Waves] (14:3) Wint 86, p. 70.
"Being Thirty Years of Memory" (for Miklos Radnoti). [SpiritSH] (52) 86, p. 28.

"Boston Common" (For Denise Levertov). [YetASM] (4) 85, p. 8.
"Boston Poet's Fall." [Poem] (56) N 86, p. 3.
"Budapest, 1985." [Abraxas] (34) 86, p. 33.
"A Cambridge Ensemble." [Amelia] (3:1) Ja 86, p. 70.
"Checkpoint Charlie." [PoeticJ] (13) 86, p. 10.
"Country Road Poet." [Poem] (56) N 86, p. 4.
"Czeslaw Milosz." [AntigR] (64) Wint 86, p. 130.
"The Drawbridge." [BallSUF] (26:4) Aut 85, p. 7.
"Haifa, 1945." [Os] (22) 86, p. 2.
"I Know You Were Here (Budapest, 1986)." [SpiritSH] (52) 86, p. 26.
"In a Cafe (Budapest, 1984)." [SpiritSH] (52) 86, p. 27.
"Looking Across My Life." [SpiritSH] (52) 86, p. 30.
"Marina Tsvetayeva." [Waves] (14:3) Wint 86, p. 70.
"Memory: Speak." [YetASM] (4) 85, p. 7.
"Miklos Radnoti." [SpiritSH] (52) 86, p. 27-28.
"Osweicim — At Dachau." [NewL] (52:2/3) Wint-Spr 86, p. 71.
"Return to Budapest, 1986." [SpiritSH] (52) 86, p. 23-24.
"Return to Budapest (Easter, 1985)." [SpiritSH] (52) 86, p. 23.
"A Russian Mass in America." [AntigR] (64) Wint 86, p. 129.
"Somnambulist Poet." [SpiritSH] (52) 86, p. 29.
"Spring Sonata." [PoeticJ] (13) 86, p. 29.
"Twin Cities (Budapest)." [SpiritSH] (52) 86, p. 24-26.
"Warsaw, 1984." [Abraxas] (34) 86, p. 34.
"Warsaw, 1984." [BallSUF] (26:4) Aut 85, p. 32.
"Warsaw, 1984." [Contact] (7:38/39/40) Wint-Spr 86, p. 83.
"Yannis Ritsos." [AntigR] (64) Wint 86, p. 129.
3892. NIEDECKER, Lorine
    "From This Condensery" (Selection). [Nat] (242:10) 15 Mr 86, p. 312.
3893. NIEDELMAN, Hilda L.
    "Nail Soup" (from a fourth grade reader). [Confr] (33/34) Fall-Wint 86-87, p. 109.
3894. NIELSEN, Gretchen
    "Hell's Getting Ready." [Sam] (46:5 [i.e. 46:1] release 181) 86, p. 20.
3895. NIELSEN, Nancy L.
    "Raven in the Winter Feels Free." [Blueline] (8:1) Sum-Fall 86, p. 46.
    "Reading *Poetry and Experience*, by Archibald MacLeish." [BelPoJ] (36:3) Spr 86,
        p. 14.
    "Seen Flying Together Wild." [BelPoJ] (36:3) Spr 86, p. 13.
    "Snake Dance." [BelPoJ] (36:3) Spr 86, p. 12.
NIEMIER, Glynis Benbow
    See BENBOW-NIEMIER, Glynis
3896. NIEVES MIELES, Edgardo
    "Federico Garcia Lorca." [Mairena] (8:21) 86, p. 20.
3897. NIGHTINGALE, Barbara
    "No Change in the Tropics." [PassN] (7:2) Spr-Sum 86, p. 11.
3898. NIGRO, Nic
    "Decisions." [BellArk] (2:4) Jl-Ag 86, p. 7.
    "Renewal." [BellArk] (2:4) Jl-Ag 86, p. 16.
3899. NILSON, Nina
    "Sun." [RagMag] (5:1) Spr 86, p. 44.
3900. NIMMO, Kurt
    "35 Cents for the First Fifteen Minutes." [SlipS] (6) 86, p. 65.
3901. NIMS, John Frederick
    "Closed for Restoration." [YaleR] (75:3) Spr 86, p. 428.
    "Finisterre." [GeoR] (40:3) Fall 86, p. 755-756.
    "From the Rapido: La Spezia-Genova." [Atlantic] (257:4) Ap 86, p. 92.
    "Mélisande at the Kaleidoscope." [GrandS] (5:3) Spr 86, p. 19.
NIORD, Chard de
    See DeNIORD, Chard
3902. NIRANJANA, Tejaswini
    "Ambition." [Jacaranda] (2:1) Fall 86, p. 32.
3903. NISETICH, Frank J.
    "Apocalypse." [KanQ] (18:1/2) Wint-Spr 86, p. 253.
3904. NISHIO, Katsuko
    "At a Cannery" (tr. by James Kirkup and Akiko Takemoto). [Translation] (17) Fall
        86, p. 202.

3905. NIXON, Colin
"A Picture Dated Nineteen Seventy-Two." [Bogg] (55) 86, p. 40.
3906. NIXON, Edward
"Swallowing Cold." [Rampike] (5:1) 86, p. 65.
3907. NIXON, John, Jr.
"Paper People." [ArizQ] (42:1) Spr 86, p. 44.
3908. NOBLES, Edward
"Till It Hurts." [ManhatPR] (6) Wint-Spr 85-86, p. 52.
"Winter." [ManhatPR] (8) Wint 86-87, p. 30-31.
NOBUO, Ayukawa
    See AYUKAWA, Nobuo
3909. NOLAN, Husam
"Peeping Tom." [PassN] (7:2) Spr-Sum 86, p. 22.
3910. NOLAN, James
"Sadhu Song." [Confr] (32) Spr-Sum 86, p. 91.
3911. NOLAND, Deborah
"Guilt." [CapeR] (21:2) Fall 86, p. 6.
3912. NOLAND, John
"Snow on the Oregon Coast." [DeKalbLAJ] (19:1) 86, p. 36.
3913. NOLL, Bink
"From the Top of Stoney Mountain" (near Huntingdon in Pennsylvania). [CreamCR]
    (11:1) 86?, p. 44-45.
"The Nap." [CreamCR] (11:1) 86?, p. 43.
3914. NOLLA, Olga
"Fiesta de Máscaras en Hatillo." [RevICP] (89) Jul-Sep 85, p. 70-71.
3915. NONAGASE, Masao
"A Cruel End to My Desire" (tr. by Junko Yoshida). [KenR] (NS 7:1) Wint 85, p.
    34-35.
"Envoy" (tr. by Junko Yoshida). [KenR] (NS 7:1) Wint 85, p. 36.
"A Japanese Old Couple" (from Old Age Blues in the Sunset, tr. by Junko Yoshida).
    [WebR] (11:2) Fall 86, p. 20-24.
"My Daughter and I" (tr. by Junko Yoshida). [KenR] (NS 7:1) Wint 85, p. 35.
"The Vestiges of Passion" (tr. by Junko Yoshida). [KenR] (NS 7:1) Wint 85, p. 36.
3916. NORDHAUS, Jean
"Happiness." [CumbPR] (6:1) Fall 86, p. 35-36.
"Like Bodies Loosely Bound" (Lake George, 1960). [CumbPR] (6:1) Fall 86, p.
    33-34.
"Salt / Snow." [CentR] (30:4) Fall 86, p. 471-473.
3917. NORDSTROM, Lars
"And Eternity?" (tr. of Rolf Aggestam, w. Erland Anderson). [InterPR] (12:1) Spr
    86, p. 11.
"Encounter" (tr. of Rolf Aggestam, w. Erland Anderson). [InterPR] (12:1) Spr 86,
    p. 11.
"The Future Sleeps" (tr. of Rolf Aggestam, w. Erland Anderson). [InterPR] (12:1)
    Spr 86, p. 15.
"I Came to Uncle Axel But Could Not Find Him" (tr. of Rolf Aggestam, w. Erland
    Anderson). [InterPR] (12:1) Spr 86, p. 13.
"Song of the Shaman in Our Time" (tr. of Rolf Aggestam, w. Erland Anderson).
    [InterPR] (12:1) Spr 86, p. 7.
"Three Tons of Rock a Day" (tr. of Rolf Aggestam, w. Erland Anderson). [InterPR]
    (12:1) Spr 86, p. 9.
"Troll Eye" (tr. of Rolf Aggestam, w. Erland Anderson). [InterPR] (12:1) Spr 86, p.
    19.
"You Shall Stare Down" (tr. of Rolf Aggestam, w. Erland Anderson). [InterPR]
    (12:1) Spr 86, p. 17.
3918. NORRIS, Emma Coburn
"Gulf Shores: Another Anglo-Saxon Attitude." [NegC] (6:4) Fall 86, p. 55.
3919. NORRIS, Gunilla
"From the Convent: A Protest." [Prima] (10) 86, p. 48-49.
3920. NORRIS, Kathleen
"Hope in Elizabeth." [LitR] (30:1) Fall 86, p. 88.
3921. NORRIS, Ken
"The Edge" (for Janet). [GreenfR] (13:3/4) Sum-Fall 86, p. 154.
"Flying out of Fiji." [AntigR] (64) Wint 86, p. 41.
"Islands" (#1-#3). [AntigR] (64) Wint 86, p. 40.
"Islands" (4 selections). [PraF] (7:2) Sum 86, p. 50-51.

"Islands" (Selections). [Quarry] (35:3) Sum 86, p. 16-17.
"It isn't a great age for art." [Event] (15:1) 86, p. 110.
"One Day." [CanLit] (108) Spr 86, p. 92.
3922. NORRIS, Leslie
"The Dream" (tr. of Dafydd ap Gwilym). [QW] (23) 86, p. 148-149.
"Islands." [TarRP] (25:1) Fall 85, p. 9-11.
3923. NORTH, Charles
"For a Cowper Paperweight." [ParisR] (28:101) Wint 86, p. 190-191.
3924. NOSSIS
"Nothing is sweeter than love" (from "The Palatine Anthology, tr. by John Gill).
[YellowS] (21) Wint 86, p. 24.
3925. NOSTRAND, Jennifer
"In a house by a river." [Amelia] (3:1) Ja 86, p. 36-37.
"The silver dressing table set." [Amelia] (3:1) Ja 86, p. 36.
3926. NOTLEY, Kathie
"Bargain Hunting." [BellArk] (2:4) Jl-Ag 86, p. 5.
"Find the Little Girl in This Picture." [BellArk] (2:3) My-Je 86, p. 2.
"Roll Models." [BellArk] (2:3) My-Je 86, p. 14.
"Rules for Rule Breaking." [BellArk] (2:4) Jl-Ag 86, p. 3.
3927. NOULLET, Michelle
"The Second Day of the Typhoon." [CrescentR] (4:1) Spr 86, p. 122.
3928. NOVAK, Christine
"Die Eindrücke einer Zuschauerin . . ." [InterPR] (12:1) Spr 86, p. 60, 62.
"The Impressions of an Observer" (tr. by the author). [InterPR] (12:1) Spr 86, p.
61, 63.
3929. NOVAK, Helga M.
"How Survive This Rain" (tr. by Agnes Stein). [IndR] (9:2) Spr 86, p. 20-21.
3930. NOVAK, Michael Paul
"The Foyer at the College." [TarRP] (24:2) Spr 85, p. 21.
"El Prat, Waiting for the Last Train from Barcelona." [ConnPR] (5:1) 86, p. 34.
3931. NOWAK, Nancy
"Green Winter." [SmPd] (23:1, #66) Wint 86, p. 26.
3932. NOYES, H. F.
"The boatman's song" (tr. of Mong Hao-Jan, ed. by H. F. Noyes, tr. by W. S.
Merwin). [Amelia] (3:2) Spr 86, p. 47.
"The hearth fire dies." [Amelia] (3:3) Sum 86, p. 44.
"The moon torn apart." [Amelia] (3:3) Sum 86, p. 10.
"No one leaning" (After a Zen koan). [Amelia] (3:1) Ja 86, p. 56.
"Sleet pelts the roof." [Amelia] (3:4) Fall 86, p. 115.
"Trawler's lantern" (tr. of Tu Fu, ed. by H. F. Noyes, tr. by W. S. Merwin).
[Amelia] (3:2) Spr 86, p. 47.
3933. NOYES, Stanley
"Discipline." [HighP] (1:1) Wint 86, p. 44-45.
3934. NUGENT, Joseph W.
"Hollywood." [Sam] (46:2 release 182) 86, p. 29.
"VNV Rap Group." [Sam] (46:2 release 182) 86, p. 119.
3935. NURKSE, D.
"1917." [MSS] (5:1) 86, p. 102.
"The Boundary." [HangL] (49) Spr 86, p. 36.
"The Crest." [WestB] (18) 86, p. 75.
"The Cult." [Epoch] (35:1) 85-86, p. 19.
"Grandmother's Arrival." [MSS] (5:1) 86, p. 100-101.
"Grandmother's Cold." [WestB] (18) 86, p. 74-75.
"Grandmother's Exile." [MSS] (5:1) 86, p. 103.
"In the Hold." [WebR] (11:2) Fall 86, p. 60.
"In the New World." [MSS] (5:1) 86, p. 104.
"The Physical." [HangL] (49) Spr 86, p. 35.
"Riohacha, 1936." [Epoch] (35:1) 85-86, p. 20.
"The Road to the Coast." [WebR] (11:2) Fall 86, p. 59-60.
"The Roof of the Handbag Factory." [WestB] (18) 86, p. 74.
"The Second Chance." [AmerPoR] (15:1) Ja-F 86, p. 20.
"Taking Counsel." [HangL] (49) Spr 86, p. 34.
"Talking in the Dark Bed." [AmerPoR] (15:1) Ja-F 86, p. 20.
"A Theft." [PaintedB] (28) Ap 86, p. 75.
"The Visitors." [IndR] (9:3) Sum 86, p. 73.
"Willed Lack." [HangL] (49) Spr 86, p. 33.

"Work Glove." [AmerPoR] (15:1) Ja-F 86, p. 20.
"Written in Dust." [AmerPoR] (15:1) Ja-F 86, p. 20.
3936. NUTTING, Leslie
"The Bird in the Word." [AntigR] (66/67) Sum-Aut 86, p. 104.
"Bird Watching." [MalR] (77) D 86, p. 102-103.
"The Boy Selling the Blue Fish." [AntigR] (66/67) Sum-Aut 86, p. 102-103.
"The Diver." [GreenfR] (13:3/4) Sum-Fall 86, p. 155.
"Turin." [AntigR] (66/67) Sum-Aut 86, p. 105-106.
"The Word Belong." [MalR] (77) D 86, p. 104.
3937. NYE, Naomi Shihab
"Dying." [PaintedB] (28) Ap 86, p. 9.
"Grateful." [Sonora] (10) Spr 86, p. 13-14.
"Leaving Texas." [PaintedB] (28) Ap 86, p. 10.
"Looking for the Cat Grave." [KenR] (NS 7:1) Wint 85, p. 47.
"News Traveling Well." [Sonora] (10) Spr 86, p. 16-17.
"Now I Am Not Afraid" (tr. of Abu Zafar Obaidullah, w. the author). [Pax] (3:1/2)
    Wint 85-86, p. 193.
"Point of Rocks, Texas." [KenR] (NS 7:1) Wint 85, p. 46.
"The Tunnel of Questions" (For Bill Wright). [MidwQ] (27:2) Wint 86, p. 209-210.
"You Have to Be Careful." [Sonora] (10) Spr 86, p. 15.
3938. OAKES, Randy W.
"Explication." [Wind] (16:57) 86, p. 1.
3939. OAKEY, Shaun
"Weekends Near the Zoo." [Event] (15:1) 86, p. 54.
3940. OAKS, Jeff
"Two Dog Faces under a Red Light." [Blueline] (7:2) Wint-Spr 86, p. 4.
3941. OANDASAN, William
"Acoma." [CrossCur] (6:2) 86, p. 131.
"Promised from the Unconscious." [Electrum] (38) Spr 86, p. 29.
3942. OATES, David
"Chopin in Winter." [YellowS] (21) Wint 86, p. 6.
3943. OATES, Joyce Carol
"Autobiography." [Chelsea] (45) 86, p. 86.
"Black Winter Day." [MalR] (73) Ja 86, p. 63.
"Burning Oak, November." [Poetry] (149:2) N 86, p. 93.
"Child Walking in Sleep." [MalR] (73) Ja 86, p. 65.
"Detroit Expressway, 1971." [MichQR] (25:2) Spr 86, p. 364-365.
"Emergency Room." [NewL] (52:2/3) Wint-Spr 86, p. 88-91.
"Father of Us All." [SewanR] (94:4) Fall 86, p. 577.
"Fish." [NewRep] (194:26) 30 Je 86, p. 39.
"Flash Flood." [Chelsea] (45) 86, p. 87.
"Green Hornet." [TriQ] (67) Fall 86, p. 126.
"Heat." [YaleR] (75:4) Sum 86, p. 588.
"The House of Mystery." [MissouriR] (9:2) 86, p. 16-17.
"In the Country of the Blue." [Chelsea] (45) 86, p. 89.
"In the Silence." [DenQ] (20:4/21:1) Spr-Sum 86, p. 64.
"The Infant's Wake." [NewL] (52:2/3) Wint-Spr 86, p. 86-87.
"Invisible Woman." [CrossCur] (6:3) 86, p. 189.
"Luxury of Being Despised." [CrossCur] (6:3) 86, p. 159-160.
"Luxury of Sin." [GeoR] (40:3) Fall 86, p. 757.
"May Elegy." [KenR] (NS 7:4) Fall 85, p. 69.
"A Miniature Elegy." [MalR] (73) Ja 86, p. 64.
"Mud-Elegy." [KenR] (NS 7:4) Fall 85, p. 67.
"New Landscape." [Chelsea] (45) 86, p. 88.
"Old Concord Cemetery." [TriQ] (67) Fall 86, p. 127.
"An Old Prayer." [SewanR] (94:4) Fall 86, p. 576-577.
"Peaches, Pineapples, Hazelnuts." [CrossCur] (6:3) 86, p. 153-154.
"Peaches, Pineapples, Hazelnuts." [Shen] (36:3) 86, p. 51.
"The Riddle." [SewanR] (94:4) Fall 86, p. 578.
"Scab." [PartR] (53:1) 86, p. 101-102.
"The Shattered Mirror." [NewL] (52:2/3) Wint-Spr 86, p. 87.
"Snowblind." [MalR] (73) Ja 86, p. 64.
"The Triumph of Gravity." [KenR] (NS 7:4) Fall 85, p. 68.
"Upstairs." [MichQR] (25:2) Spr 86, p. 365.
"Weedy Logic" (For Tess and Ray). [Poetry] (149:2) N 86, p. 92-93.
"Winter Boredom." [ParisR] (28:99) Spr 86, p. 154.

279

OATES

"Winter Love." [ParisR] (28:99) Spr 86, p. 156.
"Winter Threnody." [ParisR] (28:99) Spr 86, p. 155.
"Winter Wrath." [ParisR] (28:99) Spr 86, p. 153.
3944. OBAIDULLAH, Abu Zafar
    "All My Words" (tr. of anonymous Bangla poem). [Pax] (3:1/2) Wint 85-86, p.
    194-198.
    "Now I Am Not Afraid" (tr. by the author and Naomi Shihad Nye). [Pax] (3:1/2)
    Wint 85-86, p. 193.
3945. OBATALA, T.
    "Conjur." [LitR] (30:1) Fall 86, p. 103.
    "OilFire." [LitR] (30:1) Fall 86, p. 105.
    "Screams." [LitR] (30:1) Fall 86, p. 104.
3946. OBED-EDOM
    "Sobre el Mediodía." [RevICP] (89) Jul-Sep 85, p. 66-67.
3947. OBEJAS, Achy
    "Berlin." [Abraxas] (34) 86, p. 12-13.
    "Berlin." [Cond] (13) 86, p. 97-98.
    "By the Side of the Road This Summer." [Sam] (44:3 release 175) 86, p. 57.
    "Goodby." [AntigR] (66/67) Sum-Aut 86, p. 26.
    "Knives." [HeliconN] (14/15) Sum 86, p. 83.
    "Love." [HeliconN] (14/15) Sum 86, p. 82.
    "Monday in April." [AntigR] (65) Spr 86, p. 71.
    "Montrose Harbor." [Cond] (13) 86, p. 99.
    "Oakland." [HeliconN] (14/15) Sum 86, p. 82-83.
    "Visiting Tio Catin." [AntigR] (65) Spr 86, p. 72.
3948. O'BRIEN, Margaret
    "Perfect (Pause)." [CapeR] (21:1) Spr 86, p. 33.
    "The Uninhibiting." [CapeR] (21:1) Spr 86, p. 32.
3949. O'BRIEN, Michael
    "Bartender." [WindO] (47) Sum 86, p. 48.
    "Flying Wintertime Chicago." [WindO] (47) Sum 86, p. 47.
3950. O'BRIEN, Sean
    "Kingdom of Kiev, Rios das Muertes." [Verse] (5) 86, p. 43.
3951. O'BRIEN, Sylvia
    "Spring in Central Park - 1985." [Amelia] (3:2) Spr 86, p. 87.
3952. OCHESTER, Ed
    "Abandoned Farm, Kittatinny." [KanQ] (18:1/2) Wint-Spr 86, p. 123.
    "For the Margrave of Brandenburg." [NoAmR] (271:2) Je 86, p. 15.
    "Having Built the Coop." [Poetry] (148:3) Je 86, p. 159-160.
    "Packing Lunch." [Crazy] (31) Fall 86, p. 46-49.
3953. OCHOA, Maria de los Angeles
    "A Destiempo." [Mairena] (8:21) 86, p. 109.
    "Ando." [Mairena] (8:21) 86, p. 110.
    "Me Asocio." [Mairena] (8:21) 86, p. 109.
    "Los Poemas de Abril." [Mairena] (8:21) 86, p. 110.
3954. OCHOA, Rosa Margot
    "Poemas Helénicos." [LetFem] (12:1/2) Primavera-Otoño 86, p. 144-146.
3955. O'CONNELL, Bill (William)
    "From the Front Porch, 3/28/84" (for T. Bremer). [PikeF] (7) Spr 86, p. 7.
    "Jewel Creek." [ColR] (NS 13:1) Fall 85, p. 71.
    "Letter to Jim Grabill" (11/16/85, Worcester, MA). [MidAR] (6:2) 86, p. 109.
    "Post-Post Modernism." [ColR] (NS 13:1) Fall 85, p. 70.
    "Riversong" (for Robin). [PikeF] (7) Spr 86, p. 7.
    "Visiting Emily Dickinson's Grave." [MidAR] (6:2) 86, p. 110.
3956. O'CONNOR, Christine
    "Cathedral Setting for Memorial Service." [JINJPo] (9:1) 86, p. 17.
3957. O'CONNOR, Maryjane
    "The Treasurer" (A Rondel). [Outbr] (16/17) Fall 85-Spr 86, p. 84.
3958. O'DALY, William
    "For All to Know" (tr. of Pablo Neruda). [AnotherCM] (16) 86, p. 67.
    "Gautama Christ" (tr. of Pablo Neruda). [AmerPoR] (15:5) S-O 86, p. 56.
    "Modestly" (tr. of Pablo Neruda). [AnotherCM] (16) 86, p. 65.
    "With Quevedo, in Springtime" (tr. of Pablo Neruda). [AnotherCM] (16) 86, p. 66.
3959. O'FLAHERTY, Jamie
    "Her Egyptian Flights." [ClockR] (3:1) 85, p. 41.

OGDEN

280

3960. OGDEN, Daniel
"It Doesn't Look Nice" (tr. of Kristina Lugn). [Vis] (22) 86, p. 19.
"Telephones That Ring" (tr. of Kristina Lugn). [Vis] (22) 86, p. 19.
3961. OGDEN, Hugh
"Beginnings." [Nimrod] (30:1) Fall-Wint 86, p. 119.
"The Fox." [Nimrod] (30:1) Fall-Wint 86, p. 118.
"Hawk." [CapeR] (21:2) Fall 86, p. 33.
"The Oquossoc Poem" (for Kathy). [ManhatPR] (6) Wint-Spr 85-86, p. 57.
3962. O'GRADY, Desmond
"Hellas: Coup d'Etat" (Greece, 21 April, 1967, for Andrea Giustozzi). [Agni] (23)
86, p. 142-150.
3963. O'HALLORAN, Jamie
"After October." [BellArk] (2:1) Ja-F 86, p. 1.
"Birds." [BellArk] (2:1) Ja-F 86, p. 8.
"Fool's Month." [BellArk] (2:2) Mr-Ap 86, p. 8.
"The Shades My Sister Wore." [BellArk] (2:1) Ja-F 86, p. 16.
3964. O'HARA, Deborah
"Litost" (for Milan Kundera). [CutB] (26) Spr-Sum 86, p. 26-27.
3965. O'HEHIR, Diana
"Pattern." [Field] (34) Spr 86, p. 18.
3966. O'HERN, Phillip D.
"Trapped." [NegC] (6:4) Fall 86, p. 102.
3967. OHMAN-YOUNGS, Anne
"Cutting Wood." [TarRP] (26:1) Fall 86, p. 21-22.
3968. OIJER, Bruno K.
"Gambler's Stone" (tr. by the author). [Vis] (22) 86, p. 20.
"Let This Hard Life Cling to Us" (tr. by the author). [Vis] (22) 86, p. 21-22.
3969. OLDER, Julia
"At the Shelter" (From *Hermaphroditus in America*, a work in progress). [Confr]
(32) Spr-Sum 86, p. 70.
"Leaping." [SouthernPR] (26:2) Fall 86, p. 55-60.
"Moths." [BallSUF] (27:4) Aut 86, p. 60.
"The Night of Error" (Time: WWII, Place: Labyrinthian caves—Aleppo, Syria).
[LitR] (30:1) Fall 86, p. 32.
"Street People." [Confr] (32) Spr-Sum 86, p. 69.
"When the Wind Passes Through My Skull" (tr. of Boris Vian). [Vis] (22) 86, p.
10.
"Xichu." [BallSUF] (27:4) Aut 86, p. 59.
3970. OLDHAM, Pamolu
"Chatham County." [SouthernPR] (26:1) Spr 86, p. 40.
3971. OLDKNOW, Antony
"Confidences." [MinnR] (NS 27) Fall 86, p. 70.
"I Want a Dark Woman." [WebR] (11:2) Fall 86, p. 76.
"Love of the Rain." [WebR] (11:2) Fall 86, p. 74-75.
"The Seafarer" (tr. from Old English. In Memoriam: Edwin James Batchelor, Robert
Atchison Caldwell). [NoDaQ] (54:4) Fall 86, p. 18-21.
"The Swollen Tiger." [CreamCR] (11:1) 86?, p. 52.
"The Wanderer" (tr from Old English). [NoDaQ] (54:4) Fall 86, p. 21-24.
3972. OLDS, Sharon
"The Beetle" (for my father). [ParisR] (28:101) Wint 86, p. 242.
"The Burial." [Nat] (243:18) 29 N 86, p. 618.
"My Father's Shirt." [Atlantic] (258:3) S 86, p. 77.
"Parents Day, 1950." [Nat] (243:21) 20 D 86, p. 714.
"Psalm for a Deathbed." [PoetryE] (20/21) Fall 86, p. 158-159.
"This Hour." [ParisR] (28:100) Sum-Fall 86, p. 201-202.
3973. O'LEARY, Dawn
"A get-well note to Juan from the governor." [Comm] (113:14) 15 Ag 86, p. 429.
3974. O'LEARY, Tomas
"The Calling Home." [ColR] (NS 13:1) Fall 85, p. 73.
"A Midnight Confidence." [ColR] (NS 13:1) Fall 85, p. 74.
OLEKSA, L. Sabine
See SABINE-OLEKSA, L.
3975. OLES, Carole
"Brambles" (for my father). [DenQ] (20:4/21:1) Spr-Sum 86, p. 58-59.
"Instead of Larry Bird's Autograph" (Delta 364, Atlanta-Boston, for Rick). [QW]
(22) Spr-Sum 86, p. 52-53.

3976. OLIPHANT, Dave
"Salado." [Pax] (3:1/2) Wint 85-86, p. 103-106.
3977. OLIVA, Jorge
"Ultima Parada: Cementerio de San Rafael." [LindLM] (5:3) Jl-S 86, p. 4.
3978. OLIVE, Harry
"Demon Killer." [Confr] (32) Spr-Sum 86, p. 139.
3979. OLIVER, Mary
"Acid." [Atlantic] (257:6) Je 86, p. 64.
"At Loxahatchie." [GeoR] (40:3) Fall 86, p. 759-760.
"Death at Wind River." [Poetry] (147:6) Mr 86, p. 330.
"Every Morning." [Poetry] (147:6) Mr 86, p. 328.
"Killing the Owl." [WestHR] (40:3) Aut 86, p. 259-260.
"The Mango." [Poetry] (147:6) Mr 86, p. 329-330.
"Robert Schumann." [KenR] (NS 8:1) Wint 86, p. 14.
"Shadows." [KenR] (NS 8:1) Wint 86, p. 16.
"Skunk Cabbage." [GeoR] (40:3) Fall 86, p. 758.
"Snapping Turtle." [GeoR] (40:2) Sum 86, p. 445-446.
"The Swimmer." [KenR] (NS 8:1) Wint 86, p. 15-16.
3980. OLIVER, Michael Brian
"Nitobe Garden." [CanLit] (109) Sum 86, p. 99.
3981. OLIVEROS, Alejandro
"I. En qué pensaba, en qué pensaba, oh Tom?" [LindLM] (5:2) Ap-Je 86, p. 4.
3982. OLIVEROS, Chuck
"Don't Bother with the Younger Girls." [NegC] (6:4) Fall 86, p. 82-83.
"Monkey." [Abraxas] (34) 86, p. 50-51.
3983. OLLIVIER, Larry
"Letter to Falls Church" (From Seattle, October 1985). [BellArk] (2:2) Mr-Ap 86, p. 5.
"Nearing Equinox." [BellArk] (2:2) Mr-Ap 86, p. 8.
"Three Regrets." [BellArk] (2:2) Mr-Ap 86, p. 4.
3984. OLSEN, David
"A Palmist's Reflection." [Amelia] (3:4) Fall 86, p. 91.
3985. OLSEN, T. V.
"Gay Blades." [SpoonRQ] (11:2) Spr 86, p. 2-3.
"To a Defunct Poet." [SpoonRQ] (11:2) Spr 86, p. 4.
"Viet Retrospective." [SpoonRQ] (11:2) Spr 86, p. 1.
3986. OLSEN, William
"Eighteen Species of Hummingbirds." [HayF] (1) Spr 86, p. 61-62.
"The Leeches." [PoetryNW] (27:4) Wint 86-87, p. 4-6.
"Wherever It Goes, Wherever You Go." [PoetryNW] (27:4) Wint 86-87, p. 3-4.
3987. OLSON, Elder
"?" (The Mary Elinore Smith Poetry Prize). [AmerS] (55:3) Sum 86, p. 365-366.
3988. OLSON, Kirby
"Chain Poem." [SecC] (14:1) 86, p. 46.
3989. OLSON, Ruth
"Calves." [OntR] (24) Spr-Sum 86, p. 105.
"Turning the Cow." [OntR] (24) Spr-Sum 86, p. 104.
"Two-Headed Calf." [OntR] (24) Spr-Sum 86, p. 106.
3990. OLSON, Toby
"Shining Hour." [ParisR] (28:99) Spr 86, p. 180-181.
OLUND, Barbara Molloy
See MOLLOY-OLUND, Barbara
3991. O'MELVENY, Regina
"The Green God." [Jacaranda] (2:1) Fall 86, p. 15.
3992. ONDAATJE, Michael
"The Cinnamon Peeler" (from *Running in the Family*). [LitR] (29:4) Sum 86, p. 524-525.
"High Flowers" (from *Running in the Family*). [LitR] (29:4) Sum 86, p. 521-522.
"Sweet Like a Crow" (for Hetti Corea, 8 years old. From *Running in the Family*). [LitR] (29:4) Sum 86, p. 515.
"To Colombo" (from *Running in the Family*). [LitR] (29:4) Sum 86, p. 522.
"Women Like You" (the communal poem — Sigiri Graffiti, 5th century. From *Running in the Family*). [LitR] (29:4) Sum 86, p. 523-524.
3993. O'NEILL, Patrick
"Incognito." [SanFPJ] (9:1) 86, p. 56.
"Mushrooms." [SanFPJ] (9:1) 86, p. 28.

"Novocaine." [SanFPJ] (8:4) 85, p. 89.
3994. ONO, Tozaburo
"Monstrous Fish" (tr. by James Kirkup and Akiko Takemoto). [Translation] (17) Fall 86, p. 196.
"Tomorrow" (tr. by James Kirkup and Akiko Takemoto). [Translation] (17) Fall 86, p. 195.
ONO NO KOMACHI
See KOMACHI, Ono no
3995. OPERE, Fernando
"Ahorrar un Día." [Inti] (21) Primavera 85, p. 126-127.
"Rito Nocturno." [Inti] (21) Primavera 85, p. 125.
"Superman." [Inti] (21) Primavera 85, p. 125-126.
3996. ORBAN, Ottó
"Taproot" (tr. by Jascha Kessler, w. Maria Körösy). [MalR] (77) D 86, p. 79.
"Taproot" (tr. by Jascha Kessler, w. Maria Körösy). [MichQR] (25:1) Wint 86, p. 103-104.
3997. ORDAS, Betty
"RO." [WindO] (47) Sum 86, p. 8.
3998. OREN, Miriam
"The Fig Tree" (tr. by Ruth Whitman). [PoetL] (81:2) Sum 86, p. 107.
"I Only Wish" (tr. by Ruth Whitman). [PoetL] (81:2) Sum 86, p. 107.
"Jackal" (tr. by Ruth Whitman). [PoetL] (81:2) Sum 86, p. 108.
"Snowwhite" (tr. by Ruth Whitman). [PoetL] (81:2) Sum 86, p. 106.
3999. ORESICK, Peter
"American Landscape with Unemployed, 1934." [PoetryE] (20/21) Fall 86, p. 197-198.
"Pleasure." [ChrC] (103:1) 1-8 Ja 86, p. 13.
"The Story." [PoetryE] (20/21) Fall 86, p. 195-196.
4000. ORFALEA, Gregory
"The Onion." [Confr] (32) Spr-Sum 86, p. 92-93.
4001. O'RIORDAN, Brian
"Fenians All." [GreenfR] (13:3/4) Sum-Fall 86, p. 157.
"November 25, 1970." [GreenfR] (13:3/4) Sum-Fall 86, p. 158.
4002. ORLOWSKY, Dzvinia
"The River" (after Alexander Douzhenko, 1894-1956). [Agni] (23) 86, p. 169.
4003. ORMSBY, Eric
"The Color of the Roses in February." [Chelsea] (45) 86, p. 95.
"Fetish." [Chelsea] (45) 86, p. 94-95.
4004. ORMSBY, Frank
"Felix Peccione's Crucifixion" (St. Malachy's, Alfred Street, Belfast). [Verse] (6) 86, p. 32.
"In Retrospect." [Verse] (6) 86, p. 31.
"Sarajevo." [Verse] (6) 86, p. 31.
4005. OROZCO, Olga
"I Row Against the Night" (tr. by Mary Crow). [MidAR] (6:1) 86?, p. 61, 63, 65.
"Remo Contra la Noche." [MidAR] (6:1) 86?, p. 60, 62, 64.
4006. ORR, Ed
"A Place to Go." [EngJ] (75:1) Ja 86, p. 59.
4007. ORR, Gregory
"Sex." [Ploughs] (12:3) 86, p. 80-81.
"To the Muse." [Ploughs] (12:3) 86, p. 79.
4008. ORR, Verlena
"Landscape in Dim Light." [CreamCR] (11:1) 86?, p. 49.
"One River Story." [CreamCR] (11:1) 86?, p. 48.
"Our Mother's Mother." [SnapD] (9:2) Spr 86, p. 52-53.
4009. ORRICO, Javier
"Despues de un Largo Viaje Alguien Descansa en Aguilas." [Mairena] (8:22) 86, p. 9.
4010. ORS, Eugeni d'
"A Dancer" (Una balladora, tr. by David H. Rosenthal). [SenR] (16:1) 86, p. 22.
ORSZAG-LAND, Thomas
See LAND, Thomas
4011. ORT, Daniel
"Ophelia." [Puerto] (22:1) Fall 86, p. 23-24.

4012. ORTEGA, Julio
"Tres Canciones Rusas (Y Una en New York)." [Inti] (21) Primavera 85, p. 109-112.
4013. ORTEZA, Arsenio
"Mrs. Wendler Waits for Her Husband." [PoetryNW] (27:3) Aut 86, p. 39-40.
4014. ORTH, Kevin
"Agonia Obbligato." [NowestR] (24:2) 86, p. 21.
"Dreaming of You." [WestB] (19) 86, p. 91.
"Grenada Invasion." [Shen] (36:3) 86, p. 50.
4015. ORTIZ, Cecilia
"Es Que No Suenan los Telefonos a Estas Horas?" [LindLM] (5:2) Ap-Je 86, p. 6.
"Por Todo el Calor Que Nos Falta." [LindLM] (5:2) Ap-Je 86, p. 6.
4016. ORTIZ, Simon (Simon J.)
"Comprehension" (with thanks to N. Scott Momaday). [PoetryE] (20/21) Fall 86, p. 87.
"The Farmer in Hills, Iowa." [RedBass] (11) 86, p. 10.
"Healing." [RiverS] (19) 86, p. 44.
"Intercrossing." [RiverS] (19) 86, p. 41.
"Necessary Knowing." [RedBass] (11) 86, p. 24.
"River Ice." [RiverS] (19) 86, p. 45.
"Sharing Margins." [RiverS] (19) 86, p. 42.
"Snow and Wind Finework." [RiverS] (19) 86, p. 45.
"Time and the Horizon." [RiverS] (19) 86, p. 43.
"Turning Back." [PoetryE] (20/21) Fall 86, p. 86.
ORTIZ COFER, Judith
See COFER, Judith Ortiz
4017. ORTOLANI, Al
"Feldspar." [ManhatPR] (7) Sum 86, p. 50.
"Monday Afternoon." [ManhatPR] (7) Sum 86, p. 50.
"The Visitor." [SpoonRQ] (11:2) Spr 86, p. 9.
"Willow Jungle." [SpoonRQ] (11:2) Spr 86, p. 10.
4018. OSBEY, Brenda Marie
"The Galvez Cut." [Callaloo] (9:1, #26) Wint 86, p. 109-111.
"Geography." [AmerPoR] (15:2) Mr-Ap 86, p. 8.
"House of Bones." [AmerPoR] (15:2) Mr-Ap 86, p. 9.
"House of the Dead Remembering" (House of Mercies/Variation 2). [AmerPoR] (15:2) Mr-Ap 86, p. 9.
"How I Became the Blues." [AmerPoR] (15:2) Mr-Ap 86, p. 8.
"Little Eugenia's Lover." [AmerV] (2) Spr 86, p. 110-111.
"Setting Loose the Icons." [Callaloo] (9:1, #26) Wint 86, p. 112-115.
4019. OSBORN, Alan Rice
"Another Colonial War Sort of Thing." [Electrum] (38) Spr 86, p. 46.
4020. OSBORN, Andrew (Andrew L.)
"Big Bang of the City." [HarvardA] (120, i.e. 119:3) Mr 86, p. 27.
"A Sprig of Hope from the Depthy Crypts of Sadness." [HarvardA] (119:4) My 86, p. 25.
"Trees Like Carded Wool." [HarvardA] (120:1) D 86, p. 17.
"Xmas '86: Softly We Are." [HarvardA] (120:1) D 86, p. 41.
4021. OSBORN, Millicent
"I Can't Make Up My Mind." [AmerV] (2) Spr 86, p. 3-4.
4022. OSBORNE-McKNIGHT, Juilene
"Nuclear Holocaust (William Shakespeare's Warning)." [EngJ] (75:3) Mr 86, p. 53.
4023. OSERS, Ewald
"Medieval Synagogue, Toledo." [CrossCur] (5:4/6:1) 86, p. 43.
"Niagara Falls." [CrossCur] (5:4/6:1) 86, p. 41-42.
4024. OSHEROW, Jacqueline
"International Call." [Shen] (36:4) 86, p. 64-65.
"To an Unknown Russian Poet." [Shen] (36:4) 86, p. 65-67.
4025. OSHIRO, Hide
"Tangled Hair: Poems" (tr. of Akiko Yosano, w. Dennis Maloney). [YellowS] (18) Spr 86, p. 24-25.
4026. OSING, Gordon
"Lines Composed on a Siding in Norway." [CharR] (12:2) Fall 86, p. 78.
"Mariahilfer Strasse" (Vienna). [SouthernR] (22:4) O 86, p. 790-791.
"Upon a News Item." [NewYorker] (62:28) 1 S 86, p. 38.

4027. OSLEY, Carol Ann
"Jeffrey's Poem." [WritersL] (1986:5), p. 30.
4028. OSOINACH, John Campbell
"Dear Dad" (August 25, 1986, Monday, 7 AM). [YellowS] (21) Wint 86, p. 43.
4029. OSORIO, Amparo Inés
"Recorreme Esta Noche." [Mairena] (8:22) 86, p. 27.
4030. OSTERHUBER, Magda
"End of the World" (tr. of Christoph Meckel). [Chelsea] (45) 86, p. 48.
"Tear Animals" (tr. of Christoph Meckel). [Chelsea] (45) 86, p. 46-47.
4031. OSTRIKER, Alicia
"Everywoman Her Own Theology." [Cond] (13) 86, p. 112.
"The Hawk's Shadow." [Nat] (243:6) 6 S 86, p. 186.
"Horses." [LittleM] (15:1) 86, p. 5.
"The Idea of Making Love." [Calyx] (9:2/3) Wint 86, p. 123.
"Irises." [NewYorker] (62:12) 12 My 86, p. 38.
"Lamenting the Inevitable." [OntR] (24) Spr-Sum 86, p. 22-23.
"The Living." [DenQ] (20:4/21:1) Spr-Sum 86, p. 40-42.
"The Memory." [OntR] (24) Spr-Sum 86, p. 19.
"Mother in Airport Parking Lot." [OntR] (24) Spr-Sum 86, p. 17-18.
"The Moving Target." [LittleM] (15:1) 86, p. 8.
"Stanzas to Pythagoras." [OntR] (24) Spr-Sum 86, p. 16.
"Surviving" (A Group of Poems. A Prairie Schooner Portfolio). [PraS] (60:3) Fall
        86, p. 29-41.
"Taverna, Athens 1974." [OntR] (24) Spr-Sum 86, p. 20.
"Terror." [OntR] (24) Spr-Sum 86, p. 14-15.
"To Love Is" (Selection: iii). [Calyx] (9:2/3) Wint 86, p. 122.
"The Unsaid or What She Thinks When She Gets My Letter." [Cond] (13) 86, p.
        111.
"Warning." [Cond] (13) 86, p. 113-114.
"Whales." [LittleM] (15:1) 86, p. 7.
"Wishes." [OntR] (24) Spr-Sum 86, p. 21.
"Worms." [LittleM] (15:1) 86, p. 6.
4032. OSTROM, Cheryll K.
"My Mother Taught Me." [RagMag] (5:2) Fall 86, p. 53.
"Old Women." [SingHM] (13) 86, p. 80-81.
4033. OSTROM, Hans
"In Pompeii." [CumbPR] (5:2) Spr 86, p. 9.
"Migratory Executives." [CumbPR] (5:2) Spr 86, p. 8.
"Tornado in the Pennsylvania Hills." [CutB] (25) Fall-Wint 86, p. 36.
4034. O'SULLIVAN, Sibbie
"Looking for My Glasses." [Nimrod] (30:1) Fall-Wint 86, p. 55.
4035. OSUNA, William
"Ah! La Familia." [LindLM] (5:2) Ap-Je 86, p. 7.
4036. OTERO SILVA, Miguel
"Discovery of Stone" (tr. by Kent Johnson). [ClockR] (3:1) 85, p. 56.
4037. OTT, Gil
"Act of love learned over and over" (for Julia, 5/85). [PaintedB] (28) Ap 86, p. 8.
4038. OTTEN, Charlotte F.
"Basket." [SouthernHR] (20:3) Sum 86, p. 248.
4039. OUGHTON, John
"Last Conversation with the Prison Nun" (from Mata Hari's Lost Words). [Event]
        (15:2) 86, p. 110-111.
4040. OUTRAM, Richard
"Four Sonnets" (tr. of Severo Sarduy). [Descant] (17:4, #55) Wint 86-87, p.
        163-166.
4041. OVERTON, Ron
"Annual." [IndR] (9:2) Spr 86, p. 65.
4042. OWEN, Garnet
"Peace." [SanFPJ] (9:1) 86, p. 68.
4043. OWEN, John E.
"Black Sorrow." [SanFPJ] (9:1) 86, p. 26.
"Future." [SanFPJ] (9:1) 86, p. 27.
4044. OWER, John
"The Vulture's Good Advice." [Wind] (16:58) 86, p. 19.
"A Warning." [Wind] (16:58) 86, p. 24.

4045. OXENHANDLER, Noelle
"At Blue Mountain." [Blueline] (7:2) Wint-Spr 86, p. 43.
"Eagle Lake." [Blueline] (7:2) Wint-Spr 86, p. 42.
4046. OYAMA, Richard
"Mochi." [Contact] (7:38/39/40) Wint-Spr 86, p. 48.
4047. OZICK, Cynthia
"Sanitorium" (tr. of H. Leivick). [Translation] (17) Fall 86, p. 254-255.
4048. PACE, Rosalind
"Tingel-Tangel" (from a handcoloured lithograph, 1895, by Edvard Munch).
[ThRiPo] (27/28) 86, p. 55.
4049. PACERNICK, Gary
"Snapshots." [MemphisSR] (7:1) Fall 86, p. 48.
4050. PACEY, Michael
"The Boston Suitcoat." [AntigR] (64) Wint 86, p. 21.
4051. PACK, Robert
"Calling for Help." [KenR] (NS 8:1) Wint 86, p. 66-67.
"Clayfeld Atones." [KenR] (NS 8:1) Wint 86, p. 64-65.
"Clayfeld Renews His Vow." [ParisR] (28:99) Spr 86, p. 177-179.
"Clayfeld's Operatic Debut." [NewRep] (194:14) 7 Ap 86, p. 40.
"Quasars." [QW] (23) 86, p. 104-106.
"Trying to Separate." [GeoR] (40:3) Fall 86, p. 761-762.
4052. PACKA, Sheila
"Silver Lake." [SingHM] (13) 86, p. 35.
4053. PACKARD, Linda
"Autumn Quarter Dream: 3 Months before My Thesis Is Due." [BellArk] (2:6) N-D
86, p. 3.
"Recurring Dreams." [BellArk] (2:6) N-D 86, p. 16.
4054. PACKARD, William
"Further back I go in memory." [Contact] (8:41/42/43) Fall-Wint 86-87, p. 64.
"Who was that Roman emperor who had his opponents." [Contact] (8:41/42/43)
Fall-Wint 86-87, p. 64.
4055. PACKES, Nancy
"Once on a bleak train" ("Untitled"). [BallSUF] (26:4) Aut 85, p. 16.
4056. PACKIE, Susan
"Forest Cataclysm." [InterPR] (12:2) Fall 86, p. 57.
"Icarus in 1986." [InterPR] (12:2) Fall 86, p. 58.
"Mistaken Identity." [YetASM] (4) 85, p. 3.
4057. PADGETT, Ron
"To Woody Woodpecker." [ParisR] (28:100) Sum-Fall 86, p. 203.
4058. PADHI, Bibhu
"Calcutta" (tr. of Bibek Jena). [RiverS] (20) 86, p. 55.
"Grandmother." [AntigR] (66/67) Sum-Aut 86, p. 24-25.
"Letters to God" (tr. of Prasanna Patsani). [RiverS] (20) 86, p. 54-55.
"Trees." [Pax] (3:1/2) Wint 85-86, p. 199.
4059. PADILLA, Herberto
"Recuerdo de Wallace Stevens en la Florida." [LindLM] (5:1) Ja-Mr 86, p. 10.
4060. PADRON, Justo Jorge
"Los Caballos del Sueño." [LindLM] (5:1) Ja-Mr 86, p. 12.
"La Mano Que Te Escribe." [LindLM] (5:1) Ja-Mr 86, p. 12.
"Máscara del Deseo." [LindLM] (5:1) Ja-Mr 86, p. 12.
"Trasluz." [LindLM] (5:1) Ja-Mr 86, p. 12.
PADUA, Reynaldo Marcos
See MARCOS PADUA, Reynaldo
4061. PAGAN DE SOTO, Gladys
"El Niño Presentido." [Mairena] (8:22) 86, p. 76.
4062. PAGE, Barbara Kerr
"Coming Down Snolqualmie." [Puerto] (22:1) Fall 86, p. 54.
"Isak." [Puerto] (22:1) Fall 86, p. 55.
4063. PAGE, Deborah Carty
"Death of a Paint Broodmare." [BallSUF] (26:4) Aut 85, p. 5.
4064. PAGE, P. K.
"Deaf-Mute in the Pear Tree." [GreenfR] (13:3/4) Sum-Fall 86, p. 160-161.
"In Class We Create Ourselves — Having Been Told to Shut Our Eyes . . ." (for
Judith). [GreenfR] (13:3/4) Sum-Fall 86, p. 159.
4065. PAGE, William
"Between." [KanQ] (18:1/2) Wint-Spr 86, p. 204.

"Bones." [WindO] (47) Sum 86, p. 20.
"Change." [SouthernR] (22:1) Ja 86, p. 140-141.
"Halley's Comet." [MidwQ] (28:1) Aut 86, p. 99.
"Love." [Pembroke] (18) 86, p. 267.
"The Man Who Stayed Behind." [CharR] (12:2) Fall 86, p. 67.
"Thunder." [SouthernR] (22:1) Ja 86, p. 139-140.
4066. PAGIS, Dan
"Calendar"" (tr. by Shirley Kaufman). [PoetL] (81:2) Sum 86, p. 82.
"Diagnosis"" (tr. by Shirley Kaufman). [PoetL] (81:2) Sum 86, p. 81.
"The Grand Duke of New York" (tr. by Stephen Mitchell). [PoetL] (81:2) Sum 86,
    p. 80.
4067. PAI, M. Govinda
"The Parrots" (tr. by Sumatheendra Nadig). [SenR] (16:1) 86, p. 75.
4068. PAINCHAUD, Alain-Arthur
"Aventure Mycologique." [Rampike] (5:2) 86, p. 58.
4069. PAIZ, Frank
"Easter Rising" (Viet Nam, April 1968). [MinnR] (NS 26) Spr 86, p. 56.
4070. PALEN, John
"Exposure." [InterPR] (12:1) Spr 86, p. 98.
"Inlet." [InterPR] (12:1) Spr 86, p. 99.
4071. PALEY, Grace
"The Sad Children's Song." [Field] (34) Spr 86, p. 93-94.
PALLANT, Layeh Bock
    See BOCK/PALLANT, Layeh
PALMA, Francisco Albizurez
    See ALBIZUREZ PALMA, Francisco
4072. PALMA, Marigloria
"Reflejo de una Ternura." [Mairena] (8:22) 86, p. 88.
4073. PALMER, Audrey
"Bogg 53." [Bogg] (55) 86, p. 6.
"Madame Nettle." [Bogg] (55) 86, p. 53.
4074. PALMER, Leslie
"Cleaning Out a Lot." [CapeR] (21:2) Fall 86, p. 41.
4075. PALMER, Michael
"Baudelaire Series" (Excerpts). [Sulfur] (5:3, issue 15) 86, p. 126-129.
"Baudelaire Series" (Selections: 4 poems). [Acts] (5) 86, p. 4-7.
"Baudelaire Series" (Selections: 5 poems). [Conjunc] (9) 86, p. 27-30.
"C" (Selections: 4 poems). [Acts] (5) 86, p. 37-40.
4076. PALMER, William
"Boilermakers." [PassN] (7:1) Fall-Wint 85-86, p. 8.
4077. PANG, Bingjun
"Begin from Here" (from the poem-cycle, Part V, tr. of Jiang He, w. John Minford
    et al.). [Nimrod] (29:2) Spr-Sum 86, p. 123-124.
"Train through Qin Mountains" (tr. Luo Gengye, w. John Minford). [Nimrod]
    (29:2) Spr-Sum 86, p. 108-111.
4078. PANKEY, Eric
"The Promise." [PennR] (1:2) Fall 85, p. 37.
4079. PANKOWSKI, Elsie
"Gathering Stones." [BellArk] (2:6) N-D 86, p. 8.
"Lost near Hynek's Hill." [BellArk] (2:5) S-O 86, p. 1.
"White Earth — Circa 1950." [HiramPoR] (41) Fall-Wint 86-87, p. 37.
4080. PANTIN, Yolanda
"Vitral de Mujer Sola." [LindLM] (5:2) Ap-Je 86, p. 9.
PAOLI, Francisco Matos
    See MATOS PAOLI, Francisco
4081. PAPADAKY, Sophia Mavroeidi
"The Teacher" (tr. by Rae Dalven). [Confr] (33/34) Fall-Wint 86-87, p. 114.
PAPASSEIT, Joan Salvat
    See SALVAT-PAPASSEIT, Joan
4082. PAPE, Greg
"Children of Sacaton." [MissouriR] (9:2) 86, p. 13.
"The Clowns of Shipolovi." [MissouriR] (9:2) 86, p. 12.
"The Dogs of Chinle." [QW] (23) 86, p. 61-62.
"Tai Song." [MissouriR] (9:2) 86, p. 14-15.
4083. PAPELL, Helen
"Noon, in a Kiva (40 Years After Hiroshima)." [Vis] (21) 86, p. 21.

4084. PAPP, Tibor
"Deux Poems" (Adaptation française de András Petocz). [Rampike] (5:2) 86, p. 49.
4085. PAPPAS, Theresa
"Another." [WestHR] (40:4) Wint 86, p. 352.
"Lessons." [DenQ] (20:4/21:1) Spr-Sum 86, p. 142-144.
4086. PARADIS, Phil (Philip)
"Mosquito." [TarRP] (24:2) Spr 85, p. 23.
"Semper Fidelis." [TarRP] (26:1) Fall 86, p. 35-36.
"To C.P. from Ferrante's Bar & Grill." [TarRP] (26:1) Fall 86, p. 33-34.
"To C.P. from Ferrante's Bar & Grill: Elegy for a Juiced Electrician." [BallSUF]
   (27:4) Aut 86, p. 34-35.
4087. PARCERISAS, Francesc
"Accident" (tr. by Hardie St. Martin). [Translation] (16) Spr 86, p. 88.
"Calypso" (tr. by Hardie St. Martin). [Translation] (16) Spr 86, p. 87.
"A Day Like This" (tr. by Hardie St. Martin). [Translation] (16) Spr 86, p. 91.
"Parting" (tr. by Hardie St. Martin). [Translation] (16) Spr 86, p. 86.
"Portrait of the Poet" (tr. by Hardie St. Martin). [Translation] (16) Spr 86, p. 89.
"Shave" (tr. by Hardie St. Martin). [Translation] (16) Spr 86, p. 88.
"Variation on a Poem by Lawrence Durrell" (tr. by Hardie St. Martin). [Translation]
   (16) Spr 86, p. 85.
"Wreckers" (tr. by Hardie St. Martin). [Translation] (16) Spr 86, p. 90.
4088. PARHAM, Robert
"Belmont." [CumbPR] (5:2) Spr 86, p. 21.
"I Come Clean." [BallSUF] (27:4) Aut 86, p. 12.
"Music of the Spheres, or Last Year's Lab Turtles." [KanQ] (18:1/2) Wint-Spr 86,
   p. 164.
4089. PARINI, Jay
"For My Wife at Washing" (in Torre Gentile). [Hudson] (39:3) Aut 86, p. 460.
"The Function of Winter." [MissouriR] (9:1) 85-86, p. 127.
"The Function of Winter." [Verse] (6) 86, p. 10.
"The Mariner" (For Richard Kenney). [Poetry] (148:6) S 86, p. 311-312.
"Spring As an Example." [MichQR] (25:1) Wint 86, p. 25-27.
"Stroup Pond: a Close-Up." [Hudson] (39:3) Aut 86, p. 459-460.
"This Kampuchea." [Verse] (5) 86, p. 34-35.
"Town Life" (For Ann Beattie). [Poetry] (148:6) S 86, p. 312-314.
"The Visitors." [Hudson] (39:3) Aut 86, p. 459.
4090. PARIS, Cindy
"For a Hard Winter." [CrescentR] (4:1) Spr 86, p. 38.
4091. PARISH, Barbara Shirk
"Constituent." [Wind] (16:57) 86, p. 28.
"Meeting." [Wind] (16:57) 86, p. 39.
4092. PARK, Marian Ford
"Summer campfire." [Amelia] (3:3) Sum 86, p. 26.
4093. PARK, Tony
"W.I.A." [Sonora] (11) Fall 86 [c87], p. 76.
"When I Look." [MidwQ] (28:1) Aut 86, p. 83.
4094. PARKER, Alan Michael
"Color Theory." [Shen] (36:3) 86, p. 109-110.
"Frozen Lasagne." [Shen] (36:3) 86, p. 111.
"A Short History of Numbers." [Shen] (36:3) 86, p. 112.
"Song." [NewRep] (195:1) 7 Jl 86, p. 46.
4095. PARKER, Christopher
"Drawing a Crowd." [JINJPo] (9:1) 86, p. 21.
"Fixing the Well." [JINJPo] (9:1) 86, p. 23-24.
"Garden Creatures: Riddles." [PoetryNW] (27:3) Aut 86, p. 25.
"Hopatcong Arrival." [JINJPo] (9:1) 86, p. 22.
"The King George Hotel." [JINJPo] (9:1) 86, p. 19.
"Liquidating the Corner Candy Store." [PoetryNW] (27:2) Sum 86, p. 39-40.
"The Poet of the Last Decade." [PoetryNW] (27:2) Sum 86, p. 40-41.
"The Stick." [Outbr] (16/17) Fall 85-Spr 86, p. 74-75.
"This Is Not a Poem." [JINJPo] (9:1) 86, p. 20.
"What the Pope Dreams First Night on the Job." [PoetryNW] (27:3) Aut 86, p.
   24-25.
"The Wooden Boat." [JINJPo] (9:1) 86, p. 18.
"The Wooden Boat." [Outbr] (16/17) Fall 85-Spr 86, p. 76.

4096. PARKER, Doris
    "Appeal." [SanFPJ] (8:2) 85, p. 55-56.
    "Letter." [Wind] (16:57) 86, p. 32.
    "The Reason Why" (for Jack Elder and Stacey Merkt). [SanFPJ] (8:2) 85, p. 54.
4097. PARKER, Lizbeth
    "The Fine Line." [Bogg] (55) 86, p. 20.
4098. PARKER, Susan
    "The Rubber Band." [Rampike] (5:2) 86, p. 71.
    "Swee' Pea Appassionata." [Rampike] (5:1) 86, p. 37.
4099. PARKER-LOPEZ, Carolie
    "A Field in New Hampshire." [Jacaranda] (2:1) Fall 86, p. 35.
    "The night stumbles away." [Jacaranda] (2:1) Fall 86, p. 34.
4100. PARKIN, Andrew
    "The Fall of Paris." [CanLit] (111) Wint 86, p. 67.
4101. PARQUE, Richard A.
    "Annamese Hands." [Sam] (46:2 release 182) 86, p. 75-76.
4102. PARRIS, P. B.
    "Drowned in Bruges." [Vis] (22) 86, p. 39.
4103. PARSONS, Bruce
    "History." [AntigR] (64) Wint 86, p. 14.
4104. PARTRIDGE, Dixie
    "Absence." [StoneC] (14:1/2) Fall-Wint 86-87, p. 20.
    "Bequest" (Oregon Coast, 1983). [KanQ] (18:1/2) Wint-Spr 86, p. 236-237.
    "For the Men Who Lived at the Old 3rd West Hotel in Salt Lake City." [SnapD] (9:2)
        Spr 86, p. 4-5.
    "Nocturne, October." [CrabCR] (4:1) Fall-Wint 86, p. 3.
    "Prevailing Wind." [IndR] (9:2) Spr 86, p. 100-101.
4105. PASS, John
    "A Short Chain." [MalR] (75) Je 86, p. 49-60.
4106. PASSALACQUA, Carlos M.
    "Identidad." [Mairena] (8:22) 86, p. 120.
4107. PASTAN, Linda
    "The Animals." [DenQ] (20:4/21:1) Spr-Sum 86, p. 18-19.
    "Ars Poetica." [GrandS] (5:3) Spr 86, p. 157-158.
    "At the Loom." [Poetry] (149:1) O 86, p. 5.
    "At Xian." [Ploughs] (12:3) 86, p. 18-19.
    "Before the Hurricane." [StoneC] (14:1/2) Fall-Wint 86-87, p. 58.
    "Bird on Bough." [Ploughs] (12:3) 86, p. 20-21.
    "Degas: 'Intérieur'." [NewRep] (194:5) 3 F 86, p. 38.
    "Degas: 'Intérieur'." [StoneC] (14:1/2) Fall-Wint 86-87, p. 58-59.
    "Elegy." [Poetry] (149:1) O 86, p. 4.
    "Epilogue" (for J. I.). [GeoR] (40:3) Fall 86, p. 764.
    "Erosion." [Poetry] (149:1) O 86, p. 2-3.
    "Eve, Long Afterwards." [DenQ] (20:4/21:1) Spr-Sum 86, p. 16-17.
    "Grudnow." [Poetry] (149:1) O 86, p. 1-2.
    "The Imperfect Paradise." [Poetry] (147:6) Mr 86, p. 343-345.
    "In the Rearview Mirror." [Sonora] (10) Spr 86, p. 18.
    "The Printer" (for Roland Hoover). [GeoR] (40:3) Fall 86, p. 763.
    "Prologue." [GeoR] (40:3) Fall 86, p. 765.
    "Proverbs." [StoneC] (14:1/2) Fall-Wint 86-87, p. 59-60.
    "Root Canal." [PennR] (1:1) 85, p. 52.
    "The Safecracker." [Ploughs] (12:3) 86, p. 22.
    "Song of the Hypochondriac." [GrandS] (5:3) Spr 86, p. 159-160.
    "To a Daughter Leaving Home." [AmerV] (2) Spr 86, p. 5.
    "A Walk before Breakfast." [Atlantic] (257:1) Ja 86, p. 45.
4108. PASTOR, Ned
    "If You're Bored, Why Not Nosh on a Bit of Nash?" [Amelia] (3:4) Fall 86, p.
        80-81.
    "Let 'Em Eat Liverwurst!" [Amelia] (3:4) Fall 86, p. 81-82.
4109. PATEL, Gieve
    "The Ambiguous Fate of Gieve Patel, He Being Neither Muslim nor Hindu in India."
        [LitR] (29:4) Sum 86, p. 526.
4110. PATEL, Umang
    "Devil." [Grain] (14:2) My 86, p. 42.
    "A Ghazal." [Grain] (14:2) My 86, p. 43.

4111. PATRIKIOS, Titos
  "Foresight" (tr. by Peter Mackridge). [Verse] (5) 86, p. 57.
  "Half-Finished Letter" (tr. by Peter Mackridge). [Verse] (5) 86, p. 58.
  "The Mountains" (tr. by Peter Mackridge). [Verse] (5) 86, p. 57.
  "Secret Life" (tr. by Peter Mackridge). [Verse] (5) 86, p. 57.
4112. PATSANI, Prasanna
  "Letters to God" (tr. by Bibhu Padhi). [RiverS] (20) 86, p. 54-55.
4113. PATT, John
  "American Capillary." [StoneC] (13:3/4) Spr-Sum 86, p. 2.
4114. PATTEN, Karl
  "Flying over This Death, This Life." [LitR] (30:1) Fall 86, p. 60.
PATTERSON, Bruce Woods
  See WOODS-PATTERSON, Bruce
4115. PATTERSON, Raymond R.
  "Ars Poetica." [PaintedB] (28) Ap 86, p. 7.
4116. PATTERSON, Veronica
  "Apples of October." [SouthernPR] (26:1) Spr 86, p. 35-36.
  "Ayre Street." [ColR] (NS 13:1) Fall 85, p. 25-26.
  "The Dancer between Them." [BellR] (9:2) Fall 86, p. 48.
  "Grace" (for my daughters). [ColR] (NS 13:1) Fall 85, p. 27.
  "He." [DeKalbLAJ] (19:2) 86, p. 44.
  "The Pillar of Salt Looks Forward." [DeKalbLAJ] (19:2) 86, p. 45.
  "Scheherazade Listens to a Seagull, Once My Mother." [ColR] (NS 13:1) Fall 85, p. 28-29.
4117. PAU-LLOSA, Ricardo
  "Déjeuner sur l'Eau" (for Dominique). [ForidaR] (14:1) Spr-Sum 86, p. 81-83.
4118. PAULENICH, Craig
  "Black Lake." [SoCaR] (18:2) Spr 86, p. 54.
  "The Drift of the Hunt." [SoCaR] (18:2) Spr 86, p. 55.
PAULSON, Daria J. Montero
  See MONTERO-PAULSON, Daria J.
PAULUS SILENTIARIUS
  See SILENTIARIUS, Paulus
4119. PAVESE, Cesare
  "The Cats Will Know" (tr. by Alan Williamson). [AmerPoR] (15:6) N-D 86, p. 9.
  "I Will Pass through Piazza di Spagna" (tr. by Alan Williamson). [AmerPoR] (15:6) N-D 86, p. 9.
4120. PAVLICH, Walter
  "Wondering over Thomas James (1946-1974)." [SilverFR] (11) Sum 86, p. 34-35.
4121. PAVLOVIC, Miodrag
  "War" (tr. by Bernard Johnson). [Verse] (6) 86, p. 51.
4122. PAWLAK, Mark
  "A German Lesson" (Die Verarbeite, The Process). [HangL] (49) Spr 86, p. 37.
  "Like Butterflies" (after Charles Reznikoff, for Donna Brook). [HangL] (49) Spr 86, p. 38.
4123. PAWLOWSKI, Robert
  "Oceanic." [MemphisSR] (6:1/2) Spr 86, p. 51.
4124. PAYERAS, Mario
  "In the Chama Mountains" (tr. by John Oliver Simon). [InterPR] (12:1) Spr 86, p. 31.
  "Sierra de Chama" (from *Plural*, 1984). [InterPR] (12:1) Spr 86, p. 30.
4125. PAZ, Octavio
  "A Fable of Joan Miro" (tr. by Eliot Weinberger). [Sulfur] (6:2, issue 17) 86, p. 7-9.
  "Huatesca Woman" (tr. by Kent Johnson). [ClockR] (3:1) 85, p. 55.
  "Kostas Papaioannou" (for Nitsa and Keta, tr. by Eliot Weinberger). [MassR] (27:3/4) Fall-Wint 86, p. 571-574.
4126. PEACOCK, Molly
  "Anger Sweetened." [Boulevard] (1:3) Fall 86, p. 18.
  "Asylum House." [OntR] (24) Spr-Sum 86, p. 92.
  "The Choice." [Poetry] (147:5) F 86, p. 266-267.
  "Come Back Here, Please." [Confr] (32) Spr-Sum 86, p. 49.
  "Commands of Love." [Poetry] (147:5) F 86, p. 268.
  "Dilation, Termination, and Curettage." [PoetryE] (20/21) Fall 86, p. 116.
  "Dream Come True." [Boulevard] (1:3) Fall 86, p. 16.
  "Food for Talk." [Boulevard] (1:1/2) Wint 86, p. 16.
  "A Hot Day In Agrigento." [ParisR] (28:100) Sum-Fall 86, p. 204-205.

PEACOCK

"Jones Beach on the Mediterranean." [Boulevard] (1:3) Fall 86, p. 17.
"Living without Meaning." [PartR] (53:2) 86, p. 235-236.
"Merely by Wilderness." [PoetryE] (20/21) Fall 86, p. 115.
"Parrots of the World." [Boulevard] (1:1/2) Wint 86, p. 19-20.
"Prayer." [Poetry] (147:5) F 86, p. 267.
"Seeing What It's Like." [OntR] (24) Spr-Sum 86, p. 90-91.
"The Valley of the Monsters." [Boulevard] (1:1/2) Wint 86, p. 17-18.
4127. PEALE, W. B.
"Ideology into Action." [HarvardA] (119:4) My 86, p. 31.
"Portrait of a Young Woman." [HarvardA] (119:4) My 86, p. 34.
4128. PEARL, Dan
"Gardener's Choice." [BellArk] (2:4) Jl-Ag 86, p. 1.
"Seen through a Cane." [BellArk] (2:4) Jl-Ag 86, p. 16.
"The Teacher Discovered." [BellArk] (2:5) S-O 86, p. 4.
4129. PEARSON, Helen
"A Way of Saying Things." [BellArk] (2:6) N-D 86, p. 1.
"The Widower." [BellArk] (2:6) N-D 86, p. 3.
4130. PEATTIE, Noel
"The Missionaries Explore Central Asia." [YellowS] (18) Spr 86, p. 44.
"To the Topmost Peaks." [CapeR] (21:1) Spr 86, p. 8.
4131. PEAVLER, Janet
"Morning Ritual." [EngJ] (75:2) F 86, p. 96.
4132. PEAVY, Katherine B.
"The Prophet." [Amelia] (3:1) Ja 86, p. 72.
4133. PECK, Mary
"Promiscuity Long Term." [HolCrit] (23:1) F 86, back cover.
"Saturday Matinee." [HolCrit] (23:2) Ap 86, p. 17.
4134. PECKENPAUGH, Angela
"Leaving the Known." [Interim] (5:2) Fall 86, p. 17.
"Xmas 85." [Interim] (5:2) Fall 86, p. 16.
4135. PEDEN, Margaret Sayers
"Ode to Numbers" (tr. of Pablo Neruda). [MassR] (27:3/4) Fall-Wint 86, p.
464-466.
"Ode to the Americas" (tr. of Pablo Neruda). [MassR] (27:3/4) Fall-Wint 86, p.
461-463.
4136. PEDERSON, Cynthia (Cynthia S.)
"I Have Given Up Asking Questions." [CapeR] (21:2) Fall 86, p. 23.
"The Key." [MidwQ] (27:2) Wint 86, p. 211.
"Theories." [MidwQ] (28:1) Aut 86, p. 84-85.
4137. PEDERSON, Miriam
"Small Reminders." [PassN] (7:1) Fall-Wint 85-86, p. 14.
4138. PEELER, Tim
"Beclouded Child." [PoeticJ] (14) 86, p. 32.
PEENEN, H. J. Van
See Van PEENEN, H. J.
4139. PELIEU, Claude
"Bob Kaufman" (to Eileen & Parker, tr. by Mary Beach). [RedBass] (11) 86, p. 10.
"Mary's Latest Paintings." [ParisR] (28:101) Wint 86, p. 277-278.
4140. PELTER, Maurice A.
"Epitaph for Vincent." [InterPR] (12:2) Fall 86, p. 102.
4141. PEÑA-REYES, Myrna
"Grandmother's Jewels." [Contact] (7:38/39/40) Wint-Spr 86, p. 38.
"The Manong and His Dog." [Contact] (7:38/39/40) Wint-Spr 86, p. 38.
4142. PENARANDA, Oscar
"Peace Offering." [Contact] (7:38/39/40) Wint-Spr 86, p. 45.
"Point of Departure." [Contact] (7:38/39/40) Wint-Spr 86, p. 45.
4143. PENFOLD, Nita
"The Secret." [YetASM] (5) 86, p. 8.
4144. PENN, J. L.
"Barstow California." [Amelia] (3:4) Fall 86, p. 108.
4145. PENNANT, Edmund
"Eberhart Versus Williams." [NegC] (6:2/3) Spr-Sum 86, p. 60-61.
"Four Thirty." [Confr] (32) Spr-Sum 86, p. 71.
"The Three of You." [Confr] (32) Spr-Sum 86, p. 72.
4146. PENNER, Ralph
"To the East." [LittleM] (15:1) 86, p. 20-21.

4147. PENNY, Michael
"Last Will and Testament." [AntigR] (66/67) Sum-Aut 86, p. 169.
4148. PEPPE, Holly
"Nightsong." [ManhatPR] (7) Sum 86, p. 52.
"La Primavera." [ManhatPR] (7) Sum 86, p. 52.
4149. PERALTA, Bertalicia
"I Want to Find, Desparately I Look" (tr. by Zoe Anglesey). [MassR] (27:3/4)
Fall-Wint 86, p. 570.
4150. PERCHIK, Simon
"4. As if I could blind the man holding these leaves." [MidAR] (7:1) 86, p. 21-22.
"29. If I close my eyes." [Puerto] (22:1) Fall 86, p. 56-57.
"42: More rich foam: my first meal still warm." [Bogg] (56) 86, p. 12-13.
"81." [BallSUF] (26:4) Aut 85, p. 66.
"85." [BallSUF] (26:4) Aut 85, p. 53.
"105: Creaking with fruit and ice." [Bogg] (55) 86, p. 7.
"130. The Earth dazed from thirst." [Os] (22) 86, p. 12.
"131. All night a loneliness." [Os] (22) 86, p. 13.
"Above the Weather." [SoDakR] (24:3) Aut 86, p. 155.
"Allen's Carpet Store." [Wind] (16:58) 86, p. 36.
"I calm my table." [LitR] (29:3) Spr 86, p. 344-345.
"I held his head" ("Untitled"). [WritersF] (12) Fall 86, p. 173.
"Poem: Afraid and this stream." [ColEng] (48:7) N 86, p. 688.
"Poem: This dead root, its light." [ColEng] (48:7) N 86, p. 687.
"Tighter than a branding iorn." [Wind] (16:58) 86, p. 36.
"Where is this tree going, footsteps." [MidAR] (6:2) 86, p. 107.
"Who can loosen your wedding ring, a finger." [MidAR] (6:2) 86, p. 108.
4151. PERDIGO, Luisa M.
"Tú Refas." [Mester] (15:2) Fall 86, p. 52.
4152. PEREIRA, Teresinka (Teresinka Alves)
"Bulevares." [Mairena] (8:22) 86, p. 104.
"Es la Mujer de Este Pais." [LetFem] (12:1/2) Primavera-Otoño 86, p. 147.
4153. PERELMAN, Bob
"Let's Say." [Sulfur] (5:3, issue 15) 86, p. 139-140.
"Parts." [Temblor] (4) 86, p. 62-63.
"Person." [Sulfur] (5:3, issue 15) 86, p. 140-141.
"Sentimental Mechanics" (for Ben Friedlander). [Temblor] (4) 86, p. 66.
"Word Stimuli." [Sulfur] (5:3, issue 15) 86, p. 138-139.
4154. PEREYRA, Silvina L.
"Busco a un hombre en infinitas instancias." [Mairena] (8:21) 86, p. 111-112.
4155. PEREZ, Ilma Valenzuela de
"Brisa de Estío." [LetFem] (12:1/2) Primavera-Otoño 86, p. 150-152.
"Escritor." [LetFem] (10:1) Spr 84, p. 108.
"La Noche." [LetFem] (10:1) Spr 84, p. 107.
4156. PEREZ, Luis M.
"El Niño de Mi Calle." [Mairena] (8:22) 86, p. 108.
4157. PEREZ FIRMAT, Gustavo
"Dos Poemas." [LindLM] (5:4) O-D 86, p. 23.
4158. PEREZ VALENZUELA, Liliana
"Vuelo sobre unos Labios." [LetFem] (10:1) Spr 84, p. 104-106.
4159. PERILLO, Lucia
"First Job / Seventeen." [Ploughs] (12:4) 86, p. 155-156.
"The News (A Manifesto)." [Ploughs] (12:4) 86, p. 157-158.
"The Turtle Lovers." [Ploughs] (12:4) 86, p. 159-160.
4160. PERIN, Casey C.
"Hawk in the Wild." [WoosterR] (5) Spr 86, p. 73.
4161. PERKINS, James A. (James Ashbrook)
"Confessions of a Mid-Summer Fall Upwards into Grace." [SpoonRQ] (11:2) Spr
86, p. 22.
"Invisible Deaths." [ColR] (NS 13:1) Fall 85, p. 72.
4162. PERLBERG, Mark
"Summer." [Hudson] (39:2) Sum 86, p. 271.
4163. PERLMAN, John
"Maple." [Northeast] (series 4:3) Spr 86, p. 26.
"Reading." [Abraxas] (34) 86, p. 26-27.
4164. PERRAULT, John
"Allende's Last Letter to Pablo Neruda." [SanFPJ] (9:1) 86, p. 37.

"Apartheid." [SanFPJ] (9:1) 86, p. 37.
4165. PERREAULT, George
"November: The South Porch." [WritersF] (12) Fall 86, p. 245.
4166. PESEROFF, Joyce
"Closing Up House." [MissouriR] (9:2) 86, p. 207.
"The Local Boy." [Pequod] (22) 86, p. 42-43.
"Sentimental Pictures." [Pequod] (22) 86, p. 40-41.
4167. PESSOA, Fernando
"A Cross? On the Door of the Tobacco Shop?" (tr. by George Monteiro).
[Translation] (17) Fall 86, p. 225.
"The God Pan Did Not Die" (tr. by George Monteiro). [Translation] (17) Fall 86, p.
226.
"An Instantly Venerable Sonnet" (tr. by George Monteiro). [Translation] (17) Fall
86, p. 229.
"Self-Analysis" (tr. by George Monteiro). [Translation] (17) Fall 86, p. 230.
"Today I Read Nearly Two Pages" (tr. by George Monteiro). [Translation] (17) Fall
86, p. 227.
"Tripe, Porto Style" (tr. by George Monteiro). [Translation] (17) Fall 86, p. 228.
4168. PESSOLANO, Linda
"Monochrome." [SouthernPR] (26:1) Spr 86, p. 24.
PETER, Melanie Blackshear
See BLACKSHEAR-PETER, Melanie
4169. PETERS, Ann Marie
"The Three." [SingHM] (14) 86, p. 6.
4170. PETERS, Nancy
"White Sands." [PraS] (60:2) Sum 86, p. 120.
4171. PETERS, Patricia Claire
"Letter from Harry." [Hudson] (39:3) Aut 86, p. 462-463.
4172. PETERS, Robert
"As the Bird Wings into the Tree." [Contact] (8:41/42/43) Fall-Wint 86-87, p. 74.
"The Blood Countess: Erzebet Bathory of Hungary" (Excerpt). [ConnPR] (5:1) 86,
p. 37-39.
"Clouds." [Contact] (8:41/42/43) Fall-Wint 86-87, p. 75.
"Dear Mom." [JamesWR] (3:3) Spr 86, p. 15.
"Pansy, Rose." [Contact] (8:41/42/43) Fall-Wint 86-87, p. 74.
"Rugs and Moccasins." [Contact] (8:41/42/43) Fall-Wint 86-87, p. 75.
"Sweet Macho Nothings." [JamesWR] (3:3) Spr 86, p. 15.
4173. PETERSEN, Karen (See also PETERSON, Karen)
"False Alarm." [PraF] (7:3) Aut 86, p. 121.
"Green Folly's Reprieve." [WritersL] (1986:3), p. 18.
"Some Mistake." [PraF] (7:3) Aut 86, p. 120.
4174. PETERSON, Allan
"Atmosphere got Even." [Poem] (55) Mr 86, p. 25.
"Knight." [WebR] (11:2) Fall 86, p. 58.
"Migrations." [Poem] (55) Mr 86, p. 24.
"A Sharp." [WebR] (11:2) Fall 86, p. 58.
"Under the Moon Whose Light Grows Nothing." [WebR] (11:2) Fall 86, p. 57.
4175. PETERSON, Amy
"Tragedy at Sea: The Slave Ship" (tr. of Antonio de Castro Alves). [Translation] (17)
Fall 86, p. 268-274.
4176. PETERSON, Ann
"Footnote to the Dream." [Acts] (5) 86, p. 50.
"Ghost Bird." [Acts] (5) 86, p. 45-48.
"Steady State." [Acts] (5) 86, p. 49.
4177. PETERSON, Geoff
"Terminal." [Sam] (46:2 release 182) 86, p. 114.
4178. PETERSON, Jim
"Flight." [TarRP] (26:1) Fall 86, p. 17.
"The Prodigal Father Speaks." [NegC] (6:1) Wint 86, p. 45-46.
4179. PETERSON, John J.
"Bad." [LakeSR] (20) 86, p. 18.
"Blind at Birth." [NegC] (6:4) Fall 86, p. 97.
4180. PETERSON, Karen (See also PETERSEN, Karen)
"Advice for Anatomy Students." [Interim] (5:1) Spr 86, p. 20.
"Los Desaparecidos." [Rampike] (5:1) 86, p. 73.
"To a Painter, His Works on His Walls." [Prima] (10) 86, p. 9.

4181. PETOCZ, András
"Deux Poems" (Adaptation française par Tibor Papp). [Rampike] (5:2) 86, p. 49.

4182. PETREMAN, David A.
"December Rain." [BallSUF] (27:4) Aut 86, p. 71.
"Flying." [BallSUF] (27:4) Aut 86, p. 70.
"In the Rookery." [BallSUF] (27:4) Aut 86, p. 70.

4183. PETRIE, Paul
"The Atrocity." [SouthernR] (22:3) Sum 86, p. 560-561.
"The Battlefield." [CrossCur] (5:4/6:1) 86, p. 137-138.
"Energy Audit." [KanQ] (18:1/2) Wint-Spr 86, p. 262.
"A Footnote to Epictetus." [HolCrit] (23:5) D 86, p. 16.
"Homecoming." [LittleM] (15:1) 86, p. 30.
"The Song." [Raritan] (5:3) Wint 86, p. 79-81.
"Thoreau." [ChrC] (103:5) 5-12 F 86, p. 115.
"To the Losers All Over the World." [KanQ] (18:1/2) Wint-Spr 86, p. 266.
"The Turning Point." [KanQ] (18:1/2) Wint-Spr 86, p. 266-267.
"Under the Bridge." [NegC] (6:4) Fall 86, p. 49.

4184. PETRINI, Michael
"Nui Ba Den" (Black Virgin Mountain). [Sam] (46:2 release 182) 86, p. 65.

4185. PETRINOVIC, Deborah
"Death as the Male Pretender." [KanQ] (18:4) Fall 86, p. 41.

4186. PETRONIUS, Gaius
"In love's brief act there is quick, obscene delight" ("Untitled", tr. by Joseph
    Salemi). [Paint] (13:25/26) Spr-Aut 86, p. 33.

4187. PETROUSKE, Rosalie Sanara
"Wings." [SouthernPR] (26:2) Fall 86, p. 65-68.

4188. PETRY-ANDERSON, Maxine S.
"What They Could Not Take With Them." [MinnR] (NS 27) Fall 86, p. 23-24.

4189. PETTEYS, D. F. (David F.)
"Calendar." [ManhatPR] (6) Wint-Spr 85-86, p. 35.
"Decline and Fall." [SouthernHR] (20:1) Wint 86, p. 70.
"Terminal Moraine." [KanQ] (18:1/2) Wint-Spr 86, p. 294.

4190. PETTIT, Michael
"Girl Walking Towards Woman, Carrying Flower" (Muybridge, *The Human Figure
    . . .*, plate 184). [SouthernHR] (20:4) Fall 86, p. 343.
"The Human Figure in Motion" (after the photographs of Eadwaerd Muybridge).
    [PoetryNW] (27:2) Sum 86, p. 36-39.
"Men Wrestling" (Eadweard Muybridge, *The Human Figure in Motion*, plate 67).
    [SouthernHR] (20:4) Fall 86, p. 342.

4191. PFINGSTON, Roger
"Grady's Lunch." [WoosterR] (6) Fall 86, p. 19.
"Grady's New Relationship." [WoosterR] (6) Fall 86, p. 18-19.
"Grady's Pain." [IndR] (9:2) Spr 86, p. 58.
"Quarriers." [SpoonRQ] (11:4) Fall 86, p. 12.
"Sunday Drive, 1952." [SpoonRQ] (11:4) Fall 86, p. 14.
"Under Mid-American Stars." [SpoonRQ] (11:4) Fall 86, p. 13.

4192. PFLUEGER, Virginia
"The Journey to Grandmother Ruth's Funeral." [BellArk] (2:2) Mr-Ap 86, p. 2.
"The Potter and the Poet Have Dinner." [BellArk] (2:2) Mr-Ap 86, p. 5.

PHAKIR, Lalan Shah
See LALAN SHAH PHAKIR

4193. PHELPS, Donald
"For a Female Parole Officer." [Confr] (33/34) Fall-Wint 86-87, p. 221-222.
"Swift and Sharp." [Shen] (36:2) 86, p. 24-26.

4194. PHIFER, Marjorie Maddox
"Monday Mornings." [CrossCur] (5:4/6:1) 86, p. 136.

4195. PHILLIPPY, Patricia
"The Dress." [AmerS] (55:4) Aut 86, p. 494.
"Epistle to Posterity." [PoetryNW] (27:1) Spr 86, p. 5-6.

4196. PHILLIPS, Alice Golembiewski
"The Rapture Is Coming." [GeoR] (40:3) Fall 86, p. 766.

4197. PHILLIPS, Dennis
"The World" (Excerpts). [Acts] (5) 86, p. 75-76.
"A World" (Selections: 2 poems). [Temblor] (4) 86, p. 124-125.

4198. PHILLIPS, James
"Dance Defines." [Vis] (21) 86, p. 38.

"Drift Lens." [Vis] (21) 86, p. 38.
"A Trace of Blood." [Vis] (21) 86, p. 37.
4199. PHILLIPS, Juanita
"Black." [Amelia] (3:4) Fall 86, p. 18.
4200. PHILLIPS, Louis
"Ars Amatorio." [MidAR] (6:1) 86?, p. 38.
"Kilroy at Gettysburg." [Event] (15:2) 86, p. 174-175.
"On the Main Staircase inside the Metropolitan Museum of Art." [NoDaQ] (54:2) Spr 86, p. 185.
"One Man's Sermon on Dreaming." [AntigR] (65) Spr 86, p. 57.
"The Poet, Bearing with Him a Modicum of Pessimism & the Ideal of the Sublime Life . . ." [MidAR] (6:1) 86?, p. 37.
"Promises." [StoneC] (13:3/4) Spr-Sum 86, p. 52.
"Staking Tomato Plants by the Light of the Moon." [AntigR] (65) Spr 86, p. 56.
4201. PHILLIPS, Robert
"The Balance." [Chelsea] (45) 86, p. 92.
"The Bittersweet." [Chelsea] (45) 86, p. 93.
"Hardwood." [NewRep] (195:8) 25 Ag 86, p. 38.
4202. PHILLIPS, Walt
"Action." [SlipS] (6) 86, p. 34.
"Adventure." [SlipS] (6) 86, p. 33.
"Air Bubbles at 9:10 P.M." [SlipS] (6) 86, p. 34.
"Dina." [Sam] (45:4 release 180) 86, p. 12.
"Disabilities." [Amelia] (3:1) Ja 86, p. 76.
"Down Home." [Sam] (45:4 release 180) 86, p. 26.
"Dream." [SlipS] (6) 86, p. 33.
"Drunk on a Train." [Sam] (46:5 [i.e. 46:1] release 181) 86, p. 30.
"Homer." [CrabCR] (3:3) Sum 86, p. 27.
"How I Do It." [Amelia] (3:1) Ja 86, p. 76.
"Imagine." [Sam] (44:2 release 174) 86, p. 27.
"Let Me at That Center Ring!" [Sam] (44:3 release 175) 86, p. 16.
"One of a Number of Flavors." [Amelia] (3:2) Spr 86, p. 103.
"Perspectives." [Sam] (44:2 release 174) 86, back cover.
"Souvenirs." [Amelia] (3:1) Ja 86, p. 76.
"Transactions." [Amelia] (3:2) Spr 86, p. 103.
4203. PHILLIPS, Wendy
"Metaphor." [Jacaranda] (2:1) Fall 86, p. 31.
4204. PIAGGIO, Edda
"Adiestramiento." [Mairena] (8:22) 86, p. 95.
PIAO-YÜAN, Tai
See TAI, Piao-yüan
4205. PICANO, Felice
"In a Provincial Airport." [ConnPR] (4:1) 85, p. 24-25.
4206. PICHASKE, David
"Farm Report, Western Minnesota 10/26/85." [SpoonRQ] (11:4) Fall 86, p. 16-17.
4207. PICHON, Ulysses A.
"Festival Reminiscence." [Obs] (NS 1:1/2) Spr-Sum 86, p. 79-80.
"Lazy Man" ("Untitled"). [Obs] (NS 1:1/2) Spr-Sum 86, p. 81.
"Thought I Would Be Happy Blues." [Obs] (NS 1:1/2) Spr-Sum 86, p. 78-79.
4208. PICKARD, Deanna Louise
"Not Letting Go." [PassN] (7:2) Spr-Sum 86, p. 19.
4209. PIERCE, Kathleen
"Gofer Ned." [SlipS] (6) 86, p. 64.
"It Got Tough." [SlipS] (6) 86, p. 63.
4210. PIERCEY, Wallace, Jr.
"A Certain Past." [Dandel] (13:1) Spr-Sum 86, p. 24.
"Kissed by a Stranger." [Dandel] (13:1) Spr-Sum 86, p. 26.
"Snow on the Steeples." [Dandel] (13:1) Spr-Sum 86, p. 25.
4211. PIERCY, Marge
"Baboons in the Perennial Bed." [NegC] (6:4) Fall 86, p. 12.
"Burial by Salt." [ManhatPR] (7) Sum 86, p. 6-9.
"Dead Waters." [AmerV] (3) Sum 86, p. 77.
"The Fecund Complain They Are Not Honored." [NegC] (6:4) Fall 86, p. 16.
"The Housing Project at Drancy." [NegC] (6:4) Fall 86, p. 14-15.
"It Grows on You." [PaintedB] (29) Ag 86, p. 31.
"Nocturne." [NewL] (53:1) Fall 86, p. 30-31.

"Sleeping with Cats." [YellowS] (19) Sum 86, p. 42.
"Something to Look Forward To." [Calyx] (9:2/3) Wint 86, p. 86.
"The Whole That Is Made of Wanting." [NegC] (6:4) Fall 86, p. 13.
4212. PIERMAN, Carol J.
"The Incredible Journey." [CentR] (30:3) Sum 86, p. 349-350.
"Sincere." [RiverS] (20) 86, p. 35.
PIERO, W. S. di
See Di PIERO, W. S.
4213. PIES, Ronald
"Missing Children." [LitR] (30:1) Fall 86, p. 86.
PIETRO, Marylou di
See DiPIETRO, Marylou
4214. PIETRZYK, Leslie
"Fading." [SmPd] (23:2, issue 67) Spr 86, p. 35-37.
4215. PIJEWSKI, John
"Education." [Ploughs] (12:3) 86, p. 130-131.
"Remembering Anna." [Ploughs] (12:3) 86, p. 127-129.
"Whatever the Weather." [Ploughs] (12:3) 86, p. 132.
4216. PILCHER, Barry Edgar
"Poetry, Are You Getting Enough of It." [Bogg] (55) 86, p. 51.
"Sky mushrooms." [Bogg] (55) 86, p. 39.
"Walking upside down." [Bogg] (56) 86, p. 7.
4217. PIÑA, Cristina
"Dr. Jekill and Mr. Hyde." [Mester] (15:2) Fall 86, p. 54.
"Ficha Técnica." [Mester] (15:2) Fall 86, p. 53.
4218. PINEDA, Carlos
"On Los Leones Avenue" (tr. by Sesshu Foster). [CentralP] (9) Spr 86, p. 82-83.
4219. PINEGAR, Pat
"Holding the Hand of the Dying" (for my father). [TarRP] (24:2) Spr 85, p. 22.
PING, Chou
See CHOU, Ping
4220. PINNER, David
"Children." [InterPR] (12:2) Fall 86, p. 50.
"The Light." [InterPR] (12:2) Fall 86, p. 56.
"Sea." [InterPR] (12:2) Fall 86, p. 52-54.
"Smoke." [InterPR] (12:2) Fall 86, p. 51.
"Stunted Man." [InterPR] (12:2) Fall 86, p. 55-56.
4221. PINSKER, Sanford
"At the Astoria Hotel: Leningrad." [NoDaQ] (54:4) Fall 86, p. 74.
"On First Seeing the Golden Domes of St. Basil's Church." [NoDaQ] (54:4) Fall 86,
p. 73.
4222. PINSKY, Robert
"Incantation" (tr. of Czeslaw Milosz, w. the author). [YaleR] (76:1) Aut 86, p. 1.
"Lament for the Makers." [ParisR] (28:100) Sum-Fall 86, p. 206-208.
"The Uncreation." [NewRep] (194:15) 14 Ap 86, p. 38.
PINTO, José Rafael Blengio
See BLENGIO PINTO, José Rafael
4223. PIOMBINO, Nick
"An angel fell under a shadow of conceptions." [Sulfur] (6:2, issue 17) 86, p. 37.
"My Lady Carries Stones." [Sulfur] (6:2, issue 17) 86, p. 38.
"The Pyramids." [Sulfur] (6:2, issue 17) 86, p. 37.
"Source." [Sink] (2) 86, p. 58-61.
4224. PIPER, Janet
"One Small Head." [Iowa] (16:1) Wint 86, p. 181.
"Vista." [Iowa] (16:1) Wint 86, p. 181.
4225. PIPER, Paul
"At an Outdoor Cafe." [Sulfur] (6:2, issue 17) 86, p. 102.
"Dedoubler 1." [Sulfur] (6:2, issue 17) 86, p. 102.
"Meditation." [Sulfur] (6:2, issue 17) 86, p. 104.
"Metaphor." [Sulfur] (6:2, issue 17) 86, p. 103.
"Sorrow." [Sulfur] (6:2, issue 17) 86, p. 102-103.
4226. PITT-KETHLEY, Fiona
"1984." [Verse] (5) 86, p. 42.
4227. PITTS, R. Evan
"Cows Discovering They Are Cows." [WormR] (26:4, issue 104) 86, p. 147.
"The Dying Sun." [WormR] (26:4, issue 104) 86, p. 147.

4228. PITZER, Jack
"The Double Helix." [BallSUF] (26:4) Aut 85, p. 40.
"Phoenix (Blue)." [BallSUF] (27:4) Aut 86, p. 47.
4229. PIZAN, Christine de
"Cent Ballades XIV." [CumbPR] (5:2) Spr 86, p. 46.
4230. PIZARRO, Michelle
"Lesson." [Jacaranda] (2:1) Fall 86, p. 40.
4231. PLA, Josefina
"Cómo escribir el verso que llene este vacío?" [Mairena] (8:22) 86, p. 15.
"Puedo contar mi vida por mis noches?" [Mairena] (8:22) 86, p. 33.
"Soñé Quise contar el sueño en un poema." [Mairena] (8:22) 86, p. 43.
"Yo Te Conoci." [Mairena] (8:22) 86, p. 34.
4232. PLA BENITO, Juan Luis
"Y Siempre una Paloma Manuscrita." [Mairena] (8:22) 86, p. 107.
4233. PLAICE, Stephen
"The Battlefield (Lewes 1264)." [CumbPR] (5:2) Spr 86, p. 66.
"The Logical Thirties." [CumbPR] (5:2) Spr 86, p. 62-63.
"The Serpent." [CumbPR] (5:2) Spr 86, p. 64-65.
4234. PLANELLS, Antonio
"El Cocodrilo Azul." [Inti] (21) Primavera 85, p. 124.
"Frío." [Inti] (21) Primavera 85, p. 123.
"Ha Muerto Borges." [Inti] (21) Primavera 85, p. 121-122.
"Ha Muerto Borges." [Mairena] (8:21) 86, p. 69.
"Mutaciones" (A Jorge Luis Borges). [Mairena] (8:22) 86, p. 118.
"Suicidio en Septiembre." [Inti] (21) Primavera 85, p. 122.
4235. PLANTENGA, Bart
"Almost Church." [JINJPo] (9:1) 86, p. 25.
4236. PLANTOS, Ted
"Twain's Comet." [GreenfR] (13:3/4) Sum-Fall 86, p. 163.
4237. PLATT, Donald
"How Night Comes." [ParisR] (28:101) Wint 86, p. 276.
4238. PLATT, Teri
"Arnarwater Moor." [BellArk] (2:4) Jl-Ag 86, p. 2.
PLESSIS, Rachel Blau du
See DuPLESSIS, Rachel Blau
4239. PLIMPTON, Sarah
"The door is open." [ParisR] (28:99) Spr 86, p. 157.
"You had seen where." [ParisR] (28:99) Spr 86, p. 159.
"You opened the door." [ParisR] (28:99) Spr 86, p. 158.
4240. PLUMLY, Stanley
"Analogies of the Leaf." [Atlantic] (258:3) S 86, p. 79.
"Blossom." [GeoR] (40:3) Fall 86, p. 767-768.
"Cedar Waxwing on Scarlet Firethorn." [NewYorker] (62:22) 21 Jl 86, p. 36.
"Early and Late in the Month." [NewYorker] (62:2) 3 Mr 86, p. 38.
4241. PLUMMER, Deb
"Northeaster Tides." [PoeticJ] (13) 86, p. 21.
"The Piano." [CapeR] (21:1) Spr 86, p. 39.
4242. PLUMPP, Sterling (Sterling D.)
"Blues: The Story Always Untold" (Selections: 190, 197, 201, 216). [AnotherCM]
(15) 86, p. 68-71.
"Blues from the Bloodseed" (Two sections: 4, 5). [Epoch] (35:2) 86-87, p. 93-97.
"Sanders Bottom" (for Mattie Emmanuel). [OP] (41) Spr 86, p. 8-17.
PO, Li
See LI, Po
4243. POBO, Kenneth
"Funeral Photograph." [MSS] (5:1) 86, p. 141.
"Mulching the Roses." [IndR] (9:1) Wint 86, p. 83.
4244. POEM, Nome
"Labor Day." [DeKalbLAJ] (19:3/4) 86, p. 55.
"The Poet Goes to Word-Processing School" (for DeKalb Tech). [DeKalbLAJ]
(19:3/4) 86, p. 55-56.
"Renegade Backyard Lover." [DeKalbLAJ] (19:3/4) 86, p. 60.
"You Complain I Never Touch You." [DeKalbLAJ] (19:3/4) 86, p. 56-57.
"Yuppie Madness" (Young Urban Professionals). [DeKalbLAJ] (19:3/4) 86, p. 61.

4245. POETKER, Audrey
"She Was Beautiful Then, Dancing" (In memory of Sarah Fehr Klippenstein).
[Waves] (14:3) Wint 86, p. 72.
4246. POIRIER, Thelma
"Crabapples." [Quarry] (35:3) Sum 86, p. 12.
"Lost and Found." [Quarry] (35:3) Sum 86, p. 12.
POL, Miquel Marti i
See MARTI I POL, Miquel
4247. POLAK, Maralyn Lois
"Maté." [PaintedB] (29) Ag 86, p. 74-75.
"Physic." [Boulevard] (1:3) Fall 86, p. 86-87.
"The Visiting Poet." [Boulevard] (1:1/2) Wint 86, p. 161-162.
4248. POLAVARAPU, Malu
"Encounter." [Writ] (17) 85, c86, p. 17.
"Our Affair." [Writ] (17) 85, c86, p. 16.
4249. POLCOVAR, Carol
"Marilyn Monroe." [Contact] (7:38/39/40) Wint-Spr 86, p. 91.
4250. POLITE, Frank
"Siraj." [RiverS] (19) 86, p. 51-53.
"The Strange Ladies Next Door." [RiverS] (19) 86, p. 49-50.
4251. POLITO, Robert
"Boston." [Shen] (36:4) 86, p. 70-72.
"Nana." [YaleR] (75:4) Sum 86, p. 539-541.
4252. POLKINHORN, Harry
"Having Felt to the Botoom Right Body Tone Taps." [Sink] (2) 86, p. 44.
"Placement Violates in Saying." [Sink] (2) 86, p. 43.
"Tiny Spaces." [Sink] (2) 86, p. 42.
4253. POLLET, Sylvester
"Thaw." [BelPoJ] (37:2) Wint 86-87, p. 12-13.
"When." [BelPoJ] (37:2) Wint 86-87, p. 12.
4254. POLLITT, Katha
"Aere Perennius." [NewYorker] (62:20) 7 Jl 86, p. 32.
"Atlantis." [NewRep] (195:22) 1 D 86, p. 38.
"Epithalamion" (for J.F. and D.B.). [Atlantic] (258:3) S 86, p. 78.
"Mind-Body Problem." [NewRep] (195:14) 6 O 86, p. 44.
"Small Comfort." [NewYorker] (62:33) 6 O 86, p. 38.
"A Walk." [NewYorker] (62:1) 24 F 86, p. 85.
"The White Room." [ParisR] (28:100) Sum-Fall 86, p. 209.
4255. POMERANTZ, Marsha
"Forecast" (tr. by the author). [PoetL] (81:2) Sum 86, p. 130.
4256. POND, Judith
"Heat." [MalR] (77) D 86, p. 93.
"June Bug." [PraF] (7:3) Aut 86, p. 93.
"Three Stages of Man" (After a painting by Hans Baldung-Grien). [Descant] (17:2,
#53) Sum 86, p. 85-86.
"Tonight / This Morning." [PraF] (7:3) Aut 86, p. 92.
"Undertow." [MalR] (77) D 86, p. 92.
4257. PONS, Ponç
"The Name of Loneliness Is a Dingy Bar" (La soledat té nom de bar ombrívol, tr. by
James Eddy). [SenR] (16:1) 86, p. 49.
4258. PONSOT, Marie
"Better." [Comm] (113:18) 24 O 86, p. 566.
"Explorers Cry Out Unheard." [Comm] (113:18) 24 O 86, p. 566.
"One Is One." [Comm] (113:18) 24 O 86, p. 566.
"Sonnets." [Comm] (113:18) 24 O 86, p. 566.
"The Title's Last." [Comm] (113:18) 24 O 86, p. 566.
"Unplugged." [Comm] (113:18) 24 O 86, p. 566.
4259. POPE, Deborah
"Firstborn." [SouthernPR] (26:2) Fall 86, p. 61-64.
"Happy." [PoetryNW] (27:2) Sum 86, p. 7-8.
4260. POPE, Mary McGehee
"Astronomy." [DeKalbLAJ] (19:3/4) 86, p. 62.
4261. POPE, Naomi
"Trees." [Grain] (14:2) My 86, p. 27.
4262. PORRAS, José A.
"Tilaran en el Corazon." [Mairena] (8:22) 86, p. 57.

4263. PORRET, Erik
"Blood sight" (tr. of Thomas Bruun, w. Nina Juel Bigbie). [Os] (23) 86, p. 24-25.
"Bound up in blood" (from Masker Uden Navne, tr. of Claus Carstensen, w. Nina Juel Bigbie). [Os] (23) 86, p. 38-39.
"Come to me" (tr. of Thomas Bruun, w. Nina Juel Bigbie). [Os] (23) 86, p. 24-25.
"Copperkisses" (tr. of Claus Carstensen, w. Nina Juel Bigbie). [Os] (23) 86, p. 20.
"Echoes arose in the room" (from Totenbuch, tr. of Claus Carstensen, w. Nina Juel Bigbie). [Os] (23) 86, p. 28.
"Even Further" (tr. of Pia Tafdrup, w. Nina Juel Bigbie). [Os] (23) 86, p. 30-31.
"The Formlessness of Death" (tr. of Claus Carstensen, w. Nina Juel Bigbie). [Os] (23) 86, p. 38-39.
"Polaroid" (tr. of Claus Carstensen, w. Nina Juel Bigbie). [Os] (23) 86, p. 36-37.
"Reading Piece" (from Totenbuch, tr. of Claus Carstensen, w. Nina Juel Bigbie). [Os] (23) 86, p. 36-37.
"Shrapnel in flight" (tr. of Thomas Bruun, w. Nina Juel Bigbie). [Os] (23) 86, p. 22-23.
"The Skin" (tr. of Pia Tafdrup, w. Nina Juel Bigbie). [Os] (23) 86, p. 34-35.
"Spring Flood" (tr. of Pia Tafdrup, w. Nina Juel Bigbie). [Os] (23) 86, p. 32-33.
"With a knife" (tr. of Thomas Bruun, w. Nina Juel Bigbie). [Os] (23) 86, p. 26-27.
4264. PORRITT, R.
"Sermon in England." [CumbPR] (5:2) Spr 86, p. 82.
"Those Things Tending." [CumbPR] (5:2) Spr 86, p. 80-81.
4265. PORTA, Antonio
"Distance in Love" (tr. by Lawrence R. Smith). [Caliban] (1) 86, p. 108-110.
"Letter No. 1" (from "The King of the Storeroom"). [Caliban] (1) 86, p. 113-114.
"Letter No. 2" (from "The King of the Storeroom"). [Caliban] (1) 86, p. 114.
"Letter No. 3" (from "The King of the Storeroom"). [Caliban] (1) 86, p. 114.
4266. PORTER, Anne
"The Birds of Passage." [Comm] (113:12) 20 Je 86, p. 373.
"A night in Ireland." [Comm] (113:18) 24 O 86, p. 555.
4267. PORTER, J. S.
"Africa 1." [AntigR] (66/67) Sum-Aut 86, p. 236.
"Words I." [CanLit] (110) Fall 86, p. 28-29.
4268. PORTER, Peter
"Dies Irae." [Verse] (5) 86, p. 7-10.
"The Ones Who Do Not Matter." [Verse] (5) 86, p. 6.
"Today My Father Would be One Hundred Years Old" (November 4th., 1985). [Verse] (5) 86, p. 7.
4269. PORTER, Rosalind
"Blue night of my broken soul" ("Untitled"). [Puerto] (21:2) Spr 86, p. 126.
"The Room." [Puerto] (21:2) Spr 86, p. 127.
4270. PORTMAN, Clem
"Cocktail Party." [Wind] (16:58) 86, p. 39.
"Intermezzo." [Wind] (16:58) 86, p. 38.
"Report from the River." [Wind] (16:58) 86, p. 38.
4271. PORTWOOD, Pamela
"The Numbing Sleep of Thievery." [Prima] (10) 86, p. 47.
4272. POST, Eli
"Taking the 'A' Train." [Amelia] (3:1) Ja 86, p. 79.
4273. POSTER, Carol
"Apt." [SanFPJ] (8:3) 85, p. 59.
"Apt." [SanFPJ] (8:4) 85, p. 27.
"Arche III." [SanFPJ] (8:3) 85, p. 60.
"Breathless Times." [SanFPJ] (8:4) 85, p. 35.
"Direct Memory Access." [SanFPJ] (8:4) 85, p. 36.
"Familials." [SanFPJ] (8:3) 85, p. 85.
"November Riots" (Athens, 1973). [SanFPJ] (8:4) 85, p. 34-35.
"Transceiver." [SanFPJ] (8:3) 85, p. 57.
4274. POTASH, L.
"Frankie Goes to Washington." [SanFPJ] (8:3) 85, p. 45-46.
"His Pilgrimage." [SanFPJ] (9:1) 86, p. 70-71.
"Our Democratic License." [SanFPJ] (8:1) 85, p. 61.
"Reflection." [SanFPJ] (8:3) 85, p. 47.
"Straight from the Shoulder." [SanFPJ] (8:1) 85, p. 64.
4275. POTTER, Carol
"All the Pretty Babies." [Field] (34) Spr 86, p. 37-38.

"All the Way Home." [Iowa] (16:2) Spr-Sum 86, p. 108-111.
"Bay Mare in a Second Floor Bedroom." [Iowa] (16:2) Spr-Sum 86, p. 114-115.
"A Hum to Say I'm Missing Your Touch." [AmerPoR] (15:1) Ja-F 86, p. 32.
"It Being a Free Country." [Iowa] (16:2) Spr-Sum 86, p. 111-112.
"Notes from the New World." [Iowa] (16:2) Spr-Sum 86, p. 113-114.
"Resistance." [Iowa] (16:2) Spr-Sum 86, p. 112-113.
"Rounding Up the Babies." [AmerPoR] (15:1) Ja-F 86, p. 33.
"White Horse on the Corner of Sixth Avenue." [AmerPoR] (15:1) Ja-F 86, p. 32.
4276. POTTER, Robin
"Cher R." [PraF] (7:3) Aut 86, p. 30.
"Domesticated Moon." [Quarry] (35:1) Wint 86, p. 75-80.
"Night Train to Copenhagen." [PraF] (7:3) Aut 86, p. 31.
"She Has Breasts Too." [AntigR] (66/67) Sum-Aut 86, p. 149.
4277. POTTS, Lee W.
"From the Sky." [PaintedB] (29) Ag 86, p. 7.
"Landmarks." [PaintedB] (29) Ag 86, p. 9.
"Not Looking before Crossing" (for Nancy). [PaintedB] (29) Ag 86, p. 8.
4278. POTTS, Randall
"Safari Lounge." [Zyzzyva] (2:1) Spr 86, p. 121.
4279. POULIN, A., Jr.
"In the Sleep of Fathers." [TarRP] (25:2) Spr 86, p. 26-27.
"Late Aubade." [TarRP] (25:2) Spr 86, p. 28.
4280. POULTON, Kathian
"Though not occasioned to mirror watching." [Calyx] (9:2/3) Wint 86, p. 104.
4281. POUND, Ezra
"Canto XLIX." [Field] (33) Fall 85, p. 37-38.
"Canto LXXIX." [Field] (33) Fall 85, p. 46-54.
"Canto CXVI." [Field] (33) Fall 85, p. 60-62.
"The Garden." [Field] (33) Fall 85, p. 14.
"Homage to Sextus Propertius" (Selection: I). [Field] (33) Fall 85, p. 23-25.
4282. POUND, Omar
"Two Ships at Sea." [Paint] (13:25/26) Spr-Aut 86, p. 16.
4283. POWELL, J. R.
"Psychiatric Hospital, Locked Ward, Evening Tea & Toast." [Quarry] (35:4) Aut 86,
p. 57-58.
4284. POWELL, Jim
"The Beginning of Winter." [ParisR] (28:100) Sum-Fall 86, p. 253.
"Sappho: To Aphrodite." [NewRep] (194:6) 10 F 86, p. 38.
4285. POWELL, Joseph
"The Asparagus Field." [TarRP] (24:2) Spr 85, p. 25-26.
"Counting the Change" (For Judith Kleck). [QRL] (Poetry series 6:26) 86, 62 p.
"Ode to Sleep." [Poetry] (149:2) N 86, p. 75.
"Winter's Insomnia." [Poetry] (149:2) N 86, p. 74.
4286. POWELL, Katherine Anne
"Blue Sun" (tr. of Thor Sorheim). [Writ] (18) 86, c87, p. 56.
"The Initiation" (tr. of Thor Sorheim). [Writ] (18) 86, c87, p. 53.
"The Last Waltz" (tr. of Thor Sorheim). [Writ] (18) 86, c87, p. 58.
"Rain" (tr. of Thor Sorheim). [Writ] (18) 86, c87, p. 57.
"The Voice of the People I" (tr. of Thor Sorheim). [Writ] (18) 86, c87, p. 54.
"Working Class" (tr. of Thor Sorheim). [Writ] (18) 86, c87, p. 55.
4287. POWELL, Susan
"Peppers." [Ploughs] (12:4) 86, p. 165.
"What He Must Have Been Thinking." [Ploughs] (12:4) 86, p. 163-164.
4288. POWERS, Mark
"Dancing in the Dung" (Honorable mention, 1986 Poetry Competition). [PassN]
(7:2) Spr-Sum 86, p. 5.
4289. POYNER, Ken
"Community." [WestB] (19) 86, p. 112-113.
"The Useless Crime." [WestB] (18) 86, p. 24.
4290. POZZI, Antonia
"Time" (tr. by Deborah Woodard). [ColR] (NS 13:1) Fall 85, p. 45.
4291. PRADO, Adélia
"Concerted Effort" (tr. by Ellen Watson). [MassR] (27:3/4) Fall-Wint 86, p.
420-421.
"Denouement" (tr. by Ellen Watson). [MassR] (27:3/4) Fall-Wint 86, p. 418-419.
"Love in the Ether" (tr. by Ellen Watson). [MassR] (27:3/4) Fall-Wint 86, p. 419.

"A Man Inhabited a House" (tr. by Ellen Watson). [Writ] (18) 86, c87, p. 111.
"Passion" (tr. by Ellen Watson). [Writ] (18) 86, c87, p. 113-115.
"Professional Mourner" (tr. by Ellen Watson). [Writ] (18) 86, c87, p. 112.
4292. PRADO, Holly
"The Curtain." [Temblor] (4) 86, p. 153-155.
"Mud." [IndR] (9:2) Spr 86, p. 93.
4293. PRANGE, Marnie
"I Want Back In." [MissouriR] (9:2) 86, p. 53.
4294. PRATT, C. W.
"On the Beauty of the Universal Order." [Comm] (113:18) 24 O 86, p. 557.
4295. PRATT, Cynthia R.
"Breathing Saltwater." [CrabCR] (3:3) Sum 86, p. 9.
PREE, Don Keck du
    See DuPREE, Don Keck
4296. PREIL, Gabriel
"Memoranda in Black and White" (tr. by Grace Schulman). [Translation] (16) Spr
    86, p. 156.
"Morning Glasses" (tr. by Grace Schulman). [Translation] (16) Spr 86, p. 155.
"Not That She Doesn't Know" (tr. by Grace Schulman). [Translation] (16) Spr 86,
    p. 155.
"Province of a Line" (tr. by Grace Schulman). [Translation] (16) Spr 86, p. 154.
4297. PRESLEY, John Woodrow
"From the Houses of the Dead." [NoDaQ] (54:2) Spr 86, p. 197.
4298. PRESTON, D. S.
"For Czeslaw Milosz." [SewanR] (94:2) Spr 86, p. 210.
"Nicodemus." [SewanR] (94:2) Spr 86, p. 211.
4299. PRICE, Bobby G.
"A Philosopher's Trio." [StoneC] (14:1/2) Fall-Wint 86-87, p. 28.
4300. PRICE, Elizabeth A.
"Life of Crime." [BlackWR] (12:2) Spr 86, p. 53-54.
4301. PRICE, Gale
"Greetings from West Virginia." [SanFPJ] (8:4) 85, p. 93.
"New Cars." [SanFPJ] (8:4) 85, p. 10.
"Scabbin'." [SanFPJ] (8:4) 85, p. 8.
4302. PRICE, Phyllis E.
"At the Spring." [Poem] (56) N 86, p. 21.
"Heir to the land." [Poem] (56) N 86, p. 22-23.
4303. PRICE, Reynolds
"Before the Flood." [NewL] (52:2/3) Wint-Spr 86, p. 214-215.
"The Claim." [NewYorker] (62:14) 26 My 86, p. 34.
"For James Dean." [SouthernR] (22:2) Ap 86, p. 369.
"For Leontyne Price" (La Forza del Destino, 1984). [SouthernR] (22:2) Ap 86, p.
    369-370.
"For Viven Leigh." [SouthernR] (22:2) Ap 86, p. 370-371.
"Last Conversation" (Joel Jackson, 1945-1980). [Shen] (36:2) 86, p. 64-65.
"Three Secrets." [Poetry] (148:1) Ap 86, p. 29-35.
4304. PRICE, V. B.
"Arrangement" (for Gail and Zachariah Rieke). [ClockR] (3:1) 85, p. 18.
4305. PRICE-GRESTY, David
"On the University Quarterback." [Amelia] (3:2) Spr 86, p. 41-42.
"Reunion." [Amelia] (3:4) Fall 86, p. 25.
"South Glamorgan Blues." [Amelia] (3:2) Spr 86, p. 42.
4306. PRIEST, Robert
"The Man with the Nitroglycerine Tears." [GreenfR] (13:3/4) Sum-Fall 86, p. 164.
4307. PRIVETT, Katharine
"Don't I Know You?" [WebR] (11:2) Fall 86, p. 83.
"Outlaws' Cave" (near Ingalls, Oklahoma). [ColEng] (48:5) S 86, p. 459.
"Two Figures in Circular Dance." (Chapbook issue). [Sam] (44:1 release 173) 86,
    12 p.
4308. PROCSAL, Gloria H.
"Husbands all dead." [Amelia] (3:4) Fall 86, p. 60.
4309. PROPER, Stan
"Auction." [PoeticJ] (14) 86, p. 12.
"Dawn's Early Light." [SanFPJ] (8:3) 85, p. 28.
"Dump Fire." [SanFPJ] (9:1) 86, p. 8.
"Fall Omens." [PoeticJ] (16) Fall 86, p. 39.

301

"Garbage and Food." [SanFPJ] (8:3) 85, p. 25.
"The Night Forgets." [PoeticJ] (14) 86, p. 37.
"October Apple Orchard." [PoeticJ] (13) 86, p. 37.
"Space Echoes." [SanFPJ] (8:4) 85, p. 24.
"Town Dump." [SanFPJ] (9:1) 86, p. 48.
"Watching a Solar System." [SanFPJ] (8:4) 85, p. 47.
4310. PROPERTIUS
"Four Odes" (2.5, 2.26, 3.24, 3.25, tr. by Joseph Salemi). [Translation] (17) Fall
86, p. 317-321.
4311. PROPP, Karen
"Nothing But Heart." [Ploughs] (12:3) 86, p. 117.
"Who Sweeps the Sidewalk." [Ploughs] (12:3) 86, p. 116.
4312. PROSPERE, Susan
"House of Straw." [Field] (33) Fall 85, p. 99-100.
"Moving Pictures." [NewYorker] (61:46) 6 Ja 86, p. 75.
"Ode to the Lightning Bug." [AmerS] (55:3) Sum 86, p. 401-402.
"Saturnalia." [Field] (33) Fall 85, p. 96-98.
"Tree of Knowledge." [Field] (34) Spr 86, p. 72-73.
4313. PROUTY, Morton D., Jr.
"Wolves." [NegC] (6:4) Fall 86, p. 36.
4314. PROVENCHER, Richard
"Port Medway, Southshore." [PottPort] (8) 86-87, p. 44.
"What Else Is New." [WritersL] (1986:1), p. 23.
4315. PROVOST, Sarah
"The Frog Prince." [AmerPoR] (15:5) S-O 86, p. 36.
"An Incompleteness." [VirQR] (62:2) Spr 86, p. 261-262.
"Inland, Thinking of Waves." [VirQR] (62:2) Spr 86, p. 260-261.
"X's for Eyes." [HolCrit] (23:5) D 86, p. 17.
4316. PRUNTY, Wyatt
"The Distance into Place." [NewRep] (194:10) 10 Mr 86, p. 36.
"The Player Piano." [SewanR] (94:1) Wint 86, p. 97.
"To My Father." [SewanR] (94:1) Wint 86, p. 97-98.
"A Winter's Tale." [SewanR] (94:1) Wint 86, p. 98.
4317. PUGLISI, Steven E.
"Words for Benjamin" (Benjamin Moloise, hung to death, Pretoria, S.A., Friday,
Oct. 18, 1985). [WillowS] (18) Sum 86, p. 18-21.
4318. PULLEY, Nancy L.
"Persimmon." [PassN] (7:2) Spr-Sum 86, p. 8.
4319. PULTZ, Constance
"Displaced." [NegC] (6:4) Fall 86, p. 58.
"Divisive Cadences." [Wind] (16:57) 86, p. 21.
"The Ides of March." [Vis] (21) 86, p. 23.
"Neighbors." [TarRP] (24:2) Spr 85, p. 28-29.
"Squirrels." [SouthernPR] (26:1) Spr 86, p. 52.
4320. PUMPHREY, Patricia
"Eve Being Introduced to Grapes." [Amelia] (3:1) Ja 86, p. 27.
4321. PURDY, Al
"Double-Focus." [GreenfR] (13:3/4) Sum-Fall 86, p. 169-170.
"There Is of Course a Legend" (Domenico Theotocopoulos in the stained glass
shroud of Toledo). [GreenfR] (13:3/4) Sum-Fall 86, p. 166-168.
4322. PURDY, Lawrence
"From Pericles to Aspasia: a Letter." [AntigR] (65) Spr 86, p. 166.
4323. PURPLE, Marnie
"If the Sun Were Not Your Mistress." [WillowS] (18) Sum 86, p. 79.
"On the Flood Plain." [WillowS] (18) Sum 86, p. 78.
4324. PURSIFULL, Carmen M.
"First Stop / City of Senses." [Americas] (14:2) Sum 86, p. 49-51.
"The Migrating Bird." [Americas] (14:2) Sum 86, p. 48.
4325. PYBUS, Rodney
"Black Pansies." [KenR] (NS 7:4) Fall 85, p. 30.
"Goldfinches." [Stand] (27:1) Wint 85-86, p. 68-69.
"Out of the Blue" (After Johannes Vermeer). [KenR] (NS 7:4) Fall 85, p. 29-30.
QI, Tang
See TANG, Qi
4326. QUALLS, Becky
"Bethesda" (for F.W.). [Wind] (16:57) 86, p. 33.

4327. QUEEN, Don
"Suddenly the Wind" (For Richard Eberhart, lover of lilacs). [NegC] (6:2/3)
Spr-Sum 86, p. 52.
QUEMAIN, Jaime Suarez
See SUAREZ QUEMAIN, Jaime
4328. QUENEAU, Raymond
"Misery by My Gauge" (tr. by Elton Glaser). [ColR] (NS 13:1) Fall 85, p. 40.
4329. QUIG, Steven (Steven J.)
"30. The blurred forms of children have begun." [PoetryNW] (27:4) Wint 86-87, p.
23.
"At the Psychologist's." [BellArk] (2:4) Jl-Ag 86, p. 5.
"Love Poem at the Safeway, Wichita." [BellArk] (2:4) Jl-Ag 86, p. 3.
QUILOBRAN, Arturo Zuñiga
See ZUÑIGA QUILOBRAN, Arturo
4330. QUINLAN, Linda
"For Rita." [Cond] (13) 86, p. 132.
"Grandmother" (A cook at ten in Newfoundland). [SingHM] (13) 86, p. 90-91.
4331. QUINN, Fran
"Towards an Architecture of Beer Glasses." [PaintedB] (28) Ap 86, p. 47.
4332. QUINN, Harold
"Piecework." [NegC] (6:1) Wint 86, p. 90.
4333. QUINN, John
"Turning Back from Lok Ma Chau." [Interim] (5:1) Spr 86, p. 24.
"Valley Fog" (for Lacy). [WestB] (18) 86, p. 39.
4334. QUINN, John Robert
"D. H. Lawrence in Taos." [SpiritSH] (52) 86, p. 43.
"Porch Swings." [Wind] (16:57) 86, p. 34.
"Shutters and Vestibules." [SpiritSH] (52) 86, p. 43-44.
"A Summer Day." [SpiritSH] (52) 86, p. 44.
"Tent Meeting." [Wind] (16:57) 86, p. 34.
4335. QUINN, Philip
"Th Hungry Mental Paca Factor." [Rampike] (5:2) 86, p. 75.
4336. QUIÑONES, Magaly
"La Nueva Gesta." [Mairena] (8:22) 86, p. 17-18.
4337. R. C. (*See also* CLOKE, Richard)
5 poems. [SanFPJ] (9:1) 86.
22 poems. [SanFPJ] (8:1-4) 85.
4338. R. J. S.
"Open Letter to the Township Trustees." [Sam] (44:2 release 174) 86, p. 52.
4339. RA, Carol Hawn
"Stone Foundation." [Wind] (16:56) 86, p. 52.
4340. RAAB, Lawrence
"At Evening." [Poetry] (148:3) Je 86, p. 139-140.
"Cloud, Castle, Lake" (After a story by Vladimir Nabokov). [Poetry] (148:3) Je 86,
p. 140-141.
"Cold Spring." [DenQ] (20:4/21:1) Spr-Sum 86, p. 11.
"A Familiar Story." [QW] (23) 86, p. 137.
"Looking at Pictures." [Poetry] (148:3) Je 86, p. 138-139.
"On the Island." [QW] (23) 86, p. 135-136.
"Others." [PartR] (53:1) 86, p. 96-97.
"Scene from a Novel." [DenQ] (20:4/21:1) Spr-Sum 86, p. 10.
"What We Don't Know about Each Other." [NewYorker] (62:37) 3 N 86, p. 48.
4341. RABASSA, Gregory
"Corrected Perspective" (tr. of Joan Brossa). [Translation] (16) Spr 86, p. 25.
"Hamlet" (for the poet Stephen Spender, in remembrance of London, tr. of Joan
Brossa). [Translation] (16) Spr 86, p. 26.
"Joana" (tr. of Joan Brossa). [Translation] (16) Spr 86, p. 29.
"The People Don't Realize" (tr. of Joan Brossa). [Translation] (16) Spr 86, p. 28.
"Revolutionary Artist" (tr. of Joan Brossa). [Translation] (16) Spr 86, p. 28.
"Sack of Blood" (A Small Tale, tr. of Joan Brossa). [Translation] (16) Spr 86, p.
27.
"Untitled Short Poems" (tr. of Joan Brossa). [Translation] (16) Spr 86, p. 24-25.
4342. RABINOVITCH, Sacha
"The Problem of Pain." [CumbPR] (5:2) Spr 86, p. 26.
4343. RABORG, Frederick A., Jr.
"Scene from an Empty Sound Stage." [CimR] (76) Jl 86, p. 56.

303

RACHEL

4344. RACHEL, Naomi
"Ceremony of the Dead." [SouthwR] (71:2) Spr 86, p. 255-256.
4345. RACINE, Jean (Jean Baptiste)
"Phaedra" (Selections: Act 5, Scenes 6-7, tr. by Richard Wilbur). [Translation] (17)
Fall 86, p. 311-316.
"Phaedra" (Selections, tr. by Richard Wilbur). [Shen] (36:2) 86, p. 27-46.
4346. RACKHAM, Peter
"Countdown." [PottPort] (8) 86-87, p. 52.
4347. RADAIKIN, Norine
"Prince Edward Island." [BellArk] (2:6) N-D 86, p. 7.
4348. RADAUSKAS, Henrikas
"The Work of Mirrors" (tr. by Jurate Mazeika). [Vis] (22) 86, p. 14.
4349. RADAVICH, David
"Kansas Canticle." [Farm] (3:2) Spr-Sum 86, p. 30-32.
4350. RADIN, Doris
"Feeling Her World." [HeliconN] (14/15) Sum 86, p. 46.
"Remember." [HeliconN] (14/15) Sum 86, p. 47.
"Rivka Has a Man's Head." [HeliconN] (16) Wint 86, p. 21.
4351. RADISON, Garry
"The Improvisator." [WestCR] (21:1) Je 86, p. 83.
"In My Passing." [WestCR] (21:1) Je 86, p. 82.
4352. RADNOTI, Miklos
"Second Eclogue" (tr. by Steven Kovacs). [RedBass] (11) 86, p. 26.
4353. RADTKE, Rosetta
"Across the Canyon." [PassN] (7:2) Spr-Sum 86, p. 9.
"Dove." [Pembroke] (18) 86, p. 250.
"Lullaby." [Wind] (16:56) 86, p. 33-34.
"Statue of the Pioneers." [Wind] (16:56) 86, p. 34.
4354. RAFFA, Joseph
"Bar Writers." [WindO] (47) Sum 86, p. 35.
"Feathery Affection." [SanFPJ] (8:3) 85, p. 64.
"I Hesitate at the Gate." [SanFPJ] (8:3) 85, p. 30.
"Infantile Behavior." [SanFPJ] (8:4) 85, p. 25.
"The Latest Broadcast." [SanFPJ] (8:4) 85, p. 25.
"Lusting for Amnesia." [SanFPJ] (8:4) 85, p. 30.
"Megaton of Flowers." [SanFPJ] (8:4) 85, p. 21.
"Out Last Sunrise." [Kaleid] (13) Sum-Fall 86, p. 55.
"Puff of Dawn." [SanFPJ] (8:2) 85, p. 65.
"Purgatory." [SanFPJ] (8:2) 85, p. 28.
"They've Got to Cut Something." [Wind] (16:57) 86, p. 35.
"Window of Vulnerability." [SanFPJ] (8:4) 85, p. 22.
4355. RAFFANIELLO, Robert
"Metamorphosis." [Outbr] (16/17) Fall 85-Spr 86, p. 23.
4356. RAGAN, James
"Breath." [DenQ] (20:4/21:1) Spr-Sum 86, p. 65-66.
"A Killing in the Old Country." [NewL] (52:2/3) Wint-Spr 86, p. 72.
"The Lake Isle of Bled" (Yugoslavia, 1984). [NewL] (52:2/3) Wint-Spr 86, p. 73.
"The Midnight Strip at Faustos Beer Cafe." [Interim] (5:1) Spr 86, p. 40.
"The Painting of the Steelworks on the Old Bank Ceiling" (for RH). [DenQ]
(20:4/21:1) Spr-Sum 86, p. 67.
"Why There Are No Male Virgins" (for L.U.). [Interim] (5:1) Spr 86, p. 39.
4357. RAIL, Dewayne
"Poem for My Daughter." [WestHR] (40:4) Wint 86, p. 341-342.
4358. RAISOR, Philip
"Family Reunion" (for my son and daughter). [SouthernR] (22:4) O 86, p. 802-803.
"On Getting an Education." [TarRP] (24:2) Spr 85, p. 12-13.
"The Poet." [TarRP] (24:2) Spr 85, p. 13-14.
4359. RAKOVSZKY, Zsuzsa
"Snapshot" (tr. by Clive Wilmer and George Gömöri). [Verse] (5) 86, p. 56.
4360. RALEIGH, Richard
"Belo Horizonte." [WestCR] (21:1) Je 86, p. 43.
"Elective Surgery." [WestCR] (21:1) Je 86, p. 41.
"Errand in Winter." [Amelia] (3:4) Fall 86, p. 41.
"Lovesick Mengele." [CrabCR] (4:1) Fall-Wint 86, p. 27.
"Lovesick Mengele." [WestCR] (21:1) Je 86, p. 42.

4361. RAMKE, Bin
"After the War." [NewYorker] (62:29) 8 S 86, p. 34.
"The Attempt to Write the Last Poem of His Life." [SouthernR] (22:1) Ja 86, p. 135.
"A Father Failing." [ParisR] (28:101) Wint 86, p. 241.
"The Loves of a Lapsed Catholic." [SouthernR] (22:1) Ja 86, p. 134.
"Martyrdom: A Love Poem." [GeoR] (40:3) Fall 86, p. 769-770.
"Night Flying." [SouthernR] (22:1) Ja 86, p. 133-134.
"Syllogism." [GeoR] (40:3) Fall 86, p. 770.
"The Writer Awakened by Terror One Night." [NewEngR] (8:3) Spr 86, p. 311-312.
4362. RAMOS, Pericles Eugenio da Silva
"Future, 4" (tr. by Manoel Cardozo). [Vis] (20) 86, p. 7.
4363. RAMOS de CHING, Ines Asinc
"Carta al Hermono Prisonero." [Contact] (7:38/39/40) Wint-Spr 86, Supplement p. 9.
"A Death" (tr. by J. Jacinto, V. Sales-Gomez & J. Tagami). [Contact] (7:38/39/40) Wint-Spr 86, Supplement p. 10.
"Definiedo." [Contact] (7:38/39/40) Wint-Spr 86, Supplement p. 13.
"Defining" (tr. by J. Jacinto, V. Sales-Gomez & J. Tagami). [Contact] (7:38/39/40) Wint-Spr 86, Supplement p. 12.
"Letter to a Brother Prisoner" (tr. by J. Jacinto, V. Sales-Gomez & J. Tagami). [Contact] (7:38/39/40) Wint-Spr 86, Supplement p. 8.
"Una Muerte." [Contact] (7:38/39/40) Wint-Spr 86, Supplement p. 11.
4364. RAMSEY, Paul
"A Branch of the Tree." [SouthernR] (22:3) Sum 86, p. 562.
"The Two." [SouthernR] (22:3) Sum 86, p. 563.
4365. RANDALL, Belle
"Donner." [Thrpny] (27) Fall 86, p. 14.
"Lines from My Mother's Journal." [Contact] (8:41/42/43) Fall-Wint 86-87, p. 9.
4366. RANDALL, Margaret
"The Gloves" (for Rhoda Waller). [Calyx] (9:2/3) Wint 86, p. 129-130.
"The Gloves" (for Rhoda Waller). [OP] (42/43) Wint 86-87, p. 199-200.
"Immigration Law." [ClockR] (3:2) 86, p. 46.
"Immigration Law." [OP] (42/43) Wint 86-87, p. 200.
"These Our Hands" (for Gina). [ClockR] (3:2) 86, p. 45.
"Under Attack" (for Marian McDonald). [ClockR] (3:2) 86, p. 47-48.
4367. RANDALL-MILLS, Elizabeth
"Early Morning Concert." [SpiritSH] (52) 86, p. 36.
"January Swan." [SpiritSH] (52) 86, p. 35-36.
"Naturalist." [SpiritSH] (52) 86, p. 38.
"Root Song." [SpiritSH] (52) 86, p. 35.
"Visitation." [SpiritSH] (52) 86, p. 37.
"Yesterday's Garden." [SpiritSH] (52) 86, p. 37.
4368. RANDOLPH, Gail
"Hair Is Hair." [Obs] (NS 1:1/2) Spr-Sum 86, p. 10-11.
4369. RANDOLPH, Sally
"Body of Knowledge" (Excerpt). [Calyx] (10:1) Sum 86, p. 18.
4370. RANGEL FIGUEROA, Eduardo
"Palabra." [Mairena] (8:22) 86, p. 53.
4371. RANKIN, Paula
"Girl Passing among Trailers." [NoAmR] (271:3) S 86, p. 60.
"North Coast Spring." [MemphisSR] (7:1) Fall 86, p. 14.
4372. RANSOM, J. R.
"Judy." [PassN] (7:2) Spr-Sum 86, p. 8.
4373. RANZ HORMAZABAL, Candelas
"Asi." [Mairena] (8:22) 86, p. 38.
4374. RAO, Velcheru Narayana
"For the Lord of the Animals" (Excerpt, tr. of Dhurjati, w. Hank Heifetz). [Translation] (16) Spr 86, p. 200-202.
4375. RASH, Ron
"Like Nothing Else in Kansas." [SouthernHR] (20:4) Fall 86, p. 363.
4376. RASMUSSEN, Tamara
"My Mother." [AntigR] (64) Wint 86, p. 60.
"The New-Born Moose." [AntigR] (64) Wint 86, p. 60.
4377. RASULA, Jed
"The Field & Garden of Circe" (Excerpt). [Temblor] (4) 86, p. 165-166.

4378. RATCH, Jerry
"Sonnet 154." [Contact] (7:38/39/40) Wint-Spr 86, p. 84.
"Sunflowers, 1888. Van Gogh." [NegC] (6:4) Fall 86, p. 92.
4379. RATCLIFF, Stephen
"Distance" (Excerpts). [Sink] (2) 86, p. 48-52.
4380. RATNER, Rochelle
"The Illustrator" (for Hugh Thomas). [ManhatPR] (6) Wint-Spr 85-86, p. 10.
"Mother, Father, Daughter." [ManhatPR] (6) Wint-Spr 85-86, p. 8-9.
4381. RATTEE, Michael
"The Body of a Begger" (from a conversation with Marco Jerez). [PikeF] (7) Spr 86,
p. 7.
"The History of Someone Else." [CutB] (25) Fall-Wint 86, p. 20.
4382. RATUSHINSKAYA, Irina
"Prison Poems and Drawings" (tr. by Reginald Gibbons and Roman Durbin). [TriQ]
(66) Spr-Sum 86, p. 152-157.
4383. RATZLAFF, Keith
"The Orderly." [NewL] (52:2/3) Wint-Spr 86, p. 96.
4384. RAVIKOVITCH, Dahlia
"Australia" (tr. by Warren Bargad). [PoetL] (81:2) Sum 86, p. 99-100.
"Impoverishment" (tr. by Warren Bargad). [PoetL] (81:2) Sum 86, p. 101.
"Next Year" (tr. by Stanley F. Chyet). [PoetL] (81:2) Sum 86, p. 98-99.
4385. RAWLING, Tom
"Sloe Gin." [Verse] (5) 86, p. 46.
4386. RAWLINGS, Doug
"411 Days and Nights." [Sam] (46:2 release 182) 86, p. 98.
"Jen II." [Sam] (46:2 release 182) 86, p. 116.
"Number 7." [Sam] (46:2 release 182) 86, p. 1.
"Semper Paratus: To the Graduating Class." [Sam] (46:2 release 182) 86, p. 123.
"Survivor's Manuel." [Sam] (46:2 release 182) 86, p. 120.
4387. RAWLINS, Susan
"Still Things Change." [Shen] (36:2) 86, p. 51.
"When Two Explanations Fit All The Facts the Simpler One Tends to Be True."
[CarolQ] (38:2) Wint 86, p. 50.
4388. RAWORTH, Tom
"Notebook, January-March 1971." [Acts] (5) 86, p. 112-121.
4389. RAWSON, Eric
"Axolotl" (after reading Cortázar). [MidAR] (6:1) 86?, p. 105.
"Cherries on the Branches." [DenQ] (20:4/21:1) Spr-Sum 86, p. 61-63.
"Critique." [AmerPoR] (15:3) My-Je 86, p. 15.
"The Eclipse." [Crazy] (31) Fall 86, p. 68-69.
"Sliding to a Halt on 14th Street." [TarRP] (24:2) Spr 85, p. 29-30.
"The Spirit Room" (for Catherine). [AmerPoR] (15:3) My-Je 86, p. 14.
4390. RAY, David
"August 7: The Sanctuary at Banff." [Event] (15:2) 86, p. 19.
"August 7: the Sanctuary at Banff" (for Judy). [CreamCR] (11:1) 86?, p. 32.
"Bhopal." [ColEng] (48:4) Ap 86, p. 351.
"The Birth of Woe." [MSS] (5:1) 86, p. 60-61.
"The Conference in the Alps" (for Carl Sagan). [CreamCR] (11:1) 86?, p. 33-35.
"A Four Mile Walk." [KanQ] (18:1/2) Wint-Spr 86, p. 74-76.
"Homage to Akbar." [WritersF] (12) Fall 86, p. 61-62.
"In Eden, Minnesota." [MSS] (5:1) 86, p. 59.
"My Children Leave for the Alps." [WritersF] (12) Fall 86, p. 60-61.
"Near Cirencester" (For Rose). [CreamCR] (11:1) 86?, p. 31.
"The Parting." [MSS] (5:1) 86, p. 58.
"Ropewalk." [ColEng] (48:4) Ap 86, p. 350.
"The Weddings in the Garden." [WritersF] (12) Fall 86, p. 59.
"The Widower." [WritersF] (12) Fall 86, p. 57-58.
"Writing" (In Memoriam, Samuel Cyrus David Ray 1965-1984). [MSS] (5:1) 86, p.
57.
4391. RAY, Gene
"Fathers and Sons." [PikeF] (7) Spr 86, p. 12.
4392. RAY, Judy
"Ten Stations of the Sweet Briar Lake." [HeliconN] (16) Wint 86, p. 46-47.
"Writing in Virginia." [HeliconN] (16) Wint 86, p. 47.
4393. RAY, Tom H.
"Striptease." [JamesWR] (3:3) Spr 86, p. 14.

4394. RAYSHICH, Steve
"Lit Class, High School." [Sam] (45:4 release 180) 86, p. 27-28.
4395. RAZ, Hilda
"My Daughter Home from College Tells Me about the Gods." [PennR] (2:1)
Fall-Wint 86, p. 84.
"Yom Kippur." [NoAmR] (271:2) Je 86, p. 37.
4396. REA, Susan
"Eclipse." [PennR] (1:2) Fall 85, p. 18.
"The Man Who Waves." [PassN] (7:2) Spr-Sum 86, p. 9.
"Playing Candleland." [BelPoJ] (37:1) Fall 86, p. 31.
"Weather Report" (for Archie Ammons). [Pembroke] (18) 86, p. 218-219.
4397. REA, Tom
"387 West." [NoDaQ] (54:4) Fall 86, p. 169.
"The Dead Husband Speaks from His Photograph." [NoDaQ] (54:4) Fall 86, p. 168.
"The King Dreams Queen Q." [WillowS] (17) Wint 86, p. 74-75.
"The X Cross." [WillowS] (17) Wint 86, p. 76-77.
"Y of the Uplifted Arms." [WillowS] (17) Wint 86, p. 78.
4398. REAGLER, Robin
"Reach To / Ride To." [DenQ] (20:4/21:1) Spr-Sum 86, p. 79-81.
"This Version." [DenQ] (20:4/21:1) Spr-Sum 86, p. 77-78.
"Winter: The Problem with Music." [NoAmR] (271:4) D 86, p. 49.
4399. REANEY, James
"Animated Film, a Sequence of Emblem Poems." [GreenfR] (13:3/4) Sum-Fall 86,
p. 173-176.
"Triads II." [GreenfR] (13:3/4) Sum-Fall 86, p. 172.
4400. REARDON, Patrick
"A. Einstein." [StoneC] (14:1/2) Fall-Wint 86-87, p. 18.
"In the Land of the Black Dog." [StoneC] (14:1/2) Fall-Wint 86-87, p. 19.
4401. REBOREDO, Jorge
"Pretexto de las Palabras." [Mairena] (8:22) 86, p. 52.
4402. RECKERT, Tony
"Call." [WestCR] (21:2) O 86, p. 51.
"Down the Words." [WestCR] (21:2) O 86, p. 47.
"Hey You." [WestCR] (21:2) O 86, p. 49.
"The Long House" (for Lyell Island). [WestCR] (21:2) O 86, p. 52-54.
"Ludwig at the Wedding" (a mangle for orchestra and mouth-organ). [WestCR]
(21:2) O 86, p. 50-51.
"M." [WestCR] (21:2) O 86, p. 48.
"Outside, the Huge Planes." [WestCR] (21:2) O 86, p. 47.
4403. RECTOR, K. K.
"Circus People" (after Jonathan Holden). [KanQ] (18:1/2) Wint-Spr 86, p. 174.
4404. RECTOR, Liam
"Getting Over Cookie." [ParisR] (28:100) Sum-Fall 86, p. 254-257.
4405. RED HAWK
"For Susan, Who Could Not Play Brahms." [ManhatPR] (6) Wint-Spr 85-86, p. 7.
4406. REDEL, Victoria
"Attempts at Reckoning." [NewEngR] (9:2) Wint 86, p. 159-160.
4407. REDGROVE, Peter
"The Bible behind the Scene." [ManhatR] (4:1) Fall 86, p. 47.
"Diver." [Verse] (3:3) N 86, p. 6.
"Dress." [ManhatR] (4:1) Fall 86, p. 44.
"Mammiseum" (Dream in Truro Museum). [ManhatR] (4:1) Fall 86, p. 45-47.
"More Wet Girls." [ManhatR] (4:1) Fall 86, p. 43-44.
"The Mountain-Hut." [ManhatR] (4:1) Fall 86, p. 41-42.
"The Mudlark Poems" (Selections). [Sulfur] (5:3, issue 15) 86, p. 130-135.
"Noisy Book." [ManhatR] (4:1) Fall 86, p. 42-43.
"Odour of Magnetism." [ManhatR] (4:1) Fall 86, p. 45.
"Right Up to the Edges." [Verse] (3:3) N 86, p. 4.
"Sara's Christmas." [Verse] (3:3) N 86, p. 5.
4408. REDMAN, Blanche
"The Visit." [BallSUF] (26:4) Aut 85, p. 37.
4409. REECE, Byron Herbert
"Such Instance." [GeoR] (40:3) Fall 86, p. 771-772.
4410. REED, Alison (Alison T.)
"Alison in Bright Blue" (for Gerre). [CarolQ] (39:1) Fall 86, p. 59.

307

"At the Bedside of a Dying Grandfather Who Once Played the Violin." [NegC] (6:1)
    Wint 86, p. 76.
"Bearded Iris." [Thrpny] (25) Spr 86, p. 9.
"Birdhouse." [CarolQ] (39:1) Fall 86, p. 60.
"En Famille." [MalR] (75) Je 86, p. 88-89.
"Orientation." [MalR] (75) Je 86, p. 90-91.
"The Tea Room." [CarolQ] (39:1) Fall 86, p. 69.
"A Way of Happening, a Mouth." [Poem] (56) N 86, p. 14-19.
"Words for Russian Farmers, Puerto Rican Tourists, South American Workers,
    Words for Us." [Poem] (56) N 86, p. 12-13.
4411. REED, John R.
    "Correggio's 'Io'." [TriQ] (67) Fall 86, p. 124-125.
    "Five to Life." [CarolQ] (39:1) Fall 86, p. 26.
    "Salt Mines." [MichQR] (25:2) Spr 86, p. 349.
4412. REED, W. A.
    "Day Lilies." [Farm] (3:1) Fall 85, p. 39.
    "The War Years." [Farm] (3:1) Fall 85, p. 38.
4413. REEDER, Kathryn
    "Giacometti's Woman." [CimR] (77) O 86, p. 32.
    "Love, Once." [WebR] (11:2) Fall 86, p. 70.
4414. REES, Elizabeth
    "Dissecting a Scream." [Cond] (13) 86, p. 128.
    "Intensive Care." [HeliconN] (14/15) Sum 86, p. 142.
    "Laymen's Psychiatry." [Cond] (13) 86, p. 126-127.
    "A Matter of Perspective." [Confr] (32) Spr-Sum 86, p. 112.
    "Noticing Sleep." [StoneC] (13:3/4) Spr-Sum 86, p. 59.
4415. REES, Ennis
    "Fire in the Tree." [SouthernR] (22:3) Sum 86, p. 564.
4416. REESE, Leslie A.
    "The Trappers Alley Poem" (For Brothers). [MichQR] (25:2) Spr 86, p. 347-348.
4417. REESOR, Carol
    "10.4%* and Christmas Is Coming, or (My Best Friend's Got the Blues)"
        (*Unemployment statistic). [WebR] (11:2) Fall 86, p. 84-85.
    "Forecast." [WebR] (11:2) Fall 86, p. 85.
4418. REEVE, F. D.
    "Applefall" (tr. of Andrei Voznesensky, w. William Jay Smith). [AmerPoR] (15:6)
        N-D 86, p. 24-25.
    "The Boar Hunt" (tr. of Andrei Voznesensky). [AmerPoR] (15:6) N-D 86, p. 25-26.
    "City Yard." [SewanR] (94:2) Spr 86, p. 212.
    "The Driver" (tr. of Andrei Voznesensky). [AmerPoR] (15:6) N-D 86, p. 23.
    "The Thief of Memories" (tr. of Andrei Voznesensky). [AmerPoR] (15:6) N-D 86,
        p. 26.
4419. REEVERTS, Wanie
    "Margaret Donnegan Webster: Prairie Rose." [SpoonRQ] (11:2) Spr 86, p. 52.
    "A Song to Be Sung Before Running." [SpoonRQ] (11:2) Spr 86, p. 53.
4420. REEVES, Trish
    "Cold Wind." [PraS] (60:4) Wint 86, p. 78.
    "The Shawl Pin." [PraS] (60:4) Wint 86, p. 77-78.
4421. REGAN, J. M.
    "Aphasiac." [JamesWR] (4:1) Fall 86, p. 3.
    "Teratogenesis." [JamesWR] (3:4) Sum 86, p. 8.
4422. REGAN, Jennifer
    "Angelus" (after Millet). [Chelsea] (45) 86, p. 113.
    "Bird Houses." [Confr] (32) Spr-Sum 86, p. 41.
    "Chorus." [Hudson] (39:3) Aut 86, p. 454.
    "December, 1944." [Hudson] (39:3) Aut 86, p. 452-453.
    "The Fall." [Confr] (32) Spr-Sum 86, p. 43.
    "Freude! Freude!" [Chelsea] (45) 86, p. 111.
    "The Glass Eye." [Hudson] (39:3) Aut 86, p. 452.
    "Growing Up in the Good Old Days of Radio." [Hudson] (39:3) Aut 86, p.
        454-455.
    "Strange Departures of Men." [Confr] (32) Spr-Sum 86, p. 42.
    "Without Shadows." [Chelsea] (45) 86, p. 112.
4423. REICH, Asher
    "Our Blood is the World's Petrol" (tr. by Karen Alkalay-Gut). [MassR] (27:2) Sum
        86, p. 193.

4424. REID, Alastair
"The Web" (tr. of Jorge Luis Borges). [NewYorker] (62:15) 2 Je 86, p. 32.
4425. REID, Bethany
"An Adult Fairy Tale" (For Matthew). [BellArk] (2:4) Jl-Ag 86, p. 6.
"Aschenputtel." [BellArk] (2:4) Jl-Ag 86, p. 1.
"The Coyotes and My Mom." [BellArk] (2:5) S-O 86, p. 3.
"Dread." [BellArk] (2:4) Jl-Ag 86, p. 5.
4426. REID, Dennis
"Don't Leave Me Lily." [Dandel] (13:1) Spr-Sum 86, p. 10-11.
"Drying Out Again." [Dandel] (13:1) Spr-Sum 86, p. 9.
REID, Jasper
See WEITZEL, Selomo
4427. REID, Monty
"Entries." [PraF] (7:1) Spr 86, p. 38-39.
4428. REID, Robert Sims
"Butte Montana: Romance at the Pekin Cafe." [IndR] (9:1) Wint 86, p. 66-67.
4429. REIDEL, James
"The Prince of Dark Bodies" (for S.D.S.). [ParisR] (28:101) Wint 86, p. 267.
4430. REILLY, Kathleen I.
"The Worldcomber." [KanQ] (18:1/2) Wint-Spr 86, p. 224-225.
4431. REIN, Sonja A.
"Le Grand Masturbateur" (Excerpt, tr. of Salvador Dali, w. Frank C. Lewis).
[ClockR] (3:1) 85, p. 61-62.
4432. REINHOLD, Daniel
"On the Road Again." [Sam] (44:3 release 175) 86, p. 2.
"Poet of War." [Sam] (44:3 release 175) 86, p. 34.
4433. REISNER, Barbara
"Good Luck, Sweet Dreams." [Wind] (16:57) 86, p. 36-37.
"In October the Trees Argue." [ManhatPR] (6) Wint-Spr 85-86, p. 51.
4434. REISS, James
"Hermes Restored." [NewRep] (195:13) 29 S 86, p. 34.
"Unfinished Still Life, 1957." [PennR] (1:2) Fall 85, p. 44.
4435. REISS, Pat
"Life's Liar." [WritersL] (1986:4), p. 18.
4436. REITER, Lora K.
"Bonding." [KanQ] (18:3) Sum 86, p. 80-81.
"In a Hotel the Night before Visiting Palenque" (A Gringa's Version of Borges'
"Streetcorner Man"). [BelPoJ] (37:1) Fall 86, p. 2-3.
"Snake in the Cradle." [BelPoJ] (36:3) Spr 86, p. 10-11.
"Water in the Basement." [BelPoJ] (37:1) Fall 86, p. 4.
4437. REITER, Thomas
"Demolition: The Anniversary." [ManhatPR] (8) Wint 86-87, p. 22.
"The Dowser's Complaint." [Ascent] (11:3) 86, p. 22-24.
"Eight Days and Seven Nights." [SouthernHR] (20:3) Sum 86, p. 265.
"The Lessons." [GeoR] (40:4) Wint 86, p. 970-971.
"Piney." [BelPoJ] (36:4) Sum 86, p. 4-5.
"Spiders." [TarRP] (25:2) Spr 86, p. 20.
"To Apples." [PoetryNW] (27:4) Wint 86-87, p. 31-32.
4438. RELIN, Lou
"Earth's Rebirth After the Disaster." [SanFPJ] (8:4) 85, p. 72.
"We Are the Civilized." [SanFPJ] (8:4) 85, p. 68.
"What If?" [SanFPJ] (8:4) 85, p. 65.
4439. RENAUD, Tristan
"Domaine Du." [Rampike] (5:2) 86, p. 36.
4440. RENCHLER, R. S.
"Edward Hopper." [SouthernHR] (20:3) Sum 86, p. 222.
4441. RENNERT, Margot
"Second Escape." [SanFPJ] (8:3) 85, p. 22-24.
4442. REPISO MOYANO, José
"Plenitud." [Mairena] (8:22) 86, p. 111.
"Presagio." [Mairena] (8:22) 86, p. 111.
4443. REPOSA, Carol Coffee
"Going Home." [DeKalbLAJ] (19:3/4) 86, p. 85-86.
"January in San Antonio." [Pax] (3:1/2) Wint 85-86, p. 107.
4444. REPP, John
"Birdlike." [MalR] (77) D 86, p. 122.

"Come Home." [Outbr] (16/17) Fall 85-Spr 86, p. 6.
"In the Absence." [MalR] (77) D 86, p. 121.
"On the Water." [CrabCR] (3:3) Sum 86, p. 12.
"Out the Window." [Outbr] (16/17) Fall 85-Spr 86, p. 7.
"Unpacking to *The Magic Flute*." [MalR] (77) D 86, p. 122.
4445. RESS, Lisa
"Daybreak." [PraS] (60:4) Wint 86, p. 50-51.
"A Visit and a Desert." [PraS] (60:4) Wint 86, p. 49-50.
"Walk in October." [GWR] (6:2) 86, p. 37.
4446. REVAGLIATTI, Rolando
"Insomnio." [Mairena] (8:22) 86, p. 109.
4447. REVARD, Carter
"Over and Out." [Chelsea] (45) 86, p. 29.
4448. REVELL, Donald
"At the Exhibition of Parables." [AmerPoR] (15:6) N-D 86, p. 48.
"The Backyard in August." [CharR] (12:1) Spr 86, p. 72.
"Beloved Author and the New State." [NewEngR] (9:2) Wint 86, p. 162.
"Car Radio." [Poetry] (147:4) Ja 86, p. 211.
"Cezanne." [TarRP] (25:1) Fall 85, p. 42-43.
"Descriptive Quality." [CharR] (12:1) Spr 86, p. 73.
"Divorce Pending." [NewEngR] (9:2) Wint 86, p. 161.
"Emily Dickinson's Mirror." [PoetryE] (20/21) Fall 86, p. 103.
"Fauviste" (for Bin Ramke). [AmerPoR] (15:6) N-D 86, p. 48.
"Middle West." [MidAR] (7:1) 86, p. 134.
"To Penelope." [Poetry] (149:1) O 86, p. 6.
"Winter Coming." [MidAR] (7:1) 86, p. 135.
4449. REVERE, Elizabeth
"For My Granddaughter Maureen." [CapeR] (21:2) Fall 86, p. 36.
4450. REWAK, William J.
"Felix." [WritersF] (12) Fall 86, p. 205.
4451. REYES, Carlos
"Field Burning." [WillowS] (18) Sum 86, p. 39-40.
"Islands." [WillowS] (18) Sum 86, p. 38.
REYES, Myrna Peña
See PEÑA-REYES, Myrna
4452. REYNA, Bessy
"Uncertainty" (to my old man, tr. by Zoe Anglesey). [MassR] (27:3/4) Fall-Wint 86,
p. 643-645.
4453. REYNOLDS, Diane
"Unorganized Resistance." [StoneC] (13:3/4) Spr-Sum 86, p. 58.
4454. RHENISCH, Harold
"Biblos." [Grain] (14:2) My 86, p. 26.
"The Confessional Poets." [CanLit] (111) Wint 86, p. 82-85.
"In the Alphabet of Birds." [Grain] (14:2) My 86, p. 15-25.
"The Tree." [AntigR] (64) Wint 86, p. 12-13.
4455. RHODE, Robert T.
"Spring's Denial." [Farm] (3:2) Spr-Sum 86, p. 51.
4456. RIBOVICH, John
"Archaic Moon." [HolCrit] (23:1) F 86, p. 16.
4457. RICARDO, Cassiano
"The Ex(orbit)ant Voyage" (tr. by Manoel Cardozo). [Vis] (20) 86, p. 16-18.
4458. RICE, James A.
"They Failed to Tell Me." [Sam] (46:2 release 182) 86, p. 111.
4459. RICE, Paul
"My Soul, Escaping." [BelPoJ] (37:2) Wint 86-87, p. 31.
"On the Pine Mountain Trail." [BelPoJ] (37:2) Wint 86-87, p. 30.
"Picniking on the Indian Grounds." [GeoR] (40:2) Sum 86, p. 489.
4460. RICH, Mark
"April Oak First Green." [Poem] (55) Mr 86, p. 35.
"Carnival." [Vis] (20) 86, p. 30-32.
"Remorse." [Vis] (20) 86, p. 32.
"When She Listens after Supper." [Poem] (55) Mr 86, p. 36.
4461. RICHARD, Margaret B.
"The Brier Patch." [NegC] (6:4) Fall 86, p. 206.
4462. RICHARDS, Anne
"Changing Heraclitus." [Jacaranda] (2:1) Fall 86, p. 39.

4463. RICHARDS, Elizabeth
"Portland." [NewEngR] (9:1) Aut 86, p. 87.
4464. RICHARDSON, Marilyn
"Banner" (for Sara Poli). [Callaloo] (9:2, #27) Spr 86, p. 347-348.
4465. RICHMAN, Elliot
"After the Inquisition." [WindO] (47) Sum 86, p. 14.
"Ariel's Night Song to the Stars above Arles." [WindO] (47) Sum 86, p. 15.
"Crucifixion in Black Brook, NY." [Sam] (44:3 release 175) 86, p. 25.
"The Parting." [WindO] (47) Sum 86, p. 13.
"Saw-Toothed Feathers." [Bogg] (55) 86, p. 14.
"A Treatise on the Epistemological and Ontological Verity of Artistic Creation . . ."
[Bogg] (55) 86, p. 64.
"Winter." [CentR] (30:1) Wint 86, p. 59.
"Zen Death Song of a Maintenance Man." [Bogg] (56) 86, p. 22.
4466. RICHMOND, Judith
"Why." [BellArk] (2:3) My-Je 86, p. 3.
4467. RICHMOND, Steve
"Ah." [WormR] (26:3, issue 103) 86, p. 99.
"Dolphin." [WormR] (26:3, issue 103) 86, p. 100.
"Gagaku." [Bogg] (55) 86, p. 6.
"Gagaku: Better to see demons." [SecC] (14:1) 86, p. 57.
"Gagaku: Demons point at their own chests." [SecC] (14:1) 86, p. 59-60.
"Gagaku: Demons take a nap in their seats." [SecC] (14:1) 86, p. 61-62.
"Gagaku: no no no they signal me." [WormR] (26:3, issue 103) 86, p. 98.
"Gagaku: so many people ask him." [WormR] (26:3, issue 103) 86, p. 98.
"Gagaku: the gold fish." [WormR] (26:1, issue 101) 86, p. 34.
"Gagaku: they are hammering." [WormR] (26:1, issue 101) 86, p. 35.
"Gagaku: When one writes poetry." [Bogg] (56) 86, p. 43.
"Satie is on." [WormR] (26:3, issue 103) 86, p. 97.
"Smoking." [WormR] (26:3, issue 103) 86, p. 101.
"Things." [SecC] (14:1) 86, p. 58.
4468. RICHTER, Gregory C.
"Dark Destination" (tr. of Jóhann Hjálmarsson). [Paint] (13:25/26) Spr-Aut 86, p.
30.
"June 26" (tr. of Matthías Johannessen). [Paint] (13:25/26) Spr-Aut 86, p. 31.
4469. RICKABAUGH, René
"Brilliant Rain." [NowestR] (24:2) 86, p. 37.
"Launching the New Boat." [NowestR] (24:2) 86, p. 38.
"Remembrance." [NowestR] (24:2) 86, p. 39.
"Room Nine." [NowestR] (24:2) 86, p. 36.
4470. RICKEL, Boyer
"Night-Singing." [OhioR] (36) 86, p. 78.
"On Father's Day." [OhioR] (36) 86, p. 79.
4471. RICKERT, Mary
"My Menopause." [NegC] (6:4) Fall 86, p. 106-108.
4472. RICKETTS, Marijane G.
"Burst, Bubble, Burst." [PoeticJ] (13) 86, p. 39.
"Catch That Bus, Kids." [PoeticJ] (15) Sum 86, p. 2.
"A Lesson in Economics." [PoeticJ] (14) 86, p. 11.
"The Quiet One." [PoeticJ] (13) 86, p. 5.
4473. RIDL, Jack
"St. Paul Realized the Rapture." [ThRiPo] (27/28) 86, p. 56.
4474. RIGGS, Dionis (Dionis Coffin)
"In Prison" (tr. of Ahmet Arif, w. Ozcan Yalim & William Fielder). [InterPR] (12:1)
Spr 86, p. 65.
"Such Love" (tr. of Attilâ Ilhan, w. William Fielder and Ozcan Yalim). [StoneC]
(14:1/2) Fall-Wint 86-87, p. 16.
4475. RIGSBEE, David
"Blue Vase." [SouthernPR] (26:1) Spr 86, p. 49.
"Bugs." [Pembroke] (18) 86, p. 265.
"Crickets." [GeoR] (40:3) Fall 86, p. 773.
"Exhaustion." [SouthernPR] (26:1) Spr 86, p. 50-51.
"The Peacocks at Winter Park." [Pembroke] (18) 86, p. 263-264.
"Prisoners Bathing." [Pembroke] (18) 86, p. 264-265.
4476. RILE, Karen
"Brandywine." [PaintedB] (28) Ap 86, p. 26.

"The Fear of Being Noticed." [PaintedB] (28) Ap 86, p. 25.
"Sleight of Hand." [PaintedB] (28) Ap 86, p. 24.
4477. RILEY, Joanne M. (Joanne W.)
"Canadian Geese on New Year's Day" (for Aileen). [PaintedB] (29) Ag 86, p. 10.
"Farmwife Describes the Accident." [BelPoJ] (36:4) Sum 86, p. 32-33.
"Living in a House with Stairs." [CrossCur] (5:4/6:1) 86, p. 51.
4478. RILKE, Rainer Maria
"Autumn Day" (tr. by Edward Snow). [Thrpny] (27) Fall 86, p. 11.
"Black Cat" (tr. by Edward Snow). [AmerPoR] (15:6) N-D 86, p. 19.
"Buddha in Glory" (tr. by Edward Snow). [AmerPoR] (15:6) N-D 86, p. 19.
"Eve" (tr. by Paul Morris). [WebR] (11:1) Spr 86, p. 9.
"The Insane" (tr. by Paul Morris). [WebR] (11:1) Spr 86, p. 10.
"Landscape" (tr. by Edward Snow). [AmerPoR] (15:6) N-D 86, p. 19.
"The Last Supper" (tr. by Paul Morris). [WebR] (11:1) Spr 86, p. 10.
"Late Autumn in Venice" (tr. by Edward Snow). [AmerPoR] (15:6) N-D 86, p. 19.
"The Lute" (tr. by Edward Snow). [AmerPoR] (15:6) N-D 86, p. 19.
"Neighbor" (tr. by Paul Morris). [WebR] (11:1) Spr 86, p. 9.
"People at Night" (tr. by Paul Morris). [WebR] (11:1) Spr 86, p. 11.
4479. RILLING, Helen E.
"Men of Attica." [Amelia] (3:2) Spr 86, p. 16.
4480. RIMBAUD, Arthur
"The Drunken Boat" (adapted by Charles Behlen). [Pax] (3:1/2) Wint 85-86, p.
108-110.
RIN, Ishigaki
See ISHIGAKI, Rin
4481. RIND, Sherry
"Standing Outside a Black Rhinoceros." [CrescentR] (4:1) Spr 86, p. 65.
"Wish for a Bare Desk." [PoetryNW] (27:1) Spr 86, p. 25.
"Wish for a Bare Desk" (corrected reprint). [PoetryNW] (27:2) Sum 86, p. 25.
4482. RINGOLD, Francine
"Small Path" (tr. of Sun Jin-xuan, w. Xu Yaoping and Xia Mingshan). [Nimrod]
(29:2) Spr-Sum 86, p. 36.
4483. RIOS, Alberto
"Horses, Which Do Not Exist." [ParisR] (28:101) Wint 86, p. 270.
"I Can Stay." [Pax] (3:1/2) Wint 85-86, p. 200-201.
"Song before Song." [Pax] (3:1/2) Wint 85-86, p. 202.
"Today, Which Can Be Held, Even in Our Hands" (for M. and R.). [Pax] (3:1/2)
Wint 85-86, p. 200.
RIOS, Maria Eloísa Segovia de
See SEGOVIA DE RIOS, Maria Eloísa
4484. RITCHIE, Elisavietta
"A Secret Admirer Sends Me an Antique Venetian Greeting Card." [Amelia] (3:3)
Sum 86, p. 24.
4485. RITSOS, Yannis
"Agamemnon" (tr. by Marianthe Colakis). [WebR] (11:1) Spr 86, p. 12-28.
"Apollo's First Altar" (tr. by Edmund Keeley). [NewRep] (194:12) 24 Mr 86, p. 40.
"The Decay of the Argo" (tr. by Edmund Keeley). [NewRep] (194:12) 24 Mr 86, p.
40.
"Phaedra" (To Yannis Tsarouchis, tr. by Peter Green and Beverly Bardsley).
[SouthernHR] (20:3) Sum 86, p. 227-247.
"Requiem on Poros" (tr. by Edmund Keeley). [NewRep] (194:12) 24 Mr 86, p. 40.
4486. RITTY, Joan
"Echo." [PoeticJ] (16) Fall 86, p. 2.
"Exchange." [PoeticJ] (13) 86, p. 2.
"Predators." [PoeticJ] (13) 86, p. 40.
"Syndrome." [PoeticJ] (14) 86, p. 40.
"Young Mother." [PoeticJ] (14) 86, p. 2.
4487. RITZER, Mariann
"A Matter of Interpretation." [SpoonRQ] (11:4) Fall 86, p. 33.
4488. RIVARD, Ken
"Details of Eye." [Waves] (14:3) Wint 86, p. 62.
"Determination at the Table." [AntigR] (65) Spr 86, p. 94.
"Natural Playthings." [Waves] (14:3) Wint 86, p. 63.
"Not One Live Thing Needs Warming." [AntigR] (65) Spr 86, p. 93.
"Pinballs and the Orange Bathing Cap" (Selections). [Quarry] (35:1) Wint 86, p.
24-29.

4489. RIVERA, Etnairis
"Por unos días como siglos." [Mairena] (8:22) 86, p. 90-91.
RIVERA, Rafael Barreto
See BARRETO-RIVERA, Rafael
4490. RIVERS, J. W.
"Bound to Fidelity of Representation, Charles Willson Peale Paints Washington at Yorktown." [SoCaR] (18:2) Spr 86, p. 64-65.
"Illinois: At Night, Black Hawk's Statue Broods" (For Robt. D. Sutherland). [Poetry] (148:2) My 86, p. 73.
"In the Orange Grove." [TexasR] (7:1/2) Spr-Sum 86, p. 84-85.
4491. ROBBINS, Anthony
"Wonderland." [YellowS] (19) Sum 86, p. 14.
4492. ROBBINS, Martin
"At the Barber's" (tr. of Gevorg Emin). [WebR] (11:1) Spr 86, p. 62-64.
"At the Colorado Historical Museum." [Os] (22) 86, p. 3.
"Bridge over the Mississippi." [StoneC] (13:3/4) Spr-Sum 86, p. 20.
"Come On, Tonight Let's Have Fun" (tr. of Gevorg Emin). [WebR] (11:1) Spr 86, p. 64.
"The Firefly" (tr. of Gevorg Emin). [InterPR] (12:1) Spr 86, p. 68.
"For My American Lit. Students" (at the Winsor School for girls). [InterPR] (12:1) Spr 86, p. 78.
"Long Distance Calling." [CrossCur] (6:2) 86, p. 14-15.
"Metaphysical Question." [CrossCur] (6:2) 86, p. 16.
"Old Scar." [InterPR] (12:1) Spr 86, p. 79.
"Red Memory." [WebR] (11:1) Spr 86, p. 66.
"Say 'Good Morning' to the Old Ones" (tr. of Gevorg Emin). [WebR] (11:1) Spr 86, p. 65.
"A Sudden Change in the Wind." [CapeR] (21:1) Spr 86, p. 7.
"Twentieth Century" (tr. of Gevorg Emin). [WebR] (11:1) Spr 86, p. 59-61.
"Winter Scene" (tr. of Gevorg Emin). [InterPR] (12:1) Spr 86, p. 67.
"Your Hands" (tr. of Gevorg Emin). [InterPR] (12:1) Spr 86, p. 66.
4493. ROBBINS, Mary Susannah
"Amelie's Love." [Ploughs] (12:4) 86, p. 168-169.
"I want today to talk to you of work." [Outbr] (16/17) Fall 85-Spr 86, p. 21-22.
4494. ROBBINS, Patrick
"A Room at Daybreak." [HarvardA] (120:1) D 86, p. 43.
4495. ROBBINS, Richard
"The Oregon Coast." [MissouriR] (9:1) 85-86, p. 126.
"Walking" (Mark 8). [CrabCR] (3:2) Spr 86, p. 4.
4496. ROBBINS, Tim
"Boys." [HangL] (49) Spr 86, p. 40.
"Jubilee." [HangL] (49) Spr 86, p. 39.
4497. ROBERSON, Ed
"Changes on a Lullaby." [Callaloo] (9:1, #26) Wint 86, p. 118-119.
"The Letter of the Mathematician's Bride Afraid of War." [Callaloo] (9:1, #26) Wint 86, p. 116-117.
4498. ROBERTO, Ernesto
"En Cada Negro Nubarron de Lluvia." [Mairena] (8:22) 86, p. 113.
4499. ROBERTS, Bonnie
"Getting Close at Harry's Bar." [SlipS] (6) 86, p. 72.
"The Real Thing." [Bogg] (56) 86, p. 62.
4500. ROBERTS, Dorothy
"A River Story." [AntigR] (66/67) Sum-Aut 86, p. 52.
"The Shack." [Hudson] (39:2) Sum 86, p. 277.
4501. ROBERTS, Jim
"How Long" (tr. of Flavia Cosma, w. Roger Greenwald and the author). [Writ] (18) 86, c87, p. 109.
"If I could Be" (tr. of Flavia Cosma, w. Roger Greenwald and the author). [Writ] (18) 86, c87, p. 108.
"Toil" (tr. of Flavia Cosma, w. Roger Greenwald and the author). [Writ] (18) 86, c87, p. 107.
4502. ROBERTS, Kim
"Night Tumbles into Town by Rail." [OhioR] (36) 86, p. 93.
"Summer." [SoDakR] (24:2) Sum 86, p. 82.
4503. ROBERTS, Len
"Another Spring on Olmstead Street." [WestB] (19) 86, p. 110.

"At the Train Tracks." [OhioR] (37) 86, p. 95.
"Building the Barn Door." [VirQR] (62:2) Spr 86, p. 265.
"Cleaning the Glasses." [IndR] (9:2) Spr 86, p. 90.
"A Dish for Each Ticket." [TarRP] (24:2) Spr 85, p. 21.
"Dreaming with the Mockingbird's Song." [PaintedB] (28) Ap 86, p. 71.
"Eating the Heart." [PaintedB] (28) Ap 86, p. 72.
"First Kiss." [NowestR] (24:3) 86, p. 94.
"Following the Cat" (for Joshua). [VirQR] (62:2) Spr 86, p. 265-266.
"Hiding Places" (for Joshua). [NowestR] (24:3) 86, p. 14.
"The Moment." [Poetry] (148:6) S 86, p. 333.
"The Naming Field." [WestB] (19) 86, p. 111.
"The Night Out." [Raccoon] (20) Ap 86, p. 26.
"Nights on Olmstead Street." [Poetry] (148:6) S 86, p. 334.
"The Prank Fire Alarm at the Christmas Play." [MemphisSR] (7:1) Fall 86, p. 44.
"The Second Heaven" (for Deborah). [PaintedB] (28) Ap 86, p. 71.
"She Goes Out to Buy Groceries." [WestB] (18) 86, p. 98.
"The Shelves." [IndR] (9:2) Spr 86, p. 92.
"Shoveling Our Way Out." [WestB] (18) 86, p. 99.
"Shoveling Snow in Cohoes, New York." [NowestR] (24:3) 86, p. 15.
"Stealing." [NowestR] (24:3) 86, p. 93-94.
"The Trains" (for Walt). [VirQR] (62:2) Spr 86, p. 266-267.
"The Woodshed" (for David Johnson). [IndR] (9:2) Spr 86, p. 91.
4504. ROBERTS, Mark
"These Things Are You." [Bogg] (56) 86, p. 50.
4505. ROBERTS, Stephen R.
"Artificial Lake." [Vis] (22) 86, p. 38.
4506. ROBERTS, Steven
"Coracle" (Excerpts). [Sink] (1) 86, p. 54-58.
4507. ROBERTSON, D. C.
"Time and Tide." [Rampike] (5:2) 86, p. 66-67.
4508. ROBERTSON, James F.
"Fragments of an Autobiography." [Verse] (3:3) N 86, p. 50.
4509. ROBERTSON, William B.
"Front Page Religion." [Event] (15:2) 86, p. 98-99.
"Getting On." [MalR] (73) Ja 86, p. 76-77.
"Product of Turkey." [CanLit] (108) Spr 86, p. 44-45.
"Remembrance Day, 1983." [CanLit] (108) Spr 86, p. 91.
"Young Refugee." [Event] (15:2) 86, p. 97.
4510. ROBINSON, Alfred Eugene
"Journey Westward." [Contact] (7:38/39/40) Wint-Spr 86, p. 86.
4511. ROBINSON, Ethel Winter
"Charity." [SanFPJ] (9:1) 86, p. 92.
"Traffic Slowly Creeps." [SanFPJ] (9:1) 86, p. 89.
4512. ROBINSON, James Miller
"Big Ears and Ruddy Face" (after Horacio Quiroga). [WormR] (26:4, issue 104) 86, p. 126-127.
"Hard Times." [WormR] (26:4, issue 104) 86, p. 124-125.
4513. ROBINSON, Julia
"Ever Green Daphne." [CarolQ] (38:2) Wint 86, p. 28.
4514. ROBINSON, Kit
"Forgotten Algebra." [Sink] (1) 86, p. 21.
"Nesting of Layered Protocols." [Sink] (1) 86, p. 19.
"Rented Objects." [Sink] (1) 86, p. 20.
4515. ROBINSON, Lillian S.
"Migrations: Pennsylvania." [PennR] (1:2) Fall 85, p. 16.
4516. ROBINSON, Mark
"Buttocks." [Sam] (44:3 release 175) 86, p. 20-21.
4517. ROBINSON, Michael N.
"Kangaroo Death." [SanFPJ] (8:1) 85, p. 50.
"Little Mistakes." [SanFPJ] (8:1) 85, p. 51.
4518. ROBINSON, Peter
"Sunday Afternoons in the Abbey Grounds." [Quarry] (35:3) Sum 86, p. 54.
4519. ROBINSON, Susan
"Please Call Back." [Quarry] (35:3) Sum 86, p. 13.

4520. ROBLES, Al
"Sakurai Takamine the Kyushu Mountain Sake Hobo." [Contact] (7:38/39/40)
Wint-Spr 86, p. 74-75.
4521. ROBLES, Doreen Breheney
"A child gathers." [Amelia] (3:1) Ja 86, p. 30.
4522. ROBSON, Ruthann
"Regine's Rebuke to Kierkegaard." [NegC] (6:1) Wint 86, p. 38-39.
"Subway." [RedBass] (11) 86, p. 9.
4523. ROCA, Juan Manuel
"My Family Toyed with a Borrowed Violin" (tr. by Gary Emmons). [Pequod] (22)
86, p. 62.
4524. ROCHE, Maurice
"Mem. Mori" (An excerpt from *Compact*, tr. by Mark Polizzotti). [Rampike] (5:2)
86, p. 14-15.
4525. ROCHE, Paul
"Elegy for Sylvia Plath." [CentR] (30:3) Sum 86, p. 354-357.
ROCQUE, Emma la
See LaROCQUE, Emma
4526. RODD, Laurel
"A face bare of rouge" (tr. of Yosano Akiko). [RedBass] (10) 86, p. 20.
"An Instant" (tr. of Yosano Akiko). [RedBass] (10) 86, p. 20.
"Sozorogoto" (Excerpt, tr. of Yosano Akiko). [RedBass] (10) 86, p. 20.
4527. RODEFER, Stephen
"Anemic Cinema." [Sulfur] (6:1, issue 16) 86, p. 52-53.
"Par." [Sink] (1) 86, p. 12.
"Par." [WestHR] (40:3) Aut 86, p. 209-210.
"Passing Duration" (Selections: 3 poems). [Temblor] (3) 86, p. 54-58.
"Voluntary." [Sink] (1) 86, p. 10-11.
4528. RODITI, Edouard
"The Sybil's Complaint." [Caliban] (1) 86, p. 34.
4529. RODNING, Susan
"Silence Man." [AntigR] (66/67) Sum-Aut 86, p. 152.
4530. RODRIGUES, Charles
"From Hour Third." [SanFPJ] (8:1) 85, p. 43.
"Trinkets." [SanFPJ] (8:1) 85, p. 42.
4531. RODRIGUEZ, Magda Graniella
"Sólo una vez." [LetFem] (10:1) Spr 84, p. 103.
"To: Magda, From: La Otra, Re: Lo Que Nos Concierne." [LetFem] (10:1) Spr 84,
p. 102.
4532. RODRIGUEZ-FLORIDO, Jorge J.
"Afonico." [LindLM] (5:4) O-D 86, p. 23.
4533. ROE, Margie McCreless
"The Existence of Blue." [ChrC] (103:18) 21-28 My 86, p. 518.
4534. ROFFMAN, Rosaly DeMaios
"And Yet I'm Not Sad" (Rainer Marie Rilke's "Duino Elegy I"). [DeKalbLAJ]
(19:3/4) 86, p. 86-87.
"The Body Gives Away Secrets." [Wind] (16:58) 86, p. 29.
"For the Blind Woman Who Trusts under the Moon." [WindO] (47) Sum 86, p. 23.
4535. ROGERS, Bruce P. H.
"Heroica." [Abraxas] (34) 86, p. 20-21.
"Morning after the Storm." [Abraxas] (34) 86, p. 19.
4536. ROGERS, Del Marie
"The Animals." [Pax] (3:1/2) Wint 85-86, p. 112.
"Furniture." [Puerto] (21:2) Spr 86, p. 159.
"Looking for the Deer." [Pax] (3:1/2) Wint 85-86, p. 111-112.
4537. ROGERS, Linda
"Dream Galliard." [CanLit] (109) Sum 86, p. 33.
"Woman of the Dunes." [CanLit] (109) Sum 86, p. 56.
4538. ROGERS, Pattiann
"The Answering of Prayers." [Poetry] (147:4) Ja 86, p. 217-218.
"The Creation of the Inaudible." [GeoR] (40:3) Fall 86, p. 774.
"Dreaming the Dream of Death" (For the man who died in his sleep). [Amelia] (3:4)
Fall 86, p. 4-5.
"The Favorite Dance of the Deaf and Blind Beggar." [MissouriR] (9:2) 86, p.
146-147.
"For the Wren Trapped in a Cathedral." [MissouriR] (9:2) 86, p. 144-145.

"Geocentric." [PoetryE] (20/21) Fall 86, p. 177-178.
"The Myth: Raison d'Etre." [Amelia] (3:4) Fall 86, p. 6-7.
"The Next Story." [YaleR] (75:4) Sum 86, p. 538-539.
"Pity My Simplicity." [PraS] (60:4) Wint 86, p. 80-81.
"Rolling Naked in the Morning Dew." [PraS] (60:4) Wint 86, p. 79-80.
"The Thing in Itself." [Poetry] (147:4) Ja 86, p. 215-216.
"The Voice of the Precambrian Sea." [NewEngR] (9:1) Aut 86, p. 9-10.
"The Way of Creation." [BlackWR] (12:2) Spr 86, p. 27-28.
4539. ROGERS, Sandra
"The New and Improved Testament." [NegC] (6:1) Wint 86, p. 86.
4540. ROGERS, Timothy J.
"Muerte Arrebatada" (Selections: Poem 1-3, 8, 15, tr. of Etelvina Astrada). [WebR]
(11:1) Spr 86, p. 5-15.
ROGOFF, Jay Grover
See GROVER-ROGOFF, Jay
4541. ROJAS, Miguel A.
"Encuentro." [Inti] (21) Primavera 85, p. 130.
"Hospital." [Inti] (21) Primavera 85, p. 131.
"O?" [Inti] (21) Primavera 85, p. 129.
"Síntesis." [Inti] (21) Primavera 85, p. 130.
4542. ROJAS GUARDIA, Armando
"25. Así como a veces desearíamos." [LindLM] (5:2) Ap-Je 86, p. 5.
4543. ROLLINS, Scott
"Jan Van Goyen 1982" (tr. of Henk Bernlef). [Caliban] (1) 86, p. 41.
"Owl" (tr. of Arie van den Berg). [Vis] (21) 86, p. 17.
"Rondo" (tr. of Arie van den Berg, w. James S. Holmes). [BostonR] (11:5) O 86,
p. 18.
"Uncle Carl: a Home Movie" (tr. of J. Bernlef). [Stand] (27:2) Spr 86, p. 24.
4544. ROLSTON, Layne
"Alvaro" (For Andrew Wyeth). [BellR] (9:1) Spr 86, p. 20.
"A Boy on a Swing: Bass Creek Commune." [BellR] (9:1) Spr 86, p. 22.
"Free Climb with Granddad." [BellR] (9:1) Spr 86, p. 23.
"The Woman with Hash Brown Hair, or, Why I Don't Go to the Ox No More."
[BellR] (9:1) Spr 86, p. 21.
4545. ROMAGNOLI, Anna
"Arrival." [Northeast] (series 4:4) Wint 86-87, p. 27.
"Portrait of a Woman." [Northeast] (series 4:4) Wint 86-87, p. 28.
4546. ROMAINE, E.
"Honeycomb" (for my son). [NewL] (53:1) Fall 86, p. 84.
4547. ROMANO, Tom
"Accountability." [EngJ] (75:3) Mr 86, p. 90.
4548. ROMELL, Karen
"Midden." [Descant] (17:2, #53) Sum 86, p. 96-97.
4549. ROMTVEDT, David
"Again Yellowstone River, Way Out East." [CrabCR] (4:1) Fall-Wint 86, p. 11.
"Blytheville, Arkansas, USA." [OP] (42/43) Wint 86-87, p. 3-4.
"Endless Space." [Ascent] (11:3) 86, p. 24.
"Guatemala, The Year of Our Lord 1984." [OP] (42/43) Wint 86-87, p. 5-6.
"Headwind." [CrabCR] (3:2) Spr 86, p. 5.
"In Kibuye When a Visitor Leaves We Wave until That Visitor Is Completely Out of
Sight." [OP] (42/43) Wint 86-87, p. 2-3.
"Message from Zaïre." [OP] (42/43) Wint 86-87, p. 1.
"Night after Night Dreams." [Raccoon] (20) Ap 86, p. 22.
"Standing at the Old Bridge over the Yellowstone River, Glendive, Montana."
[CrabCR] (4:1) Fall-Wint 86, p. 11-12.
"To Say Another's Name." [OP] (42/43) Wint 86-87, p. 6-7.
4550. RONAN, John J.
"John Hews (1685-1793)." [HolCrit] (23:3) Je 86, p. 13.
4551. RONER, C. J.
"Cutoff at Lasing Source." [SanFPJ] (8:3) 85, p. 38-39.
"Flight Home to the Fatherland." [SanFPJ] (8:3) 85, p. 40.
"Hostages to Our State Department." [SanFPJ] (8:3) 85, p. 66-67.
"Nobody Ever Saw Anyone Sold." [SanFPJ] (8:1) 85, p. 37-39.
"Percussion Grenade Democracy." [SanFPJ] (8:3) 85, p. 65.
"Sure Those French Colonels Are Smooth." [SanFPJ] (8:1) 85, p. 35.
"Why Congress Must Always Vote." [SanFPJ] (8:1) 85, p. 40.

4552. RONK-LIFSON, Martha
"At First." [NewEngR] (8:3) Spr 86, p. 334.
"The Painting for My Mother." [SouthernR] (22:2) Ap 86, p. 368.
4553. ROOT, Judith
"First Anniversary of an Accidental Shooting" (For James). [Poetry] (147:6) Mr 86,
p. 336.
"Waiting Room in Missouri." [Poetry] (147:6) Mr 86, p. 335.
4554. ROOT, William Pitt
"After Kierkegaard." [Verse] (6) 86, p. 4.
ROQUE, Catherine la
See La ROQUE, Catherine
4555. RORIPAUGH, Robert
"The Beekeeper's Daughter." [Interim] (5:1) Spr 86, p. 34.
"Mary Lonebear." [Interim] (5:1) Spr 86, p. 34.
ROSADO, Beatriz Morales
See MORALES ROSADO, Beatriz
4556. ROSALIK, Timothy
"Dance." [WindO] (47) Sum 86, p. 7.
ROSARIO MARQUEZ, Nieves del
See MARQUEZ, Nieves del Rosario
4557. ROSBERG, Rose
"Funeral Procession." [KanQ] (18:4) Fall 86, p. 138.
4558. ROSCHER, Marina
"Breather" (tr. of Sarah Kirsch, w. Charles Fishman). [Vis] (22) 86, p. 11.
"Gentle Fright" (tr. of Sarah Kirsch, w. Charles Fishman). [HolCrit] (23:5) D 86, p.
14.
"Rainy Season" (tr. of Sarah Kirsch, w. Charles Fishman). [Vis] (22) 86, p. 11.
4559. ROSE, Jennifer
"Horoscope." [Nat] (242:23) 14 Je 86, p. 834.
"On Losing the Sense of Smell." [ParisR] (28:101) Wint 86, p. 235.
"Strawberries." [ParisR] (28:101) Wint 86, p. 236.
4560. ROSE, Jonathan
"Bumper Crop." [PoeticJ] (13) 86, p. 33.
4561. ROSE, Wendy
"Lenape." [Contact] (7:38/39/40) Wint-Spr 86, p. 84.
"What the Mohawk Made the Hopi Say." [Contact] (7:38/39/40) Wint-Spr 86, p. 85.
4562. ROSE, Wilga
"Fisherman." [Bogg] (55) 86, p. 38.
4563. ROSEBURY, Pauline P.
"A Logical Conclusion." [SanFPJ] (8:1) 85, p. 74.
"Octagonal Peg in Hexagonal Hole." [SanFPJ] (8:1) 85, p. 75.
"Octagonal Peg in Hexagonal Hole." [SanFPJ] (8:2) 85, p. 69.
4564. ROSEN, Kenneth
"Sheep in Wales." [Ploughs] (12:3) 86, p. 118-121.
"Talking Trash." [NewEngR] (8:4) Sum 86, p. 428-432.
"Tulips." [NewEngR] (8:4) Sum 86, p. 425-427.
4565. ROSEN, Michael J.
"Always the Deeper Meaning." [YaleR] (76:1) Aut 86, p. 125.
"Chattel." [MichQR] (25:1) Wint 86, p. 124-125.
"Fittings." [NegC] (6:4) Fall 86, p. 56-57.
"Fountain." [BostonR] (11:5) O 86, p. 15.
"Ocean City, October." [CarolQ] (38:2) Wint 86, p. 32.
"Penn's Relations." [PraS] (60:3) Fall 86, p. 112-113.
"Small Consolations" (for Janet). [HighP] (1:1) Wint 86, p. 6-7.
"Snakehandling." [Thrpny] (27) Fall 86, p. 20.
"Standing His Ground." [SenR] (16:2) 86, p. 49-50.
"A Sudden Upset." [PraS] (60:3) Fall 86, p. 115-116.
"Thoreau's House Site" (for my brother). [SenR] (16:2) 86, p. 48.
"Traveling in Notions." [PraS] (60:3) Fall 86, p. 109-110.
"Voting at His Old Elementary." [PraS] (60:3) Fall 86, p. 113-114.
"What Penn Overhears at the Health Club." [PraS] (60:3) Fall 86, p. 110-111.
4566. ROSENBAUM, Harriet
"A Visit at Breakfast" (Salvatore Dali). [StoneC] (13:3/4) Spr-Sum 86, p. 61.
4567. ROSENBERG, Liz
"The Blue-Flowered Bell." [AntR] (44:4) Fall 86, p. 428-429.
"Children: Fourth of July." [Harp] (273:1634) Jl 86, p. 33.

317

ROSENBERG

"History." [AntR] (44:4) Fall 86, p. 427.
"In the End We Are All Light." [NewYorker] (61:49) 27 Ja 86, p. 36.
"The Stolen Child." [Nat] (242:15) 19 Ap 86, p. 558.
4568. ROSENBERG, Robert
"My Grandfather's Money." [ManhatPR] (8) Wint 86-87, p. 56.
4569. ROSENBERGER, F. C. (Francis Coleman)
"Muse." [SouthernPR] (26:2) Fall 86, p. 71.
"Reliques of the Poets." [ArizQ] (42:2) Sum 86, p. 186.
4570. ROSENTHAL, David H.
"Absurdity" (tr. of Joan Salvat-Papasseit). [Translation] (16) Spr 86, p. 5.
"All My Longing for Tomorrow" (to Marià Manent, tr. of Joan Salvat-Papasseit).
[Translation] (16) Spr 86, p. 7-9.
"Alone and Dressed in Mourning" (Sol i de dol, tr. of J. V. Foix). [SenR] (16:1) 86,
p. 29.
"Between You and Me" (En mig de tu i de mi, tr. of Josep Carner). [SenR] (16:1)
86, p. 23.
"Christmas" (Nadal, tr. of Joan Salvat-Papasseit). [SenR] (16:1) 86, p. 24.
"A Dancer" (Una balladora, tr. of Eugeni d'Ors). [SenR] (16:1) 86, p. 22.
"I Like, at Random" (Em plau, d'atzar, tr. of J. V. Foix). [SenR] (16:1) 86, p. 28.
"Nightmare" (tr. of Joan Salvat-Papasseit). [Translation] (16) Spr 86, p. 11.
"Nocturne for Accordion" (To Joseph Aragay, tr. of Joan Salvat-Papasseit).
[Translation] (16) Spr 86, p. 10.
"Nothing Is Petty" (Res no és mesqui, tr. of Joan Salvat-Papasseit). [SenR] (16:1)
86, p. 25.
"Stroll" (to Joaquim Torres-Garcia, tr. of Joan Salvat-Papasseit). [Translation] (16)
Spr 86, p. 6.
4571. ROSENTHAL, M. L.
"As for Love." [SouthernR] (22:2) Ap 86, p. 372-378.
"I Got to That Town, They All Greeted Me, . . ." (tr. of J. V. Foix). [Translation]
(16) Spr 86, p. 68-69.
"It Was Growing Dark and We Stared at the Hides Scattered About . . ." (tr. of J. V.
Foix). [Translation] (16) Spr 86, p. 66.
"It's When I Sleep That I See Clearly" (tr. of J. V. Foix). [Translation] (16) Spr 86,
p. 67.
4572. ROSENWASSER, Rena
"Archaeology." [Contact] (8:41/42/43) Fall-Wint 86-87, p. 63.
"Clodia of the Claudians." [Contact] (8:41/42/43) Fall-Wint 86-87, p. 62.
"Juventas / Fire or Air." [Contact] (8:41/42/43) Fall-Wint 86-87, p. 62.
4573. ROSENZWEIG, Gerry
"Forty years in the city." [SmPd] (23:1, #66) Wint 86, p. 10.
"Heron." [PoeticJ] (16) Fall 86, p. 17.
"Island Men." [PoeticJ] (13) 86, p. 25.
"Juncoes." [PoeticJ] (13) 86, p. 24.
"Perch." [PoeticJ] (16) Fall 86, p. 16.
4574. ROSOLIO, Cristina Beatriz
"Acecho." [Mairena] (8:21) 86, p. 113.
"Por Estas Cosas." [Mairena] (8:21) 86, p. 114.
"Preguntan." [Mairena] (8:21) 86, p. 114.
"Sobrevivencias." [Mairena] (8:21) 86, p. 113.
4575. ROSS, Aden
"Many: Many for A.R. Ammons." [Pembroke] (18) 86, p. 108-109.
"River Night Rising." [CentR] (30:4) Fall 86, p. 475.
"Semaphore." [KanQ] (18:1/2) Wint-Spr 86, p. 185.
"Your Bavarian Cremes." [KanQ] (18:1/2) Wint-Spr 86, p. 186.
4576. ROSS, Michael Lance
"An Assumption of Consumption." [HarvardA] (119:4) My 86, p. 12.
"The Dancing Time." [HarvardA] (120, i.e. 119:3) Mr 86, p. 6.
4577. ROSSER, J. Allyn
"Message: Bottle #32." [PoetryNW] (27:3) Aut 86, p. 10.
"Of Green." [SoDakR] (24:2) Sum 86, p. 96-97.
"With Tigers' Teeth." [CarolQ] (39:1) Fall 86, p. 34.
4578. ROSSI, Lily
"Morir de Pie." [Mairena] (8:22) 86, p. 68.
4579. ROSSINI, Clare
"After 'Landscape with Castle,' by Jacob Grimmer, 1592." [PraS] (60:4) Wint 86,
p. 86.

"Scene between a Mother and Grandmother." [PraS] (60:4) Wint 86, p. 85.
4580. ROSSNER, Blair
"Four Songs for the Impermanent" (w. Katie Eliot). [BellArk] (2:6) N-D 86, p. 3.
4581. ROTELLA, Alexis
"Blue Umbrella Skirt." [PikeF] (7) Spr 86, p. 12.
"Haiku" (3 poems). [Northeast] (series 4:3) Spr 86, p. 40.
"A Mouse Is Swimming in the Ice Cold Stream." [BellR] (9:1) Spr 86, p. 38.
"Water Wheel." [SlipS] (6) 86, p. 65.
4582. ROTELLA, Guy
"Anniversary, with Meteors and Stars" (for Mary Jane). [HiramPoR] (40) Spr-Sum
86, p. 21.
"Wings." [WestB] (18) 86, p. 44-45.
4583. ROTH, Hal
"Winter rain." [Amelia] (3:1) Ja 86, p. 22.
4584. ROTH, Michael
"The Day Che Guevara Came to Iquique." [Electrum] (38) Spr 86, p. 9.
ROTHE, Tomi Nagai
See NAGAI-ROTHE, Tomi
4585. ROTHENBERG, Jerome
"Altar Pieces / 1986." [Caliban] (1) 86, p. 10-11.
"The Nature Theater of Oklahoma." [Sulfur] (6:1, issue 16) 86, p. 103-107.
4586. ROTHMAN, David (David J.)
"Meditation and Movement at Les Terres Neuves, La Gaude." [CrabCR] (3:2) Spr
86, p. 5-6.
"The Prayers of Theodore Parker." [TarRP] (25:1) Fall 85, p. 46.
4587. ROTHMAN, Susan Noe
"Laughter and Lemonade." [PoeticJ] (13) 86, p. 19.
4588. ROUFF, Ruth A.
"Browsing." [SanFPJ] (8:2) 85, p. 46-47.
4589. ROUNTREE, Thomas
"Necessity." [NegC] (6:4) Fall 86, p. 207.
ROUS, Peter de
See De ROUS, Peter
4590. ROY, Lucinda
"Arthur's Wife." [NegC] (6:4) Fall 86, p. 80-81.
4591. ROYAL, Richard
"When You Arrive" (for Marc-Steven Dear, 1953-1986). [CentralP] (9) Spr 86, p.
105.
4592. ROZ, Víctor
"Amor con Amor Se Paga." [Mairena] (8:22) 86, p. 96.
4593. ROZEMA, Mark
"Cattle Mutilation." [CutB] (26) Spr-Sum 86, p. 32-33.
"The Monks." [CutB] (26) Spr-Sum 86, p. 31.
4594. ROZEN, Shelley
"On the Reservation." [BellR] (9:1) Spr 86, p. 29.
4595. ROZIJ, Roman
"Halloween." [LittleM] (15:1) 86, p. 48.
"The Lady in the Blizzard." [LittleM] (15:1) 86, p. 47.
"The Narcissist." [LittleM] (15:1) 86, p. 47.
"Slo Mo." [LittleM] (15:1) 86, p. 48.
4596. ROZSA, Endre
"To Mayakovsky, in Place of an Introduction" (tr. by Timothy Kachinske). [Stand]
(27:1) Wint 85-86, p. 24-25.
4597. RUARK, Gibbons
"Glasnevin." [Raccoon] (20) Ap 86, p. 27.
"Postscript to an Elegy." [Poetry] (149:3) D 86, p. 135.
"St. Stephen's Green." [Raccoon] (20) Ap 86, p. 28.
4598. RUBENS, Philip M.
"High in the Clear Sky." [Blueline] (8:1) Sum-Fall 86, p. 15.
4599. RUBENSTEIN, David
"From the Italian." [CrabCR] (3:2) Spr 86, p. 27.
4600. RUBIA BARCIA, José
"Anxiety of Signs" (tr. of Juan Larrea, w. Clayton Eshleman). [Sulfur] (6:1, issue
16) 86, p. 123.
"On Vacation Like a Stone" (tr. of Juan Larrea, w. Clayton Eshleman). [Sulfur] (6:1,
issue 16) 86, p. 122-123.

"Risk Attraction" (tr. of Juan Larrea, w. Clayton Eshleman). [Sulfur] (6:1, issue 16) 86, p. 122.
"Thorns in the Snow" (tr. of Juan Larrea, w. Clayton Eshleman). [Sulfur] (6:1, issue 16) 86, p. 121-122.
4601. RUBIN, Anele
"The House Plant." [Lips] (12) 86, p. 18.
4602. RUBIN, Larry
"The Bachelor: Last Try." [SouthernPR] (26:1) Spr 86, p. 63.
"Crossing Victoria Ferry" (Vancouver). [SouthernR] (22:3) Sum 86, p. 565.
"Deathwatch." [SouthernR] (22:3) Sum 86, p. 565-566.
"Into the Looking Glass." [SouthernR] (22:3) Sum 86, p. 566.
"Lessons of the Beach: Possibilities of Renewal." [ManhatPR] (7) Sum 86, p. 23.
"Lines for the Parents of a Marginal Child." [NewL] (52:2/3) Wint-Spr 86, p. 237.
"Metamorphoses." [DenQ] (20:4/21:1) Spr-Sum 86, p. 37.
"Tourists from Florida Reach New Mexico" (for an elderly aunt). [AmerS] (55:4) Aut 86, p. 519.
"Transparencies." [DenQ] (20:4/21:1) Spr-Sum 86, p. 36.
4603. RUBIN, Mark
"Hope." [VirQR] (62:4) Aut 86, p. 606-608.
"Oleander." [VirQR] (62:4) Aut 86, p. 608-609.
"A Part Harmony" (for Kelsey). [Crazy] (31) Fall 86, p. 65.
"Wren." [Crazy] (31) Fall 86, p. 63-64.
4604. RUBINSTEIN, David
"The Main Course." [YetASM] (5) 86, p. 4.
"She Wakes Me from a Bad Dream." [RagMag] (5:2) Fall 86, p. 54.
4605. RUCKS, Carol
"Tortoise." [SingHM] (14) 86, p. 25.
4606. RUDD, Gail
"The Blessing." [SouthernPR] (26:1) Spr 86, p. 16.
4607. RUDMAN, Mark
"Any One Bone You Want." [LitR] (30:1) Fall 86, p. 57.
"Bad News." [Agni] (23) 86, p. 15-17.
"In Siena." [SenR] (16:2) 86, p. 92.
"Maturity." [Boulevard] (1:3) Fall 86, p. 127-128.
"Mound Building." [PoetryE] (20/21) Fall 86, p. 143-145.
"The Punch." [ParisR] (28:100) Sum-Fall 86, p. 258-259.
"Recovering from Michelangelo." [Boulevard] (1:1/2) Wint 86, p. 159.
RUE, Dorie La
See LaRUE, Dorie
4608. RUEFLE, Mary
"Alive and on Earth." [BellR] (9:1) Spr 86, p. 19.
4609. RUESCHER, Scott
"Scolding the Man in the Mirror on the First Day of Autumn, 1985." [PoetryNW] (27:1) Spr 86, p. 41-42.
4610. RUFFIN, Paul
"Baby in a Fruit Jar: Found and Returned." [PennR] (1:1) 85, p. 70.
"Bob Prater Talks about Kathy." [Pembroke] (18) 86, p. 250-251.
"The Storm Cellar" (For Walt). [ConnPR] (4:1) 85, p. 22.
"Student Housing the First Day of Spring." [MemphisSR] (6:1/2) Spr 86, p. 37.
RUGERIS, C. K. de
See DeRUGERIS, C. K.
4611. RUGO, Mariève
"Landscape As Closure." [BlackWR] (13:1) Fall 86, p. 92-93.
"To Diane Arbus." [NewL] (53:1) Fall 86, p. 20.
"To My Mother." [SenR] (16:2) 86, p. 96-97.
RUISSEAUX, Pierre des
See DesRUISSEAUX, Pierre
RUIZ, José O. Colón
See COLON RUIZ, José O.
4612. RUIZ CUMBA, Israel
"Desde ayer." [Mairena] (8:22) 86, p. 18.
4613. RUIZ DE HOYOS, Ramón
"A un Ruiseñor." [Mairena] (8:22) 86, p. 108.
4614. RUMMEL, Mary Kay
"We Could Have Walked Together." [SingHM] (13) 86, p. 32-33.

4615. RUNCIMAN, Lex
"The Biographer's Art." [Ploughs] (12:4) 86, p. 170-173.
4616. RUNEFELT, Eva
"New" (tr. by Lennart and Sonja Bruce). [Translation] (17) Fall 86, p. 309-310.
"The Slaughterhouse" (tr. by Lennart and Sonja Bruce). [Translation] (17) Fall 86, p. 307-308.
4617. RUNNING, Thorpe
"I Keep Punctuating My Madness" (tr. of Laura Cerrato). [ColR] (NS 13:1) Fall 85, p. 49.
"Madame Bovary" (tr. of Alfredo Veiravë). [ColR] (NS 13:1) Fall 85, p. 43.
"Recorres la Palabra" (Excerpt, tr. of Luis Martinez Cuitiño). [ColR] (NS 13:1) Fall 85, p. 46.
"We Were Brave" (tr. of Jorge Brega). [ColR] (NS 13:1) Fall 85, p. 47.
"Without Your Presence" (tr. of Laura Cerrato). [ColR] (NS 13:1) Fall 85, p. 48.
4618. RUSCALLEDA BERCEDONIZ, Jorge María
"La Casa." [Mairena] (8:22) 86, p. 69.
4619. RUSH, Jerry (Jerry M.)
"Horology." [Grain] (14:2) My 86, p. 34.
"Identities." [Grain] (14:2) My 86, p. 33.
"A Simple Story." [Event] (15:2) 86, p. 164-165.
4620. RUSH, Nan
"Image." [YetASM] (5) 86, p. 7.
4621. RUSS, Biff
"Later, and More Slowly (March 1985)." [IndR] (9:2) Spr 86, p. 98.
4622. RUSS, Don
"The Dance." [Poem] (55) Mr 86, p. 22.
"Florida." [Poem] (55) Mr 86, p. 21.
"Götterdämmerung." [Poem] (55) Mr 86, p. 23.
"Wild Morning Glories in a Florida Garden." [Poem] (55) Mr 86, p. 20.
4623. RUSS, Lawrence
"Nocturne with Smoke." [IndR] (9:1) Wint 86, p. 34-35.
4624. RUSS, Lisa
"Grief: A Sequence." [CarolQ] (38:2) Wint 86, p. 29-31.
"Love Poem." [VirQR] (62:3) Sum 86, p. 433-434.
4625. RUSSAKOFF, Molly
"Summer in Kensington." [PaintedB] (28) Ap 86, p. 28.
4626. RUSSELL, Carol Ann
"The Color Blue in Certain Cars." [PraS] (60:2) Sum 86, p. 62-63.
"The Fork in the Road." [PraS] (60:2) Sum 86, p. 63.
"The Last Goddess in Mankato, Minnesota." [SingHM] (13) 86, p. 34.
"Midway." [PraS] (60:2) Sum 86, p. 64-65.
"When You Are Gone." [MidwQ] (27:4) Sum 86, p. 473.
4627. RUSSELL, Hilary
"Wesley Schroder Jacking Deer." [PoetL] (81:1) Spr 86, p. 44.
4628. RUSSELL, Norman (Norman H.)
"Climbing the Mountain." [Caliban] (1) 86, p. 131.
"The Magnet" (A Cherokee Indian poem). [SmPd] (23:1, #66) Wint 86, p. 36.
"On Thursday." [Contact] (8:41/42/43) Fall-Wint 86-87, p. 53.
"The Orca and the Sea Lion." [Caliban] (1) 86, p. 130.
"Summer Night." [Caliban] (1) 86, p. 131.
"Two Trees" (A Cherokee Indian poem). [SmPd] (23:1, #66) Wint 86, p. 37.
"Yellow Pine." [Puerto] (21:2) Spr 86, p. 55.
RUSSELL, R. F. Gillian Harding
See HARDING-RUSSELL, R. F. Gillian
4629. RUSSELL, Sandra
"Sacrifice." [BallSUF] (27:4) Aut 86, p. 57.
4630. RUSSELL, Scott
"Courthouse in Menominee." [KanQ] (18:1/2) Wint-Spr 86, p. 278.
"Going for Apples." [KanQ] (18:1/2) Wint-Spr 86, p. 268.
4631. RUSSELL, Timothy
"In Gross." [PennR] (2:1) Fall-Wint 86, p. 19.
"In Medio." [PennR] (2:1) Fall-Wint 86, p. 20-22.
4632. RUSSELL, Tom
"My Father, After Midnight." [CarolQ] (38:2) Wint 86, p. 74.
4633. RUSSO, Albert
"In Palermo's Catacombs 3=mc^2." [Amelia] (3:3) Sum 86, p. 98-99.

4634. RUTHER, Barbara
"Mama." [PoeticJ] (15) Sum 86, p. 38-39.
4635. RUTHERFORD, Bonnie
"Vanishing Point." [BellArk] (2:2) Mr-Ap 86, p. 6.
"Visions of Chaos." [BellArk] (2:2) Mr-Ap 86, p. 3.
4636. RUTHERFORD, Julie
"Why Edna O'Keefe Should Run for Prime Minister." [Bogg] (55) 86, p. 44.
4637. RUTSALA, Vern
"Adelfina." [ThRiPo] (27/28) 86, p. 58-59.
"Against Telephones." [ColEng] (48:8) D 86, p. 798.
"American Names." [ThRiPo] (27/28) 86, p. 57.
"April." [Interim] (5:2) Fall 86, p. 31.
"The History of Apples." [TarRP] (24:2) Spr 85, p. 1-2.
"The History of Disappointment." [ColEng] (48:8) D 86, p. 798.
"Home Remedies." [ColEng] (48:8) D 86, p. 797.
"Louver." [CharR] (12:1) Spr 86, p. 79.
"Making a Living." [TarRP] (24:2) Spr 85, p. 3-5.
"The Other Night." [BellR] (9:2) Fall 86, p. 28.
"Shelter." [Poetry] (149:2) N 86, p. 70-71.
"Spring in McCall, Idaho." [Interim] (5:2) Fall 86, p. 30.
"White Water." [Poetry] (149:2) N 86, p. 72-73.
4638. RYAN, Gregory A.
"Santiago's Tall Ship." [CentralP] (9) Spr 86, p. 50.
4639. RYAN, Kathryn
"Stricken by the Light." [Cond] (13) 86, p. 107.
4640. RYAN, Kay
"The Animal Itself." [YaleR] (75:3) Spr 86, p. 427-428.
"At the Aquarium" (Selections: 8 poems). [PikeF] (7) Spr 86, p. 18.
"A Calling." [MassR] (27:1) Spr 86, p. 70.
"The Devil." [KenR] (NS 7:2) Spr 85, p. 84-85.
"The Fluid Core." [Zyzzyva] (2:3) Fall 86, p. 102.
"The Hinge of Spring." [MSS] (5:1) 86, p. 166.
"Houdini." [CentR] (30:4) Fall 86, p. 471.
"It Doesn't Matter." [KenR] (NS 7:2) Spr 85, p. 85.
"The New Kabbalists." [Poetry] (147:4) Ja 86, p. 225.
"Periphery." [PartR] (53:4) 86, p. 592-593.
"Renaissance." [Poetry] (147:4) Ja 86, p. 226.
"Rhinoceros." [MSS] (5:1) 86, p. 167.
"Song from the Watchtower." [KenR] (NS 7:2) Spr 85, p. 86.
"That Gentleness." [KenR] (NS 7:2) Spr 85, p. 86.
"Why We Cannot Be Oriental." [KenR] (NS 7:2) Spr 85, p. 84.
4641. RYAN, Margaret
"Black Rasberries." [Amelia] (3:4) Fall 86, p. 49.
"Shells." [Amelia] (3:3) Sum 86, p. 17-18.
4642. RYAN, Michael
"Fire." [NewYorker] (62:42) 8 D 86, p. 150.
4643. RYDER, William H., Jr.
"The Angel." [Sam] (46:2 release 182) 86, p. 57.
4644. RYERSON, Alice
"Autumn Dusk." [Prima] (10) 86, p. 11.
"Chicken Yard after the Fire." [PraS] (60:4) Wint 86, p. 41-42.
"Jester" (story taken from the diary of a French doctor working in North Yemen in
the 1930's). [BelPoJ] (36:4) Sum 86, p. 34-35.
"The Outsiders." [PraS] (60:4) Wint 86, p. 40-41.
"Peace Banner" (For a boy with many parents). [Prima] (10) 86, p. 24.
RYU, Kazuo
See KAZUO, Ryu
RYUICHI, Tamura
See TAMURA, Ryuichi
S., L. C..
See L. C. S.
S., R. J.
See R. J. S.
4645. SAARIKOSKI, Pentii (Pentti ?)
"He looks in the distance for his destination" (tr. by Michael Cole and Karen
Kimball). [Chelsea] (45) 86, p. 124.

"The wind is coming up" (tr. by Michael Cole and Karen Kimball). [Chelsea] (45) 86, p. 125.
"The world's idea that you can see the world" (tr. by Michael Cole and Karen Kimball). [WebR] (11:1) Spr 86, p. 29.
4646. SABATIER, Roland
"Lettre pour Names, Eau, Couple et Nature." [Rampike] (5:2) 86, p. 76-79.
4647. SABINE-OLEKSA, L.
"Jaime." [MidAR] (7:1) 86, p. 54-55.
4648. SACHA, Amy Harder
"The Lunar Eclipse" (for Nan Killoran). [SingHM] (14) 86, p. 54.
SACHIKO, Yoshihara
See YOSHIHARA, Sachiko
4649. SADOFF, Ira
"Autumn Elegy for the Giants." [NewYorker] (62:34) 13 O 86, p. 50.
"Blue Lights." [Ploughs] (12:3) 86, p. 87.
"Central Avenue Breakdown." [Chelsea] (45) 86, p. 14-16.
"The Convex." [Ploughs] (12:3) 86, p. 86.
"Double Elegy." [Nat] (242:12) 29 Mr 86, p. 462.
"The Girl in Red and Green" (after Balthus). [Chelsea] (45) 86, p. 11.
"In the House of the Child." [YaleR] (75:4) Sum 86, p. 535-536.
"The Man with the Blues Guitar." [Chelsea] (45) 86, p. 12-13.
"North Platte: August, 1968." [Ploughs] (12:3) 86, p. 84-85.
"The Pink Gardenia." [MissouriR] (9:2) 86, p. 60.
4650. SAEZ BURGOS, Juan
"El Relato del Encantador" (Tres prólogos, brújula y guía para traductores). [RevICP] (91) Enero-Marzo 86, p. 55-57.
4651. SAFARIK, Alan
"May Day." [CanLit] (110) Fall 86, p. 108.
"The Owl." [CanLit] (110) Fall 86, p. 29.
4652. SAGAN, Miriam
"China Basin Beach." [Sam] (44:2 release 174) 86, p. 23.
SAGAWA, Roberto Yutaka
See YUTAKA SAGAWA, Roberto
4653. SAHA, P. K.
"My Lovers' Lovers." [BellR] (9:2) Fall 86, p. 27.
"Raahu." [BellR] (9:2) Fall 86, p. 27.
4654. SAHIL, Zeeshan
"Bazaar." [Pax] (3:1/2) Wint 85-86, p. 202.
SAINT
See names beginning with ST. (filed as spelled)
4655. SAKNUSSEMM, Kristopher
"Terrible Herbst." [NewEngR] (9:2) Wint 86, p. 181-182.
"View from the Attic." [NewEngR] (9:2) Wint 86, p. 180.
4656. SALAMUN, Tomaz
"Only the Snow Stays" (tr. by Sonja Kravanja-Gross and Anselm Hollo). [Vis] (22) 86, p. 27.
"The White Angel" (tr. by Sonja Kravanja-Gross and Anselm Hollo). [Vis] (22) 86, p. 26.
4657. SALAS, Alejandro
"No Sabía." [LindLM] (5:2) Ap-Je 86, p. 5.
"La Plaza Mayor Se Sienta." [LindLM] (5:2) Ap-Je 86, p. 5.
4658. SALASIN, Sal
"No Saturday morning kiddies programming." [LittleM] (15:2) 86, p. 21.
"Under the off-track betting wire." [AnotherCM] (16) 86, p. 98.
4659. SALEH, Dennis
"1999." [Interim] (5:1) Spr 86, p. 43-44.
"Conch." [Vis] (20) 86, p. 10.
"Declivity." [SecC] (14:1) 86, p. 37.
"Di Chirico, *Mannequin*." [Vis] (20) 86, p. 10.
"Fuchsia." [SecC] (14:1) 86, p. 40-41.
"Magritte, Study for Luna." [SouthernPR] (26:1) Spr 86, p. 67-70.
"Spell." [SecC] (14:1) 86, p. 38-39.
4660. SALEMI, Joseph
"III.65. The breath of a young girl, biting an apple" (tr. of Marcus Valerius Martialis). [Paint] (13:25/26) Spr-Aut 86, p. 32.

"Four Odes" (2.5, 2.26, 3.24, 3.25, tr. of Propertius). [Translation] (17) Fall 86, p. 317-321.
"Horace, I.9" (tr. of Horace). [CumbPR] (5:2) Spr 86, p. 59.
"Horace, II.8" (tr. of Horace). [CumbPR] (5:2) Spr 86, p. 61.
"In love's brief act there is quick, obscene delight" ("Untitled", tr. of Gaius Petronius). [Paint] (13:25/26) Spr-Aut 86, p. 33.
"Three Epitaphs" (27, 31, 35, tr. of Ausonius). [Translation] (17) Fall 86, p. 322-323.
4661. SALES-GOMEZ, Victoria
"A Death" (tr. of Ines Asinc Ramos de Ching, w. J. Jacinto & J. Tagami). [Contact] (7:38/39/40) Wint-Spr 86, Supplement p. 10.
"Defining" (tr. of Ines Asinc Ramos de Ching, w. J. Jacinto & J. Tagami). [Contact] (7:38/39/40) Wint-Spr 86, Supplement p. 12.
"Farewell" (tr. of Rafael Yamasato, w. J. Jacinto & J. Tagami). [Contact] (7:38/39/40) Wint-Spr 86, Supplement p. 22.
"Imitation of Watanabe" (tr. of Rafael Yamasato, w. J. Jacinto & J. Tagami). [Contact] (7:38/39/40) Wint-Spr 86, Supplement p. 23.
"Letter to a Brother Prisoner" (tr. of Ines Asinc Ramos de Ching, w. J. Jacinto & J. Tagami). [Contact] (7:38/39/40) Wint-Spr 86, Supplement p. 8.
"Noriko" (tr. of Rafael Yamasato, w. J. Jacinto & J. Tagami). [Contact] (7:38/39/40) Wint-Spr 86, Supplement p. 16-17.
"The Snow and the Male Flower" (tr. of Rafael Yamasato, w. J. Jacinto & J. Tagami). [Contact] (7:38/39/40) Wint-Spr 86, Supplement p. 21.
"Well of Desires" (tr. of Rafael Yamasato, w. J. Jacinto & J. Tagami). [Contact] (7:38/39/40) Wint-Spr 86, Supplement p. 20.
"With Doubtful Comic Achievements" (tr. of Jose Watanabe, w. J. Jacinto & J. Tagami). [Contact] (7:38/39/40) Wint-Spr 86, Supp. p. 28-29.
"With Regard to Misadjustments . . ." (tr. of Jose Watanabe, w. J. Jacinto & J. Tagami). [Contact] (7:38/39/40) Wint-Spr 86, Supp. p. 26.
4662. SALINERO, Amelia
"Poemas de Horizonte." [Mairena] (8:22) 86, p. 104.
4663. SALING, Joseph
"Colorado." [BallSUF] (26:4) Aut 85, p. 26.
4664. SALISBURY, Ralph
"Long and Longer." [CrossCur] (6:2) 86, p. 128.
"A Name on a Tombstone." [SilverFR] (11) Sum 86, p. 30.
"Until, and After." [SilverFR] (11) Sum 86, p. 28-29.
"Vines Black upon Black Leaves." [Ploughs] (12:4) 86, p. 109.
4665. SALKEY, Andrew
"The Araucaria and the Copihue." [Stand] (27:2) Spr 86, p. 5.
"Twelve Years Afterwards (1985)." [Stand] (27:2) Spr 86, p. 4.
4666. SALLEE, Wayne Allen
"The 950 at 12:40." [SlipS] (6) 86, p. 66.
"Grievances (Dreaming of Fresh-Faced Zombies." [SlipS] (6) 86, p. 67.
4667. SALLI, Donna
"Do You See, Mummu?" [Prima] (10) 86, p. 50.
4668. SALLIS, James
"For Mandelstam." [ManhatPR] (6) Wint-Spr 85-86, p. 29.
"Lineman" (for Tony). [ManhatPR] (6) Wint-Spr 85-86, p. 28.
"Sentences." [NoDaQ] (54:2) Spr 86, p. 198-199.
"Two Poems for Kim" ("Mayday," "Trying to Surface"). [CharR] (12:2) Fall 86, p. 54-55.
4669. SALOMON, Carol
"Songs" (tr. of Lalan Shah Phakir). [BellArk] (2:1) Ja-F 86, p. 5.
4670. SALTER, Mary Jo
"The Annunciation." [YaleR] (75:3) Spr 86, p. 370.
4671. SALVADOR, Nelida
"Exorcismo." [Mairena] (8:21) 86, p. 116.
"Indicios." [Mairena] (8:21) 86, p. 115.
"Nombrar las Cosas." [Mairena] (8:21) 86, p. 116.
"Oscura Persistencia." [Mairena] (8:21) 86, p. 115.
4672. SALVAREZZA, Luis Alberto
"Emily Dickinson." [Mairena] (8:22) 86, p. 110.
4673. SALVAT-PAPASSEIT, Joan
"Absurdity" (tr. by David H. Rosenthal). [Translation] (16) Spr 86, p. 5.

"All My Longing for Tomorrow" (to Marià Manent, tr. by David H. Rosenthal).
[Translation] (16) Spr 86, p. 7-9.
"Christmas" (Nadal, tr. by David H. Rosenthal). [SenR] (16:1) 86, p. 24.
"How Like a Kite My Star Is" (Quina grua el meu estel, tr. by Nathaniel Smith and
Lynette McGrath). [SenR] (16:1) 86, p. 26-27.
"Nightmare" (tr. by David H. Rosenthal). [Translation] (16) Spr 86, p. 11.
"Nocturne for Accordion" (To Joseph Aragay, tr. by David H. Rosenthal).
[Translation] (16) Spr 86, p. 10.
"Nothing Is Petty" (Res no és mesqui, tr. by David H. Rosenthal). [SenR] (16:1)
86, p. 25.
"Stroll" (to Joaquim Torres-Garcia, tr. by David H. Rosenthal). [Translation] (16)
Spr 86, p. 6.
4674. SALZANO, Daniel
"Little Salzanos" (tr. by John Oliver Simon). [InterPR] (12:1) Spr 86, p. 25, 27.
"Salzanitos" (from Voces y Fragmentos: Poesia Argentina de Hoy, 1981). [InterPR]
(12:1) Spr 86, p. 24, 26.
4675. SAMARAS, Nicholas
"Aubade: Macedonia." [OP] (42/43) Wint 86-87, p. 82-83.
"The Road of One Thousand Trees." [OP] (42/43) Wint 86-87, p. 81.
4676. SAMMONS, Toni
"Another Life." [MalR] (75) Je 86, p. 41.
"January 21." [StoneC] (14:1/2) Fall-Wint 86-87, p. 40-41.
"January 28." [MalR] (75) Je 86, p. 42.
"Quantum Return." [MalR] (75) Je 86, p. 43.
4677. SAMPSON, Dennis
"Blue Flowers." [TarRP] (26:1) Fall 86, p. 29.
"Human Fallibility." [Hudson] (38:4) Wint 86, p. 626.
"The Message." [Hudson] (38:4) Wint 86, p. 624-625.
"Metaphors for the Dead." [TarRP] (26:1) Fall 86, p. 30.
"The Next Truth." [SoDakR] (24:3) Aut 86, p. 64.
"Water Strider, Coming into the Light." [Hudson] (38:4) Wint 86, p. 623-624.
4678. SAMSON, Sue
"A Weight of Old Voices." [Farm] (3:2) Spr-Sum 86, p. 52.
4679. SAN MARTIN, Manuel
"Aquí en la Meseta." [InterPR] (12:2) Fall 86, p. 20.
"En los Altos Desiertos de la Luz." [InterPR] (12:2) Fall 86, p. 22.
"Fluidly and by Night" (tr. by Joseph Snow). [InterPR] (12:2) Fall 86, p. 23.
"Here in the Uplands" (tr. by Joseph Snow). [InterPR] (12:2) Fall 86, p. 21.
"In the Far Reaches of the Light" (tr. by Joseph Snow). [InterPR] (12:2) Fall 86, p.
23.
"An Insect on the Moon" (tr. by Joseph Snow). [InterPR] (12:2) Fall 86, p. 25.
"Liquidamente y Nocturno." [InterPR] (12:2) Fall 86, p. 22.
"Nain" (City of Good, tr. by Joseph Snow). [InterPR] (12:2) Fall 86, p. 27.
"Nain" (ciudad del bien). [InterPR] (12:2) Fall 86, p. 26.
"Por la Luna el Insecto." [InterPR] (12:2) Fall 86, p. 24.
"Tejiendo." [InterPR] (12:2) Fall 86, p. 24.
"Weaving" (tr. by Joseph Snow). [InterPR] (12:2) Fall 86, p. 25.
SANCHEZ, Bethoven Medina
See MEDINA SANCHEZ, Bethoven
4680. SANCHEZ, Carmen
"El Reverso." [Mairena] (8:22) 86, p. 120.
SANCHEZ, Jorge Zuñiga
See ZUÑIGA-SANCHEZ, Jorge
4681. SANCHEZ, Ricardo
"Maricopa Schemas in Europa." [Pax] (3:1/2) Wint 85-86, p. 113-115.
4682. SANCHEZ, Sonia
"Philadelphia: spring, 1985." [Callaloo] (9:1, #26) Wint 86, p. 120-121.
"This Is a Torot Reading" (for Robert Buttel on the Occasion of His Retirement).
[PennR] (1:2) Fall 85, p. 3.
4683. SANDEEN, Ernest
"Dialogue at the Door." [Poetry] (149:3) D 86, p. 166.
"A Journey of the Mental Traveller." [Poetry] (149:3) D 86, p. 165.
"My Two Lives." [Poetry] (149:3) D 86, p. 167.
"The Prowler." [Poetry] (149:3) D 86, p. 167.
4684. SANDERS, Mark
"Before Rain." [KanQ] (18:1/2) Wint-Spr 86, p. 147.

"Night Fishing on the Missouri." [KanQ] (18:1/2) Wint-Spr 86, p. 146.
4685. SANDERS, Shelley
"Home Remedy." [CutB] (26) Spr-Sum 86, p. 28-29.
4686. SANDERS, Teresa
"The Cover-Up." [Amelia] (3:2) Spr 86, p. 84-85.
"Madness." [Amelia] (3:2) Spr 86, p. 85.
"Ode to the Poetry Teacher." [Amelia] (3:2) Spr 86, p. 86.
"The Submission." [Amelia] (3:2) Spr 86, p. 84.
4687. SANDRY, Ellen S.
"Autumn in the Arctic begins." [SanFPJ] (8:3) 85, p. 20.
"Wildlife on the Witness Stand." [SanFPJ] (8:3) 85, p. 20.
4688. SANDY, Stephen
"Midsummer Night." [Boulevard] (1:1/2) Wint 86, p. 166.
"On the Street." [Boulevard] (1:1/2) Wint 86, p. 167.
"To Ammons." [Pembroke] (18) 86, p. 228-229.
"The White Oak of Eagle Bridge." [NewEngR] (9:1) Aut 86, p. 69-71.
4689. SANER, Reg
"The Day Only the Trees Were Raining." [PoetryNW] (27:3) Aut 86, p. 30-31.
"Life Story." [VirQR] (62:4) Aut 86, p. 602-603.
"Orchestra." [GeoR] (40:3) Fall 86, p. 777.
"Petroglyphs at Newspaper Rock." [VirQR] (62:4) Aut 86, p. 603-604.
"Poem: Drawing closer, he reached day after day." [WestB] (19) 86, p. 67.
"Toward Solomon's Palace." [Shen] (36:3) 86, p. 89.
"What We See Is What We Are." [YaleR] (75:3) Spr 86, p. 424-425.
4690. SANFIELD, Steve
"Climbing Waganupa." [Pax] (3:1/2) Wint 85-86, p. 203-204.
"A Moment." [Pax] (3:1/2) Wint 85-86, p. 204-205.
4691. SANFORD, Christy Sheffield
"Torso." [Amelia] (3:4) Fall 86, p. 107.
"The Touching of Our Forearms More Intimate." [YellowS] (20) Aut 86, p. 7.
4692. SANFORD, William W.
"Observation of Bird Shooting." [Confr] (32) Spr-Sum 86, p. 207.
4693. SANGER, Peter
"Collocution" (Hector Saint-Denys-Garneau, 1912-1943). [AntigR] (66/67)
     Sum-Aut 86, p. 146.
"Escalade" (Paul-Emile Bourduas, 1905-1960). [AntigR] (66/67) Sum-Aut 86, p.
     147.
"The Sleeper." [AntigR] (66/67) Sum-Aut 86, p. 148.
4694. SANTATERESA, Matt
"Cottage with a View." [AntigR] (66/67) Sum-Aut 86, p. 168.
"Reveille." [Quarry] (35:1) Wint 86, p. 66-67.
4695. SantaVICCA, Ed
"How I Made Your Mother Blush" (for Bruce). [JamesWR] (3:3) Spr 86, p. 14.
SANTIAGO, José Manuel Torres
     See TORRES SANTIAGO, José Manuel
SANTIAGO BACA, Jimmy
     See BACA, Jimmy Santiago
4696. SANTIAGO IBARRA, Beatriz M.
"No Habia Nada." [Mairena] (8:22) 86, p. 93.
4697. SANTIAGO MERLO, Antonio
"Antiflor." [Mairena] (8:21) 86, p. 67.
"Ella Sensible." [Mairena] (8:21) 86, p. 67.
"Generado." [Mairena] (8:21) 86, p. 66.
"Rayoso." [Mairena] (8:21) 86, p. 66.
SANTO, Grace di
     See DiSANTO, Grace
4698. SANTOS, Sherod
"The Blinded Ring-Tail." [Nat] (242:5) 8 F 86, p. 152.
"Homage to the Impressionist Painters." [NewYorker] (62:9) 21 Ap 86, p. 69.
"Mothers & Fathers." [ParisR] (28:100) Sum-Fall 86, p. 260.
"Near the Desert Test Sites." [NewYorker] (61:48) 20 Ja 86, p. 77.
"To a Young Novitiate." [Nat] (242:18) 10 My 86, p. 644.
4699. SANTOS SILVA, Loreina
"Hijos Apocrifos." [Mairena] (8:22) 86, p. 102.

4700. SAPINKOPF, Lisa
"The Beautiful Summer" (tr. of Yves Bonnefoy). [StoneC] (13:3/4) Spr-Sum 86, p. 19.
"Coral" (Excerpt, tr. of Sophia de Mello Breyner Andresen). [AnotherCM] (15) 86, p. 5.
"Dead, How bright you are" (tr. of Sophia de Mello Breyner Andresen). [WebR] (11:1) Spr 86, p. 34-35.
"Delphi the Second Day" (tr. of Yves Bonnefoy). [StoneC] (13:3/4) Spr-Sum 86, p. 19.
"Graphic" (tr. of Sophia de Mello Breyner Andresen). [AnotherCM] (15) 86, p. 6.
"The lamp burned low" ("Untitled", tr. of Yves Bonnefoy). [AnotherCM] (15) 86, p. 8.
"Shore of Another Death" (tr. of Yves Bonnefoy). [NewOR] (13:2) Sum 86, p. 88-89.
"To a Sadness" (from Réqnant Désert, tr. of Yves Bonnefoy). [AnotherCM] (15) 86, p. 7.
"A Voice" (tr. of Yves Bonnefoy). [WebR] (11:1) Spr 86, p. 36.
4701. SAPPHIRE
"New Year's Morning January 1, 1986." [Cond] (13) 86, p. 81.
4702. SARAFINCHAN, Robin
"For Bruce." [PottPort] (8) 86-87, p. 28.
4703. SARDUY, Severo
"Four Sonnets" (tr. by Richard Outram). [Descant] (17:4, #55) Wint 86-87, p. 163-166.
4704. SAREMBOCK, Alice
"The Bad Breath of the Car." [Bogg] (55) 86, p. 52.
4705. SARGENT, Colin
"Flavors Like These." [PoetL] (80:4) Wint 86, p. 197.
"Green Ribbon Kelp." [PoetL] (80:4) Wint 86, p. 198-199.
4706. SARGENT, Michael T.
"Biting the Tongue Off a Corpse." [Sam] (46:2 release 182) 86, p. 38.
"Dying Is Forever." [Sam] (46:2 release 182) 86, p. 115.
4707. SARGENT, Robert
"Fish Galore." [BallSUF] (26:4) Aut 85, p. 41.
"Ver der Leck's Picture." [PikeF] (7) Spr 86, p. 23.
4708. SARTON, May
"The Silence Now." [Calyx] (9:2/3) Wint 86, p. 125.
"The Smile" (Stefano Sassetta). [CreamCR] (11:1) 86?, p. 41.
"To Those in the Limbo of Illness." [CreamCR] (11:1) 86?, p. 40.
4709. SASANOV, Catherine
"Crime." [ConnPR] (5:1) 86, p. 30.
4710. SASS/WRIGHT, Tish
"Transient Transit." [WritersL] (1986:2), p. 26.
"Tulips." [WritersL] (1986:4), p. 12.
4711. SATTERFIELD, Jane Marie
"The Gravity of Night." [AntR] (44:2) Spr 86, p. 197.
4712. SATYAMURTI, Carole
"Last Supper." [Bogg] (55) 86, p. 56.
4713. SAUL, George Brandon
"Wry Residuum." [ArizQ] (42:1) Spr 86, p. 52.
4714. SAUL, Lynn
"Four Poems for Georgia O'Keeffe." [PennR] (1:2) Fall 85, p. 68-69.
4715. SAVAGE, Gail
"Late Tomato Harvest." [ManhatPR] (7) Sum 86, p. 57.
4716. SAVARD, Jeannine
"Classicism on the Water." [HayF] (1) Spr 86, p. 95-96.
"How She Got Her Real Name." [CutB] (25) Fall-Wint 86, p. 19.
"On the Fourth Day / After the Second Dissolution of Strindberg's Mind." [NoAmR] (271:2) Je 86, p. 47.
"Within Eyeshot." [NoAmR] (271:1) Mr 86, p. 51.
4717. SAVINO, Robert
"The Fix." [NegC] (6:1) Wint 86, p. 66.
4718. SAVISHINSKY, Joel
"Copper on Tin." [CrossCur] (6:2) 86, p. 17.
4719. SAVITT, Lynne
"For My Husband on Our Seventh Anniversary." [SecC] (14:1) 86, p. 63.

4720. SAVOIE, Terrence
"'Nightflutterer's Dance' — Paul Klee." [Farm] (3:2) Spr-Sum 86, p. 46.
"What Were You Doing When?" [ColR] (NS 13:1) Fall 85, p. 50.
4721. SAWYER-LAUCANNO, Christopher
"No Writing Allowed" (tr. of Gloria Fuertes). [AmerPoR] (15:4) Jl-Ag 86, p. 48.
"The Thin Women" (tr. of Gloria Fuertes). [AmerPoR] (15:4) Jl-Ag 86, p. 48.
4722. SBROCCHI, Frances
"Ancient Graffiti." [Quarry] (35:4) Aut 86, p. 10-11.
"Hibiscus." [Quarry] (35:4) Aut 86, p. 12.
4723. SBROCCHI, Frances Arnett
"Eva." [AntigR] (64) Wint 86, p. 10.
4724. SCALAPINO, Leslie
"Delay Series" (The Series as Qualitative Infinity). [Temblor] (4) 86, p. 23-32.
"Walking By." [Acts] (5) 86, p. 54-69.
4725. SCAMMELL, Michael
"Artist and Model" (tr. of Veno Taufer). [Vis] (22) 86, p. 23-25.
"At the End of the Journey" (tr. of Veno Taufer). [Vis] (20) 86, p. 39.
4726. SCANLON, Dennice
"The Difference in Effects of Temperature Depending on Geographical Location . . .
." [PoetryNW] (27:1) Spr 86, p. 34-35.
4727. SCANNELL, Vicki
"Addressing the Sky." [NowestR] (24:2) 86, p. 18.
"Like a Dream to Be Brushed Away." [QW] (22) Spr-Sum 86, p. 8.
"Spicing of Life." [PoetryNW] (27:3) Aut 86, p. 11.
4728. SCARBROUGH, George
"Ice Storm" (for my father). [CumbPR] (6:1) Fall 86, p. 20.
"Postcard Woodcut." [CumbPR] (6:1) Fall 86, p. 19.
4729. SCARPE, Francis
"Metamorphosis of Narcissus" (tr. of Salvador Dali). [ClockR] (3:1) 85, p. 5-9.
4730. SCHACHNE, Mark
"I've grown to know." [SmPd] (23:1, #66) Wint 86, p. 11.
4731. SCHACHT, Ulrich
"Nowhere Is Near So Far" (Poems in German & English, tr. by Thomas Edwards,
assisted by Ulrike Aitenbichler and Ken Letko). [MidAR] (6:2) 86, p. 49-86.
4732. SCHAEFER, Ted
"The Wallace Stevens Motel." [NewL] (52:2/3) Wint-Spr 86, p. 242-243.
4733. SCHAEFFER, Susan Fromberg
"Dry Ritual No. 1." [NewL] (53:1) Fall 86, p. 24-25.
"Sunday Morning." [CharR] (12:2) Fall 86, p. 75.
"Valediction." [OntR] (25) Fall-Wint 86-87, p. 103-106.
4734. SCHANCHE, Carol
"Shuttle-Shock." [EngJ] (75:4) Ap 86, p. 39.
4735. SCHANICK, Jean
"July 4th." [PassN] (7:2) Spr-Sum 86, p. 15.
4736. SCHEELE, Roy
"A Freshening." [PraS] (60:2) Sum 86, p. 33.
"Memory." [SewanR] (94:3) Sum 86, p. 379.
"Under Magnification." [SewanR] (94:3) Sum 86, p. 380.
4737. SCHEFFLEIN, Susan
"Management." [BallSUF] (27:4) Aut 86, p. 18.
"Summer Loss." [BallSUF] (26:4) Aut 85, p. 22.
4738. SCHEIER, Libby
"Art in the Morning." [MalR] (73) Ja 86, p. 94.
"The Man." [CanLit] (108) Spr 86, p. 143.
"Poem for My Son at Age 2." [CrossC] (8:2) 86, p. 11.
"Sociology." [CanLit] (108) Spr 86, p. 104.
4739. SCHEINOHA, Gary A.
"Iceberg." [PoeticJ] (14) 86, p. 36.
"January Thaw." [PoeticJ] (14) 86, p. 36.
4740. SCHENK, Joyce
"Memories of Mrs. Heitschu." [YetASM] (5) 86, p. 6.
4741. SCHERZER, Joel
"Manhattan Skyline." [CrabCR] (3:2) Spr 86, p. 16.
4742. SCHEVILL, James
"Always We Walk Through Unknown People." [StoneC] (14:1/2) Fall-Wint 86-87,
p. 63.

"Dog-Pack." [Interim] (5:2) Fall 86, p. 22.
"Frank Lloyd Wright Desperately Designing a Chair." [StoneC] (14:1/2) Fall-Wint
    86-87, p. 65.
"The Images of Execution." [StoneC] (14:1/2) Fall-Wint 86-87, p. 64.
"The Mailman and *Das Ewig Weibliche*." [StoneC] (14:1/2) Fall-Wint 86-87, p. 63.
4743. SCHEXNAYDER, Kenneth
    "Departure." [BlackWR] (12:2) Spr 86, p. 71.
    "Distinctions." [CutB] (25) Fall-Wint 86, p. 29.
    "For the First Time." [CutB] (25) Fall-Wint 86, p. 28.
    "It Was in April." [TarRP] (25:1) Fall 85, p. 20.
    "Not All Faces." [TarRP] (25:1) Fall 85, p. 21.
4744. SCHEYE, Paula
    "Gulls." [AntR] (44:2) Spr 86, p. 206.
    "Lemmings." [AntR] (44:2) Spr 86, p. 207.
4745. SCHIFF, Jeff
    "Grackle at Dusk." [WritersF] (12) Fall 86, p. 130-131.
4746. SCHILLING, Julie Stricker
    "For William Hampton (1902-1948)." [Outbr] (16/17) Fall 85-Spr 86, p. 19.
4747. SCHIMMEL, Harold
    "And Not Wind from There" (tr. of Ya'ir Hurvitz). [PoetL] (81:2) Sum 86, p. 117.
    "And Still I Love" (tr. of Ya'ir Hurvitz). [PoetL] (81:2) Sum 86, p. 118.
    "At the Hour of Brightening" (tr. of Ya'ir Hurvitz). [PoetL] (81:2) Sum 86, p.
      117-118.
    "A Bird" (tr. of Mordechai Geldman). [PoetL] (81:2) Sum 86, p. 111.
    "Call-Up" (tr. of Meir Wieseltier). [PoetL] (81:2) Sum 86, p. 110.
    "Caution Prevents Accidents" (tr. of Meir Wieseltier). [PoetL] (81:2) Sum 86, p.
      109.
    "My Father in His Youth" (tr. of Mordechai Geldman). [PoetL] (81:2) Sum 86, p.
      112.
    "Poem about Jerusalem" (tr. of Meir Wieseltier). [PoetL] (81:2) Sum 86, p. 110.
    "With Long Hooks" (tr. of Mordechai Geldman). [PoetL] (81:2) Sum 86, p.
      111-112.
4748. SCHLOSSER, Robert
    "Bankok Sights." [Sam] (46:2 release 182) 86, p. 69.
    "Consider Clearing the Deck from the Mideast to the Midwest." [Sam] (45:4 release
      180) 86, p. 41.
    "Fear of Sky Death." [Sam] (46:2 release 182) 86, p. 7.
    "Support Troops / Our Brains Are Cooking Bugs." [Sam] (46:2 release 182) 86, p.
      91.
4749. SCHMIDT, Paul
    "The Gem of the Ocean." [GrandS] (5:4) Sum 86, p. 75-76.
    "On Swan Land" (tr. of Velimir Khlebnikov). [Temblor] (4) 86, p. 84-88.
4750. SCHMIDT, Susan
    "The Woman in the Cake." [BellR] (9:2) Fall 86, p. 10.
4751. SCHMITZ, Dennis
    "Direction: A Photo by Cartier-Bresson." [RiverS] (20) 86, p. 20.
    "Driving with One Light." [Field] (33) Fall 85, p. 75-76.
    "A Photo of Cartier-Bresson: Bread." [RiverS] (20) 86, p. 22.
    "A Photo of Cartier-Bresson: Patriot." [RiverS] (20) 86, p. 23.
    "A Photo of Cartier-Bresson: Rain." [RiverS] (20) 86, p. 21.
    "So High" (for my brother, Gerry). [Field] (33) Fall 85, p. 73-74.
4752. SCHNEIDER, Aaron
    "Animal Skins." [Germ] (10:1) Spr-Sum 86, p. 11.
    "Aquarium." [Germ] (10:1) Spr-Sum 86, p. 16.
    "Breakfast of Bears." [Waves] (14:3) Wint 86, p. 66.
    "Cutting Wood on Big Mountain: Autumn, 1973." [Germ] (10:1) Spr-Sum 86, p.
      12.
    "Daughter of Mercy." [Germ] (10:1) Spr-Sum 86, p. 13.
    "Madman's Mesa." [Germ] (10:1) Spr-Sum 86, p. 14-15.
    "Wild Honey." [Germ] (10:1) Spr-Sum 86, p. 9-10.
4753. SCHNEIDER, Lauren
    "Sending Sigosto Home." [PennR] (1:2) Fall 85, p. 19.
4754. SCHNEIDER, Pat
    "Fever" (for my brother, Sam). [MinnR] (NS 27) Fall 86, p. 73-74.
4755. SCHNEIDERMAN, Henry
    "Prayer for the Mortally Ill in Winter." [YetASM] (5) 86, p. 8.

329

4756. SCHNOEKER, Yvette A.
"Ode to the Mortal Mind." [SnapD] (9:2) Spr 86, p. 51.
4757. SCHOEBERLEIN, Marion
"Winter's Way." [Amelia] (3:1) Ja 86, p. 19.
4758. SCHOENBERGER, Nancy
"Galleria." [AntR] (44:2) Spr 86, p. 192-195.
4759. SCHOFIELD, Don
"Hagar in the Wilderness." [NewEngR] (9:1) Aut 86, p. 15.
4760. SCHOONOVER, Amy Jo
"Flee from Destruction to Come." [HiramPoR] (40) Spr-Sum 86, p. 22.
4761. SCHORR, Laurie
"Amusement." [ThRiPo] (27/28) 86, p. 62.
4762. SCHOTT, Penelope Scambly
"The Rock of This Odd Coincidence." [GeoR] (40:3) Fall 86, p. 778.
"Suspended from School." [SouthernPR] (26:1) Spr 86, p. 22.
SCHRAMA, Heleen Mendl
See MENDL-SCHRAMA, Heleen
4763. SCHRAMM, Darrell G. H.
"The Tree." [MidwQ] (27:4) Sum 86, p. 474-475.
4764. SCHRAMM, Richard
"Late Light." [QW] (23) 86, p. 108.
4765. SCHREIBER, Chris H.
"Dinner Time." [SnapD] (9:2) Spr 86, p. 56-57.
"Sister's Shamrock Plant." [SnapD] (9:2) Spr 86, p. 58.
4766. SCHREIBER, Ron
"A Florida Story." [PikeF] (7) Spr 86, p. 23.
"The Horses of Ch'en." [Abraxas] (34) 86, p. 10.
"The Seventh Parcel." [Wind] (16:56) 86, p. 35-36.
"Travel." [Wind] (16:56) 86, p. 35.
"The Wheel with Spikes & Barbs." [Lips] (12) 86, p. 40-41.
4767. SCHREIBMAN, Susan
"An Apple Once Bitten." [Amelia] (3:1) Ja 86, p. 62.
4768. SCHROEDER, Bethany
"Flinch" (for Cory Brown). [PraS] (60:4) Wint 86, p. 92.
"Forked Tale" (for Phyllis Janowitz). [PraS] (60:4) Wint 86, p. 91-92.
4769. SCHROEDER, Gary
"Mistaken Light: A Portrait of Atta." [PassN] (7:1) Fall-Wint 85-86, p. 20.
4770. SCHROEPPEL, Julia
"Swim at Brown Lake." [MemphisSR] (6:1/2) Spr 86, p. 50.
SCHULER, Else Lasker
See LASKER-SCHULER, Else
4771. SCHULER, Robert
"For Credence Clearwater Revival." [TarRP] (25:2) Spr 86, p. 14.
"July Jazz, Midsummer Meditation" (for Henri Matisse). [TarRP] (25:2) Spr 86, p. 13.
"May 1st: Matisse Time." [TarRP] (25:2) Spr 86, p. 13.
"Summer Loves." [TarRP] (25:2) Spr 86, p. 13.
"Ten Translations from the French." [SpoonRQ] (11:2) Spr 86, p. 30-34.
4772. SCHULER, Ruth Wildes
"Vincent." [PoeticJ] (15) Sum 86, p. 43.
4773. SCHULMAN, Grace
"Adam" (tr. of Celia Dropkin). [Translation] (17) Fall 86, p. 250.
"By Which to Lydda?" (Selections: 19 poems, tr. of T. Carmi). [PoetL] (81:2) Sum 86, p. 83-89.
"The Circus Dancer" (tr. of Celia Dropkin). [Translation] (17) Fall 86, p. 249.
"The Filth of Your Suspicion" (tr. of Celia Dropkin). [Translation] (17) Fall 86, p. 250.
"Julian of Norwich." [NewRep] (194:25) 23 Je 86, p. 36.
"Memoranda in Black and White" (tr. of Gabriel Preil). [Translation] (16) Spr 86, p. 156.
"Morning Glasses" (tr. of Gabriel Preil). [Translation] (16) Spr 86, p. 155.
"Not That She Doesn't Know" (tr. of Gabriel Preil). [Translation] (16) Spr 86, p. 155.
"Province of a Line" (tr. of Gabriel Preil). [Translation] (16) Spr 86, p. 154.
4774. SCHULTE, Rainer
"Villa Serpentara" (tr. of Wolfgang Bachler). [RiverS] (20) 86, p. 38.

4775. SCHULTE, Ray
  "Chinese Love Song." [CharR] (12:1) Spr 86, p. 76.
  "The Prophetess: Taipei." [CharR] (12:1) Spr 86, p. 76.
  "Statue of Kuan Yin at Keelung International Harbor." [CharR] (12:1) Spr 86, p. 76.
4776. SCHULTZ, Christine A.
  "The Religion of Willows." [HeliconN] (14/15) Sum 86, p. 145.
  "When Things Get Lost." [HeliconN] (14/15) Sum 86, p. 144.
4777. SCHULTZ, Lee
  "The End of Knitting." [CrossCur] (5:4/6:1) 86, p. 68.
  "Winterbound" (for Chi-wu Ch'ien & Liu Tsung-yüan). [CrossCur] (5:4/6:1) 86, p.
    69.
4778. SCHULTZ, Philip
  "The Hemingway House in Key West." [ClockR] (3:2) 86, p. 22.
  "The Horizon." [ClockR] (3:2) 86, p. 24.
  "My Guardian Angel Stein." [GeoR] (40:3) Fall 86, p. 779-780.
  "Stein, Goodbye." [ClockR] (3:2) 86, p. 23.
4779. SCHULTZ, Robert
  "Analysis." [Hudson] (39:2) Sum 86, p. 286-287.
  "It Is Not Yet Morning, But Morning Rises." [Hudson] (39:2) Sum 86, p. 285.
4780. SCHUYLER, James
  "Mood Indigo" (for David Trinidad). [ParisR] (28:100) Sum-Fall 86, p. 261-262.
  "Shaker." [NewYorker] (61:50) 3 F 86, p. 46.
  "Simone Signoret" (for Jane and Joe Hazan). [ParisR] (28:101) Wint 86, p.
    232-234.
4781. SCHWAGER, Elaine
  "First Child." [Writ] (17) 85, c86, p. 12.
  "Possessed." [Writ] (17) 85, c86, p. 11.
4782. SCHWAID, Alfred
  "Ten Thousand Generations." [Chelsea] (45) 86, p. 55-60.
4783. SCHWARTZ, Delmore
  "How Can He Possess." [ParisR] (28:101) Wint 86, p. 16.
  "The Maxims of Sisyphus" (Sisyphus' Success). [ParisR] (28:101) Wint 86, p. 15.
  "Poem: How Marvelous Man's Kind Is." [ParisR] (28:101) Wint 86, p. 20-21.
  "The Power and Glory of Language." [ParisR] (28:101) Wint 86, p. 18.
  "The Sequel, the Conclusion, the Endlessness." [ParisR] (28:101) Wint 86, p. 19.
  "Sonnet: I follow thought and what the world announces." [ParisR] (28:101) Wint
    86, p. 17.
4784. SCHWARTZ, Hillel
  "Cat Scan." [WebR] (11:1) Spr 86, p. 86.
  "Dance for the End of Hunger in the Ballroom of the El Cortez Hotel." [CutB] (25)
    Fall-Wint 86, p. 13.
  "The Duke and the Duchess Antique Shop." [Contact] (8:41/42/43) Fall-Wint 86-87,
    p. 56.
  "A Few Long Minutes at Lourdes." [PoetryNW] (27:2) Sum 86, p. 6.
  "Keep-away." [PraS] (60:4) Wint 86, p. 87-88.
  "A Theory of Fractions." [Thrpny] (24) Wint 86, p. 13.
  "Third Red Queen." [PraS] (60:4) Wint 86, p. 89.
4785. SCHWARTZ, Jacqueline
  "Complaint in Florence II." [RedBass] (11) 86, p. 10.
4786. SCHWARTZ, Jeffrey
  "The Habit of a Foreign Sky" (for B). [StoneC] (14:1/2) Fall-Wint 86-87, p. 21.
4787. SCHWARTZ, Stephen
  "Christmas 1985: After Robert Lowell." [LindLM] (5:3) Jl-S 86, p. 5.
4788. SCHWARTZBERG, Cindie
  "Not News." [AnotherCM] (15) 86, p. 85.
  "Speak to Me Ushas." [AnotherCM] (15) 86, p. 83-84.
4789. SCHWEIZER, Harold
  "Alzheimer's." [Ploughs] (12:4) 86, p. 140.
  "Our Faces." [Ploughs] (12:4) 86, p. 142.
  "Three Swiss Tales." [Ploughs] (12:4) 86, p. 138-139.
  "The Water on the Lake." [Ploughs] (12:4) 86, p. 141.
4790. SCHWERNER, Armand
  "Body." [NoDaQ] (54:3) Sum 86, 2nd section, p. 59-65.
  "Tablet XXV." [NoDaQ] (54:3) Sum 86, 2nd section, p. 57-58.
4791. SCOBIE, Stephen
  "The Baroness Elsa." [CanLit] (111) Wint 86, p. 127-129.

"Lethbridge, Alberta, Thursday Evening, November 25th, 1982." [GreenfR]
(13:3/4) Sum-Fall 86, p. 177.
4792. SCOFIELD, Sandra
"The Waitress." [MinnR] (NS 26) Spr 86, p. 22.
4793. SCOTELLARO, Rocco
"L'Agosto di Grassano" (per Carlo Levi). [NewRena] (6:3, #20) Spr 86, p. 50.
"L'Arancio." [NewRena] (6:3, #20) Spr 86, p. 52.
"August at Grassano" (for Carlo Levi, tr. by Ruth Feldman and Brian Swann).
[NewRena] (6:3, #20) Spr 86, p. 51.
"The Orange Tree" (tr. by Ruth Feldman and Brian Swann). [NewRena] (6:3, #20)
Spr 86, p. 53.
4794. SCOTT, Gaar
"Certain People." [YetASM] (5) 86, p. 8.
4795. SCOTT, Paul
"Annie." [RagMag] (5:2) Fall 86, p. 57.
"Arrested." [RagMag] (5:2) Fall 86, p. 56.
"Never Enough The." [RagMag] (5:2) Fall 86, p. 58.
4796. SCOTT, Robert
"For Joseph." [Amelia] (3:4) Fall 86, p. 45.
4797. SCOTT, Robert Ian
"In the Science Museum." [WestCR] (20:4) Ap 86, p. 56.
"A Little, Last Columbus." [WestCR] (20:4) Ap 86, p. 55.
"A Small World." [WestCR] (20:4) Ap 86, p. 55.
4798. SCRASE, David
"The Old World" (tr. of Ursula Krechel). [ColR] (NS 13:1) Fall 85, p. 41.
4799. SCRIMGEOUR, J. D.
"Summer 1983." [PikeF] (7) Spr 86, p. 13.
4800. SCUTELLARO, Guy
"The World Is Burning — Just Ask!" [CrossCur] (5:4/6:1) 86, p. 14-15.
4801. SEA, Gary N.
"The Old Acquaintance" (tr. of Jürg Weibel). [WebR] (11:2) Fall 86, p. 30.
4802. SEABURG, Alan
"The Joy of It." [CapeR] (21:1) Spr 86, p. 42.
"The Sign." [CapeR] (21:1) Spr 86, p. 43.
"Small Moments." [BallSUF] (26:4) Aut 85, p. 71.
4803. SEATON, J. P.
"House Cricket" (tr. of Tu Fu). [CarolQ] (39:1) Fall 86, p. 70.
4804. SEATON, Maureen
"Mortal Sins." [NegC] (6:1) Wint 86, p. 69-70.
"A Sudden Light in Columbia Heights." [PoetL] (80:4) Wint 86, p. 219.
"Woody Allen, Woody Allen." [PoetL] (80:4) Wint 86, p. 218.
4805. SEATON, Peter
"As As In." [Sink] (2) 86, p. 53.
"The Pyramids of Elysium." [Temblor] (3) 86, p. 93-97.
"Shangri-La." [Sink] (2) 86, p. 55.
"Why I Am Not a Painting" (for Larry Estridge). [Sink] (2) 86, p. 54-55.
4806. SECREAST, Donald
"Snow Ledges above the Ulta Valley." [SouthernPR] (26:1) Spr 86, p. 60.
4807. SEDGWICK, Eve Kosofsky
"The Warm Decembers" (Selection: "A letter from Trollope to his wife"). [Raritan]
(6:2) Fall 86, p. 51-62.
4808. SEEMAN, Julianne
"River Run." [BellArk] (2:4) Jl-Ag 86, p. 4.
"Strip Mining." [BellArk] (2:4) Jl-Ag 86, p. 5.
4809. SEGALEN, Victor
"Stele of the Way of the Soul" (tr. by Dorothy Aspinwall). [WebR] (11:2) Fall 86, p.
27.
4810. SEGALL, Pearl B. (Pearl Bloch)
"At the Summit." [SanFPJ] (8:1) 85, p. 33.
"Beirut: Fire-Free Zone." [SanFPJ] (8:4) 85, p. 95.
"Brother Smiled." [SanFPJ] (8:1) 85, p. 49.
"Coloring Poem." [PoeticJ] (13) 86, p. 6.
"The Image-Makers." [SanFPJ] (8:4) 85, p. 94.
"A Slight Misinterpretation." [SanFPJ] (8:4) 85, p. 96.
"Thriller?" [PoeticJ] (15) Sum 86, p. 7.
"To Satisfy a Nation." [SanFPJ] (8:1) 85, p. 34.

"To the Nth Degree." [PoeticJ] (15) Sum 86, p. 34.
"Twins' B'nai Mitzvah." [PoeticJ] (16) Fall 86, p. 36.
"The Vase." [PoeticJ] (14) 86, p. 5.
4811. SEGARRA, Samuel
"Libres Pareados para una Ilusion Amante." [Mairena] (8:22) 86, p. 105.
4812. SEGELEN, Victor
"To Get Lost Daily" (tr. by Dorothy B. Aspinwall). [CrabCR] (4:1) Fall-Wint 86, p. 5.
4813. SEGOVIA DE RIOS, Maria Eloísa
"Triste Amor." [LetFem] (12:1/2) Primavera-Otoño 86, p. 156-157.
"Ya Paso." [LetFem] (12:1/2) Primavera-Otoño 86, p. 156.
4814. SEGREST, Mab
"What the Thunder Says." [RedBass] (10) 86, p. 10.
4815. SEIDEL, Frederick
"The Blue-Eyed Doe." [AmerPoR] (15:1) Ja-F 86, p. 31.
"Morphine." [ParisR] (28:100) Sum-Fall 86, p. 263-278.
"On Wings of Song." [AmerPoR] (15:1) Ja-F 86, p. 30.
4816. SEIDMAN, Hugh
"After the Ear Inn after the Snow." [ParisR] (28:100) Sum-Fall 86, p. 279-280.
4817. SEIFERLE, Rebecca
"After Reading a Collection of Poems." [ArizQ] (42:3) Aut 86, p. 222.
"The Artist at Ninety." [YetASM] (4) 85, p. 3.
"Blond Movies." [PaintedB] (29) Ag 86, p. 19-21.
"Like Gifts." [StoneC] (13:3/4) Spr-Sum 86, p. 72.
"Movie Stars." [CarolQ] (39:1) Fall 86, p. 5.
"The Toad." [NegC] (6:1) Wint 86, p. 42-44.
"Vocabulary." [IndR] (9:1) Wint 86, p. 36-37.
4818. SEIFERT, Jaroslav
"From Bozena Nemcová's Fan" (in Czech & English, tr. by Ron D. K. Banerjee). [InterPR] (12:1) Spr 86, p. 40-46.
4819. SEILER, Sheila
"Prodding for Pitfalls." [Sam] (44:2 release 174) 86, p. 18.
4820. SELAWSKY, John T.
"Blue Racer." [Poem] (55) Mr 86, p. 7.
"First Frost." [Poem] (55) Mr 86, p. 8-9.
"June of My Thirty-Third Year." [SoDakR] (24:2) Sum 86, p. 85.
"Memory." [StoneC] (13:3/4) Spr-Sum 86, p. 29.
"Northern Pike." [WestB] (19) 86, p. 25.
"The Stream." [SoDakR] (24:2) Sum 86, p. 84.
"World Champ." [StoneC] (13:3/4) Spr-Sum 86, p. 28.
4821. SELINGER, Eric
"Queer, Poor, Demure, Hair." [HarvardA] (120, i.e. 119:3) Mr 86, p. 9.
4822. SELLAND, Eric
"Kusudama" (tr. of Minoru Yoshioka). [Temblor] (4) 86, p. 161-162.
"Mother" (tr. of Minoru Yoshioka). [Temblor] (4) 86, p. 163-164.
"Pilgrimage" (tr. of Minoru Yoshioka). [Temblor] (4) 86, p. 158-160.
"Transparencies III & IV." [Temblor] (4) 86, p. 144-147.
4823. SELLERS, Bettie M.
"If Justice Moved." [GeoR] (40:3) Fall 86, p. 781.
4824. SELMAN, Robyn
"What Matters, More of Less." [ManhatPR] (8) Wint 86-87, p. 42-44.
4825. SELVA MIRANDA, Stella
"Iraida." [Mairena] (8:22) 86, p. 112.
4826. SELVAGGIO, Marc
"The Tree of Heaven." [PennR] (1:2) Fall 85, p. 46.
4827. SEMONES, Charles
"The Revenants" (for D.S.F.). [Wind] (16:57) 86, p. 38-39.
4828. SENGHOR, Léopold Sédar
"Kaya-Magan" (Ode to the Accompaniment of African Harp, tr. by Ann Neelon). [AmerPoR] (15:1) Ja-F 86, p. 19.
4829. SERCHUK, Peter
"Waiting for Poppa at the Smithtown Diner." [IndR] (9:3) Sum 86, p. 74-76.
"What You Need." [LittleM] (15:2) 86, p. 42.
4830. SERRA DELIZ, Wenceslao
"La Luna Existe" (A mi amigo Angel Ramos). [RevICP] (91) Enero-Marzo 86, p. 53-54.

333

4831. SESHADRI, Vijay
"This Fast-Paced, Brutal Thriller." [Shen] (36:2) 86, p. 99.
"Too Deep to Clear Them Away." [Shen] (36:2) 86, p. 100.
4832. SETH, Vikram
"The Golden Gate" (Selections: 8.12-8.16). [Zyzzyva] (2:1) Spr 86, p. 142-144.
4833. SETTLE, Marty
"Winter Strains." [SpoonRQ] (11:4) Fall 86, p. 26.
4834. SEXTON, Anne
"Locked Doors." [GeoR] (40:3) Fall 86, p. 783-784.
"Snow." [GeoR] (40:3) Fall 86, p. 784.
"The Witch's Life." [GeoR] (40:3) Fall 86, p. 782-783.
4835. SEXTON, Tom
"Nagoonberries." [Interim] (5:2) Fall 86, p. 29.
"On the Russian River." [Interim] (5:2) Fall 86, p. 29.
SHADDOX, Brenda Davidson
See DAVIDSON-SHADDOX, Brenda
4836. SHADOIAN, Jack
"Spring Again, 1988." [Outbr] (16/17) Fall 85-Spr 86, p. 81-82.
4837. SHAFFER, Eric Paul
"Amusing Myself." [PoeticJ] (15) Sum 86, p. 32.
"Change." [PoeticJ] (15) Sum 86, p. 36-37.
SHALIN, Hai-Jew
See HAI-JEW, Shalin
4838. SHANAFELT, Clara
"Profile." [Bogg] (56) 86, p. 15.
4839. SHAO, Yanxiang
"Memory" (tr. by Rewi Alley). [Verse] (6) 86, p. 47.
4840. SHAPIRO, Alan
"Blue Vase." [DenQ] (20:4/21:1) Spr-Sum 86, p. 116-117.
"The Riddle." [Thrpny] (24) Wint 86, p. 4.
4841. SHAPIRO, David
"The Lost Golf Ball." [Boulevard] (1:1/2) Wint 86, p. 170-171.
"The Queen of the Metropolitan Museum." [PartR] (53:4) 86, p. 588-591.
4842. SHAPIRO, Harvey
"Considering." [PoetryE] (20/21) Fall 86, p. 122.
"East Hampton Reading." [PoetryE] (20/21) Fall 86, p. 121.
"For Charles Reznikoff." [PoetryE] (20/21) Fall 86, p. 123.
"Pleasure." [PoetryE] (20/21) Fall 86, p. 120.
4843. SHAPIRO, Karl
"At Auden's Grave." [ParisR] (28:100) Sum-Fall 86, p. 281-283.
"At Auden's Grave." [ParisR] (28:99) Spr 86, p. 217-218.
"Vietnam Memorial." [NegC] (6:4) Fall 86, p. 11.
4844. SHAPIRO, Norman R.
"Fables" (Selections, tr. of Jean de La Fontaine. Texas Review Poetry Award
Chapbook). [TexasR] (7:1/2) Spr-Sum 86, p. 33-48.
4845. SHATTUCK, Roger
"Meanwhile." [Atlantic] (257:3) Mr 86, p. 61.
4846. SHAW, Kenneth Kerr
"Tribute to Neal Cassady." [Bogg] (55) 86, p. 57-58.
4847. SHAW, Robert B.
"Safe Harbor." [Poetry] (148:4) Jl 86, p. 218.
4848. SHAWGO, Lucy
"The Answer." [KenR] (NS 8:4) Fall 86, p. 84.
"For Ingrid Bergman." [KenR] (NS 8:4) Fall 86, p. 85.
"The Letter." [HolCrit] (23:5) D 86, p. 18.
4849. SHAY, Timothy
"Eyeless Storm." [WestCR] (21:2) O 86, p. 18.
"Failed Tactics." [WestCR] (21:2) O 86, p. 17.
"So Quickly Eaten Up." [WestCR] (21:2) O 86, p. 16.
"Thanks for the Medical Care Sweetheart." [AntigR] (66/67) Sum-Aut 86, p. 234.
4850. SHDO, Tamar
"Against All That Is Missing." [BellR] (9:2) Fall 86, p. 9.
4851. SHEARD, Norma Voorhees
"Landmark." [CapeR] (21:2) Fall 86, p. 5.
"Lovers Sitting in a Car in the Parking Lot near the Boathouse . . ." [CapeR] (21:2)
Fall 86, p. 4.

4852. SHECK, Laurie
"The Annunciation." [Iowa] (16:1) Wint 86, p. 97-98.
"In the Basilica of San Francesco." [Iowa] (16:1) Wint 86, p. 96-97.
"Water." [Nat] (242:15) 19 Ap 86, p. 559.
4853. SHECTMAN, Robin
"Sarah at Bedtime." [BelPoJ] (36:3) Spr 86, p. 39.
4854. SHEEHAN, Marc J.
"The Counting Poem." [CentR] (30:1) Wint 86, p. 57-58.
"For Cello, Prepared Heart and Voices." [PennR] (1:1) 85, p. 33-34.
"Owls." [PassN] (7:1) Fall-Wint 85-86, p. 14.
4855. SHEEHAN, Thomas
"Moon Dance, Trees Coming Green, April." [KanQ] (18:3) Sum 86, p. 90-92.
"Night Forgery." [SoDakR] (24:2) Sum 86, p. 148.
"A Private Ceremony." [IndR] (9:3) Sum 86, p. 80-82.
"Thomas, Thomas." [SoDakR] (24:2) Sum 86, p. 146-147.
4856. SHEIRER, John
"Haiku" (3 poems). [WindO] (47) Sum 86, p. 4.
4857. SHEIRER, John Mark
"How I Plan to Know and Understand the Universe: Step One." [YetASM] (4) 85,
    p. 4.
4858. SHELDON, Glenn
"A Hungry Fisherman Catches More Fish" (New England adage). [DeKalbLAJ]
    (19:3/4) 86, p. 88.
"Professor at the Funeral." [WindO] (47) Sum 86, p. 12.
4859. SHELLEY, Pat
"French Movie" (formula poem). [Bogg] (56) 86, p. 11.
4860. SHELLY, Nadine
"The Faery Lady." [Grain] (14:2) My 86, p. 52.
"Lilith." [Grain] (14:2) My 86, p. 52.
4861. SHELNUTT, Eve
"Answering." [NoAmR] (271:3) S 86, p. 55.
4862. SHELTON, Mark
"Wine Day." [PassN] (7:2) Spr-Sum 86, p. 21.
4863. SHEPARD, Neil
"Astronomical" (Paxico, Kansas). [SouthernR] (22:3) Sum 86, p. 567.
"Conviction" (Brattleboro, 1899). [SouthernR] (22:3) Sum 86, p. 569.
"Of Larry Bird and Wallace Stevens." [SouthernR] (22:3) Sum 86, p. 568-569.
4864. SHEPHERD, J. Barrie
"Community Thanksgiving." [ChrC] (103:35) 19 N 86, p. 1020.
"Community Thanksgiving" (corrected printing). [ChrC] (103:36) 26 N 86, p. 1058.
"Egg Rolling." [ChrC] (103:10) 19-26 Mr 86, p. 298.
"Epiphany." [ChrC] (103:1) 1-8 Ja 86, p. 12.
"Essence." [ChrC] (103:40) 24-31 D 86, p. 1176.
"Foothold." [ChrC] (103:5) 5-12 F 86, p. 110.
"Incarnating." [ChrC] (103:38) 10 D 86, p. 1112.
"Testing." [ChrC] (103:7) 26 F 86, p. 204.
"Trade Questions." [ChrC] (103:9) 12 Mr 86, p. 264.
4865. SHEPPARD, Susan
"Crossing Water." [Wind] (16:56) 86, p. 37-38.
4866. SHER, Gail
"The Lanyard." [Notus] (1:1) Fall 86, p. 13-21.
"The Lanyard." [Sink] (1) 86, p. 13-18.
4867. SHER, Steven
"Meteor Shower, Night in the Catskills." [Outbr] (16/17) Fall 85-Spr 86, p. 85-86.
"New Year, Times Square." [Outbr] (16/17) Fall 85-Spr 86, p. 87.
"Postmarked Indiana" (on hearing from Ogden Alger). [KanQ] (18:4) Fall 86, p. 55.
"Winnemucca Pickup." [Wind] (16:58) 86, p. 40.
4868. SHERMAN, Alana
"Cape May." [PoeticJ] (16) Fall 86, p. 20.
"Hurricane Season." [PoeticJ] (16) Fall 86, p. 38.
4869. SHERMAN, G. W.
"Motorcycles" (In memory of O.J. Whitemarsh, of Bellingham, Washington). [Sam]
    (46:5 [i.e. 46:1] release 181) 86, p. 2.
"The Piper Paid." [Sam] (45:4 release 180) 86, p. 24-25.
"To a Vietnamese Student, Cramming." [Sam] (45:4 release 180) 86, p. 2.

4870. SHERRY, James
"Our Nuclear Heritage" (Excerpt). [Sink] (2) 86, p. 38-39.
"Plane and Fencing Rhetoric." [Sink] (2) 86, p. 40-41.
4871. SHIFFRIN, Nancy
"Deadly Minuet." [Amelia] (3:1) Ja 86, p. 85.
"Sunday." [Amelia] (3:1) Ja 86, p. 85-86.
SHIGEHARU, Nakano
See NAKANO, Shigeharu
4872. SHIKATANI, Gerry
"Postcards." [GreenfR] (13:3/4) Sum-Fall 86, p. 179-180.
4873. SHIKIBU, Izumi
"Did I sigh at your absence yesterday?" [YellowS] (18) Spr 86, p. 23.
"How dense love's foliage has grown." [YellowS] (18) Spr 86, p. 5.
"Remembering you." [YellowS] (18) Spr 86, p. 11.
"What wind is this." [YellowS] (18) Spr 86, p. 28.
"Why haven't I thought of it before?" [YellowS] (18) Spr 86, p. 13.
4874. SHIKITANI, Gerry
"Bird of Two Forms." [Contact] (7:38/39/40) Wint-Spr 86, p. 35.
"The Food." [Contact] (7:38/39/40) Wint-Spr 86, p. 35.
4875. SHILLING, Grant
"After Dinner." [WestCR] (21:1) Je 86, p. 39.
"At the Beach Cafeteria." [WestCR] (21:1) Je 86, p. 38.
"Black Warm." [WestCR] (21:1) Je 86, p. 34.
"Down Note." [WestCR] (21:1) Je 86, p. 40.
"Early Morning View from a Rainy Day Driveway." [WestCR] (21:1) Je 86, p. 39.
"Friday Night Sabbath." [WestCR] (21:1) Je 86, p. 34.
"Like Asphalt." [WestCR] (21:1) Je 86, p. 36-37.
"Music by the Window." [WestCR] (21:1) Je 86, p. 35.
"Naked Man Posing as a Woman, N.Y.C. 1968" (for Diane Arbus). [WestCR] (21:1) Je 86, p. 37.
"Turned-over-Tricycle." [WestCR] (21:1) Je 86, p. 38.
4876. SHINKAWA, Kazue
"Never Bind Me" (tr. by James Kirkup and Akiko Takemoto). [Translation] (17) Fall 86, p. 204-205.
4877. SHIPLEY, Vivian
"It Is Lovely to Think, Richard Eberhart, of Lovely You." [NegC] (6:2/3) Spr-Sum 86, p. 65.
"Minnie Taber." [MemphisSR] (6:1/2) Spr 86, p. 27.
4878. SHIRLEY, Aleda
"Aubade." [Poetry] (149:2) N 86, p. 63-64.
"Because of the Rose." [VirQR] (62:2) Spr 86, p. 257-258.
"Finding the Room." [Poetry] (148:3) Je 86, p. 152-153.
"Hostage to Fortune." [VirQR] (62:2) Spr 86, p. 258-260.
"A Hundred Circles." [AmerPoR] (15:1) Ja-F 86, p. 36.
"I Will Give You Three Seasons." [PraS] (60:3) Fall 86, p. 65-66.
"Idiot Savant." [PoetryNW] (27:1) Spr 86, p. 13-14.
"L'Ivresse des Grandes Profondeurs." [Poetry] (148:3) Je 86, p. 155.
"Let Me Tell You How It Happened." [PoetryNW] (27:1) Spr 86, p. 14-15.
"The Rivers Where They Touch." [AmerPoR] (15:1) Ja-F 86, p. 36.
"Small Talk." [AmerV] (4) Fall 86, p. 80-81.
"Speculations on the Pearl." [DenQ] (20:4/21:1) Spr-Sum 86, p. 12-13.
"Sunset Grand Couturier." [Poetry] (148:3) Je 86, p. 153-154.
"Voices inside Voices." [PraS] (60:3) Fall 86, p. 66-67.
"The Wandering Year." [Poetry] (147:6) Mr 86, p. 341-342.
4879. SHISLER, Barbara Esch
"Janice." [HiramPoR] (40) Spr-Sum 86, p. 23.
4880. SHIVELY, Bill
"Wherever They Go." [Contact] (8:41/42/43) Fall-Wint 86-87, p. 14.
"Wine Song." [Contact] (8:41/42/43) Fall-Wint 86-87, p. 14.
4881. SHOAF, Diann Blakely
"A Man Is Found Mauled to Death in Polar Bear Cage in Central Park" (The New York Times). [ConnPR] (5:1) 86, p. 13.
"The Sculpture Garden." [SouthernHR] (20:3) Sum 86, p. 262-263.
4882. SHOLL, Betsy
"Catechism." [BelPoJ] (37:1) Fall 86, p. 21.

4883. SHOMER, Enid
"Atlantic City Luck." [CapeR] (21:1) Spr 86, p. 28.
"Before the Wine." [StoneC] (14:1/2) Fall-Wint 86-87, p. 25.
"The Bookkeeper at H. G. Smithy's." [NewL] (52:2/3) Wint-Spr 86, p. 212.
"Burial Above Ground." [SlipS] (6) 86, p. 40-41.
"City Driving at Twilight." [SlipS] (6) 86, p. 41.
"What Eats in the Middle of the Night." [PassN] (7:2) Spr-Sum 86, p. 5.
"Woman on the Street." [SlipS] (6) 86, p. 42.
"Women Bathing at Bergen-Belsen." [NegC] (6:1) Wint 86, p. 13.
4884. SHORB, Michael
"Galloping Horse Unearthed at Leitai, China." [ManhatPR] (6) Wint-Spr 85-86, p. 42.
"Teeth White As Stars." [Vis] (22) 86, p. 31.
4885. SHORR, Kathy
"Amnesia." [NegC] (6:4) Fall 86, p. 100-101.
4886. SHORT, Kandy
"And at the Memorial: Pan In." [SnapD] (9:2) Spr 86, p. 55.
"Girl Scouts." [SnapD] (9:2) Spr 86, p. 54.
4887. SHREVE, Sandy
"Public Execution." [Event] (15:2) 86, p. 104-105.
4888. SHU, Ting
"?.!" (tr. by Carolyn Kizer). [Zyzzyva] (2:2) Sum 86, p. 56-57.
"A Boat with Two Masts" (tr. by Tao Liu). [Verse] (6) 86, p. 48.
"Dream of an Island" (tr. by Chou Ping). [Nimrod] (29:2) Spr-Sum 86, p. 97.
4889. SHUGRUE, Jim
"Again." [Wind] (16:56) 86, p. 5.
"Saturday / Sunday." [SoDakR] (24:2) Sum 86, p. 95.
4890. SHUMAKER, Peggy
"Blue Ridge Reservoir." [NoAmR] (271:3) S 86, p. 8.
"The Circle of Totems." [BlackWR] (12:2) Spr 86, p. 55-58.
"Newlywed." [HayF] (1) Spr 86, p. 97.
"Turned Wood." [PoetryNW] (27:4) Wint 86-87, p. 39.
"Wounded Science." [HayF] (1) Spr 86, p. 98.
4891. SHUMWAY, Mary
"Sussex Flight." [Northeast] (series 4:3) Spr 86, p. 6.
SHUNTARO, Tanikawa
See TANIKAWA, Shuntaro
4892. SHURBANOV, Alexander
"Medusa: Selected Poems" (tr. of Nicolai Kantchev, w. Jascha Kessler). [QRL] (Poetry series 6:26) 86, 38 p.
4893. SHURIN, Aaron
"Artery" (Selections: 1-5). [Acts] (5) 86, p. 70-74.
"Artery" (Selections: 11-15). [Conjunc] (9) 86, p. 111-112.
"Artery" (Selections: 5 poems). [Temblor] (3) 86, p. 72-76.
"City of Men." [Temblor] (4) 86, p. 11-18.
4894. SHUTTLE, Penelope
"29th February." [Verse] (5) 86, p. 47.
"The Animals from Underground." [ManhatR] (4:1) Fall 86, p. 51.
"Clouds." [Verse] (5) 86, p. 46.
"Selena." [ManhatR] (4:1) Fall 86, p. 49-50.
"Seven Mirrors." [ManhatR] (4:1) Fall 86, p. 48.
4895. SHUTTLEWORTH, Paul
"An Audience." [Sam] (44:3 release 175) 86, p. 32.
"Beneath a Cottonwood." [PraS] (60:2) Sum 86, p. 90.
"A Cartload of Afternoon." [BellR] (9:2) Fall 86, p. 19.
"Evening and a Wren Flying Home to a Dead Tree." [WestB] (18) 86, p. 92.
"Farmyard." [BellR] (9:2) Fall 86, p. 20.
"Frank James at Age Seventy in 1913." [PraS] (60:2) Sum 86, p. 88.
"A Girl As Pretty As a Painted Easter Egg." [WestB] (18) 86, p. 93.
"Isn't It Better This Way?" [Sam] (45:4 release 180) 86, p. 48.
"It Recurs." [BellR] (9:2) Fall 86, p. 20.
"The One Who Left Her Husband and Grew Her Chestnut Hair Long." [BellR] (9:2) Fall 86, p. 19-20.
"A Ring Is Less than a Home." [Sam] (44:3 release 175) 86, p. 30-31.
"A Widow's Grief, 1897." [PraS] (60:2) Sum 86, p. 89.

337

SICOLI

4896. SICOLI, Dan
"After Noon." [Amelia] (3:1) Ja 86, p. 80.
"Before the Rage." [SlipS] (6) 86, p. 73-74.
"Message." [Amelia] (3:2) Spr 86, p. 97.
"Stiff." [Amelia] (3:2) Spr 86, p. 97.
4897. SIDDHARTHA, Leonard
"After Surgery, the Small Rebirth." [BellArk] (2:6) N-D 86, p. 3.
"The Garden." [BellArk] (2:6) N-D 86, p. 8.
"The Philosopher, Stoned." [BellArk] (2:6) N-D 86, p. 16.
4898. SIDERIS, Hilary
"My Clone Won't Read Hart Crane." [MidAR] (6:2) 86, p. 17.
"Now That My Clone Has Smoked the Last of My Dope." [MidAR] (6:2) 86, p. 18.
4899. SIDNEY, Joan Seliger
"What Women Want." [YellowS] (20) Aut 86, p. 14.
4900. SIEGEL, Joan I.
"The Fawn." [InterPR] (12:2) Fall 86, p. 108.
"Te Deum." [InterPR] (12:2) Fall 86, p. 107.
"Where did They Put Him." [Sam] (44:3 release 175) 86, p. 13.
4901. SIEGEL, Robert
"Cancer Surgeon at St. Joseph's." [PraS] (60:1) Spr 86, p. 57-58.
"Distracted at the Sink." [BallSUF] (27:4) Aut 86, p. 8.
"Levity" (St. Joseph of Copertino, 1603-1663). [PraS] (60:1) Spr 86, p. 59.
"Lullaby: 'I Love You, My Plain Pine Box'." [BallSUF] (27:4) Aut 86, p. 43.
4902. SIERRA, Carmen A.
"Cuando se muere la memoria de infancia." [Mairena] (8:22) 86, p. 116.
4903. SIETECASE, Reynaldo
"Vamos a liberarnos." [Mairena] (8:22) 86, p. 58-59.
4904. SIGURDSSON, Olafur Johann
"Space Travel" (tr. by Alan Boucher). [Vis] (20) 86, p. 9.
4905. SILBERT, Layle
"Biology." [RagMag] (5:2) Fall 86, p. 70.
"The Gent." [Confr] (32) Spr-Sum 86, p. 127.
4906. SILEN, Ivan
"El Quinto Angel." [RevICP] (90) Oct-Dic 85, p. 50.
4907. SILENTIARIUS, Paulus
"They say a man bitten by a rabid dog" (from "The Palatine Anthology, tr. by John Gill). [YellowS] (21) Wint 86, p. 24.
4908. SILESKY, Barry
"Castling." [CutB] (25) Fall-Wint 86, p. 31.
"A Day in the Country." [Ascent] (11:3) 86, p. 34-35.
"The New Tenants." [GrandS] (5:2) Wint 86, p. 218-219.
"Rural Particles." [IndR] (9:2) Spr 86, p. 13.
"Some Aspects of Brooms." [SouthwR] (71:1) Wint 86, p. 120-121.
4909. SILKIN, Jon
"The Coldness." [Stand] (27:3) Sum 86, p. 46.
4910. SILLIMAN, Ron
"Demo" (from "The Alphabet," for Kit Robinson). [Temblor] (3) 86, p. 140-148.
"Lit" (Selection: V). [Sink] (1) 86, p. 22-25.
"OZ" (Excerpt). [Caliban] (1) 86, p. 80-82.
"Oz" (Excerpt). [Sulfur] (6:1, issue 16) 86, p. 124-129.
"Oz" (Excerpt). [Zyzzyva] (2:1) Spr 86, p. 146-149.
SILVA, Loreina Santos
See SANTOS SILVA, Loreina
4911. SILVA, Sam
"Material Directives from God." [Sam] (46:5 [i.e. 46:1] release 181) 86, p. 44.
4912. SILVA ACEVEDO, Manuel
"Me Han Roto el Hueso Mas Fino del Oído." [SilverFR] (11) Sum 86, p. 18.
"They've Broken the Most Delicate Bone in My Ear" (tr. by Steven F. White). [SilverFR] (11) Sum 86, p. 19.
SILVA RAMOS, Pericles Eugenio da
See RAMOS, Pericles Eugenio da Silva
4913. SILVER, William (William F.)
"After Reading Richard Holmes's Shelley." [IndR] (9:3) Sum 86, p. 45-46.
"The Cemetery at Cambria, California." [TarRP] (25:2) Spr 86, p. 25-26.
4914. SILVER-LILLYWHITE, Eileen
"The Wrecking Ball." [NowestR] (24:2) 86, p. 16.

338

4915. SILVERMAN, Stuart J.
"After This." [HolCrit] (23:2) Ap 86, p. 19.
4916. SILVERSTEIN, David I.
"Deciding What to Do with Your Life." [ChiR] (35:3) Spr 86, p. 48-49.
4917. SIMAS, Joseph
"Memorials." [Temblor] (3) 86, p. 81-84.
4918. SIMEONI, Piera
"Aquarium Fish" (tr. by Ruth Feldman). [NewRena] (6:3, #20) Spr 86, p. 55.
"Pesci in Acquario" (from Liriche ed Epigrammi). [NewRena] (6:3, #20) Spr 86, p. 54.
4919. SIMIC, Charles
"Black Coffee and Rolls." [Verse] (6) 86, p. 9.
"Dear Child." [Verse] (6) 86, p. 7.
"Early-Evening Algebra." [NewYorker] (61:46) 6 Ja 86, p. 30.
"Easter." [Field] (35) Fall 86, p. 71.
"Henri Rousseau's Bed." [Poetry] (147:4) Ja 86, p. 199-200.
"The Implements of Augury" (for Ljubinka). [Field] (35) Fall 86, p. 72.
"The Lesson." [PoetryE] (20/21) Fall 86, p. 182-184.
"March." [Verse] (6) 86, p. 8.
"The Marvels of the City" (for Bata). [Field] (35) Fall 86, p. 73.
"Matches." [Verse] (6) 86, p. 6.
"A Series of Fortuitous Circumstances." [ParisR] (28:100) Sum-Fall 86, p. 284.
"Severe Figures." [GeoR] (40:3) Fall 86, p. 785.
"The Study of Letters and Numerals." [Verse] (6) 86, p. 8.
4920. SIMKO, S. Daniel
"Afterwards." [OP] (42/43) Wint 86-87, p. 34-35.
"Coda." [OP] (42/43) Wint 86-87, p. 35.
"Coming Home." [OP] (42/43) Wint 86-87, p. 29.
"Deposition." [OP] (42/43) Wint 86-87, p. 33.
"Homage to Georg Trakl." [OP] (42/43) Wint 86-87, p. 29-30.
"Still Life: A Treatment." [OP] (42/43) Wint 86-87, p. 32-33.
"To Max Jacob in the Blue." [OP] (42/43) Wint 86-87, p. 30-32.
"Winter Music." [OP] (42/43) Wint 86-87, p. 34.
4921. SIMMONS, James
"War on Want." [NewEngR] (9:1) Aut 86, p. 28-29.
4922. SIMMS, Michael
"The Fire-Eater." [BlackWR] (13:1) Fall 86, p. 7-9.
4923. SIMON, John Oliver
"Alone Sometimes." [InterPR] (12:1) Spr 86, p. 90.
"Granzio." [InterPR] (12:1) Spr 86, p. 86.
"In the Chama Mountains" (tr. of Mario Payeras). [InterPR] (12:1) Spr 86, p. 31.
"Little Salzanos" (tr. of Daniel Salzano). [InterPR] (12:1) Spr 86, p. 25, 27.
"The New Day Dazzles You" (For Gustavo Eguren, tr. of Fayad Jamís). [InterPR] (12:1) Spr 86, p. 33-35.
"San Miguelito." [InterPR] (12:1) Spr 86, p. 89.
"Saying Kaddish for My Stepfather in Mexico City and Mendocino." [InterPR] (12:1) Spr 86, p. 87-88.
"Sea Voyages" (tr. of Guillermo Boido). [InterPR] (12:1) Spr 86, p. 21.
"A Single Syllable" (tr. of Saúl Ibargoyen). [InterPR] (12:1) Spr 86, p. 23.
"To My Father" (tr. of Maria Guerra Tejada). [InterPR] (12:1) Spr 86, p. 29.
4924. SIMON, Louise
"Pathways" (Selections). [Quarry] (35:3) Sum 86, p. 7-11.
4925. SIMON, Margaret B.
"Starweave." [Vis] (20) 86, p. 14.
4926. SIMON, Maurya
"Angle of Repose." [LitR] (30:1) Fall 86, p. 116.
"Blue Movies." [LittleM] (15:2) 86, p. 23.
"Contusion." [CumbPR] (5:2) Spr 86, p. 36.
"Encounter." [WillowS] (17) Wint 86, p. 23.
"First Light." [WillowS] (17) Wint 86, p. 20.
"Fountainbleau." [SoDakR] (24:2) Sum 86, p. 83.
"Hermosa Beach, Revisited." [LitR] (30:1) Fall 86, p. 117.
"Icarus in the Twentieth Century." [Verse] (5) 86, p. 36.
"In the Shtetl." [MissouriR] (9:2) 86, p. 192-193.
"King Midas's Daughter." [CumbPR] (5:2) Spr 86, p. 34.
"November Ellipsis." [ManhatPR] (7) Sum 86, p. 48.

"Nude Mice" (for Miroslav Holub). [LittleM] (15:2) 86, p. 24.
"Off the Island of Krk, Yugoslavia." [LittleM] (15:1) 86, p. 57.
"The Poem at the End of the World." [GeoR] (40:4) Wint 86, p. 880-881.
"Red Tide." [LittleM] (15:2) 86, p. 22.
"Seizure." [Electrum] (38) Spr 86, p. 13.
"Self Portrait." [WillowS] (17) Wint 86, p. 21-22.
"The Sibyl." [GrandS] (5:2) Wint 86, p. 134.
"Snapshot." [CumbPR] (5:2) Spr 86, p. 35.
"Sunday." [WillowS] (17) Wint 86, p. 18-19.
"Vermeer's Women." [BlackWR] (12:2) Spr 86, p. 69.
4927. SIMONI, Wanda D.
"Forever." [SanFPJ] (8:2) 85, p. 17.
"Nuclear Nightmare." [SanFPJ] (8:2) 85, p. 26-27.
4928. SIMONS, Mary Crescenzo
"Road Blocks." [Amelia] (3:3) Sum 86, p. 69-70.
4929. SIMONSUURI, Kirsti
"Bibliothèque Nationale" (tr. by Jascha Kessler and the author). [Writ] (18) 86, c87, p. 70.
"For Bowie" (tr. by Jascha Kessler and the author). [MalR] (77) D 86, p. 46.
"A Monk" (tr. by Jascha Kessler and the author). [Writ] (18) 86, c87, p. 68.
"Moving" (tr. by Jascha Kessler and the author). [Writ] (18) 86, c87, p. 73.
"Mythos" (tr. by Jascha Kessler and the author). [MalR] (77) D 86, p. 47.
"A Poetry Reading" (tr. by Jascha Kessler and the author). [Writ] (18) 86, c87, p. 71-72.
"Some Definite Laws" (tr. by Jascha Kessler and the author). [Writ] (18) 86, c87, p. 69.
"Song" (from *Kanteletar*, collected by Lonnrot in the 19th c., tr. of anonymous poem, w. Jascha Kessler). [MalR] (77) D 86, p. 45.
"Travelling Light" (tr. by Jascha Kessler and the author). [Writ] (18) 86, c87, p. 67.
4930. SIMPSON, Jak
"The Beat." [MoodySI] (16/17) Sum 86, p. 9.
4931. SIMPSON, Louis
"Drugstore Nights." [OhioR] (36) 86, p. 36-38.
"His Funny Valentine." [Hudson] (39:1) Spr 86, p. 83-86.
"The Peace March." [PoetryE] (20/21) Fall 86, p. 69.
"Publishing Days." [Hudson] (39:1) Spr 86, p. 81-82.
"Pursuit of Happiness." [Caliban] (1) 86, p. 78-79.
4932. SIMPSON, Nancy
"The Group." [SouthernPR] (26:1) Spr 86, p. 54-55.
4933. SIMRIL, C.
"Hiroshima Stopwatch." [CanLit] (109) Sum 86, p. 54.
4934. SIMS, Peter
"The Ground Is Too Fast for Us." [Quarry] (35:3) Sum 86, p. 57-58.
"Play." [Quarry] (35:3) Sum 86, p. 58-59.
4935. SINCLAIR, John
"If I Could Be With You." [MichQR] (25:2) Spr 86, p. 205-212.
"Louisiana Blues" (from *Fattening Frogs for Snakes: Delta Blues Suite*). [Notus] (1:1) Fall 86, p. 27-29.
"Spiritual" (after John Coltrane). [Notus] (1:1) Fall 86, p. 26.
4936. SINGER, Rosanne
"Picnic on the Grass." [YetASM] (4) 85, p. 2.
4937. SINGLETON, Martin
"Desert Lynx." [AntigR] (65) Spr 86, p. 142.
"Dream before Dawn." [AntigR] (65) Spr 86, p. 144.
"From a Line by Cyril Dabydeen." [GreenfR] (13:3/4) Sum-Fall 86, p. 181.
"Learning to Aim." [AntigR] (65) Spr 86, p. 141.
"Northeast." [GreenfR] (13:3/4) Sum-Fall 86, p. 182-184.
"Poet As Diver." [AntigR] (65) Spr 86, p. 143.
SISTER MAURA
See MAURA (SISTER)
4938. SIVAN, Aryeh
"One Hundred Years of Jewish Settlement Later" (tr. by Hillel Halkin). [PoetL] (81:2) Sum 86, p. 78-79.
"An Unpleasant Incident at a Memorial" (tr. by Hillel Halkin). [PoetL] (81:2) Sum 86, p. 79.

4939. SIVIY, D. Weldon
"Follow hungry wolves." [Electrum] (38) Spr 86, p. 10.
"Listen, don't reply." [Amelia] (3:1) Ja 86, p. 95.
4940. SJOGREN, Britta H.
"Innocence Abroad." [LittleM] (15:1) 86, p. 27-29.
"Song to an Intimate Stranger (II)." [LittleM] (15:1) 86, p. 27.
4941. SKAU, Michael
"Block." [YetASM] (5) 86, p. 8.
4942. SKEEN, Anita
"Making Sense of It All." [KanQ] (18:4) Fall 86, p. 74.
"Travelers." [KanQ] (18:4) Fall 86, p. 73.
"Use of Example." [YellowS] (20) Aut 86, p. 19.
"Without Words." [YellowS] (20) Aut 86, p. 18.
4943. SKEENS, Gary S.
"Reality Morning." [YetASM] (4) 85, p. 3.
4944. SKEETER, Sharyn Jeanne
"Moment: Felix with the Round Face in Windshield." [Obs] (NS 1:1/2) Spr-Sum 86,
p. 83.
"Street Encounter, Port-au-Prince." [Obs] (NS 1:1/2) Spr-Sum 86, p. 82.
4945. SKILLMAN, Judith
"Denmark in the Spring" (for Joel). [TarRP] (24:2) Spr 85, p. 9-10.
"Independence Day." [StoneC] (13:3/4) Spr-Sum 86, p. 36.
"The Librarian Decides on Cryonics." [Poetry] (148:5) Ag 86, p. 258.
"On a Stump Outside Vacation Bible School." [MalR] (77) D 86, p. 64.
"The Worship of the Visible Spectrum." [Poetry] (148:6) S 86, p. 339-340.
"Written on Learning of Arrhythmia in the Unborn Child." [Poetry] (148:6) S 86, p.
338.
4946. SKINNER, Jauneth
"Indian Pony Days." [BallSUF] (27:4) Aut 86, p. 72-73.
4947. SKINNER, Jeffrey
"A Guide to Forgetting." [Nat] (242:24) 21 Je 86, p. 866.
"Three Morning Songs." [StoneC] (13:3/4) Spr-Sum 86, p. 50.
4948. SKINNER, Knute
"Tayto Crisps" (for Dunstan and Morgan). [Amelia] (3:3) Sum 86, p. 18.
4949. SKLAREW, Myra
"Letters" (tr. of Moshe Dor, w. the author and Erella Hadar). [PoetL] (81:2) Sum
86, p. 103.
"Responsibility" (tr. of Moshe Dor, w. the author and Erella Hadar). [PoetL] (81:2)
Sum 86, p. 104.
4950. SKLOOT, Floyd
"Beat the Clock." [NowestR] (24:1) 86, p. 24.
"The House of Bric-a-brac." [Northeast] (series 4:3) Spr 86, p. 37.
"It Might." [PennR] (2:1) Fall-Wint 86, p. 14.
"The Jack London Hotel." [PennR] (2:1) Fall-Wint 86, p. 15.
"Kaleidoscope" (Chapbook). [SilverFR] (12) 86, unpaged.
"The Middle of America." [PennR] (2:1) Fall-Wint 86, p. 16.
"Second Honeymoon." [CrossCur] (5:4/6:1) 86, p. 52-53.
"Settings." [CrossCur] (5:4/6:1) 86, p. 54.
"The Spiel." [PoetryNW] (27:4) Wint 86-87, p. 26-27.
"Surfacing." [PennR] (2:1) Fall-Wint 86, p. 18.
"Swimmer." [PoetryNW] (27:2) Sum 86, p. 21-22.
SKOOT, Floyd
See SKLOOT, Floyd
4951. SKOYLES, John
"Times Square." [AmerPoR] (15:6) N-D 86, p. 29.
4952. SKRANDE, Eva
"Gabriela." [Sonora] (10) Spr 86, p. 40.
4953. SLAUGHTER, William
"Alibis." [WritersF] (12) Fall 86, p. 185-186.
4954. SLAVITT, David R.
"Canaletto's Ruin." [OntR] (25) Fall-Wint 86-87, p. 100-102.
"Jephtha's Prayer." [Boulevard] (1:1/2) Wint 86, p. 157-158.
"The Tristia of Ovid" (Selection: III, 10). [Boulevard] (1:1/2) Wint 86, p. 154-156.
4955. SLEADD, Marcie
"The Girls in Their Summer Dresses" (after a Short Story by Irwin Shaw). [KanQ]
(18:4) Fall 86, p. 102.

4956. SLEIGH, Tom
"M. on Her Thirtieth Birthday." [Poetry] (147:5) F 86, p. 270-271.
"The Porch Swing." [BostonR] (11:2) Ap 86, p. 11.
"Seventh Floor: Cancer Ward." [Poetry] (147:5) F 86, p. 269-270.
"Sunday Drive." [BostonR] (11:2) Ap 86, p. 11.
"A Vision" (for Frank Bidart). [BostonR] (11:2) Ap 86, p. 11.
"You Have Her Eyes." [Shen] (36:2) 86, p. 94.
4957. SLESINGER, Warren
"The Screed of the Flesh." [ThRiPo] (27/28) 86, p. 65.
4958. SLOAN, De Villo
"Bolinas." [SecC] (14:1) 86, p. 65.
4959. SLOAN, Gerry
"Depots" (for my father). [NegC] (6:4) Fall 86, p. 75.
"Joy of Man's Desiring" (for Nancy). [Poem] (56) N 86, p. 31.
"The Monarch Migration." [CapeR] (21:2) Fall 86, p. 30.
"Snapshot, 1956." [DeKalbLAJ] (19:3/4) 86, p. 88.
4960. SLOCUM, Bob
"Falling." [BallSUF] (27:4) Aut 86, p. 44.
4961. SLOMAN, Joel
"Giuditta." [Writ] (17) 85, c86, p. 23-24.
"I Did Forget." [Writ] (17) 85, c86, p. 25.
"Messes." [Writ] (17) 85, c86, p. 21.
"Moby Dick." [Writ] (17) 85, c86, p. 22.
4962. SLOMKOWSKA, Lusia
"Gdansk/4 AM." [Agni] (23) 86, p. 50.
"The heart-scarlet tulip." [Amelia] (3:3) Sum 86, p. 6.
"Waldek's Wedding." [Agni] (23) 86, p. 51.
"Why Cities Have Farmer's Markets" (for my mother). [Agni] (23) 86, p. 49.
4963. SLYOMOVICS, Susan
"Old Man Lampo died in Spain" (tr. of Abderrahman Abnoudy). [SenR] (16:1) 86,
p. 84-90.
4964. SMALL, Abbott
"Remaking Feet" (For my Aunt Shirley). [Wind] (16:56) 86, p. 39.
4965. SMALLWOOD, Vivian
"The Homecoming." [NegC] (6:4) Fall 86, p. 30.
4966. SMETZER, Michael
"A Man Who Told the Truth." [Wind] (16:56) 86, p. 9.
4967. SMITH, Allen
"Under the Bridge." [WritersL] (1986:4), p. 20.
4968. SMITH, Antony
"Morning Prayers." [LitR] (29:2) Wint 86, p. 250.
4969. SMITH, Arthur
"The Light of Being Winded." [NewYorker] (62:17) 16 Je 86, p. 38.
"Untitled Canvas." [MissouriR] (9:1) 85-86, p. 44-45.
4970. SMITH, Barbara
"Portrait of Foxes." [TarRP] (24:2) Spr 85, p. 26.
4971. SMITH, Bob
"Answering the Riddle." [HangL] (49) Spr 86, p. 41.
"Elegy on a Sunny Day." [Contact] (8:41/42/43) Fall-Wint 86-87, p. 54.
"Falling in Love with the Anchorwoman." [Contact] (8:41/42/43) Fall-Wint 86-87,
p. 54.
4972. SMITH, Carolyn
"The Point, Unknown." [CrossC] (8:1) 86, p. 8.
4973. SMITH, Charlie
"By Fire." [Field] (33) Fall 85, p. 85.
"Discovery." [Field] (33) Fall 85, p. 86.
"What Can Be United." [GeoR] (40:2) Sum 86, p. 447-448.
4974. SMITH, Dave
"Ancestral Farmhouse." [KenR] (NS 7:1) Wint 85, p. 10-11.
"Caravati's Salvage: Richmond, Virginia." [GeoR] (40:3) Fall 86, p. 788.
"Careless Love." [Poetry] (147:5) F 86, p. 257-258.
"Championship Fight." [Poetry] (147:5) F 86, p. 259-260.
"Driving Lesson." [Poetry] (147:5) F 86, p. 258-259.
"During the Fall." [SouthernPR] (26:1) Spr 86, p. 71-72.
"Field Music." [KenR] (NS 7:1) Wint 85, p. 11-14.
"First May Day." [SouthernPR] (26:1) Spr 86, p. 72.

"Gargoyle." [NewYorker] (62:4) 17 Mr 86, p. 36.
"Pillage." [KenR] (NS 7:1) Wint 85, p. 9-10.
"Pregnant." [KenR] (NS 7:1) Wint 85, p. 8-9.
"Snow Sundown." [NewYorker] (61:50) 3 F 86, p. 40.
"Summer House." [KenR] (NS 7:1) Wint 85, p. 7-8.
4975. SMITH, Douglas
"Letter to the Prairie, Open." [PraF] (7:1) Spr 86, p. 52-53.
"On the 401 from Waterloo to Toronto." [GreenfR] (13:3/4) Sum-Fall 86, p. 185.
4976. SMITH, Francis J.
"Palimpsest at Bibury." [ColEng] (48:5) S 86, p. 460.
4977. SMITH, Gary
"Freshman Composition" (For Janet). [Confr] (33/34) Fall-Wint 86-87, p. 54.
4978. SMITH, Iain Crichton
"Aberdeen." [Stand] (27:4) Aut 86, p. 23.
"There Are Those." [Stand] (27:4) Aut 86, p. 22.
"Villagers, in the Second World War." [Stand] (27:4) Aut 86, p. 22.
4979. SMITH, J. D.
"The Acorns Have Fallen." [StoneC] (13:3/4) Spr-Sum 86, p. 23.
"Iowa." [Poem] (56) N 86, p. 10.
"She." [CutB] (26) Spr-Sum 86, p. 14.
4980. SMITH, J. Winston
"Wartime Flightline Rhyme." [SanFPJ] (8:3) 85, p. 29.
4981. SMITH, James Steel
"Thing." [Amelia] (3:1) Ja 86, p. 75.
SMITH, James Sutherland
See SUTHERLAND-SMITH, James
4982. SMITH, Jan
"The Old Women." [NegC] (6:1) Wint 86, p. 67.
4983. SMITH, Jim
"Translations Naif" (Selections: 1, 3, 7, 11, 12). [Quarry] (35:1) Wint 86, p. 20-23.
4984. SMITH, John
"Inside Out." [InterPR] (12:2) Fall 86, p. 111.
"My Father's Stone." [InterPR] (12:2) Fall 86, p. 112.
4985. SMITH, Jordan
"For Dulcimer & Doubled Voice." [GeoR] (40:3) Fall 86, p. 789-790.
"The Hudson at Mechanicville." [QW] (23) 86, p. 15-16.
4986. SMITH, Keith
"Drills." [IndR] (9:2) Spr 86, p. 17.
4987. SMITH, Lawrence R.
"A Brief Essay on Action." [Caliban] (1) 86, p. 68-69.
"Detective." [Caliban] (1) 86, p. 70.
"Distance in Love" (tr. of Antonio Porta). [Caliban] (1) 86, p. 108-110.
"Memorial Day, 1986." [Caliban] (1) 86, p. 70-71.
4988. SMITH, Le Roy, Jr.
"Solo flight from base." [Comm] (113:12) 20 Je 86, p. 367.
4989. SMITH, Michael C.
"Night Flight." [Jacaranda] (2:1) Fall 86, p. 3-4.
4990. SMITH, Nathaniel
"Autobiography" (Autobiografia, tr. of Miquel Martí i Pol, w. Lynette McGrath). [SenR] (16:1) 86, p. 40.
"The Blind Cow" (La vaca cega, tr. of Joan Maragall). [SenR] (16:1) 86, p. 21.
"How Like a Kite My Star Is" (Quina grua el meu estel, tr. of Joan Salvat-Papasseit, w. Lynette McGrath). [SenR] (16:1) 86, p. 26-27.
"I Won't Tell You" (No et diré, tr. of Vicent Andrés Estellés). [SenR] (16:1) 86, p. 36.
"The Lovers" (Els amants, tr. of Vicent Andrés Estellés). [SenR] (16:1) 86, p. 39.
"The Man Condemned to Death" (Reu de mort, tr. of Angel Guimerà, w. Lynette McGrath). [SenR] (16:1) 86, p. 19-20.
"Metamorphosis-I" (Metamòrfosi-I, tr. of Miquel Martí i Pol, w. Lynette McGrath). [SenR] (16:1) 86, p. 41.
"The Mud, the Rain" (El fang, la pluja, tr. of Vicent Andrés Estellés). [SenR] (16:1) 86, p. 37.
"On the Way into Exile" (El camí de l'exili, tr. of Pere Oriol Costa). [SenR] (16:1) 86, p. 44.
"Secretly and Very Chastely" (Horatians, XLVI: Secretament i molt castament, tr. of Vicent Andrés Estellés). [SenR] (16:1) 86, p. 38.

"We Speak of You" (Parlem de tu, tr. of Miquel Martí i Pol, w. Lynette McGrath). [SenR] (16:1) 86, p. 42.
4991. SMITH, Patricia Keeney
"Two and Terrible." [CrossC] (8:2) 86, p. 13.
4992. SMITH, Patricia M.
"For John K. Toole." [StoneC] (14:1/2) Fall-Wint 86-87, p. 31.
4993. SMITH, R. T.
"Brides." [Pembroke] (18) 86, p. 253-255.
"Byzantine." [Puerto] (21:2) Spr 86, p. 163.
"Hinges." [KanQ] (18:1/2) Wint-Spr 86, p. 234.
"Metamorphosis." [CumbPR] (6:1) Fall 86, p. 45-46.
"Querencia" (for John Engels). [KanQ] (18:1/2) Wint-Spr 86, p. 235-236.
"Talon." [HolCrit] (23:4) O 86, back cover.
"Two Women." [Poem] (56) N 86, p. 24-25.
4994. SMITH, Roch C.
"The Hand" (tr. of Jacques Cau). [InterPR] (12:2) Fall 86, p. 31.
"Having struggled a long time with words" ("Untitled," tr. of Gilles Vigneault). [InterPR] (12:2) Fall 86, p. 29.
4995. SMITH, Ron
"Bagging Leaves in March." [Nat] (243:15) 8 N 86, p. 498.
"Running Again in Hollywood Cemetery" (Guy Owen Poetry Prize Winner). [SouthernPR] (26:2) Fall 86, p. 5-7.
"There." [CrescentR] (4:2) Fall 86, p. 34.
"Water Tower" (for Stan). [CrescentR] (4:2) Fall 86, p. 33.
4996. SMITH, Rush
"At the Bar." [CrescentR] (4:2) Fall 86, p. 22.
4997. SMITH, Sheila
"China Remembers." [Caliban] (1) 86, p. 49.
"Jean's Boy." [Caliban] (1) 86, p. 49.
"Valeria Delidow's Black Shoe Poem" (Für das Mädchen, das schwarz trägt). [Caliban] (1) 86, p. 48.
4998. SMITH, Stephen E.
"Bark." [Interim] (5:1) Spr 86, p. 19.
"Cleaning Pools" (for my father). [SouthernPR] (26:2) Fall 86, p. 45-46.
"New Shoes." [Abraxas] (34) 86, p. 54.
"Old Shoes." [Abraxas] (34) 86, p. 55-56.
"Spoons" (For Archie). [Pembroke] (18) 86, p. 175-176.
"Working for Dorsey." [SouthernPR] (26:1) Spr 86, p. 39-40.
SMITH, Sybil Woods
See WOODS-SMITH, Sybil
4999. SMITH, Thomas R.
"Young Man." [LakeSR] (20) 86, p. 34.
5000. SMITH, Tom
"Exodus 2:5" (Sestina). [CrabCR] (4:1) Fall-Wint 86, p. 9.
"Exodus 4:10" (Sestina). [CrabCR] (4:1) Fall-Wint 86, p. 9.
"Exodus 5:1" (Sestina). [CrabCR] (4:1) Fall-Wint 86, p. 9.
"Exodus 8:3" (Sestina). [CrabCR] (4:1) Fall-Wint 86, p. 10.
"Exodus 15:24" (Sestina). [CrabCR] (4:1) Fall-Wint 86, p. 10.
"Exodus 19:16" (Sestina). [CrabCR] (4:1) Fall-Wint 86, p. 10-11.
5001. SMITH, William Jay
"Applefall" (tr. of Andrei Voznesensky, w. F. D. Reeve). [AmerPoR] (15:6) N-D 86, p. 24-25.
"Autolithography" (tr. of Andrei Voznesensky, w. Vera Dunham). [AmerPoR] (15:6) N-D 86, p. 27.
5002. SMITH, Willie
"Back Home." [Amelia] (3:4) Fall 86, p. 106.
"Dawn." [Amelia] (3:2) Spr 86, p. 72.
5003. SMITH-BOWERS, Cathy
"Elegy for My Brother." [SouthernPR] (26:1) Spr 86, p. 28-29.
"The Fat Lady Travels." [GeoR] (40:3) Fall 86, p. 786-787.
5004. SMITH-SOTO, Mark
"And Then" (tr. of Alfredo Ernesto Espino). [InterPR] (12:2) Fall 86, p. 17.
"Nobody Drowns Eve" (tr. of Alfredo Ernesto Espino). [InterPR] (12:2) Fall 86, p. 15.
"Of Someone Who Is Not I" (tr. of Alfredo Ernesto Espino). [InterPR] (12:2) Fall 86, p. 19.

"Three Sisters." [Nimrod] (30:1) Fall-Wint 86, p. 83-87.
"Toulouse Lautrec" (tr. of Alfredo Ernesto Espino). [InterPR] (12:2) Fall 86, p. 13.
"Your Clothing" (tr. of Alfredo Ernesto Espino). [InterPR] (12:2) Fall 86, p. 11.
5005. SMITS, Lia
"#205. Fall while you are still shining!" (tr. of Imants Ziedonis). [Os] (23) 86, p. 2-3.
5006. SMOLINSKY, Stephanie
"I Know I Have a Tendency to Dream" (tr. of Joan Vinyoli). [Translation] (16) Spr 86, p. 102.
"In Our Gray Raincoats" (tr. of Joan Vinyoli). [Translation] (16) Spr 86, p. 103.
"Night and Day" (tr. of Joan Vinyoli). [Translation] (16) Spr 86, p. 106.
"Pietà" (tr. of Joan Vinyoli). [Translation] (16) Spr 86, p. 102.
"Ravines" (tr. of Joan Vinyoli). [Translation] (16) Spr 86, p. 101.
"The Silence of the Dead" (tr. of Joan Vinyoli). [Translation] (16) Spr 86, p. 105.
"Time Lost" (tr. of Joan Vinyoli). [Translation] (16) Spr 86, p. 101.
"Toward Nothing" (tr. of Joan Vinyoli). [Translation] (16) Spr 86, p. 104.
"Who Still Dares" (tr. of Joan Vinyoli). [Translation] (16) Spr 86, p. 104.
5007. SMYTH, Damian Barry
"A Reluctant Requiem." [Amelia] (3:2) Spr 86, p. 108-109.
5008. SNIDER, Clifton
"The Cavern Club." [ConnPR] (4:1) 85, p. 33.
5009. SNIVELY, Susan
"The Women at the Watching" (Hugo van der Goes' Portinari Altarpiece). [YaleR] (75:3) Spr 86, p. 370-372.
5010. SNODGRASS, Ann
"On Leave: Kyoto." [CrossCur] (6:2) 86, p. 35.
"Portal." [ParisR] (28:101) Wint 86, p. 269.
5011. SNODGRASS, W. D.
"The Death of Cock Robin" (After the paintings of DeLoss McGraw: Selections: 3 poems). [KenR] (NS 7:2) Spr 85, p. 48-51.
"W.D. Attempts to Swallow the Symbol" (after the painting by De Loss McGraw). [NegC] (6:4) Fall 86, p. 17.
5012. SNOTHERLY, Mary C.
"October Dichotomy." [InterPR] (12:1) Spr 86, p. 93.
"A Patchwork." [InterPR] (12:1) Spr 86, p. 94-95.
5013. SNOW, Edward
"Autumn Day" (tr. of Rainer Maria Rilke). [Thrpny] (27) Fall 86, p. 11.
"Black Cat" (tr. of Rainer Maria Rilke). [AmerPoR] (15:6) N-D 86, p. 19.
"Buddha in Glory" (tr. of Rainer Maria Rilke). [AmerPoR] (15:6) N-D 86, p. 19.
"Landscape" (tr. of Rainer Maria Rilke). [AmerPoR] (15:6) N-D 86, p. 19.
"Late Autumn in Venice" (tr. of Rainer Maria Rilke). [AmerPoR] (15:6) N-D 86, p. 19.
"The Lute" (tr. of Rainer Maria Rilke). [AmerPoR] (15:6) N-D 86, p. 19.
5014. SNOW, Joseph
"Fluidly and by Night" (tr. of Manuel San Martín). [InterPR] (12:2) Fall 86, p. 23.
"Here in the Uplands" (tr. of Manuel San Martín). [InterPR] (12:2) Fall 86, p. 21.
"In the Far Reaches of the Light" (tr. of Manuel San Martín). [InterPR] (12:2) Fall 86, p. 23.
"An Insect on the Moon" (tr. of Manuel San Martín). [InterPR] (12:2) Fall 86, p. 25.
"Nain" (City of Good, tr. of Manuel San Martín). [InterPR] (12:2) Fall 86, p. 27.
"Weaving" (tr. of Manuel San Martín). [InterPR] (12:2) Fall 86, p. 25.
5015. SNOW, Karen
"The Cat Cemetery." [BelPoJ] (37:2) Wint 86-87, p. 18-19.
5016. SNYDER, Gary
"12 August." [CrossCur] (6:3) 86, p. 213-214.
"Advice for Tourists" (from "The Market"). [TriQ] (66) Spr-Sum 86, p. 92-93.
"At the White River Roadhouse in the Yukon." [ParisR] (28:100) Sum-Fall 86, p. 319.
"Axe Handles." [CrossCur] (6:3) 86, p. 261-262.
"The Bath." [CrossCur] (6:3) 86, p. 255-258.
"Beneath My Hand and Eye the Distant Hills, Your Body." [CrossCur] (6:3) 86, p. 239-240.
"Burning Island." [CrossCur] (6:3) 86, p. 249-250.
"Control Burn." [CrossCur] (6:3) 86, p. 259-260.
"Cratershan 15 August." [CrossCur] (6:3) 86, p. 215-216.

345

"Daylight All Day, Cool North Breeze with Low Clouds, Midnight Twilight, . . ."
[Zyzzyva] (2:4) Wint 86-87, p. 114-117.
"Dullness in February: Japan." [AmerPoR] (15:6) N-D 86, p. 3.
"The Feathered Robe" (For Yaeko Nakamura). [AmerPoR] (15:6) N-D 86, p. 4.
"For George Leigh-Mallory." [AmerPoR] (15:6) N-D 86, p. 3.
"Foxtail Pine." [CrossCur] (6:3) 86, p. 237-238.
"Granite Creek Guard Station 9 July." [CrossCur] (6:3) 86, p. 211.
"It." [CrossCur] (6:3) 86, p. 253-254.
"Message from Outside." [AmerPoR] (15:6) N-D 86, p. 3.
"Milton by Firelight" (Piute Creek, August 1955). [CrossCur] (6:3) 86, p. 217-218.
"Myths and Texts" (Selections from "Logging": 1, 3, 15, "Hunting": 1, 6,
    "Burning": 1, 17). [CrossCur] (6:3) 86, p. 221-234.
"Old Rotting Tree Trunk Down." [CrossCur] (6:3) 86, p. 263-264.
"One Year." [AmerPoR] (15:6) N-D 86, p. 4.
"Out of the Soil and Rock." [AmerPoR] (15:6) N-D 86, p. 3.
"The Persimmons." [NewYorker] (62:30) 15 S 86, p. 36.
"The Rainy Season." [AmerPoR] (15:6) N-D 86, p. 4.
"Revolution in the Revolution in the Revolution." [CrossCur] (6:3) 86, p. 251-252.
"Riprap." [CrossCur] (6:3) 86, p. 219.
"A Walk." [CrossCur] (6:3) 86, p. 235-236.
"A War of Dwarfs and Birds beyond the Sea." [AmerPoR] (15:6) N-D 86, p. 4.
"Wave." [CrossCur] (6:3) 86, p. 247.
5017. SNYDER, V. Mony
"Reward of Heaven!" [WritersL] (1986:4), p. 27.
5018. SOBIN, Anthony
"Drunk in a Boat." [BelPoJ] (36:4) Sum 86, p. 30.
"Ode." [BelPoJ] (36:4) Sum 86, p. 31-32.
5019. SOBIN, Gustaf
"Escargots" (for Harris). [Temblor] (3) 86, p. 40-41.
"A Flora Beginning with Vineyards." [Temblor] (3) 86, p. 42.
"Nine Drafts from America's Edges." [Temblor] (3) 86, p. 43-45.
"Ode: For the Budding of Islands." [Temblor] (3) 86, p. 46.
"Road, Roadsides and the Disparate Frames of Sequence" (W. W.'s). [Temblor] (4)
    86, p. 3-10.
"Two Paths." [Temblor] (3) 86, p. 39.
5020. SOBKOVIAK, Patti
"Equation." [PikeF] (7) Spr 86, p. 20.
5021. SOBSEY, Cynthia
"For My Father." [NegC] (6:1) Wint 86, p. 74-75.
5022. SODERLING, Janice
"Miss Peterson." [Event] (15:1) 86, p. 17.
5023. SODOWSKY, Roland
"Ephraim Street." [Pax] (3:1/2) Wint 85-86, p. 131.
"Ninety Miles to Yaounde." [Pax] (3:1/2) Wint 85-86, p. 132.
5024. SOHNE, Karen
"Days peeled off." [Amelia] (3:4) Fall 86, p. 118.
5025. SOLDOFSKY, Alan
"Poem for Sioux City." [RiverS] (20) 86, p. 56.
5026. SOLLFREY, Stacey
"People grow in the wombs that stand between others." [Bogg] (55) 86, p. 23.
"Still Walking Around Again." [RagMag] (5:2) Fall 86, p. 71.
5027. SOLOMON, Stanley J.
"Imitations: Heroes in Our Time." [CharR] (12:2) Fall 86, p. 65-66.
5028. SOLOMOS, Dionysios
"Xanthoula" (tr. by David Mason). [Translation] (16) Spr 86, p. 143-144.
5029. SOLONCHE, J. R.
"413B." [CrossCur] (6:2) 86, p. 112-113.
"The Albino on the Bus." [ThRiPo] (27/28) 86, p. 60-61.
"Arrowhead." [LitR] (29:2) Wint 86, p. 224.
"History Lesson." [Sam] (44:2 release 174) 86, p. 29.
"Memorial Maker." [LitR] (29:2) Wint 86, p. 225-226.
"Nightgown." [LitR] (29:2) Wint 86, p. 226.
"Raking Leaves." [PoetryNW] (27:3) Aut 86, p. 6-7.
"The Shallows." [PoetryNW] (27:1) Spr 86, p. 37-38.
"Sleeping through the Quake." [PoeticJ] (15) Sum 86, p. 4.
"Two Portraits by Matthew Brady." [Sam] (44:2 release 174) 86, p. 42.

"Waiting Room." [CumbPR] (5:2) Spr 86, p. 19-20.
5030. SOLWAY, David
"Handling the Chess Pieces" (from *Chess Poems*). [AntigR] (64) Wint 86, p. 7.
"The Master" (from *Chess Poems*). [AntigR] (64) Wint 86, p. 8.
"The Pin" (from *Chess Poems*). [AntigR] (65) Spr 86, p. 106-111.
"Reminiscence of an Amateur" (from *Chess Poems*). [AntigR] (64) Wint 86, p. 9.
5031. SOMECK, Ronnie
"Johnny" (tr. by Lisa Fliegel). [PoetL] (81:2) Sum 86, p. 123.
"Welders Street. She Sings at Weddings" (tr. by Lisa Fliegel). [PoetL] (81:2) Sum 86, p. 124.
5032. SOMERVILLE, Jane
"An Illustration in a Child's Book." [SoDakR] (24:2) Sum 86, p. 124.
"Leaving Home." [LitR] (30:1) Fall 86, p. 31.
"The Man Who Killed Bugs with His Bare Hands." [HiramPoR] (41) Fall-Wint 86-87, p. 39.
"The Middle of the Night." [HiramPoR] (41) Fall-Wint 86-87, p. 38.
5033. SOMMER, Richard
"Haiku: You fear night noises." [AntigR] (66/67) Sum-Aut 86, p. 194.
"The Web." [AntigR] (66/67) Sum-Aut 86, p. 194.
5034. SOMOZA, Joseph
"Winter Advice." [Sam] (44:2 release 174) 86, p. 14.
5035. SONDE, Susan
"From 'Letters from the Baja'" (for Andi, for Daivd). [SouthernPR] (26:1) Spr 86, p. 55.
5036. SONG, Cathy
"The Age of Reptiles." [Poetry] (148:1) Ap 86, p. 17-20.
"Litany." [Poetry] (148:1) Ap 86, p. 15-16.
"A Question of Happiness." [Contact] (7:38/39/40) Wint-Spr 86, p. 26.
"A Small Light." [BlackWR] (13:1) Fall 86, p. 62-63.
"The Tree House." [Poetry] (148:1) Ap 86, p. 12-13.
"The Window and the Field." [Poetry] (148:1) Ap 86, p. 13-15.
5037. SONIAT, Katherine
"Daughter." [Poetry] (148:6) S 86, p. 335.
"Fifteenth Century Flat." [PraS] (60:3) Fall 86, p. 93.
"For the Thirteenth Year" (for Shelton). [ConnPR] (4:1) 85, p. 32.
"Lighthouse Telephone." [Poetry] (148:4) Jl 86, p. 219-220.
"Making Ghosts." [PraS] (60:3) Fall 86, p. 94.
"Rhapsody." [PraS] (60:3) Fall 86, p. 92.
"That Far from Home." [NoAmR] (271:1) Mr 86, p. 65.
"Voyeur" (For Rick). [NegC] (6:4) Fall 86, p. 59.
"Words on the Pennsylvania Turnpike." [HiramPoR] (41) Fall-Wint 86-87, p. 40.
5038. SONNENSCHEIN, Dana
"The El Platform." [IndR] (9:2) Spr 86, p. 67.
"The Morning Comes in Steel." [PassN] (7:1) Fall-Wint 85-86, p. 19.
"Retour a la Raison" (After Man Ray). [IndR] (9:2) Spr 86, p. 66.
5039. SONNEVI, Göran
"Blue Ripening" (tr. by Rika Lesser). [Writ] (18) 86, c87, p. 75.
"Dyron, 1981" (Two Poems, tr. by Rika Lesser). [Chelsea] (45) 86, p. 126-128.
"I said to you" (tr. by Rika Lesser). [Writ] (18) 86, c87, p. 76.
"The wound bleeding" (tr. by Rika Lesser). [Writ] (18) 86, c87, p. 77.
5040. SORENSEN, Sally Jo
"Alienation." [WestB] (18) 86, p. 45.
"The Redemption." [WestB] (19) 86, p. 106.
5041. SORESTAD, Glen
"Air Canada Owls." [CanLit] (108) Spr 86, p. 79-80.
"Answering the Telephone." [PraF] (7:2) Sum 86, p. 16.
"The Earthquake." [Puerto] (21:2) Spr 86, p. 116-117.
"Night Flights." [PraF] (7:2) Sum 86, p. 17.
5042. SORHEIM, Thor
"Blue Sun" (tr. by Katherine Anne Powell). [Writ] (18) 86, c87, p. 56.
"The Initiation" (tr. by Katherine Anne Powell). [Writ] (18) 86, c87, p. 53.
"The Last Waltz" (tr. by Katherine Anne Powell). [Writ] (18) 86, c87, p. 58.
"Rain" (tr. by Katherine Anne Powell). [Writ] (18) 86, c87, p. 57.
"The Voice of the People I" (tr. by Katherine Anne Powell). [Writ] (18) 86, c87, p. 54.
"Working Class" (tr. by Katherine Anne Powell). [Writ] (18) 86, c87, p. 55.

5043. SORKIN, Adam J.
"Landscape in White" (tr. of Anghel Dumbraveanu, w. Irina Grigorescu). [LitR]
(30:1) Fall 86, p. 24.
"The Sailor's Window" (tr. of Anghel Dumbraveanu, w. Irina Grigorescu). [LitR]
(30:1) Fall 86, p. 25.
5044. SORKIN, Jayne
"Ima." [SinW] (29/30) 86, p. 121-123.
5045. SORNBERGER, Judith
"Confirmation." [TarRP] (25:1) Fall 85, p. 43-44.
"February Letter." [Calyx] (9:2/3) Wint 86, p. 114-115.
"Last Week of Summer." [KanQ] (18:1/2) Wint-Spr 86, p. 210-211.
"Late Winter on the Plains." [KanQ] (18:1/2) Wint-Spr 86, p. 209.
"My Student Says She Is Not Beautiful." [Calyx] (9:2/3) Wint 86, p. 113.
"Women's Aerobics Class." [DenQ] (20:4/21:1) Spr-Sum 86, p. 96-97.
5046. SOTO, Gary
"At the All-night Cafe." [OhioR] (37) 86, p. 40-41.
"Confession to Mrs. Robert L. Snow." [Ploughs] (12:1/2) 86, p. 152-153.
"Crossing Over." [MissouriR] (9:1) 85-86, p. 187.
"Getting a Feel for the Place." [OhioR] (37) 86, p. 42-43.
"Heaven." [Poetry] (148:3) Je 86, p. 168.
"Our Days." [NewRep] (194:8) 24 F 86, p. 36.
"The Seventieth Year." [Poetry] (148:3) Je 86, p. 167-168.
SOTO, Gladys Pagan de
See PAGAN DE SOTO, Gladys
SOTO, Mark Smith
See SMITH-SOTO, Mark
5047. SOTOMAYOR, Aurea Maria
"5 Sáficas." [RevICP] (90) Oct-Dic 85, p. 49.
"Promenade o Paseo por los Parques." [RevICP] (91) Enero-Marzo 86, p. 58-59.
5048. SOUSTER, Raymond
"At the Police Station." [GreenfR] (13:3/4) Sum-Fall 86, p. 188.
"Blue Heron near the Old Mill Bridge." [GreenfR] (13:3/4) Sum-Fall 86, p. 187.
"Death of a Sunflower." [GreenfR] (13:3/4) Sum-Fall 86, p. 187.
5049. SOUTHWICK, Marcia
"What the Sun Invents." [PraS] (60:4) Wint 86, p. 22-23.
SOUZA, Eunice de
See De SOUZA, Eunice
5050. SPACKS, Barry
"Actors Exercise." [PoetryNW] (27:1) Spr 86, p. 24.
"Brief Sparrow" (For Lauren Mesa). [Poetry] (149:1) O 86, p. 30.
"Creatures." [Interim] (5:2) Fall 86, p. 20-21.
"Defining Luxury." [SewanR] (94:4) Fall 86, p. 580.
"A Gist." [MissouriR] (9:1) 85-86, p. 124.
"Living Alone." [Jacaranda] (2:1) Fall 86, p. 5-6.
"Metaphysics at the Beach." [SewanR] (94:4) Fall 86, p. 579.
"The Plant and the Coal." [GrandS] (5:2) Wint 86, p. 84.
"That Woman." [SewanR] (94:4) Fall 86, p. 579.
"Travelers' Advisory." [GrandS] (5:2) Wint 86, p. 84-85.
5051. SPARK, Muriel
"Going Up to Sotheby's." [Interim] (5:2) Fall 86, p. 3-4.
5052. SPARKS, Amy B.
"The Mourning of Icarus." [SouthernPR] (26:2) Fall 86, p. 8-9.
5053. SPEAKES, Richard
"Embodied" (For John Cooke). [Poetry] (147:4) Ja 86, p. 214.
"Heartbreak Hotel Piano-Bar." [Poetry] (147:4) Ja 86, p. 212.
"Patsy Cline." [Poetry] (147:4) Ja 86, p. 213.
"Susan Worries about the Future." [TarRP] (25:1) Fall 85, p. 26-27.
5054. SPEAR, Roberta
"Breeding Season." [MemphisSR] (7:1) Fall 86, p. 26-27.
"Chestnuts for Verdi." [MissouriR] (9:1) 85-86, p. 46-47.
"In the Moon." [Poetry] (149:3) D 86, p. 146-148.
5055. SPEARS, Heather
"Au Musée Rodin." [MalR] (77) D 86, p. 53-54.
"Dear Parents, Sorry" (from Drawing the Newborn, 1983). [MalR] (73) Ja 86, p.
72.

"Hydroce-Falus Obs" (from *Drawing the Newborn*, 1983). [MalR] (73) Ja 86, p. 75.

"Sara" (from *Drawing the Newborn*, 1983). [MalR] (73) Ja 86, p. 73.

"Theodor" (from *Drawing the Newborn*, 1983). [MalR] (73) Ja 86, p. 74.

"When You Receive Your Body." [MalR] (75) Je 86, p. 5.

5056. SPEARS, Woodridge
"The Night, a Torn-Down Thing." [Wind] (16:58) 86, p. 39.

5057. SPECTOR, Robert Donald
"Eric, the Mythographer." [Confr] (33/34) Fall-Wint 86-87, p. 159.

"Exegesis." [Confr] (33/34) Fall-Wint 86-87, p. 159.

5058. SPEER, Laurel
"Chanticleer and Pertelote Engage in a Little Medieval Debate." [NegC] (6:4) Fall 86, p. 72.

"Emily Dickinson Isn't In." [KanQ] (18:3) Sum 86, p. 70.

"An Exam." [MidAR] (7:1) 86, p. 108-109.

"Lines Written on the Beginning of a Story by Cheever." [KanQ] (18:3) Sum 86, p. 70.

"Mae West (2) of the Kissing Booth." [SecC] (14:1) 86, p. 68.

"Meeting with Dante in a Narrow Street." [PaintedB] (28) Ap 86, p. 46.

"A Movie Script of Paradise Lost." [CrabCR] (4:1) Fall-Wint 86, p. 14.

"Putting on a Girdle for the Wallace Sterling Tea" (1958). [ManhatPR] (6) Wint-Spr 85-86, p. 31.

"Roberta and Frank at the Hotel Del." [SecC] (14:1) 86, p. 66-67.

"Satyriasis." [ThRiPo] (27/28) 86, p. 67.

"Teaching Tennis and Verbs." [HolCrit] (23:5) D 86, back cover.

"Three Ways to Kill a Wolf." [CentralP] (9) Spr 86, p. 92.

"Tongue." [ThRiPo] (27/28) 86, p. 66.

"We." [Event] (15:2) 86, p. 155.

"What We Do for Entertainment on Sundays." [MidAR] (6:1) 86?, p. 82.

5059. SPENCE, Michael
"Darkmont." [CimR] (74) Ja 86, p. 31.

"Leaving the Limbo of Lost Images." [CharR] (12:1) Spr 86, p. 86-87.

"On a Raft." [CrabCR] (3:3) Sum 86, p. 27.

"Slug." [MidAR] (6:2) 86, p. 42.

5060. SPENCE, Pete
"The Cantors Foot" (Excerpt). [Sink] (2) 86, p. 24-26.

5061. SPENCER, Mary Frances
"Chapter II." [SanFPJ] (8:3) 85, p. 91.

"Leather Baby." [SanFPJ] (8:3) 85, p. 90.

5062. SPENCER, Robert
"90. Parts of his body he needed." [HangL] (49) Spr 86, p. 42.

"Little League in the Hill Towns." [StoneC] (14:1/2) Fall-Wint 86-87, p. 32.

"Town." [StoneC] (14:1/2) Fall-Wint 86-87, p. 33.

"What Can I Say, What Can Possibly Be Said." [StoneC] (14:1/2) Fall-Wint 86-87, p. 33.

5063. SPENCER, Susan
"Hot on the Trail of the Apocalypse." [BellR] (9:1) Spr 86, p. 56.

"Wanting In." [BellR] (9:1) Spr 86, p. 57.

5064. SPICHER, Julia
"Riding Bike with No Hands." [WestB] (19) 86, p. 74.

5065. SPIEGEL, Moshe
"God of Mercy" (tr. of Kadia Molodowsky). [WebR] (11:1) Spr 86, p. 41-42.

"The Grave of Rachel" (tr. of Ivan Alekseyevitch Bunin). [WebR] (11:1) Spr 86, p. 42.

5066. SPIEGEL, Robert
"My Face." [Wind] (16:56) 86, p. 40-41.

5067. SPINA, Vincent
"Hector." [BallSUF] (26:4) Aut 85, p. 17-18.

"The Lake." [YetASM] (5) 86, p. 9.

5068. SPIRES, Elizabeth
"The Needle." [YaleR] (76:1) Aut 86, p. 126.

"Stonington Self-Portrait." [PartR] (53:4) 86, p. 581-582.

"The Travellers." [GeoR] (40:3) Fall 86, p. 791-792.

"Two verticals lie down." [ParisR] (28:100) Sum-Fall 86, p. 320.

5069. SPIVACK, Kathleen
"The Bureau." [HeliconN] (14/15) Sum 86, p. 14.

"Chicken Dinner." [BelPoJ] (36:4) Sum 86, p. 8-11.
"Favorite Places" (for Paul Nagano). [HeliconN] (14/15) Sum 86, p. 16-17.
"Finding Out." [HeliconN] (14/15) Sum 86, p. 15.
"Flies." [HeliconN] (14/15) Sum 86, p. 17.
"Last Rose." [CentR] (30:4) Fall 86, p. 477-478.
"The Museum of Fine Arts." [MinnR] (NS 27) Fall 86, p. 87-88.
"St. John's River, Northern Florida." [BellR] (9:2) Fall 86, p. 50.
"To Start." [HeliconN] (14/15) Sum 86, p. 15.
"The Tree-of-Life Quilt." [BellR] (9:2) Fall 86, p. 49.
"Young Girl, Northern New Mexico." [MidwQ] (27:2) Wint 86, p. 213-214.
5070. SPIVACK, Susan Fantl
"Climbing Snowy Mountain." [Blueline] (8:1) Sum-Fall 86, p. 26-27.
5071. SPOLLEN, Anne
"Seasons." [Amelia] (3:2) Spr 86, p. 51.
5072. SPRAYBERRY, Sandra
"Year's End." [BlackWR] (12:2) Spr 86, p. 81-86.
5073. ST. ANDREWS, B. A.
"Chinese Dinner for One." [NewYorker] (62:40) 24 N 86, p. 121.
"Covenant." [DeKalbLAJ] (19:3/4) 86, p. 89.
"The Half-Life of Ulysses." [Comm] (113:11) 6 Je 86, p. 337.
"The Lesson on Lizard Mountain." [CrossCur] (5:4/6:1) 86, p. 46-47.
5074. ST. ANDREWS, Bonnie
"Shooting the Elder Poet." [PikeF] (7) Spr 86, p. 23.
5075. ST. CLAIR, Philip
"Hand." [MalR] (77) D 86, p. 98-99.
"Hawks." [PoetryNW] (27:1) Spr 86, p. 8-11.
"Pines." [MalR] (77) D 86, p. 96-97.
"Rose." [MalR] (77) D 86, p. 94-95.
5076. ST. CLAIR, Rosslyn
"Dances in the fog." [Pax] (3:1/2) Wint 85-86, p. 116.
"In Utah." [Pax] (3:1/2) Wint 85-86, p. 116.
5077. ST. GEORGE, G.
"Zero, Once Again." [CutB] (25) Fall-Wint 86, p. 44.
5078. ST. JOHN, David
"The Bells of Santa Maria in Trastevere." [OP] (42/43) Wint 86-87, p. 77.
"Brushstrokes." [SenR] (16:2) 86, p. 12-15.
"Castello (1527)." [Pequod] (22) 86, p. 60.
"The Dragon in the Lake." [SenR] (16:2) 86, p. 7-10.
"Eclogue." [MissouriR] (9:2) 86, p. 154-155.
"Francesco and Clare." [Field] (35) Fall 86, p. 105-106.
"In the Pines." [QW] (23) 86, p. 143-147.
"The *Kama Sutra* According to Fiat." [Pequod] (22) 86, p. 58-59.
"The Lake." [Field] (35) Fall 86, p. 107.
"Nothing Personal." [SenR] (16:2) 86, p. 11.
"The Photograph of J in Venice." [OP] (42/43) Wint 86-87, p. 73-75.
"Vespers: The Balcony." [MissouriR] (9:2) 86, p. 153.
"The World They Knew." [OP] (42/43) Wint 86-87, p. 76-77.
5079. ST. JOHN, Primus
"That Day / The Sun was Especially Hot." [Callaloo] (9:1, #26) Wint 86, p. 124-125.
"We Came to Know Each Other." [Callaloo] (9:1, #26) Wint 86, p. 122-123.
5080. ST. MARTIN, Hardie
"Accident" (tr. of Francesc Parcerisas). [Translation] (16) Spr 86, p. 88.
"Calypso" (tr. of Francesc Parcerisas). [Translation] (16) Spr 86, p. 87.
"A Day Like This" (tr. of Francesc Parcerisas). [Translation] (16) Spr 86, p. 91.
"Parting" (tr. of Francesc Parcerisas). [Translation] (16) Spr 86, p. 86.
"Portrait of the Poet" (tr. of Francesc Parcerisas). [Translation] (16) Spr 86, p. 89.
"Shave" (tr. of Francesc Parcerisas). [Translation] (16) Spr 86, p. 88.
"Variation on a Poem by Lawrence Durrell" (tr. of Francesc Parcerisas). [Translation] (16) Spr 86, p. 85.
"Wreckers" (tr. of Francesc Parcerisas). [Translation] (16) Spr 86, p. 90.
5081. ST. PIERRE, Marianne
"Blue Frieze: The Women." [LitR] (29:3) Spr 86, p. 342-343.
5082. STACH, Carl L.
"The Final Prospect." [GeoR] (40:3) Fall 86, p. 793.

5083. STAFFORD, Kim R.
"Feather Bag, Stick Bag." [Atlantic] (257:4) Ap 86, p. 114.
"In a Photograph, My Grandmother, Re-Shingling the Roof, Pretends to Be
Departing for Heaven." [VirQR] (62:1) Wint 86, p. 43.
"Losing One." [NowestR] (24:3) 86, p. 16.
"Nineteenth Century News." [OhioR] (36) 86, p. 65.
"Under an Oak in California." [VirQR] (62:1) Wint 86, p. 43-44.
"Walking to the Mailbox." [VirQR] (62:1) Wint 86, p. 44-45.
"Wilma Tells How They Moved Old Joseph's Bones." [MalR] (74) Mr 86, p.
109-110.
5084. STAFFORD, William
"Another Language." [Caliban] (1) 86, p. 47.
"Artist in Residence: Banff." [Paint] (13:25/26) Spr-Aut 86, p. 8.
"Bowing." [Caliban] (1) 86, p. 45-46.
"Buddha's Thoughts." [Paint] (13:25/26) Spr-Aut 86, p. 10.
"A Child of Our Century." [Interim] (5:1) Spr 86, p. 10.
"Children Still Play." [Agni] (23) 86, p. 28.
"Commitment." [QW] (23) 86, p. 97.
"Crowded Falls." [Field] (33) Fall 85, p. 94.
"Early Morning at Howard's House." [Caliban] (1) 86, p. 46.
"Étude." [MemphisSR] (7:1) Fall 86, p. 11.
"From the Afterworld" (tr. of Sachiko Yoshihara, w. Yorifumi Yaguchi). [Field]
(33) Fall 85, p. 71-72.
"Hurricane." [ForidaR] (14:1) Spr-Sum 86, p. 17.
"The Light by the Barn." [Farm] (3:2) Spr-Sum 86, p. 33.
"Local Events." [Caliban] (1) 86, p. 45.
"Old Clunker." [Paint] (13:25/26) Spr-Aut 86, p. 9.
"Outside Wichita." [Field] (33) Fall 85, p. 95.
"Pelican Flight." [ForidaR] (14:1) Spr-Sum 86, p. 18.
"Reading the Fine Print." [MemphisSR] (7:1) Fall 86, p. 12.
"Some Things the World Gave." [Iowa] (16:1) Wint 86, p. 95.
"Sometimes." [MemphisSR] (7:1) Fall 86, p. 11.
"Surrounded by Mountains." [Field] (33) Fall 85, p. 93.
"Tides." [GeoR] (40:3) Fall 86, p. 795.
"Tracks in the Sand." [GeoR] (40:2) Sum 86, p. 473.
"Trusting Each Other." [GeoR] (40:3) Fall 86, p. 794.
"Trying to Please." [Interim] (5:1) Spr 86, p. 9.
"Widow." [CrabCR] (3:3) Sum 86, p. 3.
5085. STAHL, Frieda
"Numera Una." [HolCrit] (23:3) Je 86, p. 14.
5086. STALL, Lindon
"Divertimento." [SouthernR] (22:3) Sum 86, p. 572-575.
"To Poieisthai" (After Rilke's "Buddha in der Glorie"). [SouthernR] (22:3) Sum 86,
p. 575.
"Tombeau" (for J. M. F.). [SouthernR] (22:3) Sum 86, p. 576.
5087. STALLINGS, Alicia E.
"Preparing the Garden." [DeKalbLAJ] (19:3/4) 86, p. 62-63.
"What Is Real." [DeKalbLAJ] (19:2) 86, p. 46.
5088. STAMBUK, Drago
"Atrium." [Ploughs] (12:4) 86, p. 89.
"Blurred Mirror." [Ploughs] (12:4) 86, p. 88.
"Evaporation from the Iliac Pelvis." [Ploughs] (12:4) 86, p. 87.
"Fire." [Ploughs] (12:4) 86, p. 90.
"Hegeso." [Ploughs] (12:4) 86, p. 90.
"Love abandons you" ("Untitled"). [Ploughs] (12:4) 86, p. 87.
5089. STANBRIDGE, Joanne
"In the Amber Dark (3)." [AntigR] (66/67) Sum-Aut 86, p. 172.
5090. STANDING, Sue
"Letter to Hugo from Seattle." [ConnPR] (5:1) 86, p. 29.
5091. STANDRIDGE, Rusty
"Yorick's Reply." [Thrpny] (26) Sum 86, p. 20.
5092. STANFORD, Michael
"From the Ends of the Earth." [BelPoJ] (37:2) Wint 86-87, p. 32-33.
5093. STANHOPE, Rosamund
"In May Considering the Swallow." [WebR] (11:2) Fall 86, p. 67.

351

STANIZZI

5094. STANIZZI, John L.
"Home Repairs." [StoneC] (13:3/4) Spr-Sum 86, p. 54.
5095. STANLEY, Charles M.
"Dignity." [PoeticJ] (14) 86, p. 27.
5096. STAP, Don
"A Small Joy or Sadness." [PassN] (7:1) Fall-Wint 85-86, p. 19.
"Things That Look the Same." [MassR] (27:2) Sum 86, p. 216.
"Walking at Midnight." [CharR] (12:1) Spr 86, p. 14.
"Walking at Midnight" (corrected printing). [CharR] (12:2) Fall 86, p. 70.
5097. STAPANCHEV, Stephen
"Carolus Linnaeus" (For Richard Eberhart). [NegC] (6:2/3) Spr-Sum 86, p. 46.
5098. STAPLEY, Julie N.
"Homecoming." [BellArk] (2:6) N-D 86, p. 1.
5099. STARBUCK, George
"Double Dactyls" (2 poems: "Shake-up" & "Districto Federal"). [Atlantic] (258:4) O
   86, p. 61.
"'Dr. No' for New Year's, at the Hotel Irazu." [Ploughs] (12:3) 86, p. 125.
"The Duke of Ipso's Ecological Eclogue." [GrandS] (5:3) Spr 86, p. 141.
"Oyster Bar on the Road to Mururua." [Ploughs] (12:3) 86, p. 123-124.
"Practical Shooter Comes to Downers Grove." [Iowa] (16:1) Wint 86, p. 120-122.
"S.D.I." [Ploughs] (12:3) 86, p. 126.
"To a Real Standup Piece of Painted Crockery." [Iowa] (16:1) Wint 86, p. 123.
5100. STARZEC, Larry
"The Husband of the Circus Fat Lady." [Ascent] (12:1) 86, p. 27.
5101. STEDLER, Harding
"Cabbage Hands." [InterPR] (12:2) Fall 86, p. 68.
"Freedom Riders." [Wind] (16:58) 86, p. 37.
"Tail of Woe." [PoeticJ] (14) 86, p. 20.
"Winter Sun, Summer Sun." [InterPR] (12:2) Fall 86, p. 68.
5102. STEELE, Frank
"American Males." [AmerV] (4) Fall 86, p. 136.
5103. STEELE, Leighton
"The Berkeley School of Music." [PraF] (7:2) Sum 86, p. 31.
"Evergreen Place." [PraF] (7:2) Sum 86, p. 33.
"Isla Vista (II)." [PraF] (7:2) Sum 86, p. 32-33.
5104. STEELE, Timothy
"Beatitudes, While Setting Out the Trash." [YaleR] (75:3) Spr 86, p. 372.
5105. STEEN, Elizabeth
"Poem: Don't forget to tie a string around." [EngJ] (75:6) O 86, p. 44.
5106. STEFANESCU, Isabella
"Along the Tracks" (tr. of Ionel Ciupureanu). [Descant] (17:2, #53) Sum 86, p. 115.
"L'Ecume des Jours" (tr. of Ionel Ciupureanu). [Descant] (17:2, #53) Sum 86, p.
   116.
5107. STEFANILE, Felix
"Belluccia" (Little Pretty, tr. of Giambattista Basile's *Pentameron*, III, 6). [Sparrow]
   (50) 86, p. 1-15.
"The Story-Teller of Messer Azzolino" (tr. of anonymous Italian poem). [Sparrow]
   (50) 86, p. 16-20.
5108. STEFFENS, Bradley
"The Destruction of Sodom." [BellArk] (2:2) Mr-Ap 86, p. 12-14.
"Sunset, 1967." [StoneC] (14:1/2) Fall-Wint 86-87, p. 50-51.
"The Twelve-Foot-Long Iguana." [StoneC] (14:1/2) Fall-Wint 86-87, p. 50.
5109. STEFFEY, Duane
"Letter from California" (for Stephen Dunn). [KanQ] (18:3) Sum 86, p. 81.
5110. STEIN, Agnes
"How Survive This Rain" (tr. of Helga M. Novak). [IndR] (9:2) Spr 86, p. 20-21.
5111. STEIN, Charles
"A Suite of 4 Seed Poems" (for Franz Kamin). [Temblor] (3) 86, p. 149-159.
5112. STEIN, Hannah
"Exorcism." [PraS] (60:4) Wint 86, p. 52-53.
"Fragile." [CumbPR] (5:2) Spr 86, p. 53.
"Winter in Fox-light" (for Pat Johnson). [PraS] (60:4) Wint 86, p. 51-52.
5113. STEIN, Jill
"The Hollow Place." [WestB] (19) 86, p. 89-90.
"My Mother Explains About Revelations." [WestB] (19) 86, p. 86-89.

5114. STEIN, M. D.
"Eliot at Margate." [Raritan] (6:1) Sum 86, p. 112-113.
"Sun Age." [Raritan] (6:1) Sum 86, p. 111-112.
5115. STEINARR, Steinn
"Burning Face" (from the Icelandic poem cycle "Time and Water", tr. by Alan Boucher). [Vis] (22) 86, p. 13.
"The Skies Rain" (tr. by Alan Boucher). [Vis] (20) 86, p. 8.
"Transparent Wings" (tr. by Alan Boucher). [Vis] (21) 86, p. 31.
5116. STEINBERG, Alan
"The Hudson." [CapeR] (21:1) Spr 86, p. 30.
5117. STEINBERGH, Judith W.
"Salt Marsh." [StoneC] (13:3/4) Spr-Sum 86, p. 52.
"This Wild." [Calyx] (10:1) Sum 86, p. 19.
5118. STEINEM, Robert
"An Act of Defiance." [BellArk] (2:2) Mr-Ap 86, p. 3.
"Opposition." [BellArk] (2:1) Ja-F 86, p. 16.
"The Transition to Two." [BellArk] (2:1) Ja-F 86, p. 7.
"Twice Killed." [BellArk] (2:2) Mr-Ap 86, p. 7.
5119. STEINGASS, David
"Farmer Plows Country Trunk." [SpoonRQ] (11:2) Spr 86, p. 12.
"The First Time." [PoetryNW] (27:1) Spr 86, p. 21-22.
"Indiana: Fathers." [NoAmR] (271:4) D 86, p. 45.
"Midwest Mythology." [SpoonRQ] (11:2) Spr 86, p. 11.
"The Night the Bed Broke." [Nimrod] (30:1) Fall-Wint 86, p. 88-93.
5120. STEINKE, Paul David
"Father at the Seashore." [ManhatPR] (8) Wint 86-87, p. 41.
"Vacant House." [ManhatPR] (8) Wint 86-87, p. 40.
5121. STEINKE, René
"On Matisse's 'Studio' at the Tate." [ChrC] (103:10) 19-26 Mr 86, p. 294.
5122. STEINKE, Russell
"Burchfield's *Six O'Clock*, 1936." [KanQ] (18:4) Fall 86, p. 120.
5123. STEINMAN, Lisa
"An Anatomy of Dreams." [WillowS] (17) Wint 86, p. 8-9.
"Reading for the Governor in the Ceremonial Office." [WillowS] (17) Wint 86, p. 10-11.
"The Translation of Natural Languages." [WillowS] (17) Wint 86, p. 6-7.
5124. STEPANCHEV, Stephen
"After the Third Inning." [Interim] (5:2) Fall 86, p. 42.
"Kleptomaniac." [Interim] (5:1) Spr 86, p. 12.
"Slapping Erasers." [Raccoon] (20) Ap 86, p. 23.
"A Stone Age Bowl." [Interim] (5:2) Fall 86, p. 41.
"A Village in Vojvodina." [Interim] (5:1) Spr 86, p. 11-12.
5125. STEPHANOU, Lydia
"Take Care My Child" (tr. by Rae Dalven). [Confr] (33/34) Fall-Wint 86-87, p. 115.
5126. STEPHEN, Ian
"Buddha." [WorldO] (19:3/4) Spr-Sum 85, p. 21.
5127. STEPHENSON, Shelby
"Poem for Forty Weekdays." [ChrC] (103:19) 4-11 Je 86, p. 556.
5128. STERLE, Francine
"Balance." [BellArk] (2:2) Mr-Ap 86, p. 5.
"Digging Potatoes When You're Too Mad to Talk." [StoneC] (14:1/2) Fall-Wint 86-87, p. 44.
"Dream in Black and White." [BellR] (9:1) Spr 86, p. 58.
"Feeding Yourself" (For Clifford). [BellR] (9:1) Spr 86, p. 58.
"Retreat." [BellArk] (2:2) Mr-Ap 86, p. 4.
"Seamstress." [BellArk] (2:2) Mr-Ap 86, p. 7.
"Wind Old Woman." [CutB] (26) Spr-Sum 86, p. 25.
5129. STERLING, Jane
"I walked late last night." [Amelia] (3:3) Sum 86, p. 41.
5130. STERLING, Phillip
"Good-Bye." [Blueline] (8:1) Sum-Fall 86, p. 23.
5131. STERN, Bert
"Joan Miro" (tr. of Xi Chuan, w. the author). [Nimrod] (29:2) Spr-Sum 86, p. 78.
5132. STERN, Gerald
"All I Have Are the Tracks." [NewEngR] (9:1) Aut 86, p. 95.
"Bela." [AmerPoR] (15:4) Jl-Ag 86, p. 34.

"The Blink of an Eye." [AmerPoR] (15:4) Jl-Ag 86, p. 37.
"A Garden" (For Howard and Gretchen Rogovin). [AmerPoR] (15:4) Jl-Ag 86, p. 37.
"Grapefruit." [AmerPoR] (15:4) Jl-Ag 86, p. 36.
"Hidden Justice." [GeoR] (40:3) Fall 86, p. 797.
"I Am in Love." [PoetryE] (20/21) Fall 86, p. 151-152.
"It Was a Rising." [AmerPoR] (15:4) Jl-Ag 86, p. 36.
"Knowledge Forwards and Backwards." [AmerPoR] (15:4) Jl-Ag 86, p. 33.
"Making the Light Come." [AmerPoR] (15:4) Jl-Ag 86, p. 37.
"My First Kinglet." [NewEngR] (9:1) Aut 86, p. 96-97.
"My Swallows." [GeoR] (40:3) Fall 86, p. 796-797.
"No Longer Terror." [AmerPoR] (15:4) Jl-Ag 86, p. 35.
"Nobody Else Alive." [ParisR] (28:101) Wint 86, p. 53.
"One Animal's Life" (for Rosalind Pace). [ParisR] (28:100) Sum-Fall 86, p. 321-322.
"A Pair of Hands." [ParisR] (28:101) Wint 86, p. 52.
"Richard Strauss, My Hero." [ParisR] (28:101) Wint 86, p. 50-51.
"Saturday Afternoon." [ParisR] (28:101) Wint 86, p. 54.
"A Song for the Romeos" (for my brothers Jim Wright and Richard Hugo). [ParisR] (28:101) Wint 86, p. 48-49.
"Two Moons." [AmerPoR] (15:4) Jl-Ag 86, p. 32.
5133. STERN, Joan
"Moving." [TarRP] (25:2) Spr 86, p. 38-39.
"No Warts, No Songs." [ManhatPR] (8) Wint 86-87, p. 24.
"The Ready Position" (for Jerry). [TarRP] (25:2) Spr 86, p. 39-40.
5134. STERN, Lee
"The Heart." [PaintedB] (29) Ag 86, p. 27.
5135. STERN, Robert
"For Borges." [AntigR] (66/67) Sum-Aut 86, p. 9.
"Theophrastus Bombastus von Hohenheim Paracelsus." [AntigR] (65) Spr 86, p. 50-51.
"Vienna." [AntigR] (65) Spr 86, p. 51.
5136. STERNBACH, David
"At Last, an Authoritative History of Non-Belligerent Submarine Disasters." [Sink] (1) 86, p. 47.
"More and More Green." [Sink] (1) 86, p. 49.
"Substance 24." [Sink] (1) 86, p. 48-49.
5137. STERNBERG, Ricardo
"Oriole Weather." [CanLit] (111) Wint 86, p. 100.
5138. STERNLIEB, Barry
"Hatchery System." [Sam] (44:2 release 174) 86, p. 20.
"Hawks & Doves." [Sam] (44:3 release 175) 86, p. 37.
"Homecoming." [RiverS] (20) 86, p. 86-87.
5139. STEVEN, Ida-Marie
"When Our Anger Is Over." [StoneC] (13:3/4) Spr-Sum 86, p. 33.
5140. STEVENS, Alex
"Doing the Laocoön with Kids in School." [Shen] (36:3) 86, p. 52.
"In Scorching Time." [GeoR] (40:3) Fall 86, p. 798-799.
5141. STEVENS, Lois Prante
"The Plight of Sam." [Amelia] (3:3) Sum 86, p. 48.
5142. STEVENS, Peter
"Act of Creation" (for George Steiner). [GreenfR] (13:3/4) Sum-Fall 86, p. 189.
"Aurora." [GreenfR] (13:3/4) Sum-Fall 86, p. 190.
5143. STEVENSON, Becky
"As the camels walked upon the land." [Grain] (14:2) My 86, p. 43.
5144. STEWARD, D. E.
"Lafayette." [Puerto] (21:2) Spr 86, p. 114-115.
"Mittelland." [Puerto] (22:1) Fall 86, p. 63.
"Small Press." [Bogg] (55) 86, p. 6.
5145. STEWART, Diane
"Elegy for Mother." [AmerV] (3) Sum 86, p. 108-109.
5146. STEWART, Dolores
"Going Out to Saturn." [AmerS] (55:3) Sum 86, p. 390.
"The Observer." [BelPoJ] (36:3) Spr 86, p. 1.
5147. STEWART, Frank
"The Boarder." [BellR] (9:1) Spr 86, p. 40.

"The Firebombing" (for L.F. and J.M. and SNCC, 1965). [BellR] (9:1) Spr 86, p. 39-40.
"Honolulu, Winter Morning." [BellR] (9:1) Spr 86, p. 41.
5148. STEWART, Ginny Lowe
"M.C." [YetASM] (4) 85, p. 6.
5149. STEWART, Pamela
"The Edge of Things." [HighP] (1:1) Wint 86, p. 42-43.
"Modesty." [HighP] (1:1) Wint 86, p. 40-41.
5150. STEWART, Pat
"Over Your Shoulder." [Bogg] (56) 86, p. 50.
5151. STEWART, Susan
"The Cardinal." [MissouriR] (9:1) 85-86, p. 123.
"A Garland." [SenR] (16:2) 86, p. 55-62.
"In the Novel." [MemphisSR] (7:1) Fall 86, p. 31.
"Mouth of the Wolf." [MemphisSR] (7:1) Fall 86, p. 30.
5152. STIBER, Alex
"Wading River, July 1954." [AmerV] (4) Fall 86, p. 17.
5153. STICKNEY, John
"Nailing Down the Night." [WestB] (18) 86, p. 94-95.
"There's More to Soup Than Meets the Eye." [Vis] (20) 86, p. 27.
5154. STIFFLER, Randall
"Deer Crossing." [LitR] (29:2) Wint 86, p. 196.
5155. STILL, James
"Apples in the Well." [AmerV] (5) Wint 86, p. 73.
5156. STILLMAN, Lisa
"David." [BelPoJ] (36:3) Spr 86, p. 29.
5157. STILLWELL, Marie
"Christmas at Blue Spring." [WebR] (11:2) Fall 86, p. 78.
"Red." [WebR] (11:2) Fall 86, p. 77.
5158. STILLWELL, Mary Kathryn
"Moving to Malibu." [MidAR] (6:2) 86, p. 31.
5159. STIRLING, Dale
"Nerve." [YetASM] (4) 85, p. 3.
5160. STOCK, Norman
"Holy bless the subway mob." [HangL] (49) Spr 86, p. 44.
"I Only Remember the Good Parts." [HangL] (49) Spr 86, p. 43.
"The Power of Prayer." [NewEngR] (8:4) Sum 86, p. 453-454.
"The rabbi in my head." [HangL] (49) Spr 86, p. 45.
5161. STOCKLAND, Will
"Comets and Madness." [SanFPJ] (8:3) 85, p. 82-83.
"Endless Road." [SanFPJ] (9:1) 86, p. 49.
"Four More Years." [SanFPJ] (8:3) 85, p. 80.
"Lawrence." [SanFPJ] (9:1) 86, p. 42-43.
"Martyrdom." [SanFPJ] (8:4) 85, p. 41.
"Mind Cycle — The Word from Phase A." [SanFPJ] (9:1) 86, p. 43.
"Nothin' Else Is Goin' That Well Either." [SanFPJ] (8:3) 85, p. 24.
"On My Appointment as Bishop." [SanFPJ] (8:4) 85, p. 41.
"The Season of the Scientist." [SanFPJ] (8:3) 85, p. 94.
5162. STOFFER, Jeff
"Cattle Talk." [SnapD] (9:2) Spr 86, p. 60.
5163. STOLOFF, Carolyn
"The Countess." [PoetryNW] (27:4) Wint 86-87, p. 33-34.
"Facts." [Chelsea] (45) 86, p. 42-43.
"The Sneeze, Notes for an Essay." [Contact] (8:41/42/43) Fall-Wint 86-87, p. 55.
"There's a Hidden Door to the Closet." [ConnPR] (5:1) 86, p. 31-32.
5164. STONE, Arlene
"Oracle." [YellowS] (19) Sum 86, p. 40.
5165. STONE, Arthur
"The Death of Lorca." [HayF] (1) Spr 86, p. 65.
5166. STONE, Carole
"A Mother to a Daughter." [PassN] (7:2) Spr-Sum 86, p. 20.
5167. STONE, John
"Transplant." [DenQ] (20:4/21:1) Spr-Sum 86, p. 89.
5168. STONE, Ken
"The Enigma" (To R. Eberhart). [NegC] (6:2/3) Spr-Sum 86, p. 51.
"From Dusk to Dawn: Night Watch II." [Sam] (46:2 release 182) 86, p. 63-64.

"The Fury" (To R.E.). [NegC] (6:2/3) Spr-Sum 86, p. 50.
"The Premonition: To T. R." [PoeticJ] (16) Fall 86, p. 13.
"Teotihuacans, 26 July 1974." [WritersL] (1986:6), p. 19.
"Three Things." [WritersL] (1986:2), p. 22.
"You Ask About Vietnam!" [Sam] (46:2 release 182) 86, p. 125.
5169. STONE, Reynold
"That Centrifugal Swing." [AntigR] (66/67) Sum-Aut 86, p. 230.
5170. STORACE, Patricia
"Runners." [NewYRB] (33:11) 26 Je 86, p. 10.
5171. STORK, Gerry
"For Helen." [NewL] (53:1) Fall 86, p. 82.
5172. STORY, Gertrude
"IX. Ophelia Was a Woman." [Waves] (14:3) Wint 86, p. 44.
"IXX. Under a Hot White Moon." [Waves] (14:3) Wint 86, p. 45.
5173. STOUT, Robert Joe
"The Job on Battery Street." [CapeR] (21:2) Fall 86, p. 35.
"The Magic." [CentR] (30:3) Sum 86, p. 350.
"No One Really Lives in California." [NewRena] (6:3, #20) Spr 86, p. 67.
"Valley of Death." [TexasR] (7:1/2) Spr-Sum 86, p. 82.
5174. STOVALL, Paul B.
"Progress." [PikeF] (7) Spr 86, p. 22.
5175. STOVER, Dean
"A Personal Day of Judgment in Norway." [HayF] (1) Spr 86, p. 48-49.
5176. STOVER, Lois
"The Preposition Love." [EngJ] (75:5) S 86, p. 69.
5177. STOVICH, Raymond J.
"Walking the street." [Wind] (16:57) 86, p. 15.
5178. STOWELL, Deborah Pappas
"San Miguel de Allende." [InterPR] (12:2) Fall 86, p. 101.
"Zenophobia." [InterPR] (12:2) Fall 86, p. 100.
5179. STRAHAN, Bradley R.
"Archilochos." [CrossCur] (6:2) 86, p. 36-37.
"Carnival" (tr. of Anrique Paco d'Acos). [Vis] (22) 86, p. 17.
"Moonstone." [Vis] (20) 86, p. 12.
"Palm Sunday." [StoneC] (13:3/4) Spr-Sum 86, p. 69.
"Poem with a Line from James Wright." [CrabCR] (3:2) Spr 86, p. 6.
"The Rose." [Wind] (16:56) 86, p. 42.
"Routines." [HolCrit] (23:1) F 86, p. 19.
"We Touch Here." [WritersL] (1986:1), p. 15.
5180. STRAHAN, Jack
"Vietnam." [Sam] (46:2 release 182) 86, p. 9-10.
5181. STRAND, Mark
"A Story You Know." [GeoR] (40:3) Fall 86, p. 800.
"Viewing the Coast." [GrandS] (5:4) Sum 86, p. 15-16.
5182. STRATO
"Now you're ready!" (from "The Palatine Anthology, tr. by John Gill). [YellowS] (21) Wint 86, p. 24.
"Yesterday, in the baths" (from "The Palatine Anthology, tr. by John Gill). [YellowS] (21) Wint 86, p. 24.
5183. STRAUS, Austin
"Conscience." [PoeticJ] (13) 86, p. 14.
"Dictators and Poets." [PoeticJ] (13) 86, p. 15.
"Fog, New York." [SmPd] (23:2, issue 67) Spr 86, p. 25.
"Gardeners." [PoeticJ] (14) 86, p. 28.
"Ghost." [Wind] (16:56) 86, p. 43.
"K." [Confr] (33/34) Fall-Wint 86-87, p. 162.
"Pizza Parlor / Reseda" (5/25/84). [Wind] (16:56) 86, p. 43-44.
"The Yellow Spider." [PoeticJ] (14) 86, p. 28.
5184. STRAUSS, David Levi
"Listening to Berg's Lyric Suite, the Cellist's Tearful Eye Toward Baudelaire." [Temblor] (3) 86, p. 78-80.
"Peg's House (Venice)." [Temblor] (3) 86, p. 77.
5185. STRECKER, James
"Coleman Hawkins." [Quarry] (35:3) Sum 86, p. 77.
"Tatum, Carter, and Bellson." [Quarry] (35:3) Sum 86, p. 78.

5186. STREZNEWSKI, Marylou Kelly
"Back to School." [EngJ] (75:2) F 86, p. 91.
5187. STRICKER, Meredith
"& the Fur of Rabbit." [MalR] (73) Ja 86, p. 80.
5188. STRICKLAND, Stephanie
"Visitor." [SouthernPR] (26:1) Spr 86, p. 56.
5189. STRINGER, A. E.
"The Architecture of Light." [ColR] (NS 13:1) Fall 85, p. 23.
"General Motors and the Red Army." [ColR] (NS 13:1) Fall 85, p. 22.
"Texas Rain." [ColR] (NS 13:1) Fall 85, p. 24.
5190. STROBERG, Paul
"Good Jobs Don't Grow on Trees, You Know." [WormR] (26:1, issue 101) 86, p. 6-7.
"Nightmare." [WormR] (26:1, issue 101) 86, p. 6.
"No Quarter." [WormR] (26:1, issue 101) 86, p. 7.
"Soakin Donut." [WormR] (26:1, issue 101) 86, p. 7-8.
5191. STROUS, Allen
"Spaces" (Chapbook of Poems). [OhioR] (37) 86, p. 65-80.
5192. STRUTHERS, Ann
"I Think of Virgil's Farmer." [MidAR] (7:1) 86, p. 137.
"Richard Hugo (1923-1982)." [CharR] (12:2) Fall 86, p. 74.
5193. STRUTHERS, Betsy
"First Born." [CrossC] (8:2) 86, p. 10.
5194. STRYK, Dan
"Fishing after Rain." [KanQ] (18:1/2) Wint-Spr 86, p. 212-213.
"Unfinished Symphony." [WestHR] (40:2) Sum 86, p. 163-164.
"Winds of the Midwest." [BallSUF] (26:4) Aut 85, p. 6.
5195. STRYK, Lucien
"Savants." [GeoR] (40:3) Fall 86, p. 801.
5196. STUART, Dabney
"Discovering My Daughter." [TarRP] (24:2) Spr 85, p. 28.
"The Innocent One's Last Words to the Guilty One." [SouthernPR] (26:1) Spr 86, p. 14.
"My Mother Announces She Is Pregnant." [SouthernPR] (26:1) Spr 86, p. 25.
"The People Who Sit in Chairs." [WestHR] (40:1) Spr 86, p. 51.
"Three Sisters" (for Eve Shelnutt). [TarRP] (24:2) Spr 85, p. 27.
STUBBS, John Heath
   See HEATH-STUBBS, John
5197. STUDER, Constance
"At Dusk." [Kaleid] (13) Sum-Fall 86, p. 60.
"Rachel." [Kaleid] (13) Sum-Fall 86, p. 60.
"The Waiting Room." [Kaleid] (13) Sum-Fall 86, p. 60.
5198. STULL, Denver
"The New Road." [PoeticJ] (13) 86, p. 34.
"Tip top of the oak." [Amelia] (3:1) Ja 86, p. 38.
5199. STUPP, John
"Retarded Boys in the Shower." [PennR] (2:1) Fall-Wint 86, p. 90.
5200. ST'URUA, Lia
"He Saw a Naked Women" (1980, tr. by Kevin Tuite). [LitR] (30:1) Fall 86, p. 18.
"There Must Be Something" (1984, tr. by Kevin Tuite). [LitR] (30:1) Fall 86, p. 19-20.
"The Victim of the City" (1984, tr. by Kevin Tuite). [LitR] (30:1) Fall 86, p. 17-18.
5201. SU, Shih
"Five Tz'u" (tr. by Julie Landau). [Translation] (17) Fall 86, p. 324-325.
5202. SUAREZ QUEMAIN, Jaime
"I Want a Lucid Witness from You" (tr. by Ruben Martinez). [RedBass] (11) 86, p. 8.
5203. SUBLETT, Dyan
"Simple Rituals." [GeoR] (40:3) Fall 86, p. 802-803.
5204. SUBRAMAN, Belinda
"Blood Relations." [YellowS] (21) Wint 86, p. 29.
"Demons #20" (for Steve Richmond). [Bogg] (55) 86, p. 26.
"I See Demons Too, Steve." [SecC] (14:1) 86, p. 69.
"Language." [Bogg] (56) 86, p. 13.
SUEUR, Meridel le
   See Le SUEUR, Meridel

357

5205. SUGIYAMA, Heiichi
"Ennui" (tr. by James Kirkup and Akiko Takemoto). [Translation] (17) Fall 86, p. 197.
"Going Down" (tr. by James Kirkup and Akiko Takemoto). [Translation] (17) Fall 86, p. 198.
5206. SUHOR, Charles
"The Death of Excellence." [EngJ] (75:3) Mr 86, p. 110.
5207. SULLAM, Elizabeth
"In Memory of Roberto Tinti, Called Bob, Commander of the Thirty-Fourth Garibaldi Brigade." [Vis] (21) 86, p. 30-31.
"Night Walks Unaware." [Vis] (21) 86, p. 26-27.
"The Sap of Oleander Thickened in Your Veins." [Vis] (21) 86, p. 28.
"Sunset." [Vis] (21) 86, p. 26.
5208. SULLIVAN, Francis
"Requiem." [LittleM] (15:2) 86, p. 33.
5209. SULLIVAN, James
"Israhel Van Meckenem's Engraving of *The Presentation at the Temple* (c. 1495) . . ." [BelPoJ] (37:2) Wint 86-87, p. 34-35.
5210. SULLIVAN, Janet
"Persephone at the Seed Rack." [NegC] (6:1) Wint 86, p. 83.
5211. SULLIVAN, John
"Sub-Saharan Landscape with Human Figures, Dying." [SanFPJ] (8:2) 85, p. 33-34.
5212. SULLIVAN, Mary Jane
"Going To." [Cond] (13) 86, p. 100.
"What's the Difference between a Country and a House." [Cond] (13) 86, p. 101-103.
5213. SULLIVAN, William
"Solo." [BallSUF] (26:4) Aut 85, p. 67.
SUMIO, Matsuda
See MATSUDA, Sumio
5214. SUMMERS, Thomas H.
"Dietary Dilemma." [BellR] (9:1) Spr 86, p. 52.
5215. SUMRALL, Noel
"Roses." [DeKalbLAJ] (19:3/4) 86, p. 111.
5216. SUN, Jin-xuan
"Autumn" (tr. by Xu Yaoping and Manly Johnson). [Nimrod] (29:2) Spr-Sum 86, p. 37.
"Small Path" (tr. by Xu Yaoping, Xia Mingshan and Francine Ringold). [Nimrod] (29:2) Spr-Sum 86, p. 36.
"The Winter Snow" (tr. by Xu Yaoping and Manly Johnson). [Nimrod] (29:2) Spr-Sum 86, p. 38.
5217. SUNDAHL, Daniel J.
"Hiroshima Maiden: An Imaginary Translation from the Japanese." [NewL] (53:1) Fall 86, p. 51-53.
5218. SUPERVIELLE, Jules
"The Difficult Journey" (tr. by Dorothy Aspinwall). [WebR] (11:2) Fall 86, p. 28.
"Forgetting My Body" (tr. by Dorothy Aspinwall). [WebR] (11:2) Fall 86, p. 29.
"The Point of a Flame" (tr. by Dorothy Aspinwall). [WebR] (11:2) Fall 86, p. 28.
5219. SUPRANER, Robyn
"A Time to Live" (Barbara Cantor: 1932-1941, Capt. Arthur Rubenstein: 1928-1955). [BelPoJ] (36:4) Sum 86, p. 16-17.
"Vermont Frieze." [BelPoJ] (36:4) Sum 86, p. 17.
SURIA, Violeta López
See LOPEZ SURIA, Violeta
5220. SURVANT, Joe
"August Is the Month of Spiders." [Farm] (3:2) Spr-Sum 86, p. 39.
"Brownian Movement." [Farm] (3:2) Spr-Sum 86, p. 40.
"The Cattle Are Eating the Forest." [Farm] (3:2) Spr-Sum 86, p. 41.
5221. SUSHINSKY, Mabel
"This Is How a Capricorn Gardens." [WindO] (47) Sum 86, p. 39.
"This Is How a Scorpio Gardens." [WindO] (47) Sum 86, p. 39.
5222. SUSSKIND, Harriet
"Hours." [HeliconN] (16) Wint 86, p. 55.
"Riddle." [DenQ] (20:4/21:1) Spr-Sum 86, p. 71-72.
"Selma Cantor Is Seventy-Five." [NegC] (6:1) Wint 86, p. 31-35.

"A Slow Way to Voices." [DenQ] (20:4/21:1) Spr-Sum 86, p. 73-75.
SUSSMAN, Leona Mahler
    See MAHLER-SUSSMAN, Leona
5223. SUTHER, Judith D.
    "Epitaph." [SpiritSH] (52) 86, p. 19.
    "The Fisherman" (For a burned-out academic). [SpiritSH] (52) 86, p. 18.
    "Matins." [SpiritSH] (52) 86, p. 19.
    "Non-Elective Surgery" (For a deconstructivist). [SpiritSH] (52) 86, p. 21.
    "Spiritual Exercise." [SpiritSH] (52) 86, p. 20-21.
5224. SUTHERLAND, Connie
    "Driving Out." [Paint] (13:25/26) Spr-Aut 86, p. 11.
5225. SUTHERLAND, Judith L.
    "Advent." [ChrC] (103:39) 17 D 86, p. 1140.
5226. SUTHERLAND-SMITH, James
    "Sonnets from Zawia" ("On Cooking Chickens," "Literacy"). [Confr] (33/34)
        Fall-Wint 86-87, p. 67-68.
    "To an Eleven Year Old Boy Unable to Speak More Than Two Words." [StoneC]
        (14:1/2) Fall-Wint 86-87, p. 11.
5227. SUTTER, Barton
    "Freeway." [TarRP] (24:2) Spr 85, p. 33.
    "Tools." [TarRP] (24:2) Spr 85, p. 31-33.
5228. SUTTON, Catherine
    "Graveyard Quilt" (Made by Elizabeth Mitchell, Lewis Co., Kentucky, circa 1839).
        [AmerV] (4) Fall 86, p. 129.
5229. SUTTON, Maureen D.
    "Anne Has a Satellite Dish." [CapeR] (21:2) Fall 86, p. 3.
    "Gotcha." [SanFPJ] (8:4) 85, p. 37.
    "Living Well." [SanFPJ] (8:2) 85, p. 77.
    "Speculations on Industry Near Ground Zero." [SanFPJ] (8:4) 85, p. 54-55.
    "Still Dreaming." [SanFPJ] (8:2) 85, p. 78-79.
5230. SUYEMOTO, Toyo
    "Camp Memories." [Contact] (7:38/39/40) Wint-Spr 86, p. 34.
    "Masked." [Contact] (7:38/39/40) Wint-Spr 86, p. 34.
5231. SVEHLA, John
    "Autumn's Buds." [NegC] (6:1) Wint 86, p. 93.
    "Broken Stars." [DeKalbLAJ] (19:3/4) 86, p. 90.
    "Bug Shadows." [DeKalbLAJ] (19:2) 86, p. 47.
    "Desert Year Flats." [Wind] (16:56) 86, p. 19.
    "Morning." [DeKalbLAJ] (19:1) 86, p. 37.
    "The Nation's Sun." [DeKalbLAJ] (19:3/4) 86, p. 90.
    "A Pine Bee." [DeKalbLAJ] (19:1) 86, p. 37.
    "Rose Hills." [DeKalbLAJ] (19:3/4) 86, p. 90.
    "Shampoo Seas." [DeKalbLAJ] (19:1) 86, p. 37.
    "A Shuttered Breeze." [Wind] (16:56) 86, p. 10.
    "Town Farm." [Wind] (16:56) 86, p. 48.
    "Two Broken Horses." [DeKalbLAJ] (19:2) 86, p. 47.
5232. SVOBODA, Robert
    "A Rogue's Thesaurus." [SmPd] (23:3, #68) Fall 86, p. 22-27.
5233. SVOBODA, Terese
    "Curtis, Nebraska." [PraS] (60:2) Sum 86, p. 122.
    "Electricity Fails a Whole State." [SenR] (16:2) 86, p. 89.
    "Go South, Old Man." [PraS] (60:2) Sum 86, p. 121.
    "New Lincoln Penny." [NewEngR] (9:2) Wint 86, p. 189.
    "Seeing." [SenR] (16:2) 86, p. 88.
    "Single Parent Wants to See a Film But Has No Sitter." [PennR] (2:1) Fall-Wint 86,
        p. 86-87.
    "Under the Cottonwood." [Chelsea] (45) 86, p. 90.
    "Water Ballet." [Chelsea] (45) 86, p. 91.
5234. SWAIM, Alice Mackenzie
    "Of Loss and Leaving." [BallSUF] (27:4) Aut 86, p. 37.
5235. SWANBERG, Christine
    "Byron, Illinois." [SpoonRQ] (11:2) Spr 86, p. 38.
    "The Dead of Winter." [SpoonRQ] (11:4) Fall 86, p. 29.
    "For a Brother-in-Law Leaving for Tupelo." [SpoonRQ] (11:2) Spr 86, p. 39.
    "For Robert Pirsig." [EngJ] (75:1) Ja 86, p. 78.
    "Lake." [SingHM] (13) 86, p. 27.

"Westbound on the Canadian Pacific." [SpoonRQ] (11:4) Fall 86, p. 28.
5236. SWANDER, Mary
  "Doc." [Iowa] (16:1) Wint 86, p. 39-47.
  "Novena." [GeoR] (40:3) Fall 86, p. 804.
  "Thirteen." [SouthwR] (71:2) Spr 86, p. 242.
5237. SWANGER, David
  "How Our Lives Fill the Sky." [PoetryNW] (27:1) Spr 86, p. 42-44.
  "Longer." [GeoR] (40:4) Wint 86, p. 907-908.
  "She Marries a Violinist." [LitR] (29:2) Wint 86, p. 238.
  "What the Wing Says." [GeoR] (40:3) Fall 86, p. 805.
5238. SWANN, Brian
  "August at Grassano" (for Carlo Levi, tr. of Rocco Scotellaro, w. Ruth Feldman).
    [NewRena] (6:3, #20) Spr 86, p. 51.
  "The Beginning of the World." [KenR] (NS 8:2) Spr 86, p. 76-77.
  "Flower in the Mountains." [StoneC] (14:1/2) Fall-Wint 86-87, p. 70-71.
  "Märchen." [KenR] (NS 8:2) Spr 86, p. 77.
  "Names." [KenR] (NS 8:2) Spr 86, p. 76.
  "The Orange Tree" (tr. of Rocco Scotellaro, w. Ruth Feldman). [NewRena] (6:3,
    #20) Spr 86, p. 53.
  "Six Dream Songs" (from Song of the Sky, versions of Native American songs and
    poems). [StoneC] (14:1/2) Fall-Wint 86-87, p. 71-72.
  "A Woman." [StoneC] (14:1/2) Fall-Wint 86-87, p. 69.
  "The World's Imperfect Memory" (in memoriam xxx). [LitR] (29:3) Spr 86, p. 341.
  "Wrong Number." [OhioR] (37) 86, p. 116.
5239. SWANN, Roberta M.
  "Instead." [IndR] (9:2) Spr 86, p. 96-97.
  "Ordinary Epiphanies." [YellowS] (21) Wint 86, p. 38.
  "Statistics." [StoneC] (14:1/2) Fall-Wint 86-87, p. 73-74.
  "Watching Lizards" (for Leo and Nora Lionni). [StoneC] (14:1/2) Fall-Wint 86-87,
    p. 74-75.
5240. SWANNELL, Anne
  "Poetry Reading in a (Divided) Conference Room." [CanLit] (109) Sum 86, p.
    84-85.
  "The Wrong Question." [CanLit] (109) Sum 86, p. 4.
5241. SWANSON, Catherine
  "Trains." [PassN] (7:1) Fall-Wint 85-86, p. 27.
5242. SWANSON, Robert
  "The Pottery Figures at the Museum in San Jose, Costa Rica, 1910." [TarRP] (26:1)
    Fall 86, p. 41.
  "Rejuvenation." [DeKalbLAJ] (19:2) 86, p. 48.
5243. SWANSON, Susan Marie
  "Grass." [SingHM] (13) 86, p. 94.
  "Life's First Thunderstorm." [AmerPoR] (15:1) Ja-F 86, p. 14.
  "The Reindeer of Stars." [Prima] (10) 86, p. 53-58.
5244. SWARD, Robert
  "Alpha the Dog." [GreenfR] (13:3/4) Sum-Fall 86, p. 191.
  "Name-Dropping." [GreenfR] (13:3/4) Sum-Fall 86, p. 192.
5245. SWEDE, George
  "Several Short Poems." [GreenfR] (13:3/4) Sum-Fall 86, p. 193.
5246. SWEENEY, Gael
  "Belmont Park: Ruffian." [HiramPoR] (40) Spr-Sum 86, p. 56-57.
  "Delinquency." [HiramPoR] (40) Spr-Sum 86, p. 58-61.
  "Searching for Halley's Comet." [HiramPoR] (40) Spr-Sum 86, p. 54-55.
5247. SWEENEY, Matthew
  "The Bats." [Field] (34) Spr 86, p. 55-56.
5248. SWEET, Bruce
  "Mushroom." [Blueline] (8:1) Sum-Fall 86, p. 15.
5249. SWENSON, Karen
  "Adam and His Father." [SouthernPR] (26:1) Spr 86, p. 23.
  "The Artists." [DenQ] (20:4/21:1) Spr-Sum 86, p. 148.
  "The Garden." [MichQR] (25:1) Wint 86, p. 126.
5250. SWENSON, May
  "Waterbird." [Atlantic] (257:6) Je 86, p. 38.
5251. SWIFT, Joan
  "At the Teahut." [Ploughs] (12:4) 86, p. 35-36.
  "Flying." [Ploughs] (12:4) 86, p. 33-34.

5252. SWISHER, Robert K.
"The moon is out again tonight." [RagMag] (5:2) Fall 86, p. 72.
5253. SWISS, Thomas
"The Music Box." [AmerS] (55:2) Spr 86, p. 178-180.
5254. SWIST, Wally
"Pay day." [Amelia] (3:3) Sum 86, p. 60.
"Three Haiku." [Amelia] (3:1) Ja 86, p. 67.
5255. SWOH-ALLEN-BOLT
"A Silver." [JamesWR] (3:2) Wint 86, p. 8.
5256. SYED, Abdul Mannan
"Fish" (tr. by Kabir Chowdhury). [Pax] (3:1/2) Wint 85-86, p. 205.
"Moonlight Like a Ghost Stands at the Door" (tr. by Kabir Choudhury). [SenR]
(16:1) 86, p. 78.
5257. SYLVESTER, Santiago E.
"Hamlet in the Market-Place" (tr. by Anthony Edkins). [WebR] (11:1) Spr 86, p. 29.
5258. SZE, Arthur
"Evil Grigri." [NewL] (52:2/3) Wint-Spr 86, p. 69.
"The Negative." [NewL] (52:2/3) Wint-Spr 86, p. 70-71.
"The Silence." [Contact] (7:38/39/40) Wint-Spr 86, p. 43.
5259. SZEMAN, Sherri
"Counting the Thunder." [NewL] (53:1) Fall 86, p. 26-27.
"Fireflies." [CarolQ] (38:3) Spr 86, p. 55-57.
"Fireflies." [DeKalbLAJ] (19:2) 86, p. 49-51.
"Learning the New Language." [ChiR] (35:3) Spr 86, p. 50-51.
"Letter to Sylvia." [WritersF] (12) Fall 86, p. 186-188.
"The Toast." [SouthernPR] (26:1) Spr 86, p. 10-11.
"Vin Ordinaire, Vin Chaud." [KanQ] (18:1/2) Wint-Spr 86, p. 278-279.
5260. SZINETAR, Vasco
"Esto Que Gira" (a Silvana). [LindLM] (5:2) Ap-Je 86, p. 7.
5261. SZUMIGALSKI, Anne
"Desire." [MalR] (75) Je 86, p. 39.
"His Method." [MalR] (75) Je 86, p. 40.
"A Pineal Casement." [MalR] (75) Je 86, p. 38.
"Procession — The Poem as a Dark Familar." [Grain] (14:2) My 86, p. 10-11.
"A Woman Gets Up." [MalR] (75) Je 86, p. 37.
5262. TABIOS, Presco
"Battling Bonifacio — the North Star." [Contact] (7:38/39/40) Wint-Spr 86, p. 39.
5263. TADA, Chimako
"A Dirge" (tr. by James Kirkup and Akiko Takemoto). [Translation] (17) Fall 86, p.
203.
5264. TAFDRUP, Pia
"Even Further" (in Danish and English, tr. by Nina Juel Bigbie and Erik Porret).
[Os] (23) 86, p. 30-31.
"The Skin" (in Danish and English, tr. by Nina Juel Bigbie and Erik Porret). [Os]
(23) 86, p. 34-35.
"Spring Flood" (in Danish and English, tr. by Nina Juel Bigbie and Erik Porret).
[Os] (23) 86, p. 32-33.
5265. TAFOYA, Terry
"Christmas." [CutB] (25) Fall-Wint 86, p. 70.
"Grandmother." [CutB] (25) Fall-Wint 86, p. 68-69.
5266. TAFT, David
"Some Boys Must Know." [Bogg] (56) 86, p. 45.
5267. TAGAMI, Jeff
"A Death" (tr. of Ines Asinc Ramos de Ching, w. J. Jacinto & V. Sales-Gomez).
[Contact] (7:38/39/40) Wint-Spr 86, Supplement p. 10.
"Defining" (tr. of Ines Asinc Ramos de Ching, w. J. Jacinto & V. Sales-Gomez).
[Contact] (7:38/39/40) Wint-Spr 86, Supplement p. 12.
"Farewell" (tr. of Rafael Yamasato, w. J. Jacinto & V. Sales-Gomez). [Contact]
(7:38/39/40) Wint-Spr 86, Supplement p. 22.
"Imitation of Watanabe" (tr. of Rafael Yamasato, w. J. Jacinto & V. Sales-Gomez).
[Contact] (7:38/39/40) Wint-Spr 86, Supplement p. 23.
"Letter to a Brother Prisoner" (tr. of Ines Asinc Ramos de Ching, w. J. Jacinto & V.
Sales-Gomez). [Contact] (7:38/39/40) Wint-Spr 86, Supplement p. 8.
"Noriko" (tr. of Rafael Yamasato, w. J. Jacinto & V. Sales-Gomez). [Contact]
(7:38/39/40) Wint-Spr 86, Supplement p. 16-17.

"The Snow and the Male Flower" (tr. of Rafael Yamasato, w. J. Jacinto & V.
    Sales-Gomez). [Contact] (7:38/39/40) Wint-Spr 86, Supplement p. 21.
"Well of Desires" (tr. of Rafael Yamasato, w. J. Jacinto & V. Sales-Gomez).
    [Contact] (7:38/39/40) Wint-Spr 86, Supplement p. 20.
"With Doubtful Comic Achievements" (tr. of Jose Watanabe, w. J. Jacinto & V.
    Sales-Gomez). [Contact] (7:38/39/40) Wint-Spr 86, Supp. p. 28-29.
"With Regard to Misadjustments . . ." (tr. of Jose Watanabe, w. J. Jacinto & V.
    Sales-Gomez). [Contact] (7:38/39/40) Wint-Spr 86, Supp. p. 26.
5268. TAGGART, John
    "Not Quite Parallel Lines" (With Drawings by Bradford Graves). [Conjunc] (9) 86,
        p. 99-107.
    "Rule 14L." [Epoch] (35:1) 85-86, p. 44-47.
    "Three." [Epoch] (35:1) 85-86, p. 48.
5269. TAGLIABUE, John
    "After Breakfast Contentment." [BellR] (9:2) Fall 86, p. 47.
    "At an Henri Rousseau Exhibit." [ConnPR] (5:1) 86, p. 11-12.
    "At the Henri Rousseau Exhibit." [ConnPR] (5:1) 86, p. 10-11.
    "Pear Blossoms Handscroll" (circa 1235). [MemphisSR] (6:1/2) Spr 86, p. 22.
    "Tai-yang means Sun and Yuan Chen's poetry means pleasure." [CentR] (30:3) Sum
        86, p. 353.
    "The Tenor of My Climbing." [BellR] (9:2) Fall 86, p. 47.
    "To My Father." [CrossCur] (6:2) 86, p. 160.
    "Twelve Hanging Scrolls by Yuan Chiang" (circa 1691). [MemphisSR] (6:1/2) Spr
        86, p. 23.
    "Unfinished Ache or All the People in All of the Nursing Homes . . ." [NewL]
        (53:1) Fall 86, p. 21.
    "While reading 'To the Waters of Chia-ling' by Yuan Chen." [CentR] (30:3) Sum
        86, p. 353.
5270. TAHANA
    "July 4 — Anytime." [SanFPJ] (8:3) 85, p. 68.
5271. TAHIR, M. Athan
    "Indus Horses." [CrossCur] (5:4/6:1) 86, p. 24.
5272. TAI, Piao-yüan
    "Cheng-Tao Temple" (tr. by Jonathan Chaves). [Translation] (17) Fall 86, p. 326.
5273. TAKAGI, Kyozo
    "How to Cook Women" (tr. by Michio Nakano and James Kirkup). [Translation]
        (17) Fall 86, p. 33.
    "A Skyline — New Year's Day" (tr. by Michio Nakano and James Kirkup).
        [Translation] (17) Fall 86, p. 32.
    "Snowy Night" (tr. by James Kirkup and Michio Nakano). [Translation] (17) Fall
        86, p. 31.
    "To the Sea" (tr. by Michio Nakano and James Kirkup). [Translation] (17) Fall 86,
        p. 34.
5274. TAKAMURA, Kotaro
    "Whale Spouting" (tr. by James Kirkup and Akiko Takemoto). [Translation] (17)
        Fall 86, p. 184-185.
5275. TAKEMOTO, Akiko
    "The Ancient Pine Tree on Mt. Tempai" (tr. of Hitoshi Anzai, w. James Kirkup).
        [Translation] (17) Fall 86, p. 116.
    "Appetite" (tr. of Sachiko Yoshihara, w. James Kirkup). [Translation] (17) Fall 86,
        p. 207.
    "At a Cannery" (tr. of Katsuko Nishio, w. James Kirkup). [Translation] (17) Fall
        86, p. 202.
    "A Dirge" (tr. of Chimako Tada, w. James Kirkup). [Translation] (17) Fall 86, p.
        203.
    "Do Not Get Up" (tr. of Takuboku Ishikawa, w. James Kirkup). [Translation] (17)
        Fall 86, p. 186.
    "Early Winter" (tr. of Mokuo Nagayama, w. James Kirkup). [Translation] (17) Fall
        86, p. 209.
    "The Electric Car" (tr. of Masao Nakagiri, w. James Kirkup). [Translation] (17) Fall
        86, p. 199.
    "Emperor" (tr. of Ryuichi Tamura, w. James Kirkup). [Translation] (17) Fall 86, p.
        201.
    "Ennui" (tr. of Heiichi Sugiyama, w. James Kirkup). [Translation] (17) Fall 86, p.
        197.

"Fist" (tr. of Takuboku Ishikawa, w. James Kirkup). [Translation] (17) Fall 86, p. 187.
"Frozen Love" (tr. of Mokuo Nagayama, w. James Kirkup). [Translation] (17) Fall 86, p. 208.
"Going Down" (tr. of Heiichi Sugiyama, w. James Kirkup). [Translation] (17) Fall 86, p. 198.
"The Governor" (tr. of Shigeharu Nakano, w. James Kirkup). [Translation] (17) Fall 86, p. 194.
"Gray Gulls" (tr. of Tatsuji Miyoshi, w. James Kirkup). [Translation] (17) Fall 86, p. 192-193.
"High-Pressure Chart" (tr. of Jun Honda, w. James Kirkup). [Translation] (17) Fall 86, p. 210-211.
"Monstrous Fish" (tr. of Tozaburo Ono, w. James Kirkup). [Translation] (17) Fall 86, p. 196.
"Mount Fuji" (tr. of Mitsuharu Kaneko, w. James Kirkup). [Translation] (17) Fall 86, p. 188-189.
"My Eye" (tr. of Hitoshi Anzai, w. James Kirkup). [Translation] (17) Fall 86, p. 115.
"My Father" (tr. of Jukichi Yagi, w. James Kirkup). [Translation] (17) Fall 86, p. 191.
"The Name" (tr. of Sachiko Yoshihara, w. James Kirkup). [Translation] (17) Fall 86, p. 206.
"Never Bind Me" (tr. of Kazue Shinkawa, w. James Kirkup). [Translation] (17) Fall 86, p. 204-205.
"One Day" (tr. of Jukichi Yagi, w. James Kirkup). [Translation] (17) Fall 86, p. 190.
"Overhang" (tr. of Mokuo Nagayama, w. James Kirkup). [Translation] (17) Fall 86, p. 209.
"Rain" (tr. of Jukichi Yagi, w. James Kirkup). [Translation] (17) Fall 86, p. 191.
"Sorrow" (tr. of Jukichi Yagi, w. James Kirkup). [Translation] (17) Fall 86, p. 190.
"Sorrow Piling Up Within Me" (tr. of Jukichi Yagi, w. James Kirkup). [Translation] (17) Fall 86, p. 190.
"A Thought in Autumn" (tr. of Nobuo Ayukawa, w. James Kirkup). [Translation] (17) Fall 86, p. 200.
"Tomorrow" (tr. of Tozaburo Ono, w. James Kirkup). [Translation] (17) Fall 86, p. 195.
"Whale Spouting" (tr. of Kotaro Takamura, w. James Kirkup). [Translation] (17) Fall 86, p. 184-185.

5276. TAKSA, Mark
"Choice at the Blossom Cafe." [CimR] (75) Ap 86, p. 14.
"Mill Worker's House." [YetASM] (4) 85, p. 8.
"Sweating Out the Enemy." [Wind] (16:56) 86, p. 45.

TAKUBOKU, Ishikawa
See ISHIKAWA, Takuboku

5277. TALAL, Marilynn
"Balloons." [YetASM] (4) 85, p. 4.
"Mrs. Suzuki, Japanese Tea Master." [Pax] (3:1/2) Wint 85-86, p. 134.
"Pomegranate." [Pax] (3:1/2) Wint 85-86, p. 133.

TALIANA
See TAHANA

5278. TALLMOUNTAIN, Mary
"Nuliajuk, a Sequence." [Calyx] (9:2/3) Wint 86, p. 124.

5279. TALLOSI, Jim
"Islands Awakening." [PraF] (7:2) Sum 86, p. 54.
"March 4/84." [PraF] (7:2) Sum 86, p. 52.
"Night Establishes Itself." [PraF] (7:2) Sum 86, p. 53.

5280. TAMER, Ulkü
"History of the Vanquished" (tr. by Talat S. Halman). [Verse] (5) 86, p. 49.

5281. TAMM, Riina
"Elder-trees that thrushes have sown" (tr. of Jaan Kaplinski, w. the author and Sam Hamill). [WillowS] (18) Sum 86, p. 77.
"I could have said: I stepped from the bus" (tr. of Jaan Kaplinski, w. the author and Sam Hamill). [WillowS] (18) Sum 86, p. 75.
"It gets cold in the evening" (tr. of Jaan Kaplinski, w. the author and Sam Hamill). [WillowS] (18) Sum 86, p. 76.

"Once I got a postcard from the Fiji Islands" (tr. of Jaan Kaplinski, w. the author and Sam Hamill). [WillowS] (18) Sum 86, p. 74.

5282. TAMMARO, Thom
"I and the Village." [BallSUF] (26:4) Aut 85, p. 58-59.
"Lyrids." [MidwQ] (27:3) Spr 86, p. 314-315.

5283. TAMMINGA, Frederick W.
"The Breasts of Almatricia" (after Pierre Louÿs). [YellowS] (20) Aut 86, p. 15.
"The Passing Past Surviving" (after Pierre Louÿs). [YellowS] (20) Aut 86, p. 15.

5284. TAMURA, Ryuichi
"Emperor" (tr. by James Kirkup and Akiko Takemoto). [Translation] (17) Fall 86, p. 201.

5285. TANA, Patti
"Birds and Leaves." [ManhatPR] (7) Sum 86, p. 28.
"Vanishing Point." [ManhatPR] (7) Sum 86, p. 28.

5286. TANG, Chao
"By the Dream Ocean" (tr. of Gu Cheng). [Verse] (6) 86, p. 50.
"By the Dream Ocean" (tr. of Gu Cheng, w. Tony Barnstone). [Nimrod] (29:2) Spr-Sum 86, p. 28.
"Many Years" (tr. of Bei Dao, w. Tony Barnstone). [Nimrod] (29:2) Spr-Sum 86, p. 96.
"Memory" (on an exhibition of Ling Fengmian's Paintings, tr. of Tang Qi). [Verse] (6) 86, p. 47.
"Memory" (on an exhibition of Ling Fengmian's paintings, tr. of Tang Qi, w. Tony Barnstone). [Nimrod] (29:2) Spr-Sum 86, p. 35.

5287. TANG, Qi
"Memory" (on an exhibition of Ling Fengmian's Paintings, tr. by Tang Chao). [Verse] (6) 86, p. 47.
"Memory" (on an exhibition of Ling Fengmian's paintings, tr. by Tony Barnstone and Tang Chao). [Nimrod] (29:2) Spr-Sum 86, p. 35.

5288. TANIKAWA, Shuntaro
"Drawing a Picture" (tr. by Harold Wright). [Translation] (17) Fall 86, p. 61-66.

5289. TANNEN, Deborah
"Does Life Extend?" (tr. of Erling Indreeide). [Vis] (22) 86, p. 14.

5290. TANNENBAUM, Judith
"December." [Electrum] (38) Spr 86, p. 11.

5291. TAO, Liu
"A Boat with Two Masts" (tr. of Shu Ting). [Verse] (6) 86, p. 48.

5292. TAPSCOTT, Stephen
"The Ailanthus." [YaleR] (75:4) Sum 86, p. 534-535.
"A Choice." [PraS] (60:1) Spr 86, p. 88.
"Comrade" (for A.R. Ammons). [Pembroke] (18) 86, p. 212-214.
"Contact." [PraS] (60:1) Spr 86, p. 89.
"Daylilies in August." [AmerPoR] (15:4) Jl-Ag 86, p. 11.
"Gathering." [Agni] (23) 86, p. 130.
"The Jump." [PraS] (60:1) Spr 86, p. 90.
"Love Sonnets" (Selections: II, VI, XXII, XXXIII, tr. of Pablo Neruda). (for Mary Oliver). [Atlantic] (257:2) F 86, p. 62-63.
"Mud." [YaleR] (75:4) Sum 86, p. 534.
"One Hundred Love Sonnets" (Selections: I, XX, LI, LII, XCII, C, tr. of Pablo Neruda). [AmerPoR] (15:3) My-Je 86, p. 21-22.

5293. TARABA, M. S.
"Days Like These." [Cond] (13) 86, p. 130-131.

5294. TARN, Nathaniel
"Gisants" (Three poems: "Convoy," "Tale," "Dialogues," tr. of Michel Deguy). [Conjunc] (9) 86, p. 24-26.
"The Land in Question." [Conjunc] (9) 86, p. 125-127.
"The Life-Sitter" (hommage to J.R.). [Os] (22) 86, p. 15.
"Metamorphosis of Spider into Crab." [Conjunc] (9) 86, p. 122-124.
"Remission Bardo." [Conjunc] (9) 86, p. 121-122.
"Winter Oasis." [Os] (22) 86, p. 14.

5295. TATE, Diana
"For the Barley Sower." [PraS] (60:2) Sum 86, p. 65.

5296. TATE, James
"Aunt Sophie's Morning." [Ploughs] (12:3) 86, p. 70.
"Neighbors." [Sonora] (11) Fall 86 [c87], p. 79.
"Poem: The angel kissed my alphabet." [Ploughs] (12:3) 86, p. 69.

TATSUJI, Miyoshi
   See MIYOSHI, Tatsuji
5297. TAUFER, Veno
   "Artist and Model" (tr. by Michael Scammel). [Vis] (22) 86, p. 23-25.
   "At the End of the Journey" (tr. by Michael Scammell). [Vis] (20) 86, p. 39.
5298. TAUS, Roger
   "Blues for Anna." [Electrum] (38) Spr 86, p. 15.
5299. TAYLOR, Ana Ortiz de Montellano
   "In Reality" (Response to Katha Politt's "Drinking from a cup of shadows").
   [SingHM] (13) 86, p. 14.
5300. TAYLOR, Bruce
   "Father Lewis." [NowestR] (24:3) 86, p. 21.
   "With Cho at the Lower Han." [PassN] (7:2) Spr-Sum 86, p. 19.
5301. TAYLOR, Dabrina
   "Captiva." [SouthernHR] (20:4) Fall 86, p. 355.
5302. TAYLOR, Eleanor Ross
   "Limits." [BostonR] (11:4) Ag 86, p. 12.
   "A Little Obituary." [BostonR] (11:4) Ag 86, p. 12.
   "March 9." [PartR] (53:4) 86, p. 580-581.
   "Motherhood, 1880." [BostonR] (11:4) Ag 86, p. 12.
   "New Girls." [BostonR] (11:4) Ag 86, p. 12.
   "Rachel Plummer's Dream" (Winter 1836). [BostonR] (11:4) Ag 86, p. 12.
5303. TAYLOR, Keith
   "Banshee." [PassN] (7:2) Spr-Sum 86, p. 15.
   "Landed Immigrants." [Notus] (1:1) Fall 86, p. 69.
5304. TAYLOR, Kent
   "4 A.M." [Abraxas] (34) 86, p. 10.
   "7-18-83." [Abraxas] (34) 86, p. 7.
   "A Belated Touché for D.A. Levy." [Abraxas] (34) 86, p. 9.
   "Family Matters." [Abraxas] (34) 86, p. 6-7.
   "For the Destroyed Poets of Ohio." [Abraxas] (34) 86, p. 5.
   "Heading North." [Abraxas] (34) 86, p. 8.
5305. TAYLOR, Louis
   "A Moment of Darkness." [Bogg] (55) 86, p. 54.
5306. TAYLOR, Perry
   "Always Lighter Than Expected." [Quarry] (35:4) Aut 86, p. 60.
   "A Sense of Proportion." [Quarry] (35:4) Aut 86, p. 59.
5307. TAYLOR, Ross
   "Dragon Story." [VirQR] (62:4) Aut 86, p. 598-599.
   "Green Complaint." [VirQR] (62:4) Aut 86, p. 599-600.
5308. TAYLOR, Sally
   "Family Tones." [DeKalbLAJ] (19:1) 86, p. 38.
   "Summer Term." [Vis] (21) 86, p. 16.
5309. TEDESCO, Cosmo
   "A Love Hope." [WritersL] (1986:3), p. 11.
   "New World." [WritersL] (1986:5), p. 25.
5310. TEILLIER, Jorge
   "The Exorcisms" (tr. by Carolyne Wright). [AmerV] (5) Wint 86, p. 37.
   "Nieve Nocturna." [InterPR] (12:1) Spr 86, p. 38.
   "Night Snow" (tr. by Mary Crow). [InterPR] (12:1) Spr 86, p. 39.
   "Seated Before the Fire" (tr. by Mary Crow). [InterPR] (12:1) Spr 86, p. 37.
   "Sentados Frente al Fuego." [InterPR] (12:1) Spr 86, p. 36.
TEJADA, Maria Guerra
   See GUERRA TEJADA, Maria
5311. TEJERINA, Elina M.
   "Cancion Desalmada." [Mairena] (8:21) 86, p. 117.
   "Canciones del Abandonado." [Mairena] (8:21) 86, p. 117.
5312. TELLMAN, Susan
   "Reason of Two." [BallSUF] (26:4) Aut 85, p. 12.
Ten BERGE, H. C.
   See BERGE, H. C. ten
5313. TENNENT, Cheryl Ervin
   "Final Moments." [Paint] (13:25/26) Spr-Aut 86, p. 7.
5314. TENNYSON, Alfred
   "When the schemes of all the systems, kingdoms and republics fall" (Excerpt).
   [SanFPJ] (8:3) 85, p. 6.

365

5315. TERASHIMA, Robert
"The Robin." [HangL] (49) Spr 86, p. 47.
"The Warning." [HangL] (49) Spr 86, p. 48.
5316. TERPSTRA, John
"Naked Trees" (10 selections). [MalR] (76) S 86, p. 55-60.
5317. TERRANOVA, Elaine
"Autumn Moths." [PoetryNW] (27:2) Sum 86, p. 24.
"A Holy Day." [Boulevard] (1:3) Fall 86, p. 92.
"Pearls." [PassN] (7:1) Fall-Wint 85-86, p. 22.
"Picking Strawberries." [PennR] (1:2) Fall 85, p. 15.
5318. TERRILL, Richard
"Two Calendars." [NoAmR] (271:1) Mr 86, p. 37.
5319. TERRIN BENAVIDES, Manuel
"Corazon Armonico." [Mairena] (8:22) 86, p. 46.
5320. TERRIS, Virginia
"December." [ManhatPR] (6) Wint-Spr 85-86, p. 13.
5321. TERRY, Arthur
"Autumn Room" (tr. of Gabriel Ferrater). [Translation] (16) Spr 86, p. 113.
"Landscape with Figures" (tr. of Gabriel Ferrater). [Translation] (16) Spr 86, p. 117.
"Maîtresse de Poète" (tr. of Gabriel Ferrater). [Translation] (16) Spr 86, p. 118.
"October" (tr. of Gabriel Ferrater). [Translation] (16) Spr 86, p. 116.
"A Small War" (tr. of Gabriel Ferrater). [Translation] (16) Spr 86, p. 114.
"Solstice" (tr. of Gabriel Ferrater). [Translation] (16) Spr 86, p. 112.
"Time Was" (tr. of Gabriel Ferrater). [Translation] (16) Spr 86, p. 119.
"An Uncertain Step" (tr. of Gabriel Ferrater). [Translation] (16) Spr 86, p. 115.
5322. TERRY, Patricia
"Tropical Architecture." [Hudson] (39:2) Sum 86, p. 291.
5323. TESSIERI, Enrique
"Cold Turkey Night." [Amelia] (3:4) Fall 86, p. 98.
5324. TETI, Zona
"Grass and light." [Comm] (113:7) 11 Ap 86, p. 220.
5325. THALMAN, Mark
"Black Canyon." [PennR] (1:2) Fall 85, p. 71.
"Rings." [Blueline] (8:1) Sum-Fall 86, p. 3.
5326. THAYER, Carl
"The Drunken Boat" (after Rimbaud's "Bateau ivre"). [HiramPoR] (41) Fall-Wint 86-87, p. 41-45.
5327. THERRIEN, Debbie
"Haiku for Raindrops." [WritersL] (1986:2), p. 18.
"Listener's Song." [WritersL] (1986:2), p. 23.
5328. THESEN, Sharon
"The Green Wind." [MalR] (77) D 86, p. 21-22.
"Nevado Del Ruiz." [MalR] (77) D 86, p. 23.
"Nucleus Vibrating." [MalR] (77) D 86, p. 24.
"The Same Trophy." [MalR] (77) D 86, p. 27-28.
"Woman Reading." [MalR] (77) D 86, p. 25-26.
5329. THIBAUDEAU, Colleen
"The Tin Shop." [GreenfR] (13:3/4) Sum-Fall 86, p. 194. .
5330. THIEL, Robert
"Corfu: Afternoon" (Manoulis from an Ikon). [PottPort] (8) 86-87, p. 28.
"Jacaranda Shimmering." [Quarry] (35:4) Aut 86, p. 13-14.
5331. THOMAS, Daniel B.
"Testament." [Lips] (12) 86, p. 23.
5332. THOMAS, Gail
"Amulet." [Calyx] (10:1) Sum 86, p. 28-29.
"Custodian." [Calyx] (10:1) Sum 86, p. 26-27.
5333. THOMAS, George
"Mirage" (for the movie actor, Marion Morrison). [BellArk] (2:6) N-D 86, p. 4.
5334. THOMAS, James M.
"Quite a Large Rock." [AntigR] (64) Wint 86, p. 131.
5335. THOMAS, Jim
"Cissy's *Ciseaux*." [MidwQ] (27:2) Wint 86, p. 212.
"Dove Hunting, Corporation Style." [BallSUF] (27:4) Aut 86, p. 13.
"Loner." [Paint] (13:25/26) Spr-Aut 86, p. 13.
"On Grace." [KanQ] (18:1/2) Wint-Spr 86, p. 112.

"Thirteen Wheels." [Paint] (13:25/26) Spr-Aut 86, p. 12.
5336. THOMAS, John
"For Philomene" (after Lady Ise). [Temblor] (3) 86, p. 160.
"He Despairs of the Poems He Reads." [Temblor] (3) 86, p. 162.
"He Despairs of the Thoughts He Thinks." [Temblor] (3) 86, p. 161.
"He Reflects on the History and the Irrelevance of Absolution." [Temblor] (3) 86, p. 162.
"The Knight Rides Slowly Through the Green Wood." [Temblor] (3) 86, p. 163.
"Our Old Age, a Joyous Vision." [Temblor] (3) 86, p. 161.
"Poem for Her Birthday, Love Poem to Her Mind." [Temblor] (3) 86, p. 160.
5337. THOMAS, Joyce
"The Last Snowman." [Blueline] (8:1) Sum-Fall 86, p. 18.
5338. THOMAS, Judy
"A Poem for Sad Eyes." [Wind] (16:58) 86, p. 34.
"What Made Sad Eyes." [Wind] (16:58) 86, p. 34.
5339. THOMAS, M. J.
"The Fisher." [AmerPoR] (15:4) Jl-Ag 86, p. 11.
"For Halina, a Refugee." [AmerPoR] (15:4) Jl-Ag 86, p. 11.
5340. THOMAS, Stephen
"For My Grandmother." [Contact] (8:41/42/43) Fall-Wint 86-87, p. 9.
5341. THOMASON, Wanda
"That Sort of Dream." [KanQ] (18:1/2) Wint-Spr 86, p. 135.
5342. THOMPSON, Brent
"The Kingdom of Canada" (Selections: I-III). [Quarry] (35:1) Wint 86, p. 58-63.
5343. THOMPSON, Carol
"Dreams." [PoeticJ] (16) Fall 86, p. 12.
5344. THOMPSON, Catherine
"Dry Spring." [SpoonRQ] (11:4) Fall 86, p. 35.
"Looking into a Mirror at Thirty-Five." [SpoonRQ] (11:4) Fall 86, p. 34.
5345. THOMPSON, Douglas H.
"Computer Program." [SanFPJ] (8:1) 85, p. 13.
"In the Year of the Robot Cabinet." [SanFPJ] (8:1) 85, p. 12.
5346. THOMPSON, Hilary
"Turtle Talk." [Germ] (10:1) Spr-Sum 86, p. 17.
5347. THOMPSON, John
"Absent Friends" (Lt. Randolph Smith USAAF, 1919-1943). [NewYRB] (33:9) 29 My 86, p. 29.
5348. THOMPSON, Judith
"Remembering and Forgetting." [KanQ] (18:1/2) Wint-Spr 86, p. 147.
5349. THOMPSON, Kent
"The Doctor's Postcard." [MalR] (74) Mr 86, p. 74.
"Farm for Sale." [MalR] (74) Mr 86, p. 74.
5350. THOMPSON, Nigel
"Outermost Outgoing" (tr. of Andrea Zanzotto). [Verse] (3:3) N 86, p. 49.
5351. THOMPSON, Olav
"Harvest Warning" (tr. of Sigrid Undset, w. Ron Wakefield). [LitR] (29:3) Spr 86, p. 358.
"The Thorn Tree" (tr. of Johan Sebastian Welhaven, w. Ron Wakefield). [LitR] (29:3) Spr 86, p. 359.
5352. THOMPSON, Perry
"Death of the Hero." [DeKalbLAJ] (19:3/4) 86, p. 91.
"Gardeners." [DeKalbLAJ] (19:1) 86, p. 46.
"In Gravity's Thousand Arms." [DeKalbLAJ] (19:1) 86, p. 46.
"No Longer Burned by Passion." [DeKalbLAJ] (19:1) 86, p. 47.
"One for Tony, America's Guest." [DeKalbLAJ] (19:3/4) 86, p. 91-92.
"Tell the Monkey in the Street." [DeKalbLAJ] (19:3/4) 86, p. 92.
"Through the Drinking Moon." [DeKalbLAJ] (19:3/4) 86, p. 93.
"The World Dearly Loves Cages." [DeKalbLAJ] (19:1) 86, p. 47.
5353. THOMPSON, Sue Ellen
"Moths." [SenR] (16:2) 86, p. 85-86.
5354. THOMSON, David
"At the Water." [NegC] (6:4) Fall 86, p. 110.
5355. THORBURN, Alexander
"The House." [Nat] (242:17) 3 My 86, p. 620.
5356. THORNDIKE, Jon
"Poet Lore." [SlipS] (6) 86, p. 42.

367

5357. THORNE, Evelyn
"For a Time and a Time" (Standing before the facade of a cathedral in Mexico).
[HiramPoR] (40) Spr-Sum 86, p. 24.
5358. THORNTON, Russell
"Ravine Creek in December." [Germ] (10:1) Spr-Sum 86, p. 24.
"Song." [Germ] (10:1) Spr-Sum 86, p. 23.
5359. THORPE, Michael
"Brave New Lovers." [PottPort] (8) 86-87, p. 45.
"Monody in Pioneer's Rest." [Germ] (10:1) Spr-Sum 86, p. 26.
"The Space between the Stars." [Germ] (10:1) Spr-Sum 86, p. 25.
"The Week's Major Poet." [AntigR] (64) Wint 86, p. 104.
5360. THRASHER, Shelley
"Parents." [PoeticJ] (13) 86, p. 22.
5361. TICHY, Susan
"At a P.C. Sergeant's House" (Zambales Mountains, Philippines). [AmerV] (3) Sum
86, p. 29-30.
"At a Place of Ambush" (Philippines). [BelPoJ] (37:2) Wint 86-87, p. 8-9.
"Letter from Palestine" (for Salim). [BelPoJ] (37:2) Wint 86-87, p. 10-11.
"Orpheus" (from Africa, for Suzanne in Asia). [BelPoJ] (36:3) Spr 86, p. 27-29.
5362. TIEMAN, John Samuel
"The Concise History of Original Sin." [RiverS] (19) 86, p. 56-57.
"Poem Lesson." [EngJ] (75:2) F 86, p. 94.
"Poem to Be Read When Older" (for Laura Rose Kennedy). [RiverS] (19) 86, p. 54.
"Simplicity." [RiverS] (19) 86, p. 55.
5363. TIERNEY, Nelia
"Co-creation" (WQ Editors' Second Prize Winner, Poetry). [CrossC] (8:1) 86, p.
17.
5364. TIERNEY, Terry
"The Boxer's Choice." [KanQ] (18:1/2) Wint-Spr 86, p. 214.
"The Empty Bottle." [Puerto] (21:2) Spr 86, p. 119.
"The Poet's Garage." [PoetryNW] (27:1) Spr 86, p. 31.
"Widow's Peak." [Contact] (7:38/39/40) Wint-Spr 86, p. 82.
5365. TIGER, Madeline
"Ars Poetica." [NewRep] (195:4) 28 Jl 86, p. 38.
"Night Breathing." [Amelia] (3:4) Fall 86, p. 58.
"What the Brother of the Man Married to the Twin of the Woman Who Died Did."
[Shen] (36:4) 86, p. 81-82.
5366. TIHANYI, Eva
"Escaping Hypnosis" (WQ Editors' First Prize Winner, Poetry). [CrossC] (8:1) 86,
p. 16.
5367. TILLMAN, Albert
"My new matins violate the sabbath." [Bogg] (55) 86, p. 25.
5368. TIM, Henry
"The Partings." [NegC] (6:2/3) Spr-Sum 86, p. 49.
5369. TIMEWELL, Lary
"Chi." [CapilR] (41) 86, p. 52-53.
"Cosmos & October Tent." [CapilR] (41) 86, p. 54-55.
"Creation / Theatre." [CapilR] (41) 86, p. 56-57.
"Misogynist Eme / & Victor Man." [CapilR] (41) 86, p. 58-59.
"La Mort / & Le Party Fou." [CapilR] (41) 86, p. 48-49.
"Once / The." [CapilR] (41) 86, p. 44-45.
"Open City / & Pink Megaphone." [CapilR] (41) 86, p. 46-47.
"Votre Liberté / & Space Flowers." [CapilR] (41) 86, p. 50-51.
TING, Shu
See SHU, Ting
5370. TINGUELY, Vince
"Point of Exit." [PottPort] (8) 86-87, p. 44.
5371. TIO, Elsa
"De Mano de los Hombres." [Mairena] (8:22) 86, p. 92.
"De Mano de los Hombres." [RevICP] (88) Abril-Junio 85, p. 54.
5372. TIPPING, Richard Kelly
"Nanao Sakaki on the Roof at Bondi." [Verse] (5) 86, p. 18.
5373. TIPTON, Paul W.
"War." [Sam] (46:2 release 182) 86, p. 122.
"Webs." [Sam] (46:2 release 182) 86, p. 42.

5374. TISERA, Mary
"The Embattled Warrior Is." [LittleM] (15:2) 86, p. 32.
"You Had Your Ways" (for Wilhelmina Steinbacher). [WestB] (19) 86, p. 103.
5375. TOBIN, Daniel
"Italian Journal." [Amelia] (3:3) Sum 86, p. 103-104.
5376. TODD, Albert
"Disbelief in Yourself Is Indispensable" (tr. of Yevgeny Yevtushenko). [NegC] (6:4)
Fall 86, p. 9-10.
5377. TODD, Theodora
"Topographia." [BelPoJ] (37:2) Wint 86-87, p. 2-3.
5378. TOKARCZYK, Michelle M.
"Leaving the Subway, Approached by a Pornographer." [LitR] (30:1) Fall 86, p.
106.
5379. TOLL, Chris
"The Dark Pages" (for Ruth Pettus). [Bogg] (55) 86, p. 30.
5380. TOLOUI, Karen
"Celebrant." [ColEng] (48:5) S 86, p. 462.
5381. TOME, Jesús
"El Amor Duerme en el Pecho del Poeta" (Spanish tr. of French tr. of Federico
García Lorca). [Mairena] (8:21) 86, p. 46.
5382. TOMLINSON, Charles
"Fountain." [Hudson] (39:1) Spr 86, p. 93.
"In the Borghese Gardens" (For Attilio Bertolucci). [Hudson] (39:1) Spr 86, p.
92-93.
"The Return" (To Paolo Bertolani). [Hudson] (39:1) Spr 86, p. 87-91.
5383. TOMLINSON, Rawdon
"Fat People at the Amusement Park." [HiramPoR] (40) Spr-Sum 86, p. 25.
"A Good Night's Sleep." [HiramPoR] (40) Spr-Sum 86, p. 26.
"The Photograph at the County Fair." [WritersF] (12) Fall 86, p. 188-189.
"Raggedy Ann." [Abraxas] (34) 86, p. 15.
"The Young Cambodian Doctor Explains Social Engineering." [Abraxas] (34) 86, p.
14.
5384. TOMPKINS, Leslie
"Reach for the Moon." [SingHM] (14) 86, p. 33.
5385. TONGUE, Margaret
"Dream of the Hunt." [StoneC] (13:3/4) Spr-Sum 86, p. 30-31.
5386. TORNEO, David
"His Nightmare" (For Matthew Peake). [SilverFR] (11) Sum 86, p. 36.
"Saint Francis in Whittier." [ManhatPR] (7) Sum 86, p. 40.
"The Surface of Water." [ManhatPR] (7) Sum 86, p. 41.
5387. TORNES, Elizabeth (Beth)
"Cant." [Ploughs] (12:3) 86, p. 33.
"Ensenada Maternity Ward." [Ploughs] (12:3) 86, p. 30-31.
"November, Mesnil-en-Thelle." [Ploughs] (12:3) 86, p. 32.
"O Tourist" (tr. of Mohamed Al Magut, w. Saheb Meshtet). [SenR] (16:1) 86, p. 72.
"Orphan" (tr. of Mohamed Al Magut, w. Saheb Meshtet). [SenR] (16:1) 86, p. 69.
"Tattoo" (tr. of Mohamed Al Magut, w. Saheb Meshtet). [SenR] (16:1) 86, p.
70-71.
"Thirst." [Ploughs] (12:3) 86, p. 29.
5388. TORRES, Graciela
"Asi Llegaron." [Mairena] (8:22) 86, p. 54.
5389. TORRES SANTIAGO, José Manuel
"Cancion Apagada." [Mairena] (8:22) 86, p. 72.
5390. TORRESON, Rodney
"The Childhood Mare." [Farm] (3:2) Spr-Sum 86, p. 34.
"Vernon Dahl." [PassN] (7:1) Fall-Wint 85-86, p. 19.
5391. TOSTESON, Heather
"Myths." [BelPoJ] (37:2) Wint 86-87, p. 6-7.
"Quatrains for Jeremy." [Wind] (16:56) 86, p. 46.
"Sundew." [SmPd] (23:2, issue 67) Spr 86, p. 24.
5392. TOURTIDIS, Ilya
"Gregarious Lovers." [WestCR] (20:4) Ap 86, p. 48-49.
"The Shore Life." [WestCR] (20:4) Ap 86, p. 50-51.
5393. TOUSTER, Eva
"Academic Discourse: An Abstract." [Poem] (56) N 86, p. 62.

"The Ides of March" (To a young woman in psychotherapy). [CapeR] (21:2) Fall 86, p. 38.
"In a Clear Intellectual Light." [Poem] (56) N 86, p. 59.
"On Listening to the Resurrection Symphony, December 28, 1982" (For my father, 1886-1982). [Outbr] (16/17) Fall 85-Spr 86, p. 20.
"A Perte de Vue: A Fugue Piece for Precarious Lovers." [Poem] (56) N 86, p. 58.
"A Word on Words: Response to the Outcry against *Ouroboros*." [Poem] (56) N 86, p. 60-61.
5394. TOWELL, Larry
"White Rags." [CanLit] (111) Wint 86, p. 114-115.
5395. TOWLE, Parker
"Our Winter." [StoneC] (13:3/4) Spr-Sum 86, p. 53.
5396. TOWNS, Jeanne R.
"If." [SanFPJ] (9:1) 86, p. 64.
"The Morning After." [BlackALF] (20:3) Fall 86, p. 271-272.
"A Prayer." [SanFPJ] (9:1) 86, p. 61.
"The Thief." [BlackALF] (20:3) Fall 86, p. 271.
"To Michael." [SanFPJ] (9:1) 86, p. 61.
5397. TOWNSEND, Cheryl
"Early Morning." [PoeticJ] (13) 86, p. 38.
"One Week." [PoeticJ] (13) 86, p. 38.
"Seduction Across a Fence." [SlipS] (6) 86, p. 69.
"Want Dreams to Wake Reality." [PoeticJ] (13) 86, p. 38.
"When You." [Bogg] (55) 86, p. 8.
5398. TOWNSLEY, Thomas
"Tesserae." [Rampike] (5:2) 86, p. 22.
TOZABURO, Ono
See ONO, Tozaburo
5399. TRACHTENBERG, Paul
"Laguna Beach Types: Les Isaacs." [ConnPR] (4:1) 85, p. 27.
5400. TRAINER, Yvonne
"The Blind Man Speaks." [WestCR] (21:1) Je 86, p. 77.
"Mentor." [WestCR] (21:1) Je 86, p. 78.
"My Father." [WestCR] (21:1) Je 86, p. 78.
5401. TRALE, Marianne
"Talking the Song Over with a Friend." [PennR] (1:1) 85, p. 65-66.
5402. TRAMMELL, Robert
"Fire Clings to Air." [AnotherCM] (15) 86, p. 97.
"Malakoff Man." [AnotherCM] (15) 86, p. 87.
"Mass of Confusion." [AnotherCM] (15) 86, p. 86.
5403. TRANSTROMER, Tomas
"Molokai" (tr. by John F. Deane). [Verse] (6) 86, p. 18-19.
5404. TRANTER, John
"Having Completed My Fortieth Year" (for Peter Porter). [Verse] (5) 86, p. 12-14.
"Luck." [Verse] (3:3) N 86, p. 44.
"Red Cruise." [Verse] (5) 86, p. 12.
5405. TRAUNSTEIN, Russ
"In Memoriam." [SanFPJ] (8:3) 85, p. 78-79.
"Kenny." [SanFPJ] (8:2) 85, p. 93.
5406. TRECHOCK, Mark
"Vermont." [Poem] (55) Mr 86, p. 19.
5407. TREGEBOV, Rhea
"Foot Soldier." [GreenfR] (13:3/4) Sum-Fall 86, p. 195.
5408. TREININ, Avner
"Initials" (tr. by Shirley Kaufman). [PoetL] (81:2) Sum 86, p. 91.
"Potash" (tr. by Shirley Kaufman). [PoetL] (81:2) Sum 86, p. 92.
"The Recurrence Theorem (Poincaré Cycle)" (tr. by Shirley Kaufman). [PoetL] (81:2) Sum 86, p. 92-94.
5409. TREITEL, Margot
"Anne Hutchinson: Dissenter." [NewRena] (6:3, #20) Spr 86, p. 30.
"Beethoven's Pastoral: Side Two." [Wind] (16:56) 86, p. 47.
"Edible Roots." [NewRena] (6:3, #20) Spr 86, p. 31.
"Feast Day." [HolCrit] (23:2) Ap 86, back cover.
"Food Chain." [WindO] (47) Sum 86, p. 17-18.
"Forsaking All Others." [RagMag] (5:2) Fall 86, p. 73.
"Interiors." [RagMag] (5:2) Fall 86, p. 73.

"North Light." [PassN] (7:1) Fall-Wint 85-86, p. 13.
"Romance in West Africa" (Nigeria, 1965). [ColEng] (48:1) Ja 86, p. 43.
"Stay with Me." [Wind] (16:56) 86, p. 48.
"Teaching English As a Second Language." [WebR] (11:2) Fall 86, p. 71.
"The War Bride's Story." [WebR] (11:2) Fall 86, p. 72-73.
5410. TREMBLAY, Bill
"After the Movietone News of the Week." [PikeF] (7) Spr 86, p. 28.
"The Kid in the Carriage House." [PikeF] (7) Spr 86, p. 28.
"Marie-Paul to Frances about Duhamel." [TarRP] (24:2) Spr 85, p. 20.
"Parole Board Asks Duhamel: Ever Had a Decent Job?" [TarRP] (24:2) Spr 85, p. 19-20.
"Where Things Stood." [MidAR] (6:2) 86, p. 35-37.
"Whither Goest Thou." [PikeF] (7) Spr 86, p. 28.
5411. TREMBLAY, Gail
"Falling, Gloria Looks Up" (for G.M.Y.). [Calyx] (9:2/3) Wint 86, p. 96-97.
5412. TREMMEL, Robert
"General Delivery: August." [Ascent] (12:1) 86, p. 49-50.
"Watching *Poltergeist* on Cable TV after the Ball Game and a Few Beers." [Ascent] (12:1) 86, p. 51-52.
"You Will Become Like One of Us." [Ascent] (12:1) 86, p. 50-51.
5413. TRENTHAM, Edwina
"An Unceasing Flow of Tears." [AmerV] (2) Spr 86, p. 102.
5414. TRESTON, Myrna
"Burial." [Wind] (16:56) 86, p. 51-52.
"Weeds." [Wind] (16:56) 86, p. 49-50.
5415. TRETHEWEY, Eric
"In the Landscape of Opinion." [Poetry] (149:2) N 86, p. 80-81.
"Luck." [Poetry] (149:2) N 86, p. 80-81.
"The Open Door." [SouthernHR] (20:4) Fall 86, p. 324.
"Where Were You Headed?" [Poetry] (149:2) N 86, p. 82.
5416. TRIBUNE, George
"A Handful of Ashes." [SanFPJ] (8:3) 85, p. 89.
"Negotiate." [SanFPJ] (8:3) 85, p. 92.
"A November 22nd Poem." [SanFPJ] (8:1) 85, p. 52.
"Rancid Cheese." [SanFPJ] (8:2) 85, p. 20.
"Realization." [SanFPJ] (8:3) 85, p. 49.
"Smog." [SanFPJ] (8:1) 85, p. 56.
"Soldier's Burden." [SanFPJ] (8:3) 85, p. 52.
"The Star-Wars Charade." [SanFPJ] (8:2) 85, p. 85.
"The Turgid Brook." [SanFPJ] (8:1) 85, p. 53.
5417. TRIEM, Eve
"Litany for Today." [Calyx] (10:1) Sum 86, p. 39.
5418. TRINIDAD, David
"Great-Grandmother Smith." [ParisR] (28:99) Spr 86, p. 171-174.
5419. TRITTO, Michael
"Church." [CumbPR] (6:1) Fall 86, p. 37-39.
"Flights." [PoetL] (80:4) Wint 86, p. 209-210.
"Radiance." [CumbPR] (6:1) Fall 86, p. 40-41.
5420. TRIVELPIECE, Laurel
"Aggie, Leaving the Field." [ManhatPR] (8) Wint 86-87, p. 12.
"Arrangements." [ManhatPR] (8) Wint 86-87, p. 13.
"Climbing in Thinner Air." [ManhatPR] (8) Wint 86-87, p. 14.
"Night Harvest." [PraS] (60:1) Spr 86, p. 87.
"One of Sibyl's Songs." [IndR] (9:3) Sum 86, p. 44.
5421. TRIVERS, Mildred Raynolds
"The Farm Wife." [BallSUF] (26:4) Aut 85, p. 52.
"Song." [BallSUF] (26:4) Aut 85, p. 72.
5422. TROISE, Donald
"Architecture." [JamesWR] (3:3) Spr 86, p. 10.
"Clouds." [LittleM] (15:1) 86, p. 31-32.
"Part Company." [LittleM] (15:1) 86, p. 31.
5423. TROLL, Tim
"Aurora and Orion." [PaintedB] (29) Ag 86, p. 12.
"The Passing of Gus Mike." [PaintedB] (29) Ag 86, p. 11.
5424. TROTMAN, Harvey
"Hindsight." [MoodySI] (16/17) Sum 86, p. 36.

5425. TROWBRIDGE, William
"Bad Birds." [TarRP] (26:1) Fall 86, p. 18-19.
"Bearing Gifts" (December 22, 1985). [NewL] (53:1) Fall 86, p. 100-101.
"The Book of Kong" (Special issue). [PoetC] (17:3) 86, p. 1-44.
"Endangered Species." [TarRP] (25:1) Fall 85, p. 27.
"Father and Son Project 22: Model Airplane Building." [KenR] (NS 8:4) Fall 86, p. 68.
"Late Fall Night." [KenR] (NS 8:4) Fall 86, p. 67.
"Suppose." [TarRP] (25:1) Fall 85, p. 28.
"Walking Back." [Poetry] (148:6) S 86, p. 315.
5426. TROWELL, Ian Douglas
"Brighton & Hove." [InterPR] (12:2) Fall 86, p. 95.
"Emptying of Change." [InterPR] (12:2) Fall 86, p. 94.
5427. TRUDELL, Dennis
"Green Tomatoes." [GeoR] (40:3) Fall 86, p. 806.
"A Liberation." [MinnR] (NS 26) Spr 86, p. 57.
"Nicaraguan." [PraS] (60:4) Wint 86, p. 68.
"To the Young Man Who Said 'Nuke 'em' When I Offered a Central American Flier." [MinnR] (NS 27) Fall 86, p. 92-93.
"Watch Them Die." [GeoR] (40:3) Fall 86, p. 807.
"We All Came Out." [PraS] (60:4) Wint 86, p. 67-68.
5428. TRUER, Jere
"Every Morning." [Germ] (10:1) Spr-Sum 86, p. 43.
"From One Side of the Soul to Another." [Germ] (10:1) Spr-Sum 86, p. 47.
"The Lover." [Germ] (10:1) Spr-Sum 86, p. 44.
"The Voice of Water." [Germ] (10:1) Spr-Sum 86, p. 46.
"Watching the Coot Swim." [Germ] (10:1) Spr-Sum 86, p. 42.
"The Window." [Germ] (10:1) Spr-Sum 86, p. 45.
5429. TRUHLAR, Richard
"Vehicle of the Parasite." [Rampike] (5:1) 86, p. 56-57.
5430. TRULLEN, Guadalupe
"En Imposible Vuelo." [LetFem] (12:1/2) Primavera-Otoño 86, p. 162.
"Regreso." [LetFem] (12:1/2) Primavera-Otoño 86, p. 162.
5431. TRUSSELL, Robert C.
"They Do It All on Purpose." [KanQ] (18:3) Sum 86, p. 82.
TU, Fu
See DU, Fu
5432. TUCKER, Jean
"Interrogating the Fact." [ThRiPo] (27/28) 86, p. 64.
"Patrick's Day Note for Mary Garvey." [ThRiPo] (27/28) 86, p. 63.
5433. TUCKER, Martin
"Alfred al Fresco." [Boulevard] (1:3) Fall 86, p. 89-90.
"The Apple in His Eye." [Boulevard] (1:1/2) Wint 86, p. 160.
"College Confrontations." [Confr] (33/34) Fall-Wint 86-87, p. 102.
5434. TUCKER, Memye Curtis
"After the Eclipse, Sacatepequez." [SingHM] (14) 86, p. 9.
"Solution." [NegC] (6:1) Wint 86, p. 97-98.
5435. TUCKER, Sally
"Downstaged." [EngJ] (75:6) O 86, p. 56.
"What I Learned in the Five Minutes between Classes." [EngJ] (75:3) Mr 86, p. 90.
5436. TUDOR, Stephen
"Detroit River, North to South." [MichQR] (25:2) Spr 86, p. 153-154.
5437. TUITE, Kevin
"By the Aragvi" (1980, tr. of Ana K'alandadze). [LitR] (30:1) Fall 86, p. 21.
"The Cathedral Glowed" (1960, tr. of Ana K'alandadze). [LitR] (30:1) Fall 86, p. 23.
"A Cool Spring's Cut-Crystal" (tr. of Ana K'alandadze). [LitR] (30:1) Fall 86, p. 23.
"He Saw a Naked Women" (1980, tr. of Lia St'urua). [LitR] (30:1) Fall 86, p. 18.
"January Flowers at Uplistesikhe" (1961, tr. of Ana K'alandadze). [LitR] (30:1) Fall 86, p. 21.
"Speak, Ladybug!" (1945, tr. of Ana K'alandadze). [LitR] (30:1) Fall 86, p. 22.
"There Must Be Something" (1984, tr. of Lia St'urua). [LitR] (30:1) Fall 86, p. 19-20.
"The Victim of the City" (1984, tr. of Lia St'urua). [LitR] (30:1) Fall 86, p. 17-18.

5438. TULLOSS, Rod
"After a Period of Great Stress, a Letter from My Old Teacher" (vi.9.83, Hopewell,
for Mr. Carroll Royer). [LitR] (29:3) Spr 86, p. 343.
"Lying on My Back in the Assunpink." [Nimrod] (30:1) Fall-Wint 86, p. 82.
5439. TULLY, John
"Election Day." [ColEng] (48:6) O 86, p. 558.
5440. TUMBALE, Elkion
"Searings and Roefish." [Bogg] (55) 86, p. 12.
"Take wing nightcrease." [HiramPoR] (40) Spr-Sum 86, p. 27.
5441. TURCO, Lewis
"An Amherst Calendar" (from lines in Emily Dickinson's letters). [Chelsea] (45) 86,
p. 108-110.
"Passages" (from lines in Emily Dickinson's letters). [Chelsea] (45) 86, p. 106-107.
"The Winter Garden" (On lines from Emily Dickinson's letters). [LitR] (30:1) Fall
86, p. 89.
5442. TURCOTTE, Paulette
"On a Voyageur Bus" (between Peterborough and Ottawa). [Waves] (14:3) Wint 86,
p. 73.
5443. TURGEON, Gregoire
"The Memory of Snow." [PaintedB] (29) Ag 86, p. 24.
"Seurat: Bathing at Asnières." [PaintedB] (29) Ag 86, p. 25.
"Two Winters." [PaintedB] (29) Ag 86, p. 23.
5444. TURKI, Fawaz
"A Discussion." [SenR] (16:1) 86, p. 103.
"In Search of Yacove Eved." [SenR] (16:1) 86, p. 105-106.
"Moments of Ridicule and Love." [SenR] (16:1) 86, p. 104.
"Palestinians in Exile." [SenR] (16:1) 86, p. 101-102.
5445. TURNBULL, Harry
"Stable Dilemma" (A one-act play in three seminarial lines). [Bogg] (55) 86, p. 15.
5446. TURNER, Alberta
"The Mystery Won't Insist." [PraS] (60:1) Spr 86, p. 64-65.
"Nubs." [PraS] (60:1) Spr 86, p. 63.
"Sad Chair." [Stand] (27:1) Wint 85-86, p. 71.
"Simple Simon." [Stand] (27:1) Wint 85-86, p. 71.
5447. TURNER, Frederick
"Fiat Lux." [SouthernR] (22:2) Ap 86, p. 379-381.
"Incarnateness." [SouthernR] (22:2) Ap 86, p. 381-382.
5448. TURNER, Myron
"Playing the Numbers" (poems). [NoDaQ] (54:3) Sum 86, 55 p.
5449. TURON, Mercedes
"Voy salpicando de versos." [LetFem] (12:1/2) Primavera-Otoño 86, p. 153-154.
5450. TUSIANI, Joseph
"Black and White." [SpiritSH] (52) 86, p. 16.
"Falsetto." [SpiritSH] (52) 86, p. 14-15.
"Oxygen." [SpiritSH] (52) 86, p. 16.
"To 'The Worm, Our Busy Brother'" (Robert Browning, Sordello). [SpiritSH] (52)
86, p. 17.
5451. TUSSMAN, Malka Heifetz
"Arrived" (tr. by Marcia Falk). [AmerPoR] (15:6) N-D 86, p. 20.
"Thou Shalt Not" (for Yudka, tr. by Marcia Falk). [AmerPoR] (15:6) N-D 86, p. 20.
5452. TWICHELL, Chase
"Words for Synthesizer." [PennR] (1:1) 85, p. 59.
5453. TYLER, Robert L.
"Birth of a Poet." [CrossC] (8:1) 86, p. 25.
"Glasgow, 1944." [Descant] (17:2, #53) Sum 86, p. 84.
"Glasgow, 1944." [Lips] (12) 86, p. 19.
"Real Life in the Global Village." [AntigR] (65) Spr 86, p. 121-122.
5454. TYNES, Maxine
"En Route: For Bob Bradford." [PottPort] (8) 86-87, p. 27.
5455. UBA, George
"Arriving in Los Angeles, 1955." [Jacaranda] (2:1) Fall 86, p. 11.
"This Room." [Jacaranda] (2:1) Fall 86, p. 10.
5456. UCEDA, Julia
"Condemned to Silence" (For Ramón Sender, tr. by Noël M. Valis). [AmerPoR]
(15:6) N-D 86, p. 10.
"The Stranger" (tr. by Noël M. Valis). [AmerPoR] (15:6) N-D 86, p. 11.

5457. UCHMANOWICZ, Pauline
"Doing 'The Loop'." [OhioR] (37) 86, p. 81.
"The Sore Ankle." [IndR] (9:2) Spr 86, p. 22-23.
5458. ULLMAN, Leslie
"My Mother Is Not Watching." [Poetry] (148:6) S 86, p. 316-317.
5459. ULVEN, Tor
"Along the leaf-nerves" (tr. by Siri Hustvedt). [Writ] (18) 86, c87, p. 65.
"I try to write faster" (tr. by Siri Hustvedt). [Writ] (18) 86, c87, p. 64.
"Let the door stand wide open" (tr. by Siri Hustvedt). [Writ] (18) 86, c87, p. 63.
"Slush" (tr. by Siri Hustvedt). [Writ] (18) 86, c87, p. 62.
"They dance far into the woods" (tr. by Siri Hustvedt). [Writ] (18) 86, c87, p. 60.
"You can't be silent enough" (tr. by Siri Hustvedt). [Writ] (18) 86, c87, p. 61.
5460. UMPIERRE, Luzma
"The Statue." [Cond] (13) 86, p. 108-109.
5461. UNDERWOOD, Robert
"Bukowski, how do you do?" [OroM] (4:1-4) My 85, p. 49.
5462. UNDSET, Sigrid
"Harvest Warning" (tr. by Ron Wakefield and Olav Thompson). [LitR] (29:3) Spr 86, p. 358.
5463. UNGER, Barbara
"Sonya." [CarolQ] (39:1) Fall 86, p. 85-86.
5464. UNTERECKER, John
"Bent Light." [Blueline] (7:2) Wint-Spr 86, p. 44.
"First Trip to the Fun House: Crystal Beach." [SouthernR] (22:2) Ap 86, p. 386-387.
"Honolulu Zoo: October." [SouthernR] (22:2) Ap 86, p. 383-386.
5465. UNWIN, Peter
"Oedipus." [Quarry] (35:1) Wint 86, p. 95-98.
5466. UPDIKE, John
"Airport." [OntR] (25) Fall-Wint 86-87, p. 23.
"Another Dog's Death." [ConnPR] (5:1) 86, p. 3.
"From Above." [OntR] (25) Fall-Wint 86-87, p. 24.
"Hymn." [Harp] (273:1638) N 86, p. 35.
"Munich." [NewRep] (194:16) 21 Ap 86, p. 38.
"Oxford, Thirty Years After." [NewYorker] (62:22) 21 Jl 86, p. 32.
"A Pear Like a Potato." [NewYorker] (61:48) 20 Ja 86, p. 26.
"Somewhere." [NewRep] (195:11/12) 15-22 S 86, p. 48.
5467. UPTON, Lee
"Aide-Mémoire." [YaleR] (75:3) Spr 86, p. 425-427.
"Dark Ages." [AmerPoR] (15:6) N-D 86, p. 12.
"Hotel Life." [Field] (34) Spr 86, p. 78-79.
"The Imagination of Flowers." [Field] (34) Spr 86, p. 82-83.
"Kirsten's Winter Adventure." [AmerV] (5) Wint 86, p. 137-138.
"New Year's Eve on a Train." [Field] (34) Spr 86, p. 80.
"Note in Rain." [AmerPoR] (15:6) N-D 86, p. 12.
"Scroll." [Field] (34) Spr 86, p. 84.
"Solicitation." [Field] (34) Spr 86, p. 76-77.
"Sudden Childhood." [Field] (34) Spr 86, p. 81.
5468. URRUTIA, Angel
"Tu Sol Es un Guadiana." [Mairena] (8:22) 86, p. 20.
5469. URTADO, Gori
"No puedo cantar la luz cascabelera de vuestros bares." [Mairena] (8:22) 86, p. 78.
5470. USCHUK, Pamela
"The Flies" (tr. of Antonio Machado). [AnotherCM] (16) 86, p. 101-102.
"For the Horseman of the Crass and Vulnerable Word." [AnotherCM] (16) 86, p. 99-100.
"Praying Mantis." [WritersF] (12) Fall 86, p. 191-192.
"Waiting for Rain." [HighP] (1:1) Wint 86, p. 8-15.
"Who Gathers Honey." [WritersF] (12) Fall 86, p. 189-190.
5471. UU, David
"Calm Seas." [Rampike] (5:2) 86, p. 20-21.
5472. VAISH, Yogi Nandan
"Bearer serves me the food" ("Untitled"). [Amelia] (3:2) Spr 86, p. 107.
"Christmas eve." [Amelia] (3:4) Fall 86, p. 95.
5473. VALDES, Natasha
"Divertimento." [Mairena] (8:22) 86, p. 44.

"Explicacion." [Mairena] (8:22) 86, p. 44.
"Mesalina." [Mairena] (8:22) 86, p. 44.
"Mitologia." [Mairena] (8:22) 86, p. 44.
"Reflejo." [Mairena] (8:22) 86, p. 44.
VALENZUELA, Liliana Pérez
    See PEREZ VALENZUELA, Liliana
VALENZUELA DE PÉREZ, Ilma
    See PEREZ, Ilma Valenzuela de
5474. VALERY, Paul
    "The Graves by the Sea" (tr. by John Finlay). [SouthernR] (22:1) Ja 86, p. 118-122.
    "Intérieur." [Amelia] (3:4) Fall 86, p. 99.
    "Interior" (tr. by Michael L. Johnson). [Amelia] (3:4) Fall 86, p. 99.
5475. VALIS, Noël M.
    "Condemned to Silence" (For Ramón Sender, tr. of Julia Uceda). [AmerPoR] (15:6) N-D 86, p. 10.
    "The Stranger" (tr. of Julia Uceda). [AmerPoR] (15:6) N-D 86, p. 11.
VALLE, Máximo Gonzalez del
    See GONZALEZ DEL VALLE, Máximo
5476. VALLE, Victor
    "Mazatl." [Americas] (14:2) Sum 86, p. 44-45.
    "Remedio." [Americas] (14:2) Sum 86, p. 46-47.
    "Wedding." [Americas] (14:2) Sum 86, p. 43.
5477. VALLS, Jorge
    "All of a sudden: — Look!" (tr. by James Maraniss). [AmerPoR] (15:3) My-Je 86, p. 29.
    "Discovery" (tr. by James Maraniss). [AmerPoR] (15:3) My-Je 86, p. 29.
    "I spoke that word to create it from the air" (tr. by James Maraniss). [AmerPoR] (15:3) My-Je 86, p. 29.
    "Like a wounded beast" (tr. by James Maraniss). [AmerPoR] (15:3) My-Je 86, p. 29.
    "Where I am there is no light" (tr. by James Maraniss). [AmerPoR] (15:3) My-Je 86, p. 29.
Van . . .
    See also names beginning with "Van" without the following space, filed below in their alphabetic positions, e.g., VANDERSEE
5478. Van BRUNT, H. L.
    "Have a Nice Day." [SouthernPR] (26:1) Spr 86, p. 11.
    "On Looking at a Raphael." [SouthernPR] (26:1) Spr 86, p. 12.
5479. Van BRUNT, Lloyd
    "Liebesliedchen" (from "The Wyoming Suite"). [Vis] (21) 86, p. 32.
    "Mandrake into Merlin." [Confr] (33/34) Fall-Wint 86-87, p. 202.
    "Passing Strange." [NewL] (52:2/3) Wint-Spr 86, p. 165.
    "Taking a Bearing." [Blueline] (7:2) Wint-Spr 86, p. 26-27.
Van den BERG, Arie
    See BERG, Arie van den
5480. Van DUYN, Mona
    "First Trip through the Automatic Car Wash." [NewYorker] (61:47) 13 Ja 86, p. 30.
    "In Bed with a Book." [Poetry] (149:2) N 86, p. 76.
    "Late Loving." [Atlantic] (258:3) S 86, p. 80.
    "Misers" (for James Merrill). [NewRep] (195:20) 17 N 86, p. 47.
    "Near Changes" (From "The Year's Top Trivia," Sanford Teller, Information Please Almanac, 1979). [Poetry] (149:2) N 86, p. 77-78.
    "Views." [Poetry] (149:2) N 86, p. 79.
5481. Van MATRE, Connie
    "Budget Cut Blues." [SanFPJ] (8:3) 85, p. 77.
    "Counting in Millions." [SanFPJ] (8:3) 85, p. 15.
    "It's real big of Stockman." [SanFPJ] (8:3) 85, p. 35.
    "A Peaceful Prayer." [SanFPJ] (8:3) 85, p. 33.
    "People sleep." [SanFPJ] (8:3) 85, p. 47.
    "Shouldn't people who want more bombs." [SanFPJ] (8:3) 85, p. 50.
    "When nuclear dumps." [SanFPJ] (8:3) 85, p. 13.
5482. Van PEENEN, H. J.
    "Poems for a Second Wife." [BellArk] (2:6) N-D 86, p. 8.
5483. Van WALLEGHEN, Michael
    "The Age of Reason." [Iowa] (16:1) Wint 86, p. 92-94.
    "Hidden Meaning." [AnotherCM] (16) 86, p. 103-104.

"Meat." [Iowa] (16:1) Wint 86, p. 91-92.
"The Spoiled Child." [AnotherCM] (16) 86, p. 105-107.
5484. Van WERT, William F.
"Images." [LitR] (30:1) Fall 86, p. 56.
5485. Van WINCKEL, Nance
"Children Too Near the Freeway." [PoetryNW] (27:3) Aut 86, p. 43.
"Coming Home from the Big Game." [PoetryNW] (27:3) Aut 86, p. 44.
"In the Fifth Season." [WillowS] (18) Sum 86, p. 26.
"The Last Trial of Kepler's Mother." [MinnR] (NS 27) Fall 86, p. 84.
"Quotidian Rain." [AnotherCM] (15) 86, p. 98.
"She Who Hunts." [PoetryNW] (27:3) Aut 86, p. 41-42.
"What Makes Her Think So." [ChiR] (35:3) Spr 86, p. 52.
"You Get So." [GeoR] (40:4) Wint 86, p. 938.
5486. Van ZUTPHEN, Carmen
"Thoughts." [PottPort] (8) 86-87, p. 49.
5487. VANDERSEE, Charles
"Eve." [SewanR] (94:3) Sum 86, p. 381-382.
"Spring at Arm's Length." [GeoR] (40:3) Fall 86, p. 808-809.
"The Tables of the Things of This Earth." [SewanR] (94:3) Sum 86, p. 383.
5488. VANDO, Gloria
"Chimayo." [HeliconN] (14/15) Sum 86, p. 105-106.
"Promesas." [HeliconN] (14/15) Sum 86, p. 104-105.
"Return to the City of Holy Faith." [HeliconN] (14/15) Sum 86, p. 106-107.
5489. VANDORFER, Ron
"Folded and Refolded: A State of Being." [Ploughs] (12:4) 86, p. 180-182.
5490. VANDRE, Maryann
"Children of Hunger." [SanFPJ] (8:1) 85, p. 76.
"Data Processed." [SanFPJ] (8:1) 85, p. 76.
VANMATRE
    See Van MATRE, Connie
5491. VARGA, Jon
"Photograph." [PoeticJ] (14) 86, p. 18.
"Postcard." [PoeticJ] (14) 86, p. 7.
"Postcard." [RagMag] (5:1) Spr 86, p. 14.
5492. VARNADO, S. L.
"The Dissolution of the Aardvark" (After Richard Eberhart). [NegC] (6:2/3)
    Spr-Sum 86, p. 66-67.
5493. VASCONCELLOS, Cherry Jean
"All Animals Out." [WormR] (26:2, issue 102) 86, p. 69.
"Call from Mom." [WormR] (26:2, issue 102) 86, p. 69.
"On the Chase." [WormR] (26:2, issue 102) 86, p. 69.
5494. VASQUEZ, Timmy
"Anglo Saxon." [SanFPJ] (8:4) 85, p. 18.
"Someday I'm Gonna Flip." [SanFPJ] (8:4) 85, p. 11.
5495. VAVRA, Linda
"Landing" (for Cathy S.). [PennR] (1:2) Fall 85, p. 39.
5496. VAZQUEZ, Lourdes
"Azul." [LindLM] (5:4) O-D 86, p. 27.
"Clasificado." [LindLM] (5:4) O-D 86, p. 27.
"Luz Redonda." [LindLM] (5:4) O-D 86, p. 27.
5497. VEACH, Cindy
"This Summer." [CrossCur] (6:2) 86, p. 61-62.
5498. VEGA, Jose Luis
"Nueva Canción de las Antillas." [RevICP] (88) Abril-Junio 85, p. 58.
VEGA, Luz Méndez de la
    See MENDEZ de la VEGA, Luz
5499. VEINBERG, Jon
"Martha." [Poetry] (148:1) Ap 86, p. 9.
"Next to Tut." [Poetry] (148:1) Ap 86, p. 10-11.
"Sparrows As Ghosts." [Poetry] (148:1) Ap 86, p. 7-9.
5500. VEIRAVE, Alfredo
"Madame Bovary" (tr. by Thorpe Running). [ColR] (NS 13:1) Fall 85, p. 43.
5501. VELASCO, Angelita
"The Saga of Oppression." [SingHM] (13) 86, p. 20-21.
5502. VELEZ, Lydia
"A Julia de Burgos." [Americas] (14:2) Sum 86, p. 53.

"Mi Abuela." [Americas] (14:2) Sum 86, p. 52.
5503. VENUTI, Lawrence
"July Arrives for the Dead" (tr. of Milo De Angelis). [Stand] (27:3) Sum 86, p. 17.
"The Slowness" (tr. of Milo De Angelis). [Stand] (27:3) Sum 86, p. 17.
Ver ELLEN, Patricia
See VerELLEN, Patricia
5504. VERACRUZ, Margo
"Twilight in Texas." [Jacaranda] (2:1) Fall 86, p. 16.
5505. VERE, John
"Krystel." [Bogg] (56) 86, p. 56.
5506. VerELLEN, Patricia
"A Day the Day Owned." [BellArk] (2:1) Ja-F 86, p. 16.
"Sex Films for Medical Students." [BellArk] (2:1) Ja-F 86, p. 12.
5507. VERMA, Neeru
"Searching." [Grain] (14:2) My 86, p. 46.
"Tall green grass with a large lake to the south." [Grain] (14:2) My 86, p. 46.
5508. VERNON, William (William J.)
"American Beauty." [Sam] (44:3 release 175) 86, p. 58.
"Blindness." [Bogg] (55) 86, p. 11.
"Hiyasa." [CrabCR] (3:3) Sum 86, p. 24.
5509. VERSHEL, Larry
"The Volunteers at Geva" (Selections: 6 poems). [LitR] (29:3) Spr 86, p. 318-320.
5510. VERSTEEG, Tom
"Spring." [NegC] (6:1) Wint 86, p. 67.
5511. VERTREACE, Martha M.
"Black Tulips." [Outbr] (16/17) Fall 85-Spr 86, p. 83.
"Celestial Navigation." [MidwQ] (28:1) Aut 86, p. 86.
"Trade Secrets." [ColEng] (48:7) N 86, p. 686.
"Tycho's Ghost, 1572." [MidwQ] (28:1) Aut 86, p. 87.
5512. VESZI, Endre
"Dreaming of the Castle" (tr. by Jascha Kessler w. Maria Korosy). [Vis] (22) 86, p. 12.
5513. VIAN, Boris
"When the Wind Passes Through My Skull" (tr. by Julia Older). [Vis] (22) 86, p. 10.
VICCA, Ed Santa
See SantaVICCA, Ed
VICENTE, Arminda Arroyo
See ARROYO VICENTE, Arminda
5514. VIDAS, Gregory
"Swallowing Silence." [CrossCur] (5:4/6:1) 86, p. 88-89.
5515. VIDOTTO, Leonice Pesci
"Cartas." [LetFem] (12:1/2) Primavera-Otoño 86, p. 148.
"Na Condição Igual." [LetFem] (12:1/2) Primavera-Otoño 86, p. 149.
"Nesta Noite Mutilada." [LetFem] (12:1/2) Primavera-Otoño 86, p. 148-149.
"Somos Estrelas." [LetFem] (12:1/2) Primavera-Otoño 86, p. 149.
5516. VIEBAHN, Fred
"Doing Dishes" (tr. by the author). [SenR] (16:2) 86, p. 83.
5517. VIERECK, Peter
"Auschwitz (Nietzsche Contra Wagner" (excerpted from *Archer in the Marrow: The Applewood Cycles*). [LitR] (29:2) Wint 86, p. 209-214.
"The Crossbow Cycle" (closing cycle of *Archer in the Marrow: The Applewood Cycles*). [NewL] (52:2/3) Wint-Spr 86, p. 121-135.
"Waltz." [PraS] (60:1) Spr 86, p. 91-101.
5518. VIEYRA, Antonio
"Imagen." [Mairena] (8:22) 86, p. 113.
VIGNE, Steven la
See LaVIGNE, Steven
5519. VIGNEAULT, Gilles
"Après avoir longtemps peiné de mots" ("Sans titre," from *Exergues*, 1977). [InterPR] (12:2) Fall 86, p. 28.
"Having struggled a long time with words" ("Untitled," tr. by Roch C. Smith). [InterPR] (12:2) Fall 86, p. 29.
5520. VILLALBA, Susana
"El Oro Caido" (fragmentos). [Mairena] (8:22) 86, p. 25.

5521. VINCENT, Gwendolyn
"Dances." [Amelia] (3:4) Fall 86, p. 63.
"Minotaur." [StoneC] (13:3/4) Spr-Sum 86, p. 20.
"Shadow Pictures." [Amelia] (3:2) Spr 86, p. 68.
5522. VINCENT, Paul
"Brassempouy" (tr. of H. C. ten Berge, w. Theo Hermans). [Stand] (27:2) Spr 86,
p. 22.
"Lübeck" (tr. of H. C. ten Berge, w. Theo Hermans). [Stand] (27:2) Spr 86, p. 23.
5523. VINNER, Shlomo
"Jerusalem As She Is" (tr. by Seymour Mayne). [Writ] (18) 86, c87, p. 117-125.
"Pneumatic Drills on the Ninth of Ab" (tr. by Seymour Mayne). [PoetL] (81:2) Sum
86, p. 105.
5524. VINYOLI, Joan
"I Know I Have a Tendency to Dream" (tr. by Stephanie Smolinsky). [Translation]
(16) Spr 86, p. 102.
"In Our Gray Raincoats" (tr. by Stephanie Smolinsky). [Translation] (16) Spr 86, p.
103.
"Night and Day" (tr. by Stephanie Smolinsky). [Translation] (16) Spr 86, p. 106.
"Pietà" (tr. by Stephanie Smolinsky). [Translation] (16) Spr 86, p. 102.
"Ravines" (tr. by Stephanie Smolinsky). [Translation] (16) Spr 86, p. 101.
"The Silence of the Dead" (tr. by Stephanie Smolinsky). [Translation] (16) Spr 86,
p. 105.
"Time Lost" (tr. by Stephanie Smolinsky). [Translation] (16) Spr 86, p. 101.
"Toward Nothing" (tr. by Stephanie Smolinsky). [Translation] (16) Spr 86, p. 104.
"Who Still Dares" (tr. by Stephanie Smolinsky). [Translation] (16) Spr 86, p. 104.
5525. VINZ, Mark
"The Biggest Tree in North Dakota." [SoDakR] (24:3) Aut 86, p. 21.
"Holiday Greetings." [SpoonRQ] (11:2) Spr 86, p. 15.
"Katy Knows." [SpoonRQ] (11:2) Spr 86, p. 13.
"The Love Song of J. Alfred Professor" (for Roland Dille). [BallSUF] (27:4) Aut
86, p. 55.
"Minnesota Gothic" (for Bud and Little Bingo). [SpoonRQ] (11:2) Spr 86, p. 14.
"Norwegian Joke." [SpoonRQ] (11:4) Fall 86, p. 11.
"Psalm: Toward Winter's End" (for John Judson). [SpoonRQ] (11:2) Spr 86, p. 16.
"Still Life on the South Shore." [SpoonRQ] (11:2) Spr 86, p. 17.
"Still Life with Old Man." [BallSUF] (26:4) Aut 85, p. 11.
"Touring Lyon County." [SpoonRQ] (11:4) Fall 86, p. 10.
"The Trouble with Poems." [PassN] (7:2) Spr-Sum 86, p. 19.
"Unfinished Business." [BallSUF] (27:4) Aut 86, p. 16.
5526. VIRGILIO, Peter
"Debris." [SlipS] (6) 86, p. 37.
"Yet Another After Bukowski." [SlipS] (6) 86, p. 38-39.
VITO, E. B. de
See De VITO, E. B.
5527. VIZCAYA, Lydia
"Powder Sugar Donut." [CutB] (25) Fall-Wint 86, p. 46-47.
5528. VLASAK, Keith
"Goodwill." [YetASM] (4) 85, p. 8.
5529. VLASOPOLOS, Anca
"The Break." [Interim] (5:1) Spr 86, p. 18.
"Eurydice Speaks." [Interim] (5:1) Spr 86, p. 17.
"Fit." [Interim] (5:1) Spr 86, p. 17-18.
5530. VOGELSANG, Arthur
"Cahuenga Pass." [Epoch] (35:2) 86-87, p. 120.
"How to Deal Fairly with Men and Love Them." [ColEng] (48:3) Mr 86, p. 268.
"One Girl Was Chosen. How Tall Was She?" [ColEng] (48:3) Mr 86, p. 267.
"Romantic & Modern." [ColEng] (48:3) Mr 86, p. 266.
"Tongue and Eyes." [Epoch] (35:2) 86-87, p. 118.
"A True Account." [Epoch] (35:2) 86-87, p. 119-120.
"Why You're a Dog and I'm Wonderful." [ColEng] (48:3) Mr 86, p. 267.
5531. VOIGT, Ellen Bryant
"Fairy Tale." [Atlantic] (258:1) Jl 86, p. 44.
"The Fence." [NewYorker] (62:30) 15 S 86, p. 106.
"A Fugue" (for Tom Moore). [GeoR] (40:3) Fall 86, p. 810-811.

5532. VOLDSETH, Beverly
"After Visiting My Grandfather's Farm and Finding Nothing Is the Same."
[RagMag] (5:2) Fall 86, p. 74.
5533. VOLLMER, Judith
"The Bracelet." [WestB] (19) 86, p. 27.
"Sara's Terrace." [WestB] (19) 86, p. 26.
5534. VOLOSHIN, Maksimilian
"Over the Fields of Alsace" (tr. by Eugene Dubnov and John Heath-Stubbs). [Event]
(15:2) 86, p. 115.
Von DASSANOWSKY-HARRIS, Robert
See DASSANOWSKY-HARRIS, Robert von
5535. VORONCA, Ilarie
"I am like you, O Wind!" ("Untitled", tr. by Dorothy Aspinwall). [WebR] (11:2) Fall
86, p. 26.
"Tale (Fragment)" (tr. by Dorothy B. Aspinwall). [CrabCR] (4:1) Fall-Wint 86, p.
4.
5536. VOSK, D. M.
"New Recipe for *Terra Nova*." [Vis] (20) 86, p. 35.
5537. VOZNESENSKY, Andrei
"Applefall" (tr. by William Jay Smith and F. D. Reeve). [AmerPoR] (15:6) N-D 86,
p. 24-25.
"Autolithography" (tr. by William Jay Smith and Vera Dunham). [AmerPoR] (15:6)
N-D 86, p. 27.
"The Boar Hunt" (tr. by F. D. Reeve). [AmerPoR] (15:6) N-D 86, p. 25-26.
"The Driver" (tr. by F. D. Reeve). [AmerPoR] (15:6) N-D 86, p. 23.
"Portrait" (tr. by Diana Der Hovanessian). [AmerPoR] (15:6) N-D 86, p. 23.
"The Thief of Memories" (tr. by F. D. Reeve). [AmerPoR] (15:6) N-D 86, p. 26.
VRIES, Carrow de
See De VRIES, Carrow
VRIES, Peter de
See De VRIES, Peter
VRIES, Peter Hugh de
See DeVRIES, Peter Hugh
VRIES, Rachel de
See DeVRIES, Rachel (Rachel Guido)
VRIES, Rachel Guido de
See DeVRIES, Rachel (Rachel Guido)
5538. WADDINGTON, Miriam
"Babies." [PraF] (7:3) Aut 86, p. 17.
"Knives and Ploughshares." [PraF] (7:3) Aut 86, p. 16.
"The Life of a Woman." [PraF] (7:3) Aut 86, p. 18.
"Mechanics for Women." [CanLit] (111) Wint 86, p. 99-100.
"Peace Notes I." [PraF] (7:3) Aut 86, p. 14.
"Peace Notes, II" (for Lyubomir). [PraF] (7:3) Aut 86, p. 15.
"Reflections." [GreenfR] (13:3/4) Sum-Fall 86, p. 196.
5539. WADE, Sidney
"The Church and the Steeple." [Shen] (36:2) 86, p. 63.
"Father Uda." [GrandS] (5:4) Sum 86, p. 137.
5540. WADSWORTH, William
"Jealousy" (after Sappho). [WebR] (11:2) Fall 86, p. 53.
"The Need for Attention." [Shen] (36:4) 86, p. 68-69.
"The River Twice." [Shen] (36:4) 86, p. 67-68.
"To a Catholic Friend in the Tropics" (for Patricia, who died after childbirth).
[WebR] (11:2) Fall 86, p. 52.
5541. WAGNER, Anneliese
"The Future." [BellR] (9:1) Spr 86, p. 24.
"The Trip." [BellR] (9:1) Spr 86, p. 24.
5542. WAGNER, Cathy
"Moonrise." [SecC] (14:1) 86, p. 70.
5543. WAGNER, Diana
"In a Dream." [RagMag] (5:1) Spr 86, p. 39.
5544. WAGNER, Kathleen
"Living Alone." [Amelia] (3:1) Ja 86, p. 78.
5545. WAGNER, Shari
"How to Find a Dinosaur." [IndR] (9:1) Wint 86, p. 64-65.

379

5546. WAGONER, David
   "The Art of Surrender." [GeoR] (40:3) Fall 86, p. 812.
   "The Astronomer's Apprentice." [Poetry] (148:1) Ap 86, p. 3-4.
   "Catching the Big One at Lone Lake" (A Memory of Richard Hugo). [KenR] (NS
      8:1) Wint 86, p. 68-69.
   "The Excursion of the Speech and Hearing Class." [Agni] (23) 86, p. 131.
   "Five Dawn Skies in November." [NewRep] (194:9) 3 Mr 86, p. 40.
   "For a Third Anniversary." [Poetry] (148:1) Ap 86, p. 2.
   "Looking for Nellie Washington." [KenR] (NS 8:1) Wint 86, p. 69-70.
   "Lullaby through the Side of the Mouth." [YaleR] (75:2) Wint 86, p. 315.
   "Ode to Twelve Yards of Unscreened Fill Dirt." [Poetry] (148:1) Ap 86, p. 1-2.
5547. WAGSTAFF, Blanche Shoemaker
   "Pageants." [Bogg] (56) 86, p. 15.
5548. WAH, Fred
   "The Bird Part of It." [MalR] (77) D 86, p. 30.
   "Elite 2." [Contact] (7:38/39/40) Wint-Spr 86, p. 36.
   "Maybe My Grandmothers Went North." [MalR] (77) D 86, p. 29.
   "The Poem Called Syntax." [MalR] (77) D 86, p. 29.
5549. WAINWRIGHT, Andy
   "Flight of the Falcon" (Selections: 6 poems). [AntigR] (65) Spr 86, p. 16-22.
5550. WAKEFIELD, Kathleen
   "Sisters." [ThRiPo] (27/28) 86, p. 68.
   "Stories." [PassN] (7:1) Fall-Wint 85-86, p. 21.
5551. WAKEFIELD, Ron
   "Harvest Warning" (tr. of Sigrid Undset, w. Olav Thompson). [LitR] (29:3) Spr 86,
      p. 358.
   "Lineage" (tr. of Olav H. Hauge, w. Katherine Hanson and the author). [LitR]
      (29:3) Spr 86, p. 357.
   "The Thorn Tree" (tr. of Johan Sebastian Welhaven, w. Olav Thompson). [LitR]
      (29:3) Spr 86, p. 359.
5552. WAKOSKI, Diane
   "The Archeology of Movies & Books." [Caliban] (1) 86, p. 22-26.
   "Carol's Sweetheart Fingers." [Interim] (5:2) Fall 86, p. 10-11.
   "Clint's Bottle of 1977 Chateauneuf du Papes." [ManhatPR] (6) Wint-Spr 85-86, p.
      12.
   "Memory." [ManhatPR] (7) Sum 86, p. 17.
   "Seeing Robert in the Crystal Ball." [ManhatPR] (6) Wint-Spr 85-86, p. 11.
   "The Slap." [NegC] (6:4) Fall 86, p. 18-19.
   "A Snowy Winter in East Lansing." [Sulfur] (6:1, issue 16) 86, p. 89-90.
   "Some Pumpkins." [ManhatPR] (6) Wint-Spr 85-86, p. 11.
   "Wearing Cheryl's Gift." [NegC] (6:4) Fall 86, p. 20-21.
   "What Would Tennessee Williams Have Said." [Sulfur] (6:1, issue 16) 86, p. 86-89.
5553. WAKULICH, Bob
   "Bearings." [Rampike] (5:1) 86, p. 65.
5554. WALCOTT, Derek
   "Gros-Ilet." [LitR] (29:3) Spr 86, p. 256.
   "A Latin Primer" (for H. D. Boxill). [TriQ] (65) Wint 86, p. 188-191.
   "The Light of the World." [ParisR] (28:101) Wint 86, p. 192-195.
   "On the Indian Trail." [PartR] (53:4) 86, p. 612.
   "Roman Peace." [NewRep] (195:19) 10 N 86, p. 46.
   "Steam" (for Leslie Epstein). [TriQ] (65) Wint 86, p. 194-195.
   "The Whelk-Gatherers." [TriQ] (65) Wint 86, p. 192-193.
5555. WALCZAK, Rene
   "Walls, Windows & Doors" (Without Music). [NegC] (6:4) Fall 86, p. 74.
5556. WALDEN, Edith M.
   "Epilogue: Hermione's Canto" (Book Seven). [Iowa] (16:3) Fall 86, p. 284-296.
5557. WALDMAN, Anne
   "How I Became Biblical." [Acts] (5) 86, p. 97.
   "Iovis Omnia Plena" (Excerpts). [Notus] (1:1) Fall 86, p. 41-52.
   "Lad of the Malign" (after Seken Chung). [Acts] (5) 86, p. 98.
   "Loud Concerts." [Acts] (5) 86, p. 96.
5558. WALDROP, Rosemarie
   "The Reproduction of Profiles" (Excerpts). [Sink] (1) 86, p. 45-46.
5559. WALKER, Brenda
   "Absurd Chess" (tr. of Mircea Dinescu, w. Andrea Deletant). [Translation] (16) Spr
      86, p. 215.

"Cold Comfort" (tr. of Mircea Dinescu, w. Andrea Deletant). [Translation] (16) Spr 86, p. 215.
"A Couple" (tr. of Mircea Dinescu, w. Andrea Deletant). [Translation] (16) Spr 86, p. 214.
"How the Natives on the Reservation Lost the Right . . ." (tr. of Mircea Dinescu, w. Andrea Deletant). [Translation] (16) Spr 86, p. 216.
5560. WALKER, David
"On the Lawn near Dark" (For James Wright, 1927-1980). [BelPoJ] (36:3) Spr 86, p. 17.
5561. WALKER, Eric
"And Not Before." [Pax] (3:1/2) Wint 85-86, p. 136.
"Quixote Commission." [Pax] (3:1/2) Wint 85-86, p. 135.
5562. WALKER, Jeanne Murray
"Driving Home in the Blizzard." [PraS] (60:3) Fall 86, p. 99-100.
"Inspecting the Garden after Dark." [Poetry] (148:6) S 86, p. 332.
"Seizure." [Poetry] (148:6) S 86, p. 331-332.
5563. WALKER, Leon
"April." [PoeticJ] (16) Fall 86, p. 3.
"Relic." [PoeticJ] (15) Sum 86, p. 40.
5564. WALKER, Margaret
"A Poem for Farish Street" (Excerpts). [Iowa] (16:1) Wint 86, p. 127-129.
5565. WALKER, Sue
"Micanopy Cemetery" (For R.E.). [NegC] (6:2/3) Spr-Sum 86, p. 58-59.
5566. WALLACE, Bronwen
"Lonely for the Country." [GreenfR] (13:3/4) Sum-Fall 86, p. 197-198.
5567. WALLACE, Bruce
"Dandelion Time" (for Abbey). [SouthernR] (22:2) Ap 86, p. 388.
"The Flowerbed" (for Iphigenia). [SouthernR] (22:2) Ap 86, p. 389.
"Postscript from a Letter to a Twenty-Two-Year-Old Daughter." [SouthernR] (22:2) Ap 86, p. 390.
"Someone Knows." [SouthernR] (22:2) Ap 86, p. 390.
5568. WALLACE, Mark
"Entering." [InterPR] (12:1) Spr 86, p. 101.
"Flying Westward." [InterPR] (12:1) Spr 86, p. 100.
5569. WALLACE, Naomi
"Americana." [OP] (42/43) Wint 86-87, p. 138.
"Another Time: Hands" (Managua 1985). [OP] (42/43) Wint 86-87, p. 139.
"The Vow." [HayF] (1) Spr 86, p. 58.
5570. WALLACE, Robert
"The Fear." [AmerS] (55:3) Sum 86, p. 400.
5571. WALLACE, Ronald
"Basketball." [TarRP] (25:1) Fall 85, p. 29-30.
"Class of 1963: Matheny." [TarRP] (25:1) Fall 85, p. 29.
"Fall." [PoetryNW] (27:4) Wint 86-87, p. 25.
"Frogs." [PoetryNW] (27:4) Wint 86-87, p. 24.
"Letter to My Father." [CutB] (26) Spr-Sum 86, p. 30.
"Old Man on Sidewalk." [HiramPoR] (40) Spr-Sum 86, p. 28.
"Poet in the Goat Yard." [PoetryNW] (27:2) Sum 86, p. 47.
"The Poet Reclining" (After Chagall). [CapeR] (21:2) Fall 86, p. 26.
"Wiffle Ball." [Atlantic] (257:6) Je 86, p. 60.
"Wild Strawberries." [NowestR] (24:1) 86, p. 109.
5572. WALLACE, T. S.
"Ambivalence." [PaintedB] (29) Ag 86, p. 76.
"Beyond Ourselves, or Crossing to Macedonia." [TarRP] (25:1) Fall 85, p. 45.
"Beyond the Neat Houses Cheap Talk Built." [NegC] (6:1) Wint 86, p. 101.
"In a Miserable Age." [CrescentR] (4:1) Spr 86, p. 88.
"Mengele Drowns." [CumbPR] (6:1) Fall 86, p. 30-31.
"Merton." [CrabCR] (4:1) Fall-Wint 86, p. 13.
"The Snowblind." [SoDakR] (24:3) Aut 86, p. 23.
"Thomas." [SoDakR] (24:3) Aut 86, p. 156.
"Ways and Means." [NegC] (6:4) Fall 86, p. 48.
5573. WALLACE-CRABBE, Chris
"A Glimpse of Shere Khan." [Verse] (5) 86, p. 14.
5574. WALLACH, Martin
"Hunting Rabbits with a Dog." [Poem] (55) Mr 86, p. 2-3.

WALLEGHEN, Michael van
  See Van WALLEGHEN, Michael
5575. WALLENSTEIN, Barry
  "At Ground Zero." [BelPoJ] (36:4) Sum 86, p. 1.
  "A Family Affair." [Outbr] (16/17) Fall 85-Spr 86, p. 8.
5576. WALLIN, Lori Ann
  "Stop-Light Poem." [SnapD] (9:2) Spr 86, p. 3.
5577. WALLS, Doyle Wesley
  "The Sanctity." [Puerto] (22:1) Fall 86, p. 70-71.
5578. WALRATH, Norma
  "Outside (Or My Own Rum Running)." [EngJ] (75:7) N 86, p. 86.
5579. WALSH, Arlene
  "Fire and Smoke." [ManhatPR] (8) Wint 86-87, p. 32-33.
5580. WALSH, John
  "H. D. at the Beinecke." [Iowa] (16:3) Fall 86, p. 125.
5581. WALSH, Phyllis
  "Burial Mounds at the Foot of Bluffs." [SpoonRQ] (11:4) Fall 86, p. 45.
  "Difficulties of Cultivating Shooting Stars." [SpoonRQ] (11:4) Fall 86, p. 43.
  "Her Paisley Shawl." [SpoonRQ] (11:4) Fall 86, p. 44.
5582. WALSH, William J., III
  "Gogo Boots and Ponytails." [DeKalbLAJ] (19:3/4) 86, p. 94.
5583. WALTER, Robert R.
  "Goldfinches at the Feeder." [SoCaR] (19:1) Fall 86, p. 59.
5584. WAMPLER, Pamela
  "Since the Invention of the Telescope: A Phone Call." [Crazy] (31) Fall 86, p.
    41-42.
WANG, C. H.
  See YANG, Mu
5585. WANG, Chiu-ssu
  "After Reading the Poems of Master Han Shan" (Two poems, tr. by Jonathan
    Chaves). [Translation] (17) Fall 86, p. 329.
  "Living in the Woods" (In the Manner of Yao Ho, tr. by Jonathan Chaves).
    [Translation] (17) Fall 86, p. 330.
  "The Robber of Kuan-Shan" (tr. by Jonathan Chaves). [Translation] (17) Fall 86, p.
    330.
5586. WANG, Wei
  "Suffering from Heat" (tr. by Tony Barnstone, Willis Barnstone and Xu Haixin).
    [Nimrod] (29:2) Spr-Sum 86, p. 20.
  "Visiting the Mountain Courtyard . . ." (tr. by Tony Barnstone, Willis Barnstone and
    Xu Haixin). [Nimrod] (29:2) Spr-Sum 86, p. 23.
  "Weeping for Ying Yao" (tr. by Tony Barnstone, Willis Barnstone and Xu Haixin).
    [Nimrod] (29:2) Spr-Sum 86, p. 22.
  "Written When Climbing the City Tower . . ." (tr. by Tony Barnstone, Willis
    Barnstone and Xu Haixin). [Nimrod] (29:2) Spr-Sum 86, p. 23.
5587. WANG, Xin-Di
  "Butterfly, Bee, and Evergreen Trees" (tr. of Xin Di). [Verse] (6) 86, p. 46.
WANGUSA, Hellen G. Akwii
  See AKWII-WANGUSA, Hellen G.
5588. WANIEK, Marilyn Nelson
  "It's All in Your Head" (for Deborah M.). [GeoR] (40:3) Fall 86, p. 813-815.
5589. WANLESS, James
  "Façons d'Endormi, Façons d'Eveillé" (Selections, tr. of Henri Michaux). [Notus]
    (1:1) Fall 86, p. 72-75.
5590. WARD, Jerry W., Jr.
  "D.C./Dispossessed." [OP] (41) Spr 86, p. 29.
  "The Dancer's Zoo." [CapeR] (21:2) Fall 86, p. 16.
  "Mr. Wright's Return." [CapeR] (21:2) Fall 86, p. 15.
  "Southern Towns." [CapeR] (21:2) Fall 86, p. 14.
  "Summoning: Unprinted Negative of a Neocon Woman." [OP] (41) Spr 86, p.
    30-31.
5591. WARD, Robert
  "Jim Hearst: Farmer, Poet, Teacher." [Farm] (3:2) Spr-Sum 86, p. 19.
5592. WARD, Robert R.
  "All This and the Stupid Moon." [BellArk] (2:1) Ja-F 86, p. 14-15.
  "Can You Sense the First Stirrings of Blood?" [YellowS] (20) Aut 86, p. 22.
  "Covering Your Blind Side." [BellArk] (2:3) My-Je 86, p. 4.

"Darkness Is the Absence of Light." [BellArk] (2:6) N-D 86, p. 8.
"How Abstract, the Idea of Mulberries." [BellArk] (2:3) My-Je 86, p. 6.
"In Any Other Context." [BellArk] (2:5) S-O 86, p. 5.
5593. WARD, Tom
    "Todd." [WoosterR] (6) Fall 86, p. 65.
5594. WARLAND, Betsy
    "Serpent (W)rite" (An excerpt from "turn three"). [PraF] (7:3) Aut 86, p. 24-25.
    "Turn Five" (from *Serpent (W)rite*). [Event] (15:2) 86, p. 107-109.
5595. WARN, Emily
    "Harvest." [Contact] (8:41/42/43) Fall-Wint 86-87, p. 11.
5596. WARNE, Candice
    "The Broken Iris" (For Elaine). [HiramPoR] (40) Spr-Sum 86, p. 29.
5597. WARNER, Val
    "The Afterglow." [Verse] (3:3) N 86, p. 51.
5598. WARNER, Yolanda
    "America, Your Hands are Filthy!" [SanFPJ] (9:1) 86, p. 33.
    "Coming of Age in Nicaragua." [SanFPJ] (9:1) 86, p. 35-36.
5599. WARNING, Margaret
    "Enemies in Africa." [InterPR] (12:2) Fall 86, p. 97.
    "Sunday Afternoon, Baroda, India." [InterPR] (12:2) Fall 86, p. 96.
5600. WARREN, Charlotte Gould
    "India: Silver." [LitR] (30:1) Fall 86, p. 115.
5601. WARREN, Chris
    "The Mind Dressed in Skins." [Quarry] (35:4) Aut 86, p. 15.
5602. WARREN, Robert Penn
    "Caribou." [PartR] (53:4) 86, p. 609-610.
    "Debate: Question, Quarry, Dream" (from *You, Emperors, and others*). [YaleR]
       (75:2) Wint 86, p. 317-318.
    "Garland for You: Poem" (from *You, Emperors, and others*). [YaleR] (75:2) Wint
       86, p. 316-317.
    "Muted Music." [GeoR] (40:3) Fall 86, p. 818.
    "Seasons." [GeoR] (40:3) Fall 86, p. 816-817.
    "Tell Me a Story." [PartR] (53:4) 86, p. 611.
5603. WARREN, Rosanna
    "Painting a Madonna." [GeoR] (40:3) Fall 86, p. 819-820.
    "Season Due." [Atlantic] (258:2) Ag 86, p. 56.
5604. WARWICK, Joanna
    "Stages of Prayer." [AntigR] (66/67) Sum-Aut 86, p. 219-220.
5605. WAS, Elizabeth
    "Onion Leaves, Her Map Untended." [Sink] (2) 86, p. 62-65.
5606. WASHBURN, Katharine
    "Last Poems" (Selections, tr. of Paul Celan, w. Margret Guillemin). [AmerPoR]
       (15:3) My-Je 86, p. 3-5.
5607. WASSERBURG, Charles
    "Eaton Canyon." [SouthwR] (71:4) Aut 86, p. 439-440.
5608. WASSON, Kirsten
    "Admonition." [Ascent] (11:3) 86, p. 48.
    "Bedtime Story." [Confr] (32) Spr-Sum 86, p. 137.
    "Calling Home." [MSS] (5:1) 86, p. 139.
    "In the Shower." [ManhatPR] (8) Wint 86-87, p. 55.
5609. WATANABE, Jose
    "A Proposito de los Desajustes, O Algo Parecido a Ser or No Ser." [Contact]
       (7:38/39/40) Wint-Spr 86, Supplement p. 27.
    "Con Dudosos Logros Cómicos." [Contact] (7:38/39/40) Wint-Spr 86, Supplement
       p. 30-31.
    "With Doubtful Comic Achievements" (tr. by J. Jacinto, V. Sales-Gomez & J.
       Tagami). [Contact] (7:38/39/40) Wint-Spr 86, Supp. p. 28-29.
    "With Regard to Misadjustments . . ." (tr. by J. Jacinto, V. Sales-Gomez & J.
       Tagami). [Contact] (7:38/39/40) Wint-Spr 86, Supp. p. 26.
5610. WATERHOUSE, Philip A.
    "Intervals." [Amelia] (3:4) Fall 86, p. 88-89.
5611. WATERMAN, Cary
    "Porthmadog, Wales, 1983." [Prima] (10) 86, p. 34.
5612. WATERS, Mary Ann
    "Cowboy." [Poetry] (147:4) Ja 86, p. 193.
    "Home Cooking." [Poetry] (147:4) Ja 86, p. 192.

"The Quarry: A Dialogue from Above and Below." [Poetry] (147:4) Ja 86, p. 191.
"Snowstorm." [Poetry] (147:4) Ja 86, p. 189-190.
5613. WATERS, Michael
"The Conversion of Saint Paul." [Poetry] (149:3) D 86, p. 150-151.
"The Faithful." [GeoR] (40:3) Fall 86, p. 821.
"The Lighthouse Keeper at Thomas Point." [QW] (22) Spr-Sum 86, p. 32-35.
"Lipstick." [OhioR] (37) 86, p. 86-87.
"On the Afternoon of the Prom." [PaintedB] (29) Ag 86, p. 73.
"Photographs of the Depression." [TarRP] (25:1) Fall 85, p. 17-18.
"Punks." [PaintedB] (29) Ag 86, p. 71-72.
"Romance in the Old Folks' Home." [Poetry] (149:3) D 86, p. 151-152.
"Snakes" (for Mary Oliver). [MissouriR] (9:2) 86, p. 150-151.
"Thunder above Ardsley-on-Hudson." [PaintedB] (29) Ag 86, p. 72.
"Yellow Stars." [NoAmR] (271:3) S 86, p. 46.
5614. WATSON, Craig
"Belief." [Sink] (1) 86, p. 4.
"Door." [Sink] (1) 86, p. 3.
"Space." [Sink] (1) 86, p. 3.
5615. WATSON, Ellen
"Concerted Effort" (tr. of Adélia Prado). [MassR] (27:3/4) Fall-Wint 86, p. 420-421.
"Denouement" (tr. of Adélia Prado). [MassR] (27:3/4) Fall-Wint 86, p. 418-419.
"Film Short" (tr. of Jotamario). [MassR] (27:3/4) Fall-Wint 86, p. 626-628.
"Love in the Ether" (tr. of Adélia Prado). [MassR] (27:3/4) Fall-Wint 86, p. 419.
"A Man Inhabited a House" (tr. of Adélia Prado). [Writ] (18) 86, c87, p. 111.
"Passion" (tr. of Adélia Prado). [Writ] (18) 86, c87, p. 113-115.
"Professional Mourner" (tr. of Adélia Prado). [Writ] (18) 86, c87, p. 112.
"Visit to Weimar" (tr. of Ernesto Cardenal). [MassR] (27:3/4) Fall-Wint 86, p. 506-509.
"Wandering from Sleep." [OP] (42/43) Wint 86-87, p. 166-167.
"We Misfits Don't Forget You, Marilyn" (tr. of Jotamario). [MassR] (27:3/4) Fall-Wint 86, p. 624-626.
5616. WATSON, Lawrence
"Melancholy." [ManhatPR] (6) Wint-Spr 85-86, p. 27.
5617. WATSON, W. Karl
"Elegy for My Grandfather D. 1919." [BallSUF] (27:4) Aut 86, p. 20-21.
5618. WATSON, Wilfred
"Re Ezra Pound" (for Donna Grulhke). [GreenfR] (13:3/4) Sum-Fall 86, p. 199.
5619. WATT, F. W. (Frank)
"In Translation." [CanLit] (110) Fall 86, p. 58-59.
"Letter to My Parents." [GreenfR] (13:3/4) Sum-Fall 86, p. 200.
"On a Gestapo Photograph Purported to be of the Captured Spy 'Madeleine'." [GreenfR] (13:3/4) Sum-Fall 86, p. 201.
5620. WATTEN, Barrett
"Conduit" (for Kit Robinson). [Temblor] (3) 86, p. 117-127.
"The Word." [Zyzzyva] (2:3) Fall 86, p. 27-38.
5621. WAUGAMAN, Charles A.
"Potts Point." [CapeR] (21:2) Fall 86, p. 28.
5622. WAUGH, Robert H.
"The Bud." [InterPR] (12:2) Fall 86, p. 64.
"The Side of the Road." [InterPR] (12:2) Fall 86, p. 62-63.
5623. WAYMAN, Tom
"Another Poem about Solitude." [ColR] (NS 13:1) Fall 85, p. 12.
"Beetle." [ColR] (NS 13:1) Fall 85, p. 15-16.
"Breath." [ColR] (NS 13:1) Fall 85, p. 17.
"Defective Parts of Speech." [OntR] (24) Spr-Sum 86, p. 102-103.
"Defective Parts of Speech: 'An Auxiliary Used to Express Necessity, Duty, Obligation, etc.'." [MassR] (27:1) Spr 86, p. 35-36.
"Defective Parts of Speech: Found." [MassR] (27:1) Spr 86, p. 36.
"Defective Parts of Speech: Official Errata." [MinnR] (NS 26) Spr 86, p. 26.
"Defective Parts of Speech: Sunday." [MassR] (27:1) Spr 86, p. 37-39.
"Defective Parts of Speech: Technical Manual." [MassR] (27:1) Spr 86, p. 33-34.
"Defective Parts of Speech: Translations." [MassR] (27:1) Spr 86, p. 34-35.
"Defective Parts of Speech: Two Visitors." [Event] (15:2) 86, p. 100-101.
"Holding the Line." [ColR] (NS 13:1) Fall 85, p. 13-14.
"It's an Impossible Situation." [CrossC] (8:1) 86, p. 9.

"Mine." [CrossC] (8:1) 86, p. 9.
"The Nationalism of the Trees." [ColR] (NS 13:1) Fall 85, p. 18.
"The Runners." [CanLit] (108) Spr 86, p. 66-67.
5624. WAYNE, Jayne
"Headache." [SouthernPR] (26:1) Spr 86, p. 51.
5625. WEARNE, Alan
"Elise" (Excerpt, from chapter eight of the verse-novel *The Nightmarkets*). [Verse]
(5) 86, p. 15-16.
5626. WEATHERS, Winston
"The Aeneid, Book VI: A Reenactment." [SouthernR] (22:3) Sum 86, p. 571.
"Fantasia in a Minor Key." [SouthernR] (22:3) Sum 86, p. 570.
"The Wreck of the Heart, As Painted by a Flemish Master." [SewanR] (94:4) Fall
86, p. 581-582.
5627. WEAVER, Richard
"Rain." [BlackWR] (12:2) Spr 86, p. 70.
5628. WEBB, Charles
"Hope Chest." [BellR] (9:2) Fall 86, p. 18.
"Weeb Dreams He's Thrown in Jail for Becoming Discouraged in Public." [CimR]
(76) Jl 86, p. 61-62.
"A Weekend at the Rest Easy Motel." [SlipS] (6) 86, p. 72.
"What the Clouds See." [SouthernPR] (26:1) Spr 86, p. 46.
5629. WEBB, Phyllis
"Pepper Tree" (for Breyten Breytenbach). [MalR] (77) D 86, p. 16.
"Performance." [GreenfR] (13:3/4) Sum-Fall 86, p. 202-203.
"Thinking Cap." [MalR] (77) D 86, p. 17.
5630. WEBER, Elizabeth
"My Grandmother's Hands." [Calyx] (9:2/3) Wint 86, p. 94-95.
5631. WEBER, Marc
"Day of the Dead." [ColR] (NS 13:1) Fall 85, p. 37.
5632. WEBSTER, Diane
"Dance." [YetASM] (4) 85, p. 6.
"Heritage." [YetASM] (5) 86, p. 9.
"Siamese Twins." [PoeticJ] (14) 86, p. 38.
5633. WEDDLE, Mike
"City." [PassN] (7:1) Fall-Wint 85-86, p. 28.
5634. WEDGE, Philip
"Prayer." [HighP] (1:1) Wint 86, p. 37-38.
5635. WEEDON, Syd
"October's Rain." [RagMag] (5:2) Fall 86, p. 75.
5636. WEEKLEY, Richard J.
"11:30 P.M." (La Coruna, Spain, July 13, 1984). [Wind] (16:57) 86, p. 40.
"Against the Hard Wet Pails." [Electrum] (38) Spr 86, p. 14.
"You Make the Morning Broom." [Wind] (16:57) 86, p. 40.
5637. WEEKS, Ramona
"Working Piggybank." [ForidaR] (14:1) Spr-Sum 86, p. 48.
5638. WEEKS, Robert Lewis
"Anatomy." [NegC] (6:4) Fall 86, p. 44.
"But God Is a Great Singer." [NegC] (6:4) Fall 86, p. 45.
"Calling the Cats." [WebR] (11:2) Fall 86, p. 68.
"The Cat in the Window." [HiramPoR] (41) Fall-Wint 86-87, p. 46.
"Classification." [HiramPoR] (41) Fall-Wint 86-87, p. 47.
"A Cruet the Color of Your Eyes." [NegC] (6:4) Fall 86, p. 42.
"The Difference." [NegC] (6:4) Fall 86, p. 43.
"Double Entendre." [InterPR] (12:2) Fall 86, p. 113-114.
"Study of Sun XI." [SoDakR] (24:2) Sum 86, p. 94.
"They Said." [WebR] (11:2) Fall 86, p. 69.
"Waiting for Rain." [NegC] (6:4) Fall 86, p. 44.
WEI, Wang
See WANG, Wei
5639. WEIBEL, Jürg
"The Old Acquaintance" (tr. by Gary N. Sea). [WebR] (11:2) Fall 86, p. 30.
5640. WEIDMAN, Phil
"Balance." [WormR] (26:3, issue 103) 86, p. 102.
"Be Somebody." [WormR] (26:3, issue 103) 86, p. 103.
"Bronchobuster." [WormR] (26:1, issue 101) 86, p. 11.
"Buffer, Gretel & Bear." [WormR] (26:1, issue 101) 86, p. 11.

"Cat Lady." [WormR] (26:3, issue 103) 86, p. 103.
"Cut." [WormR] (26:3, issue 103) 86, p. 102.
"Feeling the Pressure." [WormR] (26:1, issue 101) 86, p. 11.
"Finding Myself." [WormR] (26:3, issue 103) 86, p. 103.
"Lecture." [WormR] (26:1, issue 101) 86, p. 11-12.
"Mole." [WormR] (26:3, issue 103) 86, p. 103.
"Next Best." [WormR] (26:3, issue 103) 86, p. 102.
"No Bad Example." [WormR] (26:1, issue 101) 86, p. 11.
"Numbers Game." [WormR] (26:3, issue 103) 86, p. 102.
"Playing Nazi Soldier, 1944." [WormR] (26:3, issue 103) 86, p. 103.
"Quicker Than a Snake." [WormR] (26:1, issue 101) 86, p. 11.
"Small Talk." [WormR] (26:3, issue 103) 86, p. 104.
"Something Like a Prayer." [WormR] (26:3, issue 103) 86, p. 103.
"Trip." [WormR] (26:1, issue 101) 86, p. 12.
5641. WEIER, John
"Jed." [PraF] (7:2) Sum 86, p. 47.
"Welland Stockyards 1955." [PraF] (7:2) Sum 86, p. 46.
5642. WEIGEL, Tom
"It Might As Well Be Spring." [LittleM] (15:2) 86, p. 56.
"Orange Crush." [LittleM] (15:2) 86, p. 57-63.
"Twenty Four Hours from Tulsa" (to Tony Towle). [LittleM] (15:2) 86, p. 55.
"West of Lunch." [LittleM] (15:2) 86, p. 63.
"The Will of the Curves." [LittleM] (15:2) 86, p. 54.
5643. WEIGL, Bruce
"Amigo del Corazón." [TriQ] (65) Wint 86, p. 199-200.
"Apparition of the Exile." [TarRP] (25:1) Fall 85, p. 8.
"Breakdown." [TriQ] (65) Wint 86, p. 201.
"Dialectical Materialism." [OP] (42/43) Wint 86-87, p. 150-151.
"The Husband." [AmerPoR] (15:6) N-D 86, p. 28.
"In the Autumn Village." [TriQ] (65) Wint 86, p. 202.
"The Kiss." [TriQ] (65) Wint 86, p. 196-197.
"LZ Nowhere" (for Bill and Anne). [OP] (42/43) Wint 86-87, p. 153.
"The Offices of Loss." [OP] (42/43) Wint 86-87, p. 151-153.
"Regret for the Mourning Doves Who Failed to Mate." [WestHR] (40:1) Spr 86, p. 79.
"The Soldier's Epistle." [TarRP] (25:1) Fall 85, p. 7.
"Some Thoughts on the Ambassador: Bong Son, 1967." [OP] (42/43) Wint 86-87, p. 153-154.
"They Name Heaven" (Managua, December 1984). [AmerPoR] (15:6) N-D 86, p. 29.
"The Third Person." [AmerPoR] (15:6) N-D 86, p. 28.
"This Man." [TriQ] (65) Wint 86, p. 198.
"The Years Without Understanding." [TarRP] (25:1) Fall 85, p. 6.
5644. WEINBERG, Jeffrey H.
"Used Book Store." [MoodySI] (16/17) Sum 86, p. 31.
5645. WEINBERGER, Eliot
"A Fable of Joan Miro" (tr. of Octavio Paz). [Sulfur] (6:2, issue 17) 86, p. 7-9.
"Kostas Papaioannou" (for Nitsa and Reia, tr. of Octavio Paz). [MassR] (27:3/4) Fall-Wint 86, p. 571-574.
5646. WEINBERGER, Florence
"The Power in My Mother's Arms." [Calyx] (9:2/3) Wint 86, p. 92-93.
5647. WEINER, Rebecca
"Dead Man's Float." [SenR] (16:2) 86, p. 66.
"On the Road to Blue Earth." [SenR] (16:2) 86, p. 65.
5648. WEINGARTEN, Roger
"Barn Cat Summer" (For Mark Cox). [Poetry] (148:3) Je 86, p. 129-130.
"Border Minstrel." [SewanR] (94:2) Spr 86, p. 213-214.
"Daycare Daydream." [NoAmR] (271:4) D 86, p. 41.
"The Emperor's New Formalist Hunt for the Here and Now." [PoetryE] (20/21) Fall 86, p. 186-187.
"Invisible Fire." [SewanR] (94:2) Spr 86, p. 214-215.
"It's Like That." [Poetry] (147:6) Mr 86, p. 340.
"A Late Twentieth-Century Afternoon with the Dead." [Poetry] (147:6) Mr 86, p. 338-339.
"My Brain Tumor." [Poetry] (147:6) Mr 86, p. 337-338.
"Northern Gothic." [NewRep] (195:9) 1 S 86, p. 38.

"Then My Father's Insomnia Will Break Like the Wine Glass I Crushed Underfoot at My Wedding." [Poetry] (149:3) D 86, p. 153-155.
5649. WEINMAN, Paul
"Certain Shellfish." [SanFPJ] (8:4) 85, p. 53.
"Foot Thrust." [Sam] (44:3 release 175) 86, p. 14.
"Hardball Ain't All Bucolic." (Chapbook issue). [Sam] (45:3, release 179) 86, 15 p.
"It's a Wonder." [DeKalbLAJ] (19:1) 86, p. 40-41.
"Not So Familiar." [Contact] (7:38/39/40) Wint-Spr 86, p. 88.
"Splintered Windows." [SanFPJ] (8:4) 85, p. 56.
"Towns Touching." [CrabCR] (3:2) Spr 86, p. 8.
5650. WEINSTEIN, Debra
"All Summer Long." [HeliconN] (14/15) Sum 86, p. 147.
"Broadview Drive." [HeliconN] (14/15) Sum 86, p. 146.
"Withhold My Name." [HeliconN] (14/15) Sum 86, p. 146.
5651. WEINSTEIN, Lucie
"Premonitions of Death" (tr. of Adele Krebs, w. Jennifer Krebs). [SinW] (29/30) 86, p. 101.
5652. WEIRATHER, Larry
"Van Gogh Tumulus, Newgrange, Ireland." [Comm] (113:11) 6 Je 86, p. 347.
5653. WEIRICH, Clo
"Invitation." [Amelia] (3:4) Fall 86, p. 28.
5654. WEISS, David
"Grass." [PoetryNW] (27:4) Wint 86-87, p. 30-31.
"On the Marshes at Dawn." [GeoR] (40:3) Fall 86, p. 822.
5655. WEISS, Irving
"Sens-Plastique" (Selections, tr. of Malcolm de Chazal). [Rampike] (5:1) 86, p. 27.
5656. WEISS, Sigmund
"Ethnic Cynicism." [SanFPJ] (9:1) 86, p. 60.
"The Final Tally." [SanFPJ] (8:1) 85, p. 72.
"The Gods of War." [SanFPJ] (9:1) 86, p. 77.
"Melody in Black." [SanFPJ] (8:1) 85, p. 72.
"Neutronic Explosion." [SanFPJ] (8:1) 85, p. 69.
5657. WEITZEL, Selomo (Jasper Reid)
"To Yevgeny Yevtushenko" (tr. by Will Kirkland). [NewOR] (13:4) Wint 86, p. 37.
5658. WELBOURN, Cynthia
"Mississippi Music Cruise." [Amelia] (3:2) Spr 86, p. 86.
"Summer in New Orleans." [DeKalbLAJ] (19:1) 86, p. 41.
"Transformation." [DeKalbLAJ] (19:1) 86, p. 41.
5659. WELBURN, Ron
"Bones and Drums" (for Lewis McMillan). [Callaloo] (9:1, #26) Wint 86, p. 126.
"Plaid Jumper in the Window." [YetASM] (4) 85, p. 2.
5660. WELCH, Don
"Borges." [WillowS] (17) Wint 86, p. 45.
"Steel-Worker." [CutB] (25) Fall-Wint 86, p. 37.
"Three Small Letters to the Coast." [WillowS] (17) Wint 86, p. 46-47.
5661. WELCH, Liliane
"Cairns." [Quarry] (35:3) Sum 86, p. 50.
"I Sail to Italy Not of My Own Free Will." [PraF] (7:3) Aut 86, p. 125.
"Names." [PraF] (7:3) Aut 86, p. 124.
"September 1983" (Alpine Rescue on the Pala del Rifugio). [Quarry] (35:3) Sum 86, p. 51.
"The Wind on Manstorna Peak" (for Ghigno Timillero). [Quarry] (35:3) Sum 86, p. 50.
5662. WELHAVEN, Johan Sebastian
"The Thorn Tree" (tr. by Ron Wakefield and Olav Thompson). [LitR] (29:3) Spr 86, p. 359.
5663. WELISH, Marjorie
"The Last Vaudeville." [Conjunc] (9) 86, p. 162-163.
"Two Studies of a Man's Head and One of a Kneeling Woman." [Conjunc] (9) 86, p. 164.
5664. WELLS, Nigel
"Isle of Arvon Sonnets" (Selections: "That Fence Over There," "Bricks and Tongues"). [Stand] (27:4) Aut 86, p. 7.
5665. WELLS, Stan
"What Did You Do Today?" [Bogg] (55) 86, p. 54.

5666. WELLS, Will
"Doing Donuts." [WritersF] (12) Fall 86, p. 239-240.
"Weak Heart." [CimR] (75) Ap 86, p. 13.
5667. WEN, Yi-duo
"Dusk" (tr. by Robert Dorsett). [SenR] (16:1) 86, p. 97.
"Last Day" (tr. by Robert Dorsett). [SenR] (16:1) 86, p. 99.
"Quiet Night" (tr. by Robert Dorsett). [SenR] (16:1) 86, p. 98.
5668. WENDELL, Julia
"Possibly So." [QW] (22) Spr-Sum 86, p. 10.
5669. WENNER, Mary
"The Flowering Peach." [BellArk] (2:3) My-Je 86, p. 7.
"In Hawaii." [BellArk] (2:4) Jl-Ag 86, p. 4.
"In Hawaii 2." [BellArk] (2:4) Jl-Ag 86, p. 4.
"Moving Pictures" (for Randy). [BellArk] (2:4) Jl-Ag 86, p. 8.
"To Kathy Who Found My Shoe on the Boulevard." [BellArk] (2:3) My-Je 86, p. 14.
WERT, William F. van
See Van WERT, William F.
5670. WESLEY, Marilyn
"The Covenant." [SingHM] (14) 86, p. 5.
5671. WESLOWSKI, Dieter
"After Aphrodite's Damage." [PaintedB] (29) Ag 86, p. 65.
"And There Was Bread." [PikeF] (7) Spr 86, p. 12.
"Bacchanalia for the Old Homestead." [KanQ] (18:1/2) Wint-Spr 86, p. 46.
"Be with Me Now." [MalR] (77) D 86, p. 119.
"The Brain of the Fat Woman." [ThRiPo] (27/28) 86, p. 69.
"Brujería." [CrossCur] (6:2) 86, p. 63.
"Crazy the Sun." [BallSUF] (27:4) Aut 86, p. 61.
"The Draw of Winter." [MalR] (77) D 86, p. 120.
"An Envelope of Moonlight." [PennR] (1:1) 85, p. 73.
"The Fall." [KenR] (NS 7:1) Wint 85, p. 93.
"A Few Crumbs." [MalR] (77) D 86, p. 119.
"Heavens!" [MalR] (77) D 86, p. 120.
"If Janos Starker." [PaintedB] (29) Ag 86, p. 66.
"Inventory." [KenR] (NS 7:1) Wint 85, p. 92.
"Laslo." [PaintedB] (29) Ag 86, p. 66.
"Open Letter to My Country." [BallSUF] (26:4) Aut 85, p. 34.
"Prayer for My Room." [NewEngR] (8:4) Sum 86, p. 468.
"The Torturer." [SouthernPR] (26:1) Spr 86, p. 53.
"When the Knight Looked into the Eyes of Death." [KanQ] (18:1/2) Wint-Spr 86, p. 45.
5672. WESSEL, Peter
"After Saint Valentine." [WritersF] (12) Fall 86, p. 239.
"The Palm Tree." [WebR] (11:1) Spr 86, p. 81.
5673. WEST, Ann J.
"Belief." [CanLit] (111) Wint 86, p. 85.
5674. WEST, John Foster
"Heart of Night." [SouthwR] (71:3) Sum 86, p. 401.
5675. WEST, Kathleene
"The Bush Baby at the Henry Dorley Zoo." [PraS] (60:2) Sum 86, p. 20-21.
"Mother, Mother, Tell about Olden Times." [PraS] (60:2) Sum 86, p. 22-24.
"Proving Ground." [PraS] (60:2) Sum 86, p. 21.
5676. WEST, Michael
"Eating My Words." [KanQ] (18:1/2) Wint-Spr 86, p. 50.
5677. WEST, Richard M.
"At Last Report the Devil's in Seattle." [BellR] (9:2) Fall 86, p. 33.
5678. WEST, Ruth Green
"In the Flood of the Moon." [Poem] (56) N 86, p. 41.
"The Intruder." [Poem] (56) N 86, p. 40.
5679. WEST, Steve
"After the Flood, 1983." [CapeR] (21:2) Fall 86, p. 11.
5680. WESTERFIELD, Nancy G.
"The Album." [Comm] (113:1) 17 Ja 86, p. 25.
"Arenas." [Nimrod] (30:1) Fall-Wint 86, p. 120.
"Going Somewhere in Nebraska." [PraS] (60:2) Sum 86, p. 72.
"Migrators." [Nimrod] (30:1) Fall-Wint 86, p. 120.

"Not Calling Margaret Tonight." [ChrC] (103:29) 8 O 86, p. 854.
"Topiary Arts." [Confr] (33/34) Fall-Wint 86-87, p. 140.
5681. WESTERGAARD, Diane
"A Christmas Card I Have Often Received." [CapeR] (21:2) Fall 86, p. 43.
"English Rose Garden." [CapeR] (21:1) Spr 86, p. 17.
"Isaac Smells Bacon." [ThRiPo] (27/28) 86, p. 70.
"The Yellow Christ by Gauguin." [CapeR] (21:1) Spr 86, p. 16.
5682. WESTWOOD, Norma
"Falling." [Interim] (5:1) Spr 86, p. 29.
"The Garden." [Vis] (20) 86, p. 34.
"Wild Plum." [Interim] (5:1) Spr 86, p. 30.
5683. WETTEROTH, Bruce
"In Memory of Quintus Horatius Flaccus." [CharR] (12:1) Spr 86, p. 77.
"Just After." [PoetryNW] (27:1) Spr 86, p. 40.
"Moving On in November." [OhioR] (37) 86, p. 33.
"Night of the Lyrids." [OhioR] (36) 86, p. 10-11.
"On a Bright Windy Day in Nebraska." [OhioR] (36) 86, p. 12.
"Rig Song." [OhioR] (36) 86, p. 6-7.
"Seeing by Night." [OhioR] (36) 86, p. 8-9.
"Stalled at the Windmill." [MidAR] (6:2) 86, p. 150-151.
"Tansy at Dachau." [OhioR] (37) 86, p. 34-35.
"Watching the Dancers from Peking." [AmerPoR] (15:5) S-O 86, p. 35.
5684. WEVILL, David
"Animula." [GreenfR] (13:3/4) Sum-Fall 86, p. 209-210.
"Child Sketch in Crayon." [GreenfR] (13:3/4) Sum-Fall 86, p. 207-208.
"Her Seasons." [GreenfR] (13:3/4) Sum-Fall 86, p. 205-206.
"Polonaise." [GreenfR] (13:3/4) Sum-Fall 86, p. 208.
"Snow Country." [GreenfR] (13:3/4) Sum-Fall 86, p. 211-212.
"Visitors." [GreenfR] (13:3/4) Sum-Fall 86, p. 204.
5685. WEXELBLATT, Robert
"A Guerrilla." [CapeR] (21:2) Fall 86, p. 12.
"Love Makes of Its Expectancies." [Poem] (55) Mr 86, p. 40.
"Twenty Lines on Metaphor." [CapeR] (21:2) Fall 86, p. 13.
"Variations on a Theme of Paganini." [SmPd] (23:1, #66) Wint 86, p. 27-28.
5686. WEXLER, Philip
"Slipping through Your Hands." [PoeticJ] (13) 86, p. 16-17.
5687. WF. H.
"All evening insects danced furiously on the lawn." [RagMag] (5:2) Fall 86, p. 18.
5688. WHALEN, Damien
"Hosting the Beavers." [CutB] (26) Spr-Sum 86, p. 17-19.
5689. WHARTON, Calvin
"End of a Season." [Event] (15:1) 86, p. 115.
5690. WHATLEY, Wallace
"Princess." [SouthernPR] (26:2) Fall 86, p. 44.
5691. WHEATCROFT, John
"The Caryatids." [Poem] (56) N 86, p. 48-49.
"Erysichthon." [Poem] (56) N 86, p. 50.
"My Father's House." [Confr] (32) Spr-Sum 86, p. 128.
"Night Landing." [ColEng] (48:2) F 86, p. 144.
5692. WHEATLEY, Pat (Patience)
"In Convoy — November 1944." [Event] (15:2) 86, p. 167-168.
"A Lamp of Earth." [Germ] (10:1) Spr-Sum 86, p. 18.
"Telescope — May 8 1945." [Event] (15:2) 86, p. 168-169.
WHEATON, Heather Holland
See HOLLAND-WHEATON, Heather
5693. WHEELER, Emily
"The Mechanic's Wife." [SenR] (16:2) 86, p. 87.
5694. WHEELER, Sylvia Griffith
"Leaving the Hague." [Paint] (13:25/26) Spr-Aut 86, p. 14.
"Let Us Consider the Wanton Apathy among Our People." [Paint] (13:25/26)
Spr-Aut 86, p. 15.
5695. WHIPP, Les
"August in Nebraska." [PraS] (60:2) Sum 86, p. 69-70.
5696. WHISLER, Robert F.
"The Analogue." [BallSUF] (27:4) Aut 86, p. 48.
"Daddy-Longlegs." [DeKalbLAJ] (19:3/4) 86, p. 95.

"Gathering Bones." [BallSUF] (26:4) Aut 85, p. 63.
"Linda's Lindy." [BallSUF] (27:4) Aut 86, p. 7.
5697. WHITCOMB-NELSON, Katharine
"What My Bridesmaid Said at the Reception." [SingHM] (13) 86, p. 42.
5698. WHITE, Gail
"At Seventy-Seven." [SpoonRQ] (11:2) Spr 86, p. 54-55.
"Dinner at the Dracula Hilton." [PikeF] (7) Spr 86, p. 23.
"Late, When the Light Strikes." [SpoonRQ] (11:2) Spr 86, p. 56.
"The Letters." [AmerS] (55:1) Wint 85-86, p. 44.
"Toward Home, Alone." [SpoonRQ] (11:2) Spr 86, p. 57.
"Viewpoints." [ChrC] (103:28) 1 O 86, p. 836.
5699. WHITE, J. P.
"Answering Your Last Letter." [Agni] (23) 86, p. 177-178.
"Bushwhacking through Bear Country." [MemphisSR] (6:1/2) Spr 86, p. 36-37.
"On the Return of Halley's Comet." [Poetry] (147:4) Ja 86, p. 221.
"Thanksgiving Night, Old Town, Portland, Oregon." [Poetry] (149:2) N 86, p. 85.
"Walking Pound's Canals." [Poetry] (147:4) Ja 86, p. 222-224.
"Walking to the Theater, I Tell You a Story about a Runaway." [Poetry] (149:2) N 86, p. 83-84.
5700. WHITE, James L.
"25 Cent Movies" (from Del Rio Hotel). [JamesWR] (3:4) Sum 86, p. 12.
"Butcher's Dance" (from Del Rio Hotel). [JamesWR] (3:4) Sum 86, p. 12.
"Voyeur" (from Del Rio Hotel). [JamesWR] (3:4) Sum 86, p. 12.
"Wolf Waiting" (from Del Rio Hotel). [JamesWR] (3:4) Sum 86, p. 12.
5701. WHITE, Janet S. (JSWhite)
"Dateline Inner City." [SanFPJ] (8:2) 85, p. 13.
5702. WHITE, Marnelle R.
"Home." [EngJ] (75:2) F 86, p. 42.
5703. WHITE, Mary Jane
"Hawaii As a Cure" (for William Carlos Williams). [AmerPoR] (15:3) My-Je 86, p. 28.
5704. WHITE, Mike
"The Bridge." [WestHR] (40:3) Aut 86, p. 210-211.
"Thinking of Missouri." [MissouriR] (9:1) 85-86, p. 26-27.
5705. WHITE, Mimi
"Climbing the Ladder." [StoneC] (13:3/4) Spr-Sum 86, p. 62.
"Dreamer" (for Charles Simic). [CrabCR] (3:2) Spr 86, p. 14.
5706. WHITE, Sarah
"Galileo and Other Renegades" (for Jack Amariglio). [MassR] (27:1) Spr 86, p. 141-142.
"Through Phases of Plum." [MassR] (27:1) Spr 86, p. 142-143.
5707. WHITE, Steven F.
"CIII. Awakened suddenly in dreams I heard him beyond the night" (tr. of Raúl Zurita). [SilverFR] (11) Sum 86, p. 15.
"The City" (Selection: Poem 60, tr. of Gonzalo Millan). [SilverFR] (11) Sum 86, p. 21, 23.
"Heartbreak Hotel" (Music of Elvis Presley, R.I.P., tr. of Oscar Hahn). [SilverFR] (11) Sum 86, p. 13.
"Is There Anyone" (tr. of Walter Hoefler). [NewOR] (13:2) Sum 86, p. 31.
"The Place You Inhabit" (tr. of Walter Hoefler). [NewOR] (13:2) Sum 86, p. 57.
"Poem of the Foreigners' Moment in Our Jungle" (for several voices, tr. of Pablo Antonio Cuadra). [AmerV] (5) Wint 86, p. 107-109.
"Reincarnation of the Butchers" (tr. of Oscar Hahn). [SilverFR] (11) Sum 86, p. 11.
"Secret Police." [WillowS] (18) Sum 86, p. 17.
"Stumbling Home Past Curfew in Santiago, Chile." [WillowS] (18) Sum 86, p. 15-16.
"Survivor" (tr. of Walter Hoefler). [NewOR] (13:2) Sum 86, p. 48.
"They've Broken the Most Delicate Bone in My Ear" (tr. of Manuel Silva Acevedo). [SilverFR] (11) Sum 86, p. 19.
"Wishing" (tr. of Omar Lara). [SilverFR] (11) Sum 86, p. 17.
5708. WHITE, William M.
"The Lamb Is Dead on Broadway." [NegC] (6:1) Wint 86, p. 71-72.
"Oh Yes You Lovely Grew." [SouthernR] (22:4) O 86, p. 801.
"Sue Ellen in the Morning." [Bogg] (55) 86, p. 18.

5709. WHITEHEAD, Jeffrey
"Looking under the Hood of a 1951 Car & Finding My Brother." [PoetryNW] (27:4)
Wint 86-87, p. 34-35.
"Wishbone in the Slaughterhouse." [PoetryNW] (27:4) Wint 86-87, p. 35.
5710. WHITEHILL, Karen
"Apology." [VirQR] (62:1) Wint 86, p. 50.
5711. WHITEMAN, Bruce
"The Invisible World Is in Decline, Book II" (8 selections). [MalR] (76) S 86, p.
118-121.
5712. WHITESIDE, James C.
"Workman." [SanFPJ] (8:1) 85, p. 26-27.
5713. WHITING, Nathan
"Chalk Dribs Down on Large Concrete." [Contact] (8:41/42/43) Fall-Wint 86-87, p.
57.
"Stall King's Tools." [HangL] (49) Spr 86, p. 49.
"Wrap the Cavelike." [Contact] (8:41/42/43) Fall-Wint 86-87, p. 57.
5714. WHITING, Shirley
"Huntsy, the Guide." [SingHM] (13) 86, p. 88.
5715. WHITMAN, Ruth
"A Brand Snatched from Anti-Tank Fire" (in . . . Ramban Hospital, Haifa, tr. of
Rami Ditzani). [PoetL] (81:2) Sum 86, p. 134-135.
"Bubba Esther, 1888." [SinW] (29/30) 86, p. 92.
"Coming Home during the Second World War." [AmerV] (4) Fall 86, p. 26.
"The Fig Tree" (tr. of Miriam Oren). [PoetL] (81:2) Sum 86, p. 107.
"Hellas, 1952." [ManhatPR] (7) Sum 86, p. 18.
"I Only Wish" (tr. of Miriam Oren). [PoetL] (81:2) Sum 86, p. 107.
"Jackal" (tr. of Miriam Oren). [PoetL] (81:2) Sum 86, p. 108.
"Net, Lake, Sieve." [CrossCur] (5:4/6:1) 86, p. 105.
"The Shepherd." [ManhatPR] (7) Sum 86, p. 19.
"Snowwhite" (tr. of Miriam Oren). [PoetL] (81:2) Sum 86, p. 106.
"The Young Scholar." [ManhatPR] (7) Sum 86, p. 18.
5716. WHITMAN, Walt
"The Song of the Broad-axe" (Selection: Part 3). [AmerPoR] (15:2) Mr-Ap 86, p. 6.
5717. WHITTEN, Hubert N.
"Einstein at Work." [PikeF] (7) Spr 86, p. 13.
5718. WHYTE, Jon
"The Road to Olduvai." [Dandel] (13:1) Spr-Sum 86, p. 5-8.
5719. WICKELHAUS, Martha
"Aftermath." [Ascent] (12:1) 86, p. 14.
"I Fear." [Ascent] (12:1) 86, p. 13.
"In This Year of Dust and Rain." [QW] (22) Spr-Sum 86, p. 7.
"Woman at a Sphygmomanometer." [CutB] (25) Fall-Wint 86, p. 45.
5720. WICKLESS, Harrison
"Decoy." [ForidaR] (14:1) Spr-Sum 86, p. 58.
"Porch: An American Twilight" (for Donald Cook). [AntR] (44:3) Sum 86, p.
338-344.
5721. WIDERKEHR, Richard
"Sundays." [YetASM] (5) 86, p. 8.
5722. WIDERSHIEN, Marc
"Mozart." [YetASM] (5) 86, p. 8.
5723. WIEDER, Laurence
"Emblem." [Boulevard] (1:1/2) Wint 86, p. 172.
"Wound Down." [Boulevard] (1:1/2) Wint 86, p. 173.
5724. WIELAND, Liza
"Fall." [ManhatPR] (6) Wint-Spr 85-86, p. 45.
"Love Poem." [ManhatPR] (6) Wint-Spr 85-86, p. 45.
5725. WIER, Dara
"Old Fashioned." [NoAmR] (271:4) D 86, p. 62.
5726. WIERZYNSKI, Kazimierz
"Ballad of the Table" (tr. by Chris Gladun). [Writ] (18) 86, c87, p. 138-140.
"Fair Play, a Morality Play" (tr. by Chris Gladun). [Writ] (18) 86, c87, p. 137.
"Scientific Expedition" (tr. by Chris Gladun). [Writ] (18) 86, c87, p. 136.
5727. WIESELTIER, Meir
"Call-Up" (tr. by Harold Schimmel). [PoetL] (81:2) Sum 86, p. 110.
"Caution Prevents Accidents" (tr. by Harold Schimmel). [PoetL] (81:2) Sum 86, p.
109.

"Poem about Jerusalem" (tr. by Harold Schimmel). [PoetL] (81:2) Sum 86, p. 110.
5728. WIGGINS, Jean
"A Crisis of Faith." [CapeR] (21:2) Fall 86, p. 1.
5729. WIGHT, Doris
"The Ballad of Sally Ward." [Amelia] (3:4) Fall 86, p. 51-53.
5730. WIGHT, Ernest
"The Endings Are True." [NewEngR] (8:3) Spr 86, p. 299.
5731. WIKLE, Lynn
"Confessional." [PoetryNW] (27:1) Spr 86, p. 15-16.
5732. WILBORN, William
"Four Corners" (Montana, 20 years later). [Thrpny] (26) Sum 86, p. 16.
"Rooms" (for the 'sixties). [WebR] (11:1) Spr 86, p. 82-83.
5733. WILBUR, Richard
"Phaedra" (Selections: Act 5, Scenes 6-7, tr. of Jean Racine). [Translation] (17) Fall
86, p. 311-316.
"Phaedra" (Selections, tr. of Jean Baptiste Racine). [Shen] (36:2) 86, p. 27-46.
5734. WILD, Peter
"Columbus Day." [SouthernPR] (26:1) Spr 86, p. 5.
"The Convert." [NoAmR] (271:4) D 86, p. 12.
"Cortez." [HiramPoR] (40) Spr-Sum 86, p. 30.
"Crystal Elephants." [Raccoon] (20) Ap 86, p. 12.
"Elotes." [BellArk] (2:2) Mr-Ap 86, p. 8.
"Evangelism." [OhioR] (37) 86, p. 111.
"Firemen." [NoDaQ] (54:1) Wint 86, p. 71.
"Gerolamo Cardano." [MemphisSR] (7:1) Fall 86, p. 45.
"Gospel Singers." [LittleM] (15:2) 86, p. 43.
"Horticulturist." [OhioR] (37) 86, p. 110.
"Hotel Owners." [MemphisSR] (6:1/2) Spr 86, p. 38.
"House Painters." [BellArk] (2:1) Ja-F 86, p. 12.
"Mayflies." [ClockR] (3:1) 85, p. 34.
"New Careers." [TarRP] (25:2) Spr 86, p. 12.
"Profitable Businesses." [MemphisSR] (6:1/2) Spr 86, p. 39.
"Promises." [Confr] (32) Spr-Sum 86, p. 82.
"Quotes." [NoDaQ] (54:1) Wint 86, p. 70.
"Rangers." [ClockR] (3:1) 85, p. 32-33.
"Real Forests." [NoDaQ] (54:1) Wint 86, p. 68.
"Roy Rogers." [CharR] (12:2) Fall 86, p. 71.
"Snails." [HiramPoR] (40) Spr-Sum 86, p. 31.
"Storms." [Confr] (32) Spr-Sum 86, p. 83.
"Trains." [BellArk] (2:1) Ja-F 86, p. 3.
"Trees." [ClockR] (3:1) 85, p. 31.
"Washing Windows." [NoDaQ] (54:1) Wint 86, p. 69.
"Zouaves." [LittleM] (15:2) 86, p. 44.
5735. WILDER, Rex
"Lonely Man Confronts the World's Problems from His Living Room." [BlackWR]
(12:2) Spr 86, p. 72.
5736. WILDING, Margo
"Earth's Instrument" (Miles Davis, San Diego, April, 1985). [Electrum] (38) Spr 86,
p. 12.
5737. WILJER, Robert
"Mole." [KanQ] (18:1/2) Wint-Spr 86, p. 12.
5738. WILKINSON, Claude
"Capturing Evanescence." [Wind] (16:58) 86, p. 41-42.
"Ephemerida." [Poem] (55) Mr 86, p. 11-13.
"For an Uncle." [Poem] (55) Mr 86, p. 14-15.
"Raking Leaves." [Wind] (16:58) 86, p. 41.
5739. WILKINSON, Davi
"Apples." [Puerto] (21:2) Spr 86, p. 124.
5740. WILL, Fred
"Pockets of Power." [MassR] (27:2) Sum 86, p. 202.
WILL, Yee Kim
See KIM, Will Yee
5741. WILLERTON, Chris
"At Five." [KanQ] (18:1/2) Wint-Spr 86, p. 303-304.
"Nightmare." [TarRP] (24:2) Spr 85, p. 30-31.
"Slow Blink." [KanQ] (18:1/2) Wint-Spr 86, p. 304.

5742. WILLEY, Edward
"Continuities." [Interim] (5:1) Spr 86, p. 16.
"Still Stone Child." [DeKalbLAJ] (19:3/4) 86, p. 63.
5743. WILLIAM, N. Sean
"At the zoo this afternoon." [SmPd] (23:3, #68) Fall 86, p. 19.
5744. WILLIAMS, Barbara
"Imprints." [Quarry] (35:3) Sum 86, p. 49.
5745. WILLIAMS, Beryle
"Lost Boys Lodge." [LakeSR] (20) 86, p. 16-17.
5746. WILLIAMS, C. K.
"Anger." [Ploughs] (12:3) 86, p. 56.
"Bishop Tutu's Visit to the White House." [TriQ] (65) Wint 86, p. 211.
"Blame." [Ploughs] (12:3) 86, p. 57.
"Carpe Diem." [OP] (42/43) Wint 86-87, p. 84-85.
"Chorus — The Bacchae" (tr. of Euripides, w. Herbert Golder). [Translation] (16)
    Spr 86, p. 254-262.
"Como." [TriQ] (65) Wint 86, p. 206.
"Conscience." [TriQ] (65) Wint 86, p. 205.
"The Dream." [TriQ] (65) Wint 86, p. 207.
"Easter." [TriQ] (65) Wint 86, p. 208.
"End of Drought." [Sulfur] (6:2, issue 17) 86, p. 90-91.
"Fire." [TriQ] (65) Wint 86, p. 203.
"First Desires." [NewYorker] (62:27) 25 Ag 86, p. 26.
"The Fountain." [MissouriR] (9:1) 85-86, p. 165.
"Ice." [MissouriR] (9:1) 85-86, p. 163.
"The Junior High School Concert: Salle Rossini." [OP] (42/43) Wint 86-87, p. 85.
"Kin." [OP] (42/43) Wint 86-87, p. 87.
"The Latin Quarter." [OP] (42/43) Wint 86-87, p. 84.
"Love: Beginnings." [NewYorker] (62:27) 25 Ag 86, p. 26.
"Love: Habit." [NewYorker] (62:27) 25 Ag 86, p. 26.
"The Modern." [Sulfur] (6:2, issue 17) 86, p. 90.
"New Car." [Ploughs] (12:3) 86, p. 58.
"Noise: Sinalunga." [MissouriR] (9:1) 85-86, p. 164.
"The Park." [TriQ] (65) Wint 86, p. 209.
"Le Petit Salvié" (for Paul Zweig, 1935-1984). [ParisR] (28:100) Sum-Fall 86, p.
    323-332.
"The Prodigy" (for Elizabeth Bishop). [OP] (42/43) Wint 86-87, p. 86.
"Racists." [TriQ] (65) Wint 86, p. 210.
"Religious Thought." [Ploughs] (12:3) 86, p. 55.
"Repression." [TriQ] (65) Wint 86, p. 204.
"Second Persons: Café de l'Abbaye." [OP] (42/43) Wint 86-87, p. 88-89.
"The Storm." [OP] (42/43) Wint 86-87, p. 88.
"USOCA." [Sulfur] (6:2, issue 17) 86, p. 89-90.
"Vehicle: Violence." [OntR] (25) Fall-Wint 86-87, p. 40.
"War." [OP] (42/43) Wint 86-87, p. 86-87.
"Will." [Sulfur] (6:2, issue 17) 86, p. 89.
5747. WILLIAMS, David
"Keeping Faith." [SanFPJ] (8:4) 85, p. 33.
"Refugee Toast." [SanFPJ] (8:3) 85, p. 88.
"Song for a Child Dead in Lebanon." [SanFPJ] (8:4) 85, p. 36.
5748. WILLIAMS, Diane
"She Dances." [MalR] (74) Mr 86, p. 63-64.
5749. WILLIAMS, Elaine
"India Journey: Five Sedokas." [ManhatPR] (6) Wint-Spr 85-86, p. 32-33.
5750. WILLIAMS, John
"At the Theatre." [DenQ] (20:3) Wint 86, p. 127-128.
"Cold Coffee." [DenQ] (20:3) Wint 86, p. 125.
"Flight." [DenQ] (20:3) Wint 86, p. 132.
"Four Letters" (Selection: IV. "To a Friend," Oscar Offerle, killed in the Philippines,
    1942). [DenQ] (20:3) Wint 86, p. 133-137.
"Memories: Texas, 1932." [DenQ] (20:3) Wint 86, p. 129-131.
"An Old Actor to His Audience" (Ford Madox Ford: 1873-1939). [DenQ] (20:3)
    Wint 86, p. 123-124.
"The Skaters." [DenQ] (20:3) Wint 86, p. 126.
5751. WILLIAMS, Mark
"Landed." [Bogg] (55) 86, p. 51.

"Warm toilet seat." [Bogg] (55) 86, p. 51.
5752. WILLIAMS, Miller
"After the Funeral for a Young Woman Who Played Her Guitar on the Corner."
[NegC] (6:4) Fall 86, p. 23.
"The Aging Actress Sees Herself a Starlet on the Late Show." [Poetry] (148:3) Je
86, p. 156.
"Despairing of Understanding We Fall into Decadence." [NegC] (6:4) Fall 86, p. 22.
"Divorce." [SouthernR] (22:3) Sum 86, p. 546.
"In a Time of Tribulation." [SouthernR] (22:3) Sum 86, p. 549.
"In Extremis in Hardy, Arkansas." [NewEngR] (8:4) Sum 86, p. 455-456.
"Mecanic on Duty at All Times." [KenR] (NS 7:4) Fall 85, p. 76.
"On a Trailways Bus a Man Who Holds His Head Strangely Speaks to the Seat
Beside Him." [Poetry] (148:3) Je 86, p. 157-158.
"One Day a Woman." [KenR] (NS 7:4) Fall 85, p. 75.
"One of Those Rare Occurrences on a City Bus." [KenR] (NS 7:4) Fall 85, p.
75-76.
"The Promotion." [SouthernR] (22:3) Sum 86, p. 547-548.
"Stopping to Look at a Crèche in a Jewelry Store Window . . ." [KenR] (NS 7:4)
Fall 85, p. 77.
"A Summer Afternoon an Old Man Gives Some Thought to the Central Question."
[KenR] (NS 7:4) Fall 85, p. 77-78.
"Tearing Down the Hotel." [Poetry] (148:3) Je 86, p. 156-157.
5753. WILLIAMS, Norman
"The Tremors at Balvano" (6 December 1980). [GeoR] (40:3) Fall 86, p. 823.
5754. WILLIAMS, Phil
"Bones." [CumbPR] (6:1) Fall 86, p. 62.
"Christa." [Poem] (56) N 86, p. 36.
"The Confederate Cemetery in Madison, Georgia." [CumbPR] (6:1) Fall 86, p. 63.
"Flying Dutchman." [Poem] (56) N 86, p. 37.
"Something New." [Poem] (56) N 86, p. 35.
5755. WILLIAMS, Sherley Anne
"Oral History Project." [Callaloo] (9:1, #26) Wint 86, p. 127-129.
5756. WILLIAMS, Susan
"Hitchhiker — December." [SingHM] (13) 86, p. 44-45.
5757. WILLIAMSON, Alan
"The Cats Will Know" (tr. of Cesare Pavese). [AmerPoR] (15:6) N-D 86, p. 9.
"The City." [YaleR] (75:4) Sum 86, p. 591-593.
"I Will Pass through Piazza di Spagna" (tr. of Cesare Pavese). [AmerPoR] (15:6)
N-D 86, p. 9.
5758. WILLIAMSON, Don T.
"Blues for Mr. Monday." [WebR] (11:2) Fall 86, p. 64.
"Leaving Wichita: The Wind." [WebR] (11:1) Spr 86, p. 77.
5759. WILLIAMSON, Janice
"Tell Tale Signs" (No. 12). [Rampike] (5:1) 86, p. 45.
5760. WILLIAMSON, Tharin
"In the Horizons Where the Racing Hills." [HolCrit] (23:1) F 86, p. 18.
5761. WILLSON, Robert
"Latest Dream Research." [NewL] (53:1) Fall 86, p. 75.
5762. WILMARTH, R.
"Memory." [PoeticJ] (14) 86, p. 4.
5763. WILMARTH, Richard
"Bicycle." [YetASM] (4) 85, p. 7.
"Paranoia." [YetASM] (5) 86, p. 9.
5764. WILMER, Clive
"Autumn Breakfast" (tr. of Dezsö Kosztolányi, w. George Gömöri). [Verse] (5) 86,
p. 55.
"Snapshot" (tr. of Zsuzsa Rakovszky, w. George Gömöri). [Verse] (5) 86, p. 56.
"What Man Can Do on This Planet" (tr. of László Kálnoky, w. George Gömöri).
[Verse] (5) 86, p. 55-56.
5765. WILNER, Eleanor
"The Astronomer's Valentine." [AmerPoR] (15:1) Ja-F 86, p. 7.
"Homage to the River" (and to Emily Grosholz). [AmerPoR] (15:1) Ja-F 86, p. 8.
"Improving the Night." [AmerPoR] (15:1) Ja-F 86, p. 8.
"Minor Epic." [AmerPoR] (15:1) Ja-F 86, p. 7.
"Why Are Men So Sad?" [AmerPoR] (15:1) Ja-F 86, p. 6.

5766. WILOCH, Thomas
"Suggestions for the Broken Child." [Bogg] (56) 86, p. 24.
5767. WILSON, Alan R.
"Counting to 100" (Selections: 1-10). [MalR] (76) S 86, p. 92-95.
5768. WILSON, Andrew L.
"Hui-Tsung (1082-1135)." [NewL] (53:1) Fall 86, p. 50.
5769. WILSON, B. H.
"Connections." [StoneC] (13:3/4) Spr-Sum 86, p. 10.
5770. WILSON, Bill
"The Ball." [Sulfur] (6:1, issue 16) 86, p. 31.
"Chosen." [Sulfur] (6:1, issue 16) 86, p. 27.
"Crawler." [Sulfur] (6:1, issue 16) 86, p. 28.
"Crib in the Rock." [Sulfur] (6:1, issue 16) 86, p. 29.
"Poem: Life is like a bobsled run." [Sulfur] (6:1, issue 16) 86, p. 32.
"To Deplane." [Sulfur] (6:1, issue 16) 86, p. 26.
"Tooth of Blond." [Sulfur] (6:1, issue 16) 86, p. 30.
5771. WILSON, Carletta
"Caribbean Gold." [Contact] (8:41/42/43) Fall-Wint 86-87, p. 22.
"This Countryside of Ghetto." [Contact] (8:41/42/43) Fall-Wint 86-87, p. 23.
5772. WILSON, Duane
"Easter Island." [ArizQ] (42:2) Sum 86, p. 140.
5773. WILSON, Harry
"Post Cards from Nicaragua." [Amelia] (3:3) Sum 86, p. 34-35.
5774. WILSON, Miles
"Night Beach Snake." [PoetryNW] (27:1) Spr 86, p. 36-37.
5775. WILSON, Paul
"Spoils." [Event] (15:2) 86, p. 178.
5776. WILSON, Ralph
"The Hesitation Pitch" (for Luis Tiant). [ThRiPo] (27/28) 86, p. 72-73.
"Running the Dog." [ThRiPo] (27/28) 86, p. 71.
5777. WILSON, Robley, Jr.
"Hanging Curtains" (Variations on a Theme of Tolstoy). [Poetry] (148:3) Je 86, p.
142-144.
"Moving Out." [GeoR] (40:3) Fall 86, p. 824.
"Sunday at the Shore." [Poetry] (148:3) Je 86, p. 144-146.
5778. WILSON, Steve
"First, the Auto Shop." [LitR] (30:1) Fall 86, p. 90.
"Thirteen Ahau" (tr. from the Book of Chilam Balam, a Mayan volume of prophecy).
[WebR] (11:1) Spr 86, p. 43.
5779. WILSUN, Don
"Blue Whale Moon." [Contact] (8:41/42/43) Fall-Wint 86-87, p. 10.
5780. WIMP, Jet
"The Discovery of Infinity." [WestB] (19) 86, p. 104-105.
"Seance." [PoetryNW] (27:3) Aut 86, p. 27-28.
5781. WINANS, A. D.
"For J. Whitebird." [CapeR] (21:2) Fall 86, p. 37.
"For Jack Micheline's Poem on Bukowski." [OroM] (4:1-4) My 85, p. 55.
"For Joanie." [YetASM] (4) 85, p. 2.
"Heat Wave." [Abraxas] (34) 86, p. 41.
"I Paid $3 to See Bukowski Read." [OroM] (4:1-4) My 85, p. 39-41.
"Saint Anthony's." [Abraxas] (34) 86, p. 40.
5782. WINBURN, Rae
"Morning." [Amelia] (3:1) Ja 86, p. 82.
"Night Chant." [Bogg] (56) 86, p. 11.
WINCKEL, Nance van
See Van WINCKEL, Nance
5783. WINDER, Barbara D.
"The Destroying Angel." [KanQ] (18:4) Fall 86, p. 154.
5784. WINDSOR, Cooley
"Prayers and Voices That Pray" (to Maura Stanton). [AmerPoR] (15:3) My-Je 86, p.
33-41.
"Saving Lot" (for Robert Castleberry). [BlackWR] (12:2) Spr 86, p. 51-52.
"The Workhouse" (for Roger Mitchell, with thanks). [IndR] (9:2) Spr 86, p. 48-49.
5785. WING, Linda
"For Julie Waiting Tables." [RagMag] (5:1) Spr 86, p. 10.
"Hot." [RagMag] (5:1) Spr 86, p. 11.

"In the Spirit." [RagMag] (5:1) Spr 86, p. 12-13.
WING, Tek Lum
    See LUM, Wing Tek
5786. WINGRAVE, Ariel Celeste
    "Psalm of South Africa." [Sam] (44:2 release 174) 86, p. 57.
5787. WINN, Howard
    "Winter Accident." [BallSUF] (27:4) Aut 86, p. 9.
5788. WINTER, Jonah
    "Childhood." [Field] (35) Fall 86, p. 102.
    "The Peaceable Kingdom." [Field] (35) Fall 86, p. 100-101.
    "Still Lives." [Field] (35) Fall 86, p. 99.
5789. WINWOOD, David
    "Sow." [ForidaR] (14:1) Spr-Sum 86, p. 59.
5790. WISCHNER, Claudia March
    "The Baba Yaga Poems." [Nimrod] (30:1) Fall-Wint 86, p. 61-68.
    "The First Year." [KanQ] (18:1/2) Wint-Spr 86, p. 282.
    "Her Reverie." [PennR] (2:1) Fall-Wint 86, p. 89.
5791. WITHERUP, William
    "Promontory: San Quentin: 6/11/84." [Abraxas] (34) 86, p. 25.
5792. WITT, Harold
    "American Lit: Moby." [WebR] (11:1) Spr 86, p. 75.
    "American Lit: Of Mice and Men." [NewL] (52:2/3) Wint-Spr 86, p. 163.
    "Ars Poetica." [CharR] (12:1) Spr 86, p. 87.
    "McTeague." [CharR] (12:1) Spr 86, p. 88.
    "Montreux Mit Musik." [LitR] (29:2) Wint 86, p. 176.
    "More Fair." [KanQ] (18:1/2) Wint-Spr 86, p. 37.
    "The Scarlet Letter." [CharR] (12:1) Spr 86, p. 87-88.
    "Strange, in a Beesmelling Dream." [Hudson] (38:4) Wint 86, p. 636.
    "The Sun Also Rises." [CharR] (12:1) Spr 86, p. 88.
    "A Tarzan." [WritersF] (12) Fall 86, p. 77.
    "A Vampire." [WritersF] (12) Fall 86, p. 77-78.
5793. WITTE, John
    "To the Poet, Mei Yao-ch'en." [Ploughs] (12:4) 86, p. 114.
    "Ultrasound." [Ploughs] (12:4) 86, p. 112.
    "With Child." [Ploughs] (12:4) 86, p. 113.
5794. WITTLINGER, Ellen
    "The Responsibility of the Hero." [MinnR] (NS 27) Fall 86, p. 85-86.
5795. WOESSNER, Warren
    "Wet Spring." [Abraxas] (34) 86, p. 29.
WOFFORD, Jan Bailey
    See BAILEY-WOFFORD, Jan
5796. WOJAHN, David
    "Dates, for Example." [NewEngR] (8:3) Spr 86, p. 332-333.
    "For Charles Bovary." [Sonora] (10) Spr 86, p. 11-12.
    "Grillework" (New Orleans, 1981). [QW] (23) 86, p. 58-60.
    "Lot's Wife." [MissouriR] (9:1) 85-86, p. 42-43.
    "The Paris Cinema." [Sonora] (10) Spr 86, p. 10.
    "Particular Words" (for Richard Hugo). [Crazy] (31) Fall 86, p. 30-31.
    "Pentecost." [Poetry] (148:2) My 86, p. 94-95.
    "Santorini." [NewEngR] (8:3) Spr 86, p. 330-331.
    "Song of the Burning" (Jim Morrison). [Crazy] (31) Fall 86, p. 27-29.
    "Students" (Port Townsend, Washington). [SenR] (16:2) 86, p. 67-68.
5797. WOLCOTT, Jamie
    "Drawing Off." [PoetL] (81:1) Spr 86, p. 46-47.
5798. WOLF, Carol E.
    "The Cookbook" (for Jean Tucker). [Amelia] (3:1) Ja 86, p. 66.
5799. WOLF, Janis T. B.
    "Allelic Diversity at Home." [Kaleid] (13) Sum-Fall 86, p. 58.
    "Cygnet Song." [Kaleid] (13) Sum-Fall 86, p. 58.
    "Rehabilitation Blues." [Kaleid] (13) Sum-Fall 86, p. 57.
5800. WOLFE, Ellen
    "Bodies of Water." [Nimrod] (30:1) Fall-Wint 86, p. 117.
5801. WOLFF, Daniel
    "All down, drowned and wasted." [PartR] (53:4) 86, p. 583-584.
    "All the ingredients of violence." [AnotherCM] (16) 86, p. 115.
    "Cigarettes, pop songs, TV, billboards." [AnotherCM] (16) 86, p. 117.

"A Great Prince in Prison Lies" (— John Donne, *The Extasie*). [Thrpny] (27) Fall 86, p. 8.
"I see what I think is a shadow inside." [GrandS] (5:3) Spr 86, p. 68.
"Interest-bearing, brilliant sun." [AnotherCM] (16) 86, p. 116.
"So looking through the dusty air." [GrandS] (5:3) Spr 86, p. 68.
"Sonnet: And if it worked, what?" [Thrpny] (25) Spr 86, p. 5.
"There's the form of the House." [GrandS] (5:3) Spr 86, p. 67.
"We're a false color." [ParisR] (28:101) Wint 86, p. 268.
5802. WOLFF, Rebecca
"Run Catch Kiss." [HangL] (49) Spr 86, p. 66.
"Seduction Theory." [HangL] (49) Spr 86, p. 65-66.
"Sleephood." [HangL] (49) Spr 86, p. 64.
5803. WOLLACH, Yona
"Drawing Nearer" (tr. by Warren Bargad). [PoetL] (81:2) Sum 86, p. 115.
"I Couldn't" (tr. by Warren Bargad). [PoetL] (81:2) Sum 86, p. 116.
5804. WOLYNN, Mark
"Nothing But Snow." [NewYorker] (61:49) 27 Ja 86, p. 40.
5805. WOO, Merle
"The Subversive" (for Nellie Wong). [Contact] (7:38/39/40) Wint-Spr 86, p. 41.
5806. WOOD, Harriett
"Under the Seed." [InterPR] (12:2) Fall 86, p. 75.
5807. WOOD, Monica
"Grace." [AmerS] (55:3) Sum 86, p. 348.
5808. WOOD, Renate
"Before School." [AmerPoR] (15:4) Jl-Ag 86, p. 3.
"The Button." [AmerPoR] (15:4) Jl-Ag 86, p. 3.
"Cabbages." [AmerPoR] (15:4) Jl-Ag 86, p. 4.
"First Love." [AmerPoR] (15:4) Jl-Ag 86, p. 5.
"The Landing." [AmerPoR] (15:4) Jl-Ag 86, p. 3.
"Landscape with Cat." [AmerPoR] (15:4) Jl-Ag 86, p. 4.
"The Mound of Eggs" (For B.). [AmerPoR] (15:4) Jl-Ag 86, p. 6.
"The Pig." [AmerPoR] (15:4) Jl-Ag 86, p. 5.
"The Pilot." [AmerPoR] (15:4) Jl-Ag 86, p. 6.
"Solitaire." [AmerPoR] (15:4) Jl-Ag 86, p. 6.
"The Suitcase." [AmerPoR] (15:4) Jl-Ag 86, p. 5.
"The Woman Who Wanted No Comfort." [AmerPoR] (15:4) Jl-Ag 86, p. 4.
5809. WOOD, Robert E.
"Circus Accident." [Wind] (16:58) 86, p. 43.
"The Prodigal Daughter." [Wind] (16:58) 86, p. 43.
5810. WOOD, Susan
"Campo Santo." [MissouriR] (9:2) 86, p. 30-32.
"Dear Everyone." [MissouriR] (9:2) 86, p. 196.
"Distances." [Poetry] (148:6) S 86, p. 324-327.
"Eggs" (For Steve Dunn). [Poetry] (148:6) S 86, p. 323-324.
"Hollow." [MissouriR] (9:2) 86, p. 194-195.
"Late-Bloomers" (For Caitlin). [Poetry] (148:6) S 86, p. 321-322.
"A Woman and Her Car." [FloridaR] (14:2) Fall-Wint 86, p. 108.
5811. WOODARD, Deborah
"In This Silence." [CarolQ] (39:1) Fall 86, p. 22.
"Now I Wear." [CarolQ] (39:1) Fall 86, p. 21.
"Time" (tr. of Antonia Pozzi). [ColR] (NS 13:1) Fall 85, p. 45.
5812. WOODRUFF, Jennifer Lynn
"My eyes can see your wrecked body" ("Untitled"). [PikeF] (7) Spr 86, p. 20.
5813. WOODS, Christopher
"Night Cafes." [CrossCur] (5:4/6:1) 86, p. 109.
"North Sea Galley Duty." [Confr] (32) Spr-Sum 86, p. 61.
"A Place between Mountains." [PoeticJ] (14) 86, p. 25.
5814. WOODS, John
"After the Late Riots." [PoetryNW] (27:4) Wint 86-87, p. 8.
"The Birthmark." [PoetryNW] (27:4) Wint 86-87, p. 10.
"The Fourth Morning in September" (for Dave Pugh, 1986). [PoetryNW] (27:3) Aut 86, p. 3-4.
"The Karma Cycle." [Field] (35) Fall 86, p. 86.
"Long Days and Changing Weather." [PoetryNW] (27:3) Aut 86, p. 4-5.
"Poetry Seen As the Shuffling of Stones." [PoetryNW] (27:4) Wint 86-87, p. 9-10.
"The Religion of Snow." [Field] (35) Fall 86, p. 87.

"Thing Love." [Field] (35) Fall 86, p. 85.
5815. WOODS, Phil
"Fort Rock." [NowestR] (24:1) 86, p. 26.
5816. WOODS-PATTERSON, Bruce
"Living next door to desperation" ("Untitled"). [JamesWR] (3:4) Sum 86, p. 5.
5817. WOODS-SMITH, Sybil
"Treatment." [CumbPR] (5:2) Spr 86, p. 15-17.
5818. WOODWARD, Tom
"They told her how, upon St. Agnes' Eve." [NegC] (6:1) Wint 86, p. 8.
5819. WOODY, Elizabeth
"A Warrior and the Glass Prisoners." [Contact] (8:41/42/43) Fall-Wint 86-87, p. 70-73.
5820. WORLEY, Jeff
"After the Move to South Clifton, 1965." [ColEng] (48:1) Ja 86, p. 42.
"Cornucopia." [CutB] (25) Fall-Wint 86, p. 30.
"High Noon." [MidAR] (6:1) 86?, p. 106-107.
"Interview." [WritersF] (12) Fall 86, p. 221-222.
"The Rookie Gets a Hit." [WestB] (18) 86, p. 64.
"The Valedictorian, Lost and Broken Down on His Way to the 20-Year Reunion." [WebR] (11:1) Spr 86, p. 74-75.
"Voyeur." [PoetL] (80:4) Wint 86, p. 215-217.
5821. WORMHOUDT, Sarah M.
"Geranium and Bones." [Poem] (55) Mr 86, p. 16.
"Landscape." [Poem] (55) Mr 86, p. 18.
"Venezia! Venezia!" [Poem] (55) Mr 86, p. 17.
5822. WORMSER, Baron
"1967." [ParisR] (28:100) Sum-Fall 86, p. 333.
"Delmore Schwartz." [ManhatR] (4:1) Fall 86, p. 6-7.
"Great Minds." [ManhatR] (4:1) Fall 86, p. 5-6.
"Homage to Thomas Eakins." [ManhatR] (4:1) Fall 86, p. 10.
"Intellectual Beauty." [ManhatR] (4:1) Fall 86, p. 7.
"James Dean" (for Maisie and Owen). [ManhatR] (4:1) Fall 86, p. 8.
"A Reply to the Journalist Who Informed the Russian People in *Izvestia* That There Was No Santa Claus." [Poetry] (149:3) D 86, p. 149.
"Social Security." [ManhatR] (4:1) Fall 86, p. 8-9.
"Starting the First Fire, Autumn" (for Janet). [YaleR] (75:4) Sum 86, p. 589.
5823. WOROZBYT, Theodore, Jr.
"Canteen." [KanQ] (18:4) Fall 86, p. 101.
"Lunch in Nancy Creek Park." [NegC] (6:4) Fall 86, p. 88-89.
"Okra." [CarolQ] (39:1) Fall 86, p. 4.
"The Pecans." [NowestR] (24:1) 86, p. 25.
5824. WORTH, Douglas
"April 14." [CrabCR] (3:2) Spr 86, p. 26-27.
"Peace Maker" (for Daniel Berrigan). [NewL] (52:2/3) Wint-Spr 86, p. 126-137.
5825. WORTH, Jan
"My Father Gives Me Stilts." [PassN] (7:2) Spr-Sum 86, p. 8.
5826. WRAY, Bettye K.
"Sitting on the Steps of Arlington" (An Ante-bellum Home). [Amelia] (3:1) Ja 86, p. 87.
5827. WREGGITT, Andrew
"Ceremony of Brown Bottles." [Event] (15:1) 86, p. 20-21.
"Going Down the Highway Backwards." [AntigR] (64) Wint 86, p. 123-124.
"Killer Whales in the Harbour." [Event] (15:1) 86, p. 26.
"Smiles Cafe." [Event] (15:1) 86, p. 24-25.
"Southeasterly" (for Randy Morrison). [CanLit] (111) Wint 86, p. 7-9.
"This Is How Poor You Are." [Event] (15:1) 86, p. 22-23.
5828. WREN, Brian
"Sing Praise to God Who Reigns Above." [ChrC] (103:14) 23 Ap 86, p. 413.
5829. WRIGHT, A. J.
"Heartblade." [YetASM] (4) 85, p. 5.
"Miranda's Hands." [Poem] (56) N 86, p. 20.
5830. WRIGHT, Anyon
"On Table Mountain." [PottPort] (8) 86-87, p. 45.
5831. WRIGHT, C. D.
"Carla." [PoetryE] (20/21) Fall 86, p. 166.
"The Lesson." [ThRiPo] (27/28) 86, p. 74.

"Slag." [PoetryE] (20/21) Fall 86, p. 165.
5832. WRIGHT, Carolyne
"Closing the Circle" (for Harriet Pappas). [IndR] (9:1) Wint 86, p. 84-85.
"Eulene Enters the Me Generation." [WillowS] (17) Wint 86, p. 14-15.
"Eulene Stays the Course." [WillowS] (17) Wint 86, p. 12-13.
"The Exorcisms" (tr. of Jorge Teillier). [AmerV] (5) Wint 86, p. 37.
"Exurban Spell." [MichQR] (25:3) Sum 86, p. 506-507.
"Heat Wave: Liberty, Missouri." [MissouriR] (9:2) 86, p. 44-45.
"Historical Site." [VirQR] (62:4) Aut 86, p. 601-602.
"Love Affair in a Small Town." [Poetry] (148:4) Jl 86, p. 209-211.
"Post-Revolutionary Letter." [Poetry] (148:4) Jl 86, p. 208-209.
"Return to Seattle: Bastille Day." [Poetry] (148:4) Jl 86, p. 211-212.
"Return to Sender." [PennR] (2:1) Fall-Wint 86, p. 35-36.
"Return to Sender?" [WillowS] (17) Wint 86, p. 16-17.
"Victor Jara (1938-1973)." [Poetry] (148:4) Jl 86, p. 213-214.
5833. WRIGHT, Charles
"Autumn Firestorm." [NewYorker] (62:36) 27 O 86, p. 40.
"From a Journal of the Year of the Ox." [NewYorker] (62:24) 4 Ag 86, p. 26-27.
"From a Journal of the Year of the Ox." [YaleR] (76:1) Aut 86, p. 46-48.
"A Journal of the Year of the Ox" (2 selections). [OP] (42/43) Wint 86-87, p. 64-71.
"A Journal of the Year of the Ox" (Excerpts). [Ploughs] (12:3) 86, p. 42-46.
"A Journal of the Year of the Ox" (Selections). [ParisR] (28:100) Sum-Fall 86, p. 334-337.
5834. WRIGHT, D. J.
"Pressure / Relief." [InterPR] (12:2) Fall 86, p. 70.
"What a Relief It Is." [InterPR] (12:2) Fall 86, p. 70.
5835. WRIGHT, Dorothy Winslow
"In Loggers' Wake." [ManhatPR] (8) Wint 86-87, p. 23.
"Mauna Ulu." [ManhatPR] (8) Wint 86-87, p. 23.
5836. WRIGHT, Franz
"The Talk." [Ploughs] (12:3) 86, p. 102.
"To the Hawk." [ParisR] (28:100) Sum-Fall 86, p. 338.
"Winter Entries." [Ploughs] (12:3) 86, p. 101.
5837. WRIGHT, Harold
"At the Public Bath" (tr. of Rin Ishigaki). [Translation] (17) Fall 86, p. 13.
"Drawing a Picture" (tr. of Shuntaro Tanikawa). [Translation] (17) Fall 86, p. 61-66.
"In the Stomachs of One Hundred Persons" (tr. of Rin Ishigaki). [Translation] (17) Fall 86, p. 10.
"Land & House" (tr. of Rin Ishigaki). [Translation] (17) Fall 86, p. 14.
"Song" (tr. of Rin Ishigaki). [Translation] (17) Fall 86, p. 11.
"Tsuetsuki Pass" (tr. of Rin Ishigaki). [Translation] (17) Fall 86, p. 12.
5838. WRIGHT, James
"Honey." [GeoR] (40:3) Fall 86, p. 827.
"To the Cicada" (Anacreon). [GeoR] (40:3) Fall 86, p. 825-827.
5839. WRIGHT, Jay
"Ann Street." [Callaloo] (9:2, #27) Spr 86, p. 309.
"Dandelion." [Callaloo] (9:2, #27) Spr 86, p. 313.
"Guadalajara." [Callaloo] (9:1, #26) Wint 86, p. 140-141.
"Guadalupe - Tonantzin." [Callaloo] (9:1, #26) Wint 86, p. 131-137.
"Orchid." [Callaloo] (9:2, #27) Spr 86, p. 311-312.
"Passionflower." [Callaloo] (9:2, #27) Spr 86, p. 310.
"Tlazoltéotl." [Callaloo] (9:1, #26) Wint 86, p. 138-139.
5840. WRIGHT, Jeffrey
"Okay So Make Me an Offer." [LittleM] (15:1) 86, p. 56.
"Old Score." [LittleM] (15:1) 86, p. 54.
"Play Along." [LittleM] (15:1) 86, p. 55-56.
5841. WRIGHT, T. M.
"Desserts." [WritersL] (1986:6), p. 16.
5842. WRIGLEY, Robert
"Apology." [KenR] (NS 7:2) Spr 85, p. 70.
"The Big Dipper." [MissouriR] (9:2) 86, p. 204.
"The Chore." [Iowa] (16:2) Spr-Sum 86, p. 58-50.
"The Crèche." [KenR] (NS 7:2) Spr 85, p. 69-70.
"Fixing the Window." [Iowa] (16:2) Spr-Sum 86, p. 58.
"Flight." [YellowS] (19) Sum 86, p. 38.

399

"Man with Lantern, Approaching" (from a painting, anonymous, circa 1920). [Iowa]
(16:2) Spr-Sum 86, p. 62.
"Parking." [Iowa] (16:2) Spr-Sum 86, p. 57-58.
"Steelhead" (in memoriam: R.H.). [CutB] (25) Fall-Wint 86, p. 17.
"Tapers." [Iowa] (16:2) Spr-Sum 86, p. 60-61.
5843. WRONSKY, Gail
"The Almost Live and Frightened Woman" (Selections, for Leonora Carrington).
[VirQR] (62:1) Wint 86, p. 38-41.
5844. WYATT, David
"Entry" (poem beginning with a line by Czeslaw Milosz). [NowestR] (24:2) 86, p.
17.
5845. WYNAND, Derk
"Heat Wave." [CanLit] (109) Sum 86, p. 55-56.
"Heat Wave." [Quarry] (35:3) Sum 86, p. 24-25.
"Heat Waves." [MalR] (74) Mr 86, p. 75-86.
5846. XI, Chuan
"I Don't Need It" (tr. of Bei Ling, w. Tony Barnstone). [Nimrod] (29:2) Spr-Sum
86, p. 94.
"Joan Miro" (tr. by Bert Stern and the author). [Nimrod] (29:2) Spr-Sum 86, p. 78.
"There Beyond the River" (tr. by Tony Barnstone and the author). [Nimrod] (29:2)
Spr-Sum 86, p. 70.
"To Jeffers" (tr. of Bei Ling, w. Tony Barnstone). [Nimrod] (29:2) Spr-Sum 86, p.
95.
"Twilight Has No Voice" (tr. of Bei Ling, w. Tony Barnstone). [Nimrod] (29:2)
Spr-Sum 86, p. 93.
5847. XIA, Mingshan
"Small Path" (tr. of Sun Jin-xuan, w. Xu Yaoping and Francine Ringold). [Nimrod]
(29:2) Spr-Sum 86, p. 36.
5848. XIN, Di
"Butterfly, Bee, and Evergreen Trees" (tr. by Wang Xin-Di). [Verse] (6) 86, p. 46.
XIN-DI, Wang
See WANG, Xin-Di
XING, Gu Zhong
See GU, Zhong Xing
5849. XU, Haixin
"Suffering from Heat" (tr. of Wang Wei, w. Tony Barnstone and Willis Barnstone).
[Nimrod] (29:2) Spr-Sum 86, p. 20.
"Visiting the Mountain Courtyard . . ." (tr. of Wang Wei, w. Tony Barnstone and
Willis Barnstone). [Nimrod] (29:2) Spr-Sum 86, p. 23.
"Weeping for Ying Yao" (tr. of Wang Wei, w. Tony Barnstone and Willis
Barnstone). [Nimrod] (29:2) Spr-Sum 86, p. 22.
"Written When Climbing the City Tower . . ." (tr. of Wang Wei, w. Tony Barnstone
and Willis Barnstone). [Nimrod] (29:2) Spr-Sum 86, p. 23.
5850. XU, Yaoping
"Autumn" (tr. of Sun Jin-xuan, w. Manly Johnson). [Nimrod] (29:2) Spr-Sum 86,
p. 37.
"Small Path" (tr. of Sun Jin-xuan, w. Xia Mingshan and Francine Ringold).
[Nimrod] (29:2) Spr-Sum 86, p. 36.
"The Winter Snow" (tr. of Sun Jin-xuan, w. Manly Johnson). [Nimrod] (29:2)
Spr-Sum 86, p. 38.
5851. YAGI, Jukichi
"My Father" (tr. by James Kirkup and Akiko Takemoto). [Translation] (17) Fall 86,
p. 191.
"One Day" (tr. by James Kirkup and Akiko Takemoto). [Translation] (17) Fall 86, p.
190.
"Rain" (tr. by James Kirkup and Akiko Takemoto). [Translation] (17) Fall 86, p.
191.
"Sorrow" (tr. by James Kirkup and Akiko Takemoto). [Translation] (17) Fall 86, p.
190.
"Sorrow Piling Up Within Me" (tr. by James Kirkup and Akiko Takemoto).
[Translation] (17) Fall 86, p. 190.
5852. YAGUCHI, Yorifumi
"From the Afterworld" (tr. of Sachiko Yoshihara, w. William Stafford). [Field] (33)
Fall 85, p. 71-72.

5853. YALIM, Ozcan
"In Prison" (tr. of Ahmet Arif, w. William Fielder & Dionis Riggs). [InterPR] (12:1)
Spr 86, p. 65.
"Such Love" (tr. of Attilâ Ilhan, w. Dionis Coffin Riggs and William Fielder).
[StoneC] (14:1/2) Fall-Wint 86-87, p. 16.
5854. YAMAMOTO, Doug
"From Ridgetop to Ridgetop." [Contact] (7:38/39/40) Wint-Spr 86, p. 76.
5855. YAMASATO, Rafael
"Farewell." [Contact] (7:38/39/40) Wint-Spr 86, Supplement p. 22.
"Farewell" (tr. by J. Jacinto, V. Sales-Gomez & J. Tagami). [Contact] (7:38/39/40)
Wint-Spr 86, Supplement p. 22.
"Imitacion de Watanabe." [Contact] (7:38/39/40) Wint-Spr 86, Supplement p. 23.
"Imitation of Watanabe" (tr. by J. Jacinto, V. Sales-Gomez & J. Tagami). [Contact]
(7:38/39/40) Wint-Spr 86, Supplement p. 23.
"La Nieve y el Estambre." [Contact] (7:38/39/40) Wint-Spr 86, Supplement p. 21.
"Noriko." [Contact] (7:38/39/40) Wint-Spr 86, Supplement p. 18-19.
"Noriko" (tr. by J. Jacinto, V. Sales-Gomez & J. Tagami). [Contact] (7:38/39/40)
Wint-Spr 86, Supplement p. 16-17.
"Pozo de los Deseos." [Contact] (7:38/39/40) Wint-Spr 86, Supplement p. 19.
"The Snow and the Male Flower" (tr. by J. Jacinto, V. Sales-Gomez & J. Tagami).
[Contact] (7:38/39/40) Wint-Spr 86, Supplement p. 21.
"Well of Desires" (tr. by J. Jacinto, V. Sales-Gomez & J. Tagami). [Contact]
(7:38/39/40) Wint-Spr 86, Supplement p. 20.
5856. YAMASHITA, Karen Tei
"Banzai" (tr. of Roberto Yutaka Sagawa). [Contact] (7:38/39/40) Wint-Spr 86,
Supplement p. 36.
"Coming from the Other Continent" (tr. of Roberto Yutaka Sagawa). [Contact]
(7:38/39/40) Wint-Spr 86, Supplement p. 39.
"Fifth-Column" (tr. of Roberto Yutaka Sagawa). [Contact] (7:38/39/40) Wint-Spr
86, Supplement p. 34.
"Midwifs." [Contact] (7:38/39/40) Wint-Spr 86, p. 29.
"Portrait of Myself" (tr. of Roberto Yutaka Sagawa). [Contact] (7:38/39/40)
Wint-Spr 86, Supplement p. 37.
"Who Is Who?" (tr. of Roberto Yutaka Sagawa). [Contact] (7:38/39/40) Wint-Spr
86, Supplement p. 38.
"Yoko" (tr. of Roberto Yutaka Sagawa). [Contact] (7:38/39/40) Wint-Spr 86,
Supplement p. 40.
5857. YAMRUS, John
"Every Time." [Bogg] (55) 86, p. 12.
YAÑEZ, Juan José Irarrazabal
See IRARRAZABAL YAÑEZ, Juan José
5858. YANG, Mu
"The Calm: Ars Poetica." [Caliban] (1) 86, p. 57.
"Prophecy." [Caliban] (1) 86, p. 56.
5859. YANNONE, Denise Stamp
"The Mirror's Other Side." [CrossCur] (5:4/6:1) 86, p. 124.
YANXIANG, Shao
See SHAO, Yanxiang
YAOPING, Xu
See XU, Yaoping
5860. YARALIAN, Sevag
"The Card Players." [Poetry] (147:4) Ja 86, p. 196-197.
"Winter Rain." [Poetry] (147:4) Ja 86, p. 198.
5861. YARMAL, Ann
"Port Antonio (Jamaica)." [YetASM] (4) 85, p. 4.
5862. YARROW, Susan
"Believing in the World" (Selections). [MalR] (73) Ja 86, p. 97.
"I(sabelle) in Love." [MalR] (73) Ja 86, p. 95.
"Where Anyone Can Come to Eat." [MalR] (73) Ja 86, p. 96.
5863. YASUTOME, Kay
"Two Runs." [Kaleid] (12) Wint 86, p. 24.
5864. YATES, J. Michael
"Centre." [WestCR] (20:4) Ap 86, p. 14.
"Deer Lake." [WestCR] (20:4) Ap 86, p. 15-18.
"The Queen Charlotte Islands Meditations" (Selections: 63, 76-79). [GreenFR]
(13:3/4) Sum-Fall 86, p. 213-215.

401

YAU

5865. YAU, John
"All This Changing Trouble Luck and Suddenness." [Sulfur] (6:2, issue 17) 86, p. 39.
"Double Feature." [Notus] (1:1) Fall 86, p. 53.
"Double Feature (2)." [Notus] (1:1) Fall 86, p. 54.
"Dragon's Blood" (1-4). [Sulfur] (6:2, issue 17) 86, p. 40-42.
"Faded Crossbow." [Notus] (1:1) Fall 86, p. 55.
"For You." [Notus] (1:1) Fall 86, p. 56.
"No One Ever Kissed Anna May Wong." [Notus] (1:1) Fall 86, p. 57.
"Seance Music." [Sulfur] (6:2, issue 17) 86, p. 39-40.
"Three Poems from Li Ho." [Contact] (7:38/39/40) Wint-Spr 86, p. 40.
"Two Voices for Li Ho." [Contact] (7:38/39/40) Wint-Spr 86, p. 40.
YBARRA, Ricardo Means
    See MEANS-YBARRA, Ricardo
5866. YEASTING, J. E.
"Ken Cloud and His Orchestra Play Their Best." [Contact] (8:41/42/43) Fall-Wint 86-87, p. 11.
5867. YELIN, Shulamis
"Gaston Miron Reads." [Quarry] (35:3) Sum 86, p. 34-35.
5868. YENSER, Pamela
"Holiday Blues." [Ascent] (12:1) 86, p. 25.
"Provisions." [PoetryNW] (27:1) Spr 86, p. 27-28.
5869. YERBURGH, Rhoda
"Amaryllis." [StoneC] (14:1/2) Fall-Wint 86-87, p. 14.
"A Casual Alien Orthography." [ManhatPR] (7) Sum 86, p. 29.
5870. YEVTUSHENKO, Yevgeny
"Disbelief in Yourself Is Indispensable" (tr. by Albert Todd). [NegC] (6:4) Fall 86, p. 9-10.
"Fuku" (Fragment, tr. by Antonina W. Bouis). [Nat] (242:11) 22 Mr 86, p. 365.
5871. YONATAN, Natan (YONATHAN, Natan)
"Another Song on Absalom" (tr. by Karen Alkalay-Gut). [PoetL] (81:2) Sum 86, p. 90.
"Terminal" (tr. by Karen Alkalay-Gut). [MassR] (27:2) Sum 86, p. 198-199.
YORIFUMI, Yaguchi
    See YAGUCHI, Yorifumi
5872. YOSANO, Akiko
"A face bare of rouge" (tr. by Laurel Rodd). [RedBass] (10) 86, p. 20.
"An Instant" (tr. by Laurel Rodd). [RedBass] (10) 86, p. 20.
"Sozorogoto" (Excerpt, tr. by Laurel Rodd). [RedBass] (10) 86, p. 20.
"Tangled Hair: Poems" (In Japanese & English, tr. by Dennis Maloney and Hide Oshiro). [YellowS] (18) Spr 86, p. 24-25.
5873. YOSEF, Hamutal bar
"Kitchen Table" (tr. by Shirley Kaufman, w. Rivka Ma'oz). [PoetL] (81:2) Sum 86, p. 97.
"Palestine" (tr. by Shirley Kaufman, w. Rivka Ma'oz). [PoetL] (81:2) Sum 86, p. 97.
5874. YOSHIDA, Junko
"A Cruel End to My Desire" (tr. of Masao Nonagase). [KenR] (NS 7:1) Wint 85, p. 34-35.
"Envoy" (tr. of Masao Nonagase). [KenR] (NS 7:1) Wint 85, p. 36.
"A Japanese Old Couple" (from Old Age Blues in the Sunset, tr. of Masao Nonagase). [WebR] (11:2) Fall 86, p. 20-24.
"My Daughter and I" (tr. of Masao Nonagase). [KenR] (NS 7:1) Wint 85, p. 35.
"The Vestiges of Passion" (tr. of Masao Nonagase). [KenR] (NS 7:1) Wint 85, p. 36.
5875. YOSHIHARA, Sachiko
"Appetite" (tr. by James Kirkup and Akiko Takemoto). [Translation] (17) Fall 86, p. 207.
"From the Afterworld" (tr. by Yorifumi Yaguchi and William Stafford). [Field] (33) Fall 85, p. 71-72.
"The Name" (tr. by James Kirkup and Akiko Takemoto). [Translation] (17) Fall 86, p. 206.
5876. YOSHIOKA, Minoru
"Kusudama" (tr. by Eric Selland). [Temblor] (4) 86, p. 161-162.
"Mother" (tr. by Eric Selland). [Temblor] (4) 86, p. 163-164.
"Pilgrimage" (tr. by Eric Selland). [Temblor] (4) 86, p. 158-160.

5877. YOTS, Michael
"The Builders." [Wind] (16:57) 86, p. 41.
"The Veteran." [Wind] (16:57) 86, p. 41-42.
5878. YOUMANS, Marlene
"Inside the Village Limits." [Blueline] (8:1) Sum-Fall 86, p. 25.
"The Retreat." [SoCaR] (18:2) Spr 86, p. 112.
"Scene with Cows." [SoCaR] (18:2) Spr 86, p. 113.
"Spring Melt." [CrescentR] (4:1) Spr 86, p. 38.
5879. YOUMANS, Rich
"Landslide." [JINJPo] (9:1) 86, p. 26.
5880. YOUNG, Al
"22 Moon Poems" (Selections: 20-21). [Ploughs] (12:3) 86, p. 66-68.
"Invitation" (In memory of Papa Jo Jones & Philly Joe Jones). [Callaloo] (9:1, #26)
    Wint 86, p. 142-143.
"Invitation" (In memory of Papa Jo Jones & Philly Joe Jones). [Zyzzyva] (2:2) Sum
    86, p. 78-79.
5881. YOUNG, Bernard
"American Poem." [Bogg] (56) 86, p. 9.
5882. YOUNG, David
"Crush Syndrome" (tr. of Miroslav Holub, w. the author). [Field] (33) Fall 85, p.
    77.
"Hemophilia" (tr. of Miroslav Holub, w. the author). [Field] (33) Fall 85, p. 80-81.
"Vanishing Lung Syndrome" (tr. of Miroslav Holub, w. the author). [Field] (33)
    Fall 85, p. 78-79.
5883. YOUNG, Dean
"Catalogues." [NowestR] (24:2) 86, p. 13-14.
"Design with X's." [IndR] (9:1) Wint 86, p. 86.
"Shallows." [ManhatPR] (8) Wint 86-87, p. 57.
"Trace Elements." [PoetryNW] (27:3) Aut 86, p. 31-32.
"Wind." [PoetryNW] (27:3) Aut 86, p. 32-33.
5884. YOUNG, Frederic
"Actaeon: the Last Breath." [ManhatPR] (6) Wint-Spr 85-86, p. 20.
"Lilies." [ManhatPR] (6) Wint-Spr 85-86, p. 19.
"Oration: against Long Walls." [ManhatPR] (6) Wint-Spr 85-86, p. 18-19.
5885. YOUNG, Gary, C.R.
"Solatio." [EngJ] (75:3) Mr 86, p. 82.
5886. YOUNG, George
"Camping at Pawnee Grasslands." [Wind] (16:58) 86, p. 44-45.
5887. YOUNG, Mary Brownsberger
"Matins." [ChrC] (103:9) 12 Mr 86, p. 270.
5888. YOUNG, Patricia
"After Breakfast." [Dandel] (13:1) Spr-Sum 86, p. 27.
"All I Ever Needed Was a Beautiful Room" (Selections). [Quarry] (35:1) Wint 86, p.
    15-19.
"Before My Time." [PraF] (7:2) Sum 86, p. 15.
"Either or Both, Your Fathers." [PraF] (7:2) Sum 86, p. 14.
"Grandmother." [AntigR] (65) Spr 86, p. 80.
"Julia." [Event] (15:1) 86, p. 107-108.
"Sasha." [Event] (15:1) 86, p. 108-109.
"Topanga Canyon." [PraF] (7:2) Sum 86, p. 13.
5889. YOUNG, Ree
"Mountain Dream." [Wind] (16:58) 86, p. 26.
5890. YOUNG, Roberta
"The Meaning of Life: Student Level." [EngJ] (75:2) F 86, p. 57.
5891. YOUNG, Sheldon"
"Haiku" (2 poems). [AntigR] (64) Wint 86, p. 24.
5892. YOUNG, Tom
"Christmas Whispered" (for David and Kevin). [JamesWR] (3:2) Wint 86, p. 5.
"Tubs." [JamesWR] (3:2) Wint 86, p. 8.
5893. YOUNG, Virginia Brady
"Connecticut State Law." [WestCR] (20:4) Ap 86, p. 32.
"Gregorian Chants." [WestCR] (20:4) Ap 86, p. 31.
"The Letters of Fanny Brawne." [WestCR] (20:4) Ap 86, p. 34-38.
"Thinking in Oblique." [WestCR] (20:4) Ap 86, p. 33.
5894. YOUNG, William
"The Mountain Cantos" (Selection: 14). [MidAR] (6:2) 86, p. 123-124.

YOUNGS, Anne Ohman
    See OHMAN-YOUNGS, Anne
5895. YU, Han
    "Rebellion" (tr. by Carolyn Kizer). [TarRP] (25:2) Spr 86, p. 8-9.
5896. YUAN, Mei
    "Fog at Liang-Hsiang" (tr. by Jonathan Chaves). [Translation] (17) Fall 86, p. 331.
    "The Next Day the Fog Was Even Worse" (tr. by Jonathan Chaves). [Translation]
        (17) Fall 86, p. 331.
    "Things Seen" (tr. by Jonathan Chaves). [Translation] (17) Fall 86, p. 332.
    "Things Seen on Spring Days" (tr. by Jonathan Chaves). [Translation] (17) Fall 86,
        p. 332.
5897. YUNG, Grant
    "The Three Easter Bunnieses." [Grain] (14:2) My 86, p. 29.
5898. YURKIEVICH, Saúl
    "Grasp" (tr. by Cola Franzen). [Conjunc] (9) 86, p. 201-203.
    "So Then" (tr. by Cola Franzen). [Conjunc] (9) 86, p. 203-204.
5899. YURMAN, Rich
    "How to Meet Your Poem." [PoeticJ] (15) Sum 86, p. 17.
    "The Language of Anger." [YetASM] (4) 85, p. 5.
    "Spectrum." [YetASM] (5) 86, p. 11.
    "To My Daughter Joining the Coast Guard." [PoeticJ] (14) 86, p. 19.
5900. YUTAKA SAGAWA, Roberto
    "Banzai." [Contact] (7:38/39/40) Wint-Spr 86, Supplement p. 36.
    "Banzai" (tr. by Karen Tei Yamashita). [Contact] (7:38/39/40) Wint-Spr 86,
        Supplement p. 36.
    "Coming from the Other Continent" (tr. by Karen Tei Yamashita). [Contact]
        (7:38/39/40) Wint-Spr 86, Supplement p. 39.
    "Fifth-Column" (tr. by Karen Tei Yamashita). [Contact] (7:38/39/40) Wint-Spr 86,
        Supplement p. 34.
    "Portrait of Myself" (tr. by Karen Tei Yamashita). [Contact] (7:38/39/40) Wint-Spr
        86, Supplement p. 37.
    "Quem E Quem?" [Contact] (7:38/39/40) Wint-Spr 86, Supplement p. 38.
    "Quinta-Coluna." [Contact] (7:38/39/40) Wint-Spr 86, Supplement p. 35.
    "Retrato de Mim." [Contact] (7:38/39/40) Wint-Spr 86, Supplement p. 37.
    "Vindo do Outro Continente." [Contact] (7:38/39/40) Wint-Spr 86, Supplement p.
        39.
    "Who Is Who?" (tr. by Karen Tei Yamashita). [Contact] (7:38/39/40) Wint-Spr 86,
        Supplement p. 38.
    "Yoko." [Contact] (7:38/39/40) Wint-Spr 86, Supplement p. 40.
    "Yoko" (tr. by Karen Tei Yamashita). [Contact] (7:38/39/40) Wint-Spr 86,
        Supplement p. 40.
5901. ZABLE, Jeffrey
    "Dali." [Wind] (16:57) 86, p. 43-44.
    "There." [Wind] (16:57) 86, p. 43.
    "This Poem." [Wind] (16:57) 86, p. 43.
    "Thoughts of Suicide." [Wind] (16:57) 86, p. 43.
5902. ZABYTKO, Irene
    "I Watched Them Dance for Their Rosh Chodesh" (for R.S.). [SingHM] (14) 86, p.
        7.
5903. ZACH, Natan
    "Script" (tr. by Karen Alkalay-Gut). [MassR] (27:2) Sum 86, p. 196-197.
5904. ZACHARIN, Noah
    "Famous Afflictions 2." [Rampike] (5:1) 86, p. 77.
5905. ZANA
    "I Walk to the Garden Today." [Kaleid] (12) Wint 86, p. 54.
    "Passing, on a Trip to Town." [Kaleid] (12) Wint 86, p. 54.
    "Telling." [Kaleid] (12) Wint 86, p. 54.
5906. ZANZOTTO, Andrea
    "Outermost Outgoing" (tr. by Nigel Thompson). [Verse] (3:3) N 86, p. 49.
ZAPATA, Rafael Castillo
    See CASTILLO ZAPATA, Rafael
5907. ZAPPALA, Robyn
    "The Hermaphrodite's Wedding Cake." [HayF] (1) Spr 86, p. 11.
    "In Another Country." [HayF] (1) Spr 86, p. 13.
    "To a New Lover." [HayF] (1) Spr 86, p. 12.

5908. ZARAGOZA, Enrique
"Grandmother." [HiramPoR] (40) Spr-Sum 86, p. 32.
"The Mask." [TriQ] (66) Spr-Sum 86, p. 167.
5909. ZARANKA, William
"The Big One." [TriQ] (66) Spr-Sum 86, p. 170-172.
5910. ZARCO, Cyn.
"Cultural Exchange." [Contact] (7:38/39/40) Wint-Spr 86, p. 31.
5911. ZARIN, Cynthia
"His First Love Speaks." [NewYorker] (62:31) 22 S 86, p. 42.
"Kate Smith in the Grandstand." [NewYorker] (62:23) 28 Jl 86, p. 28.
"Midnight in February, Green River, Vermont." [NewYorker] (61:51) 10 F 86, p.
42.
"Our Listening Audience." [GrandS] (5:3) Spr 86, p. 194.
5912. ZAUHAR, David
"Cartoons Demystified." [RiverS] (19) 86, p. 64.
"Genetic Revolution." [RiverS] (19) 86, p. 63.
"Jazz Perfume, Solo." [RiverS] (19) 86, p. 62.
5913. ZAVARZADEH, Mas'ud
"The Critic As Archivist." [Rampike] (5:2) 86, p. 16-19.
5914. ZAVATSKY, Bill
"Bald." [HangL] (49) Spr 86, p. 50-51.
5915. ZAWADIWSKY, Christina (Christine)
"Desire." [PaintedB] (29) Ag 86, p. 64.
"Inheritance." [Abraxas] (34) 86, p. 23.
"Names." [Raccoon] (20) Ap 86, inside back cover.
"Nothing Changes." [Raccoon] (20) Ap 86, inside front cover.
"Sacrifice." [Abraxas] (34) 86, p. 24-25.
5916. ZEIDNER, Lisa
"Bat and Skyscraper." [Boulevard] (1:1/2) Wint 86, p. 163-164.
"Gypsy Moths." [MissR] (15:1/2, #43/44) Fall-Wint 86, p. 35-41.
5917. ZEIGER, David
"Dancers." [Poem] (56) N 86, p. 57.
5918. ZELDA (Shneurson Mishkovsky)
"In the Dry Riverbed" (tr. by Marcia Falk). [AmerPoR] (15:6) N-D 86, p. 20.
"Then My Soul Cried Out" (tr. by Marcia Falk). [AmerPoR] (15:6) N-D 86, p. 20.
5919. ZELENIUK, Raul
"Cafe Concert." [Mairena] (8:21) 86, p. 119.
"Los Exiliados." [Mairena] (8:21) 86, p. 119.
"Felicidad." [Mairena] (8:21) 86, p. 120.
5920. ZELLEFROW, Ken
"Defiant Callings." [SmPd] (23:2, issue 67) Spr 86, p. 23.
5921. ZEMAIDUK, Nick R.
"The Higher Flight." [PoeticJ] (15) Sum 86, p. 14.
"Normal at the Front: At Peace with War." [PoeticJ] (15) Sum 86, p. 10-11.
"Whatever." [DeKalbLAJ] (19:3/4) 86, p. 95.
5922. ZENITH, Richard
"As from the Shadows" (tr. of Roger Giroux). [InterPR] (12:1) Spr 86, p. 49.
"By Itself" (tr. of Roger Giroux). [InterPR] (12:1) Spr 86, p. 55.
"The Desertion" (tr. by René Daumal). [Translation] (17) Fall 86, p. 305.
"The Disillusion" (tr. by René Daumal). [Translation] (17) Fall 86, p. 306.
"Here a Lake, Blue" (tr. of Roger Giroux). [InterPR] (12:1) Spr 86, p. 51.
"I'm Dead" (tr. by René Daumal). [Translation] (17) Fall 86, p. 304.
"Night Passes through the Heart" (tr. of Roger Giroux). [InterPR] (12:1) Spr 86, p.
53.
"The Sermon on Salt." [LitR] (29:3) Spr 86, p. 338-339.
"Somewhere" (tr. of Roger Giroux). [InterPR] (12:1) Spr 86, p. 55.
"This Phrase Which Doubts" (tr. of Roger Giroux). [InterPR] (12:1) Spr 86, p. 57.
"We Will Never Know" (tr. of Roger Giroux). [InterPR] (12:1) Spr 86, p. 53.
"What Is This Place?" (tr. of Roger Giroux). [InterPR] (12:1) Spr 86, p. 59.
5923. ZEPPER, Kevin
"Next War." [SanFPJ] (9:1) 86, p. 93.
5924. ZETH, Jeff
"Capital." [SanFPJ] (8:4) 85, p. 69.
"News at 6:00." [SanFPJ] (8:4) 85, p. 85.
5925. ZETTELL, Susan
"Minutes to Write." [PottPort] (8) 86-87, p. 4.

5926. ZHOU, Jia-ti
"A Letter" (In Chinese & English, tr. by Chou Ping). [Nimrod] (29:2) Spr-Sum 86,
p. 68-69.
5927. ZIEDONIS, Imants
"#205. Fall while you are still shining!" (in Latvian and English, tr. by Lia Smits).
[Os] (23) 86, p. 2-3.
ZIMARDI, Joselyn Ignacio
See IGNACIO-ZIMARDI, Joselyn
5928. ZIMMER, Paul
"Sitting with Lester Young" (for Michael Harper). [DenQ] (20:4/21:1) Spr-Sum 86,
p. 147.
"Zimmer to His Students." [GeoR] (40:3) Fall 86, p. 828.
5929. ZIMMERMAN, Jean
"Ceremonial" (for Gil). [AmerPoR] (15:3) My-Je 86, p. 7.
"Ode to a Friend Complaining of Her Loneliness." [AmerPoR] (15:3) My-Je 86, p.
7.
"One Hand Startles the Other with Its Touch." [AmerPoR] (15:3) My-Je 86, p. 6.
"Reading the Paper after Reading Ovid." [AmerPoR] (15:3) My-Je 86, p. 6.
5930. ZIMMERMAN, Ken
"Domestique." [Puerto] (21:2) Spr 86, p. 165.
"Night." [Puerto] (21:2) Spr 86, p. 164.
5931. ZIMMERMAN, Robert N.
"Dear Marie." [PoeticJ] (15) Sum 86, p. 20.
"Little Game." [PoeticJ] (16) Fall 86, p. 29.
"Purple at Dusk." [PoeticJ] (14) 86, p. 16.
"Zebra Stripes and Dawn" (For Jean). [PoeticJ] (13) 86, p. 20.
5932. ZIMMERMAN, Ruth
"Picture Perfect." [YetASM] (4) 85, p. 4.
"Picture Perfect" (corrected reprint). [YetASM] (5) 86, p. 9.
5933. ZIMROTH, Evan
"Morning Coffee on Isle la Motte." [Hudson] (38:4) Wint 86, p. 633-634.
5934. ZIRLIN, Larry
"Epitaph." [HangL] (49) Spr 86, p. 53-54.
"The Rubber Dagger." [HangL] (49) Spr 86, p. 52.
5935. ZISQUIT, Linda
"Alive." [PoetL] (81:2) Sum 86, p. 133.
"Correspondence." [PoetL] (81:2) Sum 86, p. 131.
"Song of Myself." [PoetL] (81:2) Sum 86, p. 132.
5936. ZIVKOVIC, Peter D.
"Fallout Children." [SanFPJ] (8:1) 85, p. 18.
"Reaping This Year's Harvests." [SanFPJ] (8:1) 85, p. 17.
5937. ZOLLER, Ann
"Imprinted Landscapes" (Selection: "The Vision of Rain"). [Nimrod] (30:1)
Fall-Wint 86, p. 94-95.
"Inside the Dark Sea." [NegC] (6:1) Wint 86, p. 100-101.
5938. ZUCKER, Jack
"In That House" (Chekhov's Mikhail: "Nothing passes"). [BallSUF] (26:4) Aut 85,
p. 70.
5939. ZUCKERMAN, Anne
"Night." [Ploughs] (12:3) 86, p. 106-107.
"Saint Francis." [Ploughs] (12:3) 86, p. 108-109.
5940. ZULAUF, Sander
"Economy, August 31st." [JINJPo] (9:1) 86, p. 27.
"The Roller Coaster at Bertrand's Island." [JINJPo] (9:1) 86, p. 28.
5941. ZUÑIGA QUILOBRAN, Arturo
"Pule Tus Silencios." [Mairena] (8:22) 86, p. 38.
5942. ZUÑIGA-SANCHEZ, Jorge
"Ante el Ojo." [Mairena] (8:22) 86, p. 95.
5943. ZURITA, Raúl
"CIII. Awakened suddenly in dreams I heard him beyond the night" (tr. by Steven F.
White). [SilverFR] (11) Sum 86, p. 15.
"CIII. Despertado de pronto en sueños lo oí tras la noche." [SilverFR] (11) Sum 86,
p. 14.
ZUTPHEN, Carmen van
See Van ZUTPHEN, Carmen

ZVI, Moshe-ben
See MOSHE-BEN-ZVI
5944. ZWEIG, Paul
"Anything Long and Thin." [AmerPoR] (15:1) Ja-F 86, p. 22.
"Bless the Earth, Bless the Fire." [AmerPoR] (15:1) Ja-F 86, p. 22.
"Breaking." [AmerPoR] (15:1) Ja-F 86, p. 22.
"The Correspondence." [AmerPoR] (15:1) Ja-F 86, p. 23.
"One Summer before Man." [AmerPoR] (15:1) Ja-F 86, p. 22.
"Piero." [AmerPoR] (15:1) Ja-F 86, p. 23.
"Poem: I don't know if I can bear this suddenly." [AmerPoR] (15:1) Ja-F 86, p. 26.
"Poem: The farmers are pumping water from the river." [AmerPoR] (15:1) Ja-F 86, p. 25.
"Poem: To know it all deeply, to know every detail." [AmerPoR] (15:1) Ja-F 86, p. 26-27.
"Poem: Why can't anything stay still?" [AmerPoR] (15:1) Ja-F 86, p. 25.
"Skywriting." [AmerPoR] (15:1) Ja-F 86, p. 24.
"Space Is the Wake of Time." [AmerPoR] (15:1) Ja-F 86, p. 23.
"The Thick World." [AmerPoR] (15:1) Ja-F 86, p. 24.
5945. ZYCHLINSKY, Rajzel
"What Has Become of" (tr. by Aaron Kramer). [Vis] (21) 86, p. 24.
5946. ZYCK, Melanie
"Under Our Window." [CarolQ] (39:1) Fall 86, p. 23.
5947. ZYDEK, Fredrick
"After a Storm." [Poem] (56) N 86, p. 34.
"Honey and Apples." [Amelia] (3:1) Ja 86, p. 38.
"Legend of the Lakes." [Amelia] (3:1) Ja 86, p. 39.
"Meeting the Missoula Poet." [SoDakR] (24:3) Aut 86, p. 101.
"Monogamy." [Poem] (56) N 86, p. 33.
"Second Meditation: Black-Mint Dreams." [PraS] (60:2) Sum 86, p. 119.
"Tell the Wet November." [Poem] (56) N 86, p. 32.

Title Index

Titles are arranged alphanumerically, with numerals filed in numerical order before letters. Each title is followed by one or more author entry numbers, which refer to the numbered entries in the first part of the volume. Poems which were untitled are represented by first lines.

And Yet I'm Not Sad : 4534.
And You Are Here Now : 822.
And You'll Break Your Mother's Back : 937.
Ando : 3953.
Andrew Maksimuk : 903.
Andrew Ramsay at the Somme : 754.
Androgynous : 2918.
Andromeda : 2858.
Anemic Cinema : 4527.
Un Ange un Peu Fou : 3088.
Angel : 3190.
An Angel : 219.
The Angel : 4643.
An angel fell under a shadow of conceptions :
    4223.
Angel in the House : 2500.
Angel Triptych : 16, 1882.
Los Angeles after the Rain : 1909.
Angelita : 1168.
Angels : 584.
Angels and Lovers : 3486.
Angels of Snow : 1150.
Angelus : 1451, 4422.
Anger : 1786, 5746.
Anger Madonna : 3140.
Anger Sweetened : 4126.
Angle of Repose : 4926.
Anglo-Canadian : 3038.
Anglo Saxon : 5494.
The Angry Woman Who Married God : 1170,
    3032.
Anguish of the Heart : 1293.
Anhelo : 3719.
Anima Poems : 1386.
Animadversions : 1819.
The Animal Itself : 4640.
Animal Skins : 4752.
Animal Story : 1205.
The Animals : 4107, 4536.
The Animals from Underground : 4894.
The Animals of That Country : 2763.
Animated Film, a Sequence of Emblem
    Poems : 4399.
Animula : 5684.
Ann : 3296.
Ann Street : 5839.
Anna Akhmatova : 3891.
Annamese Hands : 4101.
Annapolis : 977.
Anne Frank Dreams at Bergen-Belsen : 3708.
Anne Frank's House : 3112.
Anne Has a Satellite Dish : 5229.
Anne Hutchinson: Dissenter : 5409.
Annette — the Ninth Month : 1332.
Annie : 197, 4795.
Anniversary : 1389, 2388.
The Anniversary of Fidelity : 3355.
Anniversary, with Meteors and Stars : 4582.
Announcement : 409.
Annual : 4041.
Annunciation : 2220, 3450.
The Annunciation : 4670, 4852.
Anoint the Ariston : 678, 1524.
Anonymous : 2394.

Another : 4085.
Another Autumn, And : 3043.
Another Bedside History of Angst : 136.
Another Castle : 1236.
Another Clarity : 2441.
Another Colonial War Sort of Thing : 4019.
Another Dawn : 1380.
Another Dog's Death : 5466.
Another Foot of Water in the Basement :
    1656.
Another for the Same : 3430.
Another Kind of Outdoor Game : 3481.
Another Language : 5084.
Another Life : 1076, 4676.
Another Poem about Solitude : 5623.
Another Song : 2057.
Another Song on Absalom : 83, 5871.
Another Spring on Olmstead Street : 4503.
Another Sunday : 2108.
Another Time: Hands : 5569.
Another Troy : 1787.
Another Way of Seeing : 2158.
Another Wedding : 1926.
Another year enters : 188.
Another Young Woman Disappears in the
    Trees : 3140.
Anselm Hollo : 662.
Answer : 3675.
The Answer : 1886, 4848.
Answer to a Letter from Boulder : 2111.
Answer to 'The Suicide' : 1910.
Answering : 4861.
The Answering of Prayers : 4538.
Answering the Riddle : 4971.
Answering the Telephone : 5041.
Answering Your Last Letter : 5699.
Ante el Ojo : 5942.
Anthem : 206, 3793.
Anthropometric Summer Landscape : 2085.
Antiflor : 4697.
The Antigone : 2772.
Antigua : 1810.
Antropolis : 3837.
Anxiety of Signs : 1556, 3001, 4600.
Any Night : 3110.
Any One Bone You Want : 4607.
Any Time Now : 2580.
Anybody Home? : 2586.
Anyone Can Stand : 285, 1882, 1998.
Anything Long and Thin : 5944.
Anza Borrego : 241.
Apartheid : 333, 2794, 4164.
The Apartment Is Centrally Located : 3249.
Apartment on 22nd St : 1096.
Aphasiac : 4421.
Aphrodisiac : 49.
The Aphrodisiac : 607.
Apis Mellifera : 3504.
Apocalypse : 1604, 3903.
Apocryphal Journalism : 611, 1149, 3679.
Apollo's First Altar : 2758, 4485.
Apology : 1642, 2459, 5710, 5842.
An Apology to Wallace Stevens : 3283.
Apotheosis : 1556.

Autumn Scenes : 2467.
Autumn Song : 1409, 3436.
Autumn Thoughts : 3149.
Autumn's Buds : 5231.
Ave : 1704.
Ave Nocturna : 3014.
Aventure Mycologique : 4068.
Aversions : 914, 2076.
Aviva at the Crossroads : 3269.
Avowal : 1505.
Awake : 589.
Awakened suddenly in dreams I heard him
    beyond the night : 5707, 5943.
An Awakening : 371.
Away from Any Uniform : 3355.
Away from You : 1882.
A.W.O.L : 445.
Axe Handles : 5016.
Axolotl : 4389.
Ayre Street : 4116.
Azaleas and the Circus : 1062.
El Azar Organiza los Sueños : 2614.
Azul : 5496.
Ba-Lue Bolivar Ba-Lues Are : 3451.
The Baba Yaga Poems : 5790.
Babel : 1032, 1219, 1219.
Babies : 5538.
Baboons in the Perennial Bed : 4211.
Baby in a Fruit Jar: Found and Returned :
    4610.
Babyskin: Notes for a Grandchild : 25.
Bacchanalia for the Old Homestead : 5671.
Bach, Winter : 3541.
The Bachelor: Last Try : 4602.
The Back : 2931.
Back Aches Like Certain Men : 3140.
Back from the City : 2782.
Back Home : 5002.
Back Then : 1431.
Back to Life : 997.
Back to School : 5186.
Back to the Caves : 244.
Backcasting : 115.
The Background : 465.
Backpacking the San Juan : 3481.
Backstore Neighbors : 3578.
Backstroking at Thrushwood Lake : 91.
The Backyard in August : 4448.
A Backyard in California : 839.
Backyard Lyric : 3629.
Bad : 4179.
Bad Birds : 5425.
The Bad Breath of the Car : 4704.
A Bad Day : 2241.
The Bad Days : 3080.
Bad Heart : 1193.
Bad Lands : 1878.
Bad-Mouthed : 1028.
The Bad Music : 2596.
Bad News : 715, 4607.
Badger on the Loose : 3735.
Badlands : 2379, 2751.
Bag Lady Marsupials : 1883.
Baggage : 1059.

Bagging Leaves in March : 4995.
Bagomoyo, 1862 : 1684.
Bahia : 3317.
Bait : 2264.
Baked : 3488.
The Bakers' Wind : 935.
Bakersfield U.S.A : 1039.
Balance : 5128, 5640.
The Balance : 4201.
Bald : 5914.
Bald Mountain Cemetery : 2219.
The Ball : 5770.
The Ball Park : 1793.
Ballad of a Sabra : 1683, 2837.
Ballad of Dead Actresses : 885.
The Ballad of Emotion : 1301.
The Ballad of English Literature : 1455.
The Ballad of Insane Love : 1301.
The Ballad of Riddle : 1301.
The Ballad of Sally Ward : 5729.
Ballad of the Table : 1918, 5726.
Ballad of the Washed Hair : 112.
Ballade for Richard Wilbur : 2412.
Ballet Class : 1775, 3140.
Balloons : 5277.
Bamboo : 2673.
Banana leaves : 1928.
A Bang-Up Christmas : 855.
Bank Building : 1025.
Bankok Sights : 4748.
The Banks Brigade : 2286.
Banner : 4464.
Banner of Fish : 3365.
Banshee : 5303.
Banzai : 5856, 5900, 5900.
The Baptists Cut a Tree : 1024.
Bar Escargot: A Story : 2145.
Bar Writers : 4354.
Barbed-wire Winter : 2039, 2574.
Bare Hands : 2998.
Bargain Day / 1943 : 244.
Bargain Hunting : 3926.
Bark : 4998.
A Bark at the Moon : 1274, 2076.
The Barn : 2087.
A Barn Burnt in Ohio : 2392.
Barn Cat Summer : 5648.
Barn Fire : 3457.
The Barn Owl : 2068.
Barnacle Dick : 1374.
The Barometric Witch : 3491.
The Baroness Elsa : 4791.
Barra : 3034.
Barracuda : 3246.
Barred from the Polo Lounge : 731.
Barren : 212.
Barricade : 808, 1720.
Barstow California : 4144.
Bartender : 3949.
Bartending Bears in Roxbury : 3555.
Basho Awake at Night : 991.
Basia : 3722.
Basket : 4038.
A Basket of Eggs : 1358.

The Body Invisible : 3714.
The Body of a Begger : 4381.
Body of a Man : 1723.
The Body of Elisha Mitchell : 3731.
Body of Knowledge : 4369.
A Body of Water : 3379.
The Body Opulent : 1787.
Bogg 53 : 4073.
Boilermakers : 4076.
Bok and the Tree : 1974.
Bolinas : 4958.
Bolts : 610.
Bombs fell somewhere : 1006.
Bonding : 4436.
The Bone Hunter : 3737.
A Bone of Doggerel for the Dons : 3417.
Bone Scan : 39.
Bones : 4065, 5754.
Bones and Drums : 5659.
Bone's Edge : 3890.
The Bones of Potter's Field : 3688.
Boneyard : 1350.
Bonfire Joana : 3341, 3535.
Bongao Wedding : 771.
Bonus : 1525.
Bonzai for Beginners : 444.
Boogie Woogie : 1672.
The Book of Dialogue : 2559.
The Book of Forms : 779.
A Book of Hours : 2907.
The Book of Kong : 5425.
The Book of Silences : 653.
The Book of Who Are Was : 2410.
The Bookkeeper : 2491.
The Bookkeeper at H. G. Smithy's : 4883.
Books close buds : 3248.
Boot Hill : 3422.
Boot Tracks : 1162.
Border Minstrel : 5648.
Borges : 5660.
Borinquen : 423.
The Borrowed Poem : 2993.
Borrowed Things : 1009.
Boschka Layton 1921-1984 : 3038.
Boston : 4251.
Boston Common : 3891.
Boston Poet's Fall : 3891.
The Boston Suitcoat : 4050.
Boswell likes you : 742.
Boswell on Dr. Johnson's Friend, Mrs. Anna
    Williams : 1086.
Botticelli: From Bryher's Imagined Notes :
    1743.
The Bottle Woman : 3140.
Bottles : 3126.
Bought by the N.R.A : 3471.
Boughten Rooms : 1837.
The Boulevard of Broken Dreams : 3827.
Bound to Fidelity of Representation, Charles
    Willson Peale Paints Washington at
    Yorktown : 4490.
Bound up in blood : 488, 843, 4263.
Boundaries : 2186.
The Boundary : 3935.

A Bouquet of Objects : 1549.
Bourbon and Firelight : 1439.
Boustrophedon : 528.
Bowing : 5084.
A Bowl of Wine : 789.
Bowlers' Anonymous : 1350.
The Boxer's Choice : 5364.
The Boy Dreams His Destiny : 985.
The Boy in the Black Leather Jacket : 1768.
Boy on a Ledge : 3863.
A Boy on a Swing: Bass Creek Commune :
    4544.
Boy on Curb : 147.
Boy Poem : 2155.
The Boy Selling the Blue Fish : 3936.
Boy Wearing a Dead Man's Clothes : 2882.
Böyle Bir Sevmek : 2530.
Boys : 4496.
The Bracelet : 5533.
The Brain of the Fat Woman : 5671.
The Brain to the Heart : 2882.
Brambles : 3975.
A Branch of the Tree : 4364.
Branches, Scattered, Strewn: I Lie Alone :
    2272.
A Brand Snatched from Anti-Tank Fire :
    1343, 5715.
Brandywine : 4476.
Brassempouy : 436, 2318, 5522.
Brave New Lovers : 5359.
Brave Poets : 3853.
Bravo : 2066.
Brazil : 2433.
La Brea Woman : 3277.
Bread : 1095.
The Bread Sellers, Kano City, Nigeria : 500.
The Break : 5529.
Breakdancing : 2001.
Breakdown : 5643.
Breakfast Anytime : 3801.
Breakfast at the Mount Washington Hotel :
    2782.
Breakfast in Betws-y-coed : 2587.
Breakfast of Bears : 4752.
Breakfast Stop in Gallup : 2477.
Breaking : 5944.
Breaking and Entering : 1999.
Breaking Down : 545.
Breaking for the Broken : 115.
Breaking the Cup : 417.
Breaking the Sound Barrier : 1788.
Breakneck : 3510.
Breakthrough : 1425, 3811.
The Breast : 1479.
Breastfeeding at the Art Gallery of Ontario
    Alex Colville Retrospective, 1983 : 431.
The Breasts of Almatricia : 5283.
Breath : 4356, 5623.
The breath of a young girl, biting an apple :
    3383, 4660.
Breathe Deeply, and Relax : 3481.
Breather : 1675, 2839, 4558.
Breathing : 1463, 1942.
Breathing Saltwater : 4295.

Finding Myself : 5640.
Finding Our Names : 3351.
Finding Out : 5069.
Finding Silence : 3507.
Finding the Room : 4878.
Finding the Wallet : 1319.
A Fine Line : 2663.
The Fine Line : 4097.
Finger Curls : 3006.
Fingerprints : 1451.
Fingers : 1318.
The Finish : 2392.
Finisterre : 3901.
Fire : 853, 1201, 3856, 4642, 5088, 5746.
The Fire : 2675.
Fire and Smoke : 5579.
Fire Clings to Air : 5402.
Fire Eater : 1990.
The Fire-Eater : 4922.
Fire in the Tree : 4415.
Fire on the Island : 576.
The Firebombing : 5147.
Fireflies : 3185, 5259, 5259.
The Fireflies : 2039, 2574.
The Firefly : 1530, 4492.
Firemen : 5734.
Firewalk : 495.
First : 1942.
First Anniversary: Divorce : 821.
First Anniversary of an Accidental Shooting : 4553.
The First Autumn after Your Death : 2766.
First Blizzard, Worst Blizzard : 3229.
First Born : 5193.
First Child : 4781.
First Cold Night of Fall : 644.
First Communion : 20.
First Credo : 466.
The First Day of Winter : 192.
The first dead leaves fall : 189.
First Desires : 5746.
First Fire of the Season : 1325.
First Fountains : 1460.
First Frost : 4820.
First Grade, Austin, 1958 : 853.
First Hand : 2068.
First I want to make you come in my hand : 2108.
First Ice : 1380.
First Job / Seventeen : 4159.
First Kingdom : 3630.
First Kiss : 4503.
First Kisses : 1176.
First Light : 3714, 4926.
First Love : 753, 5808.
First May Day : 4974.
First Night Back : 2111.
The First of May : 2513.
The First One : 2302.
First Penmanship Lesson : 43, 761.
First Shell : 1517.
First Snow : 3446.
First Snow at Freezing Point : 3831.
First Snow in the Garden of the Geishas : 3538.
First Solo : 3481.
First Solo in Thunderstorms : 3481.
First Stop / City of Senses : 4324.
Th First Terrorism : 501.
First, the Auto Shop : 5778.
The first thing I noticed : 3568.
The First Time : 3885, 5119.
First Trip through the Automatic Car Wash : 5480.
First Trip to the Fun House: Crystal Beach : 5464.
The First Year : 5790.
Firstborn : 4259.
Firsts, Seconds, and Thirds : 585.
Fish : 951, 1620, 3943, 5256.
Fish Galore : 4707.
Fish Leaves : 2049.
Fish Poem : 2875.
The Fisher : 5339.
Fisher Day : 928.
Fisherman : 4562.
The Fisherman : 5223.
Fisherman's Lyric : 907, 924.
Fishing : 3517.
Fishing after Rain : 5194.
Fishing at Night : 2940.
Fishing Black River, Wisconsin, 1953 : 2934.
Fishing Men : 337.
Fishing with Grandfather: July 1958 : 477.
Fishing with Scudder Bates : 1402.
Fist : 2551, 2838, 5275.
Fit : 5529.
Fit for Survival? : 1272.
The Fitting : 2491.
Fittings : 4565.
Five Cats and a Discussion of the Soul after a Trip to South Carolina : 99.
Five Dawn Skies in November : 5546.
Five Embarrassing Laws of Physics : 334.
The Five Rooms of the Dream : 3740.
Five Speeches for Pygmalion : 1909.
Five Teeth Grin on the Gnawed Jawbone : 1903.
Five Things for a Friend Who Wants a Poem for His Painting : 2513.
Five to Life : 4411.
Five Tz'u : 2977, 5201.
Five Years Hence : 75.
The Fix : 4717.
Fixing the Well : 4095.
Fixing the Window : 5842.
The Flamboyance of Memory : 522.
Flash Flood : 3078, 3943.
Flashback : 1262.
Flat Box with Glass Cover : 261.
Flavors Like These : 4705.
Flea Market : 848.
Flee from Destruction to Come : 4760.
La Fleur Sauvage : 3247.
Flies : 1451, 5069.
The Flies : 3273, 5470.
Flight : 408, 1088, 1568, 4178, 5750, 5842.
Flight Home to the Fatherland : 4551.

Flight: Listening to Brubeck, Reading
    Aksyanov : 1032.
The Flight of Starlings : 2151.
Flight of the Falcon : 5549.
Flight of the Geese : 324.
Flight Preparation : 2175, 2626.
Flight to Canada : 2198.
Flights : 5419.
Flinch : 4768.
Flint : 1274, 2076.
The Flint from Mississquoi : 706.
Floating : 2765.
Floating Town : 1654.
The Floating World : 1342.
Flood : 3426.
The Flood of '82 : 1609.
The Flooding of the Swift River Valley : 918.
Flooding Pittsburgh, 1985 : 2897.
Flor Inesperada : 2542.
Flora : 3837.
Flora Baum, Historian : 722.
A Flora Beginning with Vineyards : 5019.
Flora Obbligata : 3241.
Florence Interlude : 35.
Florida : 1669, 4622.
Florida, 1984 : 3437.
Florida — Full Moonrise : 3592.
A Florida Story : 4766.
The Flower : 61.
Flower in the Mountains : 5238.
Flower Picking with Vincent van Gogh :
    1972.
The Flowerbed : 5567.
The Flowering Peach : 5669.
Flowering Plum : 3537.
Flowering Privet : 1680.
The Fluid Core : 4640.
Fluidly and by Night : 4679, 5014.
The Flutist : 91.
The Fly : 558, 2526.
Flyers : 2278.
Flying : 4182, 5251.
Flying Cloud : 597.
Flying Dutchman : 5754.
Flying Home from the Prairies : 1073.
Flying into Dusk : 788.
Flying Low, near France, among Birds : 3796.
Flying out of Fiji : 3921.
Flying over This Death, This Life : 4114.
Flying Westward : 5568.
Flying Wintertime Chicago : 3949.
Fog at Liang-Hsiang : 924, 5896.
Fog Boy : 389.
The Fog Comes In on Free Verse : 3172.
Fog, New York : 5183.
Fog Township : 1812.
Fogbound, Sailing Toward Buoy #6 : 145.
Folded and Refolded: A State of Being : 5489.
Folk Tales : 1037.
The Folkie Blues : 927.
The Folks Perform : 490.
Follow hungry wolves : 4939.
Following the Cat : 4503.
Following the Dog to Water : 3481.

Following Tracks : 3511.
Fond Memory : 556.
Fontanelle : 729, 2231.
The Food : 4874.
Food Chain : 5409.
Food for Talk : 4126.
Food for the Winter : 1060.
Food for Thought : 1677.
The Food Pickers of Saigon : 3481.
The Fool, Let them say what they want : 58,
    2837.
The Fool of the Dark Goddess Utters One of
    Her Many Names : 2456.
The foolish animal : 1503.
Fool's Gold Madonna : 3140.
Fool's Month : 3963.
Foot Hold : 3030.
Foot Soldier : 5407.
Foot Thrust : 5649.
Footage : 2214.
Football Addicts Madonna : 3140.
The Footbridge : 1032.
Foothold : 4864.
A Foothold on the Land : 3474.
A Footnote to Epictetus : 4183.
Footnote to the Dream : 4176.
Footprints : 393, 602.
Footprints at Laetoli, Tanzania : 3277.
For 2 Cents : 147.
For a Brother-in-Law Leaving for Tupelo :
    5235.
For a Cowper Paperweight : 3923.
For A.D. : 731.
For a Female Parole Officer : 4193.
For a Friend in the Hospital : 2212.
For a Friend Lacking Faith : 719.
For a Hard Winter : 4090.
For a Third Anniversary : 5546.
For a Time and a Time : 5357.
For a Whitewaterer — On His 16th Birthday :
    659.
For a Woman in Texas : 1001.
For a Woman Who Lowered Her Head : 1292.
For A.D. : 731.
For Alice : 315.
For All to Know : 3860, 3958.
For an Exchange of Rings : 2127.
For an Uncle : 5738.
For Balthus : 2712.
For Barbara : 671.
For Beethoven : 1891.
For Borges : 5135.
For Bowie : 2793, 4929.
For Bruce : 4702.
For Cello, Prepared Heart and Voices : 4854.
For Charles and Mary Lamb : 3496.
For Charles Bovary : 5796.
For Charles Reznikoff : 4842.
For Costas : 2706.
For Credence Clearwater Revival : 4771.
For Czeslaw Milosz : 4298.
For Drunks, in the Nighttime : 3796.
For Dulcimer & Doubled Voice : 4985.
For Felix E. Goodson Jr : 2168.

From Evansville to Hollywood : 2258.
From far inside what only I can know : 2558.
From Hour Third : 4530.
From 'Letters from the Baja' : 5035.
From Monochrome/ to Circuits on Full Gush :
  1208.
From One Side of the Soul to Another : 5428.
From Pericles to Aspasia: a Letter : 4322.
From Ridgetop to Ridgetop : 5854.
From Room to Room : 2636.
From Small Beginnings : 2416.
From Star to Star : 3296.
From the Afterworld : 5084, 5852, 5875.
From the Air : 3251.
From the Ballad of 'The Two Corbies' : 1086.
From the bedroom with the door closed : 844.
From the Beginning : 3227.
From the Cave : 3836.
From the Convent: A Protest : 3919.
From the East, Light : 849.
From the Ends of the Earth : 5092.
From the Family Album : 2515.
From the Free World : 74.
From the Front Porch, 3/28/84 : 3955.
From the Houses of the Dead : 4297.
From the Immense Curriculum : 776.
From the Infinite Names of the Center : 2435.
From the Italian : 4599.
From the M.P.'s Office : 2092.
From the People's Memorial Association :
  1265.
From the Rapido: La Spezia-Genova : 3901.
From the Same Theater : 856, 1563.
From the Shore: Toronto : 1547.
From the Sky : 4277.
From the Source, We Flow : 1564.
From the Top of Stoney Mountain : 3913.
From the Walls : 2156.
From This Condensery : 3892.
From Translating Translating Apollinaire :
  3883.
From underneath the radioactive mushroom :
  623.
Front Page Religion : 4509.
Front Porch : 3536.
Frost as Morning Goes On : 1590.
Frozen Lake at Midnight : 2493.
Frozen Lasagne : 4094.
Frozen Love : 2838, 3817, 5275.
The Frozen Sea : 399.
Fruit : 97, 3220, 3365.
Fuchsia : 4659.
Fuck the New syntax : 987.
The Fugitive Years : 1129.
A Fugue : 5531.
Fuku : 592, 5870.
Full Circle : 3247.
The Full Moon Follows : 1650.
Full of Night and Weeping : 1079, 3354.
Full of the Moon : 3731.
Full round bowls of flowers : 1503.
Fullness : 894.
Fun House : 330.
The Function of Winter : 4089.

Fundamentum Divisionis : 1760.
Funeral : 1350.
The Funeral : 3163.
Funeral Photograph : 4243.
Funeral Procession : 4557.
Fur : 358, 1938.
Furlough : 3525.
A Furnished Room : 3351.
Furniture : 4536.
Further back I go in memory : 4054.
The Fury : 5168.
Future : 4043.
The Future : 253, 5541.
Future, 4 : 810, 4362.
The Future as a Cow : 660.
The Future of Beauty : 3629.
The Future Sleeps : 34, 127, 3917.
Gabriela : 4952.
Gagaku : 4467.
Gagaku: Better to see demons : 4467.
Gagaku: Demons point at their own chests :
  4467.
Gagaku: Demons take a nap in their seats :
  4467.
Gagaku: no no no they signal me : 4467.
Gagaku: so many people ask him : 4467.
Gagaku: the gold fish : 4467.
Gagaku: they are hammering : 4467.
Gagaku: When one writes poetry : 4467.
Gail Pollock : 1851.
Galactite : 1556.
Galileo and Other Renegades : 5706.
Galleria : 4758.
Galleries — To Helena at Fourteen : 1811.
Gallery : 731.
Galloping Horse Unearthed at Leitai, China :
  4884.
Galveston by Dark : 3603.
The Galvez Cut : 4018.
Gambler's Stone : 3968.
The Game : 2429.
Garage Door : 546.
Garbage and Food : 4309.
Garden : 2037.
A Garden : 5132.
The Garden : 182, 578, 4281, 4897, 5249,
  5682.
The Garden and Its Owners : 1999.
The Garden and the Sea: An Essay for Helen :
  2473.
Garden Creatures: Riddles : 4095.
The Garden of St. Dymphna : 1286.
Garden Scene : 1429.
The Garden Statues : 1367.
The Gardener Envies Henri Rousseau : 1771.
Gardener in Spring : 1607.
Gardeners : 5183, 5352.
Gardener's Choice : 4128.
Gardens and Walkways : 1902.
The Gardens of Flora Baum : 722.
Gare Montparnasse (The Melancholy of
  Departure), 1914, 1983 : 3135.
Gargoyle : 4974.
Gargoyle Song : 3454.

High Canyon Recital : 3028.
High Flowers : 3992.
High Holiday at Mt. Hope : 3625.
High in the Clear Sky : 4598.
High Interest Rate Madonna : 3140.
High Noon : 5820.
High-Pressure Chart : 2426, 2838, 5275.
High Society : 927.
Higher Education : 174.
The Higher Flight : 5921.
Highway Department : 1491.
Hijos Apocrifos : 4699.
Hilda Doolittle Analyzes Sigmund Freud :
    648.
Hilderman's Store, Cape Girardeau, Missouri
    : 2765.
Hill 190, August '69 : 2352.
Hill Street, the First Walls I Slept In : 3006.
Hillsboro 1966 : 2304.
Himself the Poet : 1859.
Hindsight : 5424.
Hindu Illumination : 3587.
The Hinge of Spring : 4640.
Hinges : 4993.
Hinton's Silkscreens : 2198.
Hints for Pilgrimage : 3490.
Hired Man, the (Life and) : 3784.
Hiroshige's 'Hiratsuka: Path through a Paddy
    Field' : 2811.
Hiroshima Blooms : 3714.
Hiroshima Maiden: An Imaginary Translation
    from the Japanese : 5217.
Hiroshima Stopwatch : 4933.
His Bathrobe Pockets Stuffed with Notes :
    849.
His Daughter : 3041.
His Depression : 2943.
His First Love Speaks : 5911.
His Funny Valentine : 4931.
His Matisses, 1938 : 2757.
His Method : 5261.
His Nightmare : 5386.
His Pandemonium : 274.
His Pilgrimage : 4274.
His Pillow : 2202.
His Prayer : 1227.
His Sign Is Pisces : 456.
Historic Present : 3306.
Historic Properties, Halifax : 393.
Historical Site : 5832.
History : 3590, 4103, 4567.
History Lesson : 724, 5029.
The History of a Tough Motherfucker : 731.
The History of Apples : 4637.
The History of Disappointment : 4637.
The History of Human Sacrifice : 970.
History of Pier Paolo Pasolini : 174.
The History of Someone Else : 4381.
History of the Twentieth Century : 664.
History of the Vanquished : 2142, 5280.
The History of the Wedge : 2401.
History Repeats Itself : 2066.
Hitchhiker — December : 5756.
Hiyasa : 5508.

Ho : 3848.
Hobbled : 3197.
The Hobbyist : 2145.
Hobo Trains : 1703.
Hogan's Bar, Galway : 2068.
Holcomb County Poems : 721.
Hold Me : 1181.
Holderlin : 3725.
Holding Animals : 3140.
Holding Back the Flame : 784.
The Holding Rocks : 269.
Holding the Hand of the Dying : 4219.
Holding the Line : 5623.
The Hole in the Ceiling : 320.
The Hole in the Wall : 1172.
Hole in the Wall : 3406.
Hole to China : 3174.
The Holes in the Trees : 2134.
Holiday Blues : 5868.
Holiday Greetings : 5525.
Hollow : 5810.
The Hollow Place : 5113.
Hollywood : 3934.
Hollywood Canteen : 679.
Hollywood Jazz : 2491.
Holocaust Poems : 935.
Holy bless the subway mob : 5160.
A Holy Day : 5317.
Holy Eucharist with Dick : 1196.
Homage to Akbar : 4390.
Homage to Alice Neel : 328.
Homage to an Unknown Self : 2835.
Homage to Bukowski : 1728.
Homage to Georg Trakl : 4920.
Homage to Jose Garcia Villa : 1691.
Homage to Little Roy Lewis : 589.
Homage to Sextus Propertius : 4281.
Homage to the Impressionist Painters : 4698.
Homage to the River : 5765.
Homage to Thomas Eakins : 5822.
El hombre camina esta calle del día sin ocupar
    los ojos en el paisaje : 183.
Un Hombre Levanta o Repara Su Casa : 525.
El Hombre por el Hombre : 1820.
Home : 494, 732, 1884, 2191, 2650, 3533,
    3774, 3843, 5702.
Home Again : 2698.
Home and Away : 2353.
Home Cooking : 5612.
Home, Early Summer : 2498.
Home for Boys and Girls : 520.
Home from Hospital: Holiday : 3.
Home Movies : 184, 1766, 2130, 2513.
Home of the Razorbacks : 2563.
Home Remedies : 4637.
Home Remedy : 4685.
Home Repairs : 5094.
Home Rivers : 157.
Home Tides : 408.
Homecoming : 769, 853, 1759, 4183, 5098,
    5138.
The Homecoming : 1909, 4965.
Homecoming for Gonzalo : 2755.
Homenaje : 908.

How I Plan to Know and Understand the
    Universe: Step One : 4857.
How I See Things : 2882.
How I'll Live Then : 2585.
How It Begins : 1943.
How It Comes : 320.
How It Goes On : 1405.
How Like a Kite My Star Is : 3500, 4673,
    4990.
How Long : 1108, 2039, 4501.
How Night Comes : 4237.
How Not to Die : 228.
How Now Brown Cow : 2850.
How Our Lives Fill the Sky : 5237.
How She Got Her Real Name : 4716.
How She Knew It Was Over: A Summary :
    359.
How Suicide Fails to Seduce Dr. Rose : 3568.
How Survive This Rain : 3929, 5110.
How the Ground Rises! : 1354.
How the Moon Got Its Handle : 1924.
How the Natives on the Reservation Lost the
    Right . . : 1273, 1334, 5559.
How the Poet Works : 3838.
How the Waiting Ends : 2011.
How They Build Their Fires : 3226.
How to Be a Hedonist : 3013.
How to Be Your Own Butcher : 3486.
How to Cook Women : 2838, 3824, 5273.
How to Deal Fairly with Men and Love Them
    : 5530.
How to Find a Dinosaur : 5545.
How to Get Along with Charles Bukowski :
    3172.
How to Leave Nothing : 3043.
How to Meet Your Poem : 5899.
How to Report on What You've Seen or Read
    : 311.
How to Write a Grandmother Poem : 2438.
How We Are Born : 129.
How We Are Diminished by the Deaths of
    Strangers : 1654.
How Will You Know It's Eden? : 1984.
How You Get an Appointment at the Pre-Paid
    Health Care Center : 3172.
Howard Hughes Leaves Managua: Peacetime,
    1972 : 76.
However Did You Guess? : 3221.
How's That Again? : 2305.
How's the City Treating You : 1946.
Huatesca Woman : 2643, 4125.
The Hubbub : 115.
HUD-Section 231/8: Federal Housing for the
    Elderly : 1506.
The Hudson : 5116.
The Hudson at Mechanicville : 4985.
Hudson Bay Bill : 158.
The Hudson River : 3240.
La Huella de los Cisnes : 107.
Huerfano : 266.
Huesped de las Sombras : 3398.
Hugo Wolf Wanders Through Nocturnal
    Vienna Asking the Way to Himself :
    949.

Hui-Tsung (1082-1135) : 5768.
A Hum to Say I'm Missing Your Touch :
    4275.
Human Fallibility : 4677.
The Human Figure in Motion : 4190.
Human Time : 1943.
Humiliation as Grist : 1774.
Humility : 912.
Humoresque : 1952, 2273.
Humpback Whales : 3.
A Hundred Circles : 4878.
Hunger : 1293, 2993.
The Hunger : 659.
A Hungry Fisherman Catches More Fish :
    4858.
Th Hungry Mental Paca Factor : 4335.
Hunt : 724, 2098.
Hunter in the Snow : 2907.
Hunting Doves at Matador : 3481.
Hunting on Hardscrabble : 3481.
Hunting Rabbits with a Dog : 5574.
The Huntress : 3494.
Huntsy, the Guide : 5714.
Hurricane : 5084.
Hurricane from a Distance : 1041.
Hurricane Season : 4868.
The Hurt of Pleasure : 2270.
The Husband : 5643.
Husband and Wife : 1974.
The Husband of the Circus Fat Lady : 5100.
A Husband Pleads His Case : 2388.
Husbanding : 2689.
Husbandry : 460.
Husbands all dead : 4308.
The Husband's Letter, 1969 : 92.
Hustler : 2840.
Hyacinth : 2054.
Hydroce-Falus Obs : 5055.
Hydroponic Madonna : 3140.
Hylas : 174.
Hymn : 5466.
Hymn-Singer : 1974.
Hymns from the Time of the Conquest : 159,
    2363.
Hymns to a Tree : 2388.
Hypochondria : 3227.
Hypothermia : 1319.
I-80 with Charles Darwin : 2424.
I Always Thought of You as a Delicate Vase
    : 2726.
I am great American dying : 3254.
I Am in Love : 5132.
I am like you, O Wind! : 209, 5535.
I Am Natural : 1190.
I am neither Arab nor Jew : 159, 2837.
I Am Not Rich, But for You : 943.
I Am the Friendless Child : 159, 1729.
I Am the Same : 1274, 2076.
I and the Village : 5282.
I Arrive in a Small Boat, Alone : 3227.
I calm my table : 4150.
I Came to Uncle Axel But Could Not Find
    Him : 34, 127, 3917.
I Can Stay : 4483.

Let's Make a Baby : 2606.
Let's Say : 4153.
Letter : 1093, 4096.
A Letter : 950, 5926.
The Letter : 2653, 4848.
Letter Accompanying the Specimen of an
    Amazing Bird : 1812.
Letter before Leaving for a Reforestation
    Brigade : 1720.
Letter: Blues : 73.
Letter from a Friend : 1946.
Letter from Berlin : 3743.
Letter from California : 5109.
Letter from Harry : 4171.
Letter from Moscow : 3454.
Letter from Mother : 3767.
Letter from My Porch : 1263.
Letter from My Sister, the Tattooist : 735.
Letter from Outremer : 3105.
Letter from Palestine : 5361.
Letter from Paris : 774.
Letter from Spain : 111.
Letter from the Italian Kitchen : 3879.
Letter Home : 1416.
A Letter Home : 1690.
Letter in Early March : 2028.
Letter No. 1 : 4265.
Letter No. 2 : 4265.
Letter No. 3 : 4265.
The Letter of the Mathematician's Bride
    Afraid of War : 4497.
Letter Resembling Things : 3537.
Letter to a Brother Prisoner : 2561, 4363,
    4661, 5267.
Letter to a Censor : 930.
Letter to a Dying Scholar : 3748.
Letter to a Woman in a Wheat Field : 3281.
Letter to an Exile : 2870.
Letter to A.R. Ammons : 122.
Letter to Etheridge : 2738.
Letter to Falls Church : 3983.
Letter to Hugo from Seattle : 5090.
Letter to Jim Grabill : 3955.
Letter to Lynn : 3120.
Letter to Me of a Year Ago : 3620.
Letter to Miss Glasser : 1292.
Letter to My Father : 5571.
Letter to My Mother : 1825.
Letter to My Parents : 5619.
A Letter to Nietzsche : 2764.
Letter to Sylvia : 5259.
Letter to the Board : 1730.
Letter to the Prairie, Open : 4975.
Letter with Blurred Postmark : 1999.
Letters : 164, 1373, 2110, 4949.
The Letters : 5698.
Letters from a Lost Brother : 2123.
Letters from a Season : 1260.
Letters in the Dark : 3177.
Letters of Discipline : 1033.
The Letters of Fanny Brawne : 5893.
Letters to God : 4058, 4112.
Letters to John Berryman : 3250.
Letting Go : 1731, 3356.

Lettre pour Names, Eau, Couple et Nature :
    4646.
Levels : 2477.
Leviticus : 1034.
Levity : 4901.
The Liar : 1067.
Liar's Poker : 876.
Lib Bristol's : 753.
Liberation : 456.
A Liberation : 5427.
The Librarian Decides on Cryonics : 4945.
The Library Reading Room, Batavia, New
    York : 2476.
Libres Pareados para una Ilusion Amante :
    4811.
Los libros : 799.
Libyan Pantoum : 1176.
Liebesliedchen : 5479.
Life in the Fast Lane : 3732.
Life is boundless : 988.
Life Moves Outside : 1497.
The Life of a Woman : 5538.
Life of Crime : 4300.
The Life of Flowers : 2980.
Life on the Moon : 129.
The Life-Sitter : 5294.
Life Sources : 3556.
Life Story : 4689.
The Life We Share : 729.
Lifeless Heart : 994.
Life's First Thunderstorm : 5243.
Life's Liar : 4435.
Life's Undelivered Letter : 174.
Light : 584, 3296.
The Light : 3041, 4220.
The Light by the Barn : 5084.
Light (Culinary) Touch in a Heavy Book :
    3718.
The Light Going Down : 3043.
The Light of Being Winded : 4969.
Light of the Moon / Dark of the Moon : 647.
The Light of the World : 5554.
A Light Outside : 220.
Light Tasks : 1096.
The Light Within : 2247.
The Lighter That Never Fails : 332.
The Lighthouse Keeper at Thomas Point :
    5613.
Lighthouse Telephone : 5037.
Lightning : 1574.
The Lightning : 513.
Lightning fell like bombs last night : 2363.
Lightning near the Tower : 82.
Lights Out : 579.
The Light's True Inertia : 399.
Lightshow : 2882.
Like : 1093.
Like a Dream to Be Brushed Away : 4727.
Like a Lover : 3140.
Like a wounded beast : 3340, 5477.
Like April in Paris : 117.
Like Asphalt : 4875.
Like Being Called 'Cat' That Saturday in
    Montreal : 3140.

The Negative : 5258.
Negotiate : 5416.
Negotiations : 2207.
Neighbor : 3743, 4478.
Neighbors : 4319, 5296.
The Neighbors : 3481.
A Neighbor's Goat Reminds Me of Socrates :
     1375.
Neither Out Far Nor In Deep : 1772.
Neither Victim Nor Muse : 1375.
Nelligan : 2516.
Nelson Mandela : 1006.
The Neo-Life Temple of Health Shop : 2259.
Neolithic Man Without a Fravarti : 987.
A Neon Body : 1606.
Nerve : 5159.
Nesta Noite Mutilada : 5515.
Nesting : 3543.
Nesting of Layered Protocols : 4514.
The Nestling : 1880.
Nestus Gurley : 2596.
The Net : 3833.
Net, Lake, Sieve : 5715.
Nets : 1244.
Netting the Pond : 500.
Neutronic Explosion : 5656.
Nevada : 888, 3148.
Nevado Del Ruiz : 5328.
Never Bind Me : 2838, 4876, 5275.
Never Enough The : 4795.
Never Married : 702.
Never-Never-Land : 2394.
New : 704, 705, 4616.
New address book : 3248.
The New Affluence : 1787.
The New and Improved Testament : 4539.
The New-Born Moose : 4376.
New Car : 5746.
New Careers : 5734.
New Cars : 4301.
The New Dance of Death : 2271.
The New Day Dazzles You : 2590, 4923.
The New Days : 3525.
New Ecology : 808, 1021.
New England Koan : 428.
New Girls : 5302.
New Guy, 1969 : 3481.
A New Image : 335.
A New Jacket : 2557.
The New Jerusalem : 2150.
The New Kabbalists : 4640.
New Landscape : 3943.
A New Language : 2867.
New Law : 1739.
New Lincoln Penny : 5233.
New Lives for Old : 3053.
New Mall Restaurant : 2857.
New Nose Is Good Nose : 1066.
New Paint : 1930.
New Recipe for *Terra Nova* : 5536.
The New Road : 5198.
New Shoes : 4998.
New South : 28.
The New Tenants : 4908.

New World : 5309.
The New World : 285, 1882, 3030.
A new world order : 681.
New World Overture : 2295.
New Year : 263.
New Year, Times Square : 4867.
New Year's Eve on a Train : 5467.
New Year's Morning January 1, 1986 : 4701.
New York Summer : 1447.
Newborn : 2526.
Newfangleness : 1118.
Newly Installed Still a Novelty : 3128.
Newly stacked firewood : 2183.
Newlywed : 4890.
The News (A Manifesto) : 4159.
The News about Ray : 3251.
News at 6:00 : 5924.
News Clips: Black Women Today : 1235.
News Hooks : 1699.
News Item : 2905.
News of the Abolition of Nuclear Weapons :
     2713.
News Traveling Well : 3937.
Newsmakers : 1677.
Next Best : 5640.
The Next Birthday : 1346.
Next Day Madonna : 3140.
The Next Day the Fog Was Even Worse :
     924, 5896.
Next Door : 3654.
The Next Step : 1489.
The Next Story : 4538.
Next to Tut : 5499.
The Next Truth : 4677.
Next War : 5923.
Next Year : 965, 4384.
Next Year in Jerusalem : 2927.
The Nexus of Rain : 3647.
Niagara Falls : 4023.
Nica-Anáhuac: Recuerdos de un Viaje por
     Nicaragua durante la Guerra Civil :
     3452.
Nicaraguan : 3221, 5427.
Nicodemus : 4298.
Nieve Nocturna : 5310.
La Nieve y el Estambre : 5855.
Nifty Fifty Madonna : 3140.
Nigh Noon Summer : 1675.
Night : 3443, 5930, 5939.
The Night : 3505.
The Night, a Torn-Down Thing : 5056.
Night after Long Practice : 1330.
Night after Night Dreams : 4549.
Night and Day : 5006, 5524.
Night and Joy : 3850.
A Night at the Opera : 3020.
Night Beach Snake : 5774.
The Night before the First Day of School :
     3464.
Night-Blooming Prophecy : 2035.
Night Breathing : 5365.
Night Cafes : 5813.
Night Chant : 5782.
Night/Day : 3517.

Hamlet : 527.
On the Nolichucky : 1892.
On the Olympic Peninsula : 1488.
On the Passing of Heidegger : 2466.
On the Pine Mountain Trail : 4459.
On the Porch in the Evening : 3682.
On the Promontory : 2346.
On the Puna : 1808, 2597.
On the Pythagorean Theorem : 3117.
On the Removal of the Fascist American
    Right from Power : 2862.
On the Reservation : 4594.
On the Return of Halley's Comet : 5699.
On the Road Again : 4432.
On the Road to Blue Earth : 5647.
On the Roof : 781.
On the Russian River : 4835.
On the Sea Float Chestnut Trees : 1108, 2039.
On the Street : 4688.
On the Sundeck : 1392.
On the Truck Route in Eastern Oregon : 1051.
On the Twenty-Fifth Anniversary of the
    Mother Superior's Drowning : 2278.
On the University Quarterback : 4305.
On the Untersberg : 2057.
On the Water : 4444.
On the wave : 3869.
On the Way : 2743, 2899, 2992.
On the Way Back : 1914, 2846.
On the Way into Exile : 1110, 4990.
On the Way to Them : 667.
On Things Predictable : 656.
On Thursday : 4628.
On Turning 50 Years : 3853.
On Turning Forty : 3403.
On Turning Thirty-Five : 1645.
On Two Feet : 2791.
On Vacation Like a Stone : 1556, 3001, 4600.
On Visiting Herbert Hoover's Birth and
    Burial Place : 3246.
On Watching Challenger : 1890.
On Wednesday : 3517.
On Wings of Song : 4815.
Onan Bound : 1791.
Once : 762, 1153.
Once Again Blackberry Warheads : 637.
Once Again — Time : 744.
Once Bonded : 1976.
Once I got a postcard from the Fiji Islands :
    2152, 2728, 5281.
Once on a bleak train : 4055.
Once Removed : 2660.
Once / The : 5369.
Once Upon a Time : 3450.
Ondine : 1380.
One : 432.
One Animal's Life : 5132.
One Bitch Grieves Another : 3366.
One Day : 608, 2838, 2937, 3921, 5275, 5851.
One Day a Woman : 5752.
One Dog, One Rabbit : 1760.
One Don't : 739.
One Evening : 472.
One for Tony, America's Guest : 5352.

One from the East and One from the West :
    3591.
One Generation : 264, 2072.
One Gesture : 928.
One Girl Was Chosen. How Tall Was She? :
    5530.
One Hand Startles the Other with Its Touch :
    5929.
One Hundred Love Sonnets : 3860, 5292.
One Hundred Years of Jewish Settlement
    Later : 2125, 4938.
The One Is Neither at Rest Nor in Motion :
    2375.
One Is One : 4258.
One-Liners : 2131.
One Man's Sermon on Dreaming : 4200.
One More Winter on Sinclair : 3118.
One Night on Guard Duty : 1489.
One of a Number of Flavors : 4202.
One of Japan's Earliest Musical Instruments,
    the Biwa : 1654.
One of Sibyl's Songs : 5420.
One of the Reasons : 3456.
One of the Suitors' Harlots : 3164.
One of the World's Five Most Exciting
    Professions : 1654.
One of Those Rare Occurrences on a City Bus
    : 5752.
One of Us : 463.
One Other Thing : 3260.
One Rainy Saturday Morning : 3836.
One River Story : 4008.
One Shining Day : 2048.
One Size Fits Most : 657.
One Small Head : 4224.
One Summer before Man : 5944.
One Threat Aborted, One Not : 3172.
One Volume Missing : 1389.
One Way It Happens : 3597.
One Week : 5397.
The One Who Left Her Husband and Grew
    Her Chestnut Hair Long : 4895.
The One Who Tells : 3037.
The One with the Spoon in Her Mouth : 1939.
One Year : 5016.
The Ones Who Do Not Matter : 4268.
The Onion : 4000.
Onion Evenings : 461.
Onion Leaves, Her Map Untended : 5605.
Only Felt Just Now : 667.
Only Hours in Wadi Halfa : 3472.
The Only Pasture We Can Graze In : 1227.
The Only Reason : 650.
Only the Ego Can Pick Up a Pencil : 144.
Only the Order of Events Has Been Changed :
    3491.
Only the Snow Stays : 2414, 2911, 4656.
Only the Voice : 3153, 3622.
Opal's Dream : 2187.
Open City / & Pink Megaphone : 5369.
Open Country : 14.
The Open Door : 5415.
An Open Else : 1076.
An Open Form : 2965.

Parting : 4087, 5080.
The Parting : 4390, 4465.
Parting in Tivon : 83, 3557.
The Partings : 5368.
Partition : 175.
Parts : 4153.
Parts of his body he needed : 5062.
The Parts of Speech : 2989.
Party : 560, 1093.
The Party : 1350, 2478.
Party Damage : 202.
Pas de Deux : 390.
El Paso : 3675.
Pass It On : 2111.
Pass It On, III : 2111.
Passages : 5441.
Passeggiata Tridimensionale : 811.
Passim : 3625.
Passing : 1839.
The Passing : 1251.
Passing Away : 526.
Passing by a Village on Foot in Summer, I
    Was Amused by a Group of Children
    Playing . . : 950.
Passing by the Black Hole at Cygnus X-1 :
    1750.
Passing Cat City : 2066.
Passing Duration : 4527.
The Passing of Eden: Pomona, California :
    1226.
The Passing of Gus Mike : 5423.
Passing, on a Trip to Town : 5905.
The Passing Past Surviving : 5283.
Passing Strange : 5479.
Passing Through : 1974.
Passing through the Torrid Zone : 960.
Passing Through Walls : 296.
Passing Trees by Twilight : 3784.
Passion : 2144, 3859, 4291, 5615.
The Passionate Shopping Mall : 359.
Passionflower : 5839.
The Passover Set Was Glass : 184.
Passports : 1939.
The Password Is Elegance : 1818.
The Past : 253.
Past Present : 1897, 3410.
Pastor for a Day : 3479.
Pastoral : 1392.
Pastures : 3590.
Pataphysics : 454.
Patchwork : 3866.
A Patchwork : 5012.
Pathways : 4924.
Patience : 2560, 3298.
Patio, November, First Snow : 1430.
Patois : 3525.
Patrick's Day Note for Mary Garvey : 5432.
Patrimony : 1062.
Patsy Cline : 5053.
Pattern : 3965.
Patterns of Sleep : 1539.
Patty : 3172.
Paul Blackburn, Again : 1507.
Paul Celan : 150.

Paul Klee *They're Biting* : 3770.
Paulina : 2849.
Paulo Mia : 347.
Pause at Forty : 46.
Pavane pour les Bains Défunts : 591.
Pay day : 5254.
Peace : 4042.
Peace and Conciliation : 374.
Peace Banner : 4644.
Peace Lyric : 3626.
Peace Maker : 5824.
The Peace March : 4931.
Peace Notes I : 5538.
Peace Notes, II : 5538.
Peace Offering : 4142.
The Peaceable Kingdom : 3004, 5788.
A Peaceful Prayer : 5481.
Peach : 1868.
Peach Preserves : 2518.
Peaches, Pineapples, Hazelnuts : 3943.
The Peacock Flounder : 2212.
The Peacocks at Winter Park : 4475.
Peakload Labor : 2330.
The Pear : 95.
Pear Blossoms Handscroll : 5269.
A Pear Like a Potato : 5466.
Pearl : 2846.
Pearls : 5317.
Pears : 3442.
The Pecans : 5823.
Peeping Tom : 3909.
Peg's House (Venice) : 5184.
Pelican : 1525.
Pelican Flight : 5084.
Peligro : 3014.
The Pelvis of the Shark : 1330.
Pemba : 1684.
Pen : 1821.
Penance : 992.
Pencil and Charcoal Nectarine : 989.
Pendragon : 1735.
The Pendulum Swings : 2305.
The Pendulum's Weight : 2595.
The Penguin Jane Austen : 2041.
Penn's Relations : 4565.
Pentecost : 5796.
Pentimento : 335.
People at Night : 3743, 4478.
The People Don't Realize : 674, 4341.
People grow in the wombs that stand between
    others : 5026.
The People in These Houses : 3423.
People of the Dog : 707.
People Say Bukowski Has Sold Out : 3172.
People sleep : 5481.
The People Who Come to Save Me : 3654.
The People Who Sit in Chairs : 5196.
Pepper Tree : 5629.
Peppers : 4287.
Perch : 2594, 4573.
Percival : 2767.
Percussion Grenade Democracy : 4551.
Perennials : 2841.
The Perfect Flower of Human Time : 1541.

Te Deum : 4900.
Tea Dance : 2874.
The Tea Room : 4410.
The Teacher : 1189, 4081.
The Teacher Discovered : 4128.
The Teaching : 2952.
Teaching English As a Second Language :
    5409.
Teaching My Son Solitude : 2388.
Teaching My Students Prosody : 2068.
Teaching Tennis and Verbs : 5058.
Tear Animals : 3547, 4030.
Tearing Down the Hotel : 5752.
Tease : 756.
The Technology of Disquiet and Distance :
    3313.
The Technology of Inspiration : 1526.
The Technology of Introspection : 3313.
The Technology of Love : 1526.
The Technology of Metal, Turning : 3313.
The Technology of Nausea, and Ecstacy,
    Which, Having Flared a Moment,
    Remain Like a Blue Flame . . : 3313.
The Technology of Spring : 1526.
Teed : 2286.
The Teenage Strut : 575.
Teenagers Cruise This Street Saturday Nights
    : 3353.
The Teeth Mother Naked at Last : 538.
Teeth White As Stars : 4884.
Tejiendo : 4679.
Telegram : 67, 3148.
A Telegram, Unsigned : 147.
Telephone Poets : 2064.
Telephones That Ring : 3230, 3960.
Telescope — May 8 1945 : 5692.
Tell Me : 3416.
Tell Me a Story : 5602.
Tell Me You Love Me, Jean-Paul Sartre :
    3732.
Tell Tale Signs : 5759.
Tell the Clouds to Wait : 159, 1729.
Tell the Monkey in the Street : 5352.
Tell the Wet November : 5947.
Telling : 2111, 5905.
Telling Moves : 115.
Telling My Granddaughter about the Til-
    lamook Burn : 1331.
The Temple of Mars : 174.
The Temple of the Sun Tiger : 65.
Tempo : 1476.
The Ten-Inch Ordinance : 1656.
Ten Marriages / The Reasons : 1263.
Ten-Mile Run : 3448.
Ten Stations of the Sweet Briar Lake : 4392.
Ten Thousand Generations : 4782.
Ten Thousand Jaws : 2503.
Ten Translations from the French : 4771.
Ten Years' Apprenticeship in Fantasy : 660.
The Tenant : 1085, 2560, 3298.
Tender Glass : 2358.
Tending the Fire : 653.
Tenements : 1193.
Tennis Elbow : 2131.

Tennis Lessons : 1243.
Tennyson under the Yews : 553.
The Tenor of My Climbing : 5269.
Tent Meeting : 4334.
Tenth Fragment, Curtain of Sound : 1617.
Tenuous Mortality : 2480.
Teosofica : 3349.
Teotihuacans, 26 July 1974 : 5168.
Tepid Tea Since the Samovar Would not :
    1139.
Teratogenesis : 4421.
Tercina: Winter in Vermont : 1096.
Term : 3590.
Terminal : 83, 4177, 5871.
Terminal Hotel : 2243.
Terminal Moraine : 4189.
The Terrace : 95.
Terrapin : 314.
Terrible Herbst : 4655.
Terricciola 1968 : 1806.
Territories : 2886, 3836.
Territory : 750.
Terror : 4031.
Terrorism II : 1806.
Tesserae : 5398.
Test Flight : 3435.
Testament : 1142, 5331.
Testimoniamos sombra : 1907.
Testimony : 1680.
The Testimony : 1977.
Testing : 4864.
Testing the Tomatoes : 3782.
Texas Aubade : 751.
Texas Rain : 5189.
Telephones That Ring with a Sequence from
    Imagines : 2769.
Text, White Paper : 1814.
Textile Mill on the Charles : 1007.
Th First Terrorism : 501.
Th Hungry Mental Paca Factor : 4335.
Th Lovr Sighs If It All Revolvs around Yu :
    501.
Thanatopsis 1001 : 1128.
Thanatos : 1468, 1563.
Thanks for the Medical Care Sweetheart :
    4849.
Thanksgiving : 104, 253.
Thanksgiving, Growing Older : 1375.
Thanksgiving Night, Old Town, Portland,
    Oregon : 5699.
That : 1498.
That ain' a blowout, boy, that just natural :
    3102.
That Centrifugal Swing : 5169.
That Day / The Sun was Especially Hot :
    5079.
That Electricshock Glow : 3845.
That Evening in a Fair : 3768.
That Far from Home : 5037.
That Final Meeting : 1463.
That Gentleness : 4640.
That November : 3471.
That Rock : 826.
That Sort of Dream : 5341.

That Summer : 1422.
That Uncertain Age : 3221.
That Woman : 5050.
Thaw : 4253.
Theater of the Absurd : 3858.
A Theft : 3935.
Their Eyes Always Open : 570, 3382.
Their Sex Life : 115.
Theme Park : 1133.
Then : 2, 2108.
Then & Now : 1256.
Then My Father's Insomnia Will Break Like
    the Wine Glass I Crushed Underfoot at
    My Wedding : 5648.
Then My Soul Cried Out : 1594, 5918.
Theodor : 5055.
Theogony : 1761.
Theology : 2262.
Theophrastus Bombastus von Hohenheim
    Paracelsus : 5135.
Theorem : 1172.
Theories : 4136.
The Theory : 1479.
The Theory and Practice of Rivers : 2213.
A Theory of Fractions : 4784.
Therapy : 253, 297, 1555.
The Therapy of Joseph Small : 253.
There : 270, 4995, 5901.
There Are Poems : 1153.
There Are Ripe Moments That Sing : 669.
There Are Salt Marshes Here That Seem to :
    1139.
There Are Those : 4978.
There Beyond the River : 306, 5846.
There is a rough compassion in the rain :
    1901.
There Is No Advocate for Down and Out :
    1361.
There Is No Southern Island : 2793, 2888,
    3819.
There is no way to know what I miss : 988.
There Is Nothing : 156.
There Is of Course a Legend : 4321.
There Is Only One of Everything : 219.
There Must Be Something : 5200, 5437.
There Once was a thing named Fred : 1158.
There Was an Angel : 1053.
There Was Something I Wanted to Tell You.
    Why? : 283.
There'll Always Be : 825.
There's a difference between : 1228.
There's a Hidden Door to the Closet : 5163.
There's More to Soup Than Meets the Eye :
    5153.
There's Some Stuff That Is Always Poetry :
    1893.
There's the form of the House : 5801.
Theresa : 2489.
Thersites, after His Tirade at Agamemnon :
    1086.
These Are Not Brushstrokes : 856.
These Days : 306, 307, 2073, 3324.
These Friendly Streets : 2408.
These Our Hands : 4366.

These Things Are You : 4504.
Theseus within the Labyrinth : 1350.
The Thespians at Thermopylae : 789.
They : 865, 1733.
They dance far into the woods : 2512, 5459.
They Do It All on Purpose : 5431.
They Don't Put the Same Value on Human
    Life As We Do : 3172.
They Failed to Tell Me : 4458.
They Keep House : 3305.
They Name Heaven : 5643.
They Needed Each Other Song : 2178.
They offered us some of the finest sites in the
    world : 2725, 2837.
They Said : 5638.
They Sailed for Home : 69.
They say a man bitten by a rabid dog : 1896,
    4907.
They told her how, upon St. Agnes' Eve :
    5818.
They Want : 1246.
They've Broken the Most Delicate Bone in
    My Ear : 4912, 5707.
They've Got to Cut Something : 4354.
They've Nuked You Without Asking Me :
    741.
Thick Skins : 422.
The Thick World : 5944.
The Thief : 2078, 5396.
The Thief of Memories : 4418, 5537.
Thin Ice : 2453.
The Thin Women : 1778, 4721.
Thing : 4981.
A Thing Forgotten : 2455.
The Thing in Itself : 4538.
Thing Love : 5814.
The Thing We Fear the Most Has Already
    Happened (3) : 2014.
The Thing You Love Most : 2887.
Things : 4467.
Things Found on a Path : 2635.
Things I can't See : 365.
The Things I Did : 1583.
Things I Don't Know : 1908.
The Things of the Dead : 1067.
Things Once Human : 1693.
Things Seen : 924, 5896.
Things Seen on Spring Days : 924, 5896.
The Things That Catch the Fish : 1974.
Things That Look the Same : 5096.
Things We Could Have Been : 2567.
Think Japanese : 3217.
Thinking Cap : 5629.
Thinking in Oblique : 5893.
Thinking It's Monday, Waking Up Alone :
    3140.
Thinking of Literary Friends : 1375.
Thinking of Missouri : 5704.
Thinking of Mum : 1484.
Thinking on Medicine Street : 2014.
The Third Party : 1039.
The Third Person : 5643.
Third Person Singular : 2368.
Third Red Queen : 4784.

Who Sweeps the Sidewalk : 4311.
Who was that Roman emperor who had his
     opponents : 4054.
Who We Are : 2544.
The Whole Soul : 3110.
The Whole Sun : 3166.
The Whole That Is Made of Wanting : 4211.
A Whore : 1506.
Whose Move : 3505.
Why : 4466.
Why Are Men So Sad? : 5765.
Why Cities Have Farmer's Markets : 4962.
Why Congress Must Always Vote : 4551.
Why Edna O'Keefe Should Run for Prime
     Minister : 4636.
Why haven't I thought of it before? : 4873.
Why I Am Not a Painting : 4805.
Why I Got Pregnant in 1984 : 2787.
Why I Like My Father : 1196.
Why I Wear the Socks I Do : 1285.
Why Kids Shouldn't Wear Braces : 1194.
Why Plates Are Round : 1403.
Why She Died : 2741.
Why the Chinese Never Discovered Europe :
     1086.
Why the HG Is Holy : 2140.
Why the Word 'Homesick' Cannot Be
     Translated : 1654.
Why There Are No Male Virgins : 4356.
Why There Is No True Artificial Intelligence :
     921.
Why We Cannot Be Oriental : 4640.
Why We Have Daughters : 1862.
Why Women Cry When Plates Break : 2029.
Why You're a Dog and I'm Wonderful :
     5530.
W.I.A. : 4093.
The Wicked One : 2405.
Widow : 5084.
The Widow : 2926.
Widow Garden : 2045.
Widow under a New Moon : 978.
The Widower : 4129, 4390.
The Widower Grows Lustful : 1016.
Widower, New Hampshire, 1954 : 3139.
Widower: Year Two : 821.
A Widow's Grief, 1897 : 4895.
Widow's Peak : 5364.
Widows Travel : 996.
The Wife of Ramon : 1086.
Wiffle Ball : 5571.
Wiglaf's Tale : 2473.
The Wild and Real Agency : 3810.
Wild Animals on the Blacktop : 1117, 3334.
Wild Apples : 2067.
Wild Carrot : 1096.
Wild Country : 1201.
The Wild Garden : 434.
Wild Honey : 4752.
Wild Morning Glories in a Florida Garden :
     4622.
Wild Plum : 5682.
Wild Plums in August : 551.
Wild Radish : 3537.

The Wild, Soft Air : 1086.
The Wild Spray : 556.
Wild Strawberries : 5571.
The Wild Years : 1086.
Wilderness : 2153.
Wildflowers : 1882.
Wildflowers bobbing in open fields : 3534.
Wildlife on the Witness Stand : 4687.
Will : 5746.
The Will of the Curves : 5642.
Will This Thought Do? : 1844.
The Will to Perfection : 3405.
Willard's Coat, by Andrew Wyeth : 1380.
Willed Lack : 3935.
William Waking : 1510.
The Williamstown Gulf : 1411.
Willow Jungle : 4017.
Willows Leaning : 1558.
Wilma Tells How They Moved Old Joseph's
     Bones : 5083.
The Wimp : 1331.
Wind : 5883.
The Wind : 1236.
Wind and Banners : 194, 3694.
Wind in My Mind : 685.
The wind is coming up : 1032, 2812, 4645.
Wind Old Woman : 5128.
The Wind on Manstorna Peak : 5661.
Wind Rising from the Water's Back : 306,
     307, 2073, 3324.
Wind / Switch : 3641.
Wind Unlashes : 2137.
Windmill : 490.
The Window : 5428.
The Window and the Field : 5036.
Window of Vulnerability : 4354.
Windows : 1316.
Winds : 1369.
The Wind's Code : 570, 3382.
Winds of the Midwest : 5194.
Windsurfers : 3486.
Windward in the Rubble : 1847.
Wine Day : 4862.
Wine Song : 4880.
The Wine Tasting : 1145.
Wine, Women & 'Dream Song 291' : 1791.
Wine, Women & Weddings : 159.
The Wing of Springtime : 1274, 2076.
Wing Road : 2045.
A Wingbeat of Hope : 2822.
Wings : 753, 3462, 4187, 4582.
Wings of Dust : 3563.
Winnemucca Pickup : 4867.
Winstons : 954.
Winter : 1943, 3170, 3908, 4465.
A Winter : 677.
Winter, a Walk in Pinewoods : 2495.
Winter Accident : 5787.
Winter Advice : 5034.
Winter Boredom : 3943.
Winter Central : 1305.
Winter Coming : 4448.
Winter Day : 1462.
Winter Entries : 5836.